TEXAS COURTS
A SURVEY

CASES & MATERIALS

Ninth Edition

D1027587

ALEX WILSON ALBRIGHT
PARTNER, ALEXANDER DUBOSE JEFFERSON & TOWNSEND LLP
SENIOR LECTURER (RETIRED), UNIVERSITY OF TEXAS SCHOOL OF LAW

DUSTIN B. BENHAM
PROFESSOR OF LAW
TEXAS TECH UNIVERSITY SCHOOL OF LAW

IMPRIMATUR PRESS

A DIVISION OF

GRAIL & TUCKER LEGAL PUBLISHING, L.L.C.

8111 LYNDON B. JOHNSON FREEWAY, SUITE 1325
DALLAS, TEXAS 75251
TELEPHONE: (800) 811-6725
FACSIMILE: (214) 879-9939
www.ImprimaturPress.com

Copyright © 1996-2018 by Alex Wilson Albright

All rights reserved. No part of this work may be reproduced or copied in any form or by any means, graphic, electronic or mechanical, including photocopying, recording, taping, or information and retrieval systems without prior written permission of the copyright holder who may be contacted through the publisher.

Printed in the United States of America

ISBN 978-1-60503-123-1

These materials are prepared for classroom use. It is not a substitute for specific legal research. The cases and laws are discussed generally and the author's comments should not be relied on for the basis of a legal opinion or course of action, without careful review of applicable authorities including those cases decided since the publication of this book.

TABLE OF CONTENTS

CHAPTER 1
INTRODUCTION TO TEXAS COURTS

CHAPTER 2
THE TEXAS TRIAL COURTS

CHAPTER 3
PERSONAL JURISDICTION

CHAPTER 4
VENUE

CHAPTER 5
PLEADING

CHAPTER 6
JOINDER

CHAPTER 7
SCOPE OF DISCOVERY

CHAPTER 8
DISCOVERY MECHANICS

CHAPTER 9
DISCOVERY SANCTIONS

CHAPTER 10
EXPERTS

CHAPTER 11
SUMMARY JUDGMENTS

CHAPTER 12
SETTINGS & TRIAL

CHAPTER 13
THE JURY

CHAPTER 14
JURY CHARGE

CHAPTER 15
VERDICTS

CHAPTER 16
JUDGMENTS AND POST JUDGMENT MOTIONS

CHAPTER 17
APPEALS

CHAPTER 18
DEFAULTS AND DISMISSALS

CHAPTER 19
COMPLEX LITIGATION

CHAPTER 20
SETTLEMENTS

Chapter 1. Introduction to Texas Courts

A. The Texas Rules of Civil Procedure

Read Rules 1, 3a; Tex. Const. art. V § 31; Gov't Code § 22.004.

Texas civil practice is primarily governed by the Texas Rules of Civil Procedure, the rules promulgated by the Texas Supreme Court under its rulemaking power.[1] Pursuant to that grant of power, the Supreme Court adopted the Texas Rules of Civil Procedure in 1941. The Rules were generally amended every two years, although no amendments were made from 1990 to 1997. Since then, the Supreme Court made some significant changes to the Rules. New appellate rules and a new summary judgment rule became effective September 1, 1997. New discovery rules became effective January 1, 1999. Significant rule changes were made in response to the 2003 tort reform legislation. And the Court has adopted new electronic filing rules, rules providing expedited procedure for smaller cases, and a rule allowing an early motion to dismiss on the pleadings.

Although the original 1941 Texas Rules of Civil Procedure ("TRCP") were adopted in response to the same movement that produced the Federal Rules of Civil Procedure (adopted in 1939), and the Federal Rules were used somewhat as a guide, significant differences exist between the two. A quick look through the table of contents to the Texas Rules of Civil Procedure shows the first difference between the Texas and Federal Rules—there are many more rules in Texas than in the federal courts. The Texas rules appear to be well-organized. Further study will reveal, however, that while the organization may have made sense in 1941, the many amendments since have created a hodgepodge of rules. Often, a series of rules share the same number, but are entirely unrelated. For instance, Rule 166 governs pretrial conferences and Rule 166a governs summary judgments. Large groups of rules are missing, having been repealed for one reason or another, such as the separate codification of the Texas Rules of Appellate Procedure ("TRAP"). Moreover, although many of the rules are quite modern, others are clearly antiquated, causing only confusion in today's practice.

Many Texas courts also have a set of local rules that further define practice before them. The Texas Supreme Court adopted the current version of Rule 3a after determining that many courts had unwritten local rules, known only to the judges and local lawyers who practiced before them, that changed significant deadlines set out in the Texas Rules of Civil Procedure. Local rules often establish local procedures for handling the court's docket, pretrial matters and motions dealing with such matters as default judgments and withdrawal of counsel.[2] Rule 3a requires all local rules to be published and approved by the Supreme Court, and prohibits local rules that alter the time limits imposed by the Texas Rules of Civil Procedure.[3] It is extremely important that you become familiar with the local rules applicable to any court in which you practice. Nearly every county has a set of rules and there is little uniformity.

---

[1] The Rules Enabling Act of 1939, now codified as Gov't Code § 22.004.

[2] *See e.g.,* United Business Machines v. Southwestern Bell Media, Inc., 817 S.W.2d 120 (Tex. App.—Houston [1st Dist.] 1991, no writ) (approving Harris County local rules that allowed sanctions to be imposed after written submission without oral hearing).

[3] *See* United Marketing Technology, Inc. v. First USA Merchant Services, Inc., 812 S.W.2d 608, 611 (Tex. App.—Dallas 1991, writ denied) (holding that Dallas Civil District Court local rule allowing amended pleading only with leave of court not less than 14 days before trial is inconsistent with TRCP 63 and violates TRCP 3a).

Texas civil practice is also governed by a number of statutes. Most of these statutes can be found in the Texas Civil Practice and Remedies Code ("CPRC") and the Government Code. Sometimes, the legislative agenda differs from the rules promulgated by the Supreme Court. For example, in the 1995 legislative session significant changes were made to the venue statutes, effective for cases filed on or after September 1, 1995. The *rules* concerning venue, however, have not been revised. A sanctions bill also became law in 1995, creating significant conflicts with the sanctions practice that is now part of the rules.

Appellate practice in Texas is governed by the Texas Rules of Appellate Procedure ("TRAP"), which were adopted in 1997, and apply to both civil and criminal appeals. Before 1997, the civil appellate rules were contained in the Texas Rules of Civil Procedure. The appellate rules present more of a "cookbook" approach than do the civil rules—they provide a fairly detailed description of what one has to do when appealing a case.

The Texas Rules of Evidence ("TRE") govern the admission of evidence at trial. However, a few of these affect civil procedure, and discovery practice in particular, (such as the rules governing relevance and privilege). Thus, some of the evidence rules are also included in the materials.

B. The Adversary System and Civil Procedure

To understand any system of civil procedure, one must have a basic understanding of the adversary process, an essential element in the American judicial system. In an adversary system, neutral and passive decision-makers adjudicate disputes after hearing evidence and arguments presented by both sides. The parties and their client-dedicated legal representatives, rather than the judge, control much of the progress of the proceedings. They gather and evaluate facts and legal theories and present them to the decision-maker in the most persuasive manner possible. The system thus creates competition between the parties, encouraging each to marshal all of the law and facts favorable to its side and to attack unreliable information presented by the opponent. Although the incentives created are not so much to seek the truth as to seek success for their partisan position, in theory the competition between the two sides results in a complete and accurate account of the dispute. The adversary system creates incentives to thoroughly investigate, but it also creates incentives to keep the results of investigations confidential to prevent any benefit from accruing to the opponent.

The rules of procedure govern this adversary system, and a successful litigant must obey them. And sometimes a party wins the dispute despite the true merits of the case. Rule 1 of the TRCP, however, proclaims that "[t]he proper objective of rules of civil procedure is to obtain a just, fair, equitable and impartial adjudication of the rights of litigants under established principles of substantive law. To the end that this objective may be attained with as great expedition and dispatch and at the least expense both to the litigants and to the state as may be practicable, these rules shall be given a liberal construction." This book will explore whether our rules of civil procedure have achieved these goals of justice and efficiency.

C. An Overview of Texas Pretrial Procedure

Pretrial procedure is the process by which parties prepare for the trial in which their dispute will be resolved. While a trial may last only a few days or weeks, the pretrial portion of modern civil litigation usually consumes months or years. During the pretrial portion, the case is likely to be settled by agreement between the parties. Thus, the primary purpose, to prepare for trial, is often forgotten.

Before a lawsuit is commenced, the plaintiff must make many decisions. Most importantly, the plaintiff must decide that filing suit is worth the time, effort, and expense that it will cost to pursue it. Litigation is only one of many dispute resolution processes, and is perhaps the most expensive and time-consuming. It usually should be resorted to only when other informal methods of dispute resolution have failed.

Assuming that a party decides to pursue litigation, the litigant must decide in which court to bring the action. First, the plaintiff must determine which courts have subject matter jurisdiction over the dispute, and choose the forum accordingly. As you will see, some of the Texas trial courts have limited subject matter jurisdiction, governed by a complicated statutory scheme. The plaintiff must also determine in which of the 254 Texas counties suit should be filed. This concept, called venue, is also governed by statute, and usually gives the plaintiff several options from which to choose.

The plaintiff commences suit by filing a pleading, called the "Plaintiff's Original Petition," rather than the "Complaint" as it is called in some other courts, including the federal courts. In this written document, the plaintiff identifies the defendant and gives the defendant notice of the claims being asserted against it. The plaintiff can bring multiple claims against multiple parties. The court obtains power over the defendant when the defendant is served with process and a copy of the plaintiff's pleadings. Texas courts have power over all persons who reside in Texas as well as limited power over nonresidents. Therefore, if the plaintiff seeks to sue a nonresident, the court must consider whether it has personal jurisdiction, necessary to hear the case.

Following service of process, the defendant must respond to the petition, usually by filing an answer that denies the plaintiff's allegations, and sets forth any defensive allegations upon which the defendant wants to rely. These pleadings (the petition and answer) provide the blueprint of the lawsuit, from which decisions regarding relevance are determined in discovery and at trial. When the rules were originally promulgated, pleadings were the primary vehicle by which parties obtained information from their opponents about the litigation. Accordingly, the rules provide a vehicle for the defendant to ask the plaintiff to plead more specifically—called special exceptions in Texas. In addition, the defendant may want to contest the court's subject matter jurisdiction, personal jurisdiction, or venue. The rules provide for special pleadings that have the specific purpose of objecting to the assertion of jurisdiction or venue. The defendant may seek to dismiss one or more of the plaintiff's claims as legally or factually baseless. Last, but not least, the defendant may want to bring in additional parties or assert his own claims against the plaintiff. There are rules of procedure allowing for each of these as well.

The most time-consuming pretrial matter is discovery, where the parties formally obtain information relevant to the lawsuits from the other parties to the lawsuit and from nonparties. Over the course of time, the scope of discovery had broadened substantially, with the goal of revealing relevant facts and prohibit trial by surprise. Broad discovery has significant implications for pleading practice—as more facts are revealed through discovery, the use of pleadings as a tool to reveal facts becomes superfluous. More recent reform efforts have attempted to limit discovery practice to reduce pretrial litigation costs.

The Texas rules set out particular permitted forms of discovery. Parties are required, upon request, to provide disclosures to opponents, with standardized categories of information in every case. Parties can also take oral depositions of parties and witnesses (where the lawyers question a witness under oath, and the proceedings are recorded and transcribed for later use). Additionally, parties can make inquiries to other parties through written interrogatories (written questions that require a written answer made under oath). One of the most useful discovery vehicles is the request for documents and things (where parties are required to produce requested and relevant documents and things for inspection and copying). The rules also provide for various privileges and exemptions from discovery, which, when properly asserted by the responding party, can protect that party from having to disclose particular information in discovery. Although the 1999 rule amendments attempted to make discovery less contentious, because our system uses the adversary system to accumulate facts in discovery, disputes over discovery are a common feature of pretrial litigation. The Texas Rules of Civil Procedure provide detailed guidelines for the resolution of these disputes.

D. An Overview of Texas Trial and Appellate Procedure

The advocate in a jury trial must cultivate a split personality. He or she is almost always working the case at two levels, trying to coax a favorable verdict out of the jury while at the same time making a record of trial court errors so that the case can be reversed if the result is bad. These objectives do not always live in harmony. Often, trial counsel is so caught up in the demands of the moment—where to go with the witness when the court has excluded critical testimony, for example—that the need to "preserve error" is forgotten until it is too late.[4] Sometimes the emphasis on persuasion causes counsel to deliberately forego the preservation of error. An improper closing argument may be even more damaging if highlighted by objection. Repeated objections, though sometimes necessary, can be seen by the jury as a suspicious bent toward concealment. If you make the right objection every time you can to "protect the record" you will undoubtedly have preserved all errors for appeal—where you will surely need them, the judge and jury having long since decided that you are an obstructionist intent on defeating an open trial. In a typical trial, no more than two or three bad rulings will be critical. The rest will be harmless (that is, not reversible error) and can be seen as such when they occur. So the best advocates, who know how to preserve error, sometimes decide not to do it.

It is perhaps unfair, but it is the case that almost everything that goes wrong at a trial can and will be laid at the feet of the judge. Why? Because the judge's control of the trial is both preventative and curative. The judge can prevent unfairness by excluding certain evidence before it comes in, for example, or by preparing a correct jury charge, or, in some cases, by granting a motion for directed verdict and ending the trial early. But the judge can sometimes *cure* unfairness after the fact by such actions as striking improper comments and instructing the jury to disregard them, admonishing overzealous counsel, declaring a mistrial, or taking the case away from an errant jury.

---

[4] The term "preserving error" places an unfortunate emphasis on the negative. We should be concerned with stamping out error rather than preserving it. What is meant, of course, is that the errors which occurred during the trial are preserved in the record for appellate review.

And, at the end of the day, when the trial is over and the jury has gone home, the court can cure *all* trial errors by ordering a new trial and starting over.

Procedure is not advocacy and knowledge of procedure does not aid in persuasion. In fact, procedural rules are often devised precisely for the purpose of blunting persuasion that goes past the limits of fair advocacy. Advocacy is salesmanship. It attempts to win the favor of the court or jury and to make them do what the advocate wants. Procedural rules set the boundaries for advocacy, controlling and channeling it into an orderly (and presumably fair) contest and providing appellate recourse to those aggrieved by the trial court's actions. The trial counsel's mission is to use advocacy to win, but failing that, to protest errors with the required formalities so that the record will support a reversal on appeal. This secondary or conditional goal—preserving a basis for reversal if the verdict goes the wrong way—sometimes tempts counsel to ignore ethical obligations and to "seed the record with error" or "sandbag"; that is, to hide the real objection in a barrage of bogus complaints, so that the judge is tricked into overruling it. The judge's error can then form the basis of a reversal if the sandbagger loses, giving his client the chance to return to fight another day. One of the missions of procedure is to protect the judge—and the system—from such deception.

So, procedure sets the rules and advocacy operates within them to persuade. Many procedural disputes lie almost entirely within the trial court's discretion. The court will decide on whatever grounds it wishes, constrained only by some rather vague prohibitions against completely arbitrary behavior. If it wants to consider irrelevancies or appeals to emotion or even competing hairstyles it will do so.[5] Advocacy is an art, and whatever persuades—within the limits of ethical behavior—is right. Therefore, in this book, once we have identified a matter for decision as one within the court's discretion, we will have little more to say about it. We will leave the techniques of persuading the judge to advocacy courses and will concentrate instead on the rules and strictures which the trial court must follow or else risk reversal.

What should be the criteria for overturning the judgment of the trial court? The litigant is entitled to a fair trial but not necessarily a perfect one. The system will not compel a second contest simply because inconsequential mistakes were made in the first. The concept of "no harm no foul" informs the idea of harmless error. Unless the mistake was "calculated to cause and probably did cause" an improper judgment; that is, unless it changed the outcome of the case, the error will be said to be harmless and there will be no reversal. The harmless error rule is ignored in some situations where the system presumes that there is harm and the judgment will be reversed.

But there is another reason that not all errors are fatal. Many legitimate complaints about trial conduct are waived. Trial counsel is charged with seeing that his client's rights are protected by placing on the record the right protest at the right time and in the right form. The idea of "fundamental" or "incurable" error—a mistake requiring reversal even though no one complained of it at the time it was made—has almost completely disappeared.

Before an appellate court will reverse a trial court's actions it will want to see (1) that counsel clearly pointed out what the court was doing wrong (or was about to do wrong), (2) that counsel gave the "grounds" for the complaint—the rule or precept being violated, (3) that counsel told the court how to avoid or correct the error (unless that was clear from the nature of the protest), and (4) that the court clearly rejected the protest (e.g., overruled an objection). None of this counts for anything, of course, if it does not appear in the written record that goes to the appellate court.

[5] This is merely an example. In practice almost all judges will make a good faith attempt to decide discretionary matters in accordance with accepted standards.

These general requirements for preserving error are no more than common sense would suggest. In certain instances, however, the requirements are more detailed. The rules and cases require that the complainant follow a step-by-step sequence of motions and related actions. The best advocates, in time, master these requirements and it is important to do so. But those who must react immediately to an adverse ruling made in the heat of battle would do well to be sure the record reflects at least that the judge was told precisely what was wrong, told which rule or precept made it wrong, and then told how to fix it, and that the judge then refused to take the appropriate action.

In determining how to deal with adverse rulings or findings a careful advocate must answer some hard questions. Is the offending action one in which the court or the jury has unlimited discretion? Broad discretion? Limited discretion? Almost no discretion? Are there only two courses available either of which the trial court can take with impunity? Or is there a single right ruling, all others being wrong and potentially reversible? Furthermore, if the ruling is wrong, either as an error of law or an abuse of discretion, can it be shown to have changed the outcome? Is it a ruling that may, under special circumstances, give rise to a kind of presumed harm which overrides the usual harmless error rule? Is the complaint that the jury has acted contrary to the evidence before it and, if so, what curative action is available to the court? And finally, must an appellate review await the conclusion of the case or is the error one that may be corrected by *mandamus* or some form of interim appeal?

It may seem that this book gives short shrift to appellate procedure. But in fact, the book addresses appellate issues in every chapter. An appellate lawyer's job is not only to ensure that appellate deadlines are satisfied and the brief is written. She must also ensure that error is preserved, the record is complete, and the standards of review are well understood—all things that are included throughout this book.

E. Quick Note on Materials

In addition to this casebook, you should also have a copy of the Texas Rules of Civil Procedure, Appellate Procedure and Evidence, and the statutes that are discussed here. It is important to have a current version.

Throughout this book, "Rule ___" refers to one of the Texas Rules of Civil Procedure, which will also be abbreviated as "TRCP." The appellate rules will be abbreviated as "TRAP," and the evidence rules will be abbreviated as "TRE." The statutes will be referred to by the name of the Texas statutory code from which the statute comes (i.e. "Government Code"), but the Texas Civil Practice and Remedies Code will usually be referred to as "CPRC."

The opinions in the text are substantially edited from the original. Footnotes and string cites are often deleted without noting the deletion. Large text deletions are noted with "* * *". However, occasionally courts use "* * *" as an indication of a break in the opinion. Texas Supreme Court opinions are used whenever possible, and the Texas Supreme Court is often referred to as "the Court" or "Supreme Court."

CHAPTER 2. THE TEXAS TRIAL COURTS

A. Court Structure of Texas

October 1, 2017

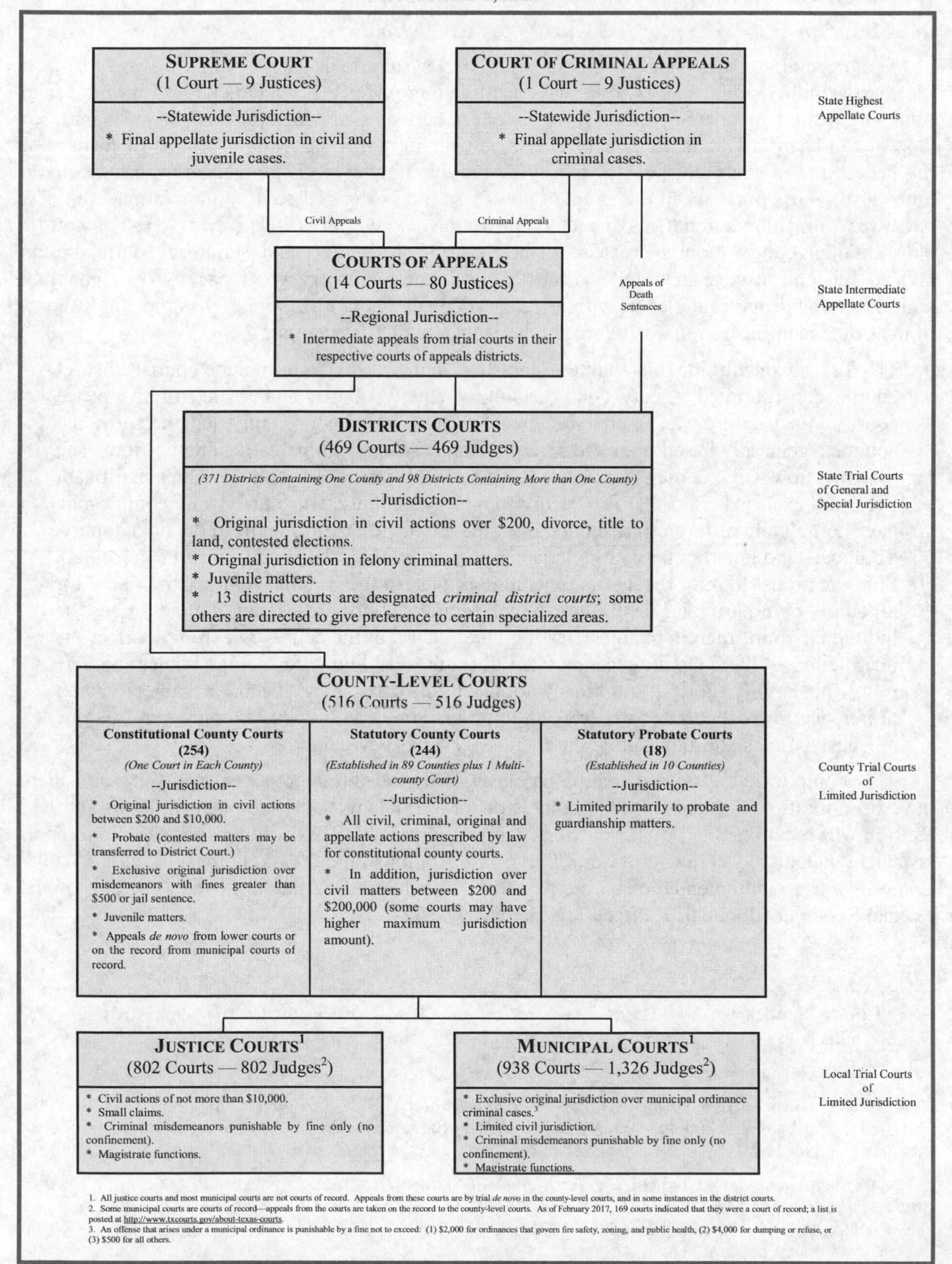

SUPREME COURT
(1 Court — 9 Justices)
--Statewide Jurisdiction--
* Final appellate jurisdiction in civil and juvenile cases.
COURT OF CRIMINAL APPEALS
(1 Court — 9 Justices)
--Statewide Jurisdiction--
* Final appellate jurisdiction in criminal cases.
State Highest Appellate Courts
Civil Appeals
Criminal Appeals
COURTS OF APPEALS
(14 Courts — 80 Justices)
--Regional Jurisdiction--
* Intermediate appeals from trial courts in their respective courts of appeals districts.
Appeals of Death Sentences
State Intermediate Appellate Courts
DISTRICTS COURTS
(469 Courts — 469 Judges)
(371 Districts Containing One County and 98 Districts Containing More than One County)
--Jurisdiction--
* Original jurisdiction in civil actions over $200, divorce, title to land, contested elections.
* Original jurisdiction in felony criminal matters.
* Juvenile matters.
* 13 district courts are designated criminal district courts; some others are directed to give preference to certain specialized areas.
State Trial Courts of General and Special Jurisdiction
COUNTY-LEVEL COURTS
(516 Courts — 516 Judges)
Constitutional County Courts
(254)
(One Court in Each County)
--Jurisdiction--
* Original jurisdiction in civil actions between $200 and $10,000.
* Probate (contested matters may be transferred to District Court.)
* Exclusive original jurisdiction over misdemeanors with fines greater than $500 or jail sentence.
* Juvenile matters.
* Appeals de novo from lower courts or on the record from municipal courts of record.
Statutory County Courts
(244)
(Established in 89 Counties plus 1 Multi-county Court)
--Jurisdiction--
* All civil, criminal, original and appellate actions prescribed by law for constitutional county courts.
* In addition, jurisdiction over civil matters between $200 and $200,000 (some courts may have higher maximum jurisdiction amount).
Statutory Probate Courts
(18)
(Established in 10 Counties)
--Jurisdiction--
* Limited primarily to probate and guardianship matters.
County Trial Courts of Limited Jurisdiction
JUSTICE COURTS1
(802 Courts — 802 Judges2)
* Civil actions of not more than $10,000.
* Small claims.
* Criminal misdemeanors punishable by fine only (no confinement).
* Magistrate functions.
MUNICIPAL COURTS1
(938 Courts — 1,326 Judges2)
* Exclusive original jurisdiction over municipal ordinance criminal cases.3
* Limited civil jurisdiction.
* Criminal misdemeanors punishable by fine only (no confinement).
* Magistrate functions.
Local Trial Courts of Limited Jurisdiction
1. All justice courts and most municipal courts are not courts of record. Appeals from these courts are by trial de novo in the county-level courts, and in some instances in the district courts.
2. Some municipal courts are courts of record—appeals from the courts are taken on the record to the county-level courts. As of February 2017, 169 courts indicated that they were a court of record; a list is posted at http://www.txcourts.gov/about-texas-courts.
3. An offense that arises under a municipal ordinance is punishable by a fine not to exceed: (1) $2,000 for ordinances that govern fire safety, zoning, and public health, (2) $4,000 for dumping or refuse, or (3) $500 for all others.

1. *The Civil Subject Matter Jurisdiction of the Texas Trial Courts*

Read Tex. Const., art. V, §§ 1, 3, 31; art. II, § 1; see Appendix.

The preceding chart[1] makes the Texas trial court system look fairly straightforward. In fact, the chart is highly simplified. The Texas Constitution provides that the judicial power of the state "shall be vested in one Supreme Court, in one Court of Criminal Appeals, in the Courts of Appeals, in District Courts, in County Courts, in Commissioner's Courts, in Courts of Justices of the Peace, and in such other courts as may be provided by law."[2] The legislature has created a number of courts pursuant to this grant of power, so the Texas trial court system is made up of a patchwork of constitutional and statutory provisions. Thus, Texas has two types of courts: constitutional courts (courts created by the Texas Constitution) and statutory courts (courts created by legislative enactment). Each newly created statutory court has its own enabling legislation that provides the court with its unique subject matter jurisdiction. As the 2008 Report of the Court Administration Task Force of the State Bar of Texas put it:[3]

> The Texas Constitution and statutes establish a four-tiered system of state courts: district courts, constitutional county courts, statutory county courts, and justice of the peace courts. Each court was intended to have its own jurisdiction, consistent between the counties, generally based upon the severity of the civil or criminal issues in question. The system, however, actually presents a patchwork array of courts with significant overlapping jurisdiction that differs from county to county. A court in one county may have completely different jurisdiction from the identically named court in the next county. To understand a particular court's jurisdiction, no less than six sources must be consulted. First, one must look to the Texas Constitution, then to the general statutory provision for all courts on a particular level, then to the specific statutory provision that authorizes the individual court, then to statutes creating other courts in the county which may affect the jurisdiction of the court in question, then to statutes dealing with specific subject matters (e.g., the Family Code), and finally to local rules that may specify a subject matter preference for particular courts (e.g., child protection cases). If this exercise can frustrate a licensed Texas attorney, surely the average Texan is bewildered.

This complicated system of courts has been criticized throughout Texas history, and there have been multiple attempts to address the structural problems that have plagued Texas courts.[4] Reform was recommended by the Citizens' Commission on the Texas Judicial System in a report issued in January 1991 and the State Bar Court Administration Task Force in October 2008. Some of these recommendations were passed by the Texas Legislature at the very end of the Special Session of June 2011, effective September 1, 2011.

---

[1] COURT STRUCTURE OF TEXAS, prepared by the Texas Office of Court Administration. *See* www.txcourts.gov.

[2] TEX. CONST. art. V, § 1.

[3] State Bar of Texas, *Court Administration Task Force Report,* Oct. 2008, http://www.texasbar.com/Content/ContentGroups/Judiciary/Supreme_Court_of_Texas/Court_Administration_Task_Force_Report.htm.

[4] *See e.g.*, C. Raymond Judice, *The Texas Judicial System: Historical Development and Efforts Towards Court Modernization*, 14 S. TEX. L.J. 295, 314 (1973); Thomas M. Reavley, *Court Improvement: The Texas Scene*, 4 TEX. TECH. L. REV. 269, 269-270 (1973).

How did we end up with this bewildering array of courts with differing subject matter jurisdictions? The Texas trial court system was developed for an essentially rural population. Counties were the basic governmental units, and the Constitution provides that each county has a county court. The county judge was the chief administrative officer of the county as well as the judge of the county court. The legislature gave the county court jurisdiction over probate matters and relatively minor civil litigation. Smaller areas within a county were served by justices of the peace who served as magistrates for various duties, such as conducting marriages and resolving breaches of the peace and petty civil disputes. District courts were the courts of general jurisdiction (having jurisdiction over all matters not within the jurisdiction of the county and justice courts). The legislature created enough to serve the population, which meant that one district court might serve several counties; and, perhaps because lawyers were scarce on the frontier, only district court judges were required to be lawyers.

As the state became more populous, the legislature created more courts. Most newly created district courts, which are funded by the state, served a single metropolitan area; now many counties have several district courts, and some of these district courts are limited to a particular specialty, such as the family and criminal district courts in Dallas and Harris County. However, some district courts still have jurisdiction over multiple counties.[5] The legislature also created new statutory courts, primarily county courts at law and probate courts to relieve the county judge of some or all the judicial duties of office. Over time, county courts at law were created to assist with the increasing caseloads of district courts as well. If the county needed another court and was willing to provide the needed resources, the legislature would create a county court at law (funded by the county) rather than a district court (largely funded by the state). Therefore, while all county courts at law have the same minimum subject matter jurisdiction, a number of them have more jurisdiction.[6] For example, the maximum amount in controversy jurisdiction of the county courts at law range from $200,000 (the minimum as of September 1, 2011) to $500,000 to $750,000 to $1 million to the unlimited dollar amount of the district court. One can never be certain of the full jurisdiction of a statutory court without consulting its own enabling statute.

The best way to determine whether a particular court has subject matter jurisdiction over a particular controversy is to check the amount in controversy. If the amount in controversy is within the court's jurisdictional limits, it has jurisdiction *unless* the particular type of controversy is excluded from its jurisdiction or another court has been granted exclusive jurisdiction over the controversy. Finally, be sure the court can grant the type of relief that you are requesting.

a. *Local Trial Courts of Limited Jurisdiction*

Read Rules 500-510; Gov't Code §§ 27.031, .032, .033; §§ 28.001, .002, .003, 30.00003.

(1) *Justice Courts*

Justice courts are the lowest ranking civil courts.[7] They have amount in controversy jurisdiction for amounts from $0.01 to a maximum of $10,000, and their jurisdiction is exclusive for amounts of $200 and less.[8] Their original jurisdiction is concurrent with district and county

---

5 *See* In re McGuire, 134 S.W.3d 406 (Tex. App.—Waco 2004, no pet.)(stating that both the 278th and 87th district courts had jurisdiction over Leon County). See also www.txcourts.gov for an updated map of all Texas district courts.

6 *See* GOV'T CODE §25.003.

7 TEX. CONST. art. V; GOV'T CODE § 27.031-032.

8 TEX. CONST. art. V, §19.

courts in civil cases involving more than $200 (county court) or more than $500 (the district court) up to the $10,000 Justice court limit.[9] Appeal from a judgment of the justice court is to the county court where a trial de novo is held, which can then be appealed to the court of appeals.[10] In cases involving claims for debt, an appeal may be taken to the statutory county court or, if there is no statutory county court within the jurisdiction, the district court.[11]

Justice courts have unique and exclusive original jurisdiction over forcible entry and detainer cases. Generally known as "FED", they are brought to determine the right of possession of premises, almost always involving landlord-tenant disputes. A claim for unpaid rent or damages is not part of the justice court's FED case and cannot be heard at the justice court level if the amount in controversy is outside the justice court's jurisdiction.[12] Moreover, the district court has exclusive jurisdiction if title to real property is at issue.[13]

Justice courts can grant relief as follows: They can foreclose mortgages and enforce liens on *personal* property, so long as the amount in controversy is within their jurisdiction.[14] They can issue writs of attachment, garnishment, and sequestration in cases otherwise within their jurisdiction.[15] They cannot issue injunctions or writs of mandamus or hear suits on behalf of the state for penalties, forfeitures, and escheats; and they cannot hear suits for divorce, defamation, declaration of title to land, or enforcement of liens on land.[16]

The Texas Supreme Court adopted new rules governing justice courts, effective August 31, 2013. The rules abolish the former division of the Justice Courts into a Small Claims Court and a Justice Court and take other steps to simplify Justice Court procedure. The new rules divide cases into four categories: (1) Small claims cases for damages of $10,000 or less, excluding statutory interest and court costs, but including attorney's fees; (2) Claims for debt payment of $10,000 or less, excluding statutory interest and court costs but including attorney's fees; (3) Repair and remedy suits brought by a residential tenant under the Texas Property Code to enforce a landlord's duty to repair or remedy a condition that materially affects the physical health and safety of an ordinary tenant, with a related claim for damages of $10,000 or less; (4) Eviction cases by a landlord to recover possession of real property under the Texas Property Code, with a related claim for unpaid rent of $10,000 or less.[17]

---

9 GOV'T CODE § 27.031.

10 *See* Rule 506.

11 *See* Rule 509.8.

12 *See* Rule 500.3.

13 *See* Mitchell v. Armstrong Capital Corp., 911 S.W.2d 169 (Tex. App.—Houston [1st Dist.] 1995, writ denied); Martinez v. Daccarett, 865 S.W.2d 161 (Tex. App.—Corpus Christi 1993, no writ); Orange Laundry Co. v. Stark, 179 S.W.2d 841, 842 (Tex. App.—Amarillo 1944, no writ).

14 GOV'T. CODE § 27.031(a)(3).

15 GOV'T CODE § 27.032.

16 GOV'T CODE §§ 27.031(b); 27.032.

17 *See* Rule 503.3.

(2) *Municipal Courts*

Municipal courts serve primarily as the lowest-ranking *criminal* courts with exclusive jurisdiction over criminal cases that arise under the ordinances of the municipality and are punishable by a fine not to exceed $2,000 in all cases arising under ordinances that govern fire safety, zoning, or public health and sanitation or $500 in all other cases arising under a municipal ordinance.[18] Municipal courts have concurrent jurisdiction with the justice court in criminal cases that are punishable by fine only.[19] They have very narrow civil jurisdiction for the purpose of enforcing certain municipal ordinances.[20]

b. *Constitutional County Courts*

Read Gov't Code §§ 26.021, .022, .041, .043, .044, .050, .051.

Article 5, §16 of the Texas Constitution provides for the creation of county courts with jurisdiction "as provided by law." Therefore, their full jurisdiction is set forth in the statutes.[21]

Constitutional county courts have amount in controversy jurisdiction over amounts in excess of $200 ($200.01) through $10,000.[22] Therefore, they have concurrent jurisdiction with justice courts ($200.01-$10,000) and district courts ($500.01-$10,000). In some counties, they may have probate jurisdiction (outlined below). The constitutional county courts also have appellate jurisdiction over cases originating in justice or small claims court where the amount in controversy exceeds $20. All appellate review is by trial de novo.[23]

Constitutional county courts can grant the following relief: injunctions, mandamus, certiorari and all other writs necessary to enforce their jurisdiction.[24] They cannot hear suits for defamation, divorce, eminent domain, for forfeiture of a corporate charter, for the right to property valued at $500 or more and levied on under a writ of execution, for sequestration or attachment, for recovery of land, to enforce liens on land, or suits by the state for escheat.[25]

c. *District Courts*

Read Gov't Code §§ 24.007-.011.

District courts are the courts of general jurisdiction in Texas, presumed to have jurisdiction unless a contrary showing is made.[26] They have "residual jurisdiction"—by constitutional mandate they have jurisdiction in all cases unless exclusive jurisdiction is conferred on some other court.[27] Often the district court's "residual jurisdiction" can be determined only by checking the jurisdiction granted to other courts serving the same county or counties.

---

18 TEX. CODE CRIM. PROC. art. 4.14(a) (2009); TEX. GOV'T CODE § 29.003.

19 TEX. CODE CRIM. PROC. art. 4.14(b) (2009); TEX. GOV'T CODE § 29.003.

20 TEX. GOV'T CODE § 30.00005(d).

21 *See* GOV'T CODE §§ 26.042-44, 26.051, 26.101-.354; CPRC §§ 51.001-002, 61.021-022.

22 GOV'T CODE §§ 26.042(a), 27.031(a)(1).

23 TEX. CONST. art. V., § 6, CPRC §51.001; GOV'T CODE § 28.052.

24 TEX. CONST. art. V, § 16; GOV'T CODE §§ 26.044, 26.051; CPRC §§ 61.021, 62.021, 63.002, 65.021.

25 GOV'T CODE § 26.043.

26 Dubai Petroleum Co. v. Kazi, 12 S.W.3d 71, 75 (Tex. 2000).

27 *See* TEX. CONST. art. V, § 8; GOV'T. CODE §§ 24.007-008, 24.011.

2011 legislation attempted to make clear that the lower limit of the district court's jurisdiction is $500.01.[28] But because the statute does not confer exclusive jurisdiction of cases with an amount in controversy below $500, district courts continue to have jurisdiction over cases over $200. There is no upper limit to the district court's amount-in-controversy jurisdiction and district courts can grant all types of relief.

d. *Statutory or Legislative Courts*

By virtue of the Constitution's grant of legislative power to "establish such other courts as it may deem necessary," the Legislature has from time to time created special statutory courts.[29] The Legislature can create a statutory court with limited jurisdiction or jurisdiction equal to the constitutional dimensions of a district court.[30] The legislature may not, however, reduce the constitutional jurisdiction of a district court.[31]

(1) *County Courts at Law*

Read Gov't Code §§ 25.0001, .0003, .0004.

As noted above, each of these courts is created by a separate statute and with distinct jurisdictional parameters. In order to determine the exact jurisdiction of a county court at law, one must consult Chapter 25 of the Government Code for the specific statute that created the court.[32] GOV'T. CODE § 25.0003 provides some *minimum* jurisdictional parameters for statutory county courts. It gives all statutory county courts jurisdiction over civil cases in which the amount in controversy exceeds $500 but does not exceed $200,000 (excluding interest, punitive damages, attorney's fees, and costs), and over worker's compensation appeals, regardless of the amount in controversy,[33] as well as the jurisdiction of a constitutional county court (making the amount in controversy jurisdiction extend from $200.01 to $100,000).

(2) *Probate Courts*

Read Probate Code § 3(e), (f) and (g), § 4, § 5, § 5A, § 5B.

Even the Texas Supreme Court admits that, "Texas probate jurisdiction is, to say the least, somewhat complex."[34] The constitutional county court has general probate jurisdiction,[35] but it is often delegated by statute to other courts, usually the county court at law or a statutory court that only exercises probate jurisdiction called the "probate court." One jurisdictional scheme applies for counties that have a statutory probate court (any court to which probate jurisdiction is

---

28 GOV'T CODE § 24.007(b)(as amended, effective Sept. 1, 2011). Before the amendment, there was some question concerning whether the lower limit was $200.01 or $500.01. *See* Dubai Petroleum Co. v. Kazi, 12 S.W.3d 71, 75 n.4 (Tex. 2000)(noting uncertainty about the district court's jurisdictional minimum).

29 TEX. CONST. art. V, § 2.

30 *See* Cook v. Nelius, 498 S.W.2d 455, 456 (Tex. Civ. App.—Houston [1st Dist.] 1973, no writ)(noting the civil jurisdiction of the court has not been extended by statute and dismissing the criminal case for want of jurisdiction).

31 Lord v. Clayton, 352 S.W.2d 718, 721-22 (Tex. 1962).

32 *See e.g.,* GOV'T. CODE § 25.0732 (El Paso); Comancho v. Samaniego, 831 S.W.2d 804 (Tex. 1992).

33 Thus, the amount in controversy jurisdiction of the county court at law ranges from in excess of $200 through $100,000.

34 *See* Palmer v. Coble Wall Trust Co., 851 S.W.2d 178 n.3 (Tex. 1992).

35 PROBATE CODE § 4.

delegated); another applies to those without a statutory probate court (the constitutional county court is the only one with probate jurisdiction).

(a) *Counties with No Statutory Probate Court*

In the counties in which there is no statute expressly giving probate jurisdiction to any court, the constitutional county court exercises general probate jurisdiction. Probate matters are handled in the constitutional county court until the matter becomes contested, in which case the county judge may (and on motion of a party, must) assign a sitting statutory probate judge to hear the contested matter or transfer the contested matter to the district court.[36] If the county has a county court at law in addition to the constitutional county court, the county court at law exercises both the probate jurisdiction of the constitutional county court, and the district court's jurisdiction to hear contested probate matters.[37] The court's amount in controversy jurisdiction for civil cases does not limit its probate jurisdiction.[38]

(b) *Counties with Statutory Probate Court*

In the counties in which a statute gives probate jurisdiction to a particular court, *either* that court (which is called the statutory probate court) *or* the constitutional county court may hear probate matters. But, if a probate matter filed in the constitutional county court becomes contested, the county judge may (and on motion of a party must) transfer the entire proceeding to the statutory probate court which will hear the matter as if originally filed there.[39]

(c) *Jurisdiction of the Statutory Probate Court*

All probate courts with original probate jurisdiction have "the power to hear all matters *incident to* an estate,"[40] matters in which the controlling issue is the settlement, partition, or distribution of an estate. Furthermore, the Probate Code grants to probate courts the jurisdiction to hear actions by or against a personal representative in probate, whether or not such matter is "appertaining to or incident to an estate."[41]

---

[36] PROBATE CODE § 5(b).

[37] *See* GOV'T. CODE §§ 25.0003(c)(2); 25.1863.

[38] Hailey v. Siglar, 194 S.W.3d 74 (Tex. App.—Texarkana 2006, pet. denied).

[39] *See* PROBATE CODE § 5(c).

[40] PROBATE CODE §§ 5(e), 5A; Seay v. Hall, 677 S.W.2d 19, 25 (Tex. 1984).

[41] *See* PROBATE CODE §§ 5A(b), (c), and (e). This provision was added to the Probate Code by the Legislature in response to the Supreme Court decision in Seay v. Hall, *supra*. In Palmer v. Coble Wall Trust Co., 851 S.W.2d 178 (Tex. 1992), the Texas Supreme Court held that under the amended statute, so long as a personal representative is a defendant, probate courts have jurisdiction over the matter, without respect to whether the suit is "appertaining to or incident to" an estate. *Id.* Therefore, the probate court has jurisdiction over wrongful death and survival actions brought by the decedent's estate's personal representative. The probate court also has jurisdiction over a divorce proceeding where one party to the divorce is a ward of the probate court and the proceeding directly impacts the "assimilation, distribution, and settlement" of the ward's estate through issues such as property division and child support. In re Graham, 971 S.W.2d 56 (Tex. 1998, orig. proceeding). However, the probate court does not have jurisdiction over a writ of garnishment proceeding against an heir to an estate because it is neither "incident" nor "appertaining to" the estate; the writ does not affect *how* the estate is administered, only *where* the funds should be directed. Falderbaum v. Lowe, 964 S.W.2d 744 (Tex. App.—Austin 1998, no pet.).

The probate court has "dominant jurisdiction" over any matters "appertaining to or incident to an estate pending" in that court. As a result, a claim filed in any other court that is "appertaining to or incident to" an estate under probate in the probate court is subject to dismissal upon the filing of a plea to the jurisdiction.[42] Furthermore, probate courts can transfer to themselves cases pending in other courts which are "appertaining to or incident to" an estate already under the probate court's jurisdiction or in which personal representative is a party.[43]

(3) *Eminent Domain Jurisdiction*

Read Prop. Code §§ 21.001-.003; 21.013.

The Property Code gives concurrent jurisdiction over eminent domain matters to the county court at law and the district court.[44] If the eminent domain proceeding involves a question of title or some other matter that the county court at law cannot adjudicate, the county court at law judge must transfer the case to the district court.[45] The county court at law has primary responsibility over eminent domain matters. Therefore, if the county has a county court at law, the case should be filed there.[46]

2. *Calculating Amount in Controversy*

The amount in controversy is determined by the amount that the plaintiff seeks to recover. Thus, when the jurisdictional statute values the amount in controversy on the amount of damages "alleged" by the plaintiff, the amount in controversy is determined by the pleadings. Rule 47(b) requires the petition to state that the damages sought are within the jurisdictional limits of the court, which is sufficient to put the case within the court's jurisdiction. The rule also provides that the opponent can object to the general allegation and require the pleading party to "specify the maximum amount claimed," which must be within the jurisdictional limits of the court. Or if there is no jurisdictional pleading, the court should look at the amount in controversy proved at trial.[47] All damages are included in the amount in controversy, even though some of the claimed damages are "speculative" and not likely to be recovered.[48]

---

42 *See* Speer v. Stover, 685 S.W.2d 22, 23 (Tex. 1985).

43 PROBATE CODE § 5B. *See* Gonzalez v. Reliant Energy, Inc., 159 S.W. 3d 615 (Tex. 2005) (holding probate court cannot transfer survivor action when probate court not in county of proper venue); In re SWEPI, L.P., 85 S.W.3d 800 (Tex. 2002) (finding probate court lacked authority to transfer case that was not "appertaining to or incident to" decedent's estate).

44 PROP. CODE §§ 21.001-003.

45 *See* Christian v. City of Ennis, 830 S.W.2d 326 (Tex. App.—Waco 1992, no writ) (county court at law erred in ruling on motion to strike intervention that required determination of title to real property at issue). But note that county courts at law in some counties may be given the jurisdiction to determine title to real property in eminent domain matters by statute.

46 PROP. CODE § 21.013.

47 Peek v. Equipment Service Co., 779 S.W.2d 802 (Tex. 1989).

48 *See* United Services Automobile Association v. Brite, 215 S.W.3d 400, 402 (Tex. 2007) (holding that claims for recovery of front pay are included in amount in controversy although they were speculative and not likely recoverable).

a. *Multiple Parties*

Ordinarily the claims of multiple plaintiffs against a single defendant are aggregated—the separate claims are added together to determine the amount in controversy.[49] However, aggregation should not apply to divest a court of jurisdiction on counterclaims asserted by multiple defendants.[50] On the other hand, if one plaintiff asserts separate, independent and distinct, though joinable, claims against multiple defendants, each claim is judged on its own and must independently satisfy the jurisdictional standards.[51]

b. *Other General Rules for Calculating Amount in Controversy are as follows:*

(1) Include attorney's fees and punitive damages.[52] Note, however, that Government Code §25.0003(c), which fixes minimum jurisdictions for county courts at law, and some other jurisdictional statutes *exclude* attorney's fees, penalties, and statutory or punitive damages from amount in controversy.[53]

(2) Include interest, except interest "eo nomine", interest as interest. The jurisdictional statutes specifically exclude "interest" in determining the amount in controversy.[54] However, only interest *eo nomine* is actually excluded. Interest "as damages" *is* included. Interest *eo nomine* is interest sought in litigation that is provided for by a specific agreement or a statute for the detention of money. It is considered part of the debt to be recovered, although, strangely, it is not counted as part of the amount in controversy. Interest "as damages" is interest recoverable in addition to the amount of the debt as damages resulting from the failure to pay a sum when due. Equitable pre-judgment interest is considered interest "as damages."[55]

(3) Do not include costs of court. Filing fees, deposition costs, etc., that are taxed against the losing party at the end of the litigation are not part of the amount in controversy.[56]

(4) Multiple claims. A court can assert jurisdiction over claims *below* its minimum limits when they arise from the same transaction as the primary case.[57] The converse is not true: a court cannot acquire jurisdiction over claims in excess of its maximum jurisdictional limit.

---

[49] Texas City Tire Shop, Inc. v. Alexander, 333 S.W.2d 690, 693 (Tex. Civ. App.—Houston 1960, no writ); Tejas Toyota, Inc. v. Griffin, 587 S.W.2d 775, 776 (Tex. Civ. App.—Waco 1979, writ ref'd n.r.e.); Box v. Assoc. Inv. Co., 389 S.W.2d 687, 689 (Tex. Civ. App.—Dallas 1965, no writ).

[50] Smith v. Clary Corp., 917 S.W.2d 796 (Tex. 1996).

[51] Borrego v. del Palacio, 445 S.W.2d 620, 622 (Tex. Civ. App.—El Paso 1969, no writ).

[52] *See* Bybee v. Fireman's Fund Ins. Co., 331 S.W. 2d 910 (Tex. 1960) (attorney's fees included in amount in controversy).

[53] *See* Sears, Roebuck & Co. v. Big Bend Motor Inn, Inc., 818 S.W.2d 542 (Tex. App.—Fort Worth 1991, writ denied) (attorney's fees and treble damages available under DTPA properly excluded from amount in controversy under GOV'T CODE § 25.2222 which excludes attorney's fees and "mandatory damages and penalties").

[54] *See* GOV'T CODE §§ 25.003; 26.042; 27.031.

[55] Barnes v. U.S. Fidelity and Guaranty Company, 279 S.W.2d 919, 921 (Tex. Civ. App.—Waco 1955, no writ).

[56] MCDONALD & CARLSON, TEXAS CIVIL PRACTICE § 3.26.

[57] Andel v. Eastman Kodak Company, 400 S.W.2d 584, 586 (Tex. Civ. App.—Houston 1966, no writ).

(5) Amendments increasing or decreasing claim. If the pleadings properly set out an amount in controversy within the court's jurisdictional limits, subsequent amendments *increasing or decreasing* the plaintiff's claim have no effect upon the court's jurisdiction if the increase is the result of the passage of time.[58] If, however, the amendments involve damages which could have been claimed at the time of the original filing, the amendment will defeat the court's jurisdiction. If a plaintiff has asserted a single claim, but alleged multiple theories of recovery, jurisdiction is determined by looking to the theory that would yield the largest award.[59]

(6) Non-monetary relief. Often, a suit for non-monetary relief will have no amount in controversy. Then, jurisdiction is in the district court under its residual jurisdiction.[60] When a recovery or foreclosure on property is sought in addition to monetary damages, the amount in controversy is the greater of the fair market value of the property sought or the amount of the underlying debt.

In re UNITED SERVICES AUTOMOBILE ASSOCIATION

307 S.W.3d 299

(Tex. 2010)

CHIEF JUSTICE JEFFERSON delivered the opinion of the Court.

Texas has some 3,241 trial courts[1] within its 268,580 square miles. Jurisdiction is limited in many of the courts; it is general in others. *Compare* TEX. GOV'T CODE § 25.0021 (describing jurisdiction of statutory probate court), *with id.* § 24.007-.008 (outlining district court jurisdiction); *Thomas v. Long,* 207 S.W.3d 334, 340 (Tex.2006) (noting that Texas district courts are courts of general jurisdiction). We have at least nine different types of trial courts,[3] although that number does not even hint at the complexities of the constitutional provisions and statutes that delineate jurisdiction of those courts. *See* OFFICE OF COURT ADMINISTRATION, 2008 ANNUAL REPORT, TEXAS JUDICIAL SYSTEM, SUBJECT-MATTER JURISDICTION OF THE COURTS *passim* (2008), *available at http:// www. courts. state. tx. us/ pubs/ AR 2008/ jud branch/2a-subject-matter-*

---

58 *See* Mr. W. Fireworks Inc. v. Mitchell, 622 S.W.2d 576 (Tex. 1981); Flynt v. Garcia, 587 S.W.2d 109, 110 (Tex. 1979) (additional delinquent amounts that accrued under terms of agreement from date suit filed to trial date did not oust court of jurisdiction).

59 Lucey v. Southeast Texas Emergency Physician Assn., 802 S.W.2d 300, 302 (Tex. App.—El Paso 1990, writ denied).

60 Super X Drugs, Inc. v. State, 505 S.W.2d 333, 336, (Tex. Civ. App.—Ft. Worth 1974, no writ).

1 Texas Courts Online Home Page, *http:// www. courts. state. tx. us/* (all Internet materials as visited March 24, 2010 and copy available in Clerk of Court's file). This figure includes municipal courts, whose jurisdiction is generally limited to criminal matters, although they may also hear certain civil cases involving dangerous dogs. *See* TEX. HEALTH & SAFETY CODE § 822.0421. [Editor's Note: only to determine that a dog is dangerous.] It also includes statutory probate courts.

3 Those courts include district courts, criminal district courts, constitutional county courts, statutory county courts, justice of the peace courts, small claims courts, statutory probate courts, and municipal courts. They also include family district courts which, although they are district courts of general jurisdiction, have primary responsibility for handling family law matters. OFFICE OF COURT ADMINISTRATION, 2008 ANNUAL REPORT, TEXAS JUDICIAL SYSTEM, SUBJECT-MATTER JURISDICTION OF THE COURTS 1, 3-18 (2008), *available at http:// www. courts. state. tx. us/ pubs/ AR 2008/ jud branch/2a-subject-matter-jurisdiction-of-courts.pdf.*

jurisdiction-of-courts.pdf;[4] GEORGE D. BRADEN ET AL., THE CONSTITUTION OF THE STATE OF TEXAS: AN ANNOTATED AND COMPARATIVE ANALYSIS 367 (1977). Statutory county courts (of which county courts at law are one type)[5] usually have jurisdictional limits of $100,000, *see* TEX. GOV'T CODE § 25.0003(c)(1), unless, of course, they do not, *see, e.g.,* TEX. GOV'T CODE §§ 25.0732(a) (El Paso County), 25.0862(a) (Galveston County), 25.0942(a) (Gregg County), 25.1322(a) (Kendall County), 25.1802(a) (Nueces County), 25.2142(a) (Smith County); *see also Sultan v. Mathew,* 178 S.W.3d 747, 756 (Tex. 2005) (HECHT, J., dissenting) (observing that "[m]onetary jurisdictional limits on statutory county courts are generally from $500 to $100,000, but they vary widely from county to county, and many such courts have no monetary limits"). Appellate rights can vary depending on which court a case is filed in, even among trial courts with concurrent jurisdiction, and even when the same judge in the same courtroom presides over two distinct courts. *See, e.g., Sultan,* 178 S.W.3d at 752 (holding that there was no right of appeal to courts of appeals from cases originating in small claims courts, but recognizing that justice court judgment would be appealable); *see also id.* at 754-55 (HECHT, J., dissenting) (noting that the same justice of the peace hears small claims cases and justice court cases).[6] Consider the five-step process involved in determining the jurisdiction of any particular trial court:

> [R]ecourse must be had first to the Constitution, second to the general statutes establishing jurisdiction for that level of court, third to the specific statute authorizing the establishment of the particular court in question, fourth to statutes creating other courts in the same county (whose jurisdictional provisions may affect the court in question), and fifth to statutes dealing with specific subject matters (such as the Family Code, which requires, for example, that judges who are lawyers hear appeals from actions by non-lawyer judges in juvenile cases).

OFFICE OF COURT ADMINISTRATION, SUBJECT-MATTER JURISDICTION OF THE COURTS at 1.

Our court system has been described as "one of the most complex in the United States, if not the world." BRADEN, THE CONSTITUTION OF THE STATE OF TEXAS, at 367; *see also Continental Coffee Prods. Co. v. Cazarez,* 937 S.W.2d 444, 449 (Tex. 1996) (voicing "concern[ ] over the difficulties created for the bench, the bar, and the public by the patchwork organization of Texas' several trial courts"); *Sultan,* 178 S.W.3d at 753 (HECHT, J., dissenting) (noting that Texas courts' "jurisdictional scheme . . . has gone from elaborate . . . to Byzantine"); *Camacho v. Samaniego,* 831 S.W.2d 804, 807 n. 4, 811 (Tex. 1992) (stating that "confusion and inefficiency are endemic to a judicial structure with different courts of distinct but overlapping jurisdiction" and observing that "there are still more than fifty different jurisdictional schemes for the statutory county courts"); TEXAS JUDICIAL COUNCIL, ASSESSING JUDICIAL WORKLOAD IN TEXAS' DISTRICT COURTS 2 (2001), *available at http:// www. courts. state. tx. us/ tjc/ TJC Reports/Final Report.pdf*

---

[4] In a page-and-a-half, this report explains the subject matter jurisdiction of our appellate courts. OFFICE OF COURT ADMINISTRATION, SUBJECT-MATTER JURISDICTION OF THE COURTS at 1-2. The remainder of the eighteen-page, dual column, single-spaced document identifies, in painstaking detail, the various jurisdictional schemes governing our trial courts. *Id.* at 3-18.

[5] TEX. GOV'T CODE § 21.009(2) (" 'Statutory county court' means a county court created by the legislature under Article V, Section 1, of the Texas Constitution, including county courts at law, county criminal courts, county criminal courts of appeals, and county civil courts at law, but does not include statutory probate courts as defined by Section 3, Texas Probate Code.").

[6] Section 28.053 of the Government Code, at issue in *Sultan,* was recently amended to allow appeals to the court of appeals from de novo trials in county court on claims originating in small claims court. *See* Act of June 19, 2009, 81st Leg., R.S., ch. 1351, section 8, 2009 Tex. Gen. Laws 4274, 4274.

(observing that " 'the Texas trial court system, complex from its inception, has become ever more confusing as ad hoc responses are devised to meet the needs of an urban, industrialized society' " (quoting CITIZENS' COMMISSION ON THE TEXAS JUDICIAL SYSTEM, REPORT AND RECOMMENDATIONS INTO THE TWENTY-FIRST CENTURY 17 (1993))).

Proposals to modernize this antiquated jurisdictional patchwork have failed, but the Legislature has attempted to address one of its most worrisome aspects. In 1931, the Legislature passed "[a]n act to extend the period of limitation of any action in the wrong court." Act approved Apr. 27, 1931, 42d Leg., R.S., ch. 81, 1931 Tex. Gen. Laws 124, 124, current version at TEX. CIV. PRAC. & REM. CODE § 16.064. This statute tolls limitations for those cases filed in a trial court that lacks jurisdiction, provided the case is refiled in a proper court within sixty days of dismissal. TEX. CIV. PRAC. & REM. CODE § 16.064(a). The tolling provision does not apply, however, to those cases in which the first filing was made with "intentional disregard of proper jurisdiction." *Id.* § 16.064(b). We must decide today whether the plaintiff intentionally disregarded the jurisdictional limits applicable to county courts at law in Bexar County. Because we conclude that he did, in a way that cannot be cured by ordinary appellate review, we conditionally grant relief.

I. Background

James Steven Brite sued USAA, his former employer, alleging that it had illegally discriminated against him based on his age, violating the Texas Commission on Human Rights Act (TCHRA). *See generally United Servs. Auto. Ass'n v. Brite,* 215 S.W.3d 400 (Tex.2007) (" *Brite I* "). He filed suit in the Bexar County Court at Law No. 7, which has jurisdiction concurrent with that of the district court in "civil cases in which the matter in controversy exceeds $500 but does not exceed $100,000, excluding interest, statutory or punitive damages and penalties, and attorney's fees and costs, as alleged on the face of the petition . . . ." TEX. GOV'T CODE § 25.0003(c)(1). Brite asserted in his original petition that his damages exceeded the $500 statutory minimum, but he did not plead that his damages were below the $100,000 maximum. He pleaded that "[i]n all reasonable probability, [his] loss of income and benefits will continue into the future, if not for the balance of [his] natural life" and sought "compensation due Plaintiff that accrued at the time of filing this Petition" (back pay), "the present value of unaccrued wage payments" (front pay), punitive damages, and attorney's fees. *Id.*

Before limitations expired, USAA filed a plea to the jurisdiction, contending that Brite's damage claims exceeded the $100,000 jurisdictional limit of the statutory county court, excluding interest, statutory or punitive damages, and attorney's fees and costs. USAA argued that because Brite's annual salary was almost $74,000 when he was terminated, his front pay and back pay allegations alone exceeded the county court's jurisdictional maximum. Brite opposed, and the trial court twice denied, USAA's jurisdictional plea. Shortly thereafter, Brite amended his petition to seek damages of $1.6 million, and subsequently claimed in discovery responses that " 'his lost wages and benefits in the future, until age 65, total approximately $1,000,000.00.' " After a jury trial, the trial court awarded Brite $188,406 in back pay, $350,000 in front pay, $300,000 in punitive damages, $129,387 in attorney's fees, and prejudgment interest.

A divided court of appeals affirmed the trial court's judgment. We reversed, concluding that the amount in controversy at the time Brite filed suit exceeded $100,000, depriving the county court at law of jurisdiction over the matter. We dismissed the underlying suit for want of jurisdiction.

Within sixty days of our judgment dismissing the county court case, Brite refiled his claim in Bexar County district court. [The trial court denied defendant's summary judgment motion on the statute of limitations defense and the court of appeals denied mandamus relief.] USAA now petitions this Court for mandamus relief.

* * *

IV. Was Brite's first suit filed with "intentional disregard of proper jurisdiction"?

Section 16.064 will not save a later-filed claim if the first action was filed "with intentional disregard of proper jurisdiction." TEX. CIV. PRAC. & REM. CODE § 16.064(b). USAA contends that is what happened here, while Brite asserts that a jury must decide whether he intended to evade jurisdiction, given that he vigorously denies doing so. We agree with USAA.

Noting "[t]he importance of simplifying Court procedure," the Texas Judicial Council in 1930 drafted the tolling statute. *See* SECOND ANNUAL REPORT OF THE TEXAS CIVIL JUDICIAL COUNCIL TO THE GOVERNOR AND SUPREME COURT, Bill No. 6, at 10-12 (1930). The Legislature made a single change—extending the refiling period from thirty to sixty days—and passed the bill. In its recommendation accompanying the bill, the Council noted

> [t]hat the wrong court is frequently and in good faith chosen by capable lawyers, [as] evidenced by the hundreds of cases cited in the annotations upon the subject given in Vernon's Annotated Texas Statutes, 9 pages upon Justice Court, 17 pages upon county court and 29 pages upon district court jurisdiction.

SECOND ANNUAL REPORT, at 11. The Council explained that the Texas bill was based on a Kentucky statute that tolled limitations for actions "commenced in due time and in good faith" in a court that lacked jurisdiction. *Id.* (citing CARROLL'S KY. STAT. § 2545 (1922)). The Council stated that its bill was "like that of Kentucky in substance, but . . . a definition of 'good faith' [is] supplied." *Id.* at 11-12. It is that definition that is at issue here.

As we noted in *Brite I,* "[t]he jurisdictional statute for county courts at law values the matter in controversy on the amount of damages 'alleged' by the plaintiff . . . ." *Brite I,* 215 S.W.3d at 402-03 (quoting TEX. GOV'T CODE § 25.0003(c)(1)). Here, Brite's petition omitted the statement required by our rules—that the "damages sought are within the jurisdictional limits of the court," TEX. R. CIV. P. 47(b)—and instead pleaded only that his damages exceeded $500. Brite has never contended that he was unaware of or confused about the county court's jurisdictional limitation. While such confusion would be understandable, as other statutory county courts (even those in one county adjacent to Bexar County)[10] have no such restriction, he instead argued that "the amount in controversy should not be calculated by the damages originally sued for, but instead by the amount of damages that, more likely than not, the plaintiff would recover." *Brite I,* 215 S.W.3d at 402. We rejected that argument, concluding that "[t]he amount in controversy in this case exceeded $100,000 at the time Brite filed suit."

The parties disagree about the proper standard for intentional disregard under the tolling statute, which requires that USAA "show[ ] in abatement that the first filing was made with intentional disregard of proper jurisdiction." TEX. CIV. PRAC. & REM. CODE § 16.064(b). Brite contends that intent is always a fact issue, inappropriate for resolution on summary judgment, while USAA asserts it has met its burden through circumstantial evidence of Brite's intent and that Brite is charged with knowledge of the law. We have never before addressed this issue.

---

[10] *See* TEX. GOV'T CODE § 25.1322(a) (providing that county courts at law in Kendall County have concurrent jurisdiction with the district court); *see also* TEXAS ALMANAC 2010-11, at 221, 306.

We agree, in part, with USAA. Once an adverse party has moved for relief under the "intentional disregard" provision, the nonmovant must show that he did not intentionally disregard proper jurisdiction when filing the case. As it is the nonmovant who has this information, he should bear the burden of producing it.

We disagree, however, that a plaintiff's mistake about the court's jurisdiction would never satisfy the requirement. Section 16.064's intent standard is similar to that required for setting aside a default judgment, *see Craddock v. Sunshine Bus Lines, Inc.,* 134 Tex. 388, 133 S.W.2d 124, 126 (1939) (requiring new trial if defendant proves three elements, the first of which is that default was neither intentional nor due to conscious indifference), and we have held that a mistake of law may be a sufficient excuse. Moreover, section 16.064 was drafted precisely because "capable lawyers" often make "good faith" mistakes about the jurisdiction of Texas courts.

But while the tolling statute protects plaintiffs who mistakenly file suit in a forum that lacks jurisdiction, it does not apply to a strategic decision to seek relief from such a court-which is what happened here. Because Brite unquestionably sought damages in excess of the county court at law's jurisdiction, it matters not that he subjectively anticipated a verdict within the jurisdictional limits. For that reason, limitations was not tolled. His second suit, filed long after the expiration of the two year statute, is therefore barred.

V. Is USAA entitled to mandamus relief?

Finally, we must decide whether mandamus relief is appropriate. Deciding whether the benefits of mandamus outweigh the detriments requires us to weigh public and private interests, recognizing that-rather than categorical determinations—"the adequacy of an appeal depends on the facts involved in each case." *In re McAllen Med. Ctr., Inc.,* 275 S.W.3d 458, 469 (Tex. 2008); *In re The Prudential Ins. Co. of Am.,* 148 S.W.3d 124, 136-37 (Tex. 2004).

In *CSR Ltd. v. Link,* 925 S.W.2d 591, 596-97 (Tex. 1996), we conditionally granted mandamus relief ordering the trial court to grant CSR's special appearance in a toxic tort case. We held that "extraordinary circumstances" (namely the enormous number of potential claimants and the most efficient use of the state's judicial resources) warranted extraordinary relief, even though it was typically unavailable for the denial of a special appearance.

And although "mandamus is generally unavailable when a trial court denies summary judgment, no matter how meritorious the motion," that rule is based in part on the fact that "trying a case in which summary judgment would have been appropriate does not mean the case will have to be tried twice"—a justification not applicable here. USAA has already endured one trial in a forum that lacked jurisdiction (and then a subsequent appeal to the court of appeals and this Court) and is facing a second trial on a claim that we have just held to be barred by limitations. Two wasted trials are not "[t]he most efficient use of the state's judicial resources." Denying mandamus relief here would thwart the legislative intent that non-tolled TCHRA claims be brought within two years (as well as the tolling provision's inapplicability to suits filed with intentional disregard of proper jurisdiction), and we should not "frustrate th[at] purpose[ ] by a too-strict application of our own procedural devices."

Because the extraordinary circumstances presented here merit extraordinary relief, we conditionally grant the writ and direct the trial court to grant USAA's motion for summary judgment. We are confident the trial court will comply, and our writ will issue only if it does not.

---

3. *Procedure for Raising Lack of Subject Matter Jurisdiction*

a. *Plea to the Jurisdiction*

It is astounding that the subject matter jurisdiction of the trial courts is so difficult to determine when the consequences are so important—a court without subject matter jurisdiction has no power to act and any actions taken are void. The proper challenge to a court's subject matter jurisdiction is a "plea to the jurisdiction,"[61] not a "motion to dismiss", as in federal court. A motion for summary judgment may also be used to raise lack of subject matter jurisdiction.[62] Because a court without subject matter jurisdiction has no power over the controversy, subject matter jurisdiction can be raised at any time, by the parties or by the court. The court must dismiss the case because it has no power to do anything else. If the case was filed in the wrong court in good faith, the statute of limitations is tolled for 60 days from the date of dismissal to allow the plaintiff to refile in the proper court.[63]

b. *Appeal/Mandamus*

Plaintiff can appeal from a trial court's determination of lack of subject matter jurisdiction and the resultant dismissal and, if successful, the appellate court will remand for a full trial. If, however, the trial court erroneously asserts jurisdiction, defendant's only remedy is an appeal after final judgment, except that "governmental units" asserting immunity are allowed an interlocutory appeal by statute.[64] The Texas Supreme Court has held that mandamus is not available for review of a trial court's determination of subject matter jurisdiction before a trial on the merits.[65] But the mandamus standards have changed, and mandamus might be allowed in the appropriate case.[66]

c. *No Waiver*

Subject matter jurisdiction is unusual in that it cannot be waived. It can be raised for the first time on appeal or, even later, when the judgment is being attacked collaterally (in a separate proceeding). This is sometimes called "fundamental error." A court lacking jurisdiction over subject matter has no power over the controversy and must dismiss. Unless there is some statutory scheme involving subordinate and dominant jurisdictions (e.g., eminent domain[67] and probate[68] jurisdiction), a court without jurisdiction may not transfer the case, but can only dismiss so that the case can be refiled.

---

61 *See* Rule 85.

62 Thomas v. Long, 207 S.W.3d 334 (Tex. 2006).

63 CPRC § 16.064.

64 *See* CPRC § 51.014(8) (1997 amendment). Moreover, immunity from suit, an issue of subject matter jurisdiction, can be raised for the first time in an interlocutory appeal. Rusk County State Hospital v. Black, 392 S.W.3d 88 (Tex. 2012).

65 Bell Helicopter Textron Inc. v. Walker, 787 S.W.2d 954, 955 (Tex. 1990). *But see* Geary v. Peavy, 878 S.W.2d 607 (Tex. 1994); In re Graham, 971S.W.2d 56 (Tex. 1998, orig. proceeding) (competing jurisdiction in family law disputes addressed by mandamus).

66 *See* In re McAllen Med. Ctr., Inc., 275 S.W.3d 458, 469 (2008).

67 PROP. CODE § 21.001.

68 PROP. CODE § 5b.

4. *Standing, Ripeness and Immunity*

Subject matter jurisdiction is not limited to issues concerning whether the type of case and amount in controversy fit the limits set out in the court's creating statute. A court does not have subject matter jurisdiction when the plaintiff lacks standing, when the suit is not yet ripe for decision, and when the defendant is immune from suit (as distinguished from immune from liability). Often, these issues involve complex factual inquiries far different from the amount in controversy type issues.

5. *Cases Filed in the Texas Courts*

What kinds of civil cases are filed in the Texas courts? First of all, the numbers are again increasing after a short period of decreasing filings. The 2017 annual report of the Office of Court Administration[69] reports that in 2014, 1,415,000 new civil cases were added to the dockets of the state's courts. Approximately 75% of these new cases were filed in the municipal and justice Family law cases (including divorce proceedings) comprised one-half of the civil caseload.

Of civil cases filed in district courts (excluding those related to criminal matters) in 2017, 27% were tax collection cases. 21% were debt and contract cases, and 22% injury or damage cases. How many of these civil cases went to trial? In 2017, overall, only 0.6% of civil cases went to a jury and 10% were tried to a judge without a jury.

About 10,000appeals were filed in the courts of appeals, more than half of them civil cases, in 2017. The Supreme Court of Texas disposed of 910 petitions for review in 2017, and granted only 13% of them.

Problems

What court or courts have jurisdiction in the following situations? Explain your answer.

1.(a) A landlord wants to evict a tenant for nonpayment of rent and to recover $12,000 in rent owed.

(b) If filed in justice court, what happens if the alleged tenant responds that she is the owner of the property and the alleged landlord has no right to the property?

2. A divorce action with an estate worth no more than $500.

3. A creditor wants to file suit to recover a debt of $400 and to foreclose on the automobile that is worth $20,000 that secures the debt.

4. Trespass to try title action. (*See* Rules 783-809. What is the purpose of this special proceeding?)

5. The plaintiff alleges that he was bitten by the defendant's dog. The plaintiff files suit to recover $300 for medical expenses and to enjoin the defendant from letting the dog out.

---

[69] Found at www.txcourts.gov.

6. Two plaintiffs, each suing to recover $20,000 (two separate debts) against a single defendant.

7. In a class action, each of 50 named plaintiffs (purporting to represent a class of 10,000 plaintiffs) claims $200 damages from a single defendant.

8. A single plaintiff sues two defendants for $4500 each (two promissory notes).

9.(a) A creditor sues to recover the amount due under the terms of a promissory note. She seeks to recover $495 principal; $50 interest charged until the date the debt was due as provided in the note; $1000 interest from the date the note was due until suit was filed; and $1000 attorney's fees.

(b) Does your answer change if the case doesn't go to trial for another 4 years and immediately before trial the plaintiff amends her pleadings to seek another $3000 in interest that has accrued during the time the case has been pending and an additional $1000 in attorney's fees that have accrued during this time?

10.(a) The county wants to put a road through a piece of property. The county has offered $10,000 for the property it seeks to condemn, but the owner has refused, claiming the property is worth more.

(b) Does your answer change if everyone agrees that the property is worth $10,000, but there is a dispute over who gets the money because two parties each claim that they own the property?

11.(a) Probate of a will.

(b) If one of the assets of the estate is the deceased's survival action concerning the accident in which he died, where can that action be tried?

(c) The beneficiaries of the will want to file suit against the personal representative of the estate for fraud committed against the estate.

B. Judges in Texas

1. *Judicial Administration*

The Texas Supreme Court has constitutional responsibility for the efficient administration of the judicial system and possesses the authority to make rules of administration applicable to the courts.[1] Under the direction of the chief justice, the Office of Court Administration aids the Supreme Court in carrying out its administrative duties by providing administrative support and technical assistance to all courts in the state.

The chief justice of the Supreme Court, presiding judge of the Court of Criminal Appeals, chief justices of each of the 14 courts of appeals, and judges of each of the trial courts are generally responsible for the administration of their respective courts. Furthermore, there is a local administrative district judge in each county, as well as a local administrative statutory county court judge in each county that has a statutory county court. In counties with two or more district courts, a local administrative district judge is elected by the district judges in the county for a term not to exceed two years.[2] Similarly, in counties with two or more statutory county courts, a local administrative statutory county court judge is elected by the statutory county court judges for a term not to exceed two years. The local administrative judge is charged with implementing the local rules of administration, supervising the expeditious movement of court caseloads, and other administrative duties.[3]

In addition to these locally elected administrative judges, the Governor, with the advice and consent of the Senate, appoints presiding judges for each of nine administrative judicial regions to aid in the administration of the trial courts of the state. A map of the administrative regions appears on the next page. The appointed presiding judge must be one of the active or retired district judges in the region, or a retired appellate court judge who has district court experience residing in each region. The presiding judge of an administrative judicial region may assign a judge to handle a case or docket of an active judge in the region who is unable to preside (due to recusal, illness, vacation, etc.) or who needs assistance with a heavy docket or docket backlog. These "assigned judges" may be active judges of other courts in the region or may be individuals residing in the region who used to serve as active judges.[4]

The chief justice of the Supreme Court may convene periodic conferences of the chief justices of the courts of appeals, as well as periodic conferences of the nine presiding judges to ensure the efficient administration of justice in the courts of the state.

---

1 TEX. CONST., art. V, §31.

2 GOV'T CODE, §§74.091, 74.0911.

3 GOV'T CODE, §74.092 (detailing administrative responsibilities of local administrative judge).

4 GOV'T CODE, §§74.054, 74.056, 74.057 (discussing assignment of judges).

Administrative Judicial Regions

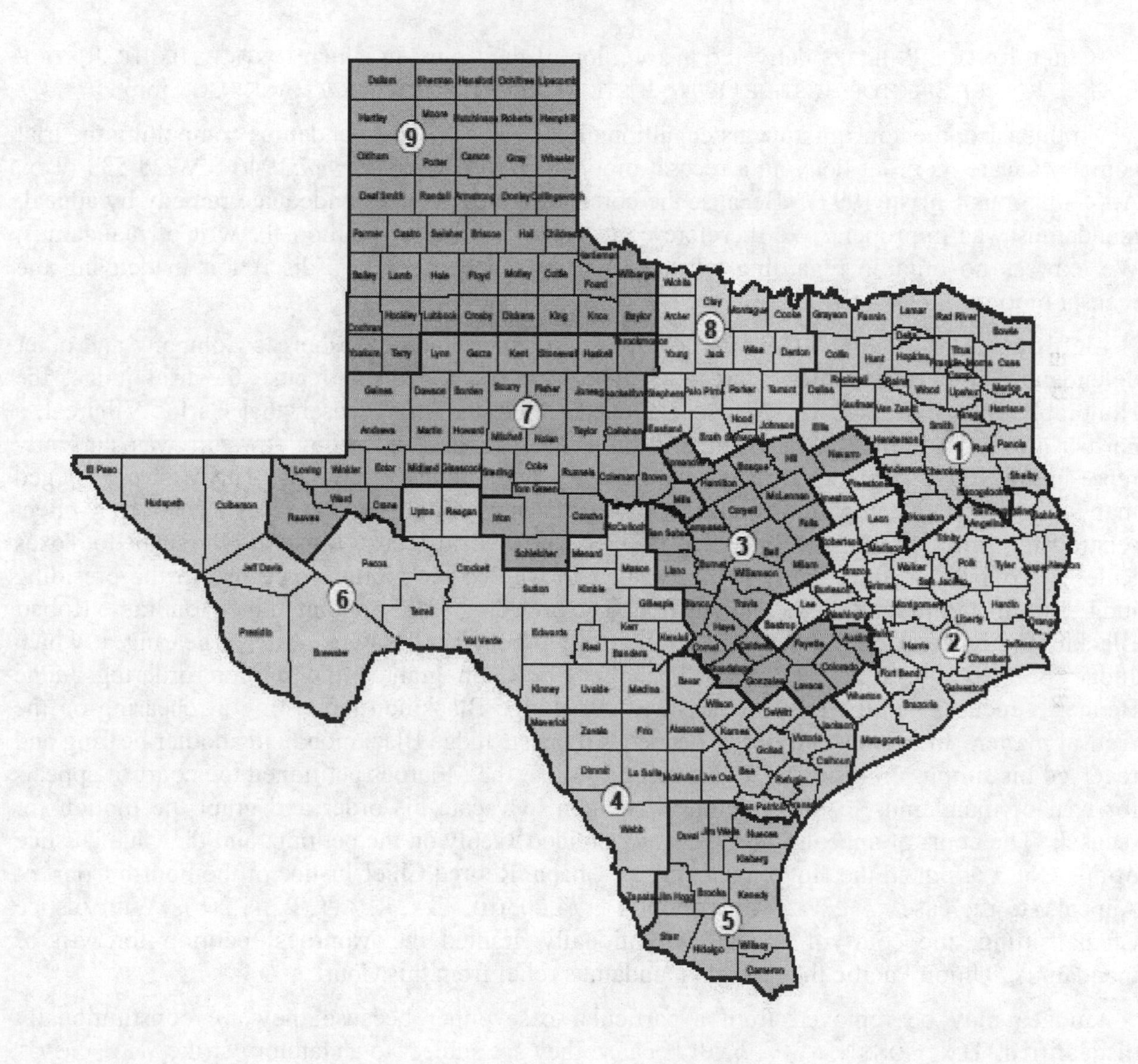

2. *Disqualification and Recusal*

Read Rule 18a, 18b; Tex. Const. Art. V., § 11; Gov't Code § 74.053; CPRC § 30.016.

In Re UNION PACIFIC RESOURCES COMPANY
969 S.W.2d 427
(Tex. 1998)

CHIEF JUSTICE PHILLIPS delivered the opinion of the Court, in which JUSTICE HECHT, JUSTICE ENOCH, JUSTICE SPECTOR, JUSTICE OWEN, JUSTICE ABBOTT, and JUSTICE HANKINSON join.

In this case, the court of appeals conditionally issued a writ of mandamus compelling the trial court to vacate its order denying a recusal motion. *Monroe v. Blackmon*, 946 S.W.2d 533 (Tex. App.—Corpus Christi 1997). Because the complaining party has an adequate remedy by appeal, mandamus was improper. We therefore conditionally grant the petition for writ of mandamus. We express no opinion regarding whether the trial court abused its discretion in denying the recusal motion.

Jeffrey Lee Monroe and Gena Jo Monroe sued Union Pacific Resources Company and other defendants for personal injury damages. The Monroes moved to recuse the trial judge, the Honorable Max Bennett. The Monroes alleged, as grounds for recusal, that Carlos Villareal, a partner in the law firm representing Union Pacific in the underlying lawsuit, was currently representing Judge Bennett, in his official capacity, in an unrelated lawsuit. The Monroes alleged that Judge Bennett's impartiality might reasonably be questioned because of the attorney-client relationship with Mr. Villareal. Judge Bennett declined to recuse himself. Pursuant to Texas Rule of Civil Procedure 18a(d) Judge Bennett forwarded the motion to recuse to the presiding judge for the administrative judicial district. The presiding judge appointed the Honorable Robert Blackmon, Nueces County district judge, to hear the recusal motion. After a hearing at which Judge Bennett appeared and testified, Judge Blackmon granted the motion ordering Judge Bennett's recusal. Judge Bennett then wrote to Judge Blackmon requesting a rehearing on the recusal matter. In response to Judge Bennett's request, Judge Blackmon held another hearing and reversed his ruling. In response to this second ruling, the Monroes petitioned the court of appeals for writ of mandamus to direct Judge Blackmon to vacate his order and grant the motion for recusal. The court of appeals sitting en banc divided evenly on the petition, and the Chief Justice of this Court assigned the Honorable Alfonso Chapa, Retired Chief Justice of the Fourth Court of Appeals, to the case. *See* TEX. GOV'T CODE § 74.003(b); TEX. R. APP. P. 41.2(b). With Justice Chapa sitting, the court of appeals conditionally granted the Monroes' petition for writ of mandamus. Union Pacific then sought mandamus relief from this Court.

Judges may be removed from a particular case either because they are constitutionally disqualified, TEX. CONST. art. V, § 11, because they are subject to a statutory strike, TEX. GOV'T CODE § 74.053(d), or because they are recused under rules promulgated by this Court. TEX. R. CIV. P. 18a, 18b; TEX. R. APP. P. 16. The grounds and procedures for each type of removal are fundamentally different. *See generally* Kilgarlin & Bruch, *Disqualification and Recusal of Judges*, 17 ST. MARY'S L.J. 599 (1986). When a judge continues to sit in violation of a constitutional proscription, mandamus is available to compel the judge's mandatory disqualification without a showing that the relator lacks an adequate remedy by appeal. This makes sense, because any orders or judgments rendered by a judge who is constitutionally disqualified are void and without effect. Likewise, on timely objection, the disqualification of an assigned judge who is not a retired judge is mandatory under section 74.053(d) of the Texas Government Code and any orders entered by a trial judge in a case in which he is disqualified are void. Therefore, the objecting party is also entitled to mandamus relief without a showing that there is no adequate remedy by appeal.

In contrast, the erroneous denial of a recusal motion does not void or nullify the presiding judge's subsequent acts. While a judgment rendered in such circumstances may be reversed on appeal, it is not fundamental error and can be waived if not raised by proper motion. Recognizing this distinction, our Rules of Civil Procedure expressly provide for appellate review from a final judgment after denial of a recusal motion. *See* TEX. R. CIV. P. 18a(f). If the appellate court determines that the judge presiding over the recusal hearing abused his or her discretion in denying the motion and the trial judge should have been recused, the appellate court can cure any harm by reversing the trial court's judgment and remanding for a new trial before a different judge. This procedure is no different than the correction of any trial court error through the normal appellate process. As we have observed, "an appellate remedy is not inadequate merely because it may involve more expense or delay than obtaining an extraordinary writ . . . . [T]he 'delay in getting questions decided through the appellate process . . . will not justify intervention by appellate courts through the extraordinary writ of mandamus.' " *Walker v. Packer*, 827 S.W.2d 833, 842 (Tex. 1992).

The court of appeals abused its discretion by issuing writ of mandamus when the complaining party has an adequate remedy by appeal. *See* TEX. R. CIV. P. 18a(f). We therefore conditionally grant the petition for writ of mandamus and direct the court of appeals to withdraw its order conditionally granting writ of mandamus against the trial court. TEX. GOV'T CODE § 22.002(a).

JUSTICE HECHT delivered a concurring opinion.

JUSTICE GONZALEZ did not participate in the decision.

Notes & Questions

1. *Constitutional Disqualification*. TEX. CONST. art. V, § 11 provides: "No judge shall sit in any case wherein he may be interested, or where either of the parties may be connected with him, either by affinity or consanguinity, within such a degree as may be prescribed by law, or when he shall have been counsel in the case." Should any of these situations arise, the judge is said to be constitutionally disqualified from sitting. Notice that the disqualification standards set out in Rule 18b(1) are identical to those stated in the Constitution. Any order involving judicial discretion by a constitutionally disqualified judge is "absolutely void" or a "nullity."[1] Thus, disqualification cannot be waived, and can be raised at any point in the proceeding, for the first time on appeal, or by collaterally attacking the order issued by the disqualified judge. Grounds for disqualification are narrow and seldom invoked.

2. *Recusal*. The rules provide for broader grounds for removing a judge called "recusal." Actually, Rule 18b contains grounds for both disqualification and recusal. The grounds for recusal, set out in Rule 18b(2) are different from those for disqualification. For instance, a judge who is biased or prejudiced concerning the subject matter or a party involved in a proceeding is

---

[1] Freedom Communications, Inc. v. Coronado, 372 S.W.3d 621, 624 (Tex. 2012); Buckholts Indep. School Dist. v. Glaser, 632 S.W.2d 146, 148 (Tex. 1982).

not *disqualified,* but the bias or prejudice may be grounds for recusal. The orders rendered by a trial judge who should be recused are not void—they are simply reviewable on appeal. And recusal, unlike disqualification, may be waived.

3. *Statutory strikes*. Judges may also be disqualified from sitting if a party files a proper statutory strike under § 74.053 of the Texas Government Code. This statutory strike may be used only to disqualify a retired or former judge who has been assigned to a particular court as a visiting judge—a judge assigned to hear matters filed in a court to which the judge has not been elected or appointed.

4. *Procedure.* Rule 18a contains the procedure that must be followed when filing a motion for disqualification or recusal. Read it carefully. Remember, for non-constitutional "recusals," not constitutional "disqualifications," any complaint is waived if not made timely in writing.[2] Also note that after a motion is filed, if the judge refuses to voluntarily recuse himself or herself from the case, the judge under attack must request the presiding judge to assign another judge to hear the motion.[3] Except for "good cause," the judge may take no further action in the case once the motion is filed until after the motion has been resolved in favor of allowing the judge to proceed. Because trial procedures stop, a frivolous recusal motion may be used as a stalling mechanism. To limit this tactic, CPRC § 30.016 allows a judge to continue to preside over a case after a tertiary (third or subsequent) recusal motion. (The statute is invoked whether the motion is the first against a third new judge or the third against the same judge.)[4] In this situation, the parties go forward with simultaneous "parallel" proceedings: both the trial in the primary cause of action and the recusal/disqualification hearing. If it is found that that the judge should be recused, what happens in the trial court? It is likely that the trial proceeding must be started over.

5. *Availability of mandamus.* What is "mandamus" and why might a party seek mandamus? We will address that issue more broadly later. But be sure that you understand what *In re Union Pacific* holds with respect to mandamus in the context of disqualification and recusal.

6. *Judge Bennett's mandamus proceeding.* The mandamus proceeding in which the Hunt Hermansen firm represented Judge Bennett raises another interesting event in Texas procedure. Here is what happened: Counsel represented approximately 700 Peruvian plaintiffs claiming injuries from exposure to toxic gases and chemicals, and filed 17 lawsuits in Nueces County. Each petition named different groups of plaintiffs, and each was randomly assigned to one of the eight district courts in the county. The first was assigned to Judge Bennett's court; the last (and only the last) was assigned to the 105th. Two hours later, counsel filed an amended petition in the 105th adding approximately 700 plaintiffs and instructed the clerk to issue citation for service upon the defendants in that case. Five days later counsel filed motions to nonsuit the other 16 lawsuits. Judge Bennett did not sign the order of nonsuit in the case pending in his court, but instead signed a "Sua Sponte Order Abating Dismissal and Setting Hearing on Transfer,

---

[2] Pettit v. Laware, 715 S.W.2d 688 (Tex. Civ. App.—Houston 1986, writ ref'd n.r.e.); Buckholts Indep. School Dist. v. Glaser, 632 S.W.2d 146 (Tex. 1982).

[3] Rule 18a (c) and (d); McLeod v. Harris, 582 S.W.2d 772 (Tex. 1979). The "presiding judge" has administrative duties over the courts in the administrative judicial region. *See* Court Administration Act, GOV'T. CODE §§ 74.001 et seq. The presiding judge is appointed by the Governor. *See* State Bar of Texas, *Court Administration Task Force Report,* Oct. 2008, http://www.texasbar.com/Content/ContentGroups/Judiciary/Supreme_Court_of_Texas/Court_Administration_Task_Force_Report.htm (recommending changes to method of selection of presiding judge).

[4] As an additional disincentive: the party making the tertiary motion will be assessed the opposing party's costs and attorney's fees if the motion is denied. CPRC § 30.016(c).

Consolidation and Sanctions." Meanwhile, the defendants removed all of the cases to federal court where they were dismissed on grounds of forum non conveniens. Nevertheless, Judge Bennett held his sanctions hearing, and ordered plaintiffs' counsel to pay $10,000 each as sanctions for abusing the judicial process. The San Antonio Court of Appeals overturned the sanctions order, holding that Judge Bennett did not have the power to sanction after the motion for nonsuit was filed. The Texas Supreme Court reversed, upholding the sanctions order.[5]

7. *"Interested" judge.* A judge is "interested" in a case, and thus constitutionally disqualified, "if an order or judgment in the case will directly 'affect him to his personal or pecuniary loss or gain.' "[6] The court further noted that, even in cases where a judge may not be legally subject to disqualification, the judge's "sense of propriety" is often a good reason for voluntary recusal.

8. *After-acquired knowledge.* Suppose you try a case against X Company before Judge Snarley. You lose and a judgment is rendered against your client, Y Company, for $100,000. No appeal is taken and the judgment becomes final. Six months later, you learn that Judge Snarley owned 60 shares of X Company at the time of trial. Is there anything you can do at this late date? The judge is "interested" and thus constitutionally disqualified. Therefore, the judgment is "absolutely void," "a nullity," and may be collaterally attacked.[8] However, this consequence does not attach to recusals based on non-constitutional grounds, and they may be waived by failure to timely protest. What is to be done if a non-constitutional basis for recusal is discovered after the trial is completed? For instance, what if it was determined after judgment that the trial judge was the first cousin to a party's attorney, and related to that attorney's client "in the fourth degree?"[9] Should the opponent be given the opportunity to raise it at that time? Should such a situation be excepted from the time periods mandated in Rule 18b? What if the lawsuit was pending in a rural county with a small population, and the parties had been in business together for almost 50 years?[10] Do you see any problem with allowing a party to raise such a point after the trial is completed?

9. *Judge as counsel in the case.* The disqualification affecting a judge who has been a counsel in the case operates to disqualify a judge whose law firm has been a counsel while he was a member.[11]

10. *Proof of judicial bias.* Bias relevant to recusal must be from an extra-judicial source. That is, it cannot be proven from the judge's conduct during the case in which the question is raised.[12]

---

5 *See* In Re Bennett, 960 S.W.2d 35 (Tex. 1997).

6 Freedom Communications, Inc. v. Coronado, 372 S.W.3d 621, 624 (Tex. 2012) (holding that a judge who took a bribe for denying defendant's motion for summary judgment was "interested" and constitutionally disqualified). *See also* Rio Grande Valley Gas Co. v. City of Pharr, 962 S.W.2d 631 (Tex. App.—Corpus Christi 1997, petition dism'd w.o.j.) (holding that the judge's status as taxpayer alone is not sufficient to rise to the level of interest necessary for constitutional disqualification).

8 *See* Fry v. Tucker, 202 S.W.2d 218 (Tex. 1947).

9 *See* Sun Exploration and Production Co. v. Jackson, 783 S.W.2d 202 (Tex. 1989)(SPEARS, J. concurring)(stating that the trial judge who was related to each of the defendants in the fourth degree should have disclosed the familial relationships).

10 *Id.* (GONZALEZ, J. concurring).

11 Tesco American, Inc. v. Strong Industries, Inc., 221 S.W.3d 550 (Tex. 2006); In re O'Connor, 92 S.W. 3d 446 (Tex. 2002).

11. *Degrees of kinship—consanguinity (blood relatives).* Under Rule 18b(1)(c) and (2)(g), the judge may not be related to a party by affinity (marriage) or consanguinity (blood) within the third degree nor to an attorney in the case within the first degree.[13]

12. *Degrees of kinship—affinity (relatives by marriage).* The judge and the judge's spouse are related by affinity in the first degree, but other relationships are treated as if the judge had the same relatives as the spouse. So, if the spouse and X are related in the third degree of consanguinity (that is, by blood), then the judge and X are related in the third degree of affinity.[14]

CAPERTON
v.
A. T. MASSEY COAL COMPANY, INC.

United States Supreme Court
129 S.Ct. 2252 (2009)

JUSTICE KENNEDY delivered the opinion of the Court.

In this case the Supreme Court of Appeals of West Virginia reversed a trial court judgment, which had entered a jury verdict of $50 million. Five justices heard the case, and the vote to reverse was 3 to 2. The question presented is whether the Due Process Clause of the Fourteenth Amendment was violated when one of the justices in the majority denied a recusal motion. The basis for the motion was that the justice had received campaign contributions in an extraordinary amount from, and through the efforts of, the board chairman and principal officer of the corporation found liable for the damages.

Under our precedents there are objective standards that require recusal when "the probability of actual bias on the part of the judge or decision maker is too high to be constitutionally tolerable." Applying those precedents, we find that, in all the circumstances of this case, due process requires recusal.

I

In August 2002 a West Virginia jury returned a verdict that found respondents A. T. Massey Coal Co. and its affiliates (hereinafter Massey) liable for fraudulent misrepresentation, concealment, and tortious interference with existing contractual relations. The jury awarded petitioners Hugh Caperton, Harman Development Corp., Harman Mining Corp., and Sovereign Coal Sales (hereinafter Caperton) the sum of $50 million in compensatory and punitive damages.

In June 2004 the state trial court denied Massey's post-trial motions challenging the verdict and the damages award, finding that Massey "intentionally acted in utter disregard of [Caperton's] rights and ultimately destroyed [Caperton's] businesses because, after conducting cost-benefit analyses, [Massey] concluded it was in its financial interest to do so." In March 2005 the trial court denied Massey's motion for judgment as a matter of law.

---

[12] *See* Dow Chem. Co. v. Francis, 46 S.W.3d 237 (Tex. 2001) (judicial remarks during trial ordinarily do not support bias or impartiality challenge); Grider v. Boston Co., 773 S.W.2d 338 (Tex. App.—Dallas 1989, writ den.).

[13] GOV'T CODE § 573.025.

[14] *Id.*

Don Blankenship is Massey's chairman, chief executive officer, and president. After the verdict but before the appeal, West Virginia held its 2004 judicial elections. Knowing the Supreme Court of Appeals of West Virginia would consider the appeal in the case, Blankenship decided to support an attorney who sought to replace Justice McGraw. Justice McGraw was a candidate for reelection to that court. The attorney who sought to replace him was Brent Benjamin.

In addition to contributing the $1,000 statutory maximum to Benjamin's campaign committee, Blankenship donated almost $2.5 million to "And For The Sake Of The Kids," a political organization formed under 26 U. S. C. §527. The §527 organization opposed McGraw and supported Benjamin. Blankenship's donations accounted for more than two-thirds of the total funds it raised. This was not all. Blankenship spent, in addition, just over $500,000 on independent expenditures-for direct mailings and letters soliciting donations as well as television and newspaper advertisements-" 'to support … Brent Benjamin.' "

To provide some perspective, Blankenship's $3 million in contributions were more than the total amount spent by all other Benjamin supporters and three times the amount spent by Benjamin's own committee. *Id.,* at 288a. Caperton contends that Blankenship spent $1 million more than the total amount spent by the campaign committees of both candidates combined. Brief for Petitioners 28.

Benjamin won. He received 382,036 votes (53.3%), and McGraw received 334,301 votes (46.7%). App. 677a.

In October 2005, before Massey filed its petition for appeal in West Virginia's highest court, Caperton moved to disqualify now-Justice Benjamin under the Due Process Clause and the West Virginia Code of Judicial Conduct, based on the conflict caused by Blankenship's campaign involvement. Justice Benjamin denied the motion in April 2006. He indicated that he "carefully considered the bases and accompanying exhibits proffered by the movants." But he found "no objective information . . . to show that this Justice has a bias for or against any litigant, that this Justice has prejudged the matters which comprise this litigation, or that this Justice will be anything but fair and impartial." *Id.,* at 336a-337a. In December 2006 Massey filed its petition for appeal to challenge the adverse jury verdict. The West Virginia Supreme Court of Appeals granted review.

In November 2007 that court reversed the $50 million verdict against Massey. The majority opinion, authored by then-Chief Justice Davis and joined by Justices Benjamin and Maynard, found that "Massey's conduct warranted the type of judgment rendered in this case." It reversed, nevertheless, based on two independent grounds-first, that a forum-selection clause contained in a contract to which Massey was not a party barred the suit in West Virginia, and, second, that res judicata barred the suit due to an out-of-state judgment to which Massey was not a party. *Id.,* at 345a. Justice Starcher dissented, stating that the "majority's opinion is morally and legally wrong." Justice Albright also dissented, accusing the majority of "misapplying the law and introducing sweeping 'new law' into our jurisprudence that may well come back to haunt us."

Caperton sought rehearing, and the parties moved for disqualification of three of the five justices who decided the appeal. Photos had surfaced of Justice Maynard vacationing with Blankenship in the French Riviera while the case was pending. Justice Maynard granted Caperton's recusal motion. On the other side Justice Starcher granted Massey's recusal motion, apparently based on his public criticism of Blankenship's role in the 2004 elections. In his recusal memorandum Justice Starcher urged Justice Benjamin to recuse himself as well. He noted that "Blankenship's bestowal of his personal wealth, political tactics, and 'friendship' have created a cancer in the affairs of this Court." Justice Benjamin declined Justice Starcher's suggestion and denied Caperton's recusal motion.

The court granted rehearing. Justice Benjamin, now in the capacity of acting chief justice, selected Judges Cookman and Fox to replace the recused justices. Caperton moved a third time for disqualification, arguing that Justice Benjamin had failed to apply the correct standard under West Virginia law-*i.e.*, whether "a reasonable and prudent person, knowing these objective facts, would harbor doubts about Justice Benjamin's ability to be fair and impartial." Caperton also included the results of a public opinion poll, which indicated that over 67% of West Virginians doubted Justice Benjamin would be fair and impartial. Justice Benjamin again refused to withdraw, noting that the "push poll" was "neither credible nor sufficiently reliable to serve as the basis for an elected judge's disqualification."

In April 2008 a divided court again reversed the jury verdict, and again it was a 3-to-2 decision. Justice Davis filed a modified version of his prior opinion, repeating the two earlier holdings. She was joined by Justice Benjamin and Judge Fox. Justice Albright, joined by Judge Cookman, dissented: "Not only is the majority opinion unsupported by the facts and existing case law, but it is also fundamentally unfair. Sadly, justice was neither honored nor served by the majority." The dissent also noted "genuine due process implications arising under federal law" with respect to Justice Benjamin's failure to recuse himself.

Four months later-a month after the petition for writ of certiorari was filed in this Court-Justice Benjamin filed a concurring opinion. He defended the merits of the majority opinion as well as his decision not to recuse. He rejected Caperton's challenge to his participation in the case under both the Due Process Clause and West Virginia law. Justice Benjamin reiterated that he had no " ' direct, personal, substantial, pecuniary interest' in this case.' Adopting "a standard merely of 'appearances,' " he concluded, "seems little more than an invitation to subject West Virginia's justice system to the vagaries of the day-a framework in which predictability and stability yield to supposition, innuendo, half-truths, and partisan manipulations."

II

It is axiomatic that "[a] fair trial in a fair tribunal is a basic requirement of due process." As the Court has recognized, however, "most matters relating to judicial disqualification [do] not rise to a constitutional level." The early and leading case on the subject is *Tumey* v. *Ohio*, 273 U. S. 510 (1927). There, the Court stated that "matters of kinship, personal bias, state policy, remoteness of interest, would seem generally to be matters merely of legislative discretion."

The *Tumey* Court concluded that the Due Process Clause incorporated the common-law rule that a judge must recuse himself when he has "a direct, personal, substantial, pecuniary interest" in a case. This rule reflects the maxim that "[n]o man is allowed to be a judge in his own cause; because his interest would certainly bias his judgment, and, not improbably, corrupt his integrity." Under this rule, "disqualification for bias or prejudice was not permitted"; those matters were left to statutes and judicial codes. Personal bias or prejudice "alone would not be sufficient basis for imposing a constitutional requirement under the Due Process Clause."

As new problems have emerged that were not discussed at common law, however, the Court has identified additional instances which, as an objective matter, require recusal. These are circumstances "in which experience teaches that the probability of actual bias on the part of the judge or decision maker is too high to be constitutionally tolerable."

* * *

III

. . . This problem arises in the context of judicial elections, a framework not presented in the precedents we have reviewed and discussed.

Caperton contends that Blankenship's pivotal role in getting Justice Benjamin elected created a constitutionally intolerable probability of actual bias. Though not a bribe or criminal influence, Justice Benjamin would nevertheless feel a debt of gratitude to Blankenship for his extraordinary efforts to get him elected. That temptation, Caperton claims, is as strong and inherent in human nature as was the conflict the Court confronted in *Tumey* and *Monroeville* when a mayor-judge (or the city) benefited financially from a defendant's conviction, as well as the conflict identified in *Murchison* and *Mayberry* when a judge was the object of a defendant's contempt.

Justice Benjamin was careful to address the recusal motions and explain his reasons why, on his view of the controlling standard, disqualification was not in order. In four separate opinions issued during the course of the appeal, he explained why no actual bias had been established. He found no basis for recusal because Caperton failed to provide "objective evidence" or "objective information," but merely "subjective belief" of bias. Nor could anyone "point to any actual conduct or activity on [his] part which could be termed 'improper.' " In other words, based on the facts presented by Caperton, Justice Benjamin conducted a probing search into his actual motives and inclinations; and he found none to be improper. We do not question his subjective findings of impartiality and propriety. Nor do we determine whether there was actual bias.

* * *

The difficulties of inquiring into actual bias, and the fact that the inquiry is often a private one, simply underscore the need for objective rules. Otherwise there may be no adequate protection against a judge who simply misreads or misapprehends the real motives at work in deciding the case. The judge's own inquiry into actual bias, then, is not one that the law can easily superintend or review, though actual bias, if disclosed, no doubt would be grounds for appropriate relief. In lieu of exclusive reliance on that personal inquiry, or on appellate review of the judge's determination respecting actual bias, the Due Process Clause has been implemented by objective standards that do not require proof of actual bias. In defining these standards the Court has asked whether, "under a realistic appraisal of psychological tendencies and human weakness," the interest "poses such a risk of actual bias or prejudgment that the practice must be forbidden if the guarantee of due process is to be adequately implemented."

We turn to the influence at issue in this case. Not every campaign contribution by a litigant or attorney creates a probability of bias that requires a judge's recusal, but this is an exceptional case. We conclude that there is a serious risk of actual bias-based on objective and reasonable perceptions-when a person with a personal stake in a particular case had a significant and disproportionate influence in placing the judge on the case by raising funds or directing the judge's election campaign when the case was pending or imminent. The inquiry centers on the contribution's relative size in comparison to the total amount of money contributed to the campaign, the total amount spent in the election, and the apparent effect such contribution had on the outcome of the election.

Applying this principle, we conclude that Blankenship's campaign efforts had a significant and disproportionate influence in placing Justice Benjamin on the case. Blankenship contributed some $3 million to unseat the incumbent and replace him with Benjamin. His contributions eclipsed the total amount spent by all other Benjamin supporters and exceeded by 300% the amount spent by Benjamin's campaign committee. Caperton claims Blankenship spent $1 million more than the total amount spent by the campaign committees of both candidates combined.

* * *

Whether Blankenship's campaign contributions were a necessary and sufficient cause of Benjamin's victory is not the proper inquiry. Much like determining whether a judge is actually biased, proving what ultimately drives the electorate to choose a particular candidate is a difficult endeavor, not likely to lend itself to a certain conclusion. This is particularly true where, as here, there is no procedure for judicial factfinding and the sole trier of fact is the one accused of bias. Due process requires an objective inquiry into whether the contributor's influence on the election under all the circumstances "would offer a possible temptation to the average . . . judge to . . . lead him not to hold the balance nice, clear and true." In an election decided by fewer than 50,000 votes (382,036 to 334,301), Blankenship's campaign contributions-in comparison to the total amount contributed to the campaign, as well as the total amount spent in the election-had a significant and disproportionate influence on the electoral outcome. And the risk that Blankenship's influence engendered actual bias is sufficiently substantial that it "must be forbidden if the guarantee of due process is to be adequately implemented."

The temporal relationship between the campaign contributions, the justice's election, and the pendency of the case is also critical. It was reasonably foreseeable, when the campaign contributions were made, that the pending case would be before the newly elected justice. The $50 million adverse jury verdict had been entered before the election, and the Supreme Court of Appeals was the next step once the state trial court dealt with post-trial motions. So it became at once apparent that, absent recusal, Justice Benjamin would review a judgment that cost his biggest donor's company $50 million. Although there is no allegation of a *quid pro quo* agreement, the fact remains that Blankenship's extraordinary contributions were made at a time when he had a vested stake in the outcome. Just as no man is allowed to be a judge in his own cause, similar fears of bias can arise when-without the consent of the other parties-a man chooses the judge in his own cause. And applying this principle to the judicial election process, there was here a serious, objective risk of actual bias that required Justice Benjamin's recusal.

. . . On these extreme facts the probability of actual bias rises to an unconstitutional level.

IV

Our decision today addresses an extraordinary situation where the Constitution requires recusal. Massey and its *amici* predict that various adverse consequences will follow from recognizing a constitutional violation here-ranging from a flood of recusal motions to unnecessary interference with judicial elections. We disagree. The facts now before us are extreme by any measure. The parties point to no other instance involving judicial campaign contributions that presents a potential for bias comparable to the circumstances in this case.

* * *

One must also take into account the judicial reforms the States have implemented to eliminate even the appearance of partiality. Almost every State—West Virginia included-has adopted the American Bar Association's objective standard: "A judge shall avoid impropriety and the appearance of impropriety." The ABA Model Code's test for appearance of impropriety is "whether the conduct would create in reasonable minds a perception that the judge's ability to carry out judicial responsibilities with integrity, impartiality and competence is impaired."

* * *

These codes of conduct serve to maintain the integrity of the judiciary and the rule of law. The Conference of the Chief Justices has underscored that the codes are "[t]he principal safeguard against judicial campaign abuses" that threaten to imperil "public confidence in the fairness and integrity of the nation's elected judges." This is a vital state interest: . . . It is for this reason that States may choose to "adopt recusal standards more rigorous than due process requires."

. . . Because the codes of judicial conduct provide more protection than due process requires, most disputes over disqualification will be resolved without resort to the Constitution. Application of the constitutional standard implicated in this case will thus be confined to rare instances.

* * *

The judgment of the Supreme Court of Appeals of West Virginia is reversed, and the case is remanded for further proceedings not inconsistent with this opinion.

It is so ordered.

CHIEF JUSTICE ROBERTS, with whom JUSTICE SCALIA, JUSTICE THOMAS, and JUSTICE ALITO join, dissenting.

I, of course, share the majority's sincere concerns about the need to maintain a fair, independent, and impartial judiciary-and one that appears to be such. But I fear that the Court's decision will undermine rather than promote these values.

* * *

Today, however, the Court enlists the Due Process Clause to overturn a judge's failure to recuse because of a "probability of bias." Unlike the established grounds for disqualification, a "probability of bias" cannot be defined in any limited way. The Court's new "rule" provides no guidance to judges and litigants about when recusal will be constitutionally required. This will inevitably lead to an increase in allegations that judges are biased, however groundless those charges may be. The end result will do far more to erode public confidence in judicial impartiality than an isolated failure to recuse in a particular case.

* * *

II

In departing from this clear line between when recusal is constitutionally required and when it is not, the majority repeatedly emphasizes the need for an "objective" standard. The majority's analysis is "objective" in that it does not inquire into Justice Benjamin's motives or decision making process. But the standard the majority articulates—"probability of bias"—fails to provide clear, workable guidance for future cases. At the most basic level, it is unclear whether the new probability of bias standard is somehow limited to financial support in judicial elections, or applies to judicial recusal questions more generally.

But there are other fundamental questions as well. With little help from the majority, courts will now have to determine:

1. How much money is too much money? What level of contribution or expenditure gives rise to a "probability of bias"?

2. How do we determine whether a given expenditure is "disproportionate"? Disproportionate *to what*?

3. Are independent, non-coordinated expenditures treated the same as direct contributions to a candidate's campaign? What about contributions to independent outside groups supporting a candidate?

4. Does it matter whether the litigant has contributed to other candidates or made large expenditures in connection with other elections?

5. Does the amount at issue in the case matter? What if this case were an employment dispute with only $10,000 at stake? What if the plaintiffs only sought non-monetary relief such as an injunction or declaratory judgment?

6. Does the analysis change depending on whether the judge whose disqualification is sought sits on a trial court, appeals court, or state supreme court?

7. How long does the probability of bias last? Does the probability of bias diminish over time as the election recedes? Does it matter whether the judge plans to run for reelection?

8. What if the "disproportionately" large expenditure is made by an industry association, trade union, physicians' group, or the plaintiffs' bar? Must the judge recuse in all cases that affect the association's interests? Must the judge recuse in all cases in which a party or lawyer is a member of that group? Does it matter how much the litigant contributed to the association?

9. What if the case involves a social or ideological issue rather than a financial one? Must a judge recuse from cases involving, say, abortion rights if he has received "disproportionate" support from individuals who feel strongly about either side of that issue? If the supporter wants to help elect judges who are "tough on crime," must the judge recuse in all criminal cases?

10. What if the candidate draws "disproportionate" support from a particular racial, religious, ethnic, or other group, and the case involves an issue of particular importance to that group?

* * *

These are only a few uncertainties that quickly come to mind. Judges and litigants will surely encounter others when they are forced to, or wish to, apply the majority's decision in different circumstances.

* * *

It is an old cliché, but sometimes the cure is worse than the disease. I am sure there are cases where a "probability of bias" should lead the prudent judge to step aside, but the judge fails to do so. Maybe this is one of them. But I believe that opening the door to recusal claims under the Due Process Clause, for an amorphous "probability of bias," will itself bring our judicial system into undeserved disrepute, and diminish the confidence of the American people in the fairness and integrity of their courts. I hope I am wrong.

I respectfully dissent.

JUSTICE SCALIA's dissenting opinion is omitted.

Notes & Questions

1. *Campaign contributions in Texas.* All judges in Texas are elected through partisan elections, and each election, especially the Texas Supreme Court's state-wide elections, can cost vast amounts of money. Most of the political contributions for these elections come from lawyers who practice before the court and litigants who either have or may have cases pending there. Thus, it should be of no surprise that allegations of bias and political favoritism are rampant in our system. The partisan election of judges in Texas had long been criticized, and judicial election reform has been on the legislative agenda several times.[1] The judicial election bills have never gotten far in the legislature, however. Many do not agree that any proposed system is any better than the current one. What are the benefits of our current system?

2. *Judicial elections after* Caperton. How may *Caperton* affect judicial politics in Texas? Will we see a rush of "*Caperton* motions" for recusal as Chief Justice Roberts fears? How will the trial courts deal with them? The excerpt reprints only the first ten of forty questions that "quickly came to mind" to the Chief Justice. Similar questions remain unanswered anytime that a new procedural rule is announced. Should rules and judicial opinions attempt to answer all of these questions or is it better to leave the answers to the lower courts?

3. *Recusal after* Caperton. Thus far Texas has held to the view that campaign contributions from lawyers or litigants do not justify a disqualification under the Texas or United States Constitution.[2] In the appeal of the famous Texas case of *Texaco v. Pennzoil*, where Pennzoil was awarded a multi-billion dollar judgment, Texaco claimed that its due process rights were violated because of campaign contributions. The record showed that Pennzoil's lead counsel, Joe Jamail, had contributed $10,000 to the judge's campaign after the lawsuit was filed and assigned to the judge's court. Moreover, Mr. Jamail served on the judge's campaign steering committee. The court found no due process violation. Might the result be different under *Caperton*?

4. *Non-constitutional grounds for recusal.* In *Caperton*, the United States Supreme Court notes that most campaign contribution recusal cases will be decided under the state's standards for recusal rather than the Constitution. The Texas decisions rejecting disqualification for campaign contributions did not address the broader recusal grounds stated in Rule 18b, which was adopted after the cases were tried. Do you see any non-constitutional grounds in Rule 18b on which a judge might be asked to step aside if one of the lawyers made a large contribution to the judge's reelection campaign and served on the judge's steering committee? Could impartiality reasonably be questioned under these circumstances? *See* Rule 18b(2)(a). Could it be argued that the judge has a "financial interest or other interest" in that a victory for his former campaign supporters would enhance their ability to contribute more money in the next campaign? *See* Rule 18b(2)(e).

---

[1] For a discussion of these proposals, *see, e.g.,* Chief Justice Wallace Jefferson, The State of the Judiciary in Texas (Feb. 11, 2009); C. Bleil, *Can a Twenty-First Century Texas Tolerate Its Nineteenth Century Judicial Selection Process?*, 26 ST. MARY'S L.J. 1089 (1995): Hill, *Taking Texas Judges Out of Politics: An Argument for Merit Election*, 40 BAYLOR L. REV. 339, (1988); O.W. Johnson and L. Johnson Urbis, *Judicial Selection in Texas: A Gathering Storm?*, 23 TEX. TECH L. REV. 525 (1992); *But see*, District Judge T. Poe and T.R. Clark, *Elections Still Work Best*, HOUSTON CHRONICLE, March 24, 1996, at 1.

[2] *See* J-IV Investment Co. v. David Lynn Machinery Co., 784 S.W.2d 106 (Tex. Civ. App.—Dallas 1990, no writ); Texaco v. Pennzoil Co., 729 S.W.2d 768 (Tex. App.—Houston [1st Dist.] 1987, writ ref'd n.r.e.), *cert. denied* 485 U.S. 994 (1988). River Road Neighborhood Ass'n v. South Texas Sports, Inc., 673 S.W.2d 952 (Tex. Civ. App.—San Antonio 1984, no writ).

Does it matter if the contribution exceeds the limits of the Election Code?[3] The Supreme Court Advisory Committee has considered amendments to Rules 18a and 18b that would address these issues, but none have been adopted.

5. *After* Caperton. In *Williams-Yulee v. Florida Bar*,[4] the United States Supreme Court applied Caperton, and upheld a state's regulation of judicial campaign financing. The Court held that the First Amendment permits the Florida Bar's ban on personal solicitation of campaign funds by judicial candidates because Florida's interest in preserving public confidence in the integrity of its judiciary was compelling.

In re CANALES

52 S.W.3d 698
(Tex. 2001)

JUSTICE ENOCH delivered the opinion of the Court.

In these consolidated mandamus petitions, we must decide whether real party in interest Cynthia Barrera's objection to a visiting judge under section 74.053 of the Texas Government Code was timely although not made until after the judge had heard and ruled on pretrial matters in the case. Because we conclude that the statute contemplates that objections be made before the first hearing over which the visiting judge is to preside in a case rather than to a particular assignment order, Barrera's objection was untimely and the trial court properly rejected it. The court of appeals therefore abused its discretion in conditionally granting Barrera a writ of mandamus.

On April 27, 1999, Barrera sued relators Judge Terry A. Canales and the county of Jim Wells in the 79th Judicial District Court of Jim Wells County. Canales, who is the district judge of that court, accordingly requested that the matter be assigned to another judge. By order of May 24, 1999, the presiding judge of the Fifth Administrative Judicial Region assigned visiting Judge Woody Densen to preside over the 79th District Court in Jim Wells County from May 24, 1999 to May 26, 1999. A separate order dated the same day assigned Judge Densen to preside over the 79th District Court in Brooks County from May 27, 1999 to May 29, 1999.

On May 25, 1999, Judge Densen heard and granted Canales's motion for a protective order in the underlying case. Two days later, on May 27, Judge Densen conducted a telephone hearing with the parties, in which he denied Barrera's motion to quash her deposition.

On July 9, 1999, the presiding judge issued another assignment order, this time assigning Judge Densen specifically to preside over the underlying case. On August 13, 1999, Barrera for the first time filed an objection to Judge Densen's assignment, invoking section 74.053 of the Texas Government Code. Judge Densen overruled her objection on August 20, 1999. That same day, Judge Densen granted Canales's motion for summary judgment against Barrera and severed the claims against Canales into a separate case. Thereafter, Judge Densen sustained the County's plea to the jurisdiction and dismissed the case with prejudice.

---

3 *See* Election Code § 251.001 *et seq.*

4 135 S.Ct. 1653 (2015).

Barrera petitioned the court of appeals for a writ of mandamus based on Judge Densen's refusal to remove himself from the case. The court of appeals concluded that Judge Densen's authority under the first assignment order expired on May 26 and that the June 9 order was necessary for him to preside further over the case. Because the two assignment orders were distinct, the court reasoned, Barrera's objection complied with section 74.053's requirement that objections be filed before the first hearing over which the assigned judge is to preside as long as Judge Densen had not taken any action under the second assignment. Thus, the court of appeals instructed Judge Densen to disqualify himself from any further proceedings in the case and declared void the orders he entered after Barrera filed her objection. Canales and the County then sought our review by mandamus.

* * *

The Court Administration Act, chapter 74 of the Government Code, divides the state into nine administrative judicial regions and empowers the presiding judge of each region to assign visiting judges to the courts in that region. Section 74.053 of that Act allows the parties to a civil case to object to an assigned judge and sets out the procedure for doing so:

> (a) When a judge is assigned under this chapter, the presiding judge shall, if it is reasonable and practicable and if time permits, give notice of the assignment to each attorney representing a party to the case that is to be heard in whole or in part by the assigned judge.
>
> (b) If a party to a civil case files a timely objection to the assignment, the judge shall not hear the case . . . .
>
> (c) An objection under this section must be filed before the first hearing or trial, including pretrial hearings, over which the assigned judge is to preside.[7]

* * *

If an objection is timely, the assigned judge's disqualification is automatic. When an assigned judge overrules a timely objection to his assignment, all of the judge's subsequent orders are void and the objecting party is entitled to mandamus relief. This Court has never before considered whether an objection would be timely in the circumstances presented here.

Canales and the County contend that Barrera waived her objection to Judge Densen because she waited to file it until after he had conducted two pretrial hearings. The statute, they argue, dictates that objections be filed before the assigned judge presides over any matter in the case, independent of the extent of the judge's authority under a particular assignment order. Otherwise, parties could "test out" a judge and then object if they disagree with the judge's preliminary rulings. Alternatively, Canales and the County maintain that Judge Densen's authority under the May 24 assignment order extended to the entire case, so that the June 9 assignment order was superfluous and did not give Barrera another opportunity to object.

Barrera counters that her objection was timely because she filed it before Judge Densen conducted any hearings under the authority of the June 9 assignment order. She argues that Judge Densen's authority under the first assignment order expired on May 26, and that he had no authority thereafter to act in the case until he received a new assignment. Because a new assignment was necessary, she reasons, a new opportunity to object arose.

---

7 TEX. GOV'T CODE § 74.053(a)-(c).

To resolve this issue, we turn to section 74.053. When we construe a statute, our primary goal is to ascertain and give effect to the Legislature's intent in enacting it. If a statute is clear and unambiguous, we need not resort to rules of construction or other aids to construe it. Even then, however, we may consider, among other things, the statute's objectives, its legislative history, and the consequences of a particular construction.

The statute's plain language convinces us that Canales and the County read it accurately. To begin with, section 74.053(a) requires notice (if practicable) to the parties to any case "that is to be heard in whole *or in part* by the assigned judge." And section 74.053(c) says that "[a]n objection under this section must be filed *before the first hearing or trial, including pretrial hearings,* over which the assigned judge is to preside." Finally, if a party files a timely objection, section 74.053(b) provides that the assigned judge "shall not hear the case." Read together, these sections preclude the argument that a new chapter 74 assignment order carries with it a new right to object. The statute explicitly recognizes the possibility that a visiting judge may be assigned to preside over only part of a case. Yet it does not say that objections must be filed before the judge presides over any hearing *under the assignment.* It says, rather, that to be timely an objection must be filed before the judge presides over *any* hearing. There is simply no basis in the statute to tie the timeliness of an objection to a judge's authority under any given assignment order.

This conclusion is reinforced by the statute's legislative history and objectives. Section 74.053 first came into being in 1985 as part of the Court Administration Act.[16] That Act's purpose was to provide a statewide framework for court administration and case management, in order to give the civil courts greater control over their dockets and speed the progress of cases through the court system. As originally enacted, section 74.053 did not restrict the number of objections that parties could make to visiting judges.

In 1987, the Legislature limited each party to one objection per case, to prevent either side from being able to put off trial indefinitely by filing one objection after another. In 1991, the statute was amended again to allow unlimited objections to former judges who are not retired judges. Legislators discussing both of these changes expressed concern that the visiting judge system was being abused because judges who were defeated in elections were continuing to sit as visiting judges. Section 74.053 answers that concern by protecting a party's interest in having its case heard by the locally-elected judge instead of one who had been rejected by the voters. The Legislature balanced this interest against its desire to create a uniform system of administration and prevent delay by carefully limiting the right to object.

Construing the statute to permit objections to a second assignment after the assigned judge has presided over some part of the case upsets this balance and is inconsistent with the statute's objectives in several ways. First, it increases delay and disrupts the judicial process if a party can remove a judge without cause in the middle of a case. And in many cases, whether an objection is timely would depend on interpreting the assignment order involved. Consequently, we would sacrifice a straightforward application of the statute for one that would inevitably cause even more delay while the parties argue about the scope of assignment orders.

Moreover, section 74.053 protects only a party's interest in having a locally-elected judge hear its case—not a party's ability to choose which judge will sit. As soon as a party knows that a visiting judge has been appointed, that party knows that the locally-elected judge will not hear at least part of the case. An immediate objection thus furthers the policy concerns reflected in section 74.053. Allowing either party to sample the visiting judge first doesn't. Of course, we

---

16 *See* Court Administration Act, 69th Leg., R.S., ch. 732, § 2, 1985 Tex. Gen. Laws 2534.

recognize that in this case Barrera has no interest in having her case tried by the locally-elected judge of Jim Wells County, whom she is suing. But we can't read the statute contrary to its language and legislative history on that basis.

The statute means exactly what it says. An objection to a judge assigned under chapter 74 is timely if it is filed before the very first hearing or trial in the case, including pretrial hearings, over which the assigned judge is to preside—without regard to the terms of the particular order under which the judge is assigned. The statute does not confer a new opportunity to object when a visiting judge who has already heard matters in the case is reassigned by a new assignment order. Once an assigned judge has heard any matter in a case, the parties have waived the right to object to that judge under section 74.053 of the Government Code.

Because Barrera's objection was untimely, Judge Densen did not abuse his discretion in overruling it. We therefore conditionally grant the writ of mandamus against the court of appeals. The writ will issue only if the court of appeals does not vacate its mandamus judgment.

Notes & Questions

1. *Who can preside?* A wide range of judges are qualified and authorized to preside in a district court. First, the "active judge" who is the current judicial officeholder of the court presides in that court.[1] Second, administrative rules provide for the appointment of "visiting judges" to preside in a court. A visiting judge may be another district judge in the county[2] or an active, former, retired or senior judge.[3] Chapter 74 of the Texas Government Code provides a number of limitations on the appointment of visiting judges, most of which we will not go into here.

2. *Striking visiting judges.* Since *Canales* and *Union Pacific* were decided, Section 74.053 has been amended. The statute now provides that each party to a civil case may assert one objection to an assigned judge, in which instance "the judge shall not hear the case."[4] Also, the parties may no longer object to an active judge—they may only object to a retired judge or a former judge.[5] But each party has unlimited objections to an assigned judge who was defeated in the judge's last judicial election.[6]

---

[1] *See* TEX. GOVT. CODE § 74.041 (defining "active judge").

[2] *See* Rule 330(e); Tex. Const. Art. V,§ 11; TEX. GOVT. CODE § 24.303.

[3] A "former judge" is a person who has served as an active judge in a district, statutory probate, statutory county court, or appellate court, but is not a retired judge; a "retired judge" is a retiree or person who served as an inactive judge for at least 96 months in the statutory probate or statutory county court and has retired under the retirement system; a "senior judge" is a retiree who has elected to be a judicial officer TEX. GOVT. CODE § 74.041 (definitions).

[4] TEX. GOVT. CODE § 74.053(b).

[5] A "former judge" either resigned or lost an election before retirement. A "retired judge" has to qualify for retirement under applicable statutes, but generally the judge must be 65 years old and have 10 years of service to be retired. *See* Mitchell Energy Corp. v. Ashworth, 943 S.W.2d 436 (Tex. 1997)(holding that a judge's status as retired or not for purposes of former § 74.053 is determined at the time the judge leaves office.)

[6] Before the 2003 amendments, parties had unlimited strikes over all former judges who were not retired judges, which included those who had resigned or lost an election before retirement.

3. *Procedure.* Read GOV'T CODE § 74.053 carefully as it specifies the procedure that must be followed to object to a visiting judge. Most importantly, it requires that the objection be filed not later than 7 days after the party receives the notice of the assignment or before the first hearing or trial, including pretrial hearings, over which the assigned judge is to preside, whichever is earlier.[7] An oral motion to excuse the visiting judge, followed by a hand written motion filed only after the objecting party's motion for continuance is denied is untimely.[8] The statute also requires that notice of a visiting judge's assignment be given if it is reasonable and practical to do so and if time permits.[9] However, parties have been unsuccessful in using this provision to excuse late filed objections.[10]

4. *Assignment to hear recusal motion.* The Supreme Court has held that a judge designated by the presiding judge of the administrative judicial district to hear a recusal motion under Rule 18a is an assigned judge subject to objection and mandatory disqualification under GOV'T. CODE § 74.053.[11] But a presiding judge who assigns himself to hear the recusal motion, rather than designating another judge to do so, is *not* subject to objection under Chapter 74.[12]

---

7 TEX. GOV'T CODE ANN. § 74.053(c). *See* O'Connor v. Lykos, 960 S.W.2d 96 (Tex. App.—Houston [1st Dist.] 1997, orig. proceeding) (signing of an order granting a new trial ends an assigned judge's authority; when the same judge was assigned to hear the retrial, the party's objection under Texas Government Code § 74.053 was timely where party made the objection before the first hearing in the second trial).

8 Money v. Jones, 766 S.W.2d 307 (Tex. App.—Dallas 1989, writ denied).

9 TEX. GOV'T CODE ANN. § 74.053(a).

10 *See Money*, 766 S.W. 2d 307 (attorney not told of assignment when called to docket call, but hand-written objection was available). *See also* Flores v. Banner, 932 S.W.2d 500 (Tex. 1996)(objection to "any former judge" was valid despite failure to name particular judge because identity not known until judge took the bench).

11 In re Perritt, 992 S.W.2d 444 (Tex. 1999).

12 In re Flores, 53 S.W.3d 428 (Tex. App.—San Antonio 2001, no pet.).

C. Attorneys in Texas

1. *Professionalism*

Read the Texas Lawyers Creed; CPRC, Ch. 10; Rule 13.

---

2. *Withdrawal of Counsel*

Read Rules 8, 9, and 10.

MOSS
v.
MALONE
880 S.W.2d 45
(Tex. App.—Tyler 1994, writ denied)

HOLCOMB, JUSTICE.

This appeal is from a denial of a motion for new trial after the court allowed Appellant's original attorney to withdraw and Appellant being pro se, dismissed her case.

Appellant brings four points of error complaining of the trial court's actions: in allowing her original counsel to withdraw and thereafter resetting the case for trial too quickly to enable her to secure counsel and then dismissing her case in violation of the Fifth, Sixth and Fourteenth Amendments to the UNITED STATES CONSTITUTION; in granting her counsel's motion to withdraw one day prior to trial violating TEXAS RULES OF CIVIL PROCEDURE 10 and TEXAS DISCIPLINARY RULES OF PROFESSIONAL CONDUCT 1.15; refusing to allow Appellant to put on evidence at the hearing on Appellant's motion for new trial in violation of TEXAS RULES OF CIVIL PROCEDURE 324(b)1; and in overruling Appellant's motion for new trial after evidence reflected Appellee's counsel had unduly harassed and coerced Appellant who was without counsel immediately prior to the dismissal of the case in violation of TEXAS DISCIPLINARY RULES OF PROFESSIONAL CONDUCT 4.01, 4.03, and 4.04, thereby violating her constitutional right to trial and rendering the dismissal involuntary and void. We will reverse the case and remand it to the trial court.

While there were no statement of facts filed, from the transcript and uncontradicted statements contained in the briefs, we find the following to be the essential facts.

Appellant's son had died as a result of an accident that had occurred between a vehicle driven by Appellee and the bicycle he was riding in Van Zandt County on March 26, 1988. Appellant brought suit through her attorney, Ted Beatty, on March 23, 1990, alleging negligence on the part of Appellee which had resulted in the death of the child. It appears there had been extensive discovery at various times during the preparation of the case for trial.

On December 9, 1991, Appellee filed a request for setting asking the court to set the case on the jury docket for March or April 1992. The court complied and the case was set for jury trial on March 9, 1992. On February 5, 1992, Appellee withdrew her request for a jury and asked the case be set for trial on the nonjury docket on March 11th or 12th, 1992. On February 10, 1992, Appellant, through her attorney, paid a jury fee. On February 24, 1992, Appellee filed her motion to strike jury demand and requested a hearing on this motion, which was set on March 5, 1992. On March 2, 1992, Appellee filed her designation of exhibits and requested jury questions, instructions, and definitions in preparation for a jury trial. On March 3, 1992, Appellant did the same. On March 5, 1992, a hearing was held on Appellee's motion to strike jury demand. Appellant's attorney announced that both parties were ready for trial on the jury docket for March 9, 1992. The court however, moved the case from the jury docket and placed the case on the nonjury docket for March 12, 1992. On March 11, 1992, one day prior to the non-jury trial, Appellant's attorney filed a motion to withdraw which reads as follows:

> TED BEATTY, attorney for JEANNIE MOSS, Plaintiff in this cause, moves this court to enter an order permitting him to withdraw as counsel of record, and in support of this motion shows: There exists a material difference of opinion between Movant and Plaintiff as to the presentation of this case. The granting of this motion will not have a material adverse effect on the interests of the Defendant and will not result in an unreasonable delay in the proceedings. WHEREFORE, movant prays the court grant this motion and order that he be released as counsel of record in this cause.

A telephone conference hearing was held between Appellant's attorney, Appellee's attorney, and the court. The trial judge orally allowed Appellant's attorney to withdraw; the order was not signed until March 23, 1992. There also appears an identical second order signed by the trial judge on April 21, 1992. The court then set the case for non-jury trial on April 9, 1992. At this setting Appellant appeared without counsel, and the following transpired:

> THE COURT: 90-156, Jeannie Moss versus Jan Heard Malone. Ma'am, you mentioned the possibility of getting a lawyer.
>
> MS. MOSS: E. Ray Andrews.
>
> THE COURT: You mentioned E. Ray Andrews.
>
> MS. MOSS: I talked to him this morning.
>
> THE COURT: Have you retained him to represent you?
>
> MS. MOSS: Yes, sir, I have. He has the records. I just need some more time.
>
> THE COURT: Did he say anything about why he didn't file a motion for continuance? How long ago did you retain him?
>
> MS. MOSS: Last week.
>
> THE COURT: Mr. McSwane.
>
> McSWANE: [Attorney for Appellee] Your Honor, I think the Court recalls the facts of this case. At the time that Mr. Beatty withdrew, when I checked back was March 10th. She was told that it would go to trial on the 9th. It had been set twice before. In fact, they had announced ready at the time of the last setting when counsel withdrew. We are ready to proceed. We are ready to go this afternoon. I mean, if she can call Mr. Andrews and he can be here, we will be ready to go.
>
> MS. MOSS: He can't be here. When he received this date—
>
> THE COURT: Did Mr. Beatty tell you back on March the 10th when we had a telephone conference and when I allowed him to withdraw that the case was set for today?

MS. MOSS: No, he didn't. He said he would call me and get the files to me. And I received the files in the mail a week ago. And he had a little card pinned in there that said be sure to be there on the 9th. And E. Ray said he could not possibly—

McSWANE: Your Honor, I beg to differ. She was in the room at the time the Court concluded the hearing. She came in, the Court specifically stated it was set April the 9th at the time. If I need to testify to that, I will.

MS. MOSS: I'm sorry. I did not hear that.

THE COURT: Were you in the room when Mr. Beatty was on the phone to me and Mr. McSwane?

MS. MOSS: No, sir. I just walked in as you were hanging up. He told you I just walked in.

THE COURT: We are going to call Mr. Andrews and we will take the case up in a few moments. [Brief recess.]

THE COURT: Let me see everyone again on Jeannie Moss versus Jan Heard Malone, please. We have talked to Mr. Andrews' office and he says that what he said was that if you could get a continuance that he would look over your paperwork and tell you after that whether he would take the case, not that he had been retained to represent you.

MS. MOSS: That's not what he told me because he was reading—

THE COURT: I will give you a chance to talk in just a minute. I will grant you a continuance until the 7th day of May, 1992. That's roughly thirty days from today's date. I knew when I let Mr. Beatty withdraw that we were going to get into this situation. But according to his motion, you don't want him to be your lawyer anymore and that's fine. But you have the right to a lawyer of your choice. But on May the 7th, 1992, I will write that date down for you, May the 7th, 1992, at 9 a.m., I will call the case for trial. Whether you get him or any other lawyer to represent you, be present with your lawyer and tell your lawyer the case has been pending. This is not the first setting. So he's going to have to come up here ready to try the lawsuit, not just get some sort of first setting on a hearing. Do you understand?

MS. MOSS: Yes. The reason I let Ted Beatty go is because he didn't ever notify me when he would get a letter. I would call his office. He did not do me a good job.

THE COURT: That's fine. And that's what I'm saying. That's between you and your lawyer and you have the right to have any lawyer you want to. And that's what I have done. But there won't be any other continuances. So on May 7, 1992, we will try the case.

McSWANE: I would like to have the witnesses sworn. Everyone that's present on the lawsuit styled Jeannie Moss versus Jan Heard Malone, will you stand at this time, please, if you are here on that lawsuit and raise your right hands, please. [Witnesses sworn.]

THE COURT: Ladies and gentlemen, this case has been continued until the 7th day of May, 1992. That's May 7, 1992 at 9 o'clock in the morning. At that time, the case will be tried. You will not receive any other subpoenas from any of the lawyers or from the clerk's office in this case because this case will be carried over. So you will have to come back on May 7, 1992 at 9 o'clock without having received any other paperwork or notifications. I just want to make you aware of that and please mark it on your calendar or make a note so you won't overlook it. But the case will be tried on May 7, 1992 at 9 a.m. Thank you for being present. [Hearing recessed.]

On May 7, 1992, the parties again appeared before the trial court and the following transpired:

THE COURT: Jeannie Moss and Jan Heard Malone.

MS. MOSS: May we come to the bench?

THE COURT: You may.

MS. MOSS: E. Ray couldn't be here today. He said he needed at least thirty more days and I've got the file and that whatever you wanted to do, for me to play it by ear. And if you needed to talk to him, you could call him. But he said for me to—to represent me fairly, he needed at least thirty more days because it wasn't being fair to me because he didn't know that much about the case. And that Ted was let off too quick and that the trial was set too quick after Ted was off. So I don't know.

THE COURT: The trial was set before Mr. Beatty was released. Well, we've already been through the same circumstances—

MS. MOSS: I've got the file and everything. He said, you know, whatever you thought was right, what you wanted to do so. For me just to play it by ear and go along with you and see what happens. We could just start over. He said he had no other choice. But he didn't know that much about the case and for him to—like I said, to represent me fairly. He said it wouldn't be fair to me, it wasn't fair to them.

THE COURT: What says the Defendant?

McSWANE: We are opposed to it, Your Honor.

THE COURT: Very well. The request for continuance will be overruled.

MS. MOSS: So what's going to happen, I'm going to be without a lawyer today?

THE COURT: That's correct.

MS. MOSS: I won't drop the case, I won't.

THE COURT: This Court is not going—

MS. MOSS: But he's trying to make me look like a criminal. This woman took my child away from me. And I can't—

McSWANE: Judge, we're ready.

MS. MOSS: She wants me to pay her $500.

THE COURT: You may take your seats.

[Hearing briefly recessed.]

THE COURT: 90-156, Jeannie Moss versus Jan Malone.

McSWANE: Your Honor, may we approach the bench?

THE COURT: You may.

McSWANE: Judge, it's my understanding, I won't speak for Ms. Moss. But my understanding is she wished to dismiss the case—well, I will let her speak.

MS. MOSS: Well, I'm not really happy about the decision up here and I don't want to be crucified. I don't want them to make me look like I'm bad. She's the one in the wrong. So to let everybody rest and let my son rest, I guess I will just drop it.

THE COURT: Any opposition by anyone?

McSWANE: No, Your Honor.

MR. RAY: [Attorney for Appellee] By drop, do you mean to dismiss the case, is that what you mean by dropping it?

MS. MOSS: Yes.

THE COURT: Very well. That request will be granted. Thank you. This case will be in recess.

[Hearing concluded.]

There appears in the record two orders of dismissal, one filed on May 12, 1992, and another signed on May 20, 1992. These orders to dismiss are identical except for the date. On June 5, 1992, Appellant obviously having then found counsel, filed her motion for new trial. Over Appellant's objection to the court and upon the urging of Appellee, the court did not hear any evidence but considered only the affidavits which were attached to the motion for new trial. The trial court did not rule on the motion and allowed it to be overruled as a matter of law on August 11, 1992. The trial court formally overruled the motion for new trial on October 5, 1992.

Appellant claims the court committed reversible error by granting the motion to withdraw by Appellant's former attorney one day prior to trial in violation of TEXAS RULES OF CIVIL PROCEDURE 10 and TEXAS DISCIPLINARY RULES OF PROFESSIONAL CONDUCT 1.15. The pertinent portions of Rule 10 read as follows:

> An attorney may withdraw from representing a party only upon written motion for good cause shown . . . . If another attorney is not to be substituted as attorney for the party, the motion *shall* state: that a copy of the motion has been delivered to the party; *the party has been notified in writing of his right to object to the motion; whether the party consents to the motion*; the party's last known address and all pending settings and deadlines. If the motion is granted, the withdrawing attorney shall immediately notify the party in writing of any additional settings or deadlines of which the attorney had knowledge at the time of the withdrawal and has not already notified the party. *The Court may impose further conditions upon granting leave to withdraw.* Notice or delivery to a party shall be either made to the party in person or mailed to the party's last known address by both certified and regular first class mail. If the attorney in charge withdraws and another attorney remains or becomes substituted, another attorney in charge must be designated of record with notice to all other parties in accordance with Rule 21a.

TEX. R. CIV. P. 10 (emphasis added).

The motion to withdraw failed to comply in the following regard:

(1) It does not appear that a copy of the motion was sent or attempted to be sent to Appellant; or

(2) that she had any notice of the motion being filed and being heard by the court;

(3) Appellant was not notified of her right to object to the motion;

(4) it does not appear that Appellant consented to the motion; and

(5) Appellant's last known address and all pending settings and deadlines, including a trial setting, were not given to her.

We are called upon to decide whether it is error for a court to allow an attorney to withdraw from representation of a client without complying with the provisions of Rule 10 of the TEXAS RULES OF CIVIL PROCEDURE requiring adequate notice to that client. This appears to be a case of first impression in Texas. Appellee, while acknowledging the motion to withdraw does not technically comply with Rule 10, argues that the trial court's decision to allow the withdrawal was not an abuse of discretion. And in this regard, Appellee states a reading of the above record shows that Appellant was aware of the withdrawal, acquiesced in it, and that it was her desire for Beatty to withdraw. We, however, decline to read the record with the same expansiveness. We read it to imply she had differences with her attorney because he failed to keep her apprised of settings, etc., and that she received her file from him one week prior to the April 9th setting.

In *Villegas v. Carter,* 711 S.W.2d 624 (Tex. 1986), the Supreme Court found that it was an abuse of discretion for the trial court to allow the attorney for the appellant to withdraw two days prior to the trial. The court stated that:

> [T]he right to counsel is a valuable right; its unwarranted denial is reversible error. (citations omitted) Therefore when a trial court allows an attorney to voluntarily withdraw, it must give the party time to secure new counsel and time for the new counsel to investigate the case and prepare for trial.

Villegas, 711 S.W.2d at 626.

In *Villegas,* the Appellant's file was turned over to him only six days prior to the date the case was set for hearing and that the last withdrawal of the two attorneys was only two days prior to the time he was required to proceed to trial.

The rules governing withdrawal contain provisions which are obviously placed there to protect the client's interest. In this case, the motion to withdraw as counsel, filed by Appellant's attorney, in addition to the stated defects, makes no reference to the effect of the withdrawal on his client. Allowing the attorney to improperly withdraw, however, did affect, and cause, the events which took place on April 9th and May 7th. On May 7, 1992, Appellant was involved in a lawsuit to fix liability for the death of her son, in which she was not represented by counsel against an adversary represented by at least two attorneys.

The court could have protected the Appellant's interests and ordered the attorney to continue to represent Appellant even though good cause may have existed for terminating the representation. He also could have ordered the Appellant, as a client, to have appeared with the attorney to determine the underlying facts of the withdrawal. *See* TEX. DISC. RULES OF PROF. CON. 1.15. A motion of continuance, which Appellant presented in the May 7th hearing, is within the trial court's sound discretion to either grant or deny. *State v. Crank,* 666 S.W.2d 91, 94 (Tex. 1984); *Hernandez v. Heldenfels,* 374 S.W.2d 196, 202 (Tex. 1963). While the trial court's course of action will not be disturbed unless the record discloses a clear abuse of discretion; when the ground for the continuance is the withdrawal of counsel, the movant must show that the failure to be represented at trial was not due to their own fault or negligence. *State v. Crank,* 666 S.W.2d at 94. We find the record negates either fault or negligence on Appellant's part. Generally when movants fail to comply with TEX. R. CIV. P. 251, we will presume that the trial court did not abuse his discretion in denying the motion. *Garcia v. Texas Employers Insurance Assn.,* 622 S.W.2d 626, 630 (Tex. App.—Amarillo 1981, writ ref'd n.r.e.). It would be unrealistic, however, to apply this presumption to lay movants, whose attorneys were allowed to withdraw. *Robinson v. Risinger,* 548 S.W.2d 762, 765 (Tex. Civ. App.—Tyler 1977, writ ref'd n.r.e.). This was a case of wrongful death. During both the April and May hearings it is clear that Appellant not only wished to continue her lawsuit, but that she was having problems getting another attorney to take the case because of the imminent trial setting. There is nothing in the record to suggest that Appellant was seeking delay in order to injure Appellee or that Appellant was negligent in failing to secure counsel.

We hold, under Rule 10 of the TEXAS RULES OF CIVIL PROCEDURE, the court erred in allowing Appellant's then trial counsel to withdraw with a deficient motion to withdraw without taking steps to protect this party litigant's valuable right. A fundamental element of due process is that every litigant is entitled to be heard in court by counsel of his own selection. This is a valuable right and an unwarranted denial of it is fundamental error where the litigant without negligence or default on his part is deprived of the right of counsel on the eve of trial. *See also* 17 C.J.S. *Continuances,* § 23. Under the narrow circumstances of this case, we find there was an abuse of discretion for the trial court to allow Appellant's attorney to withdraw as counsel. As our finding under the evidence available to us is dispositive of the case, we will not address the remaining points of error.

On the basis of the facts in the record of this case and the application of cited authorities to such facts, we have concluded that the judgment of the trial court should be reversed and the case remanded to the trial court for further proceedings in accordance with this opinion.

OPINION ON MOTION FOR REHEARING

In her motion for rehearing, Appellee accuses this Court of misapplying the standard of review enunciated in *Villegas v. Carter,* 711 S.W.2d 624 (Tex. 1986).

By order, on April 24, 1990, the Supreme Court amended TEXAS RULE OF CIVIL PROCEDURE 10 to be effective September 1, 1990. By that Rule change, the mandatory word "shall" imposes a duty on the trial court to require a motion to withdraw to comply with the requirements placed there to protect the party litigant. This altered the discretion trial courts may have previously enjoyed. When the trial court granted a motion to withdraw which failed to meet the mandatory requirements of Rule 10, the court abused its discretion. The court was aware that it was doing an act that would be a problem later when he said, "I knew when I let Mr. Beatty withdraw that we were going to get into this situation." (See original opinion for context). We have applied the reasoning in *Villegas* which reads:

> Before a trial court allows an attorney to withdraw, it should see that the attorney has complied with the Code of Professional Responsibility: (A) lawyer should not withdraw from employment until he has taken reasonable steps to avoid foreseeable prejudice to the rights of his client, including giving due notice to his client, allowing time for employment of other counsel, delivering to the client all papers and property to which the client is entitled and complying with applicable laws and rules. Supreme Court of Texas, Rules Governing the State Bar of Texas art. XII, § 8 (Code of Professional Responsibility) DR 2-110(A)(2); *Smith v. State,* 490 S.W.2d 902, 909-10 (Tex. Civ. App.—Corpus Christi 1972, writ ref'd n.r.e.).

Villegas was decided in 1986. It is noted that TEXAS RULE OF CIVIL PROCEDURE 10, as amended in 1990, appears to adopt essentially the requirements of Article XII, section 8 of the then CODE OF PROFESSIONAL RESPONSIBILITY which is quoted above. The court could have made the error harmless if he had followed the guiding rules and principles of *Villegas.* That is, he should have "give[n] the party time to secure new counsel and time for the new counsel to investigate the case and prepare for trial." *Villegas,* 711 S.W.2d at 626 (emphasis added).

Appellee attributes importance to the fact that the original counsel was prepared to go to trial two days before he withdrew. However, the trial court did not sign the order allowing counsel to withdraw until March 23, 1992, and the original counsel did not release the file until after that date. Appellant had, at most, sixteen days to "secure new counsel to investigate the case and prepare for trial" before the date set for trial, April 9, 1992. The trial court must allow meaningful time for the party to find new counsel and prepare for trial.

Appellee also assigns great importance to the 57 days that elapsed between the withdrawal of counsel and the docket call on May 7, 1992. She argues that this is sufficient time to secure new counsel. We do not believe this interpretation of the record is realistic. Appellant was forced to try to find counsel to represent her in a wrongful death action within two weeks, obtain a continuance, and then "investigate the case and prepare for trial" in twenty-eight days. If the trial court had given Appellant fifty-seven straight days to "secure new counsel to investigate the case and prepare for trial" then the equities would be significantly altered.

Appellee argues that since Appellant found an attorney willing to file a motion for new trial within thirty days of the dismissal, it conclusively shows that she was not diligent and could have found counsel who would try the case during the twenty-eight days before the dismissal. We hold this argument to be without merit.

We hold that the effect of an erroneous ruling on the motion to withdraw, when combined with the failure on two occasions to give adequate time for the party to secure new counsel and prepare for trial, amounted to harmful error.

Appellee's motion for rehearing is overruled.

Notes & Questions

1. *Client's Discharge of Counsel.* The client's discharge of counsel must be distinguished from voluntary withdrawal by the attorney. In *Rogers v. Clinton,*[1] the Texas Supreme Court noted that a "client may discharge his attorney at any time even without cause." In fact, an attorney may be sanctioned for taking actions on behalf of the client after being fired.[2] However, as illustrated by *Moss,* an attorney may withdraw from representation of a client only if the requirements of Rule 10 have been satisfied. In particular, the attorney must show good cause for withdrawal in a written motion filed with the court.[3] Is it necessary for the attorney to ensure that the client has substitute counsel in order to establish good cause in the motion to withdraw? Late withdrawal of counsel creates problems for judges who are trying to get cases to trial. Some judges will make a lawyer stay in the case until the parties have completed alternate dispute resolution, hoping that the case will be settled.

2. *Accepting employment.* When approached to become substituted counsel, what are some important considerations? Why was Ms. Moss able to find counsel after the case had been dismissed, but unable to do so before trial?

---

[1] 794 S.W.2d 9, 10 n. 1 (Tex. 1990).

[2] *See* Bloom v. Graham, 825 S.W.2d 244, 248 (Tex. App.—Fort Worth 1992, writ denied). *See also* In re News America Pub., Inc., 974 S.W.2d 97 (Tex. App.—San Antonio 1998, orig. proceeding) (opposing attorney sanctioned for meeting with party when client had not informed own counsel that counsel was discharged).

[3] *See* TRCP 10.

3. *Texas disciplinary rules governing withdrawal.* The Texas Disciplinary Rules of Professional Conduct must also be considered when an attorney considers withdrawing as counsel. Rule 1.15(d) requires a lawyer who terminates representation to take reasonable steps to protect the client's interests, including:

(a) giving reasonable notice to the client;

(b) allowing time for employment of another attorney;

(c) surrendering papers and property to which the client is entitled; and

(d) refunding any advance payments not yet earned by the attorney.[4]

4. *Attorney in Charge.* Rule 57 requires all pleadings of a party represented by an attorney, including the plaintiff's petition and the defendant's answer, to be signed by at least one attorney of record in his individual name.[5] When more than one attorney represents a party, one attorney must be designated as the "attorney in charge" pursuant to Rule 8. This designation may be accomplished by default through listing such attorney's name and signature first in the signature block; or, when not listed first, the attorney in charge must be specifically designated in the pleadings. All communications from the court or other counsel with respect to the action must be sent to the attorney in charge.[6] But motions filed by attorneys other than the attorney in charge are not void.[7] What steps must be taken, if any, to change the designation of the attorney in charge? In addition, Rule 9 generally limits a party to two counsel during trial.[8] An exception may be made in "important" cases, or upon special leave of court.

5. *Disqualification.* Sometimes an opponent will move to disqualify counsel.[9]

---

[4] *See* TDRPC 1.15(d); *see also* W. DORSANEO, 1 TEXAS LITIGATION GUIDE § 3.05 [2] (1995) [hereinafter DORSANEO].

[5] *See* TRCP 57; *see also* TRCP 45.

[6] See Morin v. Boecker, 122 S.W.3d 911, 914-16 (Tex. App.—Corpus Christi 2003, no pet.) (reversing judgment when notice sent to party instead of attorney in charge).

[7] City of Tyler v. Beck, 196 S.W.3d 784 (Tex. 2006) (per curiam).

[8] *See* TRCP 9.

[9] *See e.g.* Nat'l Medical Enterprises, Inc. v. Godbey, 924 S.W.2d 123 (Tex. 1996)(finding that plaintiffs' lawyers were disqualified).

D. Rulings on Pretrial Matters

1. *Pretrial Rulings and Appellate Review*

Read CPRC § 51.012, § 51.014.

SAFETY-KLEEN CORP.
v.
GARCIA

945 S.W.2d 268
(Tex. App.—San Antonio 1997, orig. proceeding)

GREEN, JUSTICE.

Relator, Safety-Kleen Corp. ("Safety-Kleen"), seeks a writ of mandamus to require the Respondent, The Honorable Ricardo H. Garcia, to set a hearing on Safety-Kleen's motion to compel answers to interrogatories, which was filed on January 20, 1997.[1] We conditionally grant the writ to compel Judge Garcia to act.

PROCEDURAL HISTORY.

Safety-Kleen is one of 254 defendants originally sued by 72 plaintiffs for personal injuries allegedly caused by exposure to cement products. Safety-Kleen served the plaintiffs with its first set of interrogatories between November 14, 1996 and December 6, 1996. The plaintiffs filed a joint answer to the interrogatories on January 15, 1997. On or about January 20, 1997, Safety-Kleen filed a motion to compel contending the plaintiffs "refused to submit any of the information specifically requested by [certain] interrogatories."[2]

On January 27, 1997, Safety-Kleen sent a letter to the court coordinator requesting that a hearing be set on its motion. On February 11, 1997, Safety-Kleen forwarded a second written demand to the court coordinator to set the motion for hearing. The letter notes that Safety-Kleen previously contacted the court several times regarding its request. Safety-Kleen has also included in our record an affidavit from its attorney stating that the court coordinator refused to set the motion for a hearing. The last time the court coordinator was contacted, she informed Safety-Kleen's attorney that "no motions [would] be set for hearing until October of 1997."

DISCUSSION.

A trial court is required to consider and rule upon a motion within a reasonable time. "When a motion is properly filed and pending before a trial court, the act of giving consideration to and ruling upon that motion is a ministerial act," and mandamus may issue to compel the trial judge to act.

---

[1] The real parties in interest did not file a written response and were not represented at oral argument.

[2] Safety-Kleen contends it is entitled to the discovery under the precedent established in Able Supply Co. v. Moye, 898 S.W.2d 766 (Tex. 1995). We are not called upon to address the merits of Safety-Kleen's motion in this proceeding.

Although Judge Garcia's refusal to act is evident in his failure to set Safety-Kleen's motion for hearing, Judge Garcia has also expressly indicated in recorded statements made at a preliminary hearing that he will refuse to act in regard to such motions:

MR. EDWARDS [Plaintiffs' Attorney]: Your Honor, Don Edwards. As Mr. Gonzalez was stating earlier, we have conducted discovery towards the defendants in response to their motion for transfer, and I believe—roughly, it was five to ten percent of the defendants have responded to this discovery. So at this point until the defendant—

THE COURT: I'm not responsible for the defendants not responding to your motions.

MR. EDWARDS: Yes, sir.

THE COURT: Now, don't ask me to participate in your pretrial discovery because I'm not. I don't have the time.

* * *

MR. KELLY [Plaintiffs' Attorney]: * * * But the frustration of the Plaintiff is that there's no response whatsoever. We're being asked to go forward and prove our venue facts when there's no corporation [sic] at all on the part of the defendants to give us those very venue facts. And that is why the motion to postpone was filed. It was filed in good faith to advise the Court that if we can have a sufficient period of time and the Court's help in obtaining the venue.

THE COURT: No. Don't ask for my help. You're not going to get it. I'm not going to get involved in the discovery. That's your problem.

MR. KELLY: All right. The second part of my statement, if we could have efficient [sic] time at which to obtain the venue facts, then we will be able to go forward.

THE COURT: And supposedly [sic] they won't answer then what will you do?

MR. KELLY: At that point we would have to use the Court's measures and motions to compel and have hearings before the court.

THE COURT: No, no. That's exactly what I want to avoid. If you're going—Don't you even think for one minute that you're going to pretrial me to death in this case because it won't happen. I'm telling you it won't happen.

* * *

THE COURT: Okay. Anybody else? Okay. What else on this motion? Okay. Let me rule on this motion then. The Court is going to grant this motion. I'm going to give extended time for the hearing on the motion to transfer venue. It's set for when you say?

MR. GONZALEZ: February 6.

THE COURT: No. I'm going to set it. Don't tell me. Don't even suggest. You wanted a ruling from me, you're going to get it. This case is set for the motion to transfer for October the 14th. That'll give you enough time to complete everything. And if you haven't done it by then, by golly, you better get this case out of here.

MS. HOUSTON: Your Honor, could you repeat that.

THE COURT: October the 14th. That's going to be a Tuesday. Now, what other motion.

MS. HOUSTON: Thank you, Your Honor.

THE COURT: What other motion?

> MR. GONZALEZ: Clarification. What was the discovery limited to?
>
> THE COURT: I'm not going to limit any of the discovery. I'm not going to get involved in the discovery. That's up to you. Don't get me involved in that.

It is clear from the record before us that Judge Garcia simply does not want to be involved in this case:

> THE COURT: Well, now venue facts should have already been investigated before you filed suite [sic]. Why are you taking my time? Listen. I didn't ask for you guys—for the Plaintiffs to file in my Court. I didn't ask for this case. I didn't beg you to file it in my Court. My god. I don't want it take it out. And if there's any legal grounds of taking this case out of here, you bet you I'm going to grant it. You bet you I'm going to grant it. I don't want this case. I'm not begging for it so don't ask me to rule on your side just because you filed it here. You weren't doing me any favors.

Despite Judge Garcia's misgivings, he is the elected official assigned to hear this cause, and neither the case law previously cited nor the Texas Code of Judicial Conduct give Judge Garcia the discretion to refuse to hear or rule on Safety-Kleen's motion within a reasonable period of time. *See* TEX. CODE JUD. CONDUCT, Canon 3 (1994), reprinted in TEX. GOV'T CODE ANN., tit. 2, subtit. G app. B (Vernon Supp. 1997) ("judge shall hear and decide matters;" "judge shall dispose of all judicial matters promptly, efficiently and fairly").

Safety-Kleen's right to discovery cannot be abated or otherwise affected by the pendency of a motion to transfer venue. TEX. R. CIV. P. 88. We therefore conditionally grant Safety-Kleen's petition for writ of mandamus. The writ shall issue only upon certification to this court that Judge Garcia has failed to hear and rule on Safety-Kleen's motion to compel by May 12, 1997.

Concurring opinion by JUSTICE RICKOFF omitted.

Notes & Questions

1. *Interlocutory Appeal.* Ordinarily, a party may not obtain immediate appellate review of a trial court's pretrial decision because courts of appeals generally have appellate jurisdiction only over final judgments.[1] A final judgment is a judgment that disposes of all parties and claims in a lawsuit. Therefore, review of pretrial rulings usually occurs only when the losing party appeals the judgment and points to an error that the trial judge made in a pretrial ruling that probably caused the rendition an improper judgment.[2]

However, if allowed by statute, immediate review may be available through an interlocutory appeal. The interlocutory appeal statute, § 51.014 of the Texas Civil Practice & Remedies Code, lists eight different orders that may be appealed immediately to the court of appeals. In this course, we will study two of those orders—orders ruling upon the special appearance[3] and the plea to the jurisdiction.[4] We will also study the interlocutory appeals currently available for venue

---

1 CPRC § 51.012.

2 *See* TRAP 44.1.

3 *See* CPRC § 51.014(7).

4 *See* CPRC § 51.014(8).

rulings.[5] Remember, only those orders made subject to interlocutory appeal by statute can be appealed before final judgment.

2. *Mandamus*. If your order is not included in a statute allowing interlocutory appeals, you nevertheless may be able to obtain immediate review through the extraordinary writ of mandamus. Mandamus is an original proceeding in the appellate court that seeks an order compelling a state official, such as the trial judge, to refrain from acting contrary to law. To successfully obtain mandamus relief in the court of appeals when complaining about a trial court's interlocutory order, the party must show (1) a clear abuse of discretion or legal error, and (2) no adequate remedy by appeal. In this course you will read many mandamus opinions—when you do so, be sure to consider each of these requirements.

WALKER
v.
PACKER
827 S.W.2d 833
(Tex. 1992)(orig. proceeding)

PHILLIPS, CHIEF JUSTICE.

* * *

Having concluded that the trial court erred in denying the discovery . . . we now must determine whether the appropriate remedy lies by writ of mandamus. "Mandamus issues only to correct a clear abuse of discretion or the violation of a duty imposed by law when there is no other adequate remedy by law." We therefore examine whether the trial court's error in the present case constituted a clear abuse of discretion and, if so, whether there is an adequate remedy by appeal.

1. Clear Abuse of Discretion

Traditionally, the writ of mandamus issued only to compel the performance of a ministerial act or duty.

Since the 1950's, however, this Court has used the writ to correct a "clear abuse of discretion" committed by the trial court.

A trial court clearly abuses its discretion if "it reaches a decision so arbitrary and unreasonable as to amount to a clear and prejudicial error of law." This standard, however, has different applications in different circumstances.

With respect to resolution of factual issues or matters committed to the trial court's discretion, for example, the reviewing court may not substitute its judgment for that of the trial court. The relator must establish that the trial court could reasonably have reached only one decision. Even if the reviewing court would have decided the issue differently, it cannot disturb the trial court's decision unless it is shown to be arbitrary and unreasonable.

On the other hand, review of a trial court's determination of the legal principles controlling its ruling is much less deferential. A trial court has no "discretion" in determining what the law is or

---

5 CPRC § 15.003(c).

applying the law to the facts. Thus, a clear failure by the trial court to analyze or apply the law correctly will constitute an abuse of discretion, and may result in appellate reversal by extraordinary writ.

In determining whether the trial court abused its discretion in the present case, we treat the trial court's erroneous denial of the requested discovery on the sole basis of *Russell* as a legal conclusion to be reviewed with limited deference to the trial court. This is consistent with our approach in previous mandamus proceedings arising out of the trial court's interpretation of legal rules. Under this analysis, the trial court's erroneous interpretation of the law constitutes a clear abuse of discretion.

2. Adequate Remedy by Appeal

In order to determine whether the writ should issue, however, we must further decide whether the Walkers have an adequate remedy by appeal.

Mandamus will not issue where there is "a clear and adequate remedy at law, such as a normal appeal." Mandamus is intended to be an extraordinary remedy, available only in limited circumstances. The writ will issue "only in situations involving manifest and urgent necessity and not for grievances that may be addressed by other remedies." The requirement that persons seeking mandamus relief establish the lack of an adequate appellate remedy is a "fundamental tenet" of mandamus practice.

* * *

The requirement that mandamus issue only where there is no adequate remedy by appeal is sound, and we reaffirm it today. No mandamus case has ever expressly rejected this requirement, or offered any explanation as to why mandamus review of discovery orders should be exempt from this "fundamental tenet" of mandamus practice. Without this limitation, appellate courts would "embroil themselves unnecessarily in incidental pre-trial rulings of the trial courts" and mandamus "would soon cease to be an extraordinary writ." . . .

We further hold that an appellate remedy is not inadequate merely because it may involve more expense or delay than obtaining an extraordinary writ. As we observed in *Iley v. Hughes,* the "delay in getting questions decided through the appellate process . . . will not justify intervention by appellate courts through the extraordinary writ of mandamus. Interference is justified only when parties stand to lose their substantial rights." 158 Tex. at 368, 311 S.W.2d at 652.

On some occasions, this Court has used, or at least mentioned, the more lenient standard first articulated in *Cleveland v. Ward,* 116 Tex. 1, 14, 285 S.W. 1063, 1068 (Tex. 1926), that the remedy by appeal must be "equally convenient, beneficial, and effective as mandamus." This standard, literally applied, would justify mandamus review whenever an appeal would arguably involve more cost or delay than mandamus. This is unworkable, both for individual cases and for the system as a whole. Mandamus disrupts the trial proceedings, forcing the parties to address in an appellate court issues that otherwise might have been resolved as discovery progressed and the evidence was developed at trial. Moreover, the delays and expense of mandamus proceedings may be substantial. This proceeding, for example, involving rulings on collateral discovery matters, has delayed the trial on the merits for over two years. The impact on the appellate courts must also be considered. . . . We therefore disapprove of *Cleveland, Crane, Jampole* and any other authorities to the extent that they imply that a remedy by appeal is inadequate merely because it might involve more delay or cost than mandamus.

* * *

For the above reasons, we conclude that the Walkers have not established their right to relief by mandamus on either discovery matter. Therefore, we deny the Walkers' petition for writ of mandamus.

DOGGETT, JUSTICE, dissenting.

Them that's got shall get
Them that's not shall lose
—God Bless The Child[1]

With a double standard, the majority strikes a devastating blow at the most direct method of curbing abuses of judicial power. Many judicial excesses far beyond the scope of anything alleged in this particular case will henceforth receive only an official nod and wink from the Texas Supreme Court.

Mandamus is the legal tool by which appellate courts can promptly correct arbitrary and capricious rulings by trial judges. Today's opinion announces that this remedy will be available to support concealment of the truth but not its disclosure. Mandamus is officially declared a one-way street in the Texas courts—our judiciary can help to hide but not to detect.

* * *

Today's opinion reflects the radical change in philosophy which has taken firm hold in this court—discovery is no longer a search for truth, it is merely a game of hide and seek. No longer may appellate courts intercede through mandamus even for the trial court's complete abuse of discretion in denying access to vital data; under the newly-announced double standard, intervention can, however, be accorded for those who persevere in evasion.

In re PRUDENTIAL INSURANCE COMPANY

148 S.W.3d 124
(Tex. 2004)

HECHT, JUSTICE.

* * *

III

Having concluded that the parties' contractual jury waiver is enforceable, we turn to whether Prudential is entitled to relief by mandamus. Prudential must meet two requirements. One is to show that the trial court clearly abused its discretion. We have concluded as a matter of law that Prudential was entitled to enforcement of the jury waiver. Since "[a] trial court has no 'discretion' in determining what the law is or applying the law to the facts," even when the law is unsettled, the trial court's refusal to enforce the jury waiver was a clear abuse of discretion. Thus, Prudential has met the first requirement.

---

1 Billie Holiday, *God Bless the Child* (Okeh Records 1941) (words and music by Arthur Herzog, Jr. & Billie Holiday).

The other requirement Prudential must meet is to show that it has no adequate remedy by appeal. The operative word, "adequate", has no comprehensive definition; it is simply a proxy for the careful balance of jurisprudential considerations that determine when appellate courts will use original mandamus proceedings to review the actions of lower courts. These considerations implicate both public and private interests. Mandamus review of incidental, interlocutory rulings by the trial courts unduly interferes with trial court proceedings, distracts appellate court attention to issues that are unimportant both to the ultimate disposition of the case at hand and to the uniform development of the law, and adds unproductively to the expense and delay of civil litigation. Mandamus review of significant rulings in exceptional cases may be essential to preserve important substantive and procedural rights from impairment or loss, allow the appellate courts to give needed and helpful direction to the law that would otherwise prove elusive in appeals from final judgments, and spare private parties and the public the time and money utterly wasted enduring eventual reversal of improperly conducted proceedings. An appellate remedy is "adequate" when any benefits to mandamus review are outweighed by the detriments. When the benefits outweigh the detriments, appellate courts must consider whether the appellate remedy is adequate.

This determination is not an abstract or formulaic one; it is practical and prudential. It resists categorization, as our own decisions demonstrate. Although this Court has tried to give more concrete direction for determining the availability of mandamus review, rigid rules are necessarily inconsistent with the flexibility that is the remedy's principal virtue. Thus, we wrote in *Walker v. Packer* that "an appellate remedy is not inadequate merely because it may involve more expense or delay than obtaining an extraordinary writ." While this is certainly true, the word "merely" carries heavy freight. . . . In *In re Masonite Corp.,* 997 S.W.2d 194, 195-196 (Tex. 1999), the trial court on its own motion and without any authority whatever, split two cases into sixteen and transferred venue of fourteen of them to other counties. We held that the defendants were not required to wait until appeal to complain:

> *Walker* does not require us to turn a blind eye to blatant injustice nor does it mandate that we be an accomplice to sixteen trials that will amount to little more than a fiction. Appeal may be adequate for a particular party, but it is no remedy at all for the irreversible waste of judicial and public resources that would be required here if mandamus does not issue.

These cases, among a great many others that could be cited, serve to illustrate that whether an appellate remedy is "adequate" so as to preclude mandamus review depends heavily on the circumstances presented and is better guided by general principles than by simple rules.[1]

* * *

Prudent mandamus relief is also preferable to legislative enlargement of interlocutory appeals.[2] The unavailability of mandamus relief increases the pressure for expanded interlocutory

---

[1] *See also* 16 CHARLES ALAN WRIGHT, ARTHUR R. MILLER, & EDWARD H. COOPER, FEDERAL PRACTICE AND PROCEDURE § 3934.1, at 572, 574 (1996) (stating that "[w]rit review that responds to occasional special needs provides a valuable ad hoc relief valve for the pressures that are imperfectly contained by the statutes permitting appeals from final judgments and interlocutory orders", and that "[i]mportant questions of procedure often are difficult to review by appeal, and at times may demand appellate intervention to secure uniformity between different judges, or simply to bring the balancing perspective that appellate review is intended to provide in controlling the practices as well as the substantive decisions of trial courts.").

[2] *See also* George C. Pratt, *Extraordinary Writs,* in 19 MOORE'S FEDERAL PRACTICE § 204.01[2][b], at 204-7 (3d ed. 2004) ("In order to meet the demands of justice in individual cases, discretionary review is preferable

appeals. For example, when this Court refused to review venue decisions by mandamus, the Legislature responded by authorizing mandamus review of all decisions involving mandatory venue provisions. When we held that the denial of a special appearance would ordinarily not warrant mandamus review, the Legislature responded by creating an interlocutory appeal from the denial of a special appearance. . . . Interlocutory appeals lie as of right and must be decided on the merits, increasing the burden on the appellate system. "Mandamus," on the other hand, "is an extraordinary remedy, not issued as a matter of right, but at the discretion of the court. Although mandamus is not an equitable remedy, its issuance is largely controlled by equitable principles." As a selective procedure, mandamus can correct clear errors in exceptional cases and afford appropriate guidance to the law without the disruption and burden of interlocutory appeal. Appellate courts must be mindful, however, that the benefits of mandamus review are easily lost by overuse.

The issue before us in the present case—whether a pre-suit waiver of trial by jury is enforceable—fits well within the types of issues for which mandamus review is not only appropriate but necessary. It is an issue of law, one of first impression for us, but likely to recur (it has already arisen in another case in the court of appeals, also on petition for mandamus. [citation omitted]. It eludes answer by appeal. In no real sense can the trial court's denial of Prudential's contractual right to have the Secchis waive a jury ever be rectified on appeal. If Prudential were to obtain judgment on a favorable jury verdict, it could not appeal, and its contractual right would be lost forever. If Prudential suffered judgment on an unfavorable verdict, Prudential could not obtain reversal for the incorrect denial of its contractual right "unless the court of appeals concludes that the error complained of ... probably caused the rendition of an improper judgment". Even if Prudential could somehow obtain reversal based on the denial of its contractual right, it would already have lost a part of it by having been subject to the procedure it agreed to waive.

* * *

Finally, we note that other courts have granted mandamus relief to enforce contractual jury waivers, including the only other Texas court to have addressed the issue. We are not aware of a published decision denying such relief.

* * *

For these reasons, we direct respondent, the Honorable Sally Montgomery, to vacate her order of June 6, 2003, and the prior order of June 19, 2002, to grant Prudential's motion to quash the jury demand and payment of jury fee, and to return the case to the nonjury docket. We are confident she will promptly comply. Our writ will issue only if she does not.

---

to enlarging by judicial interpretation the categories of interlocutory orders that are appealable as of right. General categories of orders that are appealable as of right often include many orders that should not be appealable at all. Review by extraordinary writ allows the circuit courts to retain the final judgment rule and avoid piecemeal appeals, yet be able to respond to the exceptional case that should be reviewed prior to final judgment. Thus, [mandamus] affords an avenue of relief to litigants and a tool for the courts to supervise the proper administration of justice.").

CHIEF JUSTICE PHILLIPS, joined by JUSTICE O'NEILL, JUSTICE JEFFERSON, and JUSTICE SCHNEIDER, dissenting.

Mandamus is an extraordinary remedy available "only in situations involving manifest and urgent necessity and not for grievances that may be addressed by other remedies." *Walker v. Packer,* 827 S.W.2d 833, 840 (Tex. 1992). . . . Although the Court's mandamus jurisprudence has not always strictly adhered to these tenets, we have endeavored to apply them more consistently since our decision in *Walker.* Because the Court retreats from that approach today, I respectfully dissent.

* * *

Admittedly, Prudential's appellate remedy is not as efficient or economical as mandamus, but that has never been the test.

* * *

But the Court now surprisingly suggests that the second prong of our mandamus standard has no fixed meaning. (The word " 'adequate' has no comprehensive definition."). Instead, the Court says we must weigh all the public and private interests implicated by the lower court ruling at issue and then decide on balance whether a remedy other than mandamus is adequate or not. . . .

I see no need to inject even greater uncertainty into an already difficult and frequently subjective process. In the past, we have emphasized that the writ of mandamus should not issue absent "compelling circumstances." But today, in circumstances far from compelling, the Court uses mandamus as a substitute for appeal, an approach rejected even by the federal procedure the Court purports to emulate. Whether today's ruling has fundamentally altered these traditional rules, or is merely an anomaly, remains to be seen.

* * *

Notes & Questions

A trial judge's discretion. In *Walker*, the Supreme Court defined a "clear abuse of discretion" necessary for mandamus relief. The court distinguishes between the trial judge's factual decisions and the trial judge's application of law. A decision can be an abuse of discretion if the trial judge's view of the facts is wholly unsupported by the evidence, or if the trial judge does not correctly apply the law to the facts. Mandamus is available if the decision was a clear abuse of discretion and there is no adequate appellate remedy.

Appellate courts also often consider whether a trial judge abused discretion in ordinary appeals. Some of a trial judge's decisions are mandated by clear and inflexible rules that the trial court must apply as written, with no discretion in applying or modifying them. But in most situations, the law gives the trial judge discretion in interpreting and applying the legal rules. The judge committed error only if that discretion was abused.

Discretion means that within broad limits the judge has leeway or flexibility. Discretion means that on a given set of facts, one judge might rule one way and another judge another way, and either ruling would be affirmed on appeal as within the court's discretion. In this sense, legal discretion is much like the deference given to baseball referees: when the officials make a judgment call on the field, it will not be overruled on instant replay unless the video shows clearly and indisputably that the wrong call was made. And like the baseball referee, the judgment call might be wrong because the referee made a mistake about the facts (the video replay shows that the runner's foot was on the base when tagged) or because the referee made a mistake about the applicable rule.

The field of trial court discretion is wide and broad. But it is not unlimited, and it may be abused. Still, trial court discretion is one of the pervasive realities of litigation. As you go through this course, remember to think about whether the trial court's decision is one of law (where there is only one correct ruling), of fact (which will be discussed in more detail later in the course) or of discretion (which can involve both law and fact).

---

2. *Requesting Action from the Trial Court: Motions, Pleas and Other Requests*

Read Rules 4, 5, 8, 21, 21a, 21b, 74, 75; TRAP 33.1.

MICHIANA EASY LIVIN' COUNTRY, INC.
v.
HOLTEN

168 S.W.3d 777
(Tex. 2005)

[James Holten bought a recreational vehicle from Michiana, an outlet store that did business only in Indiana. He sued Michiana in Texas state court for fraud, and Michiana filed a special appearance contesting personal jurisdiction. The trial court denied the special appearance, holding that Michiana was subject to the jurisdiction of the Texas courts. The Texas Supreme Court disagreed, but first the court had to deal with the absence of a record of the proceedings in the special appearance hearing.]

JUSTICE BRISTER delivered the opinion of the Court, in which CHIEF JUSTICE JEFFERSON, JUSTICE HECHT, JUSTICE OWEN, and JUSTICE GREEN joined.

* * *

B. The Record in Pretrial Hearings

[T]he appellate record contains no reporter's record of the special appearance hearing. Though candidly conceding that no oral testimony or new exhibits were presented at that hearing, Holten nevertheless argues we must presume evidence was presented that supports the trial court's order.

It is difficult to state a bright-line rule regarding unrecorded pretrial proceedings, as they come in so many shapes and sizes. Many pretrial "hearings" take place entirely on paper, while others involve a personal appearance in court. In some the parties must file all evidence with the clerk; in others they must present it in open court; in most the manner of presentation is discretionary; in at least one the answer is unclear.

What is clear is that a reporter's record is required only if evidence is introduced in open court; for nonevidentiary hearings, it is superfluous. If all the evidence is filed with the clerk and only arguments by counsel are presented in open court, the appeal should be decided on the clerk's record alone.

The difficulty of course is that the absence of a reporter's record does not tell us whether a pretrial hearing was nonevidentiary, or evidentiary but not preserved. Presuming them all the former unfairly penalizes a party that presents evidence in open court that the other party does not bother to preserve. But presuming them all the latter would require *every* hearing to be recorded—whether evidentiary (to show what was presented) or not (to show nothing was). Besides being wasteful, this would frustrate the intent of our appellate rule requiring a reporter's record only "if necessary to the appeal."[13]

For some years now the trend has been away from full evidentiary hearings in open court for most pretrial matters. While we have generally encouraged oral hearings when arguments may be helpful, both the Legislature and this Court have discouraged oral presentation of testimony and evidence when they can be fairly submitted in writing. Counsel can almost always direct the trial court's attention to pertinent deposition excerpts, discovery responses, or affidavits in less time than it takes to recreate them in open court. Presuming that most pretrial proceedings are evidentiary would not only discourage this trend, but would encumber thousands of routine hearings by requiring formal proof that no proof was offered.

Accordingly, we have in the past presumed that pretrial hearings are nonevidentiary absent a specific indication or assertion to the contrary. If the proceeding's nature, the trial court's order, the party's briefs, or other indications show that an evidentiary hearing took place in open court, then a complaining party must present a record of that hearing to establish harmful error. But otherwise, appellate courts should presume that pretrial hearings are nonevidentiary, and that the trial court considered only the evidence filed with the clerk.

* * *

Either party, of course, may allege that a hearing was evidentiary, but that allegation must be specific. Merely asserting that the trial court "considered evidence at the hearing" is not enough—trial courts do that when a hearing is conducted entirely on paper, or based solely on affidavits and exhibits filed beforehand. Instead, there must be a specific indication that exhibits or testimony was presented in open court *beyond* that filed with the clerk. As the rules of professional conduct prohibit assertions that a hearing was evidentiary when it was not,[22] and as events in open court can usually be confirmed by many witnesses, there is no reason to expect that such assertions will be lightly fabricated.

Our appellate rules are designed to resolve appeals on the merits, and we must interpret and apply them whenever possible to achieve that aim. Accordingly, we decline to presume the special appearance hearing here was evidentiary when everyone concedes it was not.

---

13 TEX.R.APP. P. 34.1.

22 Tex. Disciplinary R. Prof'l Conduct 3.03 (requiring candor toward tribunal); Tex. Lawyer's Creed: A Mandate for Professionalism IV(6) ("I will not knowingly misrepresent, mischaracterize, misquote or miscite facts or authorities to gain an advantage.").

Notes & Questions

1. *Record.* Parties request courts to act through pleadings, motions, and other requests, most of which are covered in the rules of procedure. Courts in turn act through orders, judgments, and other rulings. These requests, rulings, and all of the evidence and circumstances relevant to the decisions made are available to the appellate court only through the "record." Thus, it is very important to get everything needed for appellate review on the record, either through a writing that is filed in the trial court's records (which ultimately becomes the "clerk's record" on appeal), or orally in front of the court reporter, whose notes of the proceedings can be transcribed and put into the appellate record (called the "court reporter's record").[1] Appellate Rule 13.1(a) requires the court reporter to attend and record all proceedings unless a party expressly waives his or her right to have a court reporter record the proceedings.[2] However, GOV'T CODE §52.046(a) provides that the court reporter attends sessions of court and records the proceedings "on request." The courts of appeals disagree as to which controls.[3]

2. *Preserving error.* Generally, an appellate court may review a trial court's judgment only for errors that have been properly "preserved" in the trial court—the party has to have asked the trial court to make the correct ruling before it complain that the trial court's action was error. TRAP 33.1 governs preservation of error. It requires "as a prerequisite to presenting a complaint for appellate review" that "the record must show" that the complaining party presented the matter to the trial court by a "timely request, objection, or motion" that states "the grounds for the ruling" with "sufficient specificity to make the trial court aware of the complaint" and that the trial court ruled (or if there was no ruling, the party must object to the failure to rule). There are a few errors, called "fundamental errors," that do not require preservation. We have already addressed two important fundamental errors: subject matter jurisdiction and judicial disqualification.

3. *Reversible error.* Another general rule is that an appellate court may not reverse a trial court's judgment for an erroneous ruling unless "the error complained of … probably caused the rendition of an improper judgment." TRAP 44.1(a)(1). This is called the "harmless error rule" because it prevents reversals for harmless errors. A judgment may also be reversed if the error "probably prevented the appellant from properly presenting the case to the court of appeals." TRAP 44.1(a)(2). There are a few errors that require reversal without a showing of harm, such as venue, and others that require a lesser showing of harm, such as jury selection.

4. *Evidentiary Record.* Why was it important for the Supreme Court to determine whether there was evidence presented at the special appearance hearing in *Michiana*? In reviewing the trial court's decision, it had to determine what evidence was before the court and whether the decision was supported by that evidence. If there was no evidence presented at the hearing, the evidence before the court was limited to the written evidence presented with the defendant's special

---

1 TRAP 34 governs the clerk's and court reporter's record.

2 *See* Rittenhouse v. Sabine Valley Ctr. Found., Inc., 161 S.W.3d 157, 161-62 (Tex.App.—Texarkana 2005, no pet.)(holding that duty is mandatory and noting disagreement among courts of appeals). *See also* Reyes v. Credit Based Asset Servicing and Securitization, 190 S.W.3d 736, 740 (Tex.App.—San Antonio 2005, no pet.); Palmer v. Espey Huston & Assocs., 84 S.W.3d 345, 351 (Tex.App.—Corpus Christi 2002, pet. denied)(agreeing that Appellate Rule 13.1(a) is mandatory).

3 Polaske v. State, 16 S.W.3d 82, 88-89 (Tex.App.—Houston [1st Dist.] 2000, pet. ref'd)(holding that statute controls, so objection must be made to the absence of a court reporter to preserve error).

appearance and the plaintiff's response, and the appellate court should limit its review to the clerk's record. If there had been an evidentiary hearing, but no court reporter's record was made of that hearing (or perhaps it was made, but the complaining party did not have it transcribed and sent to the appellate court), the reviewing court has to presume that the evidence presented at the hearing supported the trial court's decision.

5. *Filing Documents.* After drafting a motion, pleading, or other request, the party must properly *file* the document with the clerk so that it is included in the clerk's record—usually through electronic filing.[4] The clerk's record is public—Rule 21c provides for redaction of "sensitive data" in filed documents. Papers presented during a hearing or trial need not be filed with the clerk[5]—Rule 74 also allows the judge to accept papers for filing.

An electronically filed document is considered timely filed if it is filed any time before midnight in the court's time zone on the filing deadline, unless it must be filed by a certain time of day. An electronically filed document is deemed filed when transmitted to the filing party's electronic filing service provider, unless the document is transmitted on a Saturday, Sunday or legal holiday; if so, it is deemed filed on the next day that that is not a Saturday, Sunday or legal holiday.[6] If an electronically filed document is deemed untimely due to technical failure, a party may seek relief from the court, and if the missed deadline is one imposed by the Rules, the court must give the party a reasonable extension.[7]

If electronic filing is not mandated, filing can be accomplished by hand-delivery to the clerk's office or by mail[8] If the document is sent to the proper clerk by first-class U.S. mail, filing is complete on the date of mailing, so long as the clerk receives the document within 10 days after the date that the document must be filed.[9] The date shown on the postmark provides prima facie evidence of the date of mailing.[10] To facilitate proof, should the date of mailing be called into question, you might consider sending the document by certified mail, return receipt requested. This would enable you to receive a receipt with a postmark, and proof of the clerk's receipt within 10 days. The party filing a paper document should get a "file-marked copy" to keep in its own file for proof of the date of filing.

6. *Serving Documents.* Anything filed with a court under Rule 21, and any notice of a hearing must be served upon opposing parties.[11] (Note that this type of service is different from service of process, by which a defendant is notified of the initial filing of a lawsuit and ordered to respond.)

---

[4] Rule 21(a) & (f).

[5] *Id.*

[6] Rule 21(f)(5).

[7] Rule 21(f)(6).

[8] Rule 5. Note that the rule no longer allows fax filing, however, fax filing is available in a few counties in which the Supreme Court has approved local rules providing for such filing.

[9] Rule 5. *See also* Stokes v. Aberdeen, 917 S.W.2d 267 (Tex. 1996) (mailing to proper court address is conditionally effective as mailing to proper court clerk's address if clerk receives a copy within 10 days). Texas Worker's Comp. Comm'n v. Hartford Accident and Indem. Co., 952 S.W.2d 949 (Tex. App.—Corpus Christi 1997, pet. denied) (mailbox rule is applicable to documents sent by first class mail only, and not those sent by private courier).

[10] *Id.*

[11] Rule 21(b), 21a(a).

If the party is represented by a lawyer, you should serve it on the lawyer.[12] Rule 21 requires all filed documents to contain a "Certificate of Service" certifying that you have served the document in accordance with the rule. You must serve notice of a hearing (and certify that you have done so) not less than three days before the hearing (unless otherwise ordered).[13] The failure to serve the other parties is a sanctionable offense.[14]

When documents are filed electronically, and the email address of the lawyer or party to be served is on file with the electronic filing manager, service must be made electronically through the electronic filing manager.[15] Where electronic service is unavailable, other methods of service are set forth in Rule 21a: in person, by mail, by commercial delivery service, by fax, by email, or by such other manner as the court . . . directs.[16] Electronic service is complete upon transmission; service by mail or commercial delivery is complete upon deposit in the mail or with the commercial delivery service; and fax service is complete upon receipt of the fax, except that receipt after 5:00 p.m. is complete the following day.[17] If the response date is calculated from the date of service, and service was provided by mail, Rule 21a(c) adds 3 days to the response time.[18]

7. *Responding to Filed and Served Documents.* The date of filing and service is important because the response date is calculated either from the date of service or the date of filing, depending upon the type of document to which the response is made. Other response dates are calculated from the date a court order is signed or other date as set forth in the rules. Often a late response is the equivalent of no response and can be devastating to your client's position. Thus, proper calculation of response dates is essential. Rule 4 sets out the rules for computation of time, and applies to *any* period of time prescribed by the rules of procedure.[19]

Under Rule 4, the day of the act or event from which you are calculating your response time *is not included* in the time you have to respond. Thus, the date of filing, service, or court order is always Day 0, not Day 1. *Do not count that day.* Then count the number of days to respond, and the last day *is included*, and is thus the day your response is due. For example, if you have 7 days from service to respond to a pleading, the date of service is Day 0, and Day 7 is the day you must respond. If the last day is a Saturday, Sunday or legal holiday, the time period runs until the next day that is not a Saturday, Sunday or legal holiday. A "legal holiday" is when the clerk's office is officially closed, regardless of whether it is an official holiday listed in a statute.[20]

Intervening Saturdays, Sundays and legal holidays are generally counted when calculating the response date. When the response time is 5 days or less, however, do not count intervening Saturdays, Sundays, or legal holidays, except Saturdays, Sundays, and legal holidays are counted

---

[12] Rule 8.

[13] Rule 21(b). *See* Approximately $1,589.90 v. State, 230 S.W.3d 871, 873 (Tex. App.—Houston [14th Dist.] 2007, no pet.) (holding that local rule may not alter time periods set by TRCP, so the trial court's 10-day notice requirement was invalid).

[14] Rule 21b.

[15] Rule 21a(a)(1).

[16] Rule 21a(a)(2).

[17] Rule 21a(b).

[18] Rule 21a(c). Note that this three-day add-on is no longer available where service is by fax.

[19] Lewis v. Blake, 876 S.W.2d 314 (Tex. 1994).

[20] Miller Brewing Co. v. Villarreal, 829 S.W.2d 770 (Tex. 1992). *See also* Hernandez v. National Restoration Technologies, L.L.C., 211 S.W.3d 309 (Tex. 2006).

for the 3-day notice of hearing period provided for in Rule 21,[21] and the 3-day extension of time for service by mail provided for in Rule 21a.

---

[21] *See* Rule 4.

CHAPTER 3. PERSONAL JURISDICTION

A. Introduction

A court may exercise power over a defendant only if the defendant is subject to the court's personal jurisdiction. A defendant not subject to the court's personal jurisdiction need not obey the court's orders, and therefore need not appear before the court to respond to a lawsuit filed there. As you learned in first-year civil procedure, a court must comport with the requirements of due process to constitutionally exercise power over a defendant. These requirements can be broadly described as notice and minimum contacts with the State. Accordingly, the Texas Rules of Civil Procedure and Civil Practice and Remedies Code contain various provisions that seek to give defendants with sufficient Texas contacts the required notice of a pending suit through service of process. Defendants challenge service of process through a motion to quash service. Defendants without "minimum contacts" with the state may challenge the exercise of jurisdiction through a "special appearance." Each of these concepts will be explored in detail in this chapter.

B. Service of Process

Read Rules 103, 105, 106, 107, 108, 108a, 109, 109a, 119.

For a Texas court to assert its power over a defendant, the Texas rules and statutes governing service of process must be followed. Further, these procedures must provide reasonable notice of suit, as required by the Due Process Clause of the United States Constitution.[1]

When the plaintiff's first original petition is filed with the clerk of the court, the plaintiff must pay a fee and request the clerk to issue a citation.[2] The clerk then completes a printed form citation with the names of the parties, the plaintiff's lawyers, and other information about the lawsuit. The citation will also contain an order directing the defendant to file a written answer "on or before 10:00 a.m. on the Monday next after the expiration of twenty days after the date of service of the citation."[3] Finally, a copy of the petition is stapled to the citation, and it is ready for service.

---

[1] Mullane v. Central Hanover Bank and Trust Co., 339 U.S. 306 (1950).

[2] Rule 6 prohibits the commencement of a civil suit and the issuance or service of process on a Sunday. *See* Morgan v. Chandler, 906 S.W.2d 584 (Tex. App.—Amarillo 1995, writ denied) (holding that objection to Sunday filing is waived unless made before answer filed).

[3] Rule 99(b). An answer may be filed by U.S. Mail, and pursuant to Rule 5, will be "filed" on the day deposited in the mail. Thomas v. Gelber Group, Inc., 905 S.W.2d 786 (Tex. App.—Houston [14th Dist.] 1995, no writ). Therefore, an answer mailed on the date due will preclude a default judgment. *But see* $429.30 in U.S. Currency v. State, 896 S.W.2d 363, 365 (Tex. App.—Houston [1st Dist.] 1995, no writ) (answer mailed day after due date not timely filed, although mailed 13 days before default judgment rendered).

After the defendant has been served with process, the person who served process must make a "return of service" pursuant to Rule 107. The return notes the date, time, and method of service. Upon completion it is filed with the clerk.[4]

1. *Methods of Service of Process*

Rule 106 provides two preferred methods for service of process—both of which provide personal service on the defendant: (1) "in hand" delivery; and (2) registered or certified mail, return receipt requested.[5] In addition, Rule 106 provides that if an affidavit is filed showing that attempts under *either* method of personal service have failed, the court can specifically authorize an alternative (or substituted) method of service.

Methods of service other than personal service are not favored because they do not provide proof that actual notice of suit was given to the defendant. Therefore, they should be used with caution. While actual notice is not required, the service must be calculated to bring the suit to the attention of the defendant under the circumstances, while complying with the United States Supreme Court's due process requirements articulated in *Mullane v. Central Hanover Bank & Trust Co.*[6] Strict compliance with Rule 106's requirement of a supporting affidavit, which describes unsuccessful attempts, must be met if the substituted service is to give the court jurisdiction over a defendant who does not personally appear.[7] A default judgment taken against a defendant without notice or without proper service is constitutionally infirm and will not stand.[8]

Service by publication is particularly suspect under the *Mullane* standard, although it may be available in some circumstances.[9] The Texas rules provide that a defaulting defendant served by publication must be represented by a court-appointed attorney ad litem.[10] Furthermore, a defaulting defendant served by publication has two years in which to file a motion for new trial challenging the default judgment.[11] Service by publication is available, however, in some circumstances, such as when the defendant's residence[12] or specific identity[13] is unknown, and in suits for delin-

---

[4] Rule 107. *See also* Rules 16, 105; Ins. Co. of the State of Pa. v. Lejeune, 297 S.W.3d 254, 256 (Tex. 2009) (holding that clerk's failure to note hour of receipt of citation was error on face of record requiring reversal of default on restricted appeal).

[5] Note that the methods for service allowed under Rule 106 are different from those allowed in federal court under Federal Rule 4(e).

[6] 339 U.S. 306 (1950). *See also* Hubicki v. Festina, 226 S.W.3d 405 (Tex. 2007) (holding that substituted service by certified mail to Mexican address was inadequate because the affidavits did not establish that the defendant received mail at that address).

[7] *See* Wilson v. Dunn, 800 S.W.2d 833, 836 (Tex. 1990).

[8] Peralta v. Heights Medical Center, 485 U.S. 80 (1988).

[9] *See* In re E.R., 385 S.W.3d 552 (Tex. 2012) (holding that service of process by publication was impermissible under the circumstances in a parental rights termination case).

[10] *See* Rule 244.

[11] Defendants served by methods other than publication have 30 days after the default judgment is signed to file a motion for new trial. *See* Rule 329b.

[12] Rule 109.

[13] Rules 111 and 112.

quent ad valorem taxes.[14] Service by publication is also a permissible alternative service when the preferred methods have failed.[15]

In Texas state courts, leave with service—service made by leaving the papers at the person's customary place of business or residence—requires a court order, different from federal court.[16] Rule 106 specifies leave-with service as a method of substituted service. But substituted service may be authorized in any manner that the evidence shows would be reasonably effective to give defendant notice of the suit.[17] The order for substituted service must specifically identify the means of substituted service authorized by the court.[18]

2. *Persons Authorized to Serve Process*

In Texas, sheriffs, constables, any other person authorized by law, or a person authorized by written order of the trial court can serve process.[19] The clerk of the court may serve process by certified mail.[20] Professional "process servers" may serve process for a fee if the process server is certified by the Texas Supreme Court.[21] No interested person may serve process; thus, the rule disqualifies the parties' attorneys and their employees.[22] Service of process is void if made by one without authority to make it.[23]

The person who serves citation must sign the return of service showing when the citation was served and the manner of service.[24] An officer's failure to sign such a return makes it fatally defective as support for a default judgment.[25] When service is by certified mail, the return receipt

---

14 *See* Rule 117a.

15 *See* Rule 106(b)(2). Forms and technical requirements are dealt with in Rules 114-117.

16 Federal Rule 4(3) allows leave-with service on.

17 *See* Rule 106(b)(1)(2); State Farm Fire & Casualty Co. v. Costley, 868 S.W.2d 298 (Tex. 1993).

18 Rivers v. Viskozki, 967 S.W.2d 868 (Tex. App.—Eastland 1998, no pet.) (default judgment reversed because the order authorizing substituted service left the method of service to the discretion of the constable delivering service in violation of TRCP 106).

19 Rule 103(e)(2)(B) allows leave-with service "at the individual's dwelling or usual place of abode with someone of suitable age and discretion who resides there."

20 Rule 106; P&H Transp., Inc. v. Robinson, 930 S.W.2d 857 (Tex. App.—Houston [1st Dist.] 1996, writ denied).

21 *See* Rules 103, 106, and HB & WM, Inc. v. Smith, 802 S.W.2d 279, 281 (Tex. App.—San Antonio 1990, no writ). Rule 103 was amended in 2005 to allow certified process servers to serve process.

22 Menon v. Water Splash, Inc., 2018 WL 344040, *5-*6 (Tex.App.—Houston [14th Dist.] 2018, no pet.). Compare Rule 103 with the more lenient rule for service of subpoenas. *See* Rule 178 permitting service of subpoenas by sheriff, constable, or any person over eighteen who is *not a party*. Thus, a server of a subpoena may be interested in the case outcome.

23 *See* Turner v. Ephraim, 28 S.W.2d 608, 609 (Tex. Civ. App.—El Paso 1930, no writ).

24 *See* Rule 107; Primate Constr. Inc. v. Silver, 884 S.W.2d 151 (Tex. 1994) (return that showed service with Original Petition, a version that did not contain allegations against defendant, was error justifying overturning default by writ of error). Rule 105 also requires the process server to endorse the day and hour on which the process server received it. *See* In re Z.J.W., 185 S.W.3d 905 (Tex. App.—Tyler 2006, no pet.) (requiring strict compliance with Rule).

25 Hot Shot Messenger Service, Inc. v. State, 818 S.W.2d 905, 907 (Tex. App.—Austin 1991, no writ).

with the addressee's signature (the "green card") must be filed.[26] Finally, when a lay person makes service of process, the server must verify the return.[27]

3. *Waiver and Acceptance of Service*

A defendant may accept or waive process and obviate the need for formal service; but to be effective, the acceptance or waiver must be in writing, filed in the case papers, and signed before a notary other than the handling attorney *after* suit has been filed.[28] The acceptance or waiver must contain the defendant's acknowledgment of receipt of a copy of the petition and, in a divorce action, must include the defendant's mailing address.[29] A waiver dated before the date suit is filed is invalid.[30]

4. *Whom to Serve*

Service of process within the State of Texas is relatively straightforward. If the defendant is an individual, that individual is personally served with process according to Rule 106 by someone authorized to serve under Rule 103. If the defendant is an entity, the entity can be served only through an individual agent or representative. Often an agent for service of process is appointed by the entity and registered with the Secretary of State's office.[31] Sometimes a statute will appoint an agent for service of process. For example, partnerships can be served by serving any partner[32] (although individual partners can be held personally liable only if they are actually named and served with process); corporations can be served by serving their registered agents or certain officers,[33] or under certain circumstances, the Secretary of State.[34]

5. *Service on Non-Residents*

Service upon non-residents is somewhat more complicated. A non-resident individual physically within the State of Texas may be served with process in Texas in the manner a Texas resident is served according to Rules 103 and 106.[35] A foreign corporation (a corporation incorpo-

---

26 Hollister v. Palmer ISD, 958 S.W.2d 956 (Tex. App.—Waco 1998, no pet.) (default judgment reversed because district clerk's failure to attach the postal service return receipt to the return of service constituted defective service).

27 Rule 107.

28 Rule 119.

29 *Id.*

30 Deen v. Kirk, 508 S.W.2d 70, 71 (Tex. 1974).

31 TEX. BUS. ORG. CODE § 5.201.

32 CPRC § 17.022.

33 TEX. BUS. ORG. CODE § 5.255.

34 TEX. BUS. ORG. CODE § 5.251.

35 At least one court has held that a nonresident individual who voluntarily comes to Texas and is served with Texas process in Texas subjects himself to the general jurisdiction of the State of Texas. *See* Goldwait v. State, 961 S.W.2d 432 (Tex. App.—Houston [1st Dist.] 1997, no writ) (Boston resident's visit to Houston at urging of his family, who wanted to convince him to voluntarily commit himself for mental health treatment, was sufficient to submit him to general jurisdiction of Texas court for purpose of involuntary commitment proceeding). *See also* Burnham v. Superior Court, 495 U.S. 604 (1990) (finding general jurisdiction over nonresident served in California).

rated under the laws of a state other than Texas) that "transacts business" in Texas is required to appoint a resident agent upon whom process may be served in Texas.[36] If there is no appointed agent, the entity can be served through an agent or clerk in the entity's Texas office or place of business.[37] Thus, because there is someone in Texas who can be served, the service of process can be made in Texas according to Rules 103 and 106.

If the non-resident defendant is not physically located in Texas and has no Texas agent for service of process, the non-resident must be served elsewhere with Texas process or served in Texas through one of Texas' long-arm statutes.[38] Rule 108 provides a method for Texas process to be served in other states by any method allowed by Rule 106, so long as that method complies with due process. Although initially there was some question about the validity of Rule 108 service, the Texas Supreme Court has confirmed that it is an appropriate method for service on non-residents.[39] This simple method of service is now the preferred method upon non-resident defendants.

Another method for service on non-residents is the Texas general long-arm statute.[40] The statute authorizes substituted service on the Secretary of State under certain circumstances, following which the Secretary mails a copy of citation and petition to the defendant by certified mail, return receipt requested.[41] Two aspects of this long-arm statute create a real possibility that a defendant may be served but never get actual notice of the suit. First, service is complete when the Secretary of State is served and has given the certified mail notice, whether or not the defendant ever receives actual notice.[42] Second, because the information about the defendant's home or office is provided to the Secretary of State by the plaintiff seeking the service, it may not be correct.[43]

---

[36] TEX. BUS. ORG. CODE § 9.001.

[37] CPRC § 17.021.

[38] If a non-resident is amenable to service of process under the long-arm statute and has contacts with the statute sufficient to afford personal jurisdiction, the non-resident is "present" in the state, preventing tolling of the statute of limitations under CPRC §16.063. That statute provides that a person's "absence" from the state suspends the statute of limitations for the period of the absence. *See* Ashley v. Hawkins, 293 S.W.3d 175, 178-79 (Tex. 2009); Kerlin v. Sauceda, 263 S.W.3d 920, 927 (Tex. 2008). Service abroad may be available under the Hague Convention. *See* Water Splash, Inc. v. Menon, ___ U.S. ___, 137 S.Ct. 1504, 1513 (2017) (holding that Hague Convention allows service by mail upon Canadian in Texas case if "first, the receiving state has not objected to service by mail; and second, service by mail is authorized under [Texas] law").

[39] Paramount Pipe & Supply Co. v. Muhr, 749 S.W.2d 491, 495-96 (Tex. 1988).

[40] CPRC §§ 17.041-45.

[41] CPRC § 17.044; *see* Whitney v. L. & L. Realty Corp., 500 S.W.2d 94, 96 (Tex. 1973); Roland Communications, Inc. v. American Communications Corpus Christi, Inc., 662 S.W.2d 145, 147 (Tex. App.—Corpus Christi 1983, no writ).

[42] *Whitney,* 500 S.W.2d at 96; Bonewitz v. Bonewitz, 726 S.W.2d 227 (Tex. App.—Austin 1987, writ ref'd n.r.e.). *See* Campus Investments, Inc. v. Cullever, 144 S.W.3d 464 (Tex. 2004) (holding that Secretary of State's certificate of showing receipt and forwarding to defendant conclusively establishes service of process on defendant.

[43] *See* CPRC § 17.045(a). Note that the pleadings must at least allege that the forwarding address is the defendant's home or office, as required by the statute. Wachovia Bank v. Gilliam, 215 S.W.3d 848, 850-51 (Tex. 2007).

At one time there was a question about whether the general long-arm statute allowed the Texas courts to reach their jurisdiction as far as due process of the United States Constitution allowed. A provision of the statute purports to confer jurisdiction on the non-resident defendant only in a "proceeding that arises out of the business done in this state."[44] This limiting language has been read out of existence by a series of Texas Supreme Court holdings, however, and it is now clear that the statute reaches as far as federal due process will allow.[45]

Texas has other long-arm statutes, in addition to the general statute, that appoint the Secretary of State or some other state official as a non-resident's agent for service of process under certain circumstances.[46]

6. *Diligence in Serving Process*

ASHLEY
v.
HAWKINS
293 S.W.3d 175
(Tex. 2008)

JUSTICE GREEN delivered the opinion of the Court.

In this case, we consider whether section 16.063 of the Texas Civil Practice and Remedies Code tolls the limitations period when a defendant leaves Texas following a motor vehicle collision, but is otherwise amenable to out-of-state service. We reverse the court of appeals' judgment and reinstate the trial court's grant of summary judgment.

I

On May 31, 2003, Gail Ashley and Doris Hawkins were involved in a motor vehicle collision in Montgomery County, Texas. After the wreck, sometime in 2004, Ashley moved to California, leaving behind no forwarding address. On April 1, 2005, approximately sixty days prior to the expiration of the two-year limitations period, Hawkins sued Ashley, alleging personal injuries and damages related to the wreck. Although Hawkins made attempts to serve Ashley, she was not actually served until May 10, 2006, by a Sacramento County sheriff, almost one year after the limitations period expired. Ashley sought summary judgment on a statute-of-limitations affirmative defense, arguing that Hawkins failed to exercise diligence in serving her. *See* TEX. CIV. PRAC. & REM.CODE § 16.003(a) (setting a two-year limitations period for personal injury actions). In response, Hawkins argued that she exercised diligence in attempting to serve Ashley . . . .

* * *

---

[44] CPRC § 17.044(b).

[45] *See* Schlobohm v. Schapiro, 784 S.W.2d 355, 357 (Tex. 1990); Guardian Royal Exchange Assurances, Ltd. v. English China Clays, PLC, 815 S.W.2d 223, 226 (Tex. 1991).

[46] *See* CPRC §§ 17.061-69 (service on Chairman of the State Highway and Public Transportation Commission for a non-resident involved in a motor vehicle accident in Texas); CPRC § 17.091 (service on a non-resident in a delinquent tax case); CPRC § 17.092 (service on non-resident utility supplier); CPRC § 17.093 (service on foreign railway); FAMILY CODE § 11.55 (service on persons outside Texas in family law cases); TEX. BUS. CORP. ACT § 8.10 (service on foreign corporation registered to do business in Texas that has not appointed a registered agent for service).

III

If a party files its petition within the limitations period, service outside the limitations period may still be valid if the plaintiff exercises diligence in procuring service on the defendant. *Gant v. DeLeon,* 786 S.W.2d 259, 260 (Tex. 1990) (per curiam). When a defendant has affirmatively pleaded the defense of limitations, and shown that service was not timely, the burden shifts to the plaintiff to prove diligence. *Proulx v. Wells,* 235 S.W.3d 213, 216 (Tex. 2007) (per curiam). Diligence is determined by asking "whether the plaintiff acted as an ordinarily prudent person would have acted under the same or similar circumstances and was diligent up until the time the defendant was served." Although a fact question, a plaintiff's explanation may demonstrate a lack of diligence as a matter of law, "when one or more lapses between service efforts are unexplained or patently unreasonable." Thus, Hawkins has the burden to "present evidence regarding the efforts that were made to serve the defendant, and to explain every lapse in effort or period of delay."

Hawkins alleges the collision occurred on May 31, 2003, setting May 31, 2005, as the date the two-year limitations period expired. TEX. CIV. PRAC. & REM.CODE § 16.003(a) (setting a two-year limitations period for personal injury actions). In her motion for summary judgment, Ashley pointed out that she was not served until May 10, 2006, almost a year after the limitations period expired. Therefore, the burden shifted to Hawkins to explain how she was diligent in attempting to serve Ashley. The record reflects that Hawkins filed suit on April 1, 2005, and the clerk first mailed service to Ashley in Conroe, Texas, at an address found on Ashley's Texas driver's license and on the accident report. This citation was returned unclaimed. Then, on June 7, 2005, Hawkins requested, and the clerk mailed, service to an address in Sacramento, California. This was returned on July 27, 2005. No other service was attempted until March 17, 2006, at which time Hawkins provided the clerk with a new address in Rio Linda, California. Almost two months later, a Sacramento County sheriff personally served Ashley at that address. However, a period of almost eight months lapsed between July 27, 2005 and March 17, 2006. During this time, the record reflects that the trial court twice set the case for dismissal based on a want of prosecution, dismissing it on January 17, 2006, only to reinstate it following a motion by Hawkins. In her response to the motion for summary judgment, Hawkins asserted that she made a diligent effort to serve Ashley, citing the two attempts at service in April and June of 2005, and also explaining:

> Counsel for [Hawkins] and his assistants have spent approximately twenty (20) hours searching for [Ashley's] whereabouts. Many search engines, including Zabasearch, Google, DCS Information Systems (a reliable intelligence source for business), People Search, Intelius, and other sources have been utilized. Counsel for [Hawkins] personally went to the last known address of [Ashley] and canvassed the apartment project where she once resided. Although [Ashley] moved to California many months before she was finally served, she never changed her address on her driver's license.
>
> [Ashley] was finally located at a different address in Rio Linda, California and served with citation.

Hawkins also attached an affidavit from her counsel, stating that he was a licensed private investigator for over fifteen years, that he is "acquainted with the resources utilized by private investigators in skip tracing," and that he utilized those resources in attempting to locate Ashley. In addition to the methods listed in the motion, the affidavit listed other websites and public records he searched. She also contended that the Montgomery County Voter Registration Database listed Ashley's address in Conroe, Texas.

We agree with the trial court and hold that, as a matter of law, Hawkins' responses do not create a fact issue as to diligence, as this eight-month gap in time is left unexplained. Hawkins stated that she spent approximately twenty hours searching for Ashley, although she does not specify when this time was spent. Either these twenty hours were expended early on, in which case, the diligence of the search later ceased; or, these hours were spread over eight months, in which case the search was never diligent. Either way, Hawkins failed to meet her burden.

As a comparison, in *Proulx,* we held that a plaintiff's thirty-seven attempts at five different addresses over the course of nine months exhibited continuing diligence to preclude summary judgment. After numerous unsuccessful attempts at effectuating service, the plaintiff in *Proulx* sought substitute service because it was clear the defendant was attempting to evade service by "moving from relative to relative and doing his best to avoid service from the courts and creditors." In *Gant,* however, we held that a plaintiff was not diligent as a matter of law where no explanation was offered for gaps in service for three different periods ranging from six to twenty months. (citing cases with seventeen, ten, six, seven, and three month gaps). These cases clarify that, while the time period is important, it is not necessarily determinative of the question of diligence. Rather, we must consider the overall effort expended over the gap in service, and whether the search ceased to be reasonable, especially when other methods of service were available.

Notably, the record does not indicate that Hawkins attempted any form of service other than service by mail or delivery. If Hawkins was unable to locate Ashley, or if Hawkins thought Ashley was evading service, other methods of service were available. In particular, no substitute service such as service by publication was attempted. *See* TEX.R. CIV. P. 109 (providing for service by publication when defendant's residence is unknown, the defendant is transient, or the defendant is absent or is a nonresident of the state). Hawkins recognized its availability by stating, in her October 11, 2005, motion to retain the case on the court's docket, that she "utilized various investigative resources to no avail" and that she "would like additional time to locate [Ashley] before resorting to service by publication [,] which is expensive." But from the time of that motion, an additional five months lapsed before service was attempted and seven months lapsed until service was achieved. Although service by publication should not be a first resort, when a plaintiff is continuously unable to locate a defendant, its availability should not be overlooked. *See Carter v. MacFadyen,* 93 S.W.3d 307, 314-15 (Tex. App.—Houston [14th Dist.] 2002, pet. denied) ("A flurry of ineffective activity does not constitute due diligence if easily available and more effective alternatives are ignored.").

C. Consequences of Failure to Properly Serve the Defendant

No judgment is valid unless the defendant has been served with process, accepted or waived service, or entered an appearance in the case.[1] Thus, when a defendant appears without service or responds to the citation by answering or otherwise appearing in the lawsuit, even if the citation or the service of process was defective, the defendant has waived any defect in the manner of service.[2]

1. *Motion to Quash*

A defendant may choose to respond to the citation, but, instead of answering and waiving service defects, challenge them by means of a motion to quash. The Rule 122 motion to quash is the proper procedural vehicle for challenging formal defects in a petition's *allegations* of jurisdiction (minimum contacts),[3] the form of process, or service of process. A motion to quash is virtually useless, however, because it does not defeat jurisdiction or result in dismissal; if it is successful, the motion merely delays the defendant's answer date. When the motion is granted, the clock begins to run towards the defendant's answer date as if the defendant were served at the time the order quashing service is signed.[4] Therefore, defendants seldom file this motion, choosing to face the inevitable, and, instead, simply file an answer.

2. *Default Judgment Overturned*[5]

The most likely result of a defendant's failure to get notice of a pending lawsuit is that the defendant will fail to appear timely and then will suffer a default judgment. The failure to appear and answer effectively admits all the liability allegations in the plaintiff's petition. Accordingly, the plaintiff will receive judgment for the amount of damages pleaded and proven. Defects in service are not waived, however, and often the defendant can successfully challenge the default judgment on that basis.[6]

In Texas state courts, there are generally three procedures used to attack a default judgment: (1) the motion for new trial, (2) the restricted appeal, formerly called the writ of error, to the court of appeals, and (3) the bill of review.[7] Each has its own special characteristics and requirements that will make it available in some cases and not in others. These methods are described below.

---

[1] Rule 124; *see* Werner v. Colwell, 909 S.W.2d 866 (Tex. 1995) (judgment not valid against employee benefit plan unless named and served with process). In the Interest of J.(B.B.)M., 955 S.W.2d 405 (Tex. App.—San Antonio 1997, no pet.) (when individual waives citation but is nevertheless served, all TRCP requirements related to notice apply).

[2] *See* City of Tyler v. Beck, 196 S.W.3d 784 (Tex. 2006) (parties involved judicial process when filed objections to condemnation award and court acquired jurisdiction without formal service of process).

[3] The Motion to Quash is *not* the proper vehicle for challenging *amenability* to the court's jurisdiction. *See* the discussion of the special appearance in this chapter.

[4] Rule 122.

[5] A more detailed discussion of these procedures is located in Chapter 18. But it is mentioned here so you will better understand the opinions following.

[6] Primate Constr. Co. v. Silver, 884 S.W.2d 151 (Tex. 1994) (requiring strict construction of service rules).

[7] A default judgment may also be subject to collateral attack, which will be discussed later in this chapter.

a. *Motion for New Trial*

If a defendant discovers a default before the judgment becomes final, generally within 30 days of the date the judgment is signed, the defendant may file a motion for new trial in the trial court that rendered the judgment.[8] The trial court must grant the motion on legal grounds if there was a legal error in the proceeding, or on equitable grounds if the defendant shows:

1. The failure to answer was not intentional or the result of conscious indifference, but from mistake or accident;

2. A meritorious defense to the plaintiff's claim;[9] and

3. The plaintiff will not be delayed or otherwise injured if the motion is granted.[10]

A trial court's order invalidating the judgment and granting a new trial is ordinarily not subject to appellate review.[11] Therefore, this method is clearly the best option for attacking a default judgment because a judge may grant the motion even though these standards are not satisfied.[12] However, the 30-day time limitation often precludes the defendant's use of this method.

b. *Restricted Appeal*

The defendant's second option for overturning a default judgment is a restricted appeal in the court of appeals.[13] This request for appellate review is available only to persons who did not participate in the trial,[14] and may be filed within *six months* of the date of the judgment. The error upon which the court of appeals reverses the judgment, however, must appear on the face of the record from the trial court. Thus, this remedy is fairly limited.[15]

c. *Bill of Review*

The defendant's third option for overturning the default judgment is the bill of review procedure.[16] The bill of review is a new lawsuit, filed within four years after the defendant knew or should have known of the default judgment.[17] The bill of review is filed in the trial court that rendered the judgment, and must show "sufficient cause" for the former judgment to be set aside and a new correct judgment substituted for it. First, the bill of review plaintiff (the defendant suffering the default) presents, in a verified pleading, facts showing (1) the default judgment was ac-

---

[8] Rule 329b(a). *See also* Rule 306a(4)(allowing clock to "restart" if no notice of judgment).

[9] This is not required if the defendant had no notice of the proceeding in which the default was rendered.

[10] *See* Craddock v. Sunshine Bus Lines, Inc., 133 S.W.2d 124 (Tex. 1939) (stating that granting the motion for new trial would cause no delay and should be granted).

[11] In re Columbia Medical Center, 290 S.W.3d 204 (Tex. 2009).

[12] Green v. McAdams, 857 S.W.2d 816 (Tex. App.—Houston [1st Dist.] 1993, no writ).

[13] TRAP 30. Under former TRAP 45, the restricted appeal was known as writ of error review.

[14] *See* Withem v. Underwood, 922 S.W.2d 956, (Tex. 1996)(holding that petitioner did not participate in a trial against him for malicious prosecution); Texaco, Inc. v. Central Power and Light Co., 925 S.W.2d 586, (Tex. 1996) (party who did not participate in the hearing of evidence may file writ of error); Flores v. H.E. Butt Grocery Co., 802 S.W.2d 53, 55-57 (Tex. App.—Corpus Christi 1990, no writ) (merely filing an answer is not participation in the trial); DORSANEO, 100.13.

[15] *See* Sanchez v. Texas Industries, Inc., 485 S.W.2d 385 (Tex. Civ. App.—Waco 1972, writ ref'd n.r.e.).

[16] TRCP 329b(f).

[17] Valdez v. Hollenbeck, 465 S.W.3d 217, 222 (Tex. 2015).

quired through "extrinsic fraud" or "official mistake" (2) a meritorious defense to the underlying cause of action and (3) freedom from negligence in permitting the judgment to be taken.[18] If these requirements are satisfied, a new trial is had on the underlying cause of action, and judgment is entered accordingly.

If the defendant had no notice of the proceeding in which the default was rendered, the defendant need not independently satisfy the "extrinsic fraud" or "official mistake" requirement.[19] Furthermore, the United States Supreme Court in *Peralta v. Heights Medical Center, Inc.*[20] held that the meritorious defense requirement of the bill of review procedure violated due process in cases where the defendant had no notice of the proceeding where the default was rendered. The Texas Supreme Court has also applied the same reasoning to the meritorious defense requirement in equitable motions for new trial where the defendant had no notice.[21]

The following opinions illustrate the types of errors in service of process that may be raised through these procedures.

ZUYUS
v.
NO'MIS COMMUNICATIONS, INC.

930 S.W.2d 743

(Tex. App.—Corpus Christi 1996, no writ)

HINOJOSA, JUSTICE

No'Mis Communications, Inc. sued Peter T. Zuyus, for fraud, negligent misrepresentation, and violations of the Texas Deceptive Trade Practices-Consumer Protection Act ("DTPA"). After Zuyus failed to answer, No'Mis Communications obtained a default judgment from which Zuyus failed to timely perfect an ordinary appeal. Zuyus requests that we review this case by writ of error. We grant in part and deny in part Zuyus's petition for writ of error.

No'Mis Communications filed suit against Zuyus and Ted Tompers on April 20, 1994. Tompers answered on August 25, 1994. When Zuyus did not file an answer, No'Mis Communications filed a motion for default judgment and a motion to sever. After a hearing, the trial court granted a default judgment against Zuyus and awarded No'Mis Communications actual damages of $163,676.00, exemplary damages of $327,352.00, and attorney's fees of $6,400.00. In addition, the court awarded pre-judgment and post-judgment interest, court costs, and attorney's fees in the event of an appeal. The trial court also granted the motion for severance.

The following four elements are necessary for review by writ of error: 1) the petition must be brought within six months of the date of judgment 2) by a party to the suit 3) who did not participate in the trial, and 4) error must be apparent from the face of the record. *Stubbs v. Stubbs*, 685

---

18 Alexander v. Hagedorn, 148 Tex. 565, 226 S.W.2d 996 (1950).

19 Texas Industries, Inc. v. Sanchez, 525 S.W.2d 870 (Tex. 1975).

20 485 U.S. 80 (1988).

21 Lopez v. Lopez, 757 S.W.2d 721 (Tex. 1988).

S.W.2d 643, 644 (Tex. 1985); *Brown v. McLennan County Children's Protective Servs.*, 627 S.W.2d 390, 392 (Tex. 1982); TEX. R. APP. P. 45. Zuyus has clearly met the first three elements. By eleven points of error, Zuyus contends that error is apparent on the face of the record.

By his first point of error, Zuyus contends that the trial court erred in rendering a default judgment against him. Zuyus argues that the trial court lacked personal jurisdiction over him. Zuyus contends that he never received a copy of the process and notice required by TEX. CIV. PRAC. & REM. CODE ANN. § 17.045.[1]

Zuyus was president of Voice Systems & Services, Inc. of Mannford, Oklahoma. Voice Systems, by and through its agents and employees, conducted business in Cameron County, Texas. After Voice Systems allegedly breached a contract, No'Mis Communications sued Zuyus and Voice Systems for negligent misrepresentation, fraud, and violations of the DTPA. No'Mis Communications alleged in its pleadings that Zuyus did not maintain a regular place of business in Texas and had not designated an agent for service of process within the state. No'Mis Communications asked that Zuyus be served with process by serving the Secretary of State of the State of Texas in accordance with TEX. CIV. PRAC. & REM. CODE ANN. § 17.044.[2] The petition listed Voice Systems' business address as Zuyus's mailing address.

The record includes a certificate from the secretary of state certifying: 1) that he received two copies of the citation and petition on July 29, 1994; 2) that on July 29, 1994, he forwarded a copy of the process to Peter T. Zuyus, Rt. 3, Box 31, Cleveland, OK 74020, via certified mail, return receipt requested; and 3) that the process was returned to him on August 23, 1994, with the notation "unclaimed." The secretary of state's certificate was filed with the clerk of the trial court on September 7, 1994. The trial court signed the default judgment on January 23, 1995.

In a writ of error proceeding directly attacking a default judgment, the record must affirmatively show that the trial court had jurisdiction over the defendant's person. To support a default judgment upon substituted service, the record must show: 1) that the pleadings allege facts, which if true, would make the defendant amenable to process and 2) that the defendant was, in fact, served in the manner required by law. Petitioner's arguments are directed only at the second prong.

---

[1] Section 17.045 states, in relevant part, as follows:

§ 17.045. Notice to Nonresident

(a) If the secretary of state is served with duplicate copies of process for a nonresident, he shall require a statement of the name and address of the nonresident's home or home office and shall immediately mail a copy of the process to the nonresident.

(d) The process or notice must be sent by registered mail or by certified mail, return receipt requested.

TEX. CIV. PRAC. & REM. CODE ANN. § 17.045 (Vernon 1986).

[2] Section 17.044 states, in relevant part, as follows:

§ 17.044. Substituted Service on Secretary of State

(b) The secretary of state is an agent for service of process on a nonresident who engages in business in this state, but does not maintain a regular place of business in this state or a designated agent for service of process, in any proceeding that arises out of the business done in this state and to which the nonresident is a party.

TEX. CIV. PRAC. & REM. CODE ANN. § 17.044(b) (Vernon 1986).

Zuyus argues that the trial court did not have personal jurisdiction over him because the secretary of state's certificate shows that the notice was returned "unclaimed." Zuyus relies on *Barnes v. Frost Nat'l Bank*, 840 S.W.2d 747 (Tex. App.—San Antonio 1992, no writ), to support his contention. Zuyus's reliance is misplaced.

* * *

The record shows that No'Mis Communications informed the trial court, in the motion for default judgment, that Zuyus's last known mailing address was Rt. 3, Box 31, Cleveland, OK 74020. No'Mis Communications also filed a "Certificate of Last Known Address" with the clerk of the trial court, in compliance with TEX. R. CIV. P. 239a, certifying that Zuyus's last known mailing address was Rt. 3, Box 31, Cleveland, OK 74020. On March 1, 1995, Zuyus received a copy of the default judgment that the clerk of the court mailed to him at Rt. 3, Box 31, Cleveland, OK 74020.

After receiving notice of the default judgment, Zuyus could have filed a motion for new trial. *See* TEX. R. CIV. P. 306a(4). Instead, on March 23, 1995, Zuyus filed a special appearance objecting to the trial court's jurisdiction. Zuyus swore, in an affidavit attached to the special appearance, that his correct address was Rt. 3, Box 31, Cleveland, OK 74020. Zuyus also attached a letter from No'Mis Communications' attorney, dated June 15, 1994, addressed to him and delivered at Rt. 3, Box 31, Cleveland, OK 74020. The letter contained No'Mis Communications' final settlement offer and warned Zuyus that suit would follow if the case was not settled immediately.

On March 30, 1995, the trial court denied Zuyus's special appearance. Zuyus did not appeal the trial court's denial of the special appearance and did not appeal the default judgment. *See* TEX. R. CIV. P. 306a(4).

A showing in the record that the secretary of state forwarded a copy of the process is essential to establish the trial court's jurisdiction. *Id.* at 96. Absent fraud or mistake, a certificate from the secretary of state's office is conclusive evidence that the secretary of state received service of process and forwarded the process as required.

Because we find no evidence in the record of fraud or mistake, the secretary of state's certificate is conclusive evidence 1) that the secretary received service of process in accordance with TEX. CIV. PRAC. & REM. CODE ANN. § 17.044 and 2) that the secretary, in accordance with TEX. CIV. PRAC. & REM. CODE ANN. § 17.045, forwarded a copy of the process to Zuyus, via certified mail, to Rt. 3, Box 31, Cleveland, OK 74020. Zuyus admits that this address is correct. We hold that Zuyus's failure to claim the certified letter did not deprive the trial court of personal jurisdiction over him.

We hold that Zuyus was served in the manner required by law and that the trial court had personal jurisdiction over him when it rendered the default judgment. We overrule petitioner's first point of error.

By his second point of error, Zuyus contends that the trial court erred in rendering the default judgment because the record affirmatively shows that he did not have notice of the lawsuit until March 1, 1995, when he received a copy of the judgment.

Lack of notice does not necessarily void a judgment. Due process requires only that the method of notice utilized be reasonably calculated, under the circumstances, to apprise an interested party of the pendency of the action and afford the party the opportunity to present objections. *Peralta v. Heights Medical Ctr.*, 485 U.S. 80, 84-85, 99 L. Ed. 2d 75, 108 S. Ct. 896 (1988). Notice should be by means "such as one desirous of actually informing the absentee might reasonably adopt to accomplish it." When a letter is returned as "refused" or "unclaimed," the notice is sufficient if it is apparent that the address was valid and could be located by the postal office.

In the instant case, the secretary of state mailed a copy of the citation and petition to Zuyus's home address. This is consistent with due process because it is a method of notice reasonably calculated to apprise petitioner of the pending action. We overrule petitioner's second point of error.

By his third point of error, Zuyus contends that the rendering of a default judgment was improper because he had no notice of the default hearing.

No'Mis Communications moved for default judgment because Zuyus did not file an answer. No advance notice of a hearing is required for a no-answer default judgment. We overrule petitioner's third point of error.

By his fourth point of error, Zuyus contends that the trial court erred by awarding damages that failed to conform to No'Mis Communications' pleadings. The trial court awarded No'Mis Communications actual damages of $163,676.00, exemplary damages of $327,352.00, and attorney's fees of $6,400.00. In addition, the court awarded No'Mis Communications pre-judgment and post-judgment interest, court costs, and attorney's fees in the event of an appeal.

After a default judgment is granted, the trial court must hear evidence of unliquidated damages. TEX. R. CIV. P. 243. Although a hearing was held in the instant case, and both parties cite to a statement of facts, the record before us does not include the statement of facts. In fact, the record does not even show that Zuyus requested a statement of facts. Without such evidence, we are unable to determine how the trial court arrived at its decision on damages.

We note that in addition to actual damages, the trial court awarded exemplary damages under the DTPA.[3]

No'Mis Communications concedes that its pleadings limited the amount of damages to $50,000, exclusive of interest and costs.[4] We sustain petitioner's fourth point of error and remand this case to the trial court for a new trial on the issue of damages only.

* * *

We GRANT Zuyus's petition for writ of error as it relates to damages. We REVERSE the trial court's judgment on damages and REMAND the case to the trial court for a new trial on damages only.

We DENY the remainder of Zuyus's petition for writ of error and AFFIRM the remainder of the trial court's judgment.

---

[3] The trial court awarded twice the amount of actual damages as exemplary damages.

[4] No'Mis Communications' pleadings aver that "the total amount in controversy in this cause of action is less than $50,000, exclusive of interest costs."

CALDWELL
v.
BARNES

154 S.W.3d 93
(Tex. 2004)

PER CURIAM.

This case arises from a bill of review proceeding that challenged a default judgment for lack of service. After holding a pretrial hearing and taking evidence on the question of whether a bill of review plaintiff had been served with process in the underlying lawsuit, the trial court issued a finding of fact that the plaintiff had been served and rendered judgment against him. The court of appeals affirmed. The issue before this Court is whether the plaintiff was entitled to submit the question of service to a jury at trial, or whether the trial court properly resolved the matter in a pretrial hearing. Because we conclude (1) that the plaintiff was entitled to submit the question of service to a jury at trial and the trial court erred by resolving the matter in a pretrial hearing, and (2) the plaintiff preserved his right to a jury trial, we reverse the court of appeals' judgment and remand the case to the trial court for further proceedings.

Robert F. Barnes sued Harold Caldwell, a Colorado resident, in Texas in 1989, alleging various causes of action stemming from a contract dispute. Barnes arranged for Caldwell to be personally served with process in Colorado through a private process server, DeWayne Perdew. The return of service filed with the trial court reflects that Perdew hand-delivered process to Caldwell in Jefferson County, Colorado on July 30, 1989. Caldwell contends that he was never served with process, and as a result, did not file an answer. When Caldwell did not answer, Barnes obtained a $15,500,000 default judgment against him.

In 1993, Caldwell filed a petition for a bill of review in the trial court, claiming he was never served with process. In support of his claim, Caldwell submitted (1) an affidavit stating that he had never been served; (2) a second affidavit from Perdew in which Perdew contradicted his earlier affidavit by stating that he had not, in fact, ever served Caldwell; (3) an affidavit from Perdew's ex-girlfriend, Lucy Lackey, corroborating Perdew's retraction by stating that Perdew could not have served Caldwell on July 30, 1989, because on that date he was attending a George Strait concert with her in Cheyenne, Wyoming; (4) the affidavits of four litigants in unrelated lawsuits, whom Perdew claimed to have served on July 30, 1989, but who similarly denied service; and (5) the affidavit of a landlord stating that no one resided at an apartment where Perdew claimed to have served a tenant with process on that same date.

Both parties moved for summary judgment. Caldwell asserted that the above-mentioned affidavits established that he was never served with process, and therefore the default judgment against him should be set aside. Barnes, however, asserted that Caldwell's bill of review should be denied because Caldwell had failed to exhaust his legal remedies in Colorado and because a bill of review was barred by laches since Caldwell had failed to diligently exercise his right to challenge notice when he was informed of the default judgment against him. The trial court granted summary judgment in favor of Barnes, and the court of appeals affirmed.

On review, this Court reversed the court of appeals' judgment and remanded the case to the trial court. This Court held that Barnes was not entitled to summary judgment because Caldwell was not required to exhaust his legal remedies in Colorado as a prerequisite to relief in Texas, and because a bill of review was not barred by laches since it was brought within the statutory limitations period. This Court further held that "because the original return of service conflict[ed] with Caldwell's, Perdew's, and the others' subsequent affidavits," a genuine issue of fact existed as to whether Caldwell had been served in the underlying proceeding.

In June 2000, on remand from this Court, the trial court conducted a pretrial hearing on the question of Caldwell's service. At the hearing, Caldwell offered evidence suggesting that he was never served with process, including the above-mentioned affidavits, Caldwell's own testimony that he was not served with process on July 30, 1989, or at any other time, and Lackey's testimony that on July 30, 1989, Perdew was with her in Wyoming and therefore did not serve process on Caldwell. During cross-examination, however, Caldwell admitted that in the past he had purposely allowed approximately a dozen default judgments to be taken against him, even after being properly served with process, because defaulting was often less costly than defending the underlying suits. In addition, during Lackey's cross-examination, she admitted that she could not remember who prepared her affidavit or where it was signed. She also testified that she could not produce receipts and concert ticket stubs supporting her trip with Perdew to Wyoming, because in 1991, she had relinquished them to Caldwell's agents after they arranged to meet with her at the Taco Bell where she worked in Colorado. Caldwell, however, never introduced any receipts or ticket stubs into evidence to support Lackey's claims.

After the pretrial hearing, the trial court made the following factual findings: (1) the credibility and interest of the witnesses present at the hearing was in issue; (2) Caldwell had a practice of being served with process and not answering, thus allowing default judgments to be entered against him; (3) Perdew gave at least two completely contradictory statements under oath regarding service; (4) Lackey's credibility had been called into question; and (5) Caldwell had been served. Based on these findings, the trial court declined to proceed to trial and denied Caldwell's bill of review. The court of appeals affirmed the trial court's judgment. Caldwell petitioned this Court for review. We must decide whether (1) Caldwell was entitled to submit the question of service of process to a jury at trial, and if the trial court therefore erred by resolving the matter in a pretrial hearing, and (2) whether the error was harmful because Caldwell preserved his right to a jury trial on the issue.

We begin by considering what a bill of review plaintiff must prove when claiming lack of service of process. A bill of review is an equitable proceeding brought by a party seeking to set aside a prior judgment that is no longer subject to challenge by a motion for new trial or appeal. *Baker v. Goldsmith,* 582 S.W.2d 404, 406 (Tex. 1979). Bill of review plaintiffs must ordinarily plead and prove (1) a meritorious defense to the underlying cause of action, (2) which the plaintiffs were prevented from making by the fraud, accident or wrongful act of the opposing party or official mistake, (3) unmixed with any fault or negligence on their own part. *Id.* at 406-08; 975 S.W.2d at 537.

Bill of review plaintiffs claiming non-service, however, are relieved of two elements ordinarily required to be proved in a bill of review proceeding. First, if a plaintiff was not served, constitutional due process relieves the plaintiff from the need to show a meritorious defense. *Peralta v. Heights Med. Ctr., Inc.*, 485 U.S. 80, 86-87, 108 S.Ct. 896, 99 L.Ed.2d 75 (1988) (holding that the meritorious defense requirement in a bill of review proceeding violates due process where the bill of review plaintiff has no notice of the proceeding in which the default judgment was rendered). Second, the plaintiff is relieved from showing that fraud, accident, wrongful act or official mistake prevented the plaintiff from presenting such a defense.

Bill of review plaintiffs alleging they were not served, however, must still prove the third and final element required in a bill of review proceeding that the judgment was rendered unmixed with any fault or negligence of their own. In *Caldwell,* we said this third and final element is conclusively established if the plaintiff can prove that he or she was never served with process. An individual who is not served with process cannot be at fault or negligent in allowing a default judgment to be rendered.[1] Proof of non-service, then, will conclusively establish the third and only element that bill of review plaintiffs are required to prove when they are asserting lack of service of process as their only defense.[2]

We next consider whether Caldwell was entitled to submit the question of service of process to a jury at trial or whether the trial court could properly resolve the question in a pretrial proceeding. In *Goldsmith,* we outlined the procedure to be utilized in a bill of review proceeding. 582 S.W.2d at 408-09. We held in *Goldsmith* that a bill of review plaintiff is required, as a pretrial matter, to present prima facie proof of a meritorious defense to the underlying cause of action. 582 S.W.2d at 408-09. This requirement, as we have stated, is dispensed with when the plaintiff is claiming lack of service of process. We further held that once prima facie proof of a meritorious defense has been established, the court should conduct a trial in which the plaintiff must negate his or her fault or negligence. *Goldsmith,* 582 S.W.2d at 409. Because proof of non-service conclusively negates a plaintiff's fault or negligence, then, the question of service is properly resolved at trial and not by the trial court in a pretrial proceeding if the material facts are disputed.

In sum, when a plaintiff seeks a bill of review based solely on a claim of non-service, the bill of review procedure outlined in *Goldsmith* must be slightly modified. *See id.* at 408-09. When a plaintiff claims lack of service, the trial court should: (1) dispense with any pretrial inquiry into a meritorious defense, (2) hold a trial, at which the bill of review plaintiff assumes the burden of proving that the plaintiff was not served with process,[3] thereby conclusively establishing a lack of fault or negligence in allowing a default judgment to be rendered, and (3) conditioned upon an affirmative finding that the plaintiff was not served, allow the parties to revert to their original status as plaintiff and defendant with the burden on the original plaintiff to prove his or her case.

Finally, we consider whether the denial of a jury trial on the issue of service of process was harmful error. Because the trial court considered conflicting evidence, made findings of fact based on the evidence, and ultimately determined that Caldwell was served with process, Barnes argues that it was harmless error for the trial court not to present the question of service to the jury. Specifically, Barnes relies on the court of appeals' holding that "in a non-jury case, the trial court's findings of fact have the same force and dignity as does a jury verdict on special issues." We do not agree with Barnes, however, that this was a "non-jury" case.

---

[1] A party who becomes aware of the proceedings without proper service of process has no duty to participate in them. Wilson v. Dunn, 800 S.W.2d 833, 836 (Tex. 1990).

[2] *Cf.* Campus Invs., Inc. v. Cullever, 144 S.W.3d 464, 466 (Tex. 2004) (holding that when bill of review plaintiffs are properly served with process, they must show they were not at fault or negligent in allowing a default judgment to be rendered); Gold v. Gold, 145 S.W.3d 212, 214 (Tex. 2004) (failure to seek reinstatement, new trial, or appeal, if available, normally would be negligence).

[3] At trial, the testimony of a bill of review plaintiff alone, without corroborating evidence, is insufficient to overcome the presumption that the plaintiff was served. *See* Primate Constr., Inc. v. Silver, 884 S.W.2d 151, 152 (Tex. 1994) ("The recitations in the return of service carry so much weight that they cannot be rebutted by the uncorroborated proof of the moving party.").

The record indicates that Caldwell never assented to a non-jury determination on the issue of service. Caldwell's attorney specifically asserted to the trial court that service of process was a "question of fact" and that Caldwell was entitled to a trial on the issue. Similarly, Barnes's attorney argued that service of process presented a fact question for the jury to decide. Further, the record reflects that the jury fee had been paid and the case had been placed on the jury trial docket. When a party timely demands a jury and pays the fee, the trial court may not remove the case from the jury docket over the objection of the opposing party. *See* TEX.R. CIV. P. 216, 220. The wrongful denial of a jury trial is harmful when the case contains a question of material fact. The question of whether Caldwell was served with process is a question of material fact, and therefore the denial of a jury trial was harmful error.

Caldwell must be given a jury trial because he preserved his right to have a jury decide whether he was served with process. At trial, he must establish by a preponderance of the evidence that he was never served. Pursuant to Rule 59.1 of the Texas Rules of Appellate Procedure, we grant Caldwell's petition for review, and without hearing oral argument, we reverse the court of appeals' judgment and remand the case to the trial court for further proceedings consistent with this opinion. *See* TEX.R.APP. P. 59.1.

Notes & Questions

1. *Service errors.* What was the error in service raised in the *Zuyus* case? Why was the writ of error unsuccessful? Might Mr. Zuyus be successful in a bill of review proceeding? Think about what constituted the "record" that is being reviewed in each type of proceeding.

2. *Peralta v. Heights Medical Center, Inc.*[1] The United States Supreme Court considered the Texas bill of review procedure in this case. The bill of review petitioner had been served with defective service—the citation had expired. (Under the law then in effect, a citation expired 90 days after its issuance.) He did not answer the lawsuit, a default judgment was rendered, of which he got no notice, and eventually his property was sold at a sheriff's sale. He later brought this bill of review, but admitted that he had no meritorious defense to the underlying suit. The Supreme Court held that "a judgment entered without notice or service is constitutionally unfirm." Thus, the meritorious defense requirement, which prevented the petitioner from invalidating the judgment, violated due process.

3. *Bill of review and no notice.* What is left of the bill of review requirements if a defendant proves lack of notice? What if the defendant was validly served through a method of substituted service (such as "leave with" service or service through the Secretary of State), but got no actual notice? What if the service was not proper (it didn't comply with the rules), but the defendant did get notice?[2]

---

[1] 485 U.S. 80 (1988).

[2] *See* Ross v. Nat'l Center for the Employment of the Disabled, 197 S.W.3d 795 (Tex. 2006) (granting bill of review when defendant was not served, never received citation, but received post card notice).

4. *Statute of limitations for bill of review.* The residual four-year statute of limitations applies to bills of review.[3] Application of the "discovery rule" can often allow commencement of a bill of review even more than four years after the date of the default judgment.

5. *Default judgments with notice.* In "no notice" cases we are largely sympathetic with the defendant's efforts to invalidate the default judgment. There are *many* Texas cases, however, where the default judgment is invalidated, not on the grounds of lack of notice, but because of technical violations of the rules and statutes governing service of process. For example, in *McKanna v. Edgar,*[4] the default judgment was overturned because the petition did not allege one of the two conditions statutorily required to authorize service upon the Secretary of State under the General Long-Arm Statute. The petition alleged that the defendant was a non-resident that had done business in Texas.[5] The petition failed to allege, however, that the defendant "does not maintain a place of regular business in this State or a designated agent upon whom service may be made."[6] Furthermore, in *Wilson v. Dunn,*[7] although the defendant admitted receiving the citation and copy of the petition, the default judgment was overturned because there was no affidavit in the record authorizing substituted service under Rule 106(b).

Young lawyers are often surprised at the number of default judgments brought through their doors. Obviously, when that happens one should first meticulously examine the record for formal and technical defects. If such a defect is found, what procedure is best suited for bringing it to the attention of the court?

6. *Amended pleading.* If an amended pleading asserts a new cause of action or requires a more onerous judgment from that called for in the pleading served upon the defendant with the citation, the amended pleading must be served upon the defendant to obtain a default judgment on the new matter. However, that service can be made under Rule 21a, rather than through new service of process.[8] The 1990 amendments to Rules 21 and 21a allow service by certified mail for all pleadings other than the original petition. Thus, when the record shows that the amended pleading is served properly on the defendant under Rule 21a by certified mail, and the record shows that the defendant received actual or constructive notice of the amended pleading, the default judgment will be upheld.

7. *Collateral Attacks.* So far we have discussed "direct" attacks on the default judgment—the equitable motion for new trial, restricted appeal, and bill of review. A direct attack on a judgment is an effort to amend, correct, reform or otherwise replace a judgment in a proceeding brought for that purpose.[9] A regular appeal is also a "direct" attack on the judgment.

---

[3] Valdez v. Hollenbeck, 465 S.W.3d 217, 222 (Tex. 2015). Note that a statute may prescribe an express limitations period that overcomes the four-year residual statute. *Id.* (finding that Probate Code's 2-year statute barred the heirs' bill of review).

[4] 388 S.W.2d 927 (Tex. 1965).

[5] *Id.* at 929.

[6] *Id.* at 929, *quoting* Art. 2031b (currently CPRC § 17.044).

[7] 800 S.W.2d 833 (Tex. 1990).

[8] In the Interest of E.A., 287 S.W.3d 1 (Tex. 2009).

[9] Austin Independent School District v. Sierra Club, 495 S.W.2d 878 (Tex. 1973). *See also* Pursley v. Ussery, 937 S.W.2d 566 (Tex. App.—San Antonio 1996, no writ) (bill of review filed in court other than court that rendered judgment was not a direct attack, but a collateral attack on judgment).

An attempt to avoid the binding effect of a judgment in a proceeding brought for some other purpose in a court that has no power to directly review the judgment is called a "collateral" attack.[10] In a collateral attack, the defendant claims that the earlier judgment is void and unenforceable. A defendant may collaterally attack a judgment on which the plaintiff is attempting to assert preclusive effect through res judicata (claim preclusion). Also, the defendant may attack the judgment when the plaintiff attempts to enforce it against the defendant's assets by using a collection proceeding, such as a garnishment action.

The judgment is void and subject to collateral attack when the court rendering the judgment "had no jurisdiction of the person of a party or his property, no jurisdiction of the subject matter, no jurisdiction to enter a particular judgment, or no capacity to act as a court."[11] Ordinarily, a judgment will state that the defendant was properly served with process. These judgment recitals cannot be challenged with contrary evidence; therefore, collateral attack is usually of no help to a resident defendant claiming invalid service. However, as we will see at the end of the chapter, a non-resident who was not amenable to the jurisdiction of the court can present extrinsic evidence to prove lack of minimum contacts even though the judgment recites proper service of process.

D. Minimum Contacts: Non-Resident Defendants and Due Process

If a plaintiff has complied with the Texas rules or statutes for obtaining service on non-resident defendants and the service meets the *Mullane* notice requirements, the only question remaining is whether the state can legitimately subject a defendant to suit in Texas. Constitutional due process requires that a foreign defendant have sufficient "minimum contacts" with the state to satisfy "traditional notions of fair play and substantial justice."[1]

The doctrine of "minimum contacts" has led to two kinds of contacts-based jurisdiction: general and specific. If the court has general jurisdiction over the defendant, it has the power to adjudicate claims that are unrelated to the defendant's activities in the forum state.

1. General jurisdiction.

The United States Supreme Court has determined that a defendant is subject to general jurisdiction only where the defendant is "at home" —for an individual, his or her state of residence; for a corporation, its state of incorporation or principal office.[2] If the court does not have general jurisdiction, it has limited power over the defendant, and, under the doctrine of specific jurisdiction, may only adjudicate claims that arise from or are related to the defendant's forum activities.[3] The parameters of due process have received substantial attention from the United States Supreme Court and we leave it to other courses to explore those opinions.

---

10 *Austin Independent School District*, 495 S.W.2d at 881.

11 *Id.*

1 International Shoe Co. v. Washington, 326 U.S. 310, 320 (1945).

2 Daimler AG v. Bauman, 571 US 117 (2014).

3 The United States Supreme Court has written many opinions discussing specific jurisdiction. However, it has not discussed the test for the required relationship between the claim and the forum contacts. The Texas Supreme Court has done so, however. *See* Moki Mac River Expeditions v. Drugg, 221 S.W.3d 569 (Tex. 2007).

One issue that remains open and almost certainly will be litigated in the state courts is whether a state has general jurisdiction over a corporation that is not "at home" in the state but is served with process in the state through its registered agent under the state's corporate registration statutes.[4] The United States Supreme Court has never addressed the question, and there is a "decades-old split among the federal courts" that has never been resolved.[5] Several federal courts have held that in-state service upon an appointed agent for service does confer general jurisdiction under the jurisdictional doctrines of "consent" and "presence."[6] But other courts, including the Fifth Circuit,[7] have concluded that the registration statutes confer general jurisdiction only when the corporation's contacts are sufficient to confer general jurisdiction under the constitutional standard.[8]

These courts conclude that any consent to suit obtained through those statutes is only for causes of action arising in that state. Under this analysis, the Due Process Clause would not condone the exercise of general jurisdiction on a non-resident corporation simply because it was served in the state through its registered agent.

The issue remains open in the Texas state courts as well. The Texas Supreme Court has never addressed the question, and some lower courts have held that foreign corporations are deemed to have consented to general jurisdiction by complying with registration statutes.[9] But the Corpus Christi Court of Appeals has rejected this view and held that "the designation of an agent for service of process in Texas does not amount to a general consent to jurisdiction, and is merely one of many factors to be considered in determining whether minimum contracts exist.[10]

It is tempting for courts to adopt consent-based general jurisdiction because it allows a local plaintiff to sue a defendant with significant contacts with the state at home. But, by definition, general jurisdiction would also allow any plaintiff to sue that defendant for any claim arising anywhere in the state where the defendant was registered to do business. *Asahi*'s "fairness" escape valve once provided an argument that the assertion of jurisdiction over such cases, which are entirely unrelated to the forum or its domiciliaries, could not be condoned under notions of Due Process. That argument, however, is now off the table, because the Court held in *Bauman* that the

4 Two federal district courts in Delaware have addressed the question and come to directly contrary conclusions concerning the same corporate defendant. *Compare* AstraZeneca AB v. Mylan Pharm., Inc., 571 F.Supp.3d 549 (D. Del. 2014) (rejecting consent-by-registration as basis for general jurisdiction), *with* Acorda Therapeutics v. Mylan Pharm. Inc., 571 F.Supp.3d (D.Del. 2015) (accepting consent-by-registration as basis for general jurisdiction).

5 Kevin D. Benish, *Note,* Pennoyer*'s Ghost: Consent, Registration Statutes, and General Jurisdiction After* Daimler AG v. Bauman, 90 N.Y.U. L. REV. 1609 (2015)(reviewing the relevant law in all states, and concluding that "consent-by-registration" is not constitutional).

6 *Id.* (citing opinions from the Third and Eighth Circuits so holding, and opinions from the Second and Ninth Circuits with dicta consistent with the constitutionality of general jurisdiction).

7 Wenche Siemer v. Learjet Acquisition Corp., 966 F.2d 179 (5th Cir. 1992).

8 The Benish note cited above notes that in addition to the Fifth Circuit, the Fourth, Seventh and Eleventh have held that consent-based general jurisdiction violates due process.

9 *See* Acacia Pipeline Corp. v. Champlin Exploration, Inc. 769 S.W.2d 719, 720 (Tex. App.—Houston [1st Dist.] 1989, no writ); Goldman v. Pre-Fab Transit Co., 520 S.W.2d 597, 598 (Tex. Civ. App.—Houston [14th Dist.] 1975, no writ).

10 Juarez v. United Parcel Service De Mexico, S.A. de C.V., 933 S.W.2d 281, 284-285 (Tex. App.—Corpus Christi 1996, no writ).

fairness factors did not apply to assertions of general jurisdiction,[11] making broad assertions of general jurisdiction less palatable.

2. *Specific jurisdiction.*

The United States Supreme Court has issued many opinions discussing the contacts necessary to constitute "purposeful availment" under the specific jurisdiction analysis. But it has not finalized the test for the required relationship between the claim and the forum contacts.[12] The Texas Supreme Court has done so, adopting the "substantial connection" test in the following opinion.

MOKI MAC RIVER EXPEDITIONS
v.
DRUGG

221 S.W.3d 569
(Tex. 2007)

JUSTICE O'NEILL delivered the opinion of the Court, in which CHIEF JUSTICE JEFFERSON, JUSTICE HECHT, JUSTICE WAINWRIGHT, JUSTICE BRISTER, JUSTICE GREEN, and Justice Willett joined.

Texas court may assert specific jurisdiction over an out-of-state defendant if the defendant's contact with this state is purposeful and the injury arises from or relates to those contacts. In this wrongful-death case against a Utah-based river-rafting outfitter, the defendant contends the plaintiff's death on a Grand Canyon hiking trail did not arise from or relate to its instate commercial activities so as to establish specific jurisdiction over it in Texas. We agree. Accordingly, we reverse and remand the case to the court of appeals to determine whether general jurisdiction exists.

I. Background

Charles and Betsy Drugg's thirteen-year-old son, Andy, died on a June 2001, river-rafting trip in Arizona with Moki Mac River Expeditions, a Utah-based river-rafting outfitter. Moki Mac did not directly solicit the Druggs to participate in the trip. Instead, the Druggs learned about Moki Mac's excursions from a fellow Texas resident, Annie Seals, who had contacted the company regarding a rafting trip in the Grand Canyon. There was no space available for her at that time, but Seals's contact information was placed on Moki Mac's computerized mailing list so that she would automatically receive a brochure for the 2001 season when it became available. Moki Mac subsequently sent two brochures to Seals in Texas detailing pricing and schedules for upcoming excursions. Seals informed Moki Mac of the interest of several others in Texas with whom she shared the literature, including Andy and members of his family.

Betsy Drugg reviewed the brochures and information from Moki Mac's website. After corresponding with Moki Mac representatives from her home in Texas, Betsy ultimately decided to

---

[11] *Daimler,* 134 S.Ct. at 764.

[12] The United States Supreme Court rejected California's "sliding scale" approach—relaxing the requisite connection between the forum and the claims if the defendant has extensive, but unrelated, contacts with the forum. It did not adopt any other test. Bristol-Myers Squibb Co. v. Superior Court of California, ___ U.S.__, 137 S.Ct. 1773 (2017).

send Andy on the rafting trip. Andy's grandmother sent Moki Mac an application and payment for herself and Andy. As was its practice, Moki Mac sent a letter confirming payment to the Druggs' home in Texas along with an acknowledgment-of-risk and release form, which the company requires participants to sign as a prerequisite to attendance. Both Andy and his mother signed the form and returned it to Moki Mac.

The Druggs allege that on the second day of Andy's fourteen-day trip, Moki Mac guides led the group up an incline on a trail that narrowed around and was obstructed by a large boulder. The guides were positioned at the head and rear of the group, but no guide was present near the boulder. As Andy attempted to negotiate the boulder-blocked path, requiring him to lean back while attempting to cross a very narrow ledge, he fell backwards approximately fifty-five feet and was fatally injured.

The Druggs filed suit in Texas for wrongful death due to Moki Mac's negligence and for intentional and negligent misrepresentation.[1] The trial court denied Moki Mac's special appearance and the court of appeals affirmed on the basis of specific jurisdiction, holding that the Druggs' misrepresentation claim arose from, and related to, Moki Mac's purposeful contacts with Texas. 2004 WL 100389. Because the court of appeals found specific jurisdiction, it did not consider whether general jurisdiction was proper. We granted Moki Mac's petition for review to consider the extent to which a claim must "arise from or relate to" forum contacts in order to confer specific jurisdiction over a nonresident defendant.[2]

* * *

III. *In Personam* Jurisdiction

The plaintiff bears the initial burden of pleading sufficient allegations to invoke jurisdiction under the Texas long-arm statute. The nonresident defendant then assumes the burden of negating all bases of jurisdiction in those allegations. Because the question of a court's exercise of personal jurisdiction over a nonresident defendant is one of law, we review a trial court's determination of a special appearance *de novo*. When, as here, the trial court does not make findings of fact and conclusions of law in support of its ruling, we infer "all facts necessary to support the judgment and supported by the evidence . . . ."

Texas courts may assert *in personam* jurisdiction over a nonresident if (1) the Texas long-arm statute authorizes the exercise of jurisdiction, and (2) the exercise of jurisdiction is consistent with federal and state constitutional due-process guarantees. Our long-arm statute describes what, "[i]n addition to other acts," may constitute doing business in this state. TEX. CIV. PRAC. & REM. CODE § 17.042. Pertinent to this case are the first two subsections, which provide that a nonresident does business in Texas if it:

> (1) contracts by mail or otherwise with a Texas resident and either party is to perform the contract in whole or in part in this state; [or]
>
> (2) commits a tort in whole or in part in this state;

---

1 The Druggs also claimed Moki Mac breached its agreement to provide the safety measures represented in its materials. Because the Druggs did not argue their breach-of-contract claim in the court of appeals and do not do so in their briefs to this Court, we only address the Druggs' wrongful-death claim.

2 We received an amicus brief supporting Moki Mac's position from Grand Canyon Outfitters Association and America Outdoors.

Id. § 17.042(1), (2). The Druggs' negligent and intentional misrepresentation claims based on Moki Mac's brochures and release form satisfy the doing-business requirement for jurisdiction under the plain language of the statute. But the exercise of jurisdiction under the statute must be consistent with federal and state constitutional guarantees of due process.

We have said that the long-arm statute's broad doing-business language allows the statute to "reach as far as the federal constitutional requirements of due process will allow." Thus, the requirements of the Texas long-arm statute are satisfied if an assertion of jurisdiction accords with federal due-process limitations.

Federal due-process requirements limit a state's power to assert personal jurisdiction over a nonresident defendant. Personal jurisdiction is proper when the nonresident defendant has established minimum contacts with the forum state, and the exercise of jurisdiction comports with " 'traditional notions of fair play and substantial justice.' " *Int'l Shoe Co. v. Washington,* 326 U.S. 310, 316, 66 S.Ct. 154, 90 L.Ed. 95 (1945). Minimum contacts are sufficient for personal jurisdiction when the nonresident defendant " 'purposefully avails itself of the privilege of conducting activities within the forum State, thus invoking the benefits and protections of its laws.' " *Hanson v. Denckla,* 357 U.S. 235, 253, 78 S.Ct. 1228, 2 L.Ed.2d 1283 (1958).

We have recently explained that there are three parts to a "purposeful availment" inquiry. First, only the defendant's contacts with the forum are relevant, not the unilateral activity of another party or a third person. Second, the contacts relied upon must be purposeful rather than random, fortuitous, or attenuated. Thus, "[s]ellers who 'reach out beyond one state and create continuing relationships and obligations with citizens of another state' are subject to the jurisdiction of the latter in suits based on their activities." Finally, the "defendant must seek some benefit, advantage or profit by 'availing' itself of the jurisdiction." In contrast, a defendant may purposefully avoid a particular forum by structuring its transactions in such a way as to neither profit from the forum's laws nor subject itself to jurisdiction there.

A nonresident defendant's forum-state contacts may give rise to two types of personal jurisdiction. If the defendant [is "at home" in] the forum, general jurisdiction is established whether or not the defendant's alleged liability arises from those contacts. In contrast, when specific jurisdiction is alleged, we focus the minimum-contacts analysis on the "relationship among the defendant, the forum [,] and the litigation." *Helicopteros Nacionales de Colombia v. Hall,* 466 U.S. 408, 414, 104 S.Ct. 1868, 80 L.Ed.2d 404 (1984). Specific jurisdiction is established if the defendant's alleged liability "aris[es] out of or [is] related to" an activity conducted within the forum. The United States Supreme Court has provided relatively little guidance on the "arise from or relate to" requirement, nor have we had occasion to examine the strength of the nexus required to establish specific jurisdiction.

IV. Jurisdictional Analysis

The Druggs assert that Moki Mac established sufficient minimum contacts with Texas by making material misrepresentations to them here, upon which they relied, regarding the nature of the services that would be provided on its trips. The wrongful death of their son, the Druggs argue, arose from or related to the fact that Moki Mac's services did not meet the standards it represented in Texas. Moki Mac's principal argument is that there is an insufficient nexus between any alleged misrepresentations that it made in Texas and Andy's wrongful death in Arizona to satisfy jurisdictional due process. According to Moki Mac, Andy's death might have arisen out of or related to alleged negligence that occurred in Arizona, but it had no meaningful connection to Moki Mac's alleged misrepresentations in Texas.

For a Texas forum to properly exercise specific jurisdiction in this case, (1) Moki Mac must have made minimum contacts with Texas by purposefully availing itself of the privilege of conducting activities here, and (2) Moki Mac's liability must have arisen from or related to those contacts. Before deciding whether Moki Mac's liability arose from or related to its forum contacts, we must first examine the nature of those contacts and whether Moki Mac purposefully availed itself of the privilege of conducting business here.

A. Purposeful Availment

A nonresident defendant that directs marketing efforts to Texas in the hope of soliciting sales is subject to suit here for alleged liability arising from or relating to that business. In *Michiana* [*Easy Livin' Country Inc. v. Holten,* 168 S.W.3d 77 (Tex. 2005)], we concluded that a single product sale stemming from a single phone call initiated from Texas to a nonresident defendant was not a purposeful contact sufficient to satisfy the due-process minimum-contacts test because the seller did not purposefully direct marketing efforts here to solicit sales. In that case, Holten, a Texas resident, called Michiana, the nonresident defendant, to purchase an RV manufactured outside of Texas, which Michiana delivered to Texas entirely at Holten's expense. Michiana did not advertise in Texas and undertook no affirmative efforts to solicit business here. We held that the alleged commission of a tort by making misrepresentations during a phone call initiated by Holten was insufficient, by itself, to establish jurisdiction. Such a test, we reasoned, would improperly focus the purposeful-availment analysis on the form of the action chosen by the plaintiff rather than on the defendant's efforts to avail itself of the forum. We also held that, standing alone, delivery of the single RV to Texas to accommodate Holten was a similarly deficient basis for jurisdiction.

The United States Supreme Court has recognized that a nonresident who places products into the "stream of commerce" with the expectation that they will be sold in the forum state is subject to the forum's jurisdiction. *World-Wide Volkswagen,* 444 U.S. at 297-98, 100 S.Ct. 559. Although the Court has also stated that a single contact can support jurisdiction if that contact creates a "substantial connection" with the forum, jurisdiction cannot be established where the contact creates only an " 'attenuated' affiliation with the forum." *Burger King,* 471 U.S. at 475 n. 18, 105 S.Ct. 2174 (quoting *World-Wide Volkswagen,* 444 U.S. at 299, 100 S.Ct. 559). Indeed, in *World-Wide Volkswagen,* the Court held that a New York dealership that did not advertise or solicit business in Oklahoma was not subject to suit there simply because it sold a car to New York residents in New York who "happened to suffer an accident while passing through" Oklahoma. The Court reasoned that this one occurrence was mere fortuity and too attenuated to support jurisdiction, given the dealership's complete lack of affiliation with Oklahoma. Similarly, Michiana's single contact with Texas was too attenuated to support jurisdiction in Texas. Michiana had no control over the point of customer contact that generated the sale and, like the defendant in *World-Wide Volkswagen,* had no say over where the RV would end up. Rather, Michiana's sale to Texas resulted from the mere fortuity that Holten happened to reside here, and Holten's unilateral activity could not subject Michiana to specific jurisdiction here.

Thus, the mere sale of a product to a Texas resident will not generally suffice to confer specific jurisdiction upon our courts. Instead, the facts alleged must indicate that the seller intended to serve the Texas market. *See Asahi Metal Ind. Co. v. Superior Court,* 480 U.S. 102, 112, 107 S.Ct. 1026, 94 L.Ed.2d 92 (1987). This rule accords with the due-process requirement that a nonresident defendant must take action that is purposefully directed toward the forum state. In determining whether the defendant purposefully directed action toward Texas, we may look to conduct beyond the particular business transaction at issue: "[a]dditional conduct of the defendant may indicate an intent or purpose to serve the market in the forum State." Examples of additional conduct that may indicate whether a defendant purposefully availed itself of a particular forum include advertising and establishing channels of regular communication to customers in the forum state.

Unlike in *Michiana*, the evidence in this case indicates that Moki Mac does intend to serve the Texas market. Moki Mac knowingly sells rafting trips to Texas residents and purposefully directs marketing efforts to Texas with the intent to solicit business from this state. In addition to sending the brochures and release to the Druggs, the evidence shows that Moki Mac regularly advertised in Texas. It has placed advertisements in a variety of nationally circulated publications that have Texas subscribers. Moki Mac also hired public relations firms to target media groups and tour operators, some of whom were located in Texas. In 1996, Moki Mac promoted its trips within Texas by taking out an advertisement in the *Austin Chronicle*. We have said that a nonresident defendant's advertising in local media "in and of itself, is a sufficiently purposeful act that is done in Texas."

Moki Mac's efforts to solicit business in Texas, however, go further. It solicited Texas residents through mass and targeted direct-marketing email campaigns. Moki Mac compiled a mailing list by collecting contact information from interested parties either by phone, email, or through the company's website. In addition, Moki Mac obtained a list of potential customers from a commercial source. Both its own mailing list and the commercial mailing list included Texas residents. The company would automatically send brochures and trip information to people who had previously expressed interest in a trip, even in years when that person had not expressed interest. As part of those promotions, Moki Mac offered "a free float" as an incentive to customers who coordinated a group of ten or more. Moki Mac provided this compensation to at least two Texas residents. Moki Mac occasionally provided musicians to accompany float trips free of charge. On one particular trip, Moki Mac permitted a string quartet from Fort Worth to accompany a Texas group on its float trip, free of charge to the musicians. Moki Mac also paid a fee to a travel agency located in Houston, resulting in multiple trips involving Texas residents.

In addition, Moki Mac established channels of regular communication with its customers in Texas. It was Moki Mac's practice to utilize particular customers, who would become *de facto* group leaders, to plan, organize, and promote its trips. Annie Seals was one such contact. By communicating with all of its customers through correspondence with a single group leader, Moki Mac streamlined its reservations process. The company kept these communication channels open; it was Moki Mac's practice to automatically send information regarding new trips, schedules, and prices to those on its mailing list who had been a customer or who had simply expressed interest in a trip within a three-year period.

We stated in *Michiana* that the contacts of "[s]ellers who 'reach out beyond one state and create continuing relationships and obligations with citizens of another state' " are purposeful rather than fortuitous. Moki Mac's contacts with Texas did not result, as did the defendant's in *Michiana,* from the mere fortuity that the Druggs happened to reside here. Rather, the contacts it had with Texas resulted from additional conduct through which it aimed to get extensive business in or from this state.

We conclude that Moki Mac had sufficient purposeful contact with Texas to satisfy the first prong of jurisdictional due process. But purposeful availment alone will not support an exercise of specific jurisdiction. Specific-jurisdiction analysis has two co-equal components. For specific-jurisdiction purposes, purposeful availment has no jurisdictional relevance unless the defendant's liability arises from or relates to the forum contacts. Moki Mac contends there was an insufficient nexus between Andy's injuries and Moki Mac's contacts with Texas to establish specific jurisdiction, an argument to which we now turn.

B. Relatedness Requirement

The "arise from or relate to" requirement lies at the heart of specific jurisdiction by defining the required nexus between the nonresident defendant, the litigation, and the forum. To support specific jurisdiction, the Supreme Court has given relatively little guidance as to how closely related a cause of action must be to the defendant's forum activities. In assessing the relationship between a nonresident's contacts and the litigation, most courts have focused on causation, but they have differed over the proper causative threshold. Some courts have pursued an expansive but-for causative approach, others have adopted a restrictive relatedness view requiring forum contacts to be relevant to a necessary element of proof, and some have applied a sliding-scale analysis that attempts to strike a balance between the two. *See* Mark M. Maloney, *Specific Jurisdiction and the "Arise From or Relate to" Requirement . . . What Does it Mean?*, 50 WASH. & LEE L.REV. 1265, 1276, 1299 (1993). Each approach has proponents and detractors, for the reasons we examine below.

* * *

4. Substantial Connection to Operative Facts

As we have said, the but-for relatedness test is too broad and conceptually unlimited in scope, the substantive-relevance/proximate-cause test poses too narrow an inquiry, and the sliding-scale analysis conflates the fundamental distinction between general and specific jurisdiction that is firmly embedded in our jurisprudence. In light of these concerns, some courts have applied alternative approaches, requiring that a cause of action "lie in the wake of the [defendant's] commercial activities" in the forum, or that the forum contacts be "critical steps in the chain of events that led to the [injury]." The Sixth Circuit has generally applied a test that falls somewhere between "proximate cause" and "but-for," requiring a "substantial connection" between the defendant's contacts and the plaintiff's claim to warrant the exercise of specific jurisdiction. The court explained that the specific jurisdiction's relatedness element "does not require that the cause of action formally 'arise from' defendant's contacts with the forum [but instead requires] that the cause of action, of whatever type, have a substantial connection with the defendant's in-state activities."

The Supreme Court has yet to explicate the degree of relatedness necessary to support specific jurisdiction over a nonresident defendant. However, in *Rush v. Savchuk*, the Court did consider the relation between forum contacts and the litigation in a case filed in Minnesota for personal injuries arising from an Indiana automobile accident. 444 U.S. 320, 324, 100 S.Ct. 571, 62 L.Ed.2d 516 (1980). The plaintiff claimed jurisdiction was proper in Minnesota because the defendant's insurance company did business there, and the insurer's obligation to defend and indemnify its insured in the accident litigation was inevitably the focus that would determine the victim's rights and obligations. *Id.* at 327-28, 100 S.Ct. 571. Holding that the insurance company's contacts could not be imputed to the defendant for the purpose of establishing jurisdiction, the Court concluded there were not "significant contacts between the litigation and the forum" because "the insurance policy is not the subject matter of the case . . . nor is it related to the operative facts of the negligence action." *Id.* at 329, 100 S.Ct. 571. The Court concluded that the insurance contract pertained only to the conduct and "not the substance of the litigation," and therefore the forum's jurisdiction was not affected. *Id.*

Our limited jurisprudence similarly suggests a middle ground, more flexible than substantive relevance but more structured than but-for relatedness, in assessing the strength of the necessary connection between the defendant, the forum, and the litigation. We [have spoken] in terms of a "substantial connection" between the nonresident defendant and Texas arising from purposeful action or conduct directed here. Considering our own jurisprudence and the Supreme Court's analysis in *Rush* [*v. Savchuk*, 444 U.S. 320, 324, 100 S.Ct. 571, 62 L.Ed.2d 516 (1980)],we believe that for a nonresident defendant's forum contacts to support an exercise of specific jurisdiction, there must be a substantial connection between those contacts and the operative facts of the litigation.

C. Relatedness of Moki Mac's Contacts

Betsy Drugg alleges she was induced to send Andy on the rafting trip by Moki Mac's direct solicitation, which included statements made in Moki Mac's brochures and in the release it sent to the Druggs. Specifically, Andy's mother claims she made the decision to send Andy on the trip based on Moki Mac's assurances that "[y]ou don't need 'mountain man' camping skills to participate in one of our trips," children age twelve or above are suited to participate, and "Moki Mac has taken reasonable steps to provide you with appropriate equipment and/or skilled guides." But for these promises, the Druggs claim, they would not have sent Andy on the rafting trip and he would not have fallen on the hiking trail.

Certainly on a river rafting trip safety is a paramount concern, and we accept as true the Druggs' claim that Andy might not have gone on the trip were it not for Moki Mac's representations about safety. However, the operative facts of the Druggs' suit concern principally the guides' conduct of the hiking expedition and whether they exercised reasonable care in supervising Andy. The events on the trail and the guides' supervision of the hike will be the focus of the trial, will consume most if not all of the litigation's attention, and the overwhelming majority of the evidence will be directed to that question. Only after thoroughly considering the manner in which the hike was conducted will the jury be able to assess the Druggs' misrepresentation claim. In sum, " the [alleged misrepresentation] is not the subject matter of the case . . . nor is it related to the operative facts of the negligence action." *Rush*, 444 U.S. at 329, 100 S.Ct. 571. Whatever connection there may be between Moki Mac's promotional materials sent to Texas and the operative facts that led to Andy's death, we do not believe it is sufficiently direct to meet due-process concerns. Analogous cases from other courts support our view.

Federal district courts in Texas have generally held that a nonresident's in-state advertising is insufficiently related to a negligence claim based on personal injury that occurs out of state to support an exercise of specific jurisdiction.

* * *

Courts in other jurisdictions have similarly addressed the issue, concluding that claims arising out of personal injury that occurs outside the forum do not arise from or relate to a defendant's forum advertising.

* * *

Somewhat analogous to advertising cases are those that concern efforts to recruit forum residents. Most courts have held that merely mailing letters and exchanging phone calls in recruitment efforts is insufficient to support specific jurisdiction over nonresidents for claims that arise outside the forum, although some courts have exercised jurisdiction when the defendant physically recruited in the forum.

* * *

V. Conclusion

We reverse the court of appeals' judgment and remand the case to that court to consider the Druggs' assertion that Moki Mac is subject to general jurisdiction in Texas.

JUSTICE JOHNSON filed a dissenting opinion, in which JUSTICE MEDINA joined, omitted.

E. Challenging Jurisdiction: The Special Appearance

Read Rule 120a.

1. *History*

Before 1962, no procedure existed in Texas state courts by which defendants could directly challenge the Texas court's exercise of personal jurisdiction. Any appearance, even for the purpose of challenging jurisdiction, was a "general appearance" that waived the jurisdictional challenge. Thus, the non-resident had no method to present the issue to the Texas court, and was left with the choice of defending the suit in Texas or taking a default judgment and challenging its validity by collateral attack in some other forum. Taking the second choice was risky for a defendant with valid defenses to the plaintiff's suit. If the Texas court was found to have jurisdiction over the defendant, the default judgment, to which the defendant posed no defense, was valid and enforceable against the defendant.

In 1962, the Texas Rules of Civil Procedure were amended to include the Rule 120a special appearance procedure. Under this rule, defendants can appear "specially" (as opposed to "generally") for the purpose of challenging jurisdiction. Nevertheless, the Rule 120a procedures must be followed strictly, as deviation may well be seen as making a general appearance waiving the special appearance, and subjecting the defendant to the jurisdiction of the Texas courts. Thus, a jurisdictional challenge in state court is still full of traps for the foreign defendant that is unfamiliar with Texas practice.

2. *Issues Presented in Rule 120a, Special Appearance*

In a special appearance, the court determines only the defendant's amenability to service of process issued by the courts of Texas.[1] As demonstrated, the Texas statutes and rules providing for service of process of non-residents have been interpreted to reach as far as due process allows under the United States Constitution. Thus, the only issue that may be addressed in a special appearance is the constitutionality of the attempted exercise of personal jurisdiction over the de-

---

1 Kawasaki Steel Corp. v. Middleton, 699 S.W.2d 199 (Tex. 1985).

fendant in the particular case. In other words, does the exercise of jurisdiction over the defendant in this case satisfy the requirements of due process?

Although the defendant may have a complaint that the method of service or the citation with which the defendant was served was defective, or that the plaintiff's pleadings fail to allege facts needed to invoke the court's jurisdiction, these defects are not properly the subject of a special appearance. Instead, these issues are properly addressed in a motion to quash under Rule 122.[2] This distinction can often be a trap for the lawyer who is unfamiliar with Texas practice. In many jurisdictions, the lack of personal jurisdiction is raised by a motion to quash service. In Texas, such a motion is a general appearance that waives the jurisdictional challenge.

3. *Requisites of the Special Appearance*

The special appearance must be made by sworn motion.[3] The rule does not state any details about the form of the verification, and the preferred practice is to have the client or a representative of the client verify it based upon personal knowledge. In 1976, Rule 120a was amended to allow a defendant to amend the special appearance to cure defects, including the addition of the proper verification.[4]

4. *Waiver: General Appearance*

According to Rule 120a, the special appearance must be filed "prior to motion to transfer venue or any other plea, pleading or motion."[5] The last sentence of Rule 120a(1) provides: "Every appearance, prior to judgment, not in compliance with this rule, is a general appearance."[6] A general appearance waives any dispute over whether the defendant is amenable to the process of the Texas courts because an appearance other than a special appearance "shall have the same force and effect as if the citation had been duly issued and served as provided by law."[7] Thus, the defendant can waive the special appearance by making a general appearance before filing the special appearance, or by making an appearance inconsistent with Rule 120a after the special appearance is filed, such as setting the case for trial, or filing a motion for summary judgment and having it heard.[8] However, filing a motion to dismiss under Rule 91A does not waive the special appearance.[9]

The rule also provides, however, that other pleadings and motions may be filed in the same instrument as the special appearance, or *subsequent* thereto without waiving the special appear-

---

2 *See id.* at 202. ("Defective service or defective process, or even an attempt to bring the defendant before the court under the wrong statute does not authorize the use of the special appearance.").

3 Rule 120a(1).

4 Rule 120a(1). *See* Dawson-Austin v. Austin, 968 S.W.2d 319 (Tex. 1998) (holding that lack of verification does not concede jurisdiction).

5 Rule 120a(1).

6 *Id.*

7 Rule 120.

8 *See* Moody National Bank v. Riebschlager, 946 S.W.2d 521 (Tex. App.—Houston [14th Dist.] 1997, writ denied)(holding that an appearance to file a motion to quash a writ of garnishment does not waive a later special appearance, noting that the motion in no way recognizes that the cause is properly pending before the court or that the court has jurisdiction, and therefore could not be viewed as conferring general jurisdiction on the court).

9 Rule 91A.8.

ance.[10] Historically, lawyers have been careful to file all subsequent pleadings "subject to the special appearance," although *Dawson-Austin* holds that the "subject to" language is *not* required to avoid a waiver of the special appearance.[11] Moreover, the Supreme Court has made clear that neither including a request to quash service in the special appearance, nor entering into an agreement extending time for the defendant to file an initial response, waive the special appearance.[12]

The rule itself provides that the use of discovery processes, such as the taking of depositions, the issuance of process for witnesses, and the serving of requests for admissions, does not constitute a waiver of a special appearance.[13] The Supreme Court has made clear that participating in discovery and discovery disputes when the discovery relates solely to the jurisdictional issues does not waive the special appearance.[14] And it appears that discovery must be limited to jurisdictional facts.[15]

Although not resolved by the Texas Supreme Court, it appears that a defendant may make a valid jurisdictional challenge after a default judgment. Courts of appeals have held that a court has the power to hear a special appearance filed with the motion for new trial.[16] The defendant must request a hearing on the special appearance before ruling on any other motion.

5. *Hearing*

The movant must obtain a timely hearing on the special appearance, which must be heard and determined before any other matter is heard or it will be waived.[17] If the defendant presents issues

---

[10] Rule 120a(1).

[11] Dawson-Austin v. Austin, 968 S.W.2d 319 (Tex. 1998) (overruling Portland Savings and Loan Ass'n v. Bernstein, 716 S.W.2d 532, 534-35 (Tex. App.—Corpus Christi 1984) to extent that *Portland Savings* held that motions for sanctions and to disqualify counsel that were not filed expressly "subject to" special appearance waived jurisdictional challenge); *see also* Hotel Partners v. Craig, 993 S.W.2d 116 (Tex. App.—Dallas 1994, pet. denied) (discovery pleading not filed "subject to" special appearance did not waive special appearance).

[12] *See* GFTA Trendanalysen B.G.A. Herrdum GMBH & Co., 991 S.W.2d 785 (Tex. 1999)(per curiam) (holding a motion to quash service does not waive right to contest jurisdiction); Exito Electronics Co. v. Trejo, 142 S.W.3d 302 (Tex. 2004) (holding that an agreement extending time does not constitute a general appearance).

[13] Rule 120a(1).

[14] *See also Exito Electronics Co.*, 168 S.W.3d 777; *Dawson-Austin*, 968 S.W.2d at 323.

[15] In re Doe, 444 S.W.3d 603, 608 (2014) (citing with approval); In re Stern, 321 S.W.3d 828, 838-840 (Tex.App.—Hous. [1st Dist.] 2010, orig. proceeding); *Exito Electronics Co.*, 168 S.W.3d at 306, n.4.

[16] *See* Lang v. Capital Res., 102 S.W.3d 861, 864 (Tex.App.—Dallas 2003, no pet.); Puri v. Mansukhani, 973 S.W.2d 701 (Tex.App.--Houston [14th Dist.] 1998, no pet.); Koch Graphics, Inc. v. Avantech, Inc., 803 S.W.2d 432, 433 (Tex. App.—Dallas 1991, no writ). *See also* Liberty Enterprises, Inc. v. Moore Transportation Co, 690 S.W.2d 570 (Tex. 1985) (defendant waived special appearance by approving new trial order).

[17] Rule 120a(2); Seeley v. Seeley, 690 S.W.2d 626, 627 (Tex. App.—Austin 1985, no writ); Bruneio v. Bruneio, 890 S.W.2d 150 (Tex. App.—Corpus Christi 1994, no writ); Mouso v. Alworth, 777 S.W.2d 795, 797 (Tex. App.—Beaumont 1989, no writ); Barrett v. Barrett, 715 S.W.2d 110, 113 (Tex. App.—Texarkana 1986, writ ref'd n.r.e.); Steve Tyrell Productions, Inc., v. Ray 674 S.W.2d 430, 437 (Tex. App.—Austin 1984); Brown v. Brown, 520 S.W.2d 571, 575 (Tex. Civ. App.—Houston [14th Dist.] 1975, writ dism'd); *but see* Stegall & Stegall, 592 S.W.2d at 429-30 (limiting *Brown* by concluding that failure to set a hearing on special appearance was not waiver).

other than the special appearance at the hearing, waiver may occur.[18] Of course, if the objection to jurisdiction is overruled by the court, the defendant may (and should) appear generally and defend the suit without waiving the jurisdictional objection.[19] Note, however, that having a motion to dismiss under Rule 91A ruled on does not waive the special appearance.[9]

6. *Proof at Hearing*

Originally, affidavits were not admissible at special appearance hearings because they denied the right of cross-examination to the opposing party.[20] The normal rules of evidence were applied at these hearings, and live testimony, usually from the defendant, was required. In 1990, however, Rule 120a was amended to make affidavits admissible for the purpose of challenging or defending personal jurisdiction.[21] Any affidavits must be filed at least seven days before the hearing.[22] The court may properly determine the special appearance from the pleadings, stipulations, affidavits and attachments, discovery products, and oral testimony.[23]

7. *Burden of Proof*

Unlike federal court, in which it is the plaintiff's burden to prove personal jurisdiction in response to a Rule 12(b)(2) motion to dismiss,[24] in Texas state court under Rule 120a, it is the defendant's burden to plead and prove that the defendant is not subject to the court's jurisdiction.[25] The defendant bears not only the burden of producing evidence in support of his jurisdictional contest, but also the burden of persuasion.[26]

---

[18] *See* Landry v. Daigrepont, 35 S.W.3d 265 (Tex. App.—Corpus Christi 2001, no pet.) (defendant waived special appearance by arguing merits of motion for new trial first); Clements v. Barnes, 822 S.W.2d 658, 659 (Tex. App.—Corpus Christi 1991) *rev'd on other grounds*, 834 S.W.2d 45 (Tex. 1992) (defendant waived timely filed special appearance by raising issues concerning merits of cause of action before court ruled on special appearance).

[19] Rule 120a(4).

[9] Rule 91A.8.

[20] Main Bank & Trust v. Nye, 571 S.W.2d 222, 223-24 (Tex. Civ. App.—El Paso 1978, writ ref'd n.r.e.).

[21] Rule 120a(3).

[22] *Id.*

[23] *Id. See* Franklin v. Geotechnical Services, Inc., 819 S.W.2d 219, 223 (Tex. App.—Fort Worth 1991, writ denied)(holding that an entire deposition was properly before the court under Rule 120a(3), even though only excerpts were read into the record, because, (1) it was a "result of discovery process," and (2) it was attached as an exhibit to the plaintiff's response to the motion challenging jurisdiction and, thus, qualified as a pleading under the rule).

[24] Walker v. Newgent, 583 F.2d 163, 166 (5th Cir. 1978), *cert. denied,* 441 U.S. 906 (1979).

[25] Kawasaki Steel Corp., 699 S.W.2d at 203; Central Texas Cattle Co. v. McGinness, 842 S.W.2d 388, 390 (Tex. App.—San Antonio 1992, no writ).

[26] Smith v. Reynolds, 533 S.W.2d 861, 862 (Tex. Civ. App.—San Antonio 1976, no writ); Hoppenfeld v. Crook, 498 S.W.2d 52, 55 (Tex. Civ. App.—Austin 1973, writ ref'd n.r.e.).

DAWSON-AUSTIN
v.
AUSTIN

968 S.W.2d 319
(Tex. 1998)

JUSTICE HECHT delivered the opinion of the Court in which CHIEF JUSTICE PHILLIPS, JUSTICE GONZALEZ, JUSTICE SPECTOR, JUSTICE OWEN, and JUSTICE HANKINSON joined.

The issues we address in this divorce action are whether the district court had in personam jurisdiction over the wife, and if not, whether the court nevertheless had jurisdiction to divide the marital estate. The court of appeals upheld personal jurisdiction. We disagree.

I

Since 1970, William Franklin Austin has been the president, chief executive officer, sole director, and sole stockholder of Starkey Laboratories, Inc., a Minnesota corporation in the business of manufacturing and distributing hearing aids. In 1977, Austin met Cynthia Lee Dawson at a seminar in Oregon, where she was living, and persuaded her to come to work for Starkey at its headquarters in Minnesota. Austin was 35 years old and divorced, and Dawson was 30 years old and separated from her husband. Dawson soon moved into Austin's Minnesota home and continued working for Starkey. On a business trip to China in 1980, Austin and Dawson recited marriage vows in a Beijing restaurant. Two years later they filed a marriage certificate in Minnesota. At some point Dawson assumed the surname, Dawson-Austin.

Dawson-Austin worked for Starkey until shortly after she and Austin separated in 1992. Over the years the business had grown. In 1980 Starkey was worth about $1.5 million with some $12 million in net revenues. By 1992 the company had become the second largest manufacturer of hearing aids in the world with sales totaling more than $200 million and a net worth of at least $40 million.

Throughout the marriage the couple's principal residence was in Minnesota, although they also owned homes elsewhere, including one they acquired in California in 1984. They never resided in Texas, and neither of them ever came to the state except on business, and then only a few times. When they separated in February 1992, Dawson-Austin was living in their California home, and she remained there. Austin moved to Texas on March 10. On April 10 Dawson-Austin filed for divorce in California but did not serve Austin until October 16. Austin filed for divorce in Texas on September 10, the first day he could do so under Texas law, TEX. FAM. CODE § 6.301 (formerly TEX. FAM. CODE § 3.21), and served Dawson-Austin four days later.

Dawson-Austin filed a special appearance and an amended special appearance, both of which the district court overruled. Dawson-Austin requested the court in dividing the couple's property to apply Minnesota law, under which she contends she would be entitled to a part of the increase in value of petitioner's Starkey stock attributable to the efforts of either spouse. The court refused and instead applied Texas law, holding that the stock was Austin's separate property subject only to any right of reimbursement of the community estate. The district court also struck Dawson-Austin's two expert witnesses retained to testify on the value of the community and its right of reimbursement, on the grounds that they were not timely identified in discovery. In a bench trial, Austin stipulated to Dawson-Austin's valuation of the community estate at $3,750,000. The court awarded Dawson-Austin 55.59% of the community—a little over $2 million.

Dawson-Austin appealed. The court of appeals in its initial opinion reversed the decree, holding that Minnesota law should have been applied in dividing the marital estate. On rehearing, however, a divided court of appeals affirmed the decree in all respects. 920 S.W.2d 776.

II

We first consider whether, as a matter of procedure, Dawson-Austin made a general appearance in the case.

Dawson-Austin filed *pro se* a single instrument including a special appearance, a motion to quash service of citation, a plea to the jurisdiction of the court, a plea in abatement, and subject to all of the above, an original answer. Only the answer was expressly made subject to the special appearance; the motion and pleas were not. The instrument contained a verification of the facts and allegations stated in each component of the instrument except the special appearance. Dawson-Austin contends that the failure to include the special appearance in the verification was a typographical error. The district court overruled Dawson-Austin's special appearance because it was not sworn as required by Rule 120a(1), TEX. R. CIV. P., and because a motion to quash service of citation, plea to the jurisdiction, and plea in abatement, all included in the same instrument with the special appearance, were not expressly made subject to the special appearance.

The day after the court's overruling of the special appearance, Dawson-Austin filed a motion for reconsideration and an amended special appearance. The court denied the amended special appearance "on the merits", in the court's words, and did not rule on the motion to reconsider.

The court of appeals held that Dawson-Austin's special appearance was properly overruled because it was unsworn. The court did not consider whether the other pleadings in the same instrument should have been expressly subjected to the special appearance. 920 S.W.2d at 782. The court also held that Dawson-Austin waived her amended special appearance because, before it was filed, Dawson-Austin argued her motion to quash and did not object to the district court's consideration of it.

Austin argues that there are yet other reasons, in addition to those given by the lower courts, for concluding that Dawson-Austin made a general appearance in the proceeding. We address each of these arguments in turn.

A

As the lower courts both held, an unsworn special appearance does not comply with Rule 120a(1), TEX. R. CIV. P., and thus is ineffectual to challenge in personam jurisdiction. The lower courts also held, however, that the lack of verification can be cured by amendment. Austin argues that an unsworn special appearance cannot be cured and is itself a general appearance. Austin's argument is contrary to the express provision of Rule 120a(1) that a special appearance "may be amended to cure defects". By "cure", the rule means to restore the special appearance. The rule does not limit the kinds of defects that can be cured. The absence of a verification is such a defect, and an amendment that adds a verification cures the special appearance. Every court that has considered the issue agrees.

Austin argues, alternatively, that even if an unsworn special appearance can be cured by amendment, the amendment must be filed before the special appearance is ruled on. This argument, too, finds no footing in Rule 120a(1). The rule simply does not require that an amendment be filed before a ruling on the special appearance, as long as the amendment is filed before there is a general appearance.

Austin's arguments are not only contradicted by both the language and silence of Rule 120a, they misperceive what constitutes a general appearance. One court has explained:

> A party enters a general appearance whenever it invokes the judgment of the court on any question other than the court's jurisdiction; if a defendant's act recognizes that an action is properly pending or seeks affirmative action from the court, that is a general appearance.

Moore v. Elektro-Mobil Technik GmbH, 874 S.W.2d 324, 327 (Tex. App.—El Paso 1994, writ denied). Another court has stated the same proposition in the negative:

> "[A]lthough an act of defendant may have some relation to the cause, it does not constitute a general appearance, if it in no way recognizes that the cause is properly pending or that the court has jurisdiction, and no affirmative action is sought from the court."

Investors Diversified Servs., Inc. v. Bruner, 366 S.W.2d 810, 815 (Tex. Civ. App.—Houston 1963, writ ref'd n.r.e.). These courts have accurately restated the principle underlying a general appearance. An unverified special appearance neither acknowledges the court's jurisdiction nor seeks affirmative action. While it cannot be used to disprove jurisdiction, it certainly does not concede it.

Thus, Dawson-Austin did not enter a general appearance by filing an unsworn special appearance or by amending it only after it was overruled.

B

Austin argues that Dawson-Austin made a general appearance by filing a motion to quash service, a plea to the jurisdiction, and a plea in abatement, all in the same instrument with the special appearance and all following the special appearance in the instrument, but none expressly made subject to the special appearance. The district court agreed with this argument; the court of appeals did not address it. The argument is contrary to Rule 120a, which states: "a motion to transfer venue and any other plea, pleading, or motion may be contained in the same instrument or filed subsequent thereto without waiver of such special appearance". The rule makes matters in the same instrument and subsequent matters subject to the special appearance without an express statement to that effect for each matter.

* * *

Because Dawson-Austin's motion and pleas fully complied with Rule 120a, they did not constitute a general appearance.

C

The hearing on Dawson-Austin's special appearance, motion to quash service of process, plea to the jurisdiction, and plea in abatement was requested by Austin, not Dawson-Austin, because he wished the Texas court to proceed before the California court. As Austin's counsel told the district court, "we can't protect ourselves against the California lawsuit if we don't proceed today." Dawson-Austin did not ask the district court for a hearing on any of the matters she filed. On the contrary, Dawson-Austin filed a motion for continuance the day of the hearing on the grounds that she had not been given the requisite notice for the hearing, her counsel had just been hired to make an appearance and he was in a jury trial at the time of the hearing, discovery was needed on the special appearance, and discovery was needed on the motion to quash. Dawson-Austin's counsel reurged the motion for continuance throughout the hearing, and also requested a postponement because of Austin's and Dawson-Austin's unavailability to testify. The district court denied the continuance.

Austin argues that Dawson-Austin's motion for continuance was not made subject to the special appearance and was therefore a general appearance. The district court appears to have rejected this argument, and the court of appeals did not address it. Austin's argument is incorrect for several reasons. First, as already discussed, Rule 120a expressly states that pleadings and motions may be "filed subsequent [to a special appearance] without waiver of such special appearance". Dawson-Austin's motion for continuance was filed subsequent to her special appearance and thus, by the plain language of the rule, was not a general appearance. Second, the motion for continuance did not request affirmative relief inconsistent with Dawson-Austin's assertion that the district court lacked jurisdiction, which, as we have noted, is the test for a general appearance. Rather, the motion asked the court to defer action on all matters. Third, the motion was particularly appropriate, given that Austin, not Dawson-Austin, set the matters for hearing. Dawson-Austin was obliged to request that hearing of her motion and pleas be deferred until after the special appearance. Rule 120a(2) states: "Any motion to challenge the jurisdiction provided for herein shall be heard and determined before a motion to transfer venue or any other plea or pleading may be heard." She could not request a postponement of the special hearing without also requesting a postponement of her other matters on which Austin, not Dawson-Austin, had requested a hearing. Dawson-Austin was also entitled to seek a postponement of the special appearance hearing until she could complete discovery, as expressly permitted by Rule 120a, and she was entitled to ask for more time for discovery on her motion to quash, provided she did not attempt to take that discovery before the special appearance was decided.

Dawson-Austin was entitled to request more time to prepare for the special appearance hearing that Austin set. Her request to postpone consideration of her other matters was required if the special appearance hearing were to be delayed. Dawson-Austin's motion for continuance in no way constituted a general appearance.

* * *

E

Finally, Austin argues and the court of appeals held that Dawson-Austin, by asserting her motion to quash service of process at the conclusion of the hearing on her special appearance, made a general appearance before filing her amended special appearance the next day. The record does not support this argument.

Again, it must be recalled that Austin, not Dawson-Austin, requested the hearing on the motion to quash, along with the special appearance and Dawson-Austin's other matters, and insisted on going forward. Dawson-Austin did not raise any of the matters at the hearing; on the contrary, Dawson-Austin, as has been noted, repeatedly requested a postponement as to all of them.

* * *

As the record shows, Dawson-Austin's counsel did not raise or argue the motion to quash or any other matter. Austin's counsel raised the motion to quash, and the court ruled it moot without a word from Dawson-Austin's counsel. Only then did the court ask Dawson-Austin's counsel whether he agreed, and he essentially conceded. Nothing else transpired before the filing and hearing of Dawson-Austin's amended special appearance. Thus, the district court properly considered the special appearance on the merits.

III

A

However, the district court erred in overruling Dawson-Austin's amended special appearance. Section 6.305(a) of the Family Code provides:

> If the petitioner in a suit for dissolution of a marriage is a resident or a domiciliary of this state at the time the suit for dissolution is filed, the court may exercise personal jurisdiction over the respondent or over the respondent's personal representative although the respondent is not a resident of this state if:
>
> (1) this state is the last marital residence of the petitioner and the respondent and the suit is filed before the second anniversary of the date on which marital residence ended; or
>
> (2) there is any basis consistent with the constitutions of this state and the United States for the exercise of the personal jurisdiction.

TEX. FAM. CODE § 6.305(a) (formerly TEX. FAM. CODE § 3.26(a)). Austin had been domiciled in Texas exactly six months to the day when he filed suit for divorce. *See id.* § 6.301 ("A suit for divorce may not be maintained in this state unless at the time the suit is filed either the petitioner or the respondent has been . . . a domiciliary of this state for the preceding six-month period . . . .") (formerly TEX. FAM. CODE § 3.21). Dawson-Austin, however, neither was nor ever had been a Texas resident. Thus the district court did not have in personam jurisdiction over Dawson-Austin unless it was under Section 6.305(a)(2).

The United States Constitution permits "a state court [to] take personal jurisdiction over a defendant only if it has some minimum, purposeful contacts with the state, and the exercise of jurisdiction will not offend traditional notions of fair play and substantial justice." Dawson-Austin had no "minimum, purposeful contacts" with Texas. At the time Austin filed suit, Dawson-Austin resided in California, as Austin's petition itself alleged. She was served in California. At the hearing on her amended special appearance, she testified unequivocally and without contradiction from Austin that her only contact with the State of Texas had been to attend a business convention nine or ten years earlier. She had never lived in Texas, and Austin had not lived here before March 1992. There was no basis for the district court to exercise personal jurisdiction over Dawson-Austin, and Austin does not contend otherwise.

B

Even though the district court did not have in personam jurisdiction over Dawson-Austin, it is possible under the United States Constitution, and thus under Texas law, for the court to have had jurisdiction to divide the marital estate located in Texas. The property in Texas in which the parties claimed an interest was Austin's Dallas home and Texas bank accounts, which the parties agreed was community property, and the stock certificate evidencing Austin's shares in Starkey. As we have previously stated, Austin contends that his Starkey stock is separate property, while Dawson-Austin claims that she is entitled under Minnesota law to part of the increase in value of the stock attributable to her and Austin's efforts during marriage.

* * *

In the present case, the location in Texas of property that either is or is claimed to be part of the marital estate does not supply the minimum contacts required for the court to exercise jurisdiction over Dawson-Austin. Austin bought his Dallas home, opened his Texas bank accounts, and brought his Starkey stock certificate to Texas after he separated from Dawson-Austin. We do not believe that one spouse may leave the other, move to another state in which neither has ever lived, buy a home or open a bank account or store a stock certificate there, and by those unilateral actions, and nothing more, compel the other spouse to litigate their divorce in the new domicile consistent with due process. One spouse cannot, solely by actions in which the other spouse is not involved, create the contacts between a state and the other spouse necessary for jurisdiction over a divorce action. *See In the Interest of S.A.V.*, 837 S.W.2d 80, 83-84 (Tex. 1992) (holding that without personal jurisdiction over one parent, a court could still decide custody of a child living in the State, but could not determine support and visitation). Moreover, Dawson-Austin's claim to a part of the value of the Starkey stock is completely unrelated to the situs of the certificate; rather, it is based on the parties' efforts to increase the value of Starkey, most of which occurred in Minnesota. In no sense can it be said that Dawson-Austin ever "purposefully availed" herself of the privilege of owning property in this State.

Thus, the district court lacked jurisdiction to adjudicate Dawson-Austin's claim to part of the value of the Starkey stock or to divide the marital estate.

* * *

The district court had jurisdiction only to grant a divorce and not to determine the parties' property claims. Accordingly, the judgment of the court of appeals is reversed and the case is remanded to the district court for rendition of judgment divorcing Austin and Dawson-Austin and dismissing all other claims for relief for want of jurisdiction.

JUSTICE BAKER, joined by JUSTICE ENOCH and JUSTICE ABBOTT, dissenting, omitted.

---

8. *Appealing the Special Appearance Decision*

If a trial court grants a defendant's special appearance, it signs an order of dismissal, which is a final order disposing of all issues and parties and is immediately appealable to the court of appeals for review. If the special appearance is denied, however, the order is an interlocutory order. In 1997, the interlocutory appeal statute was amended allowing an interlocutory appeal when a trial court "grants or denies a special appearance of a defendant under Rule 120a, Texas Rules of Civil Procedure, except in a suit brought under the Family Code."[1] Mandamus is available to review special appearance orders in family law cases.[2]

The Texas Supreme Court has jurisdiction over interlocutory appeals only if there is a dissent to the court of appeals' opinion or if the court of appeals' opinion conflicts with a prior opinion of another court of appeals or the Supreme Court.[3]

9. *Standard of Review on Appeal*

In *BMC Software Belgium N.V. v. Marchand*,[4] the Texas Supreme Court set forth the applicable standard for reviewing a trial court's order denying a special appearance, holding that the trial

---

1 *See* CPRC § 51.014(7).

2 *See* Canadian Helicopters v. Wittig, 876 S.W.2d 304, 307 (Tex. 1994).

3 TEX. GOV'T CODE § 22.225.

4 BMC Software Belgium, N.V. v. Marchand, 83 S.W.3d 789 (Tex. 2002).

court's factual findings should be reviewed for legal and factual sufficiency and the trial court's legal conclusions should be reviewed de novo.[5] The court's opinion said:

> Whether a court has personal jurisdiction over a defendant is a question of law. However, the trial court frequently must resolve questions of fact before deciding the jurisdiction question. If a trial court enters an order denying a special appearance, and the trial court issues findings of fact and conclusions of law, the appellant may challenge the fact findings on legal and factual sufficiency grounds.[6]

Questions of law are determined de novo in the appellate court—there is no deference given to the trial court's determination of legal issues. Legal and factual sufficiency challenges are different, however, and will be explored in a later chapter. In a nutshell, legal sufficiency attacks a fact finding as being supported by no probative evidence. If there is no evidence to support it, the fact finding cannot stand "as a matter of law." The Texas Supreme Court and the courts of appeals can determine that a fact finding is not supported by legally sufficient evidence. Factual sufficiency is a broader attack that asks whether a fact finding, although supported by some evidence, has such little support in the evidence that it "shocks the conscience" or "clearly indicates bias." If there is factually insufficient evidence to support fact findings in a jury trial, the losing party is entitled to a new trial. Only the court of appeals can review for factual sufficiency.

A trial court may issue findings of fact and conclusions of law with its special appearance ruling that detail its fact findings and legal analysis. If there are no findings and conclusions, all facts necessary to support the judgment and supported by the evidence are implied.[7]

F. Collateral Attack upon Judgment for Lack of Personal Jurisdiction

Appeals (restricted or regular) and bills of review are direct attacks on judgments—the judgment is attacked by asserting errors in the same proceeding in which the judgment was rendered. There are many errors that can result in a reversal of a judgment on appeal—lack of jurisdiction is only one of them. On the other hand, in a collateral attack the judgment is attacked in a proceeding different from that in which the judgment was rendered. Judgments are subject to collateral attack only if the judgment is void, such as when the court rendering the judgment "had no jurisdiction of the person of a party or his property, no jurisdiction of the subject matter, no jurisdiction to enter a particular judgment, or no capacity to act as a court."[1] Ordinarily, a judgment will state that the defendant was properly served with process. Because these judgment recitals cannot be challenged with contrary evidence, collateral attack is usually of no help to a resident defendant claiming invalid service. However, a non-resident who was not amenable to the jurisdiction of the court can present evidence in a collateral attack to prove lack of minimum contacts even though the judgment recites proper service of process.

---

[5] *Id.*

[6] *Id.* at 794 (citations omitted).

[7] *Id.* at 795.

[1] Austin Independent School District v. Sierra Club, 495 S.W.2d 878, 881 (Tex. 1973).

LAYTON
v.
LAYTON

538 S.W.2d 642
(Tex. Civ. App.—San Antonio 1976, writ ref'd n.r.e.).

CADENA, JUSTICE.

Appellant, Janet L. Layton, plaintiff below, complains of the judgment of a district court of Bexar County, Texas, refusing to enforce a judgment of a Maryland court that she recover from her former husband, appellee, Gary A. Layton, the sum of $8,233.68, representing past due installments of alimony and child support ($6,640.18) which appellee had been ordered to pay by a prior decree of the Maryland court, plus attorney's fees in the amount of $1,500.00 and court costs in the sum of $93.50.

The principal question before us is whether Article IV, Sec. 1 of the United States Constitution, which commands that full faith and credit be given in each state to the judicial proceedings of every other state, requires that a Texas court enforce the Maryland judgment for arrearages in alimony and child support, when both such judgment and the prior child support and alimony decree on which it is based were rendered by the Maryland court after a Texas court had rendered judgment, in a suit filed by appellee husband in Bexar County, dissolving the marriage between appellant and appellee, dividing the property of the parties, awarding custody of the parties' two minor children to appellant, and ordering appellee to make periodic payments toward the support of such children.

The parties were married in the State of Virginia. Thereafter, because of appellee's military service, the parties lived in several states before coming to Texas, where appellee had been assigned to duty, in 1971. After they had been in Texas some months, they finally separated, and appellant established her residence with the children in Baltimore County, Maryland. Appellee remained in Texas at his then post, Lackland Air Force Base, in Bexar County.

Appellee filed his suit for divorce in Bexar County on April 27, 1972. His petition alleged that appellant and the children were residents of Maryland. After out-of-state notice was personally served on her in Maryland, appellant entered a special appearance challenging the jurisdiction of the Texas court. Her objection to jurisdiction was overruled, and she filed no further pleadings in the Texas case. The decree of divorce entered by the Texas court on October 3, 1972, recites that, other than her unsuccessful challenge to the jurisdiction of the Texas court, appellant failed to enter her appearance in the Texas case, either in person or by attorney, and "wholly made default."

Prior to the time that she was served with notice of the Texas divorce suit, appellant filed her petition in the circuit court for the City of Baltimore, Maryland, seeking a divorce *a mensa et thoro*, custody of the minor children, child support, and alimony. On November 22, 1972, after the Texas divorce decree had been rendered and had become final, appellant filed her amended or supplemental complaint in the Maryland court, seeking the same relief as that sought in her original complaint, except that in this amended pleading she sought a divorce *a vinculo*, rather than a divorce a *mensa et thoro*.

In answer to this amended or supplemental complaint, appellee filed "preliminary objections" in the Maryland court. In this pleading appellee asked that the "service of summons returned by the Sheriff of Baltimore City as to the Supplemental Bill of Complaint and Show Cause Order appended thereto" be quashed "on the grounds of *lack of jurisdiction over the person*" of appellee "and insufficiency or illegality of service of process." (Emphasis added.)

In his "preliminary objections" appellee alleged (1) that he was a resident of Texas; (2) that while he was temporarily in the City of Baltimore, Maryland for the purpose of visiting his sick grandmother, a deputy sheriff served the summons in question on appellee's father, rather than on appellee; and (3) that the divorce proceedings in Texas, in which Janet had participated, and the divorce degree (sic) entered by the Texas court were "determinative . . . of all issues of alimony, support, custody and property."

Appellee's preliminary objections were overruled by order entered by the Maryland court on January 22, 1973. This order recites that the Maryland court had acquired in personam jurisdiction over appellee. Appellee filed no further pleadings in the Maryland case.

On August 1, 1973, the Maryland court entered a "Decree of Permanent Alimony And Other Relief." This decree recited that the Maryland court had "acquired *in personam* jurisdiction over . . . Gary A. Layton;" and that the court was satisfied that "all allegations as to the acts of . . . abandonment committed by" appellee had been proved by "clear and convincing evidence." After a recital to the effect that the Maryland court had "reviewed and considered" the prior Texas divorce decree, there follows language (1) awarding custody of the minor children to appellant; (2) ordering appellee to pay, as child support, the sum of $51.92 per week, per child; (3) awarding appellant, as permanent alimony, the sum of $57.69 per week; (4) ordering appellee to pay all arrearages in child support payments, amounting, as of the date of this decree, to $2,509.61; (5) ordering appellee to pay arrearages in alimony pendente lite in the total amount of $1,384.56; and (6) ordering appellee to pay $1,500.00 to appellant's attorney as attorney's fees.

Appellee did not appeal from this decree.

On November 23, 1973, in the same cause as that in which the August 1, 1973 decree was entered, appellant filed her petition seeking a determination of "alimony and support arrearages" and praying that the court reduce the amounts so determined to a money judgment. It was in response to this petition that the judgment, which appellant now seeks to enforce in Texas, was rendered. This judgment, entered January 3, 1974, recites appellee had personal notice of appellee's petition and that in personam jurisdiction had been acquired over appellee by the Maryland court.

There is no showing that any of the orders, decrees or judgments rendered by the Maryland court have been set aside or modified, and appellee does not suggest that such orders, decrees or judgments are not final.

The case now before us was filed by appellant in Bexar County, Texas, seeking enforcement of the money judgment rendered by the Maryland court on January 3, 1974. In his answer to such suit appellee, in addition to special exceptions not here relevant and a general denial, made the following allegations: (1) Appellant appeared in the Texas divorce case for the purpose of challenging the jurisdiction of the Texas court. (2) After her challenge to the jurisdiction was overruled, the case was set for trial on the merits but, although appellant was notified of such setting, she failed to appear at the hearing and the divorce decree was rendered by the Texas court. (3) Thereafter, appellant, "flaunting the jurisdiction of" the Texas court, "proceeded to obtain subsequent divorce decree in the State of Maryland, which decree she now seeks to enforce." (4) "Thus, by reason of these facts, (appellant) is estopped from enforcing said Maryland decree, which is subsequent in time to the Texas decree. . . ."

Nowhere in appellee's pleadings is there any language suggesting that the Maryland court lacked jurisdiction over the subject matter or the person of appellee. It should also be pointed out that the Maryland court did not enter a "divorce decree."

* * *

For the purpose of this opinion, we assume, without deciding, that the Texas divorce decree terminated appellant's right to support, although it might be argued that since the Texas courts are prevented by Texas law from ordering a husband to support his wife after the divorce, the question of permanent alimony was not litigated in the Texas court.

However, such assumption merely leads to the conclusion that the Maryland court should have given conclusive effect to the Texas decree and denied appellant's prayer for alimony. That is, the Maryland court should have given full faith and credit to the Texas judgment as finally determinative of appellant's right to support after the divorce. It is clear that the Maryland court failed to give such effect to the Texas judgment. The question, then, is whether the refusal of the Maryland court to give full faith and credit to the Texas judgment relieves the Texas courts of the obligation to enforce the Maryland decree.

It is clear that a Texas court, when asked to give full faith and credit to another state's judicial proceedings, may collaterally inquire into the jurisdiction of the foreign court to enter the judgment in question. *Williams v. North Carolina*, 325 U.S. 226, 65 S.Ct. 1092, 89 L.Ed. 1577 (1945).

Appellee insists that the Maryland court had no jurisdiction to enter the decree which appellant now seeks to enforce in Texas. There are two reasons why this argument is unpersuasive.

In the first place, as already pointed out, appellee's pleadings below raise no question concerning the jurisdiction of the Maryland court to enter the judgment. His pleadings merely assert that because the Texas divorce was rendered prior to the Maryland decree and because appellant "flaunted" the jurisdiction of the Texas court, she is "estopped" from attempting to enforce the subsequent Maryland decree. There is no allusion to the power of the Maryland court. At best, appellee's answer can be interpreted only as a plea of res judicata or, perhaps, estoppel by judgment. The pleading condemns the actions of appellant, not the action of the Maryland court.

The conclusions of law filed by the court below recite that the "parties and the issues were the same in Texas as in the State of Maryland finally," and that the Maryland court "was without jurisdiction to proceed to grant any type of relief to (appellant) on any issue decided by the Texas Court."

We know of no rule supporting the conclusion that the jurisdiction of a court of a sister state is affected by the action of a Texas court. The Texas divorce decree would not, in fact, have deprived even a Texas court of jurisdiction to entertain a subsequent suit involving the same issues. It is true, of course, that the prior decree could be successfully interposed as a defense to the subsequent litigation involving the same parties and the same issues. But this invocation of the prior judgment would be simply a resort to the doctrine of res judicata. The plea of res judicata is a plea in bar. It is not a plea to the jurisdiction. Res judicata is an affirmative defense which must be affirmatively pleaded. Rule 94, TEX. R. CIV. P. Failure to plead this defense results in its waiver. Since it is elementary that a court's lack of jurisdiction over the subject matter cannot be waived, it must be concluded that a final determination by one court of the issues before it has no effect on the power of other courts. It cannot be held that the Texas divorce decree in some manner deprived the Maryland court of jurisdiction.

The findings of fact and conclusions of law make no reference to the in personam jurisdiction of the Maryland court. They do not contain a statement to the effect that appellee was not subject to the jurisdiction of that court. The issue of in personam jurisdiction of the Maryland court was not raised by the pleadings.

In the second place, even if we give to the pleadings and the findings of fact and conclusions of law the broadest possible interpretation and conclude that the lower court concluded that the Maryland court lacked jurisdiction of the subject matter and the person of appellee, such a finding cannot stand. While, as pointed out above, a Texas court which is asked to enforce the judgment of a sister state may collaterally inquire into the jurisdiction of the court of such other state, this collateral inquiry is permissible only where the party resisting enforcement of the foreign judgment did not appear in the foreign proceedings. In the case before us, appellee appeared in the Maryland proceedings and unsuccessfully litigated the question of the jurisdiction of the Maryland court. He therefore had no right to relitigate the jurisdictional issue in Texas. In *Gunther*, *supra*, the Texas court correctly inquired collaterally into the jurisdiction of the California court, since the party resisting enforcement in Texas of the California judgment received no notice of the California proceedings, nor did he participate in such proceedings in any way.

The trial court's conclusion, if, in fact, it concluded, that the Maryland court lacked jurisdiction of the subject matter or of the parties is erroneous.

The law applicable to this case is stated in *Roche v. McDonald*, 275 U.S. 449, 451-52, 48 S.Ct. 142, 143, 72 L.Ed. 365 (1927), as follows:

> It is settled by repeated decisions of this Court that the full faith and credit clause of the Constitution requires that the judgment of a State court which had jurisdiction of the parties and the subject-matter in suit, shall be given in the courts of every other State the same credit, validity and effect which it has in the State where it was rendered, and be equally conclusive upon the merits; and that only such defense as would be good to a suit thereon in that State can be relied on in the courts of any other State.

The place to raise the defense that the Texas divorce decree should be given full faith and credit as determinative of appellant's right to support was in the Maryland court and, in fact, appellee expressly raised that issue by his pleadings in the Maryland proceedings. As the New York court of appeals pointed out in *Lynn*, *supra*, appellee's only remedy to correct the error, if any, of the Maryland court in failing to give adjudicative effect to the Texas judgment was by direct appeal through the Maryland courts and, if necessary, to the Supreme Court of the United States. Texas courts cannot sit as appellate tribunals for the purpose of correcting mistakes made by Maryland courts in applying the Full Faith and Credit Clause.

The fact that the Maryland court failed to give full faith and credit to the prior Texas judgment does not justify retaliatory action by the Texas courts.

* * *

In summary: (1) Appellee, having appeared in the Maryland proceedings and having litigated the jurisdictional question unsuccessfully there, cannot relitigate the question of the jurisdiction of the Maryland court in Texas, not in view of the final determination of that question by the Maryland court, may a Texas court collaterally review the correctness of such determination, as it would have the power to do if appellee had not appeared in the Maryland suit. (2) Even if it be assumed that the Maryland court erroneously failed to give full faith and credit to the prior Texas divorce decree, appellee's right to attack the Maryland judgment on that ground "died with his failure to appeal" from that judgment. (3) The error, if any, of the Maryland court in refusing to give full faith and credit to the Texas judgment does not justify the refusal of the Texas court to enforce the Maryland judgment. (4) The traditional Texas policy against permanent alimony does not support the refusal to enforce foreign decrees reducing unpaid alimony installments to money judgments.

The judgment of the trial court is reversed and judgment is here rendered that appellant, Janet L. Layton, recover from appellee, Gary A. Layton, the sum of $8,233.68, with interest at the rate of 9% Per annum from January 3, 1973, the date of the Maryland judgment which judicially ascertained and reduced to a liquidated amount the extent of appellee's arrearage in alimony and child support payments.

G. Forum Non Conveniens

Read CPRC §§ 71.031, 71.051.

Despite a state court's right to exercise jurisdiction over a given matter and defendant, the state court will sometimes defer to the jurisdiction of a foreign court in a more appropriate forum.[1] The doctrine of forum non conveniens does not rest on jurisdiction but gives the court discretion to decline to exercise jurisdiction by granting a defendant's motion to dismiss.[2]

Forum non conveniens is a common law doctrine. However, some states, including Texas, have statutes governing the application of the doctrine in certain cases. The Texas statute has a rather tortured history.

In the 1991 opinion in *Dow Chemical v. Alfaro*,[3] the Texas Supreme Court held that CPRC § 71.031 gave foreign plaintiffs a right to a Texas forum in personal injury and wrongful death cases, preventing courts from dismissing personal injury and wrongful death cases on the grounds of forum non conveniens. During the 1993 legislative session, the Texas Legislature enacted a new section of the Civil Practice and Remedies Code titled "Forum Non Conveniens," effective for cases filed on or after September 1, 1993.[4] The bill that ultimately became law was drafted by representatives from the Texas Trial Lawyers Association, an association representing plaintiff's lawyers, and "Jobs for Texas," a group of large corporations associated for the express purpose of challenging the Supreme Court's decision in *Alfaro*. The new statute allowed personal injury and wrongful death cases filed in Texas to be dismissed on grounds of forum non conveniens under certain circumstances. During a subsequent legislative session, the statute was amended, making it easier for courts to dismiss certain cases, and now it permits forum non conveniens dismissals in all personal injury cases. Moreover, it now appears that forum non conveniens dismissals are compelled in some cases.

---

[1] Gulf Oil Corporation v. Gilbert, 330 U.S. 501, 504 (1947).

[2] *See generally* Albright, *In Personaml Jurisdiction: A Confused and Inappropriate Substitute for Forum Non Conveniens,* 71 TEX. L. REV. 351 (1992) (discussing Texas courts' willingness to dismiss for lack of due process the same cases they would have dismissed on forum non conveniens grounds).

[3] 786 S.W.2d 674 (Tex. 1990), *cert. denied*, 498 U.S. 1024 (1991).

[4] CPRC § 71.051.

In re GENERAL ELECTRIC COMPANY

271 S.W.3d 681
(Tex. 2008)

JUSTICE JOHNSON delivered the opinion of the Court.

Although Austin Richards never lived or worked in Texas, he sued numerous defendants in Dallas County as a result of alleged exposure to asbestos at his jobsite in Maine. He alleged that he developed mesothelioma as a result of the exposure and that the defendants were liable to him because they produced or were involved in furnishing the asbestos. Several defendants moved for dismissal on the basis of forum non conveniens. The trial court denied the motions. At issue in this mandamus proceeding is whether the trial court abused its discretion by denying the defendants' motions to dismiss. We conclude that it did and conditionally grant mandamus relief.

I. Background

Aside from a period of military service, Austin Richards lived in Maine his entire life. He worked in Maine for over thirty years as a mason handling pipe-covering insulation. In December 2005, he was diagnosed with mesothelioma. Richards and his wife (collectively "Richards") filed suit in Dallas County against General Electric and over twenty other companies, three of which are headquartered in Texas. Richards alleged that the defendants mined, processed, manufactured, sold, or distributed asbestos which caused or contributed to his disease. The case was transferred to the asbestos multi-district litigation court in Harris County. *See* TEX.R. JUD. ADMIN. 13.

Seven defendants moved for dismissal of Richards's suit based on forum non conveniens. *See* TEX. CIV. PRAC. & REM.CODE § 71.051. They argued that the suit had no connection to Texas and that Maine was an adequate alternative forum for the case. Richards responded that the trial court should deny the motions to dismiss because the defendants had not met their burden of proof regarding the section 71.051 factors. He especially emphasized that the defendants had not proved the existence of an adequate alternative forum in which the claim could be tried. Richards asserted that if his case were dismissed and he refiled in Maine, the case would be vulnerable to removal to federal court and if removed, it would be transferred to the federal Multi-District Litigation Court No. 875 (MDL 875) for pretrial proceedings. Richards further argued that cases transferred to MDL 875 do not get tried and "virtually nothing happens to them at all." Richards urged that he was seriously ill from his disease and that if the Texas trial court declined to exercise jurisdiction, MDL 875 would not be adequate because he would not survive long enough to have his case tried.

At the hearing on the motion to dismiss, the judge asked whether the defendants would agree that they would not attempt to remove the case to federal court if he granted the motion to dismiss. Several defendants, including General Electric, did not agree to waive their removal rights. The judge sent a letter to the parties indicating that he would deny the motion to dismiss and expressing concern that if he granted the motion and the case were refiled in Maine, it would be removed to federal court and transferred to MDL 875 where it would "sit . . . for several years." The judge wrote that his ruling on the motion might have been different if the defendants had waived their right of removal.

The defendants filed a motion to reconsider. They asserted that even if their motions to dismiss were granted and Richards refiled his case in Maine, removal to federal court was speculative, the criticisms of MDL 875 were unfounded as recent activity there refuted any argument that it did not provide an adequate remedy, and the court's ruling should not depend on the defendants' waiver of their removal rights. After another hearing, the trial court granted the motion to reconsider, set aside the letter in which he stated the grounds for his previous ruling, and denied the motion to dismiss without stating a reason.

Three defendants-General Electric, Warren Pumps, and Ingersoll-Rand (defendants)-seek mandamus relief directing the trial court to grant their motions to dismiss. They argue that on this record, the statutory forum non conveniens factors require dismissal.

II. Discussion

A. Availability of Mandamus Review

After the parties submitted briefs in this case, we held that an adequate remedy by appeal does not exist when a motion to dismiss for forum non conveniens is erroneously denied. *See In re Pirelli Tire, L.L.C.,* 247 S.W.3d 670, 679 (Tex. 2007). Accordingly, mandamus relief is available in this case, if warranted.

B. Forum Non Conveniens

1. General

The defendants claim that the trial court had no discretion but to apply the factors found in the forum non conveniens statute and dismiss Richards's claim because those factors weigh in favor of a forum other than Texas. Richards argues that even considering the statutory factors, the trial court had discretion to determine whether a forum non conveniens dismissal would serve the interest of justice, which in this case it would not.

We review a trial court's decision about whether to dismiss a case on forum non conveniens grounds for an abuse of discretion. A court abuses its discretion if its decision is arbitrary, unreasonable, or without reference to guiding principles.

The applicable forum non conveniens statute provides:

> If a court of this state, on written motion of a party, finds that in the interest of justice and for the convenience of the parties a claim or action to which this section applies would be more properly heard in a forum outside this state, the court shall decline to exercise jurisdiction under the doctrine of forum non conveniens and shall stay or dismiss the claim or action. In determining whether to grant a motion to stay or dismiss an action under the doctrine of forum non conveniens, the court shall consider whether:
>
> (1) an alternate forum exists in which the claim or action may be tried;
>
> (2) the alternate forum provides an adequate remedy;
>
> (3) maintenance of the claim or action in the courts of this state would work a substantial injustice to the moving party;
>
> (4) the alternate forum, as a result of the submission of the parties or otherwise, can exercise jurisdiction over all the defendants properly joined to the plaintiff's claim;
>
> (5) the balance of the private interests of the parties and the public interest of the state predominate in favor of the claim or action being brought in an alternate forum, which shall include consideration of the extent to which an injury or death resulted from acts or omissions that occurred in this state; and

(6) the stay or dismissal would not result in unreasonable duplication or proliferation of litigation.

TEX. CIV. PRAC. & REM.CODE § 71.051(b).

Prior to 2003, section 71.051 provided that a case brought by a United States resident "may" be stayed or dismissed under the doctrine of forum non conveniens. In 2003, the Legislature amended the statute. Among other changes, the amended statute provided that a trial court "shall" dismiss a claim or action if the court found that in the interest of justice and for the convenience of the parties a claim or action would be more properly heard in a forum outside Texas. Before the 2005 amendments the statute also provided that when determining whether to dismiss an action based on forum non conveniens, a trial court "may" consider the factors specified in section 71.051(b). In 2005, the Legislature amended the statute to its current form. It now provides that when determining whether to dismiss an action based on forum non conveniens, a trial court "shall" consider the factors specified in section 71.051(b).

The defendants claim that the amended statute takes away much of a trial court's discretion in regard to forum non conveniens motions by requiring the court to weigh the statutory factors and decline to exercise jurisdiction if the factors weigh in favor of granting the motion. Richards claims, however, that the Legislature has always provided trial courts discretion to deny forum non conveniens motions, and the statute does not remove that discretion. Instead, the statute merely requires that dismissals serve the interests of justice-an inherently discretionary standard.

Use of the word "shall" in a statute imposes a duty. TEX. GOV'T CODE § 311.016(2). We agree with defendants that by using the word "shall" in regard to a trial court's consideration of the factors listed in section 71.051(b), the Legislature has essentially defined the terms "interest of justice" and "convenience of the parties" as they are used in section 71.051(b). The Legislature also, by use of the word "shall," requires dismissal of the claim or action if the statutory factors weigh in favor of the claim or action being more properly heard in a forum outside Texas.

Richards asserts that the defendants, as movants, had the burden to prove that each factor weighed in favor of dismissal and urges that they failed to meet the burden. We disagree. Prior to 2003, the statute provided that a trial court could stay or dismiss a claim under the forum non conveniens statute "if the party seeking to stay or dismiss proves" the enumerated factors "by a preponderance of the evidence." However, the statute was amended to provide only that a trial court "shall consider" the factors. TEX. CIV. PRAC. & REM.CODE § 71.051(b). The statute does not mandate that a movant prove each factor or that each factor must weigh in favor of dismissal to require a motion to be granted. In construing statutes we presume that each word in the statute was put there for a purpose and that each word not in the statute was omitted for a purpose. The statute does not contain language placing the burden of proof on a particular party in regard to the factors, as was the situation with the prior version. Nor does the statute require that a party prove each factor of section 71.051(b). The statute simply requires the trial court to consider the factors, and it must do so to the extent the factors apply. To the extent evidence is necessary to support the positions of the parties, the trial court must base its findings and decision on the weight of the evidence, and certainly is entitled to take into account the presence or absence of evidence as to some issue or position of a party.

With the foregoing in mind, we turn to the enumerated factors to determine whether the trial court abused its discretion in failing to grant the motions to dismiss.

2. Section 71.051(b)(1) and (2)-Adequate Alternate Forum

The first two factors in section 71.051(b) are: (1) whether an alternate forum exists where the claim may be tried, and (2) whether the alternate forum provides an adequate remedy. The defendants assert that Maine, where Richards lived and was allegedly exposed to asbestos, is such an alternate forum. Richards does not dispute that Maine state courts are an alternate forum or that those courts provide an adequate remedy. He urges in his brief that had defendants agreed not to remove the case to federal court, the Texas case would have been dismissed and the case would have been tried in Maine. But he contends the defendants have not proved the availability of an alternate forum where the claims may be *tried.* He takes that position because none of the defendants in this case maintain a principal place of business or are incorporated in Maine. Therefore, his case would be vulnerable to removal to federal court on diversity jurisdiction grounds. *See* 28 U.S.C. 1332(a)(1). He claims that once removed to federal court, his case would almost certainly be transferred to MDL 875, and it is widely accepted that cases transferred to MDL 875 do not get tried. * * * He claimed in the trial court, and continues to claim in this Court, that because of the situation in MDL 875, dismissal would not work *justice,* but would work *injustice.* Richards argued that a transfer to MDL 875 would work an injustice because he would have no chance at a trial before his death and that because claims languish in MDL 875, it is not an alternate forum in which the claim may be *tried* as required by section 71.051(b)(1).

* * *

Ordinarily, an alternate forum is shown if the defendant is "amenable to process" in the other jurisdiction. *Piper Aircraft Co. v. Reyno,* 454 U.S. 235, 254 n. 22, 102 S.Ct. 252, 70 L.Ed.2d 419 (1981). There may be circumstances where an alternate forum is not adequate because the remedies it offers are so unsatisfactory that they really comprise no remedy at all. But, comparative analyses of procedures and substantive law in different forums should be given little weight in forum non conveniens analysis because such analyses pose significant practical problems. Comparison of the "rights, remedies, and procedures" available in each forum would require complex exercises in comparative law that the forum non conveniens doctrine is designed to help courts avoid. Therefore, a comparative analysis of the procedures, rights, and remedies available in Texas, Maine, and federal courts should only be given weight if Maine (and a potential transfer to MDL 875) would in substance provide no remedy at all.

The disadvantages Richards perceives in MDL 875 proceedings are ones of comparative speed to disposition of his case. His objection is based on comparative analysis of procedural processes and times to trial. That is the type of exercise that is disfavored when forum non conveniens motions are considered. * * *

Furthermore, even if Richards's case is dismissed in Texas, filed in Maine, and transferred to MDL 875 for pretrial proceedings, Richards will not be deprived of all remedies for purposes of forum non conveniens analysis. Though Richards (and others) may be critical of the methods used and time taken to dispose of pretrial matters in the federal asbestos MDL scheme, the scheme is designed to resolve asbestos cases, not deprive injured parties of a remedy. The federal Constitution guarantees Richards the right to a jury trial and due process, and the Maine and federal courts are bound to afford those rights to Richards. U.S. CONST. amend. VII, amend XIV, § 1. We believe, therefore, that Maine, and even MDL 875, come within the Legislature's intent that the alternate forum be one "in which the claim or action may be tried." TEX. CIV. PRAC. & REM.CODE § 71.051(b).

We conclude that on balance, the factors set out in sections 71.051(b)(1) and (2) weigh strongly, if not conclusively, in favor of Richards's action being heard in a forum outside Texas.

3. Section 71.051(b)(3)-Substantial Injustice to Defendants by Litigating in Texas

The defendants point to private interest considerations in support of their assertion that litigating this case in Texas will work a substantial injustice to them. *See* TEX. CIV. PRAC. & REM.CODE § 71.051(b)(3). They also point to the increased costs of traveling to Maine to depose witnesses for trial in Texas. Richards argues that the defendants' claims in this regard are conclusory allegations which are insufficient to support dismissal. He also claims that regardless of the forum, expert witnesses in asbestos cases reside all over the country and attorneys must routinely travel to take depositions.

While some travel in this case will almost certainly occur regardless of the forum in which the case is ultimately litigated, that aspect does not override the fact that the evidence and witnesses relevant to the issue of Richards's asbestos exposure and his damages are outside the subpoena power of Texas courts. TEX.R. CIV. P. 176.3. * * * Further, while Richards argues that defendants have not identified any specific witness or evidence they are unable to obtain, such a showing is not necessary.

We conclude that the section 71.051(b)(3) factor-whether maintaining the action in Texas would work a substantial injustice to defendants-weighs strongly in favor of the claim being more properly heard in a forum outside Texas.

4. Section 71.051(b)(4)-Jurisdiction Over all Defendants

Richards claims the evidence did not show that all the defendants in this case are subject to the jurisdiction of Maine courts, or have consented to jurisdiction in Maine. *See* TEX. CIV PRAC. & REM CODE § 71.051(b)(4). The defendants that filed motions to dismiss stipulated to jurisdiction in Maine, agreed to submit to jurisdiction there, or admitted they were subject to jurisdiction under the Maine long-arm statute. Further, the defendants argue that under the Maine long-arm statute, courts in Maine will have jurisdiction over all defendants *properly* joined as parties.

* * *

The Maine long-arm statute is plain and speaks for itself. This record presents no reason to do what typically is not done in forum non conveniens analyses-perform a comprehensive comparative consideration of Maine jurisprudence in regard to each party to Richards's suit. Requiring Texas trial courts and appellate courts to engage in such exercises would slow down and complicate forum non conveniens hearings and decisions to the point that they could become major detriments to disposition of cases. This record presents no reason, for purposes of forum non conveniens analysis, to consider Maine's long-arm statute further than its plain words. The section 71.051(b)(4) factor-whether the alternate forum can exercise jurisdiction over all defendants properly joined to the plaintiff's claim-weighs in favor of the claim being more properly heard in a forum outside Texas.

5. Section 71.051(b)(5)-Public and Private Interest

Richards contends the defendants did not demonstrate that the balance of public and private interests weigh in favor of a Maine forum. Generally, the public interest factors to be considered are administrative difficulties related to court congestion, burdening the people of a community with jury duty when they have no relation to the litigation, local interest in having localized controversies decided at home, and trying a case in the forum that is at home with the law that governs the case. The private interest considerations generally are considered to be the ease of access to proof, the availability and cost of compulsory process, the possibility of viewing the premises, if appropriate, and other practical problems that make trial easy, expeditious, and inexpensive.

As to the public interest factors, the parties do not disagree that Maine law will apply in this case. Maine undoubtedly has an interest in ensuring that its citizens are not exposed to hazardous materials in the workplace. Absent some overriding consideration, the citizens of Texas should not be burdened with jury duty in a complex asbestos exposure case that has no relationship to Texas. In this case, most evidence and fact witnesses are admittedly located in Maine. Richards's treating physicians, co-worker witnesses, and family members are there. The paper mill where Richards was allegedly exposed to asbestos is in Maine. Compulsory process is unavailable to require attendance at a Dallas County trial by witnesses approximately two thousand miles away. *See* TEX. R. CIV. P. 176.3. Richards says that he has already provided or will provide copies of his medical records to the defendants. But a promise to produce some or even most evidence does not cure the logistical problems created by lack of effective compulsory process for trial. Richards also asserts the defendants' claim that there is no compulsory process for witnesses who reside in Maine is an insufficient, "unsubstantiated, conclusory allegation" because the defendants have never identified a witness whose appearance they will be unable to obtain at a Texas trial. But detail regarding which witnesses would be called and what evidence would be unavailable is not necessary in a case such as this where the practical problems of trying a personal injury case hundreds of miles from the scene of the occurrence, the place where the lay witnesses reside, and where most other evidence is located is manifest. Reasonable access to witnesses and evidence is a fundamental need in regard to any trial-asbestos or otherwise.

* * *

Section 71.051(b)(5) requires a trial judge to balance the public and private interests to determine whether those factors predominate in favor of the claim being more properly heard in a forum outside Texas, and on balance, it is clear that the factors weigh in favor of Richards's action being heard in Maine.

6. Section 71.051(b)(6)-Unreasonable Duplication of Litigation

Richards asserts that the defendants failed to show dismissal would not result in unreasonable duplication of litigation. He claims dismissal would result in two lawsuits: the Texas case against the nonmoving defendants would remain pending while a new suit would be filed against the moving defendants in Maine. We disagree that had the trial court granted the defendants' motions to dismiss, this would have resulted in unreasonable duplication of litigation. Section 71.051(b) currently provides that if a court decides "a claim or action" would be more properly heard in another forum, the court shall stay or dismiss "the claim or action." The language is broad and does not require that a trial court dismiss only the claims or actions against moving defendants. *See* TEX. CIV. PRAC. & REM.CODE § 71.051(b) (requiring dismissal of a claim or action on written motion of "a" party).

* * *

We disagree with Richards's position in regard to the section 71.051(b)(6) factor. The potential that a trial court might grant a motion to dismiss as to only part of an action and that some duplication of litigation could occur, depending on Richards's own litigation decisions, does not turn the trial court's decision to grant motions to dismiss such as the ones in this case into decisions causing unreasonable duplication of litigation. Under the circumstances, the section

71.051(b)(6) factor-that the stay or dismissal would not result in unreasonable duplication or proliferation of litigation-weighs in favor of the claim being more properly heard in a forum outside Texas.

* * *

III. Conclusion

When all section 71.051(b) factors in a case favor the conclusion that an action or claim would be more properly held in a forum outside Texas, as they do here, the statute requires the trial court to grant motions requesting that it decline to exercise its jurisdiction. The trial court's denial of the relators' motions to dismiss violated the forum non conveniens statute and was an abuse of its discretion. We conditionally grant the petition for writ of mandamus and direct the trial court to grant the relators' motions. The writ will issue only if the trial court fails to comply.

JUSTICE O'NEILL did not participate in the decision.

Notes & Questions

1. *Dismissal when plaintiff is a Texas resident.* The forum non conveniens statute prohibits dismissal of an action filed by a legal resident of Texas or a "derivative claimant" of a legal Texas resident, which is defined as "a person whose damages were caused by personal injury or wrongful death of another." A Texas resident appointed as the representative of a nonresident claimant (such as next friend, guardian, or administrator) will not provide the necessary residency to prevent dismissal.[1] Furthermore, if an action involves both plaintiffs who are legal residents of Texas and plaintiffs who are not, the court may apply the forum non conveniens factors to the nonresident's claims and dismiss or not as it is appropriate to do so.[2]

2. *Forum non conveniens and venue.* The doctrine of forum non conveniens allows a court to decline to exercise its jurisdiction and dismiss in favor of a court of another judicial system with jurisdiction. Venue, which is discussed in the next chapter, is different. It concerns the transfer of cases from a state district court in one Texas county to another district court in another Texas county. A motion to transfer venue under the venue statutes is far different from a motion to dismiss on grounds of forum non conveniens. However, the venue statute now provides for "mandatory venue" in another jurisdiction (not another Texas county) when the parties of a "major transaction" have made certain written agreements.[3]

---

[1] CPRC 71.051(e) & (h). *See* In re Mahindra, ___ S.W.3d ___ (Tex. 2018) (finding that wrongful death claims of decendent's sons, Texas residents, could not be dismissed, and trial court did not abuse its discretion in not dismissing claims brought in representative capacity); In re Bridgestone America Tire Operations, LLC, 459 S.W.3d 517 (Tex. 2015) (finding next friend's legal residency does not trigger exception, before 2015 amendments).

[2] CPRC 71.051(e) (abrogating In re Ford Motor Co., 442 S.W.3d 265 (Tex. 2014). See In re Mahindra, ___ S.W.3d ___ (Tex. 2018) (finding no abuse of discretion in not dismissing claims brought in representative capacity when claims brought in individual capacity could not be dismissed).

[3] CPRC § 15.020.

3. *Comity*. Under the doctrine of comity, the courts of one state will recognize the laws of a sister state and extend immunity to a sister sovereign as a matter of deference or respect. The Texas Supreme Court has held that the Texas courts should decline to exercise jurisdiction over a sovereign entitled to immunity in the courts of its own state.[4] This aspect of comity is similar to the forum non conveniens doctrine because the court is declining to exercise jurisdiction available to it under the United States Constitution and the laws of the State of Texas. Nevertheless, the Texas Supreme Court has indicated that the proper procedural method to raise comity is the special appearance rather than the motion to dismiss, which is the appropriate forum non conveniens procedural device.[5]

H. Forum Selection Clauses

In re ADM INVESTOR SERVICES, INC.

304 S.W.3d 371
(Tex. 2010)

JUSTICE GREEN delivered the opinion of the Court.

In this case, we consider whether the trial court abused its discretion by denying a motion to dismiss premised on a forum-selection clause. We conclude that it did. The real party in interest did not overcome the presumption against the relator's waiving its right to enforce the forum-selection clause, or satisfy her burden to demonstrate that enforcing the clause would be unreasonable and unjust. Accordingly, we conditionally grant the relator's petition for writ of mandamus and order the trial court to dismiss the case as to the relator.

I

Jetta Prescott executed an agreement in 2001 with ADM Investor Services, Inc., allowing ADM to trade commodities on Prescott's behalf. Texas Trading Company Incorporated acted as a broker and guarantor in the transaction. When Prescott's account balance reached a deficit greater than $50,000.00, ADM was authorized to close her account and collect the deficit from Texas Trading. In early 2004, Prescott's balance reached a deficit of $57,844.29. ADM closed her account and collected the deficit from Texas Trading's CEO, Charles Dawson. Dawson filed suit in his individual capacity in Hopkins County against Prescott and obtained a judgment against her.

Prescott then sued both Texas Trading and ADM in Rains County, alleging several legal theories including fraud, breach of fiduciary duty, and negligence. Texas Trading simultaneously filed an answer and a motion to transfer venue to Hopkins County. ADM responded to the suit by filing an answer, a motion to dismiss, and, alternatively, a motion to transfer venue to Hopkins

---

4 K.D.F. v. Rex, 878 S.W.2d 589 (Tex. 1994).

5 *See id.*; Hawsey v. Louisiana Department of Social Service, 934 S.W.2d 723 (Tex. App.—Houston [1st Dist.] 1996, writ denied); State of New Mexico v. Caudle, 108 S.W.3d 319 (Tex. App.—Tyler 2002, pet. Denied).

County. ADM's motion to dismiss relied on the choice-of-law and forum-selection clause in its agreement with Prescott, which reads:

> All actions or proceedings arising directly, indirectly or otherwise in connection with, out of, related to, or from this Agreement or any transaction covered hereby shall be governed by the law of Illinois and may, at the discretion and election of [ADM], be litigated in courts whose situs in [sic] within Illinois.

. . . The trial court later conducted a hearing on ADM's motion to dismiss, which it denied. The trial court explained its reasoning in a letter, stating that although the forum-selection clause would be enforceable if ADM were the lone defendant, "[i]t seems unreasonable to the Court for Plaintiff to have to pursue the same cause of action against two defendants in two different states." . . . The court of appeals denied ADM's petition for writ of mandamus on the alternative ground that ADM waived enforcement. 257 S.W.3d 817, 822 (Tex. App.—Tyler 2008).

II

* * *

Mandamus will issue if the relator establishes a clear abuse of discretion for which there is no adequate remedy by appeal. *In re Prudential Ins. Co. of Am.,* 148 S.W.3d 124, 135-36 (Tex. 2004). We have consistently granted petitions for writ of mandamus to enforce forum-selection clauses because a trial court that improperly refuses to enforce such a clause has clearly abused its discretion. *See In re AIU Ins. Co.,* 148 S.W.3d 109, 114-15 (Tex. 2004).

A party waives a forum-selection clause by substantially invoking the judicial process to the other party's detriment or prejudice. [W]e [have] adopted a test considering the totality of the circumstances. But merely participating in litigation does not categorically mean the party has invoked the judicial process so as to waive enforcement. Waiver can be implied from a party's unequivocal conduct, but not by inaction.

We disagree with the court of appeals that ADM waived enforcement. Simultaneously filing an answer and motion to transfer venue with a motion to dismiss falls short of substantially invoking the judicial process to Prescott's detriment or prejudice. ADM's approximately three-month delay in requesting a hearing also does not compel us to find waiver. We do not consider the length of any delay separate from the totality of the circumstances. Here, despite the gap between filing and requesting a hearing, ADM did nothing "unequivocal" to waive enforcement. Moreover, we have considered comparable delays before without finding waiver.

We also reject any agency theory that holds ADM as waiving enforcement because of the actions taken by Texas Trading, an initial co-defendant, or its CEO, Dawson. . . .

Prescott has also failed to establish an exception under which the trial court's refusal to enforce the forum-selection clause would be permissible. A trial court abuses its discretion in refusing to enforce a forum-selection clause unless the party opposing enforcement of the clause can clearly show that (1) enforcement would be unreasonable or unjust, (2) the clause is invalid for reasons of fraud or overreaching, (3) enforcement would contravene a strong public policy of the forum where the suit was brought, or (4) the selected forum would be seriously inconvenient for trial. The burden of proof is heavy for the party challenging enforcement. When inconvenience in litigating in the chosen forum is foreseeable at the time of contracting, the challenger must "show that trial in the contractual forum will be so gravely difficult and inconvenient that he will for all practical purposes be deprived of his day in court."

Prescott failed to meet her heavy burden to establish that enforcing the forum-selection clause will be unreasonable or unjust, or seriously inconvenient. The mere existence of another defendant does not compel joint litigation, even if the claims arise out of the same nucleus of facts. *See In re Int'l Profit Assocs., Inc.*, 274 S.W.3d 672, 680 (Tex. 2009) (per curiam) ("If all it takes to avoid a forum-selection clause is to join as defendants local residents who are not parties to the agreement, then forum-selection clauses will be of little value."). Indeed, as the case reaches us, the trial court already separated the case, isolating ADM as a defendant in Prescott's suit in Rains County. Still, our conclusion would not differ even if ADM and Texas Trading were co-defendants in a single forum. Nothing in the record establishes that Prescott could not proceed in Illinois. Moreover, while a trial in Texas is undoubtedly more convenient for a Texas resident, Prescott failed to prove that a trial in Illinois would deprive her of her day in court. Prescott's circumstances here are thus not sufficient to meet the heavy burden she has to avoid a forum-selection clause.

We observe that Prescott asserted in her brief to this Court that her "health will prevent her from prosecuting her claims in two different states." The record shows that Prescott presented an affidavit to the trial court, opposing Texas Trading's motion to transfer venue to Hopkins County. Prescott swore that she was nearing the age of 80, suffered chronic health problems including fibromyalgia and heart problems, often had difficulty walking, and had been hospitalized several times in recent months. Prescott believed that her "case will be severely prejudiced if transferred to Hopkins County." Although we are sympathetic to Prescott's health concerns, the record does not establish that requiring her to pursue her claims against ADM in Illinois, the forum to which she agreed in 2001, would be unreasonable or unjust. Further, even assuming that health concerns could render a selected forum sufficiently inconvenient to preclude enforcement of a forum-selection clause, we believe that Prescott's conclusory statements are insufficient to establish such inconvenience. *Cf. Lyon,* 257 S.W.3d at 234 ("If merely stating that financial and logistical difficulties will preclude litigation in another state suffices to avoid a forum-selection clause, the clauses are practically useless.").

By allowing for exceptions when enforcement of forum-selection clauses would be unreasonable or unjust, or seriously inconvenient, we, as the Supreme Court in *M/S Bremen,* have recognized that there may be extreme circumstances that courts cannot presently anticipate or foresee; but we have not established a bright-line test for avoiding enforcement of forum-selection clauses. *See M/S Bremen,* 407 U.S. at 17, 92 S.Ct. 1907 (speculating that exceptional circumstances could exist such as a forum-selection clause in a contract of adhesion, or a controversy that the parties could never have had in mind).[2] We have consistently refused to close the door to the possibility that exceptional circumstances could exist, even as we have chosen not to confront them in particular cases. *See, e.g., Int'l Profit Assocs.,* 274 S.W.3d at 679-80; *Lyon,* 257 S.W.3d at 231-32; *Michiana Easy Livin' Country, Inc. v. Holten,* 168 S.W.3d 777, 793 (Tex. 2005). Here, though, we need not elaborate on these exceptions any further because the sparse record in this mandamus case does not demonstrate such exceptional circumstances.

---

2 The Supreme Court clarified in *Carnival Cruise Lines, Inc. v. Shute* that its use of "serious inconvenience of the contractual forum" in *M/S Bremen* was in the context of a hypothetical agreement between two Americans to resolve a local dispute in a remote alien forum, not an agreement to resolve the dispute in another state. 499 U.S. 585, 594, 111 S.Ct. 1522, 113 L.Ed.2d 622 (1991).

III

We conclude that Prescott did not overcome the presumption against ADM's waiving its right to enforce the forum-selection clause by showing that ADM substantially invoked the judicial process. We also conclude that Prescott failed to satisfy her burden to demonstrate that enforcement of the forum-selection clause would be unjust and unreasonable. Accordingly, we hold that the trial court abused its discretion in denying ADM's motion to dismiss.

JUSTICE WILLETT filed a concurring opinion. JUSTICE WILLETT, concurring.

I join the Court's result and write separately only to add a brief word on the evidentiary burden borne by a party asserting medical hardship to escape a forum-selection clause, an issue of first impression in this Court. Also, while today's case is a sub-par vehicle given its slim record, I believe the Court should one day clarify something else in medical-hardship cases: the meaning of phrases like "seriously inconvenient" and "unreasonable or unjust"—two of the bases for avoiding a forum-selection clause—and, relatedly, whether physical ailments can qualify as "special and unusual circumstances" sufficient to defeat enforcement. Actions to enforce forum-selection clauses arrive at the Court via mandamus, and it seems unfair to conclude a lower court clearly abused its discretion by acting without reference to guiding principles if the principles they must reference supply scant guidance.

1. What sort of health-related evidence would suffice to escape a forum-selection clause?

I agree that Jetta Prescott's affidavit detailing her myriad health woes is, standing alone, insufficient to avoid the contracted-for forum. The lesson of *In re Lyon,* as the Court notes, is that the mere assertion of "financial and logistical difficulties" is not enough to negate a forum-selection clause, lest such clauses become "practically useless." Ease of evasion is certainly no less a concern when the claimed hardship is physical rather than financial. So I agree that a party asserting medical infirmities must offer more than her own testimony.

I would go a step further, however, and make clear for the bench and bar what sort of evidence *would* suffice. Boiled down, a party opposing a forum-selection clause bears a "heavy burden" of proving a heavy burden—that trial in the chosen forum would be unjustly onerous. And if the assertion is health-related, a health professional should do the asserting. In my view, first-party patient testimony is insufficient (though perhaps not always necessary), and third-party provider testimony is necessary (though perhaps not always sufficient). Specifically, a competent medical provider should attest that the patient's condition makes travel to the agreed forum not merely inconvenient or impracticable, but medically prohibited. This is the approach adopted in a recent federal-court case involving an 81-year-old New York resident who broke her hip on a cruise ship and argued "inconvenience" to defeat transfer of her personal-injury suit to Washington State under a forum-selection clause. Both the plaintiff and her orthopedic surgeon described her condition, the surgeon testifying she could tolerate a plane flight, although it would be difficult and she would suffer discomfort. The court held that while this plaintiff failed to make the requisite showing—she proved only that travel would be unpleasant, not unfeasible—a plaintiff whose physical limitations bar travel can satisfy the heavy burden of proof required to set aside a forum-selection clause on grounds of inconvenience. If health concerns are ever held to preclude enforcement, this type of proof, at minimum, seems necessary.

2. In a forum-selection clause case involving a medically infirm party, what do "seriously inconvenient" and "unreasonable or unjust" mean?

* * *

Cases involving medical hardship strike me as somewhat unique. Financial or logistical burdens may be easily anticipated; not so with many medical burdens.[10] The Court notes that when a forum's inconvenience is foreseeable at the time of contracting, the party opposing enforcement must "show that trial in the contractual forum will be so gravely difficult and inconvenient that he will for all practical purposes be deprived of his day in court." True, but in conducting that analysis we must also confront what we confirmed just last year: a party asserting inconvenience can avoid enforcement by proving that "special and unusual circumstances developed *after* the contracts were executed" such that litigation in the chosen forum would work a deprivation of its day in court. So can exacting evidence of severe medical ailments constitute "special and unusual circumstances" in certain cases?

The Court never mentions this "special and unusual circumstances" basis for negating a forum-selection clause, but that is immaterial here. Mrs. Prescott's only evidence of post-contract medical problems is her lone affidavit, which even if wholly persuasive, is wholly insufficient. Accordingly, we need not consider the affidavit's substance (or lack thereof) and whether Mrs. Prescott's ailments qualify as "special and unusual circumstances."

In sum, this Court has never addressed, nor has *any* Texas appellate court, whether medical concerns can negate a forum-selection clause. Given the ubiquity of such clauses in everyday contracts, both commercial and consumer, I hope a future case with a more-developed record gives us an opportunity to clarify how the various bases for avoiding enforcement apply when a party asserts serious medical hardship. This seems only fair. . . .

Notes & Questions

1. *Forum-selection agreements versus venue-selection agreements*. As will be discussed in the chapter on venue, forum-selection agreements are different from venue-selection agreements. While the former is generally enforceable in Texas, the latter is not.

---

[10] Parties ought not bear an expectation of prognostication when it comes to their health, required to foretell whether future maladies might make a potential out-of-state trial too onerous. Infirmities are inevitable, but that doesn't make them foreseeable such that healthy parties who execute a forum-selection clause must consider whether health woes years or decades down the road might pose a travel problem. Cross-country travel may be undemanding for a healthy 60-year-old who signs a forum-selection clause but inconceivable for an ailing almost-80-year-old who contests one.

2. *Choice-of-law agreements.* Texas has adopted the Restatement for enforcing choice-of-law agreements.[1] The parties will be held to their choice when "the state of the chosen law has a sufficiently close relationship to the parties and the contract to make the choice reasonable."[2]

---

1 Exxon Mobile Corp. v. Drennen, 452 S.W.3d 319, 325 (Tex. 2014)(following *DeSantis v. Wackenhut Corp.,* 793 S.W.2d 670, 677 (Tex.1990)). The RESTATEMENT(SECOND) OF CONFLICT OF LAWS § 187(2), provides:

> The law of the state chosen by the parties to govern their contractual rights and duties will be applied, even if the particular issue is one which the parties could not have resolved by an explicit provision in their agreement directed to that issue, unless either
>
> (a) the chosen state has no substantial relationship to the parties or the transaction and there is no other reasonable basis for the parties' choice, or
>
> (b) application of the law of the chosen state would be contrary to a fundamental policy of a state which has a materially greater interest than the chosen state in the determination of the particular issue and which, under the rule of § 188, would be the state of applicable law in the absence of an effective choice of law by the parties.

2 Exxon Mobile Corp. v. Drennen, 452 S.W.3d 319 (Tex. 2014) (upholding choice-of-law provision where Texas had a materially greater interest in contract, the New York law was not contrary to a fundamental policy of Texas, and Exxon's need for uniformity in construing its employment contracts was a logical rationale for the choice).

CHAPTER 4. VENUE

A. Introduction

Read Venue Statute, Chapter 15, CPRC; Rules 86-89.

"Subject matter jurisdiction" determines which court in the hierarchy of Texas courts is authorized to hear the particular case. "Personal jurisdiction" determines whether the Texas state courts have power over a particular defendant. "Forum non conveniens" determines the appropriate judicial system in which the matter should be litigated. These concepts can all be distinguished from the subject of this chapter—venue. "Venue" determines which of the 254 Texas counties in Texas are permissible locations for the litigation.

Texas venue is one of the most important considerations in evaluating a Texas lawsuit. It is largely governed by statute, and the statutory scheme has changed dramatically over the last 25 years as tort reform swept Texas. But the current scheme is built on the old scheme, and venue can get very complicated. The venue statute sets out proper venue alternatives. The rules of procedure, Rules 86 through 89, set out the procedure for challenging a plaintiff's venue choice as not being within the statutory alternatives. There are several procedural provisions in the statute as well, however. To make matters even more complicated, the Rules governing venue have not caught up to the most recent statutory changes. Therefore, much of venue procedure is learned through caselaw.

Before 1983, the plaintiff's choice of venue could be challenged through the "plea of privilege" practice, by which defendants asserted the "privilege" to be sued in the county of their domicile. However, there were numerous mandatory and permissive exceptions to this privilege, which the plaintiff could invoke. Whenever a defendant put venue at issue, the issues were presented in a full evidentiary hearing, and the parties had a right to insist on a jury to determine fact questions. The trial could very well resemble a full trial on the merits because, if the plaintiff relied on an exception allowing venue in the county where the cause of action accrued, the plaintiff was required to prove the cause of action by a preponderance of the evidence. Therefore, the merits of the case often were tried at the venue hearing stage and then again at the trial. Moreover, a party dissatisfied with the results of the venue hearing had the right to an interlocutory appeal. The inefficiencies of this system caused widespread criticism, eventually leading to the 1983 reforms.[1]

The 1983 statutes and rules made major changes. The 1983 version of Chapter 15 of the Civil Practice and Remedies Code set out the plaintiff's permissible venue options, which were far less complicated than the previous statute. The procedure for venue challenges was simplified as well, making it much easier for a plaintiff to sustain venue in the county of suit.

The 1983 Texas venue scheme was attacked also, this time as being subject to abuse by plaintiffs. The popular press frequently discussed this type of abuse, subjecting the entire system to ridicule. My personal favorite was reported in *The Dallas Observer* in early 1994.[2]

In January 1991, a Taco Bell in Irving was held up by two teenagers, who shot four people to death. Police caught the teenagers less than a mile away, and they were soon convicted of murder. The families of the victims filed a civil wrongful death suit in San Diego, Duval County, Texas, against Jerome Green, the teenager serving a 50-year sentence in prison for the crime (the

---

1 *See generally*, Guittard & Tyler, *Revision of the Texas Venue Statute: A Reform Long Overdue*, 32 BAYLOR L. REV. 563 (1980); Price, *Texas Venue Statute: Legislative History*, 15 ST. MARY'S L.J. 855 (1984).

2 *See* John MacCormack, *Hot Gun, Did Top Plaintiff's Lawyer John Cracken Go Too Far To Squeeze Millions Out of Taco Bell?,* DALLAS OBSERVER, January 6, 1994, at 16.

other received the death penalty), and American Security Products Co., the company that manufactured the safe in the Taco Bell. The petition claimed that venue was proper in Duval County because "Defendant Jerome Green is a citizen and resident of Duval County, Texas." Green's had lived in the Dallas area when the crime occurred, and his current address was listed as Tennessee Colony, Texas, where he was in prison. Green, represented by the Dallas lawyer who was his appointed counsel in the criminal trial, did not challenge venue. American Security did file a motion to transfer venue, but the motion was overruled at a hearing held in chambers. Nine minutes after the motion was overruled, the plaintiffs amended their lawsuit, adding Taco Bell as a third-party defendant. Taco Bell filed a motion to transfer, claiming that Green's alleged residence in Duval County "was obviously manufactured and originates from some type of agreement with the Plaintiffs concerning venue in this case." In a subsequent deposition, Green testified that he planned to move to Duval County after getting out of prison, although he had never been to Duval County, did not know anyone who lived there, and could not place it on the map. Taco Bell lost the venue challenge, ultimately settled the case for $8.25 million, and sued the plaintiffs' lawyer, Green, and Green's lawyer in federal court for conspiracy to defraud. The federal claims were eventually dismissed. When you hear these tales of venue abuse, it is not surprising that venue became an important issue in the tort reform proposals presented in the 1995 legislative session.

Perhaps the most significant change brought by the 1995 statute is the addition of the concepts of "convenience" and "fairness" to Texas venue. Traditionally, the statutory venue scheme of proper and improper venue had been concerned strictly with the mechanical application of the statute, rather than with the subjective concerns such as "convenience" and "fairness" that constitute the federal courts' concept of venue.

Note that a venue challenge concerning any party's inability to receive a fair trial in a given county (an "unfair forum") is governed by Rules 257 through 259, not the venue statute and Rules 86-89. "Transferring venue" under Rule 86 et seq. and "changing venue" under Rule 257 *et seq.* involve different procedures and will be considered separately.

B. The Venue Statute: Permissive, Mandatory, and Improper Venue

The Texas venue statute will usually provide several alternatives for venue in a particular lawsuit. The statutory scheme envisions a hierarchy of proper venues.[1] On the bottom rung are counties for which there is no statutory venue justification, and thus "improper venues," unless defendant fails to assert its venue rights. On the next rung are "permissive venues," which are the venues permitted under the statutory "general rule"[2] *and* its exceptions.[3] On the top rung are "mandatory venues."[4] Each of the statutes contains the "venue facts" (such as "residence," "principal office") under which the venue alternatives of that statute are available. It is extremely important to read the statutes carefully to identify the "venue facts" that must be pleaded and proved if venue is challenged.

Many statutes that create causes of action have their own venue provision, setting forth mandatory or permissive venue.[5] We will not discuss these provisions in this course but be aware of their presence.

1. *The General Rule*

The "general rule" was changed in 1983 and again in 1995. In the "plea of privilege" practice, there was one general rule: the county of defendant's residence. In 1983, there were two: the county of defendant's residence (if defendant was a natural person) or the county where all or part of the cause of action accrued.[6] Now there are five, which can be placed into three general categories: (1) a county of residence[7] (either an individual defendant's residence, a non-individual defendant's principal office, or, in certain circumstances, the plaintiff's residence); (2) a county where the cause of action occurred;[8] and (3) a county of proper venue where the court chooses to transfer the action "for the convenience of parties and witnesses and in the interest of justice,"[9]

a. *Residence of an Individual*

"Residence" for venue purposes has been long defined as being established if a person has (1) a fixed place of abode; (2) occupied or intended to be occupied consistently over a period of time; (3) permanently rather than temporarily. An early venue opinion, *Snyder v. Pitts*,[10] held that a defendant may have more than one residence for venue purposes. For instance, in *Mijares v.*

---

[1] *See* CPRC § 15.001(b) [1995] defining "proper venue."

[2] CPRC § 15.001 [1983]; § 15.002 [1995].

[3] CPRC § 15.031 *et seq.*

[4] CPRC § 15.011 *et seq.*

[5] *See, e.g.*, In re Lopez, 372 S.W.3d 174 (Tex. 2012) (construing mandatory venue provision in arbitration statute, CPRC § 171.096(c)); Wichita County v. Hart, 917 S.W.2d 779 (Tex. 1996) (holding that venue provision in Whistleblower's Act, TEX. GOV'T CODE § 554.007 (1994) is permissive).

[6] CPRC § 15.001 [1983].

[7] CPRC § 15.002(a)(2), (3), (4) [1995].

[8] CPRC § 15.002(a)(1) [1995].

[9] CPRC § 15.002(b) [1995].

[10] 241 S.W.2d 136 (Tex. 1951).

Paez,[11] a student's college address was considered a residence for venue purposes, even though the student also resided at his parents' home (his "domicile") and did not intend to remain at his college address past graduation. Also, a defendant who is in the process of moving from one county to another, and whose affairs are in such a state that it is uncertain in which county the defendant's residence is located, may be sued in either county.[12]

The 1995 amendments did nothing to change the basic concept of "residence." However, the amendments clearly limit residence for venue purposes to residence at the time the cause of action accrued, a limitation not contained in the earlier statute.[13] While this limitation was primarily targeted toward plaintiffs who reputedly would change their residences before filing a lawsuit to acquire more favorable venue, it also clearly limits the shenanigans carried out in the *Taco Bell* case discussed above. The provision in the general rule regarding plaintiff's residence was added only after the legislators realized that there was no provision providing venue for suits filed by Texas residents when the cause of action accrued outside Texas, the individual defendants were not Texas residents, and the corporate defendants had no principal office in Texas. Ultimately, it was decided that in such circumstances plaintiffs could sue in the county of their residence.

b. *Principal Office*

One of the major changes brought about by the 1995 amendments was the addition of a non-individual defendant's "principal office" in Texas as part of the general rule.[14]

_In re_ MISSOURI PACIFIC RAILROAD COMPANY
998 S.W.2d 212
(Tex. 1999)

JUSTICE GONZALES delivered the opinion for a unanimous court.

These consolidated mandamus proceedings concern the mandatory venue statute for suits brought under the Federal Employers' Liability Act (FELA). In each case the key issue is whether the plaintiff in the underlying lawsuit sued the corporate defendant in a county where it maintains "a principal office," as defined in the venue statutes. We conclude that the plaintiffs in all of the suits failed to prove that the corporate defendant has a principal office in the county of suit, so we direct the trial courts in Jefferson County and Tarrant County to transfer the cases to a proper county.

I

These mandamus proceedings arise out of three FELA lawsuits filed in Jefferson County, and three filed in Tarrant County. Section 15.018(b) of the venue statutes gives three choices:

---

[11] 534 S.W.2d 435 (Tex. Civ. App.—Amarillo 1976, no writ)

[12] *See* Howell v. Mauzy, 899 S.W.2d 690 (Tex. App.—Austin 1994, writ denied) (venue proper in Travis County where the evidence showed Justice Mauzy and his wife had vacated their house in Dallas, although it had not yet been sold, and moved to Austin).

[13] CPRC § 15.002(a)(2), (3), (4); § 15.007 [1995].

[14] CPRC § 15.002(3) [1995]. This applies only to defendants who are not "natural persons."

(b) All suits brought under [FELA] shall be brought:
(1) in the county in which all or a substantial part of the events or omissions giving rise to the claim occurred;
(2) in the county where the defendant's principal office in this state is located; or
(3) in the county where the plaintiff resided at the time the cause of action accrued.

Subparts (b)(1) and (b)(3) do not apply here because none of the plaintiffs reside in the county of suit and none claim the cause of action arose there. All the plaintiffs in the Jefferson County cases claim damages for an injury occurring outside of Texas. Freddie Burleigh, a Louisiana resident, sued his employer, Missouri Pacific Railroad Company (Mo-Pac), for injuries he suffered in Louisiana. Terriance Spiller and Juanita Spiller, residents of Harris County, sued Mo-Pac for injuries Terriance Spiller received in Louisiana. Tamara L. Weston resides in Dalhart, Hartley County. She sued Southern Pacific Transportation Company and Mo-Pac in Jefferson County for an injury she suffered near Obar, New Mexico.

Each plaintiff in the Tarrant County suits against Union Pacific Railroad alleged he suffered an injury in his home state outside Texas. Ronald E. Smirl, a resident of Oklahoma, sued for an injury suffered in Chickasha, Oklahoma. Bobby Ray Martin, a Louisiana resident, sued for an incident occurring in Shreveport, Louisiana. Willie B. Williams is a resident of Arkansas who alleges an injury in Gurdon, Arkansas.

The venue challenges proceeded much the same in all the cases. The plaintiff alleged that the railroad maintained a principal office in the county of suit. The railroad denied that it had a principal office in the county of suit or that venue was proper there, and moved to transfer venue to Harris County where the railroad had principal offices in Texas. In each case the trial court denied the motion and retained venue, resulting in these mandamus proceedings.

* * *

III

* * *

* * * The controlling issue here is what the plaintiff's had to plead and prove to establish venue in "the county where the defendant's principal office in this state is located" under the FELA venue statute.

The railroads contend that a foreign corporation only has one principal office under the mandatory venue statutes for FELA actions. If the FELA venue statute is read in isolation, the provision for suit "in the county where the defendant's principal office in this state is located" would indicate a company's Texas headquarters. However, that view is complicated by the general definition of "principal office" in section 15.001:

In this chapter:

(a) "Principal office" means a principal office of the corporation . . . in this state in which the decision makers for the organization within this state conduct the daily affairs of the organization. The mere presence of an agency or representative does not establish a principal office.

The plaintiffs respond that the phrase "a principal office" indicates that there can be more than one principal office. Further, the plaintiffs argue, the "daily affairs" of these defendants consist of operating trains, so that a principal office is wherever a railroad official makes decisions about operating trains.

We agree with the plaintiffs that a corporation can have more than one principal office. We are bound by the statutory definition of "principal office" as "a" principal office. Thus, when we apply the general definition of "principal office" to the FELA venue statute, we must assume a defendant company could have more than one principal office.

But we reject the plaintiffs' argument that the statute clearly defines a principal office as any place where a company official makes decisions about the company's business. Such a broad definition would include agencies and representatives, which the statute expressly rejects. Agencies and representatives, as we defined them under the former venue statutes, are officials who possess broad power and discretion to act for the corporation.[35] Thus, "decision makers" who "conduct the daily affairs" are officials of a different order than agents or representatives. Morever, even though "a principal office" suggests there can be more than one office, the term "principal" indicates some sort of primacy.[36] It is unlikely that an office clearly subordinate to and controlled by another Texas office could be "a principal office." Finally, in context, "the daily affairs" of a company cannot mean relatively common, low-level managerial decisions.

Beyond these preliminary observations, the statute is not entirely clear in all its particulars. The language of the statute could support more than one reasonable interpretation and therefore is ambiguous. Because it is ambiguous, we may turn to extratextual sources such as the statute's legislative history.

IV

Sections 15.001 and 15.018 codify parts of Senate Bill 32, enacted by the 74th Legislature. The railroads contend that Senate Bill 32's legislative history supports its interpretation of the venue statutes. The plaintiffs argue to the contrary, that the bill's history supports their own interpretation. Both the House and Senate proposed changes to the venue statutes for corporations during the 74th regular session of the Legislature, House Bill 6 and Senate Bill 32. As the plaintiffs readily concede, and legislative history bears out, a major purpose of the 1995 amendments was to reduce or limit forum shopping. * * *

We find nothing in the legislative history to dissuade us from our initial observations about the meaning of section 15.001. Rather, the legislative history supports our conclusion that: (1) a company may have more than one principal office, (2) the "decision makers" who conduct the "daily affairs" of the company are officials who run the company day to day, (3) a mere agent or representative is not a "decision maker" nor is a principal office one where only decisions typical of an agency or representative are made, and (4) a principal office is not an office clearly subordinate to and controlled by another Texas office.

The debates on the floor of the House and the Senate confirm that the Legislature did not intend to limit venue to only one county where the company maintains a corporate office if the facts do not warrant it. A company may control or direct its daily affairs in Texas through decision makers of substantially equal responsibility and authority in different offices in the state. In that case each office may be a principal office of the company.

Necessarily, courts must look at the corporation's structure to determine a company's principal office or offices. The titles of the company officials in a particular office are not as informa-

---

[35] *See Ruiz*, 868 S.W.2d at 759 (holding that oil company foreman lacked discretion and authority to constitute an agency or representative for venue purposes).

[36] *See* WEBSTER'S THIRD NEW INTERNATIONAL DICTIONARY 1802 (1969) (defining the adjective "principal" as "most important, consequential, or influential: relegating comparable matters, items, or individuals to secondary rank").

tive as a description of their responsibility and authority, relative to other company officials within the state. We recognize that our interpretation does not provide a precise test. But we believe the Legislature intended a flexible test to allow for the myriad forms that corporate structures can take.

V

* * *

The plaintiffs' evidence focused largely on the extent of operations and equipment in Jefferson County, Texas. The evidence showed that the railroad's corporate headquarters were in Omaha, Nebraska, and many of the executive and administrative decisions were made there. The evidence did little to define the role of any of the decision makers in Jefferson County relative to the rest of the company in Texas. A party cannot prove a prima facie case that a county has a principal office without evidence of the corporate structure and the authority of the officers in the county of suit as compared with the remainder of the state. The only company officials in Jefferson County the plaintiffs' evidence identified were a manager of train operations, a manager of yard operations, and a "maintenance and way" foreman. There was testimony that the railroads' corporate headquarters delegated some policy-making to the local level. However, there is little evidence of the kinds of decisions the Jefferson County officials could make. More importantly, there is no evidence of how the Jefferson County officials' authority compared to others statewide, so that the court could make a meaningful determination whether Jefferson County is in any sense a "principal office."

VI

The Tarrant County plaintiffs put on more extensive evidence of Union Pacific's organization structure in Texas. Union Pacific is divided into four regions. The southern region includes most of Texas and parts of Louisiana. The southern region is further divided into six divisions. In answer to interrogatories, the railroad identified the "decision makers" who office in Harris County as a general solicitor, a vice president for transportation, a general manager, two general supervisors, a chief engineer, and two division superintendents. All but the division superintendents are considered executive officers of the company. The former general solicitor stated in a deposition that "the real policy decisions and real serious operational decisions are made by persons at the level of superintendent or above." The only official the plaintiffs claim is a "decision maker" in Tarrant County is a division superintendent for the Fort Worth service unit. He testified in his deposition that his duties included coordinating the movement of trains, staffing the crews within the area, and ensuring rules compliance and discipline. The division superintendent also said that the southern region is based in Houston, and his boss is the general manager in Harris County.

This evidence is sufficient to characterize a division superintendent as a decision maker under the statute. However, it fails to establish prima facie that the Tarrant County office is a principal office when compared to the responsibility and authority exercised by company officials elsewhere in Texas. The evidence shows that the division superintendent in Tarrant County is not an executive officer and has the least authority of any of the decision makers with any real discretion or authority. In contrast, there are six executive officers in Harris County. The two highest ranking officers in Texas, general solicitors, conduct the affairs of the railroad from offices in Harris County. They oversee legal affairs such as FELA litigation in Texas for the railroads. The general manager of transportation is responsible for the transportation plan for the southern region of the Company, which includes Texas and Louisiana. The general manager supervises the assistant general manager and the general superintendent. The general supervisor also supervises six division superintendents, two in Houston, three in other Texas offices, and one in Louisiana. The general superintendent performs the logistics for deciding train starts and yard starts. Finally, the chief engineer directs the activities of local maintenance-of-way and signal service units throughout the region.

VII

The plaintiffs failed to establish Jefferson County or Tarrant County as principal offices of the railroads. The burden shifted to the defendants to prove that Harris County is a proper venue. The venue facts bear out that Harris County is "a" principal office of the railroads, and therefore a proper venue under the mandatory FELA statute. The trial courts abused their discretion by not sustaining the motions to transfer. Accordingly, we conditionally issue writs of mandamus directing the trial courts to sustain the railroads' motions to transfer the cases to Harris County. The writs will not issue unless the trial courts fail to act in accordance with this opinion.

Notes & Questions

1. *Agency or representative.* What is a "mere agency or representative" that does not meet the requirements for "principal office?" The "agency or representative" language of the venue statute comes from CPRC §§ 15.036 and 15.037 [1983], the repealed provisions that provided a type of "residence" venue alternative for foreign and domestic corporations under both the 1983 statute and its predecessor. Section 15.036 applied to domestic corporations, which are those incorporated under the laws of the State of Texas. Section 15.037 applied to all others, which were treated as foreign corporations even if the corporations had permits to do business in Texas and might even have their home office in Texas.[1] Under these provisions, a Texas corporation could be sued in a county where it had an agency or representative if the plaintiff resided in that county. A foreign corporation could be sued *anywhere* the corporation had an agency or representative, or, if it had none, where the plaintiff resided. There were many tales of courts finding an "agency or representative" in some remote South Texas county. While the meaning of "agency and representative" for venue purposes was addressed long ago, its application was fairly fluid. The Texas Supreme Court addressed this issue in *Ruiz v. Conoco*,[2] and limited the circumstances under which "agency or representative" could be found. The court said:

> Thus, venue against a corporation may be predicated upon the presence in a county of either an agency—a more or less regular and permanent business operation—or a representative with broad powers to act for the corporation. As we held in *Milligan,* however, an ordinary employee is neither an agency nor a representative, even though the employer corporation may be liable for the employee's tortious conduct. The missing element in an ordinary employee, essential for both types of persons in the venue statute, is possession of broad power and discretion to act for the corporation.

2. *Determining "principal office."* How is a principal office different from an "agency or representative?" Not all corporations "doing business" in Texas in the jurisdictional sense have offices in Texas. If you were advising such a corporation, might you suggest that the corporation establish an office in a favorable Texas county? Would a small office be a "principal office?" How

---

1 *See e.g.,* Sumitomo Corp. v. James K. Anderson, Inc., 599 S.W.2d 117, 119 (Tex. Civ. App.—Dallas 1980, no writ).

2 868 S.W.2d 752(Tex. 1993).

would you evaluate the situation of a company that had retail stores in many counties, but no management office in Texas?

3. *A corporation's "residence."* A number of venue statutes continue to allow venue in the county of a party's "residence" without limiting the term to natural persons.[3] The Supreme Court has held that the Legislature did not intend to exclude corporations from these provisions—for example, when the defendant resides and all events occur out of state, a plaintiff corporation can bring the suit in the county of its residence.[4] A corporation's "residence" is different from its "principal office"—the county of the corporation's registered office and registered agent required by the Business Corporations Act is the corporation's statutory place of residence.[5]

---

c. *Where the Claim Occurred*

The 1983 statute and its predecessor allowed venue in counties where "a part" of a cause of action accrued. It has long been held that a cause of action accrues wherever some necessary element of the cause of action occurs.[15] The 1995 amendments, however, allow venue only in those counties where a "substantial part of the events or omissions giving rise to the claim occurred."[16]

Under the pre-1983 venue scheme, a plaintiff relying on a venue provision setting venue where the cause of action accrued had to prove that it had a cause of action and, therefore, prove all elements of the cause of action by a preponderance of the evidence. The venue facts were seen as (1) the plaintiff has a cause of action, and (2) an essential element of that cause of action occurred in the county. Because the venue hearing required live testimony and was presented to a jury, it often resembled a dress rehearsal for the trial. Requiring plaintiffs to prove their cause of action to establish venue was specifically overruled by the 1983 statutory venue changes.[17] Thus, beware of pre-1983 venue opinions holding that plaintiff must prove its cause of action by a preponderance of the evidence.

---

3 *See e.g.* CPRC §§ 15.002(a), 15.033, 15.035(b), 15.082, 15.087, 15.088, 15.092(c), 15.098; PROP. CODE § 21.013 (relating to condemnation suits).

4 In re Transcontinental Realty Investors, Inc., 271 S.W.3d 270 (Tex. 2008).

5 *Id.*

15 *See* Lubbock Manuf. Co. v. Sames, 598 S.W.2d 234, 237 (Tex. 1980) (in tort case, venue proper where the injury occurs); Humphrey v. Mays, 804 S.W.2d 328 (Tex. App.—Austin 1991, writ denied) (in contract case, venue proper in Austin where agreement allegedly modified in telephone call to plaintiffs in Austin).

16 CPRC § 15.002(a)(1) [1995]. *See* KW Construction v. Stephens & Sons Concrete, 165 S.W.3d 874 (Tex. App.—Texarkana 2005, pet. denied); Chiriboga v. State Farm Mut. Automobile Ins. Co., 96 S.W.3d 673 (Tex. App.—Austin 2003, no pet.).

17 CPRC § 15.064(a) [1983, 1995 unchanged].

In re TEXAS DEPARTMENT OF TRANSPORTATION

218 S.W.3d 74
(Tex. 2007)

PER CURIAM.

The Texas Department of Transportation (TxDOT) and Gillespie County each seek writ of mandamus directing the probate court of Travis County to transfer venue of a personal injury suit to Gillespie County. They assert that as to each of them, separately, venue is mandatory in Gillespie County. We conditionally grant relief.

On the evening of January 16, 2004 Courtney Foreman was a passenger in a car approaching a bridge over the Pedernales River in Gillespie County. As it neared the bridge the car slid off the roadway, through a gap between the guardrail and the adjacent embankment and into the river. Courtney drowned.

Courtney's parents, Barbara and Steven Foreman, sued TxDOT, the County, the Allen Keller Company, James Robbins (the car's driver) and others in Travis County probate court. Their claims against TxDOT and the County were brought pursuant to the Texas Tort Claims Act, TEX. CIV. PRAC. & REM.CODE §§ 101.001-.109. (TTCA). The Foremans classify their claims as falling into four categories: negligence, gross negligence, premises defect and special defect or injury-by-traffic-control-device. Venue is alleged to be proper in Travis County as to TxDOT pursuant to section 101.102(a) of the TTCA because part of the cause of action arose in Travis County, and as to Gillespie County under section 15.005 of the Civil Practice and Remedies Code because venue is proper in Travis County as to TxDOT. The basis for the claim that part of the cause of action arose in Travis County is that TxDOT, its bridge division, and other defendants maintained offices in Travis County and entered into and performed, at least in part, their contract and job duties in Travis County. It is alleged that the negligent performance of those duties in Travis County resulted in the defective roadway and approach to the bridge where the accident occurred.

TxDOT and the County filed motions to transfer venue to Gillespie County where the accident occurred. TxDOT asserted that the only claims which can be "properly pled" against it are claims for which sovereign immunity is waived by the TTCA, which in this instance are premises defect and special defect claims. TxDOT urges that because any actions taken and decisions made by its employees antecedent to the accident are not part of such causes of action, there is no "properly pled cause of action," part of which took place in Travis County and on which to sustain venue in Travis County. Gillespie County concurred in TxDOT's position and also asserted that regardless of whether all or some of the cause of action took place in Travis County, section 15.015 of the Civil Practice and Remedies Code made venue in Gillespie County mandatory for claims against the county.[1] The motions were denied. The court of appeals denied mandamus relief. TxDOT and the County now seek mandamus relief from this Court.

Generally, chapter 15 of the Texas Civil Practice and Remedies Code governs venue of actions. Section 15.016 provides that if an action is governed by a separate mandatory venue provision, then the action shall be brought in the county required by the separate venue provision. Section 101.102(a) is such a mandatory provision. It requires claims made pursuant to the TTCA to be brought in the county in which all or a part of the cause of action arose. Chapter 15 also authorizes parties to seek mandamus relief to enforce its mandatory venue provisions. TEX. CIV.

---

1 Because our decision is based on TTCA section 101.102(a), we do not address the effect of section 15.015.

PRAC. & REM.CODE § 15.0642. In seeking mandamus under section 15.0642, a party need not prove the lack of an adequate appellate remedy, but need only show that the trial court abused its discretion by failing to transfer the case.

The Foremans do not disagree with TxDOT's assertion that for venue to be proper in Travis County, one of the Foremans' claims under the TTCA must have arisen at least in part in Travis County. *Citing Wilson v. Texas Parks & Wildlife Department*, 886 S.W.2d 259 (Tex. 1994), they claim that negligent decisions and actions by TxDOT employees and agents in Travis County resulted in the condition of the premises at the accident site in Gillespie County and are part of a premise defect or special defect cause of action.

* * *

We have distinguished between causes of action based on negligent activities and those based on premise defects. A negligent activity claim arises from activity contemporaneous with the occurrence, whereas a premises defect claim is based on the property itself being unsafe.

* * *

The Foremans allege that TxDOT failed to use ordinary care in designing, inspecting, maintaining, and employing others to inspect and maintain the bridge and surrounding roadway. But, they do not allege that such activities were actively ongoing at the time of the accident. Taking the Foremans' allegations as true for purposes of determining the venue issue, such negligent activities would be causes of the conditions at the scene of the accident, but not contemporaneous activities proximately causing the accident. Accordingly, the Foremans properly pled only a cause of action for premises or special defect as to the roadway and bridge. They did not properly plead a contemporaneous-activity negligence cause of action which would include, as part of the cause of action, allegedly negligent actions or omissions which took place in Travis County. Thus, the Foremans failed to "properly plead" a negligence cause of action for which Travis County would be proper venue. Having failed to properly plead a negligence cause of action, they have also failed to properly plead a gross negligence cause of action for which Travis County would be proper venue.

* * *

In sum, the Foremans properly pled premise and special defect causes of action, but neither of these claims arose, in any part, in Travis County. Allegations and evidence of TxDOT's employees' knowledge, decisions, or failure to make decisions in Travis County as to the condition of the roadway and bridge in Gillespie County do not allege or constitute prima facie evidence that part of the cause of action arose in Travis County.

Without hearing oral argument we conditionally grant mandamus relief and direct the probate court to transfer venue of the underlying case as to TxDOT and Gillespie County to Gillespie County. TEX.R.APP. P. 52.8(c). The writ will issue only if the probate court fails to comply.

Notes & Questions

The Wilson case. In the opinion above, the Supreme Court distinguishes this case from *Wilson v. Texas Parks & Wildlife*, upon which the plaintiffs relied in arguing that the cause of action arose in Travis County, where decisions were made. In *Wilson* the plaintiffs were fishing on the Pedernales River when the river rose quickly and two of the party drowned trying to make it back to shore. It was disputed whether they were on park property or right off of it. The allegations were not that the premises in the park were dangerous, but that the Parks Department (in Travis County) failed to use existing systems to warn of impending flash floods. Thus, the *Wilson* case alleged contemporaneous negligent activity that occurred in Travis County, and venue was proper there.

---

d. *Transfer for Convenience and Justice*

This provision of the 1995 statute contains an entirely new concept for venue in Texas: convenience and justice![18] Before the 1995 revisions, other than motions to change venue for lack of an impartial forum,[19] defendants could seek transfer only when the plaintiff filed suit in an improper county or a county other than a mandatory county. There was no provision for transfer merely because the convenience of the parties and interests of justice compelled transfer. Although these concepts govern venue practice in the federal courts[20] and common law forum non conveniens, they had no place in Texas venue practice. Therefore, the addition of this provision is quite revolutionary. However, the concept of "proper venue" has by no means become extinct. Even this provision limits transfer for reasons of convenience and justice to a county of proper venue.[21] For the first time, however, the judge is given substantial discretion to transfer the case under circumstances that would have made transfer impossible under the old statutes.

2. *Other Permissive Venues—Exceptions to the General Rule*

The venue statutes contain seven separate *permissive* venue exceptions to the general venue rule, each of which applies to either a particular type of party or cause of action. These permissive exceptions provide additional proper venue alternatives from which the plaintiff can choose when filing the lawsuit, or from which the defendant can choose in deciding where to transfer the case.

Two of the most important permissive venue exceptions, both of which concerned corporations, were repealed in 1995 in favor of the new general rule, as was the provision relating to nonresidents. The remaining provisions changed little in the 1995 amendments—often they substituted the concepts of "principal office" and "substantial part of the events giving rise to the claim"

---

[18] *See* CPRC § 15.002(6).

[19] *See* Rules 257-259.

[20] 28 U.S.C. § 1404 (1988).

[21] Accordingly, a plaintiff cannot rely on convenience and justice to establish proper venue in an otherwise improper county. Convenience and justice concepts apply only to transfers of venue upon the motion of a defendant. Chiriboga v. State Farm Mut. Automobile Ins. Co., 96 S.W.3d 673 (Tex. App.—Austin 2003, no pet.).

where appropriate, but there are some vestiges of the old statutes, allowing venue in a county of a party's "residence" or "domicile."

Other statutes may contain venue provisions as well. And there is a "catch-all" permissive venue exception providing that actions under statutes that prescribe permissive venue may be brought in the county allowed by that statute.[22]

3. *Mandatory Venue Exceptions*

The statutes also contain nine *mandatory* venue exceptions to the general rule,[23] all of which state that the action "must" or "shall" be brought in a given county or counties. Nevertheless, if a mandatory venue exception applies to a particular case, it does not mean that the case *must* be filed in the mandatory county in a jurisdictional sense. Properly asserted mandatory venues simply trump the permissive venues.[24] Therefore, if a mandatory venue exception applies, a defendant can transfer venue to the mandatory county even if the plaintiff filed the case in a county of proper permissive venue.

Section 15.011 of the Civil Practices and Remedies Code provides that certain land-related actions, such as title disputes or suits for recovery of damages to real property, are to be brought in the county in which all or part of the property is located.[25] Similarly, under § 15.015, the county where leased real property is located is the mandatory venue for landlord-tenant suits. Section 15.012 commands that actions to stay proceedings in a suit shall be brought in the county in which the suit is pending. Actions to restrain execution of judgment based on invalidity are to be brought in the county in which the judgment was rendered (§ 15.013). Travis County is the mandatory venue for mandamus actions against state government department heads (§ 15.014) while actions against a county are to be brought in that county (§ 15.015). Libel, slander, or invasion of privacy suits and prison inmate litigation are subject to mandatory venue under §§ 15.017 and 15.018 respectively. Finally, § 15.020 allows for specification of venue by agreement in actions arising from "major transactions", where the consideration is at least $1 million.[26]

As with permissive venue, there is a mandatory venue provision providing that actions under other statutes that prescribe mandatory venue must be brought in the county specified in that statute.[27]

---

[22] CPRC § 15.038.

[23] Two were added in the 1995 amendments: § 15.0115, concerning landlord-tenant disputes; and § 15.018, concerning FELA and Jones Act cases. *See* In re Missouri Pacific, 998 S.W.2d 212 (Tex. 1999) (concerning § 15.018).

[24] *See* In re Continental Airlines, Inc., 988 S.W.2d 733 (Tex. 1998) (holding that plaintiff's choice of relief sought—declaratory judgment rather than injunction—prevents application of mandatory venue).

[25] In re Applied Chemical Magnesias Corp., 206 S.W.3d 114 (Tex. 2006) (holding that use of declaratory relief to quiet title does not preclude mandatory venue).

[26] *See Pinto Tech. Ventures, L.P. v. Sheldon*, 526 S.W.3d 428, 447 (Tex. 2017) (holding that 15.020 did not apply because there was no evidence that parties agreed to forum selection clause for claims arising from financing agreement); In re Texas Association of School Boards, Inc. 169 S.W.3d 653 (Tex. 2005) (holding that the premium amount, not the coverage limits, establishes the consideration for an insurance policy for purposes of the mandatory exception to the venue statute).

[27] CPRC § 15.106.

4. *Venue Agreements*

In re FISHER
433 S.W.3d 523
(Tex. 2014)

Opinion by JUSTICE JOHNSON.

After Nighthawk Oilfield Services, Ltd. acquired Richey Oilfield Construction, Inc. from Mike Richey, the business did not go as well as the parties had hoped and Richey filed suit in Wise County against two Nighthawk executives. In this mandamus proceeding we consider whether the trial court abused its discretion by failing to enforce venue selection clauses in the acquisition documents. Concluding that it did, we conditionally grant relief.

I. Background

On May 3, 2007, Mike Richey sold his interest in Richey Oilfield Construction, Inc. (Richey Oil), an oilfield services company that he founded and operated, to Nighthawk Oilfield Services, Ltd. (Nighthawk) for $33 million. NOSGP, L.L.C. was Nighthawk's general partner and Mark Fisher and Reece Boudreaux were limited partners. The transaction resulted in Richey Oil becoming a wholly-owned Nighthawk subsidiary, with Richey remaining employed as president of Richey Oil and becoming a limited partner in Nighthawk.

The primary agreements regarding the transaction were a Stock Purchase Agreement, an agreement for the purchase of Richey Oil's goodwill (the Goodwill Agreement), and a Promissory Note. Each contained a clause naming Tarrant County as the venue for state court actions.

In the Stock Purchase Agreement, NOSROC, Inc. agreed to pay Richey $13 million in cash for Richey Oil's issued and outstanding stock. That agreement contained the following provision:

> *Jurisdiction; Service of Process.* Any proceeding arising out of or relating to this Agreement may be brought in the courts of the State of Texas, Tarrant County, or if it has or can acquire jurisdiction, in the United States District Court for the Northern District of Texas, and each of the parties irrevocably submits to the non-exclusive jurisdiction of each such court in any such proceeding, waives any objection it may now or hereafter have to venue or to convenience of forum, agrees that all claims in respect of the proceeding may be heard and determined in any such court and *agrees not to bring any proceeding arising out of or relating to this Agreement in any other court.* (Emphasis added)

In the Goodwill Agreement, Richey sold his goodwill interest to Nighthawk. That interest was defined as his "right, title and interest in and to all of [Richey's] knowledge, experience and rights relating to the Business, and [Richey's] personal relationships and experience with the customers of the Business and further including the trade name 'Richey' to the extent and as used in conjunction with the Business." The Goodwill Agreement provided that Richey would receive $7 million in cash, a $6.5 million promissory note, and $6.5 million in Nighthawk limited partnership interest units. The Goodwill Agreement contained the same venue selection clause as the Stock Purchase Agreement.

The $6.5 million promissory note (the Note) was signed by Fisher as president of Nighthawk. It provided that "[Nighthawk] . . . irrevocably agrees that any legal proceedings in respect of this note . . . or other writing relating hereto shall be brought in the district courts of Tarrant County, Texas, or the United States District Court for the Northern District of Texas."

A month after Nighthawk purchased Richey Oil, Nighthawk made a $20 million "special distribution" to its partners. The distribution was contemplated in the Goodwill Agreement, which provided: "[I]t has been represented to [Richey] that a distribution to the owners or holders of all units of [Nighthawk] is anticipated to be made contemporaneously with or subsequent to the Closing and [Richey] shall participate in such distribution on a pro rata basis."

Six months later, Richey paid $1 million to Nighthawk at Fisher's request. According to Richey, Fisher related that he was seeking similar amounts from all the limited partners, Nighthawk would treat the money as loans, and in six months the loans plus ten percent would be paid back. Fisher claims that the other limited partners made similar contributions totaling $3.9 million, but they agreed that those contributions would be treated as equity, not loans.

Richey asserts that when he asked Fisher to repay the $1 million as agreed, Fisher denied his request and claimed the money was a capital contribution for which Richey would receive preferred equity units. Richey has never been repaid the $1 million.

In connection with the acquisition, Nighthawk opened a controlled-disbursement account so Richey Oil could access Nighthawk's revolving line of credit. As part of that process, Richey and Fisher executed a Deposit Account Signature Card at Bank of America that gave Richey check signing authority. In May and June 2009, Fisher authorized Richey to pay Richey Oil vendors from the account. However, when Richey did so, Bank of America rejected several of the checks for insufficient funds in the account. According to Richey, Fisher told some payees of the rejected checks that Richey created the problem. Several payees referred their returned checks to collection agencies, attorneys, and authorities, who sent demand letters threatening civil and criminal prosecution. Shortly thereafter, Nighthawk and Richey Oil filed for bankruptcy.

Richey soon sued Fisher and Boudreaux in Wise County where Richey resided. He sued both of them for breach of fiduciary duty, common law fraud, statutory fraud, and violations of the Texas Securities Act. He sued Fisher separately for defamation, common law fraud, negligent misrepresentation, and interference with prospective business relations related to the statements Fisher allegedly made to him about availability of money in the Richey Oil account and communications made to third parties regarding the returned checks. He sued Boudreaux separately for aiding and abetting Fisher's breaches of fiduciary duty, acts of fraud, and violations of the Texas Securities Act.

Fisher and Boudreaux responded by moving the trial court to transfer venue to Tarrant County or dismiss the suit pursuant to the mandatory venue selection clauses in the Stock Purchase Agreement and the Goodwill Agreement. . . .

The trial court denied Fisher's and Boudreaux's motions . . . .

* * *

IV. The Venue Selection Clauses

We next consider whether the trial court abused its discretion by refusing to transfer Richey's claims pursuant to venue selection clauses in the agreements under Texas Civil Practice and Remedies Code § 15.020. Mandamus relief is specifically authorized to enforce a statutory mandatory venue provision. TEX. CIV. PRAC. & REM. CODE § 15.0642.

A. Section 15.020—Major Transactions

Relators assert that by its plain language—"Notwithstanding any other provisions of this title"—Texas Civil Practice and Remedies Code § 15.020 overrides other venue provisions and required the trial court to enforce the venue agreements. Section 15.020 applies to a "major transaction," which is defined as a transaction evidenced by a written agreement and which involves $1 million or more:

> (c) Notwithstanding any other provision of this title, an action arising from a major transaction may not be brought in a county if:
>
> > (1) the party bringing the action has agreed in writing that an action arising from the transaction may not be brought in that county, and the action may be brought in another county of this state or in another jurisdiction; or
> >
> > (2) the party bringing the action has agreed in writing that an action arising from the transaction must be brought in another county of this state or in another jurisdiction, and the action may be brought in that other county, under this section or otherwise, or in that other jurisdiction.

Id. § 15.020(c). Richey argues that section 15.020 and the venue selection clause in the Goodwill Agreement do not apply for the following reasons: (1) his tort claims do not "arise from" the purchase of Richey Oil; (2) the only agreement that relates to Richey's claims is the Partnership Agreement which has no forum or venue selection clause; (3) the contractual venue selection clause is permissive, not mandatory; and (4) venue is mandatory in Wise County under the statutory provision requiring a suit for libel or slander to be brought in the county where the plaintiff resided at the time of the accrual of the cause of action. *See id.* § 15.017. We address the arguments in turn.

B. Does Section 15.020 Apply?

The parties do not dispute that the Richey Oil acquisition, which included the sale of Richey's goodwill, constitutes a "major transaction" as defined by section 15.020. Richey urges, however, that section 15.020 does not apply because his claims against Relators are not claims "arising from" the purchase of Richey Oil; rather, he asserts, his claims arise from the operation or management of Nighthawk. We have not previously addressed when an action "arises from" a major transaction under section 15.020, but we have previously addressed similar issues as to forum selection agreements.

In *In re International Profit Assocs.*, 274 S.W.3d 672 (Tex. 2009) (per curiam), we analyzed whether a forum selection clause in a contract applied to tort claims between the contracting parties. In determining whether the claims were within the scope of the clauses, we called for a "commonsense" examination of the substance of the claims made to determine if they "arise" from the contract. *Id.* at 677. We explained that a court should consider whether a claimant seeks a direct benefit from a contract and whether the contract or some other general legal obligation establishes the duty at issue. *Id.* We concluded that no matter how the claimant characterized or pleaded the claims, the tort claims in that case—including fraud and negligent misrepresentation—"arise from the contractual relationship between the parties, not from obligations imposed by law." *Id.* at 678.

In *Lisa Laser,* 310 S.W.3d 880, we applied the same type of analysis to determine the scope of a forum selection clause and whether it applied to the plaintiffs' contract claims. In that case, HealthTronics had a contract with Lisa Laser for exclusive distribution rights of certain medical devices. *Id.* at 882. The agreement also provided HealthTronics with rights of first refusal to distribute new products if certain requirements were met. *Id.* An exhibit to the agreement provided that the terms and conditions that followed, including a California forum selection clause that applied to "any dispute arising out of this agreement," applied to sales by Lisa Laser to HealthTronics. *Id.* HealthTronics sued Lisa Laser in Travis County for breach of contract, alleging that Lisa Laser breached its obligation to afford HealthTronics the first right to distribute new products, and for tortious interference with a contract. *Id.* Lisa Laser sought mandamus relief after the trial court denied its motion to dismiss based on the forum selection clause. *Id.* at 882-83. HealthTronics argued that the forum selection clause only applied to part of the contract, that is, sales transactions between it and Lisa Laser. *Id.* at 884. Applying the reasoning from *International Profit Associates,* we concluded that Lisa Laser's obligation, if any, to inform HealthTronics of new products and to offer it a right of first refusal to distribute those products "only arises from the Distribution Agreement." *Id.* at 884-86. The obligations were not imposed under general law, they would not exist but for the agreement, and therefore they arose out of the agreement. *Id.* at 886. We concluded that the forum selection clause itself applied more broadly than to mere sales transactions because it applied to "any dispute arising out of" the agreement and the trial court erred in refusing to enforce the forum selection clause. *Id.* at 887.

Turning to the case at hand, we see no reason to deviate from the type of analysis we used in *International Profit Associates* and *Lisa Laser.* Similarly to our method of analysis in those cases, we will use a common-sense examination of the substance of the claims to determine whether the statute applies. *See Int'l Profit Assocs.,* 274 S.W.3d at 677.

Richey alleged in his live pleadings that "[a] substantial part of the acquisition was deferred consideration in the form of a $6,500,000 Promissory Note." He further alleged that he suffered substantial damages caused by Relators' authorization of the $20 million special distribution and that "[t]he effect of the distribution was to severely impair [Nighthawk's] ongoing operations and ultimately to render [Nighthawk] insolvent and incapable of continuing its business and affairs." Richey brought a claim for breach of fiduciary duty related to that $20 million distribution of Nighthawk assets. He alleged that his damages included "benefit of the bargain losses." And in a response to Relators' supplemental motion to dismiss in the trial court, he explained that he sought damages for "the loss of the promissory note issued [to] him individually."

Applying a common-sense analysis, we conclude that Richey in substance is seeking to recover the $6.5 million owed to him under the Note and for actions flowing directly from the acquisition and actions anticipated to flow from it.

First, the Note was consideration for his transfer of goodwill and was specifically provided for under the Goodwill Agreement. His claim for Nighthawk's failure to pay the Note, regardless of whether it is labeled as a breach of fiduciary duty claim or otherwise, arises from that major transaction. . . . Because Richey's claims substantively arise from commitments in the Goodwill Agreement, we disagree with his claim that the only agreement that relates to his claims is the Partnership Agreement.

* * *

Here, Richey's claims do more than "touch matters" included in the Goodwill Agreement and the Note. Liability for failure to pay him on the Note must be determined by reference to those agreements. *See id.* And when an injury is to the subject matter of a contract, the action is ordinarily "*on the contract.*" *Sw. Bell Tel. Co. v. DeLanney,* 809 S.W.2d 493, 494 (Tex. 1991) (emphasis added).

C. Is the Venue Selection Clause Mandatory?

Richey next argues that even assuming his claims arise from Nighthawk's purchase of Richey Oil, section 15.020 is inapplicable because he did not agree in writing that an action arising from the transaction "must" be brought in Tarrant County or "may not be brought" in Wise County. He claims that the acquisition documents and the Note include permissive, not mandatory venue selection clauses. He references the Goodwill Agreement's provisions that "any proceeding arising out of or relating to this Agreement *may* be brought in the courts of the State of Texas, Tarrant County, or if it has or can acquire jurisdiction, in the United States District Court for the Northern District of Texas" and that the parties "submit[ ] to the *non-exclusive* jurisdiction of each such court," and "the proceeding *may* be heard and determined in any such court." (Emphasis added). Richey argues that this permissive language controls over the mandatory language providing that each of the parties "agrees not to bring any proceeding arising out of or relating to this Agreement in any other court." He asserts that finding the clause mandatory would render all of the permissive language meaningless. Relators counter that the permissive language applies to consent to jurisdiction, but the mandatory language applies to require venue. We agree with Relators.

The beginning of the jurisdiction clause at issue here provides that "[a]ny proceeding arising out of or relating to this Agreement may be brought in the courts of the State of Texas, Tarrant County . . . and each of the parties irrevocably submits to the non-exclusive jurisdiction of each such court in any such proceeding." Objections to personal jurisdiction may be waived, so a litigant may consent to the personal jurisdiction of a court through a variety of legal arrangements. *Burger King Corp. v. Rudzewicz,* 471 U.S. 462, 472 n. 14, 105 S.Ct. 2174, 85 L.Ed.2d 528 (1985). For example, a contractual "consent-to-jurisdiction clause" subjects a party to personal jurisdiction, making an analysis of that party's contacts with the forum for personal jurisdiction purposes unnecessary. *RSR Corp. v. Siegmund,* 309 S.W.3d 686, 704 (Tex. App.—Dallas 2010, no pet.) (concluding a contract provision that claims "may be heard" in Dallas courts was a "consent-to-jurisdiction" clause and the trial court erred by granting the defendant's special appearance); *see Ramsay v. Tex. Trading Co.,* 254 S.W.3d 620, 629 (Tex. App.—Texarkana 2008, pet. denied) (explaining that a permissive forum selection clause is one under which the parties consent to the jurisdiction of a particular forum but do not require suit to be filed there); *see also Granados Quinones v. Swiss Bank Corp. (Overseas), S.A.,* 509 So.2d 273, 274 (Fla. 1987) ("Permissive clauses constitute nothing more than a consent to jurisdiction and venue in the named forum.").

The provision here providing that the parties irrevocably submit to the non-exclusive jurisdiction of the courts in Tarrant County is a consent-to-jurisdiction clause. But the parties not only submitted themselves to jurisdiction of the Tarrant County courts, each party also "irrevocably . . . agree[d] not to bring any proceeding arising out of or relating to this Agreement in any other court." Our primary goal in construing this contractual language is to determine the parties' intent as reflected by the language they used. *El Paso Field Servs., L.P. v. MasTec N. Am., Inc.,* 389 S.W.3d 802, 805 (Tex. 2012). The contract reflects intent that the parties submit to the jurisdiction of the state or federal courts in Tarrant County *and* that they will not file suit "arising out of or relating to this Agreement" anywhere else. The requirement that if the parties file suit it will be in Tarrant County is not diluted by their agreement to submit to jurisdiction there, and we disagree with Richey's position that construing the venue selection clause as mandatory would render his agreement to submit to personal jurisdiction in Tarrant County meaningless. Simply put, Richey clearly agreed in the Goodwill Agreement that an action arising from that transaction must be brought in Tarrant County. *See* TEX. CIV. PRAC. & REM. CODE § 15.020(c).

Richey also asserts that when a venue provision such as the one involved here includes the term "non-exclusive," it is not mandatory, even if the provision includes other language reflecting that it is mandatory. . . .

[W]e conclude that where the phrase "non-exclusive jurisdiction" is in a venue selection clause that also includes language reflecting intent that the venue choice is mandatory, the non-exclusive language does not necessarily control over the mandatory language. We agree with the court's decision in *Muzumdar v. Wellness International Network, Ltd.,* 438 F.3d 759, 762 (7th Cir.2006) where the court rejected a party's contention that the phrase "non-exclusive jurisdiction"—which the court noted required the parties to submit to personal jurisdiction—rendered a forum selection clause permissive. There the court concluded that it could not "find that a provision which requires appellants to submit to the 'non-exclusive' jurisdiction of Texas courts somehow undermines a very strongly worded forum selection clause containing mandatory language: 'SHALL BE PROPER ONLY' or 'SHALL BE PROPER' in Dallas County, Texas." *Id.* Similarly, the phrase "non-exclusive jurisdiction" in the Goodwill Agreement does not control over the plainly worded mandatory language.

D. Venue in Wise County

Finally, Richey argues that venue in Wise County is proper even if it is not mandatory, so the trial court did not err by denying Relators' motion to dismiss. First, Richey points to Texas Civil Practice and Remedies Code § 15.017 which provides that:

> A suit for damages for libel, slander, or invasion of privacy shall be brought and can only be maintained in the county in which the plaintiff resided at the time of the accrual of the cause of action, or in the county in which the defendant resided at the time of filing suit, or in the county of the residence of defendants, or any of them, or the domicile of any corporate defendant, at the election of the plaintiff.

TEX. CIV. PRAC. & REM. CODE § 15.017. He asserts that because he resided in Wise County at the time his cause of action for defamation accrued, this mandatory provision applies.

We have already concluded that section 15.020 applies, mandating that Richey's actions must be brought in Tarrant County. Venue may be proper in multiple counties under mandatory venue rules, and the plaintiff is generally afforded the right to choose venue when suit is filed. *Wilson v. Tex. Parks & Wildlife Dep't,* 886 S.W.2d 259, 260 (Tex. 1994). But in this case, the language of section 15.020 applies to an action arising from a major transaction "[n]otwithstanding any other provision of this title." TEX. CIV. PRAC. & REM. CODE § 15.020(c). This indicates that the Legislature intended for it to control over other mandatory venue provisions. *See Molinet v. Kimbrell,* 356 S.W.3d 407, 413-14 (Tex. 2011) (holding that the phrase "notwithstanding any other law" indicates a legislative intent that the provision prevail over conflicting law).

Next, Richey alternatively argues that if section 15.017 does not apply, venue is proper in Wise County under the general venue statute because a substantial part of the events giving rise to his claim occurred there. *See* TEX. CIV. PRAC. & REM. CODE § 15.002(a)(1) (providing that a lawsuit shall be brought in various enumerated places including "in the county in which all or a substantial part of the events or omissions giving rise to the claim occurred"). He cites *Acker v. Denton Publishing,* 937 S.W.2d 111, 115 (Tex. App.—Fort Worth 1996, no writ) for the proposition that if a plaintiff's choice of venue is proper, it is reversible error for a trial court to transfer venue even if the county of transfer would also have been proper if chosen by the plaintiff. But *Acker* did not address whether a case should be transferred when a mandatory venue provision for a different county was applicable. And we long ago explained that "[i]f the plaintiff's chosen venue rests on a *permissive* venue statute and the defendant files a meritorious motion to transfer based on a *mandatory* venue provision, the trial court must grant the motion." *Wichita Cnty. v. Hart,* 917 S.W.2d 779, 781 (Tex. 1996) (emphasis added). The permissive venue statute does not control over the mandatory venue provision applicable in this case.

V. The Remainder of Richey's Claims

Having determined that Richey's claims seeking his benefit of the bargain losses arose out of a major transaction, we conclude that all of Richey's claims against Relators must be transferred to Tarrant County because Texas Civil Practice and Remedies Code § 15.004 provides that:

> In a suit in which a plaintiff properly joins two or more claims or causes of action arising from the same transaction, occurrence, or series of transactions or occurrences, and one of the claims or causes of action is governed by the mandatory venue provisions . . . , the suit shall be brought in the county required by the mandatory venue provision.

It is not necessary for us to analyze Richey's claims to determine whether they arise from the same transaction, occurrence, or series of transactions: the parties affirmatively assert that they do.

* * *

VII. Conclusion

The trial court abused its discretion by failing to enforce the mandatory venue selection clauses in the Stock Purchase Agreement and Goodwill Agreement. We conditionally grant relief. We direct the trial court to vacate its order denying Relators' motion to transfer venue and to grant the motion. The writ will only issue if the trial court fails to comply with our directive.

Notes & Questions

1. *Venue agreements versus forum agreements*. The terms "venue" and "forum" are often used interchangeably (in fact, the *Fisher* opinion did so when it was first issued, but then was corrected), and can create much confusion. As one court of appeals[1] said:

> In this case, the parties have used "forum" and "venue" interchangeably. We pause to note the difference between the two terms to avoid any confusion about our holding. Each term has a distinct legal meaning that must be carefully observed, even though in some instances, Texas case law has muddled the distinction between the two. . . .
>
> "Forum" generally refers to a sovereign or a state. In contrast, "[a]t common law, 'venue' meant 'the neighborhood, place, or county in which the injury is declared to have been done or in fact declared to have happened." In Texas, "venue" refers to the county in which suit is proper within the forum state. Thus, a "forum"-selection agreement is one that chooses another state or sovereign as the location for trial, whereas a "venue"-selection agreement chooses a particular county or court within that state or sovereign.

Contractual provisions, such as the one in *Fisher*, may contain both forum-selection (selecting Texas as the proper forum) and venue selection agreements (selecting Tarrant County as the county of venue if suit is filed in the Texas state courts).

---

1 In re Great Lakes Dredge & Dock Co. L.L.C., 251 S.W.3d 68, 73-74 (Tex. App.—Corpus Christi 2008, no et.).

As discussed in the previous chapter, *forum* selection clauses are presumptively valid.[2] However, for almost 100 years this Texas Supreme Court has held that "the fixing of *venue* by contract, except in such instances as [specifically permitted by statute] is invalid and cannot be the subject of private contract."[3]

2. *Mandatory venue for major transactions*. § 15.020, at issue in *Fisher*, allows for specification of venue by written agreement in actions arising from "major transactions", where the consideration is at least $1 million.[4] The provision does not apply to agreements for personal, household or family purposes, and does not apply to settlements of personal injury or wrongful death claims. The statute is worth reading carefully as it actually applies to "forum selection" as well as "venue" agreements. After you study venue procedure, consider what kind of motion you would bring if you sought to enforce a forum selection clause that required suit to be filed in a state other than Texas.

3. *Permissive venue for place of performance in contract.* An important permissive exception that gives parties some ability to provide contractually for venue alternatives is §15.035, which applies to suits for violation of a written obligation. This provision allows parties to agree on a *specific place of performance*, which, if breached, will provide a permissive venue alternative in that county.[5] Consider this: Supplier sells Retailer $50,000 of widgets, and there is a written contract that the payment is to be made "at the Alamo." Retailer fails to pay. Retailer's principal office is in Austin; Supplier's principal office is in San Marcus. The contract was negotiated at a convention in Dallas. What are the proper venues for Supplier's lawsuit?

Note, however, that in an action based on a contractual obligation of the defendant to pay money based on a consumer transaction, venue is not proper in the place specified for performance. Suit by the creditor on such a consumer obligation may be brought only in the county where the contract was signed or where the defendant resides when the suit is commenced.[6]

---

[2] *See* Ch. 3, Sec. H, *supra*.

[3] Fidelity Union Life Insurance Co. v. Evans, 477 S.W.2d 535, 536 (Tex. 1972) (emphasis added)(noting agreement with Int'l Travelers' Ass'n v. Branum, 109 Tex. 543, 212 S.W.630, 631-32 (1919)). *See also* Leonard v. Paxon, 654 S.W.2d 440, 441 (Tex. 1983, no writ)(holding that mandatory venue provisions in the family code could not be negated by contract); Fleming v. Ahumada, 193 S.W.3d 704, 712-13 (Tex. App.—Corpus Christi 2006, no pet.)(holding contractual provision to fix venue in Bexar County invalid); In re Great Lakes Dredge & Dock Co., L.L.C., 251 S.W.3d at 75-79 (holding that venue agreement fixing venue in Harris County was unenforceable); In re Calderon, 96 S.W3d 711, 722 (Tex. App.—Tyler 2003, orig. proceeding) (holding that venue provision in mediated settlement agreement was void).

[4] *See* In re Texas Association of School Boards, Inc. 169 S.W.2d 653 (Tex. 2005) (holding that the premium amount, not the coverage limits, establishes the consideration for an insurance policy for purposes of the mandatory exception to the venue statute).

[5] *See* WTFO, Inc. v. Braithwaite, 899 S.W.2d 709 (Tex. App.—Dallas 1995, no writ) (note providing for payment in Dallas County or "at such other county that the holder may designate in writing" makes place of performance uncertain and § 15.035 inapplicable).

[6] CPRC §15.035(b).

5. *Venue in Cases with Multiple Parties or Claims*

a. Multiple plaintiffs.

Two of the most important venue provisions of the 1983 venue statute provided for venue in lawsuits with multiple parties or multiple claims.. These provisions sought to have all claims and parties involved in a single transaction or occurrence joined in one lawsuit. Therefore, the statute provided that if venue was proper as to one claim, it was proper as to all claims properly joined with it. Similarly, if venue was proper as to one defendant, it was proper as to all defendants properly joined. Likewise, counterclaims, cross-claims and third-party claims did not affect venue. Plaintiff's pleadings in the primary case set venue for all other claims properly joined.[29] As a result, the plaintiff's initial choice of defendants and claims was often significant as far as venue choices are concerned.

Under these venue provisions, multiple plaintiffs often joined together to assert multiple claims or causes of action against multiple defendants, especially in toxic tort cases. All of the plaintiffs could sue in a county in which the only basis for venue was that one of them resided in the county of suit.

The 1995 amendments substantially changed venue in multiple plaintiff cases. Section 15.003 requires plaintiffs to establish venue independently, significantly restricting joinder in Texas state courts. The purpose is to prevent multiple plaintiffs from filing suits in far-flung counties, relying on venue as established by their co-plaintiff (*e.g.,* the one resident of the county of suit). Instead, the plaintiffs must sue in a county in which the defendant has a significant presence, such as the county of its principal office. But the statute does allow plaintiffs who cannot independently establish venue to join an ongoing lawsuit if they can establish four criteria, including an "essential need" to try the claim in the county of suit. Also, parties are given a right to take an accelerated interlocutory appeal of the trial court's decision on multiple plaintiff venue issues.[30]

b. Multiple defendants.

The 1995 amendments, however, retain the 1983 provisions regarding multiple defendants.[31] Like the 1983 version of § 15.061, the new § 15.005 allows a plaintiff to join multiple defendants without independently proving venue for each. Thus, if venue is proper over one defendant (*e.g.,* the defendant's "principal office" is in the county of suit), venue is proper over all defendants properly joined in claims arising from the same transaction, occurrence, or series of transactions or occurrences.[32] The statute thus arguably contains an incentive for plaintiffs to join marginal defendants that can establish proper venue for the entire case. Is there any relief for defendants who believe this has happened in their case? The Texarkana Court of Appeals has held that the individual defendant whose residence in Harrison County established venue for the case "was not a proper defendant" where the plaintiffs "offered no evidence whatsoever to substantiate a cause of action against [the resident defendant]," and "the trial court directed a verdict in favor of [the

---

[29] *See* Arthur Brothers, Inc. v. U.M.C., Inc., 647 S.W.2d 244, 245 (Tex. 1982) (venue of primary action proper against third-party contribution defendant).

[30] *See* Surgitek v. Abel, 997 S.W.2d 598 (Tex. 1999). Section 15.003 which was amended in 2003, will be discussed later in this chapter.

[31] CPRC § 15.005 (1995).

[32] This is the standard for proper joinder of multiple defendants.

resident defendant] because of the absence of any evidence against him," which was not challenged on appeal.[33] The court held that venue was improper in Harrison County, requiring reversal.

c. Multiple claims with mandatory venue.

The 1983 statute did not tell the judge what to do if a defendant asserted a mandatory venue exception that governs only one of several causes of action pending in an otherwise proper permissive county. Should she transfer the whole case to the county of mandatory venue or sever the claims, retaining the part of the case not controlled by the mandatory exception? Prior law said that the result depended upon whether the action involved joint (not severable) or joint and several (severable) causes of action. The 1995 amendments specifically addressed the matter in § 15.004. A mandatory venue provision that controls one claim or cause of action controls all claims and causes of action that a plaintiff joins in any lawsuit that arises from the same transaction, occurrence or series of transactions or occurrences as the mandatory cause of action. The concept of "same transaction, occurrence or series of transactions or occurrences" comes from the joinder provisions of the rules.[34] However, a mandatory provision that applies to a third-party defendant (not joined by the plaintiff) does not affect venue.[35] What if the third-party claim is subject to a mandatory venue provision?

PERRYMAN
v.
SPARTAN TEXAS SIX CAPITAL PARTNERS, LTD.
546 S.W. 3d 110
Tex. 2018

BOYD, JUSTICE.

. . .

III.

Venue

We now address the Perrymans' conditional cross-point that the trial court should have transferred venue to Montague County. Spartan filed its suit against EOG in Harris County in May 2011. In October 2012, EOG joined the Perrymans as third-party defendants and filed a cross-claim for a declaratory judgment regarding the apportionment of the royalty interests. The Perrymans filed a motion to transfer venue in November 2012, arguing that because EOG's claim

---

[33] ACF Industries, Inc. v. Carter, 903 S.W.2d 423 (Tex. App.—Texarkana 1995, writ dism'd by agr); *see also* Pines of Westbury, Ltd. v. Paul Michael Const., Inc., 993 S.W.2d 291 (Tex. App.—Eastland 1999, no pet.)(holding that summary judgment against venue defendant destroyed venue); Acker v. Denton Publishing Co., 937 S.W.2d 111 (Tex. App.—Ft Worth 1996, no writ) (holding that review revealed that venue defendant was not a proper defendant because there is no genuine issue of material fact that would support a cause of action against venue defendant); In re Valetutto, 976 S.W.2d 893 (Tex. App.—Austin 1998, orig. proceeding) (holding that pleadings showed lack of standing for cause of action governed by mandatory venue).

[34] *See* Rule 40.

[35] In re County of Galveston, 211 S.W.3d 879 (Tex. App.—Houston [14th Dist.] 2006, no pet.).

against them involved real property, the mandatory venue statute requires that the case be transferred to the county where the property is located—Montague County. *See* TEX. CIV. PRAC. & REM. CODE § 15.011.

The trial court denied the motion. Although venue would normally be determined under section 15.011 as the Perrymans argue, the trial court noted that section 15.062 states that third-party claims arising out of the same transaction "shall be" determined in the same venue as the original suit. *See id.* § 15.062. . . .

Venue may be proper under general, mandatory, or permissive venue rules. *See* TEX. CIV. PRAC. & REM. CODE §§ 15.001–.040. Mandatory venue rules may also designate multiple counties as proper. *See In re Fisher*, 433 S.W.3d 523, 533 (Tex. 2014). The plaintiff makes the first choice of venue by filing the lawsuit. *Wilson v. Tex. Parks & Wildlife Dep't*, 886 S.W.2d 259, 260 (Tex. 1994). When the plaintiff files in a "proper" venue, "that choice of venue should be honored absent a mandatory venue statute that requires transfer." *In re Omni Hotels Mgmt. Corp.*, 159 S.W.3d 627, 629 (Tex. 2005) (citing *GeoChem Tech Corp. v. Verseckes*, 962 S.W.2d 541, 544 (Tex. 1998)). "Proper" venue is defined by statute as

> (1) the venue required by the mandatory provisions of Subchapter B ["Mandatory Venue"] or another statute prescribing mandatory venue; or
>
> (2) if Subdivision (1) does not apply, the venue provided by this subchapter or Subchapter C ["Permissive Venue"].

TEX. CIV. PRAC. & REM. CODE § 15.001(b). Thus, when both a mandatory and a permissive venue statute apply to a suit, the permissive statute must yield to the mandatory statute. *See Langdeau v. Burke Inv. Co.*, 163 Tex. 526, 358 S.W.2d 553, 556 (1962). A trial court's erroneous denial of a motion to transfer venue requires the judgment's reversal and a remand for new trial. *Wichita Cty. v. Hart*, 917 S.W.2d 779, 781 (Tex. 1996) (citing TEX. CIV. PRAC. & REM. CODE § 15.064(b); *Ruiz v. Conoco, Inc.*, 868 S.W.2d 752, 757 (Tex. 1993)).

Here, Spartan sued EOG for breach of contract and for an accounting in Harris County, EOG's principal place of business, under the general venue statute. *See* TEX. CIV. PRAC. & REM. CODE § 15.002(a) ("Except as otherwise provided by this subchapter or Subchapter B or C, all lawsuits shall be brought: . . . in the county of the defendant's principal office in this state, if the defendant is not a natural person . . . ."). EOG did not complain that venue was improper, although when it added the Perrymans as third-party defendants, it noted that Montague County was the mandatory and proper venue for its claims against the Perrymans. However, it asserted that the Harris County court had jurisdiction over the third-party claims "because Spartan's and Menser's claims regarding the lease are already pending in this action." It went on:

> Because this pleading raises the issue of title to the royalty interest for the first time in this action, and because the Third Party Defendants are now joined as parties for the first time, EOG anticipates that the Third Party Defendants will likely move to transfer venue of this action to Montague County, Texas. If they do move for venue transfer, EOG submits that this action should be transferred to Montague County, Texas.

Although the Perrymans did indeed move to transfer venue, EOG never contested venue on its own motion and nothing in the record indicates that it filed anything in support of the Perrymans' motion.

If the Perrymans were the original defendants to the main action, our statutes would have required the trial court to transfer venue on the Perrymans' motion. *See GeoChem*, 962 S.W.2d at 544. However, the Perrymans were joined as third-party defendants. And the venue statutes also state: "Venue of the main action shall establish venue of a counterclaim, cross claim, or third-party claim properly joined under the Texas Rules of Civil Procedure or any applicable statute." TEX. CIV. PRAC. & REM. CODE § 15.062(a). The Perrymans were properly joined by EOG, which then filed a proper third-party claim against them. Thus, section 15.062(a) appears to apply.

This raises the question of whether section 15.062(a) is also a mandatory provision like section 15.011 (the real property venue statute). By its plain and common meaning, "shall" denotes mandatory action. *See* TEX. GOV'T CODE § 311.016(2) (" 'Shall' imposes a duty."). And we have held that the phrase "shall bring suit" is "unmistakably mandatory." *Wichita Cty.*, 917 S.W.2d at 783 (citing *Mingus v. Wadley*, 115 Tex. 551, 285 S.W. 1084, 1087 (1926), *overruled on other grounds by Dubai Petroleum Co. v. Kazi*, 12 S.W.3d 71 (Tex. 2000)); *see Fid. Union Life Ins. Co. v. Evans*, 477 S.W.2d 535, 536 (Tex. 1972) (holding that venue provision stating that case "shall be returnable to and tried in" a certain county was "mandatory and is controlling over other statutory exceptions to the venue statute"). However, we have noted that the use of "shall" "is not necessarily determinative that a statute is mandatory." *Cassidy v. Fuller*, 568 S.W.2d 845, 847 (Tex. 1978) (holding that venue provision in the Family Code "clearly" intended its use of "shall" to be mandatory) (citing *Chisholm v. Bewley Mills*, 155 Tex. 400, 287 S.W.2d 943 (1956)). In *Langdeau*, for instance, we held that "a declaration that 'venue shall lie' in a certain county is not equivalent to a command that the suit 'must be brought' in that county. 358 S.W.2d at 555. It merely signifies an intention to give the plaintiff the legal right, if he chooses, to maintain such a suit there." *See id.* at 555–56 ("While that subdivision is expressed in mandatory terms, it does not convert a merely permissive venue provision, wherever it may be found, into a mandatory prescription."). Importantly, though, we noted that the venue statute at issue in *Langdeau* did not provide "that the actions mentioned therein shall or must be brought in the county." *Id.* at 554.

The third-party-venue statute states that the main action "shall establish venue" for properly joined third-party claims. TEX. CIV. PRAC. & REM. CODE § 15.062(a). "Shall establish" is not similar to "shall lie"; it does not indicate permission, it denotes a requirement. *See Establish*, BLACK'S LAW DICTIONARY (10th ed. 2014) ("To settle, make, or fix firmly; to enact permanently."). We therefore hold that section 15.062(a) is a mandatory venue provision.

The Perrymans argue, however, that section 15.062(a) is limited by section 15.062(b). Subsection (b) states:

> If an original defendant properly joins a third-party defendant, venue shall be proper for a claim arising out of the same transaction, occurrence, or series of transactions or occurrences by the plaintiff against the third-party defendant if the claim arises out of the subject matter of the plaintiff's claim against the original defendant.

TEX. CIV. PRAC. & REM. CODE § 15.062(b). The Perrymans argue that subsection (b) means that the main dispute's venue determines the venue of third-party claims only when the third-party claims "aris[e] out of the same transaction, occurrence, or series of transactions or occurrences by the plaintiff." This reading is not persuasive.

The Perrymans joined this suit as third-party defendants brought in by EOG. Our Rules of Civil Procedure allow "a defending party, as a third-party plaintiff, [to] cause a citation and petition to be served upon a person not a party to the action who is or may be liable to him or to the plaintiff for all or part of the plaintiff's claim against him." TEX. R. CIV. P. 38(a). When brought in as a third-party defendant, a third party may assert defenses against the defendant's claim against him and the plaintiff's claim against the defendant. *Id.* Rule 38(a) also states

> The third-party defendant may also assert any claim against the plaintiff arising out of the transaction or occurrence that is the subject matter of the plaintiff's claim against the

> third-party plaintiff. *The plaintiff may assert any claim against the third-party defendant arising out of the transaction or occurrence that is the subject matter of the plaintiff's claim against the third-party plaintiff*, and the third-party defendant thereupon shall assert his defenses and his counterclaims and cross-claims.

Id. (emphasis added). Rule 38(a) makes clear that if a plaintiff wishes to bring a claim against a third-party defendant, that claim must arise out of the transaction or occurrence forming the basis of the plaintiff's claim against the original defendant. *See id.* (defining "third-party plaintiff" as the "defending party" to the original suit). This limitation prevents plaintiffs from gaming the system to avoid strictures such as venue by waiting until a defendant joins a third-party before the plaintiff asserts a claim against him.

Read in light of our rules of civil procedure, subsection 15.062(b) allows proper venue for "a claim . . . by the plaintiff against the third-party defendant" if the claim against the third-party defendant arises out of the same transaction or occurrence *and* the same subject matter as the plaintiff's claim against the original defendant. TEX. CIV. PRAC. & REM. CODE § 15.062(b) (emphasis added). In this case, the original plaintiffs, Spartan and Menser, brought no claim against the Perrymans. Only EOG did. Thus, subsection (b) does not apply here.

We are therefore presented with two counties of mandatory venue. At least twice before we have faced competing mandatory venue provisions. In *Brown v. Gulf Television Co.*, 157 Tex. 607, 306 S.W.2d 706, 709 (1957), the plaintiff sought to quiet title to land and also requested injunctive relief. We noted that the "directions" of two relevant venue articles of the former statutes were "stated in mandatory terms." *Id.* at 708. We held that they did not conflict, however, because the request for injunctive relief was "merely ancillary" to the "primary and principal relief sought." *Id.* Our holding in *Brown* indicates that the plaintiff's choice of "primary relief" dictates the governing venue provision. *Id.* at 709.

In *Fisher*, we again faced two competing mandatory venue provisions. 433 S.W.3d at 533-34. The causes of action concerned both a "major transaction," requiring venue in the county on which the parties had agreed in writing, *see* TEX. CIV. PRAC. & REM. CODE § 15.020(c), and defamation, requiring venue in the home county of the plaintiff or the defendant, *see id.* § 15.017. However, in that case, the major-transaction statute include language stating that it was to apply "[n]otwithstanding any other provision of this title." *Id.* § 15.020(c). This proviso, we held, indicated "that the Legislature intended for it to control over other mandatory venue provisions." *Fisher*, 433 S.W.3d at 534 (citing *Molinet v. Kimbrell,* 356 S.W.3d 407, 413-14 (Tex. 2011)).

In reconciling these two provisions, our analysis in *Wilson* is useful. There, we considered the venue statutes together with our rules of civil procedure to hold that "if the plaintiff chooses a county of proper venue, . . . no other county can be a proper venue in that case." 886 S.W.2d at 261. Such a reading, we held, "gives effect to the plaintiff's right to select a proper venue." *Id.* (citing *Maranatha Temple, Inc. v. Enter. Prods. Co.*, 833 S.W.2d 736, 741 (Tex. App.—Houston [1st Dist.] 1992, writ denied)). Similarly, holding here that the third-party-venue provision controls over other mandatory venue provisions gives effect to both provisions while honoring the general rule that the plaintiff makes the first choice of appropriate venue. *See Omni Hotels Mgmt. Corp.*, 159 S.W.3d at 629. We therefore hold that venue was proper in Harris County and the trial court did not err in denying the Perrymans' motion to transfer venue.

Notes & Questions

Occasionally, more than one mandatory venue provision may apply to a case. How should that conflict be resolved? Generally, the plaintiff may choose between the two proper mandatory venues.[1] However, as referenced in the *Perryman* opinion, the Texas Supreme Court has held that mandatory venue provision relating to major transactions, § 15.020, controls over other mandatory venue provisions.[2] And one court of appeals applied the principles of statutory construction to determine which mandatory venue provision governed.[3] That court reasoned that if two mandatory venue statutes conflict and neither originates under the main venue statute, it is not the plaintiff's choice that controls, but rather it is a matter of statutory construction—a specific, later statute controlled over an earlier, general statute.

C. Procedure for Challenging Venue

1. *Trial Court Procedure*

Read Rules 86, 87.

Heretofore, we have focused on what counties are possible venues for a plaintiff's lawsuit; and at the same time, what counties may be available for a defendant who seeks transfer. However, when a defendant challenges the plaintiff's venue choice, venue procedure is essential to making the determination of where is proper venue.

Venue procedure starts when the plaintiff files suit. The plaintiff makes the initial venue choice by filing suit in the county that the plaintiff has chosen. Although there is no formal requirement, it is good practice for a plaintiff to plead the venue facts in the original petition reflecting how venue is proper in the county of suit.

The defendant may challenge venue with a timely-filed motion to transfer.[1] The motion must be filed in due order (after a special appearance, but before any other pleading or motion but not a Rule 91A motion to dismiss) or it is waived.[2] The motion should allege that transfer is required because the county of suit is not a proper county or because mandatory venue is prescribed in another county.[3] It should further request that the case be transferred to a specific proper county and allege the necessary venue facts for that county. Although not included in Rule 86, a defendant

---

[1] Perryman v. Spartan Texas Six Capital Partners, Ltd, 546 S.W.3d 110 (Tex. 2018); In re Fisher, 433 S.W.3d 523 (2014); Wilson v. Texas Parks and Wildlife Dept., 886 S.W.2d 259 (Tex. 1994); Marshall v. Mahaffey, 974 S.W.2d 942 (Tex. App.—Beaumont 1998, pet. denied).

[2] In re Fisher, 433 S.W.3d at 533.

[3] In re Sosa, 370 S.W.3d 79, 81(Tex. App.—Houston [14th Dist.] 2012, orig. proceeding).

[1] *See* Rule 86.

[2] Rule 86(1); 91A.8. Waiver, venue is much like waiver of the special appearance.

[3] Rule 86(3).

seeking transfer on grounds of "convenience and justice" should allege that basis for transfer and the three required fact findings set out in CPRC § 15.002(b).

Rule 87(2) provides that after a venue challenge, each party has the burden of establishing venue. Thus, the plaintiff has the burden of establishing that venue is proper in the county of suit, and the defendant has the burden of establishing that venue is proper in the county to which defendant seeks transfer. Rule 87(3)(a) provides that "all venue facts, when properly pleaded, shall be taken as true, unless specifically denied by the adverse party." Therefore, if all venue facts are alleged in the petition, the plaintiff will have satisfied its burden *unless* the defendant, in its motion to transfer, specifically denies one or more of those venue facts. Clearly, then, the defendant will need to include specific denials in the motion, unless the motion seeks transfer from a proper county to a mandatory county or one that is more convenient pursuant to the "county non conveniens" theory.

What if the plaintiff did not initially allege venue facts, or later wants to add additional bases for venue other than those initially pleaded? One court of appeals has held that plaintiffs can amend their petitions for venue purposes "as many times as they like and so can the defendants."[4] In that case, the plaintiff had pleaded incorrectly that the accident occurred in Brooks County, although it had in fact occurred in neighboring Hidalgo County. When the defendant specifically denied the allegation, seeking transfer to Harris County, the plaintiff amended its petition to allege that the defendant had an "agency or representative" in Brooks County. The plaintiff also added a cause of action under the Deceptive Trade Practices Act to take advantage of the special, and arguably broader, venue provision in that statute. The court of appeals held this to be proper, and agreed that venue could be maintained in Brooks County.

If a defendant has specifically denied venue facts, the plaintiff is put to its burden of prima facie proof[5] and must present evidence by affidavit or discovery products authenticated by affidavit.[6] The affidavit must be made on personal knowledge (not mere "information and belief") and contain specific facts that would be admissible in evidence.[7] The plaintiff may also want to specifically deny some of the defendant's venue facts, putting the defendant to its proof. In that case, the defendant must respond with its own affidavits. Note the strict deadlines set out in Rule 87(1).

At the venue hearing, the court considers the motion, any response, and affidavits to determine whether the parties have satisfied their burdens of proof. If the transfer is sought because the county of suit is improper, the court looks at plaintiff's proof. If the plaintiff successfully satisfies its prima facie proof burden, there is no transfer. If the defendant satisfies its prima facie proof burden of a mandatory county, the suit is transferred to that county. Likewise, if the plaintiff fails to make prima facie proof, the case is transferred, provided the defendant has satisfied its burden of showing that the county to which it seeks transfer is a proper county. No oral testimony may be considered and the court may not consider the credibility of the witnesses.

---

4 Nabors Loffland Drilling Co. v. Martinez, 894 S.W.2d 70, 73 (Tex. App.—San Antonio 1995, writ denied) (*citing* Tex. R. Civ. P. 62-67; Chapin & Chapin, Inc. v. Texas Sand & Gravel Co., 844 S.W.2d 664, 665 (Tex. 1992)). *See also* In re Pepsico, Inc., 87 S.W.3d 787, 784 (Tex. App.—Texarkana 2002, no pet.)(holding that an original timely motion to transfer venue may be amended to cure defects in the original motion if the amended motion is filed before the trial court rules on the original motion).

5 Rule 87(3).

6 *See* Rule 86(3)(a); Kimmell v. Leoffler, 791 S.W.2d 648, 653 (Tex. App.—San Antonio 1990, writ denied).

7 Rule 86(3)(a).

When venue is based upon where the cause of action arose, Rule 87 and CPRC § 15.064(a) make clear that proof of the merits of the cause of action is not required. The existence of the cause of action is established if pleaded properly in plaintiff's petition. The defendant may then specifically deny that a part of the cause of action occurred in the county of suit, to which the plaintiff would respond with an affidavit establishing that a "substantial part" arose in the county. The defendant can also claim that the events or omissions that occurred in the county of suit are not "a substantial part" of those giving rise to plaintiff's claim, and assert that "a substantial part" occurred elsewhere.

---

2. *Hearings and Motions*

GENTRY
v.
TUCKER
891 S.W.2d 766
(Tex. App.—Texarkana 1995, no writ)

GRANT, JUSTICE.

Larry Gentry appeals the granting of injunctive relief and a declaratory judgment against him. Gentry contends: (1) that the trial court erred in ruling that Gentry waived his motion to transfer venue by filing a motion for continuance for a temporary injunction hearing and by proceeding to a trial on the merits; (2) that the trial court erred in refusing to allow Gentry to have forty-five days' notice, as required by TEX. R. CIV. P. 87 for the transfer of venue hearing; and (3) that the trial court erred in setting the trial date three weeks after the answer was due.

Gordon G. Tucker, Fred E. Tucker, Jr., and Huel H. Weaver (the Tuckers) sued Larry Gentry seeking injunctive relief and a declaratory judgment relating to a dispute involving a partnership. A temporary injunction hearing was scheduled for September 17, 1993. On that day, Gentry filed a motion for continuance of that hearing. The hearing was rescheduled for September 24, 1993. On the answer day, September 20, 1993, Gentry filed an answer subject to a motion to transfer venue. On September 24, 1993, the trial court granted the temporary injunction and set the trial date for October 11, 1993, three weeks from Gentry's answer day. At trial, final judgment, including a permanent injunction, was entered in the Tuckers' behalf.

In his first point of error, Gentry contends that the trial court erred in ruling that he waived his motion to transfer venue. On September 17, 1993, a hearing on a temporary injunction was scheduled. Gentry filed a motion for continuance. The trial court then rescheduled the hearing for September 24, 1993. On September 20, 1993, Gentry filed a motion to transfer venue. The trial court determined that the motion for continuance waived Gentry's right to a motion to transfer venue.

An objection to improper venue is waived if not made by written motion filed prior to or concurrently with any other plea, pleading, or motion, except a special appearance motion provided by Rule of Civil Procedure 120a. TEX. R. CIV. P. 86(1). However, Gentry argues that his motion for continuance was a preliminary motion and, therefore, did not waive error. Courts have held that appearing in other matters prior to the main suit will not waive the plea. * * *

In the case at bar, Gentry filed a motion for continuance on a preliminary matter. This did not invoke the court's general jurisdiction in the main suit, nor was it a motion for continuance of the entire case. Therefore, Gentry's motion for continuance of a hearing on a temporary injunction did not waive his right to transfer venue.

The Tuckers also contend that the right to contest venue was waived by Gentry because he tried the case on the merits. A pending motion to transfer will be waived by actions invoking the judicial power of the court in a manner inconsistent with a continuing intention to insist upon the motion. The motion will be waived if the defendant who is filing it, without first insisting upon its disposition, tries the case on the merits.

Gentry did participate in the trial on the merits. Because the statement of facts was not timely filed, it is not before this Court. Therefore, there is no confirmation to Gentry's assertion in his brief that he insisted upon its disposition, nor does the record reflect that he objected to the court's failure to address the motion to transfer venue. Hence, the motion was waived when the case was tried on the merits. The trial court did not abuse its discretion in determining that Gentry waived his right to transfer venue. This point of error is overruled.

By his second point of error, Gentry contends that the trial court erred in refusing to allow Gentry to have forty-five days' notice as required by TEX. R. CIV. P. 87 for the transfer of venue hearing. Rule 87 indicates that, except on leave of court, each party is entitled to at least forty-five days' notice of a hearing on the motion to transfer. A party, however, must move for continuance to preserve error on Rule 87 grounds that he was not given either sufficient notice of the hearing or reasonable time to prepare for trial after the hearing. Because the movant has an affirmative duty to request a setting on a motion to transfer for lack of venue, he must pursue a hearing thereon in order to later rely upon his motion on appeal. It is the plaintiff's responsibility to see that this matter was resolved before a trial on the merits.

In the case at bar, there is no showing that Gentry did anything beyond requesting a hearing on the motion to transfer venue. Without a record of an objection or motion for continuance of the trial setting, Gentry has not shown that he directed the trial court's attention to this matter. Therefore, no error is preserved.

* * *

The judgment of the trial court is affirmed.

Notes & Questions

1. *Refusal to hold hearing.* In *Marshall v. Mahaffey*[1], the judge overruled the venue motion without a hearing. On appeal the Beaumont Court of Appeals found that the defendant had preserved its venue rights by requesting a hearing, even though the defendant did not "demand" that the judge follow the rules and hold a hearing.

2. *Waiver.* As with the special appearance, a defendant may waive its venue rights if it fails to follow the procedures of Rules 86-88. The most obvious way to waive venue is to fail to file a timely motion to transfer.[2] Defendants also have the obligation to get their venue motions heard

---

1 974 S.W.2d 942, 945 (Tex. App.—Beaumont 1998, pet. denied).

2 *See* Rule 86, CPRC § 15.063 [1983] [same as 1995].

within a reasonable time before the trial on the merits[3] and to get a ruling on the motion.[4] Filing an answer before a motion to transfer will waive the motion, but the cautious practitioner will file an answer subject to the motion to transfer to prevent a default judgment should the motion be denied.[5]

3. *Waiver of others' venue rights.* Under the 1983 statute, there was some concern that one defendant could fail to file a motion to transfer, thereby waiving venue for itself and all other defendants.[6] This concern has been put to rest with the 1995 statute. Section 15.0641 specifically provides that one defendant's "action or omission" does not "impair or diminish the right of any other party to properly challenge venue."

4. *Discovery subject to venue motion.* Similar to the practice under Rule 120a, it has been held that the venue motion can be waived if the defendant takes action after filing the motion to transfer that is construed as inconsistent with the venue challenge.[7] The venue rules, however, explicitly provide that discovery is to proceed regardless of the motion to transfer and that such discovery does not constitute waiver.[8] Although many defendants continue the ritual of adding to every pleading filed subsequent to the motion to transfer the words "subject to our motion to transfer venue," it is almost certainly unnecessary.[9]

5. *Further Motions.* Rule 87(5) is a rather strange provision, entitled "Motion for Rehearing." Interestingly, there is no reference to a rehearing anywhere in the paragraph. However, this paragraph does clearly provide that once a motion to transfer is sustained or denied, no further motions to transfer can be considered.[10] This prevents late-added defendants from having their motions to transfer considered *unless* the motion is on grounds of an unfair forum under Rules 257-59, or on the ground of a mandatory exception unavailable to the other movants.[11] Late-added defendants with other venue claims merely are permitted to file a motion to transfer in order to

---

[3] Rule 87(1); Whitworth v. Kuhn, 734 S.W.2d 108, 111 (Tex. App.—Austin 1987, no writ).

[4] Cliff Jones, Inc. v. Ledbetter, 896 S.W.2d 417 (Tex. App.—Houston [1st Dist.] 1995, no writ).

[5] *See* Glover v. Moser, 930 S.W.2d 940 (Tex. App.—Beaumont 1996, writ denied). *But see* Dawson-Austin v. Austin, 968 S.W.2d 319 (Tex. 1998) (holding that a motion filed subsequent to but not expressly "subject to" a special appearance did not waive the special appearance).

[6] *See* S. Fortney, *Commentary: Civil Procedure Rules Committee Should End Venue Ambiguity,* 10 TEXAS LAWYER Sept. 5, 1994 at 25; WTFO, Inc. v. Braithwaite, 899 S.W.2d 709 (Tex. App.—Dallas 1995, no writ) (holding that a defendant could not waive venue for another under the 1983 statute); Brookshire Grocery Co. v. Smith, 99 S.W.3d 819 (Tex. App.—Beaumont 2003, pet. denied)(holding that one defendant's failure to file motion to transfer waived venue for other defendant under 1983 statute).

[7] *See* Nacol v. Williams, 554 S.W.2d 286, 288 (Tex. Civ. App.—Eastland 1977, writ dism'd) (defendant waived venue under pre-1983 statute by presenting motion to require plaintiff to post security for costs after plea of privilege filed).

[8] Rule 88. *See* Nabors Loffland Drilling Co. v. Martinez, 894 S.W.2d 70 (Tex. App.—San Antonio 1995, writ denied) (defendant did not waive venue by asking the court for affirmative relief on discovery and procedural matters after motion filed).

[9] *Id.*

[10] Rule 87(5). *See* Dorchester Master Ltd. Partnership v. Anthony, 734 S.W.2d 151, 152 (Tex. App.—Houston [1st Dist.] 1987, orig. proceeding); U.S. Resources, Inc. v. Placke, 682 S.W.2d 403, 405 (Tex. App.—Austin 1984, orig. proceeding).

[11] Rule 87(5). *See also* Gilcrease v. Garlock, Inc. 211 S.W.3d 448 (Tex. App.—El Paso 2006, no pet.) (holding that venue is fixed after motion to transfer denied, preventing refilling elsewhere after nonsuit).

preserve grounds for reversal on appeal. What if the first venue challenge on permissive venue is lost despite its merit because of the incompetence of the initial defendant? Under the 1983 venue scheme, the second defendant could only file a motion to preserve error for appeal. Look at § 15.0641 [1995]. Does this make a difference?

6. *Reconsideration*. If a court cannot hear a second motion to transfer, can it nevertheless properly *reconsider* its prior ruling? Rule 87(5) was originally titled "No rehearing," which indicated not. In 1990, however, the title was changed to "Motion for Rehearing." The courts of appeals that addressed the question before the amendment gave differing answers.[12] In *HCA Health Services of Texas, Inc. v. Salinas,*[13] the Supreme Court addressed a situation where the trial court *inadvertently* signed an order granting a motion to transfer to another county. When the order was called to his attention, he immediately signed an order vacating the first one, and after hearing on the motion the next day, signed an order denying the motion. The Supreme Court held that the first order was invalid because it was made without notice, and that the trial court had the power to vacate the order. More recently, in *Orion Enterprises, Inc. v. Pope*,[14] the San Antonio Court of Appeals held that the trial judge could reconsider the order, so long as the court's plenary power over the proceeding had not expired.

7. *Consent*. The trial court must transfer an action to another county of proper venue if the parties file a written consent to such transfer pursuant to CPRC § 15.063. Rule 86(1) states that this written consent may be filed "at any time." However, the language at the first part of the statute seems to allow transfer only when requested "before the filing of the answer." Applying this language literally to preclude transfer after the parties have agreed to seems absurd. Therefore, the better view is that the motion based on consent can be filed after the answer is filed or even after the trial has begun, given the language stating that the consent may be filed "at any time." On the other hand, Rule 87 requires the court to decide a motion to transfer within a reasonable time before commencement of trial, which is also arguably applicable to all types of motions, including motions based on consent. Using this reasoning, the written consent would need to be filed prior to the beginning of trial.[15]

Note that written consent to transfer is different from an agreement to set venue that is entered into *before* suit is filed. As we have seen, the latter agreements are generally ineffective.

---

[12] *See* Tenneco Inc. v. Salyer, 739 S.W.2d 448, 450 (Tex. App.—Corpus Christi 1987, orig. proceeding) (trial court cannot reconsider prior ruling); Dorchester Master Ltd. Partnership v. Anthony, 734 S.W.2d 151, 152 (Tex. App.—Houston [1st Dist.] 1987, orig. proceeding) (same); U.S. Resources Inc. v. Placke, 682 S.W.2d 403, 405 (Tex. App.—Austin 1984, orig. proceeding) (court can reconsider prior ruling before actual transfer takes place).

[13] 838 S.W.2d 246 (Tex. 1992).

[14] 927 S.W.2d 654 (Tex. App.—San Antonio 1996, org. proceeding).

[15] DORSANEO § 61.20[3][c].

GEOCHEM TECH CORPORATION
v.
VERSECKES

962 S.W.2d 541
(Tex. 1998)

Opinion

OWEN, JUSTICE, delivered the opinion of the Court, in which PHILLIPS, CHIEF JUSTICE, GONZALEZ, HECHT, ENOCH, SPECTOR, ABBOTT and HANKINSON, JUSTICES, join.

The issue in this case is whether a nonsuit fixes venue in the county to which transfer is sought when the nonsuit is taken after a motion to transfer has been filed but before a ruling on venue has been made. The court of appeals concluded that the effect of a nonsuit under our current rules of procedure is the same as it was under the former venue rules and held that venue was fixed in the county to which transfer was sought. 929 S.W.2d 85. We hold that the effect of a nonsuit depends on the state of the record at the time it is filed and that under the facts of this case, venue was not fixed solely in Stephens County, a county to which transfer was sought.

In December 1993, GeoChem Tech Corporation sued GeoServ Company and Michael Verseckes in Dallas County. GeoChem sought damages and injunctive relief. GeoServ filed a motion to transfer asserting that venue was mandatory in Stephens County under TEX. CIV. PRAC. & REM. CODE § 65.023(a) (requiring a suit for injunctive relief to be tried in county of defendant's domicile). The same day, Verseckes filed a motion to transfer, relying on the same mandatory venue provision, but requested that the lawsuit be transferred to Van Zandt County, a county in which he claimed to reside. Subsequently, Verseckes filed an amended motion to transfer venue and sought to have the case transferred to Stephens County instead of Van Zandt County, still asserting mandatory venue, but claiming that he was a resident of Stephens County as well as Van Zandt County. GeoChem then amended its petition, adding three other defendants.

Before the Dallas County trial court ruled on the motions to transfer, GeoChem nonsuited the entire case. On that same day, GeoChem refiled its suit in Van Zandt County against all defendants. The defendants filed motions to transfer to Stephens County, and the Van Zandt County trial court granted those motions. The Stephens County trial court ultimately rendered final judgment against GeoChem. GeoChem appealed the venue ruling as well as other adverse determinations. The court of appeals reversed and remanded in part, but held that the case was properly transferred to Stephens County. We reverse the judgment of the court of appeals and remand to the trial court for further proceedings in accordance with this opinion.

Under our former venue practice, the filing of a proper plea of privilege constituted prima facie proof of a defendant's right to obtain a transfer. The plea of privilege was required to be verified and was required to affirmatively assert certain facts. If a plaintiff took a nonsuit while the plea of privilege was pending, venue was fixed in the county to which transfer was sought. Because the plea of privilege was prima facie proof of the right to transfer, the dismissal was deemed an admission that venue was improper in the original county of suit and that the defendant had the right to transfer venue.

We no longer have a "plea of privilege" under our venue statutes and rules. Instead, a party seeking to transfer a suit must file a motion objecting to venue. *See* TEX. R. CIV. P. 86. Verification of the motion is not required, and the motion may be, but is not required to be, supported by affidavits at the time it is filed. *See* TEX. R. CIV. P. 86(3). As the court of appeals correctly observed, all venue facts, when properly pleaded, shall be taken as true unless specifically denied by the adverse party. *See* TEX. R. CIV. P. 87(3)(a). When a venue fact is specifically denied, the party pleading the fact must submit supporting affidavits or otherwise make prima facie proof. *See id.* A party who seeks to maintain venue in the county of suit under certain sections of the Civil Practice and Remedies Code has the burden to make prima facie proof that venue is maintainable in that county. *See* TEX. R. CIV. P. 87(2)(a). A party seeking a transfer has the burden to make prima facie proof that venue is maintainable in the county to which transfer is sought. *Id.* Thus, the pleadings at any given point in time after a motion to transfer is filed may or may not establish a prima facie case of proper venue, depending on what has been filed by the plaintiff and what has been filed by the defendant.

When a nonsuit is filed, we must consider the state of the record at that point. Under our current rules of procedure, if an objection to venue in the county of suit has been filed, with or without supporting affidavits, and the plaintiff then takes a nonsuit and has not specifically denied the venue facts averred by the party seeking transfer, the venue facts alleged in the motion to transfer are taken as true. *See* TEX. R. CIV. P. 87.

At the time GeoChem filed its notice of nonsuit, Verseckes had filed a motion to transfer and an amended motion to transfer in which he stated that he resided in Van Zandt and Stephens Counties. GeoChem never met its burden of proving that venue was proper in Dallas County. As discussed above, the venue facts alleged by Verseckes were taken as true under Rule 87(3)(a) until specifically denied, and GeoChem had not specifically denied them. Those mandatory venue facts became established when the nonsuit was filed.

Further, mandatory venue facts had been established by prima facie proof at the time the nonsuit was taken. Verseckes had filed affidavits in which he stated that he resided in both Van Zandt and Stephens Counties. We note that for venue purposes, an individual may have more than one residence. *See Snyder v. Pitts,* 150 Tex. 407, 241 S.W.2d 136, 140 (1951); *Rosales v. H.E. Butt Grocery Co.,* 905 S.W.2d 745, 748 (Tex. App.—San Antonio 1995, writ denied). There is no contention in this case that the affidavits filed by Verseckes were insufficient to establish prima facie proof of residences in two counties.

The court of appeals concluded that although venue was proper in Van Zandt County, once GeoChem had made its "first choice" by filing in a county in which venue was improper, GeoChem was not entitled to refile in a second county of its choice over the objection of a defendant. 929 S.W.2d at 89. The court of appeals reasoned that "there can be only one first choice" because "any other posture would be to promote rather than prevent the very type of legal 'gamesmanship' sought to be prevented under the old venue law." *Id.* We conclude that the venue statutes do not support this conclusion.

The court of appeals recognized that under the current venue statutes, the plaintiff has the "first choice" of venue. 929 S.W.2d at 89 (citing *Wilson v. Texas Parks & Wildlife Dep't,* 886 S.W.2d 259, 260 (Tex. 1994)). However, the statutes do not say that the plaintiff may choose venue only once. They simply say that if the county chosen is not proper, the case must be transferred if a sufficient motion is filed and ruled upon. *See* TEX. CIV. PRAC. & REM. CODE § 15.063.

In this case, the mandatory venue provision regarding injunctions requires that the suit be tried in a county in which a defendant against whom the injunction is sought is domiciled. *See* TEX. CIV. PRAC. & REM. CODE § 65.023. When GeoChem filed its second suit in Van Zandt County, it did so in full compliance with the mandates of the venue statutes. *See id.* GeoChem did not lose the right, under the facts of this case, to choose between two counties in which mandatory venue is proper by filing its first suit in a county in which venue was improper. Because venue in Van

Zandt County was proper under TEX. CIV. PRAC. & REM. CODE § 65.023, the trial court erred in transferring the case to Stephens County. *See* TEX. R. CIV. P. 87(3)(c) (providing that if a claimant has made prima facie proof that venue is proper in the county of suit, the cause shall not be transferred unless the motion to transfer is based on a mandatory exception or on grounds that an impartial trial cannot be had in the county where the action is pending).

Under Rule 59.1 of the Texas Rules of Appellate Procedure, the Court grants GeoChem's application for writ of error and, without hearing oral argument, reverses the judgment of the court of appeals and remands this case to Van Zandt County for further proceedings.

BAKER, J., noted his dissent.

Notes & Questions

Nonsuit to get second bite at the venue apple. *Geochem* holds that a nonsuit is filed *before* venue is determined, the plaintiff may be able to file suit and maintain venue in another county, depending upon the state of the record at the time the nonsuit is filed. In that case, the record supported venue in both Van Zandt and Stephens Counties, so the plaintiff could choose to refile in either. Likewise, if the plaintiff nonsuits before a motion to transfer is filed, the plaintiff can choose to refile in another proper county.[1] What if *after* losing the venue challenge, and facing trial in the defendant's chosen county, the plaintiff files a nonsuit under Rule 162 and refiles the case in another proper county, but one that the plaintiff prefers over the defendant's county? No, it won't work. The Supreme Court has held that once venue has been determined in a case, it is fixed and conclusively decided as to those parties and claims.[2]

---

3. *Appellate Review*

Read CPRC §§ 15.063, 15.064.

ROSALES
v.
H.E. BUTT GROCERY CO.
905 S.W.2d 745
(Tex. App.—San Antonio 1995, writ denied)

CHAPA, CHIEF JUSTICE.

Appellants Rolando Rosales and Esmeralda Cruz appeal a summary judgment granted in favor of appellees, H.E. Butt Grocery Company, Harvey Mabry, and Eva Wallace. Appellants originally filed suit in Maverick County, alleging causes of action of defamation, negligent and intentional infliction of emotional distress, and invasion of privacy. The trial court granted appellees' motion to transfer venue to Bexar County, where this summary judgment was granted against appellants.

---

1 Peysen v. Dawson, 974 S.W.2d 377, 380 (Tex.App.—San Antonio 1998, no pet.).

2 In re Team Rocket, L.P., 256 S.W.3d 257, 260 (Tex. 2007).

The dispositive issue before this court is whether the trial court erred in granting the motion to transfer venue. TEX.R.APP.P. 90.

* * *

In *Ruiz v. Conoco, Inc.,* 868 S.W.2d 752 (Tex.1993), the Texas Supreme Court recognized that the procedure for appellate review mandated by section 15.064(b) of the Texas Civil Practice and Remedies Code "is fundamentally flawed because it allows appellate review of venue on a basis different from that on which it was decided." Apparently concerned with this "fundamental flaw," the supreme court thereafter in *Wilson v. Texas Parks & Wildlife Dep't,* 886 S.W.2d 259 (Tex. 1994), analyzed the venue statute and established the current standard of review, which "strikes a balance between the competing interests of the plaintiff and the defendant." The court stated:

> Venue selection presupposes that the parties to the lawsuit have choices and preferences about where their case will be tried. Venue may be proper in many counties under general, mandatory, or permissive venue rules. The plaintiff is given the first choice in the filing of the lawsuit. If the plaintiff's venue choice is not properly challenged through a motion to transfer venue, the propriety of venue is fixed in the county chosen by the plaintiff. If a defendant objects to the plaintiff's venue choice and properly challenges that choice through a motion to transfer venue, the question of proper venue is raised. The burden is on the plaintiff to prove that venue is maintainable in the county of suit. If the plaintiff fails to meet this burden, the trial court must transfer the lawsuit to another specified county of proper venue [if the defendant then proves that venue is maintainable in the county to which transfer is sought]. If the plaintiff meets the burden, the trial court must maintain the lawsuit in the county where it was filed. TEX.R.CIV.P. 87-3(c) ("If a claimant has adequately pleaded and made prima facia [sic] proof that venue is proper in the county of suit . . . then the cause shall not be transferred but shall be retained in the county of suit . . . .").
>
> Together, Rule 87-3(c) and section 15.063(1) require that a lawsuit pleaded and proved to be filed in a county of proper venue may not be transferred. Therefore, if the plaintiff chooses a county of proper venue, and this is supported by proof as required by Rule 87 [prima facie proof], no other county can be a proper venue in that case. This rule gives effect to the plaintiff's right to select a proper venue.

* * *

Appellant Rosales, plaintiff below, chose to file his claim in Maverick County as the county of his residence.[2] The appellees, defendants below, challenged the venue. This required appellant Rosales to present "prima facie proof" that Maverick County was a county of his residence by "any probative evidence." The venue statute provides that venue shall be determined by the trial court from the pleadings and affidavits. When deciding a motion to transfer venue, the trial court must take as true those facts which the party with the burden of proof has presented by prima facie proof. If the record before us reflects that appellant Rosales carried his burden, "no other county can be a proper venue" as a matter of law.

In *Mills v. Bartlett,* 377 S.W.2d 636 (Tex. 1964), the court stated the following regarding "residence":

---

2 Appellant's county of **residence** was an appropriate **venue** of this claim under the provisions of section 15.017 of the civil practice and remedies code, which dictates venue in libel, slander, and invasion of privacy cases. *See* TEX.CIV.PRAC. & REM.CODE ANN. § 15.017 (Vernon 1986).

> The term "residence" is an elastic one and is extremely difficult to define. The meaning that must be given to it depends upon the circumstances surrounding the person involved and largely depends upon the present intention of the individual. Volition, intention and action are all elements to be considered in determining where a person resides and such elements are equally pertinent in denoting the permanent residence or domicile.

Moreover, it is well-settled law in Texas that for venue purposes a person may have a residence in two or more counties. Thus, it is possible under Texas venue law for Rosales to have a residence in Maverick County along with a residence in Bexar County, as alleged by appellees.

Because appellees properly challenged Rosales's venue choice, he was required to plead and make prima facie proof that his venue selection was proper. "A prima facie case represents the minimum quantum of evidence necessary to support a rational inference that the allegation of fact is true. The party with the burden of proof must produce at least this much evidence to avoid a finding that the allegation is not true as a matter of law." In discussing prima facie evidence, the Texas Supreme Court opined:

> The term "prima facie evidence" is ambiguous at best. As Professor Wigmore points out, it sometimes is used "as equivalent to the notion of a presumption," i.e., it entitles the proponent to an instructed verdict on the issue in the absence of evidence to the contrary. The term is also used to mean that the proponent has produced sufficient evidence to go to the trier of fact on the issue.

Coward v. Gateway Nat'l Bank, 525 S.W.2d 857, 859 (Tex. 1975).

To determine whether appellant Rosales carried his burden of presenting prima facie proof of his Maverick County residence, we must review the entire record before us. The record reflects sworn evidence from appellant Rolando Rosales (1) that he was born in Maverick County and thereafter attended primary and secondary schools in Maverick County and graduated from high school in Maverick County; (2) that he attended college away from Maverick County only because there was no college in Maverick County; (3) that he grew up at 350 Concho St., Eagle Pass, Maverick County, was married in Maverick County, and baptized all his children in Maverick County; (4) that he has owned by inheritance a share of the 350 Concho St. home since 1981 when his mother died and has continued to help pay the bills connected with the home; (5) that 350 Concho St. has always been his permanent residence which he has occupied for substantial periods of times in the past and intends to continue to occupy in the future; (6) that he has voted and is registered to vote in Maverick County; (7) that his driver's license and social security card show his residence as 350 Concho St., Maverick County; (8) that he had to obtain employment away from Maverick County because unemployment is at forty percent in Maverick County; (9) that had H.E.B. offered to transfer him to one of its stores in Maverick County, he would have welcomed the offer; (10) that he has continuously returned to his residence in Maverick County over a substantial period of time; and (11) that his intentions are and have always been to return to his residence in Maverick County. The record also discloses an exhibit with copies of Rosales's driver's license and social security card reflecting his residence as 350 Concho St., Eagle Pass, which is in Maverick County. Moreover, the record reflects sworn deposition testimony of Lorena Rosales, wife of appellant Rolando Rosales. In the deposition, Mrs. Rosales stated that she and her husband have a residence in Maverick County on Concho St., Eagle Pass, where they have lived in the past and where they intend to return permanently in the future. She also stated that if her husband could find an equivalent-paying job in Maverick County, they would return permanently to their residence there. We conclude that the foregoing evidence constitutes probative evidence and prima facie proof that appellant Rosales is a resident of Maverick County.

Appellees contend on appeal, as they did in the trial court, that appellants have engaged in a "thinly veiled attempt to manufacture venue in Maverick County." In support of this claim appellees point to evidence suggesting that appellant Rosales had little contact with Maverick County other than the fact that it was his boyhood home. Indeed, appellees cite a long list of evidence from which they argue that Rosales maintained his only residence in Bexar County.

The evidence cited by appellees challenges the validity of Rosales's evidence produced in response to the motion to transfer venue. This is exactly the type of conflict in evidence that would be decided by the trier of fact in a typical civil trial. This is a venue challenge, however, and the rules applicable to a typical civil trial do not apply. Rule 87 of the rules of civil procedure requires trial courts to make venue determinations on the basis of prima facie proof only, and does not require, or even affirmatively permit, trial courts to assess the credibility of conflicting affiants. The trial courts are further limited in their venue determinations since "[p]rima facie proof is not subject to rebuttal, cross-examination, impeachment or even disproof," no matter whether the evidence as a whole shows the prima facie proof was wrong or misleading. *Ruiz v. Conoco, Inc.,* 868 S.W.2d at 757. Thus, trial courts must maintain venue in the county selected by the plaintiff if the plaintiff selects a county of proper venue and supports the selection with prima facie proof of venue. *Wilson v. Texas Parks & Wildlife Dept.,* 886 S.W.2d 259, 261 (Tex. 1994); *Ruiz v. Conoco, Inc.,* 868 S.W.2d at 757.

Trial courts are thereby greatly restricted in their usual fact-finding abilities, and although appellate courts are "obliged to conduct an independent review of the entire record to determine whether venue was proper in the ultimate county of suit," appellate courts cannot be fact-finders. *See Ruiz v. Conoco, Inc.,* 868 S.W.2d at 758. The limitations on the trial court's typical fact-finding functions are highlighted in cases involving allegations of misrepresentation of venue facts.

Perhaps the trial court in the instant case engaged in a credibility assessment, but we have no way of knowing because there is nothing in our record to so indicate. If the trial court did engage in such an assessment, how are we to review it—our "independent review" is not to be a factual sufficiency review. *Ruiz,* 868 S.W.2d at 758. Further, we must uphold the trial court's determination if there is any "probative evidence" in the entire record that venue was proper in the county where judgment was rendered, while at the same time upholding the legislative dictate that the plaintiff is given the first choice in the filing of the lawsuit.

The complexities and apparent conflicts presented in venue review are perhaps solved by *Ruiz*'s dictate that if there is any probative evidence in the entire record that destroys the prima facie proof relied upon by the trial court, then the appellate court must reverse. Commentators have suggested that *Ruiz* and other cases, along with the venue statute and rule, distill down into the following "rules":

> (1) *prima facie* proof is to be considered by the appellate court, and standing alone, is sufficient to constitute "probative evidence," and
>
> (2) only conclusive evidence to the contrary can "destroy" probative evidence.

We have determined that appellants provided prima facie proof establishing Rosales's Maverick County residence. The question thus becomes whether our independent review of the entire record reveals any conclusive proof to destroy the prima facie proof presented by appellants. Appellees presented controverting evidence, but their evidence did not "destroy" appellants' prima facie proof. At best, appellees presented evidence that challenged appellants' evidence and raised fact questions. Under the parameters presented by current venue law, the trial court was not free to disregard appellants' prima facie proof, and this court cannot engage in a fact-finding review.

Thus, although appellees presented conflicting evidence regarding the residence of appellant Rosales, the previously detailed evidence constitutes probative evidence and prima facie proof that appellant Rosales is a resident of Maverick County. Accordingly, venue was proper in Maverick County, and the court erred in transferring the case to any other county, because under these circumstances "no other county can be a proper venue . . . ."

* * *

The judgment of the trial court is reversed and the cause is remanded, and the trial court is ordered to transfer the cause to Maverick County for a new trial.

Notes & Questions

1. *The standard of appellate review for venue.* Clearly, appellate review in venue is far different from ordinary appellate review. It all begins with the statute, CPRC § 15.064(b), which states:

> On appeal from the trial on the merits, if venue was improper it shall in no event be harmless error. In determining whether venue was or was not proper, the appellate court shall consider the entire record, including the trial on the merits.

Many courts had come up with various interpretations of this statute, and the conflict was ultimately resolved by the Supreme Court in *Ruiz v. Conoco*:[1]

> The procedure mandated by this statute is fundamentally flawed because it allows appellate review of venue on a basis different from that on which it was decided. In deciding a motion to transfer venue, the trial court is required by Rule 87, TEX. R. CIV. P., to take as true those facts of which prima facie proof is made by the party with the burden of such proof; yet in reviewing the trial court's decision, an appellate court must reverse (there cannot be harmless error) if other evidence in the record, even evidence adduced after venue was determined, destroys the prima facie proof on which the trial court relied. Prima facie proof is not subject to rebuttal, cross-examination, impeachment or even disproof. The evidence as a whole may well show that prima facie proof was misleading or wrong. But while the wisdom of the statute may be challenged, there is no misunderstanding its plain language: an appellate court is obliged to conduct an independent review of the entire record to determine whether venue was proper in the ultimate county of suit.
>
> * * *
>
> Therefore, if there is any probative evidence in the entire record, including trial on the merits, that venue was proper in the county where judgment was rendered, the appellate court must uphold the trial court's determination. If there is no such evidence, the judgment must be reversed and the case remanded to the trial court. The error cannot be harmless, according to the statute. If there is any probative evidence that venue was proper in the county to which transfer was sought, the appellate court should instruct the trial court to transfer the case to that county. Only if there is no probative evidence that venue was proper either in the county of suit or in the county to which transfer was sought should the appellate court remand the case to the trial court to conduct further proceedings on the issue of venue. This is one instance in which remand cannot be avoided. Rule 87(3)(d), TEX. R. CIV. P., contemplates that

---

1 868 S.W.2d 752 (Tex. 1993).

additional proof may be ordered in connection with a motion to transfer if neither party makes the required showing at first. In the unusual instance where there is no probative evidence in the record that venue is proper anywhere, a remand is unavoidable.

The issue for us, then, is whether there is any probative evidence in the record to support the trial court's determination that venue was proper in Starr County. As in any other situation, we view the record in the light most favorable to the trial court's ruling. We do not defer, however, to the trial court's application of the law.

Ruiz was refined in *Wilson v. Texas Parks & Wildlife*, quoted at length in the *Rosales* opinion. Specifically, *Wilson* made clear that venue choice was important in determining whether venue is proper or not—if a plaintiff files in a permissive venue and a court transfers to another permissive venue, only the original county is "proper" for purposes of appellate review. The transferee county is not "proper" and any judgment rendered from that county is reversed for improper venue.

2. *No interlocutory appeal and no harmless error.* Because one of the primary motivations for venue reform in 1983 was to eliminate the expense and delay of interlocutory venue appeals, the 1983 procedural statutes and rules, which largely remain in effect after the 1995 amendments, generally forbid interlocutory appeal.[2] As a political compromise, § 15.064(b) was written to provide that if an appellate court should find that venue in the trial court was improper, "it shall in no event be harmless error and shall be reversible error." Thus, when a trial court makes a blatant error in its venue ruling, the parties must try the case but are assured of reversal on appeal.

Notice that this concept of "no harmless error" is abrogated for decisions a trial court makes on a motion to transfer for "convenience and justice." The statute provides that this ruling is *not* grounds for appeal and can never be reversible error.[3] What does this do to the trial court's discretion with regard to rulings on these motions? Under what circumstances can a trial courts' decision based on county non conveniens be reversed?

---

4. *Convenience and Justice Review*

GARZA
v.
GARCIA
137 S.W.3d 36
(Tex. 2004)

JUSTICE BRISTER delivered the opinion of the Court, in which JUSTICE HECHT, JUSTICE OWEN, JUSTICE O'NEILL, JUSTICE SCHNEIDER and JUSTICE SMITH joined.

The Legislature amended the venue statutes in 1995 to allow a trial court to transfer venue "[f]or the convenience of the parties and witnesses and in the interest of justice." At the same time, the Legislature mandated that a trial court's order granting or denying such a transfer for convenience is "not grounds for appeal or mandamus and is not reversible error."

---

2 *See* Rule 87(b); CPRC § 15.064(a).

3 CPRC § 15.002(c) [1995].

In this case, a defendant filed a motion asserting both improper venue and inconvenience, which the trial court granted without specifying the grounds. Generally, we must affirm such general orders if any ground in the accompanying motion is meritorious. Because the motion here asserted convenience as one ground, and the statute precludes reversal of any ruling made on convenience grounds, we hold the court of appeals erred in considering and reversing the trial court's venue order.

* * *

II

The record reflects that petitioner Ines Gonzalez Garcia (a resident of Hidalgo County) brought suit against J & R Valley Oilfield Services, Inc. (a business in Hidalgo County) and Ramiro Garza (a resident of either Hidalgo or Starr County) concerning an auto accident occurring in Hidalgo County. Of sixteen potential lay and expert witnesses designated by the parties, fourteen were residents of Hidalgo County, and two of Mexico. None resided in Starr County. Nevertheless, suit was brought in Starr County, based on evidence that Garza lived there.

J & R's motion to transfer venue (which Garza joined) argued that Starr County was not a county of proper venue, and added "[a]lternatively, your Defendant would show that venue should be transferred to Hidalgo County for the convenience of the parties." The trial court's order stated that "after considering the motion, the pleadings, the affidavits, the responses as well as arguments of counsel and after a hearing, the Court grants Defendants' Motion to Transfer Venue."

At the trial in Hidalgo County, the jury awarded Garcia $120,000. Unsatisfied, she appealed seeking automatic reversal and a new trial based on the venue transfer.

The court of appeals reversed, refusing to presume a venue order was granted on convenience grounds unless the order specifically said so. In addition to reversing the traditional presumption applicable to all other orders, this rule would sometimes do just what the Legislature prohibited. Because the transfer order here includes no reasons, we cannot be certain on which of the two grounds it was granted; one ground was convenience, and the evidence showed most of the witnesses and all of the events took place in Hidalgo County. As the Starr County judge certainly might have intended to grant it on convenience grounds, we cannot ignore the Legislature's ban on reviewing such orders by adopting a new presumption so we can review them anyway.

The court of appeals refused to imply a finding on convenience grounds because the statutory prohibition on appellate review precluded reviewing the record for evidence that might support such an implied finding. But the statute precludes review not just of the evidence, but of the order itself. As a result, it is irrelevant whether a transfer for convenience is supported by *any* record evidence. Hypothetically, a trial judge could state there was no evidence for a convenience transfer, but grant it nonetheless, and (except for perhaps reporting it to the Judicial Conduct Commission) there is very little we could do about it.

We acknowledge the court of appeals' concern that the usual presumption in favor of nonspecific orders will make many venue orders "immune from review." But in transfer orders based on convenience, that appears to have been precisely the Legislature's intent. And even under the court of appeals' bright-line test, trial judges who are so inclined may make any venue order immune from review simply by adding "granted on convenience grounds."

Nor do we believe the potential for error or injustice here justifies making an exception to the general rule that trial judges and lawyers need not detail specific findings in every order. When a defendant files a motion based on both convenience and another venue ground, a trial judge may grant the motion on the former ground and we cannot review it. Or the judge may deny both, in which case we may review only the latter. The court of appeals was concerned a trial judge might intend to deny a motion based on convenience while granting (erroneously) the motion on an alternative ground. But most venue provisions are based on notions of convenience. As the county where the parties reside or the events occurred will often be the most convenient, we decline to change our usual presumption rules to presume the opposite.

* * *

Finally, we do not believe the movant's convenience motion must be more specific than the one here, at least when it is part of a motion asserting other venue grounds and there is no special exception. For example, under the general venue rule in section 15.002(a), the movant must plead venue facts (and support them with affidavits if necessary) that show no individual defendant resides in the forum county, no defendant business has its principal Texas office there, and a substantial part of the events did not occur there.[22] While a movant has every reason to add more facts in an effort to prevail, if those reasons alone are enough to convince the trial judge that the case would be more conveniently tried elsewhere, it would be mere formalism to reverse because they were not stated under two different headings.

While appellate justices may chafe at restrictions on appellate review, the Texas Constitution generally allows the Legislature to expand or limit such review as it sees fit. Nor is the restriction here unreasonable under these circumstances. Debates in the Legislature indicate the transfer for convenience statute was intended "to make sure that venue is not a game any longer" by giving trial judges some power to ensure cases were tried where they sensibly belonged, but without adding reversible error or additional delays. This case was tried four years ago, and has been on appeal ever since. The Legislature might reasonably have concluded that discretionary transfers would make litigation more convenient only if they did not have to be re-fought on appeal. Accordingly, we hold the court of appeals erred by reversing the venue order here.

III

Because the court of appeals should have affirmed the trial court's transfer order on convenience grounds, we reverse the court of appeals' judgment. Because Garcia failed to present her factual sufficiency point to the trial court (by failing to ever pay the filing fee), she has failed to preserve her remaining point, and we render judgment reinstating the trial court's judgment.

---

5. *Mandamus and Interlocutory Appeal*

In re TEAMROCKET, L.P.
256 S.W.3d 257
(Tex. 2008)

JUSTICE GREEN delivered the opinion of the Court.

In this case, we decide whether a plaintiff who was denied his initial venue of choice can nonsuit his case in the transferee county and refile in a third county. We hold that a plaintiff cannot avoid a venue ruling in such a way. Because the trial court in the third county refused to enforce

[22] *See* TEX. CIV. PRAC. & REM.CODE § 15.002(a); TEX.R. CIV. P. 86(3), 87(3)(a).

the prior order setting venue in the transferee county, we conditionally grant the writ of mandamus.

I

Thomas Creekmore died when the airplane he was flying crashed in Fort Bend County. His family brought negligence, strict liability, survival, and wrongful death claims in Harris County against Team Rocket, L.P., MLF Airframes, Inc., and Mark L. Frederick (collectively, Team Rocket), related to Team Rocket's manufacture and sale of the plane kit that Creekmore had purchased. Team Rocket moved to transfer venue, arguing that venue was improper in Harris County because they did not deliver the kit parts to Creekmore's residence there. The Harris County trial court agreed and transferred the case to Williamson County, Team Rocket's principal place of business and the residence of its representative. After the transfer, the Creekmores voluntarily nonsuited the case and immediately refiled the same claims against the same defendants in Fort Bend County. Team Rocket moved to transfer venue to Williamson County based on the Harris County trial court's prior venue order and the doctrine of collateral estoppel. The Fort Bend County trial court denied the motion. Team Rocket then sought mandamus relief in the court of appeals, which denied the petition.

II

We grant the extraordinary relief of mandamus only when the trial court has clearly abused its discretion and the relator lacks an adequate appellate remedy. *In re Prudential Ins. Co. of Am.,* 148 S.W.3d 124, 135-40 (Tex. 2004).

A

[The Supreme Court held that the Fort Bend County erred in denying the motion to transfer because venue was fixed in Williamson County after the Harris County court made its venue ruling.]

B

The adequacy of an appellate remedy must be determined by balancing the benefits of mandamus review against the detriments. *Prudential Ins. Co. of Am.,* 148 S.W.3d 124, 136 (Tex. 2004). In evaluating benefits and detriments, we consider whether mandamus will preserve important substantive and procedural rights from impairment or loss. Our venue statutes create a balance: a plaintiff has the first choice of venue when he files suit, and a defendant is restricted to one motion to transfer that venue. By defying the Harris County trial court's venue ruling by nonsuiting and refiling elsewhere, the Creekmores disrupted that balance in their favor and thereby impaired Team Rocket's procedural rights.

In addition to impairment of rights, we consider whether mandamus will "allow the appellate courts to give needed and helpful direction to the law that would otherwise prove elusive in appeals from final judgments." *Prudential,* 148 S.W.3d at 136. This petition involves a legal issue-the construction of Texas venue statutes and related rules in the context of voluntary nonsuit-that is likely to recur, as demonstrated by the court of appeals' decisions that have already addressed it.

Finally, we consider whether mandamus will spare litigants and the public "the time and money utterly wasted enduring eventual reversal of improperly conducted proceedings." *Prudential,* 148 S.W.3d at 136. Although we generally do not grant a petition for mandamus for venue determinations absent extraordinary circumstances, we have granted mandamus relief when the trial court issued an improper order transferring venue that "wrongfully burdened fourteen other courts in fourteen other counties, hundreds of potential jurors in those counties, and thousands of taxpayer dollars in those counties." When, as in this case, a trial court improperly applied the venue statute and issued a ruling that permits a plaintiff to abuse the legal system by refiling his case in county after county, which would inevitably result in considerable expense to taxpayers and defendants, requiring defendants to proceed to trial in the wrong county is not an adequate remedy. *See Prudential,* 148 S.W.3d at 137. "[A]n appellate remedy is not inadequate merely because it may involve more expense or delay than obtaining an extraordinary writ," *Walker,* 827 S.W.2d at 842, but extraordinary relief can be warranted when a trial court subjects taxpayers, defendants, and all of the state's district courts to meaningless proceedings and trials. *See Prudential,* 148 S.W.3d at 137.

We have granted mandamus relief in the context of Rule 87 venue rulings where, as here, the trial court made no effort to follow the rule. In this case, the Creekmores defied the Harris County trial court's venue order by attempting to have another court revisit the question of venue, which had already been decided. To say that the Fort Bend County trial court, which violated statutory venue procedure and Rule 87(5), committed reversible error while declining to correct the injustice would compromise the integrity of the venue statute and result in an irreversible waste of resources. We hold that Team Rocket has no adequate appellate remedy.

III

For the reasons described above, we conditionally grant the writ of mandamus directing the Fort Bend County trial court to vacate its venue order and transfer the Creekmores' case to Williamson County. If the court fails to do so, the writ will issue.

JUSTICE WAINWRIGHT filed a concurring opinion, in which CHIEF JUSTICE JEFFERSON and JUSTICE O'NEILL joined. JUSTICE WAINWRIGHT, concurring, joined by CHIEF JUSTICE JEFFERSON and JUSTICE O'NEILL.

For the reasons expressed in my dissent in *In re McAllen Medical Center,* --- S.W.3d ----, ---- (Tex. 2008), I respectfully disagree with the Court's expansion of its mandamus jurisdiction beyond established legal tenets. Because the Court has indeed crossed that bridge, I reluctantly join the Court's opinion.

Notes & Questions

1. *General prohibition of interlocutory review.* Because CPRC 15.064(a) generally prohibits interlocutory review of venue decisions, appellate courts usually denied mandamus when parties sought to correct venue errors by mandamus.[1] In fact, mandamus was denied in one case that was strikingly similar to the *Team Rocket* case.[2] But it now appears that courts are to treat mandamus in venue the same as any other mandamus.[3] What is left of the venue statute's prohibition of interlocutory review? When should parties losing venue motions seek mandamus relief?

2. *Exceptions to prohibition of interlocutory review.* Despite the general prohibition discussed above, the 2003 amendments to the venue statute provided for interlocutory review in two specific situations: (1) an interlocutory appeal for joinder of multiple plaintiffs, discussed in the next sec-

1 *See* Polaris Inv. Mgmt. Corp. v. Abascal, 892 S.W.2d 860 (Tex. 1995)(refusing to consider venue errors by mandamus).

2 *See* Tenneco v. Salyer, 739 S.W.2d 448 (Tex.App.—Corpus Christi 1987, orig. proceeding).

3 *See also* In re Masonite, 997 S.W.2d 194 (Tex. 1999).

tion; and (2) mandamus to enforce mandatory venue, under CPRC 15.0642. The Supreme Court held that because of the "near impossibility of showing that appeal is inadequate to remedy an erroneous venue decision" due to the "no harmless error rule," the adequacy of an appellate remedy is not a prerequisite of this mandamus.[4]

---

6. *Statutory Interlocutory Appeal—Joinder*

SURGITEK, BRISTOL-MEYERS SQUIBB CO.
v.
ABEL
997 S.W.2d 598
(Tex. 1999)

JUSTICE ENOCH delivered the opinion for a unanimous court.

This case presents several issues concerning section 15.003 of the Texas Civil Practice and Remedies Code. Section 15.003 limits when a plaintiff may join an action in a venue that would otherwise be improper for that plaintiff. Here, 104 plaintiffs who could not independently establish venue in Bexar County attempted to join two plaintiffs in a Bexar County action against makers of silicone-gel breast implants. Concluding that the 104 plaintiffs were improperly joined, the trial court granted the defendants' motion to transfer venue of those plaintiffs' claims. A divided court of appeals reversed, with one justice concurring and one justice dissenting. We conclude that: (1) the court of appeals had jurisdiction to hear the appeal; (2) a trial court may limit the scope of evidence on its section 15.003(a) joinder determination to pleadings and affidavits, but it has discretion to consider a broader range of evidence, including live testimony; (3) appellate courts should conduct a de novo review of the propriety of a trial court's section 15.003 joinder decision; and (4) the plaintiffs here did not establish an "essential need" to have their claims tried in Bexar County. Consequently, we reverse the court of appeals' judgment and reinstate the trial court's venue transfer order.

BACKGROUND

One-hundred-six plaintiffs sued Surgitek, Bristol-Myers Squibb Co., and Medical Engineering Corp. (Surgitek) for injuries they allegedly sustained from defective breast implants. Surgitek moved to transfer venue of 104 of these plaintiffs' claims, asserting that none could establish proper venue in Bexar County and that none could establish that they were entitled to join the Bexar County suit under section 15.003.

Section 15.003(a) provides:

> In a suit where more than one plaintiff is joined each plaintiff must, independently of any other plaintiff, establish proper venue. Any person who is unable to establish proper venue may not join or maintain venue for a suit as a plaintiff unless the person, independently of any other plaintiff, establishes that:
>
> (1) joinder or intervention in the suit is proper under the Texas Rules of Civil Procedure;

---

[4] *In re* Missouri Pacific Railroad Co. 998 S.W.2d 212(Tex. 1999).

(2) maintaining venue in the county of suit does not unfairly prejudice another party to the suit;
(3) there is an essential need to have the person's claim tried in the county in which the suit is pending; and
(4) the county in which the suit is pending is a fair and convenient venue for the person seeking to join in or maintain venue for the suit and the persons against whom the suit is brought.

The trial court agreed with Surgitek that 104 plaintiffs did not establish that their joinder in the Bexar County suit was proper. The trial court transferred venue of 103 of these plaintiffs to Dallas County, Surgitek's principal place of business in Texas, and one plaintiff to Tarrant County, that plaintiff's residence. (While this action was pending in this Court, 45 plaintiffs, including the Tarrant County plaintiff, have, through settlement or nonsuit, ceased being parties to this appeal. Fifty-nine plaintiffs remain, and our opinion and judgment apply only to those parties.)

The plaintiffs appealed the trial court's order to the court of appeals, which, after determining that it had jurisdiction to hear the appeal, reversed and remanded.

* * *

BURDEN OF PROOF

The parties disagree about which party has the burden of proof, and the nature of that burden, under section 15.003(a). The court of appeals concluded that the Legislature, in enacting section 15.003(a), did not intend to alter pre-existing statutory standards for venue hearings and proof. Thus, it stated that in a section 15.003(a) determination, a trial court is to look only to the pleadings and affidavits, and not to any other proof, such as live testimony. And it determined that the trial court should consider only whether the plaintiff presented prima facie proof that joinder under section 15.003(a) is appropriate; if so, the plaintiff has established her right to join. We disagree that a trial court is so limited in conducting a section 15.003(a) hearing and determination.

The fact that section 15.003(a) appears in the venue chapter of the Civil Practice and Remedies Code informs but does not control what type of hearing or standard of proof governs a section 15.003(a) joinder determination. Ultimately, we resolve the issue of what quantum-of-proof and nature-of-proof standards are established by section 15.003(a) not just by looking at where it was placed in the Civil Practice and Remedies Code, but also by considering legislative intent as reflected in its plain language.

Section 15.003(a) takes as its starting point a "person who is unable to establish proper venue." Thus, before the trial court even reaches the joinder elements, it first has to determine whether a plaintiff can independently establish proper venue. This determination, of course, is made using venue proof standards—if the plaintiff offers prima facie proof through pleadings and affidavits that venue is proper, the inquiry is over.

But when a plaintiff cannot establish proper venue, section 15.003(a) expressly places the burden on the plaintiff to "establish" four elements before she can join venue for the suit. The plaintiffs urge that we construe this requirement to mean only that they must offer the same quantum of prima facie proof required to establish venue. Surgitek argues that the plaintiffs must prove the four elements by a preponderance of the evidence, and that the trial court should conduct a full evidentiary hearing as it would in a normal joinder matter.

We conclude that the plain language of section 15.003(a) places the burden on the plaintiff in the first instance to offer prima facie proof of the four elements, but that it contemplates the admission, in some instances, of a broader range of evidence than would be admissible in a venue hearing. The Legislature used the same word—establish—in section 15.003(a) to describe both venue proof ("Any person who is unable to *establish* proper venue . . . ") and joinder proof (" . . . unless the person . . . *establishes* [the four elements.]"). Because a plaintiff need only offer prima facie proof to "establish" venue, it follows that, at least initially, a plaintiff must offer prima facie proof of each joinder element. And if the defendant offers no rebuttal evidence, the inquiry is over.

But Surgitek is correct that the four elements a plaintiff must establish under section 15.003(a) do not lend themselves readily to the prima facie standard applied in venue hearings. The usual types of prima facie proof in a venue determination—pleadings and affidavits establishing places of residence, principal offices, and even where the cause of action accrued—are usually objective enough that pleadings and affidavits can fairly be said to enable the trial court to correctly decide the issue. But the section 15.003(a) elements—joinder under the Texas Rules of Civil Procedure, unfair prejudice, essential need, and fairness and convenience—are relatively subjective and not as readily susceptible to proof by affidavit or pleading. Thus, the defendant must be afforded the opportunity to rebut the plaintiff's prima facie proof.

Accordingly, we conclude that the trial court has discretion to allow a broader range of proof in making a section 15.003(a) joinder determination than it would in a venue hearing. Specifically, a trial court may allow the parties to offer testimony, if the trial court believes it would be useful to its determination. Moreover, a trial court may order limited discovery on the joinder elements, affording the parties the opportunity to more fully develop evidence on the issues raised. To the extent that a defendant's joinder evidence rebuts the plaintiff's prima facie proof on any of the joinder elements, a trial court has discretion to consider all available evidence to resolve any disputes that the parties' proof creates. A trial court's decision to limit the scope of evidence is an abuse of discretion only if a party is materially prejudiced by its inability to offer further proof.

SCOPE AND STANDARD OF REVIEW

The court of appeals expressly limited its review in this case to the affidavits and pleadings. Its decision to do so logically followed from its conclusion that under section 15.003(a) a trial court could only consider affidavits and pleadings. But just as that determination was error, so too was the standard of review the court of appeals employed.

Section 15.003(c)(1) describes the proper standard for the court of appeals to apply:

> The court of appeals shall . . . determine whether the joinder or intervention is proper based on an independent determination from the record, and not under either an abuse of discretion or substantial evidence standard.

Construing this language, as we must, by its plain meaning, we conclude that a court of appeals should conduct a de novo review of the entire record to determine whether a trial court's section 15.003(a) joinder determination was proper. The phrase "independent determination," coupled with the admonition not to conduct an abuse of discretion or a substantial evidence review, suggests that the court of appeals should make its own determination of the propriety of joinder under section 15.003(a), with no deference to the trial court's ruling. Thus, its review of the merits of the joinder determination should be de novo. And the phrase "from the record" indicates that the court of appeals is not constrained solely to review the pleadings and affidavits, but should consider the entire record, including any evidence presented at the hearing.

On the other hand, the court of appeals should employ an abuse of discretion standard to review a party's contention that it was improperly denied the opportunity to present further proof. While the plain language of section 15.003(c)(1) prevents a court of appeals from using an abuse of discretion standard when reviewing the propriety of a trial court's section 15.003(a) joinder determination, nothing in section 15.003(c)(1) precludes employment of that standard for reviewing the trial court's decision to limit the scope of evidence.

ANALYSIS

With the proper burden of proof and scope and standard of review in mind, we turn now to the record in this case.

The evidence plaintiffs offered to establish their right to join the Bexar County litigation consisted of affidavits from the two plaintiffs who could independently establish venue in Bexar County, pleadings Surgitek filed in the multi-district federal breast implant litigation, an affidavit from the plaintiffs' counsel, and Surgitek's witness designations. The plaintiffs offered Surgitek's MDL pleadings as evidence that in another proceeding Surgitek took the position that some common questions of fact and law exist across breast implant cases, thus showing that joinder was proper under Rule 40 of the Texas Rules of Civil Procedure. Plaintiffs' counsel's affidavit reiterated the commonality of fact questions, and further stated that Surgitek designated the same expert witnesses in each case. Finally, the plaintiffs offered Surgitek's witness list to demonstrate that these witnesses were located all over the country, thus showing that no matter where the cases are tried the witnesses will have to travel.

The court of appeals held that this evidence was sufficient to satisfy all four section 15.003(a) elements for joinder. We disagree.

Section 15.003(a)(3) requires the plaintiff to establish that "there is an essential need to have the person's claim tried in the county in which the suit is pending." The court of appeals held that the plaintiffs established their "essential need" to try their claims against Surgitek in Bexar County "by proving the need to pool resources against common experts and issues." But that is not enough. The trial court's order in this case kept all of the remaining plaintiffs together in a single action, thereby allowing them to pool resources. Thus, if the need to pool resources were dispositive, the plaintiffs could have no complaint.

We agree with Surgitek that the "essential need" element requires each plaintiff seeking joinder to demonstrate that there is an "essential need" for her claim *to be tried in Bexar County*. The plain language of section 15.003(a)(3) compels this result: "[the person seeking joinder must establish that] there is an essential need to have the person's claim tried *in the county in which the suit is pending*." Citing a legal dictionary definition of "essential," Surgitek argues that an "essential need" is one that is "indispensably necessary." Another dictionary likewise defines "essential" as "necessary, such that one cannot do without it." We recognize that this burden is very high, but the language of the statute makes it so. Here, the plaintiffs did not establish that it was "indispensably necessary" to try their claims in Bexar County. Because we conclude that the plaintiffs failed to establish this joinder element, we need not consider whether they established the other three.

Accordingly, we reverse the court of appeals' judgment and reinstate the trial court's order transferring venue of the 59 remaining plaintiffs' claims to Dallas County.

Notes & Questions

1. *What is "essential need"?* Only one opinion has found "essential need" to exist. In *Teco-Westinghouse Motor Co. v. Gonzalez,*[1] the Corpus Christi Court of Appeals found that the evidence established an essential need to try the case in Cameron County because the testimony of an indispensable witness was only available in Cameron County. The witness had filed an affidavit saying that he resided in Cameron County and worked in Monterrey, Mexico, and the demands of his job "do not allow for travel to Travis or Williamson County" to testify.

2. *2003 amendments to § 15.003.* The 2003 amendments to § 15.003 made clear that interlocutory appeal is available to review a trial court's determination that "a plaintiff did or did not independently establish proper venue" or "a plaintiff that did or did not establish proper venue did or did not establish the items prescribed by Subsections (a)(1)-(4)." This amendment effectively overruled the Supreme Court's opinion in *American Home Products Corp. v. Clark,*[2] which held that the statute did not give interlocutory appeal jurisdiction over the trial courts initial determination of whether the additional plaintiffs could independently establish proper venue. Interlocutory review was available only for issues concerning proper joinder of additional plaintiffs who could *not* independently establish venue. Concurring and dissenting opinions in *American Home Products* asked for legislative action because the statute prevented the appellate court from stopping what these justices perceived as blatant forum shopping. The trial court found that all plaintiffs in the phen-fen case independently established venue in Johnson County because all alleged negligent representation by the doctor who resided in Johnson County. However, only one of eleven plaintiffs was alleged to be treated by that doctor. Because the trial judge allowed joinder because all plaintiffs independently established proper venue in Johnson County, interlocutory appeal was not available.

---

1 54 S.W.3d 910, 917 (Tex. App.—Corpus Christi 2001, no pet.).

2 38 S.W.3d 92 (Tex. 2000).

D. Motions to Change Venue Because of Unfair Forum

Read Rules 257-259.

Rules 257 through 259 concern a venue motion based on the impossibility of obtaining a fair trial in the forum, a concept that is far different from the traditional concept of statutory venue. The procedure for these motions is also far different from that contemplated for statutory venue, perhaps necessarily so. These rules have remained virtually unchanged since they were adopted in 1941.

Under Rule 257, the motion claiming an unfair forum must be supported by the movant's own affidavit and by affidavits of at least three credible residents of the county. If the opponent fails to controvert such affidavits, the trial court must transfer the case. If the affidavits are controverted by a credible person, the judge must address the question of whether a fair and impartial trial can actually be held in the county. One unresolved issue is what kind of hearing to hold.

UNION CARBIDE CORP.
v.
MOYE

798 S.W.2d 792
(Tex. 1990)

SPEARS, JUSTICE.

This mandamus proceeding arises out of a suit in which over two thousand plaintiffs are alleging harm from exposure to toxic chemicals around the Lone Star Steel plant in Morris County. Relators here are Union Carbide Corporation and most of the four hundred defendants in the underlying suit (hereinafter referred to as Union Carbide). Union Carbide filed in the trial court a motion to transfer venue on the ground that an impartial trial could not be had in Morris County. *See* TEX. R. CIV. P. 257. The trial judge conducted a hearing based on a written record only and refused to allow live testimony. The trial judge overruled the motion to transfer venue.

Union Carbide contends that, under TEX. R. CIV. P. 258, it was entitled to a full evidentiary hearing with the presentation of live testimony in support of its motion to transfer venue. Alternatively, Union Carbide contends it was entitled to a continuance in order to better prepare for the written submission of its venue motion. We address only the second contention.

After the motion to transfer venue was filed in September 1988, the parties engaged in discovery relevant to the motion. Interrogatories were sent to the plaintiffs in order to identify their relatives in Morris County. Depositions of corporate representatives were noticed. Expert witnesses were designated and deposed.

On January 13, 1989, the trial court handed down an order reciting the parties' agreement "regarding the designation of expert witnesses and persons having knowledge of relevant facts *to be called to testify at the venue hearing* . . . ." (emphasis added). The order further stated that it applied "only to potential witnesses *who may testify at the hearing* on Defendants' Motion to Transfer Venue . . . ." The record also reflects that, when the trial judge was scheduling the venue hearing, he stated his expectation that the hearing might last as long as eight weeks. All of the above circumstances led Union Carbide to believe that the court would conduct an evidentiary hearing at which witnesses would be allowed to testify.

On the day the venue hearing was scheduled to begin, plaintiffs filed a motion opposing oral testimony. After allowing Union Carbide less than twenty-four hours to respond, the trial court sustained the plaintiffs' motion and ruled that no oral testimony would be permitted at the venue hearing.

Union Carbide was taken by surprise. Because it had anticipated an eight-week venue hearing, Union Carbide had not arranged to have all of its evidence immediately available at the start of the hearing. Many of the witnesses Union Carbide had expected to call were not in Morris County at that time. Numerous deposition transcripts were not yet available. And, because the trial court had previously extended plaintiffs' deadline for responding to interrogatories to a date after the hearing would be concluded, the defendants had intended to call certain plaintiffs as live witnesses. Thus, Union Carbide had made preparations to assemble its proof in format for a lengthy evidentiary hearing, and its plans were effectively blocked by the trial court's sudden change.

Union Carbide moved for a continuance and requested additional time in order to supplement the record with more affidavits and discovery products. The trial judge denied the continuance and instructed Union Carbide to "present what you have now." Thus, Union Carbide was left unprepared and was unable to present for consideration numerous affidavits and depositions that it might otherwise have had ready.

Given these circumstances, we conclude that the trial court abused its discretion in denying a continuance. TEX. R. CIV. P. 258 provides that "reasonable discovery" in support of a motion to change venue "shall be permitted" and expressly provides that deposition testimony and other discovery products may be attached to affidavits on the motion. Since the trial court ruled before most of Union Carbide's discovery products were even available, it effectively denied Union Carbide this right to reasonable discovery set forth in Rule 258.[1] Moreover, because the trial court implicated itself in misleading Union Carbide as to the format for proof, we conclude that the court effectively deprived Union Carbide of its fundamental due process right to notice and a hearing. Having been misled as to the form of proof that would be acceptable, Union Carbide was placed in the untenable position of being allowed to attend the hearing without being able to submit its proof. Union Carbide cannot be penalized for relying on the court's own order as to the form of proof that would be acceptable. Justice requires that Union Carbide be afforded a reasonable opportunity to supplement the venue record with appropriate affidavits and discovery products prior to the trial court's ruling on the venue motion.

We conditionally grant the writ of mandamus. The trial judge must vacate his order overruling defendants' motion to change venue and, prior to ruling on the venue motion, must permit a reasonable period of time for supplementation of the record. The writ will issue only if the trial judge fails to act in accordance with this opinion.

---

[1] While it is clear that TEX. R. CIV. P. 258 requires a trial judge to allow deposition testimony, we do not at this time address the question of whether or in what circumstances Rule 258 also requires that a trial judge allow live testimony on an application to transfer venue.

HECHT, JUSTICE, concurring.

I join the Court in holding that the trial court clearly abused its discretion by denying relators a fair opportunity to present written evidence—affidavits, depositions and discovery responses—on their motion to transfer venue of the underlying litigation on the ground that an impartial trial cannot be had in Morris County. Thus, I agree that the trial court must vacate its order denying relators' motion and must afford them a reasonable opportunity to present evidence in support of their motion. On this score the Court is unanimous.

Whether the trial court can, should or must hear live testimony in connection with relators' motion remains unclear. The Court says only: "While it is clear that TEX. R. CIV. P 258 requires a trial judge to allow deposition testimony [on a motion made under rule 257], we do not at this time address the question of whether or in what circumstances Rule 258 also *requires* that a trial judge allow live testimony on [such motion]. Significantly, the Court expresses no similar reservation regarding the trial court's *power* to hear live testimony, as distinguished from its *duty* to do so. Nor does the Court respond to JUSTICE GONZALEZ' compelling arguments for allowing the trial court to hear live testimony in at least some cases. On these issues, which have been fully briefed and argued and are ripe for decision, the Court sends the participants away in the same uncertainty in which they came to us, leaving them to read between the lines.

I agree with JUSTICE GONZALEZ that the trial court is authorized and even obliged by rule 258 to hear live testimony when it is necessary to resolve issues that cannot be determined on a written record. A witness' credibility, for example, may be an important consideration in deciding a motion under rule 257 that is difficult to ascertain from affidavits or transcribed deposition testimony. Other issues, however, may readily be resolved upon written evidence. Again as an example, the strengths and weaknesses of surveys or demographic data, often evidence material to the possibility of an impartial trial in the forum, are sometimes, although not always, of course, apparent from entirely written evidence. I do not agree with JUSTICE GONZALEZ, therefore, that live testimony is necessary whenever the availability of an impartial trial in the forum is disputed. I would hold that under 258 a trial court may hear live testimony and must do so if, but only if, the issues cannot fairly be tried on a written record.

In my view, proceedings under rule 258 are similar to those under rule 120a as amended this year. Rule 120a permits affidavits and the results of discovery processes to be considered in determining a special appearance. The rule also allows the trial court to consider oral testimony, particularly when it appears from the affidavits filed that the facts cannot fairly be presented otherwise. This procedure offers reasonable flexibility in resolving preliminary issues like personal jurisdiction and the availability of an impartial trial while assuring a full and fair presentation of the facts. Its viability depends, however, upon the wise exercise of discretion by the trial court.

This is the procedure the rules prescribed for determining relators' motion to change venue based upon their claim that they cannot receive an impartial trial in Morris County, and the Court says nothing to the contrary. The trial court as well as the parties apparently considered at one point that live testimony would be appropriate on relators' motion and prepared for such a hearing. Nothing in the record indicates that the trial court ever reconsidered the appropriateness of hearing live testimony. The trial court's eventual refusal to hear live testimony appears to have been based upon its view that live testimony was not allowed under rule 258. The Court today does not endorse that construction of rule 258. Accordingly, the trial court should feel free to hear live testimony on relators' motion if necessary to resolve the issues raised. At the same time the trial court should not feel constrained to hear oral testimony on issues which can be decided on the written evidence offered. It is not our prerogative to specify the issues on which oral testimony should be offered, or to set time limits for the hearing. These matters are committed to the sound discretion of the trial court in conducting a fair trial of the issues raised. I am compelled to add, however, that I see no justification for a hearing on relators' motion that would take more than a small fraction of the six or eight weeks once planned for it.

I therefore concur in the Court's opinion as far as it goes, and in its judgment.

GONZALEZ, JUSTICE, concurring.

I concur with the court that the trial judge abused his discretion in not allowing relators an opportunity to supplement the record. I am more concerned, however, with the trial judge's refusal to conduct a hearing with live testimony. The court today does not prohibit the trial court from hearing live testimony on relators' motion; rather it chooses not to reach the issue. I would hold that when there is a controversy over whether an impartial trial can be had in the county where the action is pending, the parties have a right to an oral hearing under rule 258 of the TEX. R. CIV. P.

This mandamus proceeding is ancillary to over two thousand personal injury and wrongful death claims pending in Morris County, Texas. The plaintiffs allege that they were injured by exposure to a "toxic mushroom cloud" around the Lone Star Steel plant in Morris County. Plaintiffs claim that each of the four hundred defendants at some time manufactured or sold a product or provided a service at the Lone Star plant and that these products or services contributed to the toxic environment in and around the plant. Approximately thirty per cent of the 2,061 plaintiffs reside in Morris County.

The defendants moved for a change of venue on the grounds that they could not receive a fair and impartial trial in Morris County. TEX. R. CIV. P. 257(c). The defendants sought to show that there are fewer than 6,000 citizens of the county qualified for jury duty and that the vast majority of potential jurors are plaintiffs, relatives of plaintiffs, or employees of Lone Star Steel. The defendants also asserted that the litigation was widely known among the county's citizens and that a significant number of citizens had formed fixed opinions about the merits of the case. Further, Lone Star Steel's recent layoffs of most of the work force allegedly generated strong local resentment towards Lone Star Steel and anyone connected with it. Finally, a proposed hazardous waste incinerator to be located in Morris County and owned by a sister company of Lone Star Steel allegedly created "near-hysteria" over environmental matters.

The defendants supported their motion for change of venue with affidavits as required by rule 258 of the TEX. R. CIV. P. The plaintiffs attacked the motion by controverting affidavits, thus forming an issue to be "tried" by the judge under rule 258.

The preparations for the venue hearing reasonably led defendants to believe that there would be an oral hearing with live testimony on the venue motion. Plaintiffs allegedly fostered this impression, stipulating to an order setting deadlines for designating witnesses. The trial judge set aside six to eight weeks for the hearing. A January 13, 1989 order recited the parties' agreement "regarding the designation of expert witnesses and persons having knowledge of relevant facts to be called to testify at the venue hearing," stating that the order applied "only to potential witnesses who may testify at the hearing on Defendant's Motion to Transfer Venue." Because the courtroom was not big enough to accommodate all of the parties and their counsel, arrangements were made to conduct the hearing in the local high school auditorium.

On the day the hearing was to begin, as defendants sought to call their first witness, plaintiffs filed a "Motion Opposing Introduction of Oral Testimony at the Hearing." Plaintiffs argued that the 1983 revisions to TEX. REV. CIV. STAT. art. 1995 (now recodified at TEX. CIV. PRAC. & REM. CODE §§ 15.063 and 15.064) were meant to do away with evidentiary hearings not only for "conventional venue" but for all types of venue issues. Plaintiffs' last minute motion was the first mention of any opposition to live testimony at the hearing. The trial judge allowed defendants less than 24 hours to respond, and then granted the motion.

Defendants claim that they were ambushed by this tactic. All along the plaintiffs and the trial judge led them to believe that there would be an opportunity to present evidence by live testimony at an oral hearing, and the defendants prepared accordingly. Defendants were not prepared to submit their evidence to the court on a paper record. Because the hearing was expected to be lengthy, some of the witnesses had yet to arrive. Defendants also lacked several deposition transcripts, but had expected to receive these before the hearing concluded. Defendants assert that they lacked relevant discovery responses from plaintiffs, which, as a result of the trial court's extension of time, were not due until after the scheduled end of the hearing. Defendants state that they had planned to overcome this situation by calling several plaintiffs as witnesses.

After the trial judge refused to allow oral testimony, the defendants requested a continuance so that they could supplement the record. The trial judge denied the continuance, and ordered defendants to proceed with what they had. While the judge indicated that he would take defendants' request to supplement the record under advisement, he concluded the hearing without allowing supplementation. The judge eventually denied the motion to transfer without ruling on the request to supplement the record, and in a written order recited that he had considered only the "affidavits filed by each party prior to the hearing on May 17, 1989."

The plaintiffs based their opposition to the oral hearing on section 15.064(a) of the Texas Civil Practice and Remedies Code, which provides:

> In all venue hearings, no factual proof concerning the *merits of the case* shall be required to establish venue. The court shall determine venue questions from the pleading and affidavits. No interlocutory appeal shall lie from the determination.

(Emphasis added.) This section of the Practice and Remedies Code was enacted as part of the comprehensive reform of venue practice in 1983. Reading the venue statutes as a whole, in light of the historical distinction between ordinary venue determinations and transfer for local prejudice, I am convinced that section 15.064 was never intended to supplant practice under TEX. R. CIV. P 257.

In 1941, the only statute dealing with transfer for local prejudice was repealed by the promulgation of rule 257 of the Texas Rules of Civil Procedure. Thereafter, transfer for prejudice was governed by rule, while establishing proper venue was determined by statute, principally TEX. REV. CIV. STAT. art. 1995 (repealed 1985).

In former "plea of privilege" practice under article 1995, whenever venue was put in issue, the parties were entitled to a hearing resembling a full trial, including the right to a jury. As a result, the merits of the case were often tried twice, once to establish venue and again on the trial on the merits. A party dissatisfied with the venue ruling had the right to an interlocutory appeal. The inefficiency of dual trials and appeals caused wide-spread criticism and was one of the principle reasons for the reforms found in the 1983 changes.

Nothing in the scant legislative history of section 15.064 indicates that it is to apply to venue determinations under rule 257. The venue statutes do not purport to set forth the exclusive circumstances which would entitle a transfer for lack of a fair and impartial forum.[7] The vice that the legislature intended to correct—dual trials on the merits of the case—is no way implicated when the only issue to be tried in the venue hearing is the availability of an impartial forum. The silence from the legislature on this subject should not be viewed as an oversight. Rather, it is consistent with the historical treatment of ordinary venue determinations and transfer of venue for local prejudice as entirely different concepts.

The venue statutes address the question present in every case, which is to determine where the case can best be tried, balancing the interests of all the parties. These interests are largely a matter of the convenience of the parties. The issue in a motion to transfer pursuant to rule 257 based on alleged prejudice in the county where the suit is pending is one of fundamental fairness and integrity of the judicial process. Its resolution has implications far beyond the particular controversy in question.

In an ordinary venue hearing, the plaintiff's pleading of venue facts are taken as true unless specifically denied. If challenged, the plaintiff must make prima facie proof of the facts denied. The cause must remain in the county of suit once the plaintiff has met the burden of proper pleading and prima facie proof, "unless the motion to transfer is based on the grounds that an impartial trial cannot be had in the county were the action is pending as provided in rules 257-259," or cases of mandatory venue. TEX. R. CIV. P. 87(3)(c).

TEXAS RULE OF CIVIL PROCEDURE 258 provides that the movant may file affidavits to show local bias or similar grounds for transfer, and if uncontroverted the motion must be granted. If the motion is controverted "the issue thus formed shall be *tried* by the judge." *Id.* (emphasis added). Certainly the "trial" contemplated by the rule must be more than another round of affidavits.

In a determination of statutory venue, the parties are not deprived of all opportunity to develop venue facts in open court. In statutory venue the issue is whether the facts of the cause of action fit the fact situations described by statute. To a very large extent there is an overlap of the facts necessary to establish venue and the merits of the case. *Id.* The facts that come out during the trial on the merits will be considered in reviewing venue on appeal. TEX. CIV. PRAC. & REM. CODE § 15.064(b). Thus there is some opportunity to show statutory venue facts in open court. The facts to support a motion under Rule 257, however, will rarely, if ever, be further developed at the trial on the merits.

The facts in a statutory venue hearing are relatively objective. On the other hand, the existence of prejudice, favoritism and partiality so great that a fair trial cannot be had in the county where suit is pending is more subjective, with proof resting ultimately on opinion. Affidavits,

[7] The only reference in the statutes to change of venue for lack of an impartial trial is section 15.063, which provides:

> The court, on motion filed and served concurrently with or before the filing of the answer, shall transfer an action to another county of proper venue if:
>
> (1) the county in which the action is pending is not a proper county as provided by this chapter;
>
> (2) an impartial trial cannot be had in the county in which the action is pending; or
>
> (3) written consent of the parties to transfer to any other county is filed at any time.

TEX. CIV. PRAC. & REM. CODE § 15.063 (1986). If this statute is the exclusive source of authority for transferring venue for lack of an impartial forum, then prejudice which only manifests itself after an answer has been filed can never be grounds for transfer. I do not view this reference to a specific situation as indication of intent to supplant our rules and decisions on transfers for local prejudice with this provision of the Texas Civil Practice and Remedies Code.

depositions, and other documentary proof may shed some light on the scope of the alleged problem, but they are a poor substitute for an oral hearing. With an oral hearing, the trial judge can listen and observe the testimony of the witnesses in full view of the interested parties.

It is difficult, if not impossible, for the trial judge to evaluate the credibility of the witnesses and the weight to be given their testimony from reading the cold record. The importance of the issues at stake and the difficulty of adjudication by reading the record, require that the parties have the right to a hearing in open court. This procedure is not only superior to that advocated by the respondents but it is the procedure mandated by TEXAS RULE OF CIVIL PROCEDURE 258.

For these reasons, I concur that the trial judge must vacate the order overruling the defendants change of venue and I would order that he conduct an evidentiary hearing before ruling on the motion to transfer.

Notes & Questions

1. *Live testimony?* The question addressed by Justices Hecht and Gonzalez in their concurring opinions in *Union Carbide* remains unresolved. Prudent advocates will tender affidavits, authenticated discovery products, *and* live testimony, making an appropriate bill of exceptions for any trial court exclusion of evidence. But consider the opinion in *Surgitek* concerning venue joinder—might it provide some direction for unfair forum hearings? What about hearings when the defendant seeks a convenience and justice transfer?

2. *Waiver.* The venue statute[1] also seems to say that even a claim of unfair forum must be made in the defendant's first pleading (other than a Rule 120a special appearance which must be filed before a motion to transfer venue), or the venue right will be waived. This interpretation is suspect, however, because publicity adverse to a defendant can make a fair forum unfair *after* a defendant has answered, or can be discovered by the defendant after the answer is filed. It seems unlikely that a defendant will be held to have waived a venue claim which arises after the original answer is filed.[2] Moreover, Rule 86(1) seems to say that Rule 257 has its own time limits.

3. *Harmless error.* Does the no-harmless error provision of §15.064(b) apply to Rule 257 unfair forum motions to change venue? Probably not.[3] Of course, trial in an unfair forum invites constitutional attack under the due process clauses of both the Texas and United States Constitutions. Such an error is always harmful and reversible.

4. *Transfer.* Note that the defendant's "choice" of venues after transfer under Rule 257 is prescribed by the rule, giving preference to the same or adjoining districts (for district courts), and to adjoining counties (for county courts).[4] Rule 259(d)(2) also provides that if a motion to transfer on the grounds of unfair forum is granted, the parties may agree to the particular county to which venue will be transferred.

---

1 CPRC § 15.063.

2 *See* Lone Star Steel Co. v. Scott, 759 S.W.2d 144 (Tex. App.—Texarkana 1988, writ denied) (court considered motion to change venue for unfair forum filed after the defendant announced ready for trial).

3 *See id.* at 146 (the failure to grant an uncontroverted motion for change of venue was harmless).

4 *See* Rule 259.

CHAPTER 5. PLEADING

A. Pleadings Generally

Read Rules 45-50, 52-59.

Pleading is the art of composing the written instruments (the pleadings) that set forth the litigants' contentions in the litigation. In most lawsuits in Texas, a pleading known as an "Original Petition" initiates the litigation. Defendants respond to the petition with pleadings of their own, that can assert a variety of defensive matters, including a defensive pleading on the merits known as the "Answer."

Pleadings serve primarily to inform the court and the opponent about the facts and legal theories that are at issue in the lawsuit. The pleadings limit the evidence, the jury questions, and the discovery in the case. Thus, plaintiffs typically seek to have their pleadings interpreted broadly, while defendants typically seek a narrow interpretation of the plaintiff's pleadings in order to have the case dismissed.[1] If a case survives a motion to dismiss, defendants typically continue to seek a narrow construction of plaintiffs' pleadings to limit the scope of discovery, evidence, and jury questions.

1. *Plaintiffs' Pleadings*

Read Rules 78-82.

As mentioned above, the plaintiff's initial pleading, which commences the action, is called the "petition" in Texas practice.[2] In federal practice, it is called the "complaint."[3] Filing the petition with bona fide intent that process be issued and served institutes the action. It also tolls the statute of limitations, provided that the plaintiff exercises reasonable diligence in serving the defendant.[4]

The petition begins with the caption, which states the file number (filled in upon filing), the style ("Plaintiff's name vs. Defendant's name"), the county in which suit is filed and the name of the court.[5] The initial paragraphs state the names of the parties[6] and allegations necessary for service of process, personal jurisdiction and venue, along with discovery level for the case.[7] The petition then states the "cause of action" sufficient to give "fair notice" of the claim.[8]

---

1 *See* Rule 91a.

2 Rule 22.

3 FRCP 7(a).

4 *See, e.g.*, Rigo Manuf. Co. v. Thomas, 458 S.W.2d 180 (Tex. 1970). *See also* Flour Bluff I.S.D. v. Bass, 133 S.W.3d 272 (Tex. 2004) (concerning mis-identification of defendant in pleadings).

5 *E.g.*, 191st District Court of Dallas County. In counties with multiple courts, the clerk will assign the court at the same time the file number is assigned.

6 The Supreme Court has held that the inadvertent omission of the name of a party in an amended petition does not automatically operate as a nonsuit to the omitted party. American Petrofina, Inc. v. Allen, 887 S.W.2d 829, 831 (Tex. 1994).

7 *See, e.g.*, Rules 47, 79, 190.

8 Rule 47.

Fair notice is a relatively low pleading standard, enabling plaintiffs to put matters at issue with a plain statement of the wrong and relief sought. But the pleading landscape has changed in recent years. Indeed, Rule 91a allows defendants to dismiss cases on the pleadings where the causes of action alleged are "baseless."[9] The impact of Rule 91a on pleading practice is discussed in more detail later in the Chapter. Also, as this Chapter discusses in more depth below, Texas has long required heightened pleading for some matters, like special damages or an action for recision of a contract.

The Rules also require that pleadings contain certain other specific non-merits content, like signatures and certificates of service. The petition should also include a jury demand if the plaintiff wants a jury trial.[10]

2. *Defendants' Pleadings*

Read Rules 83-85, 92-95.

a. *Appearance*

When served with a citation, the defendant must appear before the court on or before the "appearance date" or risk judgment by default.[11] Therefore, the defendant's answer initially serves to enter an appearance on behalf of the defendant that entitles the defendant to notice of subsequent proceedings and prevents entry of a default judgment without notice.[12] The defendant must file a written answer by Monday at 10:00 am following the expiration of 20 days after the defendant was served with citation.[13]

Defendants should take care, however, that there are no non-merits (also known in Texas as "dilatory") matters to take up with the court before filing an answer. Certain dilatory pleas – e.g., a special appearance or motion to transfer venue – must be filed before or at the same time as the answer.[14] If a defendant answers first and tries to challenge personal jurisdiction or venue later, those matters are typically waived. Dilatory pleas, however, are not the subject of this Chapter and were taken up in depth in, e.g., Chapters 3 and 4. Still, it is good to be mindful of the rules governing the order of pleading to avoid waiving an important procedure or process defense.

b. *Denials*

One of the most important functions of the defendant's answer is the denial of the plaintiff's allegations of liability, putting the allegations at issue so that the plaintiff has to satisfy its burden of proof to prevail. A denial is simply a negation of the plaintiff's allegation—the defendant says that the allegation is not true, and thereby puts the plaintiff to its proof. In Texas, the defendant can deny all of the plaintiff's allegations by using a Rule 92 "general denial." As a practical matter, all answers in Texas state court should include a general denial. Although it is unlikely that

---

[9] Rule 91a.

[10] Rules 216, 217.

[11] *See* Rules 120, 237, 238, 239.

[12] *See* LBL Oil Co. v. International Power Services, Inc., 777 S.W.2d 390, 390-91 (Tex. 1989) (letter to court treated as appearance that entitled defendant to notice of subsequent hearings).

[13] *See* Rule 99(c), *see also* Rule 237.

[14] Rules 83, 86, 120a.

the defendant actually believes that every allegation in the petition is untrue, there is no ethical constraint that prevents a defendant from making a general denial.[15]

A general denial may not be sufficient, however, to put all of plaintiff's allegations in issue. Certain matters must be denied specifically, using what is called a "special denial." For example, the defendant must specifically deny the plaintiff's allegation that all conditions precedent have been satisfied in order to put the satisfaction of those conditions in issue.[16] Some special denials must be verified, pursuant to Rule 93.[17] If a defendant fails to specially deny matters that must be specially denied under the rules, the defendant will not be allowed to present evidence that contradicts the plaintiff's allegations on that issue.[18]

c. *Affirmative Defenses*

Rule 94 requires defendants to specifically plead all affirmative defenses upon which the defendant may rely. An affirmative defense is different from a denial. Instead of negating the plaintiff's allegations, the affirmative defense says, "Even if the plaintiff's allegations are true, I am not liable." The affirmative defense is a matter of "confession and avoidance." Many affirmative defenses are listed in Rule 94, but do not assume that it is a complete list.[19]

---

[15] *See* Rule 13, CPRC § 10.004(f). *Compare* FRCP 8(b)(3) (requiring defendants to admit or deny each allegation in plaintiff's complaint).

[16] *See* Rule 54.

[17] *See* Rule 93. A rule verified denial must be based on the affiant's personal knowledge. Cantu v. Holiday Inns, Inc., 910 S.W.2d 113 (Tex. App.—Corpus Christi 1995, writ denied). *See also* In re Dobbins, 247 S.W.3d 394, 397 (Tex. App.—Dallas 2008)(distinguishing a verification from an affidavit).

[18] *See* The Ray Malooly Trust v. Juhl, 186 S.W.3d 568 (Tex. 2006) (per curiam). *See also* Basic Capital Management, Inc. v. Dynex Commercial , Inc., 348 S.W.3d 894, 899 (Tex. 2011) (holding that verified denial of capacity was not needed where lack of standing was pleaded and no objection to lack of pleading was made at summary judgment where issue was clearly presented and acknowledging confusion in caselaw about whether a party is claiming standing or capacity). Another special denial rule is Rule 52 (verified denial of existence of a corporation).

[19] *See also,e.g.*, Rules 54, 95 (requiring special pleadings to deny that the plaintiff satisfied all conditions precedent or to assert a payment defense).

B. Pleading Standards

As the previous discussion mentioned, Texas courts generally require only fair notice of claims and defenses when pleading and do not require litigants to plead with heightened specificity. There are, however, exceptions to this rule and this Chapter discusses heightened pleading scenarios after a basic exploration of what it means to provide fair notice in a pleading.

1. *Fair Notice Standard*

PARAMOUNT PIPE & SUPPLY CO.
v.
MUHR
749 S.W.2d 491
(Tex. 1988)

KILGARLIN, JUSTICE.

These causes concern the validity of two default judgments. Paramount Pipe & Supply Co., Inc. and Winters Flexline Service Company are oil and gas field equipment suppliers. In separate lawsuits (consolidated for argument in our court), Paramount Pipe and Winters Flexline sued Western International Petroleum Corporation and Ulrich Muhr, seeking payment for materials and services furnished in connection with the drilling and operation of oil and gas wells. Paramount Pipe and Winters Flexline also sought foreclosure of mechanics' and materialmen's liens.

Neither Western International nor Ulrich Muhr filed an answer. The trial court rendered default judgments in both cases ($16,825.21 plus interest, and $4,000 attorney's fees for Paramount Pipe; $21,688.98 plus interest, and $7,000 attorney's fees for Winters Flexline). Ulrich Muhr appealed by writ of error. Western International did not seek relief from the default judgments. The court of appeals reversed and remanded for new trial Paramount Pipe's claims against Muhr on the basis that the pleadings failed to provide fair notice to Ulrich Muhr of the claims asserted. 737 S.W.2d 385. In a separate unpublished opinion, the court of appeals similarly reversed and remanded Winters Flexline's claims. We reverse the judgments of the court of appeals and affirm the judgments of the trial court.

Our initial inquiry is whether Ulrich Muhr had fair notice of the claims against him. Paragraph II of Paramount Pipe's original petition alleged that "[t]he cause of action asserted by Plaintiff arises from and is connected with purposeful acts committed by Defendant Western International Petroleum Corporation, acting for itself and as agent for Defendant Ulrich Muhr." Paragraph III alleged:

> Between the dates of October 29, 1985 and November 14, 1985 the Plaintiff, at the special instance and request of Defendant Western International Petroleum Corporation, performed services and provided materials to mineral leasehold properties situated in Callahan County, Texas, identified as the "Moon Lease", and described in EXHIBIT "A", attached hereto and incorporated herein by reference, and Defendant Western International Petroleum Corporation, acting for itself and for Defendant Ulrich Muhr, accepted such services and materials and became bound to pay the reasonable charges therefor. Defend-

ants' breach of said obligation to pay for such services and materials is the basis for the filing of Plaintiff's Sworn Statement of Lien and of Plaintiff's cause of action herein.

Paragraphs IV and V alleged full performance and presentment by Paramount Pipe. Paragraphs VII - X made the same allegations with respect to the Creswell Lease. Paragraph XI alleged:

> Plaintiff would further allege and show, independently of and alternatively to the matters contained hereinabove, that the Defendants are acting in concert to preclude Plaintiff from recovery herein for the sums due and owing to Plaintiff. Defendant Western International Petroleum Corporation has executed certain Assignments of Oil, Gas and Mineral Leases, which expressly cover the Moon and Creswell Leases, and which Assignments serve to transfer all of Western International Petroleum Corporation's rights in the leases to Ulrich Muhr, as security for a certain indebtedness owed to Ulrich Muhr. Plaintiff would allege that the Defendant, Ulrich Muhr, knew or reasonably should have known of the business activities of Defendant Western International Petroleum Corporation in connection with mineral development of the Moon and Creswell Leases, and that Western International Petroleum Corporation was acting as agent for and under the authority of Ulrich Muhr.

Paramount Pipe sought, among other forms of relief, a judgment against "Defendants, jointly and severally." Paramount Pipe attached invoices and lien statements to the petition, neither of which mentioned Ulrich Muhr.

Drafted by the same attorney, Winters Flexline's original petition used virtually identical language . . . .

* * *

In *Stoner v. Thompson*, 578 S.W.2d 679, 684-85 (Tex. 1979), we wrote that while a petition which serves as the basis for a default judgment may be subject to special exceptions, the default judgment will be held erroneous only if (1) the petition (or other pleading of the non-defaulting party that seeks affirmative relief) does not attempt to state a cause of action that is within the jurisdiction of the court, or (2) the petition (or pleading for affirmative relief) does not give fair notice to the defendant of the claim asserted, or (3) the petition affirmatively discloses the invalidity of such claim. Ulrich Muhr first argues that the second of the above conditions operates to render the instant default judgment erroneous: he submits that the pleadings did not provide fair notice of the claims asserted.

Rules 45 and 47 of the Texas Rules of Civil Procedure require that pleadings give fair notice of the claim asserted. Rule 45 mandates plain and concise language and provides that the fact "[t]hat an allegation be evidentiary or be of legal conclusion shall not be grounds for objection when fair notice to the opponent is given by the allegations as a whole." Rule 47 requires that an original pleading include "a short statement of the cause of action sufficient to give fair notice of the claim involved." The purpose of the fair notice requirement is to provide the opposing party with sufficient information to enable him to prepare a defense. *Roark v. Allen*, 633 S.W.2d 804, 810 (Tex. 1982).

Rule 45 does not require that the plaintiff set out in his pleadings the evidence upon which he relies to establish his asserted cause of action. In *Stoner*, we quoted 4 MCDONALD, TEXAS CIVIL PRACTICE § 17.23.3 at 120 (1971), as follows:

> The rules expressly countenance more general allegations than formerly were permitted, and the default judgment will stand if the plaintiff has alleged a claim upon which the substantive law will give relief, and has done so with sufficient particularity to give fair

> notice to the defendant of the basis of his complaint, even though he has stated some element or elements in the form of legal conclusions which will need to be revised if attacked by special exceptions.

Stoner, 578 S.W.2d at 683.

Edwards presented facts similar to those of our case. In *Edwards*, a feedmill sued, for feed sold, a father and son on a promissory note signed only by the son. The plaintiff alleged that the father and son were partners; the son executed the promissory note; demands were made upon the defendants; and the defendants refused to pay. The prayer was for judgment against both defendants.

In our cases, two oil and gas equipment suppliers sued Western International and Ulrich Muhr for materials and services accepted by Western International. The petitions alleged that Western International acted "for itself and as agent for" Muhr; Western International "acting for itself and for" Muhr accepted such materials and services; demand was made on Western International; and defendants refused to pay. The prayers were for judgments against both defendants.

In *Edwards*, we held that the pleadings provided fair notice. Similarly, we today hold that the original petitions at issue, each as a whole, provided fair notice to Ulrich Muhr of the claims asserted. While the petitions may have been subject to attack by special exceptions, they satisfy the fair notice requirement.

Ulrich Muhr also argues that the petitions affirmatively disclosed the invalidity of Paramount Pipe and Winters Flexline's claims. *See Stoner*, 578 S.W.2d at 685. Muhr appears to base this argument on the fact that the invoices attached to the petition do not specifically mention Muhr. *See Cecil v. Hydorn*, 725 S.W.2d 781 (Tex. App.—San Antonio 1987, no writ) (where attached agreement differed from the agreement described in the petition, exhibit governed and pleadings held not to support default judgment); *Hancock v. OK Rental Equipment Co.*, 441 S.W.2d 955 (Tex. Civ. App.—San Antonio 1969, no writ) (where attached invoices showed accounts due from business entity and not individual, and petition did not otherwise allege or disclose relationship between the two, petition as a whole held not to support default judgment). Unlike the above cases, however, the petitions in our cases allege a relationship: agency. The fact that the invoices do not specifically mention Muhr is not dispositive in his favor. Rather, in light of the agency allegations, the invoices actually support the cause of action stated in each petition. We find nothing in the petitions affirmatively disclosing invalidity of the claims alleged by Paramount Pipe and Winters Flexline against Muhr.

* * *

Muhr likewise alleges error in the trial court's award of attorney's fees to Paramount Pipe and Winters Flexline. Muhr relies on TEX. CIV. PRAC. & REM. CODE § 38.002 (Vernon 1986). He urges that neither Paramount Pipe nor Winters Flexline alleged proper presentation of their claims to Muhr nor his failure to tender the just amount owed before the expiration of the thirtieth day after such presentation. However, both petitions specifically alleged that:

> Plaintiff has provided Defendant Ulrich Muhr with notice, by certified mailings, of the Liens claimed by Plaintiff on the [aforementioned leases], and Defendant Ulrich Muhr has failed and refused to pay the sums lawfully due and owing to Plaintiff.

Both petitions also specifically prayed for recovery of attorney's fees. Certainly the omission to allege that Muhr failed to tender payment within thirty days would have been subject to attack by special exception. We conclude, however, that the petitions gave Muhr fair notice that Paramount

Pipe and Winters Flexline were seeking recovery of attorney's fees. We hold there was no error in the judgments awarding attorney's fees against Muhr.

* * *

We reverse the judgments of the court of appeals and affirm the judgments of the trial court.

Notes & Questions

1. *Pleading standards*. As you may have learned in first-year civil procedure, there are three basic types of pleading practice: "issue" pleading; "fact" pleading; and "notice" pleading. Historically, "issue pleading" required strict compliance with the pleading rules governing particular legal forms of action; "fact pleading," adopted early in Texas legal history, required a "full" statement of the facts that constituted the plaintiff's cause of action or the defendant's ground of defense. Both were extremely cumbersome, and the federal system eventually rejected them during the late 1930s in favor of "notice" pleading, the culmination of which can be seen in the Federal Rules of Civil Procedure.[1] Federal Rule 8 does not even contain the terms "fact" or "cause of action." Instead, it merely requires "a short and plain statement of the claim showing that the pleader is entitled to relief."[2] Notice pleadings are intended to do "little more than indicate generally the type of litigation involved. A generalized summary of the case that affords fair notice is all that is required."[3]

Three years after the adoption of the federal rules, the Supreme Court of Texas refused to adopt the notice pleading concept to the same degree as the Federal Rules of Civil Procedure. Although the Texas pleading rules "proceeded from the spirit of the federal rules," they require the parties to allege "in plain and concise language" a "cause of action" or "ground of defense."[4] Allegations of "facts" can be made generally (a "legal conclusion") or specifically ("evidentiary"), so long as "fair notice to the opponent is given by the allegations as a whole."[5] Further, the pleadings are to be construed so as to do "substantial justice."[6]

The historical difference between the two systems may be best explained through the peculiarities of the Texas jury charge. For many years Texas submitted "special issues" to the jury, in which the jury was asked questions that elicit findings on the controverted facts, and the court determined the legal consequences of those factual findings.[7] The plaintiff had the burden of obtaining jury findings on the facts that made up each element of the cause of action, and could get a

---

1 *See* FRCP 8.

2 FRCP 8(a).

3 MCDONALD, § 7.2 (citing Moore's Federal Practice 440 (1938)).

4 Stayton, *The Scope and Function of Pleading Under the New Federal and Texas Rules: A Comparison,* 20 TEX. L. REV. 16, 17 (1941). *See* Rule 45(b).

5 Rule 45(b). *See also* Rule 47(a) (requiring plaintiff to make a "short statement of the cause of action sufficient to give fair notice of the claim").

6 Rule 45(d).

7 Hodges & Guy, TEXAS PRACTICE: THE JURY CHARGE IN TEXAS CIVIL LITIGATION, § 1 at 2.

special issue submitted on a particular fact only if it were pleaded.[8] Through the years, the number of fact questions asked the jury proliferated, and more detailed pleadings were required to support the submission of those special issues. Therefore, the short and more general federal form of pleadings were not acceptable in Texas practice. In 1973, however, the Texas Rules of Civil Procedure were amended to promote the submission of broad-form jury questions.[9] Jury questions became broader and fewer, and now most jury questions ask ultimate mixed questions of law and fact rather than single issues of controverted fact. Therefore, as a practical matter, detailed pleadings of controverted facts are no longer needed to support the submission of these broad legal questions to the jury.[10] As a result, although the pleading rules have not changed, in *Paramount Pipe* the Texas Supreme Court clearly adopted notice pleading for Texas.[11] Ironically, federal courts are moving towards more detailed pleadings.[12] And, as discussed in more detail later in this Chapter, Texas courts are now grappling with what is a sufficient pleading in light of Rule 91a's dismissal procedures.[13]

2. *Pleading example*. Consider the following plaintiff's pleading that was included in Justice Cornyn's dissent to the Texas Supreme Court's in *Krishnan v. Sepulveda*.[14] Look at all parts of the petition. Do the pleadings give the defendant "fair notice"? What more might the defendant want to know about the claims the plaintiff is asserting? How does the defendant get that additional information?

---

[8] For example, the plaintiff may claim that the automobile collision was proximately caused by the defendant's negligence in driving at an unsafe rate of speed, in failing to maintain a proper lookout, and in failing to timely apply his brakes. Under pre-1973 practice, the petition would have to contain allegations of all three theories of negligence, and the jury charge required three separate "clusters" of questions for speed, lookout, and brakes, each including questions of negligence and proximate cause. Separate clusters would be submitted if there was evidence of the defendant's contributory negligence. *See* Sampson, J., *TDHS v. E.B., The Coup de Grace for Special Issues,* 23 ST. MARY'S L.J. 221, 224 (1991).

[9] *See* Rule 277 (requiring broad form submission whenever feasible).

[10] Under current practice, the plaintiff claiming that the collision was proximately caused by the defendant's negligence in driving at an unsafe speed, in failing to maintain a proper lookout, and in failing to timely apply his brakes might merely allege generally that the defendant's negligence proximately caused the accident, and generally describe the circumstances. The jury will be asked a single question: "Did the negligence, if any, of the persons named below proximately cause the occurrence in question?" *See* STATE BAR OF TEXAS, TEXAS PATTERN JURY CHARGE, PJC 4.01B (2008).

[11] The fair notice standard does have its limits, however. In a recent case, the Supreme Court dismissed a claim that was not specifically referenced by name in a pleading. First United Pentecostal Church of Beaumont v. Parker, 514 S.W.3d 214, 224-25 (Tex. 2017).

[12] *See, e.g.*, Bell Atlantic Corp. v. Twombly, 127 S.Ct. 1955 (2007).

[13] Rule 91a (providing for dismissal of causes of action with no basis in law or fact).

[14] 916 S.W.2d 478 (Tex. 1995).

APPENDIX

Humberto Sepulveda, Jr. and Olga Sepulveda
vs.
Dr. Elizabeth G. Krishnan
CAUSE NO. C-2424-82F
July 15, 1987
In the 332nd District Court of Hidalgo County, Texas

PLAINTIFFS' ORIGINAL PETITION

NOW COME Humberto Sepulveda, Jr., and his wife Olga Sepulveda, Plaintiffs, complaining of Dr. Elizabeth G. Krishnan, Defendant, and for cause of action would show:

1. Plaintiffs are residents of Hidalgo County, Texas. Defendant, Dr. Elizabeth G. Krishnan, is a resident of Hidalgo County, Texas, and may be served with citation at her office address of 1331 E. 6th Street, Weslaco, Texas.

2. Defendant Dr. Elizabeth G. Krishnan is a practicing physician in obstetrics and gynecology, holding herself out to the general public as qualified and competent to care for patients who require medical attention with all the necessary care and precaution expected of such physicians. At all times material, Plaintiff Olga Sepulveda was a patient of Defendant Dr. Krishnan.

3. Defendant Elizabeth G. Krishnan has been notified of Plaintiffs' health care liability claim at least sixty days prior to the filing of this lawsuit, and all conditions precedent required by Article 4590i, Section 4.01, Texas Revised Civil Statutes, have been met.

4. On or about August 6, 1985, Plaintiff Olga Sepulveda presented herself at Defendant's office for prenatal care and treatment, and for the delivery of her first child. During the course of her pregnancy, Plaintiff developed preeclampsia. Defendant Dr. Krishnan was negligent in that she failed to exercise the care of an ordinary prudent obstetrician by providing the necessary diagnosis, prenatal supervision, and prompt treatment of the Plaintiff's preeclampsia.

5. As a direct and proximate result of the Defendant's negligence, Plaintiffs' daughter, Patricia Sepulveda, died, and Plaintiffs have been caused to suffer severe mental pain, anguish, grief, and sorrow. Additionally, Plaintiffs have been caused to suffer the loss of society, companionship, and affection of their daughter, Patricia Sepulveda, deceased. Plaintiffs have also incurred expenses for funeral and burial for Patricia reasonably suitable to her station in life.

6. By reason of Article 4590i, Section 5.01, Texas Revised Civil Statute, Plaintiffs are precluded from pleading a specific amount of money claimed as damages. The Plaintiffs believe and allege that they have been damaged in a sum far in excess of the jurisdictional limits of this court.

WHEREFORE, Plaintiffs pray the Defendant be cited to appear and answer, that this case be tried before a jury, that upon final trial Plaintiffs recover judgment against the Defendant in a sum far in excess of the minimum jurisdictional limits of this court, prejudgment and post-judgment interest as allowed by law, that they recover costs of court, and for such other and further relief, both general and special, at law or in equity, to which they may be justly entitled.

Respectfully submitted,

EWERS, TOOTHAKER, ABBOTT, TALBOT & HAMILTON
P.O. Box 3670
McAllen, Texas 78502
(512) 686-3771
by: /s/ Stephen P. Dietz
Stephen P. Dietz
State Bar No. 05857300
Attorneys for Plaintiffs

PLAINTIFFS DEMAND A JURY TRIAL.

---

2. *Heightened Pleading*

Fair notice pleading is generally the default in Texas courts. But there are exceptions—some causes of action and remedies require heightened pleading. Likewise, certain damages should be pled specifically.

a. *Causes of action and remedies requiring specific pleading.* Certain causes of action and legal theories require heightened pleading. Take, for instance, defamation suits (suits that seek damages for an allegedly harmful, untrue statement). The Texas Citizens Participation Act (or "TCPA") is Texas's version of what are popularly known as "anti-SLAPP" statutes—laws aimed at curbing the abusive practice of filing a frivolous lawsuit to silence or punish one's critics. The TCPA tries to achieve that goal by allowing a defendant to seek early dismissal of and sanctions for a plaintiff's claim that is "based on, relates to, or is in response to [the defendant's] exercise of the right of free speech, the right to petition, or the right of association."[1] The defendant must file the motion to dismiss within sixty days of being served, and all discovery is immediately suspended until the motion is ruled on.[2] If the Defendant can show "by a preponderance of the evidence" that the statute applies to any of the plaintiff's claims, the court must dismiss those claims unless the plaintiff can establish "by clear and specific evidence a prima facie case for each essential element of the claim."[3] If the claim is dismissed, the court must award the defendant its attorney's fees incurred in bringing the motion.[4]

Although a stated purpose of TCPA is "to encourage and safeguard the constitutional rights of persons to petition, speak freely, associate freely, and otherwise participate in government," Texas courts have been dizzyingly applying the statute to a bevy of claims not traditionally thought of as efforts to restrain those constitutional rights.[5] As the Austin Court of Appeals has observed,

---

1 TEX. CIV. PRAC. & REM. CODE § 27.003(a).

2 *Id.* at § 27.003.

3 *Id.* at § 27.005.

4 *Id.* at § 27.009(a).

5 *Id.* at § 27.002; Cavin v. Abbott, 545 S.W.3d 47, 63-64 (Tex. App.—Austin 2017, pet. filed).

the Act "has been applied in cases for fraud and barratry, a suit for contamination of a water well, a dispute between neighbors over a fence, defamation claims arising from an employment dispute, a snarl of competing claims arising from discussions among horse breeders on social media, and a host of other types of claims."[6]

While there is some debate about what constitutes "evidence" (affidavits versus pleadings) in the anti-SLAPP context, the Supreme Court has acknowledged the TCPA heightened pleading standards for those claims it encompasses:

> Fair notice of a claim under our procedural rules thus may require something less than "clear and specific evidence" of each essential element of the claim. Because the [Anti-SLAPP] Act requires more, mere notice pleading—that is, general allegations that merely recite the elements of a cause of action—will not suffice. Instead, a plaintiff must provide enough detail to show the factual basis for its claim. In a defamation case that implicates the TCPA, pleadings and evidence that establishes the facts of when, where, and what was said, the defamatory nature of the statements, and how they damaged the plaintiff should be sufficient to resist a TCPA motion to dismiss.[7]

Several tort theories require specific pleading. For instance, plaintiffs must plead negligence per se specifically (i.e. where the plaintiff seeks to recover for a breach of duty as defined in a statute instead of the duty of ordinary care).[8] Likewise, if the plaintiff plans to rely on a *res ipsa loquitur* inference (an inference of negligence even without evidence of a specific act that constitutes a breach), and if the petition raises specific instances of conduct that breaches a duty, the pleadings should specifically raise *res ipsa* in the alternative.[9]

In contract cases, certain remedies require specific pleading. Litigants should specifically request recission or modification, if they seek it.

b. *Damages requiring specific pleading.* In Texas, the *amount* of damages usually may be pled generally until a defendant complains. The *type* of damages sought may often be pled generally but must be specifically pled in some cases, depending on whether the damages sought are categorized as "general" or "special."

i. *Amount of unliquidated Damages pled generally unless defendant specially excepts.* The proper way to plead unliquidated damages[10] is not to state an amount, but merely to state that

---

6 Long Canyon Phase II and III Homeowners Assoc., Inc. v. Cashion, 517 S.W.3d 212, 216-17 (Tex. App.—Austin 2017, no pet.).

7 *See* In re Lipsky, 460 S.W.3d 579, 590–91 (Tex. 2015); *see also* Robert T. Sherwin, *Evidence? We Don't Need No Stinkin' Evidence!: How Ambiguity in Some States' Anti-SLAPP Laws Threatens to De-Fang a Popular and Powerful Weapon Against Frivolous Litigation*, 40 Colum. J. L. & Arts 431, 447-48 (2017) ("Undoubtedly, the [Lipsky] court was acknowledging that the anti-SLAPP law imposes a higher pleading standard than the normal case.").

8 *See, e.g.*, Daugherty v. S. Pac. Transp. Co., 772 S.W.2d 81, 83 (Tex. 1989) ("a party seeking to recover on the ground of negligence per se must plead a statutory violation").

9 *See* Mobil Chem. Co. v. Bell, 517 S.W.2d 245, 254 (Tex. 1974)("if the plaintiff's pleadings gives fair notice that he is not relying solely on specific acts but instead intends to also rely on any other negligent acts reasonably inferable from the circumstances of the accident, his proof is not limited to the specific acts alleged").

10 Unliquidated damages are damages that are uncertain in amount, and cannot be established from the pleadings by a mathematical calculation. Liquidated damages are damages of a sum certain, or an amount that can be

the amount sought is within the jurisdictional limits of the court.[11] This rule allows the plaintiff to satisfy the subject matter jurisdiction pleading requirements without a public document that alleges that a defendant should be made to pay an astronomical amount of damages. The rule further provides, however, that the defendant can require the plaintiff to state a maximum amount of alleged damages by filing a special exception.

Rule 47 also requires a more specific statement of relief requested, and prevents the party from conducting discovery until the pleading is amended to comply.[12] The specific statement requires the party to plead into or out of the expedited actions process governed by Rule 169, and also provides statistical information regarding the nature of cases filed. It is not intended to affect a party's substantive rights.[13]

ii. *Pleading general vs. special damages.*

Like other allegations, damages can be pleaded generally or specifically. A general allegation of damages ("plaintiff seeks to recover damages suffered as a result of defendant's conduct") or perhaps merely a general prayer (as discussed in subsection 2.c, below) will allow the plaintiff to recover "general damages," which are the damages that naturally and necessarily result from the harm alleged.[14] "Special damages," those that proximately result from the defendant's wrongful conduct and vary with the circumstances, require specific pleading.[15] How can you tell the difference between general and special damages? It is often difficult, but some general rules have emerged. In a personal injury case, pretrial pain and suffering (which all injured persons endure) is recoverable under a general claim for damages. All other damages (medical expenses, future pain and suffering, and, except in those instances where a disability naturally follows a serious injury, lost wages) must be specifically pleaded.[16] In a contract action, consequential damages must be specifically pleaded.[17] The lesson is to try to plead *all* types of damages for which the plaintiff seeks recovery. If one type of damage is omitted, perhaps it will be found in the general allegation.

What if there is no objection to recovery of the damages not pleaded? It is tried by consent. If there is an objection, what should you immediately do to try to solve the problem? Seek to amend your pleadings.

c. *Other elements of Texas pleadings*. In addition stating the causes of action and damages alleged, Texas petitions typically include several additional elements:

---

mathematically calculated from information set forth in the pleadings. Personal injury damages are unliquidated. Principal and interest due on a promissory note are liquidated damages.

[11] Rule 47(b).

[12] Rule 47(b). See In re Greater McAllen Star Properties, 444 S.W.3d 743, 750-51 (Tex. App.—Corpus Christi 2014, orig. proceeding) (holding that party need not reissue discovery requests after pleading amendment and time to respond began to run as of date amendment complying with Rule 47 was filed).

[13] Rule 47, Comment to 2013 change.

[14] Pringle v. Nowlin, 629 S.W.2d 154, 157 (Tex. App.—Fort Worth 1982, writ ref'd n.r.e.).

[15] Rule 56.

[16] *See generally* MCDONALD, § 8.41, 8.42.

[17] *See* Henry S. Miller Co. v. Bynum, 836 S.W.2d 160, 163-64 (Tex. 1992) (PHILLIPS, C.J., concurring).

i. *Discovery level.* The plaintiff should state which "discovery level" the case will proceed under (Level 1, 2, or 3).[18] The discovery-level limitations provide timelines and limitations on discovery. Which level is appropriate and the nature of the discovery limitations under each level is discussed in more detail in the discovery mechanics chapter.

ii. *Prayer for relief.* A prayer for relief is a demand for judgment of the court, identifying the kind of relief sought.[19] Like other pleadings, prayers for relief can be general or specific. A general prayer (*e.g.,* "plaintiff requests all relief at law or equity to which she may be entitled") usually will al-low monetary relief within the court's jurisdiction, justified by proof and consistent with the claims asserted in the petition.[20] A special prayer asks the court to grant additional or different relief, such as an injunction, specific performance of a contract, or the appointment of a receiver. A plaintiff may seek different kinds of relief, in the alternative or in combination. As with all other aspects of pleadings, the question to be asked is whether the defendant has "fair notice" of the relief sought.[21]

iii. *Request for pre- and postjudgment interest.* Plaintiffs should also seek recovery of prejudgment and postjudgment interest. Postjudgment interest, the interest from the day the judgment is rendered until paid, is provided for by statute.[22] Prejudgment interest, the interest from the date the claim arises until the date the judgment is rendered, may be recoverable as well. Many contracts provide for a specific prejudgment interest rate, and if there is no rate specified in the contract, a creditor may charge and receive from the obligor interest at the rate of 6% a year beginning the 30th day after the date on which the amount is due.[23] Other statutes provide for prejudgment interest in wrongful death, personal injury and property damage cases.[24]

In other cases, prejudgment interest may be recoverable in equity to encourage settlements and to discourage delay.[25]

Statutory prejudgment and postjudgment interest is recoverable under a general prayer. However, recovery of equitable prejudgment interest must be specifically included in the pleadings.[26]

---

18 Rule 190.1.

19 *See* Rule 47(d).

20 Kissman v. Bendix Home Systems, Inc., 587 S.W.2d 675, 677 (Tex. 1979).

21 *See* Stoner v. Thompson, 578 S.W.2d 679, 683-84 (Tex. 1979) (defendant did not have fair notice that trial court might award money damages).

22 *See* TEX. FIN. CODE § 304.001 et seq.

23 *See* TEX. FIN. CODE § 302.002 et seq.

24 *See* TEX. FIN. CODE § 304.101 et seq.

25 *See* Johnson & Higgins of Texas, Inc. v. Kenneco Energy, Inc., 962 S.W.2d 507 (Tex. 1998) (adopting statutory approach to equitable prejudgment interest for date of accrual and compounding); Perry Roofing Co. v. Olcott, 744 S.W.2d 929 (Tex. 1988) (awarding equitable prejudgment interest in breach of contract action where contract contained no measure by which a sum payable could be ascertained for damages); Cavnar v. Quality Control Parking, Inc., 696 S.W.2d 549 (Tex. 1985) (awarding equitable prejudgment interest in personal injury cases) (now governed by statute).

26 *See* Republic Nat'l Bank v. Northwest Nat'l Bank, 578 S.W. 2d 109, 116-17 (Tex. 1978).

iv. *Costs of court*. A plaintiff should also include in its prayer a request for costs of court. Rule 131 allows a successful party to recover costs from its adversary. No rule or statute, however, clearly defines recoverable costs; but they generally include filing fees, court reporter charges for the completion of an original deposition transcript, and other fees charged by the court.

v. *Conditions precedent*. Rule 54 allows plaintiffs to plead generally that all conditions precedent to recovery have been performed or have occurred. When conditions precedent are so pleaded, they are not at issue in the litigation (the plaintiff does not have to prove them) unless *specifically* denied by the defendant.[27]

C. Dismissal on the Pleadings

Until recently, Texas had a less potent pre-discovery dismissal mechanism than the federal system. Defendants had to rely on special exceptions to challenge causes of action and that practice, combined with Texas' liberal notice pleading regime, allowed many cases to go forward in discovery that might have failed in federal court, particularly after the *Twombly* and *Iqbal* decisions elevated the federal pleading standard. The old, pleader-friendly Texas system changed dramatically with the adoption of a new dismissal rule, Rule 91a.

1. Rule 91a – No Basis in Law or Fact

Read Rule 91a.

In 2011, the legislature directed the Supreme Court to adopt a more robust pre-discovery dismissal procedure.[1] The Supreme Court did so, promulgating Rule 91a, a procedure to dismiss causes of action with "no basis in law or fact."[2] Courts base this judgment, primarily, on the pleadings on file when a Rule 91a motion is filed.

But how do courts assess whether a pled cause of action has no basis in law or fact in light of Texas' liberal fair notice pleading standard? Has the pleading standard changed? Courts have been grappling with, among other questions, the factual specificity required in a pleading to survive Rule 91a dismissal.[3]

---

[27] *See* Community Bank & Trust S.S.B. v. Fleck, 107 S.W.3d 541 (Tex. 2002); Greathouse v. Charter National Bank—Southwest, 851 S.W.2d 173 (Tex. 1992). *See also* Ford Motor Co. v. Cammack, 999 S.W.2d 1 (Tex. App.—Houston [14th Dist.] 1999, pet. denied)(holding that a Rule 54 pleading did not apply to standing issues, so plaintiffs were required to prove standing to bring survival action).

[1] *See, e.g.*, Timothy Patton, Motions to Dismiss Under Rule 91a: Practice, Procedure, and Review, 33 Rev. Litig. 469, 473 (2014); *cf. also* Dustin B. Benham, Emerging Issues in Texas Dismissal Practice: Pleading Standards and Important Miscellany, HLRe: Off the Record (Houston L. Rev. Online) (2015).

[2] Rule 91a.1.

[3] *See, e.g.*, Wooley v. Schaffer, 477 S.W.3d 71, 84 (Tex. App.—Houston [14th Dist.] 2014, pet. denied) (FROST, J. concurring).

ZHENG
v.
VACATION NETWORK, INC.
468 S.W.3d 180
(Tex. App.—Houston [14th Dist.] 2015, pet. denied)

OPINION

DONOVAN, JUSTICE.

Appellant, Weizhong Zheng, appeals the trial court's judgment, dismissing, under Texas Rule of Civil Procedure 91a, Zheng's claims against appellees, Vacation Network, Inc. and Linh C. Dinh, and awarding attorney's fees to appellees. We reverse the portion of the judgment dismissing Zheng's claim under the Texas Timeshare Act against Vacation Network. We affirm the portion of the judgment dismissing Zheng's fraud claim against Vacation Network and all of Zheng's claims against Dinh. We remand for further proceedings, including a determination of the appropriate awards of attorney's fees.

I. BACKGROUND

Zheng alleges the following facts in his petition: On June 6, 2009, in response to solicitations from Vacation Network and after attending a presentation, Zheng entered into a timeshare contract with Vacation Network. Dinh is the president of Vacation Network. Zheng paid the full contractual price of $7,299. Appellees failed to provide the services they verbally promised and made materially false representations or concealed or failed to disclose material facts to secure Zheng's endorsement of the contract. Three days after execution, Zheng requested cancellation and a full refund. He has not used any contractual benefits. Appellees offered a modification, which Zheng declined. Appellees refused to honor Zheng's request for cancellation and retained his payment. The contract contained a waiver-of-rescission clause in violation of the Texas Timeshare Act, and appellees were not licensed to promote timeshares.

Zheng asserts two causes of action: (1) violations of the Timeshare Act; and (2) common law fraud. As we construe the petition, he seeks damages equal to the contractual price or rescission of the contract and a refund of the price.

Appellees filed a motion to dismiss each claim pursuant to Texas Rule of Civil Procedure 91a, to which Zheng responded. The trial court conducted a hearing on the motion. On September 23, 2013, the trial court signed an order granting the motion, dismissing all of Zheng's claims with prejudice, and ordering that appellees are entitled to recover their costs and attorney's fees associated with the motion. Appellees then filed a motion for award of its attorney's fees and entry of final judgment, with evidence attached to prove the amount of attorney's fees. On February 3, 2014, the trial court signed a final judgment, dismissing appellant's claims with prejudice and awarding appellees $9,806.81 in attorney's fees. After the trial court signed the dismissal order but before it signed the final judgment, Zheng filed a motion for new trial, which was overruled.

II. DISMISSAL OF ZHENG'S CLAIMS

Rule 91a, entitled "Dismissal of Baseless Causes of Action," provides in pertinent part:

> **91a.1 Motion and Grounds.** Except in a case brought under the Family Code or a case governed by Chapter 14 of the Texas Civil Practice and Remedies Code, a party may move to dismiss a cause of action on the grounds that it has no basis in law or fact. A

cause of action has no basis in law if the allegations, taken as true, together with inferences reasonably drawn from them, do not entitle the claimant to the relief sought. A cause of action has no basis in fact if no reasonable person could believe the facts pleaded.

91a.2 Contents of Motion. A motion to dismiss must state that it is made pursuant to this rule, must identify each cause of action to which it is addressed, and must state specifically the reasons the cause of action has no basis in law, no basis in fact, or both.

* * *

91a.5 Effect of Nonsuit or Amendment; Withdrawal of Motion.

(a) The court may not rule on a motion to dismiss if, at least 3 days before the date of the hearing, the respondent files a nonsuit of the challenged cause of action, or the movant files a withdrawal of the motion.

(b) If the respondent amends the challenged cause of action at least 3 days before the date of the hearing, the movant may, before the date of the hearing, file a withdrawal of the motion or an amended motion directed to the amended cause of action.

(c) Except by agreement of the parties, the court must rule on a motion unless it has been withdrawn or the cause of action has been nonsuited in accordance with (a) or (b). In ruling on the motion, the court must not consider a nonsuit or amendment not filed as permitted by paragraphs (a) or (b).

* * *

91a.6 Hearing; No Evidence Considered. Each party is entitled to at least 14 days' notice of the hearing on the motion to dismiss. The court may, but is not required to, conduct an oral hearing on the motion. Except as required by 91a.7, the court may not consider evidence in ruling on the motion and must decide the motion based solely on the pleading of the cause of action, together with any pleading exhibits permitted by Rule 59.

TEX. R. CIV. APP. 91a.1, .2, .5(a)-(c), .6.

Determinations of whether a cause of action has any basis in law and in fact are both legal questions which we review de novo, based on the allegations of the live petition and any attachments thereto. *Wooley v. Schaffer*, 447 S.W.3d 71, 76 (Tex. App.—Houston [14th Dist.] 2014, pet. filed).[1] In conducting our review, we must construe the pleadings liberally in favor of the plaintiff, look to the pleader's intent, and accept as true the factual allegations in the pleadings to determine if the cause of action has a basis in law or fact. *Id.* We apply the fair-notice pleading standard to determine whether the allegations of the petition are sufficient to allege a cause of action. *Id.; see Roark v. Allen*, 633 S.W.2d 804, 810 (Tex. 1982) ("A petition is sufficient if it gives fair and adequate notice of the facts upon which the pleader bases his claim.").[2]

---

1 In his first issue, Zheng argues that, because Rule 91a is relatively new, there is no guidance regarding the applicable standard of review, but he urges the *de novo* standard should apply. After Zheng filed his brief, our court issued *Wooley,* prescribing *de novo* review as the standard. *See* 447 S.W.3d at 76. Thus, we sustain Zheng's first issue and apply that standard.

2 Zheng, who is represented by counsel on appeal, emphasizes that he appeared pro se in the trial court. However, when considering his petition, we hold him to the same standards and rules of procedure applicable to a licensed attorney. *See* Canton-Carter v. Baylor Coll. of Med., 271 S.W.3d 928, 930 (Tex.App—Houston [14th Dist.] 2008, no pet.).

Zheng's second and third issues are interrelated and challenge the merits of the dismissal. Zheng argues the trial court improperly considered evidence outside of the pleadings and erred by dismissing both claims. We will address separately the claims against each defendant because our analysis differs somewhat for each defendant.

A. Claims against Vacation Network

1. Violations of Timeshare Act

Zheng characterizes his first claim as based on violations of the Texas Timeshare Act ("the Act"). *See generally* TEX. PROP.CODE ANN. §§ 221.001–.090 (West, Westlaw through 2013 3d C.S.) ("the Texas Timeshare Act"). Liberally construing the petition, we glean that Zheng seeks recovery of his purchase price as actual damages or rescission of the contract and refund of the purchase price for two separate reasons: (1) appellees were not licensed by the Texas Real Estate Commission to promote timeshares; *see id.* § 221.021 (generally requiring that timeshare plan be registered with the commission); and (2) the contract contained a rescission-waiver clause which is invalid under the Act, and Vacation Network refused Zheng's timely request for cancellation. *See id.* § 221.041 (providing purchaser may cancel timeshare contract within certain timeframes, purchaser may not waive right of cancellation, and contract containing a waiver is voidable by purchaser).

In the motion to dismiss, Vacation Network asserted Zheng's claim has no basis in law or fact because the contract is not a timeshare agreement. In support, Vacation Network cited various portions of the Act and attached the contract, which was not an exhibit to Zheng's petition. Vacation Network stated the contract demonstrates Zheng purchased a right to buy, at a later time, accommodations at a discounted price and did not purchase an ownership right in property or right to use accommodations. According to Vacation Network, this distinction means the contract is not a timeshare agreement. Vacation Network also relied on Zheng's answers to a questionnaire, made a part of the contract, in which he acknowledged the contract did not convey "any interest in . . . vacation timeshareing."

Thc parties dispute whether the trial court was permitted to consider the contract. Zheng maintains the trial court could not because the contract was not attached as an exhibit to the petition or filed and referred to therein. *See* TEX.R. CIV. P. 91a.6 (providing that, except as to attorney's fees, court may not consider evidence in ruling on the motion to dismiss and must decide the motion based solely on the pleading, "together with any pleading exhibits permitted by Rule 59"); *id.* 59 (providing, inter alia, that written instruments, constituting "the claim sued on" may be made a part of the pleading by originals or copies being attached, filed and referred to, or copied in the body).

In contrast, Vacation Network argues (1) Zheng waived his contention that the trial court could not consider the contract by failing to object and by presenting his own evidence in response to the motion to dismiss, and (2) the trial court was permitted to consider the contract pursuant to Rule 91a.6 because it constitutes "the claim sued on" under Rule 59, albeit attached to the motion to dismiss rather than the petition. *See id.*

We need not decide whether the trial court was permitted to consider the contract because even if it was permitted, the trial court erred by dismissing the claim based on violations of the Act. Whether the contract is a timeshare agreement involves comparison of the contractual terms and the nature of the interest purchased by Zheng against the statute, including its definitions relative to what constitutes a timeshare interest. The analysis also involves a determination of whether Zheng is bound by his answers to the questionnaire irrespective of whether the contractual terms may be construed as a timeshare agreement. Thus, these issues extend beyond a mere determination of whether the claim as pleaded is baseless under the Rule 91a standards. This is not a situation in which a court can determine based on the pleadings that "no reasonable person" could believe the contract is a timeshare agreement, as required for the claim to have no basis in fact. *See* R. 91a. 1. And, determining the claim has no basis in law would be contrary to the Rule 91a standard and our court's precedent that we take as true Zheng's allegation that the contract is a timeshare agreement.[3] *See id.; Wooley*, 447 S.W.3d at 76.[4] Instead, Vacation Network's contention seems to be a summary-judgment ground because it asserted that the evidence and authority negates the pleaded facts—which, upon proper motion, Zheng is entitled to have evaluated under summary-judgment standards. *See generally* TEX.R. CIV. P. 166a. Accordingly, the trial court erred by dismissing the claim against Vacation Network based on the Act.

2. Fraudulent Inducement

We construe the pleading as alleging Vacation Network fraudulently induced Zheng into executing the contract. The elements of fraud are (1) the speaker made a material representation, (2) it was false, (3) the speaker knew the representation was false when he made it or he made it recklessly without any knowledge of its truth and as a positive assertion, (4) the speaker made the representation with intent that the other party act upon it, (5) the other party acted in reliance on the misrepresentation, and (6) that party suffered injury thereby. *Italian Cowboy Partners, Ltd. v. Prudential Ins. Co. of Am.*, 341 S.W.3d 323, 337 (Tex. 2011). For fraudulent inducement, the elements of fraud must be established as they relate to an inducement to enter into a contract between the parties. *See Haase v. Glazner*, 62 S.W.3d 795, 798-99 (Tex. 2001).

In the motion to dismiss, Vacation Network challenged the fraud claim for several reasons. We conclude the trial court properly dismissed the fraud claim on the first ground raised by Vacation Network and thus we need not consider its remaining grounds.

In its first ground, Vacation Network contended the fraud claim has no basis in law or fact because Zheng fails to identify what false representations were allegedly made, or what material facts were allegedly concealed or undisclosed, by Vacation Network. As Vacation Network correctly asserted, Zheng recites the elements of a fraud claim but includes no supporting facts; he fails to allege any misrepresentations that were made or any facts that were concealed or undisclosed in order to induce him into executing the contract. After Vacation Network specifically raised this deficiency in its motion to dismiss, Zheng failed to amend his petition to identify any facts supporting the fraud claim, as permitted to avoid dismissal of the claim as originally pleaded. *See* TEX.R. CIV. P. 91a.5(b), (c).

In this regard, our court recently likened the standard for addressing a Rule 91a motion to the standard for addressing a motion under Federal Rule of Civil Procedure 12(b)(6), which allows dismissal if a plaintiff fails "to state a claim upon which relief can be granted." *See Wooley*, 447 S.W.3d at 75-76; FED.R.CIV.P. 12(b)(6). We emphasized that for a claim to survive a Rule

---

[3] As Vacation Network points out, Zheng does not explicitly state in his petition that the contract is a timeshare agreement, but liberally construing the petition, we construe the crux as alleging the contract is a timeshare agreement.

[4] In its motion, Vacation Network did not assert that even if the contract were a timeshare agreement, the Act does not authorize a private cause of action for damages based on violations of the Act or Zheng has no grounds for rescinding the contract and obtaining a refund.

12(b)(6) motion, it must contain " 'enough facts to state a claim to relief that is plausible on its face.' " *Id.* at 76 (quoting *GoDaddy.com, LLC v. Toups*, 429 S.W.3d 752, 754 (Tex. App.—Beaumont 2014, pet. denied), which quoted *Bell Atl. Corp. v. Twombly*, 550 U.S. 544, 570, 127 S.Ct. 1955, 167 L.Ed.2d 929 (2007)). Although a federal complaint is liberally construed in the plaintiff's favor and all well-pleaded facts are taken as true, " '[t]hreadbare recitals of the elements of a cause of action, supported by mere conclusory statements, do not suffice.' " *Id.* (quoting *GoDaddy*, 429 S.W.3d at 754, which quoted *Ashcroft v. Iqbal*, 556 U.S. 662, 678, 129 S.Ct. 1937, 173 L.Ed.2d 868 (2009)).

In the present case, Zheng's pleading contains merely a "threadbare recital [ ]" of the elements of a fraudulent inducement claim without any alleged facts. Accordingly, the trial court did not err by determining the claim has no basis in law or fact. *See id.*

B. Claims against Dinh

In the motion to dismiss, Dinh asserted that Zheng fails to plead any causes of action against Dinh personally. We agree. Zheng pleads that Vacation Network is a corporation and Dinh is its president. Although Zheng refers to the "Defendants" collectively in the petition, it is undisputed he contracted only with Vacation Network. Consequently, Zheng essentially pleads that it is Vacation Network who fraudulently induced Zheng to execute the contract, violated the Act, and holds the purchase price that Zheng seeks either as damages or as a refund if the contract is rescinded.

Zheng pleads no basis whatsoever for imposing liability against Dinh individually. In particular, Zheng alleges no theory for disregarding the corporate form and holding Dihn personally liable for the actions of Vacation Network. Zheng's only argument on appeal for retaining Dinh as a defendant is that Zheng was not required to "marshal" all his evidence in the petition. However, this is not merely a failure to "marshal" evidence but a failure to state any basis for a claim against Dinh individually. Additionally, we may uphold dismissal of the fraud claim against Dinh for the same reason we uphold dismissal of that claim against Vacation Network—Zheng pleads only a "threadbare recital[ ]" of the elements without any supporting facts. *See id.* Accordingly, the trial court did not err by concluding the claims against Dinh have no basis in law or fact.

In summary, we sustain Zheng's third issue as to the claim against Vacation Network under the Act but overrule the issue as to the fraud claim against Vacation Network and all claims against Dinh.

III. ATTORNEY'S FEES

In his fourth issue, Zheng contends that, if he prevails in this appeal, (1) we must reverse the trial court's award of attorney's fees to appellees, and (2) Zheng is entitled to recover his appellate attorney's fees.

Under Texas law, attorney's fees are not recoverable unless specifically provided by contract or statute. *MBM Fin. Corp. v. Woodlands Operating Co.*, 292 S.W.3d 660, 669 (Tex. 2009). With respect to attorney's fees, Rule 91a provides:

> **91a.7 Award of Costs and Attorney Fees Required.** Except in an action by or against a governmental entity or a public official acting in his or her official capacity or under color of law, the court must award the prevailing party on the motion all costs and reasonable and necessary attorney fees incurred with respect to the challenged cause of action in the trial court. The court must consider evidence regarding costs and fees in determining the award.

TEX. R. CIV. P. 91a.7. Undisputedly, the rule mandates an award of attorney's fees to a prevailing party, and the award is not discretionary. *See. id; see also Drake v. Chase Bank*, No. 02-13-00340-CV, 2014 WL 6493411, at *2 (Tex. App.—Fort Worth Nov. 20, 2014, no pet.) (mem.op.).

We agree that appellees are not necessarily entitled to all attorney's fees they were awarded; in light of our disposition, they are no longer prevailing parties on all claims. *See* TEX.R. CIV. P. 91a.7. Consequently, on remand, appellees must segregate the reasonable and necessary fees incurred to obtain dismissal of the fraud claim against Vacation Network and all claims against Dinh from those incurred to obtain dismissal of the claim against Vacation Network under the Act or demonstrate why segregation is not required. *See CA Partners v. Spears*, 274 S.W.3d 51, 81-82 (Tex. App.—Houston [14th Dist.] 2008, pet. denied) (recognizing that, if any attorney's fees relate solely to claims for which fees are unrecoverable, party seeking fees must segregate recoverable from unrecoverable fees, except when discrete legal services relate to both recoverable claims and unrecoverable claims, they are so "intertwined" that segregation is not required; and party seeking fees bears burden to show segregation is not required).

With respect to Zheng's request for appellate fees, appellees assert that a prevailing party on a Rule 91a motion is entitled to recover only the attorney's fees incurred in the trial court.[5] Appellees focus on the phrase "in the trial court" in Rule 91a.7, contending it means the prevailing party may recover only the fees it incurred at the trial court level. We disagree.

We note this issue is one of first impression because Rule 91a is fairly new. The parties do not cite, and we have not found, any authority addressing whether a prevailing party on a Rule 91a motion is entitled to recover appellate attorney's fees. When construing rules of procedure, we apply the same rules of construction that govern the interpretation of statutes. *Ford Motor Co. v. Garcia*, 363 S.W.3d 573, 579 (Tex. 2012). We first look to the plain language of the rule and construe it according to its plain or literal meaning. *Id.*

Applying this principle, our disposition hinges on the placement of the phrase "in the trial court" within Rule 91a.7. The phrase is not placed directly after the word "incurred." *See* TEX. R. CIV. P. 91a.7. In other words, the rule does not state that the trial court must award the prevailing party "all costs and reasonable and necessary attorney's fees incurred in the trial court . . . ." *See id.* Instead, "in the trial court" is placed after the phrase "with respect to the challenged cause of action." *See id.* Accordingly, the plain language of the rule indicates "in the trial court" refers to "the challenged cause of action." *See id.* Thus, the prevailing party is limited to recovering the fees and costs associated with the cause of action that was challenged at the trial court level—in the motion to dismiss. *See id.* Our construction regarding the reason for inclusion of "in the trial court" is supported by the comment to Rule 91a: "Attorney fees awarded under 91a.7 are limited to those associated with challenged cause of action, including fees for preparing or responding to the motion to dismiss." *See* comment to TEX.R. CIV. P. 91a.7.

There is no limitation in the rule on the fees and costs the prevailing party is entitled to recover relative to the cause of action challenged in the trial court. *See* TEX.R. CIV. P. 91a.7. Specifically, there is nothing to suggest that "all costs and reasonable and necessary attorney fees" excludes appellate costs and fees which are generally recoverable when attorney's fees are authorized. *See In re Estate of Hardesty*, 449 S.W.3d 895, 917 (Tex. App.—Texarkana 2014, no pet.); *Cessna Aircraft Co. v. Aircraft Network, LLC*, 345 S.W.3d 139, 147-48 (Tex. App.—Dallas 2011,

[5] There is no issue on whether Zheng may recover attorney's fees incurred in the trial court because he appeared *pro se* at that stage and first obtained counsel to prosecute his appeal.

no pet.); *Jones v. Am. Airlines, Inc.*, 131 S.W.3d 261, 271 (Tex. App.—Fort Worth 2004, no pet.). Rather the word "all" entails just that—"all" fees—which would include appellate fees, because they are part of the fees incurred to ultimately prevail, if the ruling is appealed. *See* TEX.R. CIV. P. 91a.7.

Our conclusion is also supported by a provision of the Texas Civil Practice and Remedies Code promulgated to correspond with the provision of the Texas Government Code requiring the Supreme Court of Texas to adopt a rule mandating the dismissal of claims that have no basis in law or fact. *See* TEX. CIV. PRAC. & REM.CODE ANN. § 30.021 (West, Westlaw through 2013 3d C.S.); TEX. GOV'T CODE § 22.004(g) (West, Westlaw through 2013 3d C.S.). Section 30.021 provides that subject to the same exceptions set forth in Rule 91a.7, the trial court, when granting or denying a motion to dismiss, in whole or part, "shall award costs and reasonable and necessary attorney's fees to the prevailing party." *Id.* This section does not restrict such costs and attorney's fees to those incurred in the trial court. *See id.*

Therefore, we conclude Zheng is entitled to recover reasonable and necessary appellate attorney's fees, but not necessarily all of his appellate fees because he is the prevailing party only relative to his claim against Vacation Network under the Act. Accordingly, on remand, Zheng must segregate his fees incurred to appeal dismissal of that claim from those incurred to appeal dismissal of his fraud claim against Vacation Network and all claims against Dinh or demonstrate why segregation is not required. *See CA Partners*, 274 S.W.3d at 81-82.

In summary, we reverse the portion of the trial court's judgment dismissing Zheng's claim against Vacation Network under the Act. We affirm the portion of the judgment dismissing Zheng's fraud claim against Vacation Network and all of Zheng's claims against Dinh. We remand for further proceedings consistent with this opinion.

Notes & Questions

Disarray on Factual Specificity Required. Other courts have provided sub-optimal guidance on whether Rule 91a elevated the fact-pleading standard. For example, in *Wooley v. Schaffer*, 447 S.W.3d 71, the court simultaneously analogized Rule 91a motions to pleas to the jurisdiction, federal plausibility pleading, and special exceptions.[1] The Supreme Court has yet to definitively weigh in, but it did provide some first clues in the following case.

---

1 *See, e.g.*, Wooley v. Schaffer, 477 S.W.3d 71, 76 (Tex. App.—Houston [14th Dist.] 2014, pet. denied); *see also* Benham, *supra* note 1 on page 194.

CITY OF DALLAS
v.
SANCHEZ
494 S.W.3d 722
(Tex. 2016)

Per Curiam

Hours before Matthew Sanchez died from a drug overdose, a 9-1-1 operator dispatched an ambulance to his apartment complex. Once on scene, however, emergency personnel provided assistance to a different drug-overdose victim at the same complex and then left the premises without aiding Sanchez, erroneously concluding that two closely timed 9-1-1 calls concerning overdose victims at the same locale were redundant. In a wrongful-death suit against the City of Dallas, Sanchez's parents allege the 9-1-1 telephone system malfunctioned and disconnected Sanchez's call before the responders could establish the overdose reports were not duplicative.

The issue in this Rule 91a dismissal proceeding is whether the Texas Tort Claims Act waives the City's immunity from suit based on allegations in the wrongful-death suit that a condition of the City's telephone system proximately caused Sanchez's death by preventing him from receiving potentially life-saving medical care. *See* TEX. CIV. PRAC. & REM. CODE § 101.021(2) (providing a limited waiver of governmental immunity arising from the "condition or use" of tangible personal property); TEX. R. CIV. P. 91a (authorizing dismissal of a cause of action that has no basis in law or fact). We hold governmental immunity is not waived and dismissal is required because the requisite causal nexus between the alleged condition and Sanchez's injury is lacking. See *Dallas County v. Posey*, 290 S.W.3d 869, 872 (Tex. 2009) (the alleged condition must actually have caused the injury to invoke the Tort Claims Act's immunity waiver; mere involvement of property is not sufficient). We therefore reverse the court of appeals' judgment and render judgment dismissing the case.

Dismissal is appropriate under Rule 91a "if the allegations, taken as true, together with inferences reasonably drawn from them, do not entitle the claimant to the relief sought . . . [or] no reasonable person could believe the facts pleaded." TEX. R. CIV. P. 91a.1. Whether the dismissal standard is satisfied depends "solely on the pleading of the cause of action." TEX. R. CIV. P. 91a.6. We review the merits of a Rule 91a motion de novo because the availability of a remedy under the facts alleged is a question of law and the rule's factual-plausibility standard is akin to a legal-sufficiency review. See *Wooley v. Schaffer*, 447 S.W.3d 71, 75-76 (Tex. App.—Houston [14th Dist.] 2014, pet. denied). . . .

The dismissal grounds under Rule 91a have been analogized to a plea to the jurisdiction, which requires a court to determine whether the pleadings allege facts demonstrating jurisdiction. See *Wooley*, 447 S.W.3d at 75. In this case, the analogy is particularly apt because the City's Rule 91a motion challenges the trial court's subject-matter jurisdiction on the pleaded facts. Whether a pleader has alleged facts affirmatively demonstrating the existence of subject-matter jurisdiction is a question of law reviewed de novo. *See Tex. Dep't of Parks & Wildlife v. Miranda*, 133 S.W.3d 217, 226 (Tex. 2004).

In the early hours of November 16, 2012, City of Dallas 9-1-1 dispatchers received two 9-1-1 calls within approximately ten minutes of one another. Both calls originated from the same apartment complex and both requested assistance for a drug-overdose victim; however, the calls were placed from different phone numbers and concerned different residents.

This wrongful-death and survival action arises from the second 9-1-1 call, which was placed at 2:55 a.m. on Matthew Sanchez's behalf. The 9-1-1 dispatcher acquired information regarding the nature of the emergency and Sanchez's address, including the apartment number, and informed the caller that emergency responders were en route. The call was subsequently disconnected and not reestablished. After emergency responders arrived at the apartment complex to assist the subject of the first 9-1-1 call, they erroneously concluded that the two 9-1-1 calls were redundant and that a single individual was the subject of both calls. Consequently, the emergency responders never went to Sanchez's apartment to provide aid. Sanchez died at approximately 8:40 a.m.

Sanchez's parents sued the City of Dallas for negligence alleging: (1) the City's 9-1-1 dispatcher misused the phone system by hanging up before emergency responders arrived to assist Sanchez, or in the alternative, the 9-1-1 phone system malfunctioned, causing the call to disconnect prematurely; (2) the 9-1-1 dispatcher failed to follow proper procedure and violated various federal, state, and local laws and regulations by either disconnecting the call or failing to redial after the call disconnected; and (3) if the emergency responders had located Sanchez before leaving the premises, they "would have most likely saved [his] life."

In a Rule 91a motion to dismiss asserting governmental immunity from suit, the City argued the allegations in the lawsuit did not invoke a waiver of immunity under the Tort Claims Act because (1) the allegations complained about communication of information and the failure to dispatch an ambulance, not a condition or misuse of tangible property, and (2) Sanchez's death was caused by a drug overdose, not the 9-1-1 telephone system. See TEX. CIV. PRAC. & REM. CODE § 101.021(2). Alternatively, to the extent immunity might otherwise be waived under the Tort Claims Act, the City asserted the pleadings failed to overcome a statutory exception making the Act inapplicable to 9-1-1 emergency services, except for actions that "violate[ ] a statute or ordinance applicable to the action." *Id.* § 101.062(b).

The trial court granted the City's motion to dismiss as to all claims except the allegation that the 9-1-1 phone system failed or malfunctioned. On interlocutory appeal, the court of appeals affirmed, holding Sanchez's parents (1) sufficiently alleged a defect in the phone system proximately caused his death and (2) adequately pleaded a violation of a statute or ordinance as an exception to section 101.062's waiver exclusion. . . .

* * *

The Texas Tort Claims Act waives governmental immunity from suit for "personal injury and death so caused by a condition or use of tangible personal or real property if the governmental unit would, were it a private person, be liable to the claimant according to Texas law." TEX. CIV. PRAC. & REM. CODE § 101.021(2). For immunity to be waived under section 101.021(2), "personal injury or death must be proximately caused by a condition or use of tangible personal or real property." *Dallas Cty. Mental Health & Mental Retardation v. Bossley*, 968 S.W.2d 339, 342-43 (Tex. 1998). To establish a waiver of the City's immunity under section 102.021(2), we must therefore determine whether the phone's condition was a proximate cause of Sanchez's death.

Proximate cause requires both "cause in fact and foreseeability." *Ryder*, 453 S.W.3d at 929. For a condition of property to be a cause in fact, the condition must "serve[ ] as 'a substantial factor in causing the injury and without which the injury would not have occurred.' " *Id.* . . . When a condition or use of property merely furnishes a circumstance "that makes the injury possible," the condition or use is not a substantial factor in causing the injury. *Bossley*, 968 S.W.2d at 343. To be a substantial factor, the condition or use of the property "must actually have caused the injury." *Posey*, 290 S.W.3d at 872 ("This nexus requires more than mere involvement of property; rather, the condition must actually have caused the injury."). Thus, the use of property that simply hinders or delays treatment does not "actually cause[ ] the injury" and does not constitute a proximate cause of an injury. See *Miller*, 51 S.W.3d at 588.

* * *

Even construing the pleadings liberally, see *Miranda*, 133 S.W.3d at 226, the alleged telephone-system malfunction was not a proximate cause of Sanchez's death. Between the alleged malfunction and Sanchez's death, emergency responders erroneously concluded separate 9-1-1 calls were redundant and left the apartment complex without checking the specific apartment unit the dispatcher had provided to them. Moreover, approximately six hours passed between the phone malfunction and Sanchez's death, further attenuating the causal connection. Although disconnection of the telephone call may have contributed to circumstances that delayed potentially life-saving assistance, the malfunction was too attenuated from the cause of Sanchez's death—a drug overdose—to be a proximate cause. See *Bossley*, 968 S.W.2d at 343 (use of property is not a proximate cause when it is too attenuated from the injury). The alleged defect did not actually cause Sanchez's death nor was his death "hastened or exacerbated" by a telephone malfunction. See *Posey*, 290 S.W.3d at 872. . . . The malfunction was merely one of a series of factors that contributed to Sanchez not receiving timely medical assistance. See *Miller*, 51 S.W.3d at 588. Sanchez's death was caused by drugs, the passage of time, and misinterpretation of information. *See id.* (concluding the death was caused by meningitis, time, and an alleged error in judgment, not by symptom-masking treatment). Accordingly, the pleadings do not establish a defect in the 9-1-1 telephone system was a proximate cause of Sanchez's death as required to establish a waiver of governmental immunity under the Tort Claims Act.

Without hearing oral argument, we reverse the court of appeals' judgment and render judgment dismissing the case. *See* TEX. R. APP. P. 59.1.

Notes & Questions

1. *No Basis in law or fact.* Rule 91a allows dismissal on the pleadings in two situations—the pleader states a claim that has no basis in law or has no basis in fact. The rule provides that a claim has "no basis in law" "if the allegations, taken as true, together with inferences reasonably drawn from them, do not entitle the claimant to the relief sought."[1] This provision of the rule is harmonious with existing Texas pleading practice—take the allegations as true, read them in favor of the pleader, and proceed to discovery so long as the pleading states a valid cause of action. The standard for "no basis in fact", on the other hand, is distinct and perhaps altogether new.

2. *Is 91a Twiqbal?* Does the *Zheng* court's reference to *Ashcroft v. Iqbal* (and presumably, by implication, *Twombly v. Bell Atlantic*) and the *Sanchez* court's reference to "factual-plausibility standard" suggest that courts ought to apply federal plausibility pleading standards in determining

[1] Rule 91a.1.

Rule 91a motions? Would this be a change to Texas' notice-pleading tradition? Assuming Rule 91a did, at least implicity, change the standard for fact pleading, what would its likely impact be, if any?

3. *Which standard?* Did the *Sanchez* court decide the case on the provision of Rule 91a that allows dismissal of claims with "no basis in law" or did it decide the case based on the "no basis in fact" provision? How do you know?

4. *Attorney fees*. As discussed in *Zheng* above, Rule 91a mandates that trial courts, in most cases, "award the prevailing party on the motion all costs and reasonable and necessary attorney fees incurred with respect to the challenged cause of action in the trial court."[2] The comments to the rule provide that Rule 91a fees "are limited to those associated with the challenged cause of action, including fees for preparing or responding to the motion to dismiss."[3] With respect to appellate attorney fees, the *Zheng* court construed Rule 91a as a mandate to award fees incurred by a party who prevails on appeal of a trial court's Rule 91a decision.

5. *Deadlines, pleading amendments, and impact on attorney fees*. The deadline to file a motion to dismiss under Rule 91a is 60 days from when the first pleading containing the challenged cause of action is served on the movant.[4] The motion must be filed 21 days before the court holds a hearing and the response 7 days before the hearing.[5] This timetable allows pleading amendments and non-suits in the face of a motion to dismiss. Both of these mechanisms allow the pleader to avoid dismissal and resultant attorney fee awards. After an amendment, the movant may, before the hearing, amend the motion or withdraw it, likewise avoiding a loss on the motion and exposure to attorney fee awards.

6. *Appellate review.* Note that *Sanchez* was an interlocutory appeal arising, in part, from the denial of an immunity-based defense. But are appellate courts able to review trial courts' denials of Rule 91a motions in ordinary, non-immunity cases that are not subject to interlocutory appeal? Ordinarily, parties may appeal only from final judgments, that is, judgments that dispose of all parties and all claims. When a trial court grants a Rule 91a motion as to all parties and all claims, the decision constitutes a final judgment, and appellate courts have jurisdiction to review it. Rule 91a denials, however, expressly do *not* dispose of claims because, by denying the motion, the trial judge has essentially ruled that the case can go forward. Nonetheless, the Supreme Court held (in the first case it decided under the rule) that erroneous denial of a Rule 91a motion is subject to mandamus review.[6]

---

2 Rule 91a.7.

3 Rule 91a.7 cmt.

4 Rule 91a.3(a).

5 *Id.* at (b).

6 *See* In re Essex Ins. Co., 450 S.W.3d 524, 528 (Tex. 2014) ("we conclude that mandamus relief is appropriate to spare the parties and the public the time and money spent on fatally flawed proceedings").

2. *Special Exceptions*

Read Rules 90, 91.

A special exception is the device used to make objections to pleadings—to point out with particularity the defect in the pleading, so that the pleading party can attempt to cure it.[1] Most of the time, a party can cure pleading defects (by, e.g., pleading with more specificity). But in some less common circumstances, even when given an opportunity to amend, parties are unable to state a valid cause of action. In those circumstances, dismissal is appropriate, and the special exception functions in some ways like the federal motion to dismiss.[2]

There are many types of pleading defects. For example, a party may object to the opponent's defective pleadings by special exception if the pleading does not give "fair notice" of any claim. This special exception is similar to the motion for more definite statement in federal practice.[3] The special exception can also be used to object to an opponent's failure to plead a claim properly (for instance, an element of the cause of action is left out, or the claim is not legally cognizable), similar to the federal motion to dismiss for failure to state a claim.[4]

The supreme court notes that the pleadings in *Paramount Pipe* "may have been subject to attack by special exception even though they satisfy the fair notice standard." What does this mean? The Court was referring to the situation where the special exception is used simply to require the other party to plead more specifically, providing more details than "fair notice" requires. Therefore, a pleading may be subject to objection by special exception, but still satisfy the "fair notice" standard.

A special exception is made in writing, filed and served, and a hearing is held in which the trial court decides whether the special exception should be sustained or denied. The special exception is often included in the defendant's answer. A special exception raises only pleading defects that appear on the face of the opponent's pleading and does not set forth new facts that do not appear in the challenged pleading. At the special exception hearing, the factual allegations in the challenged pleading are taken as true. A judge reviewing the sufficiency of a pleading balances two competing factors: (1) the intent of the rules to eliminate technicalities and to simplify pleadings, and (2) notice to the opposing party. Often, the resolution will be fairly pragmatic, based upon the situation before the court. Therefore, it is often difficult to make generalizations about what is or is not a proper pleading.

If the special exceptions are sustained, the pleading party must amend the pleading to satisfy the objection and ruling. If no amendment is filed, the objectionable part of the pleading is stricken. If the pleading, with the defective allegations stricken, fails to state a cause of action, then a final order dismissing the suit may result.

A defendant who appears and answers can overturn a judgment based on defective pleadings only if the defendant has objected to the defect at the trial court, and allowed the plaintiff an op-

---

1 *See, e.g.*, Friesenhahn v. Ryan, 960 S.W.2d 656, 658 (Tex. 1998 ("When the trial court sustains special exceptions, it must give the pleader an opportunity to amend the pleading.").

2 *Cf.* FRCP 12(b)(6).

3 FRCP 12(e).

4 FRCP 12(b)(6).

portunity to amend and correct the defect.[5] As Rule 90 says, any defects in pleadings are waived unless the defendant points to the objection through a special exception and gives the plaintiff an opportunity to amend. Thus, a defendant faced with inadequate pleadings should first file special exceptions, pointing out specific deficiencies in the pleadings. If the court agrees that the pleadings are defective, the court should grant the special exception and, if the defect is curable, order the plaintiff to amend to correct the defects. Dismissal without the opportunity to amend (when requested and denied) is error.[6] If the plaintiff fails to amend within the time the court allows, the defendant can file a motion to dismiss for the failure to satisfy the order or file a motion for summary judgment. If the defect involves the failure to plead subject matter jurisdiction, a plea to the jurisdiction may be more appropriate.

As noted, parties may raise defects in pleadings that are not fatal—the pleading gives fair notice of a legally valid claim within the jurisdiction of the court, but the pleading is vague or omits one or more elements of the cause of action. A defaulting defendant cannot successfully overturn a default judgment for these defects, but an answering defendant may be successful in getting the trial judge to require the pleading party to file a better pleading through an amended pleading.

HUMPHREYS
v.
MEADOWS

938 S.W.2d 750
(Tex. App.—Ft. Worth 1996, writ denied)

OPINION

RICHARDS, JUSTICE.

Appellant Lloyd Humphreys was convicted in federal court on various counts of tax evasion. Humphreys's conviction was affirmed on direct appeal. The Texas Supreme Court subsequently disbarred him. On behalf of himself and his law firm, Humphreys brought this lawsuit against the attorney who represented him in the tax evasion trial, appellee Charles Meadows, and an investigator he retained to testify on his behalf at the trial, appellee Max Wayman. Humphreys's petition alleged various claims, including legal and professional malpractice, breach of contract, and fraud.

The trial court dismissed Humphreys's suit with prejudice because Humphreys allegedly refused to comply with a court order requiring him to produce certain documents in response to Meadows's and Wayman's requests for discovery and because Humphreys's pleadings contained "intolerably vague and indefinite assertions." In four points of error, Humphreys appeals the trial court's dismissal of his case. Because we find that the court abused its discretion by imposing the

[5] Not every defendant appears and answers. In such situations, courts sometimes render default judgments based upon the pleadings on file. The Paramount Pipe opinion identified three situations where pleadings would render a default judgment erroneous: (1) the pleading fails to give fair notice of the claim or defense asserted; (2) the pleading presents a claim for relief that is legally invalid; and (3) the pleading presents a claim that is outside the trial court's subject matter jurisdiction. These are sometimes called "fatal" pleading defects because the defaulting defendant can use the pleading defect as a basis upon which to overturn the default judgment.

[6] Parker v. Barefield, 206 S.W.3d 119 (Tex. 2006).

"death penalty" sanction for discovery violations without first imposing a lesser sanction and because we find that the trial court should have allowed Humphreys to further amend his amended petition to cure vagueness problems, we reverse.

* * *

II. INSUFFICIENT PLEADINGS

* * *

A trial court may not dismiss a plaintiff's case for pleading defects unless an opportunity is first afforded to amend and cure the defect. Moreover, if a plaintiff makes a good faith attempt to amend his petition in response to the trial court's sustaining of a defendant's special exceptions, the trial court may not dismiss the plaintiff's amended petition unless the defendant files special exceptions to the revised pleadings, the court sustains the new special exceptions, and the court gives the plaintiff the opportunity to amend the revised pleadings. Additionally, as a general rule, the trial court cannot dismiss a suit with prejudice when the plaintiff does not cure the objections made by special exceptions.

Humphreys filed his original petition on August 23, 1993. On April 22, 1995, Meadows filed special exceptions alleging that various paragraphs of Humphreys's petition were "vague, general, and indefinite," conclusory, and "fail[ed] to give Defendant fair notice." On August 22, 1995, the trial court sustained Meadows's special exceptions and ordered Humphreys to replead. On September 25, 1995, Humphreys filed an "Amendment to Petition." On October 30, 1995, Meadows filed a "Motion for Sanctions" alleging that Humphreys's "Amendment":

1) "does not constitute repleading or amended pleadings as contemplated by" the court's order of August 22;
2) "contains general and conclusory allegations rather than specific allegations and does not adequately respond to nor correct the deficiencies in Plaintiff's Original Petition";
3) "is not an amended petition as provided by the Texas Rules of Civil Procedure"; and
4) "fails to address all of the special exceptions of Defendant and does not replead or amend all of the allegations to which exception has been made and sustained by the Court's order."

Thereafter, the trial court entered its "Order of Dismissal With Prejudice" based in part on its conclusion that "[a]lthough . . . ordered to replead, . . . the pleadings continue to contain intolerably vague and indefinite assertions . . . and there fails to be any assertion of facts which would warrant the claimed existence of an oral contract or one implied by law."

Based on this record, we hold that the trial court abused its discretion by dismissing Humphreys's case based on insufficient pleadings. Neither Meadows nor Humphreys filed special exceptions to Humphreys's "Amendment to Petition." We find Meadows's "Motion for Sanctions" was insufficient to constitute special exceptions to the "Amendment" because it did not set out any particular deficiencies in the Amendment. *See* TEX. R. CIV. P. 91 ("special exception shall not only point out the particular pleading excepted to, but it shall also point out intelligibly and *with particularity* the . . . insufficiency in the allegations in the pleading excepted to"). Moreover, even if Meadow's "Motion for Sanctions" were sufficient to constitute special exceptions to the "Amendment," the trial court did not sustain any special exceptions to the "Amendment" or give Humphreys and opportunity to cure any deficiencies in the "Amendment."

Because the trial court abused its discretion in dismissing Humphreys's second point of error is sustained.[3] Accordingly, we reverse the trial court's order and remand this case for further proceedings consistent with this opinion.

ZEID
v.
PEARCE
953 S.W.2d 368
(Tex. App.—El Paso 1997, no petition history)

OPINION

JUSTICE JOHN G. HILL (Assigned).

Richard and Susan Zeid appeal from the trial court's order dismissing their lawsuit against Dr. William Pearce, d/b/a Coronado Animal Clinic, for veterinary malpractice. The trial court based its order upon the Zeids' failure to amend their petition to seek damages other than for pain and suffering, mental anguish, and loss of earnings. They contend in a single point of error that the trial court erred in sustaining Dr. Pearce's special exceptions and dismissing their lawsuit because pain and suffering and mental anguish are damages that are recoverable for the loss of a pet.

We affirm because one may not recover damages for pain and suffering or mental anguish for the loss of a pet.

The Zeids alleged in their original petition that they brought their dog, Persephone, to Dr. Pearce for vaccinations. They indicated that Dr. Pearce knew from previous vaccinations that the dog suffered from allergic reactions. According to the petition, Dr. Pearce was negligent and this caused the death of the dog, which went into convulsions after receiving the vaccination.

Dr. Pearce filed a special exception to the Zeids' pleading on the basis that such damages are not recoverable in Texas for the death of a dog. The trial court granted Dr. Pearce's special exception in order to afford the Zeids' an opportunity to replead and seek recoverable damages. When the Zeids declined to replead and seek other damages, the trial court dismissed the suit.

As previously noted, the Zeids' sole point of error is that the trial court erred in granting Dr. Pearce's special exception and subsequently dismissing their cause of action because pain and suffering and mental anguish are damages that are recoverable for the loss of a pet.

In Texas, the recovery for the death of a dog is the dog's market value, if any, or some special or pecuniary value to the owner that may be ascertained by reference to the dog's usefulness or services. *Heiligmann v. Rose*, 81 Tex. 222, 225, 16 S.W. 931, 932 (1891).[*] We find this longstanding Texas rule to be inconsistent with the Zeids' claim for pain and suffering and mental anguish.

* * *

---

[3] Because we reverse the trial court based on Humphreys's second point of error, we do not address his first, third, and fourth points of error.

[*] Editor's Note: The *Heiligmann* rule prohibiting recovery of non-economic damages for loss of a pet was reaffirmed in Strickland v. Medlen, 397 S.W.3d 184 (Tex. 2013).

We also note that the Texas Supreme Court has held that one may not recover damages for bystander recovery for mental anguish in medical malpractice cases. We see no reason why the same rule would not apply in cases involving death due to veterinary malpractice.

Because the Zeids did not plead for damages for the loss of their dog that are recoverable in Texas, the trial court did not err in sustaining Dr. Pearce's special exception and dismissing their cause of action. We overrule the Zeids' sole point of error.

The judgment is affirmed.

PEEK
v.
EQUIPMENT SERVICE CO.
779 S.W.2d 802
(Tex. 1989)

PHILLIPS, CHIEF JUSTICE.

These cases present the question of whether a plaintiff seeking damages under the wrongful death and survival statutes invokes the jurisdiction of a district court by filing a petition which fails to allege either a specific amount of damages or that the damages sustained exceed the court's minimum jurisdictional limits. The district court held that its jurisdiction was not invoked by such a pleading. Because plaintiffs did not file a pleading properly alleging damages until after the applicable statute of limitations had run, the district court dismissed the suit. The court of appeals, in two unpublished opinions, affirmed. We reverse the judgments of the court of appeals and remand this consolidated cause to the trial court because the original pleading, although defective, was sufficient to invoke the court's jurisdiction and prevent the running of limitations.

This matter arose out of the murder of Clyde Peek on December 18, 1984. The plaintiffs were Clyde's widow, Lucie Allen Peek, acting in her individual capacity and as representative of Clyde's estate, and Clyde's four surviving children. They brought suit on November 18, 1986, under the wrongful death and survival statutes. TEX. CIV. PRAC. & REM. CODE ANN. §§ 71.001-.003, § 71.021 (Vernon 1986). The Peeks sued six defendants: Marvin Wiley DeBerry, Jr., who shot and killed Peek; Equipment Service Company, DeBerry's employer; Victor J. Weiss, M.D. and Burton O. Neeswig, M.D., two doctors who had treated DeBerry for mental illness; Suzanne Cude, DeBerry's estranged wife; and Oshman's Sporting Goods, Inc., the owner of the store in which DeBerry purchased the murder weapon. The Peeks plead for lost care, nurture, guidance, education, wages in the past and future, pain and suffering, mental anguish, grief, loss of companionship, and loss of enjoyment of life (hedonic damages), together with interest and costs. What they did not plead, however, was the amount of damages sought, either by properly alleging that damages exceeded the minimum jurisdictional limits of the court, *see* TEX. R. CIV. P. 47(b), or by alleging a sum certain.

The Peeks amended their petition on December 16, 1986, but made no changes in their defective allegations of damages. In a second amended pleading, filed January 14, 1987, the Peeks sought $3,750,000 actual damages and $5,000,000 exemplary damages against the defendants, jointly and severally. This pleading, however, came more than two years after Clyde's death. All defendants except Oshman's Sporting Goods, Inc. filed motions to dismiss, alleging that the

Peeks had failed to invoke the jurisdiction of the district court prior to the running of the two-year statute of limitations. TEX. CIV. PRAC. & REM. CODE ANN. § 16.003(b) (Vernon 1986). The trial court granted these motions at various times, and severance orders were signed so that these judgments became final.

The Peeks timely appealed to the court of appeals, which affirmed the judgments of the trial court in two opinions. From both judgments of the court of appeals, the Peeks applied to this court for writ of error. After granting both writs, we consolidated the two causes for oral argument and decision. The parties here have assumed the minimum monetary jurisdictional limit of the district court to be $500.00. Although recent constitutional and legislative changes call this assumption into question, we will also assume, for purposes of our decision, that the jurisdiction of the district court does not extend to controversies involving sums of less than $500.00.

In this case, all parties agree that the trial court's jurisdiction was invoked not later than the filing of the Peeks' second amended petition. The respondents, however, argue that the Peeks did not invoke jurisdiction by the first two pleadings, and hence did not obtain jurisdiction until after limitations had run. The Peeks, on the other hand, assert that their original petition did invoke the trial court's jurisdiction. Although the petition did not expressly allege that the amount sought was within the court's jurisdiction, neither did anything in the petition suggest that the court lacked jurisdiction. In fact, the Peeks argue that the nature of the loss sustained and the claims asserted made it absolutely apparent that plaintiffs sought damages far in excess of five hundred dollars.

The court of appeals held, however, that the Peeks' claims were time barred because the second amended petition, which alleged sufficient jurisdictional facts, was not filed prior to the expiration of limitations. In so holding, the court of appeals rejected the Peeks' theory that their second amended petition should relate back to the date of original filing. Instead, the court concluded that a petition which does not affirmatively state that the amount in controversy is above the minimum monetary jurisdiction of the district court is, in effect, no pleading.

In reaching this conclusion, the court relied heavily on our decision in *Richardson v. First National Life Ins. Co.*, 419 S.W.2d 836 (Tex. 1967). In that case, Richardson sued for breach of contract, alleging in his petition that he believed that "at least the amount of $314.37" was due to him, and also seeking an accounting and general relief. The defendant attacked Richardson's pleading with special exceptions and, after Richardson failed to amend, the trial court dismissed his claim. The court of appeals and this court both affirmed. We held that because Richardson had specifically pleaded an amount under the minimum jurisdiction of the district court, he could not rely on his more general allegations to sustain jurisdiction. Richardson, in effect, pleaded himself out of court. In the instant case, however, the Peeks' original and first amended petitions did not affirmatively demonstrate an absence of jurisdiction. Under these circumstances, a liberal construction of the pleadings is appropriate. "In any doubtful case all intendments of the plaintiff's pleading will be in favor of the jurisdiction." Unless it is clear from the pleadings that the court lacks jurisdiction of the amount in controversy, it should retain the case. As one court recently said: "[W]e must presume in favor of the jurisdiction unless lack of jurisdiction affirmatively appears on the face of the petition."

The failure of a plaintiff to state a jurisdictional amount in controversy in its petition, without more, thus will not deprive the trial court of jurisdiction. Even if the jurisdictional amount is never established by pleading, in fact, a plaintiff may recover if jurisdiction is proved at trial. This result is consistent with our holdings in cases when a plaintiff has failed to plead facts which state a cause of action. Unless the petition affirmatively demonstrates that no cause of action exists or that plaintiff's recovery is barred, we require the trial court to give the plaintiff an opportunity to amend before granting a motion to dismiss or a motion for summary judgment. And unless defendant objects, the plaintiff may proceed to trial, however defective its allegations. So it is here. In the absence of special exceptions or other motion, defendant waives the right to complain of such a defect if plaintiff establishes the trial court's jurisdiction before resting its case.

In summary, we hold that the omission of any allegation regarding the amount in controversy from plaintiff's petition did not deprive the court of jurisdiction, but was instead a defect in pleading subject to special exception and amendment. Although defective, the original petition filed in this cause was sufficient to invoke the jurisdiction of the district court. The court of appeals therefore erred in affirming the judgments of dismissal, as the Peeks amended their petition and cured the defect prior to the rendition of the judgments which dismissed their claims. Accordingly, the judgments of the court of appeals are reversed and the causes remanded to the trial court for further proceedings.

Notes & Questions

1. *Pleadings and discovery*. The discovery rules allow parties to seek their opponent's contentions by request for disclosure,[1] interrogatory,[2] or request for admission.[3] Thus, some judges will not grant special exceptions that seek additional details when the pleading satisfies the fair notice standard. Instead, the party is encouraged to use the discovery process to obtain this information. What are the comparative advantages and disadvantages of obtaining more information about an opponent's case through discovery rather than pleadings? Why might the federal courts be moving to more detailed pleadings?[4]

2. *General demurrer*. Rule 90 prohibits the use of a general demurrer. A general demurrer *generally* excepts or objects to the pleadings without pointing out any specific defect. In the old days, parties would file a general demurrer to the opponent's pleadings that put the opponent on notice that the party expected perfect pleadings, without pointing out any particular problem. Any failure could be brought up on appeal as a reason for reversal of the judgment. The special exception is a special demurrer, which specially or *specifically* points out the pleading defect, making it much easier to cure the defect. An example of a fairly recent general demurrer appeared in *McKamey v. Kinnear*[5] as follows:

> "Plaintiff [sic, defendant] excepts . . . [naming the particular paragraph of the petition] because said allegations are too general; because said allegations are a mere conclusion of the pleader; because no facts are alleged on which said conclusions are based; because said allegations do not inform this defendant of the facts on which the plaintiff intends to rely; because said allegations do not inform this defendant of the proof that he will be required to meet on the trial of this cause and because said allegations are calculated to sur-

---

1 Rule 194

2 Rule 197.

3 Rule 198.

4 *See* Iqbal Bell Atlantic Corp. v. Twombly, 127 S.Ct. 1955 (2007).

5 484 S.W.2d 150 (Tex. Civ. App.—Beaumont 1972, writ ref'd n.r.e.)

prise and prejudice the defendant on the trial of this cause; because said allegations are calculated to cause a mistrial; said allegations should be in all things stricken and of this exception the defendant prays judgment of the Court."

D. Curing Pleading Defects Pretrial

Courts sometimes dismiss cases for pleading defects, but usually only after the pleader has been given an opportunity to cure the defect. Texas provides two primary mechanisms to cure problems in pleadings—amended and supplemental pleadings. And these methods are sometimes used to assert claims outside the statute of limitations, triggering a special provision of Texas law that allows some of these pleadings to "relate back" to an original, timely petition.

1. *Amended and Supplemental Pleadings Generally*

Read Rules 62-65, 68-70.

Most pleading defects are cured with an amended pleading. The rules provide for "amended pleadings" and "supplemental pleadings," and each raise distinct (and sometimes overlapping) procedural issues.

An amended pleading takes the place of the previously filed pleading that it amends and must be complete within itself. The previous pleading is superseded and is no longer an active pleading.[1] A supplemental pleading is not complete within itself, but only supplements a previously filed pleading. Typically, a supplemental pleading replies to allegations in an opponent's previous pleadings (*e.g.,* when a plaintiff needs to plead affirmative defenses to a defendant's affirmative defenses to the plaintiff's claims). Both the previously filed pleading and the supplemental pleading are active pleadings.[2] Each amended or supplemental pleading should be properly designated and numbered (*e.g.,* "Plaintiff's Third Amended Original Petition") so that the parties and the court can determine which are the current live pleadings. The rules also provide for a "trial amendment," which is not complete in itself, and may be simply a handwritten addition to the active pleading.[3]

Pleadings are amended to add new matters, drop old matters, and correct defects. The Texas pleading amendment rules are different from the federal rules, which allow amendments only upon leave of court.[4] In Texas, as discussed more fully later in this chapter, parties may file new pleadings at any time so long "as not to operate as a surprise to the opposite party."[5] Leave of court is required only if the pleading is sought to be filed within seven days of trial (or another time if the court specifically orders such).[6] However, the court must grant leave to amend unless

---

1 *See* Rules 64, 65.

2 *See* Rules 69, 80, 98.

3 *See* Rule 66. Trial amendments are discussed in detail in section C of this chapter.

4 FRCP 15(a).

5 Rule 63.

6 *Id.*; *see also* Rule 166.

the opponent of the new pleading shows that it will operate as a surprise.[7] Thus, a party can oppose a new pleading by filing a motion to strike the filed pleading or responding to a motion for leave to amend and presenting evidence of surprise. Nevertheless, even if the new pleading surprises the opponent, the court can allow the pleading and grant a continuance of the trial date. The additional time before trial will allow the opponent time for additional preparation that will alleviate any surprise.[8]

2. *Relation Back of Amended Pleadings Filed Outside of the Limitations Period*

Read CPRC § 16.068.

LEXINGTON INSURANCE COMPANY
v.
DAYBREAK EXPRESS, INC.
393 S.W.3d 242
(Tex. 2013)

Opinion

PER CURIAM.

The principal question in this case is whether, for purposes of Section 16.068 of the Texas Civil Practice and Remedies Code, an action for cargo damage against a common carrier, brought under the Carmack Amendment to the Interstate Commerce Act, 49 U.S.C. § 14706, relates back to an action for breach of an agreement to settle the cargo-damage claim. The answer depends on whether the cargo-damage claim is, in the words of Section 16.068, "wholly based on a new, distinct, or different transaction or occurrence" than the breach-of-settlement claim. A divided court of appeals held that a cargo-damage claim does not relate back and is therefore barred by limitations. 342 S.W.3d 795 (Tex. App.—Houston [14th Dist.] 2011). We disagree and accordingly reverse the judgment of the court of appeals and render judgment for the plaintiff.

J. Supor and Son Trucking and Rigging Company engaged respondent Daybreak Express, Inc. to transport computer equipment belonging to Burr Computer Environments, Inc. from New Jersey to Texas. When the shipment arrived, Burr claimed it was damaged. Despite Burr's contention that Daybreak's adjuster had agreed on Daybreak's behalf to settle the claim for $166,655, Daybreak would pay only $5,420. Burr also asserted a claim against Supor, whose insurer, petitioner Lexington Insurance Co., paid Burr $87,500. Then, as subrogee, Lexington sued Daybreak, but only for breaching the settlement agreement, not for damaging Burr's equipment.

An interstate carrier's responsibility for goods it transports is governed by the Carmack Amendment. Enacted in 1906, the Carmack Amendment "supersedes all state laws as to the rights and liabilities and exemptions created by such transaction." *Adams Express Co. v. Croninger*, 226 U.S. 491, 505, 33 S.Ct. 148, 57 L.Ed. 314 (1913) (internal quotation marks omitted). Because the only action against an interstate common carrier for cargo damage is under fed-

---

[7] *Id.*

[8] *See* Rule 70 (allowing court to award to the surprised party costs and expenses incurred as a result of the continuance).

eral law, Daybreak removed the case to federal court. It cited *Hoskins v. Bekins Van Lines*, 343 F.3d 769, 778 (5th Cir.2003), which states:

> Congress intended for the Carmack Amendment to provide the exclusive cause of action for loss or damages to goods arising from the interstate transportation of those goods by a common carrier. Accordingly, we hold that the complete pre-emption doctrine applies. Because the Carmack Amendment provides the exclusive cause of action for such claims, . . . claims [for such loss or damages] "only arise[ ] under federal law and [can], therefore, be removed. . . ."

(emphasis in original, citation omitted). But the federal court distinguished *Hoskins:*

> In the present case, by contrast, Lexington does not seek to impose liability on Daybreak for damages arising from the interstate transport of property. Instead, Lexington seeks to enforce an agreement it alleges Daybreak entered into in order to settle claims for damages to a shipment of electrical equipment. Resolution of this contract claim does not turn on the rights and responsibilities of Daybreak as a carrier in interstate commerce. The point of the alleged settlement agreement was precisely that Lexington's subrogor would *not* pursue the claims that may fall under the Carmack Amendment. Because this is not a suit to recover for loss or damage to property against a carrier but rather one to enforce a settlement agreement, the case will be remanded to state court.

Lexington Ins. Co. v. Daybreak Express, Inc., 391 F.Supp.2d 538, 541 (S.D. Tex. 2005) (footnote omitted).

Although Lexington successfully avoided removal by not asserting a cargo-damage claim, on remand, it amended its petition to assert one. Lexington filed its amended pleading more than four years after Daybreak rejected Burr's claim, and Daybreak contended the claim was barred by limitations. But Lexington argued that the cargo-damage claim related back to its original action for breach of the settlement agreement, which was filed within two years of Daybreak's rejection of Burr's claim and not barred by limitations. The relation-back doctrine, codified in Section 16.068, states:

> If a filed pleading relates to a cause of action . . . that is not subject to a plea of limitation when the pleading is filed, a subsequent amendment or supplement to the pleading that changes the facts or grounds of liability or defense is not subject to a plea of limitation unless the amendment or supplement is wholly based on a new, distinct, or different transaction or occurrence.

TEX. CIV. PRAC. & REM. CODE § 16.068. The trial court agreed with Lexington, and after a bench trial, rendered judgment against Daybreak for $85,800.

A divided court of appeals reversed. 342 S.W.3d 795 (Tex. App.—Houston [14th Dist.] 2011). The court held that Section 16.068 applies to a Carmack Amendment claim. *Id.* at 803-804. Since the parties do not argue to the contrary, we assume this is correct. The majority then concluded that the cargo-damage and breach-of-settlement claims were based on wholly different transactions, one centering on the transport of Burr's equipment and the other on the existence of a settlement agreement. *Id.* at 804. Further, the court reasoned, if the shipment and settlement were not different transactions, the Carmack Amendment would preempt the breach-of-settlement claim and removal would have been proper.

> The expansive reach of complete preemption under the Carmack Amendment means that any cause of action arising from the interstate transportation of goods by a common carri-

> er "is either wholly federal or nothing at all" regardless of how it is labeled . . . . Lexington's claim for breach of the purported settlement agreement cannot be both unpreempted and less than wholly distinct from the interstate transportation of goods by a common carrier.

Id. at 806 (quoting *Hoskins*, 343 F.3d at 773, emphasis in original, internal quotation marks partially omitted).

"Transaction or occurrence" is a concept fundamental to modern civil procedure. *See, e.g.*, TEX. R. CIV. P. 38 (third-party practice), 40 (joinder), 50 (pleading), 97 (counterclaims and cross-claims); TEX. CIV. PRAC. & REM. CODE § 16.068 (limitations); *Barr v. Resolution Trust Corp.*, 837 S.W.2d 627 (Tex. 1992) (res judicata). The United States Supreme Court has observed that " '[t]ransaction' is a word of flexible meaning. It may comprehend a series of many occurrences, depending not so much upon the immediateness of their connection as upon their logical relationship." *Moore v. N.Y. Cotton Exch.*, 270 U.S. 593, 610, 46 S.Ct. 367, 70 L.Ed. 750 (1926). Rule 15(c)(1)(B) of the Federal Rules of Civil Procedure employs a standard similar to Section 16.068, allowing relation back of a claim, pleaded by amendment, "that arose out of the conduct, transaction, or occurrence set out—or attempted to be set out—in the original pleading." FED. R. CIV. P. 15(c)(1)(B). "[T]he search . . . is for a common core of operative facts in the two pleadings." 6 CHARLES ALAN WRIGHT, ARTHUR R. MILLER, & MARY K. KANE, FEDERAL PRACTICE & PROCEDURE § 1497 (3rd ed.2010). "Although not expressly mentioned in the rule, the courts also inquire into whether the opposing party has been put on notice regarding the claim or defense raised by the amended pleading." *Id.*; *see also* 2 ROY W. MCDONALD & ELAINE A. GRAFTON CARLSON, TEXAS CIVIL PRACTICE § 10.18 (2d ed. 2002) ("The inquiry applied should be the pragmatic one of notice . . . .").

In the present case, the cargo-damage claim and the breach-of-settlement claim both arose out of the same occurrence: Daybreak's shipment of Burr's computer equipment. The settlement was an effort to reach agreement on the damages recoverable under the Carmack Amendment. Although Lexington might recover on the breach-of-settlement claim without proving the amount of damage to the equipment, that damage was the basis for the settlement agreement. Daybreak might well argue that it is unreasonable to believe that it agreed to pay thirty times more than it actually paid. Daybreak had fair notice that the amount of damage might be in issue, as well as whether an agreement had been reached.

The court of appeals' conclusion that the two claims are based on two separate transactions is contradicted by our decision in *Leonard v. Texaco, Inc.*, 422 S.W.2d 160 (Tex. 1967). There, a surface owner sued the mineral lessee for property damages caused by the lessee's seismic operations. Later, after limitations had run, the surface owner amended his petition to add a claim that the lessee had breached an agreement to pay for the damages, possibly to avoid having to prove negligence. *Id.* at 161, 162; *see Humble Oil & Ref. Co. v. Williams*, 420 S.W.2d 133, 134 (Tex. 1967) ("A person who seeks to recover from the lessee for damages to the surface has the burden of alleging and proving either specific acts of negligence or that more of the land was used by the lessee than was reasonably necessary."). In *Leonard,* the surface owner prevailed on the contract claim at trial, but the court of civil appeals reversed, holding under Section 16.068's predecessor, which contained the same relation-back standard, that the contract claim did not relate back to the property damage claim and was therefore barred by limitations. We disagreed. *Id.* at 162. Though the initial claim "sounded in tort and alleged an excessive use of land" and the later claim "set up a promise to pay . . . damages" that sounded in contract, we concluded: "it cannot be said" that the latter was "wholly based upon and growing out of a different transaction or occurrence." *Id.* at 163.

In *Leonard,* as in the present case, one claim centered on damage to property and the other on an alleged agreement to pay for the damage. And in each case, the requirements for proof of the two claims were somewhat different. But the claims in each cases arose out of the same occurrence and involved the same injury to property. Leonard's holding that the two claims were not based on wholly different transactions forecloses the court of appeals' contrary conclusion in this case.

The federal district court's holding that Lexington's breach-of-settlement claim is not preempted by the Carmack Amendment does not compel the conclusion that it is based on a wholly different transaction than the cargo-damage claim. Again, " '[t]ransaction' is a word of flexible meaning." *Moore*, 270 U.S. at 610, 46 S.Ct. 367. Preemption assures uniform, predictable standards of responsibility for common carriers in transactions involving interstate shipments. Relation back allows an untimely claim not wholly based on a different transaction than a timely claim. The two principles serve different purposes.

We hold that under Section 16.068, Lexington's cargo-damage claim was not barred by limitations. Accordingly, we grant Lexington's petition for review and, without hearing oral argument, reverse the judgment of the court of appeals and remand this case to that court for further proceedings. TEX. R. APP. P. 59.1.

Notes & Questions

More recently, the Supreme Court confronted the issue of whether case a post-mortem fraud claim related back to a petition that asserted medical malpractice.[1] The original petition asserted pre-death medical malpractice following the death of a patient (Jerry Carswell) against a group of defendants. Years later (and outside of the limitations period) the plaintiffs amended the petition to include, e.g., a claim for fraud in obtaining consent for a private autopsy to allegedly cover up the medical malpractice. The court held that this amendment did not relate back to the original petition:

> It is apparent from what we have set out above that the facts underlying the Carswells' pre-mortem medical malpractice claims (1) are separated in time from the facts underlying the claim for damages based on post-mortem fraud, (2) are based on facts different and distinct from those underlying the fraud claim, and (3) involve a different set of occurrences from that underlying the fraud claim. The acts and omissions underlying the medical malpractice claims allegedly caused Carswell's death. The acts underlying the post-mortem claim did not, and indeed could not, have had any causal relationship to his death.[2]

Do you agree that the post-mortem fraud claim was based on a wholly new transaction or occurrence, distinct from the alleged pre-death medical malpractice?

---

[1] Christus Health Gulf Coast v. Carswell, 505 S.W.3d 528, 530 (Tex. 2016).

[2] Christus Health Gulf Coast v. Carswell, 505 S.W.3d 528, 538 (Tex. 2016).

E. Defense Pleadings

As discussed above, Texas practice allows the defendant to generally deny the plaintiff's allegations in most cases, except where specific denial is expressly required. But how does the defendant raise defenses, particularly affirmative defenses? And how does the defendant raise that special Texas creature—the "inferential rebuttal"—to obtain a jury instruction on sole proximate cause or unavoidable accident? Moreover, the defendant may want to plead counterclaims and cross-claims, upon which the defendant has the burden, against the plaintiff or a third-party. Each of these issues is addressed in turn in this subsection.

1. *Defenses and Denials*

Sometimes it is difficult to determine who has the burden of pleading and proof. Sometimes it is difficult to determine whether a matter is a part of the plaintiff's cause of action, where the plaintiff has the burden of pleading and proof, or an affirmative defense, where the defendant must plead and prove the negative to avoid liability. The answer may be a matter of history,[1] of statutory construction,[2] or of efficiency and public policy. Consider the following opinions.

ZORRILLA
v.
AYPCO CONSTRUCTION II, LLC
469 S.W.3d 143
(Tex. 2015)

Opinion

JUSTICE GUZMAN.

In this residential construction dispute, the paramount issue on appeal is whether the statutory cap on exemplary damages is waived if not pleaded as an affirmative defense or avoidance. *See* TEX. R. CIV. P. 94 (requiring pleading and proof of affirmative defenses and avoidances); *see also* TEX. CIV. PRAC. & REM. CODE § 41.008(b) (limiting exemplary damages to the greater of $200,000 or two times economic damages plus noneconomic damages not exceeding $750,000). Our courts of appeals are split on the issue, and in this case, the lower court affirmed an exemplary damages award in excess of the statutory cap because the petitioner did not assert the cap until her motion for new trial. 421 S.W.3d 54, 68-69 (Tex. App.—Corpus Christi 2013). We hold the exemplary damages cap is not a "matter constituting an avoidance or affirmative defense" and need not be affirmatively pleaded because it applies automatically when invoked and does not require proof of additional facts. *See* TEX. R. CIV. P. 94. Here, the petitioner did not plead the statutory cap but she timely asserted the cap in her motion for new trial. We therefore reverse the

---

1 See Environmental Processing Systems, L.C. v. FPL Farming Ltd., 457 S.W.3d 414 (Tex. 2015) (lack of consent is an element of the plaintiff's trespass claim).

2 *See, e.g.*, Philadelphia Indem. Ins. Co. v. White, 490 S.W.3d 468, 485 (Tex. 2016) (construing property code to hold that tenant "carried the burden of pleading and proving the contract's invalidity as an affirmative defense" in property damage subrogation action).

court of appeals' judgment in part and render judgment capping exemplary damages at $200,000. We affirm the court of appeals' judgment in all other respects.

I. Background

[The court provides a long discussion of the facts, relevant to issues other than the pleading issue. Basically, the petitioner, Zorrilla, hired the respondent to perform construction work on two residential properties. She refused to pay invoices sent after a certain date and she claimed that she never agreed to the additional work for which the invoices sought payment.]

* * *

When Zorrilla did not pay the May invoices, Aypco Construction and Munoz sued Zorrilla for breach of contract and fraud, among other claims. Aypco and Munoz also sought attorney's fees, exemplary damages, and foreclosure of mechanic's and materialman's liens attached to the North 23rd Street and Plazas del Lago properties. The case was tried before a jury on fraud, breach-of-contract, and quantum meruit theories.

* * *

The jury found that Zorrilla defrauded Aypco Construction and awarded $56,654.15 in economic damages and $250,000 in exemplary damages. The jury also found Zorrilla breached an agreement to pay Aypco for construction services at her two homes and awarded a total of $56,654.15 in actual damages. In addition to compensatory and exemplary damages, the jury awarded Aypco Construction $150,000 in attorney's fees through trial and conditional attorney's fees in the event of an appeal.

Aypco Construction moved for judgment on the jury's verdict, electing to recover under its fraud theory. The trial court awarded fraud and exemplary damages as found by the jury, plus attorney's fees and prejudgment interest at the rate of 1.5% per month pursuant to the Prompt Payment to Contractors and Subcontractors Act (the Prompt Payment Act). In addition to money damages, the court ordered foreclosure of Aypco Construction's liens on the North 23rd Street and Plazas del Lago properties.

In a motion for new trial, Zorrilla attacked the judgment on multiple grounds, including that (1) the award of attorney's fees was inconsistent with Aypco's election of remedies; (2) the evidence was insufficient to support the misrepresentation and reliance elements of the jury's fraud finding; (3) the exemplary damages award failed for the same reason; (4) the jury's breach-of-contract finding could not be sustained in light of evidence that Zorrilla paid more than the original estimate and had specifically informed Aypco and Munoz that she would not pay for any work after April; (5) exemplary damages should be capped in accordance with section 41.008(b) of the Texas Civil Practice and Remedies Code; (6) the statutory lien on the North 23rd Street property was invalid because that property was her homestead and work had commenced on the property before a written contract was executed in accordance with the lien statute; and (7) the correct prejudgment-interest rate was 6% because the parties did not agree to any other interest rate. Zorrilla's motion was overruled by operation of law. *See* TEX. R. CIV. P. 329b(c).

The court of appeals affirmed the trial court's judgment except the award of attorney's fees. 421 S.W.3d at 58. . . . In affirming the exemplary damages award, the court concluded that (1) the statutory cap on exemplary damages did not apply because Zorrilla failed to expressly plead the cap as an affirmative defense and (2) the uncapped exemplary damages award did not exceed due-process limits. *Id.* at 69, 72.

On appeal to this Court, Zorrilla devotes most of her efforts to the exemplary damages issue, arguing that (1) she was not required to plead the statutory cap on exemplary damages and (2) if uncapped, the exemplary damages award is excessive and violates due process. . . .

II. Discussion

* * *

B. Exemplary Damages

We turn now to Zorrilla's primary argument contesting the exemplary damages award. Zorrilla argues the award of exemplary damages in the amount of $250,000 on $56,654.15 in economic damages (1) exceeds the statutory cap and should be reduced accordingly and (2) if uncapped the award violates both the United States and Texas Constitutions. Because we resolve the first issue in Zorrilla's favor, we do not reach the second issue.

Section 41.008 of the Texas Civil Practice and Remedies Code provides that:

> Exemplary damages awarded against a defendant may not exceed an amount equal to the greater of:
>
> (1)(A) two times the amount of economic damages; plus
>
> (B) an amount equal to any noneconomic damages found by the jury, not to exceed $750,000; or
>
> (2) $200,000.

TEX. CIV. PRAC. & REM. CODE § 41.008(b). Zorrilla concedes she did not specifically plead the statutory cap on exemplary damages and did not raise the issue until her motion for new trial. Aypco contends that Zorrilla therefore waived the statutory cap. The court of appeals adopted Aypco's approach, but we agree with Zorrilla.

The Texas Rules of Civil Procedure require that specific defenses and any matter "constituting an avoidance or affirmative defense" "shall [be] set forth affirmatively" in a responsive pleading. TEX. R. CIV. P. 94. If an affirmative defense or avoidance is not expressly pleaded, the party cannot rely on the defense as a bar to liability. *MAN Engines & Components, Inc. v. Shows*, 434 S.W.3d 132, 136 (Tex. 2014). Rule 94 does not explicitly require that a damages cap be affirmatively pleaded. *See* TEX. R. CIV. P. 94. We must therefore determine whether the exemplary damages cap in section 41.008(b) falls within Rule 94's residual clause, which extends the affirmative-pleading requirement to "any other matter constituting an avoidance or affirmative defense." *See id.*

The scope of a procedural rule is a question of law, which we review de novo by applying the same canons of construction applicable to statutes. *Morris v. Aguilar*, 369 S.W.3d 168, 171 n.4 (Tex. 2012). Accordingly, we start by giving Rule 94's language its plain and literal meaning. *In re Christus Spohn Hosp. Kleberg*, 222 S.W.3d 434, 437 (Tex. 2007).

Aypco and its amici argue that "affirmative defense" and "avoidance" are necessarily distinct terms of art because the inclusion of two separate terms would be redundant and serve no purpose. They suggest, without offering support, that the term "avoidance" broadly includes new matters of law and fact that are outside of the plaintiff's pleadings. We disagree.

"Avoidance" is best defined in reference to "affirmative defense." Also called a plea in avoidance, an "affirmative defense" is "[a] defendant's assertion of facts and arguments that, if true, will defeat the plaintiff's or prosecution's claim, even if all the allegations in the complaint are true." BLACK'S LAW DICTIONARY 509 (10th ed. 2009). In contrast, the term "avoidance" derives from the historic English common-law pleas of "confession and avoidance." *See* 5 Charles Alan Wright & Arthur R. Miller, *Federal Practice and Procedure* § 1270 (3d ed. 2004); *see also* BLACK'S LAW DICTIONARY at 163 (defining "avoidance" by reference to "confession and avoidance"). In its ordinary meaning, a "confession and avoidance" is "a plea in which a defendant admits allegations but pleads additional facts that deprive the admitted facts of an adverse legal effect." BLACK'S LAW DICTIONARY at 361. Essentially:

> [A confession-and-avoidance plea] is one of justification. It is based on a different set of facts from those establishing [the cause of action]. As an affirmative defense it [acknowledges] the existence of prima facie liability but [asserts] a proposition which, if established, avoids such liability. Rather than being in conflict with the [cause of action], the [confession and avoidance] admits it but asserts the existence of other facts which justify or excuse it.

Norris v. Branham, 557 S.W.2d 816, 818 (Tex. App.—El Paso 1977, writ ref'd n.r.e.) (describing self-defense, a defense long recognized as a plea in confession and avoidance); *see also Genesis Tax Loan Servs. Inc. v. Kothmann*, 339 S.W.3d 104, 108 (Tex. 2011) (defining avoidance as "an independent reason why the plaintiff should not recover"). For example, a statute of limitations is an affirmative defense, rather than a plea in confession and avoidance, because limitations defeats the plaintiff's claim without regard to the truth of the plaintiff's assertions. *See Woods v. William M. Mercer, Inc.*, 769 S.W.2d 515, 517-18 (Tex. 1988). In contrast, self-defense is a confession-and-avoidance plea because the defendant admits the conduct but seeks to avoid the legal effect by justifying an otherwise impermissible act. *Grieger v. Vega*, 271 S.W.2d 85, 90 (Tex. 1954); *see also Gibbins v. Berlin*, 162 S.W.3d 335, 340 (Tex. App.—Forth Worth 2005, no pet.) (distinguishing between self-defense in the civil context and self-defense in the criminal context). Similarly, contributory negligence is a plea in confession and avoidance because the defense allows a negligent defendant to defeat the plaintiff's recovery either partially or completely, depending on the percentage of the plaintiff's responsibility. *See, e.g., Jannette v. Deprez*, 701 S.W.2d 56, 59 (Tex. App.—Dallas 1985, writ ref'd n.r.e.).

Because "avoidance" and "affirmative defense" are closely related terms, courts frequently use the words interchangeably. *See, e.g., MAN Engines*, 434 S.W.3d at 136 (describing disclaimer as both an avoidance and an affirmative defense). Moreover, though a plea in confession and avoidance is historically distinct from an affirmative defense, the modern legal lexicon has muddled the distinction. *Compare Murray v. Gulf, C. & S.F. Ry. Co.*, 11 S.W. 125, 127 (Tex. 1889) ("If defendant relies upon contributory negligence not developed by the plaintiff's case, he must allege it. It is a defense in the nature of avoidance."), with *Keck, Mahin & Cate v. Nat'l Union Fire Ins. Co.*, 20 S.W.3d 692, 696 (Tex. 2000) ("[Defendant] denied responsibility and asserted . . . an affirmative defense against [plaintiff], based on the [plaintiff's] contributory negligence or comparative responsibility.").

Though semantically troubling, lack of precision is inconsequential here. Whether classified as an affirmative defense or an avoidance, the hallmark characteristic of both categories of defenses is that the burden of proof is on the defendant to present sufficient evidence to establish the defense and obtain the requisite jury findings. *See Denton Publ'g. Co. v. Boyd*, 460 S.W.2d 881, 882 (Tex. 1970) (holding that failure to prove and obtain favorable jury findings in support of an avoidance defense constitutes waiver); *Barfield v. Howard M. Smith Co. of Amarillo*, 426 S.W.2d 834, 839 (Tex. 1968) (concluding that estoppel did not bar the petitioner's claim because the defendant failed to prove all the essential elements of the affirmative defense); *Cameron Compress*

Co. v. Kubecka, 283 S.W. 285, 287 (Tex. Civ. App.—Austin 1926, writ ref'd) (citing *Boswell v. Pannell*, 180 S.W. 593, 595 (Tex. 1915)); *see also Ingraham v. United States*, 808 F.2d 1075, 1078-79 (5th Cir. 1987) (identifying the features of an affirmative defense).

The exemplary damages cap does not bear the characteristics of an affirmative defense or avoidance. Specifically, it does not require proof of any additional fact to establish its applicability; moreover, there is no defense to it. *See* TEX. CIV. PRAC. & REM. CODE § 41.008(b). Though certain types of claims are excluded from the statute's application, the statutory cap applies automatically to claims not expressly excepted. The cap is therefore the rule, not the exception.

A plaintiff can avoid the cap by pleading and proving the defendant intentionally or knowingly engaged in felonious conduct under criminal statutes expressly excluded from the cap under section 41.008(c). *See In re Columbia Med. Ctr. of Las Colinas*, 306 S.W.3d 246, 248 (Tex. 2010); *see also THI of Tex. at Lubbock I, LLC v. Perea*, 329 S.W.3d 548, 588 (Tex. App.—Amarillo 2010, pet. denied); *Hall v. Diamond Shamrock Ref. Co., L.P.*, 82 S.W.3d 5, 22 (Tex. App.—San Antonio 2001), rev'd on other grounds, 168 S.W.3d 164 (Tex. 2005). Nevertheless, the prospect of avoiding the cap upon plea and proof of cap-busting conduct, if possible, does not alter the fundamental principle that the statute does not impose a burden of proof on the defendant. Even in cases in which an exception is or may be invoked, the defendant bears no burden of establishing the cap's applicability; it either applies or it does not. We therefore conclude that the statutory cap on exemplary damages in section 41.008(b) is neither an affirmative defense nor an avoidance subject to Rule 94's affirmative pleading requirement.[11]

Because the statutory cap on exemplary damages automatically applies and its scope is delineated by statute, there is little concern that plaintiffs will be genuinely surprised by its application in any given case. *MAN Engines*, 434 S.W.3d at 136 ("Rule 94's purpose 'is to give the opposing party notice of the defensive issue to be tried.' It is a rule of fairness that requires the defendant to identify affirmative defenses, involving facts distinct from the elements of the plaintiff's claim, so that the plaintiff may reasonably prepare to rebut or explain them.") (quoting *Land Title Co. of Dallas, Inc. v. F.M. Stigler, Inc.*, 609 S.W.2d 754, 756 (Tex. 1980))). Section 41.008, in and of itself, provides sufficient notice of the types of claims that are excluded from the cap, allowing plaintiffs to structure their cases to avoid the cap when desired and possible. *See* TEX. CIV. PRAC. & REM. CODE § 41.008(c) (listing the crimes and intentional torts excluded from the statutory cap on exemplary damages). In the absence of a plea and proof of cap-busting conduct, the exemplary damages cap applies as a matter of law.

Zorrilla timely claimed the protection of the exemplary damages cap in her motion for new trial. *See* TEX. R. APP. P. 33. We therefore reverse the court of appeals' judgment and render judgment capping exemplary damages at $200,000. *See* TEX. CIV. PRAC. & REM. CODE § 41.008(b).

* * *

[11] Although not presented with such a scenario here, we do not foreclose the possibility that a different outcome might result if a damages cap applies only with proof of additional facts or circumstances. *See, e.g.*, Shoreline, Inc. v. Hisel, 115 S.W.3d 21, 25 (Tex. App.—Corpus Christi 2003, pet. denied) (analyzing TEX. LAB. CODE § 21.2585(d), which provides different damages caps depending on how many employees a responsible party employs.

III. Conclusion

For the reasons stated, we reverse the court of appeals' judgment as to the exemplary damages award and render judgment capping exemplary damages at $200,000. We otherwise affirm the court's judgment.

GREATHOUSE
v.
CHARTER NATIONAL BANK-SOUTHWEST

851 S.W.2d 173
(Tex. 1992)

HECHT, JUSTICE.

Section 9.504 of the Uniform Commercial Code, TEX. BUS. & COM. CODE § 9.504, requires that collateral must be disposed of in a commercially reasonable manner. The Code, however, does not allocate the burden of pleading and proving whether this requirement has been met in an action by a creditor against a debtor for the deficiency due after disposition of the collateral. We granted writ of error to resolve a split among Texas courts of appeals over this procedural issue.

Forrest Allen & Associates, Inc. defaulted on a note payable to Charter National Bank-Southwest, guaranteed by Clyde R. Greathouse, and secured by an assignment of insurance expirations, commissions, accounts receivable, furniture and fixtures. Charter took the pledged collateral and sold it for $100,000, leaving a principal balance due on the note of $151,014.95. Charter then sued Forrest Allen and Greathouse for the deficiency, interest and attorney fees. Greathouse died during the pendency of the suit, and the independent executrix of his estate was substituted as a defendant.

Charter did not plead that it had disposed of the collateral in a commercially reasonable manner, but it did plead generally that: "All conditions precedent have been performed or have occurred. All just and lawful credits, payments and offsets have been allowed." Defendants answered with a general denial. At trial before the court without a jury, Charter's sole witness established the amount due on the note after foreclosure, and Charter rested its case. Greathouse then moved for judgment on the grounds that Charter had failed to plead or prove an element of its cause of action, namely, a commercially reasonable disposition of the pledged collateral. Charter responded that it had satisfied its pleading obligation by alleging generally the performance of all conditions precedent, and that it was not required to prove the commercial reasonableness of the foreclosure absent a specific denial by Greathouse. Charter relied upon Rule 54, TEX. R. CIV. P., which states:

> In pleading the performance or occurrence of conditions precedent, it shall be sufficient to aver generally that all conditions precedent have been performed or have occurred. When such performances or occurrences have been so plead, the party so pleading same shall be required to prove only such of them as are specifically denied by the opposite party.

Charter also requested a continuance to procure evidence of the commercial reasonableness of the foreclosure sale. The trial court denied both Charter's request for a continuance and Greathouse's motion for judgment, and Greathouse rested its case without offering any evidence. After taking the case under submission, the trial court rendered judgment for Charter in the amount of $252,858.28.

Only Greathouse appealed. The court of appeals affirmed, holding "that the burden of specifically pleading a lack of commercial reasonableness or notice in a deficiency action under section 9.504 . . . rests with the debtor." Once the debtor has specifically raised the issue, the court held, the burden of proof is upon the creditor. The court reasoned: "Such an approach informs a creditor which areas (if any) are disputed and which items of proof must be produced; it does not allow a creditor to avoid proving its case . . . . Without indication of a debtor's objections, a creditor is prejudiced in the preparation of its case."

On the procedural issue before us, the Uniform Commercial Code has not achieved its purposes of simplification and uniformity of commercial law. Texas courts are severely split on the subject. Many of them indicate that the creditor must plead and prove a commercially reasonable disposition of the collateral, while others have treated commercial unreasonableness as a defense which the debtor must raise in order to shift the burden of proof to the creditor. Our sister states are equally divided. Some states place the burden on the creditor in a deficiency suit to both plead and prove compliance with the notice and commercial reasonableness requirements of section 9.504. In other states, the debtor raises the issue in pleadings as a counterclaim or a defense in order to put the creditor to proof on the matters so challenged, and the secured creditor then bears the burden of proving compliance. A few states treat the issue as an affirmative defense.

This division of authority illustrates the difficulty which attends an allocation of the burdens of pleading and proof. In discussing whether a matter should be considered an affirmative defense, Professor McDonald has observed:

> the allocation of an element to the plaintiff's case or to the defendant's affirmative pleading is not determined by abstract logic. There is no reason in logic, for instance, why a plaintiff should not be compelled as an element of his case to establish that he was free of contributory negligence or did not induce a particular contract by fraud; or that an assertedly subsisting claim has not been paid or released. Considerations of fairness and convenience, of the ease or difficulty of making proof, of the comparative likelihood that a particular defensive situation may exist in a reasonable proportion of the cases presented in court, and even of handicapping disfavored contentions, have contributed to the shaping of the concept of an "affirmative" defense.

2 ROY W. MCDONALD, TEXAS CIVIL PRACTICE IN DISTRICT AND COUNTY COURTS § 7.34.1.-C, at 221 (Frank W. Elliott ed., 1982 rev.). We employed one of these considerations in *Eckman v. Centennial Sav. Bank*, 784 S.W.2d 672, 675 (Tex. 1990), to assign the burden of pleading and proving whether a plaintiff has assets of $25 million or more and thus is excepted from the definition of business consumer under the Deceptive Trade Practices—Consumer Protection Act, TEX. BUS. & COM. CODE § 17.45(4). In assigning that burden to the defendant, we reasoned:

> The comparative likelihood that a certain situation may occur in a reasonable percentage of cases should be considered when determining whether a fact should be allocated as an element of the plaintiff's case or to the defendant as an affirmative defense. . . . Obviously, most litigants do not have assets of $25,000,000 or more. Requiring every DTPA plaintiff to prove that he is not a multimillionaire would be an inefficient and uneconomical use of judicial resources.

As Professor McDonald observed, logic alone does not dictate the assignment of the burden of pleading and proof. The division of authority throughout the country on the issue now before us demonstrates this. There is simply no clear answer to whether a creditor should be required to plead and prove that collateral has been disposed of in a commercially reasonable manner as an element of a claim for the amount due on the debt, or whether a debtor should be required to allege and show that collateral has not been so disposed of as a defense to the creditor's demand for payment. To resolve the issue, we consider factors like those Professor McDonald mentions.

A commercially reasonable disposition of collateral is in the nature of a condition to a creditor's recovery in a deficiency suit. We suggested this in *Tanenbaum v. Economics Laboratory, Inc.*, 628 S.W.2d 769, 771 (Tex. 1982), where we said: "The only limits on the creditor's disposition of the collateral is that it must be commercially reasonable, and must be made only after notification to the debtor if required by section 9.504. *Then and only then* is he entitled to sue for a deficiency." (Emphasis added.) Evidence on the issue will ordinarily be more readily available to the creditor, who takes the collateral and arranges for its disposition, than to the debtor, who ordinarily plays no role in the disposition and is absent when it occurs. In general, it is easier for a creditor to prove that a disposition of collateral was commercially reasonable than for a debtor to prove it was not. Furthermore, the creditor controls the disposition of the collateral, and the debtor often has little or no say in how it is done. Accordingly, the creditor bears greater responsibility to demonstrate that the disposition met the requirements of law. However, the commercial reasonableness of a disposition of collateral is not in dispute in most deficiency suits. To require proof of this issue in every case, even if it is not disputed, would be an unreasonable burden on the judicial process.

Based upon these considerations, we conclude that a creditor in a deficiency suit must plead that disposition of the collateral was commercially reasonable.[8] This may be pleaded specifically or by averring generally that all conditions precedent have been performed or have occurred. If pleaded generally, the creditor is required to prove that the disposition of collateral was commercially reasonable only if the debtor specifically denies it in his answer. Should the creditor plead specifically, then it must, of course, prove the allegation in order to obtain a favorable judgment.

In this case, Charter met its burden of pleading by its general allegation that all conditions precedent had been performed. In answer, Greathouse did not specifically deny that Charter's disposition of the collateral was commercially unreasonable. Consequently, Charter was not required to prove commercial reasonableness at trial. The trial court did not err in rendering judgment for Charter. Therefore, the judgment of the court of appeals is

Affirmed.

---

[8] We express no opinion on the allocation of the burdens of pleading and proof of commercial reasonableness in an action by a debtor against a creditor for wrongful foreclosure. The considerations would be different from those in deficiency actions.

2. *Inferential Rebuttals*

An inferential rebuttal is a strange animal, somewhat peculiar to Texas practice, primarily because of the Texas jury charge. An inferential rebuttal alleges a new factual theory that denies one of the elements of the plaintiff's cause of action by inference. It is different from an ordinary denial because it denies by inference instead of directly challenging the plaintiff's allegations. It is different from an affirmative defense because it does not "admit" the plaintiff's allegations, and the defendant does not assume any burden of proof. We will discuss inferential rebuttals in greater detail in the chapter on the jury charge. However, it bears some introduction here.

There are several recognized inferential rebuttals for negligence cases.[1] If the accident was "an act of God," then no one was negligent. Therefore, the accident could not be the result of defendant's negligence. If something other than the defendant's negligence was the "sole proximate cause" of the accident, the defendant's negligence was not the proximate cause. In other cases, inferential rebuttals are not so easily recognizable. For instance, a plaintiff may seek damages for breach of an employment contract, and the defendant may defend on the basis that the contract was a partnership agreement, rather than an employment agreement, under which nothing is owed. The defendant has alleged a defensive factual theory that presents an alternative to the plaintiff's theory, which therefore constitutes an inferential rebuttal. The plaintiff retains the burden of proof of its cause of action, and must disprove the defendant's inferential rebuttal theory.

---

1 The following are the inferential rebuttal instructions included in the GENERAL NEGLIGENCE volume of the TEXAS PATTERN JURY CHARGE:

PCJ 3.1 New and Independent Cause

"Proximate cause" means a cause, unbroken by any new and independent cause, that was a substantial factor in bringing about an [injury or occurrence] and without which cause such [injury or occurrence] would not have occurred. In order to be a proximate cause, the act or omission complained of must be such that a person using *ordinary care* would have foreseen that the [injury or occurrence], or some similar [injury or occurrence], might reasonably result therefrom. There may be more than one proximate cause of an [injury or occurrence].

"New and independent cause" means the act or omission of a separate and independent agency, not reasonably foreseeable, that destroys the causal connection, if any, between the act or omission inquired about and the occurrence in question and thereby becomes the immediate cause of such occurrence.

PJC 3.2 Sole Proximate Cause

There may be more than one proximate cause of an [injury or occurrence], but if an act or omission of any person not a party to the suit was the "sole proximate cause" of an [injury or occurrence], then no act or omission of any party could have been a proximate cause.

PJC 3.3 Emergency

If a person is confronted by an "emergency" arising suddenly and unexpectedly, which was not proximately caused by any negligence on his part and which, to a reasonable person, requires immediate action without time for deliberation, his conduct in such an emergency is not negligence or failure to use ordinary care if, after such emergency arises, he acts as a person of ordinary prudence would have acted under the same or similar circumstances.

PJC 3.4 Unavoidable Accident

An occurrence may be an "unavoidable accident," that is, an event not proximately caused by the negligence of any party to the occurrence.

At one time defendants were entitled to have a *question* submitted to the jury on the inferential rebuttal. Because the plaintiff retained the burden of proof, the question had to be worded in the negative (*e.g.,* "Do you find that the accident was not the result of an act of God?"), confusing the jury and often leading to inconsistent answers. Today, Rule 277 prevents a jury from being asked an inferential rebuttal question, although inferential rebuttal *instructions* may be allowed.

Because Rule 278 allows a court to submit only instructions that are raised by the written pleadings, a defendant who wants an inferential rebuttal instruction submitted to the jury should include the inferential rebuttal in its pleadings. Some courts, however, have allowed inferential rebuttal instructions based on a defendant's general denial.[2] A prudent practitioner should plead inferential rebuttals nonetheless.

3. *Counterclaims and Cross-Claims*

The answer also can contain the defendant's affirmative claims against the plaintiff or other parties where the defendant seeks to recover damages.[3] In these pleadings, the defendant becomes a "counter-plaintiff," a "cross-plaintiff," or a third-party plaintiff and must satisfy the pleading rules that apply to plaintiffs. The circumstances under which it is appropriate for defendants to file counterclaims and cross-claims will be discussed later, in the joinder chapter.

F. Curing Pleading Defects at Trial

Read Rules 63, 66, 67.

1. *Objections at Trial*

Parties often raise pleading defects before trial, by special exception. But just as often, they may be raised at trial when a party seeks to introduce evidence or requests a jury charge on matters that are not included in the pleadings—there is no "fair notice" that the party sought to introduce evidence on a certain matter or sought to recover on a particular cause of action. When evidence outside the pleadings is introduced, the opponent objects to its introduction because it is outside the pleadings. When a jury question, instruction or definition is submitted, the opponent objects to its being submitted to the jury because it is outside the pleadings.[1] If either objection is sustained, the pleading party may seek a trial amendment to conform the pleadings with the excluded evidence or jury question.[2]

---

[2] *See* Buls v. Fuselier, 55 S.W.3d 204, 211 (Tex. App. 2001) ("Evidence supporting an inferential rebuttal is admissible under a general denial, since its purpose is to rebut an element of the plaintiff's cause of action.").

[3] *See* Rule 97. No service of process is required, although the counterclaim must be served according to Rule 21a, Rule 124; Houston Crushed Concrete, Inc. v. Concrete Recycling Corp., 879 S.W.2d 258 (Tex. App.—Houston [14th Dist.] 1994, no writ).

[1] *See* Rule 278 (providing that the court shall submit questions, instructions and definitions "raised by the written pleadings and the evidence").

[2] *See* Rule 66.

MURRAY
v.
O & A EXPRESS, Inc.

630 S.W.2d 633
(Tex. 1982)

SPEARS, JUSTICE.

This action for damages arises out of a collision between an automobile and a parked truck. Plaintiffs Lawrence W. Murray and the beneficiaries under the wrongful death statute[1] of Kris Dale Christian, a deceased minor child, sued O & A Express and its employee Bill Danny Young alleging negligence and wrongful death. The trial court rendered judgment for Murray and the beneficiaries of Christian, holding that Young and O & A were negligent as a matter of law. The court of civil appeals reversed and remanded for a new trial. 614 S.W.2d 873.

The issue before this court is whether the pleadings and evidence support the trial court's finding that Young was negligent per se. We hold these findings were proper. We therefore reverse the judgment of the court of civil appeals and affirm the judgment of the trial court.

On March 29, 1974, Bill Danny Young was driving a truck owned and operated by O & A Express, Inc. on a run from El Paso, Texas to Roswell, New Mexico and back. Driving eastbound about 12 miles east of El Paso on U.S. Highway 62/180, Young experienced mechanical problems with the truck and pulled off the road onto the shoulder; however, it is uncontroverted that a portion of the truck protruded into the roadway. Young saw what he believed to be smoke coming out from the hood. First suspecting a fire, Young shut off all systems and inspected the engine. He found that almost all of the engine oil had leaked out of the truck and that the spilled oil was smoking. Young then turned on the truck's lights and attempted to start the engine. The starter functioned but the motor would not start. After several attempts to start the motor failed, Young spotted a westbound truck, turned his lights off and ran across the road to flag down the other truck. Young did not place any reflectors or warning flares on the road, nor did he activate the truck's warning flashers. While Young was across the highway talking with the other truck driver, a car driven by plaintiff Murray, in which Christian was a passenger, collided with Young's truck at the point where Young's truck protruded into the driving lane. The impact killed Christian and injured Murray.

Murray and the statutory beneficiaries of Christian brought suit against O & A Express and Bill Danny Young alleging negligence and wrongful death. The petition of Murray and Christian alleged negligence as follows:

> Plaintiff alleges that the Defendant, Bill Danny Young, was and is guilty of negligence in the following respects and particulars to wit:
>
> a. In that he then and there stopped his vehicle so that it extended into the Plaintiff's traffic lane;
>
> b. In that he then and there failed to set out any signal or warning devices;
>
> c. In other acts of negligence.

---

[1] Art. 4675. All statutory references are to Texas Revised Civil Statutes Annotated (Vernon).

O & A made no special exceptions to this petition. Murray's counsel made it clear in his opening statement to the jury that plaintiffs relied upon negligence per se in that Bill Danny Young had violated sections 93, 125, and 138 of article 6701d Texas Revised Civil Statutes.[2] Murray then introduced uncontested evidence which clearly established violations of these statutes. At the close of trial, the trial court instructed the jury in his charge that defendant Young was negligent as a matter of law. The trial court then submitted issues to the jury as to proximate cause and as to the comparative fault of Young and plaintiff Murray. The jury found that each of the three statutory violations was a proximate cause of the injury to Murray and the death of Christian. The jury also found that Murray was 10 percent responsible for the accident in failing to keep a proper lookout and that Young's negligence was 90 percent responsible. Damages were found to be $85,000 for Murray and $40,000 for the beneficiaries of Christian. After deducting for the negligence of Murray, the trial court rendered judgment on this verdict against both Young and his employer, O & A. O & A settled with Christian's beneficiaries and appealed only as to Murray.

The court of civil appeals held that Murray had not pleaded negligence per se and was therefore not entitled to recover on that theory. Thus, the court of civil appeals reversed the decision of the trial court and remanded the cause for a new trial.

The office of pleadings is to define the issues at trial. Pleadings should give fair and adequate notice of the facts upon which the pleader relies in order that the adverse party may properly prepare his defense thereto. Thus, in determining whether Murray's pleadings were sufficient to support an instruction on negligence per se, we focus upon the adequacy of the notice this pleading provided and the opportunity to prepare an adequate defense which the allegations afforded the defendants.

The unexcused violation of a penal statute constitutes negligence as a matter of law if such statute was designed to prevent injuries to a class of persons to which the injured party belongs.[3] When a defendant is alleged to be negligent as a matter of law because of the violation of a statute and a statutory violation is proven, the defendant's negligence is not at issue unless evidence of excuse is presented. The defendant in such a suit must frame his defense in terms of the recog-

---

2 Article 6701d provides in relevant part:

Sec. 93. (a) Upon any highway outside of a business or residence district no person shall stop, park, or leave standing any vehicle, whether attended or unattended, upon the paved or main-traveled part of the highway when it is practicable to stop, park, or so leave such vehicle off such part of said highway, but in every event an unobstructed width of the highway opposite a standing vehicle shall be left for the free passage of other vehicles and a clear view of such stopped vehicle shall be available from a distance of two hundred (200) feet in each direction upon such highway.

(b) This section shall not apply to the driver of any vehicle which is disabled while on the paved or main-traveled portion of a highway in such manner and to such extent that it is impossible to avoid stopping and temporarily leaving such disabled vehicle in such position.

Sec. 125. (d) Any vehicle may be equipped with lamps for the purpose of warning the operators of other vehicles of the presence of a vehicular traffic hazard requiring the exercise of unusual care in approaching, overtaking or passing.

* * *

3 It is clear in the present case that the statute involved was designed to prevent injury to persons such as Murray and Christian.

nized excuses for violation of a statute.[4] Since these excuses must be affirmatively raised by the evidence, it is important that the party alleged to be negligent as a matter of law be informed prior to trial that the opposing party relies upon the statutory violation. Thus, a party relying upon a statutory violation should plead this reliance if he is to recover on that basis. Further, the pleader should reasonably identify the statute relied upon.

Murray made no mention in his petition of the violation of a specific statute. However, this lack of a specific pleading of negligence per se was not raised by the defendants at any time during trial. O & A made no special exceptions to the pleadings of Murray even though those pleadings were general. Moreover, O & A did not object to the opening statement of Murray which made clear his reliance upon the statutes. Murray's evidence of statutory violations was likewise admitted without objection to the lack of pleadings. Finally, O & A never excepted to the lack of pleadings supporting the court's charge which instructed the jury that O & A and Young were negligent as a matter of law. Having failed to except to the lack of pleadings at any point during trial, O & A has waived any error in the pleadings of Murray.

O & A argues, and the court of civil appeals reasoned, that a trial exception to the lack of pleadings was not required because the evidence adduced at trial would have been equally consistent with the theory of common law negligence which Murray clearly alleged. However, the primary complaint of O & A is not that evidence was improperly admitted. Instead O & A complains that even though the negligence per se theory was not pleaded, the jury was instructed that the statutory violations by Young constituted negligence as a matter of law. Any ambiguity which might have existed as to the theory upon which Murray relied evaporated when Murray submitted a proposed instruction on negligence per se. By failing to make a specific objection to the lack of pleadings at the time the instruction was submitted, O & A deprived Murray of his opportunity to seek a trial amendment. TEX. R. CIV. P. 66, 274. Therefore, we see no reason why O & A should not be held to the requirement that a party complaining that an instruction is unsupported by pleadings object on that basis in the trial court.

* * *

The judgment of the court of civil appeals is reversed and the judgment of the trial court is affirmed.

---

4 In Impson v. Structural Metals, Inc., 487 S.W.2d 694, 696 (Tex. 1972), we approved the RESTATEMENT OF TORTS, SECOND § 288A as substantially stating Texas law concerning civil liability for violation of a penal statute. That section provides five categories of situations where a statutory violation is excused. They are:

(a) the violation is reasonable because of the actor's incapacity;

(b) he neither knows nor should know of the occasion for compliance;

(c) he is unable after reasonable diligence or care to comply;

(d) he is confronted by an emergency not due to his own misconduct;

(e) compliance would involve a greater risk of harm to the actor or to others.

Id. at 696.

Notes & Questions

1. *Trial by consent.* When evidence relating to a cause of action or facts not pleaded are introduced without objection, a jury question outside the pleadings is submitted to the jury without objection and the jury answers it affirmatively, the unpleaded matter is said to have been "tried by consent" under Rule 67. Thus, the plaintiff can recover on the matter, despite the lack of pleading. In effect, the defendant has waived complaint about plaintiff's failure to plead by not timely objecting when the evidence or jury question made it clear that the plaintiff was relying on unpleaded matters. If a party objects to the lack of pleading and the court sustains the objection, there can be no trial by consent, because the pleading party must amend the pleadings to recover on the unpleaded matter.[1]

2. *Notice for trial by consent.* The opposing party must have notice that an unpleaded theory is being tried in order to have trial by consent. For example, in *Boyles v. Kerr*,[2] a college coed sued a man she dated for emotional distress caused by his showing to friends videos taken by a hidden camera in his bedroom. She obtained a jury verdict for negligent infliction of emotional distress, which the Texas Supreme court reversed, refusing to recognize the negligence cause of action, but limiting emotional distress causes of action to intentional conduct. In discussing the pleadings, the Court said:

> Kerr argues that even if we do not recognize recovery for negligent infliction of emotional distress, we should recognize a cause of action for *grossly* negligent infliction of emotional distress. She contends that the judgment should be affirmed under this alternative cause of action as she obtained a jury finding, in connection with her claim for punitive damages, that Boyles was grossly negligent.
>
> Even assuming that such a cause of action were recognized in Texas, Kerr could not recover on it under the record before us because she did not plead or preserve this theory of recovery. * * *
>
> Nor was this cause of action tried by consent, as Kerr's presentation of the evidence did not put Boyles on notice that she was seeking to recover under such a theory. Although Kerr's proof was perhaps relevant to a Restatement § 46 cause of action, it was also relevant to her pled causes of action, and thus Boyles' failure to object did not constitute trial by consent.
>
> Any remaining doubt about Kerr's intention was laid to rest by her actions in response to Boyles' motion for instructed verdict. When Boyles' counsel contended that Kerr could not recover for negligence because the 'case had been tried from start to finish as an intentional tort . . . ,' Kerr's counsel objected strenuously, pointedly remarking that 'should the Court adopt counsel's suggestion, counsel would have dropped his client in the grease in that he would have gotten totally out of coverage.' Moreover, before the court ruled on Boyles' motion, Kerr's counsel abandoned her actions for intentional invasion of privacy and negligent invasion of privacy, explaining that

---

1 *See* Crosstex N. Texas Pipeline, L.P. v. Gardiner, 505 S.W.3d 580, 617 (Tex. 2016) (holding "that the trial court properly denied…request for a trial amendment to assert" a nuisance claim not supported by the evidence).

2 855 S.W.2d 593, 600-01 (Tex. 1993).

> rather than get into a complicated charge and long drawn questions that might not be clearly defined, we have reduced our offensive thrust by way of our requested submissions to negligence—*negligent infliction of emotional distress and mental anguish.*

(emphasis supplied).

Kerr thus unequivocally waived all theories other than negligent infliction of emotional distress, and the court submitted only that theory to the jury. Regardless of the proof, she cannot now claim that she either pled or tried by consent an action on any separate theory.

---

2. *Trial Amendments to Cure Defects*

If a party objects during trial for lack of pleadings, Rule 66 requires the trial judge to "freely" allow amendments to pleadings "when the presentation of the merits of the action will be subserved thereby and the objecting party fails to satisfy the court that the allowance of such amendment would prejudice him in maintaining his action or defense upon the merits." This standard is similar to Rule 63's standard for pretrial amendments.

In order for the court to have discretion to refuse to allow the amendment, there must be evidence of surprise and prejudice in the record. How does the trial court evaluate this evidence and determine whether to allow the amendment or not? The opinions discussing the exercise of discretion seem to look at three primary factors:

(1) *The time of the amendment.* An early amendment is less likely to cause surprise or prejudice than a late one. Try to avoid trial amendments by getting your pleadings into shape before the pleading deadlines. Remember that a continuance of the trial date can always cure the prejudice of a late amendment by allowing additional time for the opponent to prepare.

(2) *Type of amendment—procedural or substantive.* An amendment that changes the nature of the lawsuit (a substantive amendment) is more likely to cause surprise or prejudice than one that simply conforms the pleadings to what is going on in the lawsuit (a procedural amendment). An amendment that adds a new cause of action or defense is clearly a substantive amendment, and the amendment itself is sufficient evidence to show surprise or prejudice. No additional evidence is required to support the trial court's decision not to allow the amendment.

(3) *Implied consent—Rule 67.* If the party opposing the amendment has failed to object to matters that are not in the pleadings for some time, the party may be said to have consented to the unpleaded matters. If a party finally objects to a matter as being outside the pleadings after allowing these matters into evidence for a long time during the trial, the claim of surprise and prejudice has less credibility, and the court may allow the amendment. This concept is a little different from "trial by consent"—there is no objection to matters outside the pleading and no trial amendment when a matter is tried by consent. Here there is an objection (although late) and an amendment.

Consider the following opinions, thinking about the evidence presented and how these factors affected the court's decision.

GREENHALGH
v.
SERVICE LLOYDS INSURANCE CO.
787 S.W.2d 938
(Tex. 1990)

MAUZY, JUSTICE.

The issue in this case is whether a trial court abuses its discretion by allowing a post-verdict amendment increasing the amount of damages in Plaintiff's pleadings to conform to the amount awarded by the jury when Defendant presents no evidence of surprise or prejudice. We hold that under Texas Rules of Civil Procedure 63 and 66, a trial court must allow a trial amendment that increases the amount of damages sought in the pleadings to that found by the jury unless the opposing party presents evidence of prejudice or surprise.

Plaintiff Greenhalgh and Service Lloyds Insurance Company (Service Lloyds), his workers' compensation carrier, agreed to a settlement of Greenhalgh's workers' compensation claim. However, Service Lloyds refused to pay Greenhalgh's medical expenses as required by the settlement. Greenhalgh subsequently filed this bad-faith insurance claim against Service Lloyds. The jury found in favor of Greenhalgh on each of his theories of recovery: breach of the duty of good faith and fair dealing, bad-faith insurance practices, gross negligence, negligence, and intentional infliction of emotional distress. Greenhalgh pleaded for $10,000 in actual damages and $100,000 in punitive damages; the jury awarded $8,000 in actual damages and $128,000 in punitive damages.

Because Greenhalgh had pleaded for only $100,000 in punitive damages, he requested leave to amend his pleadings to conform the amount of damages to that found by the jury and supported by the evidence. In its responsive motion, Service Lloyds alleged that the amendment was prejudicial because Service Lloyds had relied on the $100,000 amount in Plaintiff's pleadings in preparing for trial and in deciding whether to settle the case. The trial court allowed the post-verdict amendment. The court of appeals held that the trial court abused its discretion in allowing the amendment and reduced the punitive damages to $100,000.

The court of appeals reasoned that "because a defendant receives notice of the upper limit of punitive damages only by way of pleadings, it is an abuse of discretion to allow a post-verdict trial amendment increasing punitive damages when proper objections are made." We disagree. The holding of the court of appeals ignores the mandates of the procedural rules regarding amendment of pleadings during trial. *See* TEX. R. CIV. P. 63 and 66.

Not only did the trial court not abuse its discretion in granting the amendment, it would have been an abuse of discretion if the trial court had refused the amendment. Under Rules 63 and 66 a trial court has no discretion to refuse an amendment unless: 1) the opposing party presents evidence of surprise or prejudice, TEX. R. CIV. P. 63 and 66; or 2) the amendment asserts a new cause of action or defense, and thus is prejudicial on its face, and the opposing party objects to the amendment. The burden of showing prejudice or surprise rests on the party resisting the amendment. Because Greenhalgh's amendment raised no new substantive matters and because there was no showing of surprise or prejudice by Service Lloyds, the trial court properly granted leave to file the amendment.[1]

Service Lloyds relies on appellate court holdings that a trial court abuses its discretion in allowing a post-verdict amendment increasing damages to conform to the verdict. We disapprove these holdings because they directly conflict with Rules 63 and 66.

TEXAS RULES OF CIVIL PROCEDURE 63 and 66

It is well established that a party may amend its pleading after verdict but before judgment. Rule 63 states:

> Parties may amend their pleadings, . . . as they may desire by filing such pleas with the clerk at such time as not to operate as a surprise to the opposite party; provided, that any amendment offered for filing within seven days of the date of trial *or thereafter*, . . . shall be filed only after leave of the judge is obtained, *which leave shall be granted* by the judge *unless there is a showing that such amendment will operate as a surprise* of the opposite party.
>
> (Emphasis added).

The language of Rule 63 makes it clear that without a showing of surprise the trial court must grant leave for a party to file the amendment when requested within seven days of trial or thereafter. Thus, a party's right to amend under Rule 63 is subject only to the opposing party's right to show surprise. However, the trial court may conclude that the amendment is on its face calculated to surprise or that the amendment would reshape the cause of action, prejudicing the opposing party and unnecessarily delaying the trial.

An amended pleading that changes only the amount of damages sought does not automatically operate as surprise within the contemplation of Rule 63. A party opposing an amendment increasing damages must present evidence to show that the increase resulted in surprise. Because Service Lloyds presented no evidence of surprise, the trial court properly allowed the amendment as required under Rule 63.

Rule 66 further confirms the propriety of the trial court's granting leave for Greenhalgh to file his amendment. Rule 66 provides in part:

> if during the trial any defect, fault or omission in a pleading, either of form or substance, is called to the attention of the court, the court may allow the pleadings to be amended and *shall do so freely* when the presentation of the merits of the action will be subserved thereby and the objecting party fails to satisfy the court that the allowance of such amendment would prejudice him in maintaining his action or defense upon the merits.
>
> (Emphasis added).

* * *

---

[1] Service Lloyds offered no evidence of how it was prejudiced or surprised by the trial amendment. In closing arguments Service Lloyds argued that no punitive damages should have been awarded. Service Lloyds has never argued that it would have changed its position at trial—that Plaintiff deserved zero punitive damages—if the pleadings requested $128,000 rather than $100,000. In its opposition to the amendment, Service Lloyds failed to make any showing to the trial court that an increase in punitive damages pleaded would have forced it to change its trial posture.

The "defect" that Greenhalgh sought to cure in his amendment was to conform his pleadings to the evidence and jury findings on punitive damages. Service Lloyds failed to complain in the trial court that the evidence did not support the jury's finding on punitive damages—nor has it made this argument on appeal. We have held that when objections carry neither suggestion nor hint that the opposing party was in any manner surprised or prejudiced, both the spirit and the intent of Rule 66 require that the amendment be permitted. Thus the trial court properly allowed the amendment under Rules 63 and 66.

We hold that in the absence of a showing of surprise or prejudice by an opposing party, a trial court must grant leave to a party to amend his or her pleadings to conform the amount of damages requested to that awarded by the jury. We reverse the judgment of the court of appeals and affirm the judgment of the trial court.

HECHT, JUSTICE, concurring.

I join in the Court's judgment and in much of its opinion. I am not, however, quite as convinced as the Court appears to be that the result in this case is obvious from a simple reading of the Texas Rules of Civil Procedure. I do not find a provision in the rules which expressly addresses the issue we face today and dictates the result in this case; rather, I read the pertinent rules to be somewhat conflicting and to suggest competing policy considerations, considerations which are not unique to Texas courts but are at play in the rules of other courts as well. I conclude that our decision today comports with these policies, but I add a few words to explain how and why.

Under Rule 47, a pleading for unliquidated damages may allege only "that the damages sought exceed the minimum jurisdictional limits of the court" unless specially excepted to, in which event "the court shall require the pleader to amend so as to specify the maximum amount claimed." This mandate upon the court to require a claimant to plead a specific maximum amount of unliquidated damages sought can be read, as Service Lloyds contends, to suggest that the claimant is to be held to the amount pleaded and cannot recover more, even if the evidence and findings would support a greater award. Rule 63, however, allows amendments to pleadings "at such time as not to operate as a surprise to the opposite party". And Rule 66 requires a court to allow amendments to pleadings during trial "freely when . . . the objecting party fails to satisfy the court that the allowance of such amendment would prejudice him in maintaining his action or defense upon the merits." These provisions give a broad right to amend pleadings, even during trial, provided that an opposing party is not surprised or prejudiced. The rules do not terminate this right at the close of the evidence or the return of the verdict. To complicate matters further, Rule 301 states:

> The judgment of the court shall conform to the pleadings, the nature of the case proved and the verdict, if any, and shall be so framed as to give the party all the relief to which he may be entitled in law or equity.

The rules are silent as to what judgment should be rendered when, as here, the verdict exceeds the prayer for relief in the pleadings.

If the purpose of Rule 47 were to bind the pleader to a maximum claim for unliquidated damages, it would be a significant exception to Rules 63 and 66, which allow amendments more freely. If, however, Rule 47 is intended not so much to commit the pleader to a maximum number as to provide information to his opponent to facilitate a full and fair presentation of the merits of the dispute without surprise or prejudice, the conflict between that rule on the one hand, and Rules 63 and 66 on the other, is reduced, if not eliminated, in the situation presented in this case.

This latter reading of Rule 47, which reduces the conflict between these rules, is therefore to be preferred. Moreover, it seems to me a sounder policy—and one we, as promulgators of the rules, are obliged to consider—to apply Rule 47 not strictly but with some latitude. A verdict which exceeded a prayer for relief by a few dollars would offend a strict application of Rule 47 as much as one which exceeded the other a thousandfold. The opposing party is more likely to be surprised and prejudiced, however, if an amendment of pleadings were permitted in the latter circumstances.

Surprise and prejudice would preclude a post-verdict amendment of a prayer for relief when the opposing party has taken a posture in the case premised on the damage claim as a maximum amount which could be recovered, and altering that premise would significantly undermine the party's position. For example, the amount claimed in a case involving insurance might influence decisions as to coverage, settlement, and parties to be joined. What may constitute legitimate surprise and prejudice in the abstract does not admit of easy definition. In the present case, I agree with the Court that Service Lloyds has not shown any reason why the trial court exceeded its discretion in allowing Greenhalgh to amend his claim for $100,000 exemplary damages to equal the $128,000 found by the jury. * * *

CHAPIN & CHAPIN, INC.
v.
TEXAS SAND & GRAVEL CO.

844 S.W.2d 664
(Tex. 1992)

PER CURIAM.

Texas Sand & Gravel Co., a subcontractor, sued its general contractor, Chapin & Chapin, Inc. on a sworn account, alleging that Chapin had failed to pay Texas Sand for sand and gravel delivered to a construction project. Chapin denied Texas Sand's allegations, contending that it paid for all such materials it received. The trial court refused to allow Chapin to verify its denial less than seven days before trial, thereby restricting the evidence Chapin was permitted to offer at trial. A directed verdict for Texas Sand was affirmed on appeal. 844 S.W.2d 754. We hold that the trial court's refusal to allow Chapin to amend its answer was an abuse of discretion.

Texas Sand originally filed suit for breach of contract, not on open account. Several months after suit was filed, Texas Sand requested a trial setting, representing to the district court that all of its pleadings were "now in order." The trial court scheduled trial for a date about a month later. Before that date arrived, however, Texas Sand moved for a continuance and amended its pleadings to allege a sworn account. Chapin joined in the motion for continuance, and the trial was postponed. Texas Sand again moved for a continuance, and trial was postponed a second time. Six days before the third trial setting, Texas Sand and Chapin appeared at docket call and announced ready for trial. The next day, however, Chapin moved for leave to amend its answer to include a verified denial of Texas Sand's open account allegations. The trial court considered the motion the morning of trial. Texas Sand objected, arguing that it was ready to proceed only on the assumption that its verified petition, without a verified denial, would establish a prima facie case, that it was surprised by Chapin's attempt to file a verified denial, and that it would be unprepared to proceed if the verified denial were allowed. The trial court denied Chapin's motion and proceeded to trial, prohibiting Chapin from adducing evidence of payment.

Rule 63, TEX. R. CIV. P. states that pleadings may be amended within seven days of trial "only after leave of the judge is obtained, which leave shall be granted by the judge unless there is a showing that such filing will operate as a surprise to the opposite party." . . .

Chapin argues that our recent opinion in *Greenhalgh v. Service Lloyds Ins. Co.*, 787 S.W.2d 938 (Tex. 1990), is controlling. There we held that the trial court properly allowed plaintiff to amend the amount of damages claimed after the verdict was returned in the absence of surprise or prejudice to defendant. * * *

Texas Sand argues that *Hardin*, on which we relied in *Greenhalgh*, is controlling. *Hardin* held that the trial court did not abuse its discretion in refusing to allow a defendant to amend his pleadings the day of trial in a suit on a promissory note to assert, for the first time, duress, failure of consideration, fraud, illegality and unjust enrichment. This Court concluded: "These amendments could not have been anticipated by the plaintiff, and had they been permitted, they would have prejudiced the plaintiff's presentation of the case and resulted in unnecessary delay."

The difference between *Greenhalgh*, in which we held that the amendment was not only proper but mandatory, and *Hardin*, in which we held that denial of the amendment was not an abuse of discretion, is that the amendment in the former case was of a formal, procedural nature—increasing the ad damnum—which simply conformed the pleadings to the evidence at trial and did not result in surprise or prejudice, while the amendment in the latter case was substantive—changing the bases of the defense—which rather clearly changed the nature of the trial itself. The present case—adding a verified denial—is more in the nature of a procedural change, like *Greenhalgh*, than a substantive change, like *Hardin*. By adding a verified denial in this case, Chapin did not change a single substantive issue for trial. Chapin's position throughout had been that it had already paid for all it got. The only change was procedural: Texas Sand would have been obliged to rebut Chapin's substantive defense and could not simply insist judgment on the pleadings. If Texas Sand had relied upon the absence of a verified denial to the extent that it was unprepared to proceed to trial and would thus have been prejudiced by Chapin's amendment, it would have been entitled to a continuance. However, Texas Sand's counsel stated that he was prepared to prove that all deliveries had been made or accounted for and that the amount claimed was owed. In these circumstances, following *Laughlin*, we conclude that the trial court's refusal to allow Chapin to verify its denial was an abuse of discretion.

Accordingly, a majority of this Court grants Chapin's motion for rehearing of its application for writ of error, grants that application, reverses the judgment of the court of appeals, and remands the case to the district court for further proceedings. TEX. R. APP. P. 170.

Notes & Questions

Different rule for Expedited Actions. Rule 169(b) limits recovery for a party who prosecutes an expedited action under the rule to $100,000. Thus, Comment 4 to Rule 169 says that "the rule in Greenhalgh . . . does not apply if a jury awards damages in excess of $100,000 to the party."

G. Other Pleadings Issues

There are a few other pleading matters you should keep in mind in Texas state court:

1. *Alternative pleadings.* A plaintiff may plead alternative, but inconsistent, claims. However, the plaintiff may not recover twice for the same injury in the final judgment, although the plaintiff is entitled to all relief awarded under the jury's verdict.[1]

2. *Special purpose pleadings.* There are detailed rules for some pleadings that seek specific types of remedies. A plaintiff seeking such recovery must carefully follow the specific pleading rules. Although this casebook will not cover these pleadings, a Texas lawyer should be aware of their presence in the rules. A "sworn account" action uses verified pleadings to simplify recovery for amounts due for goods and services sold on credit.[2] "Trespass to try title" is a complicated procedure used to determine ownership of real property.[3] Extraordinary relief such as injunctions and temporary restraining orders, appointments of receivers, and sequestration have their own detailed procedures.[4]

3. *Misnomer.* Rule 71 allows courts to redesignate a pleading if a party mistakenly designates it. The purpose of the rule is to prevent unintended waiver. The court is to look at the substance of the pleading, not its title or caption, to determine its purpose.

4. *Order of pleading.* Generally, once a lawsuit is initiated by plaintiff's original petition, the order of pleading is unimportant. However, the Texas Rules of Civil Procedure do make exceptions. As we have seen, a motion to dismiss under Rule 91a must be filed 60 days from when the first pleading asserting the challenged cause of action is served on the movant.[5] And a special appearance motion must be filed prior to any other plea, pleading, or motion, and a motion to transfer venue must be filed prior to or concurrently with any other plea, pleading or motion, except the special appearance.[6] Moreover, under the provisions of the Civil Practice and Remedies Code, motions to dismiss for forum non conveniens must be filed "not later than 180 days after the time required to file a motion to transfer venue."[7]

5. *Pleas in abatement.* The plea in abatement is not set out in any rule, although it is mentioned in Rule 85. Nevertheless, it is recognized as a procedural method for defendants to raise matters outside the pleadings showing that the case should not go forward in its present condition. A plea in abatement is appropriate when the plaintiff has failed to give the defendant notice of the claim as required by some statutes, such as the Deceptive Trade Practices Act.[8] Many of the situations

---

[1] *See* Birchfield v. Texarkana Memorial Hospital, 747 S.W.2d 361 (Tex. 1987).

[2] *See* Rules 185, 93(10).

[3] *See* Rule 783. Martin v. Amerman, 133 S.W.3d 262 (Tex. 2004) (holding that trespass-to-try-title is exclusive means to resolve boundary disputes).

[4] *See* Rules 680-716.

[5] Rule 91a.3.

[6] MCDONALD, TEXAS CIVIL PRACTICE § 9.4.

[7] CPRC § 71.051(d).

[8] *See* Hines v. Hash, 843 S.W.2d 464 (Tex. 1992); Falderbaum v. Lowe, 964 S.W.2d 744 (Tex. App.—Austin 1998, no pet.) (failure to submit a seasonable plea in abatement waives the objection); K.C. Roofing Co. v. Abundis, 940 S.W.2d 375 (Tex. App.—San Antonio 1997, writ denied) (abatement waived when no hearing requested and plea not verified).

under which it would be appropriate to file a plea in abatement are listed in Rule 93 as pleas to be verified. Therefore, a plea in abatement often must be sworn. The *Wyatt* case below illustrates a Rule 93(3) plea in abatement that asks the court to abate in favor of a previously filed and inherently interrelated suite.[9]

WYATT
v.
SHAW PLUMBING CO.
760 S.W.2d 245
(Tex. 1988)

OPINION

RAY, JUSTICE.

This case arises out of a dispute over the services provided by a plumbing contractor in the construction of a house in Duval County. The issue presented by this appeal involves a plea in abatement filed in a second suit in Nueces County when a prior suit was pending in Duval County. The court of appeals affirmed the Nueces County district court, holding that the decision to grant a plea in abatement was within the discretion of the Nueces County court and there was no abuse of that discretion. 736 S.W.2d 763. We hold that the Nueces County district court was required to grant the plea in abatement because a previously filed suit between the parties was pending. We, therefore, reverse the judgment of the court of appeals and remand the cause to the Nueces County district court with instructions to vacate its judgment and abate all proceedings pending final disposition of the Duval County lawsuit, which was previously filed.

This controversy involves a suit between the parties in the district court of Duval County and another suit subsequently filed in the district court of Nueces County. On Wyatt's behalf, Morgan Spear entered into an oral agreement with Shaw Plumbing Company for Shaw to perform work on the house. When Wyatt did not pay Shaw Plumbing for its services, Shaw made a written demand for payment. Following Shaw Plumbing's demand letter, Wyatt filed suit against Shaw in Duval County on February 7, 1983, alleging fraud and violation of the Deceptive Trade Practices Act.

On April 4, 1983, Shaw Plumbing filed a breach of contract suit against Wyatt and Spear in Nueces County to recover for its services. Wyatt filed a plea in abatement in the Nueces County suit based upon the pendency of the previously filed Duval County suit. The Nueces County district court signed an order denying Wyatt's plea in abatement on June 15, 1984. On February 13, 1986, Wyatt filed a second plea in abatement in Nueces County after he agreed to indemnify

---

[9] *See also* In re Red Dot Building System, Inc, 504 S.W.3d 320 (Tex. 2016); In re J.B. Hunt Transport, Inc. 492 S.W.3d 287 (Tex. 2016) (granting mandamus relief for failure to abate subsequently filed suit); Perry v. Del Rio, 66 S.W.3d 239 (Tex. 2001) (abating subsequently filed suit). Abatement in favor of a first-filed suit must be distinguished from an anti-suit injunction, where the Texas court enjoins a proceeding pending elsewhere from going forward. The principle of comity requires that courts sparingly issue anti-suit injunctions concerning suits filed in other jurisdictions. *See* Golden Rule Ins. Co. v. Harper, 925 S.W.2d 649 (Tex. 1996) (dissolving anti-suit injunction); Ex Parte Ralph Kenneth Evans, 939 S.W.2d 142 (Tex. 1997) (state courts have no power to enjoin federal court proceedings).

Spear for any claims against Spear by Shaw Plumbing. The Nueces County district court again denied the plea. Prior to the trial in Nueces County, the trial judge struck Wyatt's pleadings as a sanction for alleged discovery abuse. Judgment was rendered against Wyatt following a jury trial in Nueces County.

It has long been the policy of the courts and the legislature of this state to avoid a multiplicity of lawsuits. The need for judicial economy has recently become more acute because the dockets of our trial courts are overburdened, and litigants must wait far too long for their cases to be heard.

* * *

In the case in which Wyatt as plaintiff sued Shaw Plumbing as defendant on tort and DTPA theories, the counties in which venue was proper were: (1) Nueces County, where the defendant had its principal office situated; (2) Duval County, where the construction and plumbing was done, and thus the cause of action arose; or (3) Harris County, where the plaintiff resided at the time the cause of action arose. Wyatt's agent, Morgan Spear, was not a party to the suit brought by Wyatt. Spear was a party, however, to Shaw Plumbing's suit in Nueces County, which was based solely on breach of contract. Because there was a difference in both issues and parties, Shaw argues that the Nueces County district court was not obliged to grant the plea in abatement. We disagree.

When an inherent interrelation of the subject matter exists in two pending lawsuits, a plea in abatement in the second action must be granted. It is not required that the exact issues and all the parties be included in the first action before the second is filed, provided that the claim in the first suit may be amended to bring in all necessary and proper parties and issues. In determining whether an inherent interrelationship exists, courts should be guided by the rule governing persons to be joined if feasible and the compulsory counterclaim rule. *See* TEX. R. CIV. P. 39, 97(a).

Shaw Plumbing should have brought its compulsory counterclaim on the contract in Wyatt's tort and DTPA suit in Duval County. If Shaw Plumbing had joined Morgan Spear, venue would have been proper in the Duval County suit filed by Wyatt, where the cause of action arose. If Wyatt had sued Shaw Plumbing in Nueces County, venue would have also been proper because Shaw's principal office was situated in Nueces County. However, since Wyatt filed suit first, he chose Duval County.

It is well settled that when suit would be proper in more than one county, the court in which suit is first filed acquires dominant jurisdiction to the exclusion of other courts. *Curtis v. Gibbs*, 511 S.W.2d 263, 267 (Tex. 1974); *Cleveland v. Ward*, 116 Tex. 1, 19, 285 S.W. 1063, 1070 (1926). As long as the forum is a proper one, it is the plaintiff's privilege to choose the forum. Defendants are simply not at liberty to decline to do battle in the forum chosen by the plaintiff.

Abatement of a lawsuit due to the pendency of a prior suit is based on the principles of comity, convenience, and the necessity for an orderly procedure in the trial of contested issues. The plea in abatement must be raised in a timely manner, however, or it is waived. There has been no waiver in the present case.

There are three exceptions to the rule of *Cleveland v. Ward* that the court where suit is first filed acquires dominant jurisdiction: (1) conduct by a party that estops him from asserting prior active jurisdiction; (2) lack of persons to be joined if feasible, or the power to bring them before the court; and (3) lack of intent to prosecute the first lawsuit. None of these exceptions applies in this case.

* * *

We reaffirm that the rule of *Cleveland v. Ward* is the law regarding conflicts of jurisdiction between Texas courts of coordinate jurisdiction. In the case at bar, both lawsuits involve the same issues. Moreover, the parties in the second suit were either present in the first suit, or parties who should have been joined in the first suit. Since venue was proper in either Duval, Harris, or Nueces County, the court where suit was first filed, Duval County, acquired dominant jurisdiction. The Nueces County district court, therefore, had no discretion to deny Wyatt's plea in abatement.

Accordingly, we reverse the judgment of the court of appeals and remand the cause to the Nueces County district court with instruction to vacate its judgment and abate all proceedings pending final disposition of the Duval County lawsuit.

H. Investigating Claims and Defenses—Frivolous Pleadings*

Read Rules 13, 57, 215-2b, Chapter 10, C.P.R.C.

Texas has a rule *and* a statute requiring lawyers to investigate their claims and defenses and refrain from filing pleadings that are groundless or brought in bad faith. What is the difference between the two?

LOW v. HENRY

221 S.W.3d 609
(Tex. 2007)

JUSTICE WAINWRIGHT delivered the opinion of the Court.

Texas follows a "fair notice" standard for pleading, in which courts assess the sufficiency of pleadings by determining whether an opposing party can ascertain from the pleading the nature, basic issues, and the type of evidence that might be relevant to the controversy. However, the actual facts and evidence of a specific case limit this relatively liberal standard. Chapter 10 of the Texas Civil Practice and Remedies Code requires a pleading's signatory to certify that he or she conducted a reasonable inquiry into the allegations and concluded that each allegation or other factual contention in the pleading has or is likely to have evidentiary support. Because the attorney who filed the petition in this case obtained and directed the review of evidence that disproved some of the allegations pled against some of the defendants, the trial court correctly found that the attorney violated Chapter 10. However, we hold that the trial court abused its discretion in not providing a sufficient basis to support the imposition of a $50,000 penalty. We reverse the court of appeals' judgment and remand the case to the trial court for proceedings consistent with this opinion.

I. Factual and Procedural Background

On November 20, 1999, Henry White was admitted to Columbia North Bay Hospital after suffering a stroke. Dr. Stephen Smith treated White in the emergency room for less than one hour. Dr. Robert Low cared for him for four days before White was transferred to another hospital. White was comatose at the time of the transfer. He died in December 1999.

On January 31, 2002, Joyce White (both individually and as representative of her husband Henry White's estate) sued the alleged manufacturers, designers, and distributors of the drug known as Propulsid, Coastal Bend Hospital, Inc. d/b/a Columbia North Bay Hospital, eight physicians, and nurse Donna McMahon for damages flowing from Henry White's death. Although most of the claims involved the drug Propulsid, some alleged that the physicians and hospital were negligent in Henry White's medical treatment.

Attorney Thomas J. Henry represented Joyce White when he filed the petition. His office received copies of Henry White's medical records months before he filed the petition. Henry filed a motion to withdraw as counsel on the same day he filed the petition. Henry continued to represent Joyce White until the trial court granted the motion to withdraw on May 6, 2002.

On May 28, 2002, Dr. Smith filed a motion for sanctions against Joyce White and Henry for alleged violations of Texas Rule of Civil Procedure 13 and chapters 9 and 10 of the Texas Civil Practice and Remedies Code. Dr. Low filed the same motion.[3] Both physicians argued that none of the medical records from the hospital at which the physicians treated White contained any reference to either doctor having prescribed or provided Propulsid to White. On June 10, Joyce White nonsuited the case. The physicians' motions for sanctions remained pending.

The trial court held a hearing on the physicians' motions on July 30, 2002. Henry did not attend or testify but appeared through counsel. On July 31, 2002, the trial court granted the motions and ordered Henry to pay $25,000 in sanctions on each motion, for a total of $50,000. On August 2, 2002, the trial court entered a revised judgment that incorporated findings of fact and conclusions of law. On August 26, 2002, Henry filed a motion for new trial and a motion to vacate, modify, correct, or reform the sanctions order. On September 23, 2002, Henry filed a supplemental motion. On October 15, 2002, the trial court held a hearing on Henry's motions. After hearing more testimony, including Henry's, the trial court ultimately denied admission of all additional evidence and denied Henry's motion to modify the judgment. Henry filed a motion to reconsider, challenging the adequacy of the trial court's findings of fact and conclusions of law for the first time. The trial court denied this motion and rejected as untimely all arguments not contained in the original motion for new trial and motion to vacate, modify, correct or reform the judgment as untimely. Henry appealed.

An en banc court of appeals reversed, holding that because the allegations against the physicians were made in the alternative, sanctions under chapter 10 of the Texas Civil Practice and Remedies Code were inappropriate. The court also held that the physicians' motions did not support sanctions under Chapter 10 for unrelated prior litigation and that the trial court's order failed to meet the specificity requirements of Chapter 10. The dissenting justices argued that the trial court did not abuse its discretion and that Henry waived his other complaints. The physicians petitioned this Court for review.

---

[3] The physicians' attorney later indicated on the record that the physicians would not seek sanctions against Joyce White.

II. Applicable Law and Standard of Review

We review the imposition of sanctions here under the same standard we review sanctions under Rule 13—abuse of discretion. An appellate court may reverse the trial court's ruling only if the trial court acted without reference to any guiding rules and principles, such that its ruling was arbitrary or unreasonable. To determine if the sanctions were appropriate or just, the appellate court must ensure there is a direct nexus between the improper conduct and the sanction imposed. Generally, courts presume that pleadings and other papers are filed in good faith. The party seeking sanctions bears the burden of overcoming this presumption of good faith.

Chapters 9 and 10 of the Texas Civil Practice and Remedies Code and rule 13 of the Texas Rules of Civil Procedure allow a trial court to sanction an attorney or a party for filing motions or pleadings that lack a reasonable basis in fact or law. Chapter 9 of the Texas Civil Practice and Remedies Code only applies in proceedings in which neither Rule 13 nor Chapter 10 applies. TEX. CIV. PRAC. & REM.CODE § 9.012(h). Rule 13 authorizes the imposition of the sanctions listed in Rule 215.2(b), which only provides for a monetary penalty based on expenses, court costs, or attorney's fees. Because the trial court ordered Henry to pay $50,000 in penalties not based on expenses, court costs, or attorney's fees, and because the trial court's written order specifically orders the penalty pursuant to chapter 10 of the Texas Civil Practice and Remedies Code, we review the trial court's order in light of chapter 10. Chapter 10 provides that:

> The signing of a pleading or motion as required by the Texas Rules of Civil Procedure constitutes a certificate by the signatory that to the signatory's best knowledge, information, and belief, formed after reasonable inquiry:
>
> (1) the pleading or motion is not being presented for any improper purpose, including to harass or to cause unnecessary delay or needless increase in the cost of litigation;
>
> (2) each claim, defense, or other legal contention in the pleading or motion is warranted by existing law or by a nonfrivolous argument for the extension, modification, or reversal of existing law or the establishment of new law;
>
> (3) each allegation or other factual contention in the pleading or motion has evidentiary support or, for a specifically identified allegation or factual contention, is likely to have evidentiary support after a reasonable opportunity for further investigation or discovery; and
>
> (4) each denial in the pleading or motion of a factual contention is warranted on the evidence or, for a specifically identified denial, is reasonably based on a lack of information or belief.

TEX. CIV. PRAC. & REM.CODE § 10.001. Under Section 10.001, the signer of a pleading or motion certifies that each claim, each allegation, and each denial is based on the signatory's best knowledge, information, and belief, formed after reasonable inquiry. The statute dictates that each claim and each allegation be individually evaluated for support. The fact that an allegation or claim is alleged against several defendants-so-called " group pleadings"—does not relieve the party from meeting the express requirements of Chapter 10. Each claim against each defendant must satisfy Chapter 10.

Likewise, alternative pleading under Texas Rule of Civil Procedure 48 does not excuse noncompliance with Chapter 10. Pleading in the alternative allows multiple allegations, which may even conflict, to be alleged against a defendant, but there still must be a reasonable basis for each alternative allegation. Pleading in the alternative does not permit alleging a claim with no reasonable basis in fact or law "in the alternative" of a claim that does have support. That is simply not permitted by Texas law. *See* TEX. CIV. PRAC. & REM.CODE § 10.001. Each allegation and factual contention in a pleading or motion must have, or be likely to have, evidentiary support after a reasonable investigation.

The language of section 10.001 of the Texas Civil Practice and Remedies Code tracks much of the language in Federal Rule of Civil Procedure 11(b):

> Representations to Court. By presenting to the court (whether by signing, filing, submitting, or later advocating) a pleading, written motion, or other paper, an attorney or unrepresented party is certifying that to the best of the person's knowledge, information, and belief, formed after an inquiry reasonable under the circumstances,—
>
> (1) it is not being presented for any improper purpose, such as to harass or to cause unnecessary delay or needless increase in the cost of litigation;
>
> (2) the claims, defenses, and other legal contentions therein are warranted by existing law or by a nonfrivolous argument for the extension, modification, or reversal of existing law or the establishment of new law;
>
> (3) the allegations and other factual contentions have evidentiary support or, if specifically so identified, are likely to have evidentiary support after a reasonable opportunity for further investigation or discovery; and
>
> (4) the denials of factual contentions are warranted on the evidence or, if specifically so identified, are reasonably based on a lack of information or belief.

Although the text of Rule 11 does not specify that each claim, allegation, and denial be based on the signatory's best knowledge, information, and belief, formed after reasonable inquiry, Federal Rule of Civil Procedure 8(e), which allows pleading in the alternative, specifically subjects all such pleadings to the requirements of Rule 11. Neither Rule 8 nor Rule 11 permits a plaintiff "to intentionally ignore relevant evidence in order to assert unfounded claims."

The physicians argue that by filing the pleading in this case, Henry certified that to the best of his knowledge, information, and belief, the factual contentions in the pleading had or were likely to have evidentiary support. A reasonable inquiry into the allegations would have proven otherwise. *See* TEX. CIV. PRAC. & REM.CODE § 10.001(3). White's medical records, which were in Henry's possession before he filed the lawsuit, indicated that neither physician ever prescribed or administered the drug to White. The physicians argue that Henry violated Chapter 10 by alleging that they prescribed and administered Propulsid in spite of the information to the contrary in White's medical records. We agree with the physicians.

Undeniably, the petition focuses on Propulsid, a drug used to treat gastric reflux. The first sentence of the fact section of the petition summarizes, "The Plaintiffs are victims of the Defendants' decision to manufacture, market, design, promote, and/or distribute [Propulsid]." The petition claims that Johnson & Johnson, Janssen Pharmaceutica, and Janssen Research Foundation were negligent, negligent per se, and strictly liable for the defective design, marketing, manufacture, and distribution of the drug and for the violation of specified statutes and regulations. The petition also includes fraud and misrepresentation claims against Johnson & Johnson, Janssen Pharmaceutica, and Janssen Research Foundation regarding the safety and efficacy of the drug. The petition further alleges that collectively the "defendants" breached implied and express warranties. Finally, the petition makes the following sixteen allegations of negligence against the "Defendant Physicians and Hospital"—eight physicians and a hospital:

a. In failing to weigh the substantial risks involved in prescribing the drug against its potential benefits, if any;

b. In failing to try alternate treatments such as antacids and gastric acid reducing agents before prescribing the drug;

c. In failing to advise the Plaintiffs about changes in lifestyle before prescribing the drug;

d. In failing to obtain a careful history of the Plaintiffs and in prescribing the drug in the presence of underlying cardiac conditions and other conditions or family history that would preclude the use of the drug;

e. In failing to determine the Plaintiffs' medications and in prescribing the drug along with contraindicated medications;

f. In failing to perform ECG monitoring at baseline and in failing to refer to prior ECGs performed on the Plaintiffs;

g. In failing to warn or adequately warn the Plaintiffs concerning the contraindications, warnings; precautions, adverse reactions, and drug interactions associated with the use f[sic] the drug;

h. In failing to advise the Plaintiffs concerning any significant changes in the patient package inserts and Physicians' Desk Reference;

i. In failing to advise the Plaintiffs concerning the contents of FDA warnings and "Dear Doctor" letters;

j. In failing to advise the Plaintiffs concerning the reasons for withdrawal of the drug from the market;

k. In failing to warn the Plaintiffs concerning abnormal EGGs [sic] and prolonged QTC intervals;

l. In failing to properly diagnose the cardiac conditions caused by the drug;

m. In failing to properly read and interpret the Plaintiffs' ECGs;

n. In failing to administer the proper treatment for the cardiac conditions caused by the drug;

o. In failing to discontinue the drug; or

p. In failing to continue to monitor the Plaintiffs, including ECG monitoring, electrolyte monitoring, prescription drug monitoring, and cardiac condition monitoring.

In six places—paragraphs a, b, c, d, e, and o—the petition alleges that Drs. Low and Smith provided or prescribed the drug to White. The other paragraphs allege negligent conduct other than prescribing or providing Propulsid to White.

However, Drs. Low and Smith presented undisputed evidence at the trial court that neither doctor ever prescribed or administered Propulsid to White and that a pre-suit review of White's medical records would have confirmed that fact. Dr. Low filed an affidavit with his motion for sanctions swearing that "[a]t no time during [his] involvement with this patient did [he] ever prescribe, provide, administer or order Propulsid for Mr. White." Dr. Smith filed an affidavit making the same statement with his motion. At the July 30, 2002 hearing on the motions, the physicians again testified that they did not administer or prescribe Propulsid. The testimony established that Dr. Smith was White's doctor for less than an hour in the emergency room, and Dr. Low, an internal medicine doctor at Columbia North Bay, provided care to White for four days after he arrived at Columbia North Bay and before his transfer to a facility in Corpus Christi. Dr. Low also confirmed that "anyone familiar with reviewing a medical record could easily have confirmed [Dr. Low's] testimony and the fact that [Dr. Low] had nothing to do with Propulsid had they simply reviewed the record." Dr. Smith testified that White's medical record contains no reference to Dr. Smith's ever prescribing or administering Propulsid to White. In fact, Henry does not dispute Dr. Low's testimony that White had not been taking Propulsid approximately two weeks before his treatment by the physicians. Dr. Smith similarly testified that he was informed that White had not been taking Propulsid "for some time" before his arrival at the Columbia North Bay emergency room and his subsequent treatment by Drs. Low and Smith.

The evidence at the hearing supports the trial court's conclusion that:

> Based upon the totality of the evidence admitted during the hearing on the Motions for Sanctions, each and all of the allegations brought against Drs. Low and Smith, and therefore the lawsuit brought against these physicians, did not, on January 31, 2002, and do not now, have evidentiary support; nor were they on January 31, 2002, likely to have evidentiary support after a reasonable opportunity for further investigation . . . .

Under chapter 10 of the Texas Civil Practice and Remedies Code, the physicians were not required to specifically show bad faith or malicious intent, just that Henry certified he made a reasonable inquiry into all of the allegations when he did not and that he certified that all the allegations in the petition had evidentiary support, or were likely to have evidentiary support, when some allegations did not. We conclude that the trial court did not abuse its discretion in concluding that Henry failed to meet the standard in Chapter 10.

* * *

IV. Amount of Sanction

Henry claims that the $50,000 sanction, a $25,000 sanction for the petition filed against each doctor, is excessive. The amount of the sanction is limited by the trial court's duty to exercise sound discretion. A trial court abuses its discretion when it acts without reference to any guiding rules or principles, not when it simply exercises that discretion in a different manner than reviewing appellate courts might. In [*Transamerican v.*] *Powell* we held that a sanction under rule 215 of the Texas Rules of Civil Procedure, now rule 215.2, must relate directly to the abuse found and "be no more severe than necessary to satisfy its legitimate purpose." Texas Rule of Civil Procedure 215.2 allows a trial court to disallow any further discovery; charge certain expenses, costs, or attorney's fees of one party against the offending party; order certain facts to be established as true; limit a party's ability to defend against or bring certain claims; strike pleadings or parts of pleadings; or find a party in contempt of court. In contrast, Chapter 10 authorizes a sanction ordering the offending party to, among other things, pay a penalty into the court, as ordered in this case. TEX. CIV. PRAC. & REM.CODE § 10.004. The only restriction on the amount of the penalty in the language of the statute is that the "sanction must be limited to what is sufficient to deter repetition of the conduct or comparable conduct by others similarly situated." *Id.* § 10.004(b); The legislative history does not shed light on the question.

Generally, a sanction cannot be excessive nor should it be assessed without appropriate guidelines. Although this Court has not specifically identified factors for a trial court to consider when assessing penalties under Chapter 10, the absence of an explanation of how a trial court determined that amount of sanctions when those sanctions are especially severe is inadequate. For example, in *Cire v. Cummings*, we held the trial court was required to explain that it considered lesser sanctions before imposing severe, "death penalty" sanctions. In *Powell*, we held that the dismissal of plaintiff's case with prejudice for failing to appear for a deposition was an excessive sanction under Texas Rule of Civil Procedure 215. Because we held that the death penalty sanction at issue was "manifestly unjust," we did not identify specific factors for determining appropriate sanctions. In his concurrence, Justice Gonzalez recognized that the American Bar Association cumulated relevant factors useful to this type of analysis.[5] Although we do not require a trial court to address all of the factors listed in the report to explain the basis of a monetary sanction under Chapter 10, it should consider relevant factors in assessing the amount of the sanction. In addition, the determination of the amount of a penalty to be assessed under Chapter 10, which is not limited to attorney's fees and costs, should nevertheless begin with an acknowledgment of the costs and fees incurred because of the sanctionable conduct. This provides a monetary guidepost of the impact of the conduct on the party seeking sanctions and the burdens on the court system.

The trial court found that the claims brought against the doctors did not meet the evidentiary support requirement in Chapter 10. The trial court also concluded that the lawsuit was ground-

[5] The ABA's 1988 report was designed, in part, to help bring uniformity to the uneven application of sanctions under Federal Rule of Civil Procedure 11. American Bar Association, Standards and Guidelines for Practice Under Rule 11 of the Federal Rules of Civil Procedure, reprinted in 121 F.R.D. 101, 104 (1988). The factors are:

a. the good faith or bad faith of the offender;

b. the degree of willfulness, vindictiveness, negligence, or frivolousness involved in the offense;

c. the knowledge, experience, and expertise of the offender;

d. any prior history of sanctionable conduct on the part of the offender;

e. the reasonableness and necessity of the out-of-pocket expenses incurred by the offended person as a result of the misconduct;

f. the nature and extent of prejudice, apart from out-of-pocket expenses, suffered by the offended person as a result of the misconduct;

g. the relative culpability of client and counsel, and the impact on their privileged relationship of an inquiry into that area;

h. the risk of chilling the specific type of litigation involved;

i. the impact of the sanction on the offender, including the offender's ability to pay a monetary sanction;

j. the impact of the sanction on the offended party, including the offended person's need for compensation;

k. the relative magnitude of sanction necessary to achieve the goal or goals of the sanction;

l. burdens on the court system attributable to the misconduct, including consumption of judicial time and incurrence of juror fees and other court costs;

* * *

n. the degree to which the offended person's own behavior caused the expenses for which recovery is sought . . . .

Id. at 125-26 (cited in *Powell*, 811 S.W.2d at 920-21 (GONZALEZ, J., concurring)). This nonexclusive list of factors is helpful in guiding the often intangible process of determining a penalty for sanctionable behavior.

less, as defined in Texas Rule of Civil Procedure 13. The trial court's order stated that Henry "has consistently engaged in a similar pattern of conduct."

Dr. Low testified that he felt that Henry harassed him by filing the lawsuit. He testified that he lost a day and a half from the office because of the lawsuit but does not quantify this expense and identifies no other out-of-pocket expenses. Dr. Smith testified that he believed Henry felt "bad will toward [him] personally" because Henry filed a suit with no basis in fact against him. Two other physicians, Drs. Mastin and Canterbury, testified that Henry had named them in lawsuits in which they had never treated the plaintiff patients. Both testified about the impact of the lawsuits and intent to sue letters on their malpractice insurance rates: Dr. Mastin testified that his group's rates increased by 68% due in part to three groundless suits filed by Henry's clients; Dr. Canterbury also testified that her practice group faced increased insurance premiums due to groundless pleadings like Henry's.

Although we conclude that the trial court was within its discretion to award sanctions under Chapter 10, we cannot determine the basis of the $50,000 penalty on this record. Given the severity of the sanction, therefore, we remand this case in the interest of justice to allow the parties to present evidence responsive to our guidelines, if necessary, and to allow the trial court to consider the amount of the penalty imposed in light of the guidelines in this opinion.

V. Conclusion

We recognize that in some cases, a party may not have evidence that proves each specific factual allegation at the time a lawsuit is filed. Certainly, the law does not require proof of a case without reasonable time for discovery. However, this does not excuse the filing of claims against parties when the attorney filing the lawsuit possesses information that a reasonable inquiry would have determined negated some of the claims made. We affirm the trial court's determination that chapter 10 was violated but hold that the trial court abused its discretion in not more specifically identifying the basis for imposing a $50,000 penalty under chapter 10 of the Texas Civil Practice and Remedies Code. We reverse the judgment of the court of appeals and remand the case to the trial court for proceedings consistent with this opinion.

Notes & Questions

1. *Sanctions and the legislature.* Does Texas even need a sanctions rule for frivolous pleadings? The Texas Supreme Court Task Force on Sanctions noted that this is certainly a debatable point. Often judges disagree as to whether an argument is not "merely losing" but "losing and sanctionable," leading to inconsistent results. Moreover, there is some feeling that the basic assumption of the rule, that "frivolous" litigation is really a significant problem, is incorrect. Nevertheless, the Task Force concluded that doing away with the rule was not an option in Texas, because it is legislatively mandated.[1] During the 1995 tort reform, the Texas legislature again addressed the issue of frivolous pleadings, apparently feeling that Civil Practice and Remedies Code Chapter 9 and Rule 13 did not go far enough to deter frivolous lawsuits. The final result was Chapter 10 to the CPRC.

2. *Safe harbor.* Federal Rule 11 has a "safe harbor" procedure whereby a party can withdraw or correct a challenged pleading within 21 days of service of the motion. Rule 13 originally con-

[1] *See* TEX. CIV. PRAC. & REM. CODE §§ 9.011-.014.

tained a 90-day grace period that was eliminated in the 1990 amendments.[2] Chapter 10 of the Civil Practice and Remedies Code says nothing about a "safe harbor."

3. *When to judge pleadings*. The Texas Supreme Court has held that Rule 13 and Chapter 10 require pleadings to be judged at the time the pleading is filed.[3] Compare this to Federal Rule 11, which provides for pleading sanctions upon filing or "later advocating" a pleading. The court thus distinguished sanctions for groundless pleadings and for discovery abuse. "A claim may be likely to receive evidentiary support when filed and thus not be groundless under Chapter 10. But if a party later learns through discovery that no factual support for the contention exists and still pursues litigation, such conduct could be sanctionable. But the sanctionable conduct would like be the abuse of the discovery process, not the filing of pleadings" under rules allowing sanctions for "unreasonably frivolous, oppressive or harassing" discovery requests.[4]

4. *Delay in moving for sanctions.* When a defending party delays moving for sanctions, it has some responsibility for the overall increase in litigation costs. Thus, when the plaintiff's pleadings were frivolous from the date of filing because they were filed after the statute of limitations were filed, but the defendant did not file summary judgment and sanctions motions until years later, "the defending party cannot arbitrarily shift the entire costs on its adversary simply because it ultimately prevails on a motion for sanctions." Thus, the Supreme Court reversed a sanction award of approximately $1.4 million in attorney's fees, and remanded to the trial court to "discernably examine" one of the *Low* factors, "the degree to which the offended person's own behavior caused the expenses for which discovery is sought."[5]

5. *Sanctions after nonsuit.* A plaintiff has a right to dismiss its case, known as taking a "nonsuit."[6] The Texas Supreme Court held that a court can impose Rule 13 sanctions upon a plaintiff that has nonsuited its claims, even when the motion for sanctions was filed after the nonsuit.[7]

> Rule 13 sanctions serve both deterrent and compensatory purposes. Courts impose sanctions against parties filing frivolous claims to deter similar conduct in the future and to compensate the aggrieved party by reimbursing the costs incurred in responding to baseless pleadings. Rule 162 would frustrate these purposes if it allowed a party to escape sanctions by simply nonsuiting the aggrieved party.[8]

---

[2] *See* Univ. of Texas Health Sci. Ctr. at Houston v. Rios, 542 S.W.3d 530, 537 (Tex. 2017) (observing in dicta that "[a]mendments do not always avoid the consequences of filing. For example, filing a fictitious pleading is sanctionable under Rule 13. The rule once allowed sanctions to be avoided by amending the offensive pleading, but the rule was amended to remove that possibility. Sanctions cannot be avoided merely by amending pleadings.").

[3] Nath v. Texas Children's Hospital, 446 S.W.3d 355, 369 (Tex. 2014).

[4] *Id.* (citing TRCP 215.3).

[5] Nath v. Texas Children's Hospital, 446 S.W.3d 355, 372 (Tex. 2014).

[6] Rule 162. See discussion on nonsuits in Chapter 16.

[7] Scott & White Memorial Hospital v. Schexnider, 940 S.W.2d 594 (Tex. 1996). *See also* Villafani v. Trejo, 251 S.W.3d 466 (Tex. 2008) (holding that nonsuit did not prevent defendant from appealing order denying sanctions under Medical Liability Insurance Improvement Act).

[8] *Schexnider*, 940 S.W.2d at 596-97.

Note, however, that C.P.R.C. § 10.004(e) prevents courts from pursuing a *sua sponte* sanctions motion after nonsuit or settlement. And Rule 91A.5 gives plaintiffs until three days before the dismissal hearing to nonsuit or amend the pleadings to avoid incurring attorney fees.

6. *Sanctions by state court after removal of case to federal court.* In *In re Bennett*, the Texas Supreme Court held that state courts retain jurisdiction to sanction lawyers for pre-removal conduct once a case has been removed to federal court as long as the sanction does not operate upon the merits of the underlying case.[9]

7. *Sanctions by federal court after removal of case to federal court.* In *Tompkins v. Cyr*, a federal district court held that federal judges may apply state sanctions rules to pleading filed in state court before removal to federal court.[10] The plaintiff sued the defendants in state court for a variety of torts arising from the defendants' public campaign against the plaintiff's medical practice, which included performing abortions. The defendants removed to federal court after the plaintiff added a RICO claim. Several defendants were then dismissed from the suit, and they moved for sanctions under both Federal Rule 11 and TRCP 13. The court concluded that the defendants could seek sanctions under TRCP 13, reasoning that limiting sanctions to those provided for under the federal rules would allow a plaintiff to escape sanctions by virtue of fortuitous removal to federal court. The court, however, denied the sanctions.

8. *Order must state the reasons for sanctions with particularity.* An order for sanctions must state the good cause supporting the order with particularity, reciting the specific reasons for the order.[11] The party being sanctioned must object to the lack of particularity to preserve error.[12] This can be done by motion or by written objection.[13]

9. *Criminal liability for false pleadings.* Under Texas law, one commits the offense of tampering with a governmental record if he "makes, presents or uses a governmental record with knowledge of its falsity." Penal Code § 37.10 (a)(5). In *State v. Vasilas*,[14] the Texas Court of Criminal Appeals held that an indictment charged a felony offense by alleging that the defendant, a lawyer, drafted a petition for expunction of a criminal record, made false entries in this petition, filed this petition, and then in some unspecified way "used" that petition. The court held that any document filed with a court, including a pleading in a civil case, is a "governmental record" under the statute. If the lawyer, aware of its falsity, then used this governmental record with intent that it be taken as a genuine one, the lawyer committed a crime. If the lawyer did it with intent to defraud or harm another, the crime becomes a state jail felony. The court remanded to the court of appeals to determine whether Rule 13 controlled over the criminal statute.

10. *Verifications and affidavits.* Generally, pleadings are not made under oath, and the truthfulness of the pleading is judged under the pleading standards discussed above. However, some

---

[9] In re Bennett, 960 S.W.2d 35 (Tex. 1997, orig. proceeding).

[10] Tompkins v. Cyr, 995 F. Supp. 664 (N.D. Tex. 1998).

[11] Rudisell v Paquette, 89 S.W.3d 233 (Tex. App.—Corpus Christi 2002, no pet.); Murphy v. Friendswood Development Co., 965 S.W.2d 708 (Tex. App.—Houston [1st Dist.] 1998, no pet.)(dismissing sanctions for failure to satisfy TRCP 13's particularity requirement where order merely referenced the appellee's motion for sanctions as justification).

[12] Alexander v. Alexander, 956 S.W.2d 712 (Tex. App.—Houston [14th Dist.] 1997, petition denied)(party raising lack of particularity for first time on appeal has waived error).

[13] *Id.* at 715.

[14] 187 S.W.3d 486 (Tex. Crim. 2006).

pleadings must be verified (e.g. Rule 93 verified denials, Rule 120a special appearance), and some must be supported by affidavit (e.g. Rule 166a summary judgment). One court has distinguished between the two:

> Verification is "[a] formal declaration made in the presence of an authorized officer, such as a notary public, by which one swears to the truth of the statements in a document." An affidavit is statutorily defined as "a statement in writing of a fact or facts signed by the party making it, sworn to before an officer authorized to administer oaths, and officially certified to by the officer under his seal of office." Tex. Gov't Code Ann. § 312.011(1). Thus, a verification declares that the facts contained in a certain document are true, while an affidavit contains facts stated under oath."[15]

Another distinction must be made between a verification or affidavit and an acknowledgement. An acknowledgement is not made under oath, but is simply the notary's verification of a signature as being that of the person signing a document.[16]

11. *Contempt and inherent powers*. The rules provides for sanctions for frivolous pleadings and abusive discovery. A court can also punish lawyers and litigants through its contempt power and inherent powers.

"Contempt of court is broadly defined as disobedience to or disrespect of a court by acting in opposition to its authority. Within this definition, there are two basic types of contempt: direct contempt and constructive contempt. Direct contempt is that type of disobedience or disrespect which occurs within the presence of the court, while constructive contempt occurs outside the court's presence . . . A criminal contempt conviction for disobedience to a court order requires proof beyond a reasonable doubt of: (1) a reasonably specific order; (2) a violation of the order; and (3) the willful intent to violate the order."[17] Contempt can also be civil in nature. Civil contempt is "failing to do something which the contemnor is required to do by order of the court for the benefit or advantage of a party to the proceeding." While criminal contempt is punished by a specific term of imprisonment or fine, civil contempt is remedial in nature—the imprisonment or fine continues until the contemnor does what is required.[18]

See the following opinion for an interesting example of a court using its inherent powers.

---

15 In re Dobbs, 247 S.W.23d 394, 397 (Tex. App.—Dallas 2008).

16 Centro Juricide Instituto y Estudios Superiores de Monterrey v. Intertravel, Inc., 2 S.W.3d 446 (Tex. App.—San Antonio 1999, no pet.).

17 Ex parte Chambers, 898 S.W.2d 257 (Tex. 1995).

18 William W. Kilgarlin and Scott A. Ozmun, *Contempt of Court in Texas—What You Shouldn't Say to the Judge,* 38 BAYLOR L. REV. 297 (1986).

MARRIAGE OF POWELL

170 S.W.3d 156
(Tex.App.—Eastland 2005, no pet.)

JUSTICE WRIGHT.

This is an appeal from an order on a motion to enforce. We affirm the order of the trial court.

Michael Powell and Deborah Powell were divorced in 2001. After a hearing on a prior motion to enforce, the trial court ordered Michael Powell to pay attorney's fees in the amount of $1,000 to Kenneth N. Tarlton. Payment was due to be made on or before November 1, 2003.

On October 30, 2003, Michael Powell paid several agents to deliver 20 bank bags of unrolled pennies to Tarlton's office. After contacting several banks, Tarlton located a bank who would redeem the 100,000 pennies. The bank charged Tarlton a $100 redemption fee, and Tarlton received a cashier's check from the bank for a total of $900.

On November 4, 2003, Tarlton filed the present motion to enforce. At the hearing, Michael Powell informed the trial court that he was ordered to pay Tarlton $1,000 and that is what he did. Michael Powell further stated:

> But as far as Mr. Tarlton, which I do not respect in any shape, form, or fashion, I wanted to make a hardship upon him. He was delivered legal tender currency of $1,000. It would be several people that would love to have $1,000.

The record reflects that Michael Powell had instructed his agents to leave only the pennies at Tarlton's office and to return the bank bags to the bank. However, Michael Powell's agents were prevented from taking the bank bags from Tarlton's office. The record further reflects that each bank bag weighed between 15 and 20 pounds and that it took Tarlton 2.7496 hours to collect and redeem the pennies. Tarlton stated that his hourly rate for non-court time was $150. The record also reflects that pennies had originally been collected as a fundraiser for Graford High School and had not been rolled.

The trial court declined to hold Michael Powell in contempt and found his "choice of conduct to be frivolous and ridiculous." This trial court then ordered Michael Powell to pay the $100 bank redemption fee, an additional $350 in attorney's fees, and court costs totaling $83. The trial court further ordered that all sums be paid by Michael Powell to Tarlton by cashier's check, by money order, or by cash in the following denominations of U.S. Reserve Notes: five $100 bills, one $20 bill, one $10 bill, and three $1 bills.

In his sole issue on appeal, Michael Powell contends that the trial court had no legal basis to order him to pay the $100 bank redemption fee, the $350 in additional attorney's fees, and the $83 in court costs. We disagree.

The trial court has inherent power which it may use to aid in the exercise of its jurisdiction, in the administration of justice, and in the preservation of its independence and integrity. *Eichelberger v. Eichelberger*, 582 S.W.2d 395, 398 (Tex. 1979). The trial court has vast discretion to maintain control of the proceedings before it, to expedite the proceedings, and to prevent what it considers to be the unnecessary use of its time or resources. *See Dow Chemical Company v. Francis*, 46 S.W.3d 237, 240-41 (Tex. 2001).

The record before this court reflects that the trial court acted within its discretion. The issue is overruled.

The order of the trial court affirmed.

CHAPTER 6. JOINDER

A. Permissive Joinder of Claims and Parties

1. *Permissive Joinder*

Read Rules 37, 38, 40, 41, 43, 51, 97.

TWYMAN
v.
TWYMAN*
855 S.W.2d 619
(Tex. 1993)

CORNYN, JUSTICE.

We now consider whether the cause of action for intentional infliction of emotional distress may be brought in a divorce proceeding.

* * * [T]here appears to be no legal impediment to bringing a tort claim in a divorce action based on either negligence or an intentional act such as assault or battery. The more difficult issue is when the tort claim must be brought and how the tort award should be considered when making a "just and right" division of the marital estate. *See* TEX. FAM. CODE § 3.63(b). Of the states that have answered this question, several have held that the tort case and the divorce case must be litigated separately. Other states require joinder of the two actions.

We believe that the best approach lies between these two extremes. As in other civil actions, joinder of the tort cause of action should be permitted,[16] but subject to the principles of res judicata. *See Barr v. The Resolution Trust Corp.,* 837 S.W.2d 627, 631 (Tex. 1992) (reaffirming the transactional approach to res judicata analysis). *See also* TEX. R. CIV. P. 51. Of course, how such claims are ultimately tried is within the sound discretion of the trial court. *See* TEX. R. CIV. P. 174. But joinder of tort claims with the divorce, when feasible, is encouraged. Resolving both the tort and divorce actions in the same proceeding avoids two trials based at least in part on the same facts, and settles in one suit "all matters existing between the parties."[18]

When a tort action is tried with the divorce, however, it is imperative that the court avoid awarding a double recovery. When dividing the marital estate, the court may take into account several factors, including the fault of the parties if pleaded . . . . [A] spouse should not be allowed

---

* Editor's Note: In Boyles v. Kerr, 855 S.W.2d 593 (Tex. 1993), the Texas Supreme Court held that there was no cause of action in Texas for negligent infliction of emotional distress. Soon thereafter, in this opinion, the court expressly adopted the tort of intentional infliction of emotional distress.

16 We anticipate that most tort cases between spouses will be joined with the divorce proceeding, however, situations may exist in which the facts supporting the tort action will be different from those supporting a petition for divorce.

18 By holding that these actions may be brought in a single lawsuit we are not authorizing the use of contingent fee arrangements in family law matters. *See* TEX. DISCIPLINARY R. PROF. CONDUCT 1.04 & cmt. 9 (1989), reprinted in TEX. GOV'T CODE ANN., tit. 2, submit. G app. (Vernon Supp. 1993) (STATE BAR RULES art. 10, § 9). Rather, attorneys should enter two separate fee arrangements, one for the divorce and the other for the tort claim. *See* Andrew Schepard, *Divorce, Interspousal Torts, and Res Judicata,* 24 FAM. L.Q. 127, 151-52 (1990).

to recover tort damages and a disproportionate division of the community estate based on the same conduct. Therefore, when a fact-finder awards tort damages to a divorcing spouse, the court may not consider the same tortious acts when dividing the marital estate . . . . The court may still award a disproportionate division of property for reasons other than the tortious conduct. To avoid the potential problem of double recovery, the fact-finder should consider the damages awarded in the tort action when dividing the parties' property. If a jury is used to render an advisory division of the parties' estate, the judge should limit, by appropriate instruction, the jury's consideration of the alleged tortious acts and later consider the award of damages in determining a just and right division of the marital estate.

Notes & Questions

1. *Joinder of claims in two-party suits.* When there are only two parties to a suit, one plaintiff and one defendant, Rule 51(a) permits the parties to join in the same proceeding as many claims as each may have against the other. Therefore, in such suits there is no misjoinder—no claim joined in these suits will be in violation of Rule 51(a). There is one somewhat obscure exception: Rule 97(g) forbids tort counterclaims against contractual claims and vice versa unless one "arises out of or is incident to or is connected with same."

2. *Joinder of claims in multiple-party suits.* When there are multiple parties, however, Rule 51(a) limits joinder of claims to those situations where "the requirements of Rules 39, 40, and 43 are satisfied." The important limitation is found in Rule 40, the rule that limits the joinder of parties. Under Rule 40(a), additional parties may join or be joined in the action only if the claims asserted by or against them arise "out of the same transaction, occurrence, or series of transactions of occurrences and if any question of law or fact common to all of them will arise in the action." Thus, in multiple party suits, some claims may be subject to objection on grounds of misjoinder for noncompliance with Rule 51(a). Note that the federal rules have a broader concept of joinder. Federal Rule 18(a) is not limited by the joinder of parties rule; therefore, any claims between parties properly joined may be joined.

3. *Defendants' joinder of claims.* Defendants assert their affirmative claims against the plaintiffs by counterclaim.[1] They assert claims against co-parties (other defendants joined by the plaintiff) by cross-claim.[2] The same concepts that govern joinder of claims govern joinder of counterclaims and cross-claims. If there are only two parties, a defendant may bring any counterclaim against the plaintiff.[3] If there are multiple parties, joinder is limited. Cross-claims (which necessarily are asserted only in multiple party cases) are limited to claims "arising out of the transaction or occurrence that is the subject matter either of the original action or of a counterclaim therein."[4]

---

1 *See* Rule 97(a)-(d).

2 *See* Rule 97(e).

3 *See* Rule 97(b).

4 Rule 97(e). Because it is not expressly limited by Rule 40, this language and the language of Rule 97(b) could be construed to allow counterclaims and crossclaims that do not arise from the same transaction, even when there are multiple parties. This issue, however, has never been decided by the Texas appellate courts. The language is identical to that found in Federal Rule 13(b) and (g), and, therefore is more appropriate for the

4. *Compulsory joinder of claims.* Notice that the court in *Twyman* notes that one of "the more difficult issues" is not whether the tort claimed could be joined with the divorce action but whether the claim *must* be brought in the pending action or be barred. This is the subject of section B of this chapter.

5. *Permissive joinder of parties.* Under Rule 40, multiple plaintiffs and multiple defendants can be joined in the same suit so long as the claims asserted arise out of the same transaction, occurrence, or series of transactions or occurrences, with common questions of law and fact. A plaintiff joins multiple defendants in a suit simply by alleging claims against more than one defendant in the petition and serving process upon them. Multiple plaintiffs can join together to allege claims against the defendants, either by filing separate petitions in the same suit or filing one petition together.

6. *Defendants' joinder of parties.* Defendants primarily join additional parties via three methods: (1) a Rule 38 third-party petition; (2) a counterclaim, as allowed by Rule 97(f) (pursuant to the provisions of Rule 38, 39, and 40); or (3) a cross-claim as allowed by Rule 97(f) (same). Rule 38, however, is not the exclusive means of joining third-parties. The Supreme Court explored third-party practice against entities related to a plaintiff against whom a counter-claim had been filed in *Bennett v. Grant*.[5] In that case, Bennett sued Grant for slander and Grant counterclaimed. More than 30 days later, Grant sought to add Bonham Corporation (Bennett's cattle company) as a third-party defendant in the case. Bennett and Bonham claimed this was misjoinder because Grant was late under Rule 38, but Justice Willett writing for the court observed that Rule 38 was inapplicable because Grant did not seek to shift fault on Bennett's slander claim from Grant to Bonham, as contemplated by the rule. Further the court noted:

> [J]oinder was permissible under other rules. For instance, under Rule 37, joinder of "additional parties necessary or proper parties to the suit" is permitted. Additionally, under Rule 39, joinder of an additional party is permitted if "in his absence complete relief cannot be accorded among those already parties." Further, under Rule 40, permissive joinder of parties as defendants is allowed if a plaintiff or counter-plaintiff asserts against them "any right to relief ... arising out of the same transaction [or] occurrence."[6]

The court also held that Bonham and Bennett waived complaint about misjoinder: "Joinder is an issue that arises in the trial court, and to preserve error, Bonham Corp. was required to present its objection there. Because it failed to do so, Bonham Corp. has waived the issue in this Court."[7]

7. *No joinder of insurance companies.* Rule 38(c) specifically prevents parties from joining insurance companies in tort cases unless the company is *directly* liable to the person injured by statute or contract. There is no "direct action" statute in Texas, and insurance policies typically contain a "no action" provision that specifically prevents a third party from asserting rights

---

broader concept of joinder found in the federal rules. As a practical matter, it has made no difference because a court is likely to use its discretion to sever a claim that arises from a different transaction or occurrence than the other claims. This issue may become more important, however, because of the significance of proper joinder in venue added in the 1995 amendments.

5 525 S.W.3d 642, 653-54 (Tex. 2017).

6 *Id.*

7 *Id.* at 654.

against the insurer until the insured's liability is reduced to judgment or compromised by a settlement agreement.[8] What advantage do plaintiffs seek to gain by making insurance carriers parties to the primary liability action?

8. *Statute of limitations.* What if the plaintiff files a cause of action the day before the statute of limitations runs, and by the time the defendant has been served, the defendant's counterclaim is time barred? CPRC § 16.069 tolls the statute of limitations for counterclaims and cross-claims until the 30th day after the date on which the party filing the claim is required to answer. CPRC §16.068 is closely related, and concerns the statute of limitations for claims added by an amended or supplemental pleading.[9] The statute provides that the amended pleading will relate back to the time the original action was filed for statute of limitations purposes, unless the new pleading is "wholly based on a new, distinct or different transaction or occurrence."

9. *Recovery of attorney's fees.* Texas law does not allow recovery for attorney's fees unless authorized by statute or contract. For example, attorney's fees are recoverable by statute when a party asserts a claim for breach of an oral or written contract under Chapter 38 of the Civil Practice & Remedies Code. When a party sues another under multiple theories of recovery (for example, a breach of contract claim and a fraud claim) and seeks recovery of attorney fees under one or more (but not all) claims, the claimant must segregate fees between claims for which fees are recoverable and claims for which they are not. However, when discrete legal services advance both a recoverable and unrecoverable claim, the expended fees are so intertwined that they cannot be segregated.[10] Consider how an attorney might prove up attorney's fees when fees must be segregated (i.e. they are not inextricably intertwined). The Supreme Court suggests that the lawyer testify as to what percentage of the entire fee for the case or particular work should be attributed to the claims for which fees are recoverable.[11]

10. *Interpleader.* Plaintiffs or defendants may file a Rule 43 "interpleader," a method by which claims and parties can be joined even though the claims technically may not arise from the same transaction or occurrence and do not have common questions of law or fact. Typically, an interpleader involves a sum of money or other valuable property that is claimed by several parties. The sum of money could be insurance proceeds, with several people claiming to be the beneficiary under the policy.[12] And a bailor may hold personal property such as jewelry or collectible art with ownership claims being asserted by multiple parties. Perhaps there is a contract to purchase a piece of real property, but parties other than the possessor claim to hold an interest in the property. All of these claims are connected because they concern rights to the property, but they may have no other relationship. Party A's rights may have their genesis under completely different circumstances and at a completely different time than B's rights. The interpleader allows a party that may be subject to multiple liability from all of these competing claims (the "stakeholder") to bring them into one lawsuit for resolution. A disinterested stakeholder, one that has reasonable doubts as to the party entitled to the fund or property, and who in good faith deposits the

---

[8] *See* Getty Oil Co. v. Ins. Co. of North America, 845 S.W.2d 794, 800 (Tex. 1992).

[9] *See* Chapter 5.

[10] Tony Gullo Motors I, L.P. v. Chapa, 212 S.W.3d 299, 314 (Tex. 2006); *see also* Kinsel v. Lindsey, 526 S.W.3d 411, 427 (Tex. 2017) (to recover attorneys fees, party was "required to segregate work relating to recoverable and non-recoverable claims").

[11] Tony Gullo Motors I, L.P. v. Chapa, 212 S.W.3d 299, 314 (Tex. 2006).

[12] *See* State Farm Life Ins. Co. v. Martinez, 216 S.W.3d 799 (Tex. 2007).

fund or property with the court and interpleads the claimants, is entitled to recover attorney's fees from the interpleaded fund.[13]

---

2. *Intervention*

Read Rules 60, 61.

In re UNION CARBIDE CORP.
273 S.W.3d 152
(Tex. 2008)

PER CURIAM.

In this case, family members who survived John Hall intervened in a pending personal injury suit filed by Kenneth Moffett. Union Carbide, a defendant in both the pending suit and the intervention, filed a motion to strike the intervention. Instead of ruling on that motion, the trial court severed the Halls' claims into a new suit that then remained pending in the same court. We conclude that (1) the trial court abused its discretion by failing to rule on Union Carbide's motion to strike before considering whether to sever the intervention; (2) the trial court only had discretion to grant the motion to strike; and (3) Union Carbide does not have an adequate remedy by appeal. We conditionally grant mandamus relief.

On January 27, 2006, Kenneth Moffett filed a personal injury action in the 212th District Court of Galveston County. Moffett alleged that he was exposed to toxic chemicals distributed, marketed, or manufactured by fourteen defendants and that the exposure caused him to develop acute myelogenous leukemia. He claims to have been exposed to the chemicals from 1974 to 2000, including short periods of time in the mid-1970s and in the 1980s when he worked at the Union Carbide facility in Texas City.

On March 5, 2007, family members who survived John Hall intervened in Moffett's lawsuit. They alleged that Hall died from myelodysplastic syndrome caused by his exposure between 1963 and 1998 to toxic chemicals at Union Carbide's Texas City facility. Some, but not all of the defendants sued by the Hall survivors were also defendants in Moffett's suit. Union Carbide was a defendant in both the Moffett and Hall suits. Union Carbide filed a motion to strike the Halls' intervention because the Halls failed to show that they possessed a justiciable interest in the Moffett suit. The trial court conducted a hearing on the motion to strike but did not rule on it. Instead, the trial court severed the Halls' claims into a separate suit and directed the suit to be docketed and maintained on the regular docket of the court. Union Carbide petitioned the court of appeals for a writ of mandamus directing the trial court to rule on and grant its motion to strike. The court of appeals denied the petition.

In this Court, Union Carbide argues that the trial court abused its discretion by both refusing to rule on its motion to strike the intervention and refusing to grant the motion because the Halls

---

[13] Great American Reserve Ins. Co. v. Sanders, 525 S.W.2d 956, 958 (Tex. 1975) (overruled on other grounds by State Farm Life Ins. Co. v. Martinez, 216 S.W.3d 799 (Tex. 2007); United States v. Ray Thomas Gravel Co., 380 S.W.2d 576, 580-81 (Tex. 1964).

did not show a justiciable interest in the Moffett suit. Union Carbide also urges it does not have an adequate appellate remedy and that the benefits of mandamus review outweigh the detriments.

Texas Rule of Civil Procedure 60 provides that "[a]ny party may intervene by filing a pleading subject to being stricken out by the court for sufficient cause on the motion of any party." The rule authorizes a party with a justiciable interest in a pending suit to intervene in the suit as a matter of right. *Guar. Fed. Sav. Bank v. Horseshoe Operating Co.,* 793 S.W.2d 652, 657 (Tex. 1990). Because intervention is allowed as a matter of right, the "justiciable interest" requirement is of paramount importance: it defines the category of non-parties who may, without consultation with or permission from the original parties or the court, interject their interests into a pending suit to which the intervenors have not been invited. Thus, the "justiciable interest" requirement protects pending cases from having interlopers disrupt the proceedings. The parties to the pending case may protect themselves from the intervention by filing a motion to strike. If any party to the pending suit moves to strike the intervention, the intervenors have the burden to show a justiciable interest in the pending suit.

To constitute a justiciable interest, "[t]he intervenor's interest must be such that if the original action had never been commenced, and he had first brought it as the sole plaintiff, he would have been entitled to recover in his own name to the extent at least of a part of the relief sought" in the original suit. *King v. Olds,* 71 Tex. 729, 12 S.W. 65, 65 (1888). In other words, a party may intervene if the intervenor could have "brought the [pending] action, or any part thereof, in his own name." *Guar. Fed. Sav. Bank,* 793 S.W.2d at 657.

In this case, the Halls' petition in intervention only briefly addressed their interest in the Moffett suit:

> In the original action, Moffett claims exposure to benzene and benzene-containing products at premises including Union Carbide in Texas City and against some, if not all, of the Defendants that Intervenors are making claims. Intervenors are entitled to a recovery against the defendants and Intervenors' claims [that] arise out of the same transaction and/or series of transactions and have common questions of law and/or fact with the claims in the original action.

Neither party introduced evidence at the hearing on Union Carbide's motion to strike. In their brief the Halls claim to have met their burden of showing that they had a justiciable interest in the Moffett suit. They primarily base their argument on allegations that Hall and Moffett suffered from similar blood disorders resulting from exposure to benzene at Union Carbide's facilities. Yet the Halls do not assert that they could have brought any part of Moffett's claim. While there is a real controversy between the Halls and Union Carbide-whether John Hall's exposure to toxic chemicals while working at Union Carbide caused his disease-the Halls make no claim that their controversy will be affected or resolved by resolution of the Moffett case. Accordingly, the Halls fail to demonstrate a justiciable interest in Moffett's suit and are not entitled to intervene in the Moffett suit.

The Halls assert that even if they did not properly intervene in Moffett's suit, the trial court had discretion to sever their claims rather than striking them. First, the Halls claim that their petition met the standard for permissive joinder found in Texas Rule of Civil Procedure 40, and therefore, the trial court could properly sever their claims under Rule 41. But the joinder standard does not control here because this was an intervention, and the two are distinct. *Compare* TEX.R. CIV. P. 40(a) (providing the requirements to join in an action as a plaintiff), *with Guar. Fed. Sav. Bank,* 793 S.W.2d at 657 (providing the requirements to intervene in an action). Permissive joinder relates to "proper parties to an action who may be joined or omitted at the *pleader's* election." Permissive joinder and intervention are authorized and permitted by separate rules, and the rules provide different processes for addressing the different situations. TEX.R. CIV. P. 41, 60. Because interventions by uninvited participants have potential for disrupting pending suits, trial courts should rule on motions to strike interventions before considering other matters such as severance.

The Halls reference *Boswell, O'Toole, Davis & Pickering v. Stewart,* 531 S.W.2d 380, 382 (Tex.Civ.App.—Houston [14th Dist.] 1975, no writ), in which the court stated that a trial judge may "proceed to trial of the intervention claim; he may sever the intervention; he may order a separate trial; he may strike the intervention for good cause." However, Rule 60 does not provide for such options as equal alternatives; it provides only that an intervention is "subject to being stricken out by the court for sufficient cause on the motion of any party."

The Halls further argue that mandamus relief is not proper because the Court cannot prescribe the manner in which the trial court exercises its discretion. *See Walker v. Packer,* 827 S.W.2d 833, 839-40 (Tex. 1992) (noting that mandamus relief is available to correct a trial court's clear abuse of discretion). The Halls' argument assumes that Rule 60 afforded the trial court discretion to refuse to rule on Union Carbide's motion to strike before it considered severing the Hall case from the Moffett case. It did not. The trial court abused its discretion in failing to first rule on the motion to strike. Furthermore, the Halls did not show that they possessed any justiciable interest in the Moffett lawsuit. They did not show that they had standing to have brought and recovered for any part of Moffett's claim. Accordingly, the trial court had no discretion to deny Union Carbide's motion to strike the petition in intervention.

For mandamus to issue, a relator must show that it has no adequate remedy by appeal. *In re Prudential Ins. Co. of Am.,* 148 S.W.3d 124, 135-36 (Tex. 2004). "An appellate remedy is 'adequate' when any benefits to mandamus review are outweighed by the detriments." Union Carbide claims that the benefits of mandamus review outweigh the detriments because (1) the issue presented is one of law that is likely to recur, yet eludes an answer by appeal; (2) the trial court's action effectively establishes a template for circumventing procedures for random assignment of cases in multi-court counties; (3) it will be difficult or impossible to show on appeal that the deprivation of a randomly assigned judge entitles Union Carbide to appellate relief; (4) the effective initiation of suit by intervention and severance deprived Union Carbide of procedural rights afforded to defendants in original actions; and (5) granting mandamus will not result in any, or at most, negligible detriment. We agree with Union Carbide.

Regardless of the other benefits claimed by Union Carbide, there is significant benefit from mandamus relief in regard to the random-assignment-of-cases question. Random assignment of cases is designed to prevent forum-shopping. Practices that subvert random assignment procedures breed "disrespect for and [threaten] the integrity of our judicial system." We need not consider whether the intervention was intended to circumvent Galveston County's local rule requiring random assignment of cases because regardless of the Halls' intent, the intervention and the trial court's abuse of discretion in failing to rule on and grant the motion to strike resulted in circumvention of the random assignment rule. In regard to any detriment to the parties, the Halls' claims have now been filed as a separate lawsuit that is pending in Galveston County. There will be insignificant detriment to either party or the judicial system if mandamus relief is granted. On balance, mandamus review is warranted because the benefits of establishing the priority that trial courts must give to ruling on motions to strike interventions and re-emphasizing the importance of both appearance and practice in maintaining integrity of random assignment rules outweigh any detriment to mandamus review in this instance. Thus, Union Carbide does not have an adequate remedy by appeal.

Without hearing oral argument, we conditionally grant the writ of mandamus and direct the trial court to vacate its severance order and enter an order granting Union Carbide's motion to strike. The writ will issue only if the trial court does not do so.

Notes & Questions

1. *Intervention*. New parties can intervene in an ongoing lawsuit by filing a "plea in intervention."[1] In the *Guaranty Federal* opinion, discussed in *Union Carbide*, the Supreme Court held that the trial court properly allowed a bank customer to intervene in a lawsuit brought by a payee of a teller's check on which the bank issued a stop payment order. The court discussed interventions generally:[2]

> An intervenor is not required to secure the court's permission to intervene; the party who opposed the intervention has the burden to challenge it by a motion to strike. Without a motion to strike, the trial court abused its discretion in striking Petrolifes' plea in intervention
>
> Furthermore, under Rule 60, a person or entity has the right to intervene if the intervenor could have brought the same action, or any part thereof, in his own name, or, if the action had been brought against him, he would be able to defeat recovery, or some part thereof. The interest asserted by the intervenor may be legal or equitable. Although the trial court has broad discretion in determining whether an intervention should be stricken, it is an abuse of discretion to strike a plea in intervention if (1) the intervenor meets the above test, (2) the intervention will not complicate the case by an excessive multiplication of the issues, and (3) the intervention is almost essential to effectively protect the intervenor's interest.

The right to intervene often turns on a question of standing.[3] This is especially true in cases involving government agencies and the public interest. When a suit is brought to benefit the public at large, a citizen has no justiciable interest in the litigation, and a motion to strike the citizen's intervention must be granted unless she can show that she would be affected differently from all other citizens.[4] Delay is also a valid basis for denying intervention.[5]

---

1 *See* Rules 60, 61.

2 Guaranty Federal Savings Bank v. Horseshoe Operating Co., 793 S.W.2d 652, 657 (Tex. 1990).

3 *See* Potash Corp. v. Mancias, 942 S.W.2d 61 (Tex. App.—Corpus Christi 1997, orig. proceeding) (intervenors had no justifiable claim, so order denying motion to strike intervention was abuse of discretion); Gracida v. Tagle, 946 S.W.2d 504 (Tex. App.—Corpus Christi 1997, orig. proceeding) (third party writer claim against insured was no justifiable interest in declaratory judgment action concerning insurer's duty to defend or indemnify insured).

4 *See* Mendez v. Brewer, 626 S.W.2d 498, 499 (Tex. 1982) (foster parents did not have standing to join with Department of Human Resources in a termination suit where their sole interest was desire to adopt child if parent-child relationship with natural parents was terminated)(superceded by TEX. FAM. CODE § 11.03); Galveston County v. Lohec, 814 S.W.2d 751, 755 (Tex. App.—Houston [14th Dist.] 1992, rev'd on other grounds, 841

2. *Deadline to Intervene*. The Rules do not specify a deadline for intervention. But despite this silence, the Supreme Court recently held that "common law dictates that a party may not intervene post-judgment unless the trial court first sets aside the judgment."[6] The court went on to hold that the State of Texas attempted intervention, post-judgment, in a same-sex divorce case was too late, and thus, the state was not a party to the case.[7]

3. *Additional joinder limitations under venue statute*. Remember that Section 15.003 of the Civil Practice and Remedies Code (the venue statute) places additional limitations on joinder of multiple plaintiffs and intervening plaintiffs. In a suit where more than one plaintiff is joined, each plaintiff must, independently of any other plaintiff, establish proper venue in the county were suit was filed. A person unable to establish proper venue may not join or maintain venue for a suit as a plaintiff unless the person independently establishes that (1) joinder or intervention is proper under the Texas Rules of Civil Procedure, (2) maintaining venue in the county of suit does not unfairly prejudice another party to the suit, (3) there is an essential need to have the person's claim tried in the county in which the suit is pending, and (4) the county in which the suit is pending is a fair and convenient venue for the person seeking to join in or maintain venue for the suit *and* for the persons against whom the suit is brought.[8] Likewise, a party may not intervene or join in a pending suit as a plaintiff unless it can, independently, either establish proper venue for the county in which the suit is pending or meet the four requirements above.[9] The Supreme Court has said that the statute is a joinder statute rather than a venue statute.[10] Therefore, it appears that the proper mechanism to challenge inappropriate joinder, and the resulting venue issue, is a motion to sever. Challenges to intervening plaintiffs are made through motions to strike the intervention. Decisions of the trial court allowing or denying intervention or joinder in response to venue-statute attacks are subject to interlocutory appeal.[11] Reconsider the Problem in the venue chapter relating to intervening plaintiffs. After reading these materials, is venue the only basis upon which the defendants should challenge the intervention?

4. *Forum shopping*. The venue restrictions were intended to keep multiple plaintiffs from picking a favored county. *Union Carbide* is directed towards another type of forum shopping—picking a particular judge in a county. The intervenor in that case could satisfy the venue requirements—Texas City is located in Galveston County.

S.W.2d 361 (Tex. 1992) (taxpayer failed to establish justifiable interest in suit concerning purchasing policies of Park Board).

5 *See* Bush v. Brunswick Corp., 783 S.W.2d 724, 727 (Tex. App.—Fort Worth 1989, writ denied).

6 State v. Naylor, 466 S.W.3d 783, 788 (Tex. 2015).

7 *See id.* at 788-89.

8 TEX. CIV. PRAC. & REM. CODE § 15.003(a).

9 TEX. CIV. PRAC. & REM. CODE § 15.003(b).

10 American Home Products v. Clark, 38 S.W.3d 92 (Tex. 2001).

11 TEX. CIV. PRAC. & REM. CODE § 15.003(c). *See American Home Products*, 38 S.W.3d at 92.

3. *Bifurcation*

Read Rule 174(b), 320, TRAP 44.1(b) and 61.2.

ILEY
v.
HUGHES
311 S.W.2d 648
(Tex. 1958)

[Hancock sued Iley for injuries resulting from an assault—Iley shot Hancock with a rifle. Iley defended on grounds of defense of property, specifically to protect his pecans. The jury answered general liability questions favoring the defendant, but was unable to come to a verdict on some of the general damage questions, the malice question, and exemplary damages. Hancock offered to waive exemplary damages if the judge would render an interlocutory judgment on the general liability questions, and empanel a jury to determine damages only. The trial judge (Sarah T. Hughes, who as a federal judge in 1963 administered the presidential oath to LBJ in Dallas) granted the motion and was about to begin the damages trial when Iley sought mandamus.

CALVERT, JUSTICE.

In this proceeding Iley seeks a writ of mandamus directing the respondent District Judge to set aside her order for a separate trial of the damage issue and to declare a mistrial of the case of *Hancock v. Iley*. The respondent, Hancock, appears here by counsel in defense of the action of the District Judge. He asserts that the action of the District Judge is authorized by Rule 174(b), T.R.C.P. All parties agree that the precise question is one of first impression in this state. In deciding it we attach no controlling significance to the fact that the order for a separate trial of the damage issue was entered after a verdict was had on the liability issues. Our conclusion would be the same if the separate trial had been ordered before trial of any issue had been undertaken.

Rule 174(b) reads as follows:

> (b) Separate Trials. The court in furtherance of convenience or to avoid prejudice may order a separate trial of any claim, cross-claim, counter-claim, or third-party claim, or of any separate issue or of any number of claims, cross-claims, counter-claims, third-party claims, or issues.

There are strong arguments supporting respondents' position, some of which may be noticed.

On its face and by its literal wording the Rule would seem to authorize a separate trial of the damage and liability issues in a personal injury suit. It authorizes a trial court 'in furtherance of convenience or to avoid prejudice' to order a separate trial 'of any separate issue or of any number of . . . issues,' and we have said that the discretion to require severances and separate trials conferred on trial courts by this and other Rules is 'about as broad as language could make it.'

The Rule has been interpreted as conferring authority on trial courts to try separately certain other types of 'issues.' In a suit for damages for wrongful death, the issue of whether the plaintiff was married to the deceased and therefore entitled to maintain the suit was tried separately, apparently without question. In a suit for damages for personal injuries, the Court stated that the trial court had properly tried in limine the question of whether the plaintiff was an independent contractor and thus entitled to a recovery of damages or an employee of the defendant whose only right of recovery was under the Workmen's Compensation Law. In a suit for damages for alienation of affection, the Court specifically approved the action of the trial court in requiring a separate trial in limine of an issue of limitations. In a suit to establish a right to a share of the net profits of a business and for an accounting, the trial court, apparently without challenge, tried separately the issue of the plaintiff's right to share in the profits of the business. In [other cases] the trial court tried the issue of divorce in advance of a trial of the property rights of the parties, but separate trial of like issues was held unauthorized in [another].

* * *

Giving full weight to the foregoing arguments in support of respondents' position, we nevertheless feel that they are overborne by stronger considerations of long standing policy and practice in this state.

Our courts have always frowned upon piecemeal trials, deeming the public interest, the interests of litigants and the administration of justice to be better served by rules of trial which avoid a multiplicity of suits.

By refusing to interpret Rule 174(b) to permit separate trials of liability and damage issues in this type of case that Rule and its interpretation is kept harmonious with our interpretation of Rules 434 and 503 [now T.R.A.P. 44 and 61.2]. We have held that the broad language of those Rules directing reversal of only that part of a judgment affected by error, 'where the issues are severable,' does not permit of a disassociation on subsequent trial of liability and damage issues through severance and reversal as to only one or the other. . . .

If Rule 174(b) were now interpreted to permit separate trial of liability and damage issues, on what basis could we later deny to a trial court the right to try only the primary negligence issues? Or the contributory negligence issues? Or, more appropriately perhaps, the issue of unavoidable accident, since a finding that an accident was unavoidable would ordinarily relieve the defendant of liability?

Prior to adoption of the Rules of Civil Procedure in 1941 a separate trial of issues as here attempted would not have been countenanced. . . . It could hardly have been contemplated that Rule 174(b) would be interpreted to work such a radical departure from long settled practice.

* * *

Our conclusion is that although the discretion lodged in trial judges by Rule 174(b) in ordering separate trials of 'issues' is indeed broad and realistic, it does not authorize separate trials of liability and damage issues in personal injury litigation.

In spite of the conclusion reached and announced on the question presented by this proceeding, we, nevertheless, decline to grant the writ of mandamus [because there is an adequate remedy by appeal.]

TRANSPORTATION INS. CO.
v.
MORIEL
879 S.W.2d 10
(Tex. 1994)

CORNYN, JUSTICE.

This case requires us to clarify the standards governing the imposition of punitive damages in the context of bad faith insurance litigation. . . . We hold that Juan Moriel did not present legally sufficient evidence of gross negligence. Therefore, Moriel is not entitled to punitive damages. It necessarily follows that the constitutional issues-whether the size of the punitive damages award or the procedures the trial court followed violated Transportation's due process rights-are questions that must await another day. Because the court has not previously addressed punitive damages in the bad faith context, and because this opinion represents a substantial clarification of the gross negligence standard that will apply in all cases, we remand this case for a new trial in the interest of justice.

* * *

We held in *Lunsford v. Morris*, 746 S.W.2d 471 (Tex. 1988), that evidence of a defendant's net worth is relevant in determining the proper amount of punitive damages, and therefore may be subject to pretrial discovery. This decision aligned Texas with the overwhelming majority of other jurisdictions on this issue. As we noted in *Lunsford*, the amount of punitive damages necessary to punish and deter wrongful conduct depends on the financial strength of the defendant. "That which could be an enormous penalty to one may be but a mere annoyance to another."

However, evidence of a defendant's net worth, which is generally relevant only to the amount of punitive damages, by highlighting the relative wealth of a defendant, has a very real potential for prejudicing the jury's determination of other disputed issues in a tort case. We therefore conclude that a trial court, if presented with a timely motion, should bifurcate the determination of the amount of punitive damages from the remaining issues. Under this approach, the jury first hears evidence relevant to liability for actual damages, the amount of actual damages, and liability for punitive damages (e.g., gross negligence), and then returns findings on these issues. If the jury answers the punitive damage liability question in the plaintiff's favor, the same jury is then presented evidence relevant only to the amount of punitive damages, and determines the proper amount of punitive damages, considering the totality of the evidence presented at both phases of the trial.

At least thirteen states now require bifurcation of trials in which punitive damages are sought. Ten of these, California, Georgia, Kansas, Missouri, Montana, Nevada, Ohio, Tennessee, Utah, and Wyoming, generally follow the procedure outlined above, in which the amount of punitive damages is bifurcated from the remaining issues. The other states require bifurcation of the entire punitive damage claim, including liability and amount. We believe the former approach is preferable, as some of the evidence relevant to punitive damage liability, such as evidence of gross negligence, will also be relevant to liability for actual damages. Bifurcating only the amount of punitive damages therefore eliminates the most serious risk of prejudice, while minimizing the confusion and inefficiency that can result from a bifurcated trial.[28]

The issue in this Court is not whether bifurcation of punitive damage claims is constitutionally required, but whether our system of imposing punitive damages, on the whole, provides adequate procedural safeguards to protect against awards that are grossly excessive. Concluding that the current procedures are not adequate, we hereby adopt the requirement of bifurcated trials in punitive damage cases.

* * *

Notes & Questions

1. *Rationale*. In *Iley*, Judge Calvert uses a slippery-slope justification for the court's resistance to bifurcation. Is there a counterargument? Are damages issues intertwined with liability issues in the same way that primary negligence, comparative negligence and unavoidable accident (a finding that nobody was negligent) are intertwined? A customary argument against bifurcation is that when liability and causation are intertwined—as in, for example, a negligence case—a second jury would have to re-try liability in order to find on causation. How can a jury determine whether the injury was within the foreseeable risk created by D if it does not know what that risk was? In many cases, the second jury must know *why* the first jury found D negligent or it cannot assess causation. Note that this kind of objection to bifurcation does not apply when the same jury hears all segments.

2. *New trials and remands*. Note that *Iley* announces its rule against bifurcation in personal injury cases. The Rules incorporate *Iley* into the procedures for new trials and remands for other cases as well. Rule 320 permits the trial court to grant partial new trials on "clearly separable issues" when that can be done with fairness, but it cannot grant a separate trial on unliquidated damages alone if liability is contested. Rules 44.1, 61.1 and 61.2 of the Texas Rules of Appellate Procedure, contain similar restrictions regarding remands by appellate courts. Note that neither *Iley* nor the rules apply to cases involving liquidated damages. (Note: Liquidated damages is an amount the parties have agreed to in writing. Unliquidated damages must be proven up with evidence.) The Supreme Court reversed the court of appeals remand for trial of damages only in a breach of warranty case (unliquidated damages).[1]

3. *Motion required.* Note that bifurcation for punitive damages is not automatic. The party seeking it must timely file an appropriate motion.

4. *Statute.* The *Moriel* holding set new standards for punitive damages, and much of the substance of the *Moriel* holding was incorporated into Chapter 41 of the Texas Civil Practices and Remedies Code, effective September, 1995. The right to a bifurcated trial of the punitive damages phase is elaborated in TEX. CIV. PRAC. & REM. CODE § 41.009. The motion to bifurcate must be made be-

---

[28] Despite the authority of trial courts to order separate trials under TEX. R. CIV. P. 174(b), we have previously held that liability and damages may not be bifurcated in a personal injury action. Iley v. Hughes, 158 Tex. 362, 311 S.W.2d 648, 651 (1958). . . . Although we remain resolute that piecemeal trials as a general rule should be avoided, given the importance of the considerations we have discussed, we conclude that punitive damage cases should be the exception to the rule.

[1] Redman Homes, Inc. v. Ivy, 920 S.W.2d 664 (Tex. 1996) (Court of Appeals found that evidence supported jury findings on liability but that evidence of damages was insufficient and remanded only the damages issue).

fore voir dire, and any defendant may request it. One significant departure from *Moriel* is the statute's provision that only a defendant may move for bifurcation.

5. *Not always harmful error*. If the trial court erroneously refuses to bifurcate the punitive damage phase, the error may be harmless. In *Uniroyal Goodrich Tire Co. v. Martinez,*[2] the Supreme Court held that the error was harmless because the jury was not presented with any evidence of net worth or other prejudicial evidence that would have been admissible only in the second hearing.

6. *Same jury*. *Moriel* and the bifurcation statute both require the punitive damage phase be heard by the same jury that decided liability. The Austin Court of Appeals has held that convening a second jury violates "fundamental constitutional rights to trial by jury and to due process."[3] In that case, the plaintiff failed to object to the trial court's dismissal of the jury after the first phase. The Court of Appeals instructed the trial court to vacate its order for the second phase to be tried by a second jury. Where does that leave the plaintiff? Since the amount of punitive damages cannot be tried by a second jury in isolation from the issues of liability and actual damages, must plaintiff choose between accepting the actual damages awarded in the first trial and trying the entire case again to a second jury?

7. *Refusal to bifurcate upheld*. In *Tarrant Regional Water District v. Gragg,*[4] a landowner sought compensation for the reduction in value that a water project had caused to his property by changing the water-flow patterns. The Supreme Court upheld the trial court's refusal to bifurcate. What if the trial court had ordered bifurcation? Would the trial court's order have been upheld?

> The District argues that the trial court abused its discretion by declining to bifurcate the proceedings. According to the District, the trial court should have first conducted a bench trial on the takings issue, and then held a separate trial, if necessary, to allow a jury to assess reasonable compensation.
>
> Texas Rule of Civil Procedure 174(b) allows a trial court to order a separate trial on any issue in the interest of convenience or to avoid prejudice. We review a trial court's ruling on a motion for separate trial for an abuse of discretion. The District complains that it was prejudiced in a number of respects by the trial court's refusal to order separate trials. First, the District asserts that the failure to bifurcate left it confused about several issues, including "whether the court would find the District responsible at all," whether the court would find a temporary or permanent taking which would in turn call for different damage measures, whether a fee or an easement was taken, and how much of the Ranch was affected. The District argues that the trial court's failure to order separate trials was inherently unfair because it forced the District to present proof of damages while simultaneously contesting liability. We disagree.
>
> In nearly every case a defendant must proceed with some amount of uncertainty of the type the District describes. Defendants typically proceed generally without knowing whether they will be found liable or on what, if any, theory. And it is not at all unusual for a plaintiff to present more than one damage measure during trial. For example, a plaintiff may allege breach of contract and quantum meruit, causes of action with differ-

---

2 977 S.W.2d 328 (Tex. 1998).

3 *In re* Bradle, 83 S.W. 3d 923, 928 (Tex. App.—Austin 2002, pet. denied).

4 151 S.W.3d 546, 556-57 (Tex. 2004).

ent elements of proof and different damage measures. The District has articulated no reason why admitting damage evidence before liability is determined is any more prejudicial in the condemnation context than in any other.

On the other hand, the record supports the trial court's findings that separate trials would have resulted in considerable and unnecessary evidentiary repetition. For example, the damage questions that were submitted instructed jurors "to consider only the differences in value caused by the construction and operation of Richland-Chamber Reservoir." Whether and to what extent the Ranch was damaged by the reservoir's construction and operation were also issues central to the trial court's taking determination. Accordingly, it is likely that many, if not most, of the same witnesses would have been called to testify in both the liability and compensation trials had the trial court bifurcated the proceedings. As the trial court found, "there were several weeks of common questions of law and of fact involved in the matters that would have been considered in the first phase and the second phase of a bifurcated trial." And, as the court of appeals noted, this case had been pending in the trial court for almost seven years and had been through extensive discovery and numerous pre-trial proceedings by the time it was tried. Under these circumstances, we cannot say that the trial court abused its discretion in refusing to bifurcate the proceedings.

---

4. *Severance, Separate Trials and Consolidation*

Read Rules 40(b), 41, 174.

In re STATE OF TEXAS
355 S.W.3d 611
(Tex. 2011)

Opinion

CHIEF JUSTICE JEFFERSON delivered the opinion of the Court.

After the State sought to condemn a tract of land, the owners subdivided the property into eight separate parcels. The trial court then severed the case into eight different proceedings. The State contends that the severance was improper, and it seeks a writ of mandamus requiring the trial court to vacate the order. Because the severance would require eight trials where only one is appropriate, and because it would preclude the State from presenting relevant valuation evidence, we conditionally grant the writ.

I. Background

The State of Texas filed a petition to condemn a tract of land and a drainage easement from its owners, the Laws family. The State sought to acquire a 39.619 acre fee tract as well as a 0.23 acre drainage easement, which would come out of the Lawses' 185.835 acre property in Travis County. The property was to be used in the construction of State Highway 130. On the same day that it filed its condemnation petition, the State also filed a notice of lis pendens, giving notice of the pendency of a suit affecting the Lawses' land. *See* TEX. PROP. CODE § 12.007 (authorizing the filing of a notice of lis pendens in eminent domain actions).

A Special Commissioner's hearing was set, but five days before the hearing, nine separate limited liability corporations filed nine separate Pleas in Intervention and Suggestions of Succession. Each LLC alleged a justiciable interest in the case as successor in title to property being condemned in the suit. The assertion of interest was the result of a complex series of transactions. In all, some fifty-one acres of the Lawses' property, including all of the land subject to the condemnation petition, had been subdivided by twenty-four special warranty deeds and split among three ownership groups, each of which consisted of three investing LLCs. After these transactions, the Lawses no longer owned a direct interest in any of the land against which the State had filed, their interest now being a result only of their membership in the various LLCs. In this manner, the Lawses subdivided their original property into eight separate tracts, each of which contained some of the land being condemned.

After the subdivision, the State added the nine intervenors as parties claiming an interest in the Acquisition, but the State nonetheless continued to proceed against the Acquisition as a single plot of land. At the Special Commissioners hearing, the Lawses and the LLCs were represented by the same counsel. The State's appraisal expert testified at the hearing that because of the lack of significant retail and commercial development in the area, the property should be appraised as a single unit and that its best and highest use was to hold the frontage for future commercial use. On this basis, the State appraised the land at $0.65 per square foot and valued the whole property, including the drainage easement, at $1,155,693.

The Lawses' appraiser, rather than value the property as a single economic unit, appraised each of the eight subdivided tracts separately. He determined that the best and highest use of each of the tracts was as highway frontage commercial property. On this basis, he recommended total compensation of $4,145,000. The Special Commissioners issued an award of $2,487,991, which, at the Lawses' request, was apportioned among the eight tracts. The Lawses and the State filed various objections to the award, and the case was transferred to the County Court at Law in Travis County for trial on the appeal of the Commissioners' award. *See* TEX. PROP. CODE § 21.018. The State filed a Notice of Deposit and tendered the award into the court's registry, and the trial court granted the LLCs' motion to withdraw the funds. The Lawses filed disclaimers of interest in the Acquisition and award.

Before trial in the county court at law, the various intervening LLCs filed eight motions to sever, one for each of the tracts into which the property had been subdivided, arguing that there was no unity of ownership between the tracts. At the hearing on those motions, the LLCs did not introduce any valuation evidence. Over the State's objections, the court signed eight orders severing the single cause of action into eight separate actions. The State unsuccessfully sought mandamus relief from the court of appeals. 2010 Tex.App. LEXIS 2377, *1.

II. Mandamus

The State asks us to order the trial court to vacate its severance order. Generally, mandamus relief is appropriate only when (1) there has been a clear abuse of discretion by the trial court, and (2) there is no adequate remedy on appeal. *In re Olshan Found. Repair,* 328 S.W.3d 883, 887 (Tex. 2010). We will consider these two requirements in turn.

Courts permit severance principally to avoid prejudice, do justice, and increase convenience. *F.F.P. Oper. Partners v. Duenez,* 237 S.W.3d 680, 693 (Tex. 2007). In light of these fundamental principles, we have enumerated several requirements for proper severance: (1) the controversy must involve multiple causes of action, (2) the severed claim would be the proper subject of a lawsuit if independently asserted, and (3) the severed claim must not be so interwoven with the remaining action that they involve the same facts and issues. *Guaranty Fed. Savings Bank v. Horseshoe Oper. Co.,* 793 S.W.2d 652, 658 (Tex. 1990); *see also* TEX. R. CIV. P. 41.

Assuming the validity of the conveyances, we focus particularly on the issue of interrelatedness, *see Guaranty Fed.,* 793 S.W.2d at 658, keeping in mind the importance of doing justice and avoiding prejudice. *See F.F.P.,* 237 S.W.3d at 693. The Lawses sought to have one trial separated into eight, but in each case, the legal and factual issues would be much the same. The legal issues raised in the eight trials would be essentially identical, and, because the land was all originally part of a single plot, the factual valuation testimony would likely be very similar, even if the value of the different parcels varied somewhat. Both the Lawses and the State would thus pay the same lawyers to argue, and same experts to testify, in eight separate cases, an issue that could be tried once. Such duplication is inconvenient, and, worse, prejudicial to the State, which has a right to offer evidence that the entire property being taken should be valued as a single economic unit. *See State of Texas v. Windham,* 837 S.W.2d 73, 76 (Tex.1992).[5] Because of this, and because of the waste involved in having valuation experts give testimony eight times that they could give once, we hold that the trial court abused its discretion by ordering a severance that, by breaking up a deeply interrelated set of legal and factual issues, prejudices the parties and causes great inconvenience. *Cf. F.F.P.,* 237 S.W.3d at 693; *Guaranty,* 793 S.W.2d at 658.

Because the trial court abused its discretion, we must consider whether the State has an adequate remedy by appeal. If it does not, mandamus is proper. We assess the adequacy of an appellate remedy by "balancing the benefits of mandamus review against the detriments." *In re Team Rocket, L.P.,* 256 S.W.3d 257, 262 (Tex.2008). In performing this balancing, we look at a number of factors, among them "whether mandamus will spare litigants and the public 'the time and money utterly wasted enduring eventual reversal of improperly conducted proceedings.' " *Id.* (*quoting In re Prudential Ins. Co. of Am.,* 148 S.W.3d 124, 136 (Tex. 2004)). Thus, in *Team Rocket,* we granted mandamus where the trial court's ruling would allow a plaintiff to refile his case "in county after county . . . inevitably result [ing] in considerable expense to taxpayers and defendants." *Id.* Because the trial court's order "subject[ed] taxpayers, defendants, and all of the state's district courts to meaningless proceedings and trials," we held that "requiring defendants to proceed to trial in the wrong county" could not be considered an adequate remedy. *Id.* Similarly, in *In re Masonite Corp.,* we considered whether mandamus was appropriate to reverse a trial court's order that severed two suits into sixteen different cases that were transferred to sixteen different counties. *In re Masonite,* 997 S.W.2d 194, 196 (Tex.1999). Conditionally granting mandamus, we held that the appellate remedy was inadequate because, while some parties might be able to appeal, such appeal would be "no remedy at all for the irreversible waste of judicial and public resources that would be required here if mandamus does not issue." *Id.* at 198.

We believe that the circumstances of this case also make the appellate remedy inadequate because of the enormous waste of judicial and public resources that compliance with the trial court's order would entail. Requiring eight separate suits here, when only one is proper, would be

---

[5] Such a right might be diminished in severed suits. If the State were forced to proceed in eight separate lawsuits against eight separate owners, it is unclear on what basis it could offer *Windham* evidence that the proper economic unit by which to value a particular parcel includes other land not part of that condemnation suit and not commonly owned with the land being condemned. However, a single suit would permit the State, where it has condemned land all under common ownership at the time the condemnation petition was filed, to offer evidence that the entire condemned parcel should be valued together, thus preserving its *Windham* right.

a clear waste of the resources of the State, the landowners, and the courts. For this reason, we hold that the State lacks an adequate remedy by appeal and conditionally grant the writ of mandamus.

III. Valuation

The Lawses subdivided their property and sought severance based on a belief that its highest and best use was as multiple parcels. Though they have called the procedural wrangling in this case a waste of time and money, they pursued it out of an "abundance of caution" due to a fear that our opinions in *City of Harlingen v. Sharboneau,* 48 S.W.3d 177 (Tex. 2001), and *State of Texas v. Willey,* 360 S.W.2d 524 (Tex. 1962), would prevent them from seeking a valuation based on the subdivision. *Willey* and *Sharboneau* are distinguishable.

* * *

Similar reasoning is applicable here. The State believes that the ideal economic unit is the entire condemned tract, the highest and best use of which is to hold as investment for future development. The State is permitted under *Windham* to offer this testimony. The Lawses, like Windham, believe that the condemned tract is an inferior economic unit. Where Windham thought the proper unit was larger than the condemned tract, however, the Lawses believe that the tract to be condemned contains several self-sufficient economic units. If they have non-speculative evidence to support this contention, they should be permitted to offer it at trial. Though the State has a right to define the property being taken, it does not have the power to constrain the owners' evidence of competing conceptions of the best economic unit by which the taken property should be valued.

IV. Conclusion

The trial court's severance order prejudices the State's right to offer its valuation evidence and would cause needless duplication of legal services and expert testimony, wasting not only the parties' resources but those of the public at large. Accordingly, we conditionally grant the writ of mandamus and direct the trial court to vacate its severance order. We are confident the trial court will comply, and our writ will issue only if it does not.

Notes & Questions

1. *Misjoinder*. The remedy for misjoinder is not dismissal, but severance.[1] When claims are severed, the pending suit is divided into two or more separate suits, each with its own cause number. Each suit then proceeds independently, resulting in its own judgment.

2. *Separate trials*. When the claims are merely tried separately, as opposed to being severed, the claims remain in the original suit, but are tried and resolved separately. However, a final judgment in that suit may be rendered only upon resolution of all the claims.[2]

3. *Discretionary severance*. Claims that are properly joined may also be severed. Parties often do not want some claims joined with other claims, even if they arise from the same transaction or occurrence. This may be a matter of trial strategy. One party may believe that the evidence rele-

---

1 Rule 41.

2 *See generally* Hall, *Severance and Separate Trials in Texas*, 36 TEX. L. REV. 339 (1958).

vant to one claim will unduly prejudice that party when the fact-finder considers the other claims. Therefore, even though the claims are properly joined under Rule 51(a), the parties may object to the joinder of particular claims and seek severance of the claims under Rule 41, or separate trials under Rules 40(b), 97(h) or 174. Then, the trial judge's ruling on a motion to sever or for separate trials is subject to review only for an abuse of discretion.[3] The Texas Supreme Court has identified three elements that must be present for proper severance: (1) the controversy must involve more than one cause of action, (2) the severed cause must be one that would be the proper subject of a lawsuit if independently asserted, and (3) the severed causes must not be so intertwined as to involve the same identical facts and issues.[4] In *Guaranty Federal*, the Supreme Court approved the severance of a party's claim against the bank for wrongful dishonor of a check from the bank's claim against that party for conspiracy to defraud. But personal injury cases seem to have a different result. In *State Dep't of Highways and Public Transportation v. Cotner*,[5] the Supreme Court found an abuse of discretion. The *Cotner* trial court severed the driver-husband's claim from that asserted by the passenger-wife. The Supreme Court found that the claims were so interwoven that they involved the same facts and issues and, therefore, did not meet the third of the *Guaranty Federal* criteria. Also, in a dram shop case,[6] the Supreme Court held that the trial court abused its discretion in severing the defendant's third-party claim against the drunk driver, because the liquor provider had a contribution claim against the drunk driver.[7]

4. *Consolidation*. Rule 174(a) allows a court to consolidate suits pending before it if the suits "involve a common question of law and fact." Rule 41 seems to allow consolidation "on such terms as are just." Notice that Rule 40 requires as a predicate to permissive joinder that the claims meet both the common question test *and* the same transaction or series of transactions test. Thus, it appears that courts can consolidate cases that the parties could not have joined together. Typically, consolidation will be granted only if common questions in the lawsuits predominate over other uncommon questions. A litigant seeking consolidation must demonstrate that there are significant common questions, and that time and money can be saved by litigating the actions together. The judicial economy and convenience that may be gained by consolidation must be balanced against the likelihood that consolidation may result in delay, prejudice, or jury confusion.[8] If the judicial economy and convenience factors are substantially outweighed by the risk of an unfair outcome because of prejudice or confusion, then the trial court abuses its discretion in granting consolidation.

A Texas court's ability to consolidate is substantially more limited than a federal court's. While the federal courts can transfer suits pending all over the country to one district for consolidation so long as the suits share a "common question of law *or* fact" in the interest of efficiency

---

[3] *See* Liberty Nat'l Fire Ins. v. Akin, 927 S.W.2d 627 (Tex. 1996) (trial court did not abuse its discretion in refusing to sever insured's breach of insurance contract claim from bad faith claim).

[4] Guaranty Fed. Savings Bank v. Horseshoe Operating Co., 793 S.W.2d 652, 658 (Tex. 1990).

[5] 845 S.W.2d 818, 819 (Tex. 1993).

[6] F.F.P. Operating Partners v. Duenez, 237 S.W.3d 680 (Tex. 2007).

[7] *See also* State v. Morello, No. 16-0457, 2018 WL 1025685, at *6 (Tex. Feb. 23, 2018) (holding that claims against individual and LLC were "not so interwoven as to override proper severance" where evidence of individual's "personal actions" was presented against individual but not in case against LLC).

[8] Brentwood Fin. Corp. v. Lamrecht, 736 S.W.2d 836, 839 (Tex. App.—San Antonio 1987, writ ref'd n.r.e.).

and fairness,[9] a Texas trial judge can only consolidate those cases pending in the county in which the court is sitting. Furthermore, the Texas venue scheme substantially limits a court's ability to transfer cases from one county to another.

5. *Venue and Joinder*. Often a venue question is raised in addition to the joinder question. After severance, venue may no longer be proper over the defendants in one of the causes, so it may be transferred. Other times plaintiffs will choose to file multiple suits in different counties and the defendants want the suits consolidated. For example, in a suit involving an airplane crash, different plaintiffs may sue the airline and airplane manufacturer in different counties. Can the defendants consolidate the causes in one county? In Texas, this is largely a *venue* problem. Consider Section 15.002(b) of the venue statute, which allows transfer to another proper county for convenience and justice.

6. *Multi-District Litigation*. Pursuant to legislative mandate,[10] Rule 13 of the Texas Rules of Judicial Administration provides for statewide pretrial consolidation of cases with one or more common questions of fact, for the convenience of the parties and witnesses and to promote the just and efficient conduct of the cases. Currently, the MDL Panel decides what cases will be consolidated. MDL judges have been appointed for matters such as asbestos cases, silicosis cases, and Firestone/Ford rollover cases. Consolidated cases are sent to a "pretrial court" for pretrial matters, and then sent back to the "trial court" for trial. MDL will be considered again in the chapter on complex litigation.

7. *Default judgments*. It is common practice for a plaintiff who has sued several defendants to ask for severance of the claim against any defaulting defendant before proceeding with the pretrial activities in the case against the answering defendants. Similarly, either party may ask for severance of a claim against a single defendant who has suffered an adverse summary judgment. What advantages do these parties hope to gain by severance? The judgment in the severed cause becomes final, so it can be appealed and/or collected.

---

9 *See* Fed. R Civ. P. 42(a) (emphasis added).

10 *See* TEX. GOV'T. CODE §§ 74.161; 74.162 (providing for multidistrict litigation panel). *See* chapter on Complex Litigation for further discussion of MDL in Texas.

B. Compulsory Joinder of Claims

Read Rule 97(a).

BARR
v.
RESOLUTION TRUST CORP.

837 S.W.2d 627
(Tex. 1992)

GONZALEZ, JUSTICE.

The issue in this case is whether a claim by Sunbelt Federal Savings against George Barr based on a partnership promissory note and guarantee agreement is barred by the doctrine of res judicata. The trial court granted Barr's motion for summary judgment based on res judicata. The court of appeals, with one Justice dissenting, reversed the trial court's judgment, holding that the doctrine did not apply. We reverse the judgment of the court of appeals and affirm the trial court's judgment.

In 1985, Barr and Ron Knott were partners in the Bar III Venture. On March 14, 1985 Bar III executed a promissory note for $369,750 in favor of Sunbelt's predecessor in interest. The same day, Barr and Knott executed a personal guarantee of the note. In March 1987, Bar III defaulted on the note.

On May 24, 1988, Sunbelt filed two separate lawsuits on the note. In one suit, Sunbelt alleged liability against the partnership as maker of the note and against Knott as guarantor of the note. In the other, Sunbelt alleged that Barr was personally liable because of his unconditional guarantee of the note.

Barr moved for summary judgment in the latter lawsuit on the grounds that the terms of the guaranty agreement were too uncertain to be enforceable. Barr argued that the agreement, a standard form containing a number of options to choose and blanks to complete, was not sufficiently completed to ascertain his liability. The trial court granted the motion, and rendered a final take-nothing judgment. Sunbelt did not appeal the judgment.

Thereafter, Sunbelt amended its pleadings in the suit against the partnership and Knott by adding Barr as a defendant, alleging that his status as a partner created liability for the note. Barr's answer asserted res judicata, among other defenses.

Barr moved for summary judgment on the grounds that the take-nothing judgment in the first lawsuit barred litigation of the claims against him in the second lawsuit. Sunbelt also moved for summary judgment, requesting a judgment on the note. The trial court granted Barr's motion and denied Sunbelt's. This interlocutory judgment became final when the court rendered judgment for Sunbelt on its claims against the partnership and Knott for the full amount of the note.

Sunbelt appealed, arguing that the trial court should have granted its summary judgment instead of Barr's. The court of appeals, with one justice dissenting, determined that the first suit did not bar the second. However, the court concluded that questions of fact prevented rendition in

Sunbelt's favor, and thus remanded the case to the trial court. Both Barr and Sunbelt sought review in our court.

Much of the difficulty associated with the doctrine of res judicata is due to the confusion of several related theories. Broadly speaking, res judicata is the generic term for a group of related concepts concerning the conclusive effects given final judgments. Within this general doctrine, there are two principal categories: (1) claim preclusion (also known as res judicata); and (2) issue preclusion (also known as collateral estoppel).[1] Res judicata, or claim preclusion, prevents the relitigation of a claim or cause of action that has been finally adjudicated, as well as related matters that, with the use of diligence, should have been litigated in the prior suit. Issue preclusion, or collateral estoppel, prevents relitigation of particular issues already resolved in a prior suit.[2] Barr's argument, that Sunbelt should have brought all theories of liability in one suit, is the defense of claim preclusion.

Claim preclusion prevents splitting a cause of action. The policies behind the doctrine reflect the need to bring all litigation to an end, prevent vexatious litigation, maintain stability of court decisions, promote judicial economy, and prevent double recovery.

The question that has given courts the most difficulty is determining what claims should have been litigated in the prior suit. Early on, this Court held that res judicata "is not only final as to the matter actually determined, but as to every other matter which the parties might litigate in the cause, and which they might have decided." We have never repudiated this definition of claim preclusion, and it appears in some form in most definitions of res judicata. If taken literally, this definition of the rule would require that all disputes existing between parties be joined, regardless of whether the disputes have anything in common. This court has resorted to a wide variety of theories and tests to give res judicata a more restrictive application.

Even if only cases from more recent times are considered, our holdings with respect to res judicata are difficult to reconcile.

* * *

[I]n *Texas Water Rights Comm. v. Crow Iron Works*, 582 S.W.2d 768 (Tex. 1979), the court shifted the focus from the cause of action to the subject matter of the litigation. The question was whether a major lawsuit instigated to sort out water rights to the lower Rio Grande river precluded a subsequent suit based on the claim that during the pendency of that suit the plaintiff had purchased additional rights. The court concluded that the subsequent claim was barred, noting that:

---

1 Res judicata may be further categorized into merger and bar, because the doctrine has different applications depending on which party is successful in the prior suit. If the party asserting a claim prevails, the cause of action is merged into the judgment, and the cause of action as such ceases to exist. If the party defending a claim prevails in the prior suit, the judgment acts as a bar to matters which could have been litigated in the original suit.

2 An example of the confusion concerning collateral estoppel is the court of appeals' holding that "res judicata does not preclude relitigation of issues that the first court did not actually try and determine, unless a determination of those issues was essential to the judgment in the first suit." The court relied on RESTATEMENT (SECOND) OF JUDGMENTS § 27 (1982), which is entitled "Issue Preclusion—General Rule", i.e., collateral estoppel. *See id.* § 17(3), and comment (c). We disapprove similar language in the case cited by the court.

Our own recent holdings have contributed to the confusion by holding without elaboration that res judicata requires an "identity of issues" between the prior and subsequent suits. If an identity of issues is strictly required, then there is no basis for precluding issues that should have been raised in the prior suit but were not, and there is no distinction between claim preclusion and issue preclusion.

> The scope of res judicata is not limited to matters actually litigated; the judgment in the first suit precludes a second action by the parties and their privies not only on matters actually litigated, but also on *causes of action* or defenses which arise out of the same *subject matter* and which might have been litigated in the first suit.

Id. at 771-72 (emphasis added). * * *

A determination of what constitutes the subject matter of a suit necessarily requires an examination of the factual basis of the claim or claims in the prior litigation. It requires an analysis of the factual matters that make up the gist of the complaint, without regard to the form of action. Any cause of action which arises out of those same facts should, if practicable, be litigated in the same lawsuit.

The definition of res judicata in *Gracia* and *Crow Iron Works* is substantially similar to the rule of compulsory counterclaims embodied in the rules of civil procedure. A party defending a claim must bring as a counterclaim any claim that "arises out of the transaction or occurrence that is the subject matter of the opposing party's claim . . . ." TEX. R. CIV. P. 97.

The RESTATEMENT OF JUDGMENTS also takes the transactional approach to claims preclusion. It provides that a final judgment on an action extinguishes the right to bring suit on the transaction, or series of connected transactions, out of which the action arose. RESTATEMENT OF JUDGMENTS § 24(1). A "transaction" under the RESTATEMENT is not equivalent to a sequence of events, however; the determination is to be made pragmatically, "giving weight to such considerations as whether the facts are related in time, space, origin, or motivation, whether they form a convenient trial unit, and whether their treatment as a trial unit conforms to the parties' expectations or business understanding or usage." *Id.* § 24(2).

We conclude that the transactional approach to claims preclusion of the RESTATEMENT effectuates the policy of res judicata with no more hardship than encountered under rule 97(a) of the rules of civil procedure. Modern rules of procedure obviate the need to give parties two bites at the apple . . . to ensure that a claim receives full adjudication. Discovery should put a claimant on noticc of any need for alternative pleading. Moreover, if success on one theory becomes doubtful because of developments during trial, a party is free to seek a trial amendment.

In the case now before us, there is no valid reason to subject Barr to two different lawsuits. In the suit brought previously against Barr, the bank alleged that he executed the guarantee on the same day and as part of the "same transaction" as the promissory note. In both suits Sunbelt seeks to hold Barr primarily liable for payment of the note and seeks the same amount of damages. Both suits require proof establishing the notes of the partnership, that the notes are due, and that the partnership has defaulted. The only factual allegation that Sunbelt pleaded in the second suit that was not in the first is that Barr is a general partner of Bar III Venture.

It is clear that in this case the execution of the partnership note and Barr's guarantee of it were related in time and space and motivation, and the parties considered it as a single transaction. The issues of both claims form a convenient trial unit, whereas separate lawsuits would require significant duplication of effort of the court and the parties involved. With due diligence, the claim that Barr was liable because he is a partner could have been joined in the suit on his guarantee of the partnership note.

We reaffirm the "transactional" approach to res judicata. A subsequent suit will be barred if it arises out of the same subject matter of a previous suit and which through the exercise of diligence, could have been litigated in a prior suit. For these reasons, the judgment of the court of appeals is reversed and that of the trial court is affirmed.

Notes & Questions

1. *Res judicata*. As *Barr* discusses, the res judicata doctrine is based on the concept of the finality of judgments. Once claims or causes of action have been litigated and brought to judgment, the same parties and their privies may not litigate those claims and causes of action again. The term "res judicata" is really a generic term that includes two different theories: (1) claim preclusion (which Texans typically call "res judicata"), and (2) issue preclusion (also known as "collateral estoppel"). Claim preclusion, the doctrine at issue in *Barr*, prevents parties to a prior suit from relitigating a claim or cause of action that was brought or could have been brought (arising from the same transaction or occurrence) in that suit. Thus, when drafting pleadings, parties must consider that all claims and causes of action that arise from the transaction or occurrence upon which the suit is based—those actually asserted, as well as those not asserted, will be barred from a later suit against the same parties or their privies.

2. *Collateral estoppel*. The doctrine of collateral estoppel, or issue preclusion, prevents the relitigation of ultimate issues of fact or law (rather than entire causes of action) actually litigated (not those that could have been litigated) and essential to the judgment in a prior suit.[1] The issue decided in the first action must be identical to the issue in the pending action, and thus requires an evaluation of the jury's verdict or the judge's findings of fact. While the application of claim preclusion requires that the parties in both lawsuits be identical, collateral estoppel only requires that the party *against whom* collateral estoppel is asserted be a party in the prior litigation.[2] The function of collateral estoppel is to prevent a party from relitigating an issue that the party previously litigated and lost.[3]

3. *Compulsory counterclaims*. The compulsory counterclaim rule, a rule of joinder, like res judicata, precludes later litigation of claims that could have been brought in the prior suit. The rule requires defendants to bring same transaction and occurrence counterclaims against plaintiffs, in the forum that the plaintiff has chosen.[4] A claim is compulsory under Rule 97(a) only if it is within the court's subject matter jurisdiction, has not been filed elsewhere at the time the suit is commenced,[5] is mature, arises out of the same transaction or occurrence, doesn't require the presence of additional parties outside the court's jurisdiction and is against an opposing party. In determining whether the counterclaim is within the court's subject matter jurisdiction, remember

---

1 Getty Oil Co. v. Insurance Co. of North America, 845 S.W.2d 794, 801-02 (Tex. 1992).

2 Johnson & Higgins of Texas, Inc. v. Kenneco Energy Inc., 962 S.W.2d 507, 521 (Tex. 1998); Eagle Properties Ltd. v. Scharbauer, 807 S.W2d 714 (Tex. 1990).

3 Quinney Elec., Inc. v. Kondos Entertainment, Inc., 988 S.W.2d 212, 213 (Tex. 1999).

4 *But cf.* Klein v. Dooley, 949 S.W.2d 307, 307 (Tex. 1997)(holding that DTPA and fraud claims were not "compulsory counterclaims" to derivative statutory claims for attorney's fees and costs).

5 In re J.B. Hunt Transp., Inc., 492 S.W.3d 287, 293 (Tex. 2016) ("[A] counterclaim is compulsory if, in addition to Rule 97(a)'s other requirements, it was not the subject of a pending action when the original suit was commenced."

that a court can reach below its minimum statutory limits if the claim arises from the same transaction or occurrence. A court cannot, however, reach above its jurisdictional limits.[6]

4. *Opposing parties.* The compulsory counterclaim rule, Rule 97(a), requires a party to assert claims against an opposing party that arise out of the same transaction or occurrence that is the subject of the opposing party's claim. This rule operates to bar subsequent claims only against an "opposing party," a party that has asserted affirmative claims against the party now asserting the claims. For example: When A sues B, B must bring compulsory counterclaims against A, or they will be barred in a subsequent suit. The compulsory counterclaim rule will not bar other same transaction claims that A has against B, however, unless B asserts claims against A. Once B has asserted claims against A, B is an "opposing party" to A and the compulsory counterclaim rule comes into play.

5. *Res judicata and the compulsory counterclaim rule.* When A sues B, A is not subject to the compulsory counterclaim rule, but A is subject to the doctrine of res judicata. *Barr* substantially simplified the world of compulsory joinder by holding that the res judicata standard was identical to the standard applicable to the compulsory counterclaim rule. Before *Barr,* the standard for res judicata was narrower (barring fewer claims) than the compulsory counterclaim standard.

6. *Compulsory cross-claims.* When is a cross-claim (a claim between co-parties) that arises from the same transaction or occurrence as the main claim compulsory? Soon after *Barr* was decided, the Supreme Court was presented with a situation where a defendant, Getty Oil Co., had asserted a contractual indemnity claim against a co-defendant, NL Industries, in the plaintiff's personal injury suit.[7] Getty was found liable to the plaintiff for almost $4 million in damages, and was denied indemnity from NL. Subsequent to the conclusion of that suit, Getty sued NL and its insurers claiming that they violated an obligation to insure Getty for the loss represented by the judgment. The Supreme Court held that Getty's claims against NL were barred by res judicata. The court said:

> We do not hold that a defendant must assert a cross-claim against a co-defendant simply because it arises from the same subject matter as plaintiff's claim. TEX. R. CIV. P. 97(e) clearly makes such a cross-claim permissive; the defendant may assert it, but is not required to. Rule 97(e) comports with the principle that res judicata applies only to adverse parties. Where two parties are aligned in the first action and no issues are drawn between them, the judgment in that action does not preclude later claims between those parties. However, where a defendant does assert a cross-claim against a co-party, they become adverse, and the principles of res judicata apply. The cross-claimant becomes a plaintiff for res judicata purposes, and is required to assert all claims against the cross-defendant arising from the subject matter of the original cross-claim. *Cf.* RESTATEMENT (SECOND) JUDGMENTS § 23 (1980) ("Where a defendant interposes a claim as a counterclaim and a valid and final judgment is rendered against him on the counterclaim, the rules of bar are applicable to the judgment.").
>
> * * *
>
> Getty was not required to bring any of its cross-claims against NL in the *Duncan* suit. Once it chose to bring some of those claims, however, it was required under res judicata

6 *See* Rule 97(a); Gage v. Tom Fairey Co., 692 S.W.2d 127, 129 (Tex. App.—Dallas 1985, writ ref'd n.r.e.).

7 *See* Getty Oil Co. v. Ins. Co. of North America, 845 S.W.2d 794 (Tex. 1992).

to bring them all in the same action. Accordingly, we agree with the court of appeals' holding as to this issue.

7. *Default judgments.* If P sues D and obtains a valid default judgment, then D later sues P for claims arising from the same transaction or occurrence, what result? Are D's claims barred by the compulsory counterclaim rule? Yes. In *Jack H. Brown & Co. v. Northwest Sign Co.*,[8] the court held that the defendant's compulsory counterclaims were barred. The defaulting D had notice of the Idaho proceeding in which the default judgment was rendered, but refused to answer believing the Idaho court lacked personal jurisdiction. The Texas Supreme Court later rejected a collateral attack on jurisdictional grounds. What if the Idaho judgment had been rendered without notice? Think back to the chapter on personal jurisdiction.

8. *Settlements.* Suppose P and D are involved in an automobile collision. P sues D, and D's insurance company quickly settles the suit without informing D. D then sues P for personal injuries. Are D's claims barred by the compulsory counterclaim rule? In a 1966 opinion,[9] the Supreme Court answered yes. Rule 97(a) was then amended in response. If you represent P and reach a settlement, what provision might you require as part of the settlement agreement?

9. *Motion.* What procedural device would a defendant use to raise res judicata or the compulsory counterclaim rule? A pleading raising the affirmative defense of res judicata, then a motion for summary judgment.

C. Compulsory Joinder of Parties

Read Rule 39.

COOPER
v.
TEXAS GULF INDUSTRIES, INC.

513 S.W.2d 200
(Tex. 1974)

JOHNSON, JUSTICE

Petitioners Dr. Griffin Cooper and his wife, Dolores, appeal from summary judgment that they take nothing in a suit for cancellation and rescission of a sale of real estate to them by Texas Gulf Industries, Inc. (T.G.I.). Cooper and his wife sued T.G.I. on September 28, 1971 alleging fraud as ground for rescission and cancellation of the sale. T.G.I. moved for summary judgment asserting Dr. Cooper previously filed a suit on December 29, 1970, which suit was dismissed with prejudice on January 29, 1971, and that such dismissal with prejudice was res judicata of the instant action. The trial court granted T.G.I.'s motion for summary judgment that plaintiffs take nothing and the court of civil appeals affirmed. 495 S.W. 2d 273. We reverse and remand.

---

8 718 S.W.2d 397 (Tex. App.—Dallas 1986, writ ref'd n.r.e.).

9 Harris v. Jones, 404 S.W.2d 349, 351-52 (Tex. Civ. App.—Eastland 1966, writ refused).

In the prior suit filed December 29, 1970, Dr. Cooper was the sole plaintiff. He sought to terminate a management contract on the property at issue and alternatively sought to rescind the sale of the property. The trial court dismissed the first suit "with prejudice."

The Coopers argue that dismissal of the prior suit with prejudice is not res judicata of the instant suit because Dolores Cooper, being a grantee along with her husband in the deed to the real estate at issue, was a necessary party to a suit to cancel and rescind the sale. Accordingly, the Coopers assert, the trial court had no jurisdiction in the prior case and the judgment of dismissal with prejudice is invalid.

A decision on whether a wife is an indispensable party in an action which concerns her joint community property necessitates (1) a study of the Texas Family Code, Section 5.22 (1971), to determine the nature of the community property, (2) a reexamination of the rule that a husband can act for and represent his wife in an action concerning their joint community property under the doctrine of virtual representation, and (3) a discussion of the application of Rule 39, as amended, Texas Rules of Civil Procedure (1971), concerning the joinder of parties.

* * *

Dolores Cooper was not a party to the first suit; the doctrine of virtual representation was abolished by the new Family Code; there was no writing authorizing her husband to represent her. Accordingly, her interest in the Coopers' joint management community property is untouched by the judgment of dismissal with prejudice of the first suit.

THE JOINDER OF PARTIES

Having determined that the wife was not virtually represented by her husband, a second question is urged for consideration: was Dolores Cooper an indispensable party in the first suit? Under the traditional view, if she was an indispensable party, the judgment in the first suit would be invalid and not res judicata as to either of the Coopers; if she was not an indispensable party, then the judgment would be binding on Dr. Cooper since he was a party, although still not binding on Mrs. Cooper.

Amended Rule 39, however, initiated an entirely new method for resolving the question of joinder of parties. Amended Rule 39, effective January 1, 1971, is almost an exact copy by Texas of Federal Rule 19, Federal Rules of Civil Procedure, which is also of recent origin, having been adopted in 1966.

Prior to the amendment to Rule 39, Texas resolved questions of joinder of parties by efforts to catalogue parties as "proper," "necessary," "indispensable," "conditionally necessary," or "insistible."

That historical and classical approach to the joinder of parties has now been wholly replaced. The reasons and legal literature which impelled the adoption of the new approach are well summarized in 7 C. WRIGHT & A. MILLER, FEDERAL PRACTICE AND PROCEDURE § 1601 (1972). One of the aims of the revised rule was to avoid questions of jurisdiction. The text states:

> In addition to the failure of many courts to articulate satisfactory bases of decision prior to 1966, the Advisory Committee referred to other defects in the original version of Rule 19. Paramount among these was a problem of "jurisdiction" that arose in connection with the concept of indispensable parties. The Committee felt that the rule's [original] wording suggested that the absence of an indispensable party "itself deprived the court of the power to adjudicate as between the parties already joined." As is discussed in another section,

> failure to join a party under Rule 19 is not really a jurisdictional matter inasmuch as the court does have subject matter jurisdiction over the action before it; what is involved is a question of whether the court should decline to adjudicate the dispute because certain persons are absent. The present language of Rule 19(a) and Rule 19(b) should help eliminate this confusion.

and *see* C. WRIGHT, LAW OF FEDERAL COURTS § 70 at 298-99 (2d ed. 1970).

Contrary to our emphasis under Rule 39 before it was amended, today's concern is less that of the jurisdiction of a court to proceed and is more a question of whether the court ought to proceed with those who are present. The United States Supreme Court provides a helpful discussion of the objectives sought by its amended Rule 19 in *Provident Tradesmens Bank & Trust v. Patterson*, 390 U.S. 102, 88 Sup. Ct. 733, 19 L. Ed. 2d 936 (1968). One of the practical factors the court took into consideration in holding that an absent party was not jurisdictionally indispensable was the fact that the case had actually been tried as to those parties who were present and there was no objection at the trial level concerning the nonjoinder of a party. As expressed in *Continental Insurance Co. of New York v. Cotten*, 427 F.2d 48, 51 (9th Cir. 1970), "at the appellate stage there is reason not to throw away a judgment just because it did not theoretically settle the whole controversy."

The amended rule includes practical considerations within the rule itself, including the extent to which an absent party may be prejudiced, the extent to which protective provisions may be made in the judgment, and whether in equity and good conscience the action should proceed or be dismissed. The factors mentioned in the rule which a judge may consider are not exclusive. *Provident Tradesmens Bank & Trust Company v. Patterson, supra*; 7 C. Wright & A. Miller, FEDERAL PRACTICE AND PROCEDURE, *supra*, at 14. As expressed in *Schutten v. Shell Oil Co.*, 421 F.2d 869, 874 (5th Cir. 1970), "[the] watchwords of Rule 19 are "pragmatism" and "practicality." The court must, however, always consider the possibility of shaping a decree in order to adjudicate between the parties who have been joined."

Under the provisions of our present Rule 39 it would be rare indeed if there were a person whose presence was so indispensable in the sense that his absence deprives the court of jurisdiction to adjudicate between the parties already joined. Although not of controlling importance, the very title of the rule has been changed from "Necessary Joinder of Parties" to "Joinder of Persons Needed for Just Adjudication." Subdivision (a) provides that certain persons "shall be joined," but there is no arbitrary standard or precise formula for determining whether a particular person falls within its provisions. It is clear, moreover, that the persons described in the subdivision are to be joined only if subject to service of process. When such a person cannot be made a party, the court is required to determine "whether in equity and good conscience the action should proceed among the parties before it, or should be dismissed."

Under the foregoing analysis of Rule 39 we determine that the named parties in the first suit, Dr. Cooper and T.G.I., were properly before the court for the resolution of the issues between them; that the judgment of dismissal with prejudice resolved those issues and is necessarily res judicata as to the claims of Dr. Cooper in the second and instant suit; that the judgment of dismissal is not res judicata, however, with respect to the rights and claims of Mrs. Dolores Cooper; and finally, that the judgment of dismissal is conclusive as to Dr. Cooper except to the extent that it might have to be disregarded in giving Mrs. Cooper all the relief to which she may show herself entitled.

The judgments of the courts below are reversed and the cause remanded to the trial court for further proceedings consistent with this opinion.

Concurring opinion by JUSTICE WALKER, in which CHIEF JUSTICE GREENHILL joined, has been omitted.

Notes & Questions

1. *Fundamental error.* At one time, the case law acknowledged the existence of parties thought to be "indispensable," whose absences created reversible error, even though it was not protested at the trial court level (an example of "fundamental error"). Consequently, nonjoinder could be raised as the basis for reversal for the first time on appeal. The current view is that defect of parties must be raised at trial or it is waived.[1] The idea of "fundamental error" resulting from absent parties seems to be dead.

2. *Rare cases. Cooper* says "it would be rare indeed if there were a person whose presence was so indispensable . . . that his absence deprives the court of jurisdiction."[2] Actually, there are quite quite a few cases where courts have found this "rare" situation. For example, in *Motor Vehicle Board v. El Paso Ind. Automobile Dealers Assoc.*,[3] the court found no jurisdiction to challenge the constitutionality of a "blue law" because the enforcing board was not named as a party.

3. *Virtual representation.* The idea of "virtual representation" referred to in *Cooper* is manifested in the law of res judicata through the application of "privity." This kind of "privity" is unrelated to the privity concepts in contracts and conveyancing. Through the concept of privity, parties not present in the litigation may be bound because of their role in controlling the litigation or because the parties present adequately represented their point of view.[4] How is this concept related to compulsory joinder of parties?

4. *Motion.* What procedural device would a defendant use to raise a Rule 39 objection to absent parties? A plea in abatement.

5. *Special cases of required joinder.* Rules 30-32 and CPRC § 17.001 rules act to prevent creditors from suing an endorser or guarantors without also joining the party primarily obligated on the debt.[5] In the inverse situation, however, a "principal obligor . . . may be sued alone."[6] And a guarantor or endorser can be sued alone if he has "guaranteed" payment[7] or if the provisions of

---

1 *See, e.g.,* Provident Tradesmen Bank and Trust Co. v. Patterson, 390 U.S. 102, 118-19 (1968); Pirtle v. Gregory, 629 S.W.2d 919, 920 (Tex. 1982).

2 *See, e.g.,* Crawford v. XTO Energy, Inc., 509 S.W.3d 906, 914 (Tex. 2017) (declining to require joinder where landowners of tracts adjacent to tract at center of dispute did not "claim[] an interest relating to the subject of the action").

3 37 S.W.3d 538 (Tex. App.—El Paso 2001, no pet. h.).

4 *See* Starr v. Schoellkopf, Co., 113 S.W.2d 1227, 1228 (Tex. 1938).

5 *See* Ferguson v. McCarrell, 588 S.W.2d 895 (Tex. 1979).

6 *See* In re Red Dot Bldg. Sys., Inc., 504 S.W.3d 320, 324 (Tex. 2016) (citing CPRC 17.001(a)).

7 *See* TEX. BUS. & COM. CODE § 3.416 (a).

CPRC § 17.001(b) apply. Thus, as a practical matter the provisions of Rules 30-32 seldom are invoked.

CHAPTER 7. SCOPE OF DISCOVERY

A. Discovery in an Adversary System

Read Rules 190-193.

As discussed in Chapter 1, American courts rely upon the adversary system to resolve disputes. Before the adoption of the Federal Rules of Civil Procedure, when the adversarial nature of litigation practice was at its zenith, surprise was a primary tool of advocacy. Each side developed its own sources of information without sharing with the opposing party. The primary "discovery" tools were the detailed pleadings to be filed by each side. Pretrial discovery, as we know it today, did not exist, and there was certainly no need for discovery privileges.

The federal rules rejected the concept of trial by surprise in favor of the notion of broad pretrial discovery. The rules provided for simple notice pleading[1] and created discovery tools that allowed each party to obtain information concerning the litigation from its opponent.[2] Discovery, not pleadings, became the primary means of formulating issues and developing facts.[3]

The Texas Rules of Civil Procedure adopted in 1941 also expanded pretrial discovery, although not to the extent allowed by the federal rules.[4] Eventually, however, amendments brought the Texas rules in line with the federal rules.[5] Both systems allowed discovery of "any matter that is not privileged and is relevant to the subject matter of the pending action, whether it relates to the claim or defense of any other party." The information sought need not be admissible at the trial "if the information sought appears reasonably calculated to lead to the discovery of admissible evidence."[6]

---

[1] FED. R. CIV. P. 8, 28 U.S.C. § 723c (1940). Notice pleading is discussed in greater detail in the Pleadings chapter.

[2] The newly adopted Federal Rules permitted liberal use of depositions of parties and witnesses (Rules 26-32), interrogatories (Rule 33), requests for admissions (Rule 36), inspection of tangible evidence (Rule 34), and physical and mental examinations of parties (Rule 35). *See generally* FED. R. CIV. P. 26-36, 28 U.S.C. § 723c (1940).

[3] *See* Hickman v. Taylor, 329 U.S. 495, 501 (1947) ("The new rules, however, restrict the pleadings to the task of general notice-giving and invest the deposition-discovery process with a vital role in the preparation for trial.").

[4] As was discussed in the Pleadings chapter, the Texas rules retained a detailed pleading practice and detailed submission of special issues to the jury. *See* Rule 91, 273-79 (1942). Pretrial discovery was significantly expanded by introducing inspection of documents and tangible things, requests for admissions and interrogatories, but limited deposition practice to obtaining evidence admissible at trial, as the practice existed before 1941. *See* Rule 167, 169, 186-88, 189 (1942). *See generally,* Alex Albright, *The Texas Discovery Privileges: A Fool's Game?,* 70 TEX. L. REV. 781, 798-799 (1992) (discussing the history of the Texas discovery rules).

[5] In 1957, Texas adopted deposition rules equivalent to those in the federal rules. *See* Rule 202 (1958). During the late 1960s Texas courts began to refer to their commitment to a policy of liberal pretrial discovery. *See, e.g.*, Fisher v. Continental Ill. Nat. Bank & Trust Co., 424 S.W.2d 664, 669 (Tex. Civ. App.—Houston [14th Dist.] 1968, writ ref'd n.r.e.) ("Consistent with a policy of those rules, the courts encourage a liberal use of pre-trial discovery procedures."); Texhoma Stores, Inc. v. American Cent. Ins. Co., 424 S.W.2d 466, 472 (Tex. Civ. App.—Dallas 1968, writ ref'd n.r.e.) ("[T]he spirit of these rules requires liberal construction . . . ."). By 1973, when the scope of discovery of documents and things was made equivalent to the scope of discovery by deposition, the transformation was complete. *See* TEX. R. CIV. P. 167 (1973).

[6] Rule 192.3(a). However, Federal Rule 26(b)(1) has since been amended to allow only discovery of matters "relevant to any party's claim or defense" instead of "the subject matter of the pending action." Texas,

This concept of open discovery is clearly contrary to the confidentiality concerns of the adversary system, but it has its own advantages. Theoretically, full disclosure allows the parties and the decision-maker to learn the truth, since parties may no longer hide important facts. Thus, it is more likely that the dispute will be resolved in favor of the deserving party. As the Texas Supreme Court has often stated, "the ultimate purpose of discovery is to seek the truth, so that disputes may be decided by what the facts reveal, not by what facts are concealed."[7] Moreover, with full and early disclosure parties can better evaluate the litigation and settle the dispute based upon reasonable expectations of the evidence that will be presented at trial. Should the case proceed to trial, the trial should be more streamlined and efficient because discovery allows the issues to be narrowed and the evidence to be presented more effectively.

Discovery now is effectuated through a system of party-initiated requests and responses. Parties use interrogatories to obtain sworn answers to written questions,[8] requests for production to require other parties to produce documents and tangible things for inspection, testing, and copying,[9] and requests for admissions to require another party to admit or deny certain legal or factual matters to narrow the issues for trial.[10] The 1999 rules provide for a simple form request for a "laundry list" of discoverable items, called the "request for disclosure."[11] The rules also provide for depositions, which allow parties to directly confront witnesses and require them to answer questions under oath for use at trial under certain circumstances.[12] Formal discovery from non-parties usually is obtained through request or deposition after service of a subpoena to ensure compliance.[13] No court intervention is required to initiate or to respond to discovery unless someone requests a hearing on an objection, or files a motion to compel responses to requested discovery or a motion for protection from the requested discovery.

There are limits to discovery. Some materials, although relevant, are protected from discovery by privileges that protect the adversary system (e.g. work product) or confidential relationships (e.g. attorney-client).[14] The trial judge also can limit discovery to protect someone from "undue burden, unnecessary expense, harassment, annoyance, or invasion of personal, constitutional, or property rights."[15] Moreover, the 1999 rules allow the trial judge to limit the scope of discovery by limiting the discovery methods when unreasonably cumulative, duplicative or burdensome discovery is sought.[16]

---

to date, has rejected this change. Further federal amendments in 2015 elevated the concept of proportionality (essentially weighing the benefits vs. the burdens of discovery requests) to Federal Rule 26(b)(1)'s scope provision. The impact of this amendment on the actual scope of discovery is debatable, considering that the proportionality concept was in another Federal Rule governing discovery for years before the latest amendment. Currently, the Texas discovery scope provision does not include proportionality language, though there have been proposals in favor of a Texas rule amendment similar to the 2015 federal amendment.

[7] Jampole v. Touchy, 673 S.W.2d 569, 573 (Tex. 1984, orig. proceeding).

[8] Rule 197.

[9] Rule 196.

[10] Rule 198.

[11] Rule 194.

[12] Rule 199-203.

[13] Rules 176, 205.

[14] Rule 166b(3).

[15] Rule 192.6(b).

[16] Rule 192.4.

Obviously, the discovery rules' duty of full disclosure inevitably conflicts with the adversary system's emphasis on competition and confidentiality. Parties seek to avoid disclosure whenever possible, either by narrowly reading the request for discovery, or broadly asserting privileges.[17] Since responding to discovery is expensive, some parties request too much information in an effort to quickly exhaust the opponent's financial resources early in the litigation. Discovery disputes with the attendant motions and court intervention become the rule rather than the exception. As a result, the discovery process is often tedious, time-consuming, expensive and unpleasant. The courts have attempted to solve some of these problems by promulgating statements of professionalism.[18] Courts also impose sanctions for discovery abuse, which are often fatal to the party's position in the underlying lawsuit. Discovery itself ultimately becomes another tactic in the adversary's arsenal, threatening to overshadow the underlying substantive controversy. Remember, however, that formal discovery is not the only method for obtaining information that can be useful in a lawsuit. Old fashioned investigation, without court assistance, may reveal much relevant information. And much can be found fairly cheaply on the Internet.

Because of the pervasive feeling that discovery has gotten out of hand, legislatures (including the United States Congress)[19] and courts are seeking alternatives to our current system. Most seek to reduce the adversarial nature of discovery. These efforts resulted in amendment of the Federal Rules in December 1993 to require early, mandatory and automatic disclosure of "relevant" information, with close scrutiny by the trial judge through pretrial scheduling orders and conferences.[20] Many courts are trying to set cases on particular discovery tracks, limiting discovery based upon the complexity of the issues presented in the litigation.[21] Texas joined the discovery reform effort with new discovery rules, which became effective on January 1, 1999, seeking to decrease the cost of discovery.[22] The new rules impose judicial management of discovery in all cases through "discovery control plans." The rules also strictly limit depositions and interrogatories, limit the total time for discovery, and make significant changes to the scope of discovery. Effective March 1, 2013, the Texas Supreme Court adopted new rules to expedite smaller cases, with an amount in controversy of $100,000 or less.[23] The Federal Rules were also recently amended to, *e.g.*, expressly limit the scope of discovery to "proportional" discovery requests.[24]

---

[17] *See* Wayne D. Brazil, *Views from the Front Lines: Observations by Chicago Lawyers About the System of Civil Discovery,* 1980 AM. B. FOUND. RES. J. 217, 250 (providing evidence that attorneys make disclosures only when left no alternative by the discovery probes of opposing counsel); Wayne D. Brazil, *The Adversary Character of Civil Discovery: A Critique and Proposals for Change,* 31 VAND. L. REV. 1296, 1323 (1978) (noting that "[t]here are many standard devices used by litigators to resist the disclosure of information and to mislead the opponent through their responses to interrogatories, requests for admissions, and demands for documents").

[18] *See* TEXAS LAWYER'S CREED.

[19] CIVIL JUSTICE EXPENSE AND DELAY REDUCTION ACT, 28 U.S.C. § 471 et seq.

[20] FED. R. CIV. P. 26 (1993).

[21] *See, e.g.* CIVIL JUSTICE EXPENSE AND DELAY REDUCTION PLAN, Art. 1 (E.D. Tex. 1996).

[22] *See* Explanatory Statement Accompanying the 1999 Amendments to the Rules of Civil Procedure Relating to Discovery (preceding TRCP 176).

[23] *See* Misc. Docket No. 12-9191 (Tex. 2012) (adopting rules for expedited actions).

[24] *See* note 6, *supra*.

This chapter first will explore the scope of discovery. Then it will address written discovery requests and responses, deposition practice, discovery of expert witnesses, discovery from nonparties, and the limits the discovery rules impose on the amount of discovery sought. Finally, it will explore discovery privileges and confidentiality concerns.

B. Discovery Relevance

Read Rule 192.3, .4, .6.

Rules 192.3 and 192.4 regulate the scope of discovery. Rule 192.3 describes what information and materials are discoverable, and Rule 192.4 allows courts to restrict discovery by limiting specific methods of discovery.

The general scope of discovery under Rule 192.3 is broad, and it allows parties to seek discovery "regarding any matter that is not privileged and is relevant to the subject matter of the pending action, whether it relates to the claim or defense of the party seeking discovery or the claim or defense of any other party. The information sought need not be admissible in evidence so long as it appears "reasonably calculated to lead to the discovery of admissible evidence."[1] Rule 192.3(b) makes clear that parties may obtain discovery of relevant documents and tangible things that contain information within the scope of discovery. Rule 192.3(c) through (j) address the discoverability of specific information.

Obviously, the general scope of discovery provisions leave much for judicial interpretation, and interpretation has changed through the years. Consider the different views towards the scope of discovery represented in the following opinions.

JAMPOLE
v.
TOUCHY

673 S.W.2d 569
(Tex. 1984)

SPEARS, JUSTICE.

In this original mandamus proceeding, Stanley Jampole asks this court to direct Judge Hugo Touchy of the 129th District Court in Harris County to vacate an order denying certain pre-trial discovery. We conditionally grant the writ of mandamus.

Stanley Jampole brought a products liability suit to recover damages for the death of his wife, Judith Goodley Jampole. Mrs. Jampole died from injuries suffered on April 14, 1979, when her 1976 Chevrolet Vega caught fire after being struck from the rear by another automobile. Mr. Jampole sued the driver of the other car, General Motors Corporation, and the Chevrolet Division of General Motors, but only the latter two ("GMC") are affected by this mandamus proceeding.

---

1 Rule 192.3(a).

The type of accident forming the basis of this suit is commonly known as a post-collision, fuel-fed fire. Jampole seeks to hold GMC liable on theories of strict liability, negligence, and breach of warranty. He alleges that the 1976 Vega hatchback was defectively designed, manufactured, and marketed. Jampole maintains that placing the fuel tank of the Vega between the rear axle and bumper was unreasonably dangerous. He specifically claims that the design made the tank vulnerable to rear-end impacts, resulting in fuel leaking into the passenger compartment and igniting. Jampole alleges that GMC knew of the defect, risks, and safer alternatives, but did nothing. GMC's alleged knowledge and failure to act are asserted as grounds for punitive and exemplary damages.

Jampole seeks a writ of mandamus requiring Judge Touchy to vacate portions of an order that denied Jampole's motion to compel GMC to answer certain interrogatories and requests for production. Jampole originally sought a writ of mandamus on the same basis against Judge Thomas J. Stovall, who first heard and ruled on Jampole's motion. After this court granted Jampole leave to file his petition for writ of mandamus, Judge Touchy replaced Judge Stovall in the 129th District Court. Jampole properly asked this court to delay action on his petition while he requested that Judge Touchy reconsider Judge Stovall's order. Judge Touchy reaffirmed the prior order, and we granted Jampole's motion to amend his petition to substitute Judge Touchy as respondent.

Jampole complains that the trial court's order denied him discovery of the following types of information: (1) evidence of alternate fuel storage system designs that were known to GMC; (2) installation and assembly diagrams and specifications for 1971-77 Chevrolet Vegas and their counterpart Pontiac Astres; (3) documents revealing how GMC planned to comply with proposed federal motor vehicle safety standards that would have imposed more stringent standards for fuel storage system integrity; (4) documents pertaining to experimental, pre-production, and prototype models of the Vega; and (5) a master index listing all crash test reports available to GMC for 1971-77 Vegas and Astres and any vehicles incorporating certain design alternatives.

In deciding whether a writ of mandamus is appropriate, we recognize that mandamus will not issue unless a clear abuse of discretion is shown. Furthermore, appellate courts will not intervene to control incidental trial court rulings when there is an adequate remedy by appeal. We must first consider, then, whether Judge Touchy clearly abused his discretion by denying the requested discovery.

In making this determination, we note that the ultimate purpose of discovery is to seek the truth, so that disputes may be decided by what the facts reveal, not by what facts are concealed. For this reason, discovery is not limited to information that will be admissible at trial. To increase the likelihood that all relevant evidence will be disclosed and brought before the trier of fact, the law circumscribes a significantly larger class of discoverable evidence to include anything reasonably calculated to lead to the discovery of material evidence. This broad grant is limited, however, by the legitimate interests of the opposing party, for example, to avoid overly-broad requests, harassment, or disclosure of privileged information.

Jampole filed interrogatories to determine GMC's pre-accident knowledge of alternative designs that would have reduced the risk of fuel escaping from the Vega fuel tank on impact, entering the passenger compartment, and igniting. He specifically requested all impact tests for 1967-79 on vehicles with: (a) above-axle fuel tanks; (b) fuel tanks in other non-production locations; (c) fuel tanks containing flexible liners; (d) fuel tanks that were not made of the standard terne-plated steel (steel coated with a lead/tin alloy); (e) fuel tanks protected by deflector shields; and (f) fuel tanks equipped with break-away filler necks. Several interrogatories also asked about the design and performance of the 1973-75 Opel Kadetts, small cars manufactured by a foreign subsidiary of GMC and designed with an above-axle fuel tank.

The trial court limited discovery to knowledge and information based on records pertaining to 1971-77 Vegas and Astres. The trial court was persuaded that other vehicles were not substantially similar to the Jampoles' 1976 Vega Hatchback; therefore, he concluded that tests on those vehicles were not relevant.

Jampole contends that it was a clear abuse of discretion for the trial court to deny discovery of alternate design documents. Jampole argues that the requested documents are relevant to his strict liability claim because they could show the availability and feasibility of safer alternatives. In *Boatland of Houston, Inc. v. Bailey,* 609 S.W.2d 743, 746 (Tex. 1980), we held that whether a product is defectively designed must be determined in relation to safer alternatives; thus, evidence of the actual use of, or capacity to use, safer alternatives is relevant. The basic issue in this lawsuit is whether the 1976 Vega hatchback fuel tank design was defective because it allowed fuel to escape. Other designs that may have prevented fuel escaping are relevant to show that the Vega tank was unreasonably dangerous. Furthermore, the documents showing GMC's knowledge of alternative designs are relevant to show conscious indifference in support of Jampole's claim of gross negligence.

The trial court, in balancing the rights of the parties, took an unduly restrictive view of the degree of similarity necessary for tests on other vehicles to be relevant. The automobiles need not be identical in order for tests on one to be relevant in determining whether the design of another is defective. Design differences between vehicles that might prevent certain alternatives from being adapted to the hatchback design do not necessarily undermine the relevance or discoverability of documents relating to those alternatives. Whether a safer fuel system design suitable for one vehicle is adaptable to another is a question of feasibility to be decided by the trier of fact, not a question to be resolved in ruling on discovery requests. Moreover, if it were impossible to incorporate a safer design in the fuel system of a 1976 Vega Hatchback, the existence of that design would be relevant to establish liability for failure to warn. The time period requested is not overly broad, and Jampole has limited his request to include only tests on GMC passenger cars. There being no valid claim of privilege or limitation invoked, the trial court's denial was a clear abuse of discretion.

* * *

Having found that the trial court abused its discretion by denying discovery of alternate design and assembly documents, the remaining issue is whether Jampole has an adequate remedy by appeal. * * * The trial court's action in this case effectively prevents Jampole from proving the material allegations of his lawsuit. On appeal, it is unlikely he would be able to show that the trial court's errors were harmful . . . . Because the evidence exempted from discovery would not appear on the record, the appellate courts would find it impossible to determine whether denying the discovery was harmful. It is no answer to presume harm whenever a party can show on appeal that proper discovery was denied. . . . Moreover, requiring a party to try his lawsuit, debilitated by the denial of proper discovery, only to have that lawsuit rendered a nullity on appeal, falls well short of a remedy by appeal that is "equally efficient, convenient, beneficial, and effective as mandamus."

We expect that Judge Touchy will vacate his order denying discovery of evidence of alternate designs and assembly documents and will enter an order consistent with this opinion. Should he fail to do so, the clerk of the supreme court is directed to issue the writ of mandamus.

BARROW, JUSTICE, dissenting.

* * *

This case furnishes the court with a unique opportunity to support the efforts of Texas trial judges in curbing discovery abuses. Rather than seizing upon this opportunity and expressing confidence in trial judges, the court has now unnecessarily usurped the discretion of the trial judge. From this decision emanates a signal to the trial judge in contradiction of the court's prior attitude in this context and of the basic purpose of the amended rules of discovery.

While I or any other judge on hearing this matter might have granted more or less discovery than Judge Stovall did, it is clear that the interlocutory order signed here was the result of a full hearing by a conscientious trial judge. If this case involves a clear abuse of discretion, no trial judge is safe from the heavy hand of a mandamus action.

From a reading of the 332 page record, it is apparent that both parties in this major lawsuit had taken advocative positions that would have to be compromised during the course of discovery. Hence, Jampole's discovery requests were unnecessarily broad, and GMC's responses were unduly restrictive. Faced with the arduous task of determining the proper scope of discovery, Judge Stovall, an experienced trial judge, conducted a full two day hearing, including an actual examination of an allegedly similar vehicle, considered each request individually, and attempted to balance the interests and rights of both litigants. In fact, he granted, at least in part, substantially all the requests including all discovery requested relating to H-body type of vehicles irrespective of the model. It is obvious that Judge Stovall contemplated an ongoing discovery process, as he often stated that he would allow or disallow requested documents "at this level of the case." Moreover, at the end of the second hearing, after directing GMC to produce the requested information within sixty days, Judge Stovall reiterated that both parties were free to "come back to the well" if further discovery was desired.

* * *

It is essential that a trial judge be permitted to conduct an orderly pretrial process without the interference of the appellate court. By delaying a ruling on one aspect of the case, the trial judge may subsequently be in a better position to rule correctly since he will have had the opportunity to receive more evidence and derive more facts.

Perhaps the most disturbing aspect of the court's holding is that it promotes an attitude towards discovery with which I cannot agree. Mandamus traditionally has been an extreme measure to be utilized only when there has been a violation of a clear legal right possessed by the relator and when there is a clear legal duty to act on behalf of the respondent. Unless the law dictates "an absolute and rigid duty of the trial court to follow a fixed and prescribed course not involving the exercise of judgment or discretion," the court should be hesitant to grant relief by writ of mandamus. Thus, the discretionary nature of discovery and the amorphous notion of relevancy most often counsel against appellate court intervention into the discovery process.

The concept of relevance is not susceptible of exact definition. Nonetheless, relevance does implicate a balancing of the probative value of the information sought and the burden upon the movant if discovery is denied weighed against the burden placed upon the respondent if discovery is granted. If relevance is shown by this balancing process, the trial judge nonetheless may direct "that requested discovery not be sought in whole or in part" if the circumstances of the case so require. TEX. R. CIV. P. 166b(4)(a). Obviously, then, the trial judge may limit discovery of relevant evidence.

Less than one year ago this court observed that over the past twenty-five years it had been flooded with mandamus actions to either compel or deny discovery. Today's decision effectively insures that this flood will continue and increase into a rampage. The majority has failed to heed the warning echoed by our predecessors against "entering the thicket" by constant interruptions of the trial process. We have now not only "entered the thicket," we have become totally enshrouded in that thicket. I respectfully dissent.

Note on Mandamus of Discovery Orders

Whether appellate courts should review discovery orders through mandamus has been in the middle of the mandamus debate we explored earlier. In 1992, eight years after *Jampole*, the Supreme Court reversed course on mandamus of discovery orders in *Walker v. Packer*, where the Court specifically disapproved of Jampole's statement that an appellate remedy is inadequate because "it might involve more delay or cost than mandamus."[1] But the majority opinion scoffed at the dissenter's "claim that strict adherence to traditional mandamus standards will signal an end to effective interlocutory review for some parties or classes of litigants," and specifically identified three situations where mandamus for a discovery order might be available. The Court said:

> First, a party will not have an adequate remedy by appeal when the appellate court would not be able to cure the trial court's discovery error. This occurs when the trial court erroneously orders the disclosure of privileged information which will materially affect the rights of the aggrieved party, such as documents covered by the attorney-client privilege, or trade secrets without adequate protections to maintain the confidentiality of the information. "After the [privileged documents] had been inspected, examined and reproduced . . . a holding that the court had erroneously issued the order would be of small comfort to relators in protecting their papers." It may also occur where a discovery order compels the production of patently irrelevant or duplicative documents, such that it clearly constitutes harassment or imposes a burden on the producing party far out of proportion to any benefit that may obtain to the requesting party.
>
> Second, an appeal will not be an adequate remedy where the party's ability to present a viable claim or defense at trial is vitiated or severely compromised by the trial court's discovery error. It is not enough to show merely the delay, inconvenience or expense of an appeal. Rather, the relator must establish the effective denial of a reasonable opportunity to develop the merits of his or her case, so that the trial would be a waste of judicial resources. We recently held that when a trial court imposes discovery sanctions which have the effect of precluding a decision on the merits of a party's claims—such as by striking pleadings, dismissing an action, or rendering default judgment—a party's remedy by eventual appeal is inadequate, unless the sanctions are imposed simultaneously with the rendition of a final, appealable judgment. Similarly, a denial of discovery going to the heart of a party's case may render the appellate remedy inadequate.
>
> Finally, the remedy by appeal may be inadequate where the trial court disallows discovery and the missing discovery cannot be made part of the appellate record, or the trial court after proper request refuses to make it part of the record, and the reviewing court is unable to evaluate the effect of the trial court's error on the record before it. If the procedures of TEX. R. CIV. P. 166b(4) [now Rule 193.4] are followed, this situation should only rarely arise. If

---

[1] Walker v. Packer, 827 S.W.2d 833, 842 (Tex. 1992).

> and when it does, however, the court must carefully consider all relevant circumstances, such as the claims and defenses asserted, the type of discovery sought, what it is intended to prove, and the presence or lack of other discovery, to determine whether mandamus is appropriate.

Of course, more recently, in *In re Prudential Insurance Co.*,[2] the Supreme Court retreated from *Walker* and its relaxed the mandamus standard for an "inadequate appellate remedy." And in *In re McAllen Medical Center*,[3] the Court rejected its previous practice of identifying orders subject to mandamus as they arose or "came to mind." Instead, the Court now uses the balancing test articulated in *In re Prudential* to determine whether there is an adequate appellate remedy:

> The operative word, "adequate", has no comprehensive definition; it is simply a proxy for the careful balance of jurisprudential considerations that determine when appellate courts will use original mandamus proceedings to review the actions of lower courts. These considerations implicate both public and private interests. Mandamus review of incidental, interlocutory rulings by the trial courts unduly interferes with trial court proceedings, distracts appellate court attention to issues that are unimportant both to the ultimate disposition of the case at hand and to the uniform development of the law, and adds unproductively to the expense and delay of civil litigation. Mandamus review of significant rulings in exceptional cases may be essential to preserve important substantive and procedural rights from impairment or loss, allow the appellate courts to give needed and helpful direction to the law that would otherwise prove elusive in appeals from final judgments, and spare private parties and the public the time and money utterly wasted enduring eventual reversal of improperly conducted proceedings. An appellate remedy is "adequate" when any benefits to mandamus review are outweighed by the detriments. When the benefits outweigh the detriments, appellate courts must consider whether the appellate remedy is adequate.

Nevertheless, *Walker*'s articulation of when mandamus *is* allowed in discovery matters continues to be important. If mandamus was available in a situation that "came to mind" in *Walker*, it is certainly available under *Prudential*.

TEXACO, INC.
v.
SANDERSON

898 S.W.2d 813
(Tex. 1995)

PER CURIAM.

* * *

Tony Graffagnino Jr.'s widow and ten surviving children sued Texaco, Inc., Texaco Chemical Company, Texaco Refining and Marketing, Inc., and Star Enterprises, Inc., alleging that while Graffagnino was employed at Texaco's Port Arthur refinery from 1941 to 1984, he was exposed to toxic materials, including asbestos, from which he contracted an asbestos-related disease and died. Vernon Rieve's widow and son intervened in the action, alleging that while Rieve was

---

[2] 148 S.W.3d 124, 135-138 (Tex. 2004).

[3] 275 S.W.3d 458 (Tex. 2008).

employed at the same facility from 1933 to 1980, he, too, was exposed to toxic substances, including asbestos and benzene, resulting in his death from cancer. Both groups of plaintiffs claim damages for defendants' gross negligence under section 408.001 of the Texas Labor Code.

Plaintiffs have requested production of "all documents written by John Sexton, who was corporate safety director, that concern safety, toxicology, and industrial hygiene, epidemiology, fire protection and training." Texaco, Inc., employed Sexton from 1957 to 1987, and for the last ten of those years, Sexton was responsible for corporate safety and environmental policies and procedures, and for monitoring Texaco's compliance with safety and environmental laws. (It so happens that Sexton has sued Texaco for wrongful discharge, alleging retaliation for his efforts to identify and stop violations of safety and environmental laws. That action is pending.) Texaco objected to plaintiffs' request "in that same is a fishing expedition prohibited by [*Loftin v. Martin,* 776 S.W.2d 145, 148 (Tex. 1989)], in that it lacks specificity, requests information wholly irrelevant to any issue in this case, is overly broad, harassing and unduly burdensome." The trial court granted plaintiffs' motion to compel production. After defendants produced 2,500 pages of documents relating to benzene, butadiene, safety, toxicology, and industrial hygiene at Texaco's facilities in southeast Texas, they moved the trial court for reconsideration. The trial court denied defendants' motion. Defendants also asserted claims of privilege, which the trial court held were waived.

Defendants argue that the request is overly broad because it is not limited to information concerning employees' exposure to asbestos and benzene (the only substances specifically mentioned in plaintiffs' pleadings), or even to toxic substances generally, or to the refinery where plaintiffs' decedents worked (Texaco has facilities throughout the world), or even to facilities like that refinery, or to the time during which Sexton had safety responsibilities (he had none for the first twenty years of his employment), or to the time decedents were employed (the request calls for documents created after decedents left the company). As examples of the overbreadth of the discovery request, defendants produced for the trial court documents concerning LPG gas handling, scaffolding, fire retardant clothing, first aid instructor manuals, safety glasses, and ignition risks of flashlights, all of which are within the scope of the request. Plaintiffs acknowledge the breadth of their request but argue that they are entitled to documents showing defendants' corporate "state of mind" not just toward exposure to asbestos or other toxic substances in one refinery or others like it during any certain period of time, but toward employee safety and welfare generally.

Discovery is limited to matters relevant to the case. In *General Motors Corp. v. Lawrence,* 651 S.W.2d 732 (Tex. 1983), we held that in a case alleging the defective design of the fuel filler neck in a particular model truck, discovery requests concerning fuel filler necks in every vehicle ever made by General Motors were too broad. We granted mandamus relief directing the trial court to set aside its orders requiring compliance with the discovery requests. In *Loftin v. Martin,* we held that a request for "all notes, records, memoranda, documents and communications made that [plaintiff] contends support its allegations" was so vague, ambiguous and overbroad as to amount to "a request that [defendant] be allowed to generally peruse all evidence [plaintiff] might have." .

In the present case, too, the discovery request is overly broad. The principal issue in the underlying litigation is whether defendants were grossly negligent in exposing plaintiffs' decedents to asbestos, benzene, and other such toxic substances. Plaintiffs argue that they want to prove a general "corporate strategy to ignore safety laws." While plaintiffs are entitled to discover evidence of defendants' safety policies and practices as they relate to the circumstances involved in their allegations, a request for all documents authored by Sexton on the subject of safety, without limitation as to time, place or subject matter, is overbroad. For example, plaintiffs have not demonstrated how the requested information relating to fire training bears any relation to the case at all. Defendants have agreed to produce the documents which pertain to their attitude about the risks of which plaintiffs complain for relevant times and places. Plaintiffs are not entitled to any more.

A specific request for discovery reasonably tailored to include only matters relevant to the case is not overbroad merely because the request may call for some information of doubtful relevance. Parties must have some latitude in fashioning proper discovery requests. The request in this case, however, is not close; it is well outside the bounds of proper discovery. It is not merely an impermissible fishing expedition; it is an effort to dredge the lake in hopes of finding a fish.

The trial court's ruling requiring production beyond that permitted by the rules of procedure was a clear abuse of discretion. Defendants have no adequate remedy by appeal. Defendants are therefore entitled to relief by mandamus.

* * *

In re GRACO CHILDREN'S PRODUCTS, INC

210 S.W.3d 598
(Tex. 2006)

PER CURIAM.

We review once again a trial court's order compelling production of thousands of documents that, while they might be very relevant in some other suit, have nothing to do with this one. As we have on such occasions before, we conditionally grant the petition for writ of mandamus.

Patricia Galnares was driving on Interstate 55 near McComb, Mississippi when she veered off the road, overcorrected, and caused her Jeep Liberty to roll over. She and her 13-year-old brother Antonio suffered no permanent injury as they were wearing seatbelts. But her newborn five-week-old son Michael was found on the front seat floorboard with fatal head injuries.

Galnares sued Graco Children's Products, Inc. in Hidalgo County, alleging that defects in the harness clip of the baby's car seat failed to restrain him in the rollover. Graco's defense is that immediately after the accident investigating officers found the harness unbuckled, and that Antonio reported at the scene and later at the hospital that the baby was sitting unrestrained on the front seat while Galnares fed him.

Two weeks before trial in April 2005, the Consumer Products Safety Commission announced a provisional settlement with Graco imposing a $4 million civil penalty-the largest in the agency's history-for failing to report defects in more than a dozen products, including high chairs, swings, strollers, toddler beds, and infant carriers. The announcement listed defects such as swing trays that came unlocked, infant carrier handles that broke, high chair legs that failed, and bed slats that could entangle an infant's limbs. None of the products had five-point harnesses. None mentioned defective harness buckles. While an infant carrier was included, the defect cited was a carrying handle used only when walking, not driving.

Nevertheless, Galnares's attorneys immediately served a notice of deposition and a Fourth Request for Production on Graco, seeking 20 categories of documents including anything that mentioned or referred to any of the defects, products, complaints, or people who might have been involved with those products or the investigation. Graco objected, pointing out that the announcement had nothing to do with the carrier or defect alleged in Galnares's suit, and would involve about 20,000 pages of documents located in Pennsylvania, Ohio, and Illinois.

After two hearings, the trial court ordered Graco to produce two representatives for deposition as well as all the documents Galnares requested. The Thirteenth Court of Appeals denied relief.

"Generally, the scope of discovery is within the trial court's discretion," but "the trial court must make an effort to impose reasonable discovery limits." "[An] order that compels overly broad discovery well outside the bounds of proper discovery is an abuse of discretion for which mandamus is the proper remedy."

We have granted mandamus in several product-liability cases when a discovery order covered products the plaintiff never used. . . . In this case, there is again no apparent connection between the alleged defect and the discovery ordered.

Galnares argues that she is not required to take Graco's word that its swings, high chairs, and other products did not have harnesses like the one at issue here. But even if that were not obvious from the pictures and descriptions in the agency announcement, there are ways to find out without producing 20,000 documents. As her requests were not reasonably tailored to the relevant product defect, they were impermissibly overbroad.

Galnares asserts two reasons for production even if the sanctioned defects had nothing to do with hers. First, she says she needs discovery to show Graco did not test any of its products for rollovers. But Graco conceded as much regarding her car seat, so that issue is not rendered more or less probable if Graco also failed to do rollover testing of high chairs or strollers. *See* TEX. R. EVID. 401 (defining "relevant evidence" as that with any tendency to make consequential facts more or less probable).

Second, she asserts that the "centerpiece" of Graco's defense is its "partnership" with government agencies, during which it alleges that it never heard of children slipping from a five-point harness in a rollover. We agree that Graco cannot defend this case by proving it is generally a good corporate citizen, any more than Galnares can prosecute it by proving otherwise. *See* TEX.R. EVID. 404 (providing that party's character or other acts are inadmissible to prove "action in conformity therewith on a particular occasion"). But while a corporate defendant's "state of mind" about a particular product may be discoverable, we have rejected attempts to extend that inquiry to every product it ever made.

Any attorney would be interested in a record-breaking sanction against an adversary in an upcoming trial. But with no evidence that a defect was involved similar to the one alleged in this case, it was a blind alley. Evidence about different products and dissimilar accidents has long been inadmissible, as it generally proves nothing while distracting attention from the accident at hand. This case could have been tried more than a year ago, had not Galnares directed her attention to products she never used and defects she never alleged.

Accordingly, without hearing oral argument, we conditionally grant the writ of mandamus and direct the trial court to vacate its order compelling this discovery. TEX. R. APP. P. 52.8(c). The writ will issue only if the trial court fails to comply.

In re ALLSTATE COUNTY MUTUAL INSURANCE COMPANY
227 S.W.3d 667
(Tex. 2007)

PER CURIAM.

Discovery is a tool to make the trial process more focused, not a weapon to make it more expensive. Thus trial courts "must make an effort to impose reasonable discovery limits." In this suit alleging an insurer reneged on a $13,500 settlement offer, the trial court refused to impose any limit on the plaintiffs' 213 discovery requests. As much of this discovery has no relation or relevance to the scope of the parties' dispute, we grant mandamus relief.

Following a car accident, two plaintiffs (Jorge Karim and Teresita Manllo) brought a single suit against the other driver (Sang Cho), her carrier (Allstate County Mutual Insurance Company), and the latter's adjuster (David Gonzalez). The plaintiffs sent the insurer and its adjuster a total of 89 requests for production, 59 interrogatories, and 65 requests for admission, including requests for:

- transcripts of all testimony ever given by any Allstate agent on the topic of insurance;
- every court order finding Allstate wrongfully adjusted the value of a damaged vehicle;
- personnel files of every Allstate employee a Texas court has determined wrongfully assessed the value of a damaged vehicle; and
- legal instruments documenting Allstate's status as a corporation and its net worth.

Allstate and Gonzalez objected to the discovery and moved for summary judgment on the ground that the plaintiffs had no direct action against a third party's insurer. . . . The trial court denied the summary judgment, rejected the objections, and ordered the defendants to respond to all the requests. The Thirteenth Court of Appeals denied mandamus relief without explanation.

The plaintiffs make no effort to justify their hundreds of requests. Nor can they, given what this Court has said repeatedly in similar cases. . . .

More important, the plaintiffs' requests and the trial court's order reflect a misunderstanding about relevance. American jurisprudence goes to some length to avoid the spurious inference that defendants are either guilty or liable if they have been found guilty or liable of anything before. *See, e.g.*, TEX.R. EVID. 404 (barring proof of other crimes, wrongs, or acts "in order to show action in conformity therewith"). While such evidence might be discoverable in some cases (e.g., to prove motive or intent, *see id.*), it is hard to see why reneging on some other settlement offer makes it more or less probable that the insurer reneged on this one. TEX.R. CIV. P. 192.3; TEX.R. EVID. 401.

* * *

"Reasonable" discovery necessarily requires some sense of proportion. With today's technology, it is the work of a moment to reissue every discovery request one has ever sent to an insurer before. But by definition such a request is not "reasonably tailored." Given the limited scope of the plaintiffs' claims and the amount at issue, the trial court erred by compelling discovery of everything the plaintiffs could imagine asking in any unfair insurance practice case.

Accordingly, without hearing oral argument, we conditionally grant the writ of mandamus and direct the trial court to vacate its discovery order and reconsider the scope of permissible discovery in light of this opinion. *See* TEX.R.APP. P. 52.8(c). The writ will issue only if the trial court fails to comply.

FORD
v.
CASTILLO
279 S.W.3d 656
(Tex. 2009)

JUSTICE JOHNSON delivered the opinion of the Court.

Ford Motor Company and Ezequiel Castillo, the plaintiff in a products liability action, settled while the jury was deliberating. The settlement occurred after the presiding juror sent a note to the judge asking the maximum amount that could be awarded. Based on later discussions with jurors, Ford suspected that outside influence may have been brought to bear on the presiding juror. After Ford sought, but was refused, permission to obtain discovery on the outside influence question, it withdrew its consent to the settlement. Castillo sought summary judgment against Ford for breach of the settlement agreement. Ford's response renewed its request for discovery, but the trial court rendered summary judgment for Castillo on the breach of settlement agreement claim. We hold that the trial court erred by refusing to allow discovery on Castillo's action for breach of contract, including whether there was any outside influence on the jury. We reverse the court of appeals' judgment and remand the case to the trial court for further proceedings consistent with this opinion.

* * *

Castillo asserts that the trial court did not abuse its discretion in denying Ford's discovery request because the evidence Ford sought to develop was immaterial as it did not bear on any proper defense to the breach of contract action. Ford offers mutual mistake as one such potential defense. The parties disagree as to whether mutual mistake is applicable in this case, but a party is not required to demonstrate the viability of defenses before it is entitled to conduct discovery. Rather, a party may obtain discovery "regarding any matter that is not privileged and is relevant to the subject matter of the pending action." TEX.R. CIV. P. 192.3. The phrase "relevant to the subject matter" is to be "liberally construed to allow the litigants to obtain the fullest knowledge of the facts and issues prior to trial." *Axelson, Inc. v. McIlhany,* 798 S.W.2d 550, 553 (Tex. 1990). The trial court's preemptive denial of discovery could have been proper only if there existed no possible relevant, discoverable testimony, facts, or material to support or lead to evidence that would support a defense to Castillo's claim for breach of contract. This record does not demonstrate such a situation.

Castillo further asserts that Ford's suspicion that discovery *might* uncover relevant evidence is insufficient to render the trial court's denial of discovery an abuse of discretion. We agree that in some cases the denial of more time to conduct discovery is not an abuse of discretion when the discovery "might have" raised a fact question. *Tenneco,* 925 S.W.2d at 647. But in such cases, the parties had not been completely precluded by the trial court from conducting discovery to begin with. *See Tenneco,* 925 S.W.2d at 647. Rather, the facts in those cases were "sufficiently developed" and "all the relevant information [was] at hand." *Id.* In this case, facts and matters relevant to the question of outside influence were not developed and the question of whether follow-up discovery on the issue should be undertaken was foreclosed.

In re NORTH CYPRUS MEDICAL CENTER OPERATING CO., Ltd.
___S.W.3d ___
2018 WL 1974376
(Tex. April 27, 2018)*

JUSTICE LEHRMANN delivered the opinion of the Court, in which JUSTICE JOHNSON, JUSTICE BOYD, JUSTICE DEVINE, JUSTICE BROWN, and JUSTICE BLACKLOCK joined.

Our procedural rules allow broad discovery of unprivileged information that is "relevant to the subject matter of the pending action." TEX. R. CIV. P. 192.3(a). This includes information that may ultimately be inadmissible at trial so long as it "appears reasonably calculated to lead to the discovery of admissible evidence." *Id.* The "subject matter" of the underlying action, which involves the enforceability of a hospital lien securing payment of charges for services rendered to an uninsured patient, encompasses the reasonableness of those charges.

The trial court's order at issue in this mandamus proceeding requires the defendant hospital to produce information regarding its reimbursement rates from private insurers and public payers for the services it provided to the plaintiff. The hospital argues those reimbursement rates are irrelevant to whether its charges to the uninsured plaintiff were reasonable and that the trial court therefore abused its discretion in ordering production of that information. We disagree. The reimbursement rates sought, taken together, reflect the amounts the hospital is willing to accept from the vast majority of its patients as payment in full for such services. While not dispositive, such amounts are at least relevant to what constitutes a reasonable charge. Accordingly, we deny the hospital's petition for writ of mandamus.

I. Background

Crystal Roberts was involved in an automobile accident on June 9, 2015, and was taken by ambulance to the emergency room at North Cypress Medical Center. North Cypress released Roberts approximately three hours later after performing a series of x-rays, CT scans, lab tests, and other emergency services. Because Roberts was uninsured, North Cypress billed her for the services at its full "chargemaster" prices, which totaled $11,037.35. North Cypress also filed a hospital lien for this amount. *See* TEX. PROP. CODE § 55.002(a) ("A hospital has a lien on a cause of action or claim of an individual who receives hospital services for injuries caused by an accident that is attributed to the negligence of another person.").

The liability insurer of the driver at fault offered to settle the case for $17,380, attributing $9,404 to past medical expenses. Roberts sought reduction of North Cypress's bill, and the parties negotiated but could not reach an agreement on the bill's amount. Roberts sued, seeking a declaratory judgment that North Cypress's charges were unreasonable and its lien invalid to the extent it exceeds a reasonable and regular rate for services rendered. North Cypress counterclaimed on a sworn account for $8,278.31, the amount to which it had previously offered to reduce its bill.

Roberts served requests for production and interrogatories on North Cypress, including the following:

---

* Editor's note: at the time this book went to press, a hotly contested Motion for Rehearing was pending in the Supreme Court in *In re North Cyprus*, and the case had not been released for publication in the permanent law reports.

• Please produce all contracts regarding negotiated or reduced rates for the hospital services provided to Plaintiff in which Defendant is a party, including those with Aetna, First Care, United Healthcare, Blue Cross Blue Shield, Medicare, and Medicaid.

. . . .

• Please produce the annual cost report you are required to provide to a Medicare Administrative Contractor Medicare [sic], as a Medicare certified institutional provider for 2011, 2012, 2013, 2014 and 2015.

. . . .

• Please state the Medicare reimbursement rate for x-rays, CT scans, lab tests and emergency room services, as you performed on the Plaintiff on June 9, 2015.

• Please state the Medicaid reimbursement rate for x-rays, CT scans, lab tests and emergency room services, as you performed on the Plaintiff on June 9, 2015.

North Cypress objected to these discovery requests and moved for a protective order, asserting that they sought irrelevant information and were overly broad. Roberts filed a corresponding motion to compel. In an oral ruling on the record, the trial court ordered North Cypress to produce the requested information, though the court narrowed the scope to include only contracts "that cover the [time] period at issue in this case."

North Cypress moved for reconsideration, reiterating its relevance objection and adding that it would "suffer irreparable harm" from the disclosure of its "confidential and proprietary" negotiated insurance contracts. The trial court denied the motion, prompting North Cypress to file a petition for writ of mandamus in the court of appeals. The court of appeals denied the petition, and North Cypress now seeks mandamus relief in this Court.

II. Analysis

* * *

We address North Cypress's two challenges to the discovery order in turn.

A. Relevance

North Cypress first argues that information about reimbursement rates from insurers and government payers is not relevant to Roberts' claims about the enforceability of its hospital lien. *See* TEX. R. CIV. P. 192.3(a) (parties may obtain discovery of information that is "relevant to the subject matter of the pending action"). Evidence is "relevant" if "it has any tendency to make a fact [of consequence to the action] more or less probable than it would be without the evidence." TEX. R. EVID. 401. And as noted, evidence need not be admissible to be discoverable so long as it "appears reasonably calculated to lead to the discovery of admissible evidence." TEX. R. CIV. P. 192.3(a).

* * *

Subject to certain conditions, a hospital has a lien on the cause of action of a patient "who receives hospital services for injuries caused by an accident that is attributed to the negligence of another person." *Id.* (quoting TEX. PROP. CODE § 55.002(a). The lien also attaches to the proceeds of a settlement of the patient's cause of action. We have noted that the statute "is replete with language that the hospital recover the full amount of its lien, subject only to the right to question the reasonableness of the charges comprising the lien." *Bashara v. Baptist Mem'l Hosp. Sys.*, 685 S.W.2d 307, 309 (Tex. 1985).

* * *

1. Healthcare Pricing

This case highlights the "two-tiered" healthcare billing structure that has evolved over the past several decades. In *Haygood* [356 S.W.3d 390 (Tex. 2011)], on which North Cypress heavily relies, we described these tiers as encompassing (1) " 'list' or 'full' rates [also described as chargemaster rates] sometimes charged to uninsured patients, but frequently uncollected," and (2) "reimbursement rates for patients covered by government and private insurance." *Id.* at 393 (footnotes omitted). We noted that "[f]ew patients today ever pay a hospital's full charges," *id.* (alteration in original).

* * *

2. Evaluating Reasonableness of Hospital Charges

Citing *Haygood*, North Cypress notes that its legal right to be paid for Roberts' treatment is not offset by a negotiated agreement with an insurance carrier. The dissent similarly opines that hospitals should not be limited "to charging an uninsured patient insurer-negotiated reimbursement rates." *Post* at ——. According to North Cypress and the dissent, this renders irrelevant any adjustments that would have been applicable if Roberts were covered by private health insurance, Medicare, or Medicaid.

However, the issue is not whether Roberts may take advantage of insurance she did not have. Rather, because a valid hospital lien may not secure charges that exceed a reasonable and regular rate, the central issue in a case challenging such a lien is what a reasonable and regular rate would be. And because of the way chargemaster pricing has evolved, the charges themselves are not dispositive of what is reasonable, irrespective of whether the patient being charged has insurance. By contrast, a hospital's reimbursements from private insurers and public payers comprise the vast majority of its payments for services rendered. We fail to see how the amounts a hospital accepts as payment from most of its patients are wholly irrelevant to the reasonableness of its charges to other patients for the same services.

* * *

Roberts does not argue, and we do not conclude, that reimbursement rates standing alone are dispositive of the question of what constitutes a reasonable and regular rate for a hospital's services. And we recognize that many considerations go into negotiated rates that may explain a discount applied to a particular insurer. We further recognize that government-payer reimbursement rates are not necessarily a perfect comparator in evaluating the reasonableness of a provider's charges. But the fact that explanations exist for disparate reimbursement rates does not render them wholly immaterial. As noted, considered together, reimbursements from insurers and government payers comprise the bulk of a hospital's income for services rendered. It defies logic to conclude that those payments have nothing to do with the reasonableness of charges to the small number of patients who pay directly.

* * *

III. Conclusion

The crux of Roberts' lien claim is whether the amount secured by North Cypress's hospital lien exceeds a reasonable and regular rate for the services provided. The amounts North Cypress accepts as payment for those services from other patients, including those covered by private insurance and government benefits, are relevant to whether the charges to Roberts were reasonable and are thus discoverable. We hold that the trial court did not abuse its discretion in compelling production of this information. Accordingly, we deny North Cypress's petition for writ of mandamus.

CHIEF JUSTICE HECHT filed a dissenting opinion, in which JUSTICE GREEN and JUSTICE GUZMAN joined. [omitted]

Notes & Questions

1. *Why not allow "fishing"?* Why shouldn't adversaries be allowed to use broad requests for documents to attempt to find favorable evidence in their adversary's files? Many lawyers believe that document discovery is invasive and expensive for the producing party. Others think that document requests reveal the best evidence for trial purposes. How might the plaintiffs in these cases have more narrowly drafted requests to obtain the information they sought? Or is the information sought simply not discoverable? The Supreme Court's opinions talk about "narrowly drawn requests" and "relevance." What is the difference? Why wasn't Ford's request in *Ford v. Castillo, above*, "fishing"? How do the requests in *Cyprus Medical* compare?

2. *Relevance under the 1999 discovery rules.* When Rule 192.3(a) was adopted, there was no change in the general standard for discovery relevance. Note, however, the addition of Rule 192.4 and Comments 1 and 7 to Rule 192. Federal Rule 26(b)(1) has been amended to allow discovery of matters that are "relevant to any party's claim or defense." Texas Rule 192.3 still allows discovery of matters "relevant to the subject matter of the pending action, whether it relates to the claim or defense of the party seeking discovery or . . . of any other party." What is the significance of the difference in wording? How does the Texas Supreme Court treat "relevance" for discovery? How has technology affected attitudes towards discovery? Many of these opinions were written in tort cases—what are the different considerations concerning scope of discovery in a tort case as opposed to a business case?

3. *Limit to reasonable time.* All discovery orders must contain a reasonable time limit for discovery. In one case, the trial court limited discovery to products similar to the allegedly defective one, and the plaintiff requested production going back 15 years. But the trial court's order contained no time limitation. Because "compliance with the trial court's order would require Deere to produce documents going back decades," the order was an abuse of discretion.[1]

4. *Discovery of net worth.* In *Lunsford v. Morris*,[2] the Supreme Court held that evidence of net worth was discoverable in cases alleging claims for punitive damages and admissible in evidence as proof of punitive damages. But in 2015, the legislature enacted Texas Civil Practice and Remedies Code section 41.0115 to limit discovery of net worth information in punitive damages cases. The statute requires the requesting party to establish – before obtaining net worth discovery – "a substantial likelihood of success on the merits of a claim for exemplary damages."[3] The statute also requires courts to limit net worth discovery to the least burdensome method available.[4]

---

[1] In re Deere & Co., 299 S.W.3d 819, 821 (Tex. 2009).

[2] 746 S.W.2d 471 (Tex. 1988).

[3] CPRC § 41.0115(a).

[4] *Id.* § 41.0115(b). Because evidence of net worth is not relevant to liability, however, the Supreme Court has held that the trial should be bifurcated, with net worth evidence introduced only in a separate hearing concerning the amount of punitive damages that should be awarded after the jury makes affirmative liability findings. *See* Transportation Ins. Co. v. Moriel, 879 S.W.2d 10 (Tex. 1994) (noting that evidence about the profitability of a defendant's misconduct and about any settlement amounts for punitive damages or prior punitive damages awards that the defendant has actually paid for the same course of conduct is also admissible

5. *Discovery of insurance agreements.* Rule 192.3(f) specifically provides that insurance agreements are discoverable even though those matters are clearly *not* admissible in evidence at trial. Only insurance policies "under which any person may be liable to satisfy part or all of a judgment" are discoverable. And the Supreme Court has held that insurance policies need not be produced until the plaintiff shows that they are applicable to a potential judgment.[5] Moreover, Rule 192.3(f) only requires discovery of "the existence and contents" of policies. Related discovery, such as discovery of insurance-erosion information, is discoverable, but under Rule 192.3(a).[6] Why allow discovery of insurance information? Disclosure of insurance agreements encourages early settlement, because it lets the plaintiff know whether the defendant's liability is covered by insurance, and the limits of any policy covering the claim at issue in the lawsuit. Plaintiffs will frequently offer to settle within policy limits, which if refused, may trigger a "Stower's action." Under the reasoning of *G.A. Stowers Furniture Co. v. American Indem. Co.*,[7] an insurance company has the duty to reasonably settle a claim within policy limits. If the insurer refuses to so settle, it may be liable to the policy-holder or any excess carrier for any judgment rendered above policy limits and, perhaps, punitive damages.

6. *Discovery of settlement agreements.* Rule 192.3(g) also provides for discovery of settlement agreements, which are generally not admissible at trial. It is important for a defendant to discover settlement agreements whereby the plaintiff has entered into partial settlements in the pending case because by reason of the settlement the plaintiff may be required to credit some amount against any judgment entered against a non-settling defendant.[8] Some plaintiffs have used this rule to seek discovery of defendant's settlement agreements in other cases with other similarly situated plaintiffs. The Supreme Court rejected this argument in *Ford Motor Co. v. Leggat*.[9] The plaintiffs in a products liability action (a Bronco II roll over suit) sought discovery of the amount that Ford had paid to settle every Bronco II claim. The plaintiffs asserted that the discovery might assist a party in evaluating a case for trial or facilitating settlement, and was relevant to determining Ford's net worth and motives in handling the claims. The court granted mandamus relief and reasoned:

> We disagree with the Whites' contention that knowledge of settlement amounts is relevant to this case. Knowledge of these singular amounts paid in the past reveals nothing about Ford's current net worth. We also fail to see the relevance of Ford's motives. Unlike an insurance company, Ford is not under a duty to settle any litigation. Ford has already offered to make available to the Whites all petitions or complaints against it from accidents involving a Bronco II, from which the Whites should be able to identify any parties, attorneys, or witnesses they might wish to contact. It appears that the Whites' purpose in pursuing discovery of the amounts of settlement is to determine a settlement strategy for their own case. That is not a proper purpose of discovery, and we specifically

---

when the defendant offers it in mitigation of punitive damages. Owens-Corning Fiberglass Corp. v. Malone, 972 S.W.2d 35 (Tex. 1998) (concluding that evidence of the profitability of the defendant's misconduct was admissible).

[5] In re Dana Corp., 138 S.W.3d 298 (Tex. 2004).

[6] *Id.*

[7] 15 S.W.2d 544 (Tex. Comm'n App. 1929, holding approved).

[8] *See* CPRC § 33.012(b) (concerning settlement credits in tort cases); Stewart Title Guar. Co. v. Sterling, 822 S.W.2d 1 (Tex. 1991) (reaffirming settlement credits mandated by "one satisfaction" rule).

[9] 904 S.W.2d 643 (Tex. 1995). Rule 192 cmt. 4 confirms that *Leggatt* remains valid under the 1999 rules.

disapprove of the request for the information under these circumstances. We emphasize that we should not be interpreted to mean that the amount of a settlement could never be relevant, only that the Whites have offered no explanation of how such information is relevant to their claims in this case.

C. Privileges Preventing Discovery

Read Rule 192.5, 193.3; TRE 501-13.

Remember that Rule 192.3(a) allows discovery of all relevant matters that *are not* privileged. A privilege is a legal rule that allows a party to refuse to disclose particular documents, communications and other information. Many privileges are found in the Rules of Evidence. There are also constitutional privileges. Other privileges—like the work product privilege—are found in the Rules of Procedure. We will focus primarily on the privileges applicable to lawyers—the work product and attorney-client privileges and another privilege often confronted in civil litigation, the trade secret privileges.

---

1. *Work Product and Attorney-Client Communications—Definitions*

HICKMAN
v.
TAYLOR
329 U.S. 495
(1947)

Mr. JUSTICE MURPHY delivered the opinion of the court.

This case presents an important problem under the Federal Rules of Civil Procedure, 28 U.S.C.A. following section 723c, as to the extent to which a party may inquire into oral and written statements of witnesses, or other information, secured by an adverse party's counsel in the course of preparation for possible litigation after a claim has arisen. Examination into a person's files and records, including those resulting from the professional activities of an attorney, must be judged with care. It is not without reason that various safeguards have been established to preclude unwarranted excursions into the privacy of a man's work. At the same time, public policy supports reasonable and necessary inquiries. Properly to balance these competing interests is a delicate and difficult task.

On February 7, 1943, the tug 'J. M. Taylor' sank while engaged in helping to tow a car float of the Baltimore & Ohio Railroad across the Delaware River at Philadelphia. The accident was apparently unusual in nature, the cause of it still being unknown. Five of the nine crew members were drowned. Three days later the tug owners and the underwriters employed a law firm, of which respondent Fortenbaugh is a member, to defend them against potential suits by representatives of the deceased crew members and to sue the railroad for damages to the tug.

A public hearing was held on March 4, 1943, before the United States Steamboat Inspectors, at which the four survivors were examined. This testimony was recorded and made available to all interested parties. Shortly thereafter, Fortenbaugh privately interviewed the survivors and took statements from them with an eye toward the anticipated litigation; the survivors signed these statements on March 29. Fortenbaugh also interviewed other persons believed to have some information relating to the accident and in some cases he made memoranda of what they told him. At the time when Fortenbaugh secured the statements of the survivors, representatives of two of the deceased crew members had been in communication with him. Ultimately claims were presented by representatives of all five of the deceased; four of the claims, however, were settled without litigation. The fifth claimant, petitioner herein, brought suit in a federal court under the Jones Act on November 26, 1943, naming as defendants the two tug owners, individually and as partners, and the railroad.

One year later, petitioner filed 39 interrogatories directed to the tug owners. The 38th interrogatory read: 'State whether any statements of the members of the crews of the Tugs 'J.M. Taylor' and 'Philadelphia' or of any other vessel were taken in connection with the towing of the car float and the sinking of the Tug 'John M. Taylor'.

Attach hereto exact copies of all such statements if in writing, and if oral, set forth in detail the exact provisions of any such oral statements or reports."

Supplemental interrogatories asked whether any oral or written statements, records, reports or other memoranda had been made concerning any matter relative to the towing operation, the sinking of the tug, the salvaging and repair of the tug, and the death of the deceased. If the answer was in the affirmative, the tug owners were then requested to set forth the nature of all such records, reports, statements or other memoranda.

The tug owners, through Fortenbaugh, answered all of the interrogatories except No. 38 and the supplemental ones just described. While admitting that statements of the survivors had been taken, they declined to summarize or set forth the contents. They did so on the ground that such requests called 'for privileged matter obtained in preparation for litigation' and constituted 'an attempt to obtain indirectly counsel's private files.' It was claimed that answering these requests 'would involve practically turning over not only the complete files, but also the telephone records and, almost, the thoughts of counsel.'

* * *

Upon their refusal, the court adjudged them in contempt and ordered them imprisoned until they complied.

The Third Circuit Court of Appeals, also sitting en banc, reversed the judgment of the District Court. It held that the information here sought was part of the 'work product of the lawyer' and hence privileged from discovery under the Federal Rules of Civil Procedure. The importance of the problem, which has engendered a great divergence of views among district courts, led us to grant certiorari.

The pre-trial deposition-discovery mechanism established by Rules 26 to 37 is one of the most significant innovations of the Federal Rules of Civil Procedure. Under the prior federal practice, the pre-trial functions of notice-giving issue-formulation and fact-revelation were performed primarily and inadequately by the pleadings. Inquiry into the issues and the facts before trial was narrowly confined and was often cumbersome in method. The new rules, however, restrict the pleadings to the task of general notice-giving and invest the deposition-discovery process with a vital role in the preparation for trial. The various instruments of discovery now serve (1) as a device, along with the pre-trial hearing under Rule 16, to narrow and clarify the basic issues between the parties, and (2) as a device for ascertaining the facts, or information as to the existence or whereabouts of facts, relative to those issues. Thus civil trials in the federal courts no longer need be carried on in the dark. The way is now clear, consistent with recognized privileges, for the parties to obtain the fullest possible knowledge of the issues and facts before trial.

* * *

In urging that he has a right to inquire into the materials secured and prepared by Fortenbaugh, petitioner emphasizes that the deposition-discovery portions of the Federal Rules of Civil Procedure are designed to enable the parties to discover the true facts and to compel their disclosure wherever they may be found. It is said that inquiry may be made under these rules, epitomized by Rule 26, as to any relevant matter which is not privileged; and since the discovery provisions are to be applied as broadly and liberally as possible, the privilege limitation must be restricted to its narrowest bounds. On the premise that the attorney-client privilege is the one involved in this case, petitioner argues that it must be strictly confined to confidential communications made by a client to his attorney. And since the materials here in issue were secured by Fortenbaugh from third persons rather than from his clients, the tug owners, the conclusion is reached that these materials are proper subjects for discovery under Rule 26.

* * *

In our opinion, neither Rule 26 nor any other rule dealing with discovery contemplates production under such circumstances. That is not because the subject matter is privileged or irrelevant, as those concepts are used in these rules. Here is simply an attempt, without purported necessity or justification, to secure written statements, private memoranda and personal recollections prepared or formed by an adverse party's counsel in the course of his legal duties. As such, it falls outside the arena of discovery and contravenes the public policy underlying the orderly prosecution and defense of legal claims. Not even the most liberal of discovery theories can justify unwarranted inquiries into the files and the mental impressions of an attorney.

Historically, a lawyer is an officer of the court and is bound to work for the advancement of justice while faithfully protecting the rightful interests of his clients. In performing his various duties, however, it is essential that a lawyer work with a certain degree of privacy, free from unnecessary intrusion by opposing parties and their counsel. Proper preparation of a client's case demands that he assemble information, sift what he considers to be the relevant from the irrelevant facts, prepare his legal theories and plan his strategy without undue and needless interference. That is the historical and the necessary way in which lawyers act within the framework of our system of jurisprudence to promote justice and to protect their clients' interests. This work is reflected, of course, in interviews, statements, memoranda, correspondence, briefs, mental impressions, personal beliefs, and countless other tangible and intangible ways—aptly though roughly termed by the Circuit Court of Appeals in this case (153 F.2d 212, 223) as the 'Work product of the lawyer.' Were such materials open to opposing counsel on mere demand, much of what is now put down in writing would remain unwritten. An attorney's thoughts, heretofore inviolate, would not be his own. Inefficiency, unfairness and sharp practices would inevitably develop in the giving of legal advice and in the preparation of cases for trial. The effect on the legal profession would be demoralizing. And the interests of the clients and the cause of justice would be poorly served.

We do not mean to say that all written materials obtained or prepared by an adversary's counsel with an eye toward litigation are necessarily free from discovery in all cases. Where relevant and non-privileged facts remain hidden in an attorney's file and where production of those facts is essential to the preparation of one's case, discovery may properly be had. Such written statements and documents might, under certain circumstances, be admissible in evidence or give clues as to the existence or location of relevant facts. Or they might be useful for purposes of impeachment or corroboration. And production might be justified where the witnesses are no longer available or can be reached only with difficulty. Were production of written statements and documents to be precluded under such circumstances, the liberal ideals of the deposition-discovery portions of the Federal Rules of Civil Procedure would be stripped of much of their meaning. But the general policy against invading the privacy of an attorney's course of preparation is so well recognized and so essential to an orderly working of our system of legal procedure that a burden rests on the one who would invade that privacy to establish adequate reasons to justify production through a subpoena or court order. That burden, we believe, is necessarily implicit in the rules as now constituted.

Rule 30(b), as presently written, gives the trial judge the requisite discretion to make a judgment as to whether discovery should be allowed as to written statements secured from witnesses. But in the instant case there was no room for that discretion to operate in favor of the petitioner. No attempt was made to establish any reason why Fortenbaugh should be forced to produce the written statements. There was only a naked, general demand for these materials as of right and a finding by the District Court that no recognizable privilege was involved. That was insufficient to justify discovery under these circumstances and the court should have sustained the refusal of the tug owners and Fortenbaugh to produce.

But as to oral statements made by witnesses to Fortenbaugh, whether presently in the form of his mental impressions or memoranda, we do not believe that any showing of necessity can be made under the circumstances of this case so as to justify production. Under ordinary conditions, forcing an attorney to repeat or write out all that witnesses have told him and to deliver the account to his adversary gives rise to grave dangers of inaccuracy and untrustworthiness. No legitimate purpose is served by such production.

* * *

Denial of production of this nature does not mean that any material, non-privileged facts can be hidden from the petitioner in this case. He need not be unduly hindered in the preparation of his case, in the discovery of facts or in his anticipation of his opponents' position. Searching interrogatories directed to Fortenbaugh and the tug owners, production of written documents and statements upon a proper showing and direct interviews with the witnesses themselves all serve to reveal the facts in Fortenbaugh's possession to the fullest possible extent consistent with public policy. Petitioner's counsel frankly admits that he wants the oral statements only to help prepare himself to examine witnesses and to make sure that he has overlooked nothing. That is insufficient under the circumstances to permit him an exception to the policy underlying the privacy of Fortenbaugh's professional activities. If there should be a rare situation justifying production of these matters, petitioner's case is not of that type.

* * *

We therefore affirm the judgment of the Circuit Court of Appeals.

Affirmed.

Mr. JUSTICE JACKSON, formed by Mr. JUSTICE FRANKFURTER, concurring [omitted].

NATIONAL TANK CO.
v.
BROTHERTON

851 S.W.2d 193
(Tex. 1993)

PHILLIPS, CHIEF JUSTICE.

In this original proceeding we must determine whether accident reports and witness statements prepared by Relator and its insurer following a plant explosion are privileged from discovery. We modify our decision in *Flores v. Fourth Court of Appeals*, 777 S.W.2d 38, 40-41 (Tex. 1989), to hold that investigative documents are prepared in "anticipation of litigation" for purposes of TEX. R. CIV. P. 166b(3) if a) a reasonable person would have concluded from the totality of the circumstances surrounding the investigation that there was a substantial chance that litigation would ensue; and b) the party resisting discovery believed in good faith that there was a substantial chance that litigation would ensue and conducted the investigation for the purpose of preparing for such litigation. This approach will further the public policy underlying the investigatory privileges without unduly restricting discovery, as these privileges may be overcome where the requesting party demonstrates a substantial need for the materials and undue hardship in obtaining the substantial equivalent of the materials by other means. *See* TEX. R. CIV. P. 166b(3). Because we today alter the controlling law, we deny mandamus relief without prejudice to allow the trial court to reconsider its ruling in light of today's opinion.

I.

An explosion occurred on August 23, 1990, at a Wichita Falls manufacturing facility operated by the National Tank Company (NATCO), Relator in this proceeding. The explosion critically injured Rex Willson, a NATCO employee, and two other persons employed by independent contractors. Willson later died from his injuries. Allen Pease, NATCO's General Counsel and Secretary, learned of the explosion the day it occurred and dispatched Henry Townsend, NATCO's safety and risk control coordinator, to investigate. Although not a lawyer, Townsend was employed in NATCO's legal department under Pease's supervision. Pease also immediately notified David Sneed, a brokerage supervisor with American International Adjustment Company (AIAC), a representative of NATCO's liability insurers. Pease explained to Sneed the serious nature of the accident, and recommended that AIAC initiate its own investigation, which it did.

Willson's wife, individually and on behalf of her children and the estate, sued NATCO and several other defendants on January 15, 1991. Shortly thereafter, she requested that NATCO produce any reports prepared in connection with the accident investigation. NATCO objected, asserting the attorney-client, work-product, witness-statement, and party-communication privileges. In an order signed July 25, 1991, the trial court overruled NATCO's objections as to documents prepared prior to October 25, 1990, the date NATCO learned that it had been sued by Frank Kroupa, one of the other persons injured in the explosion. The trial court thus ordered NATCO to produce the documents prepared prior to that date. These documents are 1) the transcripts of four interviews of NATCO employees conducted by Henry Townsend shortly after the accident, 2) the transcripts of nine interviews of NATCO employees conducted by Phil Precht, an AIAC employee, shortly after the accident, and 3) three accident reports prepared by Precht and sent to Pease. The trial court, however, stayed the effect of this order to allow NATCO to seek mandamus relief.

NATCO first challenged the trial court's discovery order by a mandamus action in the Court of Appeals. That court denied relief by an unpublished order on September 20, 1991. NATCO then sought mandamus relief here on September 27, 1991. While NATCO's action was pending in this Court, the discovery dispute continued below regarding the depositions of Townsend and Don Hatfield, NATCO's Operations Manager at the Wichita Falls plant. When these individuals were deposed concerning their post-accident conversations with NATCO plant personnel, NATCO objected on the basis of the same privileges previously asserted in response to plaintiff's document requests. Consistent with its earlier ruling, the trial court by order signed November 15, 1991, held that these conversations were not privileged and ordered the depositions of Townsend and Hatfield to proceed "in line with the parameters placed upon the asserted privileges as set forth in this Court's order of July 25, 1991." The trial court did not stay the effect of this second discovery order. NATCO therefore moved for emergency relief in the mandamus action already pending in this Court involving the document requests. In addition to the relief earlier requested, NATCO asked us to immediately stay the Townsend and Hatfield depositions, arguing that the sought-after testimony would moot the issues involved in the document requests. The Court granted emergency relief on November 19, 1991, staying both the depositions and the production of documents previously ordered by the trial court.

The parties opposing mandamus relief in this Court are Bonded Inspections, Inc. and Helm Inspection Services, Inc., the independent contractors that employed two of the injured individuals, and Stephen Cook, one of those injured. The members of Willson's family have settled their claims.

* * *

IV.

A.

Texas Rule of Civil Procedure 166b(3)(c) protects from discovery witness statements "made subsequent to the occurrence or transaction upon which the suit is based and in connection with the prosecution, investigation, or defense of the particular suit, or in anticipation of the prosecution or defense of the claims made a part of the pending litigation . . . ." Texas Rule of Civil Procedure 166b(3)(d) similarly protects communications between agents, representatives or employees of a party when made in anticipation of litigation. The only issue concerning the applicability of these privileges in this case is whether the witness statements and investigative reports generated by NATCO and its insurer were made in anticipation of litigation.

An investigation is conducted in anticipation of litigation if it meets the two-prong test of *Flores v. Fourth Court of Appeals*, 777 S.W.2d 38, 40-41 (Tex. 1989). The first prong of the *Flores* test is objective. The court is required to determine whether a reasonable person, based on the circumstances existing at the time of the investigation, would have anticipated litigation. We stated in *Flores* that "[c]onsideration should be given to outward manifestations which indicate litigation is imminent." Upon further consideration, however, we conclude that the "imminence' requirement impairs the policy goals of the witness statement and party communication privileges. Serving the function filled in many jurisdictions by the work product doctrine, these privileges seek to strike a balance between open discovery and the need to protect the adversary system. As the Supreme Court noted in *Hickman*, a party[12] must be free to assemble information about the case free of undue interference from the other side:

[12] Although *Hickman* applied only to materials prepared by an attorney, the federal work product doctrine no longer distinguishes between an investigation conducted by a party and one conducted by its representative. The Texas investigative privileges likewise do not make this distinction.

> Were such materials open to opposing counsel on mere demand, much of what is now put down in writing would remain unwritten. An attorney's thoughts, heretofore inviolate, would not be his own. Inefficiency, unfairness and sharp practices would inevitably develop in the giving of legal advice and in the preparation of cases for trial. The effect on the legal profession would be demoralizing. And the interests of the clients and the cause of justice would be poorly served.

Hickman. The investigative privileges promote the truthful resolution of disputes through the adversarial process by encouraging complete and thorough investigation of the facts by both sides. At the same time, they do not unduly thwart discovery, as they are limited in scope and can be overcome by a showing of substantial need for the information and undue hardship in obtaining it from other sources.

Considering these policies, we conclude that the objective prong of *Flores* is satisfied whenever the circumstances surrounding the investigation would have indicated to a reasonable person that there was a substantial chance of litigation. The confidentiality necessary for the adversary process is not defeated because a party, reasonably anticipating future litigation, conducts an investigation prior to the time that litigation is "imminent." We accordingly modify *Flores* to the extent that it accords protection only to investigations conducted when litigation is imminent.

We agree with the dissenting justices' characterization of "substantial chance of litigation." This does not refer to any particular statistical probability that litigation will occur; rather, it simply means that litigation is "more than merely an abstract possibility or unwarranted fear." The underlying inquiry is whether it was reasonable for the investigating party to anticipate litigation and prepare accordingly.

The real parties in interest argue, and some courts of appeals have held, that the objective prong of *Flores* may be satisfied only where the plaintiff engages in some action indicating an intent to sue. *Flores*, however, does not hold this. Rather, it requires the trial court to examine the totality of the circumstances to determine whether the investigation is conducted in anticipation of litigation. Requiring that the plaintiff manifest an intent to sue would also be at odds with the policy goals of the witness statement and party communication privileges. These privileges are designed to promote the adversarial process by granting limited protection to investigations conducted in preparation for litigation. Common sense dictates that a party may reasonably anticipate suit being filed, and conduct an investigation to prepare for the expected litigation, before the plaintiff manifests an intent to sue.

We held in *Stringer v. Eleventh Court of Appeals*, that "[t]he mere fact that an accident has occurred is not sufficient to clothe all post-accident investigations . . . with a privilege." We adhere to this holding, but we disapprove *Stringer* to the extent that it holds that the circumstances surrounding an accident can never by themselves be sufficient to trigger the privilege. If a reasonable person would conclude from the severity of the accident and the other circumstances surrounding it that there was a substantial chance that litigation would ensue, then the objective prong of *Flores* is satisfied.

The second prong of the *Flores* test is subjective. There, we held that the party invoking the privilege must have had "a good faith belief that litigation would ensue." For the reasons previously discussed with respect to the objective prong, however, we conclude that the subjective prong is properly satisfied if the party invoking the privilege believes in good faith that there is a substantial chance that litigation will ensue. It does not further the policy goals of the privilege to require the investigating party to be absolutely convinced that litigation will occur. Also, although not expressly stated in *Flores*, we believe that the subjective prong plainly requires that the investigation actually be conducted for the purpose of preparing for litigation. An investigation is not conducted "in anticipation of litigation" if it is in fact prepared for some other purpose. As with the objective prong, the court must examine the totality of the circumstances to determine whether the subjective prong is satisfied.

Most courts in other jurisdictions construing "anticipation of litigation" under Federal Rule of Civil Procedure 26(b)(3) and its state counterparts likewise do not require that plaintiff have manifested an intent to sue to trigger the privilege. Rather, it is sufficient if the circumstances indicate that the materials were prepared because of the prospect of litigation. It is not necessary that litigation be threatened or imminent, as long as the prospect of litigation is identifiable because of claims that have already arisen.

The fundamental problem that has plagued other courts is determining whether a "routine" investigation is conducted in anticipation of litigation. The Advisory Committee Notes to the 1970 federal rules amendments provide that '[m]aterials assembled in the ordinary course of business, or pursuant to public requirements unrelated to litigation, or for other nonlitigation purposes" are not protected. Accordingly, many courts have recognized a bright-line "ordinary course of business' exception.

Other courts, however, have rejected a hard and fast ordinary course of business exception, recognizing that a prudent party may routinely prepare for litigation after a serious accident.

Most commentators disapprove of a bright-line ordinary course of business exception. *See* Albright, *supra*, at 845 ("Although it is true that a document routinely prepared for business purposes other than litigation is less likely to have been prepared in anticipation of litigation, it is not true that every investigation conducted on a routine basis is conducted for purposes other than litigation.").

We agree that there should be no bright-line ordinary course of business exception. It may very well be that a party routinely investigates serious accidents because such accidents routinely give rise to litigation. As with other investigations, an investigation performed in the ordinary course of business is conducted in anticipation of litigation if it passes both prongs of the *Flores* test. With regard to the subjective prong, the circumstances must indicate that the investigation was in fact conducted to prepare for potential litigation. The court therefore must consider the reasons that gave rise to the company's ordinary business practice. If a party routinely investigates accidents because of litigation and non-litigation reasons, the court should determine the primary motivating purpose underlying the ordinary business practice.

In summary, an investigation is conducted in anticipation of litigation for purposes of Rule 166b(3) when a) a reasonable person would have concluded from the totality of the circumstances surrounding the investigation that there was a substantial chance that litigation would ensue; and b) the party resisting discovery believed in good faith that there was a substantial chance that litigation would ensue and conducted the investigation for the purpose of preparing for such litigation.

* * *

The concurring and dissenting opinions by JUSTICES GONZALEZ, DOGGETT, SPECTOR and HECHT are omitted.

Notes & Questions

1. *Investigative privileges*. The investigative privileges of Former Rule 166b(3)—attorney work product and party communications—were collapsed in the 1999 discovery rule amendments into a single privilege: work product found at Rule 192.5. In 1941, Texas adopted the "investigative privilege" instead of the work product doctrine of *Hickman v. Taylor*.[1] Although the investigative privilege evolved over time, and the Texas Supreme Court cited *Hickman* often, it was not until 1999 that a rule similar to the federal work product doctrine was adopted. Although the *National Tank* opinion interprets the investigative privilege, its rule on interpreting "in anticipation of litigation" applies to Rule 192.5. The primary difference between the Texas rule and the Federal work product doctrine is that in Texas a lawyer's mental impressions are "core work product" that is singled out as not being subject to discovery under circumstances of need and hardship. Does this make a practical difference?

2. *The "litigation" that is anticipated.* The court addressed the question of what constitutes the "litigation" that must be anticipated in order for the privilege to attach. In *Flores v. Fourth Court of Appeals,*[2] the Texas Supreme Court held that "litigation" applies only to court proceedings, not proceedings before an administrative board, such as the Industrial Accident Board, that were not binding upon the subsequent district court proceeding. This distinction often was significant under the *Flores* standard, which required actual manifestation of intent to bring suit.[3] Under the *National Tank* standard, it is less of an issue. Why? Consider whether a memo drafted in preparation for an Industrial Accident Board hearing would be privileged under the *National Tank* test in the subsequent district court appeal of the Board award.

3. *Attorney-client privilege.* The attorney-client privilege of Texas Rule of Evidence 503 protects communications between a lawyer and a client concerning any legal services, and, therefore, is not limited to litigation preparations. The attorney-client privilege is absolute, not subject to the exception for need and hardship, although it can be waived. Its duration is perpetual. Might this privilege apply to any of the communications at issue in *National Tank*?

4. *Client representatives*. Until 1998, Texas used the "control group" test to determine whether communications between an attorney and a client representative were protected by the attorney-client privilege of Texas Rule of Evidence 503. The rule was revised in 1998, however, to adopt a "scope of employment" test. The amendment brings Texas' attorney-client privilege significantly closer to the "subject matter" test used in federal courts and most other states.[4]

5. *Identifying witnesses.* Rule 192.3(c), like the former rules, specifically allows discovery of persons with knowledge of relevant facts, even over a claim of privilege.[5] Notice that the discovery permitted is of *potential* witnesses, persons with knowledge of relevant facts, which is different from the witnesses that the party might use as trial witnesses. The 1999 rules also allow a party to discover the trial witnesses, which was previously considered privileged work product

---

1 329 U.S. 495 (1947).

2 777 S.W.2d 38, 39-40 (Tex. 1989, orig. proceeding).

3 *See* Albright, 70 TEX. L. REV. 781, 815 (criticizing *Flores* for excluding from privilege materials prepared for adversarial confrontation other than a formal lawsuit).

4 *See* FED. R. EVID. 502(a).

5 *See* Griffin v. Smith, 688 S.W.2d 112 (Tex. 1985) ("information concerning the identity and location of persons having knowledge of relevant facts can never be protected from discovery.")

because discovery reveals the lawyer's trial strategy.[6] Even under the former rules, however, a judge could order parties to disclose trial witnesses pursuant to a Rule 166 pretrial order.

6. *Photographs.* Photographs and other electronic images taken in anticipation of litigation are specifically excluded from the work product privilege. Under the old rules, a photograph taken for purposes of the litigation was held to be discoverable unless it was an integral part of a consulting expert's report.[7] The new rules, however, exempt from work product images that may be used as evidence and images of underlying facts.

7. *Duration of privilege.* Work product is a continuing privilege—one that a party may assert in litigation other than the litigation in which the protected materials were prepared. Under prior Texas practice, the attorney-client privilege and the attorney work product privilege were continuing privileges.[8] Because the party communications rule had language that limited its application to the specific lawsuit for which the communication was made, the party communication privilege was not continuing.[9] Consequently, while an attorney's work product was protected from discovery in later related cases, discovery was available for trial preparation materials that were party communications, but were not attorney work product. Rule 192.5 changes this, and is now like the federal rule: all work product is now protected in all subsequent cases, subject of course to the need and hardship exception for ordinary work product.

8. *Witness statements.* Rule 192.3(h) significantly changed Texas civil practice by eliminating the discovery exemption, previously found in Former Rule 166b.3.c, for witness statements made in anticipation of litigation or for trial. Rule 192.3(h) provides that statements of persons with knowledge of relevant facts are discoverable regardless of when they are made. Moreover, these witness statements are specifically excluded from the work product privilege found in Rule 192.5. However, privileges other than work product, such as the attorney-client privilege, may prevent discovery of particular statements.[10] For example, suppose that the plaintiff's lawyer in an intersection collision case has taken two statements during preparation for trial: (1) that of his client, and (2) that of a bystander witness. If the defendant requests statements through a Rule 194.2(i) request for disclosure or otherwise, the plaintiff will have to produce the bystander's statement, which is not privileged, but will not have to produce the plaintiff's statement, which the attorney-client privilege in Texas Rule of Evidence 503 protects.[11][11] Rule 192.3(h)'s definition of "witness statement" includes written statements that the witness has signed or otherwise adopted or approved in writing, as well as recordings or transcriptions of recordings of the witness's oral statements. Notes taken during a conversation or interview with the witness do not qualify as a witness statement however. As under the former rule, any person, upon written request, may obtain his or her own statement concerning the lawsuit.

9. *Lawyer's files.* Is a litigation file discoverable? The Texas Supreme Court addressed the issue in *National Union Fire Insurance v. Valdez*[12] as follows:

---

6 Alvarado v. Farah Manuf. Co., 830 S.W.2d 911 (Tex. 1992); Rogers v. Stell, 835 S.W.2d 100 (Tex. 1992); Gutierrez v. Dallas Indep. Sch. Dist., 729 S.W.2d 691 (Tex. 1987).

7 Houdaille Industries v. Cunningham, 502 S.W.2d 544 (Tex. 1973, orig. proceeding).

8 Owens Corning Fiberglass Co. v. Caldwell, 818 S.W.2d 749, 750-52 (Tex. 1991).

9 *Davis*, 856 S.W.2d at 164.

10 *See* Rule 192 cmt. 9 (noting that elimination of the "witness statement" exemption does not render all witness statements automatically discoverable).

11 TEX. R. EVID. 503.

12 863 S.W.2d 458 (Tex. 1993).

We start with the proposition, which National Union does not dispute, that a document is not privileged simply because it is contained in an attorney's files. There is no specific privilege under our rules or caselaw for "documents in an attorney's files." Thus, a party may not cloak a document with the attorney-client privilege simply by forwarding it to his or her attorney. Similarly, a file memorandum is not necessarily attorney work product, even though prepared by a lawyer. In seeking to withhold specific documents from production, a party has the burden of demonstrating the applicability of a particular privilege, notwithstanding the location of these documents in its attorney's files.

National Union contends, however, that even if some of the documents in the law firm files would not otherwise be privileged, production of an attorney's entire file necessarily reveals the attorney's mental processes, thus invoking work-product protection. We agree.

Texas Rule of Civil Procedure 166b(3)(a) protects from disclosure the "work product of an attorney." This exemption shelters the "mental processes, conclusions, and legal theories of the attorney, providing a privileged area within which the lawyer can analyze and prepare his or her case." The exemption continues even after the litigation for which the work product was prepared concludes.

An attorney's litigation file goes to the heart of the privileged work area guaranteed by the work product exemption. The organization of the file, as well as the decision as to what to include in it, necessarily reveals the attorney's thought processes concerning the prosecution or defense of the case. For example, one of the law firm files which National Union produced for in camera inspection was Schwartzberg's "trial notebook," which directly reflects his trial strategy. While a party should not be allowed to shield discoverable documents simply by placing them in an attorney's file, neither should its attorney be restricted in the organization and maintenance of his or her files by the prospect that they might have to be revealed in their entirety in either current or future litigation. As the Supreme Court recognized in *Hickman v. Taylor,*:

> Proper presentation of a client's case demands that (the attorney) assemble information, sift what he considers to be the relevant from the irrelevant facts, prepare his legal theories and plan his strategy without undue and needless interference.

Based on this doctrine, federal courts have recognized that an attorney's selection and ordering of documents in anticipation of litigation is protected work product, even where the individual documents are not privileged. . . .

Our decision today does not prevent a party from requesting specific documents or categories of documents relevant to issues in a pending case, even though some or all of the documents may be contained in an attorney's files. It does, however, prevent a party from requesting the entire file, which is almost certain to encompass numerous irrelevant and immaterial documents, such as transmittal letters and pleadings already on file with the court, as well as privileged information.

10. *Facts vs. trial preparation*: Facts are not privileged. However, a communication, compilation or organization of facts done in anticipation of litigation or for trial is privileged. Thus, a lawyer's organization of documents is protected, but the documents themselves may not be (whether a document is privileged must be determined from that document). An investigator may have uncovered new facts relating to liability during an investigation conducted in anticipation of litigation. If the opponent serves an request for disclosure or interrogatory asking for the facts

upon which the party bases its liability theory, the party must respond with all of the facts, including those uncovered in the investigation. What if the attorney has first-hand knowledge of relevant facts learned while investigating the matter now in litigation—must the facts within the lawyer's knowledge be disclosed in answer to interrogatories directed to the client? Clearly, the answer is yes. Can the opponent depose the attorney on the facts alone? The answer depends upon whether the lawyer was hired as an investigator or as a lawyer—although one court of appeals found an investigator rather than a lawyer relationship under particular facts,[13] usually it is inappropriate to depose a lawyer concerning facts within the lawyer's knowledge.[14]

> Every attorney of record in a case being litigated, or in a case where litigation is anticipated, obtains "factual, relevant information." Performing the function of a lawyer does not preclude a litigation attorney from observing, investigating, monitoring, and evaluating the facts surrounding the matter in controversy. The evidence does not show Goehringer was a fact witness divorced from the litigation. His work was reasonably related to and in furtherance of the prosecution of Baptist's case against the defendants, and also related to mitigating its damages regarding BSA and to defending against BSA's causes of action. . . . [A] trial court should not order a deposition of an attorney of record on the subject matter of the litigation without requiring a showing that less intrusive discovery methods are unavailable to obtain the information sought. Generally, an attorney of record in litigation is an advocate, not a fact witness, in the litigation process. As with compelling production of opposing counsel's litigation file, compelling a deposition of the opposing party's attorney of record concerning the subject matter of the litigation is inappropriate under most circumstances. Calling opposing counsel of record as a witness seriously disrupts the counsel's functioning as an advocate and may create a false impression that the advocate was improperly involved in the underlying issues in the litigation.

11. *Attorney-Billing Records*. The Texas Supreme Court decided in an MDL case that a bulk request for attorney billing records (requested by plaintiffs as part of an attorney-fee dispute in the litigation) sought work product.[15] Writing for the Court, Justice Guzman observed:

> Billing records constitute "communication[s] made in anticipation of litigation or for trial between a party and the party's representatives or among a party's representatives."[37] Moreover, as a whole, billing records represent the mechanical compilation of information that reveals counsel's legal strategy and thought processes, at least incidentally.
>
> * * *
>
> For example, billing records reveal when and where attorneys strategically deploy a client's resources; which issues were addressed by experienced lawyers as compared to less experienced counsel; the subject-matter expertise of an attorney working on a particular aspect of the case; and who was hired as consultants—including consulting experts and jury consultants—and when. This information provides detailed information regarding a party's litigation decisions and also illuminates the relative significance of or

---

[13] In re Texas Farmers Insurance Exchange, 990 S.W.2d 337 (Tex. App.—Texarkana 1999, orig. proceeding), *mand. denied,* 12 S.W.3d 807 (Tex. 2000).

[14] In re Baptist Hosps. Of Southeast Texas, 172 S.W.3d 136, 143 (Tex. App.—Beaumont 2005, orig. proceeding). *See also* In re ExxonMobil Corp., 97 S.W.3d 353, 358(Tex. App.—Houston [14th Dist.] 2003, orig. proceeding).

[15] In re Nat'l Lloyds Ins., 532 S.W.3d 794 (Tex. 2017).

concern about particular matters. Especially when a party is a repeat litigant, as the insurer is here, decisions revealed through billing records represent strategic choices and are pieces of "an overall legal strategy for all the cases in which it is involved," which a party must be allowed to develop without intrusion. *Owens-Corning Fiberglas Corp. v. Caldwell*, 818 S.W.2d 749, 751 (Tex. 1991) (orig. proceeding). Discovery of billing records in their entirety would provide a roadmap of how the insurer plans to litigate not only this particular case but also other MDL cases.

12. *Questions.* You represent the defendant in an automobile accident case. You have the following items in your file. Consider whether any of the following are protected by any privilege from discovery. If so, what privilege(s) would you assert?

(a) a witness' letter to you giving a short summary of what she saw. (What if the letter was from your client; your client's employee?)

(b) a typewritten transcription of the witness' description of what happened when the collision occurred as told to you when you interviewed the witness, which is signed by the witness. (What if the witness is your client? What if the transcript is not signed?)

(c) your notes taken while interviewing the witness, containing the questions asked and the answers.

(d) your memo to the file dictated after the interview discussing your impressions of the witness' demeanor and the witnesses' strong and weak points as related to the presentation of the case.

(e) a memo from the client's files dated before the incident from which the litigation arose that describes the unsafe mechanical condition of the truck that was involved in the collision. The client sent you the memo because the client considers it to be a potential "smoking gun" if it is found by the opposing side.

(f) your investigator's memo to you that specifies the length of the skid marks on the street where the crash occurred, and measurements and a description of damage done to the client's truck that was involved in the accident. Photographs, repair records for the truck, and hospital records from the driver's visit to the emergency room (which include the nurse's notes stating that your client kept saying, "I'm sorry. It was all my fault.") are attached. The truck has since been demolished.

(g) billing information in the matter, including time spent, date, and task description information.

---

2. *Discovery of Privileged Material; Need and Hardship; Exception, Waiver*

Read Rules 193.3(d); TRE 503(d)(1), 511, 512, 612

In re BEXAR COUNTY CRIMINAL DISTRICT ATTORNEY'S OFFICE

224 S.W.3d 182
(Tex. 2007)

JUSTICE WILLETT delivered the opinion of the Court, in which JUSTICE HECHT, JUSTICE O'NEILL, JUSTICE WAINWRIGHT, and JUSTICE BRISTER joined.

This case presents an issue of first impression: whether the work-product privilege protects prosecutors from testifying in a malicious prosecution suit when they have already released the prosecution file. Relator Bexar County Criminal District Attorney's Office ("DA" or "DA's Office") provided its prosecution file to real party in interest David Crudup, who had sued relator Cynthia Blank for malicious prosecution. Crudup subpoenaed DA representatives to testify, but the trial court granted the DA's Motion to Quash and For Protective Order. The court of appeals disagreed and ordered the trial court to withdraw its order.[1] The DA's Office and Blank now seek mandamus relief in this Court, and given the record and circumstances presented, we conditionally grant it.

I. Factual and Procedural Background

David Crudup and his wife were feuding neighbors of Cynthia Blank and her teenage son Travis. The Crudups and the Blanks complained repeatedly about each other to the Bexar County Sheriff's Office regarding such incivilities as barking dogs, obscenities yelled, cut cable lines, strewn grass clippings, trash left in a yard, rocks thrown at a fence, water sprayed on cars and grass, and a sprinkler that ran too long and created a puddle. Each time, the responding officer would talk to both sides and prepare an incident report.

On one occasion, Travis Blank alleged that Crudup threatened to kill him. Following this complaint, the DA charged Crudup with making terroristic threats.[2] During their investigation, members of the DA's Office interviewed Blank on several occasions. The DA's prosecution file contains sheriff's department reports, typed internal memos, letters written by Blank, and handwritten notes from interviews and telephone calls prepared by the DA's office. One set of notes detailed a series of calls between Blank and Assistant DA Robert McCabe. The file indicates that Blank refused to testify or to allow Travis to testify at trial, despite McCabe's warnings that the DA's Office would drop the charges against Crudup if they did not testify.

The DA's Office indeed dropped the charges, and Crudup sued the Blanks for malicious prosecution. The DA's Office complied with a subpoena duces tecum and turned over its prosecution file to Crudup for use in the civil case. Crudup subpoenaed McCabe, another assistant DA, and a DA investigator to testify at trial. The DA's Office and the three subpoenaed individuals filed a Motion to Quash and For Protective Order, arguing that the work-product privilege precluded the testimony Crudup sought. Crudup's response attached no evidentiary

---

[1] 179 S.W.3d 47, 51.

[2] This crime ranges from a Class B misdemeanor to a state jail felony depending upon the circumstances of the threat. *See* Tex. Penal Code § 22.07.

support other than the previously produced prosecution file. Crudup insisted the DA testimony was not work product, and in any event the DA had waived any privilege claim by disclosing the prosecution file. The trial court conducted a brief non-evidentiary hearing and granted the DA's motion from the bench. At the hearing, Crudup's counsel complained, without elaboration, that the court had "damaged my case" and "severely limited and handicapped my case." Crudup filed a motion for reconsideration, attaching a transcript of the hearing and arguing that he needed the testimony from the DA personnel "to fully develop" his case and to prove the elements of malicious prosecution. The motion also attached notes from the prosecution file written by McCabe, and purporting to "state the reasons" and "describe the reason" the criminal case was dismissed. The trial court entered a written order again granting the DA's motion and effectively denying the motion for reconsideration.

The court of appeals granted Crudup mandamus relief and directed the trial court to withdraw its order. The court of appeals concluded that under *King v. Graham*[3] Crudup must prove that Blank's provision of false information was the determining factor in the DA's decision to bring the criminal prosecution, and that "[u]nder these circumstances the work-product privilege does not operate as a blanket privilege covering all decisions made by the DA's office." The DA now seeks mandamus relief in this Court.

II. Discussion

* * *

B. The King Decision Does Not Mandate DA Testimony

Causation is an indispensable element of this malicious prosecution case. As we explained in *King*, "to recover for malicious prosecution when the decision to prosecute is within another's discretion, the plaintiff has the burden of proving that that decision would not have been made but for the false information supplied by the defendant." So Crudup must prove not only that the Blanks furnished false information, but also that this false information caused Crudup to be prosecuted.

* * *

Our reference to the district attorney's testimony in *King*, however, did not announce a blanket privilege waiver or authorize plaintiffs to subpoena prosecutors to testify whenever plaintiffs wish to bolster the causation element of their malicious prosecution lawsuit.

C. Crudup Cannot Overcome the DA's Testimonial Privilege

* * *

In the pending case, all of the DA's Office's work in connection with the criminal proceeding against Crudup, and relevant to the decision to bring criminal charges against him, constitutes work product, namely "material prepared or mental impressions developed in anticipation of litigation or for trial" or communications "made in anticipation of litigation or for trial . . . among a party's representatives" under Rule 192.5(a). The totality of the DA's work on the Crudup matter, as evidenced by the prosecution file, consisted of the preparation of a criminal charge against Crudup and the criminal litigation that followed. The trial court record indicates that Crudup was not interested in eliciting general factual testimony from DA witnesses regarding how the DA's Office receives, processes, and investigates criminal complaints. Crudup only subpoenaed DA employees who had been directly involved with his criminal case to testify in the civil case. He informed the district court, in his response to the Motion to Quash and For

[3] 126 S.W.3d 75 (Tex. 2003) (per curiam).

Protective Order, that he was interested in their testimony because "[t]he DA's office had numerous conversations with Defendant Cindy and because of these conversations they are fact witnesses to the statements made by Defendant Cindy." He stated in his motion for reconsideration that he needed the testimony in order to "present evidence of the conduct of the Defendants before the criminal case was initiated" and also "to present evidence of the conduct of the Defendants during the course of the criminal proceedings, especially as to the reason of the dismissal of the criminal case." In his briefing to this Court, he stresses that without DA testimony, he cannot prove the specific elements of malicious prosecution.

For purposes of his civil case, conversations made in the course of the criminal investigation, information learned during that investigation, and the DA's decision to drop the case all constitute work product as defined above, and while producing the prosecution file unquestionably waived protection of the documents themselves, that selective disclosure does not oblige DA staff to provide deposition and trial testimony interpreting, explaining, or otherwise elaborating on matters contained in the file. The dissent notes that Crudup may well want to quiz DA staff about various matters unrelated to the specifics of the prosecution against him: "testimony as to general procedures such as procedures of the DA's office for intake of criminal complaints, processing of those complaints, whether investigation is made into the facts of cases before criminal proceedings are instituted, and whether contacts are typically made with complaining witnesses before criminal proceedings are begun, during the proceedings, or after the proceedings are completed." Crudup, however, has never expressed the slightest interest in such general matters, which might well be fair game; the record and his briefs to this Court show him focused solely on eliciting DA testimony regarding the specific events surrounding his criminal case and insisting that without such case-specific details, "he will not be able to prove every element of malicious prosecution."

Rule 192.5(b)(1) distinguishes everyday work product from "core work product" and makes clear that the latter-defined as "the attorney's or the attorney's representative's mental impressions, opinions, conclusions, or legal theories"—is inviolate and flatly "not discoverable," subject to narrow exceptions that are inapplicable here. Core work product is sacrosanct and its protection impermeable. Assuming arguendo that the testimony Crudup seeks is non-core work product, which seems doubtful, Crudup still bears a heavy burden: he must show that he "has substantial need" for the testimony in the preparation of his case and that he "is unable without undue hardship to obtain the substantial equivalent of the material by other means."[22]

The court of appeals said it granted mandamus relief because "the DA's office has failed to meet its burden of showing any basis to quash the subpoenas." This misses the mark. In the record, briefing, and oral argument, Crudup continued to demonstrate his intention to interrogate the DAs about case-specific details. Such testimony would unquestionably require the disclosure of DA work product, which, at a minimum, places the burden on Crudup to show a "substantial need" for the testimony and the inability to obtain its substantial equivalent by other means without "undue hardship."

Addressing the first prong, "substantial need," Crudup contends that he "will not be able to prove an element of his case" (namely, causation) without testimony from the prosecutors. To be sure, granting Crudup access to live DA testimony might improve his chances in court, but improving a civil litigant's odds of winning is not enough. Substantial need is not merely substantial desire. Prosecutors could win more convictions absent the Fifth Amendment, or the priest-penitent privilege, or the marital privilege, but we safeguard these privileges and others

[22] TEX.R. CIV. P. 192.5(b)(2).

because they advance a greater societal good. Like every litigant, Crudup wants to strengthen his lawsuit, understandably so, but that cannot trump a settled privilege and justify a wide-ranging excavation of prosecutorial decision-making.

The second prong is inability to obtain the substantial equivalent of the requested material. As stated above, Crudup cannot win his malicious prosecution suit without showing that false information supplied by the Blanks to the DA's Office caused the DA to prosecute. The DA's Office, however, has already provided Crudup with the substantial equivalent of testimony: it has, pursuant to a subpoena duces tecum, turned over its entire prosecution file, which contains notes related to the investigation, sheriff's department complaint reports, Travis Blank's affidavit to the sheriff's department detailing Crudup's alleged threat, and McCabe's log of conversations with Cynthia Blank that ultimately prompted him to dismiss the criminal charges. Many if not all of these documents might come into evidence either through a non-hearsay use or as an exception to hearsay.[25] Any false statements made by the Blanks to the DA, for example, would not constitute hearsay if offered for their effect on the listener rather than for the truth of the matter asserted.[26] And Crudup has already taken a deposition on written questions of the DA's custodian of records in order to establish that the prosecution file contains records of a regularly conducted activity under Rule 803(6). Crudup is not required to produce live testimony from a prosecutor, and he might well be able to prove his case through alternative means, including (1) circumstantial evidence, (2) trial testimony and pretrial discovery from the Blanks, and (3) expert testimony on prosecutorial decision-making and whether the file suggests the DA would not have charged Crudup but for the allegedly false information. Rule 192.5 strikes a sensible balance, recognizing that a lawyer's thoughts are his own and that a party cannot invade every nook and cranny of a lawyer's case preparation, particularly when the "essence" of what the party seeks has already been revealed to him or is readily available. Indeed, while insisting he needs live testimony to prove Blank's malice, Crudup's brief concedes that the prosecution file contains all the evidence he needs: "The notes of District Attorney McCabe clearly indicate the malice of Cynthia Blank."

Understandably, Crudup desires live testimony to fortify his case, but Rule 192.5(b)(2) is not nearly so permissive. Even assuming the testimony sought is non-core work product, Crudup's burden of showing causation in his malicious prosecution suit is insufficient to constitute "substantial need." Nor has Crudup shown an inability to obtain the substantial equivalent of the testimony sought without "undue hardship." If anything, when it comes to affecting Crudup's burdens at trial, the DA's disclosure of its prosecution file did more to alleviate than to aggravate.

D. The DA Has Not Consented to Testify by Producing the File

Crudup alternatively argues that the DA waived the privilege under Texas Rule of Evidence 511(1) and cannot resist testifying. Again, we disagree. Rule 511(1) provides that a person waives a privilege against disclosure if he "voluntarily discloses or consents to disclosure of any significant part of the privileged matter . . . ." Although the DA's Office turned over its prosecution file without objection, which waived the work-product privilege as to the file's contents, the record is devoid of any indication that by doing so the DA likewise enlisted its current and former personnel to testify in Crudup's malicious prosecution suit regarding their case materials and related impressions and communications. The DA's waiver here is limited, not

---

[25] *See* TEX.R. EVID. 801(e)(2) (admission by party-opponent); *id.* 803(6) (records of regularly conducted activity); *id.* 803(8)(A), (C) (public records and reports).

[26] *See id.* 801(d).

limitless, and agreeing to produce a prosecution file does not in itself require the DA to produce its personnel so that their mental processes and related case preparation may be further probed.

We therefore hold on this record, given the protected nature of what Crudup intends to elicit, that the DA's selective disclosure of the prosecution file, while waiving the privilege as to the documents themselves, does not waive the DA's testimonial work-product privilege regarding the prosecutor's mental processes; nor did the DA's file disclosure itself give rise to a "substantial need" or "undue hardship" sufficient to overcome the privilege that protects non-core work product.

III. Conclusion

Direct prosecutor testimony is not required to prove causation and malice in malicious prosecution suits. Nor, on this record, did the DA's Office waive its work-product privilege against testifying by producing the prosecution file. Given the nature of what Crudup seeks and his inability to show both "substantial need" and "undue hardship" under Rule 192.5(b)(2), he cannot force DA personnel to discuss their mental processes or other case-related communications and preparation, even if the subpoenaed testimony relates to documents already produced.

We conditionally grant the petition for writ of mandamus and direct the court of appeals to vacate its writ of mandamus and to reinstate the trial court order quashing the subpoenas and issuing a protective order.[28] The writ will issue only if the court of appeals fails to comply.

JUSTICE WILLETT delivered a concurring opinion, omitted.

JUSTICE GREEN did not participate in the decision.

JUSTICE JOHNSON, joined by CHIEF JUSTICE JEFFERSON and JUSTICE MEDINA, dissenting.

The trial court quashed trial subpoenas and granted a protective order shortly before trial was scheduled to start in a malicious prosecution case, effectively excluding all testimony from current and former employees of the Bexar County Criminal District Attorney's office who participated in prosecuting the underlying criminal case. The trial court's action was based on an unsworn "Motion to Quash Trial Subpoenas and For Protective Order" filed by the DA's office and argued by the parties without testimony or evidence. I agree with the court of appeals that based on this record the trial court abused its discretion in quashing the subpoenas.

* * *

First, in the case before us the file was produced over a year before the DA filed the motion to quash. The subpoena duces tecum pursuant to which the Bexar County DA's office produced its file in 2003 required the production of all records relating to, and the case file for, the prosecution of David Crudup. The testimony of the assistant DA in response to the subpoena was that all the requested records had been produced. To the extent that the DA's work product was disclosed by documents, notes, trial preparatory memoranda, organization of the case file or in any other way by the file, the privilege was waived long before the DA's motion was filed in February 2005. *See* TEX.R. EVID. 511(1).

Second, the objects of the DA's motion to quash were witnesses. The work product privilege precludes testimony or discovery as to types of information; it does not make persons privileged from testifying. Witnesses are not the same as documents. Documents have fixed contents that can be analyzed to determine whether the documents and their contents are privileged. But the full knowledge of a witness as to facts and matters relevant to claims made in a lawsuit can hardly

---

28 *See* TEX.R.APP. P. 52.8(c).

ever be known, and the testimony of a witness is not fixed until after the witness has completed testifying. It is only while witnesses are testifying or after they have testified that the admissibility or privileged nature of their testimony can be determined. Witnesses occasionally are instructed, upon timely and proper motion, not to answer certain questions because the questions seek testimony as to matters which are privileged or are otherwise inadmissible. But if the questions are rephrased the witnesses then may sometimes be allowed to answer. Lawyers may be instructed not to ask witnesses about certain matters, such as privileged work product, but that does not preclude lawyers from asking, and witnesses from testifying about, other matters. For example, testimony as to general procedures such as procedures of the DA's office for intake of criminal complaints, processing of those complaints, whether investigation is made into the facts of cases before criminal proceedings are instituted, and whether contacts are typically made with complaining witnesses before criminal proceedings are begun, during the proceedings, or after the proceedings are completed would not be work product as to the Crudup prosecution. Yet such testimony was encompassed by the DA's motion and is precluded by the trial court's order.

* * *

Furthermore, to the extent a work product privilege exists, it can be waived. Texas rules and practice are in accord. If a privilege applies, it is waived if the "person or a predecessor of the person while holder of the privilege voluntarily discloses or consents to disclosure of any significant part of the privileged matter unless such disclosure is itself privileged." TEX.R. EVID. 511(1).

In disputes such as this, the burden of proceeding and producing evidence must be on one of the parties. The trial court effectively placed the burden on the Crudups to show why the DA's attorneys and employees should be required to testify and what information or facts would be elicited from them. That is different from the placement of the burden by Texas Rule of Evidence 501 and our prior cases. We have previously required the party resisting testifying or having its employees testify to shoulder the burden of properly asserting a privilege and showing that it applied to the testimony in question. . . . Because this record is clear that the DA did not make any such showing, the DA's employees were not entitled by law or rule to refuse to be witnesses and testify, even if some testimony as to their knowledge, information, and mental processes was later properly excluded upon objection. TEX.R. EVID. 501(1), (2); 511(1). Nor was the DA's office entitled to prevent its employees from being witnesses and testifying absent such showing. TEX.R. EVID. 501(4).

The Court concludes that conversations between the DA's office and Blank during the course of the criminal charge investigation were work product. But Blank was a non-party to the criminal proceeding and was not an employee of the state. The DA's office did not offer any proof that more conversations between Blank and DA employees took place than were memorialized by the DA's file. Apart from information disclosed by notes in the DA's file, for which the privilege had been waived by disclosure, the content of statements made by Blank to the DA's employees, if any, might be work product. *See* TEX.R. CIV. P. 192.3(h). But even in the absence of a record showing there were more conversations between Blank and the employees than are disclosed in the DA's file and assuming there were, statements made by the DA's employees to Blank arguably, if not conclusively, were not privileged. The DA's office did not show that any conversations between its employees and Blank not memorialized in its litigation file included work product, that is, either (1) material prepared by the DA's office or its employees for, or mental impressions of its employees developed in anticipation of, the criminal trial; or (2) communications made in preparation for the criminal trial between a party and the party's representatives. *See* TEX.R. CIV. P. 192.5(a). If the DA's employee's statements to Blank did not include work product, the statements were not privileged to start with. If the statements to Blank disclosed work product, the privilege as to the material disclosed was presumptively waived and the DA would have had the burden to prove or show why the conversations did not effect a waiver of privilege as to the disclosed matters. *See* TEX.R. EVID. 511(1); And, to the extent that documents memorializing the conversations had been produced and the privilege as to their contents thereby waived, the DA's employees had no privilege to refuse to testify about them. *See* TEX.R. EVID. 501.

Because the Crudups' response raised the question of disclosure of the DA's work product both by disclosure of the DA's litigation file and by its employees' conversations with Blank, the question of waiver of privilege was raised and the DA had the burden of proving that no waiver occurred. . . . As previously noted, the DA was representing the State in the criminal proceeding against David Crudup; Blank was neither a party to the proceeding nor an employee of the state; and the DA did not prove any reason that the content of its employees' conversations with such a non-party witness was privileged work product. If the DA's employees disclosed work product to Blank in the conversations or by disclosure of the file and if either disclosure was significant, then waiver may have occurred as to more of the DA's work product than just the amount disclosed. *See* TEX.R. EVID. 511(1). Intuitively, one could speculate that there remained some of the DA's work product for which the privilege had not been waived. But speculation is not sufficient: proof is required.

In their motion for reconsideration of the trial court's order, the Crudups attached and quoted individual notes from the DA's file setting out the contents of a conversation between Blank and the assistant DA handling the prosecution. They again urged that the contents of notes reflecting conversations were a proper subject of testimony from the subpoenaed witnesses. The DA's office still did not attempt to show authority for or offer evidence to support its employees being exempt from giving testimony as to contents of the notes. The trial court denied the Crudups' motion to reconsider.

The quashing of subpoenas by the trial court on this record turned the procedure for protecting privileged work product upside down. Instead of the DA having to show why its employees who had knowledge of relevant matters should be protected from testifying, the Crudups' attorney had to try to preserve his clients' right to call witnesses by disclosing his work product in pleadings and argument in the trial court and setting out testimony he wanted to elicit from the subpoenaed employees. He has had to continue that course through two appellate court proceedings.

* * *

The Crudups' counsel has maintained that he planned to prove that the complaint made by the Blanks to the DA was false and that the DA would not have filed the criminal proceedings absent the false complaint. Maybe he can; maybe he can't. But counsel was entitled to formulate and pursue trial strategy without having it limited by a preemptive exclusion of certain witnesses with knowledge of relevant matters or having to disclose his strategy and justify it in pretrial and appellate proceedings simply because the DA's office filed a motion such as the one it filed.

I would deny the relief sought by the DA's office.

Notes & Questions

1. *Voluntary Disclosure*. Rule 511 of the Texas Rules of Evidence provides that a person waives a privilege if the privileged matter is voluntarily disclosed. For example, in one case there was evidence that investigation materials had been disclosed to the Wall Street Journal, the FBI and the IRS—the Supreme Court held that the trial court did not abuse its discretion in finding that any privilege was waived.[1] Note, however, if materials are voluntarily, but inadvertently produced in discovery, the privilege may not be waived, pursuant to Rule 193.3(d), which was adopted in 1999.[2] 2015 amendments to Texas Rule of Evidence 511 further refined the privilege-waiver doctrines in Texas. First, the scope of a privilege waiver in a state or federal proceeding does not extend to undisclosed (but implicitly revealed) information unless the waiver is intentional, the information disclosed concerns the same subject matter as the undisclosed communication, and they ought, in fairness, be considered together.[3] Second, the principle of 193.3(d) (inadvertent disclosure in a state proceeding, often in discovery) does not waive a privilege if the holder follows Rule 193.3's provisions.[4] Third, disclosure made pursuant to a court order that states that the privilege is not waived by disclosure in that particular case is not a waiver in a Texas state court proceeding.[5] The intent of the Rule 511 amendments was to bring Texas privilege-waiver practice in line with federal practice.

2. *Crime-fraud Exception*. The attorney client and work product privileges do not apply if the lawyer's services "were sought or obtained to enable or aid anyone to commit or plan to commit with the client knew or reasonably should have known to be a crime or fraud."[6] The crime-fraud exception applies if there is prima facie proof of a crime or fraud, and if there is a relationship between the matter for which the privilege is challenged and the prima facie proof offered.[7]

3. *Refreshing recollection.* Pursuant to TRE 612, a privilege also can be waived by using a privileged writing to refresh recollection. In *Goode v. Shoukfeh*,[8] the Supreme Court applied the rule to an attorney's notes taken during voir dire, which the opponent sought during the *Batson* hearing challenging the attorney's exercise of peremptory challenges. The court held that the notes were clearly the attorney's work product, but continued:

> We hold that [a *Batson*] movant has the right to examine the voir dire notes of the opponent's attorney when the attorney relies upon these notes while giving sworn or unsworn testimony in the [*Batson*] hearing. Absent such reliance, the voir dire notes are privileged work product, and the movant may not examine them. In this case, Goode does

---

1 Axelson v. McElhanney, 798 S.W.2d 550 (Tex. 1990).

2 The Supreme Court explored the non-waiver provision in an opinion concerning expert witnesses, In re Christus Spohn Hosp. Kleburg, 222 S.W.3d 434, 440-41 (Tex. 2007), which we will read in that section of this book.

3 *See* TRE 511(b).

4 *See id.*

5 *See id.*

6 TRE 503(d)(1); TRCP 192.5(c)(5).

7 Granada Corp. v. The Honorable First Court of Appeals, 844 S.W.2d 223 (Tex. 1993).

8 943 S.W.2d 441, 449 (Tex. 1997).

> not allege that Shoukfeh's attorneys relied upon their notes during the [*Batson*] hearing, but merely claims that the notes contain evidence of the attorneys' allegedly race-based decisions. Accordingly, the notes are privileged, and the trial court properly ruled that Goode could not examine them.

4. *Waiver by offensive use.* A privilege can also be waived by offensive use—"a plaintiff who is seeking affirmative relief should not be permitted to maintain the action, and at the same time maintain evidentiary privileges that protect from discovery outcome determinative information not otherwise available to the defendant."[9] The basic principal is that a privilege should be a shield, not a sword—privilege cannot protect information that goes the heart of a cause of action asserted by the very party that simultaneously asserts the privilege. This operates as a kind of extreme "need and hardship" exception to privileges that operates in favor of defendants.

The Supreme Court first recognized waiver by offensive use in *Ginsberg v. Fifth Court of Appeals*.[10] There, the Court said: "[a] plaintiff cannot use one hand to seek affirmative relief in court and with the other lower an iron curtain of silence against otherwise pertinent and proper questions which may have a bearing upon his right to maintain his action." *Ginsberg* was a trespass to try title suit where a woman sought to establish ownership of a piece of Padre Island property against a man who claimed ownership via a deed signed by her husband, and another that she signed after his death ratifying the sale. She claimed she knew nothing of the property transfer and that the deed she allegedly signed was forged. Her psychiatrist's records, however, showed that she did know of the sale, but she sought to protect them under the physician-patient privilege. The Supreme Court held that she could either "waive her psychotherapist privilege and pursue her claim for affirmative relief or maintain her privilege and abandon her cause of action."[11]

Later the Court classified offensive use waiver as a type of sanction, and refined its application, as follows:[12]

> This Court has defined three elements necessary to conclude whether an offensive use of an evidentiary privilege is occurring:
>
> A. a party must be seeking affirmative relief;
>
> B. the party is using a privilege to protect outcome determinative information;
>
> C. the protected information is not otherwise available to the defendant.
>
> These steps identify situations where it would be unfair to allow a party to both seek relief and deny to the defense essential evidence. Once an offensive use is shown, alternative steps follow which define the courses of action a trial court may then take: Upon a finding of offensive use, the plaintiff either 1. waives the privilege or 2. risks sanction from the trial court.

Application of the doctrine has been quite restrictive. For example, in *National Union Fire Ins. v. Valdez,*[13] the Court held that a defendant's proffer of a lawyer's affidavit filed to controvert

---

[9] Tex. Dep't of Pub. Safety Officers Ass'n v. Denton, 897 S.W.2d 757, 761 (Tex. 1995).

[10] 686 S.W.2d 105 (Tex. 1985).

[11] Republic Nat'l Ins. Co. v. Davis, 856 S.W.2d 158, 161 (Tex. 1993).

[12] Dep't of Pub. Safety Officers Ass'n v. Denton, 897 S.W.2d 757, 761 (Tex. 1995). *But cf.* In re M-I L.L.C., 505 S.W.3d 569, 579 (Tex. 2016) (holding that offensive-use doctrine applies to discovery, not temporary injunction hearing).

[13] 863 S.W.2d 458, 461-62 (Tex. 1993).

the plaintiff's motion for summary judgment did not constitute offensive use waiving the work product privilege because the party "relied on information in the law firm's file only to avoid [the plaintiff's] claims. The [defendant's] assertion . . . is not even an affirmative defense, but is merely a rebuttal to the [plaintiff's] . . . cause of action."

The Court has also clarified that if the party persists in claiming the privilege, dismissing the case is not always the appropriate sanction. As we will later learn, a court may dismiss a case as a sanction only under certain circumstances set out in *Transamerican v. Powell*.[14]

The doctrine appears to apply to all types of privileges. The Court has applied it to the attorney-client privilege (which was not waived because the party claiming the privilege was not seeking affirmative relieve)[15] and the Fifth Amendment privilege against incrimination (which was being used offensively, but remanded to determine the appropriate sanction under the circumstances).[16]

5. *Exception to health care provider privileges.* In *R.K. v. Ramirez,*[17] the Texas Supreme Court compared the offensive use doctrine with the express exception to the physician-patient privilege of TRE 509 and the mental health privilege of TRE 510 for a "communication or record relevant to an issue of the physical, mental, or emotional condition of a patient in any proceeding in which any party relies upon the condition as a part of the party's claim or defense."[18] The Court concluded that this exception was not limited, as the offensive use doctrine is, to parties seeking affirmative relief. Instead, the exceptions apply "(1) when the records sought to be discovered are relevant to the conditions at issue, and (2) the condition is relied upon as a part of a party's claim or defense, meaning that the condition itself is a fact that carries some legal significance." In the case before the court, the plaintiffs alleged in their pleadings that the defendant physician's medical and mental problems (including depression and drug usage) affected his ability to care for the plaintiff, and that the clinic and hospital's selection of such an "unfit and incompetent" person caused the plaintiff's damages. Therefore, the court concluded the exception was invoked. Nevertheless, the court cautioned that the trial court has a heavy responsibility to prevent any disclosure of such highly sensitive documents that is broader than necessary.

6. *Failure to preserve privilege.* Privileges are perhaps most easily waived by a party's failure to assert the privilege properly, which we will examine in the next chapter.

7. *Disqualification when obtain opponent's privileged materials.* What happens if one lawyer obtains copies of the opponent's privileged documents outside the normal course of discovery? For example, what if your client secretly removed documents from the opponent's offices and gives them to you? This happened in *In re Meador*[19] and the defendants claimed that the plaintiff's lawyer should be disqualified. The Supreme Court held that "the trial court, after giving due consideration to the importance of the discovery privileges, must consider all the facts and circumstances to determine whether the interest of justice require disqualification."[20] The court identified six factors for the court to consider:

---

[14] 811 S.W.2d 913 (Tex. 1991).

[15] Republic Nat'l Ins. Co. v. Davis, 856 S.W.2d 158 (Tex. 1993).

[16] Dep't of Pub. Safety Officers Ass'n v. Denton, 897 S.W.2d 757 (Tex. 1995).

[17] 887 S.W.2d 836 (Tex. 1994, orig. proceeding).

[18] TRE 510(d)(5).

[19] 968 S.W.2d 346 (Tex. 1998).

[20] *Id.* at 351.

1) whether the attorney knew or should have known that the material was privileged;

2) the promptness with which the attorney notifies the opposing side that he or she has received its privileged information;

3) the extent to which the attorney reviews and digests the privileged information;

4) the significance of the privileged information; i.e., the extent to which its disclosure may prejudice the movant's claim or defense, and the extent to which return of the documents will mitigate that prejudice;

5) the extent to which movant may be at fault for the unauthorized disclosure;

6) the extent to which the nonmovant will suffer prejudice from the disqualification of his or her attorney.[21]

In *Meador* the court held that the trial court did not abuse its discretion in refusing to disqualify the plaintiff's lawyer.

The court again applied the *Meador* standards in *In re NITLA S.A. de C.V.*[22] There the court held that the trial court did not abuse its discretion in refusing to disqualify a lawyer who had received privileged documents from a judge after the judge ruled (erroneously) that the documents were not privileged.

---

3. *Trade Secrets*

Read TRE 507.

Litigation often involves corporations that depend on maintaining the exclusivity of their research, products, or processes. Texas Rule of Evidence 507 provides a qualified privilege for such "trade secrets" in an attempt to "foster technological innovation and advances in business practices while accommodating the needs of litigants."[1] The rule does not define trade secrets but is generally interpreted by courts as encompassing any information that gives its owner an improved competitive position and whose value is substantially enhanced by secrecy.[2] Specifically, the Texas Supreme Court has applied a six-factor test to determine the existence of a trade secret in *In re Bass*:

> (1) the extent to which the information is known outside of his business; (2) the extent to which it is known by employees and others involved in his business; (3) the extent of the measures taken by him to guard the secrecy of the information; (4) the value of the information to him and to his competitors; (5) the amount of effort or money expended by him in developing the information; (6) the ease or difficulty with which the information could be properly acquired or duplicated by others.[3]

---

21 *Id.* at 351-52.

22 92 S.W.3d 419 (Tex. 2002).

1 STEVEN E. GOODE ET AL., TEXAS PRACTICE: COURTROOM HANDBOOK ON TEXAS EVIDENCE, Ch. 5 (1999).

2 *Id.* at 333.

3 In re Bass, 113 S.W.3d 735, 739 (Tex. 2003).

According to the Court, litigants need not satisfy every factor to establish the existence of a trade secret, and courts may take circumstances not pertinent to any factor into consideration as well.[4]

In 2013, the legislature spoke on the definition of "trade secret" when it adopted the Texas Uniform Trade Secrets Act.[5] But that definition has not disrupted courts' application of the six-factor test in the context of Rule 507.[6]

But even if information qualifies as a trade secret, Rule 507's protection is not absolute—the trade secret privilege is qualified, and the next case lays out the framework for a requesting party to overcome it.

In re CONTINENTAL GENERAL TIRE, INC.

979 S.W. 2d 609
(Tex. 1998)

CHIEF JUSTICE PHILLIPS delivered the opinion of the Court, in which JUSTICE GONZALEZ, JUSTICE HECHT, JUSTICE ENOCH, JUSTICE SPECTOR, JUSTICE OWEN, JUSTICE BAKER, and JUSTICE ABBOTT join.

JUSTICE HANKINSON did not participate in the decision.

Under our rules of evidence, a party has a privilege to refuse to disclose its trade secrets "if the allowance of the privilege will not tend to conceal fraud or otherwise work injustice." *See* TEX. R. EVID. 507. The issue is whether Rule 507 protects from discovery a tire manufacturer's chemical formula for its "skim stock," a rubber compound used in tire manufacturing. The trial court ordered the manufacturer to produce the formula under a protective order, and the court of appeals denied the manufacturer's requested mandamus relief without opinion. We hold that, when a party resisting discovery establishes that the requested information is a trade secret under Rule 507, the burden shifts to the requesting party to establish that the information is necessary for a fair adjudication of its claim or defense. Because relator established that the formula was a trade secret, and because the real party in interest did not meet its burden of establishing necessity, we conditionally grant mandamus relief. Nothing in the relief we grant prohibits plaintiffs from seeking to discover the formula under the procedure we set forth.

I

While Kenneth Fisher was driving his pick-up truck on Highway 190, his left front tire blew out, causing him to lose control of the vehicle. Fisher's truck crossed the median and struck Dora Pratt's car, killing Pratt and her passenger. Pratt's heirs, Luz Enid Rivera, Brenda Beatriz Killens, Gilberto DeJesus Cruz, Dora Maria Cruz, and Toribio Nieves, filed the underlying products liability action against Continental General Tire, the manufacturer of the failed tire.

It is undisputed that the tire failed because its tread and outer belt separated from the inner belt. The belts are made from brass-coated steel cords encased in a skim-stock rubber compound.

---

4 *See id.* at_740.

5 *See* CPRC 134A.002(6).

6 *See, e.g.*, In re Michelin N. Am., Inc., No. 05-15-01480-CV, 2016 WL 890970, at *5 (Tex. App.—Dallas Mar. 9, 2016).

These belts, along with the other tire components, are assembled into a "green tire," to which heat and pressure are applied in a process called "vulcanization." This process causes the components in the tire, including the skim stock, to chemically bond with each other. Plaintiffs contend that either a design or manufacturing defect in the skim stock prevented the belts of Fisher's tire from properly bonding. To secure evidence to prove this claim, plaintiffs requested Continental to produce the chemical formula for the skim stock used on this tire.

Continental objected, claiming that the formula is a trade secret that Texas Rule of Evidence 507 protects. After a hearing, the trial court ordered Continental to produce the formula, subject to a protective order which the trial court had earlier entered for other confidential material produced by Continental.

The trial court stayed its order pending Continental's efforts to obtain mandamus review. After the court of appeals denied relief, we granted Continental's mandamus petition and heard oral argument.

II

Continental claims that the skim-stock formula is protected by Texas Rule of Evidence 507, which provides in full:

> A person has a privilege, which may be claimed by the person or the person's agent or employee, to refuse to disclose and to prevent other persons from disclosing a trade secret owned by the person, if the allowance of the privilege will not tend to conceal fraud or otherwise work injustice. When disclosure is directed, the judge shall take such protective measure as the interests of the holder of the privilege and of the parties and the furtherance of justice may require.
>
> TEX. R. EVID. 507.

* * *

III

Our trade secret privilege seeks to accommodate two competing interests. First, it recognizes that trade secrets are an important property interest, worthy of protection. Second, it recognizes the importance we place on fair adjudication of lawsuits. Rule 507 accommodates both interests by requiring a party to disclose a trade secret only if necessary to prevent "fraud" or "injustice." Stated alternatively, disclosure is required only if necessary for a fair adjudication of the requesting party's claims or defenses.

We therefore hold that trial courts should apply Rule 507 as follows: First, the party resisting discovery must establish that the information is a trade secret. The burden then shifts to the requesting party to establish that the information is necessary for a fair adjudication of its claims. If the requesting party meets this burden, the trial court should ordinarily compel disclosure of the information, subject to an appropriate protective order.[3] In each circumstance, the trial court must weigh the degree of the requesting party's need for the information with the potential harm of disclosure to the resisting party.

---

[3] In this case, for example, the trial court limited access to the information to the parties in this lawsuit, their lawyers, consultants, investigators, experts and other necessary persons employed by counsel to assist in the preparation and trial of this case. Each person who is given access to the documents must agree in writing to keep the information confidential, and all documents must be returned to Continental at the conclusion of the case.

IV

Before applying Rule 507 to the facts of this case, we consider various arguments the parties and amicus curiae raise.

A

Plaintiffs first argue that our decision in *Jampole v. Touchy*, 673 S.W.2d 569 (Tex. 1984), . . . require[s] Continental to produce the skim-stock formula. In *Jampole*, a products liability defendant objected to producing its assembly diagrams and instructions, contending that the documents were trade secrets. After the trial court denied discovery, this Court granted conditional mandamus relief compelling production. The Court reasoned:

> Although a valid proprietary interest may justify denying or limiting discovery requested by a direct competitor, this is not such a case. Jampole is not [the defendant's] business competitor, and [the defendant] acknowledged that, if the documents were relevant, any proprietary interest could be safeguarded by a protective order. Under these circumstances, it was an abuse of discretion for the trial court to deny discovery of the assembly documents. We do not decide whether [the defendant] has shown a sufficient proprietary interest to justify a protective order. We hold that discovery cannot be denied because of an asserted proprietary interest in the requested documents *when a protective order would sufficiently preserve that interest*.

According to plaintiffs, *Jampole* stands for the proposition that, in actions that are not between business competitors, the trial court should always require production of relevant trade secrets, subject to an appropriate protective order. This approach, however, would render the Rule 507 privilege meaningless in noncompetitor cases. Notably, the Court in *Jampole* did not consider Rule 507's effect, presumably because the defendant acknowledged that "any proprietary interest could be safeguarded by a protective order." *Jampole* thus cannot be read as limiting the privilege's scope.

* * *

Next, plaintiffs argue that a party requesting trade secret documents in a products liability case must show only that the information is relevant to the suit. However, because relevance is the standard for discovery in general, *see* TEX. R. CIV. P. 166b(2)(a), this approach likewise would render Rule 507 meaningless. Rule 507 clearly contemplates a heightened burden for obtaining trade secret information.

* * *

B

Continental and amicus curiae Product Liability Advisory Council present three other arguments about why production is not required in this case.

Continental first argues that, in general, a protective order can never adequately protect a sensitive trade secret because there is always the risk that the receiving party will either deliberately or inadvertently disclose the information. For example, Continental argues that if Robert Ochs, the plaintiffs' expert witness, learns the skim-stock formula, he will be more in demand as an expert witness in other cases, creating incentive for him to disclose the formula. Continental appears to be arguing that the risk of disclosure justifies an absolute trade secret privilege. However, Rule 507 does not support such an approach. It requires production if necessary to prevent fraud or injustice. Of course, the trial court should consider any potential inadequacies of the protective order in weighing the competing interests of the parties under Rule

507. This is especially true when the trial court has specific, fact-based grounds for believing that trade secrets may be disclosed in violation of its protective order.

* * *

Finally, the Product Liability Advisory Council argues that *Automatic Drilling Machines, Inc. v. Miller*, 515 S.W.2d 256 (Tex. 1974), controls this case. That case arose from a suit between direct competitors, in which one side sought discovery of the other side's trade secret documents. After the trial court ordered disclosure, this Court granted mandamus relief, holding that the trial court had abused its discretion. We reasoned:

> Trade secrets and confidential information are not necessarily "privileged" matters within the meaning of Rule 186a. If the information is material and necessary to the litigation and unavailable from any other source, a witness may be required to make disclosure. A public disclosure of trade secrets should not be required, however, except "in such cases and to such extent as may appear to be indispensable for the ascertainment of truth." 8 WIGMORE, EVIDENCE (McNaughton rev. 1961), § 2212(3). In acting on the motions in this case, it was necessary for the judge to weigh the need for discovery against the desirability of preserving the secrecy of the material in question.

515 S.W.2d at 259. The trial court abused its discretion in compelling disclosure because there had been no showing that the information was "so essential to respondents' investigation and development of their case as to be subject to discovery by them." 515 S.W.2d at 260.

Although the Court decided *Automatic Drilling* before it promulgated Rule 507 in 1983, the decision is consistent with the rule. We recognized in *Automatic Drilling* that trade secrets should be disclosed only where the information is "material and necessary to the litigation and unavailable from any other source." 515 S.W.2d at 259. We further recognized that the trial court must balance the need for discovery against the need for nondisclosure. As discussed previously, this mirrors the proper approach under Rule 507.

V

Accordingly, we reject the parties' alternative approaches. Instead, we apply our interpretation of Rule 507 to the facts of this case. Plaintiffs concede for purposes of this proceeding that the compound formula is a trade secret. The burden thus shifted to the plaintiffs to establish that the compound formula is necessary for a fair adjudication of this case. The only evidence that plaintiffs presented was deposition testimony from Continental's expert, Joseph Grant, that a compound that "doesn't have the right ingredients in it" could cause a belt separation. But Grant stated in his affidavit that the physical properties of a tire cannot be determined from an examination of a compound formula; rather, the finished tire itself must be tested. Further, plaintiffs do not contest Continental's assertions that the plaintiffs have no other manufacturers' compound formulas with which to compare Continental's formula. The plaintiffs contended at oral argument before this Court that their expert has found sulfur on the belt surfaces of this tire, and that plaintiffs need Continental's formula to determine whether sulfur is a regular component of the skim stock or whether it was a foreign material improperly introduced during manufacture. Regardless of whether this theory might otherwise justify discovery of the compound formula, an issue on which we express no opinion, plaintiffs presented no evidence supporting this theory to the trial court. Under these circumstances, given the highly proprietary nature of the information, the plaintiffs have not carried their burden under Rule 507 of demonstrating that the information is necessary for a fair trial.

We accordingly conclude that the trial court abused its discretion. Because the trial court has ordered Continental to produce privileged, trade secret information, Continental has no adequate remedy by appeal. *See Walker v. Packer*, 827 S.W.2d 833, 843 (Tex. 1992).

* * *

For the foregoing reasons, we conditionally grant mandamus relief directing the trial court to vacate its order compelling Continental to produce the belt skim-stock formula. We reiterate that nothing in our decision prohibits plaintiffs from seeking to discover the formula under the procedure we have set forth.

Notes & Questions

"Necessary for fair adjudication." How important must the trade secret be to opposing party's case to require discovery of it? In another tire case, the Supreme Court said:[1]

> We did not attempt to state conclusively what would or would not be considered necessary for a fair adjudication, indicating instead that the application of the test would depend on the circumstances presented. In the present case, Firestone argues that the test should be applied to preclude discovery of trade secret information unless the requesting party cannot prevail without it. While it would certainly be unfair to allow a party to prevail solely by withholding such information, our decision in *Continental General Tire* cannot be read so narrowly. It may be theoretically possible for a party to prevail without access to trade secret information and yet be unfair to put him to much weaker proof without the information. Obviously, the degree to which information is necessary in a case depends on the nature of the information and the context of the case.
>
> While it is difficult to be more specific about the test to be applied, except by demonstrating how it is properly applied in particular cases, we can say with certainty that the test cannot be satisfied merely by general assertions of unfairness. The words "fair" and "unfair" are prone to indefinite use. Just as a party who claims the trade secret privilege cannot do so generally but must provide detailed information in support of the claim, so a party seeking such information cannot merely assert unfairness but must demonstrate with specificity exactly how the lack of the information will impair the presentation of the case on the merits to the point that an unjust result is a real, rather than a merely possible, threat. The plaintiffs' evidence and argument before us fall far short of this standard.

Justice O'Neill, in a concurring opinion, would give further guidance than the majority. She said:

> First, trade secret information is generally discoverable when not allowing discovery would significantly impair a party's ability to establish or rebut a material element of a claim or defense. A party's ability is significantly impaired when the information is unavailable from any other source and no adequate alternative means of proof exist. Discovery is also necessary when the party seeking trade secret information could not knowledgeably cross-examine opposing witnesses without it, or when the party's experts would be unable to formulate opinions supported by an adequate factual foundation. On

---

[1] In re Bridgestone/Firestone Inc., 106 S.W.3d 730 (Tex. 2003).

the other hand, information that is merely cumulative is not necessary for a fair adjudication.

CHAPTER 8. DISCOVERY MECHANICS

A. Written Discovery Requests

Read Rules 194, 196, 197, 198, 215.4.

Discovery from other parties in a lawsuit can be obtained by written request, by motion and order from the trial court, and by oral or written depositions. The permissible forms of discovery are mentioned in Rule 192.1, and each has its own rule giving specifics about the form of the request and response, and other relevant information. "Written discovery" is defined in Rule 192.7(a) to include requests for disclosure, requests for production of documents and tangible things, requests for entry onto property, interrogatories and requests for admissions. Thus "written discovery" is limited to discovery between parties. The following summarizes some of the more important aspects of each rule relating to written discovery.

The discovery rules are full of details concerning *how* to request discovery and respond to those requests either by complying with the request, objecting to it, or seeking to protect privileged matters within the scope of the request. We will first learn about written discovery, then move on to other forms of discovery, including depositions.

1. *Generally Applicable Rules*

a. *Sequence.* The permissible forms of discovery can be combined in the same document and can be used in any order or sequence. Rule 192.2.

b. *Serving written requests.* A party must serve discovery upon another party by using any method available under Rule 21. The request is generally not to be filed with the clerk. Rule 191.4. Copies should be sent to all parties, including those to whom the request is not directly related. Rule 191.5. A party may serve the requests upon another party at any time after commencement of the action, but no later than 30 days before the end of the discovery period.

c. *Serving responses.* Responses generally are due 30 days after service of the request, except that a defendant served with a request before the defendant's answer is due need not respond until 50 days after service of the request. The response should be served upon the requesting party (with copies to all other parties) by a method available under Rule 21. The response is generally not filed with the clerk. Responses may contain objections and assertions of privilege, which are addressed in Rule 193.

d. *Certificate.* Every disclosure, discovery request, notice, response, and objection must be signed by the attorney or the party if not represented by an attorney. Rule 191.3. The signature constitutes a certificate that to the best of the signer's knowledge, information and belief, formed after reasonable inquiry, the request, notice, response or objection is consistent with the rules of procedure and existing law, has a good faith factual basis, is not interposed for an improper purpose, and is not unreasonably or unduly burdensome and expensive.

e. *Self-authentication.* A party's production of a document in response to written discovery authenticates that document for use against the producing party, unless the party makes a proper and timely objection to its authenticity. Rule 193.7.

2. *Rule 194 Request for Disclosure*

a. *Content of request.* The request for disclosure is a simple form request whereby a party can obtain from another party one or more of a laundry list of twelve categories of discoverable items. The laundry list includes particular matters that are specifically discoverable under Rule 192.3 (such as identifying persons with knowledge of relevant facts), contentions and damage calculations, medical records and bills, and information concerning testifying experts. Note that Rule 190.2(b)(6) contains an additional request for disclosure for cases governed by Level 1 discovery plans. This request for disclosure requires the responding party to produce "all documents, electronic information, and tangible items" that support the responding party's claims or defenses. Rule 190.2(b)(6).

b. *Content of response.* The responding party must provide the requested information within the time for response. Objections to requests for disclosure are improper, thus they are indended to provide cheap, simple and basic discovery without the hinderance or delay of objections. Privileges other than the work product privilege may be asserted and, in extremely rare cases, a motion for a protective order may be appropriate to avoid disclosure.

3. *Rule 196 Request for Production*

a. *Requests generally.* A request for production is a written request that seeks to have another party produce documents and things for inspection, copying or testing. Level 1 imposes a 15-request limit on requests for production. Level 2, however, currently imposes no limits on the number of requests that can be served upon another party, although a court can impose such a limit in a Level 3 Discovery Control Order or pursuant to its power to limit discovery under Rule 192.4. Rule 192.3(b) specifies the scope of discovery for documents and things. Parties can discover anything, regardless of form, "that constitute or contain matters relevant to the subject matter of the action," that is within the "possession, custody or control" of the person served with the request, defined to include not only physical possession, but also constructive possession (defined in Rule 192.7(b) as "a right to possession . . . that is equal or superior to the person who has physical possession.[1]

b. *Notice to nonparties.* When a party requests another to produce medical or mental health records of a nonparty, Rule 196.1(c) requires that notice of the request be served upon the nonparty unless the nonparty signs a release, the identity of the nonparty will not be disclosed, or the court, upon a showing of good cause, orders that notice is not required.

c. *Specificity of request.* Parties must request documents and things by item or category of items, and they must describe each item or category with "reasonable particularity." The Supreme Court has made it abundantly clear that parties may not use requests for production to conduct "fishing expeditions;" requests must relate specifically to the subject matter, time, and place involved in the claims serving as the basis for the lawsuit.

d. *Time, place and circumstances for production.* The requesting party must state a reasonable time and place for production on or after the date the response is due. The request must also specify the means, manner and procedure for any testing or sampling. Rule 196.1(b). If the responding party objects to the time and place for production, that party must specify a alternate time and place in the response and comply at that time and place without further request or order. Rules 196.2(3); 193.2(b). Rule 196.5 states that testing, sampling, and examination may

---

[1] *See* In re Kuntz, 124 S.W.3d 179 (Tex. 2003) (holding that "mere access" does not always constitute "physical possession.").

not destroy or materially alter an item without prior court approval. Therefore, the requesting party might file a motion seeking permission to conduct such testing, sampling or examination, or the responding party might seek a protective order prohibiting the requesting party from conducting the specified testing, sampling or examination.

e. *Response.* Responding to a request for documents and things involves two specific acts—(1) making a written response to each request that notifies the requesting party whether the responding party will comply with the request or not, and (2) producing the documents and things. The written response sets forth objections, privilege assertions, and a statement that Rule 196.2(b) requires concerning compliance with the request. The Rule 196.2(b) statement may say that the documents and things will be produced as requested or at an alternate time and place, that they are being served with the response, or that nothing responsive to the request was located after a diligent search. The production may be made at the same time as the response or at a later time designated by the requesting or producing party.

f. *Production.* The responding party produces the requested documents and things, subject to objections and privilege claims, as kept in the usual course of business or organized to correspond with the categories in the request. Rule 196.3(c). The responding party may produce copies rather than originals. Production of the original may be required, however, if the requesting party raised a question as to the authenticity of the original or circumstances make it unfair not to produce the original. Rule 196.3(b). Generally, the expense of producing the items is borne by the the responding party, and the expense of inspecting, sampling, testing, photographing and copying them is borne by the requesting party.

g. *Electronic data.* The requesting party must request data and specify the form in which it wants it produced if it seeks production of data or information that is kept in electronic or magnetic form. The responding party must produce the requested data that is available in the ordinary course of business. Data that is obtainable only through extraordinary efforts must be produced if the court orders compliance and orders the requesting party to pay the expenses of retrieval and production.[2]

h. *Request for entry upon property.* Rule 196.7 governs requests for entry onto property. A party may make a written request to another party to allow entrance onto specific property to inspect, sample, test, photograph, or survey the property or any designated object or operation on the property. Much like the request for documents or things, the request must state the time, place and other conditions for the entry, and the response may present objections or assert privileges, and must state whether the party will permit entry as requested, at a different time or place, or not at all.

4. *Rule 197 Interrogatories*

a. *Interrogatories generally.* Interrogatories are directed to a party and answered by that party in writing and under oath. They may inquire into any discoverable matter other than matters covered by Rule 195, concerning testifying experts.

b. *Limitations upon number of interrogatories.* The number of interrogatories that a party may serve on any other party is limited by the applicable discovery control plan (15 in Level 1 and 25 in Level 2). Rule 190.2, 290.3. Each "discrete subpart" of an interrogatory is considered a

---

[2] *See* In re State Farm Lloyds, 520 S.W.3d 595 (holding that requesting party may not unilaterally dictate the form of electronic production and that trial judge has discretion to order production in a form that differs from the request) (reproduced, *infra* p. 358).

separate interrogatory. There is no limit on the number of "sets" of interrogatories—thus, the 25 interrogatories may be sent in as many as 25 "sets" of only one interrogatory. Whether an interrogatory seeks "to identify or authenticate specific documents" may be unclear in some circumstances. Consider the following interrogatories, and be prepared to discuss whether they would be limited or unlimited in number:

(1) Is Exhibit 1, attached hereto, a "Memorandum" drafted by John Jones, dated Jan. 2, 2014?

(2) Identify the person who signed Exhibit 2, attached hereto.

(3) Identify all documents that support your contention that the defendant was negligent?

(4) Identify the specific documents that set forth your policies concerning maintenance and repair of the widget that is the subject of this litigation.

(5) Identify the person who authored Exhibit 3, attached hereto.

(6) Identify each person who participated in the drafting, editing, review and distribution of Exhibit 4, attached hereto.

c. *Contention interrogatories.* Rule 197.1 specifically allows parties to use contention interrogatories—those asking "whether a party makes a specific legal or factual contention" or that "ask the responding party to state the legal theories and to describe in general the factual bases for the parties claims and defenses." Rule 194 also allows discovery concerning contentions by way of request for disclosure. Here, and wherever contention discovery is allowed, the rules caution that contention discovery may not be used "to require the responding party to marshal all of its available proof or the proof the party intends to offer at trial."[3]

d. *Responses to interrogatories.* The typical interrogatory response provides a written answer to the question asked. However, a response may specify records from which an answer may be derived if the burden of deriving the answer is substantially the same for the requesting and responding parties. Rule 197.2(c). A party must answer interrogatories under oath, which generally means that the party must swear that the answers are true and correct and within the party's personal knowledge. Rule 197.2(d) excepts certain matters from the verification obligation, however. First, the responding party may qualify the verification by stating that certain answers are made upon information obtained from others. Second, the responding party need not sign interrogatory answers concerning persons with knowledge of relevant facts, trial witnesses and legal contentions, matters typically considered matters of legal investigation and strategy.

e. *Use of interrogatory answers.* A party may use answers to interrogatories directly only against the responding party at a hearing or trial. Thus, a party cannot use its own interrogatory answer to prove controverted issues. In a multi-party case, one party may use answers to another party's interrogatories against the responding party, thus obviating the need for redundant interrogatories with identical questions and answers.[4] The answer must be offered in evidence at the hearing or trial.

---

3 *See also* Rule 197.1, Rule 197 cmt. 1, Rule 194 cmt. 2, Rule 192 cmt. 5.

4 Ticor Title Ins. Co. v. Lacy, 803 S.W.2d 265, 266 (Tex. 1991).

5. *Rule 198 Requests for Admission*

a. *Requests for admission generally.* Requests for admission are written requests to a party asking the party to admit or deny certain matters. Level 1 limits the number served on another party to 15, and Level 2 imposes no limits on the number of requests that can be served upon another party, although a court can impose such a limit in a Level 3 Discovery Control Order or pursuant to its power to limit discovery under Rule 192.4. The requests may address any matter within the scope of discovery, including statements of fact, opinions, application of law to fact, and the genuineness of documents. Because the general scope of discovery rule allows discovery of "legal contentions," requests for admissions may arguably include pure questions of law (e.g. "Admit that a two-year statute of limitations governs claims for breach of fiduciary duty.").[5]

b. *Admissions on behalf of the State.* If the State of Texas is a party, requests for admissions can be problematic. The attorney general cannot bind the State of Texas by admission, agreement, or waiver.[6] Thus, requests for admission that, if admitted, would prejudice the rights of the State are ineffective.[7]

c. *Response to requests for admissions.* The response must either admit or deny the request, or state in detail the reasons why the responding party can neither admit nor deny the request. Furthermore, the response may not claim lack of information to respond unless the response states that "a reasonable inquiry was made but that the information known or easily obtainable is insufficient to enable the responding party to admit or deny." It is not proper to say that the matter presents "an issue for trial." Sanctions are available if a party's response does not comply with Rule 198 or if a party fails to admit without justification. Rule 215.4.

d. *Failure to respond to requests for admissions.* If a response is not timely served, the request automatically is deemed admitted, or, in the words of the rule, "the request is considered admitted without the necessity of a court order." Rule 198.2(c). The "deemed admission" is a sanction for the failure to timely respond to the request.

e. *Use of admissions.* Making an admission is not to be taken lightly. An admitted matter is "conclusively established" in the pending action as to the party making it,[8] unless the court allows withdrawal or amendment. Rule 198.3. These are judicial admissions, and are established without proof. No evidence, over objection, is allowed contrary to them. For example, in *Marshall v. Vise*,[9] the party who obtained deemed admissions in his favor failed to object to evidence contrary to the admissions. Thus, the Texas Supreme Court held that the evidence was properly admitted as the failure to object waived the admissions. Although the requests and responses are not ordinarily filed, a party seeking to rely on admissions at a hearing or trial should file a copy of the requests and admissions (if any) with the clerk and bring them to the court's attention.[10]

---

5 This interpretation would be different from pre-1999 practice. *See e.g.* Credit Car Ctr., Inc. v. Chambers, 969 S.W.2d 459, 464 (Tex. App.—El Paso 1996, no writ) (concluding that questions of law are improper subjects of requests for admission.)

6 TEX. GOV'T. CODE § 402.004.

7 Lowe v. Texas Tech Univ., 540 S.W.2d 297, 301 (Tex. 1976).

8 *See* United States Fidelity & Guar. Co. v. Goudeau, 272 S.W.3d 603 (Tex. 2008) (holding that an admission is binding on a party only in the capacity in which the admission was made).

9 767 S.W.2d 699 (Tex. 1989).

10 *See* Rule 191.4(c)(2) (allowing filing of discovery materials for use in a court proceeding).

B. Responding to Written Discovery

Read Rule 193.1,.2,.4,.5,.6.

Rule 193 provides the procedure for parties to respond to written discovery. Rule 193 contains the duty to timely respond to discovery requests; the duty to supplement those responses; the procedure for objecting to the form or scope of written discovery requests; and the procedure for asserting privileges.

1. *Duty to Make a Complete Response*

A party upon whom proper written discovery is served has the duty to respond completely, based on all the information reasonably available at the time of the response,[1] and to supplement incomplete or incorrect responses "reasonably promptly" upon discovering the deficiency in the original response.[2] Rule 193.5 requires "formal" supplementation—supplementation in the same form as the original response—only concerning identification of persons with knowledge of facts, expert witnesses, or trial witnesses. Otherwise, the new information can be made known to the other parties in writing, on the record at deposition, or through other discovery responses. Read carefully the rules relating to responding and supplementing discovery. The duty to respond and supplement under the current rules is a significant change from the old rules, where there was no obligation to respond completely until 30 days before trial.[3]

2. *Objections*

Rule 193.2 establishes specific obligations and procedures for objecting to written discovery requests on grounds of form and scope. A Rule 193.2 objection simply asserts that the form or scope of a written discovery request does not comply with the rules. For example, the request may be beyond the scope of discovery, be unduly burdensome, or be unreasonably duplicative or cumulative. When we discuss the rules relating to scope of discovery in Chapter 7, think about the kinds of objections that should be made to raise these issues. The objection must have a good faith factual or legal basis, which must be specifically stated in the objection. Thus, for example, the party must not only state that the request is unduly burdensome, but also explain why it is unduly burdensome. It is important to state all your objections in a timely manner, but be careful of boilerplate objections—objections obscured by numerous unfounded objections are waived. The objection must be made within the time allowed for the response—usually 30 days after service of the request—but a party may amend or supplement an objection or response to state additional objections that were inapplicable or unknown at the time of the original response. Any party may at any reasonable time request a hearing on the objection, where the party making the objection must present any evidence necessary to support the objection.[4] If the judge sustains the objection,

---

[1] Rule 193.1.

[2] Rule 193.5.

[3] *See Able Supply, v. Moye* , 898 S.W.2d 766 (Tex. 1995) (original proceeding) (finding pre-1999 rules require "full, fair discovery within a reasonable period of time," although only specific deadline was 30 days before trial).

[4] Rule 193.4(a).

there is no further obligation to respond. If the court overrules it, the responding party must respond within 30 days or such time as the court orders.[5]

3. *Protective Orders*

Although the objection is the more appropriate method by which to assert objections to form and scope of a particular discovery request, Rule 192.6 allows a party or "any other person affected" by a discovery request to file a motion for an order protecting the person from the discovery sought. The rule allows the court to use wide discretion in limiting discovery to protect the movant from "undue burden, unnecessary expense, harassment, annoyance, or invasion of personal, constitutional, or property rights." Parties often seek protective orders to pro-actively designate certain matters off-limits in discovery.

4. *Duty to Make Partial Response*

When a responding party objects to a request, Rule 193.2(b) requires that the party comply with any part of the request to which there is no objection and to state the extent to which the party is refusing to comply with the request. These provisions allow discovery to proceed despite objections, and focus the parties on real disputes. For example, if the responding party objects because the time, place, or subject matter of the request is unreasonably broad, the party has the duty to respond to as much of the request as it determines is within the permissible scope of discovery. In effect, the responding party may "blue-pencil" or rewrite the request so that it is not objectionable.

Example: Objection to Part of a Request

Interrogatory: Please describe by date and offense type any criminal conduct that occurred in the K Mart store or parking lot in the shopping center in question during the last seven years.

Response: Defendant objects to this request because it is overly broad, and exceeds the scope of discovery. Defendant refuses to respond concerning any criminal conduct other than abduction and rape from the parking lot in question as other criminal activity has no bearing on this case. Defendant also will respond only for the last five years as Defendant retains records concerning such activity for only five years. Defendant makes no response at this time, however, because it is unreasonable to do so before obtaining a ruling. All of the information necessary to respond to this request is kept in a storage facility that is not conveniently accessible. Depending upon the court's ruling on this objection, a duplicate search will be required.

5. *Unreasonable to Make Partial Response*

The rules recognize that there may be circumstances under which it is unreasonable to have to make a partial response. For example, documents are often organized in a way that requires the same search regardless of whether the party is responding to a temporally narrow or broad request. Under such circumstances, the responding party may wait to conduct the search until the

---

5 Rule 193.4(b).

parties (or the court, if necessary) resolve the scope issues.[6] Alternatively, the party may choose to make some effort to respond and provide a partial response as a tactical matter. A party given some information may not press for more. Likewise, a court may be less amenable to no response than the responding party's partial response to a "blue-penciled" request.

6. *Objection to Entire Request*

Rule 193 Comment 2 explains that some requests are entirely objectionable and deserve no response short of stating the party's legal and factual bases for the objection. These are requests that are so clearly beyond the scope of discovery, or so broad as to be called a "fishing expedition" that no response is required.

Example: Objection to the Entire Request

Request: Produce all notes, records, memoranda, documents and communications that you contend support the allegations in the plaintiff's original petition.

Response: Defendant objects to this request because it is overly broad and not in compliance with the Rule 196 requirement that a request describe each item or category of items "with reasonable particularity." Defendant refuses to respond to any part of this request.

In *Loftin v. Martin*,[7] the Supreme Court held that a similar request was objectionable and required no response because it was "merely a request . . . to generally peruse all evidence [the responding party] might have."[8]

7. *Objection to Time and Place of Production*

A Rule 193.2 objection is also appropriate when a party objects to the time or place for production of documents and things.[9] However, such an objection is a partial objection that does not relieve the responding party of any duty to respond. Instead, Rule 193.2(b) requires that the responding party state a reasonable time and date for complying with the request, and comply accordingly without further request or order.[10]

8. *Hearing*

At the hearing on the objection or motion for protective order, does the objecting party have to bring evidence to prove that the request for discovery is beyond the scope of discovery? Rule 193.4(a), states: "The party making the objection or asserting the privilege must present any evidence necessary to support the objection or privilege." The Supreme Court has held that this means that "evidence may not always be necessary to support a claim of protection from discovery."[11] When the issue is simply whether the request is "pertinent to the issues in the current liti-

---

6 *See* Rule 193 cmt. 2 (noting that partial production is required "unless that production would be burdensome and duplicative should the objection be overruled").

7 776 S.W.2d 145 (Tex. 1989) (orig. proceeding).

8 *Id.* at 148; *see also* Rule 193 cmt. 2.

9 Rule 193.2(b).

10 *Id.*

11 In re Union Pacific Resources Co., 22 S.W.3d 338 (Tex. 1999)

gation," no evidence is required, and it is not an abuse of discretion to deny discovery without evidence in the record supporting the order. In fact, the Court noted that "it is not clear what evidence *could* have been produced on the issue."

However, if the object is that the request is "overly burdensome," the objecting party should be prepared to present some evidence supporting the burden—such an estimate of the time and expense necessary to conduct the search.

C. Asserting a Privilege—Withholding Statements and Privilege Logs

Read Rule 193.3, .4

1. *Assert Privilege by Withholding, Not Objection*

Rule 193.3 presents the procedures for asserting a claim that material or information responsive to a written discovery request is privileged. A privilege is asserted when a party responds to the request, but does not allow discovery of all matters responsive to the request—the party withholds certain material or information because it is privileged. Thus, this procedure is different from the objection procedure of Rule 193.2, which is used when a party is not responding to a request because of problems with the scope and form of particular requests.[111] Furthermore, rules caution that the objection procedure should not be used to assert privileges. Nevertheless, a party that erroneously uses the objection procedure does not waive the privilege asserted, but must comply with Rule 193.3 once the error is pointed out.[122]

However, some requests on their face only request privileged information and are objectionable – no further response is required. The objection is to the form of the request as opposed to a refusal to produce privileged documents responsive to a proper request.[3] For example, if there is a request for a lawyer's litigation file, which is clearly a core work product, the request and response might look like those set out below:

Request:	Produce the entire litigation file from [a related case], including pleadings and all file indices.
Response:	Defendant objects to this request because it seeks core work product. It requests the lawyer's organization of files and selection of documents included within the file. Defendant refuses to comply with any part of this request.

---

1 *Compare* Rule 193.3 *with* Rule 193.2. An objection is appropriate when the *entire* request is objectionable because on its face it requests only privileged material. This objection is to the *form* of the request rather than an assertion that particular material responsive to the request is privileged, for which one uses the withholding procedure.

2 Rule 193.2(f). *See* In re Graco Prods. Inc., 173 S.W.3d 600 (Tex. App.—Corpus Christi 2005) (concluding that relator did not waive all privileges by objecting). *But see* In re Anderson, 163 S.W.3d 136, 140 (Tex. App.—San Antonio 2005) (noting that serving only an objection and failing to serve withholding statement may result in compelled production).

3 *See* Rule 193, Comment 2.

2. *"Withholding Statements"*

Upon responding to a request for written discovery, the responding party withholding particular privileged information or material responsive to the request must make a written withholding statement.[4] The withholding statement contains three elements: (1) a statement that information or material responsive to the request has been withheld; (2) identification of the request to which the withheld information or material relates; and (3) a statement of the privilege(s) relied upon.[5] A withholding statement may be made in an original response, an amended or supplemental response, or a separate document.

3. *When to Make a Withholding Statement*

Importantly, the withholding statement is made only when actually responding to written discovery. If an objection is made to an entire request on grounds of scope or form, and the objecting party is refusing to comply with any part of the request, a withholding statement is unnecessary.[6] Similarly, if an objection is made to part of a request but the objecting party is partially complying with the request, a withholding statement is required if the party is withholding, on grounds of privilege, specific documents responsive to the part of the request to which the party is responding.[7] If the court later overrules the scope and form objection and requires a response to the entire request, the responding party then may make a withholding statement for any additional materials responsive to the request but withheld on a claim of privilege.[8]

4. *Privilege Log*

After receiving the withholding statement, the requesting party may ask the withholding party to prepare a privilege log describing the withheld material.[9] The log, which must be provided within fifteen days after the party serves a request for it, must assert a specific privilege for each item or group of items withheld, and contain a sufficient description of the materials to enable other parties to assess the applicability of the privilege.[10] Naturally, the description should not provide so much information that it waives the privilege. The rule does not specify a standard for the level of detail required. The detail to be provided will vary depending upon the circumstances of the case and the type of material withheld. However, the description must reveal the factual basis of the privilege. For example, the description ordinarily should identify the participants to a privileged communication, the date of the communication, and the communication's general subject matter, except to the extent that doing so would waive the privilege.

---

4 Rule 193.3(a). Actually, the term "withholding statement" was used only in the Supreme Court Advisory Committee's proposals to the Supreme Court. The Supreme Court deleted this term, in part because some lawyers complained that it sounded like a tax law requirement.

5 *Id.*

6 Rule 193 cmt. 2.

7 *See* Rule 193.2(b) (setting forth a duty to respond when partially objecting).

8 Rule 193 cmt. 2. *See* Rule 193.3(a) (allowing a withholding statement with an amended or supplemental response).

9 Rule 193.3(b).

10 *Id.*

5. *Two-Step Process*

The rules envision a two-step process. First, the objection procedure resolves any dispute over the form or scope of a request to which the responding party has refused to respond. No privilege issues concerning specific responsive material are addressed at this time because a withholding statement is not appropriate until a response is made. Second, if the trial court requires a response, the responding party then asserts privileges, which are resolved through the withholding procedure. This process is intended to stop the practice of prophylactic objections. Under the prior rules, persons raising privilege claims made an objection to the request, all of which had to be made within the time for the response.[11] Because of a fear of waiving privilege objections that might arise for documents found later, parties made numerous privilege objections at the time of their response, even when the party currently had no documents subject to that privilege. Even worse, parties objecting to the scope or form of the request sometimes made prophylactic privilege objections before they even searched for documents. Thus, it was difficult to determine from the objections whether the responding party had real materials that were being withheld on grounds of privilege or the objections were being made solely to prevent waiver.

6. *Problem:*

Assume that the plaintiff in a products liability case requests from the defendant "All documents concerning repairs or the need for repair of any widget in the defendant's possession." Also assume that there are three responsive documents: (1) a repair log for the widget involved in the accident, (2) a repair log for a similar widget in another plant, and (3) the trial attorney's notes taken during an interview with a repairman who had repaired the widgets in the past. In response, the defendant makes the following objection and files no withholding statement:

> The defendant objects to the request on grounds that it is overly broad and outside the scope of discovery to the extent it requests documents concerning widgets other than the widget involved with the accident. Other widgets are not similar to the widget involved in the accident, and thus their repair records are not relevant and will not lead to the discovery of admissible evidence. Defendant will comply with the request to the extent it requests documents concerning the widget involved in the accident. Production and inspection will be permitted as requested.

Now suppose the discovery responses identify the repairman as a person with knowledge of relevant facts, but he dies before the plaintiff's attorney can interview or depose him. What should the plaintiff's attorney do? Consider Rule 193 Comment 3, which states "the rule does not prohibit a party from specifically requesting the material or information if the party has a good faith basis for asserting that it is discoverable." Also consider Rule 191.1, which allows the trial court may change any procedure pertaining to discovery for good cause.

---

[11] *See* former Rule 166b.4.

In re E.I. DuPONT DE NEMOURS & CO.

136 S.W.3d 218
(Tex. 2004)

PER CURIAM.

In the suit underlying this petition for mandamus, nearly 400 plaintiffs sued E.I. DuPont de Nemours ("DuPont") and over 100 other defendants for alleged asbestos-related injuries from 1935 to the present. In response to the plaintiffs' discovery request, DuPont asserted claims of attorney-client and/or work product privilege with respect to 607 documents.

On May 12, 2003, the trial court issued an order requiring DuPont to turn over most of the documents, ruling that DuPont had not made a prima facie showing of privilege. A divided court of appeals declined to grant mandamus relief. DuPont now seeks relief from this Court. DuPont contends that the trial court abused its discretion by holding a hearing on the plaintiffs' global challenge to all of the documents identified in its privilege log. DuPont further argues that the trial court abused its discretion by finding that DuPont had not made a prima facie showing of privilege for the documents at issue and refusing to conduct an in camera inspection of the documents before rejecting its privilege claims.

The court of appeals declined to grant DuPont mandamus relief. We agree with the court of appeals that the trial court did not abuse its discretion in holding a hearing on the plaintiffs' global challenge to DuPont's privilege claims. However, we conditionally grant the writ insofar as we conclude that DuPont made a prima facie showing of privilege for many of the approximately 530 documents that the trial court ordered produced without conducting an in camera review.

In response to plaintiffs' requests for production, DuPont produced over 55,000 pages of documents that go back more than 60 years. However, DuPont stated that it was withholding 607 documents, citing the attorney-client privilege found in Texas Rule of Evidence 503 and the work-product privilege set forth in Texas Rule of Civil Procedure 192.5. After the plaintiffs requested a privilege log,[1] DuPont timely served the log describing the documents withheld. The plaintiffs then requested a hearing challenging DuPont's privilege claims for all of the documents. In response, DuPont filed an affidavit from its paralegal Walter Connor in support of its privilege claims and tendered the documents listed on the privilege log to the court for in camera inspection. In his affidavit, Connor stated, in relevant part:

---

1 A "privilege log" is the commonly used term for a response pursuant to Texas Rule of Procedure 193.3(b) that: "1) describes the information or materials withheld that, without revealing the privileged information or otherwise waiving the privilege, enables other parties to assess the applicability of the privilege, and 2) asserts a specific privilege for each item or group of items withheld." The dissenting court of appeals opinion noted:

> The log is sufficiently detailed for the real parties in interest to assess the applicability of the specific privilege being asserted. *See* TEX.R. CIV. P. 193.3(b). For example, "DUP Bates Range 0903484-3484, Date 741029," a document from "Austin RE (DuPont Legal)" to "Mfg Environmental Committee," copied to "Bonczek RR (DuPont Legal); Galloway WR; Helmers EN; Hildrew JC; Meany DM; Reichert RJ; Schmutz JF (DuPont Legal), and Sebree DB (DuPont Legal)," is a "Memo between DuPont counsel requesting legal advice and comments re: proposed amendments to regulations concerning national emissions standards for hazardous air pollutants."

Neither the trial court nor the court of appeals majority opinion concluded that the log inadequately described the documents and the plaintiffs do not so argue in this court.

> I have reviewed all names listed on the DuPont-Brignac privilege log that are identified as "DuPont Legal." I compared each "DuPont Legal" name for each document on the privilege log with a DuPont human resources database for the legal department. Each name that is identified as "DuPont Legal" on the privilege log is a name of a person who was, at the time indicated on the document, a DuPont attorney or DuPont paralegal as confirmed by the comparison with the human resources database.

Connor further averred:

> I have reviewed and am familiar with the definitions of client, representative of client, lawyer, representative of a lawyer, and confidential as defined in Rule 503 of the Texas Rules of Evidence. Based on my review of the DuPont human resources database for the legal department, the documents listed on the DuPont-Brignac privilege log, and the definitions in Rule 503, all the documents on the DuPont-Brignac privilege log with "DuPont Legal" names associated with a claim of attorney-client privilege indicate a lawyer or a representative of a lawyer engaging in confidential communications with a client or a representative of a client regarding professional legal services, or a lawyer or representative of a lawyer rendering professional legal services or performing a requested task for a client or a representative of a client involving the rendering of professional legal services.

Finally, Connor also stated:

> I have reviewed and am familiar with the definition of "work product" as defined in Rule 192.5 of the Texas Rules of Civil Procedure. Based on my review of the DuPont human resources database for the legal department, the documents listed on the DuPont-Brignac privilege log, and the definitions in Rule 192.5, all the documents on the DuPont-Brignac privilege log with "DuPont Legal" names associated with a claim of work product indicate material prepared or mental impressions developed in anticipation of litigation or for trial by or for DuPont or its representatives, or a communication in anticipation of litigation or for trial between DuPont and its representatives or among its representatives.

On April 29, 2003, the court conducted a hearing on DuPont's assertions of privilege. The court overruled DuPont's claims of privilege except as to 76 documents, which were ordered to be delivered for in camera review. The trial court excepted those 76 documents listed on the privilege log that were associated exclusively with members of "DuPont Legal," meaning that the author, recipient, and all parties that received copies of the document were members of "DuPont Legal." The trial court ordered DuPont to produce the remainder of the documents, consisting of: 1) documents with no "DuPont Legal" names associated, and 2) documents with both "DuPont Legal" and non-"DuPont Legal" names associated.

. . . Mandamus is proper when the trial court erroneously orders the disclosure of privileged information because the trial court's error cannot be corrected on appeal. As DuPont would lose the benefit of the privilege if the documents at issue are disclosed, even if its assertions of privilege were later upheld on appeal, we conclude that this Court may provide mandamus relief in this case.

The party who seeks to limit discovery by asserting a privilege has the burden of proof. However, if a party asserting privilege claims makes a prima facie showing of privilege and tenders documents to the trial court, the trial court must conduct an in camera inspection of those documents before deciding to compel production. We have recognized:

> Generally, a trial court conducts an in camera inspection to determine if a document is in fact privileged. If it is not privileged, then it may become evidence that the factfinder

> may consider. If the document is privileged, it is not subject to discovery and may not be considered by the factfinder, even when the factfinder is the trial court.

The trial court abuses its discretion in refusing to conduct an in camera inspection when such review is critical to the evaluation of a privilege claim.

The prima facie standard requires only the "minimum quantum of evidence necessary to support a rational inference that the allegation of fact is true." The documents themselves may constitute sufficient evidence to make a prima facie showing of attorney-client or work product privilege.[2]

The plaintiffs argue that Connor's affidavit is lacking in specificity. However, an affidavit, even if it addresses groups of documents rather than each document individually, has been held to be sufficient to make a prima facie showing of attorney-client and/or work product privilege.

In *Monsanto,* the affidavit of the corporate representative asserted that a log of 117 documents involved "in-house and/or outside attorneys for Monsanto, or other Monsanto employees, representatives or agents." *In re Monsanto Co.,* 998 S.W.2d at 927. The court of appeals held that this representation constituted a prima facie showing of the attorney-client and work product privilege. In *Toyota,* the affidavit submitted by the defendant stated that one group of documents consisted of "[c]ommunications to Toyota counsel for the purpose of requesting legal advice or facilitating the rendition of professional legal service." *In re Toyota Motor Corp.,* 94 S.W.3d at 821. This representation was also found to be sufficient to establish a prima facie case of privilege. In *Shell Western E & P,* Shell established a prima facie case of attorney-client privilege where a Shell affiant swore that the "documents . . . were written by a lawyer to a client" and "consist of communications from a client to a Shell . . . lawyer . . . ." However, an affidavit is of no probative value if it merely presents global allegations that documents come within the asserted privilege. The plaintiffs contend that the affidavit at issue here is not probative because it is conclusory. The plaintiffs maintain that Connor's affidavit is indistinguishable from the affidavit found insufficient to support attorney-client privilege in *In re Temple-Inland, Inc.,* 8 S.W.3d 459 (Tex. App.—Beaumont 2000, orig. proceeding). However, the affidavit in *Temple-Inland* that was found to be conclusory merely stated that production "would violate the attorney-client privilege." *Id.* at 462. Connor's affidavit more closely resembles the affidavits in *Monsanto* and *Toyota,* as it sets forth the factual basis for the applicability of the attorney-client and/or work product privileges to the documents at issue. Additionally, while Connor did not attest to the specific contents of each of the 607 documents at issue, the plaintiffs are unable to identify any such legal requirement and do not dispute that the log submitted by DuPont contains a summary of each document. Thus, we find that the specificity of Connor's affidavit and the log taken together are reasonably adequate to establish a prima facie case of privilege given that the documents at issue go back more than 60 years.

The plaintiffs also contend that Connor's affidavit is not probative because it is not based on personal knowledge. For an affidavit to have probative value, an affiant must swear that the facts presented in the affidavit reflect his personal knowledge. Connor swore that his statements were

---

2 The dissenting court of appeals opinion examined several of the memos that were among the documents containing both "DuPont Legal" and non-"DuPont Legal" names. Both the "DuPont Legal" names and the names without designation are written with the first and middle initials before the last name. The identical format of the two types of names and the inclusion of each recipient's middle initial suggest all of the recipients were DuPont employees. Some recipients of these memos appear to have been groups, such as "Dept Occ Health Mgrs" and "Asbestos Committee." This illustrates the additional evidence that may be adduced through an in camera review.

based on his "personal knowledge of the facts stated in the affidavit." Even though Connor later explained that his determinations were "[b]ased on [his] review of the DuPont human resources database for the legal department," an affiant's acknowledgment of the sources from which he gathered his knowledge does not violate the personal knowledge requirement. Therefore, we hold that Connor's affidavit satisfies the personal knowledge requirement.

Three discrete categories of documents are in dispute. First, there are the documents which have only "DuPont Legal" names associated with them. The trial court ordered an in camera review of these 76 documents. Second, there are those documents that have both "DuPont Legal" and other names associated with them. The trial court denied DuPont's claim of privilege with respect to these documents without ordering an in camera review. Finally, there are those documents which do not have any "DuPont Legal" name associated with them. The trial court also rejected DuPont's claim of privilege concerning these documents.

We conclude that the trial court did not abuse its discretion in sustaining DuPont's privilege claims with respect to the first category of documents. The log submitted by DuPont combined with Connor's affidavit clearly make a prima facie case that those documents with only "DuPont Legal" names associated with them are covered by the attorney-client and/or work product privileges. Consequently, the trial court correctly determined that DuPont was entitled to at least an in camera review of those documents.

We also conclude that DuPont established a prima facie case of privilege with respect to the second category of documents, which contained both "DuPont Legal" and other names. Thus, we find that the trial court erroneously rejected DuPont's privilege claim as applied to these documents without at least subjecting them to an in camera review.

There is no presumption that documents are privileged, and there is no presumption that a party listed on the privilege log is an authorized person under the rule governing the privilege. Nevertheless, Connor provided sufficient indication of the relationship between the "DuPont Legal" and the non-"DuPont Legal" persons on the privilege log to establish a prima facie case of privilege. In his description of the allegedly privileged documents, Connor identified the non-"DuPont Legal" persons on the privilege log as authorized parties for purposes of attorney-client and/or work product privilege. Connor swore that the documents allegedly privileged as attorney-client materials "indicate a lawyer or representative of a lawyer engaging in communication . . . or performing a requested task . . . for a client or representative of a client." The implication of this statement is that, whatever the relationship between the "DuPont Legal" and the non-"DuPont Legal" parties listed on the privilege log, it was a relationship within the scope of the attorney-client and/or work product privilege. In light of the tests for demonstrating attorney-client and work product privilege[3] and the fact that the hundreds of documents at issue span more than 60 years,

[3] Connor did not specifically assert that each recipient was a DuPont supervisor. However, for attorney-client privilege, the subject matter test has replaced the control group test pursuant to the amendment of Rule of Evidence 503. TEX.R. EVID. 503(a)(2) & cmt; *Nat'l Tank Co. v. Brotherton,* 851 S.W.2d 193, 197-98 (Tex. 1993). The subject matter test is met where "the employee makes the communication at the direction of his superiors in the corporation and where the subject matter upon which the attorney's advice is sought by the corporation and dealt with in the communication is the performance by the employee of the duties of his employment." As such, the attorney-client privilege may apply to communications between attorneys and employees who are not executives or supervisors.

The plaintiffs point out that Connor's affidavit does not exclude the possibility that some of the recipients of documents within the second group were not DuPont employees. However, the work product privilege is not necessarily waived by disclosure to a non-employee, as there are numerous other classes of individuals who can qualify.

this statement combined with the log summarizing each document is sufficient to establish at least a prima facie case of privilege that is then subject to in camera review.[4] Because DuPont has established a prima facie case of privilege as to the second category of documents, which bear both "DuPont Legal" and non-"DuPont Legal" designations, we conclude that it was entitled to an in camera review before being required to produce these documents.

Finally, we agree with the trial court that DuPont has not established a prima facie case of privilege with respect to the third category of documents containing no "DuPont Legal" names. Connor's affidavit offers no evidence to justify privilege assertions concerning these documents. Connor's affidavit attested to the privileged nature of "[a]ll the documents on the DuPont-Brignac privilege log with 'DuPont Legal' names associated with a claim of attorney-client privilege" and "[a]ll the documents on the DuPont-Brignac privilege log with 'DuPont Legal' names associated with a claim of work product privilege." The affidavit was silent as to any claim of privilege regarding the documents that do not bear a "DuPont Legal" name. Accordingly, we agree with the appeals court that the trial court did not abuse its discretion in ruling that DuPont failed to make a prima facie case of privilege with respect to those documents containing no "DuPont Legal" names.

DuPont also argues on appeal that the plaintiffs' global challenge to their privilege claims was not sufficient to place those claims at issue. DuPont contends that the trial court abused its discretion by allowing a hearing based on the plaintiffs' global challenge to DuPont's entire privilege log. DuPont maintains that, prior to the hearing, the plaintiffs should have been required to particularize their objections to specific documents in the privilege log.

* * *

The discovery rules provide that any party may request a hearing on a claim of privilege and the party asserting the privilege must present any evidence necessary to support the privilege. TEX.R. CIV. P. 193.4(a). This provision does not contain a requirement that the party seeking discovery specify their rationale for objecting to each document before requesting a hearing.[5] Accordingly, the trial court did not abuse its discretion by holding a hearing on the plaintiffs' objection to

---

"Work product" is defined as:

(1) material prepared or mental impressions developed in anticipation of litigation or for trial by or for a party or a party's representatives, including the party's attorneys, consultants, sureties, indemnitors, insurers, employees, or agents; or

(2) a communication made in anticipation of litigation or for trial between a party and the party's representatives or among a party's representatives, including the party's attorneys, consultants, sureties, indemnitors, insurers, employees, or agents. TEX.R. CIV. P. 192.5(a).

[4] Evidence corroborating or rebutting a prima facie case of privilege could be found upon in camera review. The documents themselves may contain evidence indicating the positions held by the non-"DuPont legal" recipients and the extent to which their duties relate to the matters upon which legal advice is being given. Plaintiffs are also entitled to put on their own evidence on privilege issues. *See* TEX.R. CIV. P. 193.4. For example, plaintiffs could submit interrogatories seeking additional information about the individuals listed as authors or recipients of disputed documents.

[5] We hold simply that the trial court did not abuse its discretion by holding a hearing. We do not suggest that a trial court would abuse its discretion by requiring, at such a hearing or otherwise, that the proponent of the discovery request state their objection to the claimed privilege specifically as to each document on the privilege log. Where large numbers of documents are at issue, such an approach may promote judicial economy by focusing in camera review on those documents where there is a genuine dispute as to the application of the privilege and by clarifying the nature of the dispute so the court can hone in on the probative content of each document.

DuPont's privilege log, which challenged whether DuPont had established a prima facie case of privilege for all of the documents it withheld.

For the foregoing reasons, we conditionally grant DuPont's petition for mandamus relief from the trial court ruling insofar as the ruling denied DuPont's privilege claim without conducting an in camera review with respect to the documents containing both "DuPont Legal" and non-"DuPont Legal" names. Accordingly, pursuant to Texas Rule of Appellate Procedure 52.8 and without hearing oral argument, we direct the trial court to vacate in part its May 12, 2003 order and to conduct further proceedings consistent with this opinion. We are confident that the trial court will promptly comply, and our writ will issue only if it does not.

---

7. *Electronic Discovery*

In re WEEKLEY HOMES, L.P.
295 S.W.3d 309
(Tex. 2009)

JUSTICE O'NEILL delivered the opinion of the Court.

In this mandamus proceeding, we must decide whether the trial court abused its discretion by ordering four of the defendant's employees to turn over their computer hard drives to forensic experts for imaging, copying, and searching for deleted emails. Because the plaintiff failed to demonstrate the particular characteristics of the electronic storage devices involved, the familiarity of its experts with those characteristics, or a reasonable likelihood that the proposed search methodology would yield the information sought, and considering the highly intrusive nature of computer storage search and the sensitivity of the subject matter, we hold that the trial court abused its discretion.

I. Background

[Editor's Note: Weekley Homes, a home builder, agreed with Enclave, a developer, to purchase lots in a subdivision. The lots were to be purchased on a schedule over a period of time. Enclave later sold the lots as a group to HFG, and assigned to HFG its rights under the contract with Weekley. Weekley had signed a consent to the assignment and made various representations and warranties to HFG about Enclave's performance under the Weekley-Enclave agreement at that point.

Enclave allegedly failed to perform various obligations owed to HFG, and HFG sued Encore. Later, HFG discovered some documents that led it to believe Weekley made misrepresentations in the consent, so HFG added Weekley as a defendant, alleging various fraud claims. HFG requested that Weekley produce documents and emails to and from Weekley employees relating to Enclave, the subdivision and the contract with Enclave. Weekley produced 31 emails and a "Slope Stability Analysis" that highlighted some safety issues in the subdivision that Weekley spent $92,000 to remedy. There was only one email produced discussing the Analysis, and HFG was unconvinced that Weekley had produced them all.]

HFG moved to compel Weekley to "search for any emails stored on servers or back up tapes or other media, [and] any email folders in the email accounts of [the Employees]." At the hearing on HFG's motion, John Burchfield, Weekley's General Counsel, testified that "each [Weekley] employee has an [email] inbox that's limited in size. And once you bump that size limit, you have to start deleting things off the inbox in order to be able to receive any more emails." Burchfield further testified that "[Weekley] forces [employees] to clear out [their] inbox[es] on a regular basis," so that deleted emails will only be saved if an employee "back[s] them up on [the employee's] own personal hard drive somehow." And while deleted emails are saved on backup tapes, they are only retained "[f]or a thirty-day cycle." The trial court denied HFG's motion.

Based upon information learned at the hearing, HFG filed a "Motion for Limited Access to [Weekley's] Computers" directing its discovery efforts at the Employees' hard drives. In essence the motion would, at HFG's expense, allow any two of four named PricewaterhouseCoopers forensic experts to access the Employees' computers "for the limited purpose of creating forensic images of the hard drives." According to the motion, the experts would "make an evidentiary image of the [hard drives] using a procedure that is generally accepted as forensically sound." Once the images are created, the experts would search the images for deleted emails from 2004, the relevant year, containing twenty-one specified terms: slope stability, retaining wall, Holigan, HFG, fence, mow!, landscap!, screening wall, LSI, limited site, Alpha, entry, earnest money, Legacy, defective, lot 1, lot 8, grading, substantial completion, letter of credit, and Site Concrete. Once the responsive documents had been identified, extracted, and copied to some form of electronic media by the experts, Weekley would have the right to review the extracted data and designate which documents or information [Weekley] claims are not relevant, not discoverable, or are subject to any claim of privilege or immunity from which they are withheld under such claims, identifying such withheld documents by page identification number, directory and subdirectory identification, statement of claimed privilege or immunity from discovery, and brief description of the information in question as is required by TEX.R. CIV. PRO. 193.3.

After reviewing the extracted data, Weekley would be required to furnish HFG with any responsive documents that were not being withheld. According to the Motion, should HFG, its counsel, or the experts incidentally observe privileged or confidential information, the information would be maintained in strict confidence and otherwise valid privileges or confidentiality rights would not be waived. Failure to comply with the order's confidentiality provisions would subject the violator to penalties and contempt of court.

At the hearing on HFG's motion, Weekley complained about the intrusiveness of the suggested protocol, pointing out that the forensic experts would have access to private conversations, trade secrets, and privileged communications stored on the Employees' hard drives. Weekly also complained that requiring the Employees' hard drives to be "taken out of commission" for imaging would be burdensome and disruptive. And Weekley complained that HFG failed to show the feasibility of "obtain[ing] data that may have been deleted in 2004" using the protocol set forth in the Motion.

The trial court granted HFG's motion, and Weekley sought mandamus relief from the court of appeals. In a brief memorandum opinion, the court of appeals denied Weekley's petition. 295 S.W.3d 346. We granted oral argument in this case to determine whether the trial court abused its discretion by allowing forensic experts direct access to Weekley's Employees' electronic storage devices for imaging and searching.

II. Analysis

A. Rule 196.4's Application

1. Emails are electronic information

Texas Rule of Civil Procedure 192.3(b) provides for discovery of documents, defined to include electronic information that is relevant to the subject matter of the action. *See* TEX.R. CIV. P.

192.3(b) cmt.-1999. Rule 196 governs requests for production of documents, and Rule 196.4 applies specifically to requests for production of "data or information that exists in electronic or magnetic form." As a threshold matter, Weekley contends the trial court abused its discretion because HFG did not comply with Texas Rule of Civil Procedure 196.4 governing requests for production of electronic or magnetic data. HFG responds that Rule 196.4 does not apply because deleted emails are simply documents governed by the general discovery rules. According to HFG, Rule 196.4 only applies to spreadsheets and statistics, not emails and deleted emails.

We see nothing in the rule that would support HFG's interpretation. Emails and deleted emails stored in electronic or magnetic form (as opposed to being printed out) are clearly "electronic information." *See* Conference of Chief Justices, Guidelines for State Courts Regarding Discovery of Electronically-Stored Information v (2006). Accordingly, we look to Rule 196.4 in analyzing HFG's requests.

B. Rule 196.4's Requirements

1. Specificity

Weekley argues that HFG failed to comply with Rule 196.4 because it never specifically requested production of "deleted emails." Rule 196.4 provides that, "[t]o obtain discovery of data or information that exists in electronic or magnetic form, the requesting party must specifically request production of electronic or magnetic data and specify the form in which the requesting party wants it produced." TEX.R. CIV. P. 196.4. As we have said, email communications constitute "electronic data," and their characterization as such does not change when they are deleted from a party's inbox. Thus, deleted emails are within Rule 196.4's purview and their production was implied by HFG's request. However, for parties unsophisticated in electronic discovery, such an implication might be easily missed. Rule 196.4 requires specificity, and HFG did not specifically request deleted emails. HFG counters that it did not know how Weekley's computer system and electronic information storage worked, and thus did not know what to ask for. But it is a simple matter to request emails that have been deleted; knowledge as to the particular method or means of retrieving them is not necessary at the requesting stage of discovery. Once a specific request is made the parties can, and should, communicate as to the particularities of a party's computer storage system and potential methods of retrieval to assess the feasibility of their recovery.[6] But even though it was not stated in HFG's written request that deleted emails were included within its scope, that HFG thought they were and was seeking this form of electronic information became abundantly clear in the course of discovery and before the hearing on the motion to compel. The purpose of Rule 196.4's specificity requirement is to ensure that requests for electronic information are clearly understood and disputes avoided. Because the scope of HFG's requests was understood before trial court intervention, Weekley was not prejudiced by HFG's failure to follow the rule and the trial court did not abuse its discretion by ordering production of the deleted emails. To ensure compliance with the rules and avoid confusion, however, parties seeking production of deleted emails should expressly request them.

Weekley additionally complains that HFG's "Motion for Limited Access to [Weekley's] Computers" is not a permissible discovery device. We agree with HFG, however, that the motion was, in effect, a motion to compel and the trial court properly treated it as such.

---

6 The federal rules recognize the importance of early communication between parties on how electronic information is stored. *See* FED. R. CIV. P. 16(b), 26(f). While the Texas rules have no counterpart, early discussions between the parties or early discovery directed toward learning about an opposing party's electronic storage systems and procedures is encouraged.

C. The Trial Court Abused Its Discretion in Allowing Access to Weekley's Hard Drives on this Record

1. The appropriate procedures under the rules

Weekley next contends that, even if a motion to compel may be used to access another party's hard drives, the trial court abused its discretion by permitting the experts to rummage through the Employees' computers in search of deleted emails that may no longer exist. Such an invasive procedure is only permissible, Weekley argues, when the requesting party has produced some evidence of good cause or bad faith, together with some evidence that the information sought exists and is retrievable. According to Weekley, HFG failed to make such a demonstration. HFG responds that inconsistencies and discrepancies in a party's production justify granting access to a party's hard drives. Additionally, HFG claims it was not required to show the feasibility of retrieval because it is well-settled that deleted emails can, at least in some cases, be retrieved from computer hard drives. Once again, we turn to Rule 196.4 for guidance.

When a specific request for electronic information has been lodged, Rule 196.4 requires the responding party to either produce responsive electronic information that is "reasonably available to the responding party in its ordinary course of business," or object on grounds that the information cannot through reasonable efforts be retrieved or produced in the form requested. Once the responding party raises a Rule 196.4 objection, either party may request a hearing at which the responding party must present evidence to support the objection. TEX.R. CIV. P. 193.4(a). To determine whether requested information is reasonably available in the ordinary course of business, the trial court may order discovery, such as requiring the responding party to sample or inspect the sources potentially containing information identified as not reasonably available. *See* TEX.R. CIV. P. 193.4(a); *cf.* TEX.R. CIV. P. 196.7 & cmts.-1999; *accord* FED.R.CIV.P. 26(b)(2)(b) notes of the advisory committee to the 2006 amendments. The trial court may also allow deposition of witnesses knowledgeable about the responding party's information systems. *See* TEX.R. CIV. P. 195.1. Because parties' electronic systems, electronic storage, and retrieval capabilities will vary in each case, trial courts should assess the reasonable availability of information on a case-by-case basis.

Should the responding party fail to meet its burden, the trial court may order production subject to the discovery limitations imposed by Rule 192.4. If the responding party meets its burden by demonstrating that retrieval and production of the requested information would be overly burdensome, the trial court may nevertheless order targeted production upon a showing by the requesting party that the benefits of ordering production outweigh the costs. TEX.R. CIV. P. 192.4. Like assessing the reasonable availability of information, determining the scope of production may require some focused discovery, "which may include sampling of the sources, to learn more about what burdens and costs are involved in accessing the information, what the information consists of, and how valuable it is for the litigation in light of information that can be obtained by exhausting other opportunities for discovery." FED.R.CIV.P. 26(b)(2)(b) notes of the advisory committee to the 2006 amendments; *see also* TEX.R. CIV. P. 196.7. To the extent possible, courts should be mindful of protecting sensitive information and should choose the least intrusive means of retrieval. And when the court orders production of not-reasonably-available information, the court "must also order that the requesting party pay the reasonable expenses of any extraordinary steps required to retrieve and produce the information." TEX.R. CIV. P. 196.4.

Because HFG did not initially specifically request deleted emails as Rule 196.4 requires, Weekley had no obligation to object in its response that deleted emails were not "reasonably available . . . in its ordinary course of business." *Id.* However, because HFG's motion to compel clarified the scope of its original request, Weekley was required in its response to HFG's motion and at the subsequent hearing to make the Rule 196.4 showing. Our limited record does not reflect whether Weekley met its burden. However, the trial court's ultimate decision to order imaging of the Employees' hard drives and forensic examination implies a finding that the deleted emails were not reasonably available and required extraordinary steps for their retrieval and production. We must decide, then, whether the measures the trial court crafted for retrieving the Employees' deleted emails were proper under the circumstances presented. Although Rule 196.4 does not provide express guidelines for the manner or means by which electronic information that is not reasonably available in the ordinary course of business may be ordered produced, the federal rules and courts applying them offer some guidance.

2. The federal rules

Beginning in 2000, the federal Committee on Rules of Practice and Procedure began intensive work on the subject of computer-based discovery because of growing confusion in the area. *See* Comm. on Rules of Practice and Procedure, Summary of the Report of the Judicial Conference 22 (2005). The Committee's purpose was to "determine whether changes could be effected to reduce the costs of discovery, to increase its efficiency, to increase uniformity of practice, and to encourage the judiciary to participate more actively in case management when appropriate." *Id.* at 24. In 2005, the Committee proposed amendments to the Federal Rules to better accommodate electronic discovery. *Id.* at 22. The amendments were supported by The American Bar Association Section on Litigation, the Federal Bar Council, the New York State Bar Association Commercial and Federal Litigation Section, and the Department of Justice, and most of the amendments were unanimously approved by the Committee. *Id.* at 25. The amendments were ultimately approved by the Judicial Conference and the United States Supreme Court, and have been in effect since December 1, 2006. Although we have not amended our rules to mirror the federal language, our rules as written are not inconsistent with the federal rules or the case law interpreting them.

Under Federal Rule of Civil Procedure 26(b)(2)(B), a trial court may order production of information that is not reasonably available only "if the requesting party shows good cause." In determining whether the requesting party has demonstrated "good cause," the court must consider, among other factors, whether

> the burden or expense of the proposed discovery outweighs its likely benefit, considering the needs of the case, the amount in controversy, the parties' resources, the importance of the issues at stake in the action, and the importance of the discovery in resolving the issues.

FED.R.CIV.P. 26(b)(2)(C)(iii). The Texas rules do not expressly require a "good cause" showing before production of not-reasonably-available electronic information may be ordered, but they do require a trial court to limit discovery when

> the burden or expense of the proposed discovery outweighs its likely benefit, taking into account the needs of the case, the amount in controversy, the parties' resources, the importance of the issues at stake in the litigation, and the importance of the proposed discovery in resolving the issues.

TEX.R. CIV. P. 192.4(b). Thus, both the federal rule and ours require trial courts to weigh the benefits of production against the burdens imposed when the requested information is not reasonably available in the ordinary course of business. We see no difference in the considerations that would apply when weighing the benefits against the burdens of electronic-information production; therefore we look to the federal rules for guidance.

Providing access to information by ordering examination of a party's electronic storage device is particularly intrusive and should be generally discouraged, just as permitting open access to a party's file cabinets for general perusal would be. The comments to the federal rules make clear that, while direct "access [to a party's electronic storage device] might be justified in some circumstances," the rules are "not meant to create a routine right of direct access." FED.R.CIV.P. 34 notes of the advisory committee to the 2006 amendments. When allowing such access, the comments to Rule 34 warn courts to "guard against undue intrusiveness." *Id.*

3. Federal case law

Since the 2006 amendments to the federal rules were promulgated, federal case law has established some basic principles regarding direct access to a party's electronic storage device. As a threshold matter, the requesting party must show that the responding party has somehow defaulted in its obligation to search its records and produce the requested data. The requesting party should also show that the responding party's production "has been inadequate and that a search of the opponent's [electronic storage device] could recover deleted relevant materials." Courts have been reluctant to rely on mere skepticism or bare allegations that the responding party has failed to comply with its discovery duties.

Even if the requesting party makes this threshold showing, courts should not permit the requesting party itself to access the opponent's storage device; rather, only a qualified expert should be afforded such access. Due to the broad array of electronic information storage methodologies, the requesting party must become knowledgeable about the characteristics of the storage devices sought to be searched in order to demonstrate the feasibility of electronic retrieval in a particular case. And consistent with standard prohibitions against "fishing expeditions," a court may not give the expert carte blanche authorization to sort through the responding party's electronic storage device. Instead, courts are advised to impose reasonable limits on production. Courts must also address privilege, privacy, and confidentiality concerns.

Finally, federal courts have been more likely to order direct access to a responding party's electronic storage devices when there is some direct relationship between the electronic storage device and the claim itself. For example, in *Ameriwood Industries*, Ameriwood sued several former employees claiming they improperly used Ameriwood's computers, confidential files, and confidential information to sabotage Ameriwood's business by forwarding its customer information and other trade secrets from Ameriwood's computers to the employees' personal email accounts. Based in part on the close relationship between Ameriwood's claims and the employees' computer equipment, the trial court justified "allowing an expert to obtain and search a mirror image of [the employee] defendants" hard drives. Similarly, in *Cenveo Corp.*, Cenveo sued several former employees for improperly using its computers, confidential trade information, and trade secrets to divert business from Cenveo to themselves. Borrowing from *Ameriwood,* the district court authorized a similar order "[b]ecause of the close relationship between plaintiff's claims and defendants' computer equipment." Finally, in *Frees,* a former employee was sued for using company computers to remove certain proprietary information. Noting that the employee's computers would be "among the most likely places [the employee] would have downloaded or stored the data allegedly missing," the court allowed direct access to the employee's work and home computers. *Id.*

4. HFG did not make the necessary showing

In this case, HFG's motion relied primarily upon discrepancies and inconsistencies in Weekley's production. According to HFG, Weekley only produced "a handful of emails from Russell Rice, and one email from Biff Bailey," Weekley's Division President and Land Acquisitions

Manager respectively, while producing "no emails from the email accounts of Scott Thompson or Joe Vastano, both of whom . . . were very involved with the [s]ubdivision." Additionally, HFG expressed concern about the limited number of emails relating to the Slope Stability Analysis it received despite the importance of that report. Beyond Weekley's meager document production, HFG relied upon Burchfield's testimony that Weekley employees do not save deleted emails to their hard drives, and that Burchfield had "no earthly idea . . . whether [the deleted emails are] something a forensic specialist could go in and retrieve."

From this testimony, the trial court could have concluded that HFG made a showing that Weekley did not search for relevant deleted emails that HFG requested. But it does not follow that a search of the Employees' hard drives would likely reveal deleted emails or, if it would, that they would be reasonably capable of recovery. HFG's conclusory statements that the deleted emails it seeks "must exist" and that deleted emails are in some cases recoverable is not enough to justify the highly intrusive method of discovery the trial court ordered, which afforded the forensic experts "complete access to all data stored on [the Employees'] computers." The missing step is a demonstration that the particularities of Weekley's electronic information storage methodology will allow retrieval of emails that have been deleted or overwritten, and what that retrieval will entail. A complicating factor is the some two-and-a-half years that passed between the time any responsive emails would have been created and the time HFG requested them. Under these circumstances, it is impossible to determine whether the benefit of the forensic examination the trial court ordered outweighs the burden that such an invasive method of discovery imposed.

* * *

Because the trial court abused its discretion by granting HFG's motion without the requisite showing, we need not reach Weekley's alternative arguments that the search terms the trial court ordered are overly broad, or that the trial court's order improperly requires Weekley to create the equivalent of a "privilege log" as to irrelevant documents that the search might produce. However, because trial courts should be mindful of protecting sensitive information and utilize the least intrusive means necessary to facilitate discovery of electronic information, the trial court should consider these arguments on remand.

D. Summary of Rule 196.4 Procedure

A fundamental tenet of our discovery rules is cooperation between parties and their counsel, and the expectation that agreements will be made as reasonably necessary for efficient disposition of the case. TEX.R. CIV. P. 191.2. Accordingly, prior to promulgating requests for electronic information, parties and their attorneys should share relevant information concerning electronic systems and storage methodologies so that agreements regarding protocols may be reached or, if not, trial courts have the information necessary to craft discovery orders that are not unduly intrusive or overly burdensome. The critical importance of learning about relevant systems early in the litigation process is heavily emphasized in the federal rules. Due to the "volume and dynamic nature of electronically stored information," failure to become familiar with relevant systems early on can greatly complicate preservation issues, increase uncertainty in the discovery process, and raise the risk of disputes. FED.R.CIV.P. 26(f) notes of the advisory committee to the 2006 amendments.

With these overriding principles in mind, we summarize the proper procedure under Rule 196.4:

- the party seeking to discover electronic information must make a specific request for that information and specify the form of production. TEX.R. CIV. P. 196.4.

- The responding party must then produce any electronic information that is "responsive to the request and . . . reasonably available to the responding party in its ordinary course of business." *Id.*

- If "the responding party cannot-through reasonable efforts-retrieve the data or information requested or produce it in the form requested," the responding party must object on those grounds. *Id.*

- The parties should make reasonable efforts to resolve the dispute without court intervention. TEX.R. CIV. P. 191.2.

- If the parties are unable to resolve the dispute, either party may request a hearing on the objection, TEX.R. CIV. P. 193.4(a), at which the responding party must demonstrate that the requested information is not reasonably available because of undue burden or cost, TEX.R. CIV. P. 192.4(b).

- If the trial court determines the requested information is not reasonably available, the court may nevertheless order production upon a showing by the requesting party that the benefits of production outweigh the burdens imposed, again subject to Rule 192.4's discovery limitations.

- If the benefits are shown to outweigh the burdens of production and the trial court orders production of information that is not reasonably available, sensitive information should be protected and the least intrusive means should be employed. TEX.R. CIV. P. 192.6(b). The requesting party must also pay the reasonable expenses of any extraordinary steps required to retrieve and produce the information. TEX.R. CIV. P. 196.4.

- Finally, when determining the means by which the sources should be searched and information produced, direct access to another party's electronic storage devices is discouraged, and courts should be extremely cautious to guard against undue intrusion.

* * *

III. Conclusion

We conditionally grant the writ of mandamus and order the trial court to vacate its Order. We are confident the trial court will comply, and our writ will issue only if it does not. We note that HFG is not precluded from seeking to rectify the deficiencies we have identified.

In re STATE FARM LLOYDS

520 S.W.3d 595
(Tex. 2017)

JUSTICE GUZMAN delivered the opinion of the Court.

Electronic discovery plays an increasingly significant role in litigation and, often, at significant expense. Given the prevalence of discoverable electronic data, discovery disputes involving electronically stored information (ESI) are a growing litigation concern. With few occasions to enter the fray, we have an opportunity in these consolidated mandamus proceedings to provide further clarity regarding ESI discovery.

Though increasingly common, electronic discovery concerns manifest in variable shades and phases. In this dispute, the parties are at odds over the form in which ESI must be produced, presenting conflicting views regarding the proper interpretation and application of our discovery rules concerning such matters. The requesting party seeks ESI in native form while the responding party has offered to produce in searchable static form, which the responding party asserts is more convenient and accessible given its routine business practices. Agreeing with the requesting party, the trial court ordered production in native form, subject to a showing of infeasibility. The court of appeals denied mandamus relief.

Under our discovery rules, neither party may dictate the form of electronic discovery. The requesting party must specify the desired form of production, but all discovery is subject to the proportionality overlay embedded in our discovery rules and inherent in the reasonableness standard to which our electronic-discovery rule is tethered. The taproot of this discovery dispute is whether production in native format is reasonable given the circumstances of this case. Reasonableness and its bedfellow, proportionality, require a case-by-case balancing of jurisprudential considerations, which is informed by factors the discovery rules identify as limiting the scope of discovery and geared toward the ultimate objective of "obtain[ing] a just, fair, equitable and impartial adjudication" for the litigants "with as great expedition and dispatch at the least expense . . . as may be practicable." TEX. R. CIV. P. 1.

Delay and expense strain not only the resources of the parties, but also the judicial system. Consequently, the discovery rules imbue trial courts with the authority to limit discovery based on the needs and circumstances of the case, including electronic discovery. Thus, when a party asserts that unreasonable efforts are required to produce ESI in the requested form and a "reasonably usable" alternative form is readily available, the trial court must balance any burden or expense of producing in the requested form against the relative benefits of doing so, the needs of the case, the amount in controversy, the parties' resources, the importance of the issues at stake in the litigation, and the importance of the requested format in resolving the issues. Even without quantifying differences in time and expense, evidence that a "reasonably usable" alternative form is readily available gives rise to the need for balancing, and if these factors preponderate against production in the requested form, the trial court may order production as requested only if the requesting party shows a particularized need for data in that form and "the requesting party pay[s] the reasonable expenses of any extraordinary steps required to retrieve and produce the information." TEX. R. CIV. P. 196.4. Unless ordered otherwise, however, "the responding party need only produce the data reasonably available in the ordinary course of business in reasonably usable form." TEX. R. CIV. P. 196 cmt. 3.

Because neither the trial court nor the parties had the benefit of the guidance we seek to provide today, we deny the petitions for writ of mandamus without prejudice, affording the relator an opportunity to reurge its discovery objections to the trial court in light of this opinion.

I. Factual and Procedural Background

In these mandamus proceedings, residential homeowners sued their insurer and others alleging underpayment of insured hail-damage claims. The lawsuits assert statutory, contractual, and extra-contractual claims against the same insurer, State Farm Lloyds, in separate proceedings. We consolidated the mandamus petitions for argument because they present the same legal issues and substantially similar procedural underpinnings.

At issue are trial-court orders adopting a proposed protocol for the exchange of electronic discovery. As requested by the homeowners, the trial court ordered all ESI to be produced in its native or near-native forms rather than in the alternative, "reasonably usable" format State Farm proposed in a competing discovery protocol. The court-ordered protocol does not require State Farm to convert data stored in another form back to native form or to produce the same information in multiple forms. But it does require State Farm to produce ESI in native form regardless of whether a more convenient, less expensive, and "reasonably usable" format is readily available. If native form is "infeasible" to produce, however, a near-native form may be substituted if the parties agree on the substituted form.

Native format retains the file structure associated with and defined by the original creating application. [internal quotations omitted] For example, the native format is XLS for Microsoft Excel spreadsheets and DOC for older versions of Microsoft Word documents. The homeowners insist production in native form is vital for several reasons related to the visibility, utility, and searchability of metadata. Metadata, colloquially known as data about data, encompasses the structural information of a file that contains data about it as opposed to describing its actual substantive content. Often hidden and embedded within the original file, metadata does not normally appear on a printed page. [internal quotations omitted]

State Farm has offered to produce ESI in searchable, but "static" form. PDF, TIFF, and JPEG files are common examples of static electronic formats. Static forms of ESI are created by converting native formats into static images, which removes metadata from the native files. Static form may be searchable—to a more limited extent than native form—using optical character recognition (OCR) software.

To support ESI production in searchable static form, State Farm offered evidence that it processes more than 35,000 new claims each day and, in the ordinary course of business, information related to those claims is routinely converted into static format. When claims are being processed, claims-related information is necessarily created in native form. With regard to some types of claims-processing information, the native form is static, for example, handwritten notes and photographs. But to facilitate efficient business operations, State Farm employs a central repository—the Enterprise Claims System (ECS)—that is "the system of record" for claims handling at State Farm. Claims-related information originally created in disparate systemic locales must be uploaded to the ECS, where it is converted and stored in secure, read-only formats for data integrity and access (e.g., PDF, TIFF, or JPEG). By consolidating information from different sources into the ECS, the claims-file information becomes readily accessible for processing claims on behalf of policyholders and enables effective management of claims processes. Some ESI information exists solely in the ECS platform, but other information may also exist in native forms elsewhere within thousands of State Farm servers.

According to State Farm's discovery expert, static format is beneficial because the information can be searched, reviewed, and handled without inadvertent or intentional alteration by ECS users. With regard to litigation impacts, the expert reported that ESI in static format is easier to Bates number for discovery; allows efficient management of documents as exhibits at depositions, hearings, and trials; enables redaction, which is not possible with most native forms of ESI; and avoids intentional or unintentional alteration of the information, which may be difficult to detect or propagate further disputes about data integrity. According to a State Farm business analyst, "ECS is the most reasonably available source of claim file information in the ordinary course of business. It is the most convenient, least burdensome and least expensive means of producing the information plaintiff requested."

State Farm's expert averred that production in the native form of files "would require State Farm to engineer a new process that includes determining upstream sources of the data, validating the upstream sources, determining whether native files of the information still exist, and developing an extraction method for the native versions." Without quantifying the time or expense involved, the expert opined that "[t]hese additional steps would be an extraordinary and burdensome undertaking for State Farm" and are unnecessary because State Farm's proffered production form is "reasonably usable."

State Farm's business analyst further elaborated on the burden of native-form production relative to the convenience and cost-effectiveness of producing the information as it is maintained in the ECS, explaining that:

> forced departure from [State Farm's] standard business process for production to find other versions of information now incorporated into the claim file in ECS in other repositories . . . would require extraordinary efforts on State Farm's part . . . . Included in these additional efforts would be identifying all such repositories, finding ways to identify and match each item of information in ECS to the same information in other formats in other repositories, and then finding ways to capture, review and produce the duplicative information.

The homeowners supported their proposed electronic discovery protocol with expert testimony that static images have less utility compared to native format, which would allow them to see formulas in Excel spreadsheets, search and sort the information by data fields, analyze the relationship of data, and see information in color that may not translate as accurately to stored or printed static images. Referring to static-form production as "the electronic equivalent of a print out," the homeowner's expert explained that useful metadata would not be viewable in static form, including tracked changes and commenting in Word documents; animations, other dynamic information, and speaker notes in static printouts of PowerPoint documents; and threading information in emails that would allow construction of a reasonable timeline related to State Farm's processing of the homeowners' claims. The expert also opined that production of ESI in static form is significantly more expensive for the requesting party, due to the fact that storage costs rise with the size of the file and conversion to static form drastically increases the size of ESI files. The homeowners thus assert searchable static format is not a "reasonably usable form," as State Farm contends.

The homeowners' expert also refuted State Farm's claim of burden, testifying production would be as simple as handing over native ESI on a "thumb drive or on an external hard drive." Noting that ESI in native form has to be gathered to create static form in the first instance, the expert disclaimed the existence of any added burden on State Farm, stating: "Not only would [producing in native format not] require extraordinary steps, it would require fewer steps than those that they are employing right now. When you take the native data, you are dealing with it as it lies." Summarizing the homeowners' position, the expert explained, "[W]e're not imposing any additional duties, we're only asking that they not be allowed to dumb down, to downgrade the data for production."

* * *

II. Discussion

* * *

B. Form of Electronic Discovery

The rules of civil procedure generally extend the scope of discovery to "any matter that is not privileged and is relevant to the subject matter of the pending action, whether it relates to the claim or defense of the party seeking discovery or the claim or defense of any other party." TEX. R. CIV. P. 192.3(a). As a counterbalance rested in concerns about "unwarranted delay and expense," TEX. R. CIV. P. 192 cmt. 7. Rule 192.4 expressly constrains the scope of discovery as to otherwise discoverable matters.

* * *

So while metadata may generally be discoverable if relevant and unprivileged, that does not mean production in a metadata-friendly format is necessarily required. Indeed, as a federal district court recently observed, a weak presumption against the production of metadata has taken hold, which may be due to metadata's status as the new black, with parties increasingly seeking its production in every case, regardless of size or complexity. [internal quotations omitted]

***

In *In re Weekley Homes, L.P.*, 295 S.W.3d 309, 322 (Tex. 2009), we summarized the "proper procedure" under Rule 196.4, including the directive that the parties "make reasonable efforts to resolve the dispute without court intervention." Meeting and conferring to resolve e-discovery disputes without court intervention is essential because discovery of electronic data involves case-specific considerations and each side possesses unique access to information concerning reasonable and viable production methods, resources (technological or monetary, for instance), and needs. *In re Weekley Homes* did not consider the precise issues presented here, however—namely, whether the form requested controls and how proportionality factors into the analysis.

* * *

When a reasonably usable form is readily available in the ordinary course of business, the trial court must assess whether any enhanced burden or expense associated with a requested form is justified when weighed against the proportional needs of the case. The proportionality inquiry requires case-by-case balancing in light of the following factors:

1. Likely benefit of the requested discovery: If the benefits of the requested form are negligible, nonexistent, or merely speculative, *any* enhanced efforts or expense attending the requested form of production is undue and sufficient to deny the requested discovery. In such cases, quantifying or estimating time and expenses would not be critical, as it may be when benefits clearly exist. At the opposite end of the spectrum, a particularized need for the proposed discovery will weigh heavily in favor of allowing discovery as requested but, depending on the force of other prudential concerns, may warrant cost-shifting for any "extraordinary steps" required.

Courts should consider cumulative effects rather than viewing benefits and burdens in a vacuum. Here, for example, many similar cases arising from the same extreme weather event are currently pending against State Farm. The identification and retrieval process State Farm would have to develop for native-form production may be a ticket for one train only—exponentially increasing the burden when considered in the context of repeated litigation—or have broader utility, which could have a cumulatively reductive effect. The record does not tell us, but if there are likely uses for the identification and retrieval process beyond the instant mandamus cases, initial burden and expense may be substantially ameliorated, and if not, the burden and expense may be significantly enhanced.

2. The needs of the case: In these mandamus cases, the homeowners seek native production both for optimal search capability and to access metadata. Recognizing that metadata serves no genuinely useful purpose in many cases, many parties, local rules and courts have in current practice endorsed the use of static image production formats, principally TIFF and PDF formats. [internal quotations omitted] But metadata may be important, even dispositive in some cases.

Relevance of metadata and the relative significance to the case must be determined on a case-by-case basis. But metadata's relevance must be obvious or at least linked, more or less concretely, to a claim or defense. Hypothetical needs, surmise, and suspicion should be afforded no weight. As a general proposition, metadata may be necessary to the litigation when the who, what, where, when, and why ESI was generated is an actual issue in the case, not merely a helpful or theoretical issue. Take, for instance, a wrongful termination case where timing of the events leading up to and following termination or authorship of case-critical documents might be a central issue in the case.

Here, the homeowners have argued production in native format is necessary to ensure disclosure of all potentially relevant information. By way of example, the homeowners provided evidence that captions annotating some photographs of hail damage to a house—such as "north elevation with hail damage missed by [claims adjuster]"—were not captured when the photographs were converted to static format in the ECS. State Farm insists, however, that PDF production of photos from the ECS does not support the necessity for native-form production, as the homeowners claim, because the omitted photo captions were provided to the homeowners through an ECS "caption log" as well as via production from another database State Farm had identified as storing discoverable ESI.[49] In evaluating whether a particular form of production is required, the court should consider not only the relative importance of the information to the central issues in the case, but also availability of that information from some other source that is more convenient, less burdensome, or less expensive.

3. <u>The amount in controversy</u>: Accessibility—or relative inaccessibility—of electronic data contributes to increased costs and burdens associated with electronic discovery. "While large companies are still learning to cope with e-discovery costs, e-discovery remains costly and complex for the small company, small case, and unrepresented litigant. Because e-discovery is very expensive and quite complicated, the advent of e-discovery is forcing settlements, and thus, denying litigants an opportunity to litigate the merits of the case." Jennifer M. Smith, *Electronic Discovery and the Constitution: Inaccessible Justice*, 6 J. LEGAL TECH. RISK MGMT. 122, 141-42 (2012).

* * *

For these reasons, the amount in controversy plays a pivotal role in determining whether production in a specified form is justified given the burden or expense required to meet the demand.

4. <u>The parties' resources</u>: Whether the producing party has the means to fairly and realistically produce in the requested format is a significant proportionality consideration. An expense that is a drop in the bucket to one party, may be insurmountable to another. While this factor is important to the balancing inquiry "considerations of the parties' resources does not foreclose discovery requests addressed to an impecunious party, nor justify unlimited discovery requests addressed to a wealthy party." FED. R. CIV. P. 26 committee's note to 2015 amendment. Rather, " 'the court must apply the standards in an even-handed manner that will prevent use of discovery to wage a war of attrition or as a device to coerce a party, whether financially weak or affluent.' " *Id.* (quoting advisory committee's note to 1983 amendment).

---

[49] In addition to the ECS, State Farm identified seven other data sources for discoverable information and delineated reasonably usable formats for production from these sources: Online Reinspection Tool (searchable PDF of worksheets and photographs and other materials in the form they exist in that system); Management Closed Assignment Review (Microsoft Excel format); Messaging Archive for email and instant messages (emails in MSG, EML, or PST and attachments in native format they are archived in, such as DOC, PPT, XLS, PDF, JPEG, etc.); Enterprise Complaint Tracking (Microsoft Excel format); Fire Master Record; Information from State Farm Human Resources data sources; and Enterprise Claim Survey Tool (searchable PDF format).

But beyond financial resources, one must also consider whether the requesting party has the technological resources to make proper use of ESI in the form requested. A high-powered luxury sports car is useless to someone who lacks a license to drive it. To that point, the homeowners' discovery expert testified it would be more convenient for lawyers lacking advanced technology to use image formats, but the homeowners' counsel in this case has "invested considerably to have the tools necessary to be able to deal with advanced forms of information." This may be another way of looking at the benefit versus the burden; if the potential benefits could not be realized, any associated burden would be unwarranted.

5. Importance of the issues at stake in the litigation: Legal disputes are always important to those who are litigating them. For one side, however, the precedential value may be more significant than the other, justifying an outlay of time and expenses that would otherwise be unwarranted. Likewise, " 'many cases in public policy spheres, such as employment practices, free speech, and other matters, may have importance far beyond the monetary amount involved.' Many other substantive areas also may involve litigation that seeks relatively small amounts of money, or no money at all, but that seeks to vindicate vitally important personal or public values." *Id.* (discussing proportionality considerations, including monetary stakes versus broader societal and policy impacts and quoting a 1983 Advisory Committee Note regarding proportionality).

6. The importance of the proposed discovery in resolving the litigation: Discovery must bear at least a reasonable expectation of obtaining information that will aid the dispute's resolution. Reasonable discovery does not countenance a "fishing expedition." *In re Alford Chevrolet-Geo*, 997 S.W.2d 173, 181 (Tex. 1999) (orig. proceeding).

7. Any other articulable factor bearing on proportionality: The foregoing factors are derived directly from the discovery rules, but are certainly not exclusive. As history tells, technology is constantly evolving at rapidly increasing rates. The legal system is not nearly as agile, leaving us in a perpetually responsive posture. Trial courts have flexibility to consider any articulable factor that informs this jurisprudential inquiry.

C. Parity with the Federal Rules of Civil Procedure

Our application of proportionality principles in this context aligns electronic-discovery practice under the Texas Rules of Civil Procedure with electronic-discovery practice under the Federal Rules of Civil Procedure.

* * *

III. Conclusion

Today, we elucidate the guiding principles informing the exercise of discretion over electronic-discovery disputes, emphasizing that proportionality is the polestar. In doing so, we further a guiding tenet of the Texas Rules of Civil Procedure: that litigants achieve a "just, fair, equitable and impartial adjudication . . . with as great expedition and dispatch and at the least expense . . . as may be practicable." TEX. R. CIV. P. 1. Because the trial court and the parties lacked the benefit of our views on the matter, neither granting nor denying mandamus relief on the merits is appropriate. Accordingly, we deny the request for mandamus relief without prejudice to allow the relator to seek reconsideration by the trial court in light of this opinion.

Notes & Questions

1. *Opposing-party access and device turnover*. In 2018, the Texas Supreme Court had occasion to consider the standards to allow an opposing party direct access to an adversary's hard drives and other electronic storage media. In *In re Marion Shipman*,[1] a bank sued Marion Shipman, along with Mark and Jamie Shelton, for business-loans-gone-bad after an auto dealership owned by all three went out of business. The Shipman/Shelton ventures ended in 2010 and the bank sued.

During the litigation, Jamie Shelton brought a third-party action against Shipman alleging fraud and breach of fiduciary duty. Jamie sought—and obtained an order compelling—discovery from Shipman, including financial records and spreadsheets related to the auto business. Shipman testified at a deposition that he had produced all the documents he had, including electronic documents but that some information was on a "crashed" computer. A few days after the deposition, Shipman supplemented the document production with more electronic files, apparently recovered with the assistance of his son who found a "backup folder."

Jamie came to believe that Shipman was incompetent or unwilling to retrieve all available electronic documents and filed a new motion to compel. This time Jamie asked the court to order Shipman to turn his computer over for forensic examination. The trial court signed a broad order, compelling Shipman to turn over all computers or "media" in his possession that had been used from 2000 to the present date.[2]

The Supreme Court ultimately held that this order was an abuse of discretion. The problem with the relief the trial court granted, according to the court, was that Jamie provided insufficient proof that Shipman was incapable or unwilling to search his devices for responsive information. Though Shipman did equivocate about the existence of more documents, and though he produced information late after enlisting the help of his son, no proof indicated he was incompetent. Moreover, the court looked to the lack of evidence about the capabilities of Shipman's son—enlisted to help find documents—to find that the trial court exceeded its discretion in ordering device turnover.

In particular, the court rejected the argument that a late production is evidence of incompetence or unwillingness sufficient to support a turnover order. Producing parties "should not face the perverse incentive to conceal such information lest they be forced to hand over the underlying electronic devices for forensic examination."[3] The proof the court looked to, in contrast, was Shipman's own affidavit that he had indeed turned over all responsive information in his possession. Citing the high burden to obtain device turnover or opposing-party direct access under *Weekley*, the court found that the order for device turnover was an abuse of discretion. The court also found that the trial court's order granted broader relief than Jamie sought. In particular, the order compelled Shipman to turn over *all* devices and *media* (e.g. flash drives and external hard drives), not just his present computer.

---

1 540 S.W.3d 562 (2018).

2 The trial court also spelled out a forensic protocol meant to protect Shipman's privacy. The forensic examiner would create a list of file names without examining the content of the files. This list would be shared with Shipman's lawyer who could then lodge objections before the documents were turned over to Jamie.

3 *Id.* at 568.

Some lessons from this case: if requesting parties seek device turnover, they should seek specific testimony about the producing party's incompetence or other inability to retrieve the requested information. Moreover, if the party has conscripted the help of another person or entity to aid in searching media, the party seeking device turnover should depose or examine that person to demonstrate incompetence or inability. Lastly, draft and present an order to the court that is within the relief sought by the motion to compel and does not exceed its scope.

2. *Problem.* Tammy and Meg are involved in an intersection collision. Tammy claims that Meg was negligent and ran a red light, causing the crash. Tammy suffered several broken bones, including a broken pelvis, in the crash and incurred $120,000 in medical expenses, along with a few weeks' lost wages. Tammy sues Meg for these damages, along with pain and suffering. In Tammy's First Request for Production, she seeks "all text or other electronic messages arising from, related to, or describing the facts and circumstances of the [crash at issue] from the date of the incident to present." In response, Meg claims that no such messages exist, in part because the phone she had at the time was dropped in a swimming pool in the months following the crash (but before suit was filed). Meg still owns the phone, but it won't turn on. At a later motion to compel hearing, Tammy demands that Meg hire appropriate technicians to try to restore the data, and Tammy requests that Tammy's own experts be given access during the process (Tammy's experts believe that there is a significant chance at least some of the data can be salvaged).

Imagine that you are the judge hearing such a dispute. In light of *State Farm,* which proportionality factors are pertinent? How would you weigh them in resolving the dispute? Assuming you find that at least a portion of Tammy's request is permissible, would you give Tammy's own experts direct access to the device per *Shipman* and *Weekley?* Would it change your analysis if Meg resisted paying technicians to attempt to restore the data?

D. Depositions

Read Rules 199-203.

Depositions are one of the most valuable discovery tools, and may be used to obtain discovery from non-parties as well as parties to the litigation. Rule 199, which provides for depositions on oral examination, allows parties to interrogate a witness in person while under oath, and have the witness produce documents and tangible things. The deposition is ordinarily recorded and transcribed for use at trial. Rule 200 provides for depositions on written questions, in which parties submit written questions for a witness to answer under oath. Depositions on oral examination are clearly the most frequent, and will be the primary focus of these notes.

1. *Notice of Deposition on Oral Examination*

The party desiring to depose someone must serve written notice upon all other parties so that they can attend the deposition or seek a protective order.

a. *When to give written notice.* Rule 199.2 requires that a party give "reasonable notice" of a deposition. However, if a Request for Production is attached, 30 days notice is required because Rule 196 (Rule 205 for nonparties) applies. The deposition can be taken anytime during the discovery period, and leave of court or agreement is required if the deposition is to be taken outside of the discovery period.[1]

b. *Requirements of the notice.* The notice must be served on all parties or their attorneys according to Rule 21a. The notice must contain the name of the witness to be deposed (who can be a party or any non-party), the time and the place of the deposition, whether alternative means of conducting the deposition will be used, and, if the production of documents and tangible things is desired, a Request for Production that complies with Rule 196 (Rule 205 for nonparties). The notice should also identify persons attending the deposition other than the witness, parties, spouses of parties, counsel, counsel's employees, and officer taking the deposition.[2] Furthermore, if other parties intend to bring others into the deposition, they must give reasonable notice of their identity.[3]

c. *Depositions of organizations.* A witness must be a person. Nevertheless, the rules allow a party to name an organization as the witness and describe with reasonable particularity the matters on which examination is requested.[4] In response (a reasonable time before the deposition) the organization must designate a person or persons to testify on the organization's behalf.[5] The person must testify as to matters that are known or reasonably available to the organization, and the organization must ensure that the designated representative is competent and can give meaningful testimony on the specific topics requested.[6]

2. *Compelling Appearance*

a. *Party deponents.* Service of the notice of deposition upon the party or its attorney is sufficient to require a party, a party's agents or employees, or persons subject to the party's control to attend a deposition to give testimony and produce designated documents and tangible things.[7]

b. *Non-party deponents.* Other witnesses may be compelled to attend a deposition (or trial) to give testimony and produce designated documents upon service of a subpoena.[8] The subpoena can be issued by the clerk of the court, an attorney, or any certified court reporter, and served by anyone over 18 that is not a party.[9] Rule 176.3 provides that a subpoenaed witness cannot be compelled to appear "in a county that is more than 150 miles from where the person resides or is served."

3. *Time and Place*

Rule 199.2(2) specifies permissible times and places for depositions. The time and place of the deposition must be reasonable. A party may notice a deposition in the county of the depo-

---

1 Rule 199.2(a).

2 Rule 199.2(b)(4), 199.5(a)(3).

3 Rule 199.5(a)(3).

4 Rule 199.2(b)(1).

5 *Id.*

6 *See* Allstate Texas Lloyds v. Johnson, 784 S.W.2d 100 (Tex. App.—Waco 1989, orig. proceeding) (stating that Allstate did not produce a person able to testify as to matters described in the notice).

7 Rule 199.3.

8 Rule 176.

9 Rule 176.4, .5.

nent's residence or where the witness is employed or regularly transacts business in person. If the deponent is a party, either an individually named party or a person that an organizational party designates to testify in its behalf, the deposition may also be noticed in the county of suit.[10] Transients or nonresidents can be deposed within 150 miles of where they are served with a subpoena. The deposition can also be noticed to take place at some other convenient place directed by the court. A witness need not be present to be deposed as the rules allow the deposition to be taken by telephone or other electronic means.[11]

4. *Objections before the Deposition Begins*

Any party or a nonparty witness may object to the time, place, manner, or general scope of the deposition by filing a motion for protective order or motion to quash the notice of deposition. If the motion is filed by the third business day after service of the notice, an objection to time and place stays the oral deposition until the court rules on the motion.[12] Motions based upon other depositions do not stay the deposition—the deposition goes forward absent an agreement or court order postponing it. The ruling on the motion for protective order is within the trial court's discretion; however, if the discovery sought is within the scope of Rule 192, the party seeking protection must present evidence showing a "particular, specific and demonstrable injury by facts sufficient to justify a protective order."[13]

WAL-MART STORES, INC.
v.
STREET

754 S.W.2d 153
(Tex. 1988)

PER CURIAM.

This is a discovery mandamus proceeding. Relator Wal-Mart Stores, Inc. seeks writ of mandamus directing the Honorable John Street, Judge of the 352nd District Court, to rescind or modify his order directing that Sam Walton, the Chairman of the Board of Wal-Mart Stores, Inc., appear in Fort Worth and give his deposition in a slip-and-fall accident case pending in Judge Street's court. Andrew Carrizales, plaintiff in that suit, alleges he fell and injured himself while a business invitee in the Wal-Mart store in Sulphur Springs, Texas. Carrizales also alleges Wal-Mart was grossly negligent in failing to provide for the safety of its business invitees.

Walton was president of the corporation at the time the accident allegedly occurred. When plaintiff directed notice of deposition expressly to Walton, however, Walton was no longer an employee of Wal-Mart Stores, Inc., but was Chairman of the Board of Directors for the company. Wal-Mart moved for a protective order, asserting that it did not control Walton as an employee, that the deposition was for purposes of harassment because Walton submitted affidavits that he

---

[10] *See* Wal-Mart Stores, Inc. v. Street, 754 S.W.2d 153, 155 (Tex. 1988).

[11] Rule 199.1(b).

[12] Rule 199.4.

[13] Masinga v. Whittington, 792 S.W.2d 940 (Tex. 1990, orig. proceeding) (deponent did not make necessary showing sufficient for protection from videotaping of deposition).

had no knowledge of the particular accident or store safety procedures involved, and that Walton should not be required to travel to Fort Worth when his residence and place of business was Bentonville, Arkansas.

Our rules provide that notice may be directed to "an agent or employee who is subject to the control of a party." Judge Street conducted at least two hearings on the matter of Walton's deposition. Since the evidence is uncontroverted that Walton was not an employee when notice was served, we assume that Judge Street found as a fact that Walton as Chairman of the Board, major shareholder and past president was an agent for Wal-Mart subject to its control. As to his testimony, the test for discovery purposes is whether "the information sought appears reasonably calculated to lead to the discovery of admissible evidence." On the present record we find no clear abuse of discretion in Judge Street's decision that Walton is an agent of the corporation subject to its control and that Walton may possess knowledge reasonably calculated to lead to the discovery of admissible evidence.

Judge Street also directed that the deposition be taken in Fort Worth, Texas. Rule 201 [now Rule 199.2] provides that if the deposition notice is directed to the corporation and the corporation designates an agent or agents to give the deposition, then the deposition "may be taken in the county of suit" subject to the protective provisions of Rule 166b(4) [now Rule 192.6]. In this case, Wal-Mart did not designate Walton on its behalf. The other express provision of the rule is that the place designated "shall be reasonable" and "shall be the county of the witness' residence, or where he is employed or regularly transacts business in person or at such other convenient place as may be directed by the court in which the cause is pending." Since nothing presented to Judge Street supports any conclusion that it was reasonable or otherwise convenient for Walton to travel to Fort Worth, the express provisions of the rule require the deposition to be taken in the county containing Bentonville, Arkansas. It was clear abuse of discretion for Judge Street to order the deposition to be taken at a location directly contrary to TEX. R. CIV. P. 201(5). Since the order of Judge Street conflicts with a rule of civil procedure, a majority of the court grants leave to file the petition for writ of mandamus and, without hearing oral argument, conditionally grants writ of mandamus directing Judge Street to modify his order to provide that the deposition be taken in the county of Walton's residence. We assume Judge Street will modify his order as directed in this opinion. If not, writ of mandamus will issue.

Notes & Questions

1. *Deposition subpoena.* What is the significance of the finding that Sam Walton was Wal-Mart's "agent," subject to Wal-Mart's control? Since 1988, the Rules have been amended. Is the "agent" language the Court relies on in *Wal-Mart* still a part of the deposition rules? What is the significance of the change?[171]

2. *Place of deposition.* A deposition of a party can always be noticed for the county of suit. Although Sam Walton (under then-applicable rules) was an "agent" within Wal-Mart's control, his deposition could not be noticed for the county of suit, Tarrant County. Why?

3. *The next episode of the Sam Walton saga.* After this opinion, Judge Street issued an order directing Wal-Mart to produce Walton for his deposition at the Wal-Mart headquarters in Bentonville, Arkansas. Walton, individually, obtained a protective order from the state court in Benton-

[1] *See* In re Reaud, 286 S.W.3d 574, 582 (Tex. App.—Beaumont 2009, orig. proceeding) (per curiam).

ville directing that the deposition be taken at the Bentonville courthouse. On the day of the deposition, Walton appeared at the courthouse, and the plaintiff's attorney appeared at Wal-Mart headquarters. Although they were only one mile away from each other, neither would budge, and the deposition did not go forward. The plaintiff subsequently obtained an order from Judge Street that struck Wal-Mart's pleadings, granted a default judgment as to liability against Wal-Mart, and ordered Walton to appear for his deposition in Judge Street's courtroom in Ft. Worth. Also, in the event Walton failed to appear for the deposition, the judge imposed increasing sanctions upon Wal-Mart for each day Walton failed to appear, eventually reaching $1,280,000 for the eighth day, and $1,000,000 per day thereafter.[2] Mr. Walton fought the order requiring him to go to Fort Worth, but this time the appellate court sided with the plaintiff:

> Walton contends that rule 201(5) accords him an absolute right to have his deposition taken in the county of his residence. He refers us to the rule and to the opinion of the Texas Supreme Court in *Wal-Mart Stores, Inc.* Neither the rule nor the Supreme Court's opinion supports Walton's conclusion. Rule 201(5) of the Texas Rules of Civil Procedure provides that, in addition to the county of the witness's residence, the taking of the witness's deposition may be where the witness is employed, where he regularly transacts business in person, or at such other convenient place as may be directed by the court in which the cause is pending. In *Wal-Mart Stores, Inc.,* the Supreme Court did not find that the deposition could only be taken in Bentonville, only that the record did not offer any support of Judge Street's conclusion that it was reasonable or otherwise convenient for Walton to travel to Fort Worth. We have found that the record as it presently stands does not show that Judge Street clearly abused his discretion in making such a finding.
>
> Walton contends that there is no showing that Fort Worth is convenient to him. His argument overlooks the record as it now stands, which includes the fact of his travels to Texas and around the country doing publicity work for Wal-Mart, as well as the fact that his personal attorney practices in Dallas, a city more convenient to Fort Worth than to Bentonville.
>
> We overrule relators' amended petition for writ of mandamus and dissolve the stay order which we have previously entered in this cause.[3]
>
> JUSTICE LATTIMORE, concurring, noted:
>
> It appears that the coercive power of the trial court here lies in striking at the assets of Walton, *i.e.* the value of his stock in Wal-Mart. Even though Walton is not a party to the suit, nor is he a subpoenaed witness, nor has he ever consented to be a witness in Texas, he is being attacked by the trial court and accused of outrageous conduct. This interpretation of Walton's conduct is laid at the door of Wal-Mart, and Wal-Mart is to be punished by extreme sanctions on some theory of vicarious liability for Walton's state of mind.
>
> The drivers of this unfortunate series of events appear to be the desire of skilled and strong-willed lawyers and judge to prevail regardless of the imbalance between procedure and results. This does little to improve the standing of the civil justice system with the public.
>
> I concur only because I must follow the law as it now stands.[4]

---

2 Wal-Mart Stores, Inc. v. Street, 761 S.W.2d 587 (Tex. App.—Fort Worth 1988, orig. proceeding).

3 *Id.* at 591.

4 *Id.* at 592 (LATTIMORE, concurring).

Eventually, a total of $11.55 million in sanctions accrued before Walton appeared for his deposition. Before a final judgment was rendered in the case, a different judge assumed the bench of the 352nd District Court and entered an order withdrawing the sanctions, which was upheld by the court of appeals.[5] Only then did an ordinary slip and fall trial become a possibility.

4. *Examination and cross-examination.* When the deposition begins, the witness is placed under oath. The parties then examine and cross-examine the witness. Usually, the party noticing the deposition begins the examination of the witness, then other parties examine the witness. A party may serve written questions in lieu of participating in the oral examination.[6] No "side" may examine or cross-examine a witness for more than six hours. The discovery control plan applicable to the case may have aggregate deposition limits as well.

5. *Conduct, objections, and instructions to the witness.* Typically, there is no judge at the deposition who can rule on objections. Therefore, most objections to questions and answers are not required to be made at the deposition, because they can be made for the first time when (and if) the deposition is used at trial.[7] Nevertheless, in the past lawyers often used objections and instructions to the witness as opportunities to coach the witness and interrupt the lawyer questioning the witness. There was wide consensus that the practice had gotten so out of hand that something had to be done. As a result, the current rules severely proscribe what can be said during a deposition.

a. *Conduct restrictions, Rule 199.5(d) & (h).* The deposition is to be conducted with the same demeanor as a trial. Counsel are to cooperate and be courteous. The witness shall not be evasive or delay. Private conferences between the witness and the witness's attorney during the deposition shall not be conducted during the deposition except to determine whether a privilege should be asserted and during agreed recesses and adjournments. The rules also require good faith in conducting and defending the deposition.

b. *Objections, Rule 199.5(e).* Objections to questions are limited to "objection, leading" and "objection, form." Objections to testimony are limited to "objection, nonresponsive." These objections are waived if not stated as phrased. These objections to the form of the question or nonresponsiveness of the answer have always been appropriate, proper and required. The objections give the questioning party an opportunity to rephrase the question and the witness a chance to respond to the question during the deposition, curing any potential problem with admissibility that may arise at trial. For example, a lawyer might object to leading questions at a deposition. Although it is not improper to ask a leading question in a discovery deposition, it is improper to ask one to one's own witness at trial. Thus, parties at the deposition should make the proper objection at the deposition so that they can object to its admissibility into evidence. If they failed to make the proper objection at the deposition, the objection to the form of the question is waived, and the questioner can use the testimony at trial if it is otherwise admissible.

c. *Instructions not to answer on grounds of privilege, Rule 199.5(f).* An attorney may instruct a witness not to answer a question to preserve a privilege. The instruction on grounds of privileges from discovery are necessary to keep the witness from disclosing privileged material in an answer. Once privileged material is disclosed, the privilege is waived. Whether the privilege

---

[5] Carrizales v. Wal-Mart Stores, Inc., 794 S.W.2d 129 (Tex. App.—Fort Worth 1990, writ denied).

[6] Rule 199.5(b).

[7] *See* Rule 199.5(e) (providing that the court is not confined to objections made at the deposition other than the three required).

claimed is valid or not can be brought before the court through a motion to compel or motion for protective order while the remainder of the deposition is postponed pending restriction of the question or after the deposition is concluded. If the court determines the material is not privileged, the deposition can resume so the witness can answer the questions not answered previously.

d. *Instructions not to answer on other grounds, Rule 199.5(f).* An attorney may instruct the witness not to answer on other grounds only to comply with a court order, to protect the witness from "an abusive question or one for which any answer would be misleading," or to secure a ruling after suspending the deposition. Comment 4 to Rule 199 explains that instructions sometimes are necessary because it is unfair to require a witness to answer particular questions. The comment identifies as unduly unfair "when did you stop beating your wife?" type of questions, and questions that are "clearly beyond the scope of discovery" or that are "argumentative, repetitions, or harassing." These instructions should generally be avoided because scope of inquiry at a deposition is as broad as the scope of discovery identified in Rule 192. Nevertheless, because conference and instructions to witnesses are so severely limited, the rules use this instruction to allow attorneys to protect their witnesses from clearly irrelevant inquiries and harassment.

e. *Suspending the deposition, Rule 199.5(g).* A party or witness can suspend the deposition if the time limits have expired or the deposition is being conducted or defended in violation of the discovery rules. The deposition will be suspended for the time necessary to obtain a ruling from the trial judge on the matter in dispute.

6. *The deposition transcript.* The record of a deposition is usually a transcript, sometimes accompanied by a video.

a. *Recording the deposition.* The deposition must be before a "deposition officer."[8] By statute, the deposition generally must be recorded stenographically by a certified shorthand reporter.[9] The stenographic recording is later transcribed. At the option of the noticing party, the deposition may be recorded by nonstenographic means (e.g. audio or video).[1810] If any other party would like to record the deposition stenographically or by any other method, that party may do so upon notice and an agreement to pay for the additional method.[1911] A nonstenographic recording can be conducted without a contemporaneous stenographic recording only if the parties, their attorneys, or full-time employees of the parties or their attorneys record the deposition.[12] The deposition officer also administers the oath to the witness.

b. *Requirements.* Rule 203 sets out all the requirements for signing, certification, and delivery of the deposition transcript. The deposition officer submits the deposition transcript to the witness for review, correction and signature. The court reporter then files and serves a certificate that certifies the transcript's authenticity and the amount of time used by the parties at the deposition. The court reporter then delivers the original deposition, together with any exhibits, to the attorney or party who asked the first question at the deposition. The custodial attorney is to make the original available to other parties for inspection and copying.

c. *Motion to suppress.* A party may object to irregularities in the way the deposition officer handled the deposition by filing a motion to suppress the deposition. If the court reporter has

8 Rule 199.1(a), 203.1(a).

9 TEX. GOVT. CODE ANN. § 154.101(f).

10 Rule 199.1(c).

11 *Id.*

12 TEX. GOVT. CODE § 52.033.

complied with the delivery requirements of Rule 203.3, the motion must be filed at least one day before the case is called to trial to preserve any objections to a stenographic transcript of the deposition. A motion to suppress a nonstenographic recording must be filed at least 30 days before trial.

7. *Agreements concerning deposition procedure.* Like most discovery rules, the deposition rules may be varied by agreement.

a. *Record of agreements.* Any agreement that varies deposition procedure must be made part of the record according to Rule 11 or as part of the deposition record according to Rule 191.1 as appropriate.

b. *The "usual agreements".* Beware of situations where the court reporter and other lawyers at a deposition ask if you want the "usual agreements." These agreements may vary from county to county and from court reporter to court reporter. The rules currently provide for a procedure for objections, witness signature, and transcript delivery that is efficient and protects all of the parties and the witness. However, the usual agreements in a particular locality may be rather unusual. Be sure you understand any agreements that vary the rules' formal requirements.

8. *Supplementing the deposition.* There is no general duty to supplement deposition testimony.[13] The duty imposed by Rule 193.5 applies only to "written discovery." The deposition rules provide for the witness to make corrections when signing the transcript,[14] but make no reference to supplementing deposition testimony. Note, however, that Rule 195.6 imposes a limited duty to supplement the deposition testimony of retained experts.

9. *Using the deposition at trial.* Depositions, like other discovery, may have evidentiary value at trial.

a. *Admissibility.* A deposition is admissible at trial or in any other hearing against any party who was present or represented at the deposition or who had reasonable notice thereof, according to the rules of evidence. The deposition is admissible against a party joined after the deposition is taken if that party has an interest similar to parties who attended the deposition, or, if the party has had a reasonable opportunity to redepose the deponent, but failed to do so.[15] The depositions are read into the record in question and answer form and the rules of evidence are applied to each question and answer as though the witness were testifying live.

b. *The "same proceeding".* Depositions taken in the "same proceeding" are not hearsay, and, therefore, the deponent need not be unavailable for the deposition to be admissible.[16] The same proceeding includes any suit brought in a Texas court or a court of any other state or the United States involving the same subject matter and the same parties or their representatives or successors.[17] Depositions taken in different proceedings (or for that matter, previous testimony taken at a trial or hearing rather than a deposition) may be considered hearsay unless it falls within another hearsay exception. For instance, if the witness is "unavailable" under TRE 804(a), the witness's former testimony in another proceeding may be admitted if the party against whom the

---

[13] *See* Titus County Hospital District v. Lucas, 988 S.W.2d 740 (Tex. 1998) (no general duty to supplement depositions under old rules).

[14] Rule 203.1(b).

[15] Rule 203.6(b).

[16] TRE 801(e)(3).

[17] Rule 203.6(b).

testimony is offered or a person with a similar interest had the opportunity and similar motive to cross-examine.[18]

c. *Nonstenographic recordings.* Rule 203.6(a) directs the use of a nonstenographic recording of a deposition. Generally, the nonstenographic recording may be used to the same extent as a stenographic recording. If there is no transcript of the deposition, however, the court can require that a complete transcript be made of the nonstenographic recording by a certified court reporter. This rule addresses the unusual circumstance when a dispute exists concerning the contents of a nonstenographic recording or the written transcript of that recording.

10. *Deposition variations.* Although oral questioning, occurring during the ordinary course of litigation, usually comes to mind first when thinking about depositions, there are other forms.

a. *Depositions on written questions.* Rule 200 authorizes a party to take a deposition on written questions. The end product is similar to interrogatories in that the witness responds under oath. However, depositions on written questions are not "written discovery," so Rules 193 and 197 do not apply. The deposition notice and attached direct questions must be served 20 days before the deposition (although 30 days is required if a Request for Production is attached). Within 10 days after service, any party may object to the direct questions and serve cross-questions. Within 5 days after service of cross-questions, any party may object and serve additional questions. Within 3 days after service of these additional questions, a party may serve recross questions. Any objections to these must be served within 5 days or at the time of the deposition, whichever occurs first.

b. *Foreign depositions.* Rule 201 allows a deposition to be taken in another state or country for use in a case filed and pending in Texas state court. The deposition is noticed to be taken in the other jurisdiction before a person authorized to administer oaths according to the laws of that jurisdiction or the laws of Texas. If a subpoena is needed, the Texas court will issue a document (a commission, letter rogatory, or letter of request) to the foreign jurisdiction. Upon receipt, the foreign jurisdiction will issue and serve a subpoena. The rule also specifies the procedure for obtaining a deposition in Texas for use in a foreign proceeding.

c. *Depositions before suit or to investigate claims.* Under Rule 202, a person may file a petition for the sole purpose of taking a deposition(s) to perpetuate his own testimony or that of another person for purposes of an action that he anticipates may be filed in the future or to investigate a potential claim or suit. The petitioner joins the persons expected to be interested in the future action, and requests an order authorizing the depositions upon finding that the deposition may prevent a failure or delay of justice in the anticipated suit or the likely benefit of allowing the deposition outweighs its burden.[19] The petition must be filed in a "proper court"—one with subject-matter jurisdiction (e.g., not to investigate a claim over which the federal courts have exclusive jurisdiction) and venue (if not in the county where the witness resides) over the anticipated action, and personal jurisdiction over the potential defendant.[20] The Supreme Court has held that the rule "is not a license for forced interrogations" and requires courts to "strictly limit and carefully supervise presuit discovery to prevent abuse."[21] The Supreme Court has also held that C.P.R.C. §

---

[18] TRE 804(b)(1).

[19] *See* In re Does, 337 S.W.3d 862 (Tex. 2011) (holding that a court cannot order pre-suit discovery by agreement over objections of other interested parties without making required findings).

[20] In re Doe, 444 S.W.3d 603, 609 (Tex. 2014).

[21] In re Wolfe, 341 S.W.3d 932 (Tex. 2011).

74.351, which requires plaintiffs to file an expert report within 120 days of filing a medical liability claim, precludes taking a Rule 202 deposition before filing the report.[22]

11. *Apex depositions*. Why did the plaintiff in *Wal-Mart Stores, Inc. v. Street*,[23] want to take Sam Walton's deposition in a slip and fall case in the first place? Should plaintiffs be able to take the deposition of high-ranking executives in any lawsuit against a corporation, or does such a person deserve protection from depositions of this sort? Consider the following opinion.

CROWN CENTRAL PETROLEUM CORP.
v.
GARCIA

904 S.W.2d 125
(Tex. 1995)

HIGHTOWER, JUSTICE.

GAMMAGE, JUSTICE notes his dissent.

In this original proceeding, we consider the propriety of an "apex" deposition, the deposition of a corporate officer at the apex of the corporate hierarchy. Relators Crown Central Petroleum Corporation and Crown Central Pipe Line Company seek a writ of mandamus directing the trial court to vacate its orders of January 18 and 25, 1995 concerning the deposition of Henry Rosenberg, Jr., the chairman of the board and chief executive officer of Crown Central Petroleum Corporation (Crown Central). Today this court adopts guidelines for depositions of persons at the apex of the corporate hierarchy. Because these guidelines had not been adopted prior to the trial court's orders, we deny the writ of mandamus without prejudice so that the trial court may reconsider its ruling in light of today's opinion.

Otto L. Carl, Jr. was employed by Crown Central at its Pasadena refinery for many years. Carl retired in 1981. In 1992, Carl died of lung cancer allegedly as the result of asbestos exposure. In late 1992, Margaret Carl, individually and as representative of the estate of Otto L. Carl, Jr., deceased, Otto L. Carl, III and Margaret E. Nowak (Plaintiffs) sued Crown Central and Crown Central Pipe Line Company for gross negligence. In July 1994, Plaintiffs filed a motion to require Crown Central to produce Rosenberg for a video deposition. The motion also included a subpoena duces tecum for Rosenberg to produce sixteen categories of documents. Crown Central responded with a motion to quash deposition accompanied by Rosenberg's affidavit. Among other things, the affidavit stated: "I have no personal knowledge of Mr. Carl or his job duties, job performance, or any facts concerning alleged exposure to asbestos by Mr. Carl. I was not involved in the day-to-day maintenance decisions made at the Refinery. I have no expertise in industrial hygiene, toxicology, or the health effects of asbestos exposure."[3] Crown Central complained that

---

[22] In re Jorden, 249 S.W.3d 416 (Tex. 2008).

[23] 754 S.W.2d 153 (Tex. 1998).

[3] Rosenberg's complete affidavit stated:

> My name is Henry A. Rosenberg, Jr. I am over the age of 18 years, of sound mind, have never been convicted of a felony, and am fully competent to make this affidavit. I have personal knowledge of the facts stated herein and they are true and correct. I am Chairman of the Board and Chief Executive Officer of Crown Central Petroleum Corporation ("Crown Central"). Crown Central employs approxi-

Plaintiffs had not exhausted less intrusive means of discovery before attempting to depose Rosenberg and that the motion to produce Rosenberg for a video deposition was filed solely for harassment purposes. Concerning the subpoena duces tecum, Crown Central asserted that Rosenberg was not the custodian of the requested documents and that a substantially identical request was made by the Plaintiffs in a request for production to which Crown Central had responded and filed objections. Neither motion was heard or acted upon. In mid-December 1994, Plaintiffs filed a notice of intention to take the oral deposition of Rosenberg. The notice also included a subpoena duces tecum for Rosenberg to produce thirty-two categories of documents. Crown Central responded with a motion to quash deposition and motion for protective order. Crown Central continued to complain about Rosenberg's lack of personal knowledge, the harassment of Rosenberg and the subpoena duces tecum for Rosenberg to produce thirty-two categories of documents. In late December 1994, Plaintiffs filed their first amended notice of intention to take the oral deposition of Rosenberg which reset the date for Rosenberg's deposition. The notice also included the same subpoena duces tecum concerning production of thirty-two categories of documents. Crown Central again responded with a motion to quash deposition and motion for protective order. Crown Central continued to complain about Rosenberg's lack of personal knowledge, the harassment of Rosenberg and the subpoena duces tecum for Rosenberg to produce thirty-two categories of documents.

On January 18, 1995, after a telephone hearing, the trial court granted Plaintiffs' motion to produce Rosenberg for video deposition and denied Crown Central's motion to quash. The trial court ordered Crown Central to produce Rosenberg for deposition and that Rosenberg produce all documents requested in the subpoena duces tecum. On January 20, 1995, Crown Central filed an emergency motion for reconsideration requesting that the trial court quash the deposition, compel the Plaintiffs to serve Rosenberg with written interrogatories concerning the extent of his knowledge concerning this action which would be answered within five days, limit the duration of Rosenberg's deposition to one hour, reconsider its ruling concerning the production of documents in the subpoena duces tecum, and amend its prior order so that neither Crown Central nor Rosenberg would be required to produce any documents requested in the subpoena duces tecum until after they are afforded a reasonable opportunity to have their objections to the production considered by the court. On January 25, 1995, the trial court denied the emergency motion for reconsideration.

I.

Crown Central argues that the trial court abused its discretion when it granted Plaintiffs' motion to produce Rosenberg for video deposition and denied Crown Central's motion to quash.

It is undisputed that a "party is entitled to discovery that is relevant to the subject matter of the claim, and which appears reasonably calculated to lead to the discovery of admissible evidence." Rule 200 [now Rule 199.1] of the Texas Rules of Civil Procedure permits a party to take the dep-

---

mately three thousand employees; therefore, I do not have personal knowledge of each employee's job duties or performance. I was a member of the American Petroleum Institute in 1987, which I understand was several years after Otto Carl retired from Crown Central. The letter to Mr. Carl dated June 24, 1980, a copy of which was attached to the Plaintiffs' Motion to Produce Mr. Henry Rosenberg, Jr. for Video Deposition, was a form letter sent to all employees who worked during a work stoppage which occurred at Crown Central's Pasadena refinery (the "Refinery"). I have no personal knowledge of Mr. Carl or his job duties, job performance, or any facts concerning alleged exposure to asbestos by Mr. Carl. I was not involved in the day-to-day maintenance decisions made at the Refinery. I have no expertise in industrial hygiene, toxicology, or the health effects of asbestos exposure.

osition of "any person." However, the person noticed for deposition also has the right to protection "from undue burden, unnecessary expense, harassment or annoyance, or invasion of personal, constitutional, or property rights." TEX. R. CIV. P. 166b(5) [now Rule 192.6].

* * *

II.

As virtually every court which has addressed the subject has observed, depositions of persons in the upper level management of corporations often involved in lawsuits present problems which should reasonably be accommodated in the discovery process. From the decisions of these other courts, we distill the following guidelines for addressing the problems.

When a party seeks to depose a corporate president or other high level corporate official and that official (or the corporation) files a motion for protective order to prohibit the deposition accompanied by the official's affidavit denying any knowledge of relevant facts, the trial court should first determine whether the party seeking the deposition has arguably shown that the official has any unique or superior personal knowledge of discoverable information. If the party seeking the deposition cannot show that the official has any unique or superior personal knowledge of discoverable information, the trial court should grant the motion for protective order and first require the party seeking the deposition to attempt to obtain the discovery through less intrusive methods. Depending upon the circumstances of the particular case, these methods could include the depositions of lower level employees, the deposition of the corporation itself, and interrogatories and requests for production of documents directed to the corporation. After making a good faith effort to obtain the discovery through less intrusive methods, the party seeking the deposition may attempt to show (1) that there is a reasonable indication that the official's deposition is calculated to lead to the discovery of admissible evidence, and (2) that the less intrusive methods of discovery are unsatisfactory, insufficient or inadequate. If the party seeking the deposition makes this showing, the trial court should modify or vacate the protective order as appropriate. As with any deponent, the trial court retains discretion to restrict the duration, scope and location of the deposition. If the party seeking the deposition fails to make this showing, the trial court should leave the protective order in place.

Because these guidelines had not been adopted prior to the trial court's orders, we deny the writ of mandamus without prejudice so that the trial court may reconsider its order denying Crown Central's motion to quash Rosenberg's deposition. The stay order previously issued by this court remains in effect only so long as necessary to allow the trial court to act.

Notes & Questions

1. *Unique or superior knowledge.* In *In re Alcatel USA, Inc.*,[1] the Texas Supreme Court elaborated upon what was required to show that an executive had "unique or superior knowledge" sufficient to satisfy the *Crown Central* standard. First, the Court emphasized that proving that the deponent was "a long-time company leader who sets the company vision with lofty goals" does not satisfy the standard.[2] The opinion says:

---

[1] 11 S.W.3d 173 (Tex. 2000).

[2] *Id.* at 177.

> Virtually every company's CEO has similar characteristics. Allowing apex depositions merely because a high-level corporate official possesses apex-level knowledge would eviscerate the very guidelines established in *Crown Central*. Such evidence is too general to arguably show the official's knowledge is unique or superior.[3]

Instead, "there must be some showing beyond mere relevance, such as evidence that a high-level executive is the only person with personal knowledge of the information sought or that the executive arguably possesses relevant knowledge greater in quality or quantity than other available sources."[4]

2. Crown Central *applies to all cases.*

In *Alcatel*, the Court rejected the claim that *Crown Central* applies only to tort claims where the executive would have no reason to know about the facts relevant to the claim, and not to business cases where the executive would be expected to participate in the facts giving rise to the claim. The Court said:

> Even if a lawsuit concerns a business dispute rather than a tort claim, and regardless of whether high-level executives would be expected to participate in a decision relevant to the dispute, the *Crown Central* prerequisites must still be met. Business disputes provide no greater license than any other kind of suit to explore by apex deposition whether a high-level executive knows anything relevant to the case. It may well be true that many tort claims arise without the knowledge or involvement of a high-level officer. Conversely, it may also be true that many business disputes directly involve the decisions or actions of a high-level officer. Regardless of the truth, *vel non*, of these suppositions, the fact remains that the *Crown Central* guidelines must be applied.[5]

3. *Procedure.* When a party notices the deposition of a high-level corporate official, the official or the corporation has to object to the deposition by filing a motion for protective order under Rule 192.6. Who has the burden of proof at the hearing on the Motion for Protective Order? Does it differ from the burden in the ordinary discovery motion?

---

[3] *Id. See also* AMR Corp. v. Enlow, 926 S.W.2d 640 (Tex. App.—Fort Worth 1996, no writ); In re El Paso Healthcare Sys., 969 S.W.2d 68, 74 (Tex. App.—El Paso 1998, no writ) (both cited favorably by Supreme Court in *AMR*).

[4] *Alcatel*, 11 S.W.3d at 178.

[5] *Id.* at 179-180.

E. Discovery Control Plans

Read Rules 11, 166, 169, 190, 191.1

You may have noticed that the rules allowing discovery requests all require that discovery be conducted "before the end of the discovery period." The discovery period is defined in Rule 190. Rule 190 introduces to Texas practice discovery limitations in the form of discovery control plans and levels of discovery. Rule 190.1 says "Every case must be governed by a discovery control plan. . . ." The discovery control plans limit the time during which discovery is conducted and the amount of discovery. The expedited action rule, Rule 169, and Level 3, Rule 190.4, impose requirements and limitations on matters other than discovery in order to expedite the trial process. Read the rules carefully.

Rule 190.1 requires plaintiffs to "allege in the first numbered paragraph of the original petition" whether the plaintiff intends for the case to be governed by Level 1, 2 or 3. This does not control the applicable discovery level, however, as this is merely a notice requirement and is not binding. Rule 47(c) requires in the petition a statement of the range of monetary relief sought. Rule 169 defines "expedited actions, which are controlled by Level 1." The case is in Level 2 unless the plaintiff makes the allegations that put the case in Level 1, or a court orders the case into Level 3.

Rules 169, 190 and 166 (the pretrial conference rule) work together to provide judges and parties with tolls for planning discovery, dispositive motions, and trial. These plans may have case-specific deadlines different from those provided in the rules.

F. Discovery Agreements

Read Rules 11, 191.1

In re BP PRODUCTS NORTH AMERICA, INC.

244 S.W.3d 840
(Tex. 2008)

JUSTICE GAULTNEY delivered the opinion of the Court.[1]

This mandamus proceeding concerns the enforcement of a discovery agreement governing what is commonly referred to as an "apex" deposition. The discovery agreement was signed by the attorneys for the parties, and filed as provided by Rule 191.1 and Rule 11. We conclude the trial court abused its discretion in failing to enforce the agreement.

THE TRIAL COURT PROCEEDINGS

Fifteen people died and hundreds suffered injuries in an explosion at relator BP Products North America, Inc.'s Texas City oil refinery. The hundreds of resulting lawsuits against BP

---

[1] The Honorable David Gaultney, Justice, Ninth Court of Appeals, Beaumont, sitting by commission of the Honorable Rick Perry, Governor of Texas, pursuant to TEX. GOV'T CODE § 22.005. Justice O'Neill is recused.

Products were consolidated for discovery in the 212th District Court in Galveston County. The parties conducted extensive discovery.

The plaintiffs served notices to take the depositions of two executives of relator's parent company, BP p.l.c.: John Manzoni, the head of refining and marketing, and John Browne, the chief executive officer. BP Products moved to quash the depositions and moved for protective orders. BP Products contended the plaintiffs had not met their burden under the apex doctrine. The plaintiffs responded, alleging that both Manzoni and Browne had unique or superior knowledge of relevant facts. The trial court initially struck BP Products' supporting affidavits as insufficient, and denied the motions. BP Products sought mandamus review, and the court of appeals granted relief requiring consideration of the affidavits. The trial court again denied BP Product's motions and allowed the depositions to proceed.

Instead of attempting further mandamus review, BP Products concluded a discovery agreement with the plaintiffs regarding the executives' depositions, and the parties filed the agreement with the trial court. *See* TEX. R. CIV. P. 11, 191.1. The agreement provided that the defendants would produce Manzoni for a four-hour deposition. In return, the plaintiffs promised they would withdraw the notice of deposition of Browne and would not request the deposition of any other executive officer or board member of BP p.l.c., with one exception: paragraph four of the agreement provided that if, during the Manzoni deposition, the plaintiffs developed new evidence that John Browne had "unique and superior personal knowledge" of relevant facts, the plaintiffs would be permitted to issue a new notice of deposition for Browne. The agreement also provided that BP Products retained its right to file a motion to quash and motion for protection "on this new notice," as well as its right to seek review of the trial court's ruling on these motions. In addition, the agreement provided that "if, following appeals referenced in paragraph 4, the deposition of John Browne is not protected, the deposition of John Browne will be limited to one hour by telephone."[3]

As plaintiffs' counsel explained to the trial court, the agreement was a "quid pro quo" negotiated to avoid delay in obtaining Manzoni's testimony:

* * *

After the agreement was concluded, Browne made numerous public statements regarding the Texas City explosion, including giving interviews to Fortune and the Financial Times, providing information packets to investors, and hosting several "town hall" meetings for employees, at least one of which plaintiffs contend appeared on the internet.

Plaintiffs took Manzoni's deposition and then issued a new notice to take Browne's deposition. Despite the provision of the agreement that any deposition take place "by telephone," the notice provided that the deposition would take place in Galveston, Texas. BP Products filed a motion for protection, complaining that the deposition could not be set in Galveston, that plaintiffs could still not show that Browne had unique or superior knowledge of relevant facts as required under *Crown Central*, and that Manzoni's deposition had not produced "new evidence" Browne had "unique and superior personal knowledge" of relevant facts as required under the parties' discovery agreement. Plaintiffs responded, asserting they could satisfy both the apex standard and the standard provided in the agreement.

On October 9th, the day of the hearing on BP Products' motion for protection, plaintiffs filed a supplemental response arguing that, at the time the parties entered the agreement, "it was not

[3] For the full text of the parties' agreement, see the appendix.

anticipated" new information demonstrating Browne's knowledge would become available from Browne's public statements. Plaintiffs initially stood by the Rule 11 agreement. . . .

The trial court ended the first day of the hearing with the statement that it was not convinced "based on how Mr. Browne likes to interject himself, that he doesn't want to be deposed." The trial court continued the hearings until October 11th, to give BP Products an opportunity to examine plaintiffs' new exhibits.

BP Products argued in its written response before the trial court that Browne's public statements did not demonstrate Browne had unique or superior knowledge, and, in any event, did not justify setting aside the parties' discovery agreement. At the October 11th hearing, plaintiffs argued:

> [T]here was fraud inducement in the execution of Rule 11. And we are asking the court to dissolve the Rule 11 agreement and to allow us to proceed with the deposition of Lord Browne. Not just for the one-hour telephonic conference, but for the four to six hours individually we were originally intending to take the deposition.

BP Products responded that plaintiffs had not alleged fraud, had not made allegations attacking the Rule 11 agreement, there was no evidence of fraud, and BP Products was entitled to time "to develop it, discover it, and they have to provide some evidence which they have not."

The trial court denied BP Products' motions, and ordered Browne's deposition to proceed at a place of the parties' choosing, "without limitations and the Rule 11." In its order of October 11, 2006, the trial court found that "new circumstantial evidence developed during Mr. John Manzoni's deposition shows that Mr. Browne has unique or superior knowledge of relevant facts." In addition, the court explained its refusal to enforce the parties' Rule 11 agreement:

> The Court further finds that the parties' Rule 11 Agreement concerning the depositions of Mr. Manzoni and Mr. Browne does not prevent the deposition of Mr. Browne going forward because:
>
> (1) After the effective date, Mr. Browne personally injected himself into the case with public comments that present new evidence of his unique or superior knowledge of relevant facts;
>
> (2) The Rule 11 Agreement was based on circumstances that have changed;
>
> (3) BP made misrepresentations that induced Plaintiffs to enter into the rule 11 Agreement;
>
> (4) BP is estopped to rely on the Rule 11 Agreement; and/or
>
> (5) BP's public comments appear to be part of a continuing effort by BP to taint the jury pool.
>
> The Court orders the deposition of Mr. Browne to proceed, without limitations and the Rule 11, at a time and place within the United States to be determined by agreement of the parties, or if in London, with costs/expenses to be paid by the defendants.

Relator filed a petition for writ of mandamus with the court of appeals, and, after the court of appeals denied that petition, relator filed a petition with this Court. We granted a stay of the trial court's order pending our review of the issues.

During the pendency of this mandamus proceeding, Browne resigned from BP p.l.c., and retired. The plaintiffs then filed a motion to dismiss BP Products' petition as moot, contending that apex protections do not apply to retired officials.

* * *

THE ISSUES

BP Products contends the trial court abused its discretion by setting aside the parties' discovery agreement and ordering Browne's deposition. BP Products argues the plaintiffs have not satisfied their burden under the apex doctrine. In BP Products' view, because Browne does not have unique or superior knowledge of relevant facts, his deposition would be outside the scope of discovery permitted by the rules governing apex depositions. BP Products also asserts the plaintiffs have not made the showing required under the parties' agreement because there is no evidence that Manzoni's deposition produced "new evidence" of Browne's "unique and superior personal knowledge."

THE RULE 191.1 AGREEMENT

Rule 191.1 provides that "except where specifically prohibited" the parties may modify the "rules pertaining to discovery" by agreement. An agreement is enforceable when it complies with the terms of Rule 11, or as it affects an oral deposition, if made a part of the record of the deposition. The agreement in this case complied with the requirements of Rule 11. The parties do not argue that the agreement was specifically prohibited[5] or that the agreement was outside the scope of Rule 191.1. The question here is whether the trial court had adequate reason to set aside the parties' agreement.

This Court has not previously addressed the scope of a trial court's power to set aside an otherwise enforceable Rule 191.1 agreement. Consistent with its powers over discovery, a trial court may modify discovery procedures and limitations for "good cause." This power, however, is not "unbounded." Rule 191, cmt. 1. Wherever possible, a trial court should give effect to agreements between the parties. Discovery agreements serve an important role in efficient trial management, permitting the parties to settle their disputes without resort to judicial supervision. The Rules of Civil Procedure encourage parties to reach discovery agreements. The parties conclude an agreement, the court should not lightly ignore their bargain.

A court should be particularly reluctant to set aside a Rule 191.1 agreement after one party has acted in reliance on the agreed procedure and performed its obligations under the agreement. An easy disregard for partially performed agreements would discourage parties from committing to discovery agreements for fear that the other party would avail itself of the benefit of the bargain and then attempt to avoid its own obligations.

The trial court apparently set aside the agreement here based on the court's application of equitable and contract principles. *See Kennedy v. Hyde*, 682 S.W.2d 525, 529 (Tex. 1984) (holding that agreements complying with Rule 11 are nevertheless subject to attack on the grounds of fraud or mistake, and nonconforming agreements "may be enforced for similar equitable reasons"). The trial court found that Browne's public statements justified setting aside the discovery agreement on grounds of misrepresentation, estoppel, and changed circumstances. On this record, none of these grounds provides a valid basis for ignoring the parties' agreement.

---

5 Paragraph 1 of the agreement provided that the trial court's previous oral ruling regarding the depositions of John Browne and John Manzoni "will be deemed by the parties to be vacated and of no effect." The agreement does not set aside a court order, something specifically prohibited as noted in comment 1 to Rule 191.1. The court's original ruling did not require the plaintiffs to take Browne's deposition, and the parties could agree "to shorten the time permitted for a deposition or to change the manner in which a deposition is conducted." *See* TEX. R. CIV. P. 191.1 cmt 1.

The plaintiffs identify no specific misrepresentations on which they may have relied. Nor does the record contain evidentiary support for the assertion that BP Products made a material, false representation that could have reasonably induced the plaintiffs to enter the discovery agreement. The trial court's explanation, that Browne's public statements established plaintiffs relied on misrepresentations concerning Browne's lack of knowledge, is not supported by the record or the parties' agreement. To the contrary, plaintiffs' statements to the trial court reflect that the plaintiffs entered the agreement to avoid the delays associated with mandamus review and to obtain Manzoni's deposition testimony prior to the September trial setting. Plaintiffs have always maintained Browne has unique and superior knowledge, the trial court previously ruled plaintiffs could take Browne's deposition, and the agreement itself provides that Browne's deposition may be taken for one hour, by telephone, if Manzoni's deposition demonstrated Browne's knowledge.

Similarly, the finding that "BP is estopped to rely on the Rule 11 Agreement" does not support the order. The trial court invoked estoppel apparently to prevent BP Products from taking a position in court concerning the extent of Browne's knowledge that the court viewed as inconsistent with Browne's public statements. Even if Browne had unique or superior knowledge, that fact would not estop BP Products from insisting upon the time and manner restrictions included in the agreement; the parties expressly agreed that even if Browne's deposition was "not protected," Browne's deposition would be limited.

The record also fails to show that Browne's public statements are the kind of changed circumstance that might amount to "good cause" for setting aside the discovery agreement. Browne's public statements rendered the agreement neither impracticable nor impossible. A subsequent development reducing the usefulness of a discovery agreement to one party, without more, does not justify a refusal to enforce the agreement.

The trial court found that "BP's public comments appear to be part of a continuing effort to taint the jury pool," but nothing in the record suggests sanctions were the subject matter of the hearing before the trial court. The hearing focused on the extent of Browne's knowledge as reflected in his public statements. In the trial court, plaintiffs neither explicitly requested sanctions nor cited any supporting rule or case law. Plaintiffs make no argument and cite no authority in their brief to this Court that the order was permissible as a sanction, though in oral argument they referenced other efforts by BP Products that are not part of this record. In the absence of a motion for sanctions, proper notice and opportunity to be heard, or the trial court's invocation of the court's power to sanction, the order striking the discovery agreement is not supportable as a sanctions order. TEX. R. CIV. P. 215.3.

Rule 191.2 provides that "[p]arties and their attorneys are expected to cooperate in discovery and to make any agreements reasonably necessary for the efficient disposition of the case." The Rule also provides that, when requesting a hearing relating to discovery or when filing a discovery motion, a party must certify "that a reasonable effort has been made to resolve the dispute without the necessity of court intervention and the effort failed." To achieve "the efficient disposition of the case . . . without the necessity of court intervention," parties and their attorneys must be able to rely on agreements. We hold the trial court abused its discretion by setting aside the parties' Rule 191.1 agreement.

BP PRODUCTS' MOTION TO QUASH

BP Products asserts that the apex doctrine bars plaintiffs from taking Browne's deposition. Plaintiffs assert the issue is moot because Browne has retired. The apex doctrine, however, does not control the outcome in this case. The discovery agreement displaced the common law standard with the parties' own standard. As BP Products explained in its brief: "If new evidence was developed during Manzoni's deposition showing that Browne had unique and superior knowledge of relevant facts, then Browne would be presented at a limited deposition . . . . Both parties retained the right to appeal the trial court's ruling on the new evidence issue."

The terms of the parties' discovery agreement apply. The trial court found that "new circumstantial evidence developed during Mr. John Manzoni's deposition shows that Mr. Browne has unique or superior knowledge of relevant facts." If some evidence supports the trial court's conclusion, the trial court could order a deposition consistent with the terms of the parties' agreement.

To satisfy the "new evidence" provision, plaintiffs rely, in part, on Manzoni's inability to answer certain questions about a twenty-five percent budget cut directive issued by BP p.l.c. The trial court concluded that Manzoni's inability to answer these questions constituted new evidence that Browne would have unique and superior knowledge about the budget cuts. This inference might not normally support the taking of an apex deposition. Here, however, the trial court could reasonably construe the "new evidence" provision of the Rule 191.1 agreement to allow plaintiffs a limited deposition of Browne to answer questions Manzoni may have been unable to answer but Browne could. On this record, under that construction of the parties' agreement, the deposition of John Browne could be taken for one hour, by telephone. The court instead ordered the deposition to proceed without the limitations agreed to by the parties. Though the trial court's "new evidence" finding would support authorizing plaintiffs to take Browne's deposition consistent with the agreed limitations, the finding does not justify setting aside the agreement.

CONCLUSION

The trial court abused its discretion in setting aside a valid discovery agreement without good cause. In this case, one party had already acted in reliance on the agreed procedure, partially performing its obligations. The parties agreed to define the scope of permissible discovery under Rule 192.3(a), limiting the expense and burden of litigating a disputed issue. Delaying review until appeal, under these circumstances, would defeat not only the purpose of the discovery agreement, but also the strong public policy encouraging parties to resolve their discovery disputes without court intervention. *See* TEX. R. CIV. P. 191.2. This case presents an issue of first impression, involving an important issue of public policy. We conclude that the benefits outweigh the detriments of mandamus review. *See In re Prudential*, 148 S.W.3d at 136-38.

We conditionally grant the writ of mandamus to compel the trial court to vacate its order, and direct the trial court to enforce the parties' agreement. We are confident the trial court will comply, and our writ will issue only if the court does not.

APPENDIX

Text of the Parties' Agreement

The parties agree that, in consideration of all the agreements made herein:

1. The oral ruling of the court on August 28, 2006, regarding the depositions of John Browne and John Manzoni will be deemed by the parties to be vacated and of no effect and no order will be tendered by plaintiffs.

2. BP Products will produce John Manzoni for deposition in Chicago on September 8 for four hours of deposition time.

3. Plaintiffs will withdraw the notice of deposition of John Browne and will not again notice or request the deposition of any other executive officer or board members of BP p.l.c., with one exception set out in paragraph 4 below.

4. If, during the deposition of John Manzoni, new evidence is developed that John Browne has unique and superior personal knowledge of facts relevant to the trial of this matter, Plaintiffs may issue a new notice for the deposition of John Browne. BP Products retains its right to file a motion to quash and motion for protection on this new notice, have that motion heard at the trial court and both parties retain their right to appeal the trial court's ruling.

5. Plaintiffs agree that if, following appeals referenced in paragraph 4, the deposition of John Browne is not protected, the deposition of John Browne will be limited to one hour by telephone.

Notes & Questions

1. *Rule 11 agreements.* The Supreme Court has noted "the ubiquity of agreed docket control orders" that are "routinely used in Texas trial courts to allow parties to manage discovery, provide deadlines for dispositive motions, and set a conference or trial date."[1] Rule 191.1 allows parties to agree to modify discovery procedures and limitations if their agreement satisfies Rule 11.

Rule 11 is an additional "statute of frauds" of sorts for agreements made during the pendency of a lawsuit, and is strictly construed. An agreement that doesn't comply with the rule's requirement that it be "in writing, signed and filed with the papers as part of the record, or unless it be made in open court and entered of record" will not be enforced. The rule applies to all kinds of agreements, including agreements relating to discovery, filing deadlines, and even settlement agreements. As the Supreme Court has noted:[2]

> The reason for Rule 11 is clear. [O]ral agreements concerning suits "are very liable to be misconstrued or forgotten, and to beget misunderstandings and controversies." "The purpose of this rule is evident, and its wisdom will be readily conceded. Agreements of counsel in the course of a judicial proceeding which affect the interests of their clients should not be left to the fallibility of human recollection. . . . The rationale underlying Rule 11 is sensible and contributes to the efficient court administration. Agreements and stipulations are welcomed by courts because they limit the matters in controversy and expedited trial proceedings. Rule 11 ensures that such agreements do not themselves become sources of controversy, impeding resolution of suits. The requirements of Rule 11 are not onerous; the benefits are substantial.

2. *When to file Rule 11 agreement.* The Supreme Court has held that the Rule 11 agreement need not be filed until after the dispute arises, before it is sought to be enforced. "To require the parties to immediately rush to the courthouse with a signed document in order to quickly comply with the requirements of Rule 11 before the other party reneges on his agreement goes against the grain of the policy in Texas jurisprudence which favors the settlement of lawsuits."[3]

---

1 Spectrum Healthcare Resources, Inc. v. McDaniel, 306 S.W.3d 249 (Tex. 2010) (holding that to extend statutory deadline for expert report in healthcare liability case, the order "must explicitly indicate the parties' intention to extend the deadline and reference that specific deadline").

2 Kennedy v. Hyde, 682 S.W.2d 525 (Tex. 1984).

3 Padilla v. LaFrance, 907 S.W.3d 454, 461 (Tex. 1995).

3. *Agreements affecting depositions*. Rule 191.1 allows parties to agree to modify deposition procedures if the agreement does not satisfy Rule 11, but the agreement is "made a part of the record of the deposition."

G. Rule 204 Physical and Mental Examinations

Often a party's mental or physical condition is at issue in a lawsuit, spurring the other party to request an independent mental or physical examination. A party cannot compel another to submit to such an examination by simply requesting it--the procedure requires a motion and court order. Rule 204 governs the requirements. The court may order an examination by a "qualified physician" (or in certain circumstances a "qualified psychologist") "for good cause shown…when the mental or physical condition of a party…is in controversy." The party that is examined may request a copy of the resulting report. The following opinion was decided under the predecessor of Rule 204, but remains the leading opinion concerning the "good cause" and "in controversy" requirement.

COATES
v.
WHITTINGTON
758 S.W.2d 749
(Tex. 1988)

SPEARS, JUSTICE.

At issue in this mandamus proceeding is whether a plaintiff who claims mental anguish damages in a personal injury action may be required to submit to a mental examination. In the underlying case, relator Myrna Coates sued Drackett Products Company for injuries she sustained while using Drackett's oven cleaner. She claimed both physical and mental anguish damages, and Drackett alleged that Mrs. Coates had been contributorily negligent. Drackett moved for an order compelling Mrs. Coates to submit to a mental examination pursuant to Rule 167a of the Texas Rules of Civil Procedure. Judge Mark Whittington granted the motion and ordered Mrs. Coates to undergo the examination. The court of appeals denied Mrs. Coates' motion for leave to file petition for writ of mandamus. We hold that the trial court abused its discretion by ordering Mrs. Coates to submit to a mental examination. We therefore conditionally grant relator's petition for writ of mandamus.

Mrs. Coates was injured when she inadvertently sprayed her arm with Drackett's "Mr. Muscle Oven Cleaner" while cleaning her stove top. She suffered severe second degree burns and permanent scarring on her left forearm as a result of the incident. Mrs. Coates brought a products liability action against Drackett, seeking damages for pain and suffering, physical impairment, lost earnings, medical expenses, and mental anguish. In response, Drackett pleaded contributory negligence, misuse, and pre-existing condition. Drackett moved for an order compelling Mrs. Coates to submit to a mental examination pursuant to Rule 167a of the Texas Rules of Civil Procedure, claiming that her mental anguish was pre-existing and may have contributed to the incident with the oven cleaner. The trial judge denied the motion. Drackett then sought a rehearing of its motion, asserting that Mrs. Coates had placed her mental condition "in controversy" by pleading mental anguish damages. Drackett also claimed that there was "good cause" for the mental examination because Mrs. Coates alleged that she experienced "depression and general mental problems at the time she used the oven cleaner." Judge Whittington granted Drackett's motion and ordered that Mrs. Coates submit to a mental examination by a court appointed psychologist. Judge Whittington ordered that the examination address: (1) the relationship of Mrs. Coates' prior problems to the occurrence made the basis of the suit, if any; and (2) the relationship of Mrs. Coates' prior problems to the prayer for mental anguish damages, if any. The court of appeals denied Mrs. Coates' motion for leave to file petition for writ of mandamus.

Rule 167a of the Texas Rules of Civil Procedure provides in pertinent part:

> When the mental . . . condition . . . of a party . . . is *in controversy*, the court in which the action is pending may order the party to submit to a . . . mental examination *by a physician* . . . . The order may be made only on motion *for good cause shown* and upon notice to the person to be examined and to all parties and shall specify the time, place, manner, conditions, and scope of the examination and the person or persons by whom it is to be made.
>
> TEX. R. CIV. P. 167a. (Emphasis added.)

* * *

The more significant issue in this case, however, is whether the trial court abused its discretion by ordering Mrs. Coates to undergo a mental examination. Rule 167a was derived from Rule 35 of the Federal Rules of Civil Procedure and largely duplicates the language of the original federal rule. Federal courts' construction of Rule 35 is thus helpful to an analysis of Rule 167a. The United States Supreme Court has held that federal Rule 35 requires an affirmative showing that the party's mental condition is genuinely in controversy and that good cause exists for the particular examination. *Schlagenhauf v. Holder*, 379 U.S. 104, 118, 85 S.Ct. 234, 242, 13 L.Ed.2d 152 (1964). In *Schlagenhauf*, the Court expressly stated that these two requirements are not met "by mere conclusory allegations of the pleadings—nor by mere relevance to the case." Similarly, Rule 167a, by its express language, places an affirmative burden on the movant to meet a two pronged test: (1) the movant must show that the party's mental condition is "in controversy"; and (2) the movant must demonstrate that there is "good cause" for a compulsory mental examination. In the absence of an affirmative showing of both prongs of the test, a trial court may not order an examination pursuant to Rule 167a.

Drackett maintains that Coates' mental condition is in controversy because she has pleaded for mental anguish damages. In support of its position, Drackett relies on *Schlagenhauf*, 379 U.S. at 119, 85 S.Ct. at 243, where the United States Supreme Court stated:

> A plaintiff in a negligence action who asserts mental or physical injury . . . places that mental or physical injury in controversy and provides the defendant with good cause for an examination to determine the existence and extent of such asserted injury.

In *Schlagenhauf*, however, the court also warned that sweeping examinations of a party who has not affirmatively put his mental condition in issue may not be routinely ordered simply because the party brings a personal injury action and general negligence is alleged. Further, federal courts that have applied Rule 35 in light of *Schlagenhauf* have consistently distinguished "mental injury" that warrants a psychiatric evaluation from emotional distress that accompanies personal injury.

In her suit against Drackett, Mrs. Coates asserts that she has suffered the type of emotional distress that typically accompanies a severe second degree burn and permanent scarring. In her deposition, she described her mental anguish as feelings of embarrassment and self-consciousness because the scar is ugly and noticeable in public. She is not alleging a permanent mental injury nor any deep seated emotional disturbance or psychiatric problem. Mrs. Coates' mental anguish claim is, therefore, for the emotional pain, torment, and suffering that a plaintiff who has been burned and scarred would experience in all reasonable probability. Further, the record reflects that Mrs. Coates has not sought any type of psychiatric treatment as a result of the incident and, equally important, does not propose to offer psychiatric or psychological testimony to prove her mental anguish at trial.

To permit Drackett to compel a mental examination because Mrs. Coates has claimed mental anguish damages would open the door to involuntary mental examinations in virtually every personal injury suit. Rule 167a was not intended to authorize sweeping probes into a plaintiff's psychological past simply because the plaintiff has been injured and seeks damages for mental anguish as a result of the injury. Plaintiffs should not be subjected to public revelations of the most personal aspects of their private lives just because they seek compensation for mental anguish associated with an injury.

Drackett also contends that Mrs. Coates' mental condition has been placed in controversy by virtue of its contributory negligence claim. With regard to that claim, it is Mrs. Coates' *conduct* that is in controversy. The jury will be asked to decide whether Mrs. Coates was negligent in her use of the oven cleaner. Whatever mental processes underlay her conduct, it is the nature of that conduct, not the reasons for it, that is in issue. Rule 167a clearly does not contemplate that a plaintiff would be subjected to a probing psychiatric incursion into his or her entire psychological past on the strength of a defendant's contributory negligence claim.

The second requirement of Rule 167a is that the movant show "good cause" for compelling an examination. Drackett maintains that it showed good cause by its reference to Mrs. Coates' preexisting personal problems which, Drackett asserts, may have caused Coates to injure herself with the oven cleaner. Drackett specifically refers to Mrs. Coates' marital problems, her concerns regarding her son's medical problems, and the fact that she had to take a lower paying job when her original employer re-located. Drackett places significance on the fact that Mrs. Coates had seen a doctor two or three times before the incident with the oven cleaner and had complained of depression and problems eating and sleeping. Drackett further emphasizes that on the day of Mrs. Coates' injury, the examining physician in the hospital emergency room noted in the medical record, "Husband states patient depressed—denies suicidal tendencies." Drackett insists that this notation suggests that Mrs. Coates was suicidal and may have misused the oven cleaner intentionally or with indifference to her welfare.

The "good cause" and "in controversy" requirements of Rule 167a are necessarily related. Mrs. Coates' prior problems are clearly peripheral to the issues in this case, and, consequently, they are not "in controversy." Drackett, however, attempts to meet the "in controversy" requirement by contending that Mrs. Coates' prior problems affected her mental state at the time she used the oven cleaner and they thus provide "good cause" for compelling a mental examination. Mrs. Coates' prior problems and attendant complaints of depression are distinct from the mental anguish she claims as a result of her injury. Drackett has failed to show any connection or "nexus" between Mrs. Coates' pre-injury depression and her post-injury embarrassment.

It is well settled that a tortfeasor takes a plaintiff as he finds him. Regardless of Coates' personal problems at the time of the incident with the oven cleaner, she is entitled to recover the damages resulting from the incident "conditioned as [she] was at the time of the injury." The fact that Mrs. Coates had personal problems at the time of her injury does not, in itself, relieve Drackett of liability, and does not, absent a showing of some connection to her allegation of mental anguish, provide good cause for compelling a mental examination.

A routine allegation of mental anguish or emotional distress does not place the party's mental condition in controversy. The plaintiff must assert mental injury that exceeds the common emotional reaction to an injury or loss. Assuming it is shown that a party has put his mental condition in controversy, good cause for the compelled examination must also be shown. The "good cause" requirement of Rule 167a recognizes that competing interests come into play when a party's mental or physical condition is implicated in a lawsuit—the party's right of privacy and the movant's right to a fair trial. A balancing of the two interests is thus necessary to determine whether a compulsory examination may properly be ordered.

The requirement of good cause for a compulsory mental examination may be satisfied only when the movant satisfies three elements. First, that an examination is relevant to issues that are genuinely in controversy in the case. It must be shown that the requested examination will produce, or is likely to lead to, evidence of relevance to the case. *See Schlagenhauf*, 379 U.S. at 117-18, 85 S.Ct. at 242-43. Second, a party must show a reasonable nexus between the condition in controversy and the examination sought. Neither of these requirements has been satisfied in this case. The mere pleading of mental anguish is inadequate to establish the necessity of plaintiff's submission to a mental examination. Finally, a movant must demonstrate that it is not possible to obtain the desired information through means that are less intrusive than a compelled examination. *See Schlagenhauf*, 379 U.S. at 118, 85 S.Ct. at 242; *Marroni v. Matey*, 82 F.R.D. 371, 372 (E.D.Pa.1979). The movant must demonstrate that the information sought is required to obtain a fair trial and therefore necessitates intrusion upon the privacy of the person he seeks to have examined. *See Lowe v. Philadelphia Newspapers, Inc.*, 101 F.R.D. 296, 298 (E.D.Pa.1983). Drackett has made no showing that the information it seeks cannot be obtained by other discovery techniques. Mrs. Coates' privacy interests require, at minimum, that Drackett exhaust less intrusive means of discovery before seeking a compulsory mental examination. If, however, a plaintiff intends to use expert medical testimony to prove his or her alleged mental condition, that condition is placed in controversy and the defendant would have good cause for an examination under Rule 167a.

We hold that the trial judge abused his discretion in ordering Mrs. Coates to undergo a mental examination. We conditionally grant Mrs. Coates' petition for writ of mandamus. The writ will issue only if the trial judge refuses to rescind his order.

Notes & Questions

Mental examination by psychologist. The previous version of the rule allowed court-ordered mental examinations only if conducted by a *physician*, not a psychologist. Rule 204 now allows psychologists to conduct examinations. Moreover, when one's opponent has designated a psychologist as the testifying expert or has produced a psychologist's records for possible use at trial, a party may obtain a mental examination upon showing good cause and does not need to satisfy the "in controversy," factor.[1]

H. Discovery from Nonparties

Read Rule 176, 205; Civil Practices & Remedies Code § 22.001-22.002.

1. *Methods for discovery from nonparties.* Rule 205 allows parties to obtain discovery from persons and entities who are *not* parties to the lawsuit. The rule refers to several different methods of obtaining discovery from nonparties: (1) entry upon property under Rule 196.7 which requires a showing of "good cause;"[1] (2) depositions, including an oral deposition (Rule 199), a deposition on written questions (Rule 200), and a pre-suit deposition (Rule 202); (3) a request for production served with a deposition notice; (4) physical and mental examinations (Rule 204); and (5) a request for production of documents and things without a deposition (Rule 205.3). Before Rule 205.3 was enacted, documents could be obtained from nonparties only with a deposition notice.

2. *Compelling discovery from nonparties.* Service of a subpoena, pursuant to Rule 176, is required to compel discovery from a nonparty. Rule 205.2 requires the party seeking discovery to serve on the nonparty and all parties a copy of the notice required for the particular form of discovery sought. For a deposition, the notice must be served with or before service of the deposition subpoena. However, a notice to produce documents and things without a deposition must be served at least 10 days before service of the subpoena to give other parties time to present objections to the request.

3. ***Subpoenas generally.*** A subpoena is a court order commanding a person or entity to appear in the courtroom or other designated place to testify or produce documents or things. Rule 176 consolidates several former rules governing various aspects of trial and discovery subpoenas. Rule 176 now generally addresses the procedures by which a party may require a person to appear and to produce documents or other things for discovery, hearings or trials. The rule prescribes in detail the required form of subpoenas, the manner and proof of service, actions that may be required of the person subpoenaed, permissible range of the subpoena, response required to a subpoena, methods of objecting to and obtaining protection from subpoenas, and enforcement procedures.

---

[1] *See In re* TransWestern Publishing Co., 96 S.W.3d 501 (Tex. App.—Ft. Worth 2002, no pet.) (finding trial court abused discretion in denying motion to compel medical examination where psychologist designated to testify.)

[1] *In re* SWEPI, L.P., 103 S.W.3d 578 (Tex. App.—San Antonio 2003, no pet.).

4. *Subpoena issuance and service.* Like the federal rule,[2] the Texas rules now allow attorneys to issue subpoenas. The former rule allowed only court clerks and persons authorized to take depositions to issue subpoenas. Attorneys may also serve the subpoena, as the rule allows service by anyone over 18 and not a party to the litigation. Compare with Rule 103, which requires service of process be made by a non-party not "interested in the outcome" of the suit. The witness fee must be tendered when the subpoena is served. The failure to pay the fee precludes enforcement by fines or attachment.

5. *Subpoena range.* A subpoena may require attendance or production "in any county" that is not more than 150 miles from where the person "resides or is served." This provision makes Rule 176 consistent with CPRC 22.002. The former rule measured the subpoena range from "the courthouse." The new language appears to measure the range from the county line. Thus, if a person resides 200 miles from Presidio, but still within 150 miles of the Presidio County line, the person would be in subpoena range, even though that person would have to travel more than 150 miles to comply with the subpoena. Note that the deposition rules impose greater limitations for deposition subpoenas, as Rule 199.2 requires that depositions be taken in "the county" where the witness resides, is employed, or regularly transacts business.

6. *Enforcement.* Subpoenas are enforceable by attachment, contempt, fines, and imprisonment. The party seeking enforcement may seek relief either in the court that issued the subpoena or in the county where the subpoena was served. To ensure that the person served recognizes the subpoena's import, Rule 176.1(g) requires that every subpoena include language of this provision. A person served with a subpoena may avoid enforcement by objecting to the subpoena. An objection is made by moving for a protective order before the time specified for compliance, or if the subpoena is for a hearing or trial, by moving for protection at the time of the hearing or trial.

7. *Document production.* A subpoena need not require personal appearance. Instead, a subpoena may simply direct production of documents and things. In that event, the person subpoenaed need only produce the documents and things, and not appear personally to answer questions under oath.

8. *Voluntary appearance and cooperation.* What about the witness who agrees to appear voluntarily? It is still best to serve a subpoena to protect one's right to a continuance if the witness fails to appear.[3]

What about the witness who will cooperate by being available for trial (though outside subpoena range), but only if reimbursed for out-of-pocket expenses and lost work time? Such a witness should be entitled to reimbursement of reasonable expenses. However, what is reasonable here may be difficult to determine. What about the witness who is presently out of work but earns $20 an hour when he does have work as a carpenter? What about the witness who demands unreasonable sums as a condition to his or her appearance? In addition to the troubling ethical questions, there is also the problem of the credibility of a "paid" fact witness on cross-examination. (Although this is also a line of cross-examination of experts, it is less troubling because experts are customarily paid, whereas lay witnesses are not.)

---

2 FED. R. CIV. P. 45(a)(3).

3 *See* Rule 252 and Traders & Gen. Ins. Co. v. Gray, 257 S.W.2d 327 (Tex. Civ. App.—Waco 1953, no writ).

I. Sealing Orders

Read Rules 76a, 192.6

A Rule 192.6 protective order can be used not only to protect parties from burdensome, expensive or overly broad discovery, but also to protect the confidentiality of matters disclosed in discovery. Such a protective order may have provisions limiting dissemination of documents and information, requiring that all discovery be returned upon the conclusion of the lawsuit, and may even seal the court's file of the proceeding.[1] Confidentiality orders are quite common, because when discovery of trade secrets or other confidential information is necessary, the materials will be produced subject to a protective order that limits disclosure by the requesting party. These protective orders may be restricted, however, under the provisions of Rule 76a, which limits confidentiality and sealing orders in certain circumstances, and provides a complicated procedure that must be followed when a party seeks to seal "court records."

GENERAL TIRE, INC.
v.
KEPPLE

970 S.W.2d 520

(Tex. 1998)

HECHT, JUSTICE, delivered the opinion of the Court, in which PHILLIPS, CHIEF JUSTICE, and GONZALEZ, ENOCH, OWEN, BAKER and ABBOTT, JUSTICES, join.

After settling and dismissing Kenneth Kepple's suit against General Tire, Inc., Kepple's attorneys moved on their own behalf to vacate a protective order issued pursuant to Rule 166b(5)(c) of the Texas Rules of Civil Procedure [now Rule 192.6] which restricted their disclosure of documents General produced during discovery and designated as confidential. The district court granted the motion, holding that disclosure of the documents could not be restricted unless General complied with the procedures for sealing "court records" under Rule 76a. General then moved for protection under Rule 76a, and after an evidentiary hearing, the court denied the motion, holding that General's documents were "court records" within the meaning of Rule 76a(2)(c) and could not be sealed. The court of appeals affirmed the district court's rulings. We hold that the district court erred in invoking Rule 76a's procedures before determining whether General's documents were "court records", and that the court abused its discretion in determining that the documents were "court records". Accordingly, we reverse the court of appeals' judgment and reinstate the district court's protective order.

I

Kyle Kepple suffered severe injuries when the Ford Bronco II in which he was riding rolled over. His father Kenneth brought suit on Kyle's behalf against Ford Motor Company and General Tire, Inc., the manufacturer of the Bronco's tires. Kepple claimed that a defect in one of the tires caused the tread to separate, precipitating the rollover.

---

1 *See* In re Ford Motor Co., 211 S.W.3d 295 (Tex. 2006) (upholding confidentiality under agreed protective order despite third party disclosure).

On General's motion, the district court issued an interim protective order, pursuant to Rule 166b(5)(c), that permitted General to designate information produced during discovery as confidential after making "a bona fide determination that the material is, in fact, a trade secret or other confidential information, the dissemination of which would significantly damage [General's] competitive position." The order required Kepple to notify General if he disagreed with General's designation of any documents. Confidential information could be disclosed only to Kepple's counsel, the witnesses, the court, and the jury in this case, and to any plaintiffs' counsel, witnesses, court, or jury in any other suit against General alleging a tire defect. Confidential information could not be disclosed to any expert witness employed by one of General's competitors. General produced numerous documents under this order, including those containing design specifications, testing data, and "adjustment" reports detailing the frequency of returns under General's warranty program.

Three months after issuing the protective order, the district court stated at a pretrial conference, on its own initiative, that any order limiting dissemination of the documents must comply with Rule 76a, which governs the sealing of court records. The court indicated that the protective order would be vacated and directed General, if it desired protection, to file a motion to seal the documents under Rule 76a. Although not conceding that Rule 76a applied, General filed a "motion for protective order or, in the alternative, temporary sealing order." General asked the court to continue the terms of the interim protective order under either Rule 166b(5)(c) or Rule 76a. (General has never sought, either in the district court or on appeal, to restrict dissemination of the documents beyond the terms of the original protective order.) Before any further action was taken concerning the documents, however, the parties settled the lawsuit. The trial court signed an order dismissing the suit with prejudice, without vacating the interim protective order.

Two months later, Kepple's attorneys and their employees sought relief from the interim protective order, contending that General's documents "affect the public safety under Rule 76a" and therefore "should be made public." Over General's opposition, the court vacated the interim protective order, but two days later issued a temporary sealing order under Rule 76a. General then filed a motion to reinstate the protections of the interim protective order under either Rule 166b(5)(c) or Rule 76a. The court scheduled a hearing on General's motion, giving public notice as required by Rule 76a. Three parties intervened in the Rule 76a proceeding: Public Citizen Center for Auto Safety, Inc., Lawyers for Public Justice, and Jill Neviel, an individual.

At the Rule 76a hearing, the court first considered evidence on whether the documents were "court records" subject to Rule 76a. After determining that the documents were court records, the court heard evidence about whether they should be sealed under the standard set forth in Rule 76a(1). Based on this evidence and an *in camera* review of the documents, the court determined that General had not met its burden for sealing the documents and ordered that they "be opened to the general public" with only customer names and addresses redacted.

General appealed. Only Kepple filed a brief as appellee. The court of appeals affirmed, holding that the trial court did not abuse its discretion in concluding that the documents were court records that should not be restricted from the public. We granted General's application for writ of error.

II

Rule 166b(5)(c) authorizes a court to order "that for good cause shown results of discovery be sealed or otherwise adequately protected, that its distribution be limited, or that its disclosure be restricted." Rule 76a provides the standard and procedures for sealing court records. General first argues that Rule 76a does not apply to Rule 166b(5)(c) protective orders.

This Court promulgated Rule 76a in 1990 pursuant to legislative directive. The rule creates a presumption that all court records are open to the public and allows trial courts to seal court records only upon a showing of all of the following:

(a) a specific, serious and substantial interest which clearly outweighs:
 (1) this presumption of openness;
(2) any probable adverse effect that sealing will have upon the general public health or safety;
(b) no less restrictive means than sealing records will adequately and effectively protect the specific interest asserted.

The court must hold an oral hearing, open to the public. The party seeking a sealing order must post public notice of the hearing at least fourteen days in advance "at the place where notices for meetings of county governmental bodies are required to be posted". The notice must state the time and place of the hearing and must contain a specific description of the nature of the case and the records sought to be sealed. Any person has a right to intervene and be heard on the sealing question.

Subject to certain limited exceptions, "court records" include "all documents of any nature filed in connection with any matter before any civil court". Although the term generally does not include unfiled discovery, it does extend to "discovery, not filed of record, concerning matters that have a probable adverse effect upon the general public health or safety, or the administration of public office, or the operation of government . . . ." This application to unfiled discovery is one of the rule's most controversial aspects.

Rule 166b(5) authorizes trial courts, among other things, to issue protective orders to protect trade secrets contained in discovery. The rule provides that "the court may make any order in the interest of justice necessary to protect the movant from undue burden, unnecessary expense, harassment or annoyance, or invasion of personal, constitutional, or property rights." General argues that courts may exercise this authority independent of Rule 76a when the protection sought is less than a complete ban on disclosure of the documents.

* * *

While General's argument has logical appeal, it is undercut by the plain provision of Rule 166b(5)(c) that "[a]ny order under this subparagraph 5(c) shall be made in accordance with the provisions of Rule 76a with respect to all court records subject to that rule." This language leaves no leeway for interpretation. To the extent that discovery, whether filed or unfiled, is a "court record" under Rule 76a, the court must follow the stricter standards of that rule to limit its dissemination.

However, the rules do not specifically set forth the standards governing a trial court's threshold determination of whether particular unfiled discovery is or is not a "court record." The district court in this case apparently concluded that it was required to apply the full range of Rule 76a procedures to this threshold determination. That is, the district court required General to post public notice, and allowed any party to intervene, with regard to the "court records" determination. Also, although the district court bifurcated the court records hearing from the hearing to determine whether the documents should be sealed, it allowed intervenors to have full access to the documents at the first stage, before it determined the documents to be court records. We conclude that the court erred in part.

The special procedures of Rule 76a apply only to the sealing of "court records". The language of the rule does not authorize trial courts to also apply these special procedures to the threshold determination of whether particular unfiled discovery is, indeed, a court record subject to the rule. The rule would unnecessarily burden trial courts and litigants if it permitted a full hearing at this preliminary stage. If this were allowed, a party, merely by claiming that unfiled discovery met the standard for a court record under Rule 76a(2)(c), could trigger an elaborate, expensive process in any case where unfiled discovery has been exchanged. The opposing party would be required to post public notice, and the trial court would be required to conduct a full evidentiary hearing after at least fourteen days delay. General correctly argues that, under this interpretation, Rule 76a could easily become a tool for delay and gamesmanship. Equally likely, both courts and parties might view the rule as so cumbersome that they would make elaborate arrangements to avoid its requirements.

The rule does contemplate, however, that persons other than parties may intervene before the determination is made whether documents are "court records". Otherwise, the parties could largely control the application of the rule without regard to the public interest the rule seeks to protect. Similarly, Rule 76a(8), which allows for immediate appeal of any order "relating to sealing or unsealing court records," applies to the threshold "court records" determination. But allowing intervention before documents are determined to be "court records" does not mean that intervenors should have immediate access to the documents. On the contrary, when a party has moved to seal court records, or has filed a motion for protective order on discovery that may constitute a court record, trial courts should not allow intervenors access to the records over the moving party's objection until the court determines that they are court records which cannot be sealed. Such preliminary disclosure would compromise the effectiveness of any later sealing order, possibly even mooting the controversy. Rule 76a anticipates this problem by allowing the trial court to "inspect records *in camera* when necessary." In the present case, the district court allowed the intervenors to examine the documents General submitted *in camera* during the course of the Rule 76a hearing. While any harm caused to General cannot now be cured, we conclude that the trial court erred in this regard.

In summary, we hold that when a party seeks a protective order under Rule 166b(5)(c) to restrict the dissemination of unfiled discovery, and no party or intervenor contends that the discovery is a "court record," a trial court need not conduct a hearing or render any findings on that issue. If a party or intervenor opposing a protective order claims that the discovery is a "court record," the court must make a threshold determination on that issue. However, public notice and a Rule 76a hearing are mandated only if the court finds that the documents are court records. While a trial court is not *required* to determine whether unfiled discovery constitutes a court record until requested to do so by a party or intervenor, the court may raise this issue on its own motion. However, as previously discussed, a trial court may not apply the special procedures of Rule 76a (except for intervention) until it determines that the documents are court records. The district court in this case erred in applying the full range of Rule 76a procedures to the threshold "court records" determination.

III

Having determined that any restrictions on disclosure of General's confidential records produced during discovery must satisfy Rule 76a, we next consider the applicable standard for review of the district court's decision.

* * *

We employ an abuse of discretion standard to review a trial court's discovery rulings, including rulings on protective orders under Rule 166b. Although governed by stricter standards, a sealing order under Rule 76a is akin to a protective order, in that it requires the court to determine the extent to which information should be restricted from the public. Indeed, a trial court's threshold determination of whether unfiled discovery is a "court record" under Rule 76a will often occur in the context of a motion for protection. The nature of Rule 76a comports with an abuse of discretion review standard. In determining whether court records should be sealed, a trial court is not called upon to make a factual finding per se, but rather is required to balance the public's interest in open court proceedings against an individual litigant's personal or proprietary interest in privacy. Such a decision necessarily requires the exercise of judicial discretion, and should be reviewed on that basis. Accordingly, we hold that Rule 76a decisions must be reviewed for abuse of discretion.

IV

We turn now to the documents at issue in this case. At the outset, Kepple argues that by producing its records *in camera*, General "filed" them with the court so that they became court records, regardless of whether they would otherwise meet the "court records" standard for unfiled discovery in Rule 76a. This argument is without merit. Rule 76a specifically allows a party to submit disputed records to the trial court for *in camera* review when necessary. Were it otherwise, trial courts could not review the documents themselves in determining how to apply Rule 76a without requiring the party with the documents to relinquish the very relief sought under the rule. We therefore hold that documents do not lose their character as unfiled discovery merely because they are submitted to the trial court for *in camera* inspection in the context of a Rule 76a hearing.

***

A

"Cured tire standards" show the design specifications for certain tires General manufactured or formerly manufactured. These documents contain such information as the components and materials used in the tire, dimensions and placement of those components, the manufacturing equipment to be used, and how the tire will be cured into the final product. "Specification revisions" describe the changes General made to its cured tire standards over a period of time. Similarly, "product change proposals" describe suggested changes to the design standards, with supporting test data, which standards may or may not have been adopted. "Developmental testing documents" show testing that was performed on various models of tires. "Tire mold drawings" specify the dimensions and configurations of the metal molds used to form the tires. Finally, the category "miscellaneous documents" comprises consumer inquiries, retention records showing the length of time that certain documents were retained, and product specifications received from Ford Motor Company.

Kepple's evidence of a defect in General's tires did not link the alleged defect to any of these documents. For example, George Edwards, a consultant who specializes in tire failure analysis, testified as an expert for Kepple. Because he had acted as an expert witness in numerous cases against General, Edwards had examined the *in camera* documents at issue. Edwards testified that, in his opinion, tread separations in tires produced under these design and testing documents have been responsible for numerous serious traffic accidents. He opined that a defect in the "skim stock," which holds the steel belts together, was the root cause of the problem. Edwards reached these conclusions by analyzing actual tires involved in accidents, however, and he admitted that he could not correlate any tire defect with the information in the *in camera* documents. Dennis Carlson also testified as an expert for Kepple. Carlson testified generally that General changed its skim stock compound in 1987, and that any documents relating to that change would be important to the public safety. Like Edwards, however, Carlson was not able to correlate any defect in General's tires with a specific document or set of documents. Kepple presented other evidence through depositions and affidavits supporting its claim of product defect. None of this additional evidence, however, linked any defect to specific documents.

A party cannot demonstrate that a manufacturer's proprietary design, research, and testing records have a *probable* adverse effect on the public health or safety, as Rule 76a requires before documents are "court records", merely by producing evidence of a defect in the manufacturer's products. Rather, the party must, at a minimum, demonstrate some nexus between the alleged defect and the documents at issue. Because Kepple failed to demonstrate any such nexus, the district court abused its discretion in classifying the documents as "court records" under Rule 76a(2)(c).

* * *

For the reasons we have explained, the judgment of the court of appeals is reversed and the case is remanded to the district court for the sole purpose of reinstating the protective order issued January 14, 1994.

SPECTOR, JUSTICE, filed an opinion concurring in part and dissenting in part, in which HANKINSON, JUSTICE, joined, omitted.

Notes & Questions

1. *Trade Secrets and Rule 76a.* Might Rule 76a render a protective order protecting trade secrets ineffective? The Supreme Court does not appear to consider this a problem:[1]

> Continental argues that, if a trial court has determined that trade secrets are "necessary" to a plaintiff's personal injury case under Rule 507, it is likely that the court would also determine that they have a "probable adverse effect upon the general public health or safety" and therefore must be made public under Rule 76a. Thus, Continental argues, any protective order for the documents would be ineffective.
>
> We disagree with Continental's premise that all discoverable trade secrets will likely constitute "court records" under Rule 76a. Moreover, even if a trade secret produced under a protective order is later determined to be a court record, this does not necessarily mean that the information must be made public. Rule 76a allows the information to remain sealed upon a showing that it meets the criteria specified in Rule 76a(1). That a document contains trade secret information is a factor to be considered in applying this sealing standard.

2. *Shared discovery.* Plaintiffs' lawyers often share discovery in cases, especially products liability cases. In *Garcia v. Peeples*,[2] the Texas Supreme Court held that an order preventing dissemination of GMC's proprietary information to similarly situated plaintiffs was an abuse of discretion requiring mandamus. The Court noted that shared discovery was an "effective means to insure

---

1 In re Continental Gen. Tire, Inc., 979 S.W.2d 609 (Tex. 1998).

2 734 S.W.2d 343 (Tex. 1987).

full and fair disclosure," and therefore required that "any protective order be carefully tailored to protect GMC's proprietary interests while allowing an exchange of discovered documents."[3]

---

[3] *Id.* at 347. *See also In re* Universal Coin & Bullion, Ltd., 218 S.W.3d 828 (Tex. App.—Beaumont 2007, pet. denied) (finds that order allowing shared discovery did not adequately protect trade secrets and did not restrict the sharing to similarly situated parties nor to suits involving the same subject matter.). *Cf. also* Dustin B. Benham, Discovery Sharing in Texas: Litigant Confidentiality v. Litigation Costs, 67 Baylor L. Rev. 622 (2015) (contending that shared discovery enhances litigation efficiency).

CHAPTER 9. DISCOVERY SANCTIONS

A. "Just" Sanctions

Read Rule 215

TRANSAMERICAN NATURAL GAS CORP.
v.
POWELL
811 S.W.2d 913
(Tex. 1991)

HECHT, JUSTICE.

In this original mandamus proceeding, TransAmerican Natural Gas Corporation seeks to compel the Hon. William Powell, Judge of the 80th District Court, to set aside his orders imposing sanctions for discovery abuse. The district court struck TransAmerican's pleadings, dismissed its action against Toma Steel Supply, Inc., and granted Toma an interlocutory default judgment on its counterclaim against TransAmerican, reserving for trial only the amount of damages due Toma. We conditionally grant the writ of mandamus.

I

The underlying case is a complex, multi-party action arising out of Toma's sale of allegedly defective pipe casing to TransAmerican. TransAmerican withheld payment for the casing, apparently some $2.3 million, and sued Toma in April 1987 for damages allegedly caused by its use. Toma counterclaimed for $52 million damages resulting from TransAmerican's refusal to pay for the casing. Numerous other parties also joined in the litigation.

On July 3, 1988, the district court issued a docket control order pursuant to Rule 166 of the Texas Rules of Civil Procedure, which set a discovery cutoff date of April 3, 1989. The order allowed discovery to be conducted beyond that date only upon agreement of the parties.

On March 7, 1989, Toma noticed the deposition of TransAmerican's president, K. Craig Shephard, to take place March 16. Two days later TransAmerican's counsel, who at that time was one of the attorneys in its legal department, telephoned Toma's counsel to inform him that Shephard could not be available on March 16 because of a previously scheduled deposition in another case. When counsel could not agree on another date for Shephard's deposition, TransAmerican filed a motion for protection to quash the deposition notice and postpone the deposition. The motion stated that it would be submitted to the trial court for ruling on March 17.[1] However, the trial court did not rule on the motion on that date.

Beginning April 3, the deadline set by the district court for completion of discovery, the parties' smoldering discovery problem started to flare. On that date, counsel for TransAmerican and Toma agreed that Shephard would be deposed after April 10 on a date to be agreed upon.

---

1 The local rules governing civil cases in Harris County provide: "Motions shall state a date of submission which shall be at least 10 days from filing, except on leave of court. The motion will be submitted to the court for ruling on that date or later." Rule 3.3.2, Local Rules of the Civil Trial Division of the Harris County District Courts (1987). The March 17 submission date stated in TransAmerican's motion was only three days from the date of filing of the motion and the day after the deposition was scheduled.

Despite this understanding, counsel again failed to agree upon a date, and on April 19 Toma noticed Shephard's deposition for May 2 without TransAmerican's consent. On April 20, upon receipt of this second deposition notice, TransAmerican's counsel wrote a letter to Toma's counsel informing him that Shephard would not be available May 2 because, as before, he already had a deposition in another matter scheduled for that day. Toma's counsel replied by letter that he would not agree to reschedule the deposition. On April 27, TransAmerican reset the date for submission of its motion for protection to the trial court for ruling to May 12. By this time, of course, the motion was moot, and it is not apparent why TransAmerican continued to seek a ruling. TransAmerican did not move the trial court to postpone the May 2 deposition.

Also on April 27, Shephard's other deposition scheduled for May 2 was canceled, leaving him available to be deposed by Toma. However, TransAmerican's counsel did not advise Toma's counsel that Shephard's schedule had changed so that he could be deposed on May 2 after all, nor did Shephard appear on May 2 as noticed. TransAmerican ascribes its failure to produce Shephard for deposition to miscommunication concerning his schedule changes between attorneys in its legal department. Toma alleges that Shephard's failure to appear was purposeful and part of TransAmerican's intentional obstruction of the discovery process.

On May 8, Toma filed a response to TransAmerican's March 14 motion for protective order, even though it acknowledged that that motion was moot. Toma included in its response, however, a motion for sanctions against TransAmerican based on Shephard's failure to appear at the May 2 deposition. In return, TransAmerican filed its own sanctions motion on May 11, urging that Toma's motion for sanctions was itself an abuse of the discovery process. Toma's and TransAmerican's motions for sanctions both stated that they would be submitted to the court for ruling on May 12, the date set for submission of TransAmerican's original motion for protection.

On May 12, without hearing oral argument,[2] the district court signed an order granting Toma's motion for sanctions and striking TransAmerican's pleadings in their entirety. TransAmerican moved for reconsideration, which the district court denied after hearing argument of counsel but refusing to hear any evidence. Based upon his May 12 order striking TransAmerican's pleadings, the district court issued an order on October 6 dismissing TransAmerican's action with prejudice, rendering an interlocutory default judgment against TransAmerican and in favor of Toma on its counterclaim, and setting the case for trial solely on the issue of the damages to be awarded Toma.

TransAmerican sought mandamus relief from the court of appeals to compel the district court to set aside his May 12 and October 6 orders. A divided court of appeals denied TransAmerican leave to file its petition for writ of mandamus in an unpublished per curiam opinion. TransAmerican then moved for leave to file its petition in this Court. We granted the motion in order to review the propriety of the discovery sanctions imposed by the district court.

II

The sanctions imposed by the district court are among those authorized for various discovery abuses under Rule 215 of the Texas Rules of Civil Procedure. The district court did not specify what provision of Rule 215 it relied upon. The portions of the rule applicable to the circumstances here are paragraphs 2(b)(5) and 3. Paragraph 2(b)(5) provides in part:

---

2 Rule 3.3.4 of the Local Rules of the Civil Trial Division of the Harris County District Courts (1987) allows any party to request oral argument on a motion if the party "views it as necessary." Neither TransAmerican nor Toma appears to have requested oral argument on any of their motions before May 12.

> If a party or an officer . . . of a party . . . fails to comply with proper discovery requests or to obey an order to provide or permit discovery, . . . the court in which the action is pending may, after notice and hearing, make such orders in regard to the failure as are just, and among others the following:
>
> * * *
>
> (5) An order striking out pleadings or parts thereof, . . . or dismissing with or without prejudice the action or proceedings or any part thereof, or rendering a judgment by default against the disobedient party . . . .

At the time of the district court's rulings, paragraph 3 of Rule 215 stated in part:

> If the court finds a party is abusing the discovery process in seeking, making or resisting discovery . . . , then the court in which the action is pending may impose any sanction authorized by paragraphs (1), (2), (3), (4), (5), and (8) of paragraph 2b of this rule. Such order of sanction shall be subject to review on appeal from the final judgment.

Both paragraphs leave the choice of sanctions to the sound discretion of the trial court. However, paragraph 2(b) explicitly requires that any sanctions imposed be "just". By referring to paragraph 2(b), paragraph 3 incorporates the same requirement. Thus, whether the district court imposed sanctions under paragraph 2(b) or paragraph 3, we consider whether those sanctions were just.

In our view, whether an imposition of sanctions is just is measured by two standards. First, a direct relationship must exist between the offensive conduct and the sanction imposed. This means that a just sanction must be directed against the abuse and toward remedying the prejudice caused the innocent party. It also means that the sanction should be visited upon the offender. The trial court must at least attempt to determine whether the offensive conduct is attributable to counsel only, or to the party only, or to both. This we recognize will not be an easy matter in many instances. On the one hand, a lawyer cannot shield his client from sanctions; a party must bear some responsibility for its counsel's discovery abuses when it is or should be aware of counsel's conduct and the violation of discovery rules. On the other hand, a party should not be punished for counsel's conduct in which it is not implicated apart from having entrusted to counsel its legal representation. The point is, the sanctions the trial court imposes must relate directly to the abuse found.

Second, just sanctions must not be excessive. The punishment should fit the crime. A sanction imposed for discovery abuse should be no more severe than necessary to satisfy its legitimate purposes. It follows that courts must consider the availability of less stringent sanctions and whether such lesser sanctions would fully promote compliance.

These standards set the bounds of permissible sanctions under Rule 215 within which the trial court is to exercise sound discretion.[6] The imposition of very severe sanctions is limited, not only by these standards, but by constitutional due process. The sanctions the district court imposed against TransAmerican are the most devastating a trial court can assess against a party. When a trial court strikes a party's pleadings and dismisses its action or renders a default judgment against

---

[6] JUSTICE GONZALEZ' concurring opinion sets out guidelines for assessing sanctions which have been identified in the context of applying Rule 11, FED. R. CIV. P. *Post*, at ___. Our analysis of this case does not require us to consider whether those factors or others are appropriate considerations in imposing sanctions. However, we do subscribe to the principle, inherent in the effort to state guidelines, that the trial court's discretion in assessing sanctions must be guided by a reasoned analysis of the purposes sanctions serve and the means of accomplishing those purposes.

it for abuse of the discovery process, the court adjudicates the party's claims without regard to their merits but based instead upon the parties' conduct of discovery. "There are constitutional limitations upon the power of courts, even in aid of their own valid processes, to dismiss an action without affording a party the opportunity for a hearing on the merits of his cause." Discovery sanctions cannot be used to adjudicate the merits of a party's claims or defenses unless a party's hindrance of the discovery process justifies a presumption that its claims or defenses lack merit. However, if a party refuses to produce material evidence, despite the imposition of lesser sanctions, the court may presume that an asserted claim or defense lacks merit and dispose of it. Although punishment and deterrence are legitimate purposes for sanctions, they do not justify trial by sanctions. Sanctions which are so severe as to preclude presentation of the merits of the case should not be assessed absent a party's flagrant bad faith or counsel's callous disregard for the responsibilities of discovery under the rules.

In the present case, it is not clear whether TransAmerican or its counsel or both should be faulted for Shephard's failure to attend his deposition. Moreover, there is nothing in the record to indicate that the district court considered imposition of lesser sanctions or that such sanctions would not have been effective. If anything, the record strongly suggests that lesser sanctions should have been utilized and perhaps would have been effective. The district court could have ordered Shephard's deposition for a specific date and punished any failure to comply with that order by contempt or another sanction. He also could have taxed the costs of the deposition against TransAmerican and awarded Toma attorney fees. The range of sanctions available to the district court under Rule 215 is quite broad. The district court dismissed TransAmerican's claims against Toma and rendered default judgment for Toma on its counterclaim solely because, as the record before us establishes, TransAmerican's president failed to present himself for his deposition.[8] Nothing in the record before us even approaches justification for so severe a sanction.[9]

There are cases, of course, when striking pleadings, dismissal, rendition of default and other such extreme sanctions are not only just but necessary. In this case, however, the record before us establishes that the severe sanctions the district court imposed against TransAmerican were manifestly unjust in violation of Rule 215.

---

[8] Toma's motion for sanctions was based solely upon Shephard's failure to attend his deposition. As Toma itself stated in its response to TransAmerican's motion to refile its pleadings after they were struck: "On May 12, 1989, the Court granted [Toma's] Motion for Sanctions against [TransAmerican] for TransAmerican's refusal to agree to a date certain for Mr. Craig Shephard's deposition and for the failure of its President, Mr. Craig Shephard, to appear for a properly noticed deposition on May 2, 1989, and struck TransAmerican's pleadings in their entirety." Notwithstanding this rather clear statement in the trial court, during this mandamus proceeding Toma has suggested that the district court properly sanctioned TransAmerican because it had abused the discovery process on other occasions. TransAmerican disputes Toma's assertions. While the district court would have been entitled to consider a pattern of discovery abuse in imposing sanctions, the record does not reveal the existence of any such pattern, Toma did not complain of one, and the district court does not appear to have found one.

[9] The district court made no findings to support the sanctions imposed. Rule 215 does not require a trial court to make findings before imposing discovery sanctions, and we do not add such a requirement here. We note only that we do not have the benefit of any explanation by the district court for the severity of its ruling. It would obviously be helpful for appellate review of sanctions, especially when severe, to have the benefit of the trial court's findings concerning the conduct which it considered to merit sanctions, and we commend this practice to our trial courts. *See* Thomas v. Capital Security Services, Inc., 836 F.2d 866, 882-883 (5th Cir. 1988). Precisely to what extent findings should be required before sanctions can be imposed, however, we leave for further deliberation in the process of amending the rules of procedure.

***

Accordingly, we hold that TransAmerican is entitled to the mandamus relief it seeks. We are confident that Judge Powell will vacate his orders of May 12 and October 6, after which he may conduct further proceedings consistent with this opinion. Our writ of mandamus will issue only in the event he fails promptly to comply.

GONZALEZ, JUSTICE, concurring:

I concur with the court's opinion and judgment. The sanction in this case was clearly out of proportion to the offense committed by relator and the opinion appropriately disposes of the present controversy. However, neither our rules nor the court have set guidelines for imposing sanctions. They envision a large degree of discretion vested in the trial court and innovation should not be discouraged in attempting to fashion an appropriate sanction. However, trial judges should not be trigger happy. They should first issue orders compelling discovery. In all but the most egregious circumstances, other lesser sanctions should be tried first before imposing the ultimate sanction of the "death penalty" (dismissal of pleadings). Cases should be won or lost on their merits, not on discovery or sanctions gamesmanship. Thus I write separately to offer additional guidance to the bench and bar.

In assessing sanctions under Rule 215 of the Texas Rules of Civil Procedure, the punishment must fit the crime. Furthermore, a sanction should be a function of both the facts presented and the purpose of the rule the court is enforcing. If this is not clear from the record, the trial court is more apt to be second guessed by the appellate courts.

The Litigation Section of the American Bar Association promulgated the following standards and guidelines to be considered when determining whether to assess sanctions under Federal Rule 11:

a. the good faith or bad faith of the offender;

b. the degree of willfulness, vindictiveness, negligence, or frivolousness involved in the offense;

c. the knowledge, experience, and expertise of the offender;

d. any prior history of sanctionable conduct on the part of the offender;

e. the reasonableness and necessity of the out-of-pocket expenses incurred by the offended person as a result of the misconduct;

f. the nature and extent of prejudice, apart from out-of-pocket expenses, suffered by the offended person as a result of the misconduct;

g. the relative culpability of client and counsel, and the impact on their privileged relationship of an inquiry into that area;

h. the risk of chilling the specific type of litigation involved;

i. the impact of the sanction on the offender, including the offender's ability to pay a monetary sanction;

j. the impact of the sanction on the offended party, including the offended person's need for compensation;

k. the relative magnitude of sanction necessary to achieve the goal or goals of the sanction;

l. burdens on the court system attributable to the misconduct, including consumption of judicial time and incurrence of juror fees and other court costs;

m. the degree to which the offended person attempted to mitigate any prejudice suffered by him or her;

n. the degree to which the offended person's own behavior caused the expenses for which recovery is sought . . . .

American Bar Association, Standards and Guidelines for Practice Under Rule 11 of the Federal Rules of Civil Procedure, *reprinted in* 121 F.R.D. 101 (1988).

I recognize that Federal Rule 11 is not comparable to Rule 215 of Texas Rules of Civil Procedure and that Federal Rule 11 does not specify the types of sanctions that may be imposed. However, we do not have to re-invent the wheel. In my opinion, the ABA guidelines developed for determining when to assess sanctions under Federal Rule 11 are instructive whenever sanctions are imposed or denied under Texas Rule 215.

As the court notes, the range of sanctions available to a trial court under Rule 215 is quite broad. Some of these sanctions include:

(1) A reprimand of the offender;[2]

(2) Mandatory continuing legal education;

(3) A fine;[3]

(4) An award of reasonable expenses, including reasonable attorney's fees, incurred as a result of the misconduct;

(5) Reference of the matter to the appropriate attorney disciplinary or grievance authority;[4]

(6) An order precluding the introduction of certain evidence;

(7) An order precluding the litigation of certain issues;

(8) An order precluding the litigation of certain claims or defenses;

(9) Dismissal of the action or entry of a default judgment.[5]

ABA Standard and Guidelines, 121 F.R.D. at 124.

---

2 Although this is typically the least serious sanction available, some courts have attempted to use the reprimand as a method of embarrassing the lawyer who has committed the offense. For example the court could require the reprimanded lawyer to provide a certified copy of the reprimand order to the members of his law firm.

3 If a monetary fee is imposed, other factors should be considered by the trial court, including:

(1) The time and labor involved; (2) The novelty and difficulty of the questions involved; (3) The skill requisite to perform the legal service properly; (4) The customary fee; (5) Whether the fee is fixed or contingent; (6) Time limitations imposed by the client or the circumstances; (7) The amount involved and the results obtained; (8) The experience, reputation and ability of the attorneys; and (9) Awards in similar cases;

ABA Standards and Guidelines, 121 F.R.D. at 125-26. . . .

4 Sanctionable conduct may not necessarily be an ethical violation, however.

5 These remedies are essentially equivalent in degree depending on whether the plaintiff or the defendant is the offending party.

Sanctions are tools to be used by a court to right a wrong committed by a litigant. Any given sanction should be designed to accomplish that end. Sanctions can be compensatory, punitive or deterrent in nature. The court should assess the type of sanction most likely to prevent a recurrence of the offending conduct. The court should also consider the relative culpability of the counsel and client when selecting the appropriate sanction.

The foregoing guidelines are simply suggestions to guide a trial court in its struggle to make the punishment fit the crime.

Notes & Questions

1. *The* TransAmerican *questions.*[1] *TransAmerican* sets out the standards for determining whether sanctions are "just." The questions a reviewing court must consider are as follows:

A. Does a "direct relationship" exist between the offensive conduct and the sanction imposed?

(1) Is the sanction directed against the abuse?

(2) Is the sanction directed toward remedying the prejudice caused the innocent party?

(3) Is the sanction visited upon the offender (counsel, the party, or both)?[12]

B. Are the sanctions "not excessive"?

(1) Is the sanction no more severe than necessary to satisfy its legitimate purposes (compliance, punishment, deterrence)?

(2) Has the court considered/tested less stringent sanctions?[3]

2. *Sanctions practice.* Since *TransAmerican* was decided, the courts of appeals have regularly dealt with appeals questioning whether sanctions imposed by the trial judge meet the *TransAmerican* standards. The opinion effectively reversed the trend that began when Rule 215 was added to the Texas Rules of Civil Procedure. The 1984 amendments encouraged courts to impose sanctions freely, assuming that punishment would discourage gamesmanship in civil litigation. By the late 1980's, however, the opposite happened. The new sanctions rules were being used simply as another tool for gamesmanship. Many commentators, including former Justice William Kilgarlin who was in large part responsible for the 1984 amendments, and the Supreme Court Task Force on Sanctions chaired by Charles F. Herring, Jr., advocated movement away from sanctions practice.[4]

3. TransAmerican *applicable to all sanctions. TransAmerican* involved sanctions for discovery abuse under Rule 215. Presumably, however, the *TransAmerican* decision is applicable to any

---

[1] The following summary is quoted from Herring, Charles, Jr., and Ron H. Moss, *Sanctions and Liability,* 11TH ANNUAL ADVANCED PERSONAL INJURY LAW COURSE, STATE BAR OF TEXAS (1995).

[2] *See also, e.g.*, In re Garza, 544 S.W.3d 836, 842 (Tex. 2018) ("We conclude that the trial court acted arbitrarily and abused its discretion by imposing sanctions on Garza in the absence of evidence that she was an offender.").

[3] *See* Cire v. Cummings, 134 S.W.3d 835 (Tex. 2004) (holding that death penalty sanctions warranted without prior imposition of lesser sanctions).

[4] *See* William W. Kilgarlin, *Sanctions for Discovery Abuse: Is the Cure Worse Than the Disease?,* 54 TEX. BAR J. 658 (1991); Charles Herring, Jr., *The Rise of the "Sanctions Tort",* TEX. LAW. Jan. 28, 1991 at 22.

order that imposes severe sanctions upon litigants or lawyers,[5] and will be used to review sanctions imposed under Chapter 10 of the Civil Practice and Remedies Code. Indeed, in *Altesse Healthcare Solutions, Inc. v. Wilson*, the Supreme Court held that *TransAmerican's* "just" sanction standards apply when trial courts use their inherent authority to sanction parties for violating a temporary restraining order, observing that:[26]

> Our reasoning in *TransAmerican* stemmed primarily from Rule 215's simple requirement that discovery sanctions must be "just." Restrictions on extreme discovery sanctions also flow from the recognition that "[t]here are constitutional limitations upon the power of courts, even in aid of their own valid processes, to dismiss an action without affording a party the opportunity for a hearing on the merits of his cause." *TransAmerican*, 811 S.W.2d at 918 (quoting *Societe Internationale v. Rogers*, 357 U.S. 197, 209 (1958)). Such constitutional considerations are equally applicable to death-penalty sanctions imposed outside the scope of Rule 215. We conclude that legal standards developed to ensure "just" and constitutionally permissible sanctions for discovery violations apply to our review of the sanctions imposed in this case [for a TRO violation].

The *Altesse* court went on to strike down the trial court's "beyond-death-penalty sanctions" in the case because they put the recipient in a better position than if they prevailed fully on the merits.[37]

4. *Waiver of right to sanctions*. One must be diligent in asserting one's right to sanctions. The failure to obtain a pretrial ruling on discovery disputes that exist before trial begins will waive any claim to sanctions post-trial based on that conduct.[8] For example, the Supreme Court reversed a trial court's sanction order against a party who had lied in a deposition.[9] The court had ordered that the party pay the expenses that the opponent incurred in proving up the fact that the party had lied about. However, because the party did not raise the issue until after trial, it was not entitled to sanctions.[10]

---

5 *See* Occidental Chemical Corp. v. Banales, 907 S.W.2d 488 (Tex. 1995) (piercing work product privilege is a "severe" sanction subject to review under *TransAmerican*); Texas Dept. of Public Safety Officers Assoc. v. Denton, 897 S.W.2d 757 (Tex. 1995) (sanctions imposed by "offensive use doctrine" is reviewed under standards not unlike *TransAmerican*).

6 540 S.W.3d 570, 575 (Tex. 2018).

7 *Id.* at 576.

8 Remington Arms Co. v. Caldwell, 850 S.W.2d 167, 170 (Tex. 1993).

9 Meyer v. Cathey, 167 S.W.3d 327 (Tex. 2005)(per curiam).

10 *Id.* at 333.

B. Review of Sanctions Order

BRADEN
v.
DOWNEY

811 S.W.2d 922
(Tex. 1991)

HECHT, JUSTICE.

Respondent District Judge, Hon. Daniel M. Downey, ordered relator Don T. Braden to answer certain discovery requests and found that his earlier refusal to do so was abusive of the discovery process. As sanctions for such abuse, the district court ordered Braden to pay $10,000 to the party seeking discovery, and ordered Braden's attorney to perform ten hours community service. The deadlines ordered for payment of the monetary sanctions and completion of the community service preceded conclusion of the litigation. Braden seeks mandamus directing the district court to vacate these discovery rulings. We conclude that the district court did not clearly abuse its discretion in ordering Braden to answer the discovery requests, but that it did abuse its discretion in ordering payment of the monetary sanctions imposed and performance of community service before those sanctions, and the basis for imposing them, could be appealed. We therefore conditionally grant mandamus relief only to direct the district court to modify its order to defer compliance with the imposition of sanctions until after rendition of final judgment.

I

South Main Bank loaned a limited partnership $620,000, secured by a lien on certain commercial real estate. The borrower's general partners and most or all of its limited partners, including Braden, each personally guaranteed repayment of a portion of the loan. The part Braden guaranteed was $69,750. When the partnership became insolvent, Braden sued the Bank and others in Montgomery County, where he resided, seeking to avoid the obligation of his guaranty and to recover actual and punitive damages on various liability theories. The Bank foreclosed on its security and then sued the partnership and the guarantors in Harris County for the deficiency, alleged to be $485,767.57. Braden's lawsuit was transferred to Harris County on motion to transfer venue, where it was consolidated with the Bank's action.

After the Bank took Braden's deposition, it directed a discovery request to Braden containing eight requests for admission of facts, five requests for production of documents, and a first set of twenty-five numbered interrogatories, one with two subparts and two with five subparts each. Braden responded by objecting to most of the interrogatories and denying most of the requests. More specifically, Braden denied: that the Bank was the owner and holder of the note signed by the partnership; that the partnership had defaulted on its note and contract obligations to the Bank; that the deficiency owed by the partnership was $485,767.57; that interest on the deficiency was accruing at the rate of 11% per annum; that Braden was liable to the Bank for the partnership's debts; and that a reasonable and necessary attorney fee to collect the debt owed by the partnership would be $48,516.76. Braden admitted only that he had signed a guaranty agreement. Each request for admission was accompanied by an interrogatory asking Braden to "state all facts relied upon in denying the Request or objecting to it" if the request was not admitted. Braden answered the interrogatory relating to his denial that the Bank was the owner and holder of the partnership note by stating that he was not in a position to know one way or the other. To all the other interrogatories relating to denied requests for admission Braden repeated the following objection:

> This interrogatory is objected to because it is vague, ambiguous, overly broad, non-specific, and unduly burdensome in requesting this party to "state all facts relied upon" in denying the claim. Under the Texas Rules of Civil Procedure the number of questions including subsections in a set of interrogatories shall be limited so as not to require more than thirty answers. An interrogatory requesting a party to "state all facts" in essence requests a party to state the entire substance of all testimony, documents, and other evidence which may be offered at trial. This would of necessity involve a narrative discourse encompassing more than thirty answers and would require the disclosure of work product.

In each instance, except for the interrogatory about attorney fees, Braden added:

> This interrogatory is also objected to because Don T. Braden has been extensively examined at deposition about these very same matters. To now inquire about these same matters in interrogatories is unduly burdensome.

Braden lodged essentially the same objections to interrogatories which asked him: to "state in detail" what banking and credit review services were to be provided the partnership; to "state all facts" supporting a conclusion that such services were not properly performed; to state the content and source of information supporting his claim that banking services rendered were deficient; and to state how he was damaged as a result. Braden also objected on the same basis to several interrogatories which requested him to state in detail the factual basis for certain of his claims, including what misrepresentations were allegedly made by the Bank, who made them, and what was said. In response to an interrogatory which asked him to identify all persons with relevant or discoverable knowledge about the litigation, Braden stated:

> To the knowledge of this party, the only persons having knowledge of relevant matters are the parties to this lawsuit, the parties to Cause No. 89-04947, the persons mentioned in my deposition taken on September 20, 1988, and respective attorneys of the parties. The addresses and business affiliations of these persons are already known to you. To require this party to compile a list of addresses is unduly burdensome. If you should encounter difficulty in locating any of these persons, please contact my attorney and he will provide you with such information as I may have concerning the location of the person.

Braden responded to three of the Bank's requests for production and objected to the other two. One of the two requests to which Braden objected called for documents pertaining to a transaction which was not directly related to the litigation. The other requested Braden to "produce any and all documents which may lead to the discovery of admissible evidence in this case or which are relevant to any claim made by any party in this lawsuit." Braden objected to this request as being, among other things, improper.

The Bank moved the district court to compel Braden to answer all the discovery requests to which he objected and to award the Bank $500 attorney fees as sanctions. The district court considered the Bank's motion at a hearing at which counsel for both parties were present. The district court overruled Braden's objections to all but one of what it determined were the first thirty interrogatories, counting each subpart as a separate interrogatory.[3] The district court also

---

3 It appears from the record that the trial court actually considered only the first twenty-nine interrogatories. The one objection which the trial court did not overrule was not addressed at the hearing.

overruled Braden's relevance objection to the request for production relating to a separate transaction. The district court denied the Bank's motion as it pertained to the other interrogatories and the other request for production for all documents relevant to the claims asserted.

At the conclusion of the hearing on the Bank's motion to compel, the district court found that both parties were abusing the discovery process. As sanctions for such abuse, the district court ordered from the bench that Braden pay the Bank $10,000 and that Braden's attorney perform ten hours of community service for the Child Protective Services Agency of Harris County. The district court also ordered the Bank's attorney to perform five hours of service for the same agency. The court's subsequent order gave Braden thirty days to pay the $10,000, and gave the attorneys about six weeks to complete their community service.

Braden moved the court of appeals for leave to file his petition for writ of mandamus directing the district court to vacate its order. The court of appeals denied Braden's motion without opinion. Braden then filed his motion in this Court. We granted leave to file and, at Braden's request, stayed enforcement of the district court's order.[4]

II

* * *

Braden has failed to demonstrate that the district court clearly abused its discretion in ordering him to answer the Bank's discovery requests.

III

Braden next contends that the district court abused its discretion in sanctioning him and his attorney. Braden argues that he is entitled to mandamus relief because he has no adequate remedy at law. We examine this argument, first with regard to the monetary sanctions imposed upon Braden, and then as to the community service Braden's attorney has been ordered to perform.

A

Rule 215.3, upon which the district court relied in this case, authorizes trial courts to impose appropriate sanctions upon persons who abuse the discovery process. The rule states that orders imposing such sanctions "shall be subject to review on appeal from the final judgment." There is no provision for interlocutory appeal; "discovery sanctions are not appealable until the district court renders a final judgment." We have held this right of appeal to be an adequate remedy for review of discovery sanctions, precluding review by mandamus, in two cases involving assessment of attorney fees against a party. *Street v. Second Court of Appeals*, 715 S.W.2d 638, 639-640 (Tex. 1986) (*per curiam*); *Stringer v. Eleventh Court of Appeals*, 720 S.W.2d 801, 802 (Tex. 1986) (per curiam). In *Street*, the trial court ordered a party to pay $1,050 attorney fees as discovery sanctions. The trial court ordered the party's pleadings struck if payment was not made within four days. In an original mandamus proceeding, the court of appeals concluded that the trial court had abused its discretion and directed it to vacate its order. On petition to this Court for mandamus, we held that the sanctioned party had an adequate remedy by appeal, and that the court of appeals' issuance of its writ was contrary to Rule 215. The sanctioned party argued that appeal was an inadequate remedy because, even if the sanctions order were ultimately reversed, actual recovery from the opposing party of the amount paid was always problematic. We rejected that argument, stating that "the uncertainty of recovering the money on appeal . . . is simply not a sufficient reason for the appellate court's interference with the pre-trial stages of this action."

---

[4] The Bank's attorney has advised the Court that he performed his community service as ordered by the district court.

Street, 715 S.W.2d at 639-640. We reached the same result in *Stringer*, a case in which the court of appeals had issued mandamus to relieve a party from paying $200 attorney fees as discovery sanctions ordered by the trial court. *Stringer*, 720 S.W.2d at 802.

Our concern in both *Street* and *Stringer* was that the appeals courts not embroil themselves unnecessarily in incidental pretrial rulings of the trial courts. If all monetary sanctions like the ones in those cases were reviewable by mandamus, it would soon cease to be an extraordinary writ. The judicial system cannot afford immediate review of every discovery sanction.

However, the circumstances of the present case are far different from those in *Street* and *Stringer*. The monetary sanctions in this case are unrelated to any reasonable attorney fees incurred by any party. In its motion to compel the Bank requested that Braden be ordered to reimburse its attorney fees in the amount of only $500, a small fraction of the $10,000 sanction imposed by the district court. Assessing what amounts to a penalty against a party of the magnitude of the sanction in this case, payable before any opportunity for supersedeas and appeal, does not merely raise concerns that the amount paid may not be recouped if the sanction is eventually reversed. Rather, so severe a penalty thus imposed raises the real possibility that a party's willingness or ability to continue the litigation will be significantly impaired.

Sanctions which terminate or inhibit the presentation of the merits of a party's claims for decision are authorized by Rule 215. These include exclusion of essential evidence, striking pleadings, dismissal and default. Rule 215.2.b(3), (4), (5). The effect of such sanctions is to adjudicate claims or defenses, not on their merits, but on the manner in which a party or his attorney has conducted discovery. We recognize that severe sanctions are sometimes necessary to prevent an abusive party from thwarting the administration of justice by concealing the merits of a case. However, such sanctions must be reserved for circumstances in which a party has so abused the rules of procedure, despite imposition of lesser sanctions, that the party's position can be presumed to lack merit and it would be unjust to permit the party to present the substance of that position before the court. *TransAmerican Natural Gas Corp. v. Powell*, 811 S.W.2d 913 (Tex. 1991).

Likewise, monetary sanctions should not ordinarily be used to dispose of litigation. If the imposition of monetary sanctions threatens a party's continuation of the litigation, appeal affords an adequate remedy only if payment of the sanctions is deferred until final judgment is rendered and the party has the opportunity to supersede the judgment and perfect his appeal. The Fifth Circuit has reached the same conclusion in similar circumstances. In *Thomas v. Capital Security Services, Inc.*, 836 F.2d 866 (5th Cir. 1988), the court recognized that the assessment of sanctions, payable prior to appeal, could in some circumstances have a "preclusive effect . . . on the violating party's access to the courts." *Id.* at 882. Thus, the court held:

> We . . . believe that the imposition of sanctions must not result in total, or even significant, preclusion of access to the courts. . . . However, if a district court imposes monetary sanctions that are made payable prior to the entry of a final appealable order, a litigant may suffer a substantial restriction on his access to the courts. Financially strapped because of the sanctions award, a litigant is unable to proceed with his case on the merits. To avoid this harsh, inequitable scenario, we conclude that if a litigant contends that a monetary sanction award precludes access to the court, the district judge must either (1) provide that the sanction is payable only at a date that coincides with or follows entry of a final order terminating the litigation; or (2) makes express written findings, after a prompt hearing, as to why the award does not have such a preclusive effect.

Id. at 882-883 n. 23. This procedure allows the trial court to levy some monetary sanctions during pretrial proceedings but requires that payment of more severe sanctions be deferred until an appealable judgment is rendered. We adopt this same procedure for future cases.

In considering what monetary sanctions are appropriate, the court should consider the prejudice which the objectionable conduct has caused the opposing party. Just as sanctions should not substitute for an adjudication of the merits of the case, so also a party should not be permitted to abuse the rules of procedure so as to cause an opposing party such unnecessary delay and expense that he is forced to forsake his position. Monetary sanctions are appropriate to prevent a party from taking such unjust advantage of another.

For the present case, while we certainly do not fault the district court for not anticipating the procedures we adopt today, we nevertheless conclude on the record before us that ordering Braden to pay the discovery sanction imposed before rendition of an appealable judgment denied him an adequate remedy by appeal. Rather than review the propriety of those sanctions by mandamus, we hold instead that the district court must modify its order at least to allow Braden an opportunity to appeal before such sanctions must be paid.

B

Braden's attorney argues that if he is compelled to perform community service before an appealable judgment is rendered in the case, no relief on appeal can ever restore his time or make him whole. We agree. Time spent is different from money paid; recovery of the latter may be problematic, but recovery of the former is impossible. Nor can Braden's attorney recover damages for service the district court may have erred in requiring him to perform. Consequently, if the community service Braden's attorney is ordered to perform must be completed before he is able to obtain review of that order by appeal, his appellate remedy is plainly inadequate. If, however, the community service imposed upon Braden's attorney was not to be performed until the judgment in the case was final on appeal, Braden's attorney could fully obtain by appeal any relief to which he might be entitled. While we do not criticize this type of creative sanction, the district court should not have the discretion, by setting the time for performance of the sanctions ordered, to determine whether a party must seek relief by appeal or by mandamus. The mandate of Rule 215.3 that discovery sanctions be reviewable by appeal requires, at least in these circumstances, that the district court defer the time for performance of the community service ordered until after Braden has had an opportunity to appeal that order after final judgment is rendered. We hold therefore that the district court abused its discretion in ordering Braden's attorney to perform community service before Braden could appeal, and that it must modify its order accordingly.

IV

Finally, Braden contends that the sanctions imposed by the district court are not authorized by any rule or law. Although monetary sanctions unrelated to attorney fees and performance of community service are not among the possible sanctions enumerated in Rule 215.2b, the rule generally authorizes a trial court to sanction discovery abuse by "such orders . . . as are just". We recognize that discovery abuse is widespread and we have given trial courts broad authority to curb such abuse. We caution, however, that this authority be exercised judiciously. Justice should not tolerate abuse, but injustice cannot remedy it.

Because we have directed the district court to modify its order to allow the imposition of sanctions to be appealed, we express no opinion here whether those sanctions are authorized. That issue, as well as the basis for and propriety of those sanctions, if authorized, may be raised by Braden on appeal.

* * *

We conditionally grant Braden's petition for writ of mandamus to direct Judge Downey to modify his order to defer payment of monetary sanctions and performance of community service until final judgment is rendered to allow Braden an opportunity to appeal. In all other respects Braden's petition is denied. We are confident that Judge Downey will promptly comply with our opinion. The writ will issue only if he does not.

Notes & Questions

1. *When is mandamus available?* Rule 215(2)(b)(8) and 215(3) make clear that sanctions orders are to be reviewed on appeal from the final judgment in the case rather than by mandamus. *Braden* and *TransAmerican* create two exceptions: (1) when severe monetary sanctions are ordered paid before the final judgment is rendered, and (2) when any severe sanction is imposed that has the effect of adjudicating the dispute. In these situations, the appellate remedy is inadequate, so mandamus is available to correct a clear abuse of discretion.

2. *Standard of review*. In *Chrysler Corp. v. Blackmon*,[1] the Supreme Court held that the standard for reviewing a trial court's sanction order is whether the trial court abused its discretion in ordering the sanction, not whether there is any evidence to support the trial court's findings of fact. What is the difference? Under the latter standard, the appellate court must affirm if there is any evidence in the record supporting the trial court's finding, regardless of the contrary evidence. When an appellate court reviews for an abuse of discretion, it reviews all of the evidence, not only that supporting the trial judge's ruling, and reverses if the order was capricious, arbitrary or unreasonable in light of that evidence.

3. *Contempt*. The trial court has the power to hold someone in contempt for "disobedience or disrespect of a court by acting in opposition to its authority." Thus, courts sometimes have used the contempt power as a discovery sanction. For example, in *In re Reece*,[2] the trial court ordered a witness be put in jail for 60 days for committing perjury in a deposition. In reviewing that order, the Texas Supreme Court described the contempt powers. Contempt may occur in the presence of a court where the court has direct knowledge of the contempt (direct contempt), or outside the court's presence (constructive contempt), with constructive contempt proceedings requiring procedural safeguards that are not required in direct contempt proceedings. Furthermore, constructive contempt is limited to violations of a court's order (the most frequent contemptuous act), or acts that "impede, embarrass, or obstruct the court in the discharge of its duties."[3] Contempt orders are further classified as civil (remedial and coercive in nature) or criminal (punitive in nature). For example, a civil contempt order will usually order incarceration until the contemnor has purged the contempt (coercive incarceration), while a criminal contempt order (such as the one in *Reece)* orders incarceration as punishment (punitive incarceration). In *Reece*, the Supreme Court held that "perjury committed during a deposition does not alone constitute constructive contempt. To constitute constructive contempt, such perjury must actually

---

1 841 S.W.2d 844 (Tex. 1992).

2 341 S.W.3d 360 (Tex. 2011).

3 *Reece*, at 366.

obstruct a court in the performance of its duties."[5] The court reasoned that allowing a court to hold a litigant in contempt for misstatements during a deposition presents too high a risk for "oppression and wrong,"[6] and noted that other options are available for punishment, including discovery sanctions and referring the perjury allegation to the district attorney for criminal prosecution.[7]

C. Sanctions for Failure to Timely Respond or Supplement

How can courts enforce a party's obligation to timely respond to and supplement their responses to discovery requests. Of course, there are the Rule 215 sanctions that might be awarded for a general pattern of discovery abuse. But Rule 193.6 allows courts to impose a more specific sanction to such conduct—the "exclusion sanction." Should a party fail to timely respond to or supplement discovery, the party that failed to timely disclose may not introduce into evidence the matter not timely disclosed.[1] The rule prevents imposition of the exclusion sanction, however, if the court finds "good cause for the failure" to provide discovery, or that the failure does not "unfairly surprise or unfairly prejudice the other parties."

JACKSON
v.
MAUL

2003 WL 22295332

(Tex. App.—San Antonio [4th Dist.] 2003, no pet.) (not published in S.W.3d)

MEMORANDUM OPINION

SARAH B. DUNCAN, JUSTICE.

Kathleen P. Jackson appeals the trial court's take nothing judgment in her negligence suit against Gerald Maul. Jackson contends the trial court abused its discretion by precluding her from presenting evidence of Maul's negligence because she failed to set forth the legal theories and factual bases of her claim in response to Maul's request for disclosure pursuant to Rule 194.2(c), TEX.R. CIV. P., and then granting a directed verdict against her. We disagree and affirm the trial court's judgment.

In Request for Disclosure No. 3, Maul asked Jackson to "[s]tate the legal theories and, in general, the factual bases for your claims or defenses." Jackson responded: "Pain from injuries, past, present & future loss or earnings." On the day of trial, after both parties had announced

---

5 *Id.* at 367.

6 *Id.* at 368 (*citing* In re Michael, 326 U.S.224, 228 (1945)).

7 *Id.*

1 Rule 193.6. Note that failure to respond to a request for admission has a different sanction—a deemed admission, under Rule 198.2(c).

"ready," the trial court asked whether there were any pretrial motions that needed to be heard. Maul's attorney answered as follows:

> Yes, Your Honor. Defendant has one issue that we need to go into that's probably partially touched on in the motion in limine that doesn't need to be on the record, but in response to [Maul's request for] disclosure, [Jackson] was sent those back last year and she responded in January of this year, Judge.
>
> There's a contention disclosure that's 194.2(c) where it says state legal theories and, in general, the factual bases of your claims. All that the plaintiff handwrote in that was provided to me through counsel—original counsel, Jeff Eckols, pain for injuries past and future, loss of earnings. It doesn't list any contentions as to negligence committed by or on behalf of Gerald Maul.
>
> Under the rules of discovery, I think that they would be prohibited from putting on evidence of negligence in this case. This was a Level 2 [discovery plan case] and I have had that wagged in front of me in a motion to strike my amended pleading. There is no proper disclosure in this case. We would ask that there be no evidence of negligence against my client. And if that be the case, then the case is over.

After a discussion off the record, the trial court granted Maul's request, thus precluding Jackson from presenting evidence that Maul was negligent. Maul then moved for a directed verdict, which the trial court granted. So far as the record reflects, Jackson's attorney did not object to the form of Maul's request to exclude evidence, attempt to demonstrate that Jackson had supplemented her original response to Request No. 3 or otherwise made the requested information known to Maul in writing, attempt to demonstrate good cause for failing to have done so, or attempt to demonstrate that Maul would not be unfairly surprised or unfairly prejudiced if the trial court permitted her to introduce evidence that Maul was negligent despite her failure to supplement her discovery responses. Even if Jackson did attempt to make such a showing, the record does not reflect a ruling by the trial court.

Jackson argues the trial court imposed a "death penalty sanction" without adhering to the strictures set forth in *TransAmerican Natural Gas Corp. v. Powell,* 811 S.W.2d 913, 917 (Tex. 1991, orig. proceeding). We disagree. The trial court's action was in complete accord with Rule 193.6, TEX. R. CIV. P., which provides in relevant part:

> A party who fails to make, amend, or supplement a discovery response in a timely manner may not introduce in evidence the material or information that was not timely disclosed, or offer the testimony of a witness (other than a named party) who was not timely identified, unless the court finds that:
>
> > (1) there was good cause for the failure to timely make, amend, or supplement the discovery response; or
> >
> > (2) the failure to timely make, amend, or supplement the discovery response will not unfairly surprise or unfairly prejudice the other parties.

TEX. R. CIV. P. 193.6. "[F]ailure to supplement results in the loss of the opportunity to offer the witness' testimony. The sanction is automatic. The exception is when good cause is shown why the testimony should be allowed in spite of the discovery sanction. Determination of good cause is within the sound discretion of the trial court. That determination can only be set aside if that discretion was abused." . . . Because Jackson did not even attempt to demonstrate good cause or the absence of unfair prejudice or surprise in the trial court, the record does not reflect an abuse of discretion. The trial court's judgment is affirmed.

Notes & Questions

1. *Exceptions to exclusion.* Before 1999, the only exception to the exclusion sanction was "good cause." And the Texas Supreme Court interpreted the "good cause" provision very differently from how "good cause" has been interpreted in allowing withdrawal or amendment of admissions under Rule 198.3. In the leading case on the "good cause" exception to the exclusion sanction, the Supreme Court stated:[1]

> The good cause exception permits a trial court to excuse a failure to comply with discovery in difficult or impossible circumstances. . . . . We have repeatedly addressed what factors, standing alone, are not in themselves good cause. Included among these are inadvertence of counsel, lack of surprise, and uniqueness of the excluded evidence. The reasons in each instance are intuitive. If inadvertence of counsel, by itself, were good cause, the exception would swallow up the rule, for there would be few cases in which counsel would admit to making a deliberate decision not to comply with the discovery rules. Determining whether a party is really surprised by an offer of testimony not formally identified in discovery is difficult. The better prepared counsel is for trial, the more likely he is to have anticipated what evidence may be offered against his client, and the less likely he is to be surprised. It would hardly be right to reward competent counsel's diligent preparation by excusing his opponent from complying with the requirements of the rules. As we explained:
>
> > A party is entitled to prepare for trial assured that a witness will not be called because opposing counsel has not identified him or her in response to a proper interrogatory. Thus, even the fact that a witness has been fully deposed, and only his or her deposition testimony will be offered at trial, is not enough to show good cause for admitting the evidence when the witness was not identified in response to discovery.
>
> > Finally, if good cause could be shown simply by establishing the unique importance of the evidence to the presentation of the case, only unimportant evidence would ever be excluded, and the rule would be pointless.

In the 1999 revisions, "unfair surprise or prejudice" was added as another exception to the exclusion sanction. Obviously, it has ameliorated the effects of the Supreme Court's earlier strict interpretation of good cause, providing trial courts with some discretion to not exclude evidence in situations where the failure to timely provide discovery caused no harm to the opponent.

Of course, the sanction of excluding evidence can result in effectively preventing the party from presenting its case. This severe sanction must be used sparingly, as "absent flagrant bad faith or callous disregard for the rules, due process bars merits-preclusive sanctions."[2] Does the *Jackson* opinion satisfy that standard?

2. *Harmless error.* Remember that the case will be reversed for the admission of undisclosed evidence *only* if the admission was harmful.[3] For example, the erroneous admission of testimony may be harmless if the witness is not the only one to testify to particular facts. When a witness'

---

1 Alvarado v. Farah Manufacturing Co., 830 S.W.2d 911, 913 (Tex. 1992).

2 Wheeler v. Green, 157 S.W.3d 439, 443 (Tex. 2005).

3 TRAP 44.1.

testimony is "cumulative" of other testimony, the admission is said to be harmless.[4] As a practical matter, is cumulative evidence really harmless? What if the undisclosed witness is substantially more persuasive than the first witness?

3. *Continuance.* A trial court may postpone the trial rather than exclude the undisclosed evidence. If the trial is postponed for more than 30 days, the party can supplement its interrogatories immediately, and the supplementation will be timely for purposes of the next trial date.[5] The 1999 rules specifically allow a continuance or postponement of the trial to allow the objecting party to conduct additional discovery to meet the testimony.[6] Sometimes, this could be taken care of with early adjournment one afternoon, allowing the party time to depose the undisclosed witness.

4. *Nonsuit.* A plaintiff can escape the consequences of the automatic exclusion sanction by nonsuiting the case, which the plaintiff has an absolute right to do at any time before the plaintiff has introduced all of its evidence other than rebuttal evidence.[7] If the statute of limitations has not expired, the plaintiff can simply refile the suit, and be more careful about responding to discovery before the next trial. The exclusion sanction does not survive a nonsuit.[8]

5. *Failure to supplement "reasonably promptly."* Assume that Plaintiff responded to requests for disclosure on April 1, identifying 10 persons with knowledge of relevant facts. On May 1, Plaintiff found an additional person who saw the accident. Plaintiff interviews the witness, but does not supplement requests for disclosure until October 1. On November 1, Defendant deposes the witness. The trial is set to begin on February 1. On January 1, Defendant files a motion to exclude the witness' testimony at trial because Plaintiff failed to supplement discovery "reasonably promptly." If you are the trial judge ruling on the motion, how do you rule and why? What evidence do you want to see at the hearing?

6. *Withdrawing admissions.* The sanction for failing to respond to requests for admissions is that the admission is automatically "deemed" admitted.[9] If that happens, the party cannot introduce evidence contrary to the deemed admission, which can cause that party to lose its case. The trial court may permit withdrawal or amendment of admissions, either actual admissions or deemed admissions, if the party shows "good cause" and the court finds that the party relying on the admissions will not be "unduly prejudiced" and that "the merits of the action will be subserved" by allowing amendment or withdrawal. In an opinion concerning an older version of the rule, the Supreme Court held that a party could withdraw an admission when the party discovered that the original admission was incorrect—the defendant had admitted that he owned the premises where the plaintiff fell, but later discovered that the fall occurred on the City's right-of-way in front of his house.[10] In a more recent opinion, excerpted below, the Supreme Court has emphasized that

---

[4] Gee v. Liberty Mut. Fire Ins. Co., 765 S.W.2d 394 (Tex. 1989).

[5] *Alvarado*, 830 S.W.2d at 915; *see* Rule 215.3.

[6] *See* Rule 193.6(c).

[7] Rule 162.

[8] Schein v. American Restaurant Group, Inc., 852 S.W.2d 496 (Tex. 1993); Aetna Cas. & Sur. Co. v. Specia, 849 S.W.2d 805, 807 (Tex. 1993).

[9] Rule 198.2(c).

[10] Stelly v. Papania, 927 S.W.3d 620 (Tex. 1996).

because deemed admissions often determine the merits of a lawsuit, extra care must be taken in refusing to allow a party to change them.[11]

WHEELER
v.
GREEN
157 S.W.3d 439
(Tex. 2005)

[In this child custody case, the father was granted summary judgment terminating the *pro se* mother's custodial rights based upon unanswered requests for admissions. The father's attorney neglected to tell the court that the mother had filed responses six months before the motion for summary judgment was heard, although 2 days after the date the responses were due. She attended the summary judgment hearing, but, still *pro se*, did not file a response to the motion. After judgment was rendered, she hired an attorney, who filed a motion for new trial, which was denied.]

We [have previously held] that the standards for withdrawing deemed admissions and for allowing a late summary-judgment response are the same. Either is proper upon a showing of (1) good cause, and (2) no undue prejudice. *See* TEX.R. CIV. P. 166a(c), 198.3. Good cause is established by showing the failure involved was an accident or mistake, not intentional or the result of conscious indifference. On this record, the lower courts could have concluded that Sandra was wrong on her dates and wrong on how to correct them, but not that either was the result of intent or conscious indifference.[1]

Undue prejudice depends on whether withdrawing an admission or filing a late response will delay trial or significantly hamper the opposing party's ability to prepare for it. As Sandra's proof attached to her motion for new trial showed, Darrin's attorney received her responses two days late but six months *before* the summary judgment motion was heard. The lower courts could not have concluded on this record that Darrin would suffer any undue prejudice if the admissions were withdrawn.[2]

We recognize that trial courts have broad discretion to permit or deny withdrawal of deemed admissions, but they cannot do so arbitrarily, unreasonably, or without reference to guiding rules or principles. While requests for admissions were at one time unique in including an automatic sanction for untimely responses, failure to comply with any discovery requests now bears similar consequences. *See* TEX.R. CIV. P. 193.6(a). Nevertheless, we have held for all other forms of

---

[11] See also Marino v. King, 355 S.W.3d 629 (Tex. 2011) (finding abuse of discretion in granting summary judgment in fraud case on deemed admission because there was no evidence of bad faith or callous disregard).

[1] By contrast, if the same elementary mistakes had been made by a lawyer, such a conclusion might well be warranted.

[2] The rule governing admissions includes as part of the undue-prejudice inquiry that the "presentation of the merits [must] be subserved" by permitting withdrawal. TEX.R. CIV. P. 198.3(b). The two are different sides of the same coin, as presentation of the merits will suffer (1) if the requesting party *cannot* prepare for trial, and also (2) if the requestor *can* prepare but the case is decided on deemed (but perhaps untrue) facts anyway.

discovery that absent flagrant bad faith or callous disregard for the rules, due process bars merits-preclusive sanctions, and have applied this rule to:

- depositions;
- interrogatories;
- requests for production; and
- requests for disclosure.

When requests for admissions are used as intended—addressing uncontroverted matters or evidentiary ones like the authenticity or admissibility of documents—deeming admissions by default is unlikely to compromise presentation of the merits. *See Stelly,* 927 S.W.2d at 622 (stating requests for admissions were intended to "eliminat[e] matters about which there is no real controversy" and were "never intended to be used as a demand upon a plaintiff or defendant to admit that he had no cause of action or ground of defense"). But when a party uses deemed admissions to try to preclude presentation of the merits of a case, the same due-process concerns arise.

Of the sixty-four admissions deemed here, none sought to discover information: nine deemed circumstances changed so modification was proper, twenty-five deemed modification in the child's best interest, twenty-seven deemed Sandra liable for malicious prosecution, and three deemed her liable for child support, attorney's fees, and exemplary damages.

This record contains no evidence of flagrant bad faith or callous disregard for the rules, nothing to justify a presumption that Sandra's case lacks merit, and nothing to suggest Darrin was unable to prepare for trial without the admissions. Further, Sandra offered to pay for any expenses Darrin incurred because her responses were late. *See* TEX.R. CIV. P. 215.4. We hold under the facts presented here that the trial court should have granted a new trial and allowed the deemed admissions to be withdrawn upon learning that the summary judgment was solely because Sandra's responses were two days late.

We certainly agree that pro se litigants are not exempt from the rules of procedure. Having two sets of rules—a strict set for attorneys and a lenient set for pro se parties—might encourage litigants to discard their valuable right to the advice and assistance of counsel. But when a rule itself turns on an actor's state of mind (as these do here), application may require a different result when the actor is not a lawyer. Recognizing that Sandra did not know what any lawyer would does not create a separate rule, but recognizes the differences the rule itself contains.

Accordingly, without hearing oral argument, we reverse the court of appeals' judgment, and remand to the trial court for further proceedings consistent with this opinion. TEX.R.APP. P. 59.1.

D. Spoliation: Sanctions for Destroying Evidence

BROOKSHIRE BROTHERS, LTD.
v.
ALDRIDGE
438 S.W.3d 9
(Tex. 2014)

Opinion

JUSTICE LEHRMANN delivered the opinion of the Court, in which CHIEF JUSTICE HECHT, JUSTICE GREEN, JUSTICE JOHNSON, JUSTICE WILLETT, and JUSTICE BODY joined.

A fundamental tenet of our legal system is that each and every trial is decided on the merits of the lawsuit being tried. After all, reaching the correct verdict is the goal of a fair and impartial judiciary. However, when the spoliation of evidence is at issue, this goal is hampered in conflicting ways. First, as is the case when evidence is lost or destroyed for any reason, spoliation can deprive the factfinder of relevant evidence, which can in turn negatively impact the fairness of the trial. Trial courts therefore must have wide discretion in remedying such conduct and in imposing sanctions to deter it. However, the imposition of a severe spoliation sanction, such as a spoliation jury instruction, can shift the focus of the case from the merits of the lawsuit to the improper conduct that was allegedly committed by one of the parties during the course of the litigation process. The problem is magnified when evidence regarding the spoliating conduct is presented to a jury. Like the spoliating conduct itself, this shift can unfairly skew a jury verdict, resulting in a judgment that is based not on the facts of the case, but on the conduct of the parties during or in anticipation of litigation.

Modern technology has added another layer of complexity to these competing concerns. Due to the exponential increase in the volume of electronic data being generated and stored, maintaining the balance between the significant interest in preserving relevant evidence and the burdens associated with doing so has become increasingly difficult.

Today we enunciate with greater clarity the standards governing whether an act of spoliation has occurred and the parameters of a trial court's discretion to impose a remedy upon a finding of spoliation, including submission of a spoliation instruction to the jury. . . .

While the spectrum of remedies that may be imposed range from an award of attorney's fees to the dismissal of the lawsuit, the harsh remedy of a spoliation instruction is warranted only when the trial court finds that the spoliating party acted with the specific intent of concealing discoverable evidence, and that a less severe remedy would be insufficient to reduce the prejudice caused by the spoliation. This intent requirement is congruent with the presumption underlying a spoliation instruction—that the evidence would have hurt the wrongdoer. A failure to preserve evidence with a negligent mental state may only underlie a spoliation instruction in the rare situation in which a nonspoliating party has been irreparably deprived of any meaningful ability to present a claim or defense.

* * *

I. Background

On September 2, 2004, Jerry Aldridge slipped and fell near a display table at a Brookshire Brothers grocery store. At the time of the fall, Aldridge did not tell store employees that he was injured, and the store did not investigate the fall or complete an incident report. However, about an hour-and-a-half after leaving the store, Aldridge went to the emergency room because of pain. On September 7, Aldridge returned to the store and reported his injuries. Jon Tyler, a store manager trainee, prepared an incident report based on Aldridge's statements and the recollections of the assistant manager who was on duty at the time of Aldridge's fall. The incident report stated that "Aldridge slipped on grease that had leaked out of a container by the 'Grab N Go.' "The Grab-N-Go, which featured rotisserie chickens that were cooked and packaged in the store's deli, was located approximately fifteen feet from the area of the fall.

Aldridge's fall was captured by a surveillance camera mounted near the check-out counters. Because of the camera's placement, the floor where Aldridge fell was in the background and was obscured by a display table, which was covered with a cloth that extended to the floor. At the time of the fall, the cameras recorded surveillance video in a continuous loop that, after approximately thirty days, recorded over prior events. After Aldridge reported his injuries to Brookshire Brothers, Robert Gilmer, Brookshire Brothers' Vice President of Human Resources and Risk Management, decided to retain and copy approximately eight minutes of the video, starting just before Aldridge entered the store and concluding shortly after his fall.

Aldridge learned that Brookshire Brothers possessed video footage of the incident and, on September 13, asked the claims department for a copy so he could see his fall. Gilmer testified that he instructed the claims department not to provide the tape to Aldridge, as Gilmer believed it would be improper. The claims department wrote Aldridge a letter on September 29 stating that there was only one copy of the video at that time and that it therefore could not provide him with a copy. The camera presumably recorded over the September 2 footage by early October.

Brookshire Brothers initially paid Aldridge's medical expenses, but ceased paying by June 2005, when Gilmer wrote Aldridge a letter stating that he had reviewed the video and determined that Brookshire Brothers was going to deny responsibility. In August 2005, Aldridge's attorney sent Brookshire Brothers a letter requesting approximately two-and-a-half hours of additional footage from the store cameras. Brookshire Brothers was unable to comply with that request because the footage had been recorded over almost a year earlier.

Aldridge sued Brookshire Brothers, claiming injuries from a slip and fall under a premises-liability theory. To recover in a slip-and-fall case, a plaintiff must prove, *inter alia,* that the defendant had actual or constructive knowledge of a dangerous condition on the premises such as a slippery substance on the floor, *Keech v. Kroger Co.,* 845 S.W.2d 262, 264 (Tex. 1992), which may be accomplished with a showing that "(1) the defendant placed the substance on the floor, (2) the defendant actually knew that the substance was on the floor, or (3) it is more likely than not that the condition existed long enough to give the premises owner a reasonable opportunity to discover it," *Wal-Mart Stores, Inc. v. Reece,* 81 S.W.3d 812, 814 (Tex. 2002). Aldridge argued in the trial court that Brookshire Brothers' failure to preserve additional video footage amounted to spoliation of evidence that would have been helpful to the key issue of whether the spill was on the floor long enough to give Brookshire Brothers a reasonable opportunity to discover it. Aldridge accordingly moved for a spoliation jury instruction.

The trial court allowed the jury to hear evidence bearing on whether Brookshire Brothers spoliated the video, submitted a spoliation instruction to the jury, and permitted the jury to decide whether spoliation occurred during its deliberations on the merits of the lawsuit. The principal witness to testify on the circumstances surrounding the preservation of the video was Gilmer, who had made the decision regarding the amount of video footage to preserve after Aldridge's incident report was completed. Gilmer testified at trial that he had instructed Tyler to save the portion showing the fall and the five or six minutes before the fall so as to try to identify Aldridge entering the store. He further testified that the purpose of saving the video was to verify that Aldridge had actually fallen and that Gilmer believed the rest of the video, which he had not viewed, "[w]asn't relevant." Gilmer verified his understanding that a key legal issue in a slip-and-fall case is whether store employees knew or should have known there was something on the floor that caused the fall. However, he maintained that when the decision was made to preserve the video he "didn't know there was going to be a case." At that time, "[i]t was just a man who made a claim that he slipped and fell in the store," and the actions relating to the video were not taken "in anticipation of this trial."

The trial court submitted the following spoliation instruction to the jury:

> In this case, Brookshire Brothers permitted its video surveillance system to record over certain portions of the store surveillance video of the day of the occurrence in question. If you find that Brookshire Brothers knew or reasonably should have known that such portions of the store video not preserved contained relevant evidence to the issues in this case, and its non-preservation has not been satisfactorily explained, then you are instructed that you may consider such evidence would have been unfavorable to Brookshire Brothers.

The jury determined that Brookshire Brothers' negligence proximately caused Aldridge's fall and awarded Aldridge $1,063,664.99 in damages. The court of appeals affirmed the trial court's judgment on the verdict, holding that the trial court did not abuse its discretion in admitting evidence of spoliation or charging the jury with the spoliation instruction.

II. Spoliation Analysis

The spoliation of evidence is a serious issue. A party's failure to reasonably preserve discoverable evidence may significantly hamper the nonspoliating party's ability to present its claims or defenses, *Wal-Mart Stores, Inc. v. Johnson,* 106 S.W.3d 718, 721 (Tex. 2003), and can "undermine the truth-seeking function of the judicial system and the adjudicatory process," Justice Rebecca Simmons and Michael J. Ritter, *Texas's Spoliation "Presumption",* 43 ST. MARY'S L.J. 691, 701 (2012); *see also Trevino v. Ortega,* 969 S.W.2d 950, 954 (Tex. 1998) (BAKER, J., concurring) (observing that "[e]vidence spoliation is a serious problem that can have a devastating effect on the administration of justice"). As one federal district court has explained, "[d]ocuments create a paper reality we call proof. The absence of such documentary proof may stymie the search for the truth." *Zubulake v. UBS Warburg L.L.C.,* 220 F.R.D. 212, 214 (S.D.N.Y. 2003) (citations and internal quotation marks omitted). In some circumstances, a missing piece of evidence like a photograph or video can be irreplaceable. Testimony as to what the lost or destroyed evidence might have shown will not always restore the nonspoliating party to an approximation of its position if the evidence were available; sometimes a picture is indeed worth a thousand words.

In light of these concerns, courts have broad discretion to utilize a variety of remedies to address spoliation, including the spoliation instruction. *See* Andrew Hebl, *Spoliation of Electronically Stored Information, Good Faith, and Rule 37(e),* 29 N. ILL. U.L. REV.. 79, 86 (2008). The instruction is an important remedy, but its use can affect the fundamental fairness of the trial in ways as troubling as the spoliating conduct itself. As we have recognized, "[b]ecause the instruction itself is given to compensate for the absence of evidence that a party had a duty to preserve, its very purpose is to 'nudge' or 'tilt' the jury" toward a finding adverse to the alleged spoliator. *Wal-Mart Stores,* 106 S.W.3d at 724. Thus, an unfortunate consequence of submitting a spoliation instruction is that it "often ends litigation" because "it is too difficult a hurdle for the spoliator to overcome." *Zubulake,* 220 F.R.D. at 219. This "nudging" or "tilting" of the jury is magnified by the presentation of evidence that emphasizes the spoliator's wrongful conduct rather than the merits of the suit.

Added to these concerns are the complexities surrounding evidence preservation in today's world, as technology has advanced to allow potential litigants to store larger volumes of electronic information. *See* Simmons and Ritter, *Texas's Spoliation "Presumption",* 43 ST. MARY'S L.J. at 701. Thus, while electronic data can be a valuable source of evidence, it can also make compliance with one's responsibility to preserve and produce such data much more difficult and expensive. *See id.* at 702; Robert Hardaway, et al., *E-Discovery's Threat to Civil Litigation: Reevaluating Rule 26 for the Digital Age,* 63 RUTGERS L. REV. 521, 522 (2011). Because of the prevalence of discoverable electronic data and the uncertainties associated with preserving that data, sanctions concerning the spoliation of electronic information have reached an all-time high. Dan H. Willoughby, Jr., et al., *Sanctions for E-Discovery Violations: By the Numbers,* 60 DUKE L.J. 789, 790 (2010).

Because of these and other myriad concerns, the Federal Rules of Civil Procedure were amended in 2006 to prohibit federal courts from imposing sanctions when discoverable electronic evidence is lost "as a result of the routine, good-faith operation of an electronic information system." FED. R. CIV. P. 37(E).[3] The Texas rules do not contain a comparable provision, but the challenges facing Texas courts are just as acute. Merits determinations are significantly affected by both spoliation instructions and the conduct that gives rise to them. We have observed that when a party is inherently prevented from having the merits of its case adjudicated, constitutional due process is implicated. *TransAmerican Natural Gas Corp. v. Powell,* 811 S.W.2d 913, 917-18 (Tex. 1991) (discussing constitutional limitations on the power of courts to adjudicate a party's claims without regard to the merits, but instead based on a party's conduct in discovery). In light of these concerns, we granted review of Brookshire Brothers' petition in order to bring much-needed clarity to our state's spoliation jurisprudence.

A. Development of Spoliation Law in Texas

* * *

B. Spoliation Framework

* * *

1. The Trial Court Determines Whether Evidence Was Spoliated and the Proper Remedy

As discussed above, spoliation is an evidentiary concept, not a separate cause of action. It is well-established that evidentiary matters are resolved by the trial court. Further, spoliation is essentially a particularized form of discovery abuse, in that it ultimately results in the failure to

---

[3] Rule 37(e) is in the process of being amended again. Following the receipt of public comment, the Advisory Committee on Civil Rules recommended a proposed amended rule for adoption by the Committee on Rules of Practice and Procedure. *See* Hon. David G. Campbell, Advisory Committee on Civil Rules, *Report of Advisory Committee on Civil Rules,* 306–17 (May 2, 2014), http://www.uscourts.gov /uscourts/ RulesAndPolicies/rules/Agenda%20Books/Standing/ST2014-05.pdf# pagemode=bookmarks. The Standing Committee approved the proposal at its May 29, 2014 meeting. Thomas Y. Allman, *Standing Committee OKs Federal Discovery Amendments,* LAW TECHNOLOGY NEWS (June 2, 2014), http://www.lawtechnologynews .com/id=1202657565227? slreturn=20140505130019.

produce discoverable evidence, and discovery matters are also within the sole province of the trial court. Finally, presenting spoliation issues to the jury for resolution magnifies the concern that the focus of the trial will shift from the merits to a party's spoliating conduct. For these reasons, we agree with Justice Baker that the trial court, rather than the jury, must determine whether a party spoliated evidence and, if so, impose the appropriate remedy. *See Trevino,* 969 S.W.2d at 954 (BAKER, J., concurring). The trial court may hold an evidentiary hearing to assist the court in making spoliation findings, but not in the presence of the jury. Placing the responsibility on the trial court to make spoliation findings and to determine the proper remedy is a key mechanism in ensuring the jury's focus stays where it belongs—on the merits.

2. Spoliation Finding

With this background in mind, we turn to the elements that underlie a trial court's spoliation finding, beginning with the issue of duty. We have held that a party alleging spoliation bears the burden of establishing that the nonproducing party had a duty to preserve the evidence. *See Wal-Mart Stores,* 106 S.W.3d at 722. The standard governing the duty to preserve resolves two related inquiries: when the duty is triggered, and the scope of that duty. Specifically, we observed in *Wal-Mart Stores* that "[s]uch a duty arises only when a party knows or reasonably should know that there is a substantial chance that a claim will be filed and that evidence in its possession or control will be material and relevant to that claim." *Id.* In turn, a "substantial chance of litigation" arises when "litigation is more than merely an abstract possibility or unwarranted fear." *National Tank Co. v. Brotherton,* 851 S.W.2d 193, 204 (Tex.1993).[7]

Second, we have implicitly recognized, and now do so explicitly, that the party seeking a remedy for spoliation must demonstrate that the other party breached its duty to preserve material and relevant evidence. If a party possesses a duty to preserve evidence, it is inherent that a party breaches that duty by failing to exercise reasonable care to do so. Otherwise, the nonspoliating party would have no legitimate reason to seek a spoliation remedy. Further, we agree with Justice Baker that the breach may be either intentional or negligent. *Trevino,* 969 S.W.2d at 957 (BAKER, J., concurring).

3. Spoliation Remedies

After a court determines that a party has spoliated evidence by breaching its duty to preserve such evidence, it may impose an appropriate remedy. Rule 215.2 of the Texas Rules of Civil Procedure enumerates a wide array of remedies available to a trial court in addressing discovery abuse, such as an award of attorney's fees or costs to the harmed party, exclusion of evidence, striking a party's pleadings, or even dismissing a party's claims. These remedies are available in the spoliation context. The trial court also has discretion to craft other remedies it deems appropriate in light of the particular facts of an individual case, including the submission of a spoliation instruction to the jury.

In accordance with our well-settled precedent on remedying discovery abuse, however, the remedy must have a direct relationship to the act of spoliation and may not be excessive. In other words, the remedy crafted by the trial court must be proportionate when weighing the culpability of the spoliating party and the prejudice to the nonspoliating party. This logically follows from

[7] Federal courts have struggled with the issue of when a duty to preserve is triggered and the scope of that duty, especially as it relates to electronic data and "litigation holds." *See generally* Paul W. Grimm, et al., *Proportionality in the Post–Hoc Analysis of Pre-Litigation Preservation Decisions,* 37 U. BALT. L. REV. 381 (2008) (discussing the perplexing issue in federal courts of the duty to preserve as it relates to electronically stored information).

the remedial purpose undergirding the imposition of a spoliation remedy under Texas law, which is to restore the parties to a rough approximation of their positions if all evidence were available. *See Wal-Mart Stores,* 106 S.W.3d at 721.

The courts of appeals evaluate prejudice largely on . . . the relevance of the spoliated evidence to key issues in the case, the harmful effect of the evidence on the spoliating party's case (or, conversely, whether the evidence would have been helpful to the nonspoliating party's case), and whether the spoliated evidence was cumulative of other competent evidence that may be used instead of the spoliated evidence. These factors have proved workable in the courts of appeals, are similar to the test followed by federal courts, and provide guidance to the trial courts in analyzing prejudice in a specific case. Accordingly, we adopt them.

In light of the difficulty of conducting a prejudice analysis based on evidence that is no longer available for review, we recognize that a party's intentional destruction of evidence may, "[a]bsent evidence to the contrary," be sufficient by itself to support a finding that the spoliated evidence is both relevant and harmful to the spoliating party. This flows from the common-law spoliation presumption that all things are presumed against the wrongdoer. Conversely, negligent spoliation could not be enough to support such a finding without "some proof about what the destroyed evidence would show."[12] In any event, the trial court should of course consider all evidence bearing on the factors associated with evaluating prejudice to the nonspoliating party.

We note, however, that a trial court should exercise caution in evaluating the final prejudice factor, which accounts for the existence of cumulative evidence. For example, a spoliating party might argue that no prejudice resulted from spoliation of a video of an incident because there is also eyewitness testimony regarding the incident. But many of the inherent problems with such testimony—inaccurate memory, poor eyesight, bias, etc.—are simply not present with a video recording. Again, a picture is often worth a thousand words. The same can be true with respect to testimony regarding the contents of a destroyed document, compared to the document itself. The differences in kind and quality between the available evidence and the spoliated evidence will thus be a key factor in analyzing prejudice to the nonspoliating party.

C. Spoliation Instruction as a Remedy

Having laid out the general framework governing spoliation findings and remedies, we turn to the particular remedy at issue in this case—the submission of an instruction to the jury to presume that the missing evidence would have been unfavorable to the spoliator. Though we have generally described the purpose of a spoliation remedy in remedial rather than punitive terms, a spoliation instruction is still inherently a sanction. Further, it is among the harshest sanctions a trial court may utilize to remedy an act of spoliation. Because a spoliation instruction has the propensity to tilt a trial in favor of a nonspoliating party, it can, in some sense, be tantamount to a death-penalty sanction. At the same time, the destruction of relevant evidence can also unfairly skew the outcome of a trial. Thus, improper use of a spoliation instruction can deprive either party of the right to a fair trial on the merits of the case. It follows that an instruction should be available to address spoliation in certain circumstances, but should be used cautiously.

---

12 This does not mean that the contents of the missing evidence must be conclusively proven, as they can be demonstrated through circumstantial evidence.

1. Culpability

The competing considerations outlined above have led courts to grapple with the specific issue of whether a spoliation instruction can ever be an appropriate remedy for negligent spoliation. . . .

For several reasons, and with a narrow exception we will explain below, we conclude that a party must intentionally spoliate evidence in order for a spoliation instruction to constitute an appropriate remedy. . . . First, we have expressly stated that a spoliation instruction may be given when a party *deliberately* destroys evidence. Second, a person who merely negligently destroys evidence lacks the state of mind of a "wrongdoer," and it makes little sense to infer that a party who only negligently lost or destroyed evidence did so because it was unfavorable to the party's case. Courts that allow a negligent state of mind to warrant the submission of a spoliation instruction tend to reason that the need to deter and punish spoliation is a sufficient basis for the instruction. . . . However, in Texas, the instruction is based on the presumption of wrongdoing, so it follows that the more appropriate requirement is intent to conceal or destroy discoverable evidence.

Our analysis of Rule 215 discovery sanctions in *TransAmerican* and its progeny, in which we held that there must be a direct relationship between the offensive conduct and the sanction imposed, and that the sanction may not be excessive, also compels our conclusion. . . . To allow such a severe sanction as a matter of course when a party has only negligently destroyed evidence is neither just nor proportionate.

Finally, our approach aligns with a majority of the federal courts of appeals. . . . We believe this approach is consistent with our jurisprudence and is the most practical in this era of complex electronic discovery.

Because of the significant consequences stemming from a finding that spoliation is intentional, further discussion of the meaning of "intentional" in this context is warranted. By "intentional" spoliation, often referenced as "bad faith" or "willful" spoliation, we mean that the party acted with the subjective purpose of concealing or destroying discoverable evidence. This includes the concept of "willful blindness," which encompasses the scenario in which a party does not directly destroy evidence known to be relevant and discoverable, but nonetheless "allows for its destruction."[17]

Accordingly, we hold that a trial court's finding of intentional spoliation pursuant to the analysis set forth above is a necessary predicate to the proper submission of a spoliation instruction to the jury. In the event the trial court makes such a finding and concludes, as with

---

[17] The issue of willful blindness is especially acute in the context of automatic electronic deletion systems. A party with control over one of these systems who intentionally allows relevant information to be erased can hardly be said to have only negligently destroyed evidence, though we recognize the complexities of these determinations when a potential litigant who controls massive volumes of electronic data is attempting to determine, prelitigation, which information is likely to be discoverable. *See, e.g.,* Hardaway, et al., *E-Discovery's Threat to Civil Litigation: Reevaluating Rule 26 for the Digital Age,* 63 RUTGERS L. REV. at 529 (discussing the "staggering costs" in discovery because of the volumes of electronically stored information in computers and other databases around the country); Wright, Note, *Federal Rule of Civil Procedure 37(e): Spoiling the Spoliation Doctrine,* 38 HOFSTRA L. REV. 793, 806 (2009) (discussing the discovery problems when electronically stored information is routinely deleted from a business's computers, and the need for courts to remedy spoliation while also remembering that "[i]n a world where the very act of deletion is integral to normal operations, it is unfair to treat the inadvertent or negligent loss of [ESI] as indicative of an intent to destroy evidence and to thereby infer spoliation") (citation and internal quotation marks omitted).

any sanction, that a lesser remedy would be insufficient to ameliorate the prejudice caused by the spoliating party's conduct, the trial court is within its discretion in submitting an instruction.

2. Caveat Authorizing Instruction in Context of Negligent Spoliation

Our conclusion regarding the requisite state of mind to justify a jury instruction, however, must include a narrow caveat. On rare occasions, a situation may arise in which a party's negligent breach of its duty to reasonably preserve evidence irreparably prevents the nonspoliating party from having any meaningful opportunity to present a claim or defense. In such circumstances, the destruction or loss of the evidence, regardless of motive, could completely subvert the factfinder's ability to ascertain the truth.

* * *

We therefore conclude that, in this rare circumstance, a court should have the discretion to remedy such extreme and irreparable prejudice to the nonspoliating party with a spoliation instruction, even if the trial court determines that the evidence was only negligently lost or destroyed.

D. Admission of Spoliation Evidence at Trial

An issue that commonly arises when a party is accused of spoliation is the admissibility of evidence at trial relating to whether spoliation occurred and the culpability of the spoliating party. Under the Texas Rules of Evidence, admissible evidence must be relevant, which is defined as "having any tendency to make the existence of any fact that is of consequence to the determination of the action more probable or less probable than it would be without the evidence." TEX. R. EVID. 401. Further, a trial court may exclude even relevant evidence "if its probative value is substantially outweighed by the danger of unfair prejudice, confusion of the issues, or misleading the jury, or by considerations of undue delay, or needless presentation of cumulative evidence." TEX. R. EVID. 403. The evidentiary issue presented here is whether evidence bearing solely on whether a party spoliated evidence or the party's degree of culpability in doing so relates to a "fact that is of consequence to the determination of the action." For the reasons set out below, we hold that it does not.

Our holding that the trial court, not the jury, bears responsibility for making the required spoliation findings and imposing a remedy affects the propriety of admitting evidence regarding spoliation at trial. . . . The evidence considered by the trial court in making these findings, however, often has no bearing on the facts that are "of consequence to the determination of the action" from the jury's perspective. TEX. R. EVID. 401. . . .

That said, we recognize that all references to missing evidence, whether lost due to a party's spoliation or missing for some other reason, cannot and should not be foreclosed. For example, to the extent permitted by the Texas Rules of Evidence, parties may present indirect evidence to attempt to prove the contents of missing evidence that is otherwise relevant to a claim or defense, such as a person's testimony about the content of a missing document, photo, or recording. However, there is no basis on which to allow the jury to hear evidence that is unrelated to the merits of the case, but serves only to highlight the spoliating party's breach and culpability. While such evidence may be central to the trial court's spoliation findings, it has no bearing on the issues to be resolved by the jury.

III. Application

We review a trial court's imposition of a spoliation remedy, including the submission of a spoliation instruction to the jury, for an abuse of discretion. We similarly evaluate the court's admission of evidence under an abuse-of-discretion standard. . . .

Under the analysis set forth herein, both the admission of such evidence and the submission of the instruction were improper.

Further, based on our review of the considerable amount of record evidence surrounding the spoliation issue, we hold that the submission of a spoliation instruction in any form was an abuse of discretion. Assuming without deciding that Brookshire Brothers had and breached a duty to reasonably preserve evidence by saving an insufficient amount of video footage before allowing the additional footage to be erased, prejudicing Aldridge, there is no evidence that it did so with the requisite intent to conceal or destroy relevant evidence or that Aldridge was irreparably deprived of any meaningful ability to present his claim.

* * *

We therefore hold that the trial court abused its discretion in submitting a spoliation instruction. Further, the trial court erred in admitting evidence of the circumstances surrounding the failure to preserve additional video footage, though only to the extent such evidence was unrelated to the merits and served principally to highlight Brookshire Brothers' culpability. For example, nonspeculative testimony relating to what the missing video would have shown, such as the testimony about the cleanup, was not problematic. Further, because a portion of the video was preserved and presented at trial, some degree of questioning about the creation of the video was reasonably pursued as background for its introduction to the jury. However, testimony that is relevant only to the issues of whether Brookshire Brothers breached a duty to preserve evidence or acted with the requisite intent was improperly admitted.

The trial court's error is reversible, however, only if it "probably caused the rendition of an improper judgment." TEX. R. APP. P. 61.1(a). In *Wal-Mart Stores,* we noted that "if a spoliation instruction should not have been given, the likelihood of harm from the erroneous instruction is substantial, particularly when the case is closely contested." Such a likelihood of harm existed in this case.

The instruction capped off a trial in which both liability and the extent of Aldridge's damages were closely contested and in which significant emphasis was placed on the spoliation issue. . . . On this record, particularly when considered in conjunction with our holding in *Wal-Mart Stores* that an improper spoliation instruction presents a substantial likelihood of harm, it is "very difficult to overlook the likely impact" of the spoliation evidence and the instruction. Accordingly, we hold that the trial court's error probably caused the rendition of an improper judgment, and we reverse the judgment of the court of appeals.

We note that this case highlights the need for guidelines and clarity in our spoliation jurisprudence, as the record reflects the significant effect that the spoliation allegations had on the course of this trial. Indeed, this case typifies the manner in which the focus of the trial can impermissibly shift from the merits of the case to the spoliating conduct when such guidance is missing. Because spoliation is not directly addressed in either our rules of evidence or our rules of procedure, courts must fill in the gaps to maintain the consistency and predictability that is basic to the rule of law in our society. The continued development of the State's common law, in which we engage today, is not only the province—but the responsibility—of this Court.

* * *

V. Conclusion

We hold that the trial court abused its discretion in submitting a spoliation instruction because there is no evidence that Brookshire Brothers intentionally concealed or destroyed the video in question or that Aldridge was deprived of any meaningful ability to present his claim to the jury at trial. Accordingly, we reverse the court of appeals' judgment and remand the case to the trial court for a new trial in accordance with this opinion.

JUSTICE GUZMAN, joined by JUSTICE DEVINE and JUSTICE BROWN, dissenting, omitted.

Notes & Questions

Willful blindness. Intentional destruction of evidence encompasses the concept of "willful blindness"—where a party does not directly destroy evidence known to be discoverable, but nevertheless allows it to be destroyed. For example, a company with a seemingly innocuous document retention policy, requiring automatic destruction of electronic files after a certain amount of time, might ignore notice of circumstances likely to give rise to litigation and when litigation actually arises, the files are gone. The dissent in *Brookshire Brothers* (omitted above) criticized the majority for "render[ing] the notion of 'willful blindness' ineffective. The dissenters claim that the majority:

> … nevertheless concludes (assuming without deciding that Brookshire Brothers breached a duty to reasonably preserve evidence) "there is *no evidence* " that [Brookshire Brothers] failed to preserve the surveillance footage "with the requisite intent to conceal or destroy relevant evidence. . . ." —— S.W.3d at —— (emphasis added). Curiously, the Court reaches this result despite the fact that at the time Brookshire Brothers allowed the additional surveillance footage surrounding Aldridge's fall to automatically erase, Brookshire Brothers (particularly Gilmer) knew of Aldridge's fall, knew Aldridge had filed an incident report documenting the fall and requested a copy of the footage, and had already agreed to cover Aldridge's medical costs above and beyond the amounts Brookshire covered pursuant to its routine practice. It was Gilmer's conscious and intentional choice not to review or retain any more than the eight minutes of surveillance footage capturing the fall, a choice he made despite his admitted awareness that a key issue in a slip and fall case is whether employees had actual or constructive notice that there was a substance on the floor. And this choice inevitably resulted in the destruction of relevant evidence approximately thirty days after the fall occurred. If the concept of "willful blindness" is to have any meaning, these circumstances must give rise to at least some evidence of "willful blindness," and therefore at least some evidence that Brookshire Brothers acted with the requisite intent. But as it stands, the Court's assurances that its spoliation framework encompasses instances of "willful blindness" ring hollow given the Court's application of the concept to the facts of this case.
>
> * * *
>
> Our spoliation framework should not allow a party to pre-select the evidence that will be available against it and escape liability for the destruction of unfavorable evidence under the guise of a retention policy that preserves information for a limited time. Unfortunately, today's holding potentially provides future litigants with a blueprint for

successfully shielding themselves from spoliation liability: simply establish a document retention policy with a limited duration. Because I believe the Court's holding does not provide sufficient meaning to the concept of willful blindness given the trend toward increasing reliance on limited-duration document retention policies, I cannot join the Court in its new spoliation framework or its application to this case.

CHAPTER 10. EXPERTS

A. Consulting Expert Exemption

Read Rule 192.3(e).

Rule 192.3(e) creates three categories for expert witnesses: (1) the consulting expert—"an expert who has been consulted, retained or specially employed by a party in anticipation of litigation or in preparation for trial;"[1] (2) the "reviewed consulting expert"—a consulting expert whose opinions and mental impressions have been reviewed by the testifying expert;[2] and (3) the testifying expert—an expert who may be called to testify as an expert witness at trial.[3] Rule 192.3(e) creates an exemption from discovery for the identity, mental impressions and opinions of consulting experts. The rule also designates information that is discoverable regarding reviewed consulting experts and testifying experts.

GENERAL MOTORS CORP.
v.
GAYLE
951 S.W.2d 469
(Tex. 1997)

PHILLIPS, CHIEF JUSTICE.

In this original mandamus proceeding, we must first decide whether the trial court abused its discretion by compelling relator to designate in advance whether its crash testing was to be used for evidentiary purposes or solely for consulting purposes, and by ordering that the opposing party be allowed to attend those tests designated as evidentiary. Because we conclude that the trial court's order invades the consulting-expert privilege, and that relator lacks an adequate remedy by appeal, we conditionally grant mandamus relief compelling the trial court to vacate its crash-test order.

* * *

I

Manuel Delarosa was severely injured in 1988 when his General Motors pickup truck struck another car driven by Christopher Broussard. Delarosa's wife, a passenger in the pickup, suffered relatively minor injuries.

The Delarosas sued Broussard and General Motors in September 1990 alleging, among other things, that General Motors defectively designed the seat belts in Delarosa's pickup truck. In September 1995, after several continued trial settings, the trial court set the case for trial on January 3, 1996, on the court's "try or dismiss" docket.

* * *

---

1 Rule 192.7(d).

2 Rule 192.3(h).

3 Rule 192.7(c).

General Motors also moved to continue the January 5 trial, arguing that the case was not ready because of pending discovery issues. At that time, both the Delarosas and General Motors had discovery matters pending before the court. In particular, General Motors argued that it had not conducted critical "crash tests" because the trial court had not yet ruled on the Delarosas' motion to attend those tests.

The trial court overruled General Motors' objection to nonjury trial and its motion for continuance at a January 5 pretrial conference. Recognizing that "this case still has some discovery that needs to be done . . . ," however, the trial court decided only to hear opening statements that day, then recess the trial for three weeks before hearing testimony. The court scheduled hearings during the interim period on both sides' outstanding discovery matters, recognizing that the crash tests would have to be performed at some future date after trial recommenced. Finally, the court informed the parties that they could expect a piecemeal trial, interlaced with the completion of discovery:

> I will tell all sides also that I don't intend necessarily to commit to try this case on a continuous day-by-day basis. I may recess it for two or three weeks, hear a couple of days of testimony, and come back in a week or so. It may be that certain experts, if I allow late designations, may need to be deposed. You will have this trial finished before the spring is over and we will wrap this thing up one way or another as far as trial goes.

After hearing opening statements, the court recessed the trial in accordance with its announced plan.

The parties resolved their dispute over the Delarosas' document requests at a court hearing on January 9. After another discovery hearing the next day, the trial court granted the Delarosas' motion to attend General Motors' crash tests, subject to certain conditions. The court's order provided in pertinent part:

> 2. Plaintiffs are allowed to have representatives, i.e., a videographer, a photographer, an attorney, and one expert, present at any crash test or sled test or any test involving vehicle-to-vehicle collisions by General Motors that may pertain to this case.
>
> 3. For any test governed by this order, notices shall be given one week in advance of the test by General Motors to the plaintiffs' attorneys.
>
> 4. Plaintiffs' representatives, i.e., a videographer, a photographer, an attorney, and one expert, may attend the testing and must be afforded adequate and reasonable time prior to the test to inspect, measure, videotape, and photograph the test vehicle, dummies, cameras, instrumentation, test set-up, and other physical equipment associated with the test.
>
> 5. Plaintiffs' representatives, i.e., a videographer, a photographer, an attorney, and one expert, may photograph, videotape, and film the test itself.
>
> 6. Neither plaintiffs, their attorneys, representatives, or experts may question any of General Motors' experts, witnesses, representatives, or attorneys who may be present at the crash testing.
>
> 7. Any testing performed by purely consulting experts, whose testimony will not be offered at trial or form any basis of any testimony at trial, and whose tests and opinions will not be communicated to or form the basis of establishing any testing parameters, criteria, or conditions for any test, shall not be governed by the terms of this order and need not comply with this order. In other words, if General Motors decides to conduct

sled tests, vehicle-to-vehicle tests, or crash tests purely, solely, and strictly for consultant purposes with consulting experts, then neither the plaintiffs, their attorneys, experts, or consultants shall be allowed to be present at this consultant-only testing.

8. If any crash tests or sled tests or any test involving vehicle-to-vehicle collisions are performed with consulting experts, or any discussions occur regarding such tests, no expert designated by General Motors—that is, no testifying expert—is allowed to be present. Nor may General Motors, its representative, attorneys, consultants, or any third-parties communicate, directly or indirectly, the results, format, or testing parameters to any testifying expert or any expert whose testimony will form the basis of any trial testimony.

9. The court and any opposing party must be notified at least three working days in advance of any sled, crash, or vehicle-to-vehicle testing conducted for consulting experts only. The notices shall advise the court and any opposing party that the testing is for consultant purposes only.

10. Any test to be conducted for consultant purposes only—including (1) the parameters and set-up for the testing, (2) the criteria for the testing, (3) any measurements for the testing, (4) the speed of the testing vehicles, or sled, and (5) any other preliminary matter relating to the parameters of the testing—must be filmed or videotaped. After the testing has been filmed or videotaped, the film or videotape must be filed with the court under seal. Then, if any later crash tests, sled tests, or vehicle-to-vehicle testing is conducted, and these tests are substantially similar to the consultant-only tests in any regard involving speed, results, changes in velocity, or related matters, then the court reserves the right to disallow the use in evidence of the testing based upon the consultant-only test guidelines. The purpose of this paragraph is to prevent any party's conducting numerous tests with consulting-only experts until a favorable result is determined, and then to re-designate that testing as a sled, crash, or vehicle-to-vehicle test for designated testifying experts.

11. If the plaintiffs choose to conduct any crash test, sled test, or vehicle-to-vehicle test with dummies or anything else to simulate seat belt partings or any of the issues in this case, representatives of General Motors will be entitled to the same protections in this order, upon the filing of a proper motion.

This order effectively requires General Motors to determine beforehand whether a particular test is for evidentiary purposes or purely for consulting. Also, if General Motors runs a test for consulting purposes, it later cannot run a similar test for evidentiary purposes.

* * *

II

A

We first consider the trial court's crash-test order. General Motors argues that this order violates both the work-product privilege and the consulting-expert privilege. *See* TEX. R. CIV. P. 166b(3)(a), (b). Because we conclude that the order violates the consulting-expert privilege, we do not reach the question of whether it also infringes on protected work product.

Rule 166b exempts from discovery the following:

> The identity, mental impressions and opinions of an expert who has been informally consulted or of an expert who has been retained or specially employed by another party in anticipation of litigation or preparation for trial or any documents or tangible things

> containing such information if the expert will not be called as an expert witness, except that the identity, mental impressions and opinions of an expert who will not be called to testify as an expert and any documents or tangible things containing such impressions and opinions are discoverable if the consulting expert's opinion or impressions have been reviewed by a testifying expert.

TEX. R. CIV. P. 166b(3)(b). Like the work-product privilege, this consulting-expert privilege grants parties and their attorneys a sphere of protection and privacy in which to develop their case. Parties and counsel may consult with an expert to attempt to recreate an accident and test their litigation theories. If the expert's conclusions support the consulting party's case, that expert may be designated as a witness for trial. If, on the other hand, the expert's conclusions do not support the party's case, the identity of the expert and his or her conclusions need not be revealed to the other side. As we explained in *Tom L. Scott, Inc. v. McIlhany*, 798 S.W.2d 556, 559 (Tex. 1990): "The policy behind the consulting expert privilege is to encourage parties to seek expert advice in evaluating their case and to prevent a party from receiving undue benefit from an adversary's efforts and diligence." And as the United States Supreme Court explained in recognizing the work-product privilege: "Proper preparation of a client's case demands that [the attorney] assemble information, sift what he considers to be the relevant from the irrelevant facts, prepare his legal theories and plan his strategy without undue and needless interference. That is the historical and the necessary way in which lawyers act within the framework of our system of jurisprudence to promote justice and to protect their clients' interests." *Hickman v. Taylor*, 329 U.S. 495, 511 (1947).

Without the consulting-expert privilege, parties would be reluctant to test an uncertain theory, for fear that it would provide evidence for the other side. As one commentator has explained:

> An attorney or party consults with an expert to try out new theories or to develop new facts, all with unpredictable results. Thus, the work produced by an expert is deserving of as much protection as the work of an attorney or other agent or representative of a party. If the results are favorable, the witness will most likely become a testifying expert, whose opinions, mental impressions, and knowledge are fully discoverable. If the results are unfavorable, however, the rules allow the party to keep the expert's identity and work confidential.

Albright, *The Texas Discovery Privileges: A Fool's Game?,* 70 TEX. L. REV. 781, 848 (1992). In *Werner v. Miller*, 579 S.W.2d 455, 456 (Tex. 1979), we confirmed that the consulting-expert privilege is intended to allow "a consultant to investigate an accident without the risk of furnishing a potential expert witness or at least a theory of recovery or defense to the opposing party."

B

The trial court's crash-test order undermines General Motors' consulting-expert privilege. While the order purports to exclude tests performed by purely consulting experts, it requires General Motors to decide in advance whether a particular crash-test is evidentiary or purely consulting. Thus, if General Motors designates a test as consulting and receives a favorable outcome, General Motors cannot offer the test at trial, negating the benefit of the test. Conversely, if General Motors designates the test as evidentiary and receives an unfavorable outcome, General Motors' privilege will have been violated by plaintiffs' attendance. This approach is at odds with the rationale of the consulting-expert privilege, which is intended to allow parties to consult privately with an expert before deciding whether to designate that person as a witness.

Federal caselaw is consistent with this approach. In *Shoemaker v. General Motors Corp.*, 154 F.R.D. 235 (W.D. Mo. 1994), the court denied the plaintiffs' motion to attend defendant's litigation testing. The court concluded that "the decision about what to test and how is the embodiment of the attorney's legal theories." The court noted that, if the results of any tests are to be offered at trial, plaintiffs would have ample opportunity to depose persons knowledgeable about the tests offered.

* * *

C

The Delarosas present several arguments in support of the crash-test order. First, they argue that it is unfair to allow General Motors to conduct multiple crash tests, varying the parameters until it achieves a result favorable to its theory of the case, and then shield the earlier unfavorable tests. Rule 166b, however, does not limit the number of tests that may be run by a consulting expert. Nor should any such limit be imposed. The consulting-expert privilege is intended to allow a party to develop its factual theories fully. A party may be required to run numerous tests under different parameters where the conditions surrounding the accident, such as speed of the vehicles, angle of impact, and position of the occupants, are not precisely known. Any tests that a party does offer at trial will be admissible only if the trial court determines that there is a substantial similarity between the test conditions and the accident conditions. *See* TEX. R. CIV. EVID. 901; Thus, a party may not "rig" a test by unilaterally selecting parameters which are dissimilar from those surrounding the underlying accident.

The Delarosas next argue that because they do not have the resources to perform their own crash tests, they should have access to General Motors' tests. However, because the consulting expert privilege protects the very core of a party's thought processes and strategy regarding the litigation, there is no substantial hardship exception, such as that which exists for witness statements and party communications. *See* TEX. R. CIV. P. 166b(3). Again, effective cross-examination can expose any weaknesses in a test offered at trial, or even form a basis for excluding the test altogether.

Finally, the Delarosas rely on Rule 167(1)(b) to support their claim to attend General Motors' testing. This rule permits entry upon land in the possession or control of the opposing party "for the purpose of inspection and measuring, surveying, photographing, testing, or sampling the property or any designated object or operation thereon within the scope of Rule 166b." TEX. R. CIV. P. 167(1)(b). The key phrase is "within the scope of Rule 166b." The rule allowing entry upon land does not render discoverable items which are privileged under Rule 166b. For example, Rule 167(1)(b) obviously does not authorize a party to enter into opposing counsel's office to inspect privileged work product documents. Similarly, it does not authorize the Delarosas to enter into testing facilities under General Motors' control to view privileged tests.

For the foregoing reasons, we conclude that the trial court's crash-test order constitutes an abuse of discretion by infringing on General Motors' consulting-expert privilege.

D

We next consider whether General Motors has an adequate remedy by appeal from the crash-test order. As noted, the court of appeals reasoned that if the trial court refused to admit a crash test because of General Motors' noncompliance with its order, then General Motors could obtain review of that evidentiary ruling by ordinary appeal. As the dissenting justice below explained, however, this approach is not acceptable.

The trial court's order specifically provides that plaintiffs are to be notified of and allowed to attend any crash test which General Motors may later offer into evidence. To obtain review under the court of appeals' analysis, General Motors would have to bar the Delarosas from its testing, apparently under the pretext that all such testing was purely for consulting purposes, and then proceed to offer one or more of the tests at trial. Such conduct would flaunt the trial court's order, possibly subjecting General Motors to contempt. Such dangerous and disruptive conduct should not be a prerequisite to meaningful review of the trial court's order. General Motors lacks an adequate remedy by appeal.

* * *

For the foregoing reasons, we conditionally grant writ of mandamus compelling the trial court to vacate its January 22, 1996, crash-test order. We further direct the trial court to abort or mistry the nonjury trial commenced in January 1996, and to place the case on its jury docket in accordance with General Motors' written request and payment of jury fee, which are now timely. We are confident that Judge Gayle will act in accordance with this opinion, and the writ of mandamus will issue only if he fails to do so.

AXELSON, INC.
v.
McILHANY

798 S.W.2d 550
(Tex. 1990)

GONZALEZ, JUSTICE.

In this mandamus proceeding, we are asked to direct Judge McIlhany to vacate orders denying pretrial discovery. The court of appeals conditionally granted the petition for writ of mandamus on certain points but denied the petition on other points. Among other things, we are requested to grant relief regarding discovery of . . . "dual capacity" witnesses. We conditionally grant the writ.

The underlying suit from which this action arises involves what is believed to be the largest gas well blowout in United States history. Key Well 1-11, located in Wheeler County, blew out in October 1981 and was not brought under control for over a year. Apache Corporation operates the well and, together with El Paso Exploration Company (a/k/a Meridian Oil Production, Inc.), owns the working interest. Numerous lawsuits involving over 100 parties have been filed against Apache and El Paso, alleging that their wrongful acts caused the blowout. All suits against Apache and El Paso have been consolidated.

Plaintiffs include Arkla Exploration, Stephens Production Company and Hobart Key, all of whom own mineral interests in the same field. Tom L. Scott, Inc. and other mineral interest holders ("Scott group") intervened as plaintiffs, alleging a cause of action against Apache and El Paso only. Apache and El Paso responded by adding numerous third-party defendants. Sooner Pipe & Supply Corporation, Hydril Corporation and Babcock & Wilcox Company ("Sooner") were added because they supplied well equipment that allegedly caused the blowout. Axelson, Inc. and its parent corporation, U.S. Industries, Inc. (USI), were added because Axelson manufactured a relief valve that allegedly should have prevented the blowout. Axelson and USI are the relators herein and ask that we set aside the trial court's order denying:

> . . .
>
> (2) depositions from dual capacity witnesses (those witnesses who were active participants in the Key Well 1-11 operations or support and were later designated consulting-only experts);
>
> . . . and
>
> (4) depositions of persons who performed gas analyses at Apache's request.

We will now separately address each of the discovery requests made by Axelson and USI.

* * *

"DUAL CAPACITY" WITNESSES

Several potential witnesses in this case maintain a dual capacity—possessing firsthand knowledge of relevant facts and serving as consulting-only experts for Apache and El Paso. One of these persons, Paul Douglas Storts, is the petroleum engineer who has been in charge of the well from its inception. He also spearheaded the effort to bring the well under control after the blowout. The others include Richard Biel, Joe Fowler and Tom Hill, who were hired by Apache and El Paso to examine the wellhead equipment and have specific knowledge concerning the chain of custody of the wellhead equipment.

Axelson and USI seek to discover all facts known by Storts and his mental impressions and opinions gained while working on the well and consulting. They seek to discover only chain of custody facts from Biel, Fowler and Hill.

The trial court entered several orders from December 1984 through July 1987 limiting discovery. With regard to Storts, the trial court initially quashed his deposition, but later determined that information gained by him while working on the well was discoverable, but that information he gained while doing a combination of working on the well and consulting was not discoverable. With regard to Biel, Fowler, and Hill, the trial court allowed discovery of facts relating only to the Axelson valve. The court of appeals held that the trial court had not abused its discretion and disallowed all other discovery from these experts. We disagree.

The factual knowledge and opinions acquired by an individual who is an expert and an active participant in the events material to the lawsuit are discoverable. This information is not shielded from discovery by merely changing the designation of a person with knowledge of relevant facts to a "consulting-only expert."

The scope of discovery regarding experts who serve in the dual capacity of fact witness and consulting-only expert has not been addressed thoroughly by Texas courts. The literal text of the exemption, however, resolves the issue presented in this mandamus. The consulting expert exemption protects the identity, mental impressions and opinions of consulting-only experts; but not the facts. The rule we announce today, however, "should not extend to consulting [only] experts . . . whose only source of factual information was the consultation." *Id.* In other words, persons who gain factual information by virtue of their involvement relating to the incident or transaction giving rise to the litigation do not qualify as consulting-only experts because the consultation is not their only source of information. We now separately address Axelson's discovery requests regarding Storts, an employee designated as a consulting-only expert, and Biel, Fowler and Hill, experts designated as consulting-only who have factual knowledge of the well equipment.

Storts

An employee may be specially employed as a consulting-only expert. Nevertheless, all employees do not necessarily qualify as "consulting-only" experts. The rules provide requirements that a consulting-only expert must meet. *See* TEX. R. CIV. P. 166b(3)(b).

* * *

Under this rule, a consulting-only expert must be informally consulted or retained or specially employed in anticipation of litigation. An employee who was employed in an area that becomes the subject of litigation can never qualify as a consulting-only expert because the employment was not in anticipation of litigation. On the other hand, an employee who was not employed in an area that becomes the subject of litigation and is reassigned specifically to assist the employer in anticipation of litigation arising out of the incident or in preparation for trial may qualify as a "consulting-only" expert. In any event, a party may discover facts known by an employee acting as a "consulting-only" expert.

In this case, evidence presented to the trial court suggested that Storts was doing a combination of both working on the well and consulting. Storts was hired to work as a petroleum engineer and he worked on Key Well 1-11 before, during and after the blowout. After litigation began Apache asserted that Storts was a consulting-only expert and resisted all discovery of Storts' mental impressions, opinions and facts. On the record before him, the trial judge abused his discretion in denying discovery of Storts' mental impressions, opinions and facts because Storts did not qualify as a consulting-only expert.

Policies previously enunciated by this court support the decision we reach today. This rule aims to effectuate the ultimate purpose of discovery, which is to seek truth, so that disputes may be decided by those facts that are revealed, rather than concealed. *Jampole,* 673 S.W.2d at 573. Additionally, although Apache and El Paso are defendants in this case, they are pursuing a cross claim and "cannot use one hand to seek affirmative relief in court and with the other lower an iron curtain of silence around the facts of the case." *Ginsberg v. Fifth Court of Appeals,* 686 S.W.2d 105, 108 (Tex. 1985, orig. proceeding).

Biel, Fowler & Hill

Axelson sought only factual discovery from Biel, Fowler and Hill regarding the condition of wellhead equipment in addition to the condition of Axelson's relief valve. The trial judge limited the scope of discovery from those consulting-only experts to the Axelson valve. The trial judge abused his discretion in refusing discovery of these facts because the exemption for consulting-only experts does not extend to facts known to them.

DEPOSITION OF JACK CHISUM

The final request made by Axelson and USI is that they be allowed to depose another expert, Jack Chisum. He performed gas analyses on the well immediately after the blowout to determine the elemental content of the gas. Certain chemicals, such as hydrogen sulfide, could have caused the blowout, according to Axelson and USI. Axelson and USI took Chisum's deposition. He testified regarding tests done for Apache prior to the blowout, but he refused to testify regarding tests performed subsequent to the blowout because he was hired at the direction of Apache's attorney. Evidence suggests Chisum's tests were done at the direction of Robert Grace, who has been designated as a testifying expert by Apache and El Paso. However, the trial court denied all discovery from Chisum relating to tests conducted after the blowout. Axelson and USI sought mandamus from the court of appeals and requested production of the tests. Apache and El Paso resisted discovery, claiming the party communication exemption, the attorney work product exemption, and the consulting-only expert exemption. The court of appeals found that they were discoverable. Specifically, the court of appeals determined that because the tests were done by or at the direction of Grace, the testifying expert, they were discoverable. The court of appeals did not rule on whether Chisum could be deposed regarding the tests. After the court of appeals rendered its decision and after the tests had been disclosed, Axelson and USI noticed and subpoenaed Chisum for deposition. Apache and El Paso filed a motion to quash contending that Chisum is a consulting-only expert. The deposition never took place and was presented to this court by means of a supplemental mandamus point to this mandamus proceeding.

Since the court of appeals' decision was handed down, the trial court has not acted on whether Chisum may be deposed. He may be waiting for a decision from us on this mandamus proceeding. The parties have taken no other action in the trial court or the court of appeals and, instead, have brought this problem to our attention in a supplemental mandamus point. In order for mandamus to lie regarding this point, the respondent, Judge McIlhany, must have refused to act; that is, he must have explicitly denied motions intended to compel the deposition of Chisum. Axelson and USI cannot point to an order of the trial court refusing their most recent request to depose Chisum. *See* TEX. R. APP. P. 121. Without such a refusal by the trial judge, mandamus on this point is improper.[4] However, the principles we announce today should guide the trial court in deciding this issue.

* * *

CONCLUSION

We hold that the trial judge abused his discretion by refusing discovery of the kickback investigation without conducting an in camera inspection; denying the request to depose the six experts redesignated as consulting-only experts; denying discovery of a witness who does not qualify as a consulting-only expert; and denying discovery of facts known by consulting experts. We are confident Judge McIlhany will vacate his orders denying this discovery and will enter orders consistent with this opinion. Should he fail to do so, the clerk of the supreme court is directed to issue the writ of mandamus.

Notes & Questions

Consulting experts with knowledge of facts. Axelson makes clear that the consulting expert exemption cannot be used to shield the identity of fact witnesses from discovery. Rule 192.3(c) codifies this prohibition, requiring parties to identify as "persons with knowledge of relevant facts" experts with "first hand" knowledge of facts or with knowledge of facts obtained other than "in anticipation of litigation." This rule may require identification of a significant number of consulting experts because they acquire first-hand knowledge of facts in anticipation of litigation. For example, an expert who examines or tests physical evidence, or visits the scene and measures

---

[4] Discovery conducted while this case has been pending before the appellate courts, coupled with rule changes, might subject other experts' mental impressions and opinions to discovery. The rules have been amended, effective September 1, 1990, to allow discovery of a consulting-only expert's work product, mental impressions and opinions, if his opinions or impressions have been reviewed by a testifying expert. Because this evidence and these rule changes were not before the trial court, they do not form a basis for us to find that the trial court abused its discretion in this mandamus proceeding.

skid marks will have first-hand knowledge of relevant facts. The experts must be identified and their factual knowledge is discoverable.

B. Testifying Experts

Read Rule 192.3(e).

In re CHRISTUS SPOHN HOSPITAL KLEBERG
222 S.W.3d 434
(Tex. 2007)

JUSTICE O'NEILL delivered the opinion of the Court.

In this medical malpractice mandamus proceeding, the defendant hospital seeks to recover privileged documents that were mistakenly provided to its designated testifying expert witness. We must decide whether Texas Rule of Civil Procedure 193.3(d), known as the "snap-back" provision, preserves the privilege over Rule 192.3(e)(6)'s mandate that all documents provided to a testifying expert are discoverable. We hold that the inadvertent nature of the production in this case preserved the privilege under Rule 193.3(d) and entitled the hospital to recover the documents upon realizing its mistake, provided the hospital's designated expert does not testify at trial. The hospital has not attempted to name another testifying expert, instead indicating an intent to rely upon the expert to whom the documents were disclosed. So long as the hospital stands upon its testifying expert designation, Rule 192's plain language and purpose and the policy considerations that surrounded its amendment compel the conclusion that the documents may not be snapped back. Accordingly, we deny the hospital's petition for writ of mandamus without prejudice to any right the hospital might have to designate another testifying expert and recover the privileged documents.

I. Background

When Mona Palmer notified Christus Spohn Hospital Kleberg of her intent to file a health care liability claim arising out of her daughter Brandi Lee Palmer's death, the Hospital's internal investigator, Sandra Northcutt, conducted an investigation. That investigation generated a number of documents, labeled "CONFIDENTIAL COMMUNICATION PREPARED IN ANTICIPATION OF LITIGATION," which form the basis of this mandamus action. The Northcutt documents include Northcutt's memoranda summarizing her interviews with Hospital employees and her correspondence to and from Hospital counsel. A paralegal newly employed by the Hospital's counsel sent the Northcutt documents to the Hospital's only expert witness on standard-of-care issues, Nurse Kendra Menzies. According to the Hospital's counsel, the paralegal had recently moved to Texas from California, where she understood that all materials forwarded to an expert witness remained confidential. She assumed the same rule applied in Texas.

Menzies' expert report on Brandi Lee Palmer listed the documents she reviewed in forming her opinion; the Northcutt documents do not appear on that list. Plaintiff's counsel sought to depose Menzies, and issued a subpoena duces tecum requesting all documents furnished to and reviewed by Menzies in connection with her consultation in the lawsuit. Among the materials

Menzies brought to the deposition were the Northcutt documents. This was the first time that the Hospital's and Palmer's counsel learned the privileged documents had been forwarded to Menzies. When questioned about the documents that had been transmitted to her, Menzies testified, "I didn't read every bit. But, yes, I glanced through everything in the box."

The Hospital filed an "Objection, Assertion of Privilege, and Motion to Return Privileged Documents" pursuant to Rule 193.3(d) of the Texas Rules of Civil Procedure, known as the "snapback" provision, seeking to recover the documents mistakenly produced to Menzies. At the hearing on this issue, Menzies testified by affidavit that she did not read the documents but rather "glanced" at them "merely to identify what they were," and upon determining that they were not relevant to her needs, "tossed them back in the box." The trial court overruled the Hospital's claim of privilege, stating it was "unclear that [Menzies] did not see certain specified documents." The court of appeals denied the Hospital's request for mandamus relief. We granted the Hospital's request for mandamus review to consider the application of Rule 193.3(d)'s snap-back provision to the Northcutt documents. Mandamus is appropriate if we conclude that the documents are in fact privileged and have been improperly ordered disclosed by the trial court.

II. Discussion

A. The Parties' Arguments

The Hospital claims the Northcutt documents were created or generated in connection with the Hospital's internal investigation conducted in anticipation of litigation; therefore, the work-product privilege shields them from discovery. *See* TEX.R. CIV. P. 192.5(a), (b).[1] According to the Hospital, the privilege was not lost when the documents were transmitted to Menzies because waiver can only occur when privileged documents are voluntarily and knowingly disclosed, not when disclosure is inadvertent. The Hospital claims this principle is embodied in Rule 193.3(d)'s snapback provision, which mandates the return of privileged documents that have been inadvertently produced. Because it properly invoked Rule 193.3(d)'s snap-back provision, the Hospital argues, the trial court erred in determining that the privilege was waived. The Hospital further contends that Rule 192.3(e)(6), which mandates disclosure of all documents provided to a testifying expert, is not implicated because the Northcutt documents were not "prepared by or for the expert," and even if they were, Menzies did not read them. TEX.R. CIV. P. 192.3(c). Under these circumstances, the Hospital claims, the snap-back rule that protects the work-product privilege against inadvertent disclosure prevails.

For purposes of this appeal, Palmer does not dispute the privileged nature of the documents, nor does she challenge the Hospital's assertion that it complied with the snap-back procedures that Rule 193.3(d) requires for the return of inadvertently produced documents. Rather, Palmer contends Rule 193.3(d)'s snap-back provision does not apply to information that Rule 192.3 makes discoverable once it is provided to a testifying expert. Palmer further challenges the Hospital's statement that Menzies did not "read" the inadvertently transmitted documents, arguing a fact issue exists regarding the extent of her review. In any event, Palmer contends, whether or not Menzies actually relied upon the documents in forming her opinion is not dispositive, because implicit in Rule 192.3's disclosure requirement is the notion that documents an expert chooses to regard and those she chooses to disregard in forming an opinion are both relevant and necessary for effective cross-examination.

---

1 Because the Hospital does not assert attorney-client privilege with regard to the documents, we apply our analysis only to the work-product privilege.

We begin by examining the discovery rules in dispute, applying the same rules of construction that govern the interpretation of statutes. When a rule of procedure is clear and unambiguous, we construe the rule's language according to its plain or literal meaning.

B. Discovery from Testifying Experts

Texas Rule of Civil Procedure 192.3(e), which defines the scope of permissible discovery from experts, provides in pertinent part as follows:

> A party may discover the following information regarding a testifying expert . . . :
>
> * * *
>
> (3) the facts known by the expert that relate to or form the basis of the expert's mental impressions and opinions formed or made in connection with the case in which the discovery is sought, regardless of when and how the factual information was acquired;
>
> (4) the expert's mental impressions and opinions formed or made in connection with the case in which discovery is sought, and any methods used to derive them;
>
> (5) any bias of the witness;
>
> (6) *all documents*, tangible things, reports, models, or data compilations *that have been provided to, reviewed by, or prepared by or for the expert in anticipation of a testifying expert's testimony;* . . . .

TEX.R. CIV. P. 192.3(e) (emphasis added). We must first decide whether this rule applies to the Northcutt documents; if it does not, the documents retain their privileged nature and may be recovered pursuant to Rule 193.3(d)'s snap-back feature.

Rule 192.3(e)(6) was promulgated in 1999 to replace former Rule 166b, which permitted discovery of only those "documents . . . prepared by an expert or for an expert in anticipation of the expert's trial and deposition testimony." TEX.R. CIV. P. 166b(2)(e)(2) (repealed). Under this former rule, privileged work product lost its protected status if the material provided to the expert was, in fact, relied upon by the expert as the basis for his or her testimony. Thus, under the pre-amendment rule, if an expert did not rely on a privileged document, it was not discoverable.

To avoid the discovery disputes that frequently arose over what material an expert may or may not have relied upon, the rule was amended in 1999 to include more expansive language. In addition to documents "prepared by or for the expert," the rule now mandates discovery of documents "that have been provided to, [or] reviewed by" a testifying expert. TEX.R. CIV. P. 192.3(e)(6). The Hospital's argument that the Northcutt documents were prepared by or for the Hospital rather than by or for the expert, and that Menzies did not read them in any event, erroneously ignores the rule's disjunctive language. Whether or not the documents were actually "read" by or prepared for Menzies, they were clearly "provided to" the Hospital's testifying expert and thus fall within Rule 192.3(e)(6)'s plain language.

It is true, as the Hospital claims and Palmer does not dispute, that the Northcutt documents constitute work product under Rule 192.5, and that work product is carefully protected from discovery under our rules. TEX.R. CIV. P. 192.5(a)(1), (2). However, Rule 192.5(c)(1) specifically states that work product loses its protected status when it is provided to a testifying expert:

> (c) Even if made or prepared in anticipation of litigation or for trial, the following is not work product protected from discovery:
>
> (1) information discoverable under Rule 192.3 concerning experts . . . .

TEX.R. CIV. P. 192.5(c)(1). Because the Northcutt documents were provided to the Hospital's testifying expert, the work-product privilege does not protect them unless the snap-back provision requires their return.

C. The Snap-Back Provision

The snap-back provision was designed to protect the inadvertent disclosure of privileged material in order to reduce the cost and risk involved in document production. TEX.R. CIV. P. 193 cmt. 4. The snap-back provision states that:

> A party who produces material or information without intending to waive a claim of privilege does not waive that claim under these rules or the Rules of Evidence if-within ten days or a shorter time ordered by the court, after the producing party actually discovers that such production was made-the producing party amends the response, identifying the material or information produced and stating the privilege asserted.

TEX.R. CIV. P. 193.3(d). The rule is focused on the intent to waive the privilege, not the intent to produce the material or information. *Id.* at cmt. 4.

The snap-back provision has typically been applied when a party inadvertently produces privileged documents to an opposing party. In this case, however, the privileged material was produced by a party to its own testifying expert, invoking Rule 192.3(e)(6)'s overlapping directive that all materials provided to a testifying expert must be produced.

The tension between the snap-back provision that protects privileged documents and the expert-disclosure requirement presents an issue of first impression for our Court. In resolving this tension, we consider the respective interests the rules were designed to protect.

D. Competing Interests

As we have said, the snap-back provision was designed to ensure that important privileges are not waived by mere inadvertence or mistake. Under the rule, a party who is less than diligent in screening documents before their production does not waive any privilege that might attach to them, presuming the party complies with Rule 193.3(d)'s procedures. TEX.R. CIV. P. 193.3(d) cmt. 4. By permitting the recovery of documents inadvertently produced to the opposing side, the rule preserves the important interests that the work-product doctrine was designed to protect, while at the same time visiting no harm upon the recipient for having to return documents it was not entitled to in the first place. Under Rule 193.3(d), the production of documents without the intent to waive a claim of privilege does not waive the claim.

The concepts of waiver and the intent required to effect it, however, do not appear in our testifying-expert disclosure rule. *See* TEX.R. CIV. P. 192.5(c)(1). Rule 192.5, which governs work product, speaks not in terms of waiver but rather states that documents and tangible things provided to a testifying expert under Rule 192.3, "even if made or prepared in anticipation of litigation or for trial . . . *is not work product* protected from discovery." *Id.* (emphasis added). Thus, it appears from the rule's plain language that documents and tangible things provided to a testifying expert lose their work-product designation irrespective of the intent that accompanied their production.[2] This makes sense in light of the important interests the expert-production requirement was designed to serve.

---

[2] We note that only documents are at issue in this case. No discovery request regarding whether the Hospital's counsel provided information to Menzies orally is before us, and we voice no opinion on whether such discovery would be permitted.

The expert witness occupies a unique place in our adversarial system of justice. Considered to have "knowledge, skill, experience, training, or education," TEX.R. EVID. 702, that will "assist the trier of fact to understand the evidence or to determine a fact in issue," the expert is generally held out to be, and is seen by the jury as, an objective authority figure more knowledgeable and credible than the typical lay witness. For this reason, juries are prone to rely on experts to tell them how to decide complex issues without independently analyzing underlying factors. As the Supreme Court has noted, " '[e]xpert evidence can be both powerful and quite misleading because of the difficulty in evaluating it.' " *Daubert v. Merrell Dow Pharms., Inc.*, 509 U.S. 579, 595, 113 S.Ct. 2786, 125 L.Ed.2d 469 (1993).

Coupled with the expert's vast potential for influence is the fact that experts are generally unfettered by firsthand-knowledge requirements that constrain the ordinary witness. While lay witnesses may only testify regarding matters of which they have personal knowledge, TEX.R. EVID. 602, expert witnesses may testify about facts or data not personally perceived but "reviewed by, or made known" to them. TEX.R. EVID. 703. If the facts or data are of a type upon which experts in the field reasonably rely in forming opinions on the subject, the facts or data need not even be admissible in evidence. Thus, in many instances, experts may rely on inadmissible hearsay, privileged communications, and other information that the ordinary witness may not. *See id.* Moreover, an expert may state an opinion on mixed questions of law and fact, such as whether certain conduct was negligent or proximately caused injury, that would be off limits to the ordinary witness. TEX.R. EVID. 704.

Armed with these advantages, the expert witness paints a powerful image on the litigation canvas. And it is typically the hiring attorney who selects the materials that will provide color and hue. Just as a purveyor of fine art must examine the medium used in order to distinguish masterpiece from fake, a jury must understand the pallet from which the expert paints to accurately assess the testimony's worth. Given the importance that expert testimony can assume, the jury should be aware of documents and tangible things provided to the expert that might have influenced the expert's opinion. In terms of determining what effect documents provided to an expert had in shaping the expert's mental impressions and opinions, the attorney's intent in producing the documents is irrelevant.

In light of these important policy concerns that underlie the expert-disclosure rule, we conclude that Rules 192.3(e)(6) and 192.5(c)(1) prevail over Rule 193.3(d)'s snap-back provision so long as the expert intends to testify at trial despite the inadvertent document production. That is, once privileged documents are disclosed to a testifying expert, and the party who designated the expert continues to rely upon that designation for trial, the documents may not be retrieved even if they were inadvertently produced. Of course, inadvertently produced material that could not by its nature have influenced the expert's opinion does not evoke the concerns the expert-disclosure rule was designed to prevent and the policy concerns underlying the rule's disclosure requirement would presumably never arise. In that event, there would be nothing to prevent the snap-back rule's application, although we note that a party seeking snap-back under such circumstances would bear a heavy burden in light of the disclosure rule's underlying purpose.

Our holding comports with federal case law interpreting the federal expert-disclosure rule, which is similar to our own.

* * *

G. The Northcutt Documents

Having determined that our expert-disclosure rules preclude the snap-back of documents inadvertently produced so long as the expert remains designated to testify at trial, we must decide whether the Hospital's claim that Menzies did not read the documents affects our analysis. According to the Hospital, Menzies did not sufficiently review the Northcutt documents such that Rule 192.3(e)(6) requires their disclosure. In order to waive the privilege, the Hospital claims, the documents must have been used in arriving at the expert's mental impressions and opinions.

As we have said, Rule 192.3(e)(6) requires the production of "all documents . . . that have been *provided to*, reviewed by, *or* prepared by or for the expert . . . ." TEX.R. CIV. P. 192.3(e)(6) (emphasis added). By disjunctively requiring the production of documents "provided to" the expert, our rule appears to be broader than the federal rule, which mandates disclosure of information that is "considered by the witness in forming the opinions." FED. R. CIV. P. 26(a)(2)(B). Thus, the Hospital's claim that Menzies did not sufficiently consider the documents to warrant their production is immaterial.

We note that an expert's choice not to utilize certain information does not necessarily mean that the information plays no part in forming the expert's opinion. Materials both accepted and rejected by an expert are indicative of the process by which the expert went about forming his or her opinion and may provide an effective basis for cross-examination. Moreover, the fact that an expert chooses to ignore certain materials that have been provided may indicate a bias on the expert's part, or a proclivity toward a predetermined result.

In this case, when questioned about her review of the Northcutt documents, Menzies testified: "I didn't read every bit. But, yes, I glanced through everything in the box." In her Affidavit attached to the Hospital's First Amended Objection, Menzies attested:

> Any other documents or materials contained in that box I glanced at merely to identify what they were and when I recognized that they were not something that I would need or want to read, I tossed them back into the box. I did not, under any circumstances, read or rely upon any of the following in the formulation of my opinions, nor in the preparation of my report . . . . Frankly, I did not even know that they were in the box until Mr. Todd Taylor, at my deposition, taken on August 16, 2004, took them from my box, showed them to me and asked me if I had read or relied upon any information contained therein. It is my recollection that I testified as testifying here, that I did not.

After considering Menzies' testimony, the trial court stated that its decision to deny the Hospital's objection was based not only on delivery of the documents to Menzies, but also on her testimony "that she reviewed and glanced at some of the documents-at the documents in the box." Based on her testimony, the trial court concluded it was "unclear that she did not see certain specified documents."

We agree that it is unclear from the record to what extent Menzies reviewed the Northcutt documents, although at the very least she "glanced" at them "to identify what they were." The plain language of Rule 192.3(e)(6) makes it immaterial whether she reviewed the documents; they were discoverable because they were provided to her. Under these circumstances, the trial court did not abuse its discretion in denying the request of the Hospital, which continued to rely upon Menzies as its testifying expert, for return of the documents.

We are sympathetic to the Hospital's concerns over losing valuable work-product protections when documents are produced to a testifying expert by mistake. But the producing party in such a situation is not without a remedy. An attorney who discovers that privileged documents have been inadvertently provided to a testifying expert may presumably withdraw the expert's designation and name another. Although such a course may entail additional expense and perhaps delay, these concerns do not outweigh countervailing concerns that require full disclosure from an expert who will testify. If leave of court is necessary for an alternative designation-when, for example, the expert designation deadline has passed-courts should carefully weigh the alternatives available to prevent what may be akin to a death-penalty sanction for the party forced to trial without a necessary expert. The Hospital did not pursue such a course in this case, however, and we voice no opinion on the trial court's discretion in that regard.

Finally, the Hospital contends that, even if discoverable for purposes of deposing Menzies, the Northcutt documents should otherwise retain their privilege and not be used for other purposes or at trial. Since Menzies has already been questioned about the documents, the Hospital argues, their discovery should be confined to that context. Specifically, the Hospital seeks to quash Sandra Northcutt's deposition, which has been postponed pursuant to the parties' agreement pending the outcome of this mandamus proceeding. We decline to opine on the potential admissibility of the Northcutt documents at trial, as that issue is premature. And in light of Rule 192.5(c)'s provision that information discoverable under Rule 192.3 "is not work product protected from discovery," we cannot say that the trial court abused its discretion in denying the Hospital's motion to quash Sandra Northcutt's deposition.

III. Conclusion

For the foregoing reasons, we deny the Hospital's petition for writ of mandamus.

Read Rules 194.2(f), 195.

1. *Designating Testifying Experts*

Rule 195.1 limits discovery concerning testifying experts to requests for disclosure, depositions and reports. Experts are "designated" through responses to requests for disclosure. In fact, the request for disclosure, found in Rule 194.2(f), is the only way to initiate discovery of the identity and opinions of opposing experts, so it should be served in every case. Parties need not respond to the request for disclosure concerning experts within 30 days of service of the request as required for other disclosures. Instead, Rule 195.2 provides a standard designation schedule that should be followed unless another schedule is set by court order. The standard designation schedule requires parties "seeking affirmative relief" (plaintiffs and defendants asserting counterclaims or crossclaims) to designate experts before other parties. These parties must designate experts 90 days before the end of the discovery period. Other experts are designated 60 days before the end of the discovery period.

2. *Retained and Non-Retained Experts*

Rules 194 and 195 distinguish between experts "retained, employed by, or otherwise in control of the party" and those experts who are not. Retained experts are frequently professional witnesses who have been selected to participate in the litigation, have voluntarily agreed to become witnesses in the case, and are being paid for their voluntary participation. They can be expected to cooperate with the party that retained them. Non-retained experts are usually persons whose professions frequently bring them into contact with situations that involve litigation, such as police officers, emergency room physicians, and surgeons. These persons obtain knowledge of relevant facts and become both fact and expert witnesses, not because of any voluntary decision to be involved in a given case, but because of their involvement with the facts of the case. These witnesses may be uncooperative or even hostile to the party who seeks to offer their testimony. Rule 194 requires that parties disclose retained experts' mental impressions and opinions and a brief summary of the basis for them. For non-retained experts (who may be less apt to voluntarily cooperate), however, the party need only disclose documents, such as medical records or police reports, that reflect the expert's opinion. Also, parties must produce the retained expert's file, resume and bibliography, while there is no such requirement for non-retained experts; the provisions of Rule 195 regarding deposition scheduling and supplementation of deposition testimony apply only to retained experts.

3. *Scheduling Depositions*

Rule 195.3 contains specific provisions governing scheduling depositions of retained experts, continuing to use the "plaintiff first" model. While the expert of the party seeking affirmative relief (here called the plaintiff) will be deposed first, that deposition may occur either before or after opposing experts are designated, depending upon whether the plaintiff provides a report with its designation. If there is no report, the plaintiff designates experts 90 days before end of discovery period, and must tender experts for deposition "reasonably promptly" after designation, but no later than 15 days before opposing experts are designated. The defendant designates opposing experts 60 days before the end of the discovery period and tenders the experts "reasonably promptly" after designation and after the plaintiff's experts on the same subject are deposed. If the plaintiff chooses to provide a report when the experts are designated, the designation schedule remains the same (90 and 60 days before the end of the discovery period), but the plaintiff's experts are not deposed until after the defendant designates experts.

4. *Reports*

Although the deposition schedule encourages the plaintiff to supply an expert report, the rules do not require production of a report if the witness has not already prepared one. Moreover, if the plaintiff furnishes a report, the defendant is not required to supply one to the plaintiff in response. Rule 195.5 allows the court to order an expert to prepare a report, however.

5. *Depositions*

The only remaining method for discovery of an expert's expected testimony is the deposition. The notice may include a request for production of discoverable documents that were not included in the Rule 194 request for disclosure, such as records evidencing bias.[41] The retained expert must appear after service of a notice upon the party's attorney. Non-retained experts must be served with a subpoena to compel appearance. Expert depositions are included in the total deposition time limits of Rule 190, although in Level 2 an additional 6 hours is allotted when an opposing side designates more than two experts, for each additional expert. Rule 195.7 allocates the cost of an expert's deposition appearance to the party that retained the expert.

---

[1] *But see* In re Ford Motor Co., 427 S.W.3d 396, 398 (Tex. 2014) (holding that deposition notices to experts' employers, in attempt to prove bias, were overbroad and impermissible) (reprinted below).

6. *Discovery of Bias of Testifying Expert*

In re FORD MOTOR COMPANY
427 S.W.3d 396
(Tex. 2014)

Opinion

PER CURIAM.

In this design-defect case, the plaintiff sought to expose potential bias of the defendant's two testifying experts by inquiring at their depositions into the frequency with which they testified in favor of design-defect defendants. To further explore bias, the plaintiff now seeks to depose a corporate representative of each expert's employer. We hold that on the facts of this case, the Rules of Civil Procedure do not permit such discovery and we conditionally grant mandamus relief.

This suit arises from injuries plaintiff Saul Morales sustained after a Ford vehicle ran over him. Morales had been in his own vehicle, fleeing police who suspected he was driving drunk. Eventually, Morales stopped his vehicle and continued his flight on foot. One of the police officers likewise left his 2004 Ford Crown Victoria Police Interceptor, then pursued and apprehended Morales. While the officer attempted to handcuff Morales, the officer's vehicle began rolling backward toward the pair. The vehicle struck the officer, then ran over and came to rest on top of Morales, injuring him.

Morales sued Ford Motor Company, which designed and manufactured the police car, and the car's seller, Ken Stoepel Ford, Inc. (collectively "Ford"). In his action, Morales alleged the vehicle had a design defect that allowed the officer unintentionally to place the gear-shift selector between park and reverse, which then caused the vehicle to go into an idle-powered reverse.

To defend the lawsuit, Ford retained two expert witnesses: Erin Harley, of Exponent, Inc., and Hugh Mauldin, of Carr Engineering, Inc. After deposing both Harley and Mauldin, Morales sought corporate-representative depositions from Exponent and Carr Engineering on seventeen topics, arguing the additional depositions were necessary to prove each testifying expert's bias in favor of Ford and other automobile manufacturers.

The Rules of Civil Procedure define the scope and methods of discovery about expert witnesses. Rule 192.3(e) sets forth the scope of information that parties may discover about a testifying expert, which includes "any bias of the witness." TEX. R. CIV. P. 192.3(e). Rule 195 addresses the methods for obtaining such information, limiting testifying-expert discovery to that acquired through disclosures, expert reports, and oral depositions of expert witnesses. TEX. R. CIV. P. 195.

The official comments to Rule 195 articulate a goal of minimizing "undue expense" in conducting expert discovery. TEX. R. CIV. P. 195 cmt. 3. This goal comports with efforts by this Court and others to curb discovery abuse through the implementation of carefully crafted principles and procedures. *See In re Alford Chevrolet-Geo,* 997 S.W.2d 173, 180-81 (Tex. 1999) (orig. proceeding). We have expressed concerns about allowing overly expansive discovery about testifying experts that can "permit witnesses to be subjected to harassment and might well discourage reputable experts" from participating in the litigation process. *Ex parte Shepperd,* 513 S.W.2d 813, 816 (Tex. 1974) (orig. proceeding).

The particular deposition notices in this case highlight the danger of permitting such expansive discovery. In his deposition notices to Carr Engineering and Exponent, Morales seeks detailed financial and business information for all cases the companies have handled for Ford or any other automobile manufacturer from 2000 to 2011. Such a fishing expedition, seeking sensitive information covering twelve years, is just the type of overbroad discovery the rules are intended to prevent. *See Alford Chevrolet-Geo,* 997 S.W.2d at 180 (rules of procedure are designed to curb abusive discovery tactics, which some litigants employ simply to increase litigation costs for their adversaries); *see also Russell v. Young,* 452 S.W.2d 434, 437 (Tex. 1970) (orig. proceeding) (denying discovery of financial records from a potential medical expert witness because "[t]here is . . . a limit beyond which pre-trial discovery should not be allowed").

By holding that the requested discovery is impermissible in this case, we do not unduly inhibit discovery of an expert's potential bias. Courts have recognized that discovery into the extent of an expert's bias is not without limits. *See, e.g., In re Weir,* 166 S.W.3d 861, 865 (Tex. App.—Beaumont 2005, orig. proceeding) (per curiam) (holding expert witness did not have to testify about personal financial information because there was other evidence of bias); *Olinger v. Curry,* 926 S.W.2d 832, 834-35 (Tex. App.—Fort Worth 1996, orig. proceeding) (holding the trial court abused its discretion in ordering the production of the expert's tax returns because the expert witness had already admitted 90% of his services were provided to defendants in litigation).

Indeed, the most probative information regarding the bias of a testifying expert comes from the expert herself. In this case, for example, Harley testified that only 5% of the cases she handles are for plaintiffs and that she has never testified against an automobile manufacturer. Similarly, Mauldin testified that historically about 50% of Carr Engineering's work is done for Ford. Moreover, Mauldin admitted that in park-to-reverse cases, he has never testified that a vehicle has a design defect. Mauldin's deposition in this case also revealed that he worked at Ford for several years before becoming a consultant at Carr Engineering.

Morales argues that we have recognized at least one instance in which deposing the expert's employer was justified. In *Walker v. Packer,* we held that discovery beyond the individual expert's deposition might be permissible when extrinsic evidence, discovered after the expert's deposition, puts his credibility in doubt. 827 S.W.2d 833, 838-39 (Tex. 1992) (orig. proceeding). In that case, the expert witness, a physician, testified in his deposition that his employer had no policy restricting its doctors from testifying for plaintiffs in medical-malpractice cases. *Id.* at 837. When the deposing party discovered contrary evidence in an unrelated case, we held that deposing an employer's representative was appropriate to "narrowly seek information regarding the potential bias." *Id.* at 838.

We adopted Rule 195—establishing disclosures, expert reports, and oral depositions as the permissible methods for expert discovery—after we decided *Walker. See* TEX. R. CIV. P. 195. Assuming that this aspect of our holding in *Walker* survived the adoption of Rule 195, we disagree that *Walker* compels the result Morales seeks. Unlike *Walker*, neither expert's credibility has been impugned in this case. And Morales has not demonstrated any other circumstance to warrant deposing the witnesses' employers' corporate representatives.

Therefore, pursuant to Rule 52.8(c) of the Rules of Appellate Procedure, we conditionally grant Ford's petition for writ of mandamus without hearing oral argument and direct the trial court to vacate its discovery order. As we are confident that the trial court will comply, the writ will issue only if the trial court fails to do so.

Notes & Questions

1. *Discovery of bias.* What if the expert had refused to answer questions about how much time was spent testifying for defendants? What if the expert answered the questions, but the plaintiff felt that the expert had lied about it?[1]

2. *De-designation.* In the same well blow-out case that spawned *Axelson v. McIlhany*, the Supreme Court addressed the redesignation of testifying experts to consulting-only status to prevent discovery. In *Tom L. Scott, Inc. v. McIlhany*,[2] some defendants settled with some of the plaintiffs the day before the plaintiffs' testifying experts were to be deposed. As part of the settlement, the defendants gained control over these experts. The remaining plaintiffs sought to depose the experts, but the defendants had redesignated them as consulting-only experts and refused to present them for deposition. The Supreme Court refused to accept the redesignation, saying:

> The primary policy behind discovery is to seek truth so that disputes may be decided by facts that are revealed rather than concealed. Privileges from discovery run contrary to this policy but serve other legitimate interests. The policy behind the consulting expert privilege is to encourage parties to seek expert advice in evaluating their case and to prevent a party from receiving undue benefit from an adversary's efforts and diligence. But the protection afforded by the consulting expert privilege is intended to be only "a shield to prevent a litigant from taking undue advantage of his adversary's industry and effort, not a sword to be used to thwart justice or to defeat the salutary objects" of discovery.
>
> The redesignation of the experts in this case was an offensive and unacceptable use of discovery mechanisms intended to defeat the salutary objectives of discovery. Attorneys for Apache and El Paso even admitted to the trial judge that the settlements were "expressly contingent" on these experts not being required to give their testimony, and that there might not be a settlement agreement if the depositions were ordered. One of the settling parties expressly told the trial court that he understood the settlement offer would expire upon the depositions being taken. The legitimate purposes and policies behind the consulting expert privilege do not countenance this conduct. We hold that, as a matter of law, the redesignation of experts under the facts of this case violates the policy underlying the rules of discovery and is therefore ineffective.

Interestingly, the Court did not find that some element of the consulting expert privilege was not satisfied, but the decision was based upon a larger policy issue of "open discovery." Since *Scott* was decided, two courts of appeals have used its reasoning to compel discovery of an expert witness claimed to be consulting-only. In *Harnischfeger Corp. v. Stone*,[3] the plaintiff was

---

1 *See, e.g.* In re Plains Marketing, L.P., 195 S.W.3d 780 (Tex. App.—Beaumont 2006, no pet.) (refusing discovery of past expert reports of medical expert); In re Makris, 217 S.W.3d 521 (Tex. App.—Waco 2006, no pet.)(holding that simple denial of bias is not evidence of bias and refusing to order personal finance discovery from expert); In re Weir, 166 S.W.3d 861 (Tex. App.—Beaumont 2005, no pet.)(refusing to order additional discovery from expert who admitted testifying exclusively for defendants).

2 798 S.W.2d 556 (Tex. 1990).

3 814 S.W.2d 263, 265 (Tex. App.—Houston [14th Dist.] 1991, orig. proceeding).

prevented from hiring and redesignating as a consultant the settling defendant's expert who had been designated previously as a testifying expert. The situation was somewhat different from *Scott,* because the redesignation of the expert was not made part of the settlement agreement between the parties. In *Hardesty v. Douglas*,[4] the court allowed discovery of an expert whose affidavit had been presented in opposition to the defendant's motion for summary judgment, but was later designated as a consulting-only expert. The San Antonio Court of Appeals has twice found that de-designation does not compel discovery, noting that a "testifying expert [may] be de-designated so long as it is not part of 'a bargain between adversaries to suppress testimony' or for some other purpose."[5]

C. Duty to Supplement Expert Discovery

Read Rules 195.6, 193.5, 193.6.

Rule 195.6 prescribes explicit duties to amend and supplement expert discovery. The duty to supplement written discovery (which for experts consists only of Rule 194 requests for disclosure) is the same as the general duty imposed by Rule 193.5. A party also has a limited duty to supplement a retained expert's deposition testimony and written report—the expert's mental impressions, opinions, and the basis for them. Although the rules have changed since this case was decided, its policy analysis is instructive. Consider how the supplementation obligation of Rule 195.6 differs from that under the former rules as discussed in *Exxon.*

EXXON CORP.
v.
WEST TEXAS GATHERING
868 S.W.2d 299
(Tex. 1993)

DOGGETT, JUSTICE.

This case presents questions regarding the proper interpretation of a take-or-pay gas contract and the scope of a party's obligation to supplement discovery responses concerning expert testimony. Exxon Corp. obtained a trial court judgment for contractual damages based upon a jury verdict. The court of appeals reversed and rendered a take nothing judgment, holding both that the contract was unambiguous and that certain expert testimony regarding damages was improperly admitted. We determine that the contractual clause at issue here was ambiguous and therefore properly submitted to a jury, and that new damages calculations belatedly revealed by an expert are admissible at trial under the particular circumstances of this case. Accordingly we

---

[4] 894 S.W.2d 548 (Tex. App.—Waco 1995, orig. proceeding).

[5] Castellanos v. Littlejohn, 945 S.W.2d 236 (Tex. App.—San Antonio 1997, orig. proceeding) (*Scott* does not compel discovery of consulting only expert designated as testifying expert due to clerical error); In re Doctor's Hospital of Laredo, 2 S.W.3d 504 (Tex. App.—San Antonio 2000) (re-designation alone does not imply an improper prohibited purpose). *See also* In re State Farm Mut. Auto Ins. Co., 100 S.W.3d 338 (Tex. App.—San Antonio 2002, pet. denied) (finding no error in refusal to allow de-designation).

reverse the judgment of the court of appeals and remand to that court for consideration of other points.

* * *

III.

We next address whether the trial court was required by Texas Rule of Civil Procedure 215.5 to exclude the testimony of Exxon's damages expert, Donald Rhodes, who had been identified in interrogatory responses in January 1990. At his initial deposition in September, two months before trial, Rhodes calculated damages at approximately $28 million based on Method 1, under which he computed the baseline take-or-pay obligation of 80 percent of deliverability without accounting for either Railroad Commission allowables or WTG's nominations. While acknowledging its applicability under the terms of the contract, he chose not to employ Method 3 on the grounds that WTG's practice of nominating greater amounts than it actually took had distorted allowables and made calculation under this formula difficult. Rhodes repeatedly confirmed, however, that if he were to calculate the hypothetical allowable required to assess take-or-pay liability under Method 3, "the only way it will work" is to assume not only a hypothetical nomination of 80 percent of deliverability, but also a hypothetical take of the same amount. Otherwise, the second paragraph of section four would have no "function" or "meaning." Because such a hypothetical allowable would be "very close" to 80 percent of deliverability, he estimated that Method 3 would produce approximately the same amount of damages as already calculated under Method 1. Although Exxon had not yet decided whether to attempt the Method 3 calculations, Rhodes indicated that those "evaluations need to be done." On September 21, following this deposition and more than 30 days prior to trial, Exxon supplemented its interrogatory responses concerning this matter:

> [i]f Exxon concludes the theoretical allowable calculation described in paragraph 2 of Section 4, Article IV . . . can be calculated, those calculations will be prepared by Mr. Rhodes and may be used in take-or-pay calculations presented at trial.

On October 30, six weeks after his deposition and five days before trial, Rhodes presented his new calculations under Method 3, which totaled $23.6 million; he was immediately redeposed the following day. Although not requesting a continuance to study these calculations, after the deposition Cabot moved to "strike altered and untimely expert opinion testimony," which included any comment by Rhodes "which departs from his July 25, 1990 report, or contradicts his [original] deposition testimony." The trial court overruled the motion.

In this burgeoning technological age, modern trial practice increasingly involves complex factual issues requiring elaborate expert proof. In order to be prepared adequately for trial, both sides must be fully aware of the nature of both their own evidence and that of the opposing parties, and our procedural rules requiring full supplementation of discovery responses are designed to ensure this result. To that end, Texas Rule of Civil Procedure 166b(6)(b) requires parties to reveal the "substance of the testimony concerning which [their] expert witness is expected to testify" no less than 30 days before trial, and Rule 166b(2)(e) permits discovery of the mental impressions and opinions held by, and the facts known to, the expert. This information must be supplemented no less than 30 days before trial if it is no longer true and complete, and the failure to amend renders the substance misleading. TEX. R. CIV. P. 166b(6)(a).

Our rules do not prevent experts from refining calculations and perfecting reports through the time of trial. The testimony of an expert should not be barred because a change in some minor detail of the person's work has not been disclosed a month before trial. The additional supplementation requirement of Rule 166b(6) does require that opposing parties have sufficient information about an expert's opinion to prepare a rebuttal with their own experts and cross-examination, and that they be promptly and fully advised when further developments have rendered past information incorrect or misleading.

Here, Exxon met its obligation to report the "substance" of Rhodes' expected testimony at the time of his first deposition and its supplemental responses to interrogatories. The defendants knew how Exxon interpreted the contract and how Rhodes believed damages should be calculated. They possessed all the information necessary both for preparing to discredit his methodology and reconstructing their own damages study based on his approach to Method 3. Not having the calculations themselves does not appear to have impaired the defendants' ability to prepare for trial.

We do not imply that a party may avoid its duty to supplement by designating "multiple-choice" expert theories and opinions during the initial stages of discovery. While Rhodes had not performed the Method 3 calculations at the time of his first deposition, he maintained throughout that, to the extent calculable, Method 3 provided the only proper means by which to measure WTG's take-or-pay obligation. Exxon never maintained that Methods 1 and 3 were alternative means to calculate the same damages, but only that Method 1 might provide the best evidence of damages, given the difficulty of computing them under Method 3. And, by the end of Rhodes' first deposition, he acknowledged the need to attempt the Method 3 calculations.

Because all opposing parties were aware of both Rhodes' identity and the methodology that constituted the "substance" of his trial testimony, the trial court's decision to allow him to testify is consistent with the purposes underlying our rules of procedure. Rule 215.5 provides:

> [a] party who fails to respond to or supplement his response to a request for discovery shall not be entitled to present evidence which the party was under a duty to provide in a response or supplemental response or to offer the testimony of an expert witness or of any other person having knowledge of discoverable matter, unless the trial court finds that good cause sufficient to require admission exists.

This rule is designed to serve the "salutary purpose" of "requir[ing] complete responses to discovery so as to promote responsible assessment of settlement and prevent trial by ambush." Thus, we reiterate that [o]ur goal in promulgating Rules 166b and 215(5) and our prior opinions interpreting these rules was to encourage full discovery of the issues and facts prior to trial so that parties could make realistic assessments of their respective positions. "A trial should be based upon the merits of the parties' claims and defenses rather than on an advantage obtained by one side through a surprise attack." Recognizing the importance of full discovery of the mental impressions and opinions of experts prior to trial, this court refuses to condone "offensive and unacceptable use of discovery mechanisms [to conceal expert information] intended to defeat the salutary objective of discovery."

A last minute material alteration of expert testimony can certainly create an ambush that is every bit as damaging as that caused by the sudden appearance of an undisclosed witness. But nothing of this sort appears to have happened here. Notice of the change in damages theory was provided more than 30 days prior to trial and the expert was fully redeposed. Rhodes' final arithmetical corrections were delivered in advance of trial together with an errata sheet explaining clearly and specifically all changes that were being made. Moreover, the Method 1 analysis described during his initial four day deposition comprised a substantial component of his new calculations under Method 3. In view of all of these circumstances, excluding Rhodes' testimony would only subvert the search for truth; it would not further the important underlying purpose of Rule 215.5 that every litigant be accorded adequate notice of its opponent's proof.

CHAPTER 11. SUMMARY JUDGMENTS

A. Summary Judgments and Legal Sufficiency

Read Rule 166a

KERLIN
v.
ARIAS
274 S.W.3d 666
(Tex. 2008)

PER CURIAM.

This is another suit claiming title to a substantial part of Padre Island. . . . The heirs seek to set aside an 1847 deed (and thus all sales in the ensuing 161 years) on the basis of fraud. The trial court granted summary judgment against the heirs, but the court of appeals reversed. As the only evidence of fraud in 1847 is an affidavit by one of the current heirs-who could not possibly have personal knowledge of those events-we reverse.

The 72 alleged heirs asserted in their petition that the 1847 deed was fraudulent because it was signed by Jesus Balli's father, even though Jesus was not a minor under either Texas or Mexican law at the time. They sued Gilbert Kerlin, who apparently had no contact with them or their ancestors, but owned substantial acreage in South Padre Island from 1942 until 1961.

Kerlin moved for summary judgment on several grounds, including that the deed was valid. In support, Kerlin tendered the deed-not the original in Spanish signed in Matamoros in 1847, but a certified English translation filed in the Nueces County deed records later that same year. The translated deed affirmatively states that:

- Jesus Balli was a minor at the time the deed was signed;
- his lawful guardian was his father, who had the power to administer and convey his son's property;
- it was in his son's best interest to sell the land because the war between the United States and Mexico made it uncertain whether his title would be recognized; and
- his father accordingly sold the Padre Island property to Nicolas Grisanti on his son's behalf.

The heirs did not contest this document's authenticity. *See* TEX.R. EVID. 901(b)(7)-(8), 902(3)-(4) (authenticating ancient documents, public records, and foreign public documents). Nor did they challenge the accuracy of the translation. The statements in the translated deed are competent to prove the facts stated therein under the rules of evidence. *See* TEX.R. EVID. 803(14), (16).

The heirs' only responsive summary judgment evidence was a 2003 affidavit by Eva Castillo, in which she avers that Jesus Balli was not a minor in 1847 because he was 22 years old and had married. Kerlin objected to the affidavit on several grounds, including lack of personal knowledge and hearsay.

We agree with Kerlin that this affidavit creates no fact issue on fraud. Summary judgment affidavits "shall be made on personal knowledge, shall set forth such facts as would be admissible in evidence, and shall show affirmatively that the affiant is competent to testify to the matters stated therein." TEX.R. CIV. P. 166a(f). This affidavit fails on each count.

First, the only representation Castillo makes about the truth of her affidavit is that "[a]ll statements contained herein are true and correct to the best of my personal knowledge and belief." To have probative value, an affiant "must swear that the facts presented in the affidavit reflect his personal knowledge." An affiant's *belief* about the facts is legally insufficient.

Second, Castillo says she is competent to make the affidavit because she "heard testimony" in the Juan Jose Balli case, "reviewed documents" related to the heirs' claims, and "read historical accounts about Padre Island." Her testimony about these out-of-court sources was hearsay and carries no probative weight over Kerlin's objection. *See* TEX.R. EVID. 802.

Third, nothing in the affidavit affirmatively shows how Castillo could possibly have personal knowledge about events occurring in the 1840s. An affidavit showing no basis for personal knowledge is legally insufficient. Accordingly, Castillo's affidavit does not raise a fact issue about whether Jesus Balli was a minor at the time his father sold his interest in Padre Island.

The court of appeals held otherwise, noting first that Kerlin attached only a copy of a translation of the original deed rather than the original itself. But the heirs did not challenge the authenticity of this copy from the Nueces County deed records, and the best evidence rule does not apply to originals located outside Texas. *See* TEX.R. EVID. 1004(c).

The court of appeals also faulted Kerlin for not responding to the heirs' assertions by providing "evidence of Jesus' age or marital status at the time of the deed signing." But Kerlin presented prima facie evidence that the 1847 deed was valid; he did not have any duty to prove these additional details unless the heirs could raise a fact question regarding them. *See Centeq Realty, Inc. v. Siegler,* 899 S.W.2d 195, 197 (Tex. 1995) ("Once the defendant produces sufficient evidence to establish the right to summary judgment, the plaintiff must present evidence sufficient to raise a fact issue."). This they did not do.

The summary judgment record here raises no fact question that the 1847 deed was fraudulent. Accordingly, we grant Kerlin's petition for review, and without hearing oral argument, we reverse the court of appeals' judgment and render judgment that the heirs take nothing. TEX.R. CIV. P. 59.1.

RANDALL'S FOOD MARKETS, INC.
v.
JOHNSON

891 S.W.2d 640
(Tex. 1995)

SPECTOR, JUSTICE.

* * *

Mary Lynn Johnson, a manager of a Randall's store, purchased several items from the store, but did not pay for a large Christmas wreath that she was holding. Vernon Davis, the check-out clerk, did not charge Johnson for the twenty-five dollar wreath because, after ringing up her other items, he asked her if there was anything else, and she replied that there was nothing else. Davis reported Johnson's failure to pay him for the wreath to management. The store's security guard was then requested to investigate the incident. The guard contacted Lewis Simmons (director of the store), and Simmons reported the incident to Mike Seals (the district manager for that store).

When Johnson returned to work two days later, Simmons escorted her to an office in the back of the store and questioned her about the wreath. Johnson admitted that she left the store without paying for the wreath, explaining that she had a lot on her mind at the time. With Johnson in the room, Simmons then called Seals and reported the results of this interview to him. Because Seals wanted to meet with Johnson later that day, Simmons asked her to stay at the store. Simmons told Johnson that he did not think it would be a good idea for her to be on the store's floor; he suggested that she either remain in the office or work on a volunteer project painting a booth for a parade. Johnson chose to wait for Seals in the office. While she waited, Johnson left the office twice, once to use the restroom and the second time to visit a friend in the floral department and to pay for the wreath.

When Seals arrived at the store, he and Simmons questioned Johnson further. They asked how she could forget to pay for an item when she was checking out with several other items at the same time. This questioning caused Johnson to cry. At the end of this interview, Seals suspended Johnson for thirty days without pay and informed her that at the conclusion of the thirty days she would be transferred to another, nearby store. Johnson never reported to work at the other store. She subsequently sued Randall's, Seals, Simmons, and Davis (collectively, "Randall's"), alleging various claims, including intentional infliction of emotional distress, false imprisonment, and defamation.

* * *

The trial court granted Randall's motion for summary judgment on all of Johnson's claims. The court of appeals affirmed in part and reversed in part, reversing the judgment of the trial court on the claims of intentional infliction of emotional distress, false imprisonment, and defamation. . . .

To prevail on a motion for summary judgment, a movant must establish that there is no genuine issue as to any material fact and that he or she is entitled to judgment as a matter of law. TEX. R. CIV. P. 166a(c). A defendant who conclusively negates at least one of the essential elements of a cause of action is entitled to summary judgment as to that cause of action. Likewise, a defendant who conclusively establishes each element of an affirmative defense is entitled to summary judgment. In reviewing a summary judgment, we must accept as true evidence in favor of the non-movant, indulging every reasonable inference and resolving all doubts in his or her favor.

I.

To recover for intentional infliction of emotional distress, a plaintiff must prove that (1) the defendant acted intentionally or recklessly; (2) the defendant's conduct was extreme and outrageous; (3) the defendant's actions caused the plaintiff emotional distress; and (4) the emotional distress suffered by the plaintiff was severe. *Twyman v. Twyman,* 855 S.W.2d 619, 621-22 (Tex. 1993). In *Twyman,* we adopted the RESTATEMENT'S formulation of the tort of intentional infliction of emotional distress, including the definition of extreme and outrageous conduct as conduct that is "so outrageous in character, and so extreme in degree, as to go beyond all possible bounds of decency, and to be regarded as atrocious, and utterly intolerable in a civilized community. We hold that the summary judgment evidence establishes as a matter of law that Randall's conduct was not "extreme and outrageous," an essential element of the tort of intentional infliction of emotional distress.

The conduct that Johnson alleges was extreme and outrageous is Simmons and Seals' questioning of her regarding the wreath. Johnson maintains that during Simmons' telephone conversation with Seals, which occurred after Simmons' initial questioning of her, his tone and manner became severe and curt. She alleges that Simmons merely answered Seals' questions and did not explain the facts to him. During Simmons and Seals' subsequent meeting with Johnson, the summary judgment evidence establishes that Johnson explained her version of the wreath incident, and then she was asked how she could forget to pay for an item when she was checking out with several other items at the same time.

Accepting all evidence favorable to Johnson as true, we conclude that, as a matter of law, neither Randall's nor its agents engaged in extreme and outrageous conduct. Randall's merely asked a management-level employee to explain a report of wrongdoing. Employers act within their legal rights in investigating reasonably credible allegations of dishonesty of their employees. This conduct is not "beyond all possible bounds of decency," "atrocious," and "utterly intolerable in a civilized community"; rather, it is a managerial function that is necessary to the ordinary operation of a business organization.

* * *

We conclude that, as a matter of law, the conduct of Randall's in this case was not extreme and outrageous and did not constitute a willful detention of Johnson. On the subject of the wreath incident, we conclude that Randall's did not slander Johnson because all of the statements made by Randall's employees were both true and qualifiedly privileged. With regard to the Ketner allegations, we conclude that Randall's did not defame Johnson because all of the statements. made by Randall's employees were qualifiedly privileged. We accordingly reverse the judgment of the court of appeals and render judgment that Johnson take nothing.

PROGRESSIVE COUNTY MUTUAL INSURANCE COMPANY
v.
KELLEY

284 S.W.3d 805
(Tex. 2009)

PER CURIAM.

In this case, we consider whether two documents issued by an insurance company constitute two separate insurance policies or a single policy. We hold that this is a fact question and remand to the trial court.

Regan Kelley was struck by a car while riding her horse. Medical expenses for her injuries are alleged to have exceeded $1 million. After receiving $100,000 in benefits from the motorist's insurer, Kelley made a claim with Progressive County Mutual Insurance Company ("Progressive") for underinsured benefits under a policy issued to her parents, which also covered Kelley. At the time of the accident, Kelley was an adult living with her parents. Progressive paid the policy limit of $500,025. To cover the remaining damages, Kelley then made a claim under an alleged second policy with a limit of $500,025, also issued by Progressive. At the time of the accident, Progressive insured five of the Kelleys' vehicles. Four vehicles were listed on a two-page document, and the fifth was listed on a separate two-page document. However, the documents had separate policy numbers. Nevertheless, Progressive denied there was a second policy and refused to make any additional payments.

Kelley sued Progressive for breach of contract and Insurance Code violations, while Progressive sought a declaratory judgment requiring it to pay the maximum policy limit amount under only one policy. The suits were consolidated, and both parties filed motions for summary judgment, presenting two issues: (1) whether Progressive issued one or two policies, and (2) if two policies, whether Progressive's "Two or More Auto Policies" anti-stacking provision, found within each policy, limited recovery to one policy's maximum limits. The trial court granted Progressive's motion and denied Kelley's motion, without specifying on which ground. The court of appeals reversed and rendered judgment in favor of Kelley, holding that (1) Kelley established as a matter of law that Progressive issued two separate policies, and (2) Progressive's "Two or More Auto Policies" provision violated public policy, as it had the same effect as an "other insurance" provision previously struck down by this Court. Thus, the court of appeals held that Kelley was entitled to collect under the second policy to the extent of her actual damages. Progressive appeals to this Court, arguing that the trial court's judgment should be reinstated.

"When both parties move for summary judgment and the trial court grants one motion and denies the other, the reviewing court should review the summary judgment evidence presented by both sides and determine all questions presented and render the judgment the trial court should have rendered." "When a trial court's order granting summary judgment does not specify the grounds relied upon, the reviewing court must affirm summary judgment if any of the summary judgment grounds are meritorious."

Progressive argues it is entitled to judgment as a matter of law because it met its obligations under the single policy by paying its maximum limits, or alternatively, that the "Two or More Auto Policies" provision limits Kelley's recovery to a single policy. It argues that the documents clearly and unambiguously demonstrate Progressive only issued one policy to the Kelleys with a maximum coverage of $500,025. In support, Progressive directs the Court's attention to the multi-car discount reflected in the second document, and the affidavit of Debra Henry, Progressive's Litigation Underwriting Specialist, who explained that Progressive has specific procedures for "5+ Car" policies. According to Henry, "5+ Car" policies are split into two pages because Progressive's computer software only allows four vehicles per page, and that the two separate policy numbers generated are a product of Progressive's computer program, not an indication of two separate policies. Henry stated that had there been two policies, Progressive could have charged Kelley two policy fees, rather than the one that it did charge. Also, Henry stated that the multi-car discount reflected on the second document was applicable only because the car listed was the fifth overall under the single policy, and that this discount would not have been available if the car was covered under its own distinct policy. Conversely, Kelley argues there is no fact question as to whether two policies were issued, and that refusing to stack the two policies in these circumstances is prohibited under Texas law. In support, Kelley points to the separate policy numbers and premiums on each document, as well as Progressive's own "Product & Underwriting Guide."

Although this question deals with the interaction of two documents, the rules of construction for insurance contracts apply. The starting point of this analysis is the instrument itself. *See Coker v. Coker,* 650 S.W.2d 391, 393 (Tex. 1983) ("If the written instrument is so worded that it can be given a certain or definite legal meaning or interpretation, then it is not ambiguous and the court will construe the contract as a matter of law."). Here, the written instrument consists of two pages, and standing alone, contains the information necessary to be an insurance policy. It makes no reference to another related document or policy. In the top right corner, the document states "Page 1 of 2" and "Page 2 of 2," respectively, indicating that those are the only two pages related to that policy. These characteristics suggest the document is a single policy. However, Progressive urges the Court to consider its Product & Underwriting Guide and Henry's affidavit to explain the two documents. Extrinsic evidence is not admissible for the purpose of creating an ambiguity. But here, the document does reflect some ambiguity. The reference to the "multi-car discount" on the second document, which covers only one car, creates some ambiguity. *See Coker,* 650 S.W.2d at 394 ("A contract . . . is ambiguous when its meaning is uncertain and doubtful or it is reasonably susceptible to more than one meaning."). Also at issue here is latent ambiguity, which arises "when a contract which is unambiguous on its face is applied to the subject matter with which it deals and an ambiguity appears by reason of some collateral matter." Here, the surrounding circumstances-the existence of the two documents-creates a latent ambiguity as to the intent of the parties. Thus, we will consider extrinsic evidence, including the content of the first document. A review of the two documents together shows that each has a different policy number, policy period, premium, and listed drivers. Also, the first document reflects that it was modified more recently than the second. However, the coverage amounts and deductibles are the same in each document.

Henry addressed these discrepancies, explaining that Progressive's computer program allows only four vehicles per page, so the fifth car must be listed on a separate page. While this explanation may indicate Progressive issued a single policy, the fact that a new policy number was generated for the second document does not. Also, Henry's affidavit and Progressive's own "Product & Underwriting Guide" conflict at times. . . . Henry's affidavit, taken together with the Guide, does little to resolve the ambiguity as to whether the second document is a separate policy. That a discount was given for a fifth car could also reasonably be construed either way—Progressive may want to reward a continuing customer by offering discounts on new, additional policies in the same way it would want to offer discounts on additional coverage under the same policy. Further, while it may seem reasonable for a computer program to carry over policy information onto an additional page, the fact that each document contains a separate policy number suggests they are separate, independent policies. This evidence is sufficient to raise a fact issue as to whether Progressive issued two policies, but it falls short of establishing as a matter of law only one policy was issued. For these reasons, we hold that the documents are ambiguous as to whether one or two policies were issued.

Kelley argues that neither party claimed the contract was ambiguous. But whether a contract is ambiguous is a question of law to be decided by the Court. *J.M. Davidson, Inc. v. Webster,* 128 S.W.3d 223, 229 (Tex. 2003); *see also Sage St. Assocs. v. Northdale Constr. Co.,* 863 S.W.2d 438, 445 (Tex. 1993) (holding that a court can decide a contract is ambiguous on its own motion). We have said that in an insurance contract, where a provision is subject to two reasonable interpretations, we will adopt the interpretation that favors the insured. Here, we are not interpreting a particular exclusion or provision within an insurance policy; rather, we are determining whether two documents amount to a single or separate policies. After reviewing the face of the documents and extrinsic evidence, we hold that the documents are ambiguous, and therefore, a fact finder should resolve the meaning. *See Coker,* 650 S.W.2d at 394 ("When a contract contains an ambiguity, the granting of a motion for summary judgment is improper because the interpretation of the instrument becomes a fact issue."). Therefore, without hearing argument, we reverse the court of appeals judgment and remand to the trial court for further proceedings consistent with this opinion. TEX.R.APP. P. 59.1.

Notes on Legal Sufficiency

No tribunal reviews civil lawsuits at the time they are filed to ensure that they have merit. That is, courts do not ensure, in advance, that civil lawsuits are legally sufficient—supported by the *facts* and by the *substantive law*. Attorneys, as officers of the court, have an ethical duty to sign pleadings that advance non-frivolous factual and legal assertions. Moreover, courts do not permit juries to decide every issue that is pleaded in every lawsuit. Any litigant (usually a defendant) may ask the court to evaluate its opponent's lawsuit for legal sufficiency.[1] If the support for a cause of action is legally insufficient, the court should dismiss it. Likewise, but less often, if a defense is legally insufficient, the court should render judgment without a trial. In these situations, we say that the cause of action or defense fails "as a matter of law."

Throughout the life of a case, several procedures are available to a defendant who wants the court to screen a civil case and dismiss it. As we have seen, the defendant may challenge the plaintiff's cause of action on the pleadings by special exception—if the plaintiff cannot plead a viable cause of action, the case will be dismissed. The same challenge may be made at trial by objecting to a request for a jury question or objecting to the jury's verdict by motion for directed verdict or judgment n.o.v. But in this chapter, we address the procedure that allows courts to make a pretrial determination of the evidence that will be presented at trial—the summary judgment.

The Texas summary judgment rule, Rule 166a permits any party to obtain judgment without a trial when the case involves "patently unmeritorious claims and untenable defenses." Summary judgment is rendered only when there is no dispute in the evidence, or, as the rule says, "no genuine issue as to material fact" exists. Thus, the only issues presented in a proper summary judgment motion are issues of law. Before we look at the summary judgment procedure, it is important to have a basic understanding of the circumstances under which summary judgment is appropriate—when is a cause of action "legally insufficient."[2] There are four things to keep separate when considering legal sufficiency.

1. *The burden of production.* In every case some litigant must have the burden to produce evidence by presenting witnesses and/or documents. In most cases both parties produce evidence. But on every claim or defense, the law assigns to one party the burden of production—usually the plaintiff has the burden for its causes of action, and the defendant has the burden for its affirmative defenses and counter-claims. If, for example, the plaintiff fails to produce evidence supporting its cause of action, the plaintiff will lose.

2. *The elements of a cause of action.* For every cause of action and affirmative defense, the substantive law specifies the elements that must be proved. For example, the Supreme Court has announced the elements of the causes of action for common law intentional infliction of emotional distress and false imprisonment. In other situations, the legislature defines elements of a cause of action in a statute (e.g., the Deceptive Trade Practices Act).

---

[1] "Legal sufficiency" is to be distinguished from "factual sufficiency," which is raised by a motion for new trial. We will address factual sufficiency later in the book.

[2] We will study legal sufficiency in greater detail when we address directed verdicts and judgments notwithstanding the verdict.

3. *The concept of legal sufficiency*. Legal sufficiency consists of *factual support* and *substantive law.* When a court addresses a motion for summary judgment, the issue is whether the non-movant (e.g. the plaintiff, when the defendant files the motion for summary judgment) has satisfied her burden of production on each element of her cause of action.

a. *Historical facts*. Legal sufficiency can involve a dispute about historical facts. For example: (1) In an automobile collision case, which driver had the green light? (2) In a family law case, did a boyfriend abuse a child, and was the mother aware of the boyfriend's abuse? (3) In a family law case, did spouse *A* assault spouse *B,* or was *A* defending herself from the assault of *B*? (4) In a commercial case, was the accountant aware that the employer was committing fraud? (5) In a child support case, what is the true monthly income of the child's father, who is paid in cash and has no paper records? All these are questions that have true factual answers. Legal sufficiency often involves such factual questions about historical events. The party with the burden of production must present evidence to support the fact finding she seeks to have a legally sufficient claim. If that party presents "no evidence" of the historical fact, there is "no genuine issue of material fact," the cause of action is legally insufficient, and summary judgment is appropriate. Therefore, defendants often test whether plaintiffs can satisfy this initial burden through a motion for summary judgment. However, the burden is not high—the party with the burden need only present more than a "scintilla" of evidence to avoid summary judgment. Evidence constitutes no more than a scintilla when it is "so weak as to do no more than create a mere surmise or suspicion of [the fact's] existence." "Direct" evidence always constitutes more than a scintilla; an "unreasonable inference" from circumstantial evidence is "only a scintilla" of evidence.

Similarly, although less frequently, if the party with the burden of production manages to prove the facts essential to the claim "conclusively," there is "no genuine issue of material fact," the cause of action is proven "as a matter of law," and summary judgment may be appropriate. "Conclusive proof" is a little more elusive a concept than the "no evidence" concept described above. Conclusive proof cannot be contradicted—therefore, if there is any evidence contradicting the proponent's evidence, the evidence is not conclusive and summary judgment is not appropriate. However, even if not contradicted, it may not be conclusive—the court has to make a value judgment about whether the evidence cannot reasonably be disbelieved. For example, courts generally give more credibility to disinterested witnesses, but the unopposed testimony of an interested witness is considered conclusive if it meets a five-part test of credibility: (1) it pertains to matters reasonably capable of exact statement, (2) it is clear, direct, and positive, (3) it is internally devoid of inconsistencies, (4) it is uncontradicted either by the testimony of other witnesses or by circumstances, and (5) it is of a kind that could be readily controverted if untrue.[3]

b. *Mixed questions of law and fact*. Legal sufficiency can also involve mixed questions of law and fact. For example: (1) Was defendant's conduct on the occasion in question *negligent*? (2) Did the defendant act *reasonably* in refusing to perform a contract, (3) Did plaintiff have *good cause* for failing to perform an agreement, or for failing to give notice? (4) Was an automobile's design *unreasonably dangerous* and therefore *defective*? (5) Was the employer's conduct *extreme and outrageous*? These are not pure fact questions; they are interwoven with historical facts but they also require a degree of value judgment by the trier of fact. Usually, the issue is whether someone's conduct was "reasonable" under the circumstances. Sometimes the historical facts proven are such that they do not meet the minimum threshold for "unreasonable" conduct—no

[3] Rule 166b(c).

reasonable jury could find that the conduct was unreasonable. In such a situation, the claim is "legally insufficient" and summary judgment is appropriate.

c. *Questions of law*. Legal sufficiency also sometimes involves pure questions of law. Courts must sometimes decide whether the defendant's conduct is actionable, or whether the defendant owed plaintiff a duty to do something different. For example: (1) Do liquor distilleries have a duty to warn purchasers that excessive drinking can cause alcoholism and other physical and mental harm? (2) Does a liquor seller have a duty to the public not to serve too much alcohol to purchasers who are going to drive on the roads? If there is no duty, the plaintiff does not have a legally cognizable claim, it is "legally insufficient," and summary judgment is appropriate. There are pure questions of law in other types of cases as well—for example, is a contract unambiguous?

B. Summary Judgment Procedure

The summary judgment process begins when a party files a motion—the court has no power to render judgment without the benefit of a motion. The movant has the burden to establish entitlement to summary judgment on the issues expressly presented to the trial court, and the court cannot grant summary judgment on grounds not specifically addressed in the motion.[1] The motion is typically accompanied by summary judgment evidence—affidavits, deposition testimony and other products of discovery (e.g. answers to interrogatories, responses to requests for admissions).

The response to the motion for summary judgment seeks to show that summary judgment is not appropriate. The respondent may show that the movant is not entitled to judgment as a matter of law (attacking the movant's legal grounds for summary judgment). The respondent may also show that there is an issue of material fact that requires a trial on the merits (attacking the movant's factual grounds and including summary judgment evidence contradicting the movant's evidence).

When considering a motion for summary judgment, the trial court's duty is to determine whether there are any fact issues that need to be decided in a trial on the merits. The court is not to weigh the evidence or make credibility determinations. If there are fact issues, the court cannot grant the motion. If there are no issues of material fact, the court then must decide whether the law requires that judgment be rendered for the movant.

In Texas, we have two kinds of summary judgments: (1) Rule 166a(c) traditional summary judgments where the movant has the burden to show entitlement to summary judgment; and (2) Rule 166a(i) "no evidence" summary judgments where the defendant can cause the plaintiff to show that it has some evidence to support its cause of action. These burdens are discussed in detail below.

---

[1] McConnell v. Southside Indep. Sch. Dist., 858 S.W.2d 337 (Tex. 1993) (holding that summary judgment may not be based on grounds presented only in the brief supporting the motion for summary judgment proof).

1. *Party with the Burden of Proof Moves for Traditional Summary Judgment (Plaintiff on Causes of Action, or Defendant on Affirmative Defenses)*

When the plaintiff moves for summary judgment, the plaintiff must show that it will prevail on each element of a pleaded cause of action that entitles the plaintiff to relief under law. To do so, the plaintiff must present "conclusive proof" on each element of the valid cause of action.[2]

Likewise, a defendant that has pleaded affirmative defenses may move for summary judgment on those affirmative defenses. The defendant's burden is to prove conclusively all elements of a valid affirmative defense that bars plaintiff from the recovery sought.

2. *Party without the Burden of Proof Responds to Traditional Motion for Summary Judgment*

Once the summary judgment movant has shown entitlement to summary judgment—i.e. presented legal grounds for judgment and summary judgment evidence that would be conclusive if not controverted—the respondent has the burden to respond to the summary judgment. The response should present grounds and summary judgment evidence showing the court that summary judgment is not appropriate. Possible responses are:

a. *Present a factual dispute*. The movant can create a fact issue by presenting more than a scintilla of summary judgment evidence that contradicts the movant's evidence (e.g. an affidavit saying that D's light was green, not red). Summary judgment may not be granted when the summary judgment record presents a fact issue that the fact-finder must decide at trial.

b. *Attack quality of movant's evidence*. The respondent can show that the movant's evidence does not meet the conclusive evidence standard. Remember that conclusive evidence must be incapable of reasonable disbelief. For example, if the movant's summary judgment evidence consists entirely of the testimony of interested witnesses, the respondent can point out that the testimony does not satisfy the multi-part credibility test in Rule 166a(c), and, therefore, does not meet the summary judgment standard. The movant is entitled to summary judgment only if the summary judgment proof meets the conclusive evidence standard.

c. *Attack the movant's legal entitlement to judgment*. The respondent can show that the movant has not proven all elements of a valid cause of action or affirmative defense. Remember, the movant must be entitled to judgment as a matter of law. If the movant has failed to satisfy the law's requirements, it is not entitled to summary judgment.

d. *Attack formalities of proof*. Summary judgment evidence must be presented in a form that would be admissible in a conventional trial proceeding. Thus, summary judgment evidence is subject to the same evidentiary objections as proof at trial (e.g. hearsay). Moreover, affidavits, the most common form of summary judgment proof, must satisfy the form requirements set forth in Rule 166a(f). The summary judgment response must make the evidentiary objections and point out formal deficiencies to avoid summary judgment on the objectionable proof.

e. *Assert affirmative defenses*. The respondent may raise an affirmative defense to avoid summary judgment. However, merely pleading the affirmative defense will not defeat summary judgment. The respondent must also establish that there is a fact issue on each element of the affirmative defense through summary judgment proof. Remember, a party creates a fact issue by

---

[2] Note, however, that Rule 166a(a) specifically exempts damages from this proof burden. If the plaintiff can show entitlement to judgment on all elements of a cause of action and damages are unliquidated, the court should grant summary judgment. The amount of unliquidated damages will be determined later in a trial limited to the damages issue.

presenting more than a scintilla of evidence. The respondent does not need to conclusively prove the affirmative defense to avoid summary judgment—it just needs to present sufficient evidence to create a fact issue and necessitate a trial.

f. *What if there is no response?* The traditional motion for summary judgment must stand on its own merits, meaning that the movant must show entitlement to judgment as a matter of law to obtain summary judgment. Even if there is no response, a traditional summary judgment will not stand if the movant has not satisfied the summary judgment standard.[3] If a trial court should grant a "default" summary judgment, the non-movant may successfully attack the judgment on appeal if the motion and supporting evidence did not meet the standard. Thus, a non-movant who did not respond to the motion for summary judgment may attack for the first time on appeal the quality of the movant's summary judgment evidence and the movant's legal entitlement to judgment. But contrary evidence, affirmative defenses, and attacks on the formalities of proof must be made in a response; otherwise, they are waived.

Example—a breach of contract case:

In *Amedisys, Inc. v. Kingwood Home Health Care, LLC*,[4] the Supreme Court reviewed an order granting a traditional motion for summary judgment where the movant (Amedisys) claimed that Kingwood had breached a settlement agreement. The Court concluded that the movant had satisfied its summary judgment burden, explaining as follows:

> In this case, Amedisys had the burden to submit sufficient evidence to support each element of its breach of contract claim, and this burden required evidence that a contract in fact exists. Kingwood contends that the letter and email that Amedisys submitted to prove its acceptance of Kingwood's offer prove no such thing, but instead prove that Amedisys made a counteroffer by changing a material term of the offer. We therefore review Amedisys's letter and email to determine whether they constitute evidence that Amedisys accepted Kingwood's settlement offer. If they constitute evidence of acceptance, they were uncontroverted evidence because Kingwood did not present any evidence to disprove or create a fact issue on the acceptance element. But if the letter and email constitute no evidence of acceptance, Amedisys did not satisfy its burden of proof and was not entitled to summary judgment.
>
> * * *
>
> The shifting burden of proof in the summary judgment context is important to the disposition of this case. If the divergence in language between Kingwood's offer and Amedisys's purported acceptance was material on its face, Amedisys's letter and email would have been no evidence of acceptance and Amedisys would not have been entitled to summary judgment. Or if Amedisys's communications had been patently ambiguous about whether Amedisys intended to accept Kingwood's offer, the communications would have, themselves, created a fact issue on acceptance and Amedisys would not have been entitled to summary judgment.

Query: If the "divergence . . . was material on its face," could the trial court have granted summary judgment for *Kingwood* on Amedisys' motion? No. . . Kingwood would have to file its own motion for summary judgment. But Amedisys could file a "no evidence" motion for

---

3 *See* Rhone-Pouleme, Inc. v. Steel, 997 S.W.2d 217 (Tex. 1999); Houston v. Clear Creek Basin Auth., 589 S.W.2d 671 (Tex. 1979).

4 437 S.W.3d 507 (Tex. 2014).

summary judgment, and without further evidence of a contract, should be successful. Read further!

3. *Party without the Burden of Proof Moves for Summary Judgment*

a. *Summary Judgment for Insufficient Pleadings*

The pleadings are not summary judgment evidence, even if verified.[5] Therefore, a party generally cannot rely on statements in pleadings to support or defeat a motion for summary judgment. However, the pleadings give notice of the plaintiff's claims and the defendant's defenses. Texas (as discussed in Chapter 5) has a new mechanism – Rule 91a – to dismiss claims on the pleadings. This process, in many respects, is distinct from traditional summary judgment practice. In addition to Rule 91a, special exception practice (coupled with a motion for summary judgment if a party fails to amend pleadings in response) has long been available as a method to dismiss baseless claims in Texas. Rule 91a and special exception practice are discussed in more depth in Chapter 5.

b. *"Traditional" Motion for Summary Judgment—Disproving Facts*

The "traditional" motion for summary judgment in Texas requires the movant, even a movant that does not have a burden of proof at trial, to show entitlement to judgment. Thus, a defendant filing a traditional motion for summary judgment on the plaintiff's cause of action has the summary judgment burden of conclusively *disproving* at least one element of the plaintiff's cause of action, although the defendant has no corresponding burden of proof at trial.

Consequently, only if the defendant is able to come forward with conclusive proof disproving an element of the cause of action (an often-difficult feat) does the plaintiff have a burden to respond to the motion and come forward with evidence supporting the cause of action.[6] Often, defendants' traditional summary judgments are reversed on appeal because the defendant fails to meet this difficult summary judgment standard.

4. *"No Evidence" Motion for Summary Judgment—Putting Plaintiff to Proof of Facts*

In 1997, Rule 166a was amended to add Rule 166a(i), which allows the party without the burden of proof to move for summary judgment on the ground that the opponent lacks evidence to support an essential element of the proponent's claim. This rule is similar to the summary judgment practice in the federal courts.[7]

Under the "no evidence" rule, the defendant files the motion for summary judgment with no supporting summary judgment evidence. The motion asserts that, after an adequate time for discovery, the defendant does not believe that the plaintiff has evidence of an element (or elements) of the pleaded cause of action. The mere filing of the motion shifts the summary judgment proof burden to the plaintiff to come forward with enough evidence to take the case to a jury (more than a scintilla—this would be Zone 2 or more). If the respondent does not come forward with some evidence, the court must grant the motion for summary judgment.

---

[5] City of Houston v. Clear Creek Basis Auth., 589 S.W.2d 671, 678 (Tex. 1979).

[6] *See* Casso v. Brand, 776 S.W.2d 551, 555-56 (Tex. 1989) (holding that in the "traditional" motion for summary judgment practice "we never shift the burden of proof to the non-movant unless and until the movant has 'establish[ed] his entitlement to a summary judgment on the issues expressly presented to the trial court by conclusively proving all essential elements of his cause of action or defense as a matter of law.' ").

[7] *See* Celotex Corp. v. Catrett, 477 U.S. 317 (1986) (allowing defendant to move for summary judgment without supporting evidence).

Rule 166a(i) specifically requires that the motion state the elements as to which there is no evidence. The motion cannot be conclusory or generally allege there is no evidence to support the claims.[8] Often a defendant will move for both a traditional summary judgment and a no evidence summary judgment at the same time.[9]

Notes & Questions

1. *Kerlin, Randall's & Progressive.* These opinions consider defendants' traditional motion for summary judgment. What were the grounds for the motion—historical facts, mixed questions of law and fact or questions of law? How did the plaintiffs respond? What type of summary judgment evidence did the parties present? How would the procedure have differed if the defendants had filed no-evidence rather than traditional motions for summary judgment? The plaintiff in *Randall's* asserted a claim for intentional infliction of emotional distress. What type of motion might the defendant file if the plaintiff had alleged a claim for *negligent* infliction of emotional distress, which the Texas Supreme Court has held is not a valid cause of action in Texas?[1]

2. *Specificity of the motion.* Rule 166a(c) precludes from consideration on appeal grounds not raised in the trial court. Therefore, the motion must specifically set forth the grounds for granting summary judgment, and the response must define the controverted issues and defects in the movant's proof that would defeat the motion. If summary judgment is granted it cannot be upheld on grounds different from those set out in the motion, and cannot be defeated on grounds different from those set out in the response. However, remember that a traditional summary judgment must stand on its own—a traditional summary judgment based on legally insufficient proof will be reversed on appeal even if there was no response or the response failed to raise this failure as a ground for denial of the motion. In *City of Houston v. Clear Creek Basin Authority*,[2] Texas Supreme Court explained this rule as follows:

> The trial court may not grant a summary judgment by default for lack of an answer or response to the motion by the non-movant when the movant's summary judgment proof is legally insufficient.[3] The movant still must establish his entitlement to a summary judgment on the issues expressly presented to the trial court by conclusively proving all essential elements of his cause of action or defense as a matter of law.[4] *See Swilley v. Hughes,* 488 S.W.2d 64, 67 (Tex. 1972). Summary judgments must stand on their own merits, and the

---

[8] *See* Rule 166a cmt. to 1997 change.

[9] *See* Meriman v. XTO Energy, Inc., 407 S.W.3d 244, 248 (2013) (holding that appellate court should first consider no evidence motion if both granted).

[1] *See* Boyles v. Kerr, 855 S.W.2d 593 (Tex. 1993)(holding that while Texas recognizes a cause of action for intentional infliction of emotional distress, it does not recognize a cause of action for negligent infliction of emotional distress).

[2] 589 S.W.2d 671, 678 (Tex. 1979). *See also* Amedisys v. Kingwood Home Health Care, LLC, 437 S.W.3d 507 (Tex. 2014).

[3] The function of the summary judgment is not to deprive a litigant of his right to trial by jury, but to eliminate patently unmeritorious claims and untenable defenses. Gulbenkian v. Penn, 151 Tex. 412, 252 S.W.2d 929, 931 (1952).

[4] Editor's Note: I would add "or by conclusively disproving an essential element of his opponent's case."

non-movant's failure to answer or respond cannot supply by default the summary judgment proof necessary to establish the movant's right.

While it would be prudent and helpful to the trial court for the non-movant always to file an answer or response, the non-movant needs no answer or response to the motion to contend on appeal that the grounds expressly presented to the trial court by the movant's motion are insufficient *as a matter of law* to support summary judgment. The non-movant, however, may not raise any *other* issues as grounds for reversal. Under the new rule, the non-movant may not urge on appeal as reason for reversal of the summary judgment any and every *new* ground that he can think of, nor can he resurrect grounds that he abandoned at the hearing.

With the exception of an attack on the legal sufficiency of the grounds expressly raised by the movant in his motion for summary judgment, the non-movant must expressly present to the trial court any reasons seeking to *avoid* movant's entitlement, such as those set out in rules 93 and 94, and he must present summary judgment proof when necessary to establish a fact issue. No longer must the movant negate all possible issues of law and fact that *could* be raised by the non-movant in the trial court but were not. . . . In cases such as *Torres v. Western Cas. & Sur. Co.,* 457 S.W.2d 50 (Tex. 1970) (existence of good cause for late filing of worker's compensation claim), and *Gardner v. Martin,* 162 Tex. 156, 345 S.W.2d 274 (1961) (failure of movant to attach certified copies of prior case to establish res judicata), the non-movant must now, in a written answer or response to the motion, expressly present to the trial court those issues that would defeat the movant's right to a summary judgment and failing to do so, may not later assign them as error on appeal.

3. *Grounds specified in the motion, not the brief.* Typically, a summary judgment movant files a motion for summary judgment, which states the grounds for summary judgment and summarizes the summary judgment evidence, and a brief in support of the motion, which collects authority and makes the legal arguments supporting the judgment. However, one must be careful to include all grounds for summary judgment in the motion itself. In *McConnell v. Southside Indep. School Dist.*,[5] the Texas Supreme Court held:

Consistent with the precise language of Rule 166a(c), we hold that a motion for summary judgment must itself expressly present the grounds upon which it is made. A motion must stand or fall on the grounds expressly presented in the motion. In determining whether grounds are expressly presented, reliance may not be placed on briefs or summary judgment evidence.

If the grounds for summary judgment presented in a motion are not sufficiently specific or are unclear, the nonmovant must make a special exception, objecting to the form of the motion and giving the movant an opportunity to amend the motion, before it can claim on appeal that the summary judgment is improper because the grounds were not sufficiently specific.[6]

4. *Timing.* Rule 166a(a) allows a plaintiff to move for summary judgment anytime after the adverse party has answered. The defendant may file a motion anytime, even before filing an answer. However, a no evidence motion can be filed only "after adequate time for discovery."[7] The motion

5 858 S.W.2d 337 (Tex. 1993).

6 *Id.* at 341.

7 Rule 166a(i). This requirement is discussed in more detail in the section on no-evidence motions, *infra*.

must be filed with the clerk and served upon the opposing party at least 21 days before the time specified for the hearing.[8] The respondent must file any opposing affidavits or other response not later than 7 days before the hearing. The trial court may grant leave for longer or shorter notice periods. A longer period may be required if the responding party needs additional time to conduct discovery in order to adequately respond to the motion, and files affidavits stating the need or a verified motion for continuance.[9]

5. *Pleadings*. A summary judgment proceeding is a "trial" with respect to the time for filing amended pleadings. Thus, parties generally may amend their pleadings without leave of court more than 7 days before the summary judgment hearing.[10] Often the non-movant will amend its pleadings to add new claims or defenses to avoid a final summary judgment—while the originally pleaded claims may be disposed of by summary judgment, perhaps the newly pleaded claims will avoid summary judgment. Thus, a plaintiff may amend a pleading, adding new claims for relief after being served with a motion for summary judgment. If the defendant wants to address the newly pleaded claims, and the defendant must file an amended or supplemental motion for summary judgment. If a party seeks summary judgment on an unpleaded claim or defense, the respondent must object to the lack of pleading; otherwise, summary judgment on the unpleaded claim or defense will stand.[11]

6. *Hearing on motion for summary judgment.* No oral testimony is taken at a summary judgment hearing, and all grounds for summary judgment must be presented in writing. Therefore, the summary judgment hearing is simply an opportunity for the parties to present their arguments to the judge. As the Texas Supreme Court noted "An oral hearing on a motion for summary judgment may be helpful to the parties and the court, just as oral argument is often helpful on appeal, but since oral testimony cannot be adduced in support of or opposition to a motion for summary judgment, an oral hearing is not mandatory. Notice of hearing or submission of a summary judgment motion, however, is required, although as the court of appeals said, it is not 'jurisdictional.' "[12] Generally, a litigant cannot force a trial judge to rule on a motion for summary judgment.[13]

7. *Affidavits.* Affidavits are the most common form of summary judgment proof. In an affidavit, the witness' relevant testimony is set out in writing and followed by an oath or jurat, where the witness swears to the truth of the facts set out in the affidavit before a notary public.[14] Note that a jurat is different from the "acknowledgement" used on many legal documents—the acknowledgement simply states that the signature is that of the signer and does not contain words

---

[8] *See* Lewis v. Blake, 876 S.W.2d 314 (Tex. 1994) (discussing calculation of time for notice of summary judgment hearing).

[9] *Tenneco Inc. v. Enter. Prods. Co.,* 925 S.W.2d 640, 647 (Tex.1996). *But see* Ford v. Castillo, 279 S.W.3d 656 (Tex. 2009) (holding that when court denies responding party any discovery, party has not waived error by failing to file affidavits or motion for continuance).

[10] *See* Rule 63.

[11] *See* Roark v. Stallworth Oil & Gas, Inc., 813 S.W.2d 492, 494 (Tex. 1991).

[12] Martin v. Martin, Martin & Richards, Inc., 989 S.W.2d 357, 359 (Tex. 1999).

[13] *In re* American Media Consolidated, 121 S.W.3d 706 (Tex. App.—San Antonio 2003, no pet). *But see* Grant v. Wood, 916 S.W.2d 42 (Tex. App.—Houston [1st Dist.] 1995, orig. proceeding) (granting mandamus where refusal to rule was expressly to prevent interlocutory appeal).

[14] See Mansions in the Forest, L.P. v. Montgomery County, 365 S.W.3d 314 (Tex. 2012) (holding party must object to absence of jurat or other evidence showing affidavit was sworn by affiant, and may not be raised for first time on appeal).

indicating an oath. Affidavit proof is less expensive than a deposition, and the witness is not subject to cross-examination. However, because the testimony is not subject to cross-examination, affidavits are strictly construed, and the requirements of Rule 166a(f) must be met.

8. *Must summary judgment evidence be attached to the motion?* In *Lance v. Robinson*,[115] a property dispute involving deeds, the Supreme Court considered whether evidence must be appended to the actual summary judgment motion:

> The Lances first contend that the trial court erred in granting the Robinsons' summary-judgment motion because the Robinsons failed to attach any of the relevant deeds to that motion. At the earlier temporary-injunction hearing, the Robinsons offered certified copies of the deeds into evidence, and the trial court admitted them without objection. In their summary-judgment motion, the Robinsons expressly "referenced and specified" the injunction-hearing transcript and exhibits "as evidence in support of" the motion. At the summary-judgment hearing, the trial court judge had the temporary-injunction transcript—including the deeds and other exhibits—in front of him, reviewed the deeds, and discussed them with counsel, including the Lances' counsel, who never raised this issue or otherwise objected on the ground that the Robinsons had not re-filed the deeds as attachments to their summary-judgment motion. Nevertheless, the Lances now contend that the Robinsons failed to meet their summary-judgment burden because the deeds were not in evidence.
>
> ***
>
> The Lances acknowledge that the trial court admitted the deeds as evidence at the temporary-injunction hearing, but contend that the Robinsons had to re-file them as attachments to their summary-judgment motion. Whether this alleged error involved the "form of the summary-judgment record" or its "substance" is irrelevant because the alleged error was not error at all. Our rules require a trial court to grant a summary-judgment motion if the evidence "*on file at the time of the hearing*, or filed thereafter and before judgment with permission of the court," establishes that the movant is "entitled to judgment as a matter of law." TEX. R. CIV. P. 166a(c) (emphasis added). Here, the deeds were indisputably "on file" with the court at the time of the summary-judgment hearing. At the very end of the temporary-injunction hearing, after the Robinsons' attorney asked if he should "withdraw" the exhibits, the trial court announced, "I'm going to leave all the exhibits with the file." The court's docket sheet reflects that the court reporter filed the deeds with the court clerk that same day, just as the rules require. The record thus establishes beyond doubt that the deeds were "on file at the time of the hearing," as rule 166a requires.
>
> ***
>
> Here, while the deeds may not have been included in the "summary judgment record," the appellate record confirms that they were on file with the court at the time of the summary-judgment hearing because they had been offered and admitted at the prior temporary-injunction hearing. They thus qualified as proper summary-judgment evidence, and the trial court did not err by relying on them.

9. *Interested witness testimony and the 166a(c) credibility test.* Any interested witness testimony, even the testimony of the party, may support a traditional summary judgment if it meets the multi-part credibility test of Rule 166a(c) ("the evidence is clear, positive and direct, otherwise credible and free from contradictions and inconsistencies, and could have been readily controverted"). If it

---

[15] 543 S.W.3d 723 (Tex. 2018).

does not satisfy the test, it cannot support a summary judgment because it merely raises a fact issue—the fact-finder can believe or disbelieve the testimony. Remember, however, that interested witness testimony raising a fact issue is *always* sufficient to contradict the movant's summary judgment evidence and *defeat* a motion for summary judgment. Why? The non-movant only has to present more than a scintilla of evidence to create a fact issue.

10. *When can interested witness testimony be "readily controverted"?* The Texas Supreme Court has said that the requirement "does not mean that the summary judgment evidence could have been easily and conveniently rebutted, but rather indicates that the testimony could have been effectively countered by opposing evidence."[16] In one case, the Court held that an affidavit could have been readily controverted through discovery. Because the opponent made no attempt to controvert the affidavit through deposition testimony, interrogatories, or other discovery, the Court held that the affidavit was competent summary judgment evidence.[17]

11. *Reliability of expert testimony.* Expert testimony presented to support or defeat a summary judgment motion must be based upon a reliable foundation.[18] A party presenting expert testimony must present summary judgment proof of the expert's qualifications.[19] The trial court's determination of whether the expert is qualified or not is subject to an abuse of discretion standard of review.[20] An expert's affidavit must state the basis of the opinion, not simply conclusory statements of opinion.[21] Therefore, a plaintiff's expert's affidavit submitted in response to a defendant's motion for summary judgment may be "no evidence" if the judge determines that the expert does not meet the standards for reliability.

12. *Limitations defenses.* As we have seen, defendants can seek summary judgment on their affirmative defenses, where they conclusively prove all elements of the defense. Summary judgments on statute of limitations defenses can get complicated because plaintiffs often raise the discovery rule affirmative defense to the limitations defense. The discovery rule defers the accrual of a cause of action for limitations purposes until the plaintiff knows, or in the exercise of reasonable diligence, should have known of the facts giving rise to the cause of action.[22] What is the defendant's summary judgment burden when there is an affirmative defense to an affirmative defense?

A defendant moving for summary judgment on the affirmative defense of limitations has the burden to conclusively establish that defense. Thus, the defendant must (1) conclusively prove when the cause of action accrued, and (2) negate the discovery rule, if it applies and has been pleaded or otherwise raised, by proving as a matter of law that there is no genuine issue of material fact about when the plaintiff discovered, or in the exercise of reasonable diligence should have discovered the nature of its injury. If the movant establishes that the statute of limitations

---

16 Trico Technologies Corp. v. Montiel, 949 S.W.2d 308 (Tex. 1997), *citing* Casso v. Brand, 776 S.W.2d 551, 558 (Tex. 1989).

17 *Trico Technologies Corp.*, 949 S.W.2d at 310.

18 *See* E.I. du Pont de Nemours & Co. v. Robinson, 923 S.W.2d 549, 556-57 (Tex. 1995) (requiring expert testimony to be based upon a reliable foundation).

19 United Blood Services v. Longoria, 938 S.W.2d 29, 30 (Tex. 1997) (per curiam).

20 *Id.* at 30-31.

21 Elizondo v. Krist, 415 S.W.3d 259 (Tex. 2013); Burrow v. Arce, 997 S.W.3d 229 (Tex. 1999).

22 *See* Wagner & Brown, Ltd. v Horwood, 58 S.W.3d 732 (Tex. 2001); Computer Associates Intl, Inc. v. Altai, 918 S.W.2d 453 (Tex. 1996).

bars the action, the nonmovant must then adduce summary judgment proof raising a fact issue in avoidance of the statute of limitations.[23]

Thus, the defendant filing the motion for summary judgment has the initial burden of conclusively proving that the plaintiff filed suit outside the limitations period. Usually, this is not a difficult burden—the defendant proves up the date of the accrual of the cause of action and the date the plaintiff filed suit. However, if the plaintiff has alleged the discovery rule defense in its pleadings, the defendant must also conclusively negate the discovery rule to succeed in its motion for summary judgment. The defendant can establish that the discovery rule does not apply to the case as a matter of law (e.g. show that this is not the type of case to which the discovery rule applies),[24] or if the discovery rule does apply, conclusively negate its application in the particular case.

Can a defendant file a no evidence motion for summary judgment on the discovery rule defense to the affirmative defense of limitations?[25]

13. *Presumptions and the summary judgment burden.* In *Chavez v. Kansas City S. Railway Co.*,[226] the Supreme Court considered the impact of presumptions on the summary judgment burden. The wife and mother of two decedents, killed at a railroad crossing, sued a railroad company. During settlement negotiations, attorneys for the two sides reached a letter agreement. At a hearing to approve the agreement, the widow appeared in person to inform the court that she did not want to go forward with the settlement and would be hiring new attorneys. In later proceedings, the railroad provided summary judgment evidence that the attorneys who signed the agreement represented the widow. Though the railroad did not provide evidence that the widow expressly agreed (or authorized her attorneys to agree) to the settlement terms, it contended that courts should presume that a party consents to agreements entered into by his or her attorney. Moreover, the railroad contended that this presumption operated to satisfy its summary judgment burden.[327] The trial court granted the motion, and the court of appeals affirmed.

In a *per curiam* opinion, the Supreme Court rejected this argument, noting the rule that presumptions may shift the burden of production at trial but do not do so at the summary judgment stage. Because the railroad did not conclusively establish that the lawyers had authority from the widow to enter into the agreement, it did not meet its summary judgment burden.

14. *Conflicts in a witness' testimony and "sham" affidavits.* Suppose the witness says one thing in an affidavit, and another when she was deposed. Which one controls for summary judgment purposes? Generally, neither. The witness' conflicting testimony has created a fact issue that must be resolved by the jury and summary judgment based on either the deposition or affidavit testimony is improper. As the Texas Supreme Court has held, "if conflicting inferences may be drawn from a deposition and from an affidavit filed by the same party in opposition to a motion for summary judgment, a fact issue is presented."[28]

---

23 KPMG Peat Marwick v Harrison County Hous. Fin. Corp., 988 S.W.2d 746, 748 (Tex. 1999).]

24 The discovery rule applies only to categories of cases where the nature of the injury is inherently undiscoverable, and the injury itself is objectively verifiable. *See Computer Associates,* 918 S.W.2d at 456.

25 *See* Eslon Thermoplastics v. Dynamic Systems, Inc., 49 S.W.3d 891, 900 n.6 (Tex. App.—Austin 2001, no pet.)(not deciding whether no evidence motion may be brought on a defense to a defense).

26 520 S.W.3d 898.

27 The court assumed, without deciding, that such a presumption exists.

28 Randall v. Dallas Power & Light Co., 752 S.W.2d 4 (Tex. 1988). *See also* Gaines v. Hamman, 358 S.W.2d 557 (Tex. 1962).

But discrepancies in summary judgment proof are not always for the fact finder. Consider the following case:

LUJAN
v.
NAVISTAR, Inc.
___ S.W.3d ___
2018 WL 1974473
(Tex. Apr. 27, 2018)

JUSTICE BLACKLOCK delivered the opinion of the Court.

* * *

I. Background

Albert Lujan purchased Texas Wholesale Flower Company in 2005. The newly purchased company included aging flower delivery trucks, so Lujan purchased five new CF600 trucks manufactured by Navistar, Inc. Lujan testified in his deposition that in June 2006 he incorporated the business as Texas Wholesale Flower Co., Inc. (the Corporation). Later that year, Lujan transferred assets of his business to the Corporation in exchange for 100% of the Corporation's stock, pursuant to section 351 of the Internal Revenue Code. 26 U.S.C. § 351. He was the sole shareholder and was "in control of the corporation." *See id.* (permitting tax-free exchange if "property is transferred to a corporation by one or more persons solely in exchange for stock in such corporation and immediately after the exchange such person or persons are in control . . . of the corporation"). He also testified that after forming the Corporation he filed corporate tax returns for the Corporation.

The document reflecting the section 351 transfer indicates that Lujan transferred the five CF600 trucks to the Corporation. The Corporation's income tax returns from 2006 and 2007 list the five trucks as corporate assets and indicate that the Corporation had sales of over $4 million during that time. Lujan testified at his deposition, however, that he did not transfer ownership of the trucks to the Corporation. In 2008, the Texas Secretary of State declared the Corporation's certificate forfeited due to unpaid franchise taxes.

In 2009, Lujan sued Navistar over his dissatisfaction with the trucks, alleging breach of express and implied warranties. He claimed that the trucks had recurring mechanical problems that caused disruptions in flower deliveries and the loss of perishable products and customers. He also claimed that the trucks were unsuitable for his business despite the truck salesman's representation that they would be a good fit. Lujan sued in his individual capacity and claimed individual ownership of the vehicles.

Whether Lujan or the Corporation owned the disputed trucks eventually became a contested issue. After four years of litigation, the Corporation intervened as a plaintiff, incorporating Lujan's pleadings and adding almost $15 million to the claimed damages. Lujan's attorney also represented the Corporation. Navistar moved to strike the intervention as untimely. In response to Navistar's motion to strike, the Corporation stated equivocally that "[Lujan] made an IRS Section 351 transfer . . . [of] all of the assets and liabilities of Texas Wholesale Flower Co. to Texas Wholesale Flower Co., Inc." but that "legal title" to the trucks was not transferred to the

Corporation. The Corporation attached a copy of the section 351 transfer, which included the trucks, to its response to Navistar's motion to strike. At the hearing on the motion, the Corporation's attorney, who also represented Lujan, contradicted the Corporation's previous statement regarding the transfer of the vehicles. He claimed that the section 351 election transferred all the assets "lock, stock and barrel" to the Corporation, including the trucks—"absolutely everything [was] transferred over." During this hearing, the attorney did not distinguish between statements he made on behalf of the Corporation as opposed to Lujan. The trial court struck the Corporation's intervention as untimely.

Two months later, Navistar filed a motion for partial summary judgment against Lujan. Navistar argued that Lujan in his individual capacity did not have standing to assert claims for injury arising from the trucks that occurred after June 12, 2006, the date on which Lujan allegedly transferred ownership of the trucks to the Corporation. In his opposition to summary judgment, Lujan asserted that he "did not transfer his assets and liabilities to a corporation at any time." He supported this assertion with a sworn affidavit that stated he did not transfer ownership of the trucks to the Corporation and that the Corporation had no assets or liabilities and "never conducted business."

At the summary judgment hearing, the trial court pointed out that while Lujan's affidavit denied that the Corporation conducted any business or possessed any assets and liabilities, Lujan's attorney conceded that the Corporation filed tax returns and had assets and liabilities. The attorney admitted that those portions of the affidavit were false. He stated that when he prepared the affidavit his client "didn't recall" and "[m]isunderstood the true facts." He admitted that the Corporation had liabilities and filed tax returns. But Lujan's attorney stated that other than these falsehoods, "everything in the affidavit is true." The court was not satisfied with that explanation: "Other than where it's not true, it's true right? . . . This just goes back to my point counselor. I expect everything in here to be true. . . . I would have a little better time of this if it was a thoughtful affidavit that tried to explain" the false statements, but instead it appeared that "either you're not paying attention to what the facts of the case are, or you're just saying whatever is convenient at the time." The court expressed an interest in striking Lujan's affidavit as a sham and requested briefing on that issue. Navistar's ensuing briefing identified deposition testimony wherein Lujan admitted he incorporated the business in 2006 and filed corporate tax returns for the business in 2006 and 2007. The tax returns include the trucks as assets of the Corporation.

The trial court struck the affidavit as a sham and granted partial summary judgment. That same day, the trial court also granted summary judgment on a separate issue regarding the merits of Lujan's claims. Lujan timely appealed both rulings.

* * *

II. Analysis

A. Standard of Review

* * *

Although we generally review summary judgments de novo, a trial court's refusal to consider evidence under the sham affidavit rule should be reversed only if it was an abuse of discretion.

* * *

B. The Sham Affidavit Rule

The sham affidavit rule originated in the federal courts nearly fifty years ago.

* * *

In federal practice, the sham affidavit rule provides that "the nonmovant cannot defeat a motion for summary judgment by submitting an affidavit which directly contradicts, without explanation, his previous testimony." *Albertson v. T.J. Stevenson & Co.*, 749 F.2d 223, 228 (5th Cir. 1984). Such conflicting affidavits "indicate[ ] only that the affiant cannot maintain a consistent story or is willing to offer a statement solely for the purpose of defeating summary judgment." *Jiminez v. All Am. Rathskeller, Inc.*, 503 F.3d 247, 253 (3d Cir. 2007). The basis for the rule is that allowing manufactured affidavits to defeat summary judgment would thwart the very object of summary judgment, which "is to separate real and genuine issues from those that are formal or pretended . . . ." *Radobenko v. Automated Equip. Corp.*, 520 F.2d 540, 544 (9th Cir. 1975). Rewarding a party who seeks to defeat summary judgment by "contradicting his own prior testimony . . . would greatly diminish the utility of summary judgment as a procedure for screening out sham issues of fact." *Perma Research*, 410 F.2d at 578.

The sham affidavit rule does not authorize trial courts to strike every affidavit that contradicts the affiant's prior sworn testimony. "To allow every failure of memory or variation in a witness's testimony to be disregarded as a sham would require far too much from lay witnesses . . . ." *Tippens v. Celotex Corp.*, 805 F.2d 949, 953 (11th Cir. 1986). Sometimes a contradictory affidavit is warranted. But an explanation for the contradiction is also warranted. For example, courts have acknowledged that newly discovered evidence may justify a contradictory affidavit. Other times, an affiant "may have been confused about what was being asked" during a deposition and therefore an affidavit, though facially inconsistent, should be considered. *Pyramid Sec. Ltd. v. IB Resolution, Inc.*, 924 F.2d 1114, 1123 (D.C. Cir. 1991).

Most Texas courts of appeals have followed the federal courts by recognizing the sham affidavit rule as a valid application of a trial court's authority to distinguish genuine fact issues from non-genuine fact issues under Rule 166a. We agree. Like the federal rules of civil procedure, the Texas rules provide for summary judgment when no "genuine" fact issue exists. FED. R. CIV. P. 56(a); TEX. R. CIV. P. 166a(c). The operative clauses in federal Rule 56(a) and Texas Rule 166a(c) are materially indistinguishable. Accordingly, the overwhelming federal precedent applying the sham affidavit rule is persuasive, though not controlling, in our interpretation of Rule 166a(c). In both the federal rule and its Texas counterpart, the key word is "genuine." Not just any proffered fact issue defeats summary judgment. While a trial court must not weigh evidence, the rules of procedure require the court to determine whether a proffered fact issue is "genuine," which means "authentic or real." *Genuine*, BLACK'S LAW DICTIONARY (10th ed. 2014). A "sham" is, by definition, "not genuine." *Sham*, WEBSTER'S NEW INT'L DICTIONARY (3rd ed. 1961). The sham affidavit rule merely recognizes the authority of a trial court charged with weeding out non-genuine fact issues to require litigants to explain conflicting testimony that appears to be a sham designed to avoid summary judgment.

***

Like Rule 56 of the federal rules, Rule 166a obligates Texas trial courts to distinguish genuine fact issues, which must proceed toward trial, from non-genuine fact issues, which should not survive summary judgment. Application of the sham affidavit rule is merely one way in which trial courts have gone about discharging that obligation. We affirm this approach today. Under Rule 166a(c), a trial court may conclude that a party does not raise a genuine fact issue by submitting sworn testimony that materially conflicts with the same witness's prior sworn testimony, unless there is a sufficient explanation for the conflict. We emphasize that this rule does not contravene the long-standing principle that the trial court is "not to weigh the evidence or determine its credibility, and thus try the case on the affidavits." *Gulbenkian*, 252 S.W.2d at 931.

Rather, the sham affidavit rule is a tool that may be used to distinguish genuine fact issues from non-genuine fact issues in service of the "underlying purpose of Rule 166a [to] eliminat[e] . . . patently unmeritorious claims or untenable defenses . . . ." *Id.*

* * *

Examination of the nature and extent of the contradiction is essential. "Most differences between a witness's affidavit and deposition are more a matter of degree and details than direct contradiction. This reflects human inaccuracy more than fraud. If the differences fall into the category of variations on a theme, consistent in the major allegations but with some variances of detail, this is grounds for impeachment. If, on the other hand, the subsequent affidavit clearly contradicts the witness's earlier testimony involving the suit's material points, without explanation, then the sham affidavit rule applies. [internal quotations omitted] The sham affidavit rule is not a free-standing rule of procedure to be mechanically applied in the same way to every case. It is a flexible concept that flows from the text of Rule 166a(c) and aids courts grappling with the ultimate case-specific inquiry on summary judgment: Are the proffered fact issues genuine or not?

* * *

C. Application

We turn now to the circumstances of this case.

* * *

After disregarding Lujan's affidavit, the trial court granted partial summary judgment against Lujan because defects in the trucks injured the Corporation rather than Lujan in his personal capacity. Lujan argues that, even if the sham affidavit rule is viable, it does not apply to his affidavit. He points out that the statement in his affidavit that he did not transfer ownership of the trucks to the Corporation accords with his deposition testimony. This is true. Nevertheless, we find that under the particular circumstances of this case, the trial court did not abuse its discretion by disregarding Lujan's affidavit as a sham.

Although Lujan's affidavit and deposition testimony agree on the ownership of the trucks, Lujan fails to recognize that his deposition contradicts his affidavit on other material points, including the Corporation's activities. In his affidavit, Lujan made broad statements that "[a]t all times I did business as Texas Wholesale Flower Company . . . . At no time did a corporation conduct business as Texas Wholesale Flower Company . . . . [The Corporation] never conducted business." These statements contradict his deposition testimony that he incorporated the company in 2006 and filed tax returns as a corporation.

Q. I thought you filed corporate tax returns in '06 and '07?
A. Yeah . . . .
Q. Let me back up, though. But did you incorporate the business—
A. At some point.
Q. —in '07?
A. At some point, yes . . . .
Q. . . . And you filed as a corporation?
A. Yes.

Other sworn evidence also contradicts Lujan's affidavit, including the section 351 transfer documents and the Corporation's tax returns. Lujan stated in his affidavit that he never transferred ownership of the trucks to the corporation. However, the section 351 election states that he did transfer ownership. The Corporation's tax returns, which Lujan admitted in his deposition were filed, also included the trucks as corporate assets. These documents were "made under the penalties of perjury," 26 U.S.C. § 6065, and they contradict Lujan's affidavit. Lujan now argues that because the copies in the record of the section 351 election and the tax returns are unsigned, they should not be considered sworn statements under the sham affidavit rule. He did not make this argument to the trial court when asked about the discrepancy between the affidavit and the corporate tax returns. And he does not contend the tax documents are incorrect or not genuine. Further, in his deposition and before the trial court, Lujan admitted he filed the corporate tax returns that show the trucks as corporate assets. Under these circumstances, the district court did not abuse its discretion by relying on the tax documents as the equivalent of sworn statements for purposes of the sham affidavit rule.

In addition to the facial inconsistencies between the affidavit and Lujan's other sworn evidence, the particular circumstances of this case lend considerable support to the trial court's decision to disregard the affidavit as a sham. To begin with, Lujan's attorney openly admitted to the trial court that the affidavit was false. When the trial court pointed to the contradictions in Lujan's evidence, his attorney's only explanation for the false affidavit was that Lujan either did not recall or misunderstood the relevant facts. The trial court was not persuaded. The court stated, "either you're not paying attention to what the facts of the case are, or you're just saying whatever is convenient at the time."

The trial court also pointed to conflicting statements by Lujan's attorney during the hearing on the motion to intervene. At that hearing, the attorney stated that Lujan had transferred "absolutely everything"—"lock, stock and barrel"—to the Corporation in 2006. Then during the hearing on summary judgment, the attorney tried to limit the effect of his prior statement when confronted with the contradiction between his statement and his client's affidavit. He claimed that the statement was made on behalf of the Corporation and not Lujan. However, the record reflects that at the hearing on the intervention, the attorney appeared on behalf of plaintiff, Albert Lujan, and did not attempt to distinguish his statements on behalf of the Corporation from his statements on behalf of Lujan. Further, Lujan was the sole shareholder of the Corporation. His artful attempt to disown the Corporation's statements rang hollow to the trial court and the court of appeals, and we cannot disagree. When Lujan's attorney characterized the whole mess as a misunderstanding, the trial court justifiably responded:

> This isn't simply a situation where you said, "I misunderstood," and then you come back and then you file an affidavit that parses out specifically what the issues are as you've stated to the court right here in oral argument. Instead, there's an affidavit that says, "Look, you know, there's just this corporation that existed for all intents and purposes on paper and I never did anything with it." But that's not true.

It should be noted that the conflict between Lujan's affidavit and his attorney's statements does not alone dictate the outcome of this case. The sham affidavit rule looks to contradictions in sworn testimony, not in attorney statements. Such conflicts in sworn testimony exist in this case. What also exists in this case are other circumstances supporting the trial court's decision to disregard Lujan's affidavit as a sham. These circumstances include the admitted falsity of the affidavit and the inconsistent statements of Lujan's attorney, both of which buttress the trial court's conclusion that the late-filed and contradictory affidavit did not raise genuine fact issues sufficient to survive summary judgment. Under these circumstances, the trial court did not abuse its discretion by disregarding Lujan's affidavit.

III. Conclusion

We conclude that the sham affidavit rule is a valid component of a trial court's authority under Rule 166a to distinguish genuine fact issues from non-genuine fact issues. In the case before us, the trial court did not abuse its discretion by concluding that the affidavit in question did not raise a genuine fact issue sufficient to survive summary judgment. Therefore, we affirm the court of appeals' decision as to the partial summary judgment grant.

***

C. No Evidence Motions for Summary Judgment

FORD MOTOR CO.
v.
RIDGWAY

135 S.W.3d 598
(Tex. 2004)

PHILLIPS, CHIEF JUSTICE.

We must decide whether the evidence offered by plaintiffs in response to the defendant's Rule 166a(i) summary judgment motion created a genuine issue of material fact that a manufacturing defect in the defendant's product caused the plaintiff's injuries. Because we hold that the court of appeals erred in holding that the evidence was sufficient, we reverse the judgment of the court of appeals, and render judgment that the plaintiffs take nothing.

I

Jack Ridgway sustained serious injuries when his two-year-old Ford F-150 pick-up truck caught fire while he was driving. Ridgway was the truck's third owner. The first owner drove the truck approximately 7,000 miles and installed a spotlight on the front left "A" pillar, which is the front part of the door frame. The second owner drove the truck approximately 47,000 more miles and had the truck repaired four times at the Red McCombs Ford dealership in San Antonio ("Red McCombs"). Each repair attempted to fix a clunking noise that occurred during hard turns. Three of the four repairs also involved the fuel system and attempted to improve the truck's poor gas mileage. The Ridgways drove the truck for only one month before the fire, making no repairs or modifications.

The fire occurred when Ridgway was driving home from work on a paved county road in Bandera County. Driving at or below the speed limit, he looked into the rear-view mirror and noticed flames curling up around the cab of the truck. Before he could jump out of the truck, Ridgway sustained second-degree burns to 20 percent of his body.

Ridgway and his wife Linda sued Red McCombs and Ford, alleging products liability, breach of express and implied warranties, violations of the Texas Deceptive Trade Practices Act, and negligence. After both defendants moved for summary judgment, the Ridgways nonsuited Red McCombs, leaving only their negligence and strict products liability claims against Ford. After adequate time for discovery, Ford moved for summary judgment under Rule 166a(i) and alternatively under Rule 166a(c). The trial court granted summary judgment without specifying on which provision it relied. On appeal, a divided court of appeals affirmed the trial court's judgment on plaintiffs' negligence claim but reversed on products liability. We granted Ford's petition for review to determine whether the Ridgways presented more than a scintilla of evidence in support of their claim.

II

We first review the trial court's summary judgment under the standards of Rule 166a(i). The non-movants, here the plaintiffs, must produce summary judgment evidence raising a genuine issue of material fact to defeat the summary judgment under that provision. TEX. R. CIV. P. 166a(i). A genuine issue of material fact exists if more than a scintilla of evidence establishing the existence of the challenged element is produced. If the plaintiffs fail to produce more than a scintilla of evidence under that burden, then there is no need to analyze whether Ford's proof satisfied the Rule 166a(c) burden.

A manufacturing defect exists when a product deviates, in its construction or quality, from the specifications or planned output in a manner that renders it unreasonably dangerous. A plaintiff must prove that the product was defective when it left the hands of the manufacturer and that the defect was a producing cause of the plaintiff's injuries.

In an attempt to defeat Ford's motion, the Ridgways presented affidavits from all three of the truck's owners and from Bill Greenlees, an expert who inspected the truck after the accident. The owners explained when and where they purchased the truck, how many miles they drove it, and any modifications or repairs they made. In addition, Ridgway described when he first noticed the fire, how he reacted, and the injuries he sustained. Greenlees explained that his expert opinion was based on his visual inspection of the truck after the accident, a visual comparison of a similar but undamaged truck, a review of Ford service manuals, and a review of the National Highway Traffic Safety Administration's database. Based on the areas of greatest damage to the truck and an indication of a "hot spot in the left center area of the engine compartment," Greenlees concluded that the fire originated within the engine compartment and opined that "a malfunction of the electrical system in the engine compartment is suspected of having caused this accident." Greenlees, however, declined to eliminate all portions of the fuel system as a possible cause of the accident and conceded that "the actual cause of the fire has not been determine [sic] yet." Although Greenlees suggested that further investigation might yield a more definitive conclusion, particularly if the vehicle were disassembled, the Ridgways made no motion for further testing and did not complain that the trial court failed to allow adequate time for or sufficient scope of discovery.

When determining if more than a scintilla of evidence has been produced in response to a Rule 166a(i) motion for summary judgment, the evidence must be viewed in the light most favorable to the non-movant. We have repeatedly held that more than a scintilla of evidence exists if the evidence "rises to a level that would enable reasonable and fair-minded people to differ in their conclusions." On the other hand, "[w]hen the evidence offered to prove a vital fact is so weak as to do no more than create a mere surmise or suspicion of its existence, the evidence is no more than a scintilla and, in legal effect, is no evidence."

Both direct and circumstantial evidence may be used to establish any material fact. To raise a genuine issue of material fact, however, the evidence must transcend mere suspicion. Evidence that is so slight as to make any inference a guess is in legal effect no evidence.

The Ridgways produced no direct evidence of the fire's cause, and their circumstantial evidence that a manufacturing defect existed in the Ford F-150 when it left the manufacturer does not exceed a scintilla. Ridgway's affidavit establishes only that a fire occurred, and Greenlees could say no more than that he "suspects" the electrical system caused the fire. Because Greenlees could not rule out part of the fuel system as a possible cause and because there is no proof that identified a defect in the truck at the time it left the manufacturer, Greenlees' affidavit is not sufficient to raise a fact issue.

* * *

III

Under the circumstances of this case, the Ridgways' summary judgment proof is no more than a scintilla of evidence that a manufacturing defect was present when the truck left the manufacturer. Therefore, the Ridgways have not met their burden of showing that a genuine issue of material fact exists regarding a manufacturing defect. We accordingly reverse the judgment of the court of appeals and render judgment that the plaintiffs take nothing.

TIMPTE INDUSTRIES, INC.
v.
GISH

286 S.W.3d 306
(Tex. 2009)

JUSTICE MEDINA delivered the opinion of the Court.

Robert Gish was seriously injured when he fell from the top of a trailer into which he was attempting to load fertilizer. He sued Timpte Industries, the manufacturer of the trailer, alleging, among other things, that several features of the trailer were defectively designed, rendering the trailer unreasonably dangerous. The trial court granted a no-evidence summary judgment in Timpte's favor, but the court of appeals reversed. Finding no defect, we reverse the court of appeals' judgment and render judgment reinstating the trial court's summary judgment.

I

On the morning of June 19, 2002, Robert Gish, a long haul trucker for Scott Hinde Trucking, arrived at the Martin Resources plant in Plainview, Texas, to pick up a load of ammonium sulfate fertilizer. Gish was familiar with the plant, as he had picked up fertilizer there once or twice a week for approximately the past year. That morning Gish checked his trailer, weighed it, and waited for another customer to finish loading.

Gish's Peterbilt truck was hauling a forty-eight-foot Super Hopper trailer manufactured by Timpte Inc., a subsidiary of Timpte Industries. The Super Hopper trailer is a standard open-top, twin hopper trailer, which is loaded from above through use of a downspout or other device and is emptied through two openings on its bottom. Once the trailer is loaded, a tarp is rolled over the top to protect its contents. A ladder and an observation platform are attached to the front and rear of the trailer to allow the operator to view its contents.

After the truck ahead of him finished loading, Gish backed his trailer under the downspout attached to the fertilizer plant and yelled to a Martin employee to begin loading. In a typical delivery, an employee inside the Martin plant uses a front-end loader to drop fertilizer into a hopper. The fertilizer is then dropped onto a conveyer system that moves it to the downspout outside the plant and into the waiting trailer.

To prevent the granulated fertilizer from being blown away during the loading process, Gish attempted to lower the downspout by using a rope attached to it. The rope was attached to the downspout for that purpose, but Gish could not get it to work. He had previously complained to Martin employees about problems lowering the downspout, but he did not do so again that morning. Instead, using the ladder attached to the front of the trailer, Gish climbed atop the trailer (as he had on several other occasions when the downspout would not lower) and attempted to lower the downspout by hand while standing on the trailer's top rail. This top rail is also the top of the trailer's side wall. It is made of extruded aluminum, is between 5 and 5.66 inches wide, and is nine-and-a-half feet above the ground.

While Gish was standing on the top rail working with the downspout, a gust of wind hit him from the back, causing him to fall. This fall fractured his legs, broke his ankles, and ruptured an Achilles tendon. Gish was in a wheelchair for six months, and he still has difficulty walking and standing.

Gish sued Martin and Timpte, asserting a cause of action for premises liability against Martin and causes of action for marketing, manufacturing, and design defects, misrepresentation, and breach of warranty against Timpte. Specifically, Gish asserted that the warning labels on the Super Hopper trailer were insufficient to warn him of the danger of climbing on top of the trailer, and that the trailer contained two design defects. . . .

Timpte moved for a no-evidence summary judgment, which the trial court granted. The trial court then severed Gish's claims against Timpte from the remainder of the case, making the summary judgment final for purposes of appeal. The court of appeals affirmed the trial court's judgment as to all of Gish's claims except his claim for design defect, concluding that there was "some evidence upon which reasonable factfinders could disagree as to whether the trailer's design was both unreasonably dangerous and a cause of Gish's fall.

II

A no-evidence summary judgment motion under Rule 166a(i) is essentially a motion for a pretrial directed verdict; it requires the nonmoving party to present evidence raising a genuine issue of material fact supporting each element contested in the motion. TEX.R. CIV. P. 166a(i). When reviewing a no-evidence summary judgment, we "review the evidence presented by the motion and response in the light most favorable to the party against whom the summary judgment was rendered, crediting evidence favorable to that party if reasonable jurors could, and disregarding contrary evidence unless reasonable jurors could not."

We begin with the grounds for Timpte's no-evidence summary judgment motion. Gish contends that Timpte's motion challenged only Gish's allegation that a design defect in the Super Hopper was the producing cause of his injury, not that there was a defect rendering the product unreasonably dangerous. Because the motion did not raise this issue, Gish concludes that the trial court erred in rendering its no-evidence summary judgment in favor of Timpte.

It is well settled that a trial court cannot grant a summary judgment motion on grounds not presented in the motion. Our no-evidence summary judgment rule similarly requires that the moving party identify the grounds for the motion:

> After adequate time for discovery, a party without presenting summary judgment evidence may move for summary judgment on the ground that there is no evidence of one or more essential elements of a claim or defense on which an adverse party would have the burden of proof at trial. The motion must state the elements as to which there is no

> evidence. The court must grant the motion unless the respondent produces summary judgment evidence raising a genuine issue of material fact.

TEX.R. CIV. P. 166a(i). We have further explained that "[t]he motion must be specific in challenging the evidentiary support for an element of a claim or defense; paragraph (i) does not authorize conclusory motions or general no-evidence challenges to an opponent's case." *Id.* at Comment-1997.

The underlying purpose of this requirement "is to provide the opposing party with adequate information for opposing the motion, and to define the issues for the purpose of summary judgment." We have analogized this purpose to that of the "fair notice" pleading requirements of Rules 45(b) and 47(a). *See* TEX.R. CIV. P. 45(b) (requiring a party's pleadings to give "fair notice" to the opponent); TEX.R. CIV. P .47(a) (requiring a plaintiff's pleadings to give "fair notice of the claim involved").

After setting forth the elements of a design defect claim, Timpte's motion stated that "[p]laintiff has presented no evidence of a design defect which was a producing cause of his personal injury." In a subsequent paragraph labeled "Conclusion" Timpte restated: "There is no evidence of the product being defective or unreasonably dangerous, and there is no evidence the trailer was the proximate or producing cause of the Plaintiff's injuries." The motion thus unambiguously set out the elements of Gish's design defect claim and Timpte's belief that there was no evidence that its trailer was either unreasonably dangerous or the producing cause of Gish's injury. Although such a motion may be insufficient to give fair notice in a case involving a complex product or raising complicated issues of design defect, here the complaint was simple and straightforward; the record reveals no confusion of Gish's claim or Timpte's assertions of no evidence. Gish responded thoroughly as to both elements, indicating his understanding of Timpte's motion.

We conclude that Timpte's motion gave fair notice to Gish that it was challenging both whether the alleged defect rendered the trailer unreasonably dangerous and whether the defect was the producing cause of Gish's injury. Timpte's motion was not the type of "conclusory motion or general no-evidence challenge to an opponent's case" barred by Rule 166a(i). The issues of design defect and producing cause were clearly raised in Timpte's motion and joined in Gish's response.

FORT BROWN VILLAS III CONDOMINIUM ASSOC.
v.
GILLENWATER

285 S.W.3d 879
(Tex. 2009)

PER CURIAM

* * *

Under Rule 193.6, discovery that is not timely disclosed and witnesses that are not timely identified are inadmissible as evidence. TEX.R. CIV. P. 193.6(a). A party who fails to timely designate an expert has the burden of establishing good cause or a lack of unfair surprise or prejudice before the trial court may admit the evidence. TEX.R. CIV. P. 193.6(b). "A trial court's exclusion of an expert who has not been properly designated can be overturned only upon a finding of abuse of discretion." Before the no-evidence motion for summary judgment was introduced to Texas trial practice, courts did not apply evidentiary sanctions and exclusions for failure to timely designate an expert witness in a summary judgment proceeding. However, in 1997, the no-evidence summary judgment motion was introduced to the Texas Rules of Civil Procedure as Rule 166a(i), and in 1999, pretrial discovery rules were amended to include evidentiary exclusions under Rule 193.6. *Id.* at § 193.6. Since that time, most courts of appeals have applied Rule 193.6 to summary judgment proceedings. Because we have already held that evidentiary rules apply equally in trial and summary judgment proceedings, we also hold that the evidentiary exclusion under Rule 193.6 applies equally.

Our conclusion is based on the changes made to the pretrial discovery rules and the introduction of the no-evidence motion for summary judgment. The former pretrial discovery rules established a fluid deadline for discovery disclosure, which could be modified based on a change in the date of trial. Thus, it was possible that an exclusionary rule based on an untimely disclosure used at the summary judgment stage could exclude evidence that would later be admissible at trial. However, the new discovery rules establish a date certain for the completion of discovery, which depends on the discovery plan level and not on the trial date. *See* TEX.R. CIV. P. 190.2-.4 (providing specific time periods for the end of discovery, depending on the discovery plan level). Under the new rules, there is no longer a concern that discovery will be incomplete at the summary judgment stage. In fact, the no-evidence rule, by its very language, is to be used following discovery. TEX.R. CIV. P. 166a(i) ("*After adequate time for discovery,* a party without presenting summary judgment evidence may move for summary judgment on the ground that there is no evidence . . . .") (emphasis added). Combined with the no-evidence motion for summary judgment rule, the "hard deadline" established by the pretrial discovery rules ensures that the evidence presented at the summary judgment stage and at the trial stage remains the same. *See id.;* TEX.R. CIV. P. 190.3. Accordingly, the 193.6 exclusionary rule applies equally to both proceedings.

Here, Gillenwater did not timely disclose his expert pursuant to the deadline provided for in the agreed scheduling order and subsequent extension agreements. The trial court struck the expert's affidavit and did not consider it in granting the summary judgment. Because Rule 193.6 provides for the exclusion of an untimely expert affidavit, we hold that the trial court did not abuse its discretion in striking it. We also hold that Gillenwater failed to satisfy his burden of establishing good cause or a lack of unfair surprise or prejudice against Fort Brown. *See* TEX.R. CIV. P. 193.6(b). Gillenwater did not designate its expert until three days before the end of discovery and more than five months after the expert designation deadline.

Having held that the expert's affidavit was properly excluded, we must review the remaining evidence to determine whether the trial court appropriately granted Fort Brown's motion for summary judgment.

* * *

Notes & Questions

1. *Specificity of no evidence motion for summary judgment.* The movant need not present any evidence to support a no evidence motion for summary judgment. But Rule 166a(i) requires the movant to state the elements as to which there is no evidence. The comment to the rule further explains that the motion must be "specific in challenging the evidentiary support for an element of

a claim or defense." A "conclusory motion" or "general no-evidence challenge" is improper. Why does the rule have a specificity requirement?

2. *Response to no evidence motion.* As we have seen, the party responding to a no evidence motion must produce summary judgment evidence raising a genuine issue of material fact. Thus, once the motion is filed, the burden shifts to the respondent to produce more than a scintilla of evidence on the matter at issue. Thus, while the no evidence motion may be short, the response may be voluminous. However, the comment to the rule says that the respondent need not "marshal its proof," which courts have defined as "arranging all of the evidence in the order that it will be presented at trial."[1] Respondents should carefully point out the summary judgment evidence that creates a fact issue on each challenged element. One court of appeals found that a plaintiff's response was inadequate because "the assertion was general in nature and did not relate to the specific challenged elements. We are not required to search the record without guidance from appellant to determine whether it has produced evidence raising a genuine issue of material fact on the elements challenged. . . ."[2] However, in this case, the Supreme Court found the response to meet the minimum requirements of Rule 166a(i), although the question was "close."[3]

3. *Summary judgment evidence—the difference between federal and state practice.*[4] One of the most important distinctions between no evidence summary judgment practice in Texas state court and in federal court involves the type of evidence the respondent must present. In federal court, the respondent need not produce evidence in admissible form.[5] Under the Texas rule, however, the evidence must be in admissible form.[6] Thus, in this respect, the burden under the Texas rule exceeds that of the federal rule. As a result, a plaintiff anticipating a no evidence motion for summary judgment may need to undertake discovery to develop all necessary evidence in admissible form. Otherwise, for example, unauthenticated documents that might be needed to defeat summary judgment—and that would be provable at trial through live testimony—might be unusable.[7]

4. *Partial summary judgments.* A summary judgment that disposes of all claims and all parties in a case is a final and appealable order.[8] However, not all summary judgments dispose of all claims and all parties, as partial summary judgments are used frequently to dispose of some claims or some parties. These partial summary judgments are not final and cannot be appealed—the court

---

1 *In re* Mohawk Rubber, 982 S.W.2d 494, 498 (Tex. App.—Texarkana 1998, no pet.); Saienz v. Southern Union Gas Co., 999 S.W.2d 490, 493-94 (Tex. App.—El Paso 1999, pet. denied).

2 Brewer & Pritchard, P.C. v. Johnson, 7 S.W.3d 862, 868 (Tex. App.—Houston [1st Dist.] 1999), *aff'd on other grounds*, 73 S.W.3d 193 (Tex. 2002).

3 Johnson v. Brewer & Pritchard, 73 S.W.3d 193, 207-08 (Tex. 2002).

4 *See generally* Albright, Herring & Pemberton, HANDBOOK ON TEXAS DISCOVERY PRACTICE, § 20.7 (2008) (discussing evidentiary burdens).

5 Celotex Corp. v. Catrett, 477 U.S. 317, 324 (1986).

6 *Cf.* United Blood Servs. v. Longoria, 938 S.W.2d 29, 30 (Tex. 1997) (holding that the same evidentiary standards apply to summary judgment evidence as to evidence presented at trial). In fact, when it adopted Rule 166a(i), the Texas Supreme Court rejected a proposal that would have allowed the respondent to produce evidence in the form of a "discovery product or other material that can be reduced to summary judgment evidence."

7 Rule 193.7, which provides for self-authentication of documents produced in discovery by other parties, may remedy this problem in some cases.

8 *See* Lehmann v. Har-Con Corp., 39 S.W.3d 191 (Tex. 2001).

of appeals only has jurisdiction over "final" judgments. The issues related to finality and partial summary judgments is complicated[9] and will be considered at length in the chapter on judgments.

5. *Late response.* Rule 166a(c) provides that, except on leave of court, any response must be filed "not later than seven days prior to the day of hearing." Rule 5 allows courts to extend time periods upon a showing of "good cause." The Texas Supreme Court has held that "leave to file a late summary-judgment response should be granted when a litigant establishes good cause for failing to timely respond by showing that (1) the failure to respond was not intentional or the result of conscious indifference, but the result of accident or mistake, and (2) allowing the late response will occasion no undue delay or otherwise injure the party seeking summary judgment."[10] In that case, the Court held that the trial court did not abuse its discretion in refusing to allow the defendant to file a late response because it offered no explanation for the failure, but simply alleged that it would suffer prejudice if late filing was not permitted. Later arguments presented at a hearing on the motion for new trial indicated that the failure to timely respond was due to a calendaring error. Nevertheless, the Supreme Court refused to find an abuse of discretion.[11]

6. *No grounds stated in order*. As we saw in *Progressive v. Kelly*, a trial judge often will sign an order that simply says, "The motion for summary judgment is granted." In that situation, the order will be upheld on appeal if any theories in the motion will support summary judgment. For example, in one case the Supreme Court reasoned:[12]

> A fraud cause of action requires: (1) a material misrepresentation, (2) that was either known to be false when made or was asserted without knowledge of its truth, (3) which was intended to be acted upon, (4) which was relied upon, and (5) which caused injury. The trial court rendered summary judgment on the fraud claim without specifying the grounds. Because Dow and Hegyesi filed a no-evidence summary-judgment motion challenging each of these elements, if Francis failed to raise a "genuine issue of material fact" about any of these elements, the summary judgment for Dow and Hegyesi should stand. TEX. R. CIV. P. 166a(i). Here, the court of appeals reversed the summary judgment after determining that Francis raised a fact issue concerning a material misrepresentation, but failed to consider Dow and Hegyesi's alternative ground for summary judgment—that Francis presented no evidence of damages. "When a trial court's order granting summary judgment does not specify the ground or grounds relied on for its ruling, summary judgment will be affirmed on appeal if any of the theories advanced are meritorious." We therefore conclude that the court of appeals erred in not considering this alternative ground.

However, the appellant must raise all grounds for reversal in the appeal. "When a party fails to attack one of the grounds alleged in the motion for summary judgment, he or she waives the error and summary judgment must be affirmed."[13]

7. *Adequate time for discovery.* Rule 166a(i) promises that a no-evidence motion for summary judgment will not be granted without giving the plaintiff an adequate time for discovery to find

---

9 *Id.*

10 Carpenter v. Cimarron Hydrocarbons Corp., 98 S.W.3d 682 689 (Tex. 2002).

11 *Id.*

12 Dow Chemical Co. v. Francis, 46 S.W.3d 237, 242 (Tex. 2001).

13 Strather v. Dolgencorp of Texas, Inc., 96 S.W.3d 420, 426 (Tex. App.—Texarkana 2002, no pet.).

evidence proving up the claims. How does a court determine whether the time is adequate or not? One court of appeals has described it as follows:[14]

> Whether a nonmovant has had an adequate time for discovery for purposes of Rule 166a(i) is "case specific." Although some lawsuits that present only questions of law may require no or minimal discovery, other actions may require extensive discovery. An adequate time for discovery is determined by the nature of the cause of action, the nature of the evidence necessary to controvert the no-evidence motion, and the length of time the case has been active in the trial court. A court may also look to factors such as the amount of time the no-evidence motion has been on file and the amount of discovery that has already taken place. Furthermore, a party should not be able to abuse the discovery process, withhold key evidence from its opponents, and then use that lack of evidence to win a judgment.

In that case, the court found that the plaintiff did not have an adequate opportunity for discovery because the defendant resisted all attempts at discovery before filing the motion for summary judgment. In another case, the court of appeals applied the same factors and held that the trial court did not abuse its discretion in denying the motion for continuance of the summary judgment hearing because the case had been pending for three years, during which the plaintiff did not diligently pursue discovery.[15]

As *Fort Brown Villas* notes, Rule 166a(i) does not define "adequate time," but the comment to the rule explains that a "discovery period set by pretrial order should be adequate opportunity for discovery unless there is a showing to the contrary, and ordinarily a motion . . . would be permitted after the period but not before." However, it is not always an abuse of discretion to grant summary judgment before the discovery period closes.[16] When the facts are uncontested, or when the additional discovery sought is immaterial, the trial court can rule on the no-evidence summary judgment without allowing additional time for further discovery.[17]

8. *Combining traditional and no-evidence motions*. One can combine a traditional motion with a no evidence motion for summary judgment. Nevertheless, the Supreme Court cautions that there can be some confusion when parties combine traditional and no-evidence motions for summary judgment:[18]

> Texas Rule of Civil Procedure 166a does not prohibit a party from combining in a single motion a request for summary judgment that utilizes the procedures under either subsection (a) or (b), with a request for summary judgment that utilizes subsection (i) and

---

14 TemPay, Inc. v. TNT Concrete & Constr., Inc., 37 S.W.3d 517 (Tex. App.—Austin 2001, pet. denied).

15 Kelly v. Gaines, 181 S.W.3d 394 (Tex. App.—Waco 2005), rev'd on other grounds, 235 S.W.3d 179 (Tex. 2007).

16 *See* Branum v. Northwest Texas Healthcare System, 134 S.W.3d 340 (Tex. App.—Amarillo 2003, pet. denied) (holding that the decision is case-specific, and not a bright-line rule controlled by the expiration of the discovery period); Howard v. East Texas Baptist Univ., 122 S.W.3d 407 (Tex. App.—Texarkana 2003, no pet.) (holding affidavit seeking additional time for discovery before discovery period expired failed to show diligence, so no abuse of discretion in denying motion).

17 Daystar Residential, Inc. v. Collmer, 176 S.W.3d 24 (Tex. App.—Houston [1st Dist.] 2004, no pet.); Clawson v. Wharton County, 941 S.W.2d 267 (Tex. App.—Corpus Christi 1996, writ denied); *see also* CPRC § 41.0115(e) (creating presumption of adequate time for exemplary damages discovery when party seeks net worth information from exemplary damages defendant) (discussed in Chapter 7, Scope of Discovery).

18 Binur v. Jacobo, 135 S.W.3d, 646, 650-51 (Tex. 2004).

asserts that there is "no evidence of one or more essential elements of a claim or defense." The fact that evidence may be attached to a motion that proceeds under subsection (a) or (b) does not foreclose a party from also asserting that there is no evidence with regard to a particular element. Similarly, if a motion brought solely under subsection (i) attaches evidence, that evidence should not be considered unless it creates a fact question, but such a motion should not be disregarded or treated as a motion under subsection (a) or (b). We disapprove of decisions that hold or imply that, if a party attaches evidence to a motion for summary judgment, any request for summary judgment under Rule 166a(i) will be disregarded.

Some Texas courts have declared that when a party seeks summary judgment under subsection (a) or (b), and also under subsection (i), the better practice is to file two separate motions, or at least to include headings that clearly delineate and segregate the part of a motion relying on subsection (a) or (b) from the part that relies on subsection (i). We agree that using headings to clearly delineate the basis for summary judgment under subsection (a) or (b) from the basis for summary judgment under subsection (i) would be helpful to the bench and bar, but the rule does not require it. If a motion clearly sets forth its grounds and otherwise meets Rule 166a's requirements, it is sufficient. Here, Binur's motion for summary judgment asserted that there was no evidence of proximate cause. The court of appeals erred in concluding that this ground could be disregarded because evidence was attached to the motion.

CHAPTER 12. SETTINGS & TRIAL

A. Pretrial Conference

Read Rule 166.

Notes & Questions

1. *Practical difficulty*. In practice, the standing order that counsel meet and agree and submit joint reports or proposed pretrial orders can become a nightmare. What if your opponent will not return your calls? Will not agree to a meeting date? A desperate but sometimes effective solution is for counsel to document and outline failed attempts to set a meeting and file a unilaterally prepared proposed order.

2. *Notice*. In *Koslow's v. Mackie*,[1] the Supreme Court affirmed a dismissal for failure to file a joint status report according to the judge's order because defendants had notice that their failure to appear at the pretrial hearing might subject them to sanctions. In cases after *Koslow's*, dismissals or default judgments rendered for failure to appear have been reversed because the party had no notice that the case could be disposed of in the pretrial hearing.[2] Thus, a default judgment or dismissal rendered for failure to appear at the hearing will be valid only if the order setting the hearing states that parties may be subject to sanctions for failure to appear, or if the motions set to be heard at the hearing include a motion for dismissal or default or motion for sanctions. Also, today the death penalty sanction of dismissal or default will be judged under the standards of *TransAmerican v. Powell*.[3]

3. *Pretrial orders and discovery*. Rule 166(c) allows trial courts to order a discovery schedule as part of a pretrial order. However, it is important to remember that Rule 190 also imposes a discovery schedule in all cases, and Rule 190.4 allows the court to impose a discovery control plan by order that includes many items that are normally part of a pretrial order (e.g. trial date, deadlines for joining parties and amending pleadings). Together, Rules 166 and 190 give the trial judges substantial discretion in controlling discovery schedules and limiting discovery in civil cases.

4. *Amendment surprise*. Rule 63, unlike the Federal Rules, makes amendment to pleadings a matter of right within seven days of the trial date, if filed at a time not to operate as a surprise. The court's response to surprise is often the offer of a delayed trial, usually an unsatisfactory alternative for plaintiffs. Does Rule 166 offer help in this respect? Note that rule 166(b) allows the court to determine what amendments to pleadings will be allowed and the deadlines for filing them.

5. *Texas use of pretrial conference.* Compared to their federal counterparts, Texas courts traditionally have made little use of the pretrial conference. But in complex cases, they are an important tool to keep the case from stalling in the trial court.

---

[1] 796 S.W.2d 700 (Tex. 1990).

[2] *See* Murphree v. Ziegelmair, 937 S.W.2d 493 (Tex. App.—Houston [1st Dist.] 1995, no writ); Masterson v. Cox, 886 S.W.2d 436, 439 (Tex. App.—Houston [1st Dist.] 1994, no writ).

[3] 811 S.W.2d 913 (Tex. 1991).

B. The Jury Demand

Read Rules 216-220, Gov't Code § 51.604.

HALSELL
v.
DEHOYOS
810 S.W.2d 371
(Tex. 1991)

PER CURIAM.

In this cause, we consider whether the continuance of a trial setting affects the timeliness of a jury request. The court of appeals held that it does not, and therefore upheld the trial court's denial of Petitioner's jury request. We disagree, and therefore reverse.

Esther and George Dehoyos brought this suit against Jim B. Halsell for wrongful eviction and conversion. On the Dehoyoses' motion, the trial court set the case on the non-jury docket for final trial on the merits on September 8, 1989. Halsell filed a jury request, and paid the proper fee, on August 15, 1989.

The trial court called the case as scheduled on September 8, 1989. Thereafter, by order of September 14, 1989, the court struck Halsell's request for a jury trial on the ground that it was not timely filed. By the same order, however, the court also reset the case on the non-jury docket for final trial on the merits on October 13, 1989.

Under our rules, a request for a jury trial must be filed "a reasonable time before the date set for trial of the cause on the non-jury docket, but not less than thirty days in advance." TEX. R. CIV. P. 216. A request in advance of the thirty-day deadline is presumed to have been made a reasonable time before trial. The adverse party may rebut that presumption by showing that the granting of a jury trial would operate to injure the adverse party, disrupt the court's docket, or impede the ordinary handling of the court's business.

At the time the trial court struck Halsell's request for a jury trial, the request was timely as to the October 13, 1989, trial setting. The record contains no indication that the granting of the jury trial would have injured the Dehoyoses or caused undue disruption to the trial court. Thus, the untimely jury demand became timely when the trial court reset the case for October 13. The trial court therefore erred in denying Halsell's request for a jury trial.

A refusal to grant a jury trial is harmless error only if the record shows that no material issues of fact exist and an instructed verdict would have been justified. Here, the record reflects the existence of several material fact issues: chiefly, whether the Dehoyoses abandoned their apartment, and the extent of the Dehoyoses' damages.

We conclude that the trial court's refusal to grant a jury trial amounted to harmful error. We therefore grant Petitioner's application for writ of error and pursuant to Texas Rule of Appellate Procedure 170, without hearing oral argument, a majority of the court reverses the judgment of the court of appeals and remands this cause to the trial court for a jury trial.

CORNYN, JUSTICE, not sitting.

Notes & Questions

1. *Broad right to jury trial.* For a historical analysis of the constitutional basis for the right to a jury trial, read *Texas v. Credit Bureau of Laredo, Inc.*[1] The Texas Constitution contains two provisions regarding the right to a jury trial: the first in the Bill of Rights (Article I, Section 15) and the second in the Judiciary Article (Article V, Section 10). The Judiciary Article provision extends the right to a jury to "trial of all causes." Thus, the right to a jury in Texas is extremely broad, covering suits in equity as well as law. Only certain proceedings, where there is "some special reason that a jury has been held unsuitable," do not carry the right to a jury trial. These include civil contempt proceedings, election contests, habeas corpus proceedings for the custody of minor children, suit for removal of a sheriff, and appeals in administrative proceedings.[2]

2. *Advisory juries.* When a jury is advisory only, as in certain family law cases, the trial court's refusal to empanel a jury is not reversible error.[3]

3. *Jury fee and jury demand.* Rule 216 requires a jury demand within 30 days of trial, and payment of the fee at the same time "unless otherwise provided by law." Section 51.604 of the Government Code has a different and higher fee than the rule, and specifically says that this amount includes the amount set out in Rule 216. Thus, the statutory fee applies. The statute also says that the fee needs to be paid 10 days before trial.

4. *Waiver.* The failure to timely pay the fee and make the demand waives the right to jury trial.[4] The failure to appear at trial also waives the right to a jury even though the fee has been paid and the demand made.[5] A party's waiver of a jury in the first trial does not prevent it from timely demanding a jury if the case is remanded for a second trial.[6]

5. *Jury fee benefits.* Rule 220 provides that a party who has paid the jury fee (and thus placed the case on the jury docket) cannot take the case off the jury docket over the objection of other parties ("partics adversly interested"). Thus, Plaintiff's jury demand and fee protects the right of all parties to a jury trial.

6. *Practical note.* Most local rules and practices allow the jury fee to be paid at the time plaintiff's first pleading (usually Plaintiff's Original Petition) is filed. A common practice is to make the jury demand the last paragraph in the first pleading filed and to pay all required fees—including the jury fee—at the time of filing, forestalling the possibility that these actions will be overlooked later.

7. *Contractual jury waivers.* With increasing frequency, businesses seem not to trust the fairness of the judicial system. Some of them insist that those they do business with agree in advance that any disputes will be decided by arbitration. Others insist on contractual provisions that give up the right to a jury trial and provide that any disputes that go to court will be tried without a ju-

---

[1] 530 S.W.2d 288 (Tex. 1975).

[2] *Id.*

[3] Lenz v. Lenz, 79 S.W.3d 10 (Tex. 2002); Martin v. Martin, 776 S.W.2d 572, 575 (Tex. 1989). *See* Family Code § 105.002(c) and (d).

[4] *See* Halsell, 810 S.W.2d 371, above.

[5] *See* Chandler v. Chandler, 536 S.W.2d 260, 262 (Tex. Civ. App.—Corpus Christi 1976, writ dism.).

[6] *See* Harding v. Harding, 485 S.W.2d 297, 299 (Tex. Civ. App.—San Antonio 1972, no writ).

ry. The Texas Supreme Court has upheld such agreements, rejecting the argument that the agreement violated constitutional guarantees.[7] The court added:

> [I]f parties are willing to agree to a non-jury trial we think it preferable to enforce that agreement rather than leave them with arbitration as their only enforceable option. By agreeing to arbitration, parties waive not only their right to trial by jury, but their right to appeal, whereas by agreeing to waive only the former right, they take advantage of the reduced expense and delay of a bench trial, avoid the expense of arbitration, and retain their rights to appeal. The parties obtain dispute resolution of their own choosing in a manner already afforded to litigants in their courts. Their rights, and the orderly development of the law, are further protected by appeal. And even if the option appeals only to a few, some of the tide away from the civil justice system to alternate dispute resolution is stemmed.[8]

GENERAL MOTORS CORP.
v.
GAYLE

951 S.W.2d 469
(Tex. 1997)

PHILLIPS, CHIEF JUSTICE.

In this original mandamus proceeding, we must first decide whether the trial court abused its discretion by compelling relator to designate in advance whether its crash testing was to be used for evidentiary purposes or solely for consulting purposes, and by ordering that the opposing party be allowed to attend those tests designated as evidentiary. Because we conclude that the trial court's order invades the consulting-expert privilege, and that relator lacks an adequate remedy by appeal, we conditionally grant mandamus relief compelling the trial court to vacate its crash-test order. We must also determine whether the trial court abused its discretion by denying a continuance which would have rendered relator's jury fee timely. Because we conclude that the trial court also abused its discretion in this regard, we conditionally grant mandamus relief compelling the trial court to place this case on its jury docket.

I.

Manuel Delarosa was severely injured in 1988 when his General Motors pickup truck struck another car driven by Christopher Broussard. Delarosa's wife, a passenger in the pickup, suffered relatively minor injuries.

The Delarosas sued Broussard and General Motors in September 1990 alleging, among other things, that General Motors defectively designed the seat belts in Delarosa's pickup truck. In September 1995, after several continued trial settings, the trial court set the case for trial on Janu-

---

7 *In re* Prudential Ins. Co., 148 S.W.3d 124 (Tex. 2004). *See also* In re Frank Motor Co., 361 S.W.3d 628 (Tex. 2012) (holding that threat to terminate at will employee did not invalidate jury waiver); In re General Electric Capital Corp., 203 S.W.3d 314 (Tex. 2006) (finding that GE did not waive contractual right to non-jury trial by not objecting to first two jury trial settings).

8 *Id.*

ary 3, 1996, on the court's "try or dismiss" docket. The notice sent to the parties did not specify whether the January 3 trial was to be to a jury or to the court.

When General Motors appeared on January 3, 1996, it discovered for the first time that no party had ever paid a jury fee, so that the case was on the nonjury docket. At the docket call, the court informed the parties that it intended to try the case without a jury beginning two days later. General Motors immediately paid the jury fee and then filed an "Objection to Placement of Case on Non-Jury Docket." Although General Motors had not paid the jury fee thirty days in advance of trial as required by Texas Rule of Civil Procedure 216(a), it argued that it had been led to believe that either the Delarosas or Broussard had paid a jury fee and that the case was on the jury docket. General Motors relied on the following circumstances: 1) the parties and the court had earlier discussed the logistics of trying the case to a jury; 2) Broussard, in his original answer, asked that all matters "be properly decided by this Honorable Court and Jury;" 3) the case had been preferentially set for July 12, 1993, which according to the trial court's schedule was a civil jury week; and 4) an October 1992 letter from the Delarosas' attorney to the trial court referred to the "issues to be presented to the Court and jury." Even the trial judge, in considering General Motors' arguments, stated that he "didn't realize this was a nonjury case until right before the nonjury docket."

General Motors also moved to continue the January 5 trial, arguing that the case was not ready because of pending discovery issues. At that time, both the Delarosas and General Motors had discovery matters pending before the court. In particular, General Motors argued that it had not conducted critical "crash tests" because the trial court had not yet ruled on the Delarosas' motion to attend those tests. Finally, General Motors argued that a continuance was necessary to allow its jury fee to become timely, thereby preserving its right to a jury trial. Despite their own outstanding document discovery requests, the Delarosas opposed the continuance, announcing that they were ready to proceed to trial before the court.

The trial court overruled General Motors' objection to nonjury trial and its motion for continuance at a January 5 pretrial conference. Recognizing that "this case still has some discovery that needs to be done . . . ," however, the trial court decided only to hear opening statements that day weeks before hearing testimony. The court scheduled hearings during the interim period on both sides' outstanding discovery matters, recognizing that the crash tests would have to be performed at some future date after trial recommenced. Finally, the court informed the parties that they could expect a piecemeal trial, interlaced with the completion of discovery:

> I will tell all sides also that I don't intend necessarily to commit to try this case on a continuous day-by-day basis. I may recess it for two or three weeks, hear a couple of days of testimony, and come back in a week or so. It may be that certain experts, if I allow late designations, may need to be deposed. You will have this trial finished before the spring is over and we will wrap this thing up one way or another as far as trial goes.

After hearing opening statements, the court recessed the trial in accordance with its announced plan.

The parties resolved their dispute over the Delarosas' document requests at a court hearing on January 9. After another discovery hearing the next day, the trial court granted the Delarosas' motion to attend General Motors' crash tests, subject to certain conditions.

* * *

General Motors sought mandamus relief in the court of appeals on January 23, 1996, challenging the crash-test order and the trial court's denial of a jury trial. After initially staying the trial court proceedings, the court of appeals denied relief in June 1996, with one justice dissenting.

* * *

III

We next consider whether the trial court abused its discretion in denying General Motors' request for a jury trial. Rule 216 provides:

> No jury trial shall be had in any civil suit, unless a written request for a jury trial is filed with the clerk of the court a reasonable time before the date set for trial of the cause on the non-jury docket, but not less than thirty days in advance.

TEX. R. CIV. P. 216(a). General Motors filed a written request for a jury trial and tendered the $30.00 fee on January 3, 1996, the date the case was set for trial. General Motors also moved to continue the trial to allow its jury request to become timely. As noted, the trial court denied the motion for continuance, calling the case for nonjury trial on January 5.

"The granting or denial of a motion for continuance is within the trial court's sound discretion." General Motors argues that the trial court abused its discretion by not granting a continuance for at least thirty days, which would have rendered General Motors' jury request and payment timely. Under the unique facts of this case, we agree.

The right to jury trial is one of our most precious rights, holding "a sacred place in English and American history." Even where a party does not timely pay the jury fee, courts have held that a trial court should accord the right to jury trial if it can be done without interfering with the court's docket, delaying the trial, or injuring the opposing party.

Even as the trial court was denying General Motors' motion for continuance, it conceded that the case was not ready for trial. Because of the outstanding discovery issues, including resolution of plaintiffs' motion to attend the crash tests, the trial court decided to hear no evidence until January 29, twenty-six days after General Motors paid its jury fee. Even then, the court acknowledged that outstanding discovery issues would probably cause further multiple interruptions to the proceedings. At a discovery hearing on January 10, the court again confirmed that trial would be delayed by ongoing discovery:

> I'm going to start this case on the 29th. I'm probably going to hear from two or three or four witnesses, primarily your lay witnesses. I may even hear from your experts. I don't know, but at some point I'm going to shut this thing down for a while to let you guys finish whatever the discovery is that's still outstanding. That may be the crash tests. I don't have a problem with that.

We recognize that occasionally the exigencies of a crowded docket will require a judge to interrupt a bench trial, or even conduct it in segments. But here the trial judge commenced the nonjury trial in the teeth of a demand for a jury trial, timing the proceedings to avoid the requirements of Rule 216(a), with no expectation of reaching the heart of the case for some weeks or months. In light of such preordained delays, the Delarosas could not show that a thirty-day continuance to perfect General Motors' jury trial demand would cause them any injury or delay. In fact, the trial court's seriatim trial schedule seems only a sham to hold General Motors to its mistake in not paying the jury fee without penalizing the other side. Under these particular and unusual circumstances, we hold that the trial court abused its discretion by not granting a continuance to allow General Motors' jury request and fee to become timely.

Because the denial of a jury trial can be reviewed by ordinary appeal, mandamus is generally not available to review such a ruling. Similarly, the denial of a motion for continuance is an incidental trial ruling ordinarily not reviewable by mandamus. In the absence of any other error, we would not grant extraordinary relief merely to revise a trial judge's scheduling order, however perverse. This case, however, presents special circumstances, in that we must remedy the crash-test order by interlocutory mandamus review. Under these special circumstances, the interests of judicial economy dictate that we should also remedy the trial court's denial of the right of jury trial by mandamus.

* * *

For the foregoing reasons, we conditionally grant writ of mandamus compelling the trial court to vacate its January 22, 1996, crash-test order. We further direct the trial court to abort or mistry the nonjury trial commenced in January 1996, and to place the case on its jury docket in accordance with General Motors' written request and payment of jury fee, which are now timely. We are confident that Judge Gayle will act in accordance with this opinion, and the writ of mandamus will issue only if he fails to do so.

Judge Chides Chief Justice for Comment in Case*

Two years after the above opinion was issued, and the case had settled, Judge Gayle wrote a letter to Chief Justice Phillips responding to the Court's criticism of how he handled the case. Seldom does one see the trial judge's perspective on matters such as these. Here are some excerpts from the letter:

> This case was over five years old, and I got tired of all the excuses for not going to trial, so I set it (and not for the first time) on my try-or-dismiss docket in January 1996. This is not a sham docket, and every lawyer in this area that comes into my court knows it. Both sides received notice of the January trial setting at least four months in advance. In addition, when this case was given a preferential setting in August 1993 (which was later canceled because the lawyers were not ready), both the plaintiff's and defendant's attorneys were told in my chambers that a jury fee had not been paid.
>
> At the time of trial two-and-one-half years later, General Motors had still not paid the required jury fee under the provisions of Rule 216b, a rule which was promulgated by your court. It was not just untimely paid, it was not paid period when the case was called for trial on Wednesday morning. The trial court did not mislead them, nor did the clerk. The General Motors trial counsel, who had appeared before me numerous times, did not appear for trial, but sent word through a local attorney that the case was not ready, and he had to be "elsewhere." No one knew what "elsewhere" meant.
>
> The plaintiffs were there, as was their attorney who announced ready for trial. I could have started the trial on that day, but instead recessed the case until the following Friday

---

* TEXAS LAWYER, August 16, 1999. Reprinted by permission of TEXAS LAWYER. © 1999, TEXAS LAWYER. All rights reserved.

(two days later) to allow General Motors' attorney time to prepare for trial. I advised the plaintiff's attorney and General Motors' local counsel that I would only hear opening statements on Friday, and would not start evidence until sometime thereafter. On Friday, General Motors' lawyer (who had by now finally paid the required jury fee) requested a continuance, which I denied. However, I recessed the commencement of evidence until Jan. 29, 1996, to allow General Motors some leeway to prepare its case, designate late certain experts and to set up their crash-tests, since General Motors (at least according to their lawyer) was unprepared for trial—in short, to give General Motors a break to complete their discovery with a subsequent staggered trial schedule to allow the case to be fully developed and tried.

I did not write Rule 216. You did. I did not put the 30-day jury fee requirement in it. You did (and if you will check your history, you changed it from 10 days to 30 days several years ago). Had I granted a jury trial, it would have been a clear violation of Rule 216 and subject to mandamus by the plaintiffs. Had I granted General Motors a 30-day continuance, I would have been justifying their actions in not following Rule 216b. In short, there were no "special circumstances" as you stated on page 16 of the opinion to justify General Motors' failure to follow the law.

C. Settings

Read Rules 245-249 and 3(a).

Rule 245 gives the court power to set a case for trial upon the request of a party or on its own. Rule 245 requires all courts to give parties at least 45 days notice of the first trial setting, but only "reasonable" notice thereafter. Settings can differ greatly from one county to another—in one county a setting may mean that the case can be called anytime during the week, while in another county it may mean that it can be called anytime during the month. And when a case is set for trial, the setting does not mean that the case will be tried. Courts typically set many cases for trial for a particular setting because many of the cases on the docket will be taken off due to settlement or continuance. The practice relating to trial settings varies greatly from county to county, and it is imperative that counsel become familiar with the local rules.

LOPEZ
v.
LOPEZ
757 S.W.2d 721
(Tex. 1988)

PER CURIAM.

The issue of concern in this appeal is whether a defendant, who is not notified of a trial setting and consequently does not appear, must nevertheless set up a meritorious defense in order to obtain a new trial. * * * Because Guadalupe Lopez, the defendant in the present case, did not do this, the court of appeals held that the trial court did not err in overruling his motion for new trial and affirmed the judgment of the trial court. * * *

The judgment in this case arises out of the final distribution of assets of an estate among certain remaining heirs. Some of these heirs, as plaintiffs, claimed that two other heirs, Jesus Lopez, Jr., and Guadalupe Lopez, had profited at the expense of the estate. These plaintiffs prayed that the remaining cash assets of the estate, held in the registry of the court, be distributed with due regard to the benefits previously enjoyed by Jesus and Guadalupe.

Jesus and Guadalupe were initially represented by the same attorney, who filed answers on their behalf. Approximately eighteen months prior to trial, this attorney was permitted to withdraw as Guadalupe's counsel, although he continued in the case as attorney for Jesus. Following the withdrawal of his attorney, Guadalupe was not served with documents generated by the attorneys representing the plaintiff heirs or Jesus. Further, there is nothing in the record to suggest that any attempt was made to notify Guadalupe of the trial setting. Guadalupe apparently did not obtain the services of a new attorney until after the trial.

Although conceding that Guadalupe had no notice of the trial setting, the court of appeals nevertheless held him to the standard set forth in *Craddock v. Sunshine Bus Lines, Inc.,* 134 Tex. 388, 393, 133 S.W.2d 124, 126 (1939):

> A default judgment should be set aside and a new trial ordered in any case in which the failure of the defendant to answer before judgment was not intentional, or the result of conscious indifference on his part, but was due to a mistake or an accident; provided the motion for new trial sets up a meritorious defense and is filed at a time when the granting thereof will occasion no delay or otherwise work an injury to the plaintiff.

Although in *Craddock* the default judgment was taken because the defendant failed to answer, the same requirements apply to a post-answer default judgment.

Applying the *Craddock* standards to the facts here, the court of appeals found that Guadalupe's failure to appear was not intentional or the result of conscious indifference, because he did not have notice of the trial setting. The court of appeals, however, concluded that Guadalupe's motion for new trial was properly overruled because he did not factually set up a meritorious defense in his motion or produce evidence of a defense at the hearing on the motion.

Because the record here establishes that Guadalupe had no actual or constructive notice of the trial setting, the lower courts erred in requiring him to show that he had a meritorious defense as a condition to granting his motion for new trial. The Supreme Court has recently held that such a requirement, in the absence of notice, violates due process rights under the Fourteenth Amendment to the federal constitution. *Peralta v. Heights Medical Center, Inc.,* 485 U.S. 80, 108 S.Ct. 896, 99 L.Ed.2d 75 (1988).

The decision of the court of appeals, as it pertains to Guadalupe Lopez, is in conflict with *Peralta v. Heights Medical Center, Inc.* Pursuant to TEX. R. APP. P. 133(b), we grant Guadalupe's application for writ of error and, without hearing oral argument, a majority of the court reverses the judgment of the court of appeals and remands the cause to the trial court for new trial.

* * *

***LBL Oil Company v. International Power Services, Inc.*, 777 S.W.3d 390 (Tex. 1989) (per curiam):**

> [The defendant alleges] among other matters that he had been denied due process by the failure to serve notice of the default motion and hearing on him. Once a defendant has made an appearance in a cause, he is entitled to notice of the trial setting as a matter of due process under the Fourteenth Amendment to the federal constitution, as set forth in *Peralta v. Heights Medical Center, Inc.*, 485 U.S. 80, 108 S.Ct. 896, 99 L.Ed.2d 75 (1988). *See Lopez v. Lopez*, 757 S.W.2d 721, 723 (Tex. 1988). The record here establishes that Lindley had no actual or constructive notice of the hearing on the motion for default judgment, which effectively was his trial setting since it was dispositive of the case. The decision of the court of appeals affirming the judgment is in conflict with *Peralta* and *Lopez*.

Notes & Questions

1. *Form of notice.* In *Mansfield State Bank v. Cohn,*[1] a letter by an adversary *requesting* a trial setting was held to be sufficient notice of the setting itself.

2. *Notice of trial.* Rule 245 requires a minimum of 45 days first notice of trial setting and a reasonable notice thereafter. Rule 246 requires the clerk to give notice of trial settings upon written request of a non-resident attorney who encloses a return envelope properly addressed and stamped. The failure of such notice is ground for continuance. At one time, various local rules required that parties certify to the completion of all discovery before requesting a trial setting. Note that Rule 245 makes such local rules inoperative. All that a party is required to do in order to obtain a setting is to represent that it reasonably and in good faith expects to be ready for trial by the requested date. It violates rule 245 and the Texas Constitution for the trial court to call a case for trial without notice and dispose of it before the time a party was notified to appear.[2]

3. *Special settings.* Government Code Sections 23.101 and 23.102 mandate priority settings for temporary injunctions, criminal cases, election contests and actions under the Texas Election Code, appeals from Industrial Accident Board decision (workers' compensation) and claims under the Federal Employees Liability Act and Jones Act. Other priorities are (1) matters in which delay will

---

1 573 S.W.2d 181 (Tex. 1978).

2 *See* Rogers v. Texas Commerce Bank-Reagan, 755 S.W.2d 83 (Tex. 1988)(after giving the parties an 11:00 nonjury trial setting, on the day of trial the court called the case and heard it at 9:30)

cause physical or economic harm to the parties or to the public; (2) matters involving constitutional rights; (3) issues of public concern or affecting public welfare. Local rules often provide for "special" or preferential settings of cases on various grounds—including complexity, a great number of expert or out-of-town witnesses, statutory priority, or the fact that the case is being re-tried on remand.

4. *Local rules.* In order to avoid unfairness resulting from idiosyncratic or unpublished local rules, the Texas Supreme Court adopted Rule 3(a), making the Texas Rules of Civil Procedure govern in case of conflicts with local rules and providing for Supreme Court approval of local rules. In instances of unfairness resulting from the operation of local rules or local docket management rules, it is well to remember the dominance of Rule 3(a). Of course, such rules must comport with the due process requirements of the Texas and United States Constitutions.

5. *Docket calls and settings.* Local rules often provide for the "call of the docket," in which the cases set for trial are called out and the attorneys are asked to announce "ready" or "not ready." The "not ready" announcement is often followed by a motion for continuance. Sometimes an attorney, having announced "ready," finds that circumstances require that the announcement be withdrawn. While courts routinely accept such withdrawals, it is within their discretion to refuse to do so.[3] Similarly, when a trial court dismisses an action for want of prosecution because the attorney fails to appear for a setting, the attorney's motion to reinstate (usually containing excuses for the failure) is within the trial court's discretion to grant or deny.[4]

6. *Post-answer and no-answer default judgments.* Notice that the trial courts in *Lopez* and *LBL Oil* had granted default judgments against parties who had filed answers. The Supreme Court made clear that parties who have answered and entered an appearance are entitled to notice of any trial settings. That is, a court may grant a *post-answer* default judgment against a defendant who fails to appear for trial only if the defendant has notice of the trial setting. But different rules apply to defendants who have been served and have not filed an answer. Courts may grant *no-answer* default judgments at any time after appearance day without giving a new notice to the defendant.

---

3 *See* South Texas Lumber Stores, Inc. v. Cain, 416 S.W.2d 530, 532 (Tex. Civ. App.—Austin 1967, no writ).

4 *See* Melton v. Ryander, 727 S.W.2d 299 (Tex. App.—Dallas 1987, writ ref'd n.r.e.).

D. Continuance

Read Rules 251-254.

1. *Continuances Generally*

FORMAN
v.
FINA OIL AND CHEMICAL CO.
858 S.W.2d 498
(Tex. App.—Eastland),
rev'd on other grounds, 858 S.W.2d 373 (Tex. 1993)

MCCLOUD, CHIEF JUSTICE.

Clarence Forman sued Fina Oil and Chemical Company alleging that, while working for a third-party salvage company at Fina's refinery, he received an electrical shock while he was working on a breaker box and that the shock was a result of Fina's negligence. The jury found that plaintiff did not receive an electrical shock while working at the refinery. Plaintiff appeals a take-nothing judgment. We affirm.

Plaintiff contends in his first point of error that the trial court erred in denying his first motion for continuance so that plaintiff could take the deposition of Dr. Charles R. Baxter.

Plaintiff filed this suit on April 24, 1990. On December 16, 1991, the trial court notified both parties that the case was set for trial for February 3, 1992. The court advised the parties to appear for docket call on January 13, 1992. On January 3, 1992, Fina supplemented its answers to interrogatories by designating Dr. Baxter as an additional expert. On January 6, 1992, Fina filed a motion for continuance to postpone the February 3, 1992, trial setting. In its motion, Fina urged that additional discovery was needed and that Fina's counsel had a prior conflicting setting in another court. Plaintiff opposed Fina's motion for continuance. On January 13, 1992, the trial court overruled Fina's motion for continuance, and plaintiff announced ready for trial.

By agreement of the parties, Dr. Baxter examined plaintiff on January 14, 1992. Counsel for both parties agreed that a report of Dr. Baxter's findings would be delivered to plaintiff on January 23, 1992. Fina, however, "undesignated" Dr. Baxter as an expert in a letter sent to plaintiff's counsel on January 21, 1992. Plaintiff obtained a report directly from Dr. Baxter on January 24, 1992.

Some of the information contained in Dr. Baxter's report was beneficial to plaintiff. Plaintiff filed a motion for continuance on January 28, 1992, in order to depose Dr. Baxter. The trial court overruled this motion on February 3, 1992, and the parties went to trial.

The granting or denial of a motion for continuance is within the trial court's sound discretion. The exercise of such discretion will not be disturbed on appeal unless the record discloses a clear abuse of discretion. A trial court may be reversed for abusing its discretion only when the court of appeals finds the court acted in an unreasonable or arbitrary manner. The test for abuse of discretion is whether the trial court acted without reference to any guiding rules or principles. The mere fact that a trial judge may decide a matter within his discretionary authority in a different manner than an appellate judge in a similar circumstance does not demonstrate that an abuse of discretion has occurred.

Plaintiff's motion for continuance was made on the ground of want of testimony. TEX. R. CIV. P. 252 states the requirements for requesting a continuance on the ground of want of testimony. Plaintiff's motion for continuance was in substantial compliance with Rule 252. However, mere compliance with Rule 252 does not guarantee that a continuance will be granted. The court in *Fritsch v. J.M. English Truck Line*, 151 Tex. 168, 246 S.W.2d 856, 858 (1952), stated: "There is nothing in the rules on continuance requiring the granting of a first motion [for continuance] merely because it is in statutory form."

TEX. R. CIV. P. 251 mandates that a continuance shall not be granted except for sufficient cause. The trial court has the duty of deciding whether or not sufficient cause exists when a motion for continuance is filed. The trial court denied plaintiff's motion for continuance on the grounds that the case was filed almost two years prior to the filing of the motion and that plaintiff's counsel announced "ready" in response to Fina's prior motion for continuance.

The absence of a material witness is "sufficient cause" but only if proper diligence has been used to procure the testimony of the witness. Plaintiff knew that he would need sufficient evidence to prove his cause of action when the case was filed. Plaintiff had almost two years to find experts to testify that he had received an electrical shock. The length of time that this case had been pending supports the argument that plaintiff did not use proper diligence in securing sufficient expert testimony to prove his case.[1]

Plaintiff's announcement of ready in response to Fina's motion for continuance is also significant in reviewing the trial court's ruling. Generally, an announcement of ready waives the right to subsequently seek a delay based upon any facts which were known or with proper diligence should have been known at the time. This general rule is subject to the exception of an unforeseeable event arising through no fault of the movant. The announcement of ready by plaintiff was made after Fina designated Dr. Baxter as an expert. Plaintiff's announcement was an indication that he was prepared to try the case without the benefit, if any, of Dr. Baxter's testimony. Dr. Baxter's opinion supporting plaintiff's cause of action is not a sufficient unforeseeable event to invoke the exception to the general rule regarding an announcement of ready.

We hold that the trial court did not abuse its discretion by overruling plaintiff's motion for continuance. The trial court noted that plaintiff "strenuously" objected to Fina's motion for continuance and announced "ready . . . not having any idea at that moment what Dr. Baxter might or might not say about the facts of this case." We cannot say that the trial court acted without reference to any guiding rules or principles. Plaintiff's first point of error is overruled.

* * *

The judgment of the trial court is affirmed.

---

[1] Rule 252 sets out the requirements for the contents of a motion for continuance for want of testimony. The rule provides that, on a first application for continuance for want of testimony, it is not necessary to show that the absent testimony cannot be procured from any other source. This portion of the rule does not relieve the movant's burden of showing sufficient cause for the continuance. *See* Rule 251. A party seeking a continuance in order to obtain expert testimony cannot show due diligence in procuring the expert's testimony if he cannot show that this expert testimony cannot be obtained from another source.

***Brown v. Gage*, 519 S.W.2d 190 (Tex. Civ. App.—Ft. Worth 1975, no writ):**

It is clear that the defendants did not comply with Rule 252, Texas Rules of Civil Procedure sometimes referred to as statutory grounds for continuance. That rule and the interpretation thereof provides that before a third motion for continuance should be granted, as a matter of right, the affidavit supporting such motion must show: (1) that such testimony is material; (2) showing the materiality thereof; (3) that such movant has used due diligence to procure such testimony; (4) stating such diligence; (5) and the cause of failure, if known; (6) that such testimony cannot be procured from any other source; (7) and if it be for the absence of a witness, movant shall state the name of the witness; (8) the residence of the witness; (9) what he expects to prove by him.

It is only on the first application that it is not necessary to show that the absent testimony cannot be procured from any other source. On all subsequent applications, this must be shown.

Each of the above requirements of Rule 252 must be complied with by the defendants before they can complain of the order of the court in overruling their motion for continuance.

The facts must be alleged and the allegations cannot be made in general terms or by stating conclusions.

A general statement of the law applicable is found in 13 TEX. JUR. 2D 23, Sec. 108, 'Continuance,' which is as follows:

> The object of the statute is to prevent frivolous grounds of continuance to delay the trial. If the use of due diligence is not alleged, the application is not statutory, even though the facts stated may show diligence. It is not sufficient merely to aver that diligence has been used; the diligence that has been used must be set out. The diligence ought to be shown specifically; mere conclusions that it was used are insufficient. The application should set out the diligence with sufficient particularity and certainty to enable the court, from the application alone, to judge whether sufficient diligence has been used.

Notes & Questions

1. *First motion for continuance. Forman* makes it clear that compliance with Rule 252 does not assure a continuance. Plaintiff's motion for continuance seems to have been his first one. Should that require special consideration? Attorneys sometimes mistakenly rely on a mythical "custom" requiring courts to grant first motions for continuance. While it is true that courts are generally disinclined to allow repeated continuances, the first motion has no special status except that granted by the rule—that the missing testimony need not be unique. As the Supreme Court has noted,[1] "From the very language of the rule it will be noted that the only difference between a first and a subsequent motion is that the first motion is not required 'to show that the absent testimony cannot be procured from any other source.'"

---

1 *See* Fritsch v. English Truck Line, Inc., 246 S.W.2d 856 (Tex. 1952).

2. *Uniqueness of testimony.* If the rules do not require that a first motion based on an absent witness show that the testimony cannot be procured elsewhere, how do you explain the holding cited in footnote 1 of *Forman*? Might it rest, in part, on the idea that because expert testimony is not based on first-hand observation it is never unique? That it can always be replaced?

3. *The ready announcement.* Parties are asked for ready announcements at docket calls and again at the commencement of trial. Because of the waiver problem illustrated by *Forman*, docket call responses are sometimes equivocal: "Expect to be ready" or "Ready subject to completing the deposition of Dr. Jones."[2]

4. *Charging continuances.* Part of the *Brown* opinion not reproduced above contains this paragraph:

> "[D]efendants' attorney requested by telephone that the case be continued. By agreement of the parties, the defendants were charged with a first continuance and the case was reset . . ."

What does it matter who is "charged with" a continuance? Suppose your opponent needs a continuance. You are ready to go to trial. Will you ever agree to the continuance in this situation? What condition will you impose if you do agree? It makes sense to agree to some continuances, depending on whether the case has been delayed before and how urgently your client needs to get to trial. Why? Because it may be fair play to do so; because you may need such an agreement later, and/or because it is clear under the circumstances that the court will likely grant the continuance anyway. Because courts tend to ration the continuances allowed a given side, you want to be sure the agreed continuance is charged to your opponent. One way to do this is to require your opponent to file the motion, which you agree not to oppose.

5. *Agreed continuances.* Historically, Texas courts almost always grant agreed continuances. *See* Rule 330(d): "[T]he court shall respect written agreements of counsel for postponement and continuance if filed in the case when or before it is called for trial, unless to do so will unreasonably delay or interfere with other business of the court." This custom may be a convenience to the attorneys, but some courts are now less willing to automatically accept an agreed continuance because it allows dilatory counsel to delay a case indefinitely. Federal judges are not, as a general rule, so accommodating.

6. *Diligence and the practical consequences of procrastination.* Note *Forman's* emphasis on diligence. The failure to take necessary depositions promptly or to issue subpoenas early may hazard the right to a continuance.[3] As the Supreme Court noted, "The fact that Wood did not have an opportunity to review the depositions of his own witnesses or depose the State's witness is a predicament of his own making. That is a risk Wood took by not diligently pursuing discovery. To reward such conduct with a new trial is manifestly improper. Since Wood did not show a clear abuse of discretion [by the trial court in denying a continuance], it was error for the court of appeals to reverse the trial court."

What if Witness X, who lives within the trial court's subpoena range, is critical to your case? You have a subpoena served on him well before the trial date, but you do not take his deposition. He fails to show at trial, and you move for continuance. Your opponent resists, citing your lack of diligence in not taking the witness's deposition. Can the court deny your continuance on this basis alone? No. *See* Rule 252 (second paragraph).

---

2 *See* Reyna v. Reyna, 738 S.W.2d 772 (Tex. App.—Austin 1987, no writ).

3 *See* State v. Wood Oil Distributing, Inc, 751 S.W.2d 863 (Tex. 1988).

7. *Legal conclusions.* Legal conclusions (such as, "we have been diligent") will not do in the affidavit supporting continuance. The affidavit must set out facts and detail is recommended.

8. *Factual content of affidavits and missing testimony.* Affidavits cannot contain hearsay. What if you need a continuance and must show what you expect to prove by the witness as required by Rule 252, summarized in *Brown*? Doesn't your affidavit contain hearsay? No. It is not offered for the truth of the testimony; only to show that it exists. *See* TRCE 801(d).

9. *Religious holy days.* A statute mandates continuances when court proceedings would interfere with the observance of a religious holy day by a party, a juror or an attorney. *See* § 30.005 and Chapter 23 of the Civil Practice and Remedies Code.

---

2. *Absence of Counsel*

Read Rule 253.

VILLEGAS
v.
CARTER
711 S.W.2d 624
(Tex. 1986)

SPEARS, JUSTICE.

This case involves the trial court's discretion to deny a motion for continuance after allowing the attorney to withdraw two days before trial. As a result of the denial, the petitioner Villegas appeared pro se and prosecuted his case unsuccessfully. In an unpublished opinion, the court of appeals affirmed the judgment. We reverse the court of appeals judgment and remand to the trial court for a new trial.

In June, 1982, Jaime Lara Villegas bought a home in El Paso from Wilmot and Alicia Carter. Villegas assumed a first lien and executed a second lien for approximately $38,000. He defaulted in July 1983, and the Carters accelerated the note. Villegas and the Carters then worked out an agreement, with Villegas executing a new note for $47,000 that included accrued interest, expenses, and a higher interest rate. In January 1984, the Carters' trustee informed Villegas that he owed $1,350 in delinquent payments. Villegas paid the Carters $5,000 on March 2nd to cure the default, pay the attorney's fees, and provide a credit on future payments. On April 9th the Carters' trustee posted the property for foreclosure. On June 5th, the trustee sold the property at public auction back to the Carters.

Villegas filed suit in county court on June 25, 1984, alleging that: (1) the second promissory note was void for usury; (2) the sale was for an inordinately low amount; (3) he had not received notice of the foreclosure sale; and (4) there were other irregularities in the public sale of the property. He was represented by Paula Thomas and Miguel Cervantes. The court set the cause for trial on October 25, 1984. On October 3rd, Thomas moved to withdraw as counsel, and the motion was granted that day. Cervantes moved to withdraw as counsel on October 5th, alleging irreconcilable differences. The court granted his motion to withdraw on October 23rd.

Two days later, Villegas appeared for trial without an attorney and told the court that he wanted time to get an attorney; that he first learned about Cervantes' attempt to withdraw only six days before at his deposition; that Cervantes would not turn over his file and important evidence to him although Cervantes had not presented him with a bill; that he wanted to hire a new attorney, Jose Montez, Jr., but that Montez would not take the case until he could see the file, look over the facts, and determine the fee; and that Montez had called Cervantes to obtain the file but that Cervantes would not return his call.

The court refused Villegas' request for a continuance to obtain an attorney and his papers. The case was then tried to the court. The court denied Villegas' claim and awarded the Carters restitution of their property and a deficiency judgment of $19,700.

TEX. R. CIV. P. Rule 253 provides:

> [A]bsence of counsel will not be good cause for a continuance or postponement of the cause when called for trial, except it be allowed in the discretion of the court, upon cause shown or upon matters within the knowledge or information of judge to be stated on the record.

The granting or denial of a motion for continuance is within the trial court's sound discretion. . . . The trial court's action will not be disturbed unless the record discloses a clear abuse of discretion. When the ground for the continuance is the withdrawal of counsel, movants must show that the failure to be represented at trial was not due to their own fault or negligence. . . . Generally, when movants fail to comply with TEX. R. CIV. P. 251's requirement that the motion for continuance be "supported by affidavit," we presume that the trial court did not abuse its discretion in denying the motion. . . . It would be unrealistic, however, to apply this presumption to lay movants who without fault have their attorney withdrawn. . . .

The right to counsel is a valuable right; its unwarranted denial is reversible error. . . . Therefore, when a trial court allows an attorney to voluntarily withdraw, it must give the party time to secure new counsel and time for the new counsel to investigate the case and prepare for trial. . . . Before a trial court allows an attorney to withdraw, it should see that the attorney has complied with the Code of Professional Responsibility:

> [A] lawyer should not withdraw from employment until he has taken reasonable steps to avoid foreseeable prejudice to the rights of his client, including giving due notice to his client, allowing time for employment of other counsel, delivering to the client all papers and property to which the client is entitled and complying with applicable laws and rules.

Supreme Court of Texas, Rules Governing the State Bar of Texas art. XII, § 8 (Code of Professional Responsibility) DR 2-110(A)(2); . . .

In this case, the trial court abused its discretion because the evidence shows that Villegas was not negligent or at fault in causing his attorney's withdrawal. The court granted Villegas' attorney's motion to voluntarily withdraw two days before trial—too short a time for Villegas to find a new attorney and for that new attorney to investigate the case and prepare for trial. In addition, Villegas could not obtain a new attorney or present his case because the former attorney refused to turn over Villegas' files with his papers and evidence. The attorney did not give Villegas time to employ new counsel or deliver to Villegas the papers and property to which Villegas was entitled. In short, Villegas' attorney did not take reasonable steps to avoid foreseeable prejudice to the client.

The trial court should either have denied the attorney's motion to withdraw or granted the party's motion for continuance; it did neither. Therefore, we reverse the court of appeals judgment and remand for a new trial.

Notes & Questions

1. *Attorney's conduct.* What would be the vulnerability of Villegas' attorney if the Supreme Court had upheld the trial court's refusal of continuance and thus the judgment against Villegas? Note that there are ethical prohibitions against leaving a client in the lurch on the eve of trial.

2. *Support by affidavit.* Note that a party's failure to comply with the provisions of Rule 251 respecting supporting affidavit(s) does not mean that the motion will be denied; only that, if the trial court does deny the motion, the appellate court will presume that the trial court was operating within its zone of discretion.

3. *Absence of counsel.* In *Dancy v. Daggett,*[1] a trial court, acting in violation of local rules, denied a continuance and ignored a federal judge's telephone call advising him that the attorney was required to be in federal court in a case already in progress. Held: abuse of discretion. Note that *Villegas* and *Daggett* are exceptions to the general rule: absence of counsel does not mandate a continuance. *See* Rule 253 and *Dover Corp. v. Perez,*[2] holding that there was no abuse in denying continuance when another attorney ably represented the movant at trial.

4. *Due process.* Keep in mind that it is possible for the denial of a continuance to involve due process right to counsel under state law or under the U.S. Constitution. *See State v. Crank,*[3] in which the Texas Supreme Court recognizes the constitutional implications with respect to an administrative hearing. It holds against the client-complainant, Dr. Crank, however, who had obtained earlier continuances and delays, and who fired his attorney over "philosophical differences" on the day of the hearing. The court quotes with approval from the U.S. Supreme Court's opinion in *Ungar v. Sarafite*[4]:

> "The matter of continuance is traditionally within the discretion of the trial judge, and it is not every denial of a request for more time that violates due process even if the party . . . is compelled to defend without counsel . . . . Contrariwise, a myopic insistence upon expeditiousness in the face of a justifiable request for delay can render the right to defend with counsel an empty formality. There are no mechanical tests for deciding when a denial of a continuance is so arbitrary as to violate due process. The answer must be found in the circumstances present in every case, particularly in the reasons presented to the trial judge at the time the request is denied.

5. *Ethics rules on withdrawal.* Rule 1.15(d) of the Texas Rules of Professional Responsibility provides: "Upon termination of representation, a lawyer shall take steps to the extent reasonably practicable to protect a client's interests, such as giving reasonable notice to the client, allowing time for employment of other counsel, surrendering papers and property to which the client is en-

---

1 815 S.W.2d 548 (Tex. 1991).

2 587 S.W.2d 761 (Tex. Civ. App.—Corpus Christi 1979, writ ref'd n.r.e.).

3 666 S.W.2d 91 (Tex. 1984).

4 376 U.S. 575, 589, 84 S.Ct. 841, 849, 11 L.Ed.2d 921 (1964).

titled and refunding any advance payments of fee that has not been earned. The lawyer may retain papers relating to the client to the extent permitted by other law only if such retention will not prejudice the client in the subject matter of the representation." Rule 10 specifies the procedures that a withdrawing *attorney* should follow. Notice the last paragraph in the *Villegas* opinion, which states what the *court* should have done.

---

3. *Legislative Continuances*

Read Rule 254, CPRC § 30.003

***Waites v. Sandock*, 561 S.W.2d 772 (Tex. 1977):**

[A divorced mother filed a motion for contempt to force the child's father to pay court-ordered child support. The father's lawyer, a member of the Texas House of Representatives, filed a motion for legislative continuance, seeking postponement of the hearing from January until after May 31, when the Legislature would recess. The trial court granted the continuance without hearing the mother's evidence of her dire financial straits. The Supreme Court held that mandatory legislative continuances in such circumstances deny litigants due process of law.]

"Article I, section 13 of the Texas Constitution provides:

> . . . All courts shall be open, and every person for an injury done him, in his lands, goods, person or reputation, shall have remedy by due course of law.

This provision prohibits 'legislative bodies from arbitrarily withdrawing all legal remedies from one having a cause of action well established and well defined in the common law.' *Lebohm v. City of Galveston*, 154 Tex. 192, 197, 275 S.W.2d 951, 954 (1955). In *Lebohm*, this court went on to say:

> (L)egislative action withdrawing common-law remedies for well established common-law causes of action for injuries to one's 'lands, goods, person or reputation' is sustained only when it is reasonable in substituting other remedies, or when it is a reasonable exercise of the police power in the interest of the general welfare. Legislative action of this type is not sustained when it is arbitrary or unreasonable.

154 Tex. at 199, 275 S.W.2d at 955.

"Article 2168a effectively withdraws the common law remedy of litigants who, in emergency situations, seek to enforce court decrees and obtain other relief other than by a temporary restraining order. Although article 2168a [the predecessor to Rule 254] appears on its face merely to postpone pending suits and matters ancillary thereto, in the present case the delay in enforcement caused by the legislative continuance allegedly inflicts harm that is not susceptible to remedy at a later date. The mother here claims that the support payments are critical to her ability to feed and support her children. The trial court, after the expiration of the continuance, may force the father to pay any overdue sums, but these payments will not compensate the child for any injury resulting from the mother's present inability to care for the child. The legislative basis for withdrawing the mother's remedy—the presumption that the policy behind article 2168a outweighs a litigant's right of redress—is arbitrary and unreasonable when, in situations such as this, a party allegedly faces irreparable injury from inaction."

"The courts of other states also have rejected arguments that legislative continuance statutes are mandatory in situations of emergency or irreparable harm."

"We agree with the conclusions of these courts insofar as their decisions deal with the constitutionality of mandatory legislative continuances when the non-moving party faces irreparable harm. At the same time we reiterate the limited nature of our holding: a legislative continuance is mandatory except in those cases in which the party opposing the continuance alleges that a substantial existing right will be defeated or abridged by delay. In cases of this type the trial court has a duty to conduct a hearing on the allegations. If the allegations are shown to be meritorious the court should deny the continuance.

"Accordingly, relator's petition for writ of mandamus is conditionally granted. We assume that Judge Sondock or her successor[5] will set aside her order and proceed to trial, including any pretrial hearings or proceedings, to determine the validity of the mother's allegations. A writ will issue only if the judge of the court of domestic relations fails to do so.

In *In re Ford Motor Company*, 165 S.W.3d 315 (Tex. 2005), the Court reaffirmed *Waites v. Sondock,* (and held that the analysis remained the same under the recodified statute) but held that under the facts of this personal-injury case the trial court did not have the discretion to overrule a legislative continuance. Plaintiff Robin Fuentes sustained serious injuries, which left her a quadriplegic, when a Goodyear tire blew out on her Ford vehicle and it rolled over. The trial court scheduled the case for trial on May 16, 2005. On April 1, Ford filed a motion for legislative continuance, properly supported by an affidavit from a legislator on its litigation team. The trial court overruled the motion. The Supreme Court issued a conditional writ of mandamus ordering the trial court to grant the continuance.

The court noted that the legislator had sworn to the required facts, and therefore the *statute* gave the Court no discretion to deny the motion. Concerning the *due process* exception engrafted onto the statute for litigants who face "irreparable harm from the delay in enforcing existing rights," the Court stressed that in *Waites* the mother had a pre-existing court-ordered right to child support, and a continuance would delay enforcement and make it difficult for her to feed her children. Fuentes argued that if her case were delayed she would exhaust her right to temporary state funding for rehabilitation services; her doctor stated that without the rehabilitation her condition might worsen. But *Waites,* said the Court, involved an *existing right* to court-ordered child support, while Fuentes had only a *claim* to have Ford pay her money which she could use to purchase medical benefits. The court pointed out that the legislature has made the judgment that the public interest is served by having legislators in Austin during legislative sessions, and that legislator-lawyers should not have to choose between their duties to their clients and their duties to their constituents. The *Waites* due process exception, said the Court, requires a higher showing than Fuentes had made.

---

[5] Judge Sondock was appointed to the district court bench after the continuance in question was granted.

E. The Trial Begins

Read Rules 7-10, 265-266.

1. *Order of Proceedings*

Rule 265 sets out the order of proceedings. It is a common practice for the trial court to allow a party to call a witness "out of order"—that is, during the opponent's case-in-chief, when the witness's schedule or expert witness' fees make such a concession reasonable. Note also that the defendant may defer his opening statement until after plaintiff has rested. What if co-defendants decide that one will open at the beginning of trial and another will open after plaintiff has rested (thus presenting the defense view of the case at both opportunities)? It did not fly in *Fibreboard Corp. v. Pool.*[1] The trial court ruled that all defendants had to choose the same option and "open" at the same time, and the ruling was held on appeal to be within the trial court's discretion.

In the typical two-party case, the order of proceedings in a jury trial is something like the following:

(1) Announcements. The case is called for trial, and both parties announce ready. (If either party is not ready, the court considers and rules on that party's motion for continuance.)

(2) Pretrial motions. The court considers the motions in limine and makes rulings. Some courts consider at this time any pretrial *Daubert* objections to expert witnesses. Many courts also discuss with the attorneys how long they expect the case to take, how many witnesses they will call, and what issues they will want submitted to the jury.

(3) Voir Dire. The bailiff brings a jury panel[2] into the courtroom. The judge welcomes them and gives them some general instructions. P begins the voir dire process, followed by D. Both parties exercise their peremptory challenges, and the names of the jurors are announced. The jury is sworn and seated, and the judge gives them further instructions.

(4) Opening statements. P and D make opening statements, outlining their case for the jury. D has the option, seldom exercised, to wait and make its opening statement after P has rested.

(5) Plaintiff's case in chief. P presents witnesses and documentary evidence. D cross-examines each P witness in turn. Eventually P rests. D will sometimes make a motion for directed verdict on all or part of P's case.

(6) Defendant's case in chief. D presents witnesses and documentary evidence. P cross-examines each witness.

(7) Rebuttal. P may call witnesses to respond to matters brought out in D's case and which could not have been anticipated during P's case in chief. When P concludes her rebuttal, D may

---

[1] 813 S.W.2d 658 (Tex. App.—Texarkana 1991, writ denied).

[2] The jurors will have been "qualified" earlier by the trial judge (or in multi-judge counties, perhaps by another judge in the same jurisdiction). In other words, the jurors that are brought to the courtroom have already been screened to make sure they meet the statutory qualifications for jury service (e.g. age, residency, literacy), and they have been given an opportunity to claim statutory exemptions from jury service (e.g. students, those responsible for small children, age over 70), and to ask to be rescheduled if they have a serious conflict.

introduce evidence in response to matters brought out by P's rebuttal evidence. At some point, both sides rest and close, which means that the evidence phase of the case has concluded.

(8) Preparation of the charge. The court will prepare the charge, usually relying substantially on the requests for jury questions and instructions that the parties have previously presented. The parties are given a reasonable time to review the court's charge, and then they may object to any questions or instructions or definitions in the charge, and may officially request their own additions.

(9) Jury Argument. P sums up and argues the case to the jury. D follows. P gives rebuttal argument in reply to D's argument.

(10) Jury deliberations. The bailiff escorts the jury to the jury room. The jury chooses a presiding juror, discusses the evidence and the charge, and reaches a verdict. Eventually the presiding juror notifies the bailiff that the jury has reached a verdict, the lawyers are notified, and the jury is escorted into the courtroom.

(11) Receipt of verdict. The court reads the verdict silently and makes sure that all questions have been answered and that ten or more jurors have signed. The court then reads the answers aloud, accepts the verdict, and thanks and discharges the jury.

(12) Judgment. The winning party prepares a judgment based on the jury's answers, which states which party has won and specifies the relief granted (or states that relief is denied).

(13) Post-trial motions. The losing party may move for judgment n.o.v. or for a new trial.

As you study these chronological steps in a jury trial, ask yourself which of them would be omitted or modified in a nonjury trial.

---

2. *Invoking "The Rule"*

Read Rule 267 and TRCE 614.

DRILEX SYSTEMS, INC.
v.
FLORES
1 S.W.3d 112
(Tex. 1999)

ABBOTT, JUSTICE.

* * *

This case concerns the exclusion of an expert witness's testimony for violating "the Rule"[1] by discussing the case with a corporate representative. * * * Based on our resolution of these issues, we affirm the court of appeals' judgment, as reformed, and remand this cause to the trial court to render judgment in accordance with this opinion.

I

Jorge Flores was employed as a roughneck/floorhand for Helmerick and Payne, a drilling contractor. Jorge's hand was severely injured during a well-drilling operation for Amoco Production Company. Jorge, his wife Maria, and their three children Gina, Jose, and Georgette, sued Amoco, Drilex Systems, Inc., MASX Energy Services Group, and MASCO Industries, Inc. for Jorge's injury.

Before trial, Amoco settled with all of the plaintiffs for a total of $774,675. The case proceeded to trial against Drilex, MASX, and MASCO ("Drilex"). On the first day of trial, Drilex invoked the Rule and asked that any witnesses present in the courtroom be sworn. The trial court swore in Jorge and Maria Flores and Tom Bailey, Drilex's corporate representative. The court noted that these individuals were parties, and instructed that "anybody else" who stayed in the courtroom for a considerable time would not be allowed to testify. Although Texas Rule of Civil Procedure 267(d) requires the trial court to instruct witnesses placed under the Rule "that they are not to converse with each other or with any other person about the case other than the attorneys" and that "they are not to read any report of or comment upon the testimony in the case," TEX. R. CIV. P. 267(d), the trial court did not give such an admonishment at that time. Drilex did not attempt to have the trial court exempt its expert witnesses from the Rule.

Plaintiffs then called their first witness, Tom Bailey. During Bailey's testimony, one of Drilex's testifying expert witnesses, Randy Acock, remained present. On the second day of trial, counsel for the Flores family moved to strike Acock as a witness, arguing that Acock had violated the Rule by being present during part of Bailey's testimony. Drilex's counsel argued that Acock was exempt from the Rule because he was an expert. The trial court made no ruling at the time, and Acock left the courtroom.

---

1 *See* TEX. R. CIV. P. 267(a) (defining "placing witnesses under the rule" as the process of swearing in the witnesses and removing them from the courtroom to some place where they cannot hear the testimony of any other witness); *see also* TEX. R. EVID. 614.

When Drilex later called Acock to testify, counsel for the Flores family again objected to Acock's testimony on the basis that Acock was present for a portion of Bailey's testimony. After listening to counsel's arguments and discussing the substance of Acock's testimony, the court stated that it would allow Acock to testify. However, the court was then informed that Acock had also discussed the case with Bailey after Bailey had testified. Acock also admitted talking to another expert after hearing Bailey's testimony, but stated that they did not discuss Bailey's testimony. Based on this additional information, the trial court excluded Acock's testimony.

At the conclusion of the trial, the jury returned a verdict finding that Drilex was sixty percent responsible, Amoco was thirty percent responsible, and Jorge Flores was ten percent responsible for causing Jorge's injuries, and awarded a total of $2,145,000 in damages. After applying a credit for the Flores family's settlement with Amoco, the trial court awarded Jorge $1,929,048, and ordered that all other plaintiffs take nothing.

Drilex appealed, arguing, among other things, that the trial court improperly excluded Acock's testimony and failed to properly apply the settlement credit. * * *

II

Drilex argues that the trial court abused its discretion by excluding Acock's testimony for violating the Rule, and that this error was harmful because Acock's testimony was necessary to the presentation of its defense. We agree with the court of appeals that the trial court did not abuse its discretion, and in any event, the excluded testimony would have been cumulative.

A

Sequestration minimizes witnesses' tailoring their testimony in response to that of other witnesses and prevents collusion among witnesses testifying for the same side. The expediency of sequestration as a mechanism for preventing and detecting fabrication has been recognized for centuries. English courts incorporated sequestration long ago, and the practice came to the United States as part of our inheritance of the common law. Today, most jurisdictions have expressly provided for witness sequestration by statute or rule.

In Texas, sequestration in civil litigation is governed by Texas Rule of Evidence 614 and Texas Rule of Civil Procedure 267. These rules provide that, at the request of any party,[2] the witnesses on both sides shall be removed from the courtroom to some place where they cannot hear the testimony delivered by any other witness in the cause. TEX. R. CIV. P. 267(a); TEX. R. EVID. 614. Certain classes of prospective witnesses, however, are exempt from exclusion from the courtroom, including: (1) a party who is a natural person or his or her spouse; (2) an officer or employee of a party that is not a natural person and who is designated as its representative by its attorney; or (3) a person whose presence is shown by a party to be essential to the presentation of the cause. TEX. R. CIV. P. 267(b); TEX. R. EVID. 614.

When the Rule is invoked, all parties should request the court to exempt any prospective witnesses whose presence is essential to the presentation of the cause. The burden rests with the party seeking to exempt an expert witness from the Rule's exclusion requirement to establish that the witness's presence is essential. Witnesses found to be exempt by the trial court are not "placed under the Rule."

Once the Rule is invoked, all nonexempt witnesses must be placed under the Rule and excluded from the courtroom. Before being excluded, these witnesses must be sworn and admon-

[2] The court may also sequester the witnesses on its own motion. TEX. R. EVID. 614.

ished "that they are not to converse with each other or with any other person about the case other than the attorneys in the case, except by permission of the court, and that they are not to read any report of or comment upon the testimony in the case while under the rule." TEX. R. CIV. P. 267(a), (d). Thus, witnesses under the Rule generally may not discuss the case with anyone other than the attorneys in the case.

Witnesses exempt from exclusion under Rule 614 (and Rule 267) need not be sworn or admonished. Texas Rule of Civil Procedure 267(d) states that "[w]itnesses, when placed under Rule 614 of the Texas Rules of Civil Evidence, shall be instructed by the court that they are not to converse with each other or with any other person about the case other than the attorneys." TEX. R. CIV. P. 267(d) (emphasis added). The instruction requirement does not apply to exempt witnesses because they are not "placed under Rule 614."

A violation of the Rule occurs when a nonexempt prospective witness remains in the courtroom during the testimony of another witness, or when a nonexempt prospective witness learns about another's trial testimony through discussions with persons other than the attorneys in the case or by reading reports or comments about the testimony. When the Rule is violated, the trial court may, taking into consideration all of the circumstances, allow the testimony of the potential witness, exclude the testimony, or hold the violator in contempt. *See* TEX. R. CIV. P. 267(e). We review the trial court's action for abuse of discretion.

* * *

B

Drilex asserts that there was no Rule violation because Acock was exempt from the Rule, he spoke only to another exempt witness, and neither witness was admonished not to discuss the case with others. Thus, contends Drilex, the trial court abused its discretion by excluding Acock's testimony.

Drilex contends that the trial court "exempted" Acock from the Rule's requirement that witnesses be excluded when it ruled that Acock could testify despite the fact that he had remained in the courtroom during Bailey's testimony. Because witnesses exempt from exclusion are also exempt from Rule 267(d)'s admonishment not to discuss the case with others, Drilex argues that the trial court abused its discretion when it exempted Acock from the exclusion requirement but nevertheless excluded his testimony for discussing the case with Tom Bailey. The flaw in this argument is that Drilex never established—and the trial court never found—that Acock was in fact exempt. After being told that Acock had been present during Bailey's testimony, the trial court concluded that he would allow Acock to testify. As noted, a court may, subject to review for abuse of discretion, allow a witness to testify even though the witness has violated the Rule by remaining in the courtroom during another witness's testimony. But a decision to allow a witness to testify despite his presence in the courtroom is not the same as a finding that the witness is exempt from the Rule. Thus, although Drilex is correct that a witness who is exempt from exclusion is also exempt from Rule 267(d)'s requirement not to discuss the case with others, the trial court did not actually exempt Acock from the exclusion requirement.

Drilex also argues that all expert witnesses are exempt from the Rule under the essential presence exception in Rules 614 and 267, and therefore Acock was exempt. Drilex is correct that this exception is often relied on to allow expert witnesses to be exempt from the Rule. But nothing in Rules 614 or 267 suggests that all expert witnesses qualify for exemption. Although an expert witness may typically be found exempt under the essential presence exception,[4] experts are not automatically exempt. Instead, Rules 614 and 267 vest in trial judges broad discretion to determine whether a witness is essential. . . .

* * *

Drilex presented no evidence to the trial court to establish that Acock should have been exempt, other than its argument that experts are per se exempt. Drilex could have presented evidence that Acock needed to be present to form his opinions based on more accurate factual assumptions, *see* TEX. R. EVID. 703, but it did not do so. Moreover, Acock admitted in the bill of exceptions that he did not need to be present in the courtroom. Thus, the trial court did not abuse its discretion by failing to exempt Acock from the Rule.

* * *

Drilex further contends that Rule 614 "did not apply to Tom Bailey and it could not serve as a predicate for preventing him from discussing the case with Mr. Acock." Tom Bailey, Drilex's designated corporate representative, was exempt from exclusion, and the trial court recognized that Bailey was exempt. *See* TEX. R. CIV. P. 267(b)(2) (exempting "an officer or employee of a party that is not a natural person and who is designated as its representative by its attorney"). But the record indicates that the trial court based its decision to disqualify Acock partly on its belief that Bailey violated the Rule. The trial court stated that, although Bailey was exempt from the Rule for the purpose of exclusion from the courtroom, he was under the Rule for the purpose of discussing the case with other witnesses, and thus he violated the Rule by discussing the case with Acock. As stated previously, a witness such as Bailey who is exempt from exclusion is also exempt from the Rule for purposes of discussing the case with others. Bailey was not under the Rule for any purpose—only Acock was. Accordingly, this basis for the trial court's decision to exclude Acock was erroneous. We will nevertheless uphold the trial court's ruling if there is any legitimate basis for it in the record.

The trial court also stated that it would not allow Acock to testify because he discussed the case with another witness although he was under the Rule. The proper focus in determining whether Acock's testimony should have been excluded is whether Acock, not Bailey, was exempt from Rule 614. If Acock was not exempt, he was not free to discuss the case with Bailey, regardless of whether Bailey was exempt from the Rule. Because Acock was never exempted from Rule 614, he was not free to discuss the case with another witness, and his doing so violated the Rule. Accordingly, we conclude that the trial court's decision was not an abuse of discretion.

We acknowledge that the court never expressly placed Acock under the Rule and never instructed him not to discuss the case with others. However, a court may, in its discretion, exclude the testimony of a prospective witness who technically violates the Rule even though the witness was never actually placed under the Rule. . . .

---

[4] The Notes of the Advisory Committee to the Proposed Federal Rule, upon which the Texas rule is based, suggest that the essential presence exception contemplates an expert needed to advise counsel in the management of litigation. FED. R. EVID. 615 advisory committee's note. In addition, courts have held that expert witnesses expected to testify in an expert capacity only, and not to the facts of the case, should typically be exempt so that they can form opinions based on more accurate factual assumptions. *See, e.g., Opus 3 Ltd. V. Heritage Park, Inc.*, 91 F.3d 625, 629 (4th Cir.1996); *see also* TEX. R. EVID. 703. However, expert witnesses who are also fact witnesses provide a closer case.

Drilex invoked the Rule and was obligated to ensure that its witnesses either complied with the Rule or were exempted from it. Drilex did neither. Thus, the trial court acted within its discretion in disqualifying Acock even though the court never actually placed Acock under the Rule and failed to appropriately instruct him.

Additionally, we note that it may be an abuse of discretion in some circumstances to disqualify a witness even when the witness has violated the Rule. However, Drilex has not argued that excluding Acock's testimony was an abuse of discretion even if Acock was not exempt from the Rule, and therefore we do not decide that question.

Last, we agree with the court of appeals that the excluded testimony was largely cumulative, and thus Drilex was not harmed by Acock's disqualification.

* * *

Notes & Questions

1. *Trial court discretion.* The trial court has wide discretion in the matter of the exclusion of witnesses. It can exclude or allow a witness' testimony if the witness who has been "placed under the Rule" then hears trial testimony. Thus, when the Rule had been invoked and an investigator remained in the courtroom and heard testimony, the trial court did not abuse its discretion in refusing to allow him to testify, even though his only role would have been to authenticate a tape recording impeaching plaintiff's testimony.[1]

2. *Compliance.* Note also that a witness violating the rule may be punished by contempt, but only after the witness has been "placed under the rule," that is, sworn and instructed. In *Drilex*, the witness had not been placed under the rule, so the party, not the witness had the duty to ensure compliance.

3. *Daily copy.* You are in a trial in which you are receiving "daily copy"—transcripts of each day's testimony provided by privately paid reporters, working in relays. Your senior counsel directs that a copy of these transcripts be delivered each evening to each of three key witnesses so that they can know what the effect of the other testimony is on their own. Your senior counsel asks your opinion of this procedure. What is it? Will Rule 267d affect your opinion?

4. *"The Rule" and depositions.* What about invoking the Rule for a deposition? Rule 267 refers to "the courtroom" and Rule 614 seems to relate to testimony at trial. In *Kennedy v. Eden*,[2] the Texas Supreme Court had before it an order grounded in TRCE 614 excluding a witness from a deposition. The Court issued mandamus, holding the order to be an abuse of discretion because its duration was perpetual, expressly refusing to rule on whether a trial court can exclude witnesses from depositions *at all* under TRCE 614 (or presumably Rule 247): "If the trial court was authorized to issue such an instruction [excluding a witness from a deposition], *an issue on which we express no opinion here*, there is nothing before us to suggest that it was justified in these circumstances." (Emphasis added.) What *should* be the policy regarding invocation of "The Rule" at depositions? If witnesses are al-

---

1 *See* Southwestern Bell Telephone Co. v. Johnson., 389 S.W.2d 645 (Tex. 1965). It is also within the court's discretion to allow testimony from the offending witness. *See* Pierson v. Noon, 814 S.W.2d 506 (Tex. App.—Houston [14th Dist.] 1991, writ denied).

2 837 S.W.2d 98 (Tex. 1992).

lowed to hear each other's testimony the first time they are under oath, what good is "The Rule" at trial?

---

3. *The Right to Open and Close the Evidence*

Read Rule 265, 266, 269.

4M LINEN & UNIFORM SUPPLY CO., INC.
v.
W.P. BALLARD & CO., INC.
793 S.W.2d 320
(Tex. App.—Houston [1st Dist.] 1990, writ denied)

[Ballard sued 4M on a sworn account for the underlying debt and for attorneys' fees. By counterclaim, 4M sought damages for misrepresentation and breach of warranty. After an instructed verdict for Ballard on its account cause of action, the only remaining issues were Ballard's claim for attorneys' fees and 4M's misrepresentation and warranty claims. Over 4M's objection, the trial court allowed Ballard to open and close.]

* * *

3. Right to open and close.

In its third point of error, 4M Linen argues the trial court erred in denying it the opportunity to open and close on final argument, in violation of TEX. R. CIV. P. 266 and 269. Before trial, the court granted a motion for directed verdict on 4M Linen's stipulation of liability on the sworn account. Ballard & Co.'s only remaining issue to go to the jury was attorney's fees. 4M Linen contends the trial court should have permitted it to open and close the argument because the central issue was its DTPA claim.

There are two rules that control the order of final argument: TEX. R. CIV. P. 266, which governs both the order of presenting evidence and final argument; and TEX. R. CIV. P. 269, which governs the argument.

Rule 266, which is subject to rule 269, provides that the plaintiff has the right to open and close argument. There are two exceptions in rule 266. First, a defendant has the right to open and close if the burden of proof for the entire case under the pleadings is on defendant. TEX. R. CIV. P. 266. Second, a defendant has the right to open and close if, before trial begins, defendant admits that plaintiff is entitled to recover, subject to proof of defensive allegations in the answer.

Rule 269 provides that the party who has the burden of proof on the whole case, or the party who has the burden on all matters in the charge, has the right to open and close the argument. TEX. R. CIV. P. 269(a). There is an exception in rule 269: When there are several parties who have separate claims or defenses, the court 'shall' determine the order of argument.

4M Linen claims that it had the right to open and close the argument because it had the burden of proof on the whole case. . . . We agree with the holding in *Andrews*: when a defendant has the burden on all issues submitted to the jury, and the trial court permits defendant to open and close, we will affirm the ruling on appeal. Those are not the facts in this case.

* * *

In this case, the trial court submitted six issues to the jury, one of which was Ballard & Co.'s issue on attorney's fees. 4M Linen had the burden of proof on the remainder of the issues submitted. After looking to the pleadings of the case, we determine that Ballard & Co. carried the burden of proof on the whole case. The trial court properly denied 4M Linen's request to open and close final arguments.

We overrule 4M Linen's third point of error.

Notes & Questions

1. *Rules 265(a) and 266 v. Rule 269.* Suppose that, when the case begins, D has admitted P's entire *prima facie* case for breach of contract and damages. D disputes only the *amount* of P's claim for attorneys' fees (not P's right to reasonable attorneys' fees). D's affirmative defense to P's *prima facie* claim is limitations.

a. Who is entitled to make the first opening statement to the jury? P is under Rule 265(a). So long as D contests any part of P's case for recovery, including damages or attorneys' fees, D does not have the "burden of proof on the whole case."[1]

b. Suppose that, during the trial, D stipulates with P on a reasonable amount as P's attorneys' fees. Before closing arguments, D asks the court for leave to make the first and last final arguments under Rule 269(a), as D now has the burden of proof on all matters which are submitted by the charge. P resists, urging that Rule 265(a) controls and governs throughout the trial (based on the pleadings in force when the trial began). Who wins? D does. When the burdens on issues change during the trial so that D has the burden on each jury question at the time of final arguments, Rule 269(a) controls and D is entitled to make the first and last closing arguments.[2]

2. *Declaratory judgments.* Who gets to open and close the arguments and evidence in a declaratory judgment suit? After all, each party may have the same interest in establishing its preferred declaration of rights. In *Pace Corp. v. Jackson*,[3] the Texas Supreme Court held that one of the parties to a declaratory judgment suit (involving rights under a contract) still had the burden of proving his right to relief on a separate claim for damages. It held that "if one party is asserting a right to damages or some other active relief in his own behalf, the burden of proving his right to that relief still

---

[1] *See* Montoya v. Nueces Vacuum Service, Inc., 471 S.W.2d 110 (Tex. Civ. App.—Corpus Christi 1971, writ ref'd n.r.e.) (D's admission of liability not enough where P still has burden of proof on amount of damages); *and* Horton v. Dental Capital Leasing Corp., 649 S.W.2d 655 (Tex. App.—Texarkana 1983, no writ).

[2] *See* Community Public Service Co. v. Andrews, 590 S.W.2d 563 (Tex. Civ. App.—Houston [1st Dist.] 1979, writ ref'd n.r.e.). Note that D must be sure it has properly pled an affirmative defense. Otherwise the admission of P's prima facie case could result in rendition of judgment for P.

[3] 284 S.W.2d 340 (Tex. 1955).

rests upon him. The time sequence in the filing of pleadings can neither relieve him of his responsibilities nor deprive him of his advantages." Thus, the party who retains the burden gets the right to open and close. But suppose all parties to the case simply ask for a declaration of rights, such as the proper location of a property boundary? The problem then becomes more difficult and is not resolved by *Pace*.

---

4. *Opening Statement*

RANGER INSURANCE CO.
v.
ROGERS

530 S.W.2d 162
(Tex. Civ. App.—Austin 1975, writ ref'd n.r.e.)

SHANNON, JUSTICE.

Appellees, Sara Rogers, the administratrix of the estate of John D. Rogers, deceased, and Billie L. Arnold, individually and as next friend for William Allen Arnold, a minor, sued appellant, Ranger Insurance Company in the district court of Travis County. After a trial to a jury and upon appellees' motion, the district court entered judgment Non obstante veredicto for Billie L. Arnold and the minor child for a total of $450,000.00.

The event made the basis for this appeal was the crash of a Piper aircraft in West Texas on April 13, 1972. At the time of the crash John D. Rogers was the pilot of the aircraft and Billy J. Arnold was a passenger. Rogers was president of and a major stockholder in United Housing Corporation. Rogers had used the airplane for trips about the area in the furtherance of his business interests. On the occasion of the crash he and Arnold had flown to Lubbock in connection with the commencement of a new business venture for United Housing Corporation. Both Rogers and Arnold were killed in the crash.

* * *

By its point of error number twelve appellant claims error by the district court in permitting counsel for appellees to make an opening statement to the jury wherein he outlined in detail the names and the substance of the testimony of many witnesses he intended to call. Appellant's counsel objected repeatedly during the appellees' opening statement and moved for a mistrial. After the district court had overruled appellant's objections and motion for mistrial, appellant's counsel, in turn, gave his opening statement in terms almost as detailed as that of appellees.

TEX. R. CIV. P. 265(a) provides in part: 'The party upon whom rests the burden of proof on the whole case shall be permitted at his option to read his pleading or *to state* to the jury *briefly the nature of his claim or defense*.' (Emphasis added)

Rule 265(a) does not afford counsel the right to detail to the jury the evidence which he intends to offer, nor to read or describe in detail the documents he proposes to offer. The practice of detailing the expected testimony in the opening statement places matters before the jury without the trial court having had an opportunity to determine the admissibility of such matters. We are of the further opinion that such a practice sometimes has the effect of misleading or confusing the jurors as between the expectations of counsel and evidence actually admitted. The proper limitation of the opening statement is a matter necessarily resting in the discretion of the trial court subject to review for abuse of discretion.

The opening statements of counsel for appellees and appellant were in violation of Rule 265(a). The district court should not have tolerated counsel for either party to have detailed the evidence which he expected to introduce, and the court's failure to limit counsel was erroneous. Under the circumstances of this case, however, particularly in view of the fact that counsel for both parties violated Rule 265(a), we are not convinced that the court's failure to sustain the objections and the failure to grant the motion for mistrial was such error as was calculated to cause the rendition of an improper judgment.

* * *

The judgment is affirmed.

---

5. *Judge's General Authority to Manage the Trial*

Read Rule 265.

DOW CHEMICAL COMPANY
v.
FRANCIS
46 S.W.3d 237
(Tex. 2001)

PER CURIAM.

Renee Francis, a former employee of The Dow Chemical Company, sued Dow and its employee, Joseph Hegyesi, alleging discrimination, fraud, constructive discharge, and retaliation. The trial court granted summary judgment for Dow and Hegyesi on Francis' fraud claims and dismissed Hegyesi from the case. The remaining claims against Dow were tried to a jury. After a two-week trial, the jury rejected Francis' discrimination and constructive-discharge claims. The jury found for Francis on her retaliation claim but awarded zero damages. Based on these findings, the trial court rendered a take-nothing judgment against Francis. Francis appealed. The court of appeals reversed both the take-nothing judgment for Dow and the summary judgment for Dow and Hegyesi. In doing so, the court of appeals concluded, among other things, that the cumulative effect of the trial court's abuse of discretion with regard to its evidentiary rulings and its bias against Francis resulted in the rendition of an improper judgment. We conclude that the court of appeals erred, reverse its judgment, and remand this cause to that court for further proceedings consistent with this opinion.

In their petition for review, Dow and Hegyesi argue that the court of appeals erred in: (1) holding that the trial judge's bias resulted in an improper judgment; (2) sustaining Francis' evidentiary complaints; (3) applying incorrect legal and factual-sufficiency standards in reviewing the jury's zero damages verdict on Francis' retaliation claim; and (4) reversing the summary judgment on Francis' fraud claim. We begin with the court of appeals' bias holding.

Without citing any particular examples, the court of appeals concluded that:

> Here, the record reveals that some of the trial court's comments were not so much directed toward Francis, her attorney, or the merits of her case, as they were to the trial court's desire to expedite the proceedings. However, there are many instances of conduct by the trial court that we do not condone and which cause us concern over whether there was prejudice towards Francis.
>
> The cumulative effect of the trial court's abuse of its discretion with regard to its evidentiary rulings and its bias against the appellant resulted in the rendition of an improper judgment and constitutes reversible error.

Dow first complains that as a matter of law, the trial judge's comments were insufficient to support a finding of judicial bias or misconduct, and that the court of appeals erred in not describing the conduct it determined to be improper. Second, Dow maintains that the trial court's objectionable conduct was presumptively curable by instruction, and therefore, Francis failed to preserve her bias complaint by not objecting or requesting a jury instruction at trial. Third, Dow argues that the court of appeals failed to analyze how the alleged judicial misconduct probably caused the rendition of an improper judgment.

Francis responds with seven examples of alleged judicial bias. First, Francis claims that the trial judge assisted Dow's counsel during voir dire by commenting, "Ms. Johnson [Dow's counsel], there were a couple of other hands on your question about labor union [sic]." Second, Francis cites the following exchange as an example of the judge encouraging Dow's counsel to object:

> Counsel: "Objection, Your Honor. Remote as to time. Vague."
>
> Judge: "Go ahead."
>
> Counsel: "Not relevant."
>
> Judge: "Sustained."

Third, Francis contends that the judge frequently added additional bases to Dow's objections. Fourth, Francis asserts that the judge twice instructed Francis' counsel to "move on" "so that we can get this case to the jury." Fifth, Francis claims that the judge frequently reprimanded Francis' counsel in a condescending manner; as an example, Francis cites this response by the judge to an objection: "You can just say compound, and I can listen to the question." Sixth, Francis complains that the judge did not allow Francis' counsel to read from documents already admitted into evidence. For example, at one point, the judge said, "I instructed you not to read from the document. Would you please just direct questions to the witness? As I said, the document is in evidence and can be reviewed by the jury; and continuing to read the document at this late hour only prolongs the time we are here." And at another point in the trial, the judge again reminded Francis' counsel: "But I once again caution you that these documents are in evidence. So, rather than reviewing the documents with the jury, ask the question of the witness; and let's focus specifically on information you need to get from this witness and not information from the document that the jury has seen several times already." Francis argues that these comments were intended to prevent the impeachment of defense witnesses.

As a seventh example of alleged judicial bias, Francis describes an exchange that took place near the end of the trial, out of the jury's presence. The judge criticized Francis' counsel for calling a Dow executive to testify when counsel had not indicated his intention to do so the day before. Francis' attorney explained that he had developed his strategy just the evening before and had not made any misrepresentations to the court. The judge then apologized for her comment: "Okay. Well, I apologize. That was out of line. I shouldn't have said that. But honestly, I'm about to my limit with the conduct of how this trial has proceeded and—you know, I'm a patient person. That was out of line, and I do apologize." Francis argues the judge's improper comments spanned the two-week trial, grew increasingly caustic in nature, and were incurable by instruction. We disagree with Francis.

First, we consider whether the trial judge's comments constituted bias as a matter of law. The United States Supreme Court, when presented with similar allegations of judicial bias, has determined that "judicial rulings alone almost never constitute a valid basis for a bias or partiality motion," and opinions the judge forms during a trial do not necessitate recusal "unless they display a deep-seated favoritism or antagonism that would make fair judgment impossible. Thus, judicial remarks during the course of a trial that are critical or disapproving of, or even hostile to, counsel, the parties, or their cases, ordinarily do not support a bias or partiality challenge." Further, "[n]ot establishing bias or partiality . . . are expressions of impatience, dissatisfaction, annoyance, and even anger . . . . A judge's ordinary efforts at courtroom administration—even a stern and short-tempered judge's ordinary efforts at courtroom administration—remain immune." In short, a trial court has the inherent power to control the disposition of cases "with economy of time and effort for itself, for counsel, and for litigants."

Similarly, Texas courts have held that "the discretion vested in the trial court over the conduct of a trial is great." A trial court has the authority to express itself in exercising this broad discretion. Further, a trial court may properly intervene to maintain control in the courtroom, to expedite the trial, and to prevent what it considers to be a waste of time.

We apply these principles to this case, and after carefully examining the judge's allegedly improper comments in the context of the entire record, we conclude there is no evidence of judicial bias. The record indicates that the judge exercised her broad discretion to "maintain control and promote expedition." Thus, the court of appeals erred in concluding that the trial judge's conduct exhibited bias.

The court of appeals also erred in excusing Francis' failure to preserve her complaint. This Court [has] held that objection to a trial court's alleged improper conduct or comment must be made when it occurs if a party is to preserve error for appellate review, unless the conduct or comment cannot be rendered harmless by proper instruction. Neither Francis nor the court of appeals explain how any comments made by the trial judge were incurable or would excuse Francis' failure to preserve error. For this additional reason, the court of appeals erred in sustaining Francis' allegations of judicial bias.

* * *

Accordingly, without hearing oral argument, we grant Dow and Hegyesi's petition for review, reverse the court of appeals' judgment, and remand the case to the court of appeals for further proceedings consistent with this opinion.

---

6. *Who Can Question a Witness*

Read Rule 265.

***Pitt v. Bradford Farms*, 843 S.W.2d 705 (Tex. App.—Corpus Christi 1992, no writ.):**

Finally, appellant complains that the trial judge acted improperly by examining a witness in front of the jury. The record shows that the trial judge examined one witness, that appellant did not object during the examination, that the court immediately recessed, and that appellant requested a bench conference when the court reconvened. At that conference, the trial judge stated:

> Well, if the Court doesn't understand what the witness is doing and I don't feel that the question has been properly put to the witness so that the Court and the Jury can understand it, then I'm going to take it upon myself to ask the Jury [sic] the questions so that it can be clarified, and I do this as a matter of expediency so we can get on with the trial. I don't feel that that's embellishing the witness's testimony, I feel it's an amplification of what his answer is, and that's all, and that's the only reason it's made . . . . [T]he Court, I feel, has the right to amplify what the witness said so that everybody understands. For example—I'll give you a perfect example. When Mrs. Bradford was testifying right now there was some confusion, and I could tell from the looks on the Jury's face that there was some confusion as to what call she had reference to, and that's the reason I asked her.

We have previously held that a trial judge may examine a witness during a bench trial. . . . The Third Court of Appeals, however, [has] stated, 'If this were a jury trial, we would have to view the matter in an entirely different light.'

We agree that the examination of witnesses by a trial judge during a jury trial must be viewed in an entirely different light. A trial judge should not examine witnesses who are testifying before a jury. We disapprove of cases which suggest that trial judges may generally examine witnesses whenever they feel that the jury does not understand the evidence being presented. . . . Under our State's system of justice, the duty to present coherent evidence to the jury belongs to the advocates, not to the bench. We hold that the trial judge acted improperly by examining the witness in front of the jury.

To reverse a judgment on the ground of judicial misconduct, however, a complaining party must show either trial court bias or that he suffered probable prejudice. The record does not reflect trial court bias, and appellant has neither demonstrated nor does the record show she suffered probable prejudice from the trial court's examination of the witness. We find that the trial judge acted in a fair and impartial manner throughout the trial and that appellant did not suffer probable prejudice from the impropriety committed by the trial judge. We overrule appellant's fourth point of error.

We AFFIRM the trial court's judgment.

***Born v. Virginia City Dance Hall and Saloon*, 857 S.W.2d 951 (Tex. App.—Houston [14th Dist.] 1993, writ denied):**

[William Born, Jr. died in a car wreck after he and Nicar (the driver) had been drinking one evening at the defendant dance hall. Born's wife, children, and parents brought a dram shop suit against the dance hall, alleging that it served Born and Nicar after they were visibly intoxicated. The jury failed to find the defendant negligent, and plaintiffs appealed. One of their complaints on appeal concerned the trial judge's questioning of a witness.]

> In point of error five, appellants claim the trial court erred by instructing a witness how to answer a question on direct examination. Appellants complain about the following statements by the trial judge:
>
> Q. [Plaintiffs' counsel] Well, now, being his best friend, what would have prevented you from simply turning around and saying, 'Willie, stop it'?
>
> A. I tried.
>
> Q. What would have prevented you from turning around and saying, 'Willie, have you had too much to drink to drive the truck?'
>
> A. I know what his answer would have been.
>
> Q. What would have prevented you from turning around and really looking at this person who you say is your best friend, who you say has a drinking problem, and determining for yourself—
>
> A. I said he had a drinking problem.
>
> Q. —determining for yourself whether or not he was intoxicated?
>
> A. Like I said, you'd have to know Willie. You know, he's persistent.
>
> Q. I'm not talking about Willie. I'm talking about you.
>
> MR. COOPER: Judge, I object to him arguing with the witness. He asked him what would have prevented him, and the man answered, and he starts arguing with him.
>
> THE COURT: Overruled. The question is simply: 'Would anything have prevented you.' I take it your answer is nothing other than his personality?
>
> THE WITNESS: Yes, sir.
>
> THE COURT: Let's move along then.
>
> Appellants did not object to the trial court's action.
>
> Although the trial judge should not act as an advocate, his role is more than that of an umpire. *Henderson-Bridges, Inc. v. White*, 647 S.W.2d 375, 377 (Tex. App.—Corpus Christi 1983, no writ). For the purpose of eliciting evidence that has not otherwise been brought out, the judge may put competent and material questions to a witness, and where anything material has been omitted, it is sometimes his duty to examine a witness. *Id.* We find that the trial judge's action in this instance was to paraphrase the previous question and to clarify the witness' response. The judge did not instruct the witness to answer the question differently in any material respect than he had already answered.
>
> Appellants also complain about the trial court's answer to a question regarding the reason for the witness' termination of employment. Appellants assert that the witness previously

testified he was put on leave of absence from employment due to a criminal conviction arising out of the incident upon which this suit is based. The written transcription presented by appellants contains no testimony by this witness about this subject. Rather, the page cited by appellants contains a statement by appellants' counsel to the trial court about the witness' prior deposition testimony. Appellants' counsel was arguing that defense counsel was misleading the jury by telling them the witness was on leave of absence because of the allegations in this case. The judge addressed this issue later and the following transpired out of the jury's presence:

THE COURT: I think I'm going to rule that—Mr. Nicar, you'll need to listen to this—that you may ask him the question: 'Were you suspended because we sued you in this suit?' Your answer to that is going to be? Were you suspended because of this lawsuit?

THE WITNESS: No, sir.

We find no impropriety by the trial judge in attempting to clarify this point. Furthermore, appellants have shown no harm and we cannot perceive any harm that this action could have caused appellants. We overrule point of error five.

FAZZINO
v.
GUIDO
836 S.W.2d 271
(Tex. App.—Houston [1st Dist.] 1992, writ denied)

WILSON, JUSTICE.

Appellant, John Fazzino, appeals from a judgment entered below following a jury verdict in which a roadway bordering and/or on appellant's property was found to be dedicated for the benefit of the general public. The trial court also ordered that appellant remove any impediment placed in the roadway within his property lines. We affirm.

* * *

Appellant alleges in his sixth point of error that the trial court committed fundamental error by encouraging the questioning of witnesses by jurors during the trial. The procedure that appellant complains of is as follows:

1. After both lawyers had concluded their respective direct and cross-examination, the trial court asked the jurors for written questions.

2. The jury and witness left the courtroom while the admissibility of the question was determined.

3. The trial court read the question to both lawyers and they were given the opportunity to object to the questions.

4. The jury and witness were brought back into the courtroom and the admissible questions were read to the witness verbatim.

5. After the witness answered, both lawyers were allowed to ask follow-up questions limited to the subject matter of the juror's question.

This appears to be a case of first impression in a civil cause of action in Texas. However, two criminal cases recently decided by the Fourteenth Court of Appeals involved this same issue. . . .[T]he court in these two cases did determine that the trial court's allowing the jurors to propound questions to the witnesses was not improper.

The Fifth Circuit has stated: "There is nothing improper about the practice of allowing occasional questions from jurors to be asked of witnesses. If a juror is unclear as to a point in the proof, it makes good common sense to allow a question to be asked about it. If nothing else, the question should alert trial counsel that a particular factual issue may need more extensive development. Trials exist to develop the truth."

In the present case, both parties were afforded great procedural protection by the manner in which the questions were asked, as is outlined in the five steps describing the procedure above. Additionally, the record reveals that neither of the lawyers at trial objected to this procedure, and that neither side was injured by any of the questions from the jurors. With these procedural safeguards, there was no harm to appellant, and no fundamental error. Appellant's sixth point of error is overruled.

* * *

Appellant's final point of error is overruled, and the judgment is in all things affirmed.

Notes & Questions

1. *Current thinking*. There are many lawyers and judges who believe that jurors should be able to ask questions, provided that appropriate procedural safeguards are followed, in particular excusing the jurors when the lawyers and the judge are discussing whether the question is admissible or not.

2. *Criminal case reversals*. Since the decision in *Fazzino*, the Court of Criminal Appeals has condemned the practice of allowing jurors to propose questions in criminal cases.[1]

3. *Attorney's objections*. Note that nothing in *Fazzino* requires an attorney to object to a juror's question in front of the jury, a procedure that would be clearly prejudicial.

---

[1] *See* Morrison v. State, 845 S.W.2d 882 (Tex. Crim. App. 1992); State v. Buchanan, 846 S.W.2d 853 (Tex. Crim. App. 1993) *and* Allen v. State, 845 S.W.2d 907 (Tex. Crim. App. 1993).

7. *The Judge's Comments Before the Jury*

***Pacesetter Corp. v. Barrickman*, 885 S.W.2d 256 (Tex. App.—Tyler 1994, no writ):**

Barrickman sued his employer (Pacesetter) for wrongful discharge, claiming Pacesetter fired him for filing a worker's compensation claim. The Texas statutes make such firings actionable. A jury awarded Barrickman actual and punitive damages. One of Pacesetter's complaints on appeal concerned the trial judge's conduct in front of the jury. The appellate court described the situation as follows and then affirmed the judgment.

> Pacesetter in its fourth point maintains that the trial court erred (1) in questioning witnesses during Pacesetter's examination of the witnesses, (2) in suggesting in the presence of the jury that Pacesetter's questions were irrelevant, and (3) in commenting in the presence of the jury that Pacesetter worked "hand in glove" with its workers' compensation insurance carrier. It argues that the judge's remarks were comments on the weight of the evidence and calculated to lead the jury to infer collaboration between Pacesetter and its workers' compensation carrier in discharging plaintiff.
>
> Pacesetter cites five incidents of alleged judicial misconduct. However, Pacesetter never raised a timely objection complaining of the judge's comments or conduct, nor did it request a curative instruction or mistrial. If objectionable remarks by the judge are of the type which could have been rendered harmless by a proper instruction from the judge, failure to object to such remarks and to request a curative instruction waives error. The same rule applies in the case of a comment on the weight of the evidence. An objection must be promptly made or an instruction requested or the error is waived.
>
> The trial court has a right to inquire concerning the purpose of a line of questioning during both direct and cross-examination, since he must be granted considerable discretion in controlling the orderly progress of the trial. Even if the statements complained of constitute comments on the weight of the evidence, they must be examined in the light of the entire record to determine whether they amounted to reversible error. Even conceding for the sake of argument that the judge's comments constituted error, none were so egregious that they could not have been cured by instruction. Error, if any, was waived. Point number four is overruled.

***Brazos River Authority v. Berry*, 457 S.W.2d 79 (Tex. Civ. App.—Tyler 1970):**

The river authority condemned a tract of certain land for a reservoir project. The parties could not agree on the value of compensation owed to the landowner, and at trial a jury awarded the landowner $75,800 as compensation. On appeal, the condemnor complained that the trial judge had influenced the verdict by commenting on the weight of the evidence while a witness for the landowner was testifying. The witness had given his opinion as to the value of sand and gravel deposits underneath the surface of the condemned land. When the condemnor objected, the judge made these remarks:

> THE COURT: Well, there is no doubt in my mind that, eventually, some day, it (the sand and gravel) would have been removed.

MR. HOOPER (attorney for landowner): Yes.

MR. KULTGEN (attorney for condemnor): Of course, I object to the Court's making that statement because we have had testimony—

THE COURT: I'm sorry. I will retract that.

MR. KULTGEN: All right, sir.

The condemnor did not ask the judge to instruct the jury to disregard his remarks, but did move for a mistrial the next day. The appellate court held that error was not preserved (no ruling on the objection, no request for instruction to disregard the remark) and that any error was harmless.

Notes & Questions

1. *Objection and instruction?* Cases on prejudicial judicial comments make it clear that the judge's comments—like those of opposing counsel—must be objected to at the time they are made or the error is waived *unless* the comment could not have been cured by an instruction from the judge. Though the judicial comment cases do not expressly require counsel to follow the objection with a request for an instruction to the jury to disregard the comment, or a request for a statement to the jury by the court that the comment is withdrawn, that is the curative action contemplated by the cases[1] and is the recommended practice.[2]

2. *What objection?* The predecessor to Rule 277 forbade the judge to comment on the weight of the evidence in his charge. That prohibition was, by case law, expanded to apply to the judge's comments *during* the trial.[3] Judges cannot expressly indicate which evidence they consider credible or not credible. Nor can they indicate their views on the weight of the evidence indirectly or with subtlety in any phase of the trial. Generalizations are difficult, but almost any unfair or prejudicial comment the judge makes—whether or not it addresses any testimony or exhibit—is likely objectionable as a comment on the weight of the evidence. The objection applies to any reflection on the character of a party, reflection on a witness's honesty or ability or deportment (unless the witness deserves the judge's rebuke) and any highlighting of evidence or testimony or witnesses as more or less credible or important than other evidence. The closer the comment comes to directly evaluating or commenting on evidence, the more likely it is to be held harmful.[4] A good rule of thumb is that, if the judge goes further than a simple ruling on a motion or objection and volunteers something that is prejudicial, the correct objection is probably "comment on the weight of the evidence" and should be followed by a motion requesting that the judge withdraw the comment and instruct the jury not to consider it.

---

[1] *See also* Gillum v. Temple, 546 S.W.2d 361 (Tex. Civ. App.—Corpus Christi 1976, writ ref'd n.r.e.); *and* Pirrung v. T. & N.O. Railroad Co., 350 S.W.2d 50 (Tex. Civ. App.—Houston 1961, no writ). But it *is* required in the case of improper comments by counsel.

[2] *See*, 4 McDONALD, TEXAS CIVIL PRACTICE, Section 21:39, at p. 117.

[3] *See* 4 McDONALD, TEXAS CIVIL PRACTICE, Section 21:30, p. 111 *and* 20 TEX. L. REV. 83 (1941).

[4] *See, generally*, McDONALD, TEXAS CIVIL PRACTICE, Section 21:40, at p. 117.

8. *Making a Record—Bills of Exception*

When you object to evidence and the trial court *admits* it over your objection, the record will contain the evidence and the appellate court will be able to assess it and decide whether the trial court's ruling was erroneous and whether it was harmful. But if you are offering evidence and the court *excludes* it, you must get the evidence that you offered into the trial court's record so if you decide to appeal the appellate court will be able to assess it. This making of a record is called your "offer of proof" or your "bill of exceptions."

In the Interest of N.R.C.
94 S.W.3d 799
(Tex. App.—Houston [14th Dist.] 2002, pet. denied)

GUZMAN, Justice.

Rachel appeals from a judgment terminating her parental rights. She challenges . . . the trial court's sanctions order [which] precluded Rachel from presenting any witnesses other than herself at trial. We find the trial court abused its discretion in imposing sanctions . . . . Accordingly, we reverse and remand for a new trial.

I. FACTUAL BACKGROUND

Rachel and David divorced in 1991. At that time, the trial court named them joint managing conservators of their two children, N.R.C. and L.A.C. The children lived with David during the school year and with Rachel during the summer. [In August 2000, David brought this suit to terminate Rachel's parental rights. The trial court appointed an attorney ad litem for the children and ordered both parties to pay the ad litem's fees. Rachel did not pay, and the ad litem sought sanctions. The court granted sanctions and ordered that Rachel was "prohibited from presenting any witnesses on her behalf, save and except herself, at the trial on the merits."]

At trial, David presented evidence that Rachel had verbally and physically abused the children and that the children did not want to visit Rachel. [David introduced expert testimony that it would be in the best interest of the children to terminate Rachel's parental rights.] Rachel testified that she recognized the need to control her anger and that with appropriate psychological help, she could repair the relationship with her children. [Under the sanctions order,] Rachel was not allowed to present any other witnesses. The jury unanimously found that Rachel's parental rights should be terminated.

* * *

B. SUFFICIENCY OF THE OFFER OF PROOF

[David contended that the record does not show error because] Rachel's offer of proof was incomplete, and thus, the exclusion of her witnesses presents nothing for review. We disagree. Defense counsel began his offer of proof noting that Rachel would have called Paula Hudson, the executive director of the Jameson Center. In summarizing Hudson's proposed testimony, counsel introduced into evidence a letter in which Hudson detailed her observations of Rachel and remarked upon her progress and suitability as a parent. Hudson concluded that supervised visitation with "appropriate structuring" would provide opportunities within a safe environment to enhance both the development of positive relationships between Rachel and her children and to practice skills learned in therapy.

Defense counsel summarized the proposed testimony of Rachel's boyfriend and mother as follows:

> As further proof, had [Rachel] been allowed to call witnesses to testify in her own behalf she would have called Mr. Gregory Wassinger, who, as testimony has revealed, has been her significant other for the past four years, to testify to her actions and to the best interests of the children. Had she also been allowed to put on testimony she would have called Sameline [surname omitted] who has also been referred to in reference to this case as Grandma Sammie, also to testify to the best interests of the children.

Rule 103(a)(2) of the Texas Rules of Evidence provides that error may not be predicated upon a ruling which excludes evidence unless a substantial right of the party is affected, and the substance of the objection was made known to the trial court by offer of proof. To adequately and effectively preserve error, an offer of proof must show the nature of the evidence specifically enough so that the reviewing court can determine its admissibility. Rather than mandating formal proof, however, the Rules require only a "short, factual recitation of what the testimony would show is sufficient 'evidence' to preserve an issue for appeal." Courts prefer a concise statement over a lengthy or arduous presentation. The offer of proof may be made by counsel, who should reasonably and specifically summarize the evidence offered and state its relevance unless already apparent. If counsel does make such an offer, he must describe the actual content of the testimony and not merely comment on the reasons for it.

Counsel referenced the "best interests of the children" standard in his offer of proof. This term immediately invokes the relevant factors promulgated by the supreme court. Here, as indicated above, Rachel's attorney adequately described the substance of the proposed testimony, introduced Hudson's letter and referenced the best interest of the children. We find this showing sufficient under the circumstances.

C. CUMULATIVE NATURE OF THE TESTIMONY ON OFFER OF PROOF

In a final attempt to avoid an inquiry into the trial court's sanction, David contends the sanction was harmless, as the testimony sought to be elicited was "clearly cumulative" of that offered by Rachel. Texas courts have long recognized cumulativeness as grounds for the exclusion of probative evidence. However, the Texas Rules of Evidence discourage "*needless* presentation of cumulative evidence," not cumulativeness in and of itself. TEX. R. EVID. 403 (emphasis added). The mere fact that another witness may have given the same or substantially the same testimony is not the decisive factor. Rather, we consider whether the excluded testimony would have added substantial weight to the complainant's case.

As a litigant, Rachel retains the right to prove her case in the most persuasive manner possible. To defend herself, she may require several witnesses addressing the same material issue, as the testimony may come from disinterested sources or witnesses with differing vantage points. Indeed, litigants may, and often do, offer evidence from several different witnesses to prove one specific material fact. Often, the cumulative effect of the evidence heightens, rather than reduces, its probative force. Where, as here, different witnesses were to offer varying perspectives of the best interest of the children, the probative effect may likely have been heightened by the testimony of the stricken witnesses.

Based upon her own analysis and observations, Hudson's testimony was unique and not cumulative of any testimony given by Rachel. Though David insists that Rachel's mother and boyfriend are interested witnesses, that possibility does not automatically transform their observations into needlessly cumulative testimony unworthy of consideration. Rare indeed is the family courtroom in which multiple interested witnesses do not testify as to the best interests of the children in a termination proceeding. To say that testimony from non-party witnesses would be needlessly cumulative of the testimony of a single party witness would endorse an overly broad rule which we decline to adopt. We do not find that the testimony of the stricken witnesses would have been needlessly cumulative of that offered by Rachel.

[The court concluded that the trial court erred in striking Rachel's witnesses as a sanction for her failure to pay the ad litem's attorneys fees. It then reversed and remanded.]

LASCURAIN
v.
CROWLEY

917 S.W.2d 341
(Tex. App.—El Paso 1996, no writ)

BARAJAS, Chief Justice.

This is an appeal from a judgment rendered in a personal injury case arising out of an automobile accident. The jury returned a verdict of $110,000 for Appellant, which was reduced by credits to Appellee of $190,000. Because the amount of damages awarded to Appellant was less than the sum of the settlements reached with others prior to trial, the trial court rendered judgment that Appellant take nothing. We affirm the judgment of the trial court.

* * *

In her third point of error, Appellant alleges that because she has been unable to obtain a complete statement of facts for review, she is entitled to a new trial. During the trial, Appellant played portions of the videotape depositions of Diana Oliva, Susan Gravatt, and Chad Gillespie. Appellee showed the entire videotape depositions of these three witnesses to the jury and read portions of the Brock Perkins' deposition. None of this testimony was recorded by the court reporter. Similarly, during the direct examination of Dr. Watson, Appellant showed Dr. Watson part of the videotape deposition testimony of Dr. Misenhimer and Dr. Barron, which also was not recorded.

At our direction, the trial court held a hearing to correct the inaccuracies in the statement of facts. The trial court found that, with the consent of the parties, the official court reporter was excused during a portion of the defense presentation. Additionally, the court was unable to determine which portions of the testimony of three witnesses were utilized as evidence.

Texas Rule of Appellate Procedure 50(e) states that an Appellant is entitled to a new trial if (1) the Appellant has made a timely request for a statement of facts, (2) the court reporter's notes and records "have been lost or destroyed," and (3) the parties do not agree on a statement of facts.

Appellant cannot meet the second part of this test because the court reporter's notes are not lost or destroyed. This requirement contemplates that notes were actually made, then either lost or destroyed after coming into existence.

In the instant case, the court reporter did not make any notes when the videotapes were played to the jury; thus, there were no notes to lose or destroy. Although an Appellant is entitled to a complete statement of facts, where a witness testifies in the absence of the court reporter and the Appellant fails to object, the Appellant is not entitled to a new trial.

Moreover, Texas Rule of Appellate Procedure 11(a)(1) states that an official court reporter shall "mak[e] a full record of the evidence when requested by the judge or any party to the case . . . ." (Emphasis added). No such request was made, as Appellant and Appellee excused the court reporter during part of the defense presentation. Counsel cannot keep silent when the court reporter openly leaves the courtroom and thereby guarantee his client a new trial. Accordingly, we overrule Appellant's Point of Error No. Three.

* * *

***4M Linen & Uniform Supply Co. v. Ballard & Co.*, 793 S.W.2d 320 (Tex. App.—Houston [1st Dist.] 1990, writ denied):**

ON MOTION FOR REHEARING

* * *

There are two kinds of bills of exception: the informal bill and the formal bill. *Compare* TEX. R. APP. P. 52(b) [now see TEX. R. EVID. 103] *to* 52(c) [now see T.R.A.P. 33.2]. An informal bill of exception preserves error if: (1) an offer of proof is made before the court, the court reporter, and the opposing counsel, outside the presence of the jury; (2) it is preserved as part of the statement of facts; (3) and it is made before the charge is read to the jury. TEX. R. APP. P. 52(b) [now see TEX. R. EVID. 103].

Rule 52(b) [now see TEX. R. EVID. 103] permits a party to make an informal bill of exception before the court reads the charge to the jury. 4M Linen made its informal bill of exception after the charge was read to the jury.

Rule 52(b) [now see TEX. R. EVID. 103] states: When the court excludes evidence, *the party offering same shall as soon as practicable, but before the court's charge is read to the jury, be allowed* to make, in the absence of the jury, an offer of proof in the form of a concise statement. (Emphasis added.)

The rule is mandatory. The trial court must permit a party to make an informal bill before the jury is charged. Here, 4M Linen specifically reminded the court that it wanted to make an informal bill before the court read the charge to the jury. The court refused, and granted 4M Linen permission to make the bill after the charge was read.

Under rule 52 [now see TEX. R. EVID. 103 and T.R.A.P. 33], it was error to refuse 4M Linen permission to make an informal bill. Our task now is to determine whether the error was reasonably calculated to cause and probably did cause harm.

To appeal the trial court's exclusion of evidence, the complaining party must present the evidence that was excluded to the appellate court in a bill of exception. Because the appellate courts cannot evaluate excluded evidence unless it is preserved in a bill, it is reversible error for the trial court to refuse to permit a party to make a bill of exceptions. Here, however, although the trial court incorrectly prevented 4M Linen from making an informal bill before the charge was read to the jury, 4M Linen made a late informal bill, preserving that testimony.

On the late informal bill, Keith testified that a linen supply dealer in the Gulf Coast area would have reason to know that a linen company required a mildewcide, and that a linen supply company in this area would have run across the mildew problem many times. We hold this testimony was not relevant. There was no evidence in this case that Ballard & Co. had a duty to 4M Linen to do anything but supply the chemicals 4M Linen ordered. The laundry products were recommended to 4M Linen by Diamond Shamrock, not by Ballard & Co.

We overrule 4M Linen's second point of error."

* * *

ON SECOND MOTION FOR REHEARING

On appellant's first motion for rehearing, we held the trial court erred in refusing to allow 4M Linen to make an informal bill of exception, but we found the error was harmless. On second motion for rehearing, appellant claims the error was harmful . . . .

* * *

4M Linen complains about the timing of the bill: it was not permitted to make a bill before the trial court charged the jury, as required in TEX. R. APP. P. 52(b) [now see TEX. R. EVID. 103]. 4M Linen, however, was permitted to present the excluded evidence to the trial court after the charge was read to the jury. That evidence was brought forward for our consideration in the statement of facts.

After finding the trial court erred, we reviewed the evidence in the late bill and held the evidence was not relevant. 4M Linen now insists it has a right to a reversal and retrial because the trial court did not permit it to make a timely bill of exception.

If the purpose of the procedure for a bill of exception is to afford a party the opportunity to preserve excluded testimony for appellate review, the late informal bill did so. We find the late informal bill was the equivalent of a formal bill of exception, which can be filed as late as 60 days after the judgment is signed or, if a motion for new trial was filed, as here, 90 days after the judgment was signed.

We overrule 4M Linen's second motion for rehearing.

Notes & Questions

1. *Offers of testimonial proof.* How does one show by a bill that evidence was offered and excluded? First, the line of questioning draws an objection which is sustained. The proponent advises the judge (then or at the next convenient time, usually a recess) that he would like to "make a bill" on the excluded testimony. In order to avoid inconvenience to the jurors, bills are often made at recesses, during an extended lunch hour, or after the jury is retired for the day. (Counsel must remember to make the bill, preferably before the witness involved leaves the area.) When the time arrives, the attorney usually states for the record that this is testimony of X for a bill of exceptions, the witness is sworn (or more often reminded that he or she is still under oath), and the attorney questions the witness (in open court with no jury present) to elicit the essence of the excluded testimony, following which he "tenders" or "offers" the testimony. The opponent again objects, and the judge again sustains the objection (unless, as is sometimes the case, the judge has a change of heart and decides to allow the testimony, in which case it will be repeated before the jury).

2. *Documentary evidence.* With documentary evidence, the proper predicate should have been laid through a witness's testimony and the exhibit offered and excluded on the record. This is usually done in the presence of the jury. Thereafter, no other action is required except to state that the exhibit will be made a part of the bill of exceptions. If the predicate cannot be laid without violating a motion in limine, then it will have to be handled as with an offer of testimonial proof, that is, when the jury is absent.

3. *Formal and informal bills.* Note that error can be preserved in the "reporter's record" of the proceedings (formerly called the "statement of facts"). This is an informal bill.[1] Most appeals rely on informal bills. In unusual situations when there is no court reporter's record—or there is disagreement about the reporter's accuracy—a formal bill of exceptions may be required. Note that TRAP 33.2 is aimed at reaching a consensus on what actually took place. The judge has the final say in case of disagreement. The judge's version becomes the official bill. Then a contesting party's only recourse is to a bystander's bill under TRAP 33.2. The appellate court must choose between the competing versions based on affidavits, an unsatisfactory approach to a "fact-finding" chore. A formal bill controls over the reporter's record if the two are in conflict. *See* TRAP 33.2. Fortunately, court reporters usually record the critical events with a high degree of accuracy, so that resort to the formal bill is seldom required. TRAP 13.1 requires the court reporter to be present at all proceedings and make a record, unless excused by the agreement of the parties.

---

[1] The "reporter's record" is a written (typed) record of every utterance in the courtroom while the court is in session and includes testimony and the comments of the court and counsel.

CHAPTER 13. THE JURY

A. Assembling a Jury Panel

Read Rule 221-226a, Gov't Code Chapter 62.

In *Taylor v. Louisiana*, 419 U.S. 522, 528-30, 95 S.Ct. 692 (1975), the United State Supreme Court summarized the requirement that juries be summoned from a fair cross section of the community:

> The unmistakable import of this Court's opinions, at least since 1940 . . . is that the selection of a petit jury from a representative cross section of the community is an essential component of the Sixth Amendment right to a jury trial. Recent legislation within the federal court system [the Federal Jury Selection and Service Act of 1968, 28 U.S.C. §§ 1861-1878] has a similar thrust. . . . In passing this legislation, the Committee Reports of both the House and the Senate recognized that the jury plays a political function in the administration of the law and that the requirement of a jury's being chosen from a fair cross section of the community is fundamental to the American system of justice.

The following case applies these principles.

MENDOZA
v.
RANGER INSURANCE COMPANY
753 S.W.2d 779
(Tex. Civ. App.—Ft. Worth 1988, writ denied)

FENDER, CHIEF JUSTICE.

This is an appeal from a workers' compensation case tried before a jury primarily on the issue of the extent and duration of an injury. The trial court, based on the jury's answers to special issues, held appellant, Mary Mendoza, incurred total incapacity for a duration of four weeks. Appellant appeals from this adverse jury verdict.

We reverse and remand.

At the conclusion of the initial voir dire by the court and prior to impaneling of the jury, appellant's counsel moved for a mistrial and requested that a new panel of prospective jurors be drawn because a disproportionate number of jurors were from a single occupation. After six jurors were excused for cause and one for personal emergency, ten of the remaining twenty-one jurors identified teaching as their occupation. Appellant's motion was overruled.

In support of plaintiff's first amended motion for new trial, appellant took the sworn testimony of Thomas P. Hughes, District Clerk, and Ouida Stevens, Deputy District Clerk and Administrative Assistant to the Administrative Judge for Tarrant County. Several key facts were brought forth by the testimony. The morning the trial started, June 8, 1987, 550 jurors were called by the Administrative Judge of Tarrant County from a random list generated by data processing. Generally, those persons who postpone their jury service are placed on a transfer list, and teachers are often granted transfers in the months of March, April, and May. A transfer list was used on June 8, 1987. The computer list of 550 people and the transfer list were not mixed or shuffled prior to the first assignment to a court. The usual procedure is that the first round of jurors is drawn from the transfer list; those jurors returning to the Central Jury Room who were not selected as jurors on the first round are then randomly mixed before being sent out again to another court. Jurors are assigned to courts from the Central Jury Room in numerical order; thus, the 67th District Court on June 8, 1987, received a panel of prospective jurors composed entirely of persons on the transfer list.

Appellant's first point of error contends that she was denied her constitutional right to a fair and impartial jury by the lack of randomness in the impaneling process, and that appellant's counsel properly preserved error of the purported improper impaneling of jurors.

TEX. GOV'T CODE ANN. sec. 62.011 (Vernon 1988) provides for interchangeable juries in counties with at least three district or criminal district courts, as in Tarrant County. The Texas Supreme Court has ruled that in counties governed by the interchangeable jury statute "[o]bjection to the jury panel therefore must be presented to the judge charged with organizing and impaneling the jurors for the week."

It is the practice of the judge of the 67th District Court to conduct a preliminary voir dire at which time the court asks the occupations of the panel members. Tarrant County does not provide juror cards, nor is there any preliminary indication of whether jurors are serving pursuant to a postponement. In the instant case, the panel members' answers revealed that a substantial number of panelists were teachers. Immediately thereafter, appellant's counsel objected to the panel and moved for a mistrial on the basis that ten members of the original panel of twenty-seven were teachers. He additionally pointed out to the court that six panelists were struck for cause leaving only twenty prospective jurors. Out of this number, ten were teachers.

While there is authority holding that a party seeking to object to the randomness of a jury panel must present the objection to the judge charged with organizing and impaneling the jurors for the week, the application of this rule to the facts of the instant case results in a denial of the right to a trial before a jury that represents a cross section of the community. The rule puts an unreasonable and impractical burden on a party who is faced with a jury panel which is impermissibly selected. The first time appellant knew the basis for and had an opportunity to object to the randomness of the jury panel was during the voir dire examination in the courtroom. At this point, the time to make objections to the impaneling judge was long past; thus, appellant was denied the opportunity to preserve error in objecting to the manner in which the jury panel was assembled.

Moreover, those cases cited in support of the rule requiring that objections to the jury panel be presented to the judge charged with impaneling the jurors for the week are distinguishable from the instant case. Each of these cases contained an alleged error in the procedure of impaneling jurors which could have been detected during the initial organizing and impaneling process, but none of the cases cited dealt specifically with the lack of randomness of juror placement. *See State ex rel. Hightower*, 677 S.W.2d at 36 (the jury was not selected in compliance with the jury wheel statute); *Texas Emp. Ins. Ass'n*, 610 S.W.2d at 525 (juror excused for unauthorized and illegal reasons); *Texas & New Orleans Railroad Co.*, 306 S.W.2d at 794 (improper excuses granted for prospective jurors).

Every citizen is entitled to a fair and impartial trial before an impartial jury, fairly representative of the community. Appellant was denied this right because the panel from which she was forced to choose her jury was impermissibly assembled. The jury was not a randomly selected cross section of the community. The necessity to prevent the subtle erosion of the standards of the jury system does not require a showing by appellant of injury.

Appellant actively asserted her rights and moved for a mistrial on the proper grounds. The motion in the record is detailed and complete. We hold that the trial court abused its discretion in failing to grant the motion for mistrial. Appellant's point of error one is sustained.

In view of our holding in point of error one, it is unnecessary to address appellant's remaining points of error.

The trial court's judgment is reversed and the cause is remanded for a new trial.

Notes & Questions

1. *Harm.* How could the appellant discharge its burden of showing harm for an error in assembling the panel? How could she show that having an excess number of teachers on the panel probably changed the case outcome as required by the harmless error rule?

2. *How jurors reach the courtroom.* Government Code §§ 62.001 through 62.016 govern the selection of jury panelists. Each county is required to use a random method for selecting jurors for a panel for the week. Unless the county has elected to use a mechanical or electronic means for random selection, it is required to use a jury wheel (more like a barrel in which cards, each containing the name of a potential juror, are placed and rearranged by revolving thc barrel). Names on the cards are taken from the county's voter registration list and those persons with driver's licenses or personal identification cards issued in lieu of licenses. The sheriff and the district clerk each have a key to the wheel, and both keys are required to open it. Ten days before the first day of each term, the district clerk and the sheriff (or their deputies) draw jurors' names in the presence of a district judge for district court jurors (or the county judge for county court jurors). Parties to suits affected by the drawing may obscrvc it. Jurors whose names are drawn are listed, and summoned for duty for a given week during the term. Jurors report to the judge (or in urban areas, the judge with responsibility for jurors) and present their excuses.[1] In counties which maintain three or more district courts, the jury wheel is used to supply interchangeable panels. Jurors summoned usually report to a central jury room and lists of jurors making up the *panel for the case* are made up from the panel for the week. The panel for the case is then ordered to report to a specific courtroom where the jury panelists are seated in the order listed.[2]

3. *Challenge to the array.* Note that irregularities in making up jury lists may be attacked by a "challenge to the array" under Rule 221. However, if the jurors have been selected by jury commissioners or by drawing the names from a jury wheel, the latter being an almost universal practice, a Rule 221 challenge is inappropriate.

---

1 Note that GOV'T CODE § 62.110 provides that the court may not excuse any juror for economic reasons, unless all parties of record are present and approve.

2 For a more detailed discussion of the way jury panels are selected, *see* 4 MCDONALD & CARLSON, TEXAS CIVIL PRACTICE, §§ 21:12 through 21:14.

4. *Jury shuffle and harmless error*. Rule 223[3] prescribes the procedure for the original listing of jurors and for a "shuffle" of jurors appearing on a given jury panel. In *Rivas v. Liberty Mutual Ins. Co.*,[4] the panel for the case was apparently listed in the order in which jurors showed up in the jury room and not in the random order required by Rule 223. Furthermore, the trial judge refused counsel's request that the judge make a "drawing of the jurors' names to make up the panel for this case." The Supreme Court held that adequate randomness resulted from the procedure used to list the jurors and that the trial court's refusal was harmless error, noting that the respondent made "no attempt to show that it was required to accept a juror which it otherwise would have stricken had it not been for the trial court's ruling." The court distinguished *Heflin v. Wilson*,[5] which held that a showing that selection of potential jurors by jury commissioners instead of the mandated jury wheel was sufficient without more, to establish harm. However, the Fort Worth Court of Appeals has held that the complaining party is not required to show specific harm, but is entitled to reversal if it can show that the trial was "materially unfair" (the relaxed showing of harm that we will discuss in the context of peremptory challenges).[6] The Eastland Court of Appeals disagrees, applying the traditional harmless error analysis.[7]

5. *Juror questionnaires*. The *Mendoza* court notes that, at the time of the opinion, Tarrant County did not provide "juror cards." As of January 1, 2001, all written summonses must include a juror questionnaire developed by the Office of Court Administration of the Texas Judicial System.[8]

6. *Jury panelists instructions*. Note the juror's code of conduct in Rule 226a prescribes the conduct of attorneys and parties as well. Would the provisions of Rule 226a have any part in your pretrial instructions to your client? What if your client takes to chatting with the jurors in the hallway?

---

[3] The rule is somewhat misleadingly captioned "Jury List in Certain Counties" and is commonly referred to as the "jury shuffle" rule.

[4] 480 S.W.2d 610 (Tex. 1972).

[5] 297 S.W.2d 864 (Tex. Civ. App.—Beaumont 1956, writ ref'd).

[6] Carr v. Smith, 22 S.W.3d 128 (Tex. App.—Fort Worth 2000, pet. denied).

[7] Whiteside v. Watson, 12 S.W.3d 614 (Tex. App.—Eastland 2000, pet. dism'd by agr.).

[8] TEX. GOV'T CODE Ann. § 62.0132 (West Supp. 2001); Act of May 27, 1999, 76th Leg., R.S., ch. 539, § 2(c), 1999 Tex. Gen. Laws 3035, 3036.

B. Voir Dire Examination: Scope and Procedure

HYUNDAI MOTOR CO.
v.
VASQUEZ
189 S.W.3d 743
(Tex. 2006)

BLAND, JUSTICE*

In this case, we decide whether a trial court abuses its discretion in refusing to allow a voir dire question from counsel that previews relevant evidence and inquires of prospective jurors whether such evidence is outcome determinative. We hold that it does not. . . .

I. Background

Four-year-old Amber Vasquez died in a low-speed neighborhood traffic collision, after the passenger-side airbag in her aunt's Hyundai Accent deployed with enough force to catch Amber's chin and break her neck. The driver of the other car had turned unexpectedly in front of the Hyundai, and the force of the collision threw Amber forward in her seat. It is undisputed that Amber was not buckled into her front-seat seat belt at the time of the accident.

Amber's parents, Victor and Brenda Vasquez, sued Hyundai Motor Company and Hyundai Motor America, Inc. (together "Hyundai"), contending that Hyundai had placed the airbag incorrectly, and that the airbag had deployed with too much force in this low-impact accident. Hyundai responded that the airbag that killed Amber was not defective because a child wearing a seat belt—as state law requires—or sitting in the back seat—as the car's warnings cautioned—would not have been injured by its deployment.

In placing Amber unbuckled in the front seat, Amber's aunt, Valerie Suarez, disregarded airbag warnings on both sunvisors, a hangtag from the rearview mirror, a decal on the dashboard, and a notification in the owner's manual. Suarez ignored the warnings because she planned a short neighborhood trip and believed that the airbags would deploy only at higher speeds. Hyundai conceded that it knew some occupants would ignore the airbag warnings about placing children unbuckled in the front seat, but maintained the risk was outweighed by the benefits of the airbag to all others. Hyundai named Suarez and the driver of the other car as responsible third parties.

The trial judge dismissed two jury panels before seating the jury in the case from a third. During the first voir dire, Amber's counsel asked jurors whether the fact that Amber was not wearing her seat belt would determine their verdict.[7] After numerous jurors indicated that the

---

* The Honorable John Cayce, Chief Justice, Second District Court of Appeals, and the Honorable Jane Bland, Justice, First District Court of Appeals, sitting by commission of the Honorable Rick Perry, Governor of Texas, pursuant to the Tex. Gov't Code § 22.005. CHIEF JUSTICE JEFFERSON and JUSTICE GREEN are recused.

7 Plaintiffs' counsel asked:

> Now, what I specifically am looking for are those among you right now that will say, if [Amber] wasn't wearing a seat belt, then I don't care what the scientific evidence is. I don't care about the characteristics of this particular airbag and how it operated in this particular accident at this particular

lack of a seat belt would determine their verdict, the trial court dismissed the jury panel. During the second voir dire, the trial judge questioned the jurors along similar lines, with slightly fewer, but nonetheless significant, affirmative responses.[9] The court again dismissed the panel.

Before the third voir dire, the trial judge discussed with counsel her concern that the previous jury panels had misunderstood the inquiry about placing a child in the front seat without a buckled seat belt to be one about the weight they could give to particular evidence in the case rather than whether they could fairly consider all of the evidence presented. . . . Thereafter, the trial court allowed counsel to ask "general questions about belting" and to inquire about jurors' personal seat belt habits, but she did not allow disclosure that Amber was not wearing one at the time of the accident. Counsel asked questions about whether the jurors buckled their seat belts on short trips, before leaving the garage, before exiting a driveway, and before leaving a parking spot. At the conclusion of the third voir dire, the trial court excused 3 of the first 28 jurors for cause and seated a 12 member jury and one alternate.

The jury heard evidence for three weeks and returned a verdict in favor of Hyundai. It found no design defect and assessed liability for Amber's death to the two drivers (75 percent to Suarez, and 25 percent to the other driver). The trial court rendered a take-nothing judgment.

The Vasquezes appealed, contending the trial court erred in disallowing voir dire inquiry into whether the jurors would be "predisposed, regardless of the evidence," against the Vasquezes because "there is no seat belt in use," to a point that "[the jurors] could not be fair and impartial." Hyundai responded that the proposed voir dire inquiry is improper in that it asks jurors about the weight they would place on a particular piece of relevant evidence, and thus the trial court properly refused to allow it. . . . [T]he court of appeals reversed, holding that the trial court had abused its discretion in disallowing the inquiry because the proposed question focuses "on the ability of the jurors to be fair." . . .

II. The Purpose of Voir Dire

. . . [T]he Legislature has established general juror qualifications relating to age, citizenship, literacy, sanity, and moral character. The Legislature also has established bases for juror disqualification, including . . . anyone who "has a bias or prejudice in favor of or against a party in the case."

Voir dire examination protects the right to an impartial jury by exposing possible improper juror biases that form the basis for statutory disqualification. Thus, the primary purpose of voir dire is to inquire about specific views that would prevent or substantially impair jurors from performing their duty in accordance with their instructions and oath.

In addition, this Court recognizes that trial courts should allow "broad latitude" to counsel "to discover any bias or prejudice by the potential jurors so that peremptory challenges may be intelligently exercised." *Babcock v. Nw. Mem'l Hosp.*, 767 S.W.2d 705, 709 (Tex. 1989). "A per-

---

speed. As long as I know that she wasn't wearing an airbag—I mean a seat belt, that means that, you know, there's no way Hyundai can be responsible. If that is an attitude that you have about seat belts and about airbags, if that is an attitude that you have about accidents of this kind and the tragic results that flow from them, that's what I'm asking you about. Is there anyone here that regardless of what the evidence is, once you hear [Amber] wasn't wearing a seat belt your mind is made up?

[9] During the first voir dire, 29 out of 48 jurors indicated that the fact that Amber was not wearing a seat belt would preclude them from considering any other evidence presented. During the second panel, 18 of the 52 jurors responded affirmatively to the trial court's inquiry.

emptory challenge, commonly referred to as a 'strike,' is defined by rule 232 as one 'made to a juror without assigning any reason therefor.' " Peremptory challenges allow parties to reject jurors they perceive to be unsympathetic to their position. . . .

. . . Counsel's latitude in voir dire, while broad, is constrained by reasonable trial court control. Such control is necessary because, "[t]hough the motive of a peremptory challenge may be to protect a private interest, the objective of jury selection proceedings is to determine representation on a governmental body." *Edmonson v. Leesville Concrete Co.*, 500 U.S. 614, 626 (1991) (holding that, in civil cases, private parties may not base their peremptory challenges on a juror's race). Thus, the exercise of jury strikes is not solely a private endeavor: "[W]hen private litigants participate in the selection of jurors, they serve an important function within the government and act with its substantial assistance."

III. Voir Dire Inquiry Regarding Facts in a Case

Voir dire inquiry into potential juror bias and prejudice thus is proper to determine whether jurors are disqualified by statute and to seek information that allows counsel to intelligently exercise their peremptory strikes. Because the statute does not define "bias" or "prejudice," we defined them in *Compton v. Henrie*, 364 S.W.2d 179, 182 (Tex. 1963), using their ordinary meanings:

> Bias, in its usual meaning, is an inclination toward one side of an issue rather than to the other, but to disqualify, it must appear that the state of mind of the juror leads to the natural inference that he will not or did not act with impartiality. Prejudice is more easily defined, for it means prejudgment, and consequently embraces bias; the converse is not true.

Other sources confirm that "bias" generally relates to inclinations, while "prejudice" is associated with prejudgment. Although it expressly prohibits only bias or prejudice concerning parties, we recognized in *Compton* that the statute extends to bias or prejudice concerning types of cases. A juror who is prejudiced against all medical malpractice claims, for example, is necessarily prejudiced "against a party in the case," even if they have never met.

Although a juror may be statutorily disqualified because of a bias or prejudice against a type of claim or a general inability to follow the court's instructions regarding the law, this Court has refused to hold that statements that reflect a juror's judgment about the facts of a case as presented, rather than an external unfair bias or prejudice, amount to a disqualifying bias. In *Cortez v. HCCI-San Antonio, Inc.*, 159 S.W.3d 87, 94 (Tex. 2005), an attorney summarized the evidence during voir dire, and then inquired of the jurors whether either party was "starting out ahead." The Court held that such inquiries are improper, and that a trial court should not disqualify a juror based on an answer to an inquiry that seeks "an opinion about the evidence."

Cortez thus adopted the general rule that it is improper to ask prospective jurors what their verdict would be if certain facts were proved. Fair and impartial jurors reach a verdict based on the evidence, and not on bias or prejudice. Voir dire inquiries to jurors should address the latter, not their opinions about the former. *Cortez* involved a general summary of all the evidence, and thus we did not review whether a voir dire question addressed to the weight a juror would give a relevant piece of the evidence could be objectionable. Such an inquiry, however, raises similar concerns.

First, an inquiry about the weight jurors will give relevant evidence should not become a proxy for inquiries into jurors' attitudes, because the former is a determination that falls within their province as jurors. Just as excluding jurors who weigh summarized facts in a particular way infringes upon the right to trial by a fair and impartial jury, so too does excluding jurors who reveal whether they would give specific evidence great or little weight. *See Cortez*, 159 S.W.3d at 94. In both cases, questions that attempt to elicit such information can represent an effort to skew the jury by pre-testing their opinions about relevant evidence. And, when all of the parties to the case engage in such questioning, the effort is aimed at guessing the verdict, not at seating a fair jury.

Second, inquiring whether jurors can be fair after isolating a relevant fact confuses jurors as much as an inquiry that previews all the facts. Lawyers properly instruct jurors that voir dire is *not* evidence, yet jurors must answer whether they can fairly listen to all of the evidence based only upon the facts that counsel have revealed. In responding, jurors are unable to consider other relevant facts that might alter their responses, rendering their responses unreliable. This confusion may explain in part why jurors' voir dire reactions to the evidence have not been proven to be predictors of jury verdicts: experience tells that, whatever jurors' stated opinions about particular evidence may be at the outset, they can shift upon hearing other evidence.

Third, previewing jurors' votes piecemeal is not consistent with the jurisprudence of our sister court. In *Standefer v. State*, 59 S.W.3d 177, 183 (Tex. Crim. App. 2001), the Court of Criminal Appeals held it improper to ask jurors whether they would presume guilt if one fact [defendant refused a breath test] was proved and no others. Our sister court consistently has observed that

> [Q]uestions that are not intended to discover bias against the law or prejudice for or against the defendant, but rather seek only to determine how jurors would respond to the anticipated evidence and commit them to a specific verdict based on that evidence are not proper.

As the statutory standards for bias or prejudice in civil and criminal cases are the same, voir dire standards should remain consistent.

Finally, the Court's decision in *Babcock v. Northwest Memorial Hospital* does not dictate that a trial judge must accept questions that seek to assess jurors' opinions about the weight they will place on particular evidence. In that case, we held that counsel could question jurors about bias or prejudice resulting from a societal influence outside the case—namely, tort reform. In contrast, a question that asks jurors to judge the weight to be given an operative fact will not reveal whether jurors have potential external biases or prejudices that improperly skew their view of case facts.

Statements during voir dire are not evidence, but given its broad scope in Texas civil cases, it is not unusual for jurors to hear the salient facts of the case during the voir dire. If the voir dire includes a preview of the evidence, we hold that a trial court does not abuse its discretion in refusing to allow questions that seek to determine the weight to be given (or not to be given) a particular fact or set of relevant facts. If the trial judge permits questions about the weight jurors would give relevant case facts, then the jurors' responses to such questions are not disqualifying, because while such responses reveal a fact-specific opinion, one cannot conclude they reveal an improper subject-matter bias.

IV. Trial Court Discretion

One of the primary rules of voir dire in Texas civil cases has long been that trial courts have broad discretion in conducting it. . . . For good reason: an attorney's question is easier to parse in the courtroom than it is in an appellate record. In this case, for example, when a juror specifically asked whether questions about prejudice should take into account evidence already disclosed by counsel, the response was ambiguous:

> PROSPECTIVE JUROR NO. 7: I don't understand that question. Does that mean like that by what we have heard so far we haven't made a judgment?
>
> [PLAINTIFFS' COUNSEL]: Yeah. I don't want—Is there anyone here who has already made up their mind? Let me ask that question real, real loud again. Is there anybody here that thinks that they have already made up their mind on this case right now before you have heard any evidence whatsoever?

Without being present in the courtroom, one cannot tell whether jurors might have understood this response to be "Yes" or "No."

It can be a close question whether a juror's response indicates a prejudice due to personal animus or bias, rather than a fair judgment of the previewed evidence. Similarly, it can be a close question whether a voir dire inquiry focuses on the former or the latter, as the question presented for a ruling in this case reflects. Determining whether jurors' answers assume or ignore the evidence disclosed to them turns on the courtroom context, and perhaps the looks on their faces. So, too, does the import of counsel's questions, and whether as phrased they seek external information or a preview of a potential verdict. The trial judge is in a better position to evaluate the reasonableness of both aspects—the question and the answer.

We observed in *Cortez* that trial judges have discretion to clarify whether a juror's response is the result of confusion, misunderstanding, or mistake. Similarly, the trial judge must have discretion to exclude questions that seek to gauge the weight a juror will place on specific evidence. In *Cortez*, we held improper both (1) a juror's disqualification based on answers that previewed the juror's vote, and (2) the actual questions that sought the same.[55] Depending on the circumstances, a trial judge may choose to hear jurors' responses before deciding whether an inquiry pries into potential prejudices or potential verdicts, but if the question reaches for the latter, a trial court does not abuse its discretion in refusing to allow it. If the trial court allows a question that seeks a juror's view about the weight to give relevant evidence, then the juror's response, without more, is not disqualifying.

Permitting disclosures about the evidence the jury will hear during the case increases the potential for discovering external biases, but inquiries to jurors after doing so should not spill over into attempts to preview the verdict based on the facts as represented to the jurors. Balancing these competing concerns depends on the facts in a case and on the inquiries posited to the jury. The trial judge is in a better position to achieve the proper balance.

V. The Question

[Counsel for the Vasquezes sought permission to ask the jurors whether any of them had a "preconceived notion . . . that if there is no seat belt in use, no matter what else the evidence is, that they could not be fair and impartial." After a brief discussion, the court responded: "I'm going to sustain the objection. We are not going to go any further into seat belts. . . ."]

* * *

---

55 *Id.* at 94 (stating that "attempts to preview a veniremember's likely vote are not permitted," and that "[a] statement that one party is ahead cannot disqualify if the veniremember's answer merely indicates an opinion about the evidence").

The court of appeals held that the trial court abused its discretion in excluding the inquiry, agreeing with the Vasquezes that the proposed question "clearly focuses on the ability of the jurors to be fair," because, upon learning that Amber was not wearing a seat belt, jurors should not be so biased that they could not consider the remaining evidence in the case. Here, however, the trial court reasonably could have determined that the question seeks to gauge the jurors' verdicts and therefore we disagree with the court of appeals.

First, the question isolates a single fact material to the case: that Amber did not wear a seat belt. Hyundai's defense at trial rested in part on a theory that its airbags would not have harmed a child wearing a seat belt, as required by law, or sitting in the back seat. Assuming that placing an unbelted child in the front seat is relevant, admissible evidence, reasonable jurors could base their verdict on that fact alone. By isolating this fact, the question seeks to identify those jurors who agree that the one fact overcomes all others. As reasonable jurors, however, it is within their province to so conclude. The question thus asks the jurors' opinion about the strength of this evidence, and does not cull out any external bias or prejudice.

Jurors should not base their verdicts on matters that are irrelevant, inadmissible, or unfairly prejudicial, and counsel is entitled to frame voir dire inquiries that ensure that the seated jury will not do so. In those cases in which prejudicial evidence cannot be excluded, a party is entitled to a limiting instruction, *see* TEX. R. EVID. 105(a), and to inquire whether jurors can follow it. Here, however, both the trial court and the court of appeals concluded that evidence of the lack of a buckled seat belt was relevant and admissible; thus, the trial court could have determined that the inquiry focused upon the weight jurors would give specific evidence.

Second, incorporating phrases associated with an inquiry into whether the jurors hold a preconceived bias does not alter the basic substance of this question. Although the proposed question refers to predispositions and preconceived notions, both concepts properly relate to opinions jurors hold *before* entering the courtroom and hearing the relevant facts. Here, the question includes a relevant fact; thus, responses to it encompass more than *pre*dispositions or *pre*conceived notions. In this case, the jurors' judgments about the fact that Amber did not wear a seat belt at the time of this accident are not separable from their potential verdict. The proposed inquiry asks about these judgments, not about any separate unfair prejudice against a party or a claim jurors may have held before hearing the facts of the case.

The Vasquezes maintain that, even if the proposed question is a commitment question, it nonetheless is proper because the only commitment the question seeks is to have jurors consider all of the evidence, as the law requires. The phrases "regardless of the evidence" and "no matter what else the evidence is" included in this question, however, do not transform its substance into a commitment to listen to the evidence, because the question itself isolates one relevant piece and its impact on juror decision-making. Asking whether jurors will ignore all of the relevant facts, or all of the relevant facts *but one* are two very different questions—an affirmative answer to the former reflects bias or prejudice, but an affirmative answer to the latter, without more, reflects that jurors think a presented fact is most important, based upon what they have been told by counsel.

The emphasis of the question is not ameliorated by asking in it whether jurors could be fair and impartial. "Called as they are from all walks of life, many [jurors] may be uncertain as to the meaning of terms which are relatively easily understood by lawyers and judges." *McDonough Power Equip., Inc. v. Greenwood*, 464 U.S. 548, 555 (1984). In *Cortez*, we held that fair jurors do not leave their knowledge and experience behind, but nonetheless must approach the evidence with an open mind. However, if an inquiry suggests that, to be "fair," jurors must not decide the case based on a relevant fact, then a trial court reasonably could conclude that the question seeks a response that reveals nothing about a juror's potential fairness, but instead attempts to guess about his potential verdict.

* * *

The substance of a question, not its form, determines whether it probes for prejudices or previews a probable verdict. The trial court in this case reasonably could have concluded that the substance of the proposed question did not present a basis for disqualifying a juror for cause, and instead sought to test the weight jurors would place on the relevant fact that Amber was not wearing a seat belt at the time of the accident. Thus, the trial judge did not abuse her discretion in refusing to allow it.

VI. Further Questions

At the conclusion of the general questioning of the panel, the trial judge asked counsel to state the additional questions he sought to ask the jurors about seat belts. The Vasquezes proffered the above question. In sustaining Hyundai's objection, however, the trial judge also ruled: "We are not going to go any further into seat belts." . . . In sustaining an objection to an improper voir dire question, a trial court should not foreclose *all* inquiry about a relevant topic. The Vasquezes' complaint as to this part of the trial court's ruling, however, is not preserved.

A trial court may not foreclose a proper line of questioning, presuming that the actual questions posed are proper. In some instances, an area of inquiry may be proper, but not the particular question asked. In such circumstances, a trial court may exercise its discretion to reject the form of the question. If it is necessary to discuss the facts in the case to probe for potential biases, counsel must frame corresponding inquiries to avoid jury confusion and ensure that the question does not seek to preview the verdict. When the trial court determines that a proffered question's substance is confusing or seeks to elicit a pre-commitment from the jury, counsel should propose a different question or specific area of inquiry to preserve error on the desired line of inquiry; absent such an effort, the trial court is not required to formulate the question.

Thus, to preserve a complaint that a trial court improperly restricted voir dire, a party must timely alert the trial court as to the specific manner in which it intends to pursue the inquiry. Such a requirement provides the trial court with an opportunity to cure any error, obviating the need for later appellate review, and further allows an appellate court to examine the trial court's decision in context to determine whether error exists, and if so, whether harm resulted. In *Babcock*, we held that litigants need not present a list of each intended voir dire question, but parties must nonetheless "adequately apprise[] the trial court of the nature of their inquiry." A timely, specific presentation to the trial court of the manner of an inquiry is important because it is difficult to evaluate after a trial whether the trial court's denial of an inquiry caused a biased juror to be seated on the jury or to evaluate what additional information a party could have adduced for the exercise of peremptory strikes. Thus, the Court traditionally has adhered strictly to the principle that voir dire objections must be timely and plainly presented.

Here, in response to the trial judge's request that counsel specify the type of additional inquiry he would ask, counsel framed one inquiry. The proposed question is virtually the same inquiry that the trial court perceived had caused confusion during the second voir dire. That the trial court did not allow a similarly confusing question does not mean, though, that the trial court would have rejected a different approach had counsel proposed it. . . . Counsel does not have to present a list of questions to preserve error, but after the trial court's ruling sustaining Hyundai's objection to the one presented, it was incumbent on the Vasquezes to request alternative approaches to avoid the problems the trial court was addressing by its ruling. . . .

The Vasquezes . . . did not frame additional inquiries or convey to the trial court that the thrust of any remaining questions would be different from the single one presented for a ruling.[76] We do not know whether the trial court would have allowed other sorts of inquiries had counsel presented their substance. We therefore hold that the record does not present a sufficient basis for review of the trial court's ruling foreclosing further inquiry into seat belts.

* * *

The Texas Constitution guarantees a trial by a fair and impartial jury, and our courts use voir dire to achieve that goal. Voir dire inquiries that explore external biases and unfair prejudices further the effort, but those that test jurors' possible verdicts based on case-specific relevant evidence detract from it. The distinction between the two in some cases is a fine one. Thus, we vest trial judges with the discretion to decide whether an inquiry constitutes the former or the latter; as appellate courts, we should defer to their judgment. We hold that the trial court did not abuse its discretion. We therefore reverse the judgment of the court of appeals and remand the case to that court to consider the Vasquezes' remaining issues on appeal.

JUSTICE MEDINA, joined by JUSTICE WAINWRIGHT and JUSTICE JOHNSON, dissenting.

We can all agree that (1) litigants are entitled to fair and impartial jurors, (2) voir dire should not be used as an exercise to preview the verdict, and (3) trial courts must necessarily have broad discretion when conducting voir dire. That said, I do not agree that a trial court can totally divorce the legitimate search for bias and prejudice during voir dire from all material facts in the case. I also disagree with the Court's statement of the issue in this case because this case is not simply about the weight prospective jurors may attach to certain evidence but whether such jurors can follow their oath and the court's instructions. I believe that the issue is whether the trial court abused its discretion when it cut off questioning about seat belts; specifically questions about whether members of the venire would fairly consider all the evidence in the product liability and wrongful death suit, knowing that the decedent was not wearing her seat belt at the time of the accident.

The trial court here summarily dismissed two jury panels after approximately 60% of the first panel, and 35% of the second, initially indicated that they would not listen to any other evidence in the case upon learning that Amber was not wearing a seat belt at the time of the accident. Before beginning a third voir dire, the trial court devised a new format for questioning the panel, requiring that specific questions about seat belt attitudes be asked only during individual questioning of prospective jurors, and not to the panel as a whole, as had been done previously. When the time came to ask these questions individually, however, the trial court abandoned its plan, forbidding any further questions about seat belts. The Court agrees that this was error, but con-

[76] After the trial court had ruled on the parties' challenges for cause, the Vasquezes renewed their objection that the court improperly had restricted the voir dire, but did not frame further seat belt inquiries for a ruling. If the complaint on appeal is that a trial judge has not allowed sufficient questions about a particular subject matter, then a party should detail its areas of inquiry before challenging the juror for cause, allowing the trial judge an opportunity to cure the problem. . . .

cludes that the error was not appropriately preserved for our review. I disagree and therefore respectfully dissent.

I

* * *

I do not disagree that the question rejected by the trial court, as it was phrased, was an impermissible attempt to pre-test the weight jurors would attach to Amber not being belted. However, this improper question did not authorize the trial court to foreclose the entire area of properly-phrased seat belt usage questions. As the record reflects, there were (and are) a number of ways to pose the subject to the jury. Not all of them are improper commitment or pre-testing questions. But, when a trial court tells a party's attorney that there will be no further inquiry into a particular subject matter, as was done in this case, that party should not be prejudiced by taking the court's ruling at face value.

In re COMMITMENT OF HILL

334 S.W.3d 226

(Tex. 2011)

PER CURIAM.

A party selecting jurors for trial must be given latitude to intelligently use its peremptory challenges to seat a jury that, to the greatest extent possible, is free from bias. Here, because the trial court refused to allow two permissible lines of questioning, we reverse the court of appeals' judgment upholding the trial court's ruling and remand this case for a new trial.

This is an appeal from a civil commitment proceeding in which a jury found Seth Hill to be a sexually violent predator. *See* TEX. HEALTH & SAFETY CODE ch. 841 (providing for the civil commitment of certain violent sexual offenders). The State had the burden to prove that Hill (1) was a "repeat sexually violent offender" and (2) "suffer[ed] from a behavioral abnormality" that made him "likely to engage in a predatory act of sexual violence." *Id.* § 841.003. As such, much of Hill's trial focused on his sexual history, which formed the basis for the State's expert witness's conclusion that Hill suffered from a behavioral abnormality. During its pretrial deposition of Hill, the State explored Hill's sexual activity with other inmates in an all-male facility. In the deposition, Hill admitted to these acts. The State's expert testified at trial that "if somebody has heterosexual preferences and then they later begin practicing homosexual acts, it infers that there is an instability within their personality which again, is more evidence of why I diagnosed [Hill] with a personality disorder."

During voir dire, Hill's attorney inquired, without objection, whether potential jurors could be fair to a person they believed to be a homosexual. Several stated that they would not be able to give a fair trial to such a person. The court then instructed Hill's attorney to terminate that line of questioning. When Hill's attorney attempted several more times to raise the issue, the trial court directed him not to ask a direct question about Hill's homosexuality. Subsequently, the court stated that further questions would have to be submitted in advance.

Hill's attorney then attempted to ask the panel whether, if the State proved that Hill had committed two or more violent sexual offenses, the potential jurors would convict Hill based on that evidence alone or would also require the State to prove the statute's second element—that Hill had a behavioral abnormality predisposing him to commit such acts. The State objected to this line of questioning, calling Hill's questions improper commitment questions, and the court sustained the objection. When Hill's attorney attempted to rephrase his question, he was again told that the question was prohibited. After the jury returned its verdict that Hill met the statutory criteria, the trial court signed a judgment, and the court of appeals affirmed. 308 S.W.3d 465, 485.

Litigants have the right to question potential jurors to discover biases and to properly use peremptory challenges. *See Hyundai Motor Co. v. Vasquez*, 189 S.W.3d 743, 749-50 (Tex. 2006). This right is "constrained by reasonable trial court control." Thus, refusals to allow lines of questioning during voir dire are reviewed under an abuse of discretion standard. However, the proper discretion inquiry turns on the propriety of the question: "a court abuses its discretion when its denial of the right to ask a proper question prevents determination of whether grounds exist to challenge for cause or denies intelligent use of peremptory challenges." *Babcock v. Nw. Mem'l Hosp*., 767 S.W.2d 705, 709 (Tex. 1989). A party preserves error by a timely request that makes clear—by words or context—the grounds for the request and by obtaining a ruling on that request, whether express or implicit. TEX. R. APP. P. 33.1. Thus, in *Babcock*, we held that a party preserved error by asking a specific and proper question, stating the basis on which it sought to ask that question, and obtaining an adverse ruling from the trial court.

Hill's sexual history was part of the State's proof of his alleged behavioral abnormality, yet the trial court refused questioning that went to the potential jurors' ability to give him a fair trial. This prevented Hill from discovering the potential jurors' biases so as to strike them for cause or intelligently use peremptory challenges. *See* TEX. GOV'T CODE § 62.105(4) (naming "bias or prejudice . . . against a party in [a] case" as grounds for disqualifying a juror).

Babcock was a medical malpractice case in which the plaintiff attempted to ask the venire panel whether the "liability insurance crisis" recently in the news had resulted in improper bias in any of the jurors. The trial court repeatedly denied requests to ask such questions. *Id.* at 707-08. We held that, while the facts of the lawsuit crisis would not be evidence at trial, the media coverage surrounding the crisis "ha[d] unquestionably created the potential for bias and prejudice," and, therefore, the plaintiff should have been permitted to ask questions delving into that potential bias. We further held that the trial court abused its discretion by forbidding those questions, and error was preserved. We reversed and remanded for a new trial.

The court of appeals did not reach the abuse of discretion issue because it held that Hill failed to preserve error. However, the questions Hill asked were proper, and there was no need for him to rephrase because there were no defects for him to cure. Moreover, he made clear why he was entitled to ask the requested questions. The court instead ordered him to ask a question that did not address the issue of juror bias and then directed him to "move on" without asking any further questions on the topic. But the candid admissions of bias by the potential jurors, before the trial court suspended that line of questioning, establish both the propriety of the question and the trial court's abuse in denying Hill the right to ask it. As such, error was preserved. *Babcock*, 767 S.W.2d at 708; *Vasquez*, 189 S.W.3d at 758 (holding that a trial court "may not foreclose a proper line of questioning" where "the actual questions posed are proper").

The trial court rejected the second line of inquiry as improper commitment questions. This ruling was incorrect, however, because the "commitment" that the potential jurors were asked to make was legislatively mandated: they were asked whether they would require the state to prove both elements of a conjunctive statute. *See* TEX. HEALTH & SAFETY CODE § 841.003. Jurors swear an oath to render "a true verdict . . . according to the law . . . and to the evidence." TEX.R. CIV. P. 236. Implicit in that oath is a commitment to follow the law the Legislature enacted, and a party participating in jury selection may solicit from potential jurors that promise, essential to the empaneling of a fair jury. *See, e.g., Wainwright v. Witt*, 469 U.S. 412, 419-20, 105 S.Ct. 844, 83 L.Ed.2d 841 (1985) (recognizing, in a criminal case, that jurors may be asked to commit to follow law and statute); *see also Edmonson v. Leesville Concrete Co., Inc.,* 500 U.S. 614, 630, 111 S.Ct. 2077, 114 L.Ed.2d 660 (1991) ("Civil juries, no less than their criminal counterparts, must follow the law and act as impartial factfinders."). The trial court thus abused its discretion by refusing to permit the line of questioning. Hill preserved error by asking a proper question and receiving a direct ruling rejecting it. *See Vasquez,* 189 S.W.3d at 758 (to preserve error, a party must "adequately apprise the trial court of the nature of the inquiry" (quotations omitted)); *Babcock,* 767 S.W.2d at 708 (holding that a refusal to allow a question is an implicit ruling on a request to ask that question).

The trial court abused its discretion in rejecting these two lines of permissible questioning. Accordingly, without hearing oral argument, we grant the petition for review, reverse the court of appeals' judgment, and remand the case to the trial court for a new trial. TEX. R. APP. P. 59.1, 60.2(d).

Notes & Questions

Scope of questioning. As a general rule, counsel may inquire about anything relevant to the issues to be tried, the facts to be presented, or the parties themselves.[1] It is clear that voir dire questioning is not limited to information supporting challenges for cause, but extends to information relevant to the exercise of peremptory challenges.[2] Obviously, no questions may be asked which would introduce matters not admissible during the trial.[3] The mention of insurance, for example, is usually forbidden.[4] However, since a juror's employment by a liability insurance company would be highly relevant concerning bias about claims generally, questions eliciting that information have been allowed.[5]

Rules governing argument also apply to voir dire. Thus, counsel may not contrast the financial positions of the parties.[6] And counsel may not tell the panelists the effect of certain jury answers; that is, cannot say who will win or lose or what judgment will result from certain answers to the jury questions.[7] Another rule governing argument generally is that counsel may not attempt to foster

---

[1] Green v. Ligon, 190 S.W.2d 742, 747 (Tex. Civ. App.—Ft. Worth 1945, writ ref'd n.r.e.).

[2] Lubbock Bus Co. v. Pearson, 277 S.W.2d 186 (Tex. Civ. App.—Amarillo 1955, writ ref'd n.r.e.) *and* Greenman v. Ft. Worth, 308 S.W.2d 553 (Tex. Civ. App.—Ft. Worth 1957, writ ref'd n.r.e.).

[3] Christie v. Brewer, 374 S.W.2d 908 (Tex. Civ. App.—Austin 1964, writ ref'd n.r.e.).

[4] South Austin Drive-In Theater v. Thomison, 421 S.W.2d 933 (Tex. Civ. App.—Austin 1967, writ ref'd n.r.e.).

[5] A.J. Miller Trucking Co. v. Wood, 474 S.W.2d 763 (Tex. Civ. App.—Tyler 1971, writ ref'd n.r.e.).

[6] Texas and N.O.R. Co. v. Lide, 117 S.W.2d 479 (Tex. Civ. App.—Waco 1938, no writ).

[7] T.E.I.A. v. Loesch, 538 S.W.2d 435 (Tex. Civ. App.—Waco 1976, writ ref'd n.r.e.) (advising jurors as to the amount of recovery based on given findings in workers compensation case).

sympathy for or prejudice against a particular party, a rule equally applicable in voir dire examination.[8]

C. Statutory Disqualifications and Challenges for Cause

Read Rules 227-231 and 292, Gov't Code, Chapter 62.

CORTEZ
v.
HCCI-SAN ANTONIO, INC.

159 S.W.3d 87
(Tex. 2005)

MEDINA, Justice.

This case presents two issues: whether the trial court abused its discretion in denying a challenge to an equivocating veniremember for cause, and whether an objection to the denial was timely to preserve error. The court of appeals held that error was preserved and that the trial court did not abuse its discretion. We affirm the judgment of the court of appeals.

I

Carmen Puentes, a nursing home resident, sued HCCI-San Antonio ("HCCI"), Altman Nursing, and Jerry Tristan for negligence, gross negligence, assault, penal code violations, and intentional infliction of emotional distress related to a fall and allegations of mistreatment at the Alta Vista Nursing Center, a nursing home HCCI had purchased from Altman four months earlier. Puentes died while the suit was pending, and her heir Jesus Cortez pursued the claim.

During voir dire, counsel questioned veniremember Snider, who had handled automobile claims as an insurance adjuster. Snider said that his experience might give him "preconceived notions." "I would feel bias," he said, "but I mean, I can't answer anything for certain." When the trial judge asked him to explain his bias, he said that he had seen "lawsuit abuse . . . so many times." He said that "in a way," the defendant was "starting out ahead," and explained:

> Basically, and I mean nothing against their case, it's just that we see so many of those. It's just like, well, I don't know if it's real or not. And this type [of] case I'm not familiar with whatsoever, so that's not a bias I should have. It's just there.

Upon further questioning, he agreed that at times when he evaluated automobile claims, he found that they had merit, and that he was "willing to try" to listen to the case and decide it on the law and the evidence. Cortez challenged Snider, arguing that he had demonstrated bias, but the trial court denied the challenge. Cortez therefore had to use his last peremptory challenge to strike Snider, and veniremember 7 was empaneled. Cortez never challenged veniremember 7 for cause,

---

8 Texas and N.O.R. Co. v. Lide, 117 S.W.2d 479 (Tex. Civ. App.—Waco 1938, no writ) (classifying as highly improper attorney directing jury's attention to railroad owner's profits).

and never stated why he found 7 objectionable, but maintains that he would have struck 7 had he been able.

The jury returned a $9 million verdict against the defendants, but after reduction for settlement credits and the jury's apportionment of fault, the trial court rendered judgment against HCCI and Tristan for $87,869.36 in actual damages, and against Tristan for $250,000 in exemplary damages. Cortez, unsatisfied with the judgment, refused tender from HCCI and filed a motion for a new trial, which was denied.

Cortez appealed the judgments against HCCI and Tristan, on the ground that veniremember Snider should have been dismissed for cause. The court of appeals affirmed. We granted Cortez's petition for review, and we affirm the judgment of the court of appeals.

II

HCCI and Tristan claim that Cortez failed to preserve error by timely notifying the trial court that he would be harmed by having to use his last peremptory strike on Snider. In civil suits in Texas district courts, each side has six peremptory challenges—more than litigants in most other states.[1] TEX. R. CIV. P. 233. When a challenge for cause is denied, that error can be corrected by striking the veniremember peremptorily. Thus, the error is only harmful if this peremptory challenge would have been used on another objectionable veniremember.

Accordingly, in *Hallett v. Houston Northwest Medical Center*, we held that to preserve error when a challenge for cause is denied, a party must use a peremptory challenge against the veniremember involved, exhaust its remaining challenges, and notify the trial court that a specific objectionable veniremember will remain on the jury list. 689 S.W.2d 888, 890 (Tex. 1985). This ensures that "the court is made aware that objectionable jurors will be chosen" while there is still time "to determine if the party was in fact forced to take objectionable jurors." Our sister court applies the same test, adding that a trial court may cure the objection by granting an extra peremptory challenge. *Escamilla v. State*, 143 S.W.3d 814, 821 (Tex. Crim. App. 2004) (holding error in denying challenge for cause is harmful only if party (1) strikes that veniremember peremptorily, (2) exhausts peremptory strikes, (3) requests additional strikes, and if refused (4) identifies objectionable juror remaining on venire).

Cortez's notice served this purpose, if barely. While it is unclear whether Cortez gave his notice to the trial court before or after he delivered his strike list, it does appear that the two events were roughly contemporaneous. More importantly, notice was given before the jury was seated, and the trial court stated on the record "it's preserved." We therefore hold that error was preserved.

Nor do we find Cortez waived error by failing to state why veniremember 7 was objectionable. Peremptory challenges normally require no reason. TEX. R. CIV. P. 232. While an "objectionable" veniremember could be picked at random, the objecting party must do so before knowing who the opposing party will strike or who the actual jurors will be. If it "guesses" wrong, any error is harmless; as our sister court recently noted, if the opposing party or the court agree to re-

[1] Of the 34 states utilizing twelve jurors on civil cases, 24 allow 4 strikes per side or fewer, 7 (including Texas) allow 6 strikes per side (Alabama, California, Georgia, Louisiana, New Jersey, Texas, and Vermont), 2 allow 5 strikes per side (New York and New Mexico), and 1 (North Carolina) allows 8 strikes per side. *See* U.S. DEPARTMENT OF JUSTICE: BUREAU OF JUSTICE STATISTICS, STATE COURT ORGANIZATION 1998 at 273 (1998); *see also* ABA STANDARDS RELATING TO JUROR USE AND MANAGEMENT, Standard 9 (recommending three strikes per side in civil cases tried to twelve-member juries).

move this veniremember, the objecting party does not get to object again to the veniremember who will be seated instead.

HCCI and Tristan also contend that any error was harmless. We disagree. The fact the Cortez prevailed at trial is not relevant, because we held in *Hallett* that "harm occurs" when "the party uses all of his peremptory challenges and is thus prevented from striking other objectionable jurors from the list because he has no additional peremptory challenges." No one except the jurors themselves knows exactly what transpires in the jury room; we know only the verdict. * * * Here, we do not know why veniremember 7 was objectionable. * * * [W]e cannot know for certain that his inclusion did not affect the verdict, so we presume harm. * * *

III

Cortez next argues, citing several court of appeals opinions, that veniremembers cannot be "rehabilitated"—that once a veniremember has expressed "bias," further questioning is not permitted and the veniremember must be excused. We disagree that there is such a rule, and to the extent these decisions conflict with our opinion here, we disapprove those cases.

As a preliminary matter, we must define what we mean by "rehabilitation." We agree that if the record, taken as a whole, clearly shows that a veniremember was materially biased, his or her ultimate recantation of that bias at the prodding of counsel will normally be insufficient to prevent the veniremember's disqualification. But what courts most often mean by "rehabilitation" is further questioning of a veniremember who expressed an apparent bias. And there is no special rule that applies to this type of "rehabilitation" but not to other forms of voir dire examination. This Court has used the term only once in connection with voir dire and then with apparent approval. Similarly, our sister court has shown no special disapproval of rehabilitated veniremembers. Thus, the length and effect of efforts to rehabilitate veniremembers are governed by the same rules that apply to all of voir dire.

Of course, the rules of civil procedure contain no rule on voir dire, but a few can be gathered from case law. Among these are that voir dire examination is largely within the sound discretion of the trial judge and that broad latitude is allowed for examination. Both of these principles are completely inconsistent with the assertion that voir dire must stop at the moment a veniremember gives any answer that might be disqualifying. Certainly, just as trial judges may exclude "needless presentation of cumulative evidence," TEX. R. EVID. 403, they may place reasonable limits on questioning that is duplicative or a waste of time. But whether further questioning would be a waste of time may depend on factors that may not appear in the record, such as a veniremember's tone and demeanor. As in any other part of voir dire, the proper stopping point in efforts to rehabilitate a veniremember must be left to the sound discretion of the trial court.

At the same time, trial judges must not be too hasty in cutting off examination that may yet prove fruitful. Statements of partiality may be the result of inappropriate leading questions, confusion, misunderstanding, ignorance of the law, or merely "loose words spoken in warm debate." If a veniremember expresses what appears to be bias, we see no reason to categorically prohibit further questioning that might show just the opposite or at least clarify the statement. If the initial apparent bias is genuine, further questioning should only reinforce that perception; if it is not, further questioning may prevent an impartial veniremember from being disqualified by mistake. Similarly, we do not believe the discretion accorded trial judges in ruling on challenges for cause is arbitrarily limited in cases involving rehabilitation. Because trial judges are actually present during voir dire, they are "in a better position . . . to evaluate the juror's sincerity and his capacity for fairness and impartiality." Therefore, trial courts exercise discretion in deciding whether to strike veniremembers for cause when bias or prejudice is not established as a matter of law, and there is error only if that discretion is abused.

In reviewing such decisions, we must consider the entire examination, not just answers that favor one litigant or the other. For example, in *Goode v. Shoukfeh*, a veniremember admitted he had "a slight bias," was "leaning a little" toward the defendant, and the plaintiff was "starting off a little bit behind." Nevertheless, we affirmed the trial court's refusal to strike the veniremember for cause based on the veniremember's explanation that "both sides . . . are pretty even," that his "bias" was only because the defendant's explanation of the evidence "was just a little more clear in [his] mind[.]" The veniremember explained, "I can make my decision on the evidence that comes from the witness stand . . . . I have not made a decision just from what you two have said." Clearly, neither trial nor appellate courts are required to consider challenges for cause based on only one part of a veniremember's responses.

Nor do challenges for cause turn on the use of "magic words." Cortez argues, and we do not disagree, that veniremembers may be disqualified even if they say they can be "fair and impartial," so long as the rest of the record shows they cannot. By the same token, veniremembers are not necessarily disqualified when they confess "bias," so long as the rest of the record shows that is not the case.

Here, the challenged veniremember admitted having a better understanding of the defendant's side, having worked as an insurance adjuster. Nevertheless, his answers to the trial judge's questions revealed that any initial apparent bias he expressed was actually against lawsuit abuse. Like the veniremember in *Goode*, Snider said he was willing to listen to all the evidence and to withhold judgment until the entire case had been presented. He never indicated any inability to find for Cortez, if Cortez proved his case. More significantly, he said he was "willing to try" to make his decision based on the evidence and the law. That is all we can ask of any juror.

Many potential jurors have some sort of life experience that might impact their view of a case; we do not ask them to leave their knowledge and experience behind, but only to approach the evidence with an impartial and open mind. The veniremember here expressed willingness to do that. Any bias he did express was equivocal at most, which is not grounds for disqualification. Snider was therefore not biased as a matter of law, and it was within the trial court's discretion to refuse to strike him.

IV

Finally, we address the veniremember's affirmative response to a question by Cortez's counsel that the defendants "would be starting out ahead" of the other party before he even got into the jury box. This cannot be grounds for disqualification. As we long ago stated, "bias and prejudice form a trait common in all men," but to disqualify a veniremember "certain degrees thereof must exist." "Bias, in its usual meaning, is an inclination toward one side of an issue . . . but to disqualify, it must appear that the state of mind of the juror leads to the natural inference that he will not or did not *act* with impartiality." *Id.* at 182 (emphasis added). Accordingly, the relevant inquiry is not where jurors *start* but where they are likely to *end.* An initial "leaning" is not disqualifying if it represents skepticism rather than an unshakeable conviction.

Cortez claims his case is analogous to *Shepherd v. Ledford*, 962 S.W.2d 28 (Tex. 1998). In *Shepherd*, a veniremember agreed that "based upon [his] past experience, [he] could not be fair and objective in looking at the medical facts as they have been testified to so that both sides start out evenly[,]" and that the plaintiff was starting out "ahead." We held that the veniremember was biased as a matter of law, and that the trial court abused its discretion in failing to strike him for cause. That veniremember, unlike Snider, agreed that he "could not be fair and objective" in looking at the facts, and that is what disqualified him. Snider said he was "willing to try" to decide the case on the facts and the law.

Asking a veniremember which party is starting out "ahead" is often an attempt to elicit a comment on the evidence. *See* Scott A. Brister, *Lonesome Docket: Using the Texas Rules to Shorten Trials and Delay*, 46 BAYLOR L. REV. 525, 538 (1994). Such attempts to preview a veniremember's likely vote are not permitted. Asking which party is "ahead" may be appropriate before any evidence or information about the case has been disclosed, but here, the plaintiff's attorney gave an extended and emotional opening statement summarizing the facts of the case to the venire. A statement that one party is ahead cannot disqualify if the veniremember's answer merely indicates an opinion about the evidence. *See* Jim M. Perdue, *A Practical Approach to Jury Bias*, 54 TEX. B.J. 936, 940 (1991) (recommending that disqualification turns on follow-up question "Had you formed this opinion before you entered this courtroom?"). A statement that is more a preview of a veniremember's likely vote than an expression of an actual bias is no basis for disqualification. Litigants have the right to an impartial jury, not a favorable one.

* * *

We hold that Cortez properly preserved error and that veniremember Snider was not biased as a matter of law. The trial court therefore did not abuse its discretion in failing to strike Snider for cause. We affirm the judgment of the court of appeals.

Notes & Questions

1. *Defense lawyer juror.* Soon after *Cortez* was decided, the Supreme Court addressed another challenge for cause in *El Hafi v. Baker.*[1] In a medical malpractice case, the following exchange occurred during voir dire:

> Counsel [for plaintiffs]: Okay. Is there anybody here that feels that you could not sit on a medical case and make a decision as to whether the doctor acted within or below the standard of care? . . . How about on the third row? . . . No. 25 [hand raised] . . .
>
> Juror 25: I'm not saying I want to [sic] be impartial. If I were in your shoes, I would want to know that I have spent most of my professional career on the defense side.
>
> Counsel: Are you a lawyer?
>
> Juror 25: Yes.
>
> Counsel: Who are you with?
>
> Juror 25: Preston and Calvert.
>
> Counsel: Okay. And you actually defend health care operations?
>
> Juror 25: Correct.
>
> Counsel: Let me ask you: in all fairness, do you think that if this were a horse race so to speak, the plantiff's [sic] are starting a little bit behind in your eyes?

---

1 164 S.W.3d 383 (Tex. 2005).

Juror 25: I mean—I'm not saying that—I would do my best to be objective. I'm just saying that if I were in your shoes I might consider you towards as the attorney who spend [sic] most of his career defending malpractice lawsuits.

Counsel: You feel like you can relate very much to the defendant's [sic] lawyers in this case? Is that fair?

Juror 25: That's correct.

Counsel: You feel like you would tend to look at it from their perspective as more of the plaintiff's [sic] perspective?

Juror 25: I think it would be natural.

The trial court denied the Bakers' challenge for cause to Juror 25, and the Supreme Court held that the trial court did not abuse its discretion in doing so. The Court emphasized the juror's disagreement with every suggestion that he could not be fair and objective, and characterized the testimony as "an attempt to 'speak the truth' so that the examining counsel could intelligently exercise peremptory challenges" rather than a reflection of bias.

2. *Statutory qualifications*. Questions to members of the panel in the case will deal with the disqualification for service on that particular jury under § 62.105 of the Government Code. One is disqualified if he or she is a witness in the case;[2] is interested, directly or indirectly, in the subject matter of the case;[3] is related by consanguinity or affinity within the third degree;[4] has a bias or prejudice in favor of or against a party in the case; or has served as a juror in an earlier trial of the case, or another case involving the same fact questions. "Bias or prejudice" is by far the most important basis for disqualification of jurors, accounting for perhaps 90% or more of successful challenges for cause. By the time an attorney confronts a jury panel, it will ordinarily have been screened for the general qualifications required of jurors under § 62.102 of the Government Code. They are that the juror be at least 18 years old, a citizen of the state and county, qualified to vote in the county, of sound mind and good moral character, able to read and write, not having had specifically defined prior jury service within the preceding six months, not a convicted felon, nor under indictment for theft or a felony.[5] Those who are legally blind and those who are deaf are not automatically disqualified, but may be disqualified in a particular case, if, in the court's opinion, the impairment renders the person unfit to serve.[6]

---

2 T.R.C.E. 606 prohibits a member of the jury from testifying as a witness.

3 This usually refers to a financial or pecuniary interest. A shareholder of a party corporation is disqualified (*see* Texas Power and Light Co. v. Adams, 404 S.W.2d 930, 943 (Tex. Civ. App.—Tyler 1966, no writ), whereas a taxpayer of a governmental entity ordinarily is not (*see* City of Hawkins v. E. B. Germany and Sons, 425 S.W.2d 23, 26 (Tex. Civ. App.—Tyler 1968, writ ref'd n.r.e.). The employee of a party is also disqualified. *See* Stephens v. Smith, 208 S.W.2d 689, 691 (Tex. Civ. App.—Waco 1948, writ ref'd n.r.e.). The resident of a county is not disqualified as a juror in a case where that county is a party. *See* Local Government Code § 81.042.

4 *See* discussion of degrees of relationship in connection with recusals in Chapter 3, *and see* GOV'T CODE §§ 573.021-.025, for definitions of degrees of relationship.

5 Under § 62.103 of the Government Code, the requirement that a juror be able to read and write and the disqualification based on prior jury service may be waived in sparsely populated counties. Also, the voting requirement is based on eligibility, and the failure to register to vote does not disqualify a juror. § 62.1031, Government Code.

6 *See* § 62.104 *and* § 62.1041, Government Code.

3. *Wording of voir dire questions*. General or vague questions during voir dire are not helpful in uncovering bias or preserving error. In *Soliz v. Saenz*, 779 S.W.2d 929 (Tex. App.—Corpus Christi 1989, writ denied), plaintiffs sued a drunk driver and the business that served him liquor (Waterstreet). The jury found the driver liable but exonerated Waterstreet. One argument on appeal was that two jurors had not been truthful about their leanings and experiences. The court of appeals rejected this argument (at 933):

> During voir dire, the trial judge asked prospective jurors if they could listen to the evidence and apply the law to the facts. The prospective jurors did not respond [i.e. no juror raised a hand]. Appellants' counsel asked them if having eaten at the Waterstreet would affect their ability to sit in judgment and consider the facts and the evidence. In response, the prospective jurors shook their heads. Appellants contend that because [jurors] Adkins and Hefte did not follow the law, their answers to these voir dire questions were not truthful. Appellants also state that Adkins and Hefte failed to disclose their biases and prejudices.
>
> In certain circumstances, failure to disclose biases and prejudices during voir dire examination can amount to jury misconduct not affected by Rules 327(b) and 606(b). For instance, when a party discovers that a juror lied about a matter which reveals that the juror was clearly biased or prejudiced, this could amount to jury misconduct. * * * In order for false answers given during voir dire examination to entitle a party to a new trial, there must be a concealment by a juror in response to a specific and direct question calling for disclosure. Catch-all questions do not meet the requirement of specificity.

4. *Exemptions and excuses*. Exemptions and excuses do not disqualify the juror but provide an escape from jury duty should the holder so elect. The person may be exempted from jury services if he or she is over 70 years old; is the caretaker with legal custody of a child under ten; is a high school or college student; is an officer or employee in the legislative branch of state government; has had jury duty in the past two years (applicable to urban counties, certain restrictions apply);[7] or is the primary caretaker of an invalid.[8] Persons over 70, those with physical or mental incapacities, and those who cannot speak English may obtain permanent exemptions.[9] Jurors may also be excused if their service conflicts with a "religious holy day" as defined in § 62.112 of the Government Code. Furthermore, a court or its designated agent may excuse a juror based on "any reasonable sworn excuse," except that a juror may not be excused for "an economic reason," unless each party of record is present and approves.[10]

5. *Statutory and discretionary challenges for cause*. Once a statutory disqualification is established, the court must excuse the juror. The error is one of law and the trial court has no discretion. However, challenges for cause may prompt the trial court to excuse a juror who, though not disqual-

---

[7] *See* § 62.106(6) and (8).

[8] § 62.106, Government Code, establishes procedures for claiming exemptions.

[9] § 62.108 and § 62.109, Government Code.

[10] § 62.110, Government Code.

ified by statute, is nevertheless (in the court's opinion) unfit to serve on the jury for that case.[11] The court's decision on the second type of challenge for cause is reviewable for abuse of discretion.[12]

6. *Showing harm.* Note that *Cortez* involved the trial court's error of failing to excuse a disqualified juror after the disqualification was revealed during voir dire. It is reversible error to *refuse* to dismiss a disqualified juror if a good challenge for cause is made and if the *Hallett* steps are followed to preserve error. Be sure that you understand the *Hallett* steps described in *Cortez*. No other showing of harm is required. But erroneous *dismissal* of a qualified juror for cause is seldom reversible. Complainant must show harm, and the case law interprets that to mean that the complainant must show that he or she was denied a trial "by a fair and impartial jury," a virtually impossible burden in this circumstance.[13]

7. *The need for a record.* Following the *Hallett* steps will be futile unless they are preserved in the record for appeal. The court's action in seating a juror following a challenge results in an implied fact-finding that the juror was qualified and such a finding will not be disturbed on appeal absent a statement of facts or a formal bill of exceptions showing the challenge, the court's action and the *Hallett* steps taken to preserve error.[14]

8. *Typical sequence.* As attorneys are interrogating jurors, they may make challenges for cause, based on particular jurors' answers. Good advocacy requires that this be done outside the presence of the rest of the panel, usually at the bench, where the attorneys, the juror being questioned, and the court reporter will gather to conduct a *sotto voce* conference. Although there is a court reporter present in the courtroom, counsel sometimes overlooks the necessity for having the court reporter close enough to record the proceedings at the bench. Sometimes, to avoid keeping the rest of the panel waiting and because of the clumsiness involved in the bench proceedings, the judge will defer the questioning of suspect jurors until the end of the questions to the panel and will then declare a recess for the majority of the panelists, who are excused from the courtroom. Thereafter, individual jurors are brought up to the bench where the questioning—still *sotto voce*—proceeds, the challenges are renewed and the court rules on them. In the course of the voir dire examination, a juror will sometimes present an excuse not available earlier, and the judge will excuse the juror. It is important for counsel to keep the jury list up to date, showing the removal of jurors who have been excused, so that no peremptory challenge or "strike" will be wasted on such a juror. After all challenges for cause are disposed of, the court will allow attorneys to retire to separate locations where they can strike their lists in conference with their clients (and sometimes with counsel for other parties). Before the list is handed over to the clerk, *Hallett* requires that the aggrieved attorney make the prescribed record. The attorneys typically strike through the names of jurors on whom peremptory challenges are exercised and number those "strikes" one through six. The attorneys return their lists to the clerk, who then posts the peremptory challenges to the master list. (As we will see later, these strikes may be challenged on the basis of racial, ethnic or gender bias, requiring a hearing at this

[11] Rule 228.

[12] Moss v. Fidelity and Casualty Co., 439 S.W.2d 734 (Tex. Civ. App.—Ft. Worth 1969, no writ); Texas Power and Light Co. v. Adams, 404 S.W.2d 930 (Tex. Civ. App.—Tyler 1966, no writ); Texas Elec. Service Co. v. Yater, 494 S.W.2d 271 (Tex. Civ. App.—El Paso 1973, writ ref'd n.r.e.).

[13] City of Hawkins v. Germany and Sons, 425 S.W.2d 23 (Tex. Civ. App.—Tyler 1968, writ ref'd n.r.e.).

[14] Southwestern Bell Telephone Co. v. Sims, 615 S.W.2d 858 (Tex. Civ. App.—Houston [1st Dist] 1981, no writ); Lauderdale v. Insurance Co. of North America, 527 S.W.2d 841 (Tex. Civ. App.—Ft. Worth 1975, writ ref'd n.r.e.); City of Hawkins v. Germany and Sons, 425 S.W.2d 23 (Tex. Civ. App.—Tyler 1968, writ ref'd n.r.e.).

point.) The clerk then reads the first 12 names which remain on the list, passing over the names of jurors who have been excused or struck. At the time the list of 12 jurors chosen for service is read, attorneys may raise a *Batson* challenge, suggesting that the strikes were based on race or gender.[15] A very cautious attorney might well repeat the *Hallett* step of identifying an unacceptable juror who will be serving because a valid challenge for cause was overruled. This step will, of course, be taken outside the hearing of jurors. After the jurors are seated, the court will give the additional instructions prescribed by Rule 226(a)II.

D. Peremptory Challenges

Read Rules 232-235.

Peremptory challenges allow parties to strike jurors for no cause, any cause, or "just because." They do not have to identify why they strike a juror, and do so for any number of reasons. They originated in the English common law as an "unfettered right" to strike potential jurors.[1] Peremptory challenges are limited only by the number allocated to each party, and by the Equal Protection Clause of the United States Constitution (as we will discuss later).

Exercise of peremptory challenges is often seen as a trial lawyer's art, and more recently, as a science. In big cases, parties often hire expensive experts to assist in identifying characteristics of the "perfect juror" that are considered in putting together the voir dire examination and exercising peremptory challenges.

---

1. *Reapportioning Peremptory Challenges*

PATTERSON DENTAL COMPANY
v.
DUNN
592 S.W.2d 914
(Tex. 1979)

SPEARS, JUSTICE.

This case involves the "equalizing" by the trial court of peremptory challenges between multiple parties in a civil suit as required by TEX. REV. CIV. STAT. ANN. art. 2151a (Vernon Supp. 1978-79). Plaintiff-respondent Dunn, a dentist, sued four defendants on negligence and products liability theories for personal injuries received when a piece of equipment he was operating in his dental office exploded. The fire and explosion resulted when Dunn opened the valve of an oxygen cylinder

---

15 *Batson* challenges are discussed later in this chapter.

1 *See* Creed v. Fisher, 9 Exch. 472 (1854).

which was connected to a two-cylinder manifold system. After trial to a jury, a take-nothing judgment was rendered against Dunn. The court of civil appeals reversed and remanded the cause for a new trial. We affirm the judgment of the court of civil appeals but on different grounds.

Respondent Dunn sued Patterson Dental Company, the retail vendor of the manifold system; Fraser-Sweatman, Inc., the designer and manufacturer of the system; Western Enterprises, Inc., the manufacturer of certain component parts of the system; and Puritan-Bennett Corp. (Medicall, Inc.), the company that serviced the system. All four defendants were united in denying that there was any defective product or negligence causing the incident and in contending that the plaintiff was guilty of "misuse," but each sought indemnity and/or contribution from other defendants if there were blame placed on that defendant for the explosion. Each also alleged that another defendant's actions were the sole cause of the accident.

The trial court called a panel of forty-six jurors. The court allowed each of the defendants six peremptory challenges, a total of twenty-four, but allowed plaintiff Dunn only six. Dunn objected and moved that all defendants collectively receive only six, the same number he was allowed. The trial court denied this motion. After the evidence was presented, forty-four special issues were submitted to the jury. By a ten to two verdict, the issues were answered against plaintiff Dunn and for exoneration of the four defendants. The court of civil appeals held that under article 2151a which requires equalizing the peremptory challenges plaintiff Dunn should receive twenty-four peremptory challenges. We believe the court of civil appeals has misinterpreted the statute.

The practice of allowing peremptory challenges by parties to a civil suit was unknown to the common law. The practice in Texas began as a creature of statute and is now permitted by the Texas Rules of Civil Procedure. Rule 233 provides: "Each party to a civil suit shall be entitled to six peremptory challenges in a case tried in the district court, and to three in the county court." A peremptory challenge, commonly referred to as a "strike," is defined by rule 232 as one "made to a juror without assigning any reason therefor." These rules are derived without change from their predecessor statutes, articles 2147 and 2148, and have controlled civil trials for more than one hundred years.

The term "party" in rule 233 is not synonymous with "litigant" or "person." Rather, "party" refers to a litigant or a group of litigants having essentially common interests. Though their interests need not be completely identical, litigants on the same side of the docket are deemed to be a "party" under the rule when their interests are not antagonistic in a matter in which the jury is to be concerned.

Until article 2151a was enacted in 1971, Texas courts had engrafted into rule 233 the "single issue" test for determining the number of strikes to be allowed multiple parties aligned on the same side of a lawsuit. Under that test the presence of a solitary issue which was not common to all parties on the same side entitled each party on that side to a full set of six strikes. In other words, the community of interest of the parties on the same side must be complete before separate sets of strikes would be disallowed. Once antagonism on a single issue was found, each party received a full complement of six strikes. Application of the rule resulted in justifiable criticism of unfair results when multiple parties, each with a full set of strikes, collaborated in exercising those strikes in aid of their primary, common interest of defeating a common opponent on the other side.

The unfairness created by the single-issue rule was undoubtedly the reason article 2151a was enacted by the legislature in 1971. Intended to relax the rigidity engrafted into rule 233, the statute provides:

> After proper alignment of parties, it shall be the duty of the court to equalize the number of peremptory challenges provided under Rule 233, Texas Rules of Civil Procedure, Annotated, in accordance with the ends of justice so that no party is given an unequal advantage because of the number of peremptory challenges allowed that party.

The court of civil appeals here has interpreted the statute as requiring numerical equality of the number of strikes allowed each side. Petitioners argue that the holding conflicts with prior decisions of other courts of civil appeals. In those cases, an adjusting or proportionalizing of the strikes given to antagonistic parties on the same side was allowed by the trial court and upheld on appeal. We must determine what effect article 2151a has on the provisions of Rule 233.

The threshold question to be answered in allocating strikes when multiple litigants are involved on one side of a lawsuit is whether any of those litigants on the same side are antagonistic with respect to a question that the jury will decide. Where no antagonism exists, each side must receive the same number of strikes. * * * When antagonistic parties on the same side are required to share six strikes, it is error amounting to a violation of the basic right to trial by jury. The antagonism must exist on an issue of fact that will be submitted to the jury, not on a matter that constitutes a pure question of law. Further, the antagonism must exist between litigants on the same side, vis-à-vis each other. Antagonism does not exist because of differing conflicts with the other side; e.g., when a plaintiff sues several defendants alleging different acts or omissions against each defendant. Antagonism would exist, however, if each of the defendants alleged that the fault of another defendant was the sole cause of plaintiff's damage. . . . The existence or non-existence of cross-actions or third-party actions is not determinative. . . .

The existence of antagonism must be determined prior to the exercise of the strikes by the parties. The trial court must consider the pleadings, information disclosed by pretrial discovery, and other information brought to the attention of the trial court. * * * Information and representations made during voir dire of the jury panel also may be considered. Each case should be considered under the relevant circumstances. The existence of antagonism is not a matter within the trial court's discretion; it is a question of law whether any of the litigants aligned on the same side of the docket are antagonistic with respect to any issue to be submitted to the jury.

Here, Dunn seeks to uphold the result of the court of civil appeals' holding by arguing that no antagonism existed between the four defendants. The pleadings, however, clearly reflect that the defendants each blamed the others for the explosion of the equipment and pleaded that specific acts and omissions of others were the sole cause of plaintiff's injuries. Moreover, special issues were submitted to the jury on which defendants took opposite positions. Therefore, both the trial court and the court of civil appeals correctly concluded that there was antagonism between the defendants that entitled them to additional strikes.

Once the parties have been aligned on "sides," and it is determined that antagonism exists between parties on the same side, the provisions of article 2151a require the trial court to "equalize the number of peremptory challenges provided under Rule 233 . . . ." This task is to be done "in accordance with the ends of justice so that no party is given an unequal advantage because of the number of peremptory challenges allowed that party." Thus, article 2151a, while not involving the trial court's discretion in the determination of antagonism, does grant discretionary power to the trial court in allocating strikes.

In ascertaining whether the legislature intended that each side in a suit have an equal number of strikes after alignment, we consider the old law, the evil, and the remedy. TEX. REV. CIV. STAT. ANN. art. 10, § 6 (Vernon 1969). The application of the "single issue" rule made it possible for one side in a lawsuit, consisting of several parties each with six strikes, in effect to dictate who was on the jury. Presumably, this unfairness was the evil the legislature addressed when it enacted article 2151a in 1971.

The purpose of allowing strikes is not to allow a party to *select* a jury; instead, strikes are intended to permit a party to reject certain jurors based upon a subjective perception that those particular jurors might be unsympathetic to his position. When the number of strikes allowed to one side of the suit is grossly disproportionate to the number allowed the other side, it permits the side with the greater number to actually construct the jury. On the other hand, if the remedy provided in article 2151a was to grant each side an exactly equal number of strikes, a different evil would be substituted: the number of strikes would be unbalanced in favor of the side with a single litigant, for the antagonistic parties on the other side would have received no strikes to compensate for their antagonism between each other. The statute requires that the court equalize strikes between the parties, not the sides, of the suit. It provides that "[a]fter proper alignment of *parties* [strikes will be equalized] in accordance with the ends of justice so that no *party* is given an unequal advantage because of the number of peremptory challenges allowed that *party*." (emphasis added) The court of civil appeals incorrectly interpreted the word "party" as synonymous with "side." Moreover, had the legislature intended that each side receive the same number of strikes, it could easily have said so. Additionally, under such a construction, the last half of the statute, which speaks of the "ends of justice" and "unequal advantage," would have been superfluous. We presume the language was placed in the statute for a purpose.

We conclude that exact numerical equality between sides was not the purpose of article 2151a. Rather, the intention of the legislature was to place a duty on the trial court to equalize the positions of the parties to prevent one side, antagonistic among the parties on certain matters of fact with which the jury would be concerned but primarily united in their opposition to the other side, from selecting the jury.

Proportionalizing the strikes may be accomplished by increasing the number allotted a sole party on one side, by decreasing the number allotted the multiple parties on the other side, or by both. *King v. Maldonado*, *supra* (plaintiff allowed six; two groups of defendants allowed four each and allowed to collaborate); *Dean v. Texas Bitulithic Co.*, *supra* (plaintiff allowed six; two defendants allowed nine); *Austin Road Co. v. Evans*, *supra* (three plaintiffs allowed six each; principal defendant allowed nine). The extent to which equalizing is allowed depends upon the circumstances of the particular case, the information available to the trial court, the extent and degree of the antagonism, whether the parties collaborate in selecting jurors to be struck, the number of jurors available on the panel, and such other considerations as meet the statutory criteria of promoting the "ends of justice" and preventing "unequal advantage." The process of equalizing the strikes is not without limits, however, and is not subject to the unlimited discretion of the trial judge. Although article 2151a was intended to add an element of flexibility in awarding strikes among multiple parties and the trial court has discretionary power in determining the number of strikes awarded, in most cases a two-to-one ratio between sides would approach the maximum disparity allowable. In cases in which the disparity between strikes allowed the two sides did not exceed a two-to-one ratio, courts have held that there was no abuse of discretion. On the other hand, a disparity of four-to-one between sides as been held erroneous . . . .

In the case before us, we hold that the four-to-one disparity of strikes allowed was erroneous. Forty-six jurors were called, three of whom were excused for cause, leaving forty-three on the panel. The jury was selected from the first thirty-three jurors; that is, the twelfth juror selected was No. 33

on the panel. Plaintiff Dunn struck six of the thirty-three jurors while the four defendants struck at least fifteen, none of which had been struck by Dunn. Thus, the defendants, with twenty-four strikes, were able to exercise fifteen of them on the thirty-three member panel from which the jury was selected, effectively allowing the defendants to select the jury which would try their case. Irrespective of how they were exercised by the four defendants, the disparity of a four-to-one ratio of strikes between the two sides to the lawsuit was erroneous. The trial court had a duty to equalize the strikes in accordance with the language of article 2151a so that no party retained an unequal advantage, or, as in this case, an unequal disadvantage to Dunn.

Having determined that the trial court committed error in allocating the strikes, we must determine if the error resulted in a trial that was materially unfair, thus requiring reversal. In *Tamburello*, we held that the trial court committed reversible error in requiring two antagonistic defendants to share six strikes as against plaintiff's six strikes. After stating that the harmless error rule was applicable, we pointed out the difficulty of showing that an improper judgment probably resulted from an error of this nature. Peremptory challenges are subjective in application, are prompted by intuition, and are in spontaneous reaction to a juror's background, appearance, personality, prior contacts, and perceived attitude. We wrote in *Tamburello*, "The decision to strike is, in the last analysis, a matter of personal judgment usually based in large measure upon intangibles not susceptible of precise description and which cannot be fairly appraised by a trial or appellate court." We relaxed the requirement of the traditional "harmless error" rule by establishing the burden on the complaining party to show that "the trial which resulted against him was materially unfair" and held that the denial of strikes to each defendant, without any further showing, resulted in a trial that was so materially unfair that the judgment must be reversed.

In *Perkins v. Freeman*, *supra*, a child custody case, the plaintiff-mother was given six strikes, the defendant-father was given six, and the intervenors, paternal grandparents, were given six. Because the pleadings demonstrated that no antagonism existed between the father and his parents, we reversed and remanded, holding that their twelve strikes gave them "an unequal advantage, [that] was so materially unfair that the judgment cannot be upheld." No further showing of harm was made or discussed.

Normally, the question whether the trial was materially unfair in either the determination of antagonism or the equalizing of strikes requires that the entire record, including the statement of facts, be examined by the appellate court. The presence of error in either instance is to be viewed from the perspective of the trial judge as of the time he makes his determination. Whether any such error resulted in a materially unfair trial, however, must be decided from an examination of the entire trial record. For example, in a case in which the complaining party failed to prove his cause of action or defense, an error in allocating or equalizing strikes could not be said to have resulted in a materially unfair trial. On the other hand, when the trial is contested and the evidence is sharply conflicting, the error results in a materially unfair trial without showing more.

Here, we have no statement of facts of the testimony at the trial or of the *voir dire* examination of the jury panel. It is abundantly clear, however, from the number of special issues submitted, the ten-to-two verdict, and the absence of any motion for summary judgment or motion for instructed verdict in the record before us, that the trial was hotly contested. In these circumstances we hold that in the absence of a statement of facts that demonstrates that the non-complaining party would otherwise have been entitled to a judgment or that the case was not seriously disputed on its facts, a disparity of strikes between sides of as much as four-to-one results in a materially unfair trial as a matter of law.

The petitioners contend that Dunn did not properly preserve any error because he only objected to the trial court's action in refusing to limit the defendants collectively to six strikes, the number Dunn was allowed. We disagree. Rule 373 requires that a complaining party, "at the time the ruling or order of the court is made or sought, makes known to the court the action which he desires the court to take or his objection to the action of court and his grounds therefor; . . . ." Dunn's timely objection was essentially that the defendants received more strikes than he did, and he repeated his complaint in his motion for new trial and his amended motion for new trial, citing the specific provisions of art. 2151a. We hold that his objection was sufficient to direct the court's attention to the unequal distribution of the peremptory challenges allowed the sides and the statutory duty to equalize.

The judgment of the court of civil appeals is affirmed.

Notes & Questions

1. *Antagonism and allocation.* The existence of antagonism is a question of law. There is a right answer, and, if the trial court gets it wrong, it is error. However, once antagonism is correctly identified, then the way the trial court goes about apportioning the strikes is a matter within the court's discretion. Thus, the complaint may be that the trial court erred in determining antagonism, in which case *any* reallocation of strikes is error; or it may be that, though antagonism was correctly found, the way the strikes were allocated was unfair. In either case, however—error of law on antagonism or abuse of discretion in allocating strikes (assuming that antagonism exists)—the complainant must show harm. How does he do it?[1]

2. *The hot contest.* What about the *Patterson* "hot contest" criterion as a substitute for the record of sharply conflicting evidence required by *Tamburello*? It makes no sense. Except for a split verdict, the hot contest criterion does not identify a close case. Motions for summary judgment are routinely filed in cases presenting threshold legal questions, such as limitations, the scope of a duty, and trial court jurisdiction. These motions say nothing about the intensity of the dispute or how close the calls will be on the evidence. While motions for summary judgment resolve legal issues which may define and limit the contest, no one would suggest that the mere *filing* of such a motion means that the contest is one-sided. The same is true of motions for directed verdict, which provide even less information about the intensity of the contest or the state of the evidence. Many defense counsel make such motions as a matter of course at the close of plaintiff's evidence. The number of special issues (now jury questions) is equally uninformative. Perhaps the best refutation of the hot contest fiction is *Texaco, Inc. v. Pennzoil Co.,*[2] which is surely one of the hottest contests in the history of litigation. Because the case involved motions for summary judgment and for directed verdict, only eight jury questions, and a unanimous verdict, it would not qualify as a "hotly contested trial," even though the trial lasted several months and the verdict was for $11 billion.

---

[1] For a look at various ratios which have been held acceptable and unacceptable, *see* Patterson, Scurlock Oil Co. v. Smithwick, 724 S.W.2d 1 (Tex. 1986); Lopez v. Foremost Paving, Inc., 709 S.W.2d 643 (Tex. 1986); *and* numerous cases collected at 4 MCDONALD, TEXAS CIVIL PRACTICE 82 § 21:24 at footnote 203.

[2] 729 S.W.2d 768 (Tex. App.—Houston [1st Dist] 1987, writ ref'd n.r.e.).

3. *Antagonists confer*. Some antagonists, having been granted separate strikes, routinely confer in exercising their separate strikes and are permitted to do so.[3] Why would antagonists (usually co-defendants) combine forces in order to strike the jury? Counsel for D1 would seldom acknowledge his need for the expertise of counsel for D2 in deciding whom he should remove from the jury list. Since defendants are likely to strike the same kind of jurors, the collaboration is aimed at avoiding double strikes of the same juror. Collaboration between antagonists on strikes may be hazardous, however, if a serious question is to be raised about the existence of antagonism. In *Lopez v. Foremost Paving, Inc.*,[4] the Supreme Court found that there was not true antagonism between the defendants and reversed the case, relying in part on the fact that the "antagonistic" defendants "collaborated on the exercise of their strikes and did not have any double strikes."

4. *Antagonistic pleadings not decisive*. The Supreme Court has made clear that the trial court must look at more than just the pleadings to determine antagonism. *In Garcia v. Central Power & Light Co.*,[5] the Court struck down a 10-6 strike allocation because during the voir dire examination the defendants "asserted Garcia's contributory negligence as the sole cause of his death, and also made affirmative exculpatory representations about their co-defendants." Therefore, the Court found no antagonism between the defendants. Shortly following the *Garcia* decision, the Texas Supreme Court also found no antagonism in *Lopez v. Foremost Paving, Inc.,*[6] where the Court noted that the "antagonistic" defendants called witnesses who were asked perfunctory questions and then turned over to a co-defendant's counsel for "cross-examination" by leading questions. The Court further noted that defendants collaborated on the exercise of their strikes, had no double strikes, and neither presented motions for summary judgment nor for instructed verdict. In both *Garcia* and *Lopez,* the Court found that the trial was hotly contested *and* the evidence sharply conflicting, and reversed because of the trial court's error in awarding defendants twice the number of strikes it awarded to plaintiffs.

5. *Reviewing the entire record.* It is significant that *Lopez* held for the first time that the appellate court will look at the entire trial record (including events occurring after the judge's ruling allocating peremptory challenges) to determine antagonism. (It had previously done so to see whether the evidence was "sharply conflicting.") The trial court must determine antagonism early in the trial. Under *Lopez*, the correctness of that determination will be reviewed by taking into account events subsequent to the court's ruling—i.e., information not available to the court when the ruling was made. Is this "fair" to the judge? Perhaps not. The idea seems to be that it *is* fair to penalize the parties who have claimed to be antagonists and subsequently behaved as allies by remanding for a new trial.

6. *Waiver.* Any complaint concerning unfair allocation of strikes is waived if not timely made (ideally at the time the court reapportions strikes or refuses to do so). The point cannot ordinarily be raised for the first time on motion for new trial.[7] If, however, the complaint is based upon in-trial

---

[3] *See* King v. Maldonado, 552 S.W.2d 940 (Tex. Civ. App.—Corpus Christi 1977, writ ref'd n.r.e.). Note, however, that an unqualified agreement, such as one to dismiss a party in exchange for strikes, constitutes reversible error. *See* General Motors Corp. v. Herbert, 501 S.W.2d 950 (Tex. Civ. App.—Houston [1st Dist] 1973, writ ref'd n.r.e.).

[4] 709 S.W.2d 643 (Tex. 1986).

[5] 704 S.W.2d 734 (Tex. 1986).

[6] 709 S.W.2d 643 (Tex. 1986).

[7] Pouncy v. Garner, 626 S.W.2d 337 (Tex. App.—Tyler 1981, writ ref'd n.r.e.).

cooperation between "antagonists"—as in *Lopez*—either a motion for new trial or perhaps a motion for mistrial might be the first opportunity to complain and may preserve the error.

E. Jury Misconduct and Disqualification After Voir Dire

Read Rules 292, 327.

Previous sections discussed error resulting from the trial judge refusing to exercise a juror for cause when the voir dire revealed the error, and when the trial judge fails to properly allocate the number of peremptory strikes. In each of these situations, the error is apparent when it occurs and the opinions specify what lawyers must do to preserve error and show harm. But there are situations where the lawyers or the judge do not discover than an unqualified juror is on the panel until after the trial has begun, or even after it is completed. The verdict-loser will want to complain that the verdict is invalid because of the presence of an unqualified juror. How does this work?

PALMER WELL SERVICES, INC.
v.
MACK TRUCKS, INC.
776 S.W.2d 575
(Tex. 1989)

PER CURIAM.

Conflict with Rule 292 of the Rules of Civil Procedure and Section 62.102 of the Government Code, regarding the qualifications of jurors and the requisites of verdicts, prompts this court's examination of this case.

Suit was filed to recover for personal injuries suffered by petitioner, Paul Quinonez, as a result of an explosion and fire of a hot oil treatment unit and truck. Quinonez was employed by petitioner Palmer Well Services, Inc. (Petitioners will be referred to collectively as "Palmer"). The trial was to jury which rendered a 10-2, take-nothing verdict against the plaintiffs. Palmer filed a motion for new trial alleging the discovery, after the verdict, of a felony indictment pending against one juror. The trial court overruled the motion for new trial.

The court of appeals held that the juror should have been excluded from the panel because of the pending felony indictment and that due diligence was not lacking in failing to discover that fact earlier. However, the court of appeals held that Palmer was required to demonstrate that the unqualified juror's presence on the jury was a material factor which was reasonably calculated to, and probably did, cause the rendition of an improper judgment. The court of appeals held that Palmer failed to establish the requisite material injury[1] needed to sustain this burden and affirmed

---

[1] TEX. R. CIV. P. 327(a) provides that when a motion for new trial is sought on the ground that a juror gave an erroneous or incorrect answer on voir dire examination, the court may grant a new trial if such erroneous or

the trial court. For the reasons expressed, the court of appeals' judgment is reversed and this cause is remanded for new trial.

The only facts pertinent to this appeal regard one of the jurors, Mr. Ira Anderson. Anderson was one of the majority of 10 jurors that rendered the take-nothing verdict. During voir dire, the trial judge queried the panel as to their qualifications to serve. Conflicting evidence exists regarding whether Anderson had gone to the restroom, or remained silent when the panel was asked about pending indictments or legal accusations for a misdemeanor or felony.

Palmer contends that the verdict was not rendered by the requisite number of qualified jurors. In all but one instance,[2] where the jury is originally composed of twelve jurors, a minimum of ten members of the original jury must concur in the verdict. TEX. R. CIV. P. 292. All individuals are competent to serve as petit jurors unless disqualified by statute. TEX. GOV'T CODE Ann. § 62.101 (Vernon 1988). The general qualifications permitting jury service are set forth by statute in Texas Government Code § 62.102. That statute disqualifies a person to serve as a petit juror if he is "under indictment or other legal accusation of misdemeanor or felony theft, or any other felony." *Id.* § 62.102(8).

Respondent, Mack Trucks Inc. (Mack Trucks) concedes that Anderson was under indictment for a felony and does not argue that Palmer lacked due diligence in failing to discover that fact. Mack Trucks argues, however, that Palmer was in no way prejudiced or injured by the inclusion of Anderson on the jury. Relying on *De Leon v. Longoria,* 4 S.W.2d 222 (Tex. Civ. App.—San Antonio 1928, writ dism'd), and *Mendoza v. Varon,* 563 S.W.2d 646, 648 (Tex. Civ. App.—Dallas 1978, writ ref'd. n.r.e.), Mack Trucks asserts that showing the absence of a qualification or establishing a ground for disqualification of a juror does not render a jury verdict invalid nor require the jury verdict to be set aside. The cases of *De Leon* and *Mendoza,* however, are factually distinguishable from the instant case. In *De Leon,* although the pending felony indictment and due diligence were stipulated by the parties, a sufficient number of jurors remained that could have rendered a binding verdict. In *Mendoza,* the parties discovered the pending felony indictment during the course of the trial and agreed to allow that juror to remain empanelled and participate in the verdict. Because of the agreement to continue, the parties waived their right to complain of the disqualification of the juror.

---

incorrect answer "be material, and if it reasonably appears from the evidence both on the hearing of the motion and the trial of the case and from the record as a whole that injury probably resulted to the complaining party." TEX. R. CIV. P. 327(a). Also pertinent is TEX. R. APP. P. 81(b)(1) which provides in part:

> No judgment shall be reversed on appeal and a new trial ordered in any cause on the ground that the trial court has committed an error of law in the course of the trial, unless the appellate court shall be of the opinion that error complained of amounted to such a denial of the rights of the appellant as was reasonably calculated to cause, and probably did cause, rendition of an improper judgment in the case . . . .

[2] TEX. R. CIV. P. 292 provides:

> A verdict may be rendered in any cause by the concurrence, as to each and all answers made, of the same ten members of an original jury of twelve, or of the same five members of an original of six. However, where as many as three jurors die or be disabled from sitting and there are only nine of the jurors remaining of an original jury of twelve, those remaining may render and return a verdict. If less than the original twelve or six jurors render a verdict, the verdict must be signed by each juror concurring therein.

Thus, only in the event that *three* jurors die or become disqualified to hear a case may nine jurors render a verdict.

Palmer's plight with regard to the claim that Anderson was disqualified as a juror is distinct from either *De Leon* or *Mendoza.* First, the discovery of the pending felony indictment was not made until after the verdict was rendered. Second, the failure to discover the pending felony indictment was not due to Palmer's lack of diligence. Finally, if the rules and statutes governing the qualifications of jurors and the requisites of verdicts are to have any effect, litigants similarly situated to Palmer must be held to have suffered material injury as a matter of law. Therefore, because this is not an instance in which a verdict could have been rendered by less than ten jurors, as a matter of law Palmer was materially injured by the rendition of an unfavorable verdict by less than the requisite number of qualified jurors.

For the foregoing reasons, a majority of this court grants the application for writ of error, and without hearing oral argument, reverses the judgment of the court of appeals and remands this case to the trial court for new trial.

Notes & Questions

1. *Due diligence*. In *Palmer Well Services*, the juror's disqualification was not revealed until after trial—there was no strike for cause. The opinion requires the complaining party to be diligent in using voir dire to find disqualifications—there is no reversal without due diligence. What does due diligence require? The Austin Court of Appeals considered whether due diligence required following up with individual jurors on answers to written juror questionnaires. There the juror had answered "no" to a question about prior criminal accusations. The juror had been accused of writing bad checks, but she thought her answer was truthful because she thought no charges had been filed. The court concluded:[1]

> The justice system's use of devices to expedite the trial of cases should not become a snare for the advocates who practice within that system. We recognize that a tension exists between the justice system's desire to advance cases with dispatch and the obligation of counsel to use diligence to uncover facts that could lead to a potential juror's disqualification.
>
> We believe that these competing interests may be balanced on a case-by-case basis. The legislature has established certain minimum qualifications for jurors. *See* TEX. GOV'T CODE Ann. § 62.102 (West 1998). The supreme court has held that "the rules and statutes governing the qualifications of jurors and the requisites of [jury] verdicts" are to be given effect and that a party who suffers an adverse 10-2 verdict returned by fewer than 10 qualified jurors has suffered material injury as a matter of law.
>
> In the case before us, the question posed was unambiguous, understood by Garcia, and capable of being answered "yes" or "no." The question did not inquire into the subjective state of mind of the potential jurors or address whether they could be fair and impartial, thus perhaps requiring follow-up questions. There is no reason to believe that had additional questions been asked, Garcia would have responded differently. As was within her discretion, the district court had restricted the time available to the parties for *voir dire.* Under these particular facts, we tip the balance in favor of Preiss and hold that because he

[1] Priess v. Moritz, 60 S.W.3d 285 (Tex. App.—Austin 2001), *rev'd on other grounds*, 121 S.W.3d 715 (Tex. 2003).

> was justified in relying on Garcia's juror-questionnaire response and thus satisfied his duty of diligence, the district court abused her discretion in overruling his motion for new trial. To hold otherwise would undermine the utility of juror questionnaires and unduly extend trials by requiring counsel to unnecessarily inquire into the same information that had already been disclosed. We sustain Preiss's first issue.
>
> Because we have held that a juror who participated in the district-court verdict was not qualified to serve on the jury (a fact that was not discovered until after the verdict), that Preiss was diligent in discovering the facts forming the basis of the disqualification, and that Preiss was harmed as a matter of law when fewer than ten qualified jurors returned the verdict, we reverse the district-court judgment and remand this cause to that court for a new trial.

2. *Diligence required for peremptories.* Often lawyers will complain they were unable to properly exercise their peremptory strikes because the juror's answers during voir dire were inaccurate, misleading, or simply failed to disclose information that would be important to the lawyer in deciding how to exercise the strikes. It is extremely difficult to get reversal of a judgment and a new trial based on a juror's failure to disclose information. As one court of appeals said in refusing to reverse a judgment on these grounds:[2]

> It is counsel's responsibility to make sure that all members of the jury panel hear and understand the question asked. Baker offered no evidence to refute Mrs. Odom's assertions that she misunderstood the question and that she was unaware of her husband's claim for unemployment benefits. As the trier of fact, the trial court was entitled to believe her testimony. The trial court did not abuse its discretion by finding that no jury misconduct occurred. Even if Mrs. Odom's failure to answer the question was misconduct, Baker has not shown that such misconduct was material or that it resulted in probable harm. "To show probable harm, there must be some indication in the record that the alleged misconduct most likely caused a juror to vote differently than he 'would otherwise have done on one or more issues vital to the judgment.' " There is nothing in the record to indicate that Baker struck any of the jurors from the jury panel who responded to the question, or that it would have struck Mrs. Odom had she responded.

Voir dire questions addressed to the entire panel are particularly infirm as the basis for a reversal. Courts are prone to accept jurors' excuses for not responding because, for example, they did not hear or understand the question.[3] The case law requires that counsel ask direct questions, see that each juror hears and understands them,[4] identify for the record jurors who indicate a need to respond (by

---

2 Baker Marine Corp. v. Weatherby Engineering Co., 710 S.W.2d 690 (Tex. App.—Corpus Christi 1986, no writ).

3 *See* McCarthy Oil v. Cunningham, 255 S.W.2d 368, 372 (Tex. 1953).

4 O'Day v. Sakowitz Bros., 462 S.W.2d 119 (Tex. Civ. App.—Houston [1st Dist] 1971, writ ref'd n.r.e.); Missouri-Pacific Railroad Co. v. Cunningham, 515 S.W.2d 678 (Tex. Civ. App.—San Antonio 1974, no writ).

raising their hands), and follow up with specific questions.[5] The upshot is that reversal based on questions addressed to the entire panel will be extremely rare.[6]

3. *Less than 12 jurors and the appointment of alternate jurors.* The Texas Supreme Court was presented a case where one juror was replaced by the lone alternate juror because he realized he knew something about the case. The next day another juror called in sick. The judge proceeded with only 11 jurors, which returned a unanimous verdict.[7] The court said:

> In brief, a court need not find a juror constitutionally disabled in order to substitute an alternate when doing so does not lead to numerical diminution of a twelve-member jury.
>
> The relevant jury requirements in this proceeding are found in both the Texas Constitution and in the Texas Rules of Civil Procedure. TEX. CONST. art. V, § 13; TEX.R. CIV. P. 292. The constitution specifies that grand and petit juries in the district courts shall be composed of twelve members. TEX. CONST. art. V, § 13. As few as nine jurors may render a verdict if, during trial, as many as three jurors "die, or become disabled from sitting." *Id.* The Rules of Civil Procedure have similar language allowing as few as nine remaining jurors to return and render a verdict if "as many as three jurors die or be disabled from sitting." TEX. R. CIV. P. 292. Thus, if a trial court's dismissal of a juror results in fewer than twelve jurors, the dismissal must either be based on the juror's constitutional disability or the trial court must declare a mistrial if there was no constitutional disability.
>
> In an effort to improve efficiency by reducing mistrials, the Legislature implemented a system of alternate jurors. These alternate jurors are "drawn and selected in the same manner as regular jurors." TEX. GOV'T CODE § 62.020(c). In practice, this means that an alternate juror must have the same qualifications as a regular juror, be subjected to the same challenges, swear the same oath, and otherwise be considered equivalent to a regular juror. The plain language of this statute allows an alternate juror to substitute for a regular juror by a different and lesser standard than constitutional disability: when a regular juror is "unable or disqualified to perform their duties." *Id.* § 62.020(d); *see also Schlafly v. Schlafly,* 33 S.W.3d 863 (Tex. App.—Houston [14th Dist.] 2000, pet. denied). A juror is deemed disqualified if he "has a bias or prejudice in favor of or against a party in the case." TEX. GOV'T CODE § 62.105(4). Taking the statute and constitution together, a trial court may substitute a regular juror with an alternate if the regular juror is unable to fulfill or is disqualified from fulfilling his duties, but a trial court may only dismiss a juror and proceed with fewer than twelve jurors if the dismissed juror is constitutionally disabled.
>
> Here, the court of appeals conflated these provisions and held that the trial court wrongly proceeded with fewer than twelve jurors even though Juror Turney was not constitutionally disabled. Because the trial court substituted an alternate juror for Juror Turney, under the statute the trial court only needed to find that Juror Turney was disqualified from fulfilling his duties and that the alternate was qualified to serve. TEX. GOV'T CODE §

---

5 *See, e.g.,* Southern Truck Leasing Co. v. Manieri, 325 S.W.2d 912 (Tex. Civ. App.—Houston 1959, writ ref'd n.r.e.); Ramirez v. Wood, 577 S.W.2d 278 (Tex. Civ. App.—Corpus Christi 1978, no writ).

6 *See, e.g.,* Texaco, Inc. v. Haley, 610 S.W.2d 224 (Tex. Civ. App.—Houston [14th Dist] 1980, no writ); Liberty Cab Co. v. Green, 262 S.W.2d 522 (Tex. Civ. App.—Beaumont 1953, writ ref'd n.r.e.). *See, generally,* MCDONALD, TEXAS CIVIL PRACTICE, §§ 21:15-21:19.

7 In re M.G.N., 441 S.W.3d 246, 248-49 (2014).

62.020(c)-(d); *Schlafly,* 33 S.W.3d at 863. The parties do not brief those issues here, and we do not address them. If the court of appeals concludes the trial court did not abuse its discretion in substituting the alternate juror for Juror Turney, it must then assess whether the trial court abused its discretion in proceeding with eleven jurors after finding Juror Park constitutionally disabled. *See, e.g., McDaniel v. Yarbrough,* 898 S.W.2d 251 (Tex. 1995) (juror not disabled due to severe flooding that made travel to the courthouse difficult); *Houston & T.C. Ry. Co. v. Waller,* 56 Tex. 331, 337 (1882) ("If a juror becomes so sick as to be unable to sit longer, he is plainly disabled from sitting."). Accordingly, pursuant to Texas Rule of Appellate Procedure 59. 1, we grant the petition for review and, without hearing oral argument, reverse the court of appeals' judgment and remand for that court to consider the remaining issues in a manner consistent with this opinion.

GOLDEN EAGLE ARCHERY, INC.
v.
JACKSON

24 S.W.3d 362
(Tex. 2000)

JUSTICE GONZALES delivered the opinion of the Court, in which CHIEF JUSTICE PHILLIPS, JUSTICE HECHT, JUSTICE ENOCH, JUSTICE OWEN, JUSTICE BAKER, JUSTICE HANKINSON and JUSTICE O'NEILL joined.

The main issue in this case is whether procedural and evidentiary rules may constitutionally prohibit jurors from testifying post-verdict about statements made during deliberations, unless such statements concern outside influences. *See* TEX.R. CIV. P. 327(b); TEX.R. CIV. EVID. 606(b). Ronald Jackson obtained a verdict in a products liability case, but moved for a new trial on several grounds, including juror misconduct, juror bias, and the adequacy of the verdict. After a hearing, the trial court denied the motion. The court of appeals reversed and remanded for a new trial, holding that Texas Rule of Civil Procedure 327(b) denied Jackson his constitutional right to a fair and impartial jury trial because it prohibited him from proving jury misconduct during deliberations. Because we conclude that the rule is constitutional, we reverse the court of appeal's judgment and remand to that court to consider Jackson's other points of error that the court of appeals did not reach.

I

Jackson's wife bought him a Golden Eagle compound bow from a Wal-Mart store. When Jackson drew back the string the bow slipped out of his hand and a cable guard struck his eye, causing severe injuries. He sued Golden Eagle Archery, Inc., Coleman Company, Inc., and Wal-Mart, Inc. for negligence and products liability. The trial court dismissed the claims against Coleman and Wal-Mart, leaving Golden Eagle as the sole defendant. The jury found that Golden Eagle defectively marketed the bow but failed to find that the bow was defectively designed. The jury also found that Jackson was negligent, and attributed to him 45% of the responsibility for his injury. The jury found Jackson's damages to be approximately $25,000 for medical care, $2,500 for physical pain and mental anguish, $2,500 for vision loss, $0 for physical impairment other than vision loss, $1,500 for disfigurement, and $4,600 for past lost earnings. Ten of the twelve jurors signed the verdict. The trial court asked the ten if they agreed to the entire verdict, but neither party asked to poll the individual jurors. The trial court then rendered a judgment for approximately $20,000 damages and $6,700 prejudgment interest.

Jackson moved for a new trial. He challenged the legal and factual sufficiency of the evidence to support several of the jury's answers, contested the trial court's exclusion of certain evidence, and alleged that juror Barbara Maxwell concealed a bias during voir dire and that she and other jurors committed misconduct before and during formal deliberations. The motion attached affidavits from one of Jackson's attorneys and three jurors. Two of the affidavits were from the jurors who did not vote for the verdict, Donald Frederick and Janet Cline. A third was from the presiding juror, Shawn Lynch. The motion asserted that even though Texas Rule of Civil Procedure 327(b) prohibits consideration of juror affidavits to impeach the verdict, to ignore the evidence of misconduct during deliberations would unconstitutionally deny Jackson his right to a fair trial. Golden Eagle responded that both Rule 327(b) and Texas Rule of Civil Evidence 606(b) prohibit the court from considering the juror's affidavits, that Jackson's attorney's affidavit primarily recounted hearsay statements about what some jurors told him, and that Jackson waived any juror-bias complaint because he did not conduct a sufficient voir dire.

At the hearing on his motion for new trial, Jackson offered the four affidavits as well as juror Frederick's testimony. The trial court admitted the testimony and affidavits without limitation "to the extent they contain appropriate evidentiary matters for consideration under Rule 327," and otherwise for the purposes of Jackson's bill of exceptions. At the hearing, Jackson's attorney read passages from the voir dire questioning of the jurors to demonstrate that Maxwell had hidden her bias against lawsuits of this kind. Jackson's attorney began voir dire with a lengthy question about whether any jurors were opposed to lawsuits, or could not be fair, or simply did not want to be on a jury.[1] A panel member raised his hand. Jackson's attorney told the juror he would ask him more questions later, then asked the panel, "Anyone else?" No one responded. Jackson's attorney continued:

Is there anybody here, by the same token, who would just say, "Look, I just can't do that. I can't—I don't believe in it. I just can't give a verdict that means that somebody is going to have to pay a lot of money"? Anybody here that-again, if you do, now is the time. You owe it to yourself and you owe it to these people and to the Court to be honest about it because we-all we can do is ask you about it, but you have to tell us. Anybody here that could not do that?

---

1 [W]e're in this lawsuit concerning what we contend to be an unreasonably dangerous product that injured an unknowing consumer. And Mr. Jackson has a right to be here. He has a right to ask a Court in this county to render him a fair verdict; but there are people that, for many reasons, of their own, again, are opposed to this type of lawsuit. They just don't think that this ought to be done, that they're opposed to lawsuits. They don't think they ought to happen, that they can't render verdicts in this case, these types of cases, et cetera. If that is the case—of course, you're entitled to your opinions; and I would fight anybody for you to have that opinion. But if that's the case, you should not be on this jury because we are operating within the—within the parameters of the law; and we are doing something that Mr. Jackson has every right to do and every right to request of a Jefferson County jury.

Is there anyone on this panel that right now would say, "Look, I just don't want to sit on this kind of jury. I need out of here. I don't want to be here. I can't be fair. These type of things bother me. I don't agree with the system, too much stress," whatever; that you want to tell the Judge, tell Judge Sheffield or me and [defense counsel] right now, "I don't want to be here"? If you do, I would ask you please to be honest and do that right now because our system depends on the integrity of our jury system and the integrity of jurors. Is there anyone here that says, "I can't do this"? Anyone?

Again, no one responded. Finally, Jackson's attorney asked the panel if any of them had served on a jury. Maxwell answered that she had served on both a civil and a criminal case. She said the civil case involved a man's death in an accident. Jackson's attorney asked:

Q Did you-did you reach a verdict in that case?

A No.

Q Anything about that case that would keep you from being fair here?

A No, sir.

Frederick testified in his affidavit and at the hearing about a conversation he had with Maxwell during a trial recess. According to Frederick, Maxwell told him that previously she had served on a jury that awarded nothing for a wrongful death claim, which Frederick thought contradicted her voir dire statements, and further told him she did not believe in "awarding money in stuff like that," and that "we are the ones who end up paying for it."

The remaining juror testimony concerned events occurring after the jury retired to begin deliberating the evidence. Frederick, Cline, and Lynch all recalled that the jury bartered on the amounts to award for disfigurement and loss of vision, although their accounts contradict each other in the specifics. Frederick said that initially ten jurors had agreed to award $2,500 for disfigurement and nine had agreed to award $2,500 for loss of vision, but traded votes to award $1,500 for disfigurement and $2,500 for loss of vision. Lynch, however, claimed that initially ten jurors had agreed on $1,500 for loss of vision, and eight agreed on $2,500 for disfigurement, but ultimately decided to switch these amounts. Cline merely remembered that the jurors "traded off" on these answers.

Frederick also stated that during the jury's discussion of damages, Maxwell told other jurors that "there is too much of this going on," which he took to mean the filing of lawsuits. He said that she "held up a document which showed the name of Wal-Mart and said something to the effect that the plaintiff had probably already gotten a big settlement from Wal-Mart and did not need any more money out of this case."

Frederick and Lynch additionally testified that during jury room deliberations Maxwell speculated whether Jackson had been drinking alcoholic beverages when the accident occurred. Finally, all three juror affidavits claim that Maxwell strongly argued against Jackson's position throughout the jury room deliberations.

The trial court overruled Jackson's motion for a new trial explaining its ruling in a letter to the parties. The court advised it would not sustain Jackson's jury misconduct arguments because the jurors' affidavits and testimony all pertained to jury deliberations and were therefore incompetent. The court also rejected Jackson's complaints about undisclosed juror bias. Acknowledging that the same evidence offered to show jury misconduct "would certainly support a conclusion that the juror in question was biased against product liability suits" the court did not resolve whether Maxwell was in fact biased. Instead, the court concluded that Jackson's attorney's voir dire questioning of Maxwell was not specific enough to show she purposefully concealed any bias. Jackson did not request the trial court to make any fact findings about any of these issues.

On appeal, Jackson asserted eight points of error, any one of which, if sustained, would result in a new trial. His first six points challenged the sufficiency of the amount of the damages awarded, the weight of the evidence supporting the jury's verdict, and the exclusion of certain evidence. The court of appeals addressed only Jackson's last two points about jury misconduct and juror bias. A divided court of appeals reversed the trial court's judgment and remanded the case for a new trial. The court expressed its concern about "the ever increasing lack of veracity of jurors on voir dire . . . ." The court held that because Rule 327(b) denied Jackson the only evidence available to prove misconduct, it denied him his right to a fair and impartial trial. It concluded that the evidence established Maxwell's misconduct, and that the misconduct was material and caused harm. Golden Eagle petitioned this Court for review, and we granted the petition.

II

This case turns on whether, and to what extent, the jurors' affidavits and testimony are admissible to show juror misconduct such as undisclosed bias. The problem of jury misconduct or bias presents difficult choices about how best to promote the jury system's "purity and efficiency" under Article I, Section 15 of the Texas Constitution. On the one hand, it may be desirable in a particular case to rectify a verdict improperly decided because of juror bias or misconduct. A fair trial before an impartial tribunal is a basic requirement of due process. However, the goal of a trial by a jury free from bias or misconduct must be balanced against other legitimate interests. Courts and commentators have noted several policy reasons why losing parties should not be allowed to conduct unfettered investigations into the jury's deliberations to try to prove such allegations, in essence putting the jury on trial.

First, jury deliberations must be kept private to encourage jurors to candidly discuss the case. A verdict is a collaborative effort requiring individuals from different backgrounds to reach a consensus. A juror should feel free to raise and consider an unpopular viewpoint. To discharge their duties effectively, jurors must be able to discuss the evidence and issues without fear that their deliberations will later be held up to public scrutiny. Second, there is a recognized need to protect jurors from post-trial harassment or tampering. The losing party has every incentive to try to get jurors to testify to defects in their deliberations. The winning party would likewise want to investigate in order to protect the judgment. Jury service will be less attractive if the litigants can harass a juror after trial, call a juror to testify about jury deliberations, and make juror deliberations public. Third, a disgruntled juror whose view did not prevail in the jury room would have an avenue for vindication by overturning the verdict. This is a significant concern in Texas civil trials, in which the verdict may be less than unanimous. Fourth is the need for finality. Litigation must end at some point if the public is to have any confidence in judgments.

* * *

III

Before we consider the constitutional questions, we first determine if, and to what extent, the rules bar the evidence Jackson offered in this case. Golden Eagle argues that Rule 327(b) precludes proof of all jury misconduct except misconduct resulting from outside influences. Both Rule 327(b) and Rule 606(b) state that jurors may not testify about statements or matters occurring during deliberations, but they may testify about outside influences. A number of cases and commentators have concluded that the Texas rules forbid all proof of jury misconduct unless it involves outside influences. Many of these cases rely on a statement in *Weaver v. Westchester Fire Insurance Company:*

> [A] motion for new trial based on jury misconduct must be supported by a juror's affidavit alleging "outside influences" were brought to bear upon the jury.

739 S.W.2d 23, 24 (Tex.1987). However, our statement in *Weaver* was overly broad, because the rules' limitations on affidavits and testimony as grounds for a new trial expressly do not apply to

non-jurors. A court may, of course, admit competent evidence of juror misconduct from any other source. *See, e.g., Mayo v. State,* 708 S.W.2d 854, 856 (Tex. Crim. App. 1986) (considering testimony of witness contacted by juror); *Fillinger v.. Fuller,* 746 S.W.2d 506, 508 (Tex. App.—Texarkana 1988, no writ) (holding that rules do not require that affidavits be from jurors only); *Goode, supra,* § 606.2 & n. 42. There is no competent non-juror evidence of misconduct here, however. Jackson's attorney's affidavit relates in part to statements made in open court during voir dire; the remainder of the attorney's testimony is objected-to hearsay concerning what the jurors told him another juror said. *See Mitchell v. Southern Pac. Trans. Co.,* 955 S.W.2d 300, 322 (Tex. App.—San Antonio 1997, no writ) (holding non-juror's affidavit about what occurred in jury deliberations was hearsay). While we may consider the record of the voir dire, it alone contains no suggestion of jury misconduct.

We now turn to the juror testimony. Here three jurors testified as to (1) matters alleged to have occurred after the jury retired to begin deliberating the evidence and (2) a conversation alleged to have occurred during a trial break. We consider first the jurors' testimony about events occurring after retiring to begin deliberations.

* * *

Rule 327(b) operates to prohibit jurors from testifying about matters and statements occurring during deliberations. Harmonizing both sections, subsection (b) applies regardless of the grounds alleged for a new trial. Jackson suggests that Rule 327(a)'s provision for juror testimony would be meaningless if Rule 327(b) precludes a juror from testifying about statements made during deliberations. We disagree. Rule 327(b) does not preclude juror testimony about improper contacts with individuals outside the jury, nor juror testimony about matters or statements not "occurring during the course of the jury's deliberations." A juror may testify about jury misconduct provided it does not require delving into deliberations. For example, a juror could testify that another juror improperly viewed the scene of the events giving rise to the litigation. Likewise, a juror could testify about reasons for disqualifying another juror provided the testifying juror's knowledge was gained independent of deliberations. Juror Maxwell, had she been called to testify, could have been questioned about the facts of her prior jury service without violating Rule 327(b).

Despite the rules' prohibition against juror testimony about deliberations, both Rule 327(b) and Rule 606(b) allow jurors to testify about outside influences. Jackson argues that we should broadly interpret the exception for outside influences and consider the jurors' testimony because it falls within the exception in the rules for "outside influences." We have not defined what kind of "outside influence" a juror may testify about. . . .

Most Texas courts considering the question have held that the rules prevent a juror from testifying that the jury discussed improper matters during deliberation. We agree. The rules contemplate that an "outside influence" originates from sources other than the jurors themselves. Accordingly, here the accounts that some jurors speculated whether alcohol was involved in the accident and that Jackson may have received a settlement, or that the jurors traded answers on two issues, are all juror statements about matters occurring during their deliberations. They are not evidence of outside influences.

Jackson also argues that we should consider Maxwell herself an "outside influence" because she brought prejudices into the jury room. A number of cases have also rejected this argument, holding that the rules preclude evidence from a juror that another juror exhibited bias during jury deliberations. *See, e.g., United States v. Duzac,* 622 F.2d 911, 913 (5th Cir. 1980) (holding that the "proper time to discover such prejudices is when the jury is being selected and peremptory challenges are available to the attorneys"); *Soliz,* 779 S.W.2d at 933 (holding that evidence emanating from inside jury deliberations not admissible to show bias); *Baker Marine Corp. v. Weatherby Eng'g Co.,* 710 S.W.2d 690, 692-93 (Tex. App.—Corpus Christi 1986, no writ) (holding that juror testimony that fellow juror seemed biased during deliberation was inadmissible). Moreover, while failure to disclose bias is a form of juror misconduct that justifies a new trial under the appropriate circumstances, proof of a juror's failure to disclose bias must come from some source other than a fellow juror's testimony about deliberations.

In the same vein, Jackson contends that Maxwell was an outside influence because her bias statutorily disqualified her from serving on the jury. *See* TEX. GOV'T CODE § 62.105(4). However, Jackson did not timely raise statutory disqualification as a basis for new trial. *See* TEX.R. CIV. P. 329(b). But even if Jackson had timely raised it, Jackson must depend on proof other than matters prohibited by Rule 327(b) to establish statutory disqualification.

Finally, we consider the alleged conversation between Frederick and Maxwell during a trial break. Jackson argues that the conversation should not be considered "deliberations" and therefore barred by Rule 606(b) and Rule 327(b). We agree. The Texas Rules of Civil Procedure use the term "deliberations" as meaning formal jury deliberations-when the jury weighs the evidence to arrive at a verdict.

* * *

Juror testimony is still permitted on the issues of juror misconduct, communications to the jury, and erroneous answers on voir dire, provided such testimony does not require delving into deliberations. TEX.R. CIV. P. 327(a), (b).

Consequently, we conclude that Rules 327(b) and 606(b) do not bar Frederick's testimony about his conversation with Maxwell during a trial break. However, because this evidence does not conclusively establish that Maxwell prevaricated or concealed bias during voir dire, we do not agree that the trial court abused its discretion in failing to grant a new trial.

To warrant a new trial for jury misconduct, the movant must establish (1) that the misconduct occurred, (2) it was material, and (3) probably caused injury. Rule 327 provides that a trial court:

> may grant a new trial if . . . the erroneous or incorrect answer on voir dire examination, be material, and if it reasonably appears from the evidence both on the hearing of the motion and the trial of the case and from the record as a whole that injury probably resulted to the complaining party.

TEX.R. CIV. P. 327(a). Whether misconduct occurred and caused injury is a question of fact for the trial court. Absent findings to the contrary, we must assume that the trial court made all findings in support of its decision to deny the motion for new trial. *See id.* Consequently, Jackson had the burden to conclusively establish that Maxwell committed jury misconduct, a burden he did not discharge.

Jackson contends that juror Frederick's accounts of a casual conversation with Maxwell established that she prevaricated on voir dire and concealed her bias. Frederick's affidavit in support of Jackson's motion stated in part:

> At a recess during the trial after the testimony of the witness Mulaney, the juror Barbara Maxwell told me that she had been on a previous jury in which a family was suing for the death of another family member. Her comment was that the jury she was on awarded nothing, and that she did not believe in "awarding money in stuff like that". She also said,

"We are the ones that end up paying for it." I reminded her that she had been asked about that by [Jackson's attorney] and she gave no answer.

Frederick elaborated on this incident as a witness called by Jackson at the hearing on the motion:

Q I believe [your affidavit refers] to something that took place while the case was still being tried; is that correct?

A Yes, sir, it is.

Q Did that take place on a break of the jury?

A Yes, sir, right outside the courtroom.

Q Now, this this—I believe that you told me that you and a female juror both like to drink coffee and you-all were the only coffee drinkers?

A Yes, sir.

Q Is that right?

A That's correct.

Q And during this break this female juror made some comments; is that right?

A That's correct, yes.

Q And what was it she said?

A It was during or right after the witness Mulaney, right after his testimony. She made the comment about it being boring. She said, "Of course, the whole thing is boring." And she said, "I don't believe in lawsuits like this." And I said, "Well," I said, "I think you was asked that during voir dire." And she didn't make any comment after that. She didn't answer me one way or the other.

Q Did she in the same conversation mention to you that she had served on a wrongful death jury?

A Yes, she did. She said she had-that someone was killed in an auto accident and the family had sued and she was on the jury and she said, "We didn't award them anything because I don't believe in things like that. I don't believe in lawsuits like that."

Q And you reminded her that she'd been asked that on voir dire?

A Right, right, I reminded her. I said—I think Mr. Smith had asked that very question on voir dire, if anybody did not believe in it to say so; and she made no comment about that.

Q Now, there was one other statement in this affidavit attributed to this juror and that is, "We are the ones that end up paying for it"?

A Yes, sir, she said that.

Q She made that comment at the same time?

A Right.

Jackson contends that Frederick's testimony established that Maxwell prevaricated on voir dire. When Jackson's attorney asked the panel about prior jury service, Maxwell volunteered she had served on juries in a criminal matter and a civil matter involving a death. The attorney asked if the jury had reached a verdict in the civil case, and Maxwell answered "no". The attorney did not ask Maxwell any further questions.

We conclude that Frederick's affidavit and testimony do not conclusively establish that Maxwell failed to answer Jackson's voir dire questions truthfully. The other party to the conversation, Maxwell, did not testify at the new trial hearing nor does the record indicate that anyone called her to testify. It is at least possible that Maxwell misunderstood the voir dire question about whether the jury had reached a verdict in the wrongful death case and thought it meant whether the jury had awarded any damages in the case. There is no other evidence in the record about this conversation or the facts of Maxwell's prior jury service. This evidence does not conclusively establish that Maxwell intentionally answered incorrectly.

Jackson also contends that Frederick's testimony demonstrates that Maxwell concealed bias during voir dire. If, as Frederick testified, Maxwell said that she did not believe in "things like that" or "lawsuits like that" or in awarding money in "stuff like that" or "things like that", all referring to the wrongful death action, or that she did not believe in "lawsuits like this", referring to the present case, did she mean lawsuits that she considered to be lacking in merit or all personal injury actions? The latter is a reasonable inference, but so is the former. Frederick's testimony, if credible, was inconclusive.

But the trial court may not have considered Frederick's testimony to have been credible. It was certainly hearsay, and while no objection was made to its admission to preclude the trial court from considering it, the trial court was nevertheless free on its own to disregard the testimony.

We conclude that the evidence about discussions prior to formal deliberations does not establish jury misconduct here, and Rules 606(b) and 327(b) prohibit considering the testimony about matters and statements occurring in the course of the jury's formal deliberations. We turn now to Jackson's constitutional arguments.

IV

* * *

We conclude that Rules 327(b) and 606(b) do not deprive the litigants of a fair trial under the Texas Constitution, nor do they fail to afford litigants due process. The rules are designed to balance concerns about the threat of jury misconduct with the threat from post-verdict juror investigation and impeachment of verdicts.

V

The trial court did not abuse its discretion by denying a new trial on grounds of jury misconduct because Jackson did not present competent evidence. Accordingly, we reverse the judgment of the court of appeals and remand the case to that court to consider Jackson's other issues that it did not reach.

JUSTICE HECHT filed a concurring opinion, in which JUSTICE OWEN joined, omitted.

Notes & Questions

1. *Jury misconduct and new trial mandamus proceedings*. Since the Supreme Court decided that appellate courts could conduct a merits review of the bases for a new trial order after the trial court sets aside a jury verdict[1], new opportunities have arisen to review jury misconduct issues. In one case, the trial court granted a new trial after a verdict for the defendant because of a juror's communications about a church retreat (unrelated to the case) with an employee of the defendant. The Supreme Court held that the new trial order was an abuse of discretion because there was no showing that the communication was "material" or "probably caused injury."[2] Similarly, the Court found "no probable injury" in another case where the trial court granted a new trial after a verdict for defendant after learning that a juror failed to disclose prior lawsuits in a questionnaire provided during the jury selection process.[3]

2. *Exception to no-impeachment rule.* The United States Supreme Court has held that where a juror makes a clear statement indicating that he or she relied on racial stereotypes or animus to convict a criminal defendant, the Sixth Amendment requires that the no-impeachment rule give way in order to permit the trial court to consider the evidence of the juror's statement and any resulting denial of the jury trial guarantee.[4]

3. *Juror testimony in other contexts*. Rules 327(b) and 606 specifically refer to juror testimony in a motion for new trial hearing that seeks to invalidate a jury verdict. But the Texas Supreme Court applied the rules in another context—an action seeking to invalidate a settlement agreement. In *Ford v. Castillo*,[5] Ford settled a products liability case after the jury asked a question about the maximum amount that could be awarded. After the jury was discharged, jurors told Ford that the deliberations favored Ford, and that the presiding juror sent the question to the judge over the protest of other jurors. Ford sought to invalidate the settlement agreement for mutual mistake, and asked for discovery from the presiding juror to see if she had been subjected to outside influences. The Court held that juror testimony was discoverable, and said:

> Once the trial court discharges them, jurors are not prohibited from discussing what took place during deliberations. But there is a difference between jurors choosing to talk about their service and their being compelled to do so in discovery depositions and court hearings. We believe the better policy, in general, is to conform discovery involving jurors to those matters permitted by Rule of Civil Procedure 327 and Rule of Evidence 606. That is, discovery involving jurors should ordinarily be limited to facts and evidence relevant to (1) whether any outside influence was improperly brought to bear upon any juror, and (2) rebuttal of a claim that a juror was not qualified to serve. And although we have determined that the trial court abused its discretion by entirely depriving Ford of discovery

---

1 In re Toyota Motor Sales, U.S.A., Inc., 407 S.W.3d 746 (Tex. 2013).

2 In re Health Care Unlimited, Inc., 429 S.W.3d 600 (Tex. 2014).

3 In re Whataburger Restaurants LP, 429 S.W.3d 597 (Tex. 2014).

4 Pena-Rodriguez v. Colorado, 137 S. Ct. 855 (2017).

5 279 S.W.3d 656 (Tex. 2009). The case was ultimately tried to a jury, which found that the settlement agreement was procured by fraud. The Supreme Court affirmed. Ford Motor Co. v. Castillo, 2014 WL 2790352 (Tex. 2014) (found in Chapter 15, *infra*).

on the breach of contract claim, it remains within the trial court's discretion to reasonably control the limits of discovery and the manner in which the discovery may be obtained.

F. Constitutional Limits on the Exercise of Peremptory Challenges

GOODE
v.
SHOUKFEH
943 S.W.2d 441
(Tex. 1997)

OWEN, JUSTICE

In this case we review a determination that peremptory challenges were not based on race and consider whether two members of the venire should have been excused for cause. The trial court overruled Petitioner's objections to Respondent's peremptory challenges and also refused to excuse two veniremembers for cause. The court of appeals affirmed the trial court's take-nothing judgment. We affirm the judgment of the court of appeals.

I

James Emerson Goode died from complications following knee-replacement surgery performed at Methodist Hospital of Lubbock. Orlin Goode, as independent executor of the estate of James Goode, brought a medical malpractice suit against Mohammad F. Shoukfeh, a cardiologist who treated James Goode for a pulmonary embolism several days after his surgery. The case was tried to a jury, who failed to find Shoukfeh negligent. The trial court rendered judgment on the verdict, and Goode appealed. The court of appeals affirmed.

Goode's complaints on appeal focus on the selection of the jury. Following voir dire of the prospective jury panel, Shoukfeh peremptorily challenged six veniremembers. Goode, an African-American, objected to four of these challenges as impermissibly motivated by race under *Edmonson v. Leesville Concrete Co*. The challenged jurors included three African-Americans (jurors 7, 26, and 28) and one Hispanic (juror 9). During voir dire, Goode also alleged that Shoukfeh struck juror 9, a woman, for "gender based reasons." However, Goode has not asserted a claim of gender discrimination in this Court.

The trial court conducted a hearing on Goode's *Edmonson* challenge, which Goode's counsel began by stating that: (1) the four challenged jurors were members of a racial minority; (2) no sufficient, racially neutral reason justified these challenges; and (3) Goode would put forth evidence of his claims if the court so desired. The court declined this offer of evidence and instead called upon Shoukfeh's counsel to reply.

Responding to the court's request, Shoukfeh's counsel offered explanations for striking the four jurors in question. Juror 7 knew and had worked with either James Goode's widow or one of his children. Juror 26 was once a nurse at Methodist Hospital, and Shoukfeh's counsel expressed concern with "the reasons that she left employ there." The objection to juror 28 was that she made an "unequivocal statement . . . that she had a problem sitting in judgment" and also that she failed to disclose her prior jury service on her juror information card. Finally, juror 9 was a single mother of four who listed her occupation as "house mother," which counsel for Shoukfeh took to mean unemployed, and Shoukfeh's counsel stated that he was concerned that her service on the jury "would affect her ability to take care of four children." Shoukfeh's counsel also claimed that juror 9 would be "more of a plaintiff's juror" because she appeared to be a welfare recipient.

Following these explanations, Goode requested the opportunity to examine the voir dire notes of opposing counsel and argued that these notes should be admitted into evidence. Goode then requested the opportunity to call witnesses and eventually did call Jim Hund and Bill Moss, Shoukfeh's attorneys. The questioning of Hund and Moss focused on their respective voir dire notes. When asked whether these notes reflected any reliance on race in striking the four jurors in question, Hund invoked the work-product privilege. Moss answered "no" in response to the same question. However, both Hund and Moss asserted the work-product privilege in refusing to disclose their notes to Goode. The trial court sustained the privilege claims and refused to conduct an in camera inspection of the notes. The court then overruled Goode's Edmonson objections. Goode contends that following Shoukfeh's peremptory challenges, no African-Americans or Hispanics were left on the panel, although the record indicates that two individuals with names of Hispanic origin remained.

Goode contends that Shoukfeh failed to offer race-neutral explanations for his peremptory challenges and that the trial court erred in denying access to counsel's notes, which may have provided concrete evidence that the peremptory challenges were made with racially discriminatory intent.

II

A

Goode's challenges to the strikes exercised by Shoukfeh arise under the United States Constitution, as interpreted in decisions of both the United States Supreme Court and this Court. In *Batson v. Kentucky*, 476 U.S. 79, 106 S.Ct. 1712, 90 L.Ed.2d 69 (1986), the Supreme Court held that a criminal defendant is denied equal protection under the United States Constitution if a prosecutor uses peremptory challenges to exclude members of the jury panel solely on the basis that their race is the same as the defendant's.

The United States Supreme Court has extended the reach of *Batson* to other situations, most notably civil trials. *See Edmonson v. Leesville Concrete Co*. The Court held in *Edmonson* that race-based exclusion of civil jurors violates the equal protection rights of the excluded juror. . Other extensions of *Batson* include *J.E.B. v. Alabama* (prohibiting peremptory challenges based on sex); *Georgia v. McCollum* (prohibiting criminal defendant's exercise of peremptory challenges in a racially discriminatory manner); *Powers v. Ohio* (prohibiting racially motivated peremptory challenges even when excluded jurors are of a different race than the defendant). As in *Edmonson*, these decisions reflect the Supreme Court's recognition of the equal protection rights of both the excluded jurors and the litigants.

In the wake of *Edmonson*, this Court confirmed in *Powers v. Palacios*, 813 S.W.2d 489, 490-91 (Tex. 1991), that the use of a peremptory challenge to exclude a juror on the basis of race violates the equal protection rights of the excluded juror.

Decisions of the United States Supreme Court have delineated the substantive parameters that govern a *Batson/Edmonson* objection. In two criminal cases, *Hernandez v. New York*, and *Purkett v. Elem*, the Supreme Court explained the three-step process utilized in resolving a *Batson* objection to a peremptory challenge. At the first step of the process, the opponent of the peremptory challenge must establish a prima facie case of racial discrimination. There is no contention in this case that Goode failed to make out a prima facie case, and accordingly, we need not consider that question. In any event, once a party offers a race-neutral explanation for the peremptory challenge and the trial court has ruled on the ultimate question of intentional discrimination, the preliminary issue of a prima facie case is moot.

During the second step of the process, the burden shifts to the party who has exercised the strike to come forward with a race-neutral explanation. *Purkett*; *Hernandez*. The United States Supreme Court clarified in *Purkett* the role of an appellate court at this stage of the inquiry. The appellate court does not consider at the second step whether the explanation is persuasive or even plausible. The issue for the trial court and the appellate court at this juncture is the facial validity of the explanation. *Purkett*. In evaluating whether the explanation offered is race-neutral, a court must determine whether the peremptory challenge violates the Equal Protection Clause as a matter of law, assuming the reasons for the peremptory challenge are true. *Hernandez*. A neutral explanation means that the challenge was based on something other than the juror's race. Unless a discriminatory intent is inherent in the explanation, the reason offered will be deemed race-neutral for purposes of the analysis at step two. Thus the inquiry does not terminate at step two even if the party opposing the peremptory challenge offers a "silly or superstitious" explanation, so long as that explanation is race-neutral. *Purkett*. It is not until the third step that the persuasiveness of the justification for the challenge becomes relevant. At the third step of the process, the trial court must determine if the party challenging the strike has proven purposeful racial discrimination, and the trial court may believe or not believe the explanation offered by the party who exercised the peremptory challenge. It is at this stage that implausible justifications for striking potential jurors "may (and probably will) be found [by the trial court] to be pretexts for purposeful discrimination." Nevertheless, the Supreme Court has emphasized that "the ultimate burden of persuasion regarding racial motivation rests with, and never shifts from, the opponent of the [peremptory] strike."

The decisions of the United States Supreme Court also make clear that at the third step in the process, the issue of whether the race-neutral explanation should be believed is purely a question of fact for the trial court. In the federal system, the standard of review on appeal of a *Batson/Edmonson* challenge is whether the ruling was "clearly erroneous." Under that standard, a trial court's finding will not be disturbed unless the appellate court is " 'left with a definite and firm conviction that a mistake has been committed.' " The Texas Court of Criminal Appeals has also adopted the clearly erroneous standard of review for *Batson* issues.

Our civil jurisprudence in Texas has employed a deferential, but more familiar, "abuse of discretion" standard in reviewing many of the decisions made by a trial court. A trial court abuses its discretion if its decision "is arbitrary, unreasonable, and without reference to guiding principles." With regard to questions of fact, our abuse of discretion standard is similar, although not identical, to the federal standard of "clearly erroneous." "Where there are two permissible views of the evidence, the factfinder's choice between them cannot be clearly erroneous." In reviewing an *Edmonson* challenge, we will adhere to the abuse of discretion standard of review by which trial court rulings of this nature historically have been judged in civil cases in Texas.

However, a reviewing court will not be bound by a finding of no discrimination under either our abuse of discretion standard or the clearly erroneous standard if the justification offered for striking a potential juror is "simply too incredible to be accepted." *Hernandez*. For example, in the case of *Norris v. Alabama*, it was undisputed that no African-American had served on a grand or petit jury in the area "within the memory of witnesses who had lived there all their lives," *Hernandez*. Accordingly, the Supreme Court reversed the lower court's finding of no discrimination.

These are the parameters within which we analyze Goode's contentions that Shoukfeh gave no race-neutral explanation for his peremptory challenges and that the court of appeals applied the wrong standard in reviewing the trial court's ruling.

B

The issue of whether Goode established a prima facie case of racial discrimination is unchallenged. Accordingly, our review begins at the second step of the *Batson/Edmonson* analysis. We must determine whether, assuming the reasons Shoukfeh offered for striking the jurors at issue were true, the peremptory challenges violate the Equal Protection Clause as a matter of law. *Hernandez*. We conclude they do not. Shoukfeh's explanations were race-neutral.

Shoukfeh's counsel stated that he struck juror 7 because she knew a member of the Goode family and that he struck juror 26 because she was a former employee of Methodist Hospital. Counsel asserted that he struck juror 28 because she said she could not sit in judgment and because she made misstatements on her juror information card. Finally, Shoukfeh's counsel claimed that he struck juror 9 because she was an unmarried, unemployed, mother of four, apparently on welfare, whom he believed would be a "bad defense juror." Each of these reasons is facially race-neutral, and it cannot be said as a matter of law that there has been a violation of the Equal Protection Clause.

C

In proceeding to the third step of the *Edmonson* analysis, we address Goode's contention that the court of appeals failed to follow the *Batson/Edmonson* analytical framework. Goode argues that the court of appeals moved beyond the first step in the procedure only to improperly combine the second and third steps and summarily conclude that Shoukfeh's peremptory challenges were proper because the explanations offered by Shoukfeh's counsel were facially race-neutral. Goode contends that the court of appeals failed to determine whether the explanations were credible or were a mere pretext.

The United States Supreme Court has made it clear that whether the explanations offered for exercising peremptory challenges are credible is a fact question to be resolved by the trial court. That factual determination will be disturbed by this Court only upon a finding that the trial court abused its discretion.

Goode catalogues the factors upon which he relies to demonstrate that Shoukfeh's proffered reasons were pretextual. First, Goode contends that the pattern of Shoukfeh's peremptory strikes establishes an intent to purge the panel of racial minorities. Shoukfeh used six peremptory strikes. Three of these were used to remove African-Americans (jurors 7, 26, and 28), two were used to remove Anglos (jurors 13 and 22), and one to remove an Hispanic (juror 9). The remaining panel had no African-Americans.

Next, Goode argues that racial discrimination is established because Shoukfeh did not strike Anglo jurors who possessed characteristics similar to those of minority jurors whom he did strike. Shoukfeh struck juror 26, an African-American, allegedly because she was a former Methodist Hospital nurse, but he did not strike jurors 4 and 11, Anglos who were acquainted with one of Shoukfeh's partners, or juror 18, an Anglo who, like juror 26, was a former nurse at Methodist Hospital. Shoukfeh counters that this is irrelevant for two reasons. First, he did strike juror 13, an Anglo medical professor. Second, Shoukfeh's counsel contends that unlike juror 18, juror 26's relationship with Methodist Hospital was problematic because the reasons her employment ended concerned him.

Similarly, Goode asserts that Shoukfeh struck juror 7, an African-American, because juror 7 knew a member of the Goode family, but he did not strike juror 12, an Anglo who went to school with one of James Goode's children. Shoukfeh responds that this discrepancy is meaningless because he did strike juror 22, an Anglo who went to school with Orlin Goode.

Finally, Goode contends that Shoukfeh's failure to question three members of racial minorities before striking them (jurors 9, 26, and 28) indicates that Shoukfeh's proffered reasons for exercising these peremptory challenges were pretextual. Goode argues that the lack of questioning is particularly troubling with respect to juror 9, because the record indicates that the factors Shoukfeh identified for challenging her are ambiguous or inaccurate. Shoukfeh's stated reasons for striking juror 9 were that she was an unmarried, unemployed, mother of four, apparently on welfare, who was unlikely to be a good defense juror. Shoukfeh downplays the significance of his failure to question these minority jurors because he also did not question juror 13, one of the Anglos he peremptorily challenged.

The trial court resolved these factual disputes and chose to believe that Shoukfeh's counsel exercised the peremptory challenges for the reasons stated. The record before us does not indicate that the trial court's ruling was an abuse of its discretion. Neither this Court nor the court of appeals can second guess that decision. When, as in this case, a party offers a facially race-neutral explanation, a reviewing court cannot reweigh the evidence and reach a conclusion different from that of the trial court unless, as in *Norris*, the explanation offered is too incredible to be believed.

D

* * *

III

The court of appeals expressed some consternation that neither this Court nor the United States Supreme Court has offered guidance for the procedures to be followed in resolving *Edmonson* challenges to peremptory strikes.

Though the topic has long been the subject of judicial discourse in the criminal realm, neither of the aforementioned supreme courts expounded upon the procedures utilized in a civil proceeding. Indeed, this dearth of guidance spawned at least one jurist to wish that "some of these appellate . . . judges that turn in all this [stuff], would have to come down here and put up with it." We are generally reluctant to address issues that are not squarely before us. In this instance, however, we are persuaded that some guidance for future cases is appropriate.

Procedures for resolution of *Edmonson* challenges must adequately safeguard the constitutional rights arising under the Equal Protection Clause. However, those procedures should disrupt the trial of the case as little as reasonably possible. We are sensitive to concerns that *Edmonson* hearings will become "yet another complexity . . . to an increasingly Byzantine system of justice that devotes more and more of its energy to sideshows and less and less to the merits of the case." *Edmonson* (SCALIA, J., dissenting).

The United States Supreme Court has declined "to formulate particular procedures to be followed upon a defendant's timely objection to a prosecutor's challenges." *Batson*; *see also Powers v. Ohio* ("It remains for the trial courts to develop rules, without unnecessary disruption of the jury selection process, to permit legitimate and well-founded objections to the use of peremptory challenges as a mask for race prejudice."). Instead, the Supreme Court has continued to allow lower courts to wrestle with *Batson/Edmonson* procedures.

The state and federal courts left with the responsibility of formulating *Batson/Edmonson* procedures have produced a fairly uneven set of procedures across the country. As the court of appeals noted below, the resulting "dearth" of consistent procedural guidance is the "predicament" of the *Edmonson* rule.

The Texas criminal jurisprudence on *Batson* procedures is much more developed than civil jurisprudence. In 1987, the Legislature included a provision in the Texas Code of Criminal Procedure incorporating *Batson*.[3] Because no similar change was made to the Texas Rules of Civil Procedure, the courts of appeals have often looked to the state's criminal jurisprudence for guidance in applying *Batson* and its progeny to civil matters.

The most general procedural issue concerns the overall nature and tenor of a *Batson/Edmonson* hearing. The court of appeals in this case concluded that such a hearing is an "adversarial, evidentiary hearing" in which "the procedural and evidentiary rules normally applicable to general civil matters apply with equal force." Likewise, other Texas courts of appeals have repeatedly held that a *Batson/Edmonson* hearing should be adversarial. Other jurisdictions also require a full adversarial hearing. . . .

In contrast, courts in other jurisdictions have held that a full-blown, adversarial hearing is not required . . . .

Still other jurisdictions have specifically approved the use of ex parte, in camera proceedings in lieu of an adversarial hearing . . . .

Finally, many jurisdictions simply leave it to the trial courts to determine appropriate procedures for a given set of circumstances . . . . The trial court's choice of procedure can then be reviewed for an abuse of discretion . . . .

Consideration of an *Edmonson* challenge is by its very nature adversarial. Further, this Court has often held that ex parte, in camera procedures are disfavored. Accordingly, at a minimum, the proceedings should be held in open court. Unsworn statements of counsel may be offered to explain why the peremptory challenges were exercised. The juror information cards may be made a part of the record by inclusion in the transcript or by a formal tender into evidence. To

---

[3] The statute provides:

Art. 35.261. Peremptory challenges based on race prohibited

(a) After the parties have delivered their lists to the clerk under Article 35.26 of this code and before the court has impanelled [sic] the jury, the defendant may request the court to dismiss the array and call a new array in the case. The Court shall grant the motion of a defendant for dismissal of the array if the court determines that the defendant is a member of an identifiable racial group, that the attorney representing the state exercised peremptory challenges for the purpose of excluding persons from the jury on the basis of their race, and that the defendant has offered evidence of relevant facts that tend to show that challenges made by the attorney representing the state were made for reasons based on race. If the defendant establishes a prima facie case, the burden then shifts to the attorney representing the state to give a racially neutral explanation for the challenges. The burden of persuasion remains with the defendant to establish purposeful discrimination.

(b) If the court determines that the attorney representing the state challenged prospective jurors on the basis of race, the court shall call a new array in the case. TEX. CODE CRIM. P. art. 35.261.

the extent that any party wishes to include other information or matters in the record, the rules of evidence and procedure apply.

The more difficult questions are the extent to which the party making the *Edmonson* challenge may rebut the explanations offered and whether there is a right of cross-examination. Some jurisdictions have held that the movant does have the right to rebut the opponent's stated reason or otherwise prove that these reasons are a sham or a pretext . . . . Frequently, these jurisdictions note that the assignment to the movant of the ultimate burden of persuasion in a *Batson/Edmonson* hearing dictates that the movant have the last word . . . . However, other jurisdictions, recognizing that *Batson* itself does not mention this right, have refused to recognize it . . . .

Because the party challenging the peremptory strikes has the ultimate burden of persuasion, we conclude that the trial court should provide the party challenging the strikes under *Edmonson* a reasonable opportunity to rebut the race-neutral explanations.

Whether the movant should have the right to cross-examine the opponent's attorney in order to establish that the attorney's stated race-neutral explanations are pretextual is another much-debated issue. Some jurisdictions place the determination of the right to cross-examine within the discretion of the trial court . . . . Others deny the right on the grounds that "the disruption to a trial which could occur if an attorney in a case were called as a witness overbears any good which could be obtained by his testimony." * * * However, in *Salazar v. State*, the Texas Court of Criminal Appeals held that "[c]ross-examination [of the prosecutor] is necessary in a *Batson* hearing because once the State has met its burden of coming forward with neutral explanations for its peremptory strikes, the burden to show purposeful discrimination shifts back to the defendant to impeach or refute the neutral explanation or show that it is merely a pretext."

As with the opportunity to rebut, we conclude that the trial court should provide the party asserting objections under *Edmonson* with a reasonable opportunity to conduct cross-examination.

In sum, we acknowledge the importance of protecting equal protection rights, but also adhere to the Supreme Court's observations in *Batson* and its progeny that procedures for *Edmonson* hearings should prevent "unnecessary disruption" in the trial courts.

* * *

We affirm the judgment of the court of appeals.

DAVIS
v.
FISK ELECTRIC CO.
268 S.W.3d 508
(Tex. 2008)

CHIEF JUSTICE JEFFERSON delivered the opinion of the Court, joined by JUSTICE HECHT, JUSTICE O'NEILL, JUSTICE WAINWRIGHT, JUSTICE MEDINA, JUSTICE GREEN, JUSTICE JOHNSON, and JUSTICE WILLETT.

Our rules generally permit each party in a civil action to exercise six peremptory strikes, which are challenges "made to a juror without assigning any reason therefor." TEX.R. CIV. P. 232, 233. But peremptories exercised for an improper reason, like race or gender, are unconstitutional. In this case, the African American petitioner asserted that he was terminated based on his race. The respondents used peremptory challenges at trial to exclude five of six African Americans from the venire but contend that their reasons for doing so had nothing to do with the potential jurors' race. The stated reasons, however, when viewed in conjunction with the 83% removal rate and a comparative juror analysis, defy neutral explanation. Because we conclude that at least two of the strikes were based on race, we reverse in part the court of appeals' judgment and remand the case for a new trial.

I

Factual Background

Donald Davis, an African American, worked for Fisk Electric Company as an assistant project manager. In February 2001, Fisk was awarded the contract to install cables at Goodson Middle School, in the Cypress Fairbanks School District. After problems arose on the Goodson project, Fisk terminated Davis. Davis asserts that his termination was based on his race, as evidenced in part by his supervisor's alleged use of the "n-word" when planning Davis's termination.

Davis sued Fisk, claiming violations of 42 U.S.C. § 1981 and the Texas Labor Code. Fisk denied liability. The case was called for trial, and at the conclusion of voir dire, Fisk peremptorily struck six venire members, five of whom were African American and all of whom were minorities. Davis objected, citing *Batson v. Kentucky,* and the trial court, after a hearing, overruled the objection. The jury returned a defense verdict, the trial court signed a take-nothing judgment, and the court of appeals affirmed. We granted Davis's petition for review to apply the United States Supreme Court's most recent guidance on peremptory challenges that are allegedly race-based.

II

***Batson* Challenge**

Davis raises a single complaint: that Fisk struck prospective jurors based on race, in violation of *Batson.* We last wrote on *Batson* challenges in *Goode v. Shoukfeh,* and in the intervening years, the landscape has evolved. Significantly, after the trial in this case, the Supreme Court decided *Miller-El v. Dretke,* 545 U.S. 231 (2005) ("*Miller-El II* "), a case in which the Court concluded that a habeas petitioner was entitled to relief because prosecutors in his criminal trial peremptorily struck potential jurors based on race. Although *Miller-El II* is a criminal case, it involves many of the same factors at issue here, and we examine it in some detail.

The case began with Miller-El's 1986 capital murder trial in a Texas trial court. During jury selection, prosecutors used peremptory strikes to remove ten African Americans from the venire. Miller-El objected that the strikes were improperly based on race, given the Dallas County District Attorney's Office's historic practice of excluding blacks from criminal juries. . . .

The trial court reviewed the voir dire record, and one of the prosecutors provided his rationale for previously unexplained strikes. The trial court deemed the explanations "completely credible [and] sufficient" and found there was "no purposeful discrimination." The Court of Criminal Appeals affirmed, stating that the voir dire record provided "ample support" for the prosecutor's race-neutral explanations.

Miller-El then sought habeas relief under 28 U.S.C. § 2254, again raising his Batson claim. . . . The Supreme Court again granted certiorari, and again reversed, this time on the merits of Miller-El's *Batson* challenge.

Noting that a *Batson* challenge requires an examination of " 'all relevant circumstances,' " the Court examined five factors in determining that jury selection in Miller-El's criminal trial violated the Equal Protection Clause. The first involved an analysis of the statistical data pertaining to the prosecution's peremptory strikes. The Court noted that prosecutors used peremptory strikes to exclude 91% of the eligible African-American venire members-a percentage too great to attribute merely to "[h]appenstance."

The Court then conducted a comparative juror analysis, noting that "[m]ore powerful than these bare statistics, however, are side-by-side comparisons of some black venire panelists who were struck and white panelists who were allowed to serve." The Court explained that "[i]f a prosecutor's proffered reason for striking a black panelist applies just as well to an otherwise-similar nonblack who is permitted to serve, that is evidence tending to prove purposeful discrimination to be considered at *Batson's* third step." In conducting this analysis, the Court rejected the notion that struck venire members must be compared only to jurors who are identical in all respects (save race): "A *per se* rule that a defendant cannot win a *Batson* claim unless there is an exactly identical white juror would leave *Batson* inoperable; potential jurors are not products of a set of cookie cutters." The Court focused on the prosecution's questioning of two black venire members-Billy Jean Fields and Joe Warren-and compared their answers to those given by whites. With regard to Fields, the Court determined that:

> nonblack jurors whose remarks on rehabilitation could well have signaled a limit on their willingness to impose a death sentence were not questioned further and drew no objection, but the prosecution expressed apprehension about a black juror's belief in the possibility of reformation even though he repeatedly stated his approval of the death penalty and testified that he could impose it according to state legal standards even when the alternative sentence of life imprisonment would give a defendant (like everyone else in the world) the opportunity to reform.

As for Warren, the Court noted that the State's proffered reason-that Warren's voir dire answers were inconsistent-seemed plausible, but "its plausibility [was] severely undercut by the prosecution's failure to object to other panel members who expressed views much like Warren's." After comparing his answers to panel members who expressed similar conclusions, the Court decided that race was significant in determining who was challenged and who was not. The Court also rejected the court of appeals' independent conclusion that Warren expressed general ambivalence about the death penalty, because the prosecutor's stated reasons for striking Warren did not allude to any such ambivalence. The Court then noted:

> [T]he rule in *Batson* provides an opportunity to the prosecutor to give the reason for striking the juror, and it requires the judge to assess the plausibility of that reason in light of all evidence with a bearing on it. It is true that peremptories are often the subjects of instinct, and it can sometimes be hard to say what the reason is. But when illegitimate grounds like race are in issue, a prosecutor simply has got to state his reasons as best he can and stand or fall on the plausibility of the reasons he gives. ***A Batson challenge does not call for a mere exercise in thinking up any rational basis.*** If the stated reason does not hold up, its pretextual significance does not fade because a trial judge, or an appeals court, can imagine a reason that might not have been shown up as false. The Court of Appeals's and the dissent's substitution of a reason for eliminating Warren does nothing to satisfy the prosecutors' burden of stating a racially neutral explanation for their own actions.

A third factor the Court considered was the prosecution's use of the jury shuffle, a practice unique to Texas, and one that the Court held could "indicate decisions probably based on race." The *Miller-El* jury was shuffled some eight times, at the request of both the prosecution (three times) and the defense (five times). The Court noted that " 'the prosecution's decision to seek a jury shuffle when a predominant number of African-Americans were seated in the front of the panel, along with its decision to delay a formal objection to the defense's shuffle until after the racial composition was revealed, raise a suspicion that the State sought to exclude African-Americans from the jury.' " This was amplified by testimony that the Dallas County District Attorney's Office had previously admitted to using the shuffle to manipulate the racial makeup of juries. The Court concluded:

> The State notes in its brief that there might be racially neutral reasons for shuffling the jury, and we suppose there might be. But no racially neutral reason has ever been offered in this case, and nothing stops the suspicion of discriminatory intent from rising to an inference.

A fourth factor the Court relied on was the "contrasting voir dire questions posed respectively to black and nonblack panel members." Prosecutors gave black panel members a vivid, graphic account of the death penalty before asking about the member's feelings on the subject, while it gave nonblacks a "bland description." While the State conceded that disparate questioning occurred, it asserted that the disparity was based on panel members' differing views of the death penalty-those who expressed ambivalence received the "graphic script," while those who did not received the watered-down version. Based on the record, however, the Court concluded that black venire members were more likely to receive the graphic script regardless of their expressions of ambivalence, and the State's explanation failed for four of the eight black panel members who received that script. Additionally, four out of five nonblacks who were given the graphic script were not those who had expressed ambivalence but were instead unambiguously in favor of, or vehemently opposed to, the death penalty. The Court also noted that the State disparately used manipulative questioning regarding minimum punishments. The State conceded that practice but argued that it was premised on opposition to or ambivalence regarding the death penalty, rather than race. The Court disagreed, noting that "only 27% of nonblacks questioned on the subject who expressed these views were subjected to the trick question, as against 100% of black members. Once again, the implication of race in the prosecutors' choice of questioning cannot be explained away."

Finally, the Court considered the Dallas County District Attorney's Office's history of "systematically excluding blacks from juries." Specifically, the defense presented evidence that the DA's office had adopted a formal policy to exclude minorities from jury service, and that policy was summarized in a "manual entitled 'Jury Selection in a Criminal Case' [sometimes known as the Sparling Manual]" that was distributed to prosecutors. Although the manual was written in 1968, the evidence showed it was available to at least one of Miller-El's prosecutors. The Court also observed that prosecutors had noted the race of each prospective juror on their juror cards.

Considering the totality of the circumstances, the Court held:

> It blinks reality to deny that the State struck Fields and Warren, included in [the] 91% [of black venire members who were struck], because they were black. The strikes correlate with no fact as well as they correlate with race, and they occurred during a selection infected by shuffling and disparate questioning that race explains better than any race-neutral reason advanced by the State. The State's pretextual positions confirm Miller-El's

claim, and the prosecutors' own notes proclaim that the Sparling Manual's emphasis on race was on their minds when they considered every potential juror.

Holding that the state court's conclusion about the prosecutors' strikes of those two jurors was wrong "to a clear and convincing degree," the Court reversed the court of appeals' judgment and remanded the case for entry of judgment for Miller-El, "together with orders of appropriate relief."

* * *

V

Analysis

A

Statistical Disparity

Here, as in *Miller-El,* the statistics are "remarkable." *Miller-El II,* (noting that prosecutors used peremptory strikes to exclude 91% of eligible black venire members). Jurors were chosen from the first twenty-eight members of the venire. At the conclusion of the parties' questioning, four panelists were struck for cause or by agreement, and the parties then submitted their peremptory challenges. Fisk struck five of the six African Americans (83%) but only one (5.5%) of the eligible nonblack prospective jurors, and "[h]appenstance is unlikely to produce this disparity."

B

Comparative Juror Analysis

Beyond the raw statistics, a comparative juror analysis is similarly troubling. Fisk struck Juror No. 12, Patrick Daigle, and provided the following explanation:

> Of all the jurors, juror No. 12, who initially I thought would be good a good [sic] juror for us, reacted that corporations should be punished with the use of punitive damages. He was the most clear on that subject. In addition, I attempted to draw out of him a discussion from him about his involvement in this management-employee committee thing at Continental, something that would make me think he recognized that many of the discrimination claims that they deal with—I know he said he didn't have any personal involvement with race discrimination cases; but he seemed to be too ready to believe that Continental has discriminatory employment practices; which, you know, I could be totally wrong about this, Your Honor; but my belief is that I tend to have a high degree of skepticism about that, about Continental and the fact that he didn't have that same skepticism caused me to believe they we should exercise a challenge on him.

The trial court then immediately overruled Davis's *Batson* objection to the strike.

Davis's counsel conducted the only questioning on punitive damages, and, as is evident from the colloquy, Daigle never verbally responded to the questions about punitive damages. Fisk nonetheless asserted in the trial court that Daigle nonverbally "reacted that corporations should be punished with the use of punitive damages." Fisk did not elaborate on the type of nonverbal conduct that Daigle manifested, other than to say Daigle was "most clear" on the subject. Davis's counsel objected that "the nonverbal cues that Defense Counsel has cited throughout are not supported by the record" and also noted that Fisk never attempted to question Daigle about any alleged "nonverbal cues."

Last term, the Supreme Court decided a *Batson* case involving nonverbal conduct. In *Snyder v. Louisiana,* the Court held that the prosecution improperly struck a potential juror. The prosecution gave two reasons for its strike, one of which was that Brooks, the potential juror, looked "very nervous" throughout the questioning. The Court noted that the "record [did] not show that the trial judge actually made a determination concerning Mr. Brooks' demeanor." Absent such a finding, the Court concluded that it could not "presume that the trial judge credited the prosecutor's assertion that Mr. Brooks was nervous." Thus, while "deference [to the trial court] is especially appropriate where a trial judge has made a finding that an attorney credibly relied on demeanor in exercising a strike," here there was no such finding, and we cannot presume the trial court credited Fisk's explanation.

Additionally, the lack of further detail about Daigle's purported reaction, Fisk's failure to question Daigle about it, and the failure to strike a white juror who expressed verbally what Daigle purportedly did nonverbally, give us pause. Peremptory strikes may legitimately be based on nonverbal conduct, but permitting strikes based on an assertion that nefarious conduct "happened," without identifying its nature and without any additional record support, would strip *Batson* of meaning. Opposing counsel must have an opportunity to rebut the accusation, the trial court must be enabled to decide whether the charge accurately describes what happened during voir dire, and the appellate court must have a record on which to base its analysis. Verification of the occurrence may come from the bench if the court observed it; it may be proved by the juror's acknowledgement; or, it may be otherwise borne out by the record as, for example, by the detailed explanations of counsel. We do not think *Snyder* excludes sources of verification other than an explicit trial court finding. The point, instead, is that the communication be proved and reflected in an appellate record, and counsel must, therefore, identify that conduct with some specificity.

Nonverbal conduct or demeanor, often elusive and always subject to interpretation, may well mask a race-based strike. For that reason, trial courts must carefully examine such rationales. Our sister court which, as we have noted, has a much more developed *Batson* jurisprudence than we do, *see Goode,* 943 S.W.2d at 450,[9] has held that a prosecutor's statements that he didn't like a venireman's "attitude, his demeanor" were pretextual when his verbal answers failed to show hostility, and the prosecutor "never mentioned any specific body language, or any other nonverbal actions which led him to believe the venireman was biased against his case." *Batson* requires a "clear and reasonably specific explanation" of the legitimate reasons for a strike, and merely stating that a juror nonverbally "reacted" is insufficient.

Fisk's failure to question Daigle about his purported reaction also suggests that Daigle's reaction had little to do with Fisk's strike. Moreover, Fisk did not strike Vinzant, a white juror who stated that he would not have a problem awarding punitive damages. These factors suggest that the stated reason-Daigle's "reaction" to punitive damages—was pretextual.

Thus, we turn to the remaining reason offered for striking Daigle: that he seemed too eager to believe that his employer, Continental Airlines, discriminated against employees and that he did not express sufficient skepticism about discrimination claims. Daigle, a seventeen-year employee of Continental, listed his occupation as "customer service manager" . . . .

The court of appeals held that Fisk's explanation for striking Daigle sufficed, because even though Daigle stated he could be fair, "counsel is not required to take all voir dire answers at face

9 [footnote omitted]

value." While that is true, there is nothing in the voir dire record to support counsel's explanation that Daigle believed Continental discriminated against employees-indeed, Daigle, a longtime employee, stated that leaving his old job for Continental was "a better move for [him]," and the only thing he said about race discrimination cases was that he had never been involved with one. At best, the record shows that Daigle was neutral about employment discrimination issues, providing no support for Fisk's asserted reason for striking him. Even if Fisk were concerned about Daigle's description of his aide-of-counsel position as "like having a union without the union" (a concern that was never expressed at trial), it does not explain why Fisk failed to strike (or even question) juror 27, a white woman, about her membership in a union.

* * *

VI

Conclusion

Despite its laudable goal, *Batson* has been difficult to enforce. In *Miller-El II,* decided a year after this case was tried, the Supreme Court noted that *Batson's* "individualized focus came with a weakness of its own owing to its very emphasis on the particular reasons a prosecutor might give."

> If any facially neutral reason sufficed to answer a *Batson* challenge, then *Batson* would not amount to much more than *Swain.* Some stated reasons are false, and although some false reasons are shown up within the four corners of a given case, sometimes a court may not be sure unless it looks beyond the case at hand. Hence, *Batson's* explanation that a defendant may rely on 'all relevant circumstances' to raise an inference of purposeful discrimination.

Miller-El I's "totality of the circumstances" analysis places a heavy burden on trial courts, and we acknowledge that some of the factors that Court examined-most especially the comparative juror analysis-are perhaps more easily reviewed on appeal, with the benefit of a transcript from which such comparisons may most accurately be drawn. But without *Miller-El II*'s searching inquiry into the basis of the challenged strikes, Batson would become a "mere exercise in thinking up any rational basis."

Unlike *Miller-El II,* there is no evidence here of a historical pattern of excluding blacks from juries. But *Miller-El II* made it clear that the five factors it considered were neither exhaustive nor mandatory; courts must consider "all relevant circumstances" when reviewing *Batson* challenges. And here, the relevant circumstances include many of those pertinent in *Miller-El II*, including a statistical disparity and unequal treatment of comparable jurors.

We acknowledge that peremptory strikes, often based on instinct rather than reason, can be difficult to justify. The trial lawyer's failure to do so here does not suggest personal racial animosity on his part. A zealous advocate will seek jurors favorably inclined to his client's position, and race may even serve as a rough proxy for partiality. But whatever the strategic advantages of that practice, the Constitution forbids it.

The concurrence suggests that we ascribe sinister motives to Fisk's counsel. The question presented, however, is not whether this particular advocate harbors ill will, but whether the record explains, on neutral grounds, a statistically significant exclusion of black jurors. It is not enough, under the Supreme Court precedent we examine here, that the lawyer be pure of heart. We assume that he is. Our holding depends not on the personal sentiments of the advocate but on the state of the record. *Miller-El II* and *Snyder* emphasize that *Batson's* promise cannot be fulfilled if its requirements may be satisfied merely by ticking off a race-neutral explanation from a checklist.

After examining the totality of the circumstances, we conclude that race explains Fisk's strikes of Daigle and Pickett better than any other reason, and the trial court abused its discretion in failing to sustain Davis's *Batson* challenge. We reverse in part[15] the court of appeals' judgment and remand the case to the trial court for a new trial. TEX.R.APP. P. 60.2(d).

JUSTICE BRISTER, joined by JUSTICE MEDINA as to Part III, concurring.

I disagree with the Court's conclusion that defense counsel's peremptory strikes were racially motivated. Neutral reasons were given for them but were not properly preserved, in part because the rules changed during this appeal. The difference between not having neutral reasons and merely not preserving them is no technicality; charges of discrimination (like discrimination itself) can have far-reaching effects, including use in future trials.

* * *

I agree that peremptory strikes provide an opportunity for discrimination. But they also provide an opportunity to accuse an opponent of discrimination and get a new trial if the first one turns out badly. As these strikes have outlived their original purpose, it is time we did something about them. Rather than using this case as an opportunity to disparage one attorney, I would use it as an opportunity to discontinue a practice inherently based on stereotypes. As the Court misses that opportunity, I concur only in the judgment.

* * *

II. Scrutinizing Jurors' Shrugs

The Court also goes overboard by prohibiting peremptory strikes based on a juror's nonverbal conduct unless (1) the conduct is identified on the record "with some specificity," and (2) the juror is questioned about it. Neither has ever been required by any constitutional or procedural rule, and both exalt appellate-level clarity over trial-level reality.

* * *

The Court's new requirements are completely impractical. Most of us recognize surprise, disgust, or eagerness when we see it, but giving a "clear and reasonably specific" explanation of which muscles twitched is another matter. Yet the Court says attorneys must publicly announce any reaction they saw on the record, question the juror about it, allow opposing counsel to rebut, and obtain a ruling that the conduct occurred. This sounds like a good way to antagonize jurors; any attorney who complies can expect exchanges like the following:

Counsel: Juror No. 7, I notice that you are yawning. Why is that?

Juror No. 7: I wasn't yawning.

Counsel: Judge, I want the record to reflect that Juror No. 7 was yawning, even though he denies it.

Opposing Counsel: No he was not.

Counsel: Yes he was. Judge, may I have a ruling?

---

[15] In the trial court, Davis unsuccessfully moved for sanctions against Fisk, and the court of appeals affirmed the trial court's order. Davis does not challenge that portion of the court of appeals' judgment.

Court: I wasn't watching him, so your request is denied. And now you can't strike Juror No. 7, even though you have thoroughly embarrassed him.

This will never work. If the Court wants to prohibit peremptory strikes based on nonverbal conduct, it should say so directly rather than imposing an impractical test that does so indirectly.

III. Ending Peremptory Strikes

Yet the Court's opinion does not go far enough to ensure every American citizen the opportunity to sit on a jury.

If the composition of a jury is a matter of pure chance, neither litigants nor jurors can complain that the system has treated them unfairly. But peremptory strikes allow litigants to change the complexion of a jury, which is why they provoke charges and suspicions of discrimination. The only way to reduce or eliminate discrimination and suspicion is to reduce or eliminate these strikes.

Texas allows more peremptory strikes than most of our sister states. Twenty years after *Batson,* it is now clear we cannot always detect how many of those strikes are racially motivated, no matter how hard we try. Nor can we guarantee equal protection if we focus only on cases like this one where "too many" minority jurors were struck. In the meantime, we are doing neither the jury system nor racial harmony any favors by encouraging lawyers to accuse each other of racial motives so they can get a second trial if they lose the first one.

Haphazard success in removing race from jury selection might be the best we could expect if peremptory strikes were absolutely necessary for a fair and impartial jury. But they are not. Peremptory strikes were an important part of older jury systems in which panels were not randomly selected. Each side in ancient Rome could strike 50 jurors because each side got to propose 100 jurors for the panel. Parties needed peremptory strikes in early Texas because potential jurors were hand-picked by the local sheriff, and later by jury commissioners, and tended to reflect a limited part of the community.

But today jury venires are randomly selected, and anyone who is related to, interested in, or biased against a party or case is disqualified. It is hard to see why litigants need to remove *half* of the *unbiased* jurors to get an impartial jury—especially when peremptories are based mostly on instinct, intuition, and inference. This is especially true in civil cases, as a fractious juror or two cannot keep the rest from rendering a verdict.

There is no constitutional right to peremptory strikes. Indeed, recent cases suggest the opposite may be true, as several justices have already concluded. . . .

A majority of this Court could curb peremptory strikes today, as they stem entirely from our Rules of Civil Procedure.[33] The reason we hesitate to do so is that lawyers are tenaciously protective of them, believing they can use these strikes to mold a favorable jury. Study after study has shown this belief to be unfounded. But even if it were true, that reason is not enough: "Peremptory strikes are not intended . . . to permit a party to 'select' a favorable jury."

All these problems-discriminating against minorities, disrupting trial, and discarding perfectly good jurors—are particularly acute in Texas. Whether because of the state's diversity, the generous allowance of peremptory strikes, or something else, *Batson* challenges are far more frequent here than anywhere else. A recent Westlaw search for state court cases citing to *Batson* yields:

33

- 4 cases from Idaho,
- 17 from Alaska,
- 43 from Colorado,
- 58 from Oklahoma.
- 74 from Minnesota,
- 90 from Florida,
- 181 from Pennsylvania,
- 342 from Illinois,
- 676 from California, and
- 1,364 cases from Texas.

More than any other state, we in Texas must consider whether peremptory strikes are worth the price they impose.

G. Jury Argument

Read Rules 266, 269.

LIVING CENTERS OF TEXAS, INC.
v.
PEÑALVER

2008 WL 204502
(Tex. 2008)

PER CURIAM.

Living Centers of Texas, Inc., defendant in a wrongful death suit, stipulated liability. During final argument of the trial on damages, plaintiff's counsel compared Living Centers' lawyer's attempts to minimize damages to a World War II German program in which elderly and infirm persons were used for medical experimentation and killed. Concluding that the jury argument was improper and incurable, we reverse and remand for a new trial.

Belia Peñalver moved into a nursing home in 1997. In September 2000, a nursing home employee dropped Belia, who was then 90 years old, while transferring her from a wheelchair to a bed. She died the next day from injuries suffered in the incident. Belia's sons sued Living Centers of Texas, Inc., its administrator, and its director of nursing (collectively, "Living Centers") seeking wrongful death and survivor damages.

A first jury trial resulted in judgment in favor of the Peñalvers for $356,000 actual and $362,000 punitive damages, reduced from $500,000 when the trial court applied the statutory cap on punitive damages. The court of appeals reversed and remanded for a new trial because of improperly admitted evidence of previous falls at the nursing home. Before the second trial, Living

Centers stipulated that its negligence proximately caused Belia's injuries and death, so the only issue at trial was the amount of damages.

During closing argument at the second trial, the Peñalvers' counsel referred to Germany's World War II T-4 Project and defense counsel's trial conduct:

> In World War II the Germans had a project called T-Four. You probably read about it in history books.
>
> But what they did is they took all the people who they thought were inferior in society, primarily older people, impaired people, and they used them for experiments. They killed them. Over 400,000. That culture 60 years ago didn't consider the impaired and elderly valuable.
>
> Our culture has never looked at that. We went to war to stop that, the biggest war in the history of the world to stop those atrocities that were going on. And we're not at the point where we're tolerant today, as the defense would like you to be, of this wrongful death.
>
> * * *
>
> But [the defense lawyers'] job here is to convince you that the damages are insignificant to minimize the damages. How have they done that? At the very beginning in opening statement [they] said they only have two defenses, if you want to call it defense. She is old and she is impaired.
>
> * * *
>
> So it really goes back to that, the initial issue, where are we as a society? Have we regressed to 1944, 1945 Germany? Have we regressed or gone ahead so far now, 60 years later now, we have a different attitude, that a wrongful death of an elderly or impaired person is not every bit as significant and has every bit as significant damages as the wrongful death of anyone else?

Living Center's counsel did not object to the argument, but attempted to counter it by arguing that "there are no Nazis in this courtroom" and "I've never been accused of being a Nazi before."

The jury awarded almost three times the actual damages awarded in the first trial. The second jury awarded actual damages of $510,000 to Belia's estate and $300,000 to each of her two sons—a total of $1,110,000. Living Centers filed a motion for new trial based, in part, on allegations that the Peñalvers' jury argument as to the T-4 Project was improper, incurable, and harmful. The trial court denied the motion for new trial.

Living Centers appealed. The court of appeals affirmed, with one justice dissenting. 217 S.W.3d 44. In its petition for review, Living Centers continues to complain of the final jury argument which criticized Living Centers' counsel and referenced Germany's World War II T-4 Project.

Error as to improper jury argument must ordinarily be preserved by a timely objection which is overruled. The complaining party must not have invited or provoked the improper argument. *Standard Fire Ins. Co. v. Reese,* 584 S.W.2d 835, 839 (1979). Typically, retraction of the argument or instruction from the court can cure any probable harm, but in rare instances the probable harm or prejudice cannot be cured. In such instances the argument is incurable and complaint about the argument may be made even though objection was not timely made. *See* TEX. R. CIV. P. 324(b)(5);. To prevail on a claim that improper argument was incurable, the complaining party generally must show that the argument by its nature, degree, and extent constituted such error that an instruction from the court or retraction of the argument could not remove its effects. The test is the amount of harm from the argument:

> whether the argument, considered in its proper setting, was reasonably calculated to cause such prejudice to the opposing litigant that a withdrawal by counsel or an instruction by the court, or both, could not eliminate the probability that it resulted in an improper verdict.

But jury argument that strikes at the appearance of and the actual impartiality, equality, and fairness of justice rendered by courts is incurably harmful not only because of its harm to the litigants involved, but also because of its capacity to damage the judicial system. Such argument is not subject to the general harmless error analysis.

In *Reese,* this Court discussed different types of jury argument that constitute incurable error. For example, appeals to racial prejudice adversely affect the fairness and equality of justice rendered by courts because they improperly induce consideration of a party's race to be used as a factor in the jury's decision. Unsupported, extreme, and personal attacks on opposing parties and witnesses can similarly compromise the basic premise that a trial provides impartial, equal justice. Further, accusing the opposing party of manipulating a witness, without evidence of witness tampering, can be incurable, harmful argument.

The serious effects of arguments not based on evidence or invited by opposing counsel, such as the one under consideration here, are recognized in our Rules of Civil Procedure. Rule 269 provides that during final arguments, "[m]ere personal criticism by counsel upon each other shall be avoided, and when indulged in shall be promptly corrected as a contempt of court." TEX. R. CIV. P. 269(e). Trial courts are not required to wait for objections before correcting improper argument, but should guard against such conduct and correct it *sua sponte.* TEX. R. CIV. P. 269(g).

Incurable argument is, however, rare. Not all personally critical comments concerning opposing counsel are incurable. But arguments that strike at the courts' impartiality, equality, and fairness inflict damage beyond the parties and the individual case under consideration if not corrected. Such arguments damage the judicial system itself by impairing the confidence which our citizens have in the system, and courts countenance very little tolerance of such arguments. *See Reese,* 584 S.W.2d at 840 ("The injection of new and inflammatory matters into the case through argument has in exceptional instances been regarded as incurable by an instruction . . . . [A]n affront to the court and the equality which it must portray will be dealt with harshly.").

The argument which Living Centers complains of struck at Living Centers and its trial counsel by comparing trial counsel to perpetrators of the T-4 Project atrocities. The T-4 Project was brought up only once during trial when, upon inquiry by the Peñalvers' counsel, a witness testified that he was not familiar with the program. There was no evidence that Living Centers either intended to injure or kill Belia or that Living Centers performed medical experiments on her. The extreme final argument cannot be said to have been invited by the actions of Living Centers' counsel in pointing out what the evidence clearly showed: Belia was elderly and had certain impairments that accompanied the aging process. The Peñalvers' improper comments were not inadvertent, and the jury argument was designed to incite passions of the jury and turn the jurors against defense counsel for doing what lawyers are ethically bound to do: advocate clients' interests within the bounds of law. Counsel for Living Centers was entitled to urge a smaller damages amount than the plaintiffs sought without being painted as modern-day equivalents of T-4 Project operators who experimented on and purposefully killed humans.

The argument struck at the integrity of the courts by utilizing an argument that was improper, unsupported, and uninvited. Failure to deal harshly with this type of argument can only lead to its emulation and the entire judicial system will suffer as a result.

Our analysis and conclusion is not altered because it was Living Centers' counsel who first used the term "Nazi." The right to complain of improper, incurable jury argument is not lost by counsel's attempting to respond to and reduce the effect of such argument. *See* TEX. R. CIV. P. 269(e). We agree with the dissenting justice in the court of appeals: the argument complained of struck at the heart of the jury trial system, was designed to turn the jury against opposing counsel and his clients, and was incurable. The judgment of the court of appeals is reversed, and the case is remanded for a new trial.

In *General Motors Corporation v. Iracheta*, 161 S.W.3d 462 (Tex. 2005), the supreme court sustained General Motors' contention that there was no evidence of defect. The court reversed and rendered judgment that the plaintiff take nothing. The court then issued the following condemnation of the plaintiff's spontaneous address to the jury and held that a prompt and timely objection was not necessary:

> We are obliged by one highly unusual occurrence during summation to add this additional note. Rising to begin his argument to the jury, Iracheta's counsel stated: "Mrs. Iracheta has asked for the opportunity simply to stand and thank you for your time as well." Immediately, without leave of court or notice to opposing counsel, Mrs. Iracheta stood and said to an all-Hispanic jury: "*Muchas gracias les doy de parte de mis nietos y mi hija y de parte mia la jurado.*" ("Thank you very much to the jury on the part of my grandchildren and my daughter and on my part.") General Motors understandably did not interpose an objection at once but waited until after Iracheta's counsel had finished his argument, and then moved for a mistrial at the bench. The court denied the motion.
>
> The court of appeals concluded that General Motors' objection was untimely. We disagree. In these most unusual circumstances, General Motors' counsel was not required to object to a grandmother's expression of appreciation on behalf of her deceased daughter and deceased grandchildren, thereby risking the jury's ire, and it is entirely impractical to think otherwise. At oral argument in this Court, Iracheta's counsel concedes that it was improper for Mrs. Iracheta to address the jury but argues that the error was harmless. We think the harm is manifest to any experienced trial lawyer. A party's personal expression of gratitude to the jury at the close of a case is error that cannot be repaired and therefore need not be objected to. *Cf. Dow Chem. Co. v. Francis*, 46 S.W.3d 237, 241 (Tex. 2001) ("[O]bjection to a trial court's alleged improper conduct or comment must be made when it occurs if a party is to preserve error for appellate review, *unless the conduct or comment cannot be rendered harmless by proper instruction.*") (emphasis added).

Notes & Questions

1. *TRCP 266 & 269.* Closing argument is given after the charge is read to the jury. The party with the burden of proof on the whole case at the time of argument is entitled to open and close. This is usually the plaintiff. Rebuttal argument is limited to replying to the counsel on the other side. When there are multiple parties and multiple claims, the court has wide discretion in determining the order of argument.

2. *Limits on argument.* What is prohibited? Generally, it can be lumped into three groups: (1) don't go outside the record or law; (2) don't appeal to passion or prejudice; (3) don't insult witnesses, lawyers or litigants.

3. *Incurable error.* Most erroneous arguments either are not harmful because they don't amount to much, or they can be cured by an instruction to the jury to disregard. As you have seen in the previous opinions, however, sometimes a court finds that improper argument is so bad that it cannot be cured by an instruction. This type of error is called "incurable." As the Supreme Court said in *Standard Fire Insurance v. Reese*:[1]

> Harmless error creeps back into the practice when subjective evaluations replace a more objective and structured testing of error. For that reason, decisions since 1941 have resisted the tide of presumed harm by surrounding the decision about reversibility with several tests. In the case of improper jury argument, the complainant must prove a number of things. He has the burden to prove (1) an error (2) that was not invited or provoked, (3) that was preserved by the proper trial predicate, such as an objection, a motion to instruct, or a motion for mistrial, and (4) was not curable by an instruction, a prompt withdrawal of the statement, or a reprimand by the judge. There are only rare instances of incurable harm from improper argument. The complainant has the further burden to prove (5) that the argument by its nature, degree and extent constituted reversibly harmful error. How long the argument continued, whether it was repeated or abandoned and whether there was cumulative error are proper inquiries. All of the evidence must be closely examined to determine (6) the argument's probable effect on a material finding. (7) Importantly, a reversal must come from an evaluation of the whole case, which begins with the voir dire and ends with the closing argument. The record may show that the cause is weak, strong, or very close. From all of these factors, the complainant must show that the probability that the improper argument caused harm is greater than the probability that the verdict was grounded on the proper proceedings and evidence.

Incurable argument appeared to be limited to argument that appeals to racial or religious prejudice, but the Supreme Court appears to have expanded it recently. In a specific case an appellate court could find that just about anything was so bad that it was "incurable." (Bringing up insurance in argument used to be incurable, but now is generally treated as curable.)

4. *Incurable argument and strategic silence.* Why did counsel give up on the objections? Was he satisfied that the argument had become so egregious that it would be held incurable on appeal? If so, this is a risky course. What will be held incurable on appeal is very hard to predict during the trial. And, these days, most improper argument is considered curable by instruction.[2] The best

---

[1] 584 S.W.2d 835 (Tex. 1979).

[2] *See* MCDONALD & CARLSON, TEXAS CIVIL PRACTICE § 23:20 at fn. 178 and 23:24 at fn. 229. *See also* Alpine Tel. Corp. v. McCall, 195 S.W.2d 585, 592 (Tex. Civ. App.—El Paso 1946, writ ref'd n.r.e.).

course is to preserve error by an objection *and* a request that the jury be instructed to disregard the improper comments. The court may, in fact, sustain such objection and request, and truly limit the harm in the argument because of the jury's perception that errant counsel has acted unfairly. What is the best appellate posture for the trial court loser with respect to objections and actions by the judge? The best chance on appeal is provided when counsel objects to each improper argument and requests a curative instruction to the jury to disregard, and is overruled each time.[3] Note that a complaint of incurable argument not objected to earlier must, at the latest, be included in a motion for new trial. Rule 324(b)(5).

5. *Rule 269(g)*. Note that the court may intervene to correct improper argument without waiting for an objection. Note also the somewhat courtly procedure required (but, unfortunately, often ignored) respecting the making of objections.

6. *Hyperbole*. In *Standard Fire Insurance v. Reese*,[4] the Supreme Court distinguished improper argument, which had no support in the evidence, from hyperbole.

> Standard's argument that Reese "drove by a thousand doctors between the Astrodome and Spring Branch" to see Dr. Buning was not improper. Hyperbole has long been one of the figurative techniques of oral advocacy. Such arguments are a part of our legal heritage and language. Shakespeare wrote about "a thousand blushing apparitions" and "a thousand innocent shames," in *Much Ado About Nothing*. In *The Tempest* he wrote, "Now would I give a thousand furlongs of sea for an acre of barren ground;" in *King Richard III*, "My conscience hath a thousand several tongues, and every tongue brings in a several tale . . . ;" in *Hamlet*, "And by a sleep to say we end the heartache and the thousand natural shocks that flesh is heir to;" in *Hamlet* again, "To be honest, as this world goes, is to be one man picked out of ten thousand," and in *Romeo and Juliet*, he has Juliet saying, "A thousand times good-night!" The method has often been employed to make a point.

7. *Harmful error review*. Harmful error can occur in two situations:

A. The trial judge overruled a proper objection to an improper argument. Thus, there was no attempt to cure by instruction to the jury, and even a curable error could be harmful because there was no attempt to cure it.

B. The trial judge sustained the objection, and may have even given an instruction to disregard, but failed to grant a new trial. An incurable error would be harmful in this situation. Since they cannot be cured, the only relief available is a new trial. The new trial is sought either by a motion for mistrial when the argument was made or a motion for new trial after the judgment was signed. For incurable error, a motion for new trial after judgment alone is sufficient to preserve error. This is one of the few times that error can be preserved without making an objection at the time the error occurred. The rationale is that an objection would make no difference because the error was incurable.

8. *Preserving error for appeal review:*

A. There was error.

1) Argument was improper, and

2) Was not invited or provoked (it is not improper to respond to another's improper argument).

---

[3] *See* MCDONALD & CARLSON, TEXAS CIVIL PRACTICE § 23.24 at fn. 240.

[4] 584 S.W.2d 835 (Tex. 1979).

B. The error is properly preserved by proper trial objection.

1) For most errors, an objection to the argument at the time improper argument is made is required, and if granted then make motion for instruction to disregard.

2) For incurable error, either

a. an objection and motion for mistrial at time improper argument is made, or

b. a motion for new trial after judgment.

C. There must be harm.

1) Look at the whole record.

2) Did the improper argument affect a material jury finding? Was this a "closely contested" case or did the evidence clearly favor the appealing party? If so, the argument probably caused an improper wrong verdict.

3) Sometimes improper argument can be the straw that breaks the camel's back. Viewed in isolation, the argument might not seem harmful, but considered along with other errors it could tip the balance toward a finding of harmful error.

CHAPTER 14. JURY CHARGE

A. Origins of Broad Form Submission in Texas[1]

In any case tried to a jury in any jurisdiction, the trial judge must in some way communicate to the jurors the questions they are to decide and the instructions to be followed in deciding them. Whether written, oral, or partly written and partly oral, the charge must be framed in such a way as to require the jury to find the facts in controversy and to assist them in so doing. It is, of course, the function and responsibility of the jury to find facts, and the function and responsibility of the trial judge to determine what questions of fact shall be submitted to the jury. It is in the charge and its responsive verdict that the judge and jury must cooperate in order to carry out their respective functions and responsibilities. In framing the charge, the court must apply the theories of law relied upon as grounds of recovery and defense, and must formulate the questions of fact that are to be answered by the jury.[2]

The charge may take several forms. One extreme is the "general verdict" form, where the judge points out to the jury the factual elements to be found and by instructions directs the jury as to the method to be followed in finding the facts and giving an answer finding in favor of one party or the other. In contrast, the "special verdict" form asks the jury specific questions that elicit findings on specific controverted facts, and the judge determines the legal consequence of those findings in determining the judgment.

---

1. *The General Charge*

The old-style general charge was nothing more than a lecture delivered by the judge to the jury at the close of the evidence,[3] setting out the law applicable to the case at hand. The charge was given orally—no "hard copy" came into being[4]—and was often comparatively extemporaneous. It was sometimes elegant, sometimes learned, almost always balanced, although a federal judge might now and then comment on the weight to be given certain of the evidence. The charge would typically outline the pleadings, explain the elements of proof and the attendant burdens, and give a short treatise on the substantive law governing the case as the court saw it.

A typical general charge might begin something like this: "Members of the jury, the plaintiff—that's Mrs. Mayhew over there, as I'm sure you know—is claiming in this case that the defendant, Mr. Morrison, who was the driver of the brown Oldsmobile, was negligent just before the collision you have heard about in the following particulars: that he failed to timely apply his brakes just be-

---

[1] By Jack Ratliff, Professor Emeritus, University of Texas School of Law.

[2] Gus M. Hodges & T. Ray Guy, 34 TEXAS PRACTICE: THE JURY CHARGE IN CIVIL LITIGATION 1 (1988) (hereinafter "HODGES & GUY").

[3] Delivered after closing argument in the federal courts but before it in Texas state courts. Recent changes in Federal Rule 51 allow the judge to charge before or after closing argument (or both). *Compare* TEX. R. CIV. P. 269(a) *with* FED. R. CIV. P. 51; *see* 9 CHARLES A. WRIGHT & ARTHUR R. MILLER, FEDERAL PRACTICE & PROCEDURE § 2555, at 651 n.77 (West 1988 & Supp. 1993).

[4] *See* 9 WRIGHT & MILLER, § 2555, at 651. Federal judges *may* give the jury a copy of the instructions if they wish. *See* United States v. Standard Oil Co., 316 F.2d 884, 896 (7th Cir. 1963).

fore the collision, that he was traveling at an excessive speed under the circumstances [and so on listing the particular acts and omissions alleged]. You need to know that by 'negligence' as it is used in law we mean . . . and by 'proximate cause' we mean . . . [and so on]. You also need to know about the burden of proof: the plaintiff has the burden of proving her case by a preponderance of the evidence, that is, the greater weight of the credible evidence, or, in plain language, she has to persuade you to the point that you believe that it is more likely than not that the things she says took place did take place. [Then the defenses and the burden of defendant's proof and the effect of establishing an affirmative defense such as contributory negligence, then any inferences such as res ipsa loquitur, then agency and its effects, then the law regarding an inferential rebuttal such as sole proximate cause, and so on and so on]."

In the days before the office copier and computer, the judge would sometimes appear on the bench with a large stack of books and some random notes, stopping to read from various case opinions as he proceeded. This practice explains the apparently backward federal procedure of objecting to the court's charge after it has already been given; it was impossible to object to a charge which, immediately before its delivery, was nothing more than a handful of notes and some synapses firing away inside the judge's head. After the charge, the jury retired. It was given two slips of paper, each entitled "Verdict" and each with a signature blank for the jury foreman. One said "We find for the Defendant." The other said "We find for the Plaintiff in the sum of $___________." After the jury was out of the courtroom the judge would hear the attorneys' spoken objections to the charge and, if he acknowledged any error, he would recall the jury for additional instruction.

This process was simple, straightforward, and efficient. It invested the jurors with broad powers.[5] Contrary to a time-honored prohibition in the Texas courts, the general charge told the jury the effect of its answers, or more accurately, the jury's answer *was* the effect since it simply announced the result. It was commonly supposed, however, that the general charge was without measurable effect on the jurors; that they applied the charge at best selectively and at worst not at all.

Defense counsel hated and feared the general charge, particularly in negligence cases.[6] It allowed the jury to do what it liked about an award, fully aware of the then-fatal effect of the contributory negligence defense. Moreover, it made it easier for jurors to reach agreement, a feature thought more helpful to plaintiffs than defendants. The verdict left no clues about what specific conduct the jury had condemned or what reasoning it had employed. There were no fingerprints, and therefore, reversals of judgments based on lack of supporting evidence were hard to come by. Since plaintiffs usually have first claim on the jury's sympathies, this difficulty worked against defendants.

---

5 The choice between submitting a case to the jury under broad or narrow jury questions can be discussed in terms of judicial efficiency and practicality. For example, broad-form submissions encourage jury agreement and result in fewer conflicting jury findings. The choice between broad or narrow jury questions is, however, at bottom a philosophical choice about how much power to give the jury. The granulated special issue approach restrains the jury. The general charge empowers the jury. Although the question about how powerful we should make juries is critically important, it is ultimately a jurisprudential or philosophical question, and so is not explored in this, essentially procedural, discussion. 9 WRIGHT & MILLER, *supra* note 6, §§ 2505, 2506; *see* Leon Green, *The Submission of Special Verdicts in Negligence Cases—A Critique of the Bug Bite Case*, 17 U. MIAMI L. REV. 469, 473 (1963) (analyzing the issues submitted in Gallick v. Baltimore & O.R.R., 372 U.S. 108 (1963), and arguing that the form of the negligence issue "give[s] a jury a great power in the determination of [the] case").

6 Perhaps the past tense is misleading here. Debate over the kind of charge to be used in Texas courts continues, and the use of a general charge is often the focal point for controversy.

2. *Special Issues*

By contrast, from 1913 to 1973, Texas state courts used the special verdict form of the charge (which were called "special issues"). During this time, the Texas Supreme Court mandated the submission of each issue "distinctly and separately," requiring a separate question and separate answer for each separate act or omission upon which a party relied in making its cause of action or defense.

For example, in *Fox v. Dallas Hotel Co.*,[7], the Supreme Court held it was error to submit the plaintiff's contributory negligence to the jury in a single question: "Do you find from a preponderance of the evidence that Alexander Fox was guilty of contributory negligence in his conduct in, around, or at the elevator, or the shaft thereof, prior to or about the time he was injured?" The defendant had pleaded and presented evidence that "the injuries to Fox were proximately caused by his own contributory negligence in the following particulars: (1) That Fox in order to look under the elevator needlessly placed his body in a position where he would be injured if the elevator should descend; (2) that he failed to overcome the sticking by operating the elevator up and down; (3) that when the elevator stopped he failed to lock it in position; (4) that he went under the elevator without having locked it; and (5) that in working under the elevator he failed to get entirely in the pit."[8] The Court held that the defendant was entitled to have "[e]ach group of facts . . . which, standing alone, would, if proven, constitute a complete defense to the plaintiff's suit" submitted to the jury.[9] Thus, it was reversible error not to submit separately to the jury each of the five factual theories of negligence.

Commentators of the day described the special issue practice as follows:

> [T]he Texas special verdict system is designed as one in which jurors find facts rather than choosing the prevailing party, and theoretically are not advised of the effect of their answers; the trial judge assumes a neutral role, not summing up the evidence or commenting on the weight thereof, and the jury is not instructed as to abstract principles of law unnecessary to their determination of specific disputed factual elements.[10]

In this system, the jury made numerous findings on particularized conduct, against which specific evidence could be compared. Supporting evidence was thus "compartmentalized." The judge, not the jury, decided the outcome by interpreting the jury's "separate and distinct" findings in light of the applicable law and then, in effect, declaring the winner.

In practice, the Texas special issue system was characterized by meticulously detailed questions, pettifogging distinctions, and a Dickensian obsession with formalities. It made no concession to common sense. The gamesmanship was demanding, requiring of counsel the vigilance of an eagle and the tenacity of a snapping turtle.[11]

---

[7] 111 Tex. 461, 240 S.W. 517 (1922), *overruled* by Burk Royalty Co. v. Walls, 616 S.W.2d 911 (Tex. 1981).

[8] *Id.* at 518.

[9] *Id.*

[10] Hodges & Guy at 6.

[11] *See, e.g.,* Lewis v. Texas Employers' Ins. Ass'n, 246 S.W.2d 599 (Tex. 1952) (requiring 83 special issues for a workers' compensation case).

Negligence cases in particular required the judge to cross-examine the jury through numerous carefully crafted questions—each called a special issue—which asked about the conduct of the actor in elaborate detail.[12] The system reached its tragi-comic high point with the inferential rebuttal issues. These were essentially variants of the defendant's general denial—"I was not negligent"—but because they were statements inconsistent with but not directly denying an element of plaintiff's claim, they were accorded separate status as quasi-defenses. "The accident was unavoidable because of the ice; therefore, nobody was negligent; therefore, I was not negligent." Of course, the defendant was doing no more than repeating, by inference, his earlier and more direct general denial of the plaintiff's case.[13] Because each inferential rebuttal was presented in a separate question and because the burden of proof was to remain on the plaintiff, correct submission of unavoidable accident took this form: "Do you find from a preponderance of the evidence that the collision in question was not the result of an unavoidable accident?"[19] Juries were understandably confused by this nonsense, and were known to answer "yes" to the primary negligence question and "no" to the inferential rebuttal question, creating a conflict which required a new trial unless the judge noticed it in time to send the jury back for further deliberation.[20]

---

[12] It was not enough simply to inquire whether a party was negligent but the question was to ask, by way of a series, in what particular way was the party negligent. Thus, the simple "Was the defendant negligent?" was fatally defective. "Was the defendant negligent in failing to timely apply his brakes" did not cover his negligence with respect to speed or lookout or traffic signals, each of which were the subject of a separate question. *See* HODGES & GUY, at 85.

[13] *See, e.g.*, Yarborough v. Berner, 467 S.W.2d 188 (Tex. 1971). There were a number of inferential rebuttals, such as unavoidable accident and sole proximate cause, as well as *faux* inferential rebuttals, such as sudden emergency and failure to mitigate damages. *See* HODGES, *supra* note 18, at 40-70 (discussing different forms of inferential rebuttals); Committee on Pattern Jury Charges of the State Bar of Texas, PATTERN JURY CHARGES §§ 3.01-.05 (1989) [hereinafter TEXAS PJC]. The inferential rebuttal survives in only a few forms and is presented to the jury by instruction. But for its historical entrenchment, the inferential rebuttal would be identified as a comment on the weight of the evidence, "nudging" the jury toward a given verdict. TEXAS PJC, *supra*, §3.04 (unavoidable accident).

[19] Unavoidable accident was then defined essentially as one occurring without negligence. One interesting aspect of unavoidable accident is that it could (and can) be raised only by unusual conditions, usually weather (but including acts of small children and visual obstructions as well), which would make it more likely that an automobile collision, for example, could occur without anyone's negligence. But the jury is never informed that the conditions play any role in the rebuttal. What the jury is now told is that some accidents occur without negligence. The idea seems to be that the defendant is entitled to this "hint" from the court in unusual situations—bad weather, for example—which make negligence a less likely determinant. *See* HODGES & GUY, at 146-49; *see also* Hill v. Winn Dixie Texas, Inc., 849 S.W.2d 802 (Tex. 1992); Brown v. Goldstein, 678 S.W.2d 539 (Tex. App—Houston [14th Dist.] 1984), *rev'd on other grounds*, 685 S.W.2d 640 (Tex. 1985); WILLIAM DORSANEO & DONALD CRUMP, TEXAS CIVIL PROCEDURE: TRIAL AND APPELLATE PRACTICE, §4.02, at 230 n.3 (2d ed. 1989).

[20] *See* HODGES, at 49 (conflicting answers require a retrial); *see also* Leon Green, *Blindfolding the Jury*, 33, TEX. L. REV. 273 (1955). Gus Hodges used to call this the "Yes, we have no bananas" approach. It was not until 1971 that the supreme court acknowledged the confusion and relegated the inferential rebuttal to the status of instruction. *See* Yarborough, 467 S.W.2d at 193.

B. "Broad Form" Questions

Read Rules 277 and 278.

In the early 1970's, the Texas state courts began to move away from the mannered special issue practice, first by dropping the separate jury question on inferential rebuttals,[1] and then by abandoning, in stages, the old "separate and distinct" requirement. In 1973, Rule 277 was amended to give trial judges the discretion to use broad form questions. This amendment substantially changed the charge in negligence cases. Rather than submitting each factual theory of negligence separately, the jury could simply be asked generally whether the defendant was negligent. In *Mobil Chemical Co. v. Bell*,[2] the Supreme Court repudiated *Fox* and said, "in an ordinary negligence case, where several specific acts of negligence are alleged and evidence as to each is introduced, the submission of a broad issue inquiring generally whether the defendant was negligent is not error and not subject to the objection that the single issue inquires about several elements or issues." In 1988, Rule 277 was amended again, requiring that broad form questions be used "whenever feasible."

Eventually, the Supreme Court made clear that parties are not entitled to separate submission of the elements of a cause of action (e.g. negligence and proximate cause are submitted in the same broad form question). Moreover, the court endorsed single broad form questions that included multiple grounds of recovery or defense. For example, in one case, the court affirmed a single question ["Do you find from a preponderance of the evidence that plaintiffs performed their obligations under the commitment letter in question?"] that included both plaintiff's ground of recovery (performance) and defendant's ground of defense (waiver).[3]

The "broad-form" required "whenever feasible" by Rule 277 is not specifically identifiable without resort to specific charges approved in various cases or to the Pattern Jury Charges. It is clear that the courts and rulemakers consider the broad-form charge something short of a general charge. The broad-form charge typically asks a single question on liability and a single question on damages for each theory of recovery, though that is not invariably the case. These questions are fleshed out by instructions which typically set out the elements of proof for a cause of action or defense. Other questions may be appropriate in a broad-form submission, such as the question apportioning percentages of responsibility in negligence and products liability cases.

As the state courts moved away from special issue practice, the federal courts began to rely more frequently on the special verdict, a device that corresponds roughly to the Texas broad form submission.[4] The upshot is that Texas and federal courts, beginning at the far ends of the spectrum,

---

1 *See Yarborough*, 467 S.W.2d 188 (acknowledging that the use of inferential rebuttal questions was confusing and substituting instructions for the submission of inferential rebuttals).

2 517 S.W.2d 245,255 (Tex. 1974)

3 Island Recreational Dev. Corp. v. Republic of Texas Sav. Ass'n, 710 S.W.2d 551 (Tex. 1986).

4 These and other observations about federal practice have to do with the federal courts operating in and near Texas. Their increasing use of the special verdict may be the result of the federal judges' experience as lawyers or judges in the Texas special issue system. *See* FED. R. CIV. P. 49(a). Judge John R. Brown of the Fifth Circuit was the leading advocate for expanding the use of the special verdict and therefore his court pointed out its advantages

have now met in the middle. Both now use an approach falling somewhere between a general charge and a special issue of the old kind. Texas calls it "broad-form"; federal courts call it the "special verdict," but the differences are now so slight that the Texas-style charge should work in either venue.

Let us now look at some cases using the broad form charge and see what one looks like and consider what difference the form of the charge makes. We will also see that the pendulum has been swinging back, away from the broad form charge.

TEXAS DEPARTMENT OF HUMAN SERVICES
v.
E.B.
802 S.W.2d 647
(Tex. 1990)

COOK, JUSTICE.

* * *

The issue before this court is whether Rule 277 of the Texas Rules of Civil Procedure means exactly what it says, that is, "In all jury cases the court shall, whenever feasible, submit the cause upon broad-form questions." TEX. R. CIV. P. 277. This issue arises in the context of a suit affecting the parent-child relationship in which the Texas Department of Human Services filed suit for termination of the parent-child relationship between the parents and their two female children. After a jury trial, using broad-form questions, the trial court rendered a decree of termination based upon the jury's verdict. The court of appeals reversed and remanded the cause, holding that multiple alternative submissions were proper. We reverse the judgment of the court of appeals and affirm the judgment of the trial court.

The Texas Department of Human Services sued for termination of the parent-child relationship between the mother, Respondent E.B., and her two minor daughters.[1] The suit was based on alleged violations of the Texas Family Code § 15.02(1)(D), (E) and on the ground that the termination would be in the best interest of the children, § 15.02(2) [now § 161.001]. The district court signed a Final Decree of Termination based upon the jury's verdict. There is no complaint with respect to the sufficiency of the evidence supporting the verdict of the jury.

The judge submitted a single question for each child at trial, under the Texas Family Code § 15.02(1)(D), (E), as a broad-form submission required by this court in Rule 277. We approve of this question, which was taken from volume 5, section 218.01B of TEXAS PATTERN JURY CHARGES:

---

early and often. *See* John R. Brown, *Federal Special Verdicts: The Doubt Eliminator*, 44 F.R.D. 338, 342-44 (1967).

[1] The parent-child relationship of the father and the two children was terminated based upon the father's voluntary Affidavit of Relinquishment of Parental Rights.

Question No. 1

Should the parent-child relationship between [Respondent E.B.] and the child [E.B.] be terminated?"

Answer: "Yes" or "No"

Answer: ______

Question No. 2

Should the parent-child relationship between [Respondent E.B.] and the child [B.B.] be terminated?

Answer: "Yes" or "No"

Answer: ______

Accompanying these questions were instructions, substantially in accordance with volume 5, section 218.01A of TEXAS PATTERN JURY CHARGES, including a description of the rights, privileges, duties, and powers of a parent and definitions of the terms "termination," "clear and convincing evidence," and "endanger." The crucial instructions basically track the statutory grounds for termination as set forth in the Texas Family Code § 15.02(1)(D), (E). Additionally, the jury was given a list of "some of the factors to consider in determining the best interest of the child" taken directly from *Holley v. Adams*, 544 S.W.2d 367, 371-72 (Tex. 1976).

In *Fox v. Dallas Hotel Co.*, 111 Tex. 461, 475, 240 S.W. 517, 522 (1922), this court mandated the submission of "each issue distinctly and separately." Texas thus developed a very complicated system for issue submission. In 1973, Rule 277 was amended and provided in part: It shall be discretionary with the court whether to submit separate questions with respect to each element of a case or to submit issues broadly. It shall not be objectionable that a question is general or includes a combination of elements or issues.

By this amendment, the court replaced the previous language that required issues to be submitted "distinctly and separately." In *Mobil Chemical Co. v. Bell*, 517 S.W.2d 245, 255 (Tex. 1974), this court said the new rule meant what it said: simply ask whether the party was negligent. This court explained in a later decision that Rule 277 was designed to abolish the "distinctly and separately" requirement.

Acknowledging that there "may be some continuing question" about broad-form submissions, this court in *Burk Royalty Co. v. Walls*, 616 S.W.2d 911, 925 (Tex. 1981), expressly overruled all of the cases that arose before the 1973 revisions and which followed the decisions in *Fox*. In the 1988 amendments to Rule 277 this court said broad-form submission "shall" be used "whenever feasible" and eliminated trial court discretion to submit separate questions with respect to each element of a case.

Rule 277 mandates broad-form submissions "whenever feasible," that is, in any or every instance in which it is capable of being accomplished.

The history and struggle to recognize broad-form submission is a long one. The rule unequivocally requires broad-form submission whenever feasible. Unless extraordinary circumstances exist, a court must submit such broad-form questions. The court of appeals held that a single broad-form question incorporating two independent grounds for termination of a parent-child relationship permits the state to obtain an affirmative answer without discharging the burden that the jury conclude that a parent violated one or more of the grounds for termination under the statute. TEX. FAM. CODE § 15.02 (Vernon Supp. 1990); TEX. R. CIV. P. 292.

The charge in parental rights cases should be the same as in other civil cases. The controlling question in this case was whether the parent-child relationship between the mother and each of her two children should be terminated, not what specific ground or grounds under § 15.02 the jury relied on to answer affirmatively the questions posed. All ten jurors agree that the mother had endangered the child by doing one or the other of the things listed in § 15.02. Petitioner argues that the charge, as presented to the jury, violates her due process right by depriving a natural mother of her fundamental right to the care, custody and management of her children. Recognizing her rights does not change the form of submission. The standard for review of the charge is abuse of discretion, and abuse of discretion occurs only when the trial court acts without reference to any guiding principle. Here the trial court tracked the statutory language in the instruction and then asked the controlling question. This simply does not amount to abuse of discretion.

Broad-form questions reduce conflicting jury answers, thus reducing appeals and avoiding retrials. Rule 277 expedites trials by simplifying the charge conference and making questions easier for the jury to comprehend and answer.

Accordingly, we reverse the judgment of the court of appeals and affirm the judgment of the trial court.

Notes & Questions

1. *The Pattern Jury Charge.* Finding the correct broad-form submission has been made much easier in recent years by the Pattern Jury Charges (or "PJC") published by the State Bar of Texas. These charges represent the best thinking of distinguished lawyers, judges and teachers on how Texas statutes, rules and case law should be translated into a jury charge.

2. *The jury's role in making essential findings of fact.* In answering the questions submitted in the charge, the jury considers the evidence, which is often hotly disputed, and comes to a conclusion about what actually happened. In doing so, the jury must follow the judge's instructions about the standard to apply in determining the facts (e.g. preponderance of the evidence vs. clear and convincing evidence). The judge might also instruct the jury concerning the meaning of certain legal terms used in the charge. It is often said that the jury makes the essential findings of fact when answering the questions in the charge. What are the essential fact-findings in the *E.B.* and *B.L.D.* charge?

3. *Crafting the charge—what are the essential facts to include?* The party with the burden of proof must plead, prove with evidence, and obtain jury findings on all essential elements of the cause of action (or defense) to recover (or avoid liability). The law applicable to the pleaded causes of action determine the essential fact findings necessary for recovery (or for an affirmative defense, the applicable law determines the essential facts necessary for avoidance of liability). For common law causes of action, the judge looks to prior caselaw. For statutory causes of action, the judge looks to the statute. What are the sources of law for the parental termination charge?

4. *The 5 jurors this, 5 jurors that issue.* In a civil case, 10 of 12 jurors must agree to a verdict. How does the broad form charge affect a verdict when the plaintiff is relying on multiple factual

theories of recovery? Take *Fox v. Dallas Hotel Co.*, the elevator case discussed in the section on special issue practice above, as an example. Assume 2 jurors believed that the plaintiff was contributorily negligent in failing to lock the elevator in position, 2 believed he was negligent in failing to overcome the sticking by making it go up and down, 2 believed he was negligent in going under the elevator without locking it, and 2 believed that he was negligent in failing to get entirely in the pit. 2 jurors believe the defendant was not negligent. Thus, 10 jurors believe the defendant was negligent, but with a "distinct and separate" charge, the jury would not return a finding of negligence. Each distinct and separate question would be answered "No", with a vote of 10-2. However, a broad form question asking about the plaintiff's negligence would be answered "Yes." This argument was brought up and rejected in *E.B.*, where the Texas Supreme Court said that the jury is to be asked the "controlling question."

5. *Questions of law.* Questions of law are for the court and may not be submitted to the jury, whose job it is to decide questions of fact.[1] If the jury is asked a question containing a legal term such as "negligence" without any guidelines as to the factual elements essential to the legal conclusion, the question is one of law and is improper. In *E.B.*, the jury was asked whether to terminate the parent-child relationship, normally a legal question for the judge's ultimate decision. Why, then, are not the jury questions in *E.B.* prohibited as questions of law? Because the court provided instructions on the fact-findings and qualitative judgments (including, apparently, such things as whether continued custody would endanger the child). A question of law can be converted to a proper jury broad-form question if the factual elements leading to the legal conclusion are properly set out. A question about negligence, for example, is a question of law if the standard for negligence is not set out in lay terms by a definition (the reasonably prudent person standard). The courts have had some difficulty in fashioning a consistent view of what is and what is not a question of law. Before broad-form, jury charges that asked questions such as whether parties breached a contract were considered prohibited questions of law.[2] During the heyday of broad-form, however, a question as to whether "plaintiffs performed their obligations under the commitment letter," accompanied by appropriate instructions, was approved in the Texas Supreme Court's *Island Recreational* holding.[3]

6. *Definitions; placing the burden.* Note that broad form charges may be fatally defective if the legal terms, such as "negligence" and "proximate cause" are not defined by a separate instruction somewhere in the charge. The charge also needs a burden-placing instruction. In the earlier practice, the burden of proof was placed within each jury question (then called a "special issue"). The negligence question, for example, might read: "Do you find from a preponderance of the evidence that D was negligent in failing to timely apply his brakes on the occasion in question?" The question would be accompanied by an instruction defining "preponderance of evidence" as something like the "greater weight of the credible evidence." This way of placing the burden is still used occasionally, particularly in connection with damages questions, and is awkward but not necessarily erroneous. (The degree of detail following the word "negligent" marks this as an outdated "narrow form" or "granulated" or "separate and distinct" submission.)

---

[1] *See* National Fire Ins. Co. v. Valero Energy Co., 777 S.W.2d 501 (Tex. App.—Corpus Christi 1981, writ denied); Knutson v. Ripson, 354 S.W.2d 575 (Tex. 1962); C & C Partners v. Sun Exploration and Production Co., 783 S.W.2d 707 (Tex. App.—Dallas 1989, writ denied).

[2] *See* Barton v. Davis, 441 S.W.2d 299 (Tex. Civ. App.—El Paso 1969, writ ref'd n.r.e.) *and* Walton v. Smulcer, 222 S.W.2d 918 (Tex. Civ. App.—Ft. Worth 1949, no writ)(jury question on whether party "fully complied with their agreement").

[3] 710 S.W.2d 551 (Tex. 1986).

7. *Negligence cases.* An example of a broad-form submission of liability for a negligence case (taken from the General Negligence Volume of the Pattern Jury Charge) is as follows:

1. Did the negligence, if any, of the persons named below proximately cause the collision (occurrence) in question?

"Negligence" means failure to use ordinary carc, that is, failing to do that which a person of ordinary prudence would have done under the same or similar circumstances or doing that which a person of ordinary prudence would not have done under the same or similar conditions.

"Ordinary care" means that degree of care that would be used by a person of ordinary prudence under the same or similar circumstances."

"Proximate cause" means that which, in a natural and continuous sequence, produces an event, and without which cause such event would not have occurred. In order to be a proximate cause, the act or omission complained of much be such that a person using ordinary care would have foreseen that the event or some similar event might reasonably result therefrom. There may be more than one proximate cause of an event.

Answer "yes" or "no" for each of the following:

a. D ____________________

b. P ____________________

c. Settlor ____________________

d. Responsible Third Party ____________________

If the plaintiff seeks exemplary damages for gross negligence, the next question is as follows:

Answer the following question regarding D only if you unanimously answered "Yes" to Question 1 regarding D. Otherwise do not answer the following question regarding D.

You are instructed that, in order to answer "Yes" to the following question, your answer must be unanimous. You may answer "No" to the following question only upon a vote of ten or more jurors. Otherwise you must not answer the following question.

2. Do you find by clear and convincing evidence that the harm to P resulted from gross negligence?

"Gross negligence" means an act or omission by D,

(a) which when viewed objectively from the standpoint of D at the time of its occurrence involves an extreme degree of risk, considering the probability and magnitude of the potential harm to others; and

(b) of which D has actual, subjective awareness of the risk involved, but nevertheless proceeds with conscious indifference to the rights, safety, or welfare of others.

Answer "yes" or "no."

Answer: _______________

And the following question will be asked to determine proportionate responsibility:

If you have answered "Yes" to Question 1 for more than one of those named below, then answer the following question. Otherwise do not answer the following question.

3. What percentage of negligence that caused the collision do you find to be attributable to each of those found by you, in your answer to Question 1, to have been negligent?

The percentage you find must total 100%. The negligence attributable to a named below is not necessarily measured by the number of acts or omissions found.

a. D ____________________

b. P ____________________

c. Settlor ____________________

d. Responsible Third Party ____________________

Total 100%

These questions would be followed by a question on amount of damages (supplemented by instructions on the elements of damage to be considered) and, if appropriate, a conditional exemplary damages question. This might require a bifurcated trial if requested by a defendant. The questions, instructions and definitions used in this submission often change because the underlying substantive law changes. Significant changes were made after the 1995 and 2003 tort reform bills became law. *See* Chapter 41 CPRC.

8. *Combined charges*. Most cases involve claims under several causes of action and may involve affirmative defenses as well. A simple negligence case is not hard to submit. But when P is entitled to submission of negligence, DTPA, fraud and breach of contract against several defendants (manufacturer, retailer, installer, inspector), with several affirmative defenses requiring fact-findings (limitations, contributory fault, estoppel, waiver), things get very sticky very quickly. Several of the cases that follow explore the difficulties of appropriately combining theories and factual inquiries without confusing or misleading the jury. When one examines charges actually used it becomes apparent that the broad-form "ideal" gives way, in practice, to a hybrid submission which follows broad-form as far as possible. Keep in mind also that, in practice, the final charge is often shaped as much by what the attorneys request and complain about as what the judge might consider a perfect submission.

Do not be concerned for now with how the judge sorts out the verdict provided by the jury's answers to such a combined charge. We will consider that later, when we take up motions for judgment following the jury verdict.

CROWN LIFE INSURANCE COMPANY
v.
CASTEEL

22 S.W.3d 378
(Tex. 2000)

ABBOTT, JUSTICE.

* * *

William E. Casteel sold insurance policies as an independent agent of Crown Life Insurance Company. One of the policies sold by Casteel led to a lawsuit by policyholders against Casteel and Crown. In that lawsuit, Casteel filed a cross-claim against Crown. In this appeal from that lawsuit, we consider several issues: (1) whether Casteel, who alleges that he has been injured by the unfair and deceptive practices of Crown, has standing to sue Crown under Article 21.21 of the Texas Insurance Code; (2) whether that standing extends to Article 21.21 claims that allow recovery for Deceptive Trade Practices Act violations; and (3) whether the inclusion of invalid theories of liability submitted to the jury in a single broad-form question constitutes harmful error.

We hold that Casteel does have standing to sue Crown under Article 21.21; but Casteel does not have standing under Article 21.21 to allege DTPA-based claims that require consumer status by their terms. We also hold that submitting invalid theories of liability in a single broad-form jury question is harmful error when it cannot be determined whether the jury based its verdict on one or more of the invalid theories. We affirm in part, reverse and render judgment in part, vacate in part, and reverse and remand in part the judgment of the court of appeals.

* * *

Crown next challenges the court of appeals' conclusion that the erroneous submission of Casteel's DTPA-based Article 21.21 claims was harmless. The trial court submitted a single broad-form question on the issue of Crown's liability to Casteel. The question instructed the jury on thirteen independent grounds for liability, the first five of which were taken from the DTPA section 17.46(b) laundry list. The question requested a single answer on Crown's liability, which the jury answered affirmatively.

Casteel contends that Crown waived any defect in the liability question by failing to preserve error at the trial court. In particular, Casteel argues that Crown's objection was not specific enough because Crown objected to the question generally, instead of to each subsection. We disagree. Crown preserved error by obtaining a ruling on its timely objection to the question on the ground that Casteel did not have standing to pursue any DTPA-based Article 21.21 claims because he was not a consumer.

The court of appeals concluded that the trial court erred by submitting the DTPA-based theories of liability because Casteel did not have standing to bring them. Nevertheless, the court held that this error was harmless because Crown did not "affirmatively demonstrate that the error probably caused rendition of an improper judgment." We hold that it was error to submit four of the five DTPA-based theories of liability because Casteel was required to have consumer status to maintain an Article 21.21 cause of action under them. We now decide whether that error was harmful.

The court of appeals based its holding on the harmless error rule in former Texas Rule of Appellate Procedure 81(b)(1), which stated:

> No judgment shall be reversed on appeal and a new trial ordered [because of error] . . . unless the appellate court shall be of the opinion that the error complained of amounted to such a denial of the rights of the appellant as was reasonably calculated to cause and probably did cause rendition of an improper judgment . . . .

In addition, the court cited four decisions from three other courts of appeals holding that the submission of an invalid theory of liability in a single broad-form question is harmless if any evidence supports a finding of liability on a valid theory.

Notwithstanding that authority, the court of appeals erred by holding this error harmless. It is fundamental to our system of justice that parties have the right to be judged by a jury properly instructed in the law. Yet, when a jury bases a finding of liability on a single broad-form question that commingles invalid theories of liability with valid theories, the appellate court is often unable to determine the effect of this error. The best the court can do is determine that some evidence could have supported the jury's conclusion on a legally valid theory. To hold this error harmless would allow a defendant to be held liable without a judicial determination that a factfinder actually found that the defendant should be held liable on proper, legal grounds. Accordingly, we hold that when a trial court submits a single broad-form liability question incorporating multiple theories of liability, the error is harmful and a new trial is required when the appellate court cannot determine whether the jury based its verdict on an improperly submitted invalid theory. *See* TEX. R. APP. P. 61.1 ("No judgment may be reversed on appeal . . . unless the Supreme Court concludes that the error complained of . . . probably prevented the petitioner from properly presenting the case to the appellate courts."); *see also* TEX. R. APP. P. 44.1(a).

It is essential that the theories submitted be authorized and supported by the law governing the case. If they are not, the appellate court must, at a minimum, be able to determine whether properly submitted theories constituted the basis of the jury's verdict. Here, four of the thirteen theories in the single liability question were improperly submitted because they required that Casteel be a consumer. Yet the language of these theories was altered to remove any reference to their consumer-status requirements. Thus, the jury was confronted with four liability theories available only to consumers, but was given no indication that Casteel was required to be a consumer to succeed under any of them. Given these facts, it is possible that the jury based Crown's liability solely on one or more of these erroneously submitted theories. At any rate, it is impossible for us to conclude that the jury's answer was not based on one of the improperly submitted theories.

Although we have not considered this issue since we adopted the harmless error doctrine, we have previously held that submitting multiple independent liability theories in a single jury question is harmful when one of the theories is invalid and it cannot be determined whether liability was based on the invalid theory. *See Lancaster v. Fitch*, 112 Tex. 293, 246 S.W. 1015, 1016 (1923). In *Lancaster*, the trial court submitted a single general negligence issue with instructions regarding three distinct theories of negligence liability. The jury returned a verdict for the plaintiff. On appeal, the defendant established that the trial court should not have submitted one of the theories. The court of appeals nevertheless concluded that the error was harmless because the jury could have based its verdict on either of the properly submitted theories. We disagreed, reasoning:

> The jury may have found for [plaintiff] on each of the two issues properly submitted. On the other hand, as authorized by the pleading and the charge of the court, they may have found for [plaintiff] only on the issue that was improperly submitted. In order for courts to be able to administer the law in such cases with reasonable certainty and to lay down and maintain just and practical rules for determining the rights of parties, it is necessary that the issues made and submitted to juries, and upon which they are required to pass, be authorized and supported by the law governing the case.

Today, we reaffirm this reasoning. When a single broad-form liability question erroneously commingles valid and invalid liability theories and the appellant's objection is timely and specific, the error is harmful when it cannot be determined whether the improperly submitted theories formed the sole basis for the jury's finding. We disapprove of those courts of appeals' decisions holding that this error is harmless if any evidence supports a properly submitted liability theory.

However, when questions are submitted in a manner that allows the appellate court to determine that the jury's verdict was actually based on a valid liability theory, the error may be harmless. *See City of Brownsville v. Alvarado*, 897 S.W.2d 750, 752 (Tex. 1995) ("Submission of an improper jury question can be harmless error if the jury's answers to other questions render the improper question immaterial."); *Boatland of Houston, Inc. v. Bailey*, 609 S.W.2d 743, 749-50 (Tex. 1980) (holding that the potentially improper submission of defensive issues was harmless error when the jury also found for the defendant on independent grounds).

Casteel argues that Texas Rule of Civil Procedure 277 required the trial court to submit all liability theories in a single broad-form question, and that the verdict should not be overturned because the trial court simply followed that rule. *See* TEX. R. CIV. P. 277. Rule 277 states, "In all jury cases the court shall, whenever feasible, submit the cause upon broad-form questions. The court shall submit such instructions and definitions as shall be proper to enable the jury to render a verdict."

Rule 277 is not absolute; rather, it mandates broad-form submission "whenever feasible." *See Westgate, Ltd. v. State*, 843 S.W.2d 448, 455 n. 6 (Tex. 1992). In *Westgate*, we noted that "[s]ubmitting alternative liability standards when the governing law is unsettled might very well be a situation where broad-form submission is not feasible." Similarly, when the trial court is unsure whether it should submit a particular theory of liability, separating liability theories best serves the policy of judicial economy underlying Rule 277 by avoiding the need for a new trial when the basis for liability cannot be determined. Furthermore, Rule 277 mandates that "[t]he court shall submit such instructions and definitions as shall be proper to enable the jury to render a verdict." It is implicit in this mandate that the jury be able to base its verdict on legally valid questions and instructions. Thus, it may not be feasible to submit a single broad-form liability question that incorporates wholly separate theories of liability.

Because the error in the charge was harmful and Crown properly objected, we reverse the judgment of the court of appeals, and remand the case to the trial court for a new trial on the issue of whether Crown is liable to Casteel under Article 21.21 for unfair or deceptive practices that do not require Casteel to be a consumer.

* * *

Notes & Questions

1. Casteel *and damages questions*. In *Harris County v. Smith*, the Supreme Court applied *Casteel* to a damages question. There the trial court submitted the plaintiffs' damages in a broad form question, asking the jury to determine a single amount of damages, considering several different types of damages: physical pain and mental anguish, loss of earning capacity, physical impairment, and medical care. The County objected to the broad form question claiming there was no evidence of loss of earning capacity and physical impairment. The Supreme Court held it was error to submit a broad form question that included an element of damages on which there was no evidence and reversed and remanded citing Casteel.

> Neither our decision today nor *Casteel* is a retrenchment from our fundamental commitment to broad-form submission. This Court began moving toward modern broad-form practice in 1973, when we amended Texas Rule of Civil Procedure 277 to abolish the requirement that issues be submitted separately and distinctly, thereby granting trial courts the discretion to submit issues broadly. Over the years, we have repeatedly expressed our general preference for broad-form submission. Our current rule, amended in 1988, more strongly reflects our preference for broad-form questions, mandating that the "court shall, whenever feasible, submit the cause on broad-form questions." TEX. R. CIV. P. 277.
>
> When properly utilized, broad-form submission can simplify charge conferences and provide more comprehensible questions for the jury. But we recognize that it is not always practicable to submit every issue in a case broadly. As Professors Muldrow and Underwood observe, "broader is not always better." Muldrow & Underwood, *Application of the Harmless Error Standard to Errors in the Charge,* 48 BAYLOR L. REV. 815, 853 (1996). For example, we have suggested that broad-form submission may not be feasible when the governing law is unsettled. *See Westgate, Ltd. v. State,* 843 S.W.2d 448, 455 n. 6 (Tex. 1992). In such an instance, submitting alternative liability standards permits the appellate court to settle the law and render the correct judgment. Similarly, it would be contrary to judicial economy to insist on broad-form submission when a specific objection raises substantial concern that a particular theory of liability will infect the proposed broad-form question with error. *See Casteel.* And in a case such as this one, asking the jury to record its verdict as to each element of damages when there is doubt as to the legal sufficiency of the evidence will permit the losing party to preserve error without complicating the charge or the jury's deliberations. *See* TEXAS PATTERN JURY CHARGES—GENERAL NEGLIGENCE PJC 8.2 cmt.; *see also Muldrow & Underwood, supra*, at 855.
>
> Whether a granulated or broad-form charge is submitted, the trial court's duty is to submit only those questions, instructions, and definitions raised by the pleadings and the evidence. But using the harmless error rule to permit the indiscriminate mixture of valid and invalid liability theories or damage elements, without recourse, undermines a party's incentive to request legally correct definitions, instructions, and questions.

2. *Romero*. In *Romero v. KPH Consolidation, Inc.*,[1] the Supreme Court applied the principles of *Harris County* and *Casteel* in a different context. Plaintiff sued a hospital (owned and operated by KBH), two doctors, and a nurse for not performing a blood transfusion quickly enough. Dur-

---

[1] 166 S.W.3d 212 (Tex. 2005).

ing surgery, plaintiff had lost an enormous amount of blood before the doctors noticed and ordered the transfusion. Plaintiff alleged ordinary negligence against the four defendants concerning the transfusion (submitted by the court in Question 1). Plaintiff also sued the hospital for maliciously credentialing[2] Dr. Baker, the surgeon (submitted by the court in Question 2).

The jury answered both questions in favor of the plaintiff, and in Question 3 it apportioned the comparative negligence at 40% for the hospital, 40% for Dr. Baker, and 20% for Dr. Huie (the anesthesiologist). The Supreme Court held that there was no evidence to support the "yes" answer to Question 2, and on that cause of action it reversed and rendered a take-nothing judgment. The court then held that the jury's 40% finding against Dr. Baker was necessarily influenced by the malicious credentialing cause of action, which was not supported by the evidence. This required that the entire case be remanded for a new trial, in which the jury would assess negligence without the taint of the malicious credentialing theory and evidence.

The plaintiff argued that the evidence against the hospital, even without the evidence of malicious credentialing, was sufficient to support the 40% finding. But the court held that *Casteel* (invalid theory of liability submitted) and *Harris County* (element of damages submitted without evidence to support it) had rejected similar arguments. The court gave the following response to the plaintiff's suggestion that the court was making broad-form submission more difficult:

> The Romeros argue that to apply the rule of *Casteel* and *Harris County* in this case "encourages, if not requires, separate submission of every theory of liability, every combination of theories, and every combination of defendants together with separate apportionment and damages questions for every theory, combination of theories, and combination of defendants. In this case, the jury charge would have needed to include more than 175 issues."
>
> This is simply untrue. The jury charge in this case needed *one less question* — the question on malicious credentialing, for which there was no evidence — to be free of error, and reversal could have been avoided with *one more question*, which the trial court offered to the Romeros and they rejected.[3] The reversible error rule of *Casteel* and *Harris County* neither encourages nor requires parties to submit separate questions for every possible issue or combination of issues; the rule *does* both encourage and require parties not to submit issues that have no basis in law and fact in such a way that the error cannot be corrected without retrial. If at the close of evidence a party continues to assert a claim without knowing whether it is recognized at law or supported by the evidence, the party has three choices: he can request that the claim be included with others and run the risk of reversal and a new trial, request that the claim be submitted to the jury separately to avoid that risk, or abandon the claim altogether. The Romeros' argument assumes that it is so commonplace to come to the end of a jury trial and have no idea what claims are still le-

---

2 A statute requires heightened proof when a patient sues a hospital for wrongfully granting privileges to a doctor and allowing him to use its facilities: the patient must prove that the doctor acted with "malice," defined as acting with conscious indifference to an extreme degree of risk despite being subjectively aware of the extreme risk.

3 The trial judge had suggested a second comparative negligence question, which would have told the jury to apportion the comparative negligence a second time without considering the evidence of malicious credentialing. Had such a question been submitted, and the credentialing cause of action been set aside on appeal, the appellate courts could have disregarded the tainted percentage findings and rendered judgment using the percentages that excluded the credentialing.

gally and factually valid that the only safe course to avoid retrial is to parse out every issue in a separate jury question. Nothing in our review of thousands of verdicts rendered by juries across the State suggests that there is any validity to the assumption.

The Romeros argue that we have retreated from the mandate of Rule 277 of the Texas Rules of Civil Procedure that issues must be submitted to a jury in broad form "whenever feasible". This Court's adoption of broad-form jury submissions was intended to simplify jury charges for the benefit of the jury, the parties, and the trial court. It was certainly never intended to permit, and therefore encourage, more error in a jury charge. We continue to believe, as we stated in *Harris County*, that "when properly utilized, broad-form submission can simplify charge conferences and provide more comprehensible questions for the jury." But "it is not always practicable to submit every issue in a case broadly," and broad-form submission cannot be used to broaden the harmless error rule to deny a party the correct charge to which it would otherwise be entitled.

3. *Instructed verdicts and instructions*. Suppose in *Romero* the trial court had allowed plaintiff to present his evidence of malicious credentialing but had concluded after hearing the evidence that it was legally insufficient (as the Supreme Court ultimately held) and granted an instructed verdict on the cause of action. How could the court have prevented the jury from thinking about the evidence as it answered the ordinary negligence and comparative negligence questions? The court could of course instruct the jury not to consider the evidence. But do juries really put such evidence out of their minds? Probably not. This is why defendants in such cases will file a motion for partial summary judgment before trial and try to have the prejudicial cause of action and evidence removed from the case.

4. *Departure from broad form?* What lessons should the careful trial judge or practitioner take from *Casteel*, *Harris County*, and *Romero*? Suppose you are unsure of a particular instruction or element of a multiple theory. What if the evidence is weak on a theory or factual basis? How do these opinions fit within Rule 277's directive to use broad form whenever feasible? Can the trial court ever abuse its discretion in light of *Casteel* if it submits a charge through separate questions?

BENGE
v.
WILLIAMS

No. 14–1057, 2018 WL 2374640
(Tex. 2018)

Opinion

CHIEF JUSTICE HECHT delivered the opinion of the Court.

At the trial of this healthcare-liability case, the patient argued and offered evidence that her physician was negligent both in using an inexperienced resident to assist with performing her surgery and in not disclosing the resident's level of involvement, although she does not claim a right to recover for the nondisclosure. The jury was asked simply whether the physician was negligent without being instructed not to consider the nondisclosure. A divided court of appeals concluded that the trial court's refusal to instruct the jury as requested was harmful error, and we agree. . . . We affirm the judgment of the court of appeals remanding the case to the trial court for a new trial.

During a laparoscopic-assisted vaginal hysterectomy ("LAVH") to remove her uterus, ovaries, and fallopian tubes, Lauren Williams, 39, suffered a bowel perforation that was not immediately diagnosed, resulting in catastrophic post-surgical consequences. She sued the surgeon, Dr. Jim Benge, a board-certified obstetrician and gynecologist, and his practice group, Kelsey-Seybold Medical Group, PLLC (together referred to as "Dr. Benge"). The jury found that Dr. Benge's negligence caused Williams' injuries. We summarize the evidence in the light most favorable to the verdict.

A week before the surgery, Dr. Benge and Williams discussed the LAVH procedure and reviewed written consent forms setting out all required disclosures of risks, including damage to the bowel.

* * *

Dr. Benge testified that in explaining the consent forms, he told Williams that he "would be doing the surgery with an assistant." Williams testified that Dr. Benge did not tell her the resident would actually be performing part of the surgery.

* * *

Dr. Benge testified that the bowel perforation likely resulted from an arc of electricity from a Bovie, an electrical cutting and cauterizing instrument used during the surgery to both cut and fuse tissue and to stop bleeding. The instrument was near the weighted speculum, which was touching the bowel. Even though no immediate damage to the bowel tissue was visible at the time of the surgery, Dr. Benge testified that it was possible for an electric arc to pass from the Bovie to the speculum without being seen, causing a thermal injury to Williams' bowel tissue below.

* * *

The jury was asked a single question on liability: Did Dr. Benge's negligence proximately cause Williams' injuries? Dr. Benge objected to the question because it "allow[ed] the jury to base its finding on a violation of informed consent" that Williams did not claim. Dr. Benge requested that the jury be "instructed that in deciding whether [Dr. Benge] was negligent, you cannot consider what [Dr. Benge] told, or did not tell, [Williams] about [Dr. Giacobbe's] being involved with the surgery." The trial court overruled Dr. Benge's objection and refused to give the jury the requested instruction.

The trial court rendered judgment on the verdict for Williams for almost $2 million. On appeal, Dr. Benge argued that Dr. Patsner was not qualified under the Texas Medical Liability Act ("TMLA" or the "Act") to testify as an expert, leaving Williams with no evidence that Dr. Benge violated the standard of care, and thus requiring rendition of judgment in his favor. Dr. Benge also argued that the jury was allowed to find Dr. Benge negligent for failing to disclose Dr. Giacobbe's experience and involvement in the surgery, a basis for liability Williams had disclaimed, thus requiring a new trial. A deeply divided court of appeals agreed only with the second argument and reversed and remanded the case for a new trial. We granted Williams' and Dr. Benge's petitions for review.

* * *

III

We turn now to Dr. Benge's argument that the trial court's refusal to instruct the jury not to consider "what [he] told, or did not tell, [Williams] about [Dr. Giacobbe's] being involved with the surgery" was error requiring a new trial.

A

At trial and on appeal, Williams has steadfastly disclaimed any assertion that Dr. Benge is liable for failing to obtain her informed consent to surgery. She acknowledges that she consented in writing to the possible involvement of a resident in her LAVH procedure. She does not contend that she misunderstood the consent forms she signed. She does contend that Dr. Benge is nonetheless liable for his negligence in allowing Dr. Giacobbe in particular—with no experience in performing the surgery—to assist in the LAVH procedure, in assigning her the surgical tasks he did, and in supervising her work. Her disclaimer of an informed-consent claim does not, of course, foreclose that negligence claim.

But Williams also contends that Dr. Benge not only allowed Dr. Giacobbe to assist in surgery, he failed to disclose that Dr. Giacobbe had never performed an LAVH procedure and that she would be significantly involved in the surgery. Indeed, Williams' nondisclosure contention was front and center beginning to end. The first words out of Williams' counsel's mouth in his opening statement to the jury were that a surgeon "cannot pass off part of [a] surgery to a resident without the express permission of the patient." "[T]he reasons . . . we're bringing suit", he told the jury, were: "First, [Dr. Benge] betrayed [Williams]. He told her he was going to do the surgery. She trusted him to do the surgery. He did not, and he will admit to you he did not live up to his end of the deal." Dr. Benge betrayed Williams, counsel continued, by having "a secret surgeon, a first-time resident do a significant part of this procedure." "The first thing you must do" as a surgeon being assisted by a resident, counsel said, "is you must inform the patient." Dr. Benge "didn't tell [Williams] that [r]esident Lauren Giacobbe was going to do the procedure. He didn't tell her that the resident had never done the procedure before." "We're suing", Williams' counsel repeated, because Dr. Benge brought in "a surgeon who had no permission, who had no consent to put her hands on [Williams]." That, he reiterated, was the "[f]irst reason". The other reasons were Dr. Benge's conduct of the surgery and his post-surgical failure to promptly diagnose and treat Williams' bowel perforation.

Williams' counsel repeatedly asked Dr. Benge on the stand whether he had told Williams that Dr. Giacobbe would be involved in the surgery or her level of experience. "[Y]ou didn't tell Lauren Williams that there was going to be a first-time resident performing surgery . . . with you, correct?" Dr. Benge answered that he told Williams only that he would have an assistant who might be a resident. Dr. Benge testified that Williams had met Dr. Giacobbe just before surgery. But "[i]f someone were to . . . conclude that Lauren Williams neither had the knowledge or the consent [that a substitute surgeon was to operate], someone was deceitful, correct?" Dr. Benge agreed. "Are you going to tell me that you gave complete disclosure of who was going to be performing the operation?" counsel again asked. "I told her that I would be doing the surgery with an assistant", Dr. Benge replied. "Was there a secret surgeon used on Ms. Williams?" Dr. Benge was asked. "No", he replied. In all, Dr. Benge was asked about his nondisclosure of Dr. Giacobbe's involvement and Williams' lack of consent some 20 times. Williams' testimony likewise centered on Dr. Benge's failure to disclose, and her failure to consent to, Dr. Giacobbe's involvement.

In summation, Williams' counsel again told the jury that the "[n]umber one" reason Williams had sued was because Dr. Benge had not disclosed to her Dr. Giacobbe's lack of experience and involvement in the surgery.

Williams argues that her evidence of Dr. Benge's nondisclosure was not a claim of lack of informed consent for which he could be liable. As already noted, she disclaims any such basis for liability.[17] But Williams' argument is contradicted by the record. Dr. Patsner, Williams' expert, testified repeatedly that Dr. Benge's nondisclosure violated the standard of care—that it was negligent. Williams' counsel asked: "Would you say that [Dr. Benge] violated the standard of care if he did not explain that the third-year resident doing this her—first-time procedure—was going to be performing a part of the surgery?" "Well, yes", Dr. Patsner answered. "[T]he standard of care is to get permission from the patient for everybody who's going to be operating on them. You can't have ghost surgeons." "Period?" he was asked. "End of story?" "Period", he replied. "No question?" "No question. . . . I mean, . . . that's just the rule." Again, Williams' counsel asked Dr. Patsner: "Do you believe that Dr. Benge fell below the standard of care when he allowed someone without . . . express consent to operate on Lauren Williams?" Again, Dr. Patsner answered, "Yes." A third time, Dr. Patsner was asked: "The area of betrayal . . . the failure of Dr. Benge to explain who was doing the surgery on Ms. Williams—was that below the standard of care?" "Yes", he answered. "Was that negligent?" counsel asked. "Yes", he said.

Williams argues that her claim of nondisclosure, which she clearly makes, is not the same as a claim of lack of informed consent, which she disclaims. We fail to see the difference. Williams concedes that in her written consent, she acknowledged the possible involvement of a resident in surgery. But she contends that she was not told enough about that involvement: who the resident would be, what the resident would do, and the resident's experience. Though she acknowledges informed consent to the risks of surgery and the involvement of a resident, she has repeatedly denied informed consent to the involvement of Dr. Giacobbe, calling it a betrayal and deceitful. Her nondisclosure claim cannot be viewed as anything other than a claim of lack of informed consent.

Williams argues that evidence of Dr. Benge's nondisclosure was offered only to show that he told Williams less than he said he did—that he was not telling the truth—and therefore impugn his credibility regarding the surgery and follow-up. But Williams has not identified any fact with respect to which Dr. Benge's credibility was important. Williams contends that Dr. Benge was not truthful when he ascribed the bowel perforation to the Bovie, but that was a matter of opinion, not fact. Moreover, the repeated questions and argument were not merely about what Dr. Benge did or did not tell Williams; they were about whether he *should* have told her more—about whether he had a duty to do so under the standard of care. Williams' argument that the issue was Dr. Benge's credibility is flatly refuted by the testimony she repeatedly elicited from Dr. Patsner, not that Dr. Benge was unworthy of belief, but that he violated the standard of care and was negligent. The issues of whether Dr. Benge was negligent in involving Dr. Giacobbe and supervising her in the surgery, and whether Dr. Benge was negligent in failing to disclose to Williams what was required to obtain her informed consent, are completely different. Williams' evidence and argument at trial confused them.

---

17 The court of appeals held that "Texas law does not impose a legal duty to disclose to a patient specific information about a consented-to assisting surgeon's anticipated level of participation or experience." 472 S.W.3d 684, 709 (Tex. App.—Houston [1st Dist.] 2014). Because Williams does not claim to the contrary, we express no view on the court's holding.

B

Based on Dr. Patsner's testimony, the jury could have found that Dr. Benge was negligent in failing to disclose Dr. Giacobbe's involvement in the surgery and her lack of experience. But Williams does not assert that claim. Therefore, Dr. Benge argues, the jury should have been instructed not to consider the lack of disclosure in determining negligence, and the trial court erred in refusing the requested instruction. He contends that the error must be presumed harmful under our decision in *Crown Life Insurance Co. v. Casteel* and its progeny.

In *Casteel*, the jury was asked to find whether the defendant was liable for engaging in any of 13 practices listed in a single question . For 4 of the listed practices, the plaintiff could not recover because he was not a consumer. Hence, the question included both valid and invalid liability theories. The court of appeals held that the mixing of valid and invalid theories was error but that the error was harmless because there was some evidence to support a finding of liability under at least one of the valid theories. We disagreed, holding that "when a trial court submits a single broad-form liability question incorporating multiple theories of liability, the error is harmful and a new trial is required when the appellate court cannot determine whether the jury based its verdict on an improperly submitted invalid theory."

The jury question in the present case, unlike the one in *Casteel*, did not include multiple theories, some valid and some invalid. It inquired about a single theory: negligence. But we have twice held that when the question allows a finding of liability based on evidence that cannot support recovery, the same presumption-of-harm rule must be applied.

In *Columbia Rio Grande Healthcare, L.P. v. Hawley*, the liability question to the jury was stated the same as in the present case: Was the hospital's negligence a proximate cause of the plaintiff's injuries?[23] The jury was instructed that the hospital could "act only through its employees, agents, nurses, and servants." The charge did not define "agent". There was evidence in the case of a physician's negligence, and the hospital requested that the jury be instructed that the physician was not its agent. The trial court refused. We held that while the case presented "a different jury charge problem" than *Casteel* did, the trial court's error "effectively preclude[d] reviewing courts from determining whether the jury found liability on an invalid basis, preclude[d] determination of whether the error probably caused the rendition of an improper judgment, and [was] harmful because it prevent[ed] proper presentation of the case on appeal."

Likewise, in *Texas Commission on Human Rights v. Morrison*, the liability question to the jury asked about a single theory: employer retaliation.[29] The plaintiff complained of several adverse actions taken by her employer, including the denial of a promotion, but liability could not be based on the denied promotion because the plaintiff had not included that particular action in her EEOC complaint. Over the employer's objection, the trial court submitted a single question asking whether the employer took "adverse personnel actions" against the plaintiff. The plaintiff argued on appeal, as Williams does here, that there was no charge error because "no invalid theory was directly submitted to the jury". We rejected that argument, and even though the employer had not requested a limiting instruction, held that the error in overruling the objection was presumed harmful.

---

23 284 S.W.3d 851, 863 (Tex. 2009).

29 381 S.W.3d 533, 535 (Tex. 2012) (per curiam).

Here, as in *Hawley* and *Morrison*, while the jury was asked about a single liability theory, the plaintiff advanced multiple claims in the evidence. Dr. Benge was negligent, Williams claimed, in allowing Dr. Giacobbe to assist, failing to disclose her involvement, improperly supervising her, and failing to promptly detect the bowel perforation. Dr. Patsner testified that Dr. Benge's nondisclosure fell below the standard of care. The jury could have based its finding of negligence only on that nondisclosure or any 1 or more of Williams' other claims. Williams has disclaimed recovery for Dr. Benge's nondisclosure. Dr. Benge requested that the jury be instructed, correctly, that it could not consider the nondisclosure in deciding whether he was negligent. Because the trial court refused the instruction, we cannot determine whether it was the basis for the jury's finding. As in *Hawley* and *Morrison*, as well as *Casteel,* because an appellate court cannot determine whether the jury found liability on an improper basis, we must presume that the error in denying Dr. Benge's limiting instruction was harmful. The rule "both encourage[s] and require[s] parties not to submit issues that have no basis in law and fact in such a way that the error cannot be corrected without retrial."[34]

C

Williams argues that Dr. Benge's complaint is not about the charge but about the admission of evidence, to which he did not sufficiently object. At a pretrial hearing on the parties' motions in limine, Dr. Benge asked the court to exclude evidence on what he told or did not tell Williams about Dr. Giacobbe's involvement in the surgery. Dr. Benge argued that the evidence was irrelevant because Williams had not pleaded lack of informed consent. The trial court denied Dr. Benge's motion but granted him a running objection to questions about nondisclosure. Dr. Benge reasserted the objection early in the trial, and the trial court again allowed a running objection. But Dr. Benge did not object to each of the many questions about nondisclosure.

We need not decide whether the trial court erred by admitting evidence of Dr. Benge's failure to disclose Dr. Giacobbe's involvement to Williams, or whether Dr. Benge preserved his objection. Whether Dr. Benge has an evidentiary complaint or not, the complaint he makes is that the charge allowed the jury to consider what he did or did not tell Williams about Dr. Giacobbe's involvement in the surgery in deciding negligence, even though Williams does not seek recovery on that basis. He objected to the charge and requested a limiting instruction. In *Morrison*, we held that an objection to the charge even without a requested question or instruction preserved the complaint that the evidence would allow the jury to find liability in answer to a single broad-form question, on a theory on which the plaintiff could not recover.[35] Dr. Benge's objection and requested instruction went as far as that case requires.

The court of appeals was correct in concluding that the charge error requires a new trial.

* * *

Accordingly, the judgment of the court of appeals is *Affirmed.*

---

[34] Romero v. KPH Consolidation, Inc., 166 S.W.3d 212, 230 (Tex. 2005).

[35] 381 S.W.3d at 536.

C. Instructions and Definitions

1. *In General*

Read Rules 277, 278.

ACORD
v.
GENERAL MOTORS CORPORATION
669 S.W.2d 111
(Tex. 1984)

KILGARLIN, JUSTICE.

The principal issue presented in this products liability case is the propriety of an instruction given by the trial court in conjunction with a jury inquiry of defective design. Roy Acord, Petitioner, brought suit as a result of an accident in which his wife was killed and his minor son was injured when their vehicle was struck by a G.M.C. truck after the truck's brakes failed. Acord alleged strict liability against General Motors Corporation and common law negligence against Gilbert Johnson d/b/a Johnson's Fleet Service. The jury answers on issues of liability were favorable to both defendants and the trial court rendered a take nothing judgment against Acord. The court of appeals affirmed the judgment. 657 S.W.2d 7. We reverse the judgments as to General Motors Corporation and remand the cause to the trial court. We affirm the judgments as to Johnson.

The trial court inquired of the jury "[d]o you find from a preponderance of the evidence that at the time it was sold by General Motors, the 1970 truck involved in the accident made the basis of this suit was defectively designed because it failed to contain a dual or redundant back-up braking system." Two instructions were included with the special issue. The first stated "[b]y the term 'defectively designed' as used in this issue is meant a product that is unreasonably dangerous as designed, taking into consideration the utility of the product and the risk involved in its use." The preceding instruction follows verbatim the approved charge in *Turner v. General Motors Corp.*, 584 S.W.2d 844 (Tex. 1979).

Additionally, however, the court instructed the jury as follows: A manufacturer is not an insurer of the product he designs, and it is not required that the design adopted be perfect, or render the product accident proof, or incapable of causing injury, nor is it necessary to incorporate the ultimate safety features in the product.

Acord argues that the additional instruction was erroneous because it exceeded the guidelines of *Turner*, constituted a comment on the weight of the evidence, and injected negligence into a design defect issue. General Motors replies that the instruction does not violate *Turner*, but merely supplements it; that the giving of instructions to a jury is left to the sound discretion of the trial judge; and that the instruction has received approval by two courts of appeals. *McCants v. Salameh*, 608 S.W.2d 304 (Tex. Civ. App.—Waco 1980, writ ref'd n.r.e.); *Wenzel v. Rollins Motor Co.*, 598 S.W.2d 895 (Tex. Civ. App.—El Paso 1980, writ ref'd n.r.e.) Additionally, General Motors urges that if the instruction was erroneous, it was not harmful error and that, in any event, Acord has failed to preserve error by not obtaining a ruling from the trial court on Acord's objections to the charge.

* * *

No one questions that the disputed instruction given in this case is a correct statement of law. We have already said in *Shamrock Fuel and Oil Sales Co. v. Tunks*, 416 S.W.2d 779 (Tex. 1967), that "[a] manufacturer or distributor of products is not an insurer." We said as much in *General Motors Corp. v. Hopkins*, 548 S.W.2d 344 (Tex. 1977). *See also Duncan v. Cessna Aircraft Co.*, 665 S.W.2d 414 (Tex. 1984). We have likewise stated that a manufacturer is not required to design the safest possible product. *Henderson v. Ford Motor Co.*, 519 S.W.2d 87 (Tex. 1974). Legal scholars in early analyses of products liability have referred to such policy considerations. *See* Keeton, *Products Liability—Liability Without Fault and the Requirement of a Defect*, 41 TEX. L. REV. 855, 858 (1963); James, *Products Liability*, 34 TEX. L. REV. 192, 206 & 208 (1955). Some theorists have favored instructing the jury as to policy considerations. *See* Wade, *Strict Tort Liability of Manufacturers*, 19 SW. L.J. 5, 16-19 (1965).

In *Turner v. General Motors Corp.*, 584 S.W.2d at 849, 851, this court, in determining how strict liability cases would be submitted to a jury, relied upon Green, *Strict Liability Under Sections 402A and 402B: A Decade of Litigation*, 54 TEX. L. REV. 1185 (1976). In his article, Dean Green criticizes the "seeking [of] standards and causation doctrines that imitate those found in negligence cases." *Id.* at 1219. *Turner* was a case involving a claim of strict liability because of design defects. In *Turner*, the trial court had defined "defectively designed" as meaning that the design was unreasonably dangerous, and had defined unreasonably dangerous as being dangerous to an extent beyond that which would be contemplated by the ordinary consumer who purchased it, with the ordinary knowledge common to the community as to its characteristics. The court of appeals reversed the trial court judgment in behalf of Turner, saying that the instruction given was not proper in crashworthiness cases. The court of appeals went on to say that the jury should be instructed to balance specific factors in determining whether the design causing the injury was defective. Among those balancing factors to be included was the manufacturer's ability to eliminate the unsafe character of the product without seriously impairing its usefulness or significantly increasing its cost.

Our court disapproved the holding of the court of appeals in *Turner* that the jury was to be instructed to balance specifically enumerated factors, "*whether those listed by the Court of Appeals, or otherwise*." 584 S.W.2d at 847 (emphasis added). We also held that in future trials of strict liability cases involving design defects that the issue and instruction accompanying it "will not include either the element of the ordinary consumer or of the prudent manufacturer; to the extent of any conflicts in such respects, *Henderson* and *Hopkins* are overruled." *Id.* In a footnote to the opinion, we set out the correct special issue and instruction to be utilized. *Id.* at n. 1. Subsequently, in the *Turner* opinion, our court stated: "Accordingly, we approve the form of jury submission stated in the forepart of this opinion to be effective in the trial of design defect strict liability cases after the date on which our judgment herein becomes final." *Id.* at 851. That date was July 18, 1979, the date of the overruling of the last motion for rehearing in *Turner*.

* * *

If *Turner* was not sufficiently specific to advise the bench and bar that in strict liability cases the jury is not to be instructed with balancing factors, surely we have laid this matter to rest by our opinion in *Fleishman v. Guadiano*, 651 S.W.2d 730 (Tex. 1983), where we again endorsed the submission as approved by *Turner* and upheld the trial court's refusal to give any other instructions. The jury need not and should not be burdened with surplus instructions. Volume III of the TEXAS PATTERN JURY CHARGES (1982) utilizes for manufacturer design defect cases only the issue and instruction contained in *Turner*. We explicitly approve the *Pattern Jury Charges* issue and instruction for design defect cases, and disapprove the addition of any other instructions in such cases, however correctly they may state the law under § 402A of the RESTATEMENT (SECOND) OF TORTS.

Having resolved that the additional instruction in this case was erroneous, the paramount question becomes was such instruction harmful? The trial court's giving the additional instruction amounted to a comment on the weight of the evidence. A case similar in some respects is that of *Levermann v. Cartall*, 393 S.W.2d 931 (Tex. Civ. App.—San Antonio 1965, writ ref'd n.r.e.). Involved was a complaint of medical malpractice, in which the court's charge included the following instruction: "[y]ou are further instructed as part of the law of this case, that a medical doctor is not an insurer or guarantor of his work; neither is he responsible in law for an honest mistake in judgment, unless such mistake is due to a want of ordinary care, as the term 'ordinary care' has been defined herein before." *Id.* at 935. The court of appeals observed that with the evidence sharply conflicting on the issue of the degree of care exercised by the defendants, "this additional instruction by the trial court, that appellees were not insurers or guarantors, was a comment on the case as a whole, in that it related to the care to be exercised by appellees and was reasonably calculated to cause and probably did cause prejudicial harm to appellants so as to require remand of the case." *Id.* at 937. In a closely contested case as is the one at bar, to single out for the jury that General Motors was neither an insurer nor a guarantor of a perfect or accident-proof product, which incorporated ultimate safety features, was a comment on the case as a whole. As such, it constituted harmful error.

* * *

Thus, we sever and affirm the take nothing judgments as to Gilbert Johnson d/b/a Johnson's Fleet Service. We reverse the judgments of the courts below as to General Motors Corporation, and remand this cause for the purpose of a new trial.

LONE STAR GAS COMPANY
v.
LEMOND

897 S.W.2d 755
(Tex. 1995)

PER CURIAM.

The court of appeals held in this case that it was reversible error for the trial court to add the following sentence to the standard jury charge for marketing defects: "A seller's duty to warn arises only where the dangers to be warned of are reasonably foreseeable and are such that a consumer cannot reasonably be expected to be aware of them." We disagree because, under the record before us, any error was harmless.

Phares Lemond was injured and his wife killed in an explosion that resulted when natural gas which had accumulated in the crawl space under their home was ignited by the water heater's pilot light. Lemond sued the gas distributor, Lone Star Gas Co., claiming that it was negligent and that the gas was unreasonably dangerous as designed, manufactured, and marketed. Lemond alleged that Lone Star failed to maintain its distribution lines properly, allowing gas to leak out and up through the soil below Lemond's house, and that the odorant which should have allowed the gas to be detected was defective for a number of reasons. The trial court charged the jury on all of Lemond's theories except manufacturing defect. After a three-week trial, the jury failed to find that any negligence of Lone Star or any defect in the design and marketing of the gas caused Lemond's injuries. The trial court rendered judgment on the verdict for Lone Star.

The jury charge on marketing defect tracked the standard question and instruction prescribed by the Texas Pattern Jury Charge, 3 STATE BAR OF TEXAS, TEXAS PATTERN JURY CHARGES, PJC 71.06 (1990), except for the addition of the one sentence quoted above. Lemond does not contend, and the court of appeals did not conclude, that the additional sentence misstates the law. Rather, Lemond argues, and the court of appeals agreed, that it was error to include the sentence in the charge because it is the kind of surplus instruction discouraged by *Acord v. General Motors Corp.*, 669 S.W.2d 111 (Tex. 1984), and *Lemos v. Montez*, 680 S.W.2d 798 (Tex. 1984). The appeals court concluded that the error was not harmless because the sentence (1) conflicted with and diverted the jury's attention from other language in the charge, thereby confusing them, and (2) probably tilted or nudged the jury "one way or the other," thereby prejudicing the verdict.

Assuming, without deciding, that it was error to include the sentence in the charge, we do not agree that the error requires reversal. Besides the sentence quoted above, the trial court instructed the jury as follows:

> A "marketing defect" with respect to the product means the failure to give adequate warnings of the product's dangers that were known, or by the application of reasonably developed human skill or foresight should have been known, or failure to give adequate instructions to avoid such dangers, which failure rendered the product unreasonably dangerous as marketed.
>
> An "unreasonably dangerous" product is one that is dangerous to an extent beyond that which would be contemplated by the ordinary user of the product with the ordinary knowledge common to the community as to the product's characteristics.

The court of appeals did not identify the conflict between this language and the sentence complained of, and a comparison readily demonstrates there is none. It is not clear why the appeals court thought that the sentence diverted the jury's attention from the rest of the charge, but assuming it did, we do not see how the sentence could have misled or confused the jury. Also, because the sentence was entirely consistent with the charge as a whole, we do not see how it could have nudged the jury improperly. Unlike *Acord*, this case was not closely contended. After a three-week trial, the jury did not make a liability finding in Lemond's favor. The record does not reflect that Lemond's marketing defect claim was any stronger than his other claims, and we cannot see how the jury would have made a different finding. The court of appeals erred in reversing the trial court's judgment.

Lemond complains that he was entitled to an instruction on manufacturing defect, and that distributors of natural gas should be held to a higher standard of care because of the dangers that inhere in the product. The court of appeals addressed these complaints fully and, we believe, rejected them correctly.

Accordingly, a majority of the Court, without hearing oral argument, reverses the judgment of the court of appeals to the extent that it reverses the judgment of the trial court, affirms it in all other respects, and renders judgment that Lemond take nothing.

ENOCH, JUSTICE, took no part in the consideration or decision of this case.

FORD MOTOR CO.
v.
LEDESMA
242 S.W.3d 326
(Tex. 2007)

JUSTICE WILLETT delivered the opinion of the Court.

In this products liability case, Ford Motor Co. argues that the trial court reversibly erred in charging the jury by giving an incomplete definition of "manufacturing defect." We agree. Additionally, we hold that a frequently submitted definition of "producing cause" should no longer be used. We remand the case for a new trial under a jury charge that reflects our applicable caselaw, including our decision today.

I. Background

In March 1999, Tiburicio Ledesma, Jr. purchased a new Ford F-350 Super Duty pickup truck for his construction business. The truck had four rear tires, two on each side, surrounded by fiberglass fenders extending beyond the sides of the truck.

On June 5, 1999, Ledesma turned onto a two-lane street in Austin and began to accelerate. He testified that after shifting gears the truck suddenly began to lurch, and he lost control, striking two parked cars, a Firebird and a Civic, on the side of the street. The truck then hit the street curb and came to rest. At the time of the accident, the truck's odometer read about 4,100 miles.

Power from the truck engine is conveyed to the rear axle by the drive shaft, which connects the transmission in the front of the truck with the differential/rear axle assembly in the rear. As seen in the trial exhibit reproduced below, the rear-axle housing is attached to two sets of rear leaf springs by u-bolts, which wrap around the axle housing and are bolted to a rear spring plate that sits on top of the leaf-spring assembly. On each side of the truck, two u-bolts attach the rear-axle housing to a spring plate and set of leaf springs.

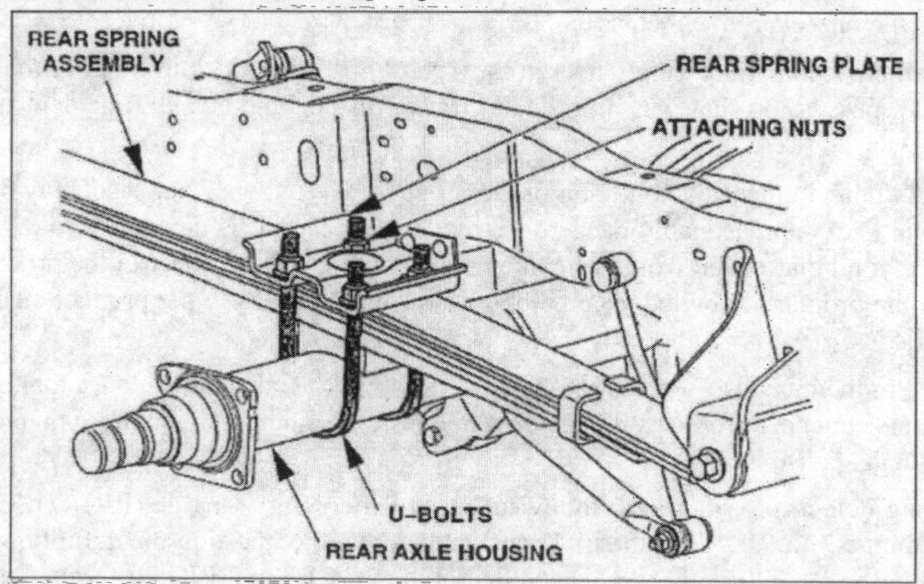

Both parties agree that the truck's rear leaf spring and axle assembly came apart and that this separation caused the drive shaft to dislodge from the transmission. The core dispute centers on *when* and *why* this malfunction occurred and whether it *caused* the collision or *resulted* from it. That is, did a manufacturing defect trigger the right rear-axle displacement and cause Ledesma to lose control of the truck and strike the parked cars (as Ledesma claims), or did the right rear axle detach when Ledesma struck the parked cars and curb (as Ford claims)?

At trial, Ledesma claimed that he lost control of the truck when its drive shaft separated from the transmission and "pronged" on the pavement, causing him to hit the parked cars. A police officer testified that he investigated the accident scene and prepared a report based on Ledesma's description of the accident. The report makes no mention of any other witnesses. Ledesma also presented two expert witnesses in support of his manufacturing defect claim, as discussed below.

Ford presented an expert, Dan May, in support of its theory that the axle-to-spring attachment failed, not because of a manufacturing defect, but because of the forces exerted on it when Ledesma struck the parked vehicles and curb. Among other efforts to discredit May, Ledesma emphasized to the jury that May was a long-time Ford employee and had never found a defect in a Ford product.

Ford also called the owner of the Firebird, Edward Plyant, who testified by deposition that he witnessed the accident from a driveway. Plyant testified that Ledesma was speeding and inattentive and struck the Firebird at a high rate of speed. Ledesma testified that Plyant did not see the accident, but came outside after hearing the ensuing commotion, and that Plyant had unsuccessfully sued Ledesma.

The jury sided 11-1 with Ledesma, finding that a manufacturing defect caused the accident and that Ledesma was not contributorily negligent, and awarding economic damages of $215,380. The court of appeals affirmed.[1]

* * *

B. Jury Charge

Ford complains that, over its objection, the trial court improperly instructed the jury on the definitions of manufacturing defect and producing cause. The jury affirmatively answered Question No. 1 of the jury charge, which asked:

> Was there a manufacturing defect in the 1999 Ford F-350 pickup truck at the time it left Ford's possession that was a producing cause of the June 5, 1999 incident in question?
>
> A "defect" means a condition of the product that renders it unreasonably dangerous. An "unreasonably dangerous" product is one that is dangerous to an extent beyond that which would be contemplated by the ordinary user of the product, with the ordinary knowledge common to the community as to the product's characteristics.
>
> "Producing cause" means an efficient, exciting, or contributing cause that, in a natural sequence, produces the incident in question. There may be more than one producing cause.

In defining defect, the trial court followed Texas Pattern Jury Charge (PJC) 71.3. As specified in the comment to PJC 71.3, the trial court included in the question the definition of producing cause found in PJC 70.1. Ford objected that both PJC 71.3 and PJC 70.1 were "not accurate

1 173 S.W.3d 78, 92.

under the law" and failed to track this Court's precedent. We agree. Ledesma may have *argued* a manufacturing defect to the jury, but the law requires the jury to determine specifically whether he had *proven* one. The jury here received a legally incorrect charge that omitted an indispensable element: that the product deviated, in its construction or quality, from its specifications or planned output in a manner that rendered it unreasonably dangerous.

1. The Court's Charge on Manufacturing Defect Failed to Include the Essential Element of a Deviation from Design

The trial court submitted the pattern jury charge's definition on manufacturing defect. We agree with Ford, however, that the model charge is erroneous, as it does not include the requirement that a manufacturing defect must deviate from its specifications or planned output in a manner that renders the product unreasonably dangerous. We established this standard in *American Tobacco Co. v. Grinnell,*[16] and in three other cases since *Grinnell* was issued a decade ago, we have recognized, with essentially identical statements, the "deviation from specifications or planned output" requirement. This requirement is separate from, and in addition to, the requirements that the product was defective when it left the manufacturer and that the defect was a producing cause of the plaintiff's injuries.

We note that the current Restatement of Torts essentially follows the same concept of a deviation from the manufacturer's design by providing that a product "contains a manufacturing defect when the product departs from its intended design even though all possible care was exercised in the preparation and marketing of the product . . . ."

The requirement of a deviation from the manufacturer's specifications or planned output serves the essential purpose of distinguishing a manufacturing defect from a design defect. PJC 71.3 refers to a "manufacturing defect" in the product "at the time it left" the manufacturer. A jury—without further guidance—may view any defect in a product at the time it leaves the manufacturer as satisfying the PJC's reference to a "manufacturing defect," rather than making the essential distinction between a manufacturing and design defect. As it stood, the court's charge merely inquired whether a "condition" of the product rendered it unreasonably dangerous. That "condition" could have been a design defect or a manufacturing defect.

The distinction is material. The danger of allowing a jury to conclude that the defect was or might have been a design defect is that "[a] design defect claim requires proof and a jury finding of a safer alternative design."[20] The charge did not make such an inquiry.

Moreover, requiring a deviation from specifications or planned output permits a jury to determine whether a specific defect caused the accident, rather than premising liability on a belief that a product failure, standing alone, is enough to find a product defect. Texas law does not generally recognize a product failure or malfunction, standing alone, as sufficient proof of a product defect. Instead, we have held that "a specific defect must be identified by competent evidence and other possible causes must be ruled out." Our law requires more than finding an undifferentiated "condition" that renders the product unreasonably dangerous, which is all the court's charge mandated. While a products liability claim does not of course require proof of manufacturer negligence, the deviation from design that caused the injury must be identified. Otherwise, the jury is

---

[16] 951 S.W.2d 420, 434 (Tex. 1997) ("Under Texas law, a plaintiff has a manufacturing defect claim when a finished product deviates, in terms of its construction or quality, from the specifications or planned output in a manner that renders it unreasonably dangerous.").

[20] Cooper Tire, 204 S.W.3d at 807 (*citing* TEX. CIV. PRAC. & REM. CODE § 82.005).

invited to find liability based on speculation as to the cause of the incident in issue.

Requiring proof of a deviation from manufacturer specifications or planned output also comports with our recognition that expert testimony is generally encouraged if not required to establish a products liability claim. If juries were generally free to infer a product defect and injury causation from an accident or product failure alone, without any proof of the specific deviation from design that caused the accident, expert testimony would hardly seem essential. Yet we have repeatedly said otherwise.

For these reasons, we hold that the court's charge was fundamentally flawed in omitting the requirement that the product deviate, in its construction or quality, from its specifications or planned output in a manner that renders it unreasonably dangerous.

2. The Erroneous Definition of Manufacturing Defect Is Reversible Error

* * *

Given that our trial courts routinely rely on the Pattern Jury Charges in submitting cases to juries, and we rarely disapprove of these charges, we conclude that the interests of justice would not be served by reversing and rendering judgment in favor of Ford. The more appropriate remedy is to reverse and remand for a new trial.

3. Producing Cause

Ford separately complains that the trial court improperly instructed the jury on producing cause. The trial court, following PJC 70.1, instructed the jury: " 'Producing cause' means an efficient, exciting, or contributing cause that, in a natural sequence, produces the incident in question. There may be more than one producing cause." Ford contends that this definition is an incorrect statement of Texas law, and that a valid definition would state that producing cause "means that cause which, in a natural sequence, was a substantial factor in bringing about an event, and without which the event would not have occurred. There may be more than one producing cause." Ford requested the trial court to use this definition.

We agree with Ledesma that the second part of the court's definition, recognizing that there may be more than one producing cause of an event, is correct. And we have seemed to sanction the first part, employing it ourselves several times in describing producing cause. But we have also described a producing cause as one "that is a substantial factor that brings about injury and without which the injury would not have occurred," the definition Ford asks us to adopt.

To say that a producing cause is "an efficient, exciting, or contributing cause that, in a natural sequence, produces the incident in question" is incomplete and, more importantly, provides little concrete guidance to the jury. Juries must ponder the meaning of "efficient" and "exciting" in this context. These adjectives are foreign to modern English language as a means to describe a cause, and offer little practical help to a jury striving to make the often difficult causation determination in a products case.

Defining producing cause as being a substantial factor in bringing about an injury, and without which the injury would not have occurred, is easily understood and conveys the essential components of producing cause that (1) the cause must be a substantial cause of the event in issue and (2) it must be a but-for cause, namely one without which the event would not have occurred. This is the definition that should be given in the jury charge.

III. Conclusion

We reverse the court of appeals' judgment and remand this case to the trial court for further proceedings.

Notes & Questions

1. *Product liability charges.* The charge in *Lone Star v. Lemond* probably included something like the following question:

> Was there a marketing defect in the gas at the time it left the possession of Lone Star Gas Company that was a producing cause of the injury in question?

Note the definition of "marketing defect" actually used in the charge, which is set out in the body of the supreme court's opinion. Compare that definition with the more general PJC definition of defect used in *Ford v. Ledesma.* What is the practical effect of the different definitions to parties trying a lawsuit?

2. *Causation.* Does the *Ledesma* opinion on producing cause mean that the PJC definition of "proximate cause" is erroneous? After *Ledesma,* the Pattern Jury Charge changed the definition of "proximate cause." How does the change to the causation definition affect the way lawyers try tort cases?

3. *Innovation in the charge.* Generally, the Supreme Court is not tolerant of judges changing charges that it has approved. This was especially true when the court was developing the law of products liability and trying to enforce the change to broad form submission, as in *Acord.* Therefore, is it any wonder that trial courts, like the trial court in *Ledesma,* feel that it is far safer to submit the charge set out in the PJC?

4. *The role of instructions generally.* As the Supreme Court has said:[1]

> The trial court must, when feasible, submit a cause to the jury by broad-form questions. TEX. R. CIV. P. 277. It is also required to give "such instructions and definitions as shall be proper to enable the jury to render a verdict." *Id.* An instruction is proper if it (1) assists the jury, (2) accurately states the law, and (3) finds support in the pleadings and evidence. Determining necessary and proper jury instructions is a matter within the trial court's discretion, and appellate review is for abuse of that discretion Rule 277 authorizes "such instructions and definitions as shall be proper to enable the jury to render a verdict."

The charge should provide definitions for legal or technical terms or common terms which have a special meaning in connection with litigation (e.g. "justification" in an intentional interference with contract case).[2] When the cause of action is grounded in statute, the statutory definition should be

---

[1] Columbia Rio Grande Healthcare, LLP, (Tex. 2009).

[2] *See, e.g.* Bell v. Missouri K.T.R. Co., 334 S.W.2d 513 (Tex. Civ. App.—Ft. Worth 1960, writ ref'd n.r.e.) *and* Texaco, Inc. v. Pennzoil Co., 729 S.W.2d 768 (Tex. Civ. App.—Houston [1st Dist.] 1987, writ ref'd n.r.e.).

followed as closely as possible.[3] Gratuitous lectures on the law are forbidden. As the court of appeals observed in *First State Bank and Trust Co. of Edinburg v. George*:[4]

> "The only function of an explanatory instruction in the charge is to aid and assist the jury in answering the issues submitted. The only requirement to be observed is that the trial court must give definitions of legal and other technical terms. Nothing else, however interesting, or, indeed, however relevant to the case in general, which does not aid the jury in answering the issue, is required."

But more recently, when reversing a trial court that refused a "loss of chance" instruction in a medical liability case,[5] the Supreme Court said:

> As this Court stated over a century ago when considering alleged charge error, "[w]e must look at the court's charge as practical experience teaches that a jury, untrained in the law, would view it." *Galveston, H. & S.A. Ry. Co. v. Washington,* 94 Tex. 510, 63 S.W. 534, 538 (1901). It asks too much of lay jurors, untrained in the law, to distill the correct Texas legal standard for loss of chance from the general proximate cause instruction given by the trial court. Columbia's requested loss of chance instruction would have assisted the jury, was an accurate statement of applicable law, and was supported by the pleadings and evidence. The trial court abused its discretion by refusing to give it.

5. *The location of definitions*. When a term appears in a single jury question, the definition should appear with the question. However, definitions and instructions relating to terms used more than once in a charge should appear at the beginning of the charge immediately after the Rule 226(a) general instructions. "It is at this location in the charge that terms such as preponderance of the evidence, negligence, ordinary care, and proximate cause are ordinarily placed."

6. *Burden of proof*. Would the following instruction, following a question, correctly place the burden of proof in a routine civil case? "Answer 'yes' or 'no' as you may determine from a preponderance of the evidence." No. It does not say who has the burden of establishing the correctness of a "yes" answer.[6] The correct instruction, authorized in the Pattern Jury Charges, is as follows:

> Answer "yes" or "no" to all questions unless you are told otherwise. A "yes" answer must be based on a preponderance of the evidence [unless you are told otherwise]. Whenever a question requires an answer other than "yes" or "no," your answer must be based on a preponderance of the evidence [unless you are told otherwise].
>
> The term "preponderance of the evidence" means the greater weight of credible evidence presented in this case. If you do not find that a preponderance of the evidence supports a "yes" answer, then answer "no." A preponderance of the evidence is not measured by the number of witnesses or by the number of documents admitted in evidence. For a fact to be

---

[3] Brown v. American Transfer and Storage Co., 601 S.W.2d 931 (Tex. 1980); *and In re* Guardianship of Dahl, 590 S.W.2d 191 (Tex. Civ. App.—Amarillo 1979, writ ref'd n.r.e.).

[4] 519 S.W.2d 198 (Tex. Civ. App.—Corpus Christi 1975, writ ref'd n.r.e.).

[5] The defendant had requested the following instruction after the definition of proximate cause: "You are instructed that Alice H. Hawley must have had greater than a fifty percent (50%) chance of survival on November 28, 2000 for the negligence of Rio Grande Regional Hospital to be a proximate cause of injury to Alice H. Hawley."

[6] Southern Pine Lumber Co. v. King, 161 S.W.2d 483, 484 (Tex. 1942).

proved by a preponderance of the evidence, you must find that the fact is more likely true than not true.[7]

7. *Burden of proof—special cases.* In juvenile cases, commitment cases, and cases involving termination of parental rights, all of which have criminal or quasi-criminal aspects, the burden of proof is greater than a preponderance of the evidence.[8] Also, when one claims that an instrument purporting on its face to be a deed is, in fact, a mortgage or deed of trust, the burden of proof is by evidence that is "clear, unequivocal and convincing."[9] And § 41.003 of the CPRC (the 1995 tort reform legislation) requires "clear and convincing" proof for punitive damages. "Clear and convincing" proof is that which produces in the mind of the trier of fact a "firm belief or conviction" as to the truth of the allegations sought to be established. § 41.001 CPRC.

8. *Rule 226a and Pattern Jury Charge additions.* Rule 226a contains required admonitory instructions that should be included in every charge. The State Bar's Pattern Jury Charges suggest additional routine or "boilerplate" charges to those set out in Rule 226a. The additions include a routine instruction on burden of proof, an instruction on the nature of the presiding juror's duties, and an instruction that, if commonly understood terms have a special meaning, that meaning is provided by definition and the jurors must accept it "in place of any other meaning."

9. *Unanimity and 10-2 verdicts.* In 1973 the Supreme Court amended the rules to allow verdicts in civil cases to be nonunanimous (that is, by 10-2 or 11-1 vote in addition to 12-0, or 5-1 in six-juror cases). In 2003, the Legislature changed this in part and required that the jury be unanimous when awarding exemplary damages. The Supreme Court has revised Rules 226a and 292 to implement the legislature's changes.

---

2. *Inferential Rebuttals*

Inferential rebuttal "defenses" are not affirmative defenses. An affirmative defense is usually one asserted by way of confession and avoidance, which takes as true the P's claim but asserts facts which, if proven—limitations, for example—will control over P's claims and defeat them. Many of such traditional defenses are listed in Rule 94. D has the burden of pleading and proving such defenses.

Inferential rebuttals, by contrast, do not confess and avoid P's claims. Neither do they attack them directly by simply denying plaintiff's allegations. (Plaintiff claims that defendant was negligent; D says he was not negligent.) Inferential rebuttal attacks an element of P's claim *inferentially* by proving something inconsistent with it. It rebuts by inference because it asserts an inconsistent truth: "X can't be true because Y is true." "I can't be negligent because the collision was *unavoidable*—that is, it happened without *anyone's* being negligent." Thus, the inferential rebuttal of unavoidable accident attacks (or rebuts by inference) P's claim that D was negligent. Similarly, the inferential rebuttal of sole proximate cause rebuts P's claim that D's negligence was *a* proximate cause. "If X's acts were the *sole* cause, how can D's acts be *a* cause?"

---

7 1 PJC 1.3.

8 *See* MCDONALD, TEXAS CIVIL PRACTICE page 208.

9 *See* Griswold v. Citizens Nat'l Bank in Waxahachie, 285 S.W.2d 791 (Tex. 1955).

As the introductory materials note, during the days of "separate and distinct" issues, inferential rebuttals caused conflict and confusion when they were submitted as jury questions, particularly in light of the need to place the burden of proof on the plaintiff. Now inferential rebuttals are submitted by instructions, not questions, reducing the confusion and eliminating the possibility of conflicting jury findings.

Some of the old inferential rebuttals, such as "assumption of the risk" and "last clear chance" have disappeared because courts abolished them when the doctrine of comparative causation was adopted in Texas—the comparative causation question "subsumed" these inferential rebuttals. And it can be argued—it *has* been argued—that the rest of these "rebuttals" are really only defensive arguments and have no place in the charge. Whatever the merits of this argument, the practice is deeply rooted and shows no sign of receding. The following cases and notes may help to clarify.

DILLARD
v.
TEXAS ELECTRIC COOPERATIVE
157 S.W.3d 429
(Tex. 2005)

O'NEILL, JUSTICE.

In this personal injury and wrongful death case, we must decide whether the trial court abused its discretion in refusing to submit one of two different instructions on the defendants' inferential rebuttal defenses. An inferential rebuttal defense operates to rebut an essential element of the plaintiff's case by proof of other facts. For example, the defendants in this case contended at trial that the fatal auto accident in issue was not caused by their negligence, but rather by the presence of cattle on the roadway or by the conduct of the cattle's owner who allowed them to be there. The jury rejected these defenses and returned a verdict for the plaintiffs, upon which the trial court rendered judgment. The court of appeals, however, reversed and remanded the case for a new trial, concluding that the jury needed more than one inferential rebuttal instruction for a full consideration of the case. Because we conclude that the trial court's instruction sufficiently informed the jury about the defendants' inferential rebuttal defenses, we reverse the court of appeals' judgment and remand the case for that court to consider other issues that the defendants raised but the court did not address.

I

Texas Electric Cooperative (TEC) of Jasper, Texas, manufactures and sells utility poles. On the evening of May 27, 1996, TEC dispatched Stephen Bumstead to deliver a load of poles to Muenster, Texas, 304 miles away. About 120 miles out, traveling west on U.S. Highway 175 at about ten o'clock at night, Bumstead crested a hill and saw several dark cows on the road. Unable to stop his loaded tractor-trailer rig quickly enough without jeopardizing control, Bumstead collided with one or more of the cows, leaving one dead in the eastbound lane about 250 feet from a bridge crossing the Neches River. Maintaining control, Bumstead proceeded over the bridge and parked his truck on the shoulder about 1,500 feet beyond the dead cow. Bumstead immediately radioed an approaching trucker to warn him of the hazard ahead. Learning that the trucker had a cell phone, Bumstead requested that he call 911 to report the accident. Bumstead turned off his headlights and waited in his truck for help to arrive.

A few minutes later, Mae Joyce Brown drove past Bumstead's rig on to the bridge heading east on Highway 175. At the same time, the Dillards were approaching the bridge from the east in the unobstructed westbound lane. Crossing the bridge, Brown saw the approaching headlights of the Dillards' vehicle but did not see the dead cow in her lane of traffic. When she hit the cow, her car was thrown into the westbound lane and into the Dillards' vehicle, killing Kenneth Dillard and injuring his wife and daughter. Brown, too, was injured in the accident.

The Dillards sued TEC and Bumstead for negligence, seeking damages for their personal injuries and for Kenneth's death. Brown intervened in the suit. The Dillards and Brown subsequently joined a number of surrounding landowners as defendants, but these claims were dismissed or abandoned before trial because the cattle involved in the accident could not be traced to any of these defendants. Also before trial, Brown settled her claims against TEC and Bumstead, leaving only the Dillards' claims for the jury.

At trial, the Dillards contended that TEC and Bumstead were negligent in operating an overloaded and top-heavy truck that could not be safely stopped when it encountered obstacles in the road, and in failing to warn approaching motorists, like Brown, of the hazard that the first accident created. TEC responded that its driver had insufficient time to take evasive action and thus could not have avoided hitting the cows despite the exercise of ordinary care. TEC also claimed that its driver was not responsible for the second accident that killed Kenneth Dillard and injured his wife and daughter because that accident was solely caused by the conduct of whatever unknown person allowed the cows to be on the roadway in the first instance.

At the charge conference, TEC requested that its defensive theories be presented to the jury in two inferential rebuttal instructions, one on unavoidable accident and the other on sole proximate cause. On sole proximate cause, TEC asked that the definition of proximate cause include the following sentence:

> There may be more than one proximate cause of an event, but if an act or omission of any person not a party to the suit was the 'sole proximate cause' of an occurrence, then no act or omission of any other persons could have been a proximate cause.

. . . The trial court refused to include this instruction, but agreed to instruct the jury on unavoidable accident, which it did in the following definition of proximate cause:

> PROXIMATE CAUSE means that cause which, in a natural and continuous sequence, produces an event, and without which cause such event would not have occurred. In order to be a proximate cause, the act or omission complained of must be such that a person using ordinary care would have foreseen that the event, or some similar event, might reasonably result therefrom. There may be more than one proximate cause of an event.
>
> An occurrence may be an "unavoidable accident," that is, an event not proximately caused by the negligence of any party to it.

See PJC 2.4 (Proximate Cause) & PJC 3.4 (Unavoidable Accident). The charge also included an instruction on spoliation based upon TEC's failure to produce Bumstead's trip logbook and any evidence of time and speed that it might contain. Guided by the court's charge, the jury returned a verdict upon which the trial court rendered judgment in the Dillards' favor.

. . . [T]he court of appeals concluded that the trial court erred in refusing TEC's sole-cause instruction because a jury could have reasonably inferred from the cows' presence on the roadway that whoever owned them was the sole cause of both accidents. The court of appeals reversed the trial court's judgment and remanded the case for a new trial. We granted the Dillards' petition for review to consider the propriety of the trial court's charge in light of the instructions that were given.

II

When defendants blame an occurrence on someone or something other than themselves, the Texas Pattern Jury Charges provide multiple alternatives. There is a sole-proximate-cause instruction if the occurrence is caused by a "person not a party to the suit."[1] There is an unavoidable-accident instruction if the occurrence is not caused by "the negligence of any party to it."[2] There is a new-and-independent-cause instruction if the occurrence is caused by someone else later.[3] There is a sudden-emergency instruction if the occurrence is caused by something other than the defendant's negligence and arises suddenly.[4] And finally, there is an act-of-God instruction if the occurrence is caused by "the violence of nature."[5] The purpose of these instructions is to advise the jurors, in the appropriate case, that they do not have to place blame on a party to the suit if the evidence shows that conditions beyond the party's control caused the accident in question or that the conduct of some person not a party to the litigation caused it.

TEC urges that it was entitled to two separate inferential rebuttal instructions here because there is evidence that the accidents may have been caused by a condition beyond its control-the cattle on the roadway—or by someone not a party to the litigation—either the unknown cattle owner or Brown. The Dillards contend, however, that there is no evidence that an unknown cattle owner did or failed to do anything to cause these accidents. They further maintain that TEC abandoned its claim that Brown caused the second accident by arguing at trial that no one involved in the accident was to blame—they were just "all in the wrong place at the wrong time." But rather than focus on whether or not there was evidence to support each of TEC's proposed inferential rebuttal defenses, we think it more appropriate to examine the adequacy of the charge that was given.

---

1 COMM. ON PATTERN JURY CHARGES, STATE BAR OF TEX., TEXAS PATTERN JURY CHARGES—GENERAL NEGLIGENCE AND INTENTIONAL PERSONAL TORTS PJC 3.2 (2003) ("There may be more than one proximate cause of an event, but if an act or omission of any person not a party to the suit was the 'sole proximate cause' of an occurrence, then no act or omission of any other person could have been a proximate cause.").

2 *Id.* PJC 3.4 ("An occurrence may be an 'unavoidable accident,' that is, an event not proximately caused by the negligence of any party to it.").

3 *Id.* PJC 3.1 ("'New and independent cause' means the act or omission of a separate and independent agency, not reasonably foreseeable, that destroys the causal connection, if any, between the act or omission inquired about and the occurrence in question and thereby becomes the immediate cause of the occurrence.").

4 *Id.* PJC 3.3 ("If a person is confronted by an 'emergency' arising suddenly and unexpectedly, which was not proximately caused by any negligence on his part and which, to a reasonable person, requires immediate action without time for deliberation, his conduct in such an emergency is not negligence or failure to use ordinary care if, after such emergency arises, he acts as a person of ordinary prudence would have acted under the same or similar circumstances.").

5 *Id.* PJC 3.5 ("An occurrence is caused by an act of God if it is caused directly and exclusively by the violence of nature, without human intervention or cause, and could not have been prevented by reasonable foresight or care.").

The trial court's charge included the following instruction: "An occurrence may be an 'unavoidable accident,' that is, an event not proximately caused by the negligence of any party to it." That instruction is a verbatim recitation from the Texas Pattern Jury Charges. . . . Although we have previously said that this instruction ordinarily applies to causes such as "fog, snow, sleet, wet or slick pavement, or obstruction of view," or to resolve a case involving "a very young child [who is] legally incapable of negligence," the instruction's language is not so limiting. The instruction merely informs the jury that it may consider causes of the occurrence other than the negligence of the parties. . . .

Under the unavoidable-accident instruction that the trial court submitted, TEC was free to argue to the jury that no one's conduct—including Brown's—caused the accident, a far easier burden than showing that others were negligent. And that's what TEC chose to do. Although TEC pled in the alternative that Brown's negligence was the sole proximate cause of the second accident, TEC did not contend during trial that Brown was to blame for the accident. . . . Whatever the conduct of an unknown cattle owner might have been, it did not justify two separate inferential rebuttal instructions on what essentially was one defense. Because the instruction the trial court gave was sufficiently broad to include all shades of TEC's inferential rebuttal theories concerning the cattle, the trial court did not err in rejecting TEC's additional request on this same issue.

Although, as we have said, the traditional instructions do not always further the jury's understanding of the defense or conform to current broad-form practices, we believe that they do serve a legitimate purpose. . . . The standard broad-form question is structured such that the jury is not asked whether any particular person was negligent, but whether "the negligence, if any," of particular persons proximately caused an occurrence. There is at least a potential implication in this phraseology that the occurrence *was* caused by *someone's* negligence. We see no harm in explaining to the jury through an inferential rebuttal instruction that no such implication is intended. But giving multiple instructions on every possible rebuttal inference has the potential to skew the jury's analysis in the other direction.

As we have noted, the Texas Pattern Jury Charges presently parse inferential rebuttal defenses into five separate instructions. . . . Many of these instructions overlap to create redundancies that encourage parties to request several so that the point can be repeatedly emphasized. . . . For example, an occurrence caused by severe weather could justify either an unavoidable-accident or an act-of-God instruction. Similarly, the instructions on new and independent cause and sole proximate cause can cover much of the same territory. Such redundancy is contrary to the spirit of broad-form submission.

More important, these instructions often draw distinctions among outside causes that are irrelevant to what jurors must decide. Under broad-form submission rules, jurors need not agree on every detail of what occurred so long as they agree on the legally relevant result. Thus, jurors may agree that a defendant failed to follow approved safety practices without deciding each reason that the defendant may have failed to do so. Similarly, the jurors here could have unanimously found Bumstead negligent, even if half believed the negligent act was overloading his truck and half believed it was failing to warn oncoming traffic—acts that preceded two different collisions.

With respect to inferential rebuttal issues, jurors need not agree on what person or thing caused an occurrence, so long as they agree it was not the defendant. If some jurors here blamed the cattle (unavoidable accident or sudden emergency) and the rest blamed the unknown cow owner (sole proximate cause), their differences would be irrelevant--they would properly return a unanimous defense verdict. Just as jurors may find against a defendant without agreeing on which precise acts were negligent, they should be able to find the opposite without agreeing on the precise reason. The trial court's instruction presented that alternative to the jury, and TEC was entitled to nothing more.

III

Because the trial court's charge adequately informed the jury about TEC's inferential rebuttal defenses, the court of appeals erred in holding that the case should be retried under a more elaborate and granulated charge. Accordingly, we reverse the judgment of the court of appeals and remand the case to that court for consideration of the other issues that TEC raised.

Notes & Questions

1. *Harm?* If a trial court erroneously includes an inferential rebuttal in the charge, is the jury really misled by this submission? Is there a real likelihood that the evil of conflicting findings lurked here as it did with the old confusing submission: "Do you find from a preponderance of the evidence that the collision in question was not the result of an unavoidable accident?" It seems unlikely.

2. *Unavoidable accident*. Some justices appear to believe that the unavoidable accident instruction doesn't much matter. Justice Brister, joined by Justices Hecht and Willett said in a concurring opinion in *Bed, Bath & Beyond*:[1]

> Accidents happen. Sometimes even when no one is negligent . . . .
>
> But I would add that the trial court did nothing wrong. It is true the unavoidable accident instruction has historically been associated only with defendants who blame children or the weather, but (as we noted recently) *that is not what it says*. All it says is that accidents may be nobody's "fault" in the legal sense. I would not presume such a truism erroneous.
>
> The assumption that such a simple instruction will "nudge" jurors toward a defense verdict reflects a very low opinion of their intelligence. Do we nudge jurors toward a plaintiff's verdict by listing the defendant *first* in every multi-party negligence or proportionate-responsibility question. Jurors may not know the secret meaning of the unavoidable-accident instruction, but the are not cattle who will be stampeded to an improper verdict by something like this.

3. *New and independent cause*. The Texas Supreme Court has discussed this inferential rebuttal instruction at least three times since *Dillard* was decided—it does not appear to be an instruction that will go away. In one case,[2] the majority held that although it was error not to submit the instruction in this case, the error was harmless. Justice Brister wrote a concurring opinion that again basically said that the instruction doesn't matter. In another,[3] the court held that the trial court did not err in refusing the instruction because the evidence did not support its submission.

---

[1] 211 S.W.3d at 760.

[2] Dew v. Crown Derrick Erectors, 208 S.W.3d 448 (Tex. 2006).

[3] Columbia Rio Grande Healthcare LLP v. Hawley, 284 S.W.3d 851 (Tex. 2009).

4. *Inferential rebuttals and Casteel.* In the third and most important new and independent cause case, the court held that including the instruction despite a lack of evidence supporting it was harmless under traditional harm analysis, and did not raise a *Casteel* issue where harm is presumed. The court said, "Inferential rebuttal issues are distinct from theories of liability and damage elements because they 'cannot be submitted in the jury charge as separate questions and instead must be presented through jury instructions.'" The "only theory of liability asserted … was negligence."[4]

5. *Inferential rebuttals and pleadings.* Generally speaking, a party must plead a claim or defense, introduce evidence on each element of it, and request appropriate jury questions and instructions on it.[5] When those steps are taken, it is reversible error to refuse an appropriate charge.[6] There must be appropriate pleadings on claims or affirmative defenses. Rule 278 says that a general denial does not entitle the pleader to the submission of a jury *question.* But what about an *instruction*? Take inferential rebuttals, for example. Is the defendant required to plead unavoidable accident in order to get an instruction on it? The courts of appeals seem to be divided on the question.[7] Similar problems arise with other theories which are not themselves claims or affirmative defenses, but are a proper subject for instructions; res ipsa loquitur, for example. What does all this suggest to the cautious pleader?

6. *Hidden inferential rebuttal questions.* In *Lemos v. Montez*,[8] the Supreme Court held that the following question was erroneous because it constituted an inferential rebuttal *question*:

Whose negligence, if any, do you find proximately caused the collision?

a. Defendant
b. Plaintiff
c. Both
d. Neither

The Court held that the inclusion of "neither" required the plaintiff to negate the inferential rebuttal of unavoidable accident. The correct way to submit the question is to ask the jury to answer "yes" or "no" as to both parties, and include the unavoidable accident instruction if raised by the evidence.

Inferential rebuttal questions can be hidden in other types of questions as well. Suppose you represent a discharged employee in a dispute regarding the amount of an agreed salary. Your client, the plaintiff ex-employee, contends that it was $3,000 per month. The defendant employer contends that it was $2,000 per month. The court has agreed to your request to submit the following jury

4 Thota v. Young, 366 S.W.3d 678 (Tex. 2012).

5 *See, e.g.,* H. E. Butt Grocery Co. v. Warner, 845 S.W.2d 258 (Tex. 1992) (holding that because the charge fairly submitted to the jury the disputed facts, the trial court refused to submit the question and instructions was not harmful error).

6 Exxon Corp. v. Perez, 842 S.W.2d 629 (Tex. 1992).

7 *Compare* Heritage Manor v. Tidball, 724 S.W.2d 952 (Tex. App.—San Antonio 1987, no writ)(pleadings required for sole cause) *with* Missouri Pacific RR Co. v. United Transports, Inc., 518 S.W.2d 904 (Tex. Civ. App.—Houston [1st Dist] 1975, writ ref'd n.r.e.) (pleadings not required for sudden emergency). *See also* Columbia Rio Grande Healthcare L.L.P. v. Hawley, 284 S.W.3d 851 (Tex. 2009) (holding that pleadings supported new and independent cause instruction).

8 680 S.W.2d 798 (Tex. 1984).

question: "Was the agreed monthly salary $3,000?" Defendant has requested in writing the following jury question: "Was the agreed monthly salary $2,000?" The defendant urges that this is necessary in order to submit his theory of the case. The judge asks you if you have an objection to the defendant's requested question. Do you? Isn't this an inferential rebuttal question inviting conflicting findings? Probably. Isn't there a problem with the burden of proof? Definitely.

---

3. *Knowing the Effect of Answers & Comments on the Weight*

Read Rule 277.

H.E. BUTT GROCERY CO.
v.
BILOTTO
985 S.W.2d 22
(Tex. 1998)

SPECTOR, JUSTICE.

The issue in this cause is whether a jury charge instruction predicating a damages question on a finding of fifty percent or less comparative negligence violates Rule 277 of the Texas Rules of Civil Procedure. The trial court submitted the jury instruction over HEB's objection and the jury found HEB and Bilotto each were fifty percent negligent. The court of appeals affirmed. We now affirm the judgment of the court of appeals.

Vinnie Bilotto suffered back injuries when he slipped and fell in an H.E. Butt Grocery Company (HEB) store. He sued HEB for negligence and gross negligence. The case was tried to a jury. Before the trial court charged the jury, HEB objected to a proposed instruction given after jury question number two. Question one read as follows:

> Did the negligence, if any, of the persons named below proximately cause the occurrence in question?

Answer "YES" or "NO" for each of the following:

> (a) H.E. BUTT GROCERY COMPANY
>
> (b) VINNIE BILOTTO

The jury answered "YES" for both HEB and Bilotto. Question two then asked the jury:

> What percentage of the negligence that caused the occurrence in question do you find to be attributable to each of those found by you, in your answer to Question No. 1, to have been negligent?
>
> (a) H.E. BUTT GROCERY COMPANY
>
> (b) VINNIE BILOTTO

The jury found both HEB and Bilotto fifty percent negligent. The instruction that followed question two, which is nearly identical to Texas Pattern Jury Charge 80.1, read:

> If, in answer to Question No. 1, you have answered "NO" for VINNIE BILOTTO, or if, in answer to Question No. 2 you have found that 50 percent or less of the negligence that

> caused the occurrence is attributable to VINNIE BILOTTO, then answer Question No. 3. Otherwise, do not answer Question No. 3.

Question three then asked the jury to assess the damages, if any, that would reasonably compensate Bilotto.

HEB objected that the instruction after question two impermissibly informed the jury of the legal effect of its answer. The trial court overruled the objection and then instructed the jury. The jury found that HEB and Bilotto were each fifty percent negligent and awarded Bilotto damages. The issue we must resolve is whether the trial court erred in submitting the jury instruction.

The trial court is given wide latitude to determine the propriety of explanatory instructions and definitions. We hold that the trial court did not err in giving this instruction.

We adopted Rule 277 in 1941. At the time, Texas courts were required by statute to submit the jury charge using special issues. Over the years, however, it became apparent that this special-issue approach had overloaded the charge with "granulated issues" and had led to more and more reversals on appeal. As a result of these problems, in 1973 we amended Rule 277 to permit the broad-form submission of jury questions.

In 1987, we again amended Rule 277 and made the broad-form submission of the jury charge mandatory. More importantly for this case, we also added language indicating that "[t]he court may predicate the damage question or questions upon affirmative findings of liability." This language determines the outcome of this dispute.

In response to question one, the jury determined that both HEB and Bilotto proximately caused Bilotto's injuries. In question two, the jury found that each party was fifty percent negligent. Because the jury found Bilotto only fifty percent negligent, in light of our comparative negligence law, the effect of the jury's answer to question two was to establish HEB's liability. The instruction that followed question two predicated the damages question on the affirmative finding of HEB's liability found in question two. The 1987 amendment to Rule 277 expressly authorizes such a conditional submission. Therefore, because this instruction is expressly authorized by Rule 277, the court did not err in giving the instruction.

HEB nevertheless contends that the instruction was improper because it informed the jury of the legal effect of its answers. However, Rule 277 states that "[t]he court's charge shall not be objectionable on the ground that it incidentally constitutes a comment on the weight of the evidence or advises the jury of the effect of their answers when it is properly a part of an instruction or definition." *Id.* (emphasis added). Thus, following the Rule, the court's charge was not objectionable on the grounds HEB asserts if it only incidentally informed the jury of the legal effect of its answers.

Initially, we note that the clear trend among states that have considered the issue is to permit the jury to know the ultimate effect of its answers. Nevertheless, when an instruction merely directs the jury to answer a damages question only if some condition or conditions have been met, it does not directly instruct the jury about the legal effect of its answers.

To be a direct comment on the weight of the evidence, the issue submitted must suggest to the jury the trial court's opinion on the matter. Similarly, to directly advise the jury of the legal effect of its answers, the issue submitted must instruct the jury how to answer each question in order for the plaintiff or defendant to prevail. PJC 80.1 does not directly inform the jury of the legal effect of its answers, but merely directs the jury to answer the damages question only if certain conditions are satisfied. Therefore, PJC 80.1 merely incidentally informs the jury of the legal effect of its answers.

HEB argues that our decision in *Grasso v. Cannon Ball Motor Freight Lines*, 81 S.W.2d 482 (Tex. 1935), controls the outcome of this case. In *Grasso*, the trial court instructed the jury:

> If, in response to the foregoing question, you have answered that the defendant's truck was operated in a negligent manner, and that such negligence, if any, caused the injury to the plaintiff, and if you have also answered that the plaintiff was not guilty of negligence, contributing to the accident, then you will answer the following question; otherwise, you need not answer the following question.

We held that this instruction impermissibly told the jury "that they must find the defendant guilty of negligence, and the plaintiff not guilty of contributory negligence, in order for the plaintiff to recover." We held that "[s]uch a charge is undoubtedly in violation of our special issue statutes."

PJC 80.1, albeit logically indistinguishable from the instruction we found impermissible in Grasso, does not violate Rule 277. The reason PJC 80.1 is permissible where the *Grasso* instruction was not is that *Grasso* predated the amendments to Rule 277.

The effect of our amendments to Rule 277 is that the rule now allows instructions such as the one at issue in *Grasso* and in this case. First, the Rule specifically authorizes courts to condition a damage question on an affirmative finding of liability. Next, this instruction only incidentally informs the jury of the legal effect of its answers. Therefore, it is in line with current Rule 277.

* * *

We do not overrule today the decades of Texas case law that holds that Texas juries cannot be directly informed of the legal effect of their answers. We do hold, however, that because conditional damages jury instructions such as PJC 80.1 are expressly permitted by Rule 277, the trial court did not err in giving the instruction. As a result, this charge is permissible under Rule 277 of the Texas Rules of Civil Procedure. Accordingly, we affirm the judgment of the court of appeals.

JUSTICE GONZALEZ, concurring.

I agree with the Court that the charge in this case is permissible because it only incidentally informed the jury of the effect of its answers. However, I think it is time to reconsider whether it makes sense to try to keep juries in the dark about the effect of their answers in these cases. When we moved from special issue practice to broad-form submissions, we dramatically reduced the number of cases in which the jury might not know for sure the effect of its answers. In the few remaining cases in which the jury might not know the legal effect of its answers, I question whether it serves the cause of justice to continue blindfolding the jury. I would join the growing number of states that allow the jury to know the legal effect of its answers.

* * *

JUSTICE BAKER, joined by JUSTICE ENOCH and JUSTICE OWEN, dissenting.

* * *

Here, the instruction informed the jury that for Bilotto to recover damages, they had to find him 50% or less responsible for his injuries. This instruction essentially told the jury what it needed to do to ensure Bilotto's recovery.

The Court concedes that PJC 80.1 is logically indistinguishable from the instruction the Court found impermissible in *Grasso*. However, the Court asserts the instruction does not violate Rule 277. The Court attempts to discount *Grasso* because it was decided before the 1988 amendments. However, the additions to Rule 277 do not affect *Grasso's* primary reasoning. The 1988 amendments did not remove the language prohibiting jury instructions from informing jurors about the legal effect of their answers. The Court does not argue that the average juror knows the 50% rule, and rightfully so because that argument cannot seriously be made. In my view, it is clear that the instruction in this case told the jury something they did not know about the findings they were making. *Grasso* clearly prohibits such an instruction. Therefore, *Grasso* is still good law and supports the proposition that the jury instruction in this case did more than incidentally inform the jury about the legal effect of their answers.

There are also policy reasons why the trial court should not condition damage findings on a finding that a plaintiff is no more than 50% negligent. That bar to recovery is only one part of a comprehensive legislative comparative negligence scheme. Without question, such an instruction provides the jury with information they can use to thwart legislative policy. Clearly, if the trial court instructs the jury on how the comparative fault system operates, then the jury can adjust its answers accordingly. This instruction to the jury is a surplus instruction that is an impermissible comment that tilts or nudges the jury one way.

JUSTICE HECHT, joined by JUSTICE OWEN, dissenting. [Omitted.]

Notes & Questions

1. *The role of the jury.* Are juries simply fact-finders, or are they representatives of the community who bring the community's values and views of justice to the legal system? Those who stress the jury as a representative democratic institution, an institution that injects a measure of humanity and justice into the dry law, usually favor broader questions and more general instructions because these allow the jury to "do justice" as the jurors see it in each case. Broad-form questions let the jury know the effect of its answers, and juries tend to favor the individual against the corporate litigant. Those who stress the uniform application of the law will usually favor more detailed jury questions and instructions because these are ways to confine the jury's discretion and promote uniform application of the law.

2. *Comments on the weight of the evidence.* Because broad form questions require instructions to properly inform the jury, it is inevitable that parties will object to some of those instructions as comments on the weight of the evidence. Remember the opinions earlier in the chapter where instructions added to approved charges were objected to as "comments on the weight of the evidence." Any party can claim that instructions that tend to nudge the jury in favor of the opponent's side of the case are impermissible comments on the weight of the evidence. But, in order to forestall complaints regarding appropriate broad-form questions, Rule 277 provides that the court "shall not in its charge comment *directly* on the weight of the evidence." (Emphasis added.) Therefore, the appropriate objection is that the charge comments *directly* on the weight of the evidence, "incidental" comments being acceptable. To be an impermissible comment on the weight of the evidence, a charge must directly comment on the evidence. How much is direct? The Court says it must suggest to the jury the trial court's opinion on the matter and/or instruct the jury how to answer the question. Given these standards, is this a viable objection to the charge in most cases?

3. *Questions containing assumptions: conditioning instructions.* A question incorporating a conclusion on a controverted matter may be made acceptable by putting it after a conditioning instruction which does not allow the jury to reach the question until it has found that the assumption is true. For example, in one case the jury was asked:

> Do you find from a preponderance of the evidence that *knowing Plaintiff to be misled as to material facts concerning insurance coverage*, Aetna intentionally kept Plaintiff misled *by concealing material facts from Plaintiff*, thereby causing Plaintiff to pay its own attorney's fees, proximately causing financial loss to plaintiff?

The Court of Appeals held that the question was an impermissible comment on the weight of the evidence. The question sought to inquire about two fact issues, (1) that Aetna knew Martin was misled as to material facts concerning insurance coverage; and (2) that Aetna concealed material facts from Martin, but it erroneously assumed the existence of (1) and inquired about (2).[1]

4. "*If any.*" There is another way to ask questions which make assumptions about controverted matters. The liberal use of such phrases as "if any" or "if any you have found" will often render the question harmless and acceptable.[2] For example, when the existence of *any* damages is challenged, the damages instruction to "answer in dollars and cents" should be followed by the term "if any," though a failure to object waives the point.[3] The practice can be overdone, however, and can itself be attacked as a comment if an uncontroverted event or injury is followed routinely by the term "if any."[4]

D. Preservation of Error

Read Rules 273-278.

1. *Form of Complaints*

Generally, if a party wants to complain on appeal that there is an error in the charge that requires reversal, that party must point out the error to the trial judge before the charge is given to the jury. Think about what those errors might be based upon the opinions we have read up to now.

The charge might be too broad or too narrow; or there may be no evidence to support the submission of a question to the jury. An instruction or definition may be legally incorrect or comment on the weight of the evidence or tell the jury the effect of its answers. The charge might omit an element of a cause of action or defense, or it may omit an entire theory upon which a par-

[1] Aetna Casualty & Surety Company v. Martin Surgical Supply Company, 689 S.W.2d 263 (Tex. App.—Houston [1st Dist.] 1985, writ ref'd n.r.e.).

[2] T.E.I.A. v. McKay, 210 S.W.2d 147 (Tex. 1948) *see* cases collected at 4 MCDONALD & CARLSON, TEX. CIV. PRAC., page 185 § 22:12, note 125 under "Qualifying Words."

[3] Justice Life Ins. Co. v. Orgain, 339 S.W.2d 230 (Tex. Civ. App.—Dallas 1960, no writ).

[4] *See, e.g.*, Gordon v. Levias, 356 S.W.2d 462 (Tex. Civ. App.—Beaumont 1962, writ ref'd n.r.e.).

ty relies. The charge may include a ground of recovery or defense that is not in the pleadings or on which there is no evidence.

Now think about how these errors might arise in the charge. The error might be an "omission"—there is something (a question, instruction or definition) that is missing from the charge. Or the error may be a "defect"—something contained in the charge is wrong and should not be there. And the error may be both a "defect" and "omission"—what is there is wrong, and something needs to be added to make it right. The concept of "defect" versus "omission" is important in the procedure for preserving error in the charge.

Parts of Rules 272, 273, 274, 276 and 278 make up a detailed and difficult procedure for preserving error in the charge. They can be summarized as follows:

a. *Object or request:*

(1) If the error is that the charge omits a *question* that the party *complaining* of the error needs to establish its claim or defense, the complaining party must *request* the needed question.

(2) If the error is that the charge omits a *question* that the *other* party needs to establish its claim or defense, the complaining party may *either request* the needed question or *object* to its omission.

(3) If the error is that the charge omits an *instruction or definition*, the complaining party must *request*, regardless of who needs it.

(4) If the error is that a *question, instruction or definition* that is submitted in the charge is *defective*, the complaining party must *object* to the defect.

b. *Form of a request:*

(1) A request must be in writing.

(2) The requests must be made separately from the objections.

(3) A request must be in "substantially correct form," which means that if the judge put what is requested in the charge, there would be no error. Failures to include the burden of proof, or including incorrect requests with correct ones has made them fail the test of being "substantially correct."

c. *Form of an objection:*

(1) An objection can be made orally or in writing (but separate from the requests).

(2) An objection must be specific, pointing out distinctly the objectionable matter and the grounds for the objection.

(3) A good objection concealed within numerous unfounded form objections will be waived.

The procedure for objecting to the charge became almost impossible, especially with the broad form charge. Often it is difficult to determine when an error is an omission or a defect, whether an omission is an omitted question or instruction, and whose question is omitted. Lawyers and judges were frustrated with the numerous opportunities for waiver. In the 1992 *Payne* case set out below, the Texas Supreme Court announced a new way to interpret the rules concerning preservation of error in the charge.

STATE DEPARTMENT OF HIGHWAYS & PUBLIC TRANSPORTATION
v.
PAYNE

838 S.W.2d 235
(Tex. 1992)

HECHT, JUSTICE.

* * *

Kenneth Payne and his wife sued the State Department of Highways and Public Transportation to recover damages for injuries which he sustained when he walked off the end of a culvert built and maintained by the State. A jury found that Payne's injuries were caused 60% by the negligence of the State and 40% by his own negligence, and the trial court rendered judgment in Payne's favor for $148,800 plus interest. The court of appeals affirmed. The two principal issues now before us are first, whether the trial court held the State to a higher standard of care than that imposed by section 101.022 of the Texas Tort Claims Act, TEX. CIV. PRAC. & REM. CODE § 101.022, and thus failed to submit the controlling question of fact to the jury, and second, whether the State has preserved this complaint for appeal. We answer both issues in the affirmative, and consequently reverse the judgment of the court of appeals and render judgment that Payne take nothing.

I

Payne's injury occurred before sunrise one morning as he walked from his home in the country across a two-lane paved road toward a deer blind he had constructed in a field. A culvert ran perpendicular to and beneath the road, ending about 22 feet from the roadbed on the deer blind side. In the dark, Payne stepped off the culvert and fell about 12 feet into a drainage ditch, sustaining injuries. Although Payne knew there was a culvert near where he was walking, he claimed that he did not see where it ended that morning because vegetation obscured it and a reflective marker was missing.

Payne alleged in his pleadings that the culvert was both a special defect and a premise defect; the State denied that the culvert was a defect of any kind. If the culvert was a premise defect, the State owed Payne the same duty a private landowner owes a licensee. TEX. CIV. PRAC. & REM. CODE § 101.022(a).[1] That duty requires that a landowner not injure a licensee by willful, wanton or grossly negligent conduct, and that the owner use ordinary care either to warn a licensee of, or to make reasonably safe, a dangerous condition of which the owner is aware and the licensee is not. *Id.*; *see* RESTATEMENT (SECOND) OF TORTS § 342 (1965). If the culvert was a special defect, the State owed Payne the same duty to warn that a private landowner owes an invitee. TEX. CIV. PRAC. & REM. CODE § 101.022(b).[2] That duty requires an owner to use ordinary care to reduce or eliminate an unreasonable risk of harm created by a premises condition of which the owner is or reasonably should be aware.

---

1 "If a claim arises from a premise defect, the governmental unit owes to the claimant only the duty that a private person owes to a licensee on private property, unless the claimant pays for the use of the premises."

2 "The limitation of duty in this section shall not apply to the duty to warn of special defects such as excavations or obstructions on highways, roads, or streets or to the duty to warn of the absence, condition, or malfunction of traffic signs, signals, or warning devices as is required by Section 101.060."

The elements of proof required to establish a breach of these two duties, absent willful, wanton or grossly negligent conduct which Payne did not plead or attempt to prove, may be compared as follows. To establish liability—

a licensee must prove that:	an invitee must prove that:
(1) a condition of the premises created an unreasonable risk of harm to the licensee;	(1) a condition of the premises created an unreasonable risk of harm to the invitee;
(2) the owner knew of the condition;	(2) the owner knew or reasonably should have known of the condition;
(3) the licensee did not actually know the condition;	
(4) the owner failed to exercise ordinary care to protect the licensee from danger;	(3) the owner failed to exercise ordinary care to protect the invitee from danger;
(5) the owner's failure was a proximate cause of injury to the licensee.	(4) the owner's failure was a proximate cause of injury to the invitee.

There are two differences between these theories. The first is that a licensee must prove that the premises owner actually knew of the dangerous condition, while an invitee need only prove that the owner knew or reasonably should have known. The second difference is that a licensee must prove that he did not know of the dangerous condition, while an invitee need not do so.

In this case, the State built the culvert and thus knew of its existence. That element under either theory of liability is not in dispute. Nor do the parties dispute that Payne knew of the existence of the culvert. The point of contention is whether Payne knew the culvert was in his path as he walked through the undergrowth in the dark. After all, Payne argues, he would hardly have stepped off the edge and fallen twelve feet to serious injury had he known, or had he been adequately warned, that the culvert was in front of him. But, the State responds, he nevertheless knew that the culvert was there somewhere, and his knowledge precludes imposition of liability on the State unless the culvert was a special defect. Both parties introduced evidence regarding Payne's knowledge of the location of the culvert.

At the close of the evidence the trial court gave the jury a charge which asked two liability questions. The first question inquired whether Payne's or the State's negligence was a proximate cause of the occurrence. The second question asked what percentage of such negligence was attributable to each. In addition to the standard definitions of negligence, proximate cause and ordinary care, the trial court gave the jury the following instructions:

> "GOVERNMENTAL LIABILITY": A governmental unit in the state is liable for personal injury and death so caused by a condition or use of tangible personal or real property if the governmental unit would, were it a private person, be liable to the claimant according to Texas law.
>
> "DUTY OWED: SPECIAL DEFECT": Where there is a special defect such as an excavation or obstruction on or adjacent to a highway, road, or street or where there is the absence or malfunction of a traffic sign, signal or warning device that is required by law, the governmental unit owes to the plaintiff a duty to warn of such special defect.

> The duty owed is a duty to use ordinary care to either warn of a dangerous condition or to make such dangerous condition reasonably safe, provided the governmental unit had knowledge of the dangerous condition, or through the exercise of ordinary care, should have had knowledge of the dangerous condition.
>
> "DANGEROUS CONDITION" means a condition other than normally connected with the use of the roadway, excavation or obstruction, and a person using ordinary care could not encounter such condition with safety.

The State's complaint is that the jury charge erroneously assumed that the culvert was a special defect and did not submit Payne's premise defect liability theory to the jury. Specifically, the State complains that the charge does not request the jury to find whether Payne knew of the location of the culvert at the time of his accident.

In effect, the trial court determined that the culvert was a special defect as a matter of law. The court of appeals agreed. To the extent they treated the issue as a question of law rather than of fact, both courts were correct. Whether a condition is a premise defect or a special defect is a question of duty involving statutory interpretation and thus an issue of law for the court to decide. However, both courts incorrectly determined the status of the culvert.

Special defects are excavations or obstructions on highways, roads, or streets. TEX. CIV. PRAC. & REM. CODE § 101.022(b). These examples set forth in the statute itself all present an unexpected and unusual danger to ordinary users of roadways. The culvert in this case was not a special defect. The end of the culvert was located far enough from the paved surface that vehicular passengers and other normal users of the roadway were unlikely to encounter it. Payne, unlike an ordinary user of the road, was walking perpendicular to the paved surface into the adjacent field. Only such a pedestrian, whose destination required him to leave the proximity of the road, was ever likely to fall off the end of the culvert. If there was a defect, it was in the field where Payne was walking. The State's duty of care with respect to such a defect is covered by the ordinary rule for premise defects under section 101.022(a).

II

Payne nevertheless argues that the State has not preserved its complaint that the trial court erred in refusing to inquire of the jury concerning his knowledge of the culvert. The State's sole objection to the charge was that the "Duty Owed" paragraph quoted above "constitutes a comment upon the weight of the evidence and amounts to an instruction to the jury that there is, in fact, a special defect, removes that issue from the province of the jury and keeps from it being a fact issue as it should be." Payne argues that this objection was not sufficiently clear to call to the trial court's attention the State's complaint that the culvert should not have been assumed to be a special defect. This argument is rather dubious in the circumstances of this case. The trial court's failure to submit Payne's premise liability theory could hardly have been an oversight. The very fact that it included instructions concerning special defects in the charge indicates that the trial court decided that the culvert was a special defect and not a premise defect. Furthermore, the trial court had allowed the parties to present evidence and argument concerning Payne's knowledge, which would have been irrelevant if the culvert was a special defect. The trial court was certainly aware that the issue was disputed.

Even if the State's objection was insufficient, the State preserved error by requesting the trial court to inquire of the jury concerning Payne's knowledge of the culvert. Specifically, the State requested the trial court to include the following question in the charge:

> Do you find from a preponderance of the evidence that Kenneth Herschel Payne had actual knowledge that the culvert was at the location in question on F.M. 1301?

Although this question places the burden of proof on the State rather than on Payne where it belongs, Payne can hardly complain. The trial court's refusal to ask the question requested by the State constituted a clear refusal to submit a premise defect theory to the jury.[4]

We do not suggest, of course, that the trial court should have submitted the case to the jury on specific questions rather than broad-form questions, as required by Rule 277, TEX. R. CIV. P. The issue is not whether the trial court should have asked the jury the specific question requested by the State; rather, the issue is whether the State's request called the trial court's attention to the State's complaint that no premise liability theory was submitted to the jury sufficiently to preserve that complaint for appeal. The State's requested question clearly called the trial court's attention to the State's complaint because it was the sole element of premise defect liability missing from the charge. Payne appears to argue that the State would have preserved error if it had plainly objected: "The charge submits only a special defect theory and not a premise defect theory." The State's request is clearer than such an objection because it calls attention to the very element of the premise defect theory omitted from the charge. The request not only objects to the omission of the theory, it suggests the missing language necessary to correct the omission. The trial court should have included the missing element in its broad-form submission in an appropriate manner.

We have received two amicus briefs concerning the proper method for preserving a complaint about the jury charge, like the State's complaint in this case. In our State's procedural jurisprudence, there are no rules more recondite than those pertaining to the preparation of the jury charge. As Professor McDonald observed forty years ago: "No aspect of procedure has developed a greater tangle of perplexities than that which embraces the rules as to the charge of the court to the jury." 3 ROY W. MCDONALD, TEXAS CIVIL PRACTICE IN DISTRICT AND COUNTY COURTS § 12.01, at 222 (Frank W. Elliott ed., 1983). The passage of time has not improved things. Dozens of cases decided since Professor McDonald wrote, many of them flatly contradictory, attest to myriad uncertainties in preserving complaints of error in the jury charge. The rules governing charge procedures are difficult enough; the case law applying them has made compliance a labyrinth daunting to the most experienced trial lawyer. Today, it is fair to say that the process of telling the jury the applicable law and inquiring of them their verdict is a risky gambit in which counsel has less reason to know that he or she has protected a client's rights than at any other time in the trial.

The preparation of the jury charge, coming as it ordinarily does at that very difficult point of the trial between the close of the evidence and summation, ought to be simpler. To complicate this process with complex, intricate, sometimes contradictory, unpredictable rules, just when counsel is contemplating the last words he or she will say to the jury, hardly subserves the fair and just presentation of the case. Yet that is our procedure. To preserve a complaint about the charge a party must sometimes request the inclusion of specific, substantially correct language in writing, which frequently requires that even well prepared counsel scribble it out in long-hand sitting in the courtroom. The rules of procedure require that the judge endorse each request with specific language, although sometimes this requirement is ignored. Sometimes a request is not sufficient and may not even be appropriate; instead, counsel must object. The objection must be specific enough to call the

---

[4] The issue of Payne's knowledge of the location of the culvert is not merely a "phase or shade" of the broad question of the State's liability, as the dissent argues. Rather, it is a key issue in dispute in the case. Nor would a finding that Payne knew of the culvert's location have conflicted with a finding that the State was negligent, as the dissent argues. Rather, such a finding would simply have precluded liability.

court's attention to the asserted error in the charge. It is not clear whether a request will serve as an objection or an objection as a request. Rather than attempt to decide under the pressure of the courtroom and in peril of losing appellate rights, whether an objection or a request is called for, cautious counsel might choose to do both in all cases—request and object. But if they are not kept separate, or if an appellate court later decides that the duplication obscured the real complaint, counsel's precaution may still result in a decision that the complaint was waived.

The procedure has been further complicated by our adoption of broad issue submission, a change intended to have the opposite effect. When special issue practice flourished in Texas, it was easier to determine which party had responsibility for submission of a particular matter to the jury, and which party had the obligation to object to misstatements in order to preserve error. That practice, however, had a host of troubles of its own, causing this Court to reject it in the last decade in favor of broad-form submission. Now, however, it is impossible to determine which party has responsibility for each part of a charge. Because many instructions in a broad-form charge bear upon elements of proof not easily divisible among the parties, it is hard to know who should complain. Recently it was argued before this Court that a party who objected to any submission at all of an issue proposed by his opponent, waived that objection if, alternatively, he proposed different language more favorable to his position. The process is becoming worse, not better.

The flaws in our charge procedures stem partly from the rules governing those procedures and partly from case law applying those rules. Last year we asked a special task force to recommend changes in the rules to simplify charge procedures, and amendments are under consideration. Rules changes must await the completion of that process; we do not revise our rules by opinion. We can, however, begin to reduce the complexity that case law has contributed to charge procedures. The procedure for preparing and objecting to the jury charge has lost its philosophical moorings. There should be but one test for determining if a party has preserved error in the jury charge, and that is whether the party made the trial court aware of the complaint, timely and plainly, and obtained a ruling. The more specific requirements of the rules should be applied, while they remain, to serve rather than defeat this principle. In this case, the State clearly met this test.

* * *

Payne was not entitled to recover on his special defect theory as a matter of law. To prevail on his premise defect theory, Payne was required to obtain a finding that he lacked knowledge of the culvert. This element of his claim was not included in the broad-form charge which the trial court submitted to the jury.[5] A finding on this one element cannot be deemed in Payne's favor because the State objected to the omission by requesting a jury question on that issue. TEX. R. CIV. P. 279;. Thus, the verdict does not support a judgment in Payne's favor.

Accordingly, the judgment of the court of appeals is reversed, and judgment is rendered that Payne take nothing.

Dissenting opinion by MAUZY, JUSTICE, joined by DOGGETT and GAMMAGE, JUSTICES omitted.

---

[5] The transcript does not reveal whether Payne requested that these elements of his claim be submitted to the jury. If he had requested them in substantially correct form, it would have been error for the trial court to refuse to submit them. TEX. R. CIV. P. 278. If any such error occurred, however, Payne has waived it because he can not demonstrate from the record that he requested submission of these elements.

Notes & Questions

1. *Charge error waiver if not properly preserved.* A party that seeks reversal of a judgment because of a charge error must have properly preserved error. Otherwise, that party will have waived the error, and there can be no reversal on that account. *Payne* does not change that rule. We have seen how confusing the preservation of error process is. Thus, waiver remains a real possibility, even after *Payne*.

2. *Waiver for failure to timely preserve error.* Rule 272 provides that error preservation must occur before the charge is read to the jury.[1] And the supreme court has held that the rule gives trial courts discretion to set a deadline for court objections that precedes the reading of the charge to the jury, so long as a reasonable amount of time is given to examine and object to the charge.[2] In that case, the court held that the trial judge did not err in refusing a last minute objection.

3. *When* Payne *saves.* *Payne's* "fully cognizant" rule will save parties from waiving charge error in many situations where parties do not comply with the charge error rules. In one case, the Supreme Court held it was error not to submit instructions to the jury limiting the jury's consideration to pre-pooling drainage. The Court then held that error was preserved when the complainant moved to bifurcate issues before trial and submitted a proposed question in response to the trial court's initial request for a proposed charge.[3] There the Court pointed to the plaintiff's consistent motions, objections and other statements throughout the trial, and concluded that the trial judge was made aware of the complaint to the charge.

---

2. *Preserving the* Casteel *objection.*

BURBAGE
v.
BURBAGE
447 S.W.3d 249
(Tex. 2014)

Opinion

JUSTICE GREEN delivered the opinion of the Court.

In this defamation case, a jury assessed compensatory and exemplary damages against Allen Chadwick Burbage (Chad) for ten statements defaming his brother, W. Kirk Burbage (Kirk). The trial court also permanently enjoined Chad from making similar statements. We are presented with three issues: (1) whether any defamatory statements fell within a qualified privilege; (2) whether evidence supports the jury's damage awards; and (3) whether the trial court abused its

---

1 *See also* Missouri Pacific Railroad Co. v. Cross, 501 S.W.2d 868 (Tex. 1973) (holding that trial court erred in approving agreement between counsel that objections could be made while jury deliberating).

2 King Fisher Marine Service, L.P. v. Tamez, 443 S.W.3d 838 (2014).

3 Southeastern Pipe Line Co. v. Tichacek, 997 S.W.2d 166 (Tex. 1999).

discretion by issuing the permanent injunction. Because we hold that Chad failed to preserve error in the charge, we do not reach the issue of qualified privilege. We also hold that the permanent injunction operates as an impermissible prior restraint on freedom of speech. Accordingly, we affirm those parts of the court of appeals' judgment. But, on damages, we hold that no evidence supports the compensatory damage award. We reverse that part of the court of appeals' judgment.

I. Factual and Procedural Background

Kirk owns and operates the Burbage Funeral Home, a centuries-old family business, in Worcester County, Maryland. Chad is Kirk's older brother. Chad and Kirk's grandmother, Anna Burbage, managed the funeral home from her husband's death in the 1940s until her death in 1985. In her will, Anna left the funeral home and all of its assets to Kirk.

Anna bequeathed the land for the Burbage family cemetery to her children, Richard Burbage, Sr., Chad and Kirk's father, and Jean Burbage Prettyman. Although primarily a family cemetery, Anna and Richard gave permission for burial or entombment of several non-family members. Richard died in 1991; in his will, he left his 50% undivided interest in the family cemetery property to Chad and Kirk's mother, Virginia Burbage Markham, but the will was never probated. Virginia conveyed this interest to Kirk by quitclaim deed in 2003. Chad felt Kirk obtained the funeral home and the family cemetery interest through manipulation, first of Anna and later of Virginia.

Although the origin of the strife between Chad and Kirk remains unclear, the "Farm Property," a 23-acre tract that Virginia inherited from Richard in 1991, aggravated any existing discord. The potential sale of the property ultimately aligned Virginia's four children against each other: Chad and Patrice Burbage Lehmann wanted to sell, while Kirk and his brother, Keith, demurred. Throughout 2006 and 2007, Chad exchanged heated emails with Kirk's attorney. In late 2007 and early 2008, Chad created a website, www.annaburbage.org, to air his grievances with Kirk. Chad placed several posters around town to publicize the website. . . .

Chad also sent letters to Shirley and Brice Phillips, family friends of the Burbages who had earlier obtained permission to place a mausoleum in the Burbage cemetery. [Chad made ten allegedly defamatory statements concerning elder abuse and fraud.]

Kirk and the Burbage Funeral Home sued Chad for defamation in Bastrop County.[1] Chad appeared pro se. The trial court submitted ten questions—one for each of the statements reproduced above—asking the jury whether Chad had proven that the statements were substantially true. The jury answered "no" to all questions. The court also asked questions on compensatory and exemplary damages for Kirk and, separately, for the Burbage Funeral Home. The court instructed the jury that all statements were defamatory per se because each statement either leveled a criminal charge or tended to cause injury to the funeral home's business or to Kirk's profession. The jury awarded Kirk $6,552,000: $250,000 for past injury to reputation; $2,500,000 for future injury to reputation; $1,000 for past mental anguish; $1,000 for future mental anguish; and $3,800,000 in exemplary damages. The jury awarded the Burbage Funeral Home $3,050,000: $50,000 for past injury to reputation; $1,000,000 for future injury to reputation; and $2,000,000 in exemplary damages. The trial court also permanently enjoined Chad from future defamatory speech in a four-page list of prohibited topics (tied to the ten defamatory statements).

---

1 Chad was a resident of Bastrop County, Texas at the time the lawsuit was filed. *See* TEX. CIV. PRAC. & REM. CODE § 15.017.

Chad appealed. The court of appeals reduced the exemplary damages to $750,000 under Texas Civil Practice and Remedies Code section 41.008(b), upheld the other damage awards, and vacated the injunction. 447 S.W.3d 291, 295, 2011 WL 6756979 (Tex. App.—Austin 2011, pet. granted) (mem.op.). Each party petitioned for review; we granted both petitions. 57 Tex. Sup.Ct. J. 53 (Nov. 22, 2013).

II. Qualified Privilege and Charge Error

We first address Chad's contention that qualified privilege barred Kirk's recovery based on Chad's defamatory statements to the Phillipses. If Chad's statements were privileged, the jury's answers on damages would rest upon invalidly submitted theories of liability. We hold that, even if the privilege applied, Chad failed to preserve jury charge error on this point.

* * *

The trial court submitted the ten statements—four unprivileged and six potentially privileged—for the jury to determine if each statement was substantially true at the time it was made. On damages, the trial court submitted broad-form questions that incorporated the jury's answers for all ten statements. If the qualified privilege applied to any statements, then, the broad-form damages questions incorporated both valid and invalid bases for liability. Such commingling may result in harmful error. *Cf. Crown Life Ins. Co. v. Casteel,* 22 S.W.3d 378, 388 (Tex. 2000) (reversing for new trial due to erroneous commingling of valid and invalid liability theories in a single broad-form liability question). To obtain reversal due to such a charge error, Chad must have preserved the error at trial. *In re B.L.D.,* 113 S.W.3d 340, 349 (Tex. 2003) ("[A]ny complaint to a jury charge is waived unless specifically included in an objection."). We now turn to this preservation question.

B. Preservation of Charge Error

The court of appeals held that Chad waived any claim of error in the submission of potentially privileged statements because he "did not object in the trial court to the submission of broad-form damages questions." 447 S.W.3d at 300-01 (citing *In re B.L.D.,* 113 S.W.3d at 349). In *In re B.L.D.,* we held that the court of appeals erred by reviewing a jury charge complaint when the parties did not object at trial to the form of submission. 113 S.W.3d at 349, 355. Chad suggests that this case differs because he raised an objection on qualified privilege, which preserved error in any derivative damages question. Kirk responds that Chad must specifically object to the damages question's form, not merely to the underlying liability issue. Kirk further argues that even Chad's qualified privilege objection failed to preserve error.

1. Charge Error Based on Valid and Invalid Liability Theories

"It is fundamental to our system of justice that parties have the right to be judged by a jury properly instructed in the law." *Casteel,* 22 S.W.3d at 388. Thus, in *Casteel,* we required a new trial when a timely and specific objection preserved the issue of erroneous commingling of valid and invalid theories of liability in a broad-form liability question, such that the appellate court could not determine whether the jury based its verdict on an improperly submitted theory. *Id.* (citing TEX.R.APP. P. 61.1). Extending this principle in *Harris County v. Smith,* 96 S.W.3d 230, 234 (Tex. 2002), we determined that a broad-form damages submission mixing valid and invalid elements of damages created the same type of harmful error. And in *Romero v. KPH Consolidation, Inc.,* 166 S.W.3d 212, 225 (Tex. 2005), where evidence supported the jury's negligence finding but *not* its malicious credentialing finding, we held that the trial court committed harmful error by submitting an apportionment question which allowed the jury to consider malicious credentialing. We explained that "[e]ven if the jury *could* still have made the same apportionment of fault [without considering malicious credentialing], the error in the question is nevertheless reversible because it effectively prevents [the appellant] from complaining on appeal that they *would not* have done so." *Id.* at 226.

We continue to adhere to these principles. Yet in addition to the common animating principle of properly instructing the jury in the law, these cases share another link: *some* timely and specific objection. *Romero,* 166 S.W.3d at 229; *Harris Cnty.,* 96 S.W.3d at 232; *Casteel,* 22 S.W.3d at 387. In other words, in situations where a party does not raise a *Casteel*-type objection, that party surely cannot raise a *Casteel* issue when it failed to preserve a claim of an invalid theory of liability that forms the basis of a *Casteel*-type error. If we allowed litigants to raise a *Casteel* issue with no valid objection, either to liability or submission form, those litigants could use a post-trial motion to raise a lack of evidence on the liability question, thus bypassing the crucial step of allowing the trial judge to correct any errors in the charge.

In *Romero,* we declined to address whether the appellant must object both to the lack of evidence to support submission of a jury question *and* the form of the submission, because in that case the appellant did both. 166 S.W.3d at 229 & n. 55 (acknowledging the difficult question of whether an additional broad-form objection is required) (citing *Pan E. Exploration Co. v. Hufo Oils,* 855 F.2d 1106, 1124 (5th Cir. 1988)). But whether or not an objection to *both* is required, *some* timely and specific objection must raise the issue in the trial court. *See Thota v. Young,* 366 S.W.3d 678, 691 (Tex. 2012) (requiring "some objection to the charge," whether to evidentiary support or to form, to preserve error for appellate review). Here, Chad objected based on qualified privilege, but he made no objection to the form of submission. If Chad's initial objection on qualified privilege did not preserve error, we need not address whether a further *Casteel*-type objection is required.

2. Specific Objections

Our rules of procedure establish the preservation requirements to raise a jury-charge complaint on appeal. *Id.* at 689. The complaining party must object before the trial court and "must point out distinctly the objectionable matter and the grounds of the objection." TEX.R. CIV. P. 274; *see also* TEX. R. APP. P. 33.1. Under Rule of Civil Procedure 274, "[a]ny complaint as to a question, definition, or instruction, on account of any defect, omission, or fault in pleading, is waived unless specifically included in the objections." TEX. R. CIV. P. 274. As a general rule, preservation requires (1) a timely objection "stating the grounds for the ruling that the complaining party sought from the trial court with sufficient specificity to make the trial court aware of the complaint, unless the specific grounds were apparent from the context," and (2) a ruling. *See* TEX. R. APP. P. 33.1. Stated differently, the test ultimately asks "whether the party made the trial court aware of the complaint, timely and plainly, and obtained a ruling." *State Dep't of Highways & Pub. Transp. v. Payne,* 838 S.W.2d 235, 241 (Tex. 1992).

Importantly, the "purpose of Rule 274 is to afford trial courts an opportunity to correct errors in the charge by requiring objections both to clearly designate the error and to explain the grounds for complaint." *Wilgus v. Bond,* 730 S.W.2d 670, 672 (Tex. 1987); *see Payne,* 838 S.W.2d at 243 (MAUZY, J., dissenting) ("Only by proper objection does a litigant afford the trial court sufficient opportunity to correct defects in the charge."). We apply these rules to Chad's objection.

3. Chad's Objection

The following dialogue occurred at the formal charge conference:

Mr. Cagle: I'm not sure if this is an objection. I apologize, Your Honor. But the matter of in the amended—defendant's amended—first amendment to the original response, defendant has requested that there be a qualified privilege relative to the letter, and the reason for the qualified privilege is it represents common interests, a continuation of a prior judicial proceeding in Maryland and a continuation of trying to resolve matters of mutual concern between the parties of the cemetery.

The Court: All right. Do you have a requested instruction that you're asking the Court to consider and to include in the charge?

Mr. A. Burbage: I have—it seems as though it would—it would require the—a question in the line after—after you find that the statement inflammatory, then there would be a question do you find the statement blah-blah-blah was false at the time it was made as it related to—

The Court: All right. Anything further on that? On that particular issue is there anything further?

Mr. A. Burbage: No. It was—it's been mentioned in the testimony.

The Court: All right. The objection is overruled. The requested instruction is denied.

Chad claims that the trial court erred in submitting liability questions on the potentially privileged statements. Therefore, Chad's objection needed to communicate to the trial court that it was improper to submit Questions 5 through 10 (on statements in the Phillips letters) to the jury. The objection does raise the subject of the qualified privilege. But, crucially, the objection must apprise the trial court of the error alleged such that the court has the opportunity to correct the problem. *See Wilgus,* 730 S.W.2d at 672. When the trial court asked Chad whether he had a requested instruction, Chad responded only with a request for a question that appears to address the falsity of the statements themselves. As Chad has argued, a qualified privilege may still apply even when the statements are false. *See O'Neil,* 456 S.W.2d at 898. It is unclear what Chad hoped to accomplish by requesting an additional question if he wanted the court to withhold Question 5 through 10 from the jury.[4] And it is uncertain even to which questions Chad referred (presumably Questions 5 through 10, but the word "inflammatory," which Chad uses to describe the placement of his proposed question, appears nowhere in the charge). Quite simply, Chad has not provided a specific objection indicating the alleged error in the charge and allowing the trial court the opportunity to correct the error.

We note that when Chad wanted to object to a specific question at the charge conference, he did so. *Before* the objection on qualified privilege at issue here, Chad objected to Question 10 because it duplicated elements of Questions 7 and 8. The trial court initially sustained this objec-

4 We cannot safely engage in assumptions about what Chad might have meant. Whether the statements were false and Chad knew of their falsity—compared with the jury's actual finding that the statements were not substantially true—would have relevance to the question of whether Chad acted with actual malice. But the trial court gave the incorrect common law definition of malice, Chad did not object to the incorrect malice definition, and, as Chad argues, the burden on actual malice falls to Kirk, not Chad. Such a confusing objection, raised during the crucial charge conference, could not have apprised the trial judge that Chad objected to the submission of the offending questions. Chad explained his desire more coherently at a hearing on his request for findings of fact and conclusions of law, but at that point it was too late.

tion (although it reversed that ruling at the end of the charge conference). Chad's objection to qualified privilege, in order to preserve error, needed to distinctly raise the issue of withdrawing Questions 5 through 10 from the jury. By its language, it does not do this. And it would make little sense for Chad to raise an objection to qualified privilege to eliminate Questions 5 through 10 when, only moments before, he eliminated Question 10 only because it was duplicative of Questions 7 and 8, *not* because the Questions 7 and 8 were improper to submit to the jury. With this in mind, we cannot conclude that Chad's intent to remove Questions 5 through 10 was "apparent from the context." TEX. R. APP. P. 31.1(a)(1)(A). We hold that Chad's objection was insufficiently specific and did not preserve his claim of error in the submission of Questions 5 through 10.

Our procedural rules are technical, but not trivial. We construe such rules liberally so that the right to appeal is not lost unnecessarily. *Arkoma Basin Exploration Co. v. FMF Assocs. 1990-A, Ltd.,* 249 S.W.3d 380, 388 (Tex. 2008). But when an objection fails to explain the nature of the error, we cannot make assumptions. Preservation of error reflects important prudential considerations recognizing that the judicial process benefits greatly when trial courts have the opportunity to first consider and rule on error. *In re B.L.D.,* 113 S.W.3d at 350 (citing *In re C.O.S.,* 988 S.W.2d 760, 765 (Tex. 1999)). Affording courts this opportunity conserves judicial resources and promotes fairness by ensuring that a party does not neglect a complaint at trial and raise it for the first time on appeal. *Id.* (citing *Pirtle v. Gregory,* 629 S.W.2d 919, 920 (Tex. 1982) (per curiam)). Nor may we stray from these rules because Chad represented himself at trial. *See Mansfield State Bank v. Cohn,* 573 S.W.2d 181, 184-85 (Tex. 1978).

4. Application

Chad argues that the court impermissibly combined valid and invalid theories of liability when the broad-form damages question incorporated privileged statements. Chad did not make a *Casteel*-type objection to form; thus, to preserve error, Chad *must* have raised some specific objection to the submission of Questions 5 through 10. *See In re B.L.D.,* 113 S.W.3d at 349-50 (holding that a complaint to a jury charge was waived because it was not specifically included in an objection). He did not. Thus, we hold that Chad's failure to object waives his right to complain of the charge on appeal.

Notes & Questions

1. *How to phrase the* Casteel *objection.* In *Thota v. Young,*[1] cited in *Burbage*, the supreme court applied *Payne* and held that a *Casteel* objection need not specifically name the *Casteel* opinion to preserve error. The court held that "a timely and specific objection that there was no evidence to support the disputed items submitted in the broad-form charge" was sufficient. Note that this objection was made at the charge conference. As *Burbage* clarifies, a no evidence objection made after the charge is read to the jury, for example by a motion for judgment notwithstanding the verdict, would not preserve error.

---

[1] 366 S.W.3d 678 (Tex. 2012).

2. *Pattern Jury Charge on error preservation.* Properly preserving error in the charge is not easy. In 2012, the Texas Pattern Jury Charge Committee included a new instruction in all volumes, hoping to assist lawyers who were trying to do it correctly. It took several years and multiple drafts to finally get a version upon which everyone could agree. It appears below:

Preservation of Charge Error (Comment)

The purpose of this Comment is to make practitioners aware of the need to preserve their complaints about the jury charge for appellate review and to inform them of general considerations when attempting to perfect those complaints. It is not intended as an indepth analysis of the topic.

Basic rules for preserving charge error.

Objections and requests. Errors in the charge consist of (1) defective questions, instructions, and definitions actually submitted (that is, definitions, instructions, and questions that, while included in the charge, are nevertheless incorrectly submitted); and (2) questions, instructions, and definitions that are omitted entirely. Objections are required to preserve error as to any defect in the charge. In addition, a written request for a substantially correct question, instruction, or definition is required to preserve error for certain omissions.

- Defective question, definition, or instruction: *Objection*

  Affirmative errors in the jury charge must be preserved by objection, regardless of which party has the burden of proof for the submission. TEX. R. CIV. P. 274. Therefore, if the jury charge contains a *defective* question, definition, or instruction, an objection pointing out the error will preserve error for review.

- Omitted definition or instruction: *Objection and request*

  If the omission concerns a definition or an instruction, error must be preserved by an objection and a request for a substantially correct definition or instruction. TEX. R. CIV. P. 274, 278. For this type of omission, it does not matter which party has the burden of proof. Therefore, a request must be tendered even if the erroneously omitted definition or instruction is in the opponent's claim or defense.

- Omitted question, Party's burden: *Objection and request*;
  Opponent's burden: *Objection*

  If the omission concerns a question relied on by the party complaining of the judgment, error must be preserved by an objection and a request for a substantially correct question. TEX. R. CIV. P. 274, 278. If the omission concerns a question relied on by the opponent, an objection alone will preserve error for review. TEX. R. CIV. P. 278. To determine whether error preservation is required for an opponent's omission, consider that, if no element of an independent ground of recovery or defense is submitted in the charge or is requested, the ground is waived. TEX. R. CIV. P. 279.

- Uncertainty about whether the error constitutes an omission or a defect:
  Objection and request

  If there is uncertainty whether an error in the charge constitutes an affirmative error or an omission, the practitioner should both request and object to ensure the error is preserved. *See State Department of Highways & Public Transportation v. Payne*, 838 S.W.2d 235, 239-40 (Tex. 1992).

Timing and form of objections and requests.

- Objections, requests, and rulings must be made before the charge is read to the jury. TEX. R. CIV. P. 272.
- Objections must—

  1. be made in writing or dictated to the court reporter in the presence of the court and opposing counsel, TEX. R. CIV. P. 272; and

  2. specifically point out the error and the grounds of complaint, TEX. R. CIV. P. 274.
- Requests must—

  1. be made separate and apart from any objections to the charge, TEX. R. CIV. P. 273;

  2. be in writing and tendered to the court, TEX. R. CIV. P. 278; and

  3. be in substantially correct wording, TEX. R. CIV. P. 278, which "does not mean that [the request] be absolutely correct, nor does it mean one that is merely sufficient to call the matter to the attention of the court will suffice. It means one that in substance and in the main is correct, *and that is not affirmatively incorrect.*" *Placencio v. Allied Industrial International, Inc.*, 724 S.W.2d 20, 21 (Tex. 1987).

Rulings on objections and requests.

- Rulings on objections may be oral or in writing. TEX. R. CIV. P. 272.
- Rulings on requests must be in writing and must indicate whether the court refused, granted, or granted but modified the request. TEX. R. CIV. P. 276.

Common mistakes that may result in waiver of charge error.

- Failing to submit requests in writing (oral or dictated requests will not preserve error).
- Failing to make requests separately from objections to the charge (generally it is safe to present a party's requests at the beginning of the formal charge conference, but separate from a party's objections).
- Offering requests "en masse," that is, tendering a complete charge or obscuring a proper request among unfounded or meritless requests (submit each question, definition, or instruction separately, and submit only those important to the outcome of the trial).
- Failing to file with the clerk all requests that the court has marked "refused" (a prudent practice is to also keep a copy for one's own file).
- Failing to make objections to the court's charge on the record before it is read to the jury (agreements to put objections on the record while the jury is deliberating, even with court approval, will not preserve error).
- Adopting by reference objections to other portions of the court's charge.
- Dictating objections to the court reporter in the judge's absence (the judge and opposing counsel should be present).

- Relying on or adopting another party's objections to the court's charge without obtaining court approval to do so beforehand (as a general rule, each party must make its own objections).
- Relying on a pretrial ruling that is the subject of a question, definition, or instruction to preserve charge error.
- Failing to assert at trial the same grounds for charge error urged on appeal; grounds not distinctly pointed out to the trial court cannot be raised for the first time on appeal.
- Failing to obtain a ruling on an objection or request.

Preservation of charge error post-*Payne*. In its 1992 opinion in *State Department of Highways & Public Transportation v. Payne*, the supreme court declined to revise the rules governing the jury charge but stated:

> There should be but one test for determining if a party has preserved error in the jury charge, and that is whether the party made the trial court aware of the complaint, timely and plainly, and obtained a ruling. The more specific requirements of the rules should be applied, while they remain, to serve rather than defeat this principle.

Payne, 838 S.W.2d at 241. The goal after *Payne* is to apply the charge rules "in a common sense manner to serve the purposes of the rules, rather than in a technical manner which defeats them." *Alaniz v. Jones & Neuse, Inc.*, 907 S.W.2d 450, 452 (Tex. 1995) (per curiam). However, in practice, *Payne* generated what amounts to an ad hoc system wherein courts decide preservation issues relating to charge error on a case-by-case basis. The keys to error preservation post-*Payne* now seem to be (1) when in doubt about how to preserve, do both (object and request); and (2) in either case, clarity is essential: make your arguments timely and plainly enough that the trial court knows how to cure the claimed error, and get a ruling on the record. *See, e.g., Wackenhut Corrections Corp. v. de la Rosa*, 305 S.W.3d 594, 610-18 & 611 n.16 (Tex. App.—Corpus Christi 2009, no pet.).

Broad-form issues. In *Crown Life Insurance Co. v. Casteel*, 22 S.W.3d 378 (Tex. 2000), the supreme court held that inclusion of a legally invalid theory in a broad-form liability question taints the question and requires a new trial. *Casteel*, 22 S.W.3d at 388. The court has since extended this rule to legal sufficiency challenges to an element of a broad-form damages question, *see Harris County v. Smith*, 96 S.W.3d 230 (Tex. 2002), and to complaints about inclusion of an invalid liability theory in a comparative responsibility finding, *see Romero v. KPH Consolidation, Inc.*, 166 S.W.3d 212 (Tex. 2005).

When a broad-form submission is infeasible under the *Casteel* doctrine and a granulated submission would cure the alleged charge defect, a specific objection to the broadform nature of the charge question is necessary to preserve error. *Thota v. Young*, 366 S.W.3d 678, 690-91 (Tex. 2012) (citing *In re A.V.*, 113 S.W.3d 355, 363 (Tex. 2003); *In re B.L.D.*, 113 S.W.3d 340, 349-50 (Tex. 2003)). But when a broad-form submission is infeasible under the *Casteel* doctrine and a granulated submission would still be erroneous because there is no evidence to support the submission of a separate question, a specific and timely no-evidence objection is sufficient to preserve error without a further objection to the broad-form nature of the charge. *Thota*, 366 S.W.3d at 690-91.

E. The Effect of an Erroneous Charge

1. *Omissions from the Charge with No Error Preserved: Deemed Findings and Waived Grounds*

Read Rules 279.

RAMOS
v.
FRITO-LAY, INC.
784 S.W.2d 667
(Tex. 1990)

DOGGETT, Justice.

The central issue in this appeal is whether an employer may be held liable in exemplary damages for the actions of its management-level employee in performing a non-managerial task. The court of appeals reversed the trial court's award of exemplary damages in this cause because Frito-Lay's sales manager was not performing a managerial task. We reverse the judgment of the court of appeals and remand the cause to that court for consideration of points it did not reach.

Liability in the trial court was premised on the intentional tort of Jose Padilla, a Frito-Lay employee, resulting in injury to Petitioner Salvador Ramos. Padilla held the title of district sales manager and had supervisory authority over twelve sales employees. On the day of the incident in question, Padilla was substituting for one of these salesmen who was on vacation, as he was unable to secure a replacement. Padilla made a route stop at Sal's Beverage Shop, a convenience store owned and operated by Ramos. A dispute arose between Padilla and Ramos concerning the ownership of a display rack, and a shoving incident ensued in which Ramos was injured.

The jury found that Padilla had committed an assault and battery proximately causing damage to Ramos and that Padilla was not deviating from the service of Frito-Lay in the furtherance of its business. The trial court entered judgment on the verdict, including an award for physical pain, medical expenses and exemplary damages. The court of appeals reversed as to medical expenses and exemplary damages but affirmed the trial court's award of damages for physical pain.

We must first consider whether error has been properly preserved. Ramos contends that Frito-Lay has waived its right to complain of the exemplary damage award because it failed to make specific objection in the trial court as to premising such award on Padilla's managerial capacity as required by Rule 52(a), Texas Rules of Appellate Procedure. Frito-Lay responds, not by pointing to a specific objection preserving error, but by contending that it was Ramos' burden to obtain affirmative jury findings on all elements necessary to predicate liability for exemplary damages. Since Ramos failed to submit issues as to managerial capacity, Frito-Lay asserts it had no obligation to object.

There can be no question that it was Ramos' burden to obtain affirmative answers to jury questions as to the necessary elements of his cause of action. If an entire theory were omitted from the charge it would be waived; and Frito-Lay would indeed have no duty to object. TEX. R. CIV. P. 279. Where, however, issues are omitted which constitute only a part of a complete and independent ground and other issues necessarily referable to that ground are submitted and answered, the omitted elements are deemed found in support of the judgment if no objection is made and they are supported by some evidence. TEX. R. CIV. P. 279.

Here, the jury found that Padilla committed an intentional tort while in the scope of his employment and awarded exemplary damages against Frito-Lay. The trial court's judgment included an award for exemplary damages. Although the question of whether Padilla was employed in a managerial capacity and acting in the scope of his employment constituted an element of Ramos' cause of action, it did not encompass an independent ground of recovery. Objection by Frito-Lay to the omission of the element of managerial capacity was thus necessary to prevent a deemed finding against it. Frito-Lay did not object, nor did it request specific findings by the trial court. If the omitted element of managerial capacity is supported by some evidence, we must deem it found against Frito-Lay under Rule 279.

We then turn to the question of whether the omitted element is supported by some evidence. The rule is well settled in Texas that an employer may be held liable in exemplary damages for the acts of an employee who is "employed in a managerial capacity and was acting in the scope of employment." In applying this rule to the facts of this case, the court of appeals found there was no evidence to support the exemplary damage award, stating that "the controlling factor is that at the time of the incident in question, Mr. Padilla was not performing the tasks of a sales manager, he was driving a delivery van and performing the usual task of a route salesman." Under the court of appeals' formulation, it is the character of the employee's act, managerial or non-managerial, and not simply whether the employee was acting in the scope of employment that determines whether exemplary damages are recoverable.

We disagree and hold that an employer may be held liable in exemplary damages for the actions of its management-level employee in performing a non-managerial task. . . . To permit an employer to escape liability for the outrageous acts of its management-level employee because the employee was performing a non-managerial task would severely undercut this purpose. Moreover, we are unwilling to draw a distinction, unsupported by the Restatement or by case law, between managerial and non-managerial tasks. This line is a very gray one indeed. In this case, Padilla testified that it was his responsibility to find someone to cover for the vacationing route salesman or to cover for the salesman himself. Padilla can be described as performing the ordinary duties of a non-managerial employee in driving the delivery van and making sales, yet he can also be described as performing the often necessary managerial duty of stepping into the breach when required. He retained his title of district sales manager and his supervisory authority over twelve employees at the time he was performing these tasks. The record contains evidence to support the deemed finding that Padilla was employed in a managerial capacity and was acting in the scope of his employment.

We reverse the judgment of the court of appeals and remand the cause to that court for consideration of points it did not reach.

Notes & Questions

1. *Careful distinctions*. Be sure to distinguish between omitted elements and waived grounds, and between deemed and expressed findings. If one of a party's grounds of recovery is entirely omitted from the charge and no objection is made to its omission, the party has waived it. If the ground of recovery is submitted in the charge, but there is an element missing and no objection is made to the

omission, the ground is not waived. Instead, the judge becomes the fact-finder—expressly (making an express finding) or by default (the finding is deemed to have been made to support the judgment). Now do you understand why a defendant may need to preserve error that appears in the questions seeking findings on the plaintiff's grounds of recovery? Should the defendant object if the ground is omitted entirely? What about when the ground is submitted, but erroneously?

2. *Improper conditioning*. What if the charge includes all necessary elements of a cause of action, but the court includes an erroneous conditioning instruction which the jury follows. Thus, it skips a critical question that should have been answered? The element (or jury question) is treated as if it had been left out of the charge altogether and Rule 279 applies so as to permit the judge to make the fact-finding *unless* the opponent has objected to the conditioning as improper.[1]

3. *Reviewing the finding*. When there is an element omitted from the charge and the finding is deemed to support the judgment, one reviews that finding on appeal as though the judge actually made the finding. Therefore, as we will see in greater detail later, it will be overturned if not supported by the evidence, and affirmed if it is supported by the evidence. Similarly, if the trial judge makes an express finding on the omitted element, the judge becomes the fact-finder and makes the finding based upon the judge's view of the evidence. Again, on appeal, the finding may be reviewed to determine whether it is supported by sufficient evidence.

4. *Other errors*. What happens when a complainant fails to object to another type of error in the charge—for example, an inferential rebuttal instruction is submitted without evidence to support it? The error is waived—it cannot be a ground for reversal of the trial court's judgment.

---

2. *Remedy for Jury Charge Error Properly Preserved—Remand or Render?*

When there is an error in the charge (properly preserved by the complainant), the appellate court must decide whether it can render judgment or must remand to the trial court for a new trial. The Supreme Court has held that in most situations the appellate court must remand to let the trial court try the case with the proper charge. However, when the error makes the jury question "immaterial" the question and answer to it should be ignored, and judgment rendered accordingly. How does one tell whether the question is "immaterial" or "merely defective?"

---

[1] *See* Little Rock Furniture Mfg. Co. v. Dunn, 222 S.W.2d 985, 991 (Tex. 1949). *See also* Archer Daniels Midland Co. v. Bohall, 114 S.W.3d 42 (Tex. App.—Eastland 2003, no pet. hist.) (holding that trial court erred in reconvening jury after dismissal to reconsider charge with conditioning instructions fixed).

BORNEMAN
v.
STEAK & ALE OF TEXAS, INC.
22 S.W.3d 411
(Tex. 2000)

PER CURIAM

In this dram shop case, Lea Borneman sued Steak & Ale of Texas, Inc. d/b/a Bennigan's (Steak & Ale) because she was injured in a car crash caused by one of its intoxicated patrons. The jury awarded her actual and punitive damages, and the trial court rendered judgment on the verdict. The court of appeals reversed and rendered a take-nothing judgment for Steak & Ale, holding that the jury charge omitted an element of Borneman's cause of action. Although we agree with the court of appeals that the charge was erroneous, the court of appeals should not have rendered judgment because the error in the charge was a defect not an omission. Accordingly, we reverse the judgment of the court of appeals and remand the case to that court for consideration of issues that it did not reach.

Nehemiah Franklin and Michael Nimon consumed a number of alcoholic drinks at a Bennigan's restaurant. Both Franklin and Nimon were underage. Over the course of a few hours, each consumed at least four or five mixed drinks and four or five beers. Franklin and Nimon left the restaurant by car. They went to Nimon's apartment, where they met Lea Borneman and Ashley Wood. The record indicates that Nimon offered Borneman and Wood a ride to a store and that Franklin drove the car with the four of them in it. The car later crashed, and the occupants, including Borneman, were injured.

Borneman sued Steak & Ale under Texas' Dram Shop Act. *See* TEX. ALCO. BEV. CODE §§ 2.01-2.03. This statute generally is the exclusive means for recovery against a provider of alcohol. The requirements set out in the Act are twofold. First, it must be "apparent" to the defendant "at the time" the alcohol is provided, sold, or served that the person consuming the alcohol is "obviously intoxicated to the extent that he present[s] a clear danger to himself and others." TEX. ALCO. BEV. CODE § 2.02(b)(1). Second, "the intoxication of the recipient" must be "a proximate cause of the damages suffered." *Id.* § 2.02(b)(2).

The jury charge contained seven questions, only the third of which is challenged. Question No. 1, tracking section 2.02(b)(1), asked whether Steak & Ale had, in fact, sold or served alcohol to Franklin when it was apparent that he was obviously intoxicated to the extent that he was a clear danger to himself and others. The jury answered "yes." Question No. 2 inquired whether Franklin's conduct was the "sole proximate cause of the occurrence in question," and the jury answered "no." Then, Question No. 3, the question challenged on appeal, asked: "Do you find the conduct of STEAK & ALE OF TEXAS, INC. D/B/A BENNIGAN'S to be a proximate cause of the occurrence in question?" The jury answered in the affirmative. Steak & Ale had objected to Question No. 3, requesting that the issue track section 2.02(b). The jury also found that Borneman's negligence was a proximate cause of the occurrence. It attributed twenty percent of the responsibility to her and eighty percent to Steak & Ale.

The trial court rendered judgment for Borneman based on the jury's verdict, but the court of appeals reversed that judgment. The court of appeals held that question three was an improper submission because the statute requires damages to be linked to the recipient's intoxication, not to mere conduct of the defendant.

We agree with the court of appeals that question three erroneously charged the jury regarding proximate cause. As a general rule, when a statutory cause of action is submitted, the charge should "track the language of the provision as closely as possible." The Dram Shop Act clearly states that the "intoxication of the recipient" must be a proximate cause of the injury. TEX. ALCO. BEV. CODE § 2.02(b)(2).

The court of appeals correctly concluded that the error in the charge required reversal. Borneman had argued to the jury that conduct by Steak & Ale—other than providing, selling, or serving alcoholic beverages to Franklin when he was "obviously intoxicated to the extent that he presented a clear danger to himself and others" and Franklin's intoxication—was a proximate cause of the injury. Among other things, Borneman argued to the jury that the conduct of Steak & Ale that proximately caused Borneman's injuries included its failure to call for a cab to take Franklin and Nimon home. The jury could thus have concluded that if only Steak & Ale had called a cab, Franklin would not have been behind the wheel in his car and would not have driven Borneman. Allowing the jury to consider that act or omission as the basis for causation would directly contravene the decision of the Legislature to define dram shop liability in reference to the patron's intoxication. The charge was therefore improper.

Borneman contends, however, that the court of appeals erred in its disposition of this case. Because the court of appeals held the error in the charge to be the omission of an element of Borneman's cause of action rather than a mere defect, it rendered judgment for Steak & Ale. We agree with Borneman that the court of appeals should not have rendered judgment against her based on this error in the charge.

In *Southeastern Pipe Line Co. v. Tichacek*, we held a jury charge to be defective and remanded the case. We noted that one kind of defective question "plainly attempts to request a finding on a recognized cause of action, but does so improperly." And in *Tichacek*, the party benefiting from the erroneous charge had not chosen to abandon its claim, but had "simply requested an improper submission of the issue to the jury." We find the present case to be analogous.

This case is also similar to the facts presented in *Spencer v. Eagle Star Insurance Co. of America*, in which we remanded a jury charge defect, rather than *State Department of Highways & Public Transportation v. Payne*, in which we rendered judgment. Borneman, like the plaintiff in *Spencer*, "plainly attempted to request a finding on a statutory cause of action." he did not, as in *Payne*, "refuse to submit a theory of recovery" by choosing one theory of recovery over another. *cf. Payne*, 838 S.W.2d. at 240-41 (rendering judgment because the charge included one of the plaintiff's theories but omitted the only legally viable theory). Nor is there any indication that Borneman was attempting to gain an advantage through submission of an improper charge. Further, this charge is not "so defective" that it warrants rendition of judgment. For these reasons, the court of appeals should not have rendered judgment against Borneman on this issue.

We grant Borneman's petition and, without hearing oral argument, *see* TEX. R. APP. P. 59.1, reverse the judgment of the court of appeals and remand the case to that court so that it may consider other of Steak & Ale's issues on appeal.

Notes & Questions

1. *Omitted elements vs. defects.* In *Borneman*, the Supreme Court notes that the Court of Appeals rendered judgment against the plaintiff because the error was an omitted element. The Supreme Court held that the error was a defect, requiring remand. Apparently, the Court of Appeals reasoned that the plaintiff has the burden to obtain affirmative findings on all elements of the cause of action. Therefore, if the plaintiff does not seek submission of the missing element, and the defendant preserves error pointing out the omitted element, the plaintiff, in effect, has waived the missing element. Obviously, the supreme court disagreed.

2. *When omitted elements matter.* "Omitted elements" in the charge do have some independent significance. Remember when *no party* preserves the error, an element omitted from the charge is deemed found to support the judgment. This is distinguished from the situation we have been discussing in this section where *the defendant preserves error* to the omitted element, and a judgment for plaintiff is reversed and remanded for new trial.

3. *Remand or render.* In 2007, in *Ford v. Ledesma*, the Supreme Court felt it necessary to provide another primer on when to remand and when to render for charge error. In that case, the error was a defective instruction. The Court said:

> Having determined that the court's charge was erroneous, . . . [and] since Ford preserved error, we turn to whether the charge error is reversible. We hold that it is. "It is fundamental to our system of justice that parties have the right to be judged by a jury properly instructed in the law." "There can be no question that it was [the plaintiff's] burden to obtain affirmative answers to jury questions as to the necessary elements of his cause of action." The jury was not asked to decide an essential element of a manufacturing defect claim, namely whether the u-bolt deviated from Ford's specifications or planned output.
>
> If a cause of action consists of more than one element, and an element is omitted from the charge "without request or objection," the missing element can be found by the trial court or deemed found if certain requirements are met. But where, as here, a proper objection is made about the omission of an essential element, the failure to include it is reversible error.
>
> Ford argues that we should reverse and render judgment in its favor because of its objected-to charge error, as we did in *State Department of Highways & Public Transportation v. Payne,* but we disagree. In *Spencer v. Eagle Star Insurance Co. of America,* we distinguished *Payne* and explained that where, as in the pending case, the theory of recovery was defectively submitted, as opposed to a situation where the plaintiff "refused to submit a theory of liability" after defendant's objection, the proper remedy is to remand for a new trial.
>
> *Spencer* distinguished cases that reversed and rendered where the plaintiff "failed to submit any jury question on a controlling issue." We further explained, in *Spencer* and in *Stutzman,* that if the plaintiff submits a jury question on his claim that is merely "defective," as opposed to "immaterial," the appropriate remedy is to remand for a new trial rather than to render judgment. In the pending case, Ledesma proffered a question on his manufacturing defect claim based on the PJC for this cause of action. He "attempted to submit a controlling issue" on his sole cause of action, and the question submitted "was the heart of [Ledesma's] case," so the question cannot be characterized as immaterial, and we cannot say that Ledesma failed to submit a jury question on a controlling issue.

Further, we "may, in the interest of justice, remand the case to the trial court even if a rendition of judgment is otherwise appropriate." "[W]e have remanded in the interest of justice when our decisions have altered or clarified the way in which a claim should be submitted to the jury." In the pending case, the trial court followed the PJC. On one occasion we not only approved a PJC issue and instruction for design defect cases, we expressly disapproved of the use of any other instructions in such cases,[1] prompting one court of appeals to remark that "[o]ur highest court has made it abundantly clear that to deviate from the pattern jury charges in products liability cases is a perilous journey."

Given that our trial courts routinely rely on the Pattern Jury Charges in submitting cases to juries, and we rarely disapprove of these charges, we conclude that the interests of justice would not be served by reversing and rendering judgment in favor of Ford. The more appropriate remedy is to reverse and remand for a new trial.

---

1 Acord v. Gen. Motors Corp., 669 S.W.2d 111, 116 (Tex. 1984).

CHAPTER 15. VERDICTS

A. Managing the Jury's Deliberations

1. *Introductory Notes*

The rules dealing with the management of jury deliberations, Rules 280 through 284, are straightforward and uncomplicated. The jurors are directed to select a leader, the "presiding juror." The written charge and all exhibits go with the jury into the jury room when deliberations begin. Although Rule 282 permits the judge to order that jurors be sequestered, that is almost never thought necessary in civil cases. However, the bailiff in charge of the jury is required to see that they remain *incommunicado* while deliberating and the bailiff is specifically forbidden to reveal the state of the deliberations.[1] Each time the jury is excused from its deliberations, the judge reminds the jurors of their oaths regarding communications with others.[2] What if the jurors disagree about the meaning of the charge or need further guidance? In such instances the presiding juror may communicate with the judge in open court (with attorneys present) either verbally or in writing.[3] However, Rule 286 requires the jurors to state any request for further instruction in writing. The court may give further instruction (always in writing) upon such a request or on its own motion.[4] Cautious judges will submit supplemental charges to counsel before giving them to the jury in order to hear any objections. Supplemental charges are often framed by agreement between all trial counsel and the court. Sometimes the only reasonable instruction is that the jurors should review the charge they already have and be guided by it. If the court gives an additional charge, it may, in its discretion, permit further argument.[5]

Rule 226a contains the rules governing a juror's conduct during deliberations and should be read carefully. The rules prohibit contact with attorneys and parties, discussion of the case with others, premature discussion by the jurors themselves, independent factual investigation or research or experimentation, the relating of personal experience, speculation about matters not in evidence (such as about attorney's fees or insurance coverage), and the reaching of a verdict by chance or by trading answers or by an agreed "quotient verdict." They also instruct against treating certain answers as unimportant or answering questions strategically in an effort to reach a predetermined outcome. The 226a "boilerplate" warns jurors that Texas law permits proof of juror misconduct and that jurors may be called to testify about it.

---

1 The bailiff may only inquire as to whether they have reached a verdict. *See* Rule 283.

2 Rule 284. Note that, while the jury deliberates, the court can proceed with other business in the courtroom as long as the deliberating jury is allowed to come and go under the court's direction. *See* Rule 288.

3 Rule 285. The requirement that jurors be instructed in open court is often waived by absent counsel who agree on the court's supplemental instruction and that it may be delivered in writing to the jury room. *See* Garza v. San Antonio Light, 531 S.W.2d 926 (Tex. Civ. App.—Corpus Christi 1975, writ ref'd n.r.e.).

4 *See* Rule 286.

5 Rule 286.

2. *Juror Note-Taking*

In 2011, the Texas Supreme Court revised the admonitory instructions following Rule 226a, which are given to prospective jurors and to jury members selected for trial. The amendments included a "plain language" revision, made clear that internet investigation and communication about the trial is prohibited, and for the first time allows jurors to take notes if they want to. Notice that the jurors cannot take the notes home, but must leave them with the bailiff when they leave the jury room. Notes can be used during deliberations only with the judge's permissions. Also, the notes will be destroyed at the end of the trial to prevent post-trial motions seeking to subpoena those notes. The instruction provides as follows:

> 10. During the trial, if taking notes will help focus your attention on the evidence, you may take notes using the materials the court has provided. Do not use any personal electronic devices to take notes. If taking notes will distract your attention from the evidence, you should not take notes. Your notes are for your own personal use. They are not evidence. Do not show or read your notes to anyone, including other jurors. You must leave your notes in the jury room or with the bailiff. The bailiff is instructed not to read your notes and to give your notes to me promptly after collecting them from you. I will make sure your notes are kept in a safe, secure location and not disclosed to anyone. [You may take your notes back into the jury room and consult them during deliberations. But keep in mind that your notes are not evidence. When you deliberate, each of you should rely on your independent recollection of the evidence and not be influenced by the fact that another juror has or has not taken notes. After you complete your deliberations, the bailiff will collect your notes.] When you are released from jury duty, the bailiff will promptly destroy your notes so that nobody can read what you wrote.

One concern about juror notes is that it gives the note-taking juror more power in deliberations—if there is a conflict about certain testimony, jurors may defer to the notes of one juror. If jurors cannot agree about testimony, they may have the testimony in question read back to them by the court reporter as prescribed by Rule 287.[6] In the reporter's absence, the court may recall the witness and have him or her repeat the testimony. The same procedure is available (and much easier to implement) with respect to deposition testimony. This rule is seldom employed except in the case of a potentially hung jury. The charge does not advise the jurors of its provisions and the judge and the lawyers are often apprehensive about its use. Court reporters, understandably, find it a pain. The frequent result is that the jurors, unaware of the rule, do not request testimony to be read back. Note that the jury cannot simply say, "We want to hear witness Smith's testimony again." Rule 287 requires the jury to state that they disagree about a witness's testimony on a specified point. There must be disagreement, not mere desire to hear the testimony again. And the jury must specify the disputed area of testimony. When the jury makes such a request, the court will have the reporter locate and read to the jury Smith's testimony on that disputed point only.

---

[6] Note that nothing in Rule 287 permits the *judge* to address the jurors directly in the jury room and it has been held reversible error for him to do so. Ross v. T.E.I.A., 267 S.W.2d 541 (Tex. 1954).

B. Defective Verdicts

When the jury returns its verdict (i.e. the court's charge with the jury's answers filled in), the presiding juror will hand it to the bailiff, who will then carry it to the judge. The judge will read the verdict to make sure that it is complete and that the same ten or more jurors have signed it, as Rule 292 requires. Occasionally the court will notice a mistake and after calling it to the jury's attention will send the jury back for further deliberation. If the verdict is complete, most courts will then ask whether either attorney wishes to inspect it. If the case is complicated and the charge contains many questions, it is advisable for attorneys to take this opportunity to inspect the verdict for mistakes before the court receives it and discharges the jury.

If the jury has not answered all the questions, the unanswered questions could be immaterial in the sense that one side may be victorious no matter how the remaining questions might be answered. In this situation, the court may accept the partial verdict and render the appropriate judgment.

---

1. *Hung Juries*

Read Rule 289.

SHAW
v.
GREATER HOUSTON TRANSPORTATION COMPANY
791 S.W.2d 204
(Tex. App.—Corpus Christi 1990, no writ)

NYE, CHIEF JUSTICE.

Coy Shaw and Richard Allen Hall appeal a jury verdict in favor of Greater Houston Transportation Company and Kenny Hamilton, the driver of the Yellow Cab, in an automobile collision case.

This case was brought by appellants Coy Shaw (the driver) and Richard Allen Hall (the passenger) against Greater Houston Transportation Company and Kenny Hamilton (Yellow Cab) for injuries received when the truck Shaw was driving collided with a Yellow Cab driven by Hamilton. The evidence was contested on all issues, particularly damages. Shaw alleged that Hamilton unlawfully changed lanes, striking the side of Shaw's pickup. Yellow Cab asserted the accident happened when a two lane road narrowed to one lane. Hamilton, Yellow Cab's driver, was in the left lane; Shaw was in the right lane. Ultimately, the jury found Hamilton (Yellow Cab) 70% negligent and Shaw 30% negligent. This case is an example of how a case should not be tried.

The testimony on damages was hotly contested. Shaw introduced testimony that he suffered lacerations and bruises. He had back pain which persisted. He was diagnosed as having herniated cervical and lumbar discs which culminated in a lumbar fusion and laminectomy. Hall received head lacerations and was unconscious at the scene of the accident. Expert testimony, introduced by Shaw, showed that he had suffered pain and would continue to have pain in the future. He had a

25% permanent disability. According to testimony by Shaw's physician the injuries were probably caused by this accident.

Shaw had a history of severe back problems, including a laminectomy prior to the accident. According to Yellow Cab's evidence, much of the doctor's testimony was based on the allegedly unreliable history Shaw gave. Yellow Cab cited evidence showing that Shaw had been seen by a doctor and was released as being without discomfort or disability. Yellow Cab also introduced evidence showing Shaw back at work.

The jury finally gave no damages to Shaw on each element. It awarded Hall $180.00 for past loss of earning capacity and $250.00 for past medical expenses.

Appellants raise eight points. By point one they complain that the trial court erred in coercing and unduly influencing the jury by the judge's supplemental charges, behavior and instructions during deliberations and throughout the trial. We look at this issue from two perspectives. First, were the actual supplemental charges given by the trial court coercive as that word is defined in law? Second, was the trial court's requirement that the jury continue deliberations for days and days unduly coercive?

The definitive case dealing with trial court coercion in the deliberation process is *Stevens v. Travelers Insurance Co.*, 563 S.W.2d 223 (Tex. 1978). In *Stevens*, the Supreme Court held that in order to test a particular charge for coerciveness, the supplemental charge must be broken down into its particulars and analyzed for possible coercive statements. A potentially coercive statement will not invalidate the charge, unless it retains its coercive nature as a whole when all of the circumstances surrounding its rendition are considered. In analyzing any verdict where additional instructions are urged, we must balance the need for the expeditious administration of justice with the appellate court's concern for impartiality in the fact-finding process. The *Stevens* court dealt solely with the coercive nature of a supplemental charge. It did not deal with the issue of the coercive effect of repeatedly returning a jury to deliberate further. Both aspects of coercion are raised in appellants' point of error.

TEX. R. CIV. P. 289 indicates that a jury to whom a case has been submitted may be discharged when they cannot agree and the parties consent to their discharge; or when they have been kept together for such time as to render it altogether improbable that they can agree; or when any calamity or accident may, in the opinion of the court, require it. There are not many cases under this rule from which to draw guidance. However, a few general rules have emerged from the cases which have arisen. The length of time the jury is to be held in an effort to secure an agreement is left to the sound discretion of the trial judge. On appeal that discretion is tested. A trial judge must have considerable latitude, short of genuine prejudice to a party. There must be substantial evidence to suggest that it was altogether improbable that the jury would reach a verdict. . . .

In the case at bar, the jury began its deliberations on February 2, 1988. Apparently, the jury sent a note to have testimony read back to them that same day. The statement of facts reflects that the court reporter read parts of testimony to the jury panel on many occasions. On February 3, 1988 additional testimony was read to the jury. At 12:45 p.m., the jury sent the following note:

> We are going to need some assistance or guidance from the court. We are at an *impasse* regarding the percentage of fault associated with each driver. Please advise if we have to agree on a set breakdown or if we can use a preponderance (51% = 100% negligence on special issue No. 5) of the facts to assign percentage of negligence.

There appears to be a written response from the judge suggesting that the jury read over the explanatory instructions set out at the beginning of the charge as well as Special Issue No. 5.

At 1:20 p.m., the jury sent out the following note:

> *We cannot come to an agreement* on the percentage. We have a majority of people who believe one party is over 51% negligent. We do not, however, have 10 people who can agree on a percentage over 51%. Is it lawful for jurors to compromise and come to an agreement on percentage.

Over objection, the Court sent back the following written response at 1:45 p.m.

> Yes so long as you do not violate instructions 5 and 6 in the Charge.

These questions each related to the liability issues which were submitted. At 3:25 p.m. on February 3, 1988, the jury sent out another note:

> *We cannot come to a conclusion* regarding the amounts of damages (in dollars), if any, that Mr. Shaw should receive from the accident. Please advise—is dollar amount necessary? If so, we are a hung jury unless you have suggestions.

This question related to the damage questions that were submitted. The court responded in writing at 3:32 p.m. that the jury should please continue deliberating.

At some point after this note was received, the trial court allowed the attorneys to each argue five additional minutes. This was after the jury had requested additional testimony recalled. The arguments ended at approximately 5:00 p.m. on February 3, 1988. The jury adjourned for the day.

At 11:00 a.m. on February 4, 1988, the jury sent out the following note:

> We are at the same impasse today as we were yesterday. We cannot get 10 people to agree on the amount of injuries (in dollars), if any, sustained by Mr. Shaw in the occurrence. *A majority of the jurors feel that further deliberation is pointless.*

At that point appellant's attorney moved for a mistrial. It is apparent that at this point the jury had deliberated on the damage issues many hours. Instead of granting a mistrial, the trial court returned the panel to the courtroom and gave the jury the following supplemental charge:

> THE COURT: Ladies and gentlemen, you all have spent a lot of time working in there, and I know that you've continued to work. I think that it would be wrong to shut this trial down, now, and after you've worked so hard, and so long, and you're almost through. If you stopped now, we would have to start all over, again, with another jury, and with another trial, and all of these people's time and effort, and all of your time and effort, would have been wasted, and I realize that it's hard because each and everyone of you have worked, and you've listened, and you've worked hard. Very hard, and you've struggled, and you've really—well, I have not had a jury work as hard as you all have, and I think because each and everyone of you are the kind of people that are thinking and caring, well, that maybe you all need to give it some more thought, and if you want further testimony that will assist you in getting your job done, tell me what it is, and then Don will take the time to find it. We've come too far, and if it takes a while, let's do it. Okay? Whatever you need, you tell me. Now, have you all got a lot of issues to go.
>
> THE JUROR: Number Seven is the one we're having problems with. It's Issue Number Seven. (This was the damage issue concerning appellant Shaw). Can I tell you the problem?

THE COURT: No.

THE JUROR: Okay.

THE COURT: Well, then are you telling me that you're through with all of the others, and you have just this one to go?

THE JUROR: Yes.

THE COURT: Well, you've worked hard.

* * *

If necessary, well, we will—well, I didn't give all of you a copy of the charge, but if that would help, and to give all of you a copy of the charge, and so that you can read it, and read the instructions, and if that might help, but I don't know if that would help, or not, but we sometimes give all twelve of you a copy of the charge, but I don't know. We just didn't do it.

But, you all just need to let me know what you need. Okay? And, you all are called the "VIP's," and because you are very important people. You are very important people to this Court, and to this country, and for what it stands for, and you, *yes, sometimes reach a point where you can't go on, but I'm not a quitter. I'm not one to throw in the towel, at all. You know that I'm "cold hearted Hannah" sometimes, and you know that I make my son come down here when he's sick, and when he shouldn't be here, and he should be in school, and I come down here when I'm sick, and because I—well, I've made you all come down here, and when you've had problems. You all have pushed me, and I've pushed you, but what I really want is to have this trial resolved as fairly as possible.*

* * *

THE COURT: Well anyway, I think you all know what I'm saying, and that you've got a responsibility, and I hope that you will take care of that responsibility, and that you can handle it, but I know that it's not easy. I mean, *I would invite—invite anyone of you all to come down here any day and to take my job for a couple of—well, for six months. And then, I would love to sit over there and to argue with you all for a couple of hours, you know, of for a couple of days.*

But, anyway, if you all need another pot of coffee, or cokes, or whatever, we'll send out for them, or for whatever you need. If you want to take a—well, it's nice and cold outside, and if you want to take a brisk walk outside, well, that's fine with me.

But, anyway, why don't you all go back there and try it, again.

(Thereupon the jury panel was removed from the courtroom.)

At 1:45 p.m. on Thursday, February 4, 1988, the jury sent to the court the following note:

We cannot come to a decision! *Tempers are heated and people are* (getting) *frustrated. Based upon the evidence, we cannot abide by the instructions and reach a verdict. At this point, we feel the case will have to be retried.*

This note was given to the Court approximately three hours after the last supplemental charge. Thereafter, the Court called the jury back into the courtroom. The following occurred:

THE COURT: All right. Bring the jury out.

(Thereupon the jury panel was returned to the courtroom.)

> THE COURT: I'm of the opinion that everybody needs a rest, and I'm going to recess the trial until Monday morning. You all will have to come back at ten o'clock, and I'll see you all Monday morning at ten o'clock. Think about it and consider it over the weekend, and come back Monday.
>
> THE JUROR: What? *Why?*
>
> THE COURT: Everybody be back here at ten o'clock Monday morning.
>
> MR. VECCHIO: Your Honor, at this time, and in view of what the juror said, we would object to further deliberations and move for a mistrial.

The court recessed the trial until Monday morning, February 8, 1988 at 10:00 o'clock. The jury returned to deliberate as instructed by the trial court. At about 5 o'clock p.m. on Monday evening the jury reached a verdict. The jury found zero damages for Mr. Shaw and $430 damages for Mr. Hill.

In reviewing the trial court's supplemental charges to the jury, (which is previously set forth in the opinion) we look first to the individual passages of the charge as suggested by the Supreme Court in *Stevens*. The trial court's first questionable supplemental charge was as follows:

> If you stopped now, we would have to start all over again, with another jury, and with another trial, and all of these people's time and effort, and all of your time and effort, would have been wasted . . . .
>
> This statement, standing alone, would not be coercive.
>
> The trial court's second supplemental charge is as follows:
>
> I want you to know exactly how important you are . . . and work it out, and to resolve this case, and if *there's any possibility that you can do that, then, I would like for you to do it. It's very important.*

This statement, standing alone, may be classified as possibly coercive. A jury is aware of the position of the trial court and its power over it. The jury is aware that only the judge can allow them to end their deliberations. The court's next supplemental charge:

> You are very important people to this Court, and to this country, and what it stands for . . . but I'm not a quitter. I'm not one to throw in the towel, at all. You know that I'm cold hearted Hannah sometimes.

This statement is potentially coercive. The Court is inferring that she is not a quitter and the jury should not quit either, until it reaches a verdict. She indicated that she was suffering personally by allowing her sick child to come to the courtroom. In other words, the trial court wanted a verdict reached by the jury.

The fourth supplemental charge to the jury is as follows:

> Well, anyway, I think you all know what I'm saying, and that you've got a responsibility, and I hope that you will take care of that responsibility . . . .

Again, this statement appears also to be potentially coercive. It informs the jury that the Court wanted a verdict reached and believed it to be the jury's responsibility to do it.

There are three charges which clearly indicate that the trial court would not allow a hung jury. It was becoming clear that the trial court was not going to let the jury quit, because she (the judge) was not a quitter. She stated that they would have breached their responsibility in not reaching a verdict.

The various disorganized "dynamite" charges as a whole were without a doubt coercive in nature. When the trial judge refused to allow the jury to cease deliberations after they had stated three times in their notes that they were deadlocked on the damage issue was, without a doubt, coercion reasonably calculated to cause the rendition of an improper verdict.

We find egregious the trial court's insistence that the jury continue their deliberations beyond a point in which they had affirmatively stated, "Tempers are heated and people are frustrated"—"we cannot abide by the instruction and reach a verdict. At this point, we feel the case will have to be retried." Even before this took place, on February 3, 1988 at 3:25 p.m., it was apparent that the jury was unable to reach a conclusion with regard to the damage issue. On February 4 at 11:00 a.m., the jury had made no progress on the damage issue. The note stated that the jury felt further deliberation was pointless. The jury was still deadlocked after the court's supplemental "dynamite" charge. At 1:45, the jury sent another note indicating deadlock. We view it as particularly significant that the jurors stated that they could not abide by the trial court's instructions. We find it was at this point that the trial court abused its discretion by returning the jury on Monday, February 8, to deliberate further. By refusing to release the jury, the jury surely knew that it would not be released until it reached a verdict. This action was coercive in nature and was harmful error. The action of the trial judge was reasonably calculated to cause the rendition of an improper verdict. We sustain point one.

* * *

There were many problems and much animosity between appellants' lawyer and the trial judge. Even though many of these incidents occurred outside the presence of the jury, the cumulative effect of all of these acts deprived appellants of a fair trial. We sustain the eighth point of error.

. . . This case was so flawed in the manner tried that a retrial is necessary. We REVERSE and REMAND this case to the trial court for new trial.

Notes & Questions

1. Stevens *and the dynamite charge*. The leading Texas case is *Stevens v. Travelers Ins. Co.*,[1] quoted in detail on the second page of *Shaw*. (*Stevens* refers to *Allen v. U.S.*,[2] in which the Supreme Court upheld a verdict-urging charge which has since become known as an "*Allen charge*" or a "*dynamite charge*.") The general rule nationwide is that the judge may, within reasonable limits, mention such matters as the time and expense already spent on the case, the number of times it has been tried, and the fact that if the jury remains deadlocked the case will have to be tried again on the same pleadings and probably the same evidence.[3]

2. *Hung jury*. Rule 289 allows a deadlocked jury to be discharged by agreement of counsel or "when they have been kept together for such time as to render it altogether improbable that they can agree" or when calamity or accident, in the court's opinion, requires it, or when by sickness or other

---

1 563 S.W.2d 223 (Tex. 1978).

2 164 U.S. 492 (1896).

3 *See* cases collected at 109 ALR 72; Pope, *Instructing Deadlocked Juries*, 3 TEX. TECH L. REV. 313 (1972) *and* 4 MCDONALD, TEXAS CIVIL PRACTICE, 376.

cause the number of jurors falls below the required number. *See* Government Code § 62.020 regarding the use of alternate jurors, who can step up when a regular juror drops out or is removed.

---

2. *Gaps and Conflicts*

Read Rule 295.

FLEET
v.
FLEET
711 S.W.2d 1
(Tex. 1986)

PER CURIAM.

This is a suit against an executor for breach of fiduciary duties. The trial court rendered a take nothing judgment against Peggy Fleet based on an incomplete verdict. In an unpublished opinion, the court of appeals affirmed the judgment.

The issue on appeal is whether the trial judge properly rendered judgment based on an incomplete verdict, and whether the court of appeals properly affirmed. We grant the application for writ of error and, pursuant to Rule 483 without hearing oral argument, reverse the judgment of the court of appeals and remand the cause for a new trial.

Claud Fleet's former mother-in-law, Irene Lewis, died on September 17, 1970, leaving a will which named Claud Fleet independent executor. In 1982, Peggy Fleet, Claud Fleet's former wife and Irene Lewis' surviving daughter, sued Claud Fleet for various breaches of fiduciary duties. The trial judge presented the acts alleged as breaches in one issue, lettered "A" through "K." Each lettered question contained a different act. The jury found "We Do Not" to questions "D" and "H," and "We Do" to questions "I," "J," and "K." The jury left the remaining questions unanswered.

Issue number seven, lettered to correspond to issue number one, asked the jury to find when "Peggy Fleet discovered or by reasonable diligence should have discovered Respondent Claud Fleet's acts . . . ." The jury left blank questions "A" through "H," and found dates for "I" through "K" of April 15, 1977, February 4, 1975, and September 14, 1973 respectively.

The trial judge rendered a take nothing judgment against Peggy Fleet, concluding, based on the jury's answers to issue seven, that Peggy Fleet was barred by the applicable statute of limitations. The court of appeals affirmed the judgment. Peggy Fleet brings two complaints to this court: (1) that the court of appeals erred in holding that the statute of limitations barred her claim; and, (2) that the trial court erred in rendering judgment and not declaring a mistrial when the jury could not agree to answers to material issues in issue number one.

Peggy Fleet's second complaint is correct and dispositive of the case because the trial court's and court of appeal's judgments conflict directly with our prior opinion in *Powers v. Standard Acc. Ins. Co.*, 144 Tex. 415, 191 S.W.2d 7 (1945). We held in *Powers* that a judgment cannot be based on a verdict containing unanswered issues, supported by some evidence, unless the issues are immaterial. Issues are only immaterial if their answers can be found elsewhere in the charge or if they cannot alter the effect of the verdict. The issues this jury left unanswered are material, for each issue inquires about a different act; none duplicate. Further, while the jury found that Peggy Fleet discovered the acts in the answered issues outside of the applicable statute of limitations period, it may have found that she discovered the unanswered acts within the applicable statute of limitations period.

Faced with a verdict which leaves material issues supported by some evidence unanswered, the trial court must instruct the jury to deliberate further on the issues. If upon further deliberation the jury cannot agree on answers to the issues, the trial court may declare a mistrial, but the trial court may not render judgment based on the incomplete verdict. The trial court will not be reversed for rendering judgment, however, unless the party who would benefit from answers to the issues objects to the incomplete verdict before the jury is discharged, making it clear that he desires that the jury redeliberate on the issues or that the trial court grant a mistrial.

Peggy Fleet properly objected to the incomplete verdict before the court discharged the jury by asking that the jury be instructed to further deliberate or that the trial judge grant a mistrial. Rather than instructing the jury to deliberate further, the trial court asked each juror if further deliberations would help them agree to answers. When the jurors said "no," the judge discharged the jury. The trial court later denied Peggy Fleet's motion for mistrial and rendered the take nothing judgment against her.

We hold that the trial court erred by rendering judgment on the incomplete verdict and not ordering a mistrial when it realized that the jury could not agree to answers to material, evidenced issues. Because the resolution of this point of error fully disposes of this case, we do not reach Peggy Fleet's point on the statute of limitations. Accordingly, we reverse the judgment of the court of appeals and remand the cause to the probate court for a new trial.

***Osterberg v. Peca*, 12 S.W.3d 31 (Tex. 2000):**

> . . . Peca complains that the court of appeals erred in holding that he waived recovery of attorney's fees. Section 253.131 entitles an opposing candidate who proves a violation of Chapter 253 to recover, in addition to damages based on the value of the unlawful contribution or expenditure, "reasonable attorney's fees incurred in the suit." TEX. ELEC.CODE § 253.131(d)(2). The trial court submitted a question asking the jury to "[f]ind, in dollars and cents, the total amount that would be a reasonable attorney's fee for the services by 'Plaintiff's attorney' incurred in this case." The jury informed the trial court that it was deadlocked on that question. After that disclosure, Peca failed to object or request an answer to his attorney's fees question. Instead, Peca asked the trial court to accept the incomplete verdict, and then asked the court to enter judgment as a matter of law for his attorney's fees. The trial court refused, and the court of appeals affirmed, holding that Peca had waived the issue for appeal. Peca argues that his failure to request a jury answer did not waive his right to attorney's fees because his uncontroverted evidence entitled him to attorney's fees as a matter of law.
>
> In finding that Peca waived his right to attorney's fees, the court of appeals relied on this Court's decision in *Fleet v. Fleet*, 711 S.W.2d 1 (Tex. 1986). In *Fleet*, we held that a trial court will not be reversed for rendering judgment on an incomplete verdict unless the party who would benefit from answers to the unanswered issues objects to the incomplete verdict before the jury is discharged. *Fleet* followed *Continental Casualty* in which the

plaintiff did not object to the jury's failure to answer questions regarding the amount he was entitled to under an insurance policy. Because the plaintiff in *Continental Casualty* failed to object before the jury was discharged, this Court held that "[t]he trial court had no alternative under the jury verdict but to render judgment for [Continental Casualty], and [the plaintiff] waived any benefit he might have claimed under the unanswered issues, and any right to have them answered." . . . Elliott, *Jury Trial: Verdict, in* 4 MCDONALD TEXAS CIVIL PRACTICE § 25:7, at 415-16 (Allen et al. eds., 1992 ed.) ("[E]very material question must be answered by the jury and the court cannot, in any circumstances, supply findings on unanswered or incompletely answered material questions . . . . A party who . . . silently allows the verdict to be accepted and the jury to be discharged waives the right to complain that the questions are unanswered, and the trial court may disregard the unanswered questions and render judgment for the party entitled to prevail under the findings made."); . . . . Peca, by failing to object when the jury did not return an answer, waived any benefit from the jury question, waived any right to have the trial judge supply his own factfinding or grant a new trial on the issue, and waived his right to appeal a judgment on the issue of attorney's fees. We affirm the court of appeals' judgment regarding attorney's fees.

Notes & Questions

1. *Gaps*. Peggy Fleet's counsel made a timely objection to the missing jury answers. Peca's did not. If the jury leaves out a critical answer and the proponent fails to complain before the jury is discharged (so that the jury can be sent back to deliberate further) the answer is waived. Its proponent loses the benefit of it. Wouldn't Rule 279 allow the judge to make the findings in place of the jury? No. The Rules make the judge the fact-finder for missing *questions* but not for missing *answers*.[1] But as we saw in connection with the charge, there is an exception: a missing jury answer is not waived, even though the proponent has not complained, if an erroneous conditioning instruction has withheld it from the jury's consideration. In such a case the question is treated exactly as if it had never been in the charge at all. Rule 279 applies, and the trial judge can supply the missing answer.[2]

Waiver of a jury's answer makes a difference only if the omitted answer is material, that is, capable of determining the outcome. Otherwise, the trial court must ignore the omission and enter judgment on the partial verdict.[3]

---

1 Under Rule 279, the judge can supply the missing answer only if there has been a partial submission—that is, if some elements "necessarily referable" to a claim or defense have been submitted. If a missing question incorporates an entire (independent) ground of recovery or defense and no one complains, that claim or defense is waived.

2 *See, e.g.* Jones, *Waiver of Unanswered Special Issues*, 38 TEX. L. REV. 93 (1959) *and* Bankers Standard Life Ins. Co. v. Atwood, 205 S.W.2d 74 (Tex. Civ. App.—Austin 1947, no writ). Despite the fact that Rule 279 deals only with elements of a cause of action or defense, *omitted from the charge*, some courts have allowed the judge to supply the answers the jurors failed to give, provided no one has objected to the jury's default. *See* Horn v. A.T. & S.F. Ry. Co., 519 S.W.2d 894, 898 (Tex. Civ. App.—Beaumont 1975, writ ref'd n.r.e.); Boyer v. G.C. & S.F. Ry. Co., 306 S.W.2d 215 (Tex. Civ. App.—Houston 1957, writ ref'd n.r.e.).

3 *See* Jones, *Waiver of Unanswered Special Issues*, 38 TEX. L. REV. 93 (1959) *and* Garza v. San Antonio Light, 531 S.W.2d 926 (Tex. Civ. App.—Corpus Christi 1975, writ ref'd n.r.e.).

2. *Conflicts*. Before the mandate for broad-form submissions, jury questions often produced conflicting answers.[4] Broad form jury questions should prevent most, but certainly not all, conflicts. The first problem is to determine whether the two answers are materially and fatally conflicting. The test, established in *Little Rock Furniture Mfg. Co. v. Dunn*,[5] is as follows. If jury answer #4 seems to conflict with answer #8, the court first considers the case outcome by placing answer #4 (but not #8) with the rest of the jury's answers and determines the case outcome dictated by those answers. It then reverses the answers (#8 in, #4 out) and determines the outcome. If the outcomes are different, there is a material conflict. Say, for example, a jury had found (a) that X was D's employee in the course of his employment and (b) that X was an independent contractor (defined, in part, as a non-employee). D's asserted liability is based on *respondeat superior*. If the court honors finding (a) P wins. If it honors finding (b) D wins. This illustration employs a conflict so obvious that "the test" would seem unnecessary. But many conflicts are more subtle and difficult to identify, and the court has a duty to "reconcile apparent conflicts in the jury's findings if reasonably possible in light of the pleadings and evidence, the manner of submission, and the other findings considered as a while."[6] As with gaps, Rule 279 allows the trial judge to ask the jury to deliberate further with further written instructions to resolve the conflict.

3. *Preserving error regarding conflicts*. There is some uncertainty about when a party must preserve error to a judgment rendered on conflicting findings. on appeal. The Texas Supreme Court addressed the issue in *USAA Texas Lloyd Co, v. Menchaca,*[7] but failed to reach a majority decision. The plurality held that the defendant could complain of the judgment without having objected to the conflict before the judge discharged the jury. The plaintiff, as the party with the burden to obtain findings to support the judgment seems to have the burden to request further deliberations to resolve the conflict. The minority would hold that the error must be preserved by an objection asserted before the court discharges the jury. The appellant bears the burden of objecting—a judgment based on conflicting answers will not be reversed unless the appellant has preserved error.

---

3. *Verdict Rendered by Less than Twelve Jurors*

Read Rule 292-95

Rule 292 allows non-unanimous verdicts, with the same ten of twelve jurors concurring with each answer in the charge. The rule also allows a unanimous verdict when any jurors have been discharged during the trial, but at least nine jurors remain. Note, however, that other law may require a unanimous verdict. For example, CPRC §41.003 requires that a jury be "unanimous in regard to finding liability for and the amount of exemplary damages."

---

4 A well-constructed charge could avoid such conflicts by submitting the "controlling issues" only once and by avoiding "phases or shades" of the same question.

5 222 S.W.2d 985 (Tex. 1949). *See also* USAA Texas Lloyd Co, v. Menchaca, 545 S.W.3d 479 (Tex. 2018) (finding material and fatal conflict); Arvizu v. Estate of Puckett, 364 S.W.3d 273 (Tex. 2012) (following *Little Rock*, and finding no fatal conflict).

6 Anderson v. Durant, ___ S.W.3d ___, No. 16-0842 (Tex. June 22, 2018).

7 545 S.W.3d 479 (Tex. 2018).

YANES
v.
SOWARDS
996 S.W.2d 849
(Tex. 1999)

PER CURIAM.

The issue here is whether the trial court abused its discretion by dismissing a juror whose grandfather was ill and not expected to live, and proceeding with only eleven jurors. We hold that it did not. We therefore reverse the court of appeals' judgment and render judgment that respondent take nothing.

Mollie and G.A. Sowards sued Hector O. Yanes, M.D., alleging that Yanes operated on the wrong artery during Mollie's coronary artery bypass surgery. During the second day of testimony, juror Christopher Obregon notified the trial court that his grandfather was in the hospital dying from an E-coli infection. The trial court interviewed Obregon about his grandfather's condition and the effect it would have on his ability to concentrate on the evidence at trial:

MR. OBREGON: My grandpa, Robert H. Williams, was in the hospital a week and a half ago, and we found out last night that he has E-coli, and they think he might pass away from—Anyway, it was supposed to be from last night to whenever it last until he get worse to where he can't handle it.

THE COURT: And are you telling me that you think that could be today?

MR. OBREGON: Yes.

THE COURT: All right. And where were you last night?

MR. OBREGON: All Saints Hospital.

THE COURT: All right. Is that where he is?

MR. OBREGON: Uh-huh.

THE COURT: The one over here in the medical district, a mile or so away?

MR. OBREGON: Uh-huh.

THE COURT: All right. Is the rest of your family there?

MR. OBREGON: Uh-huh. My mom has been there every day.

* * *

THE COURT: All right. Is this circumstance going to or not going to interfere with your ability to listen to and understand and pay attention to the evidence that you are hearing?

MR. OBREGON: It'll distract me.

THE COURT: I mean, is that a, yes, it is going to interfere, or it is not going to interfere?

MR. OBREGON: Yes, sir.

THE COURT: All right. Are you telling me that you don't think that you can pay attention due to the problem that has developed?

MR. OBREGON: Yes.

Based on the foregoing interview, the trial court found that Obregon was disabled under Rule 292 because he would be unable to concentrate, understand, or appreciate the evidence.[1] Counsel for both parties objected to this finding. They complained that the trial court's questions were overly suggestive and that Obregon's responses to them did not show that he would be absolutely unable to concentrate on the case. Nevertheless, both parties refused the trial court's invitation to question Obregon themselves.

The trial court denied the Sowards' mistrial motion, and the trial proceeded before the remaining eleven jurors. The remaining eleven jurors found unanimously for Yanes, and the trial court rendered judgment on the verdict. The court of appeals reversed and remanded the case for a new trial.

The Texas Constitution and Texas Rules of Civil Procedure require a district-court jury to consist of twelve original jurors, but as few as nine may render and return a verdict if the others die or become "disabled from sitting." "[T]rial courts have broad discretion in determining whether a juror is 'disabled from sitting' when there is evidence of constitutional disqualification."[3] But not just any inconvenience or delay is a disability. A constitutional disability must be in the nature of "an actual physical or mental incapacity."[4] In *McDaniel,* we held that a juror who was temporarily unable to return to the courthouse because of heavy flooding was not thereby disabled from sitting.

The present case is distinguishable from *McDaniel.* In *McDaniel,* the juror was "temporarily detained by flooding caused by heavy rain, which is at most a transient physical barrier." It did not affect the juror's mental capacity to understand or concentrate on the evidence at trial. Also, the trial could have resumed as soon as the flooding receded. Here, by contrast, the sickness and impending death of Obregon's grandfather affected Obregon's mental capacity indefinitely.

In *McDaniel,* this Court cited extensively to *Houston & Texas Central Ry. Co. v. Waller*[7] in which the trial court dismissed a juror because of the illness of a loved one, as in this case. The court of appeals interpreted *Waller* to categorically state "that an illness in the family is not a constitutional disqualification that will allow the trial to continue after the juror's dismissal." We disagree.

In *Waller,* juror Thomas Bradbury's wife wrote to inform him that one of their children was sick and asked him "to come home *if he could.*" The trial court, after reading the letter, asked Bradbury if the letter "satisfied him that it was necessary for him to be at home to attend his sick child." Bradbury answered, with apparent distress, that it did. Over the objection of the defendant's attorneys the trial court discharged Bradbury and continued the trial with the remaining eleven jurors. This Court reversed, stating that:

> the causes which disable the juror from sitting, and justify the extreme course of allowing, over a party's objection, a verdict to be rendered by the remainder of the jury, must be of a nature more directly showing his physical or mental incapacity than mere mental dis-

---

[1] *See* TEX. R. CIV. P. 292.

[3] McDaniel v. Yarbrough, 898 S.W.2d 251, 253 (Tex. 1995).

[4] *See id.; see also* Carrillo v. State, 597 S.W.2d 769, 771 (Tex. Crim. App. 1980) (holding that only jurors who suffer a physical, emotional, or mental disability are constitutionally disabled within the meaning of Article 5, Section 13 of the Texas Constitution).

[7] 56 Tex. 331 (1882).

> tress occasioned by the sickness of others, and the feeling that duty to the sick demanded his presence elsewhere.

The present case is distinguishable from *Waller*. In *Waller,* the trial court asked Bradbury only about his sense of paternal duty, not what effect the knowledge of his child's sickness would have on his mental capacity to fully and fairly perform his jury duty. Although Bradbury was mentally distressed, there was no evidence that his distress prevented him from discharging his job as a juror. Here, by contrast, the trial court elicited testimony from juror Obregon indicating that he would be distracted and unable to pay attention due to his grandfather's condition. Moreover, the trial court gave the Sowards the opportunity, which they declined, to question Obregon further to support their contention that Obregon was not "absolutely" unable to concentrate or act fairly. The trial court's finding of disability is supported by Obregon's testimony, which tended to show that he not only suffered "mere mental distress," but also was emotionally and psychologically disabled from sitting.

* * *

In summary, we conclude if the death or serious illness of a family member renders a juror unable to discharge his responsibilities, trial may proceed with fewer than twelve jurors. Obregon's responses to the trial court's questions support the conclusion that he was emotionally disabled and unable to discharge his responsibilities because of the serious illness of his grandfather. Therefore, we hold that the trial court did not abuse its discretion by concluding that Obregon was disabled from sitting, dismissing him, and continuing with eleven jurors. Accordingly, this Court grants Yanes's petition for review, and under Texas Rule of Appellate Procedure 59.1, without hearing oral argument, reverses the court of appeals' judgment and renders judgment that the Sowards take nothing.

C. Attacking the Jury's Verdict for Sufficiency of Evidence

The Chapter on Summary Judgments discussed circumstances under which a party could obtain a summary judgment and introduced the concept of legal sufficiency of the evidence. Legal sufficiency concepts are also important during and after trial—if the evidence does not support a finding or if the evidence compels a finding, the claim should not go to the jury, or if it does go to the jury, and the jury answers wrong, the finding should be disregarded. A party can make a legal sufficiency challenge at trial by objecting to a request for a jury question or by a motion for directed verdict or by a motion for judgment notwithstanding the verdict. If a legal challenge in sustained, the court takes the case from the jury and renders judgment.

A jury's verdict can also be attacked for "factual sufficiency"—when the evidence is not so clear as to make the resolution of the case a matter of law, but nevertheless is clear enough that a jury's finding can be said to be factually insufficient or against the weight of the evidence, requiring a new trial. If a factual challenge is sustained, the court orders a new trial before another jury. The factual sufficiency challenge is made only by a motion for new trial after a verdict.

Understandably, the circumstances under which a judge (trial or appellate) can take a case from the jury and render judgment or require a new trial, is incapable of exact definition, constantly changing, and highly controversial. We will explore the concept of legal and factual sufficiency in greater depth than before, and then take a look at the methods available to preserve error for a legal or factually sufficiency challenge to the trial court's judgment.

---

1. *The Texas Scheme—Zones of Evidence*

From William Powers, Jr. and Jack Ratliff, *Another Look at "No Evidence" and "Insufficient Evidence,"* 69 TEX. L. REV. 515 (1991):

* * *

II. "No Evidence" and "Insufficient Evidence" Points of Error

A. Clarification of Nomenclature

Texas courts customarily speak of dividing attacks on jury findings into two groups: "insufficient evidence" points and "no evidence" points. In fact, the Texas scheme is more complex. It consists of a five-zoned spectrum, with the strength of the proponent's evidence increasing in each successive zone.

In zone 1, there is no evidence (or no more than a "scintilla" of evidence) supporting a fact issue; therefore, the proponent—the party with the burden of proof on the issue—is not entitled to have that issue submitted to the jury. Such a finding will be set aside on appeal, and ordinarily the appellate court will render judgment in favor of the opponent. In zone 2, there is some evidence on the issue, and consequently it must be submitted to the jury, but there is not enough evidence to support a jury finding in the proponent's favor. A reviewing court will set aside such a finding and order a new trial. In zone 3, there is enough evidence to support a jury verdict, but not so much that a court would be justified in interfering with a contrary finding. The vast majority of cases fall into this zone, where the issue is left entirely to the finder of fact. In zone 4, the evidence favoring the proponent is even stronger, so although the issue must go to the jury, a reviewing court will set aside a jury finding against the proponent and order a new trial. In zone 5, the proponent has introduced evidence strong enough to prove a fact conclusively—that is, "as a matter of law." Accordingly, a reviewing court will set aside a contrary finding and render judgment for the proponent. As with zone 1, when the evidence falls into zone 5 there is no issue of fact for the jury to decide.

When the evidence falls into zone 1, the accepted terminology is that there is "no evidence" or "legally insufficient evidence" to support a finding in favor of the proponent. Sometimes courts also say in these instances that the proponent has failed to carry its burden "as a matter of law." This terminology is ambiguous, because courts also refer to evidence in zone 5 as establishing a fact "as a matter of law." Consequently, it should be discarded in favor of the terms "no evidence" (for zone 1) and "conclusive evidence" (for zone 5), both terms being encompassed in a reference to "legal sufficiency" points of error.

When the evidence falls into zone 2, the proper terminology is that there is "insufficient evidence" or "factually insufficient evidence" to support an affirmative finding. In zone 4, the clearest terminology is that a finding contrary to the evidence is against the "great weight and preponderance of the evidence," although this terminology is occasionally (and we think confusingly) used to refer to evidence in zone 2. Despite the differences between zones 2 and 4, attacks on jury findings in these zones are usually called "factual sufficiency" points. The preferred terminology has the proponent claim that an unfavorable (negative) finding should be set aside because it is "contrary to the great weight and preponderance of the evidence," and has the opponent claim that an unfavorable (affirmative) finding was based on "insufficient evidence."

This scheme is summarized by the chart on this page.

B. *Identifying Evidence in Zone 1*

When the record contains absolutely no evidence on a fact issue, or when the trial or appellate court determines that the only supporting evidence should not have been admitted, the case clearly falls into zone 1. But sometimes a record contains only a "scintilla" of evidence. These cases are more difficult to identify.

ZONES OF EVIDENCE

ZONE 1	ZONE 2	ZONE 3	ZONE 4	ZONE 5
	← SOME EVIDENCE		→	
NO EVIDENCE	INSUFFICIENT EVIDENCE		GREAT WEIGHT AND PREPONDERANCE OF EVIDENCE	CONCLUSIVE EVIDENCE
"a scintilla of evidence" "No Duty" case				
LEGAL SUFFICIENCY POINT "as a matter of law"	FACTUAL SUFFICIENCY POINT	**Jury Finding Will Be Upheld**	FACTUAL SUFFICIENCY POINT	LEGAL SUFFICIENCY POINT "as a matter of law"
Raised by Motion for Summary Judgment* Motion for Directed Verdict Objection to Jury Charge Motion to Disregard Findings Motion for Judgment *n.o.v.* Motion for New Trial	*Raised by* Motion for New Trial		*Raised by* Motion for New Trial	*Raised by* Motion for Summary Judgment* Motion for Directed Verdict Objection to Jury Charge Motion to Disregard Findings Motion for Judgment *n.o.v.* Motion for New Trial

Increasing Quantum of Proof Favoring Proponent →

Evidence in these zones must go to jury

* But no error is preserved if a Motion for Summary Judgment is overruled.

Evidence constitutes no more than a scintilla when it is "so weak as to do no more than create a mere surmise or suspicion of [the fact's] existence." "Direct" evidence always constitutes more than a scintilla; the "scintilla rule" applies only to cases in which the proponent attempts to establish a critical fact through an inference from other proof and the reviewing court finds the inference unreasonable.

The "scintilla rule" disqualifies evidence that is simply so weak that it does not rise to the level of "some," or zone 2, evidence. To conclude that proof on a given issue falls into zone 1, the court must be persuaded that reasonable minds could not differ on the matter, or, in Judge Calvert's words, "that the vital fact may not reasonably be inferred from the meager facts proved in the particular case." When applying this test, an appellate court must consider the evidence in the light most favorable to the proponent, considering only the supporting evidence and inferences and ignoring all contrary evidence and inferences.

* * *

C. Identifying Evidence in Zone 5

Zone 5, at the other end of the spectrum from zone 1, comprises cases in which the evidence on a fact issue is conclusive. The evidence here is so strong that the critical fact has been proved "as a matter of law," leaving nothing for the jury to decide.

Ultimately, the test for "conclusive evidence" in zone 5 is similar to the test for "no evidence" in zone 1; the court asks whether reasonable minds could differ about the fact determination to be made by the jury. Reflecting this basic similarity, the trial or appellate court's mental process in zone 5 is similar to the court's mental process in zone 1. In both instances, the process begins with a search for "some" evidence. With "no evidence" points, the search stops once the court finds enough evidence to place the issue in zone 2. Similarly, when a proponent attacks a jury's refusal to find in its favor, arguing that the evidence on a fact question is conclusive (zone 5), the reviewing court looks to see whether some evidence, which would support the jury finding, opposes that which is urged as conclusive. If so, the inquiry stops. Whatever the proponent's evidence, it cannot be conclusive if opposing evidence is in the record. But if the court finds no opposing evidence, it then goes further and looks at the record to see whether the evidence supporting the proponent's issue is enough to make it conclusive.

The unopposed testimony of an interested witness is considered conclusive if it meets a five-part test of credibility: (1) it pertains to matters reasonably capable of exact statement, (2) it is clear, direct, and positive, (3) it is internally devoid of inconsistencies, (4) it is uncontradicted either by the testimony of other witnesses or by circumstances, and (5) it is of a kind that could be readily controverted if untrue. In short, evidence meets this test when nothing in the record causes a reasonable suspicion as to its truth. Interested testimony that is not an admission or does not meet the credibility test does not qualify as conclusive, and consequently cannot place evidence supporting an issue in zone 5, even if the evidence is uncontroverted.

The Texas holdings have yielded a good deal of confusion on the effect of uncontradicted testimony by a disinterested witness. Must the jury accept it? That is, does such testimony, if uncontradicted, advance automatically to zone 5? The prevailing and better view is that the reasonable minds test should apply here. If there is nothing to cast suspicion on the testimony—that is, if reasonable minds could not differ—then the jury must accept it. But, if the testimony is impeached, inconsistent, or otherwise suspect (even though not directly controverted)—that is, if reasonable minds might or might not accept it—then the jury may reject it. McDonald aptly observes that disinterested testimony is, in fact, treated much the same as interested testimony, except that courts are more inclined in the case of interested testimony to find suspicious circumstances that would allow the jury to reject it. If either kind of testimony fails the five-part credibility test, it is not conclusive.

What if the uncontroverted testimony of a party witness is an admission against interest? Then it can be conclusive without the application of the five-part credibility test. The fact that the admission is against interest is enough to vouch for its credibility.

D. Identifying Findings in Zones 2 and 4

Zones 2, 3, and 4 make up the "some evidence" spectrum. The dividing lines separating these zones are more difficult to identify than those dividing zone 1 from zone 2, or zone 4 from zone 5. Here, no "reasonable mind" test applies, there is no concern for identifying "scintillas," and the court does not indulge inferences or confine its view to evidence favoring one side of the case. Rather, it looks at all the evidence on both sides and then makes a predominantly intuitive judgment: is the evidence—already identified as "some evidence" (zone 2, 3, or 4)—in satisfactory harmony with the fact-finding it supports?

In making this determination, courts have little guidance other than the elusive precedent furnished by other cases with similar facts. A reviewing court may not substitute its judgment for the jury's merely because it would have found the facts differently, but the court must nevertheless review the entire record to determine whether the evidence was so one-sided that the verdict will not be allowed to stand.

The difficulty of devising a clear test for zones 2 and 4 has long troubled judges and commentators. The decision necessarily turns on a process that is incapable of formulation, because its purpose is to allow the judge to correct a miscarriage of justice even when no formula or specific standard compels the correction. The language from appellate opinions offers little help. Courts are told that the jury's findings should not be disturbed unless the verdict is "manifestly unjust," or such as to "shock the conscience" or "clearly demonstrate bias." Yet, these are findings on questions which have gone to the jury only because reasonable minds could differ on the answers. Furthermore, courts of appeals are told to "weigh all of the evidence" but not "reweigh" it. Perhaps the most helpful description of limits on the granting of new trials for factual insufficiency is the one suggested by Professors Wright and Miller for federal courts. They suggest that although a trial court does not "sit to approve miscarriages of justice," it should have a "decent respect for the collective wisdom of the jury" and accept the verdict in most cases.

E. Appropriate Remedies

When the jury has made a negative finding and a proponent successfully attacks it because the evidence falls in zone 5, or when an opponent successfully attacks an affirmative jury finding because the evidence falls in zone 1, the proper remedy in the trial court is usually the entry of a judgment notwithstanding the verdict, or "n.o.v."

When the trial court has erroneously rendered a judgment based on jury findings that are contrary to zone 1 or zone 5 evidence, the appellate court will usually reverse the trial court and render a judgment that is in harmony with the evidence. The question is taken from the jury and decided as a matter of law.

When the trial court has rendered judgment n.o.v., erroneously disregarding a jury finding because the court believes that the evidence on it falls into zone 1 or zone 5, the appellate court will usually reverse and render judgment on the verdict, unless the appellee has preserved by cross-point its conditional prayer for a new trial.

But when the trial judge erroneously believes that a given fact question is governed by zone 1 or zone 5 evidence and short-circuits the process by rendering a summary judgment, directing a verdict, or withholding a fact question from the jury, there is no jury finding in place. In that event, the appellate court must remand for a new trial.

Sometimes, however, an appellate court will order a new trial even when the jury has made findings that are set aside because the evidence falls into zone 1 or zone 5. For example, if the appellate court changes the substantive law or holds that some of the proponent's evidence should not have been admitted, the proper remedy may be a new trial that gives the proponent a chance to introduce or fully develop evidence compatible with the new standard.

* * *

When the evidence on an issue falls into zone 2 or zone 4, the trial court must submit the issue to the jury; a directed verdict or judgment notwithstanding the verdict is improper. Nevertheless, the jury will be allowed to make only one finding—the "correct" finding—and, if it does not, the trial judge will grant a motion for a new trial. If the evidence is in zone 2, the trial court will order a new trial because the evidence in favor of the proponent is "factually insufficient" to support a verdict for the proponent. If the evidence is in zone 4, the trial court will order a new trial because a jury finding against the proponent is "contrary to the great weight and preponderance of the evidence." According to Rule 326, the trial court (and presumably the courts of appeals) can order a new trial based solely on a factual sufficiency point only twice. A third verdict must be permitted to stand, even if the court finds that the evidence still falls into zone 2 or zone 4.

When an appellate court finds that the trial court has improperly denied a motion for new trial—that is, when the verdict was not supported by factually sufficient evidence or was against the great weight and preponderance of the evidence—the appellate court should reverse the trial court's judgment and remand the case for a new trial. . . .

The Texas Supreme Court is the court of last resort on whether evidence constitutes "some evidence" (zones 2, 3, and 4), no evidence (zone 1), or conclusive evidence (zone 5). It has no authority—absent a mistake by the court of appeals in applying the correct legal standard—to subdivide "some evidence" into zones 2, 3, and 4. That is the exclusive province of the trial courts and the courts of appeals.

When the supreme court determines, contrary to a court of appeals' holding, that the record contains some evidence to support a finding, and the appellant has attacked the jury finding on both legal and factual sufficiency grounds, the supreme court should remand the case to the court of appeals for review of any factual sufficiency points in accordance with *Pool v. Ford Motor Co.* If the supreme court determines that the facts asserted by the plaintiff do not show a breach of the defendant's duty, it should render judgment, or remand the case to the court of appeals if the "no duty" point does not dispose of the entire case and there are further matters to be resolved consistent with the supreme court's opinion. But where the parties have not raised any factual sufficiency points and the supreme court's holding on the legal sufficiency points determines the outcome, the supreme court should render judgment, setting aside or reinstating fact-findings as appropriate. Thus, where the evidence conclusively establishes a fact that disposes of the case, the supreme court need not remand to the court of appeals for factual insufficiency points.

If, however, the court of appeals has applied the wrong legal standard in determining a "no evidence" point—if it has considered evidence contrary to the jury's fact-finding, for example—the supreme court will remand to the court of appeals for disposition of properly preserved factual sufficiency points or will render judgment if no factual sufficiency points have been preserved by cross-point. If the court of appeals mistakenly concludes that the facts alleged by the plaintiff do not constitute a ground of recovery (or do not establish a breach of duty on the part of the defendant) and disposes of the case on a "no evidence" point, the supreme court should reverse the court of appeals and affirm the trial court judgment unless there remain factual sufficiency points that require attention by the court of appeals.

---

2. *Evolution of Legal Sufficiency Standard of Evidentiary Review*

All courts agree that legal sufficiency of the evidence review requires the judge to view the evidence in the light favorable to the verdict (or to the non-movant if there is no verdict). They disagree, however, as to whether to consider only the evidence supporting the verdict, or to also consider contrary evidence in the record.[1] The Powers & Ratliff article above describes what is known as the "scintilla rule"—only the evidence supporting the verdict is considered, and if there is "more than a scintilla" of evidence, the jury's verdict is upheld. Another view, adopted by most federal courts, requires judges to consider not only the evidence supporting the verdict, but also any uncontradicted and unimpeached evidence contrary to the verdict. Thus, if there is some evidence supporting the verdict, but contrary evidence shows that this evidence is not reasonably believed, the jury's verdict cannot stand. Obviously, the first option is less intrusive into the jury's fact-finding process—it eliminates any judicial weighing of the evidence and a jury verdict that is "unreasonable" is cured by a new trial, decided by a new jury, not by a judge. The second option, of course, is embraced by those less enamored with juries, and allows judges to overturn patently unreasonable jury verdicts and render judgment without a new trial.

In 2005, the Texas Supreme Court issued its opinion in *City of Keller v. Wilson*,[2] addressing these two different approaches, but not deciding between them. Instead, the court says that:

> [A]ppellate courts must view the evidence in the light favorable to the verdict, crediting favorable evidence if reasonable jurors could, and disregarding contrary evidence unless reasonable jurors could not.

In describing this rule, the court says:

> Whether a court begins by reviewing all the evidence or disregarding part in a legal-sufficiency review, there can be no disagreement about where that review should end. If the evidence at trial would enable reasonable and fair-minded people to differ in their conclusions, then jurors must be allowed to do so. A reviewing court cannot substitute its judgment for that of the trier-of-fact, so long as the evidence falls within this zone of reasonable disagreement.
>
> Similarly, there is no disagreement about how a reviewing court should view evidence in the process of that review. Whether a reviewing court starts with all or only part of the record, the court must consider evidence in the light most favorable to the verdict, and indulge every reasonable inference that would support it. But if the evidence allows of only one inference, neither jurors nor the reviewing court may disregard it. . . .
>
> This is not to say judges and lawyers will always agree whether evidence is legally sufficient. As discussed more fully below, reasonable people may disagree about what reasonable jurors could or must believe. But once those boundaries are settled, *any* stand-

---

1 *See, e.g.*, Glannon, et al., CIVIL PROCEDURE: A COURSEBOOK 1084 (2d ed. 2014).

2 168 S.W.3d 802 (Tex. 2005).

> ard of review must coincide with those boundaries—affirming jury verdicts based on evidence within them and reversing jury verdicts based on evidence that is not. Any standard that does otherwise is improperly applied.

* * *

While judges and lawyers often disagree about legal sufficiency in particular cases, the disagreements are almost always about what evidence jurors can or must credit and what inferences they can or must make. It is inevitable in human affairs that reasonable people sometimes disagree; thus, it is also inevitable that they will sometimes disagree about what reasonable people can disagree about. This is not a new problem; Justice Calvert noted it almost fifty years ago:

> The rule as generally stated is that if reasonable minds cannot differ from the conclusion that the evidence lacks probative force it will be held to be the legal equivalent of no evidence. The application of the rule can lead to strange results. It is theoretically possible, and sometimes not far from actual fact, that five members of the Supreme Court will conclude that the evidence supporting a finding of a vital fact has no probative force, and in reaching the conclusion through application of the rule will thus hold, in effect, that the trial judge who overruled a motion for instructed verdict, the twelve jurors who found the existence of the vital fact, the three justices of the Court of Civil Appeals who overruled a "no evidence" point of error and four dissenting justices of the Supreme Court are not men of "reasonable minds."

It is not hubris that occasionally requires an appellate court to find a jury verdict has no reasonable evidentiary basis. As Justice Frankfurter stated long ago:

> Only an incompetent or a wilful judge would take a case from the jury when the issue should be left to the jury. But since questions of negligence are questions of degree, often very nice differences of degree, judges of competence and conscience have in the past, and will in the future, disagree whether proof in a case is sufficient to demand submission to the jury. The fact that [one] thinks there was enough to leave the case to the jury does not indicate that the other [is] unmindful of the jury's function. The easy but timid way out for a trial judge is to leave all cases tried to a jury for jury determination, but in so doing he fails in his duty to take a case from the jury when the evidence would not warrant a verdict by it. A timid judge, like a biased judge, is intrinsically a lawless judge.

We will consider several opinions where judges have different views about what evidence jurors must credit or not. In fact, in *City of Keller* case itself, the justices disagreed on whether the verdict had a reasonable evidentiary basis. While the majority felt that it did not and reversed for "no evidence," two dissenters, while agreeing with the standard articulated by the majority, found that the opinion "misapplies the standard . . . by crediting [contrary] evidence the jury could reasonably disregard."

Of course, most cases involve conflicting evidence, where one party introduces evidence showing that the fact is true and the other introduces evidence showing that the fact is not true. As *City of Keller* acknowledges, "It is the province of the jury to resolve conflicts in the evidence. Accordingly, courts reviewing all the evidence in a light favorable to the verdict must assume that jurors resolved all conflicts in accordance with that verdict. . . . [I]n every circumstance in which reasonable jurors could resolve conflicting evidence either way, reviewing courts must presume they did so in favor of the prevailing party, and disregard the conflicting evidence in their legal sufficiency review."

Likewise, "jurors are the sole judges of the credibility of the witnesses and the weight to give their testimony. They may choose to believe one witness and disbelieve another." But, "of course, the jury's decisions regarding credibility must be reasonable." They may not ignore "undisputed testimony that is clear, positive, direct, otherwise credible, free from contradictions and inconsistencies, and could have been readily controverted. . . . They are not free to believe testimony that is conclusively negated by undisputed facts."

Most cases turn on circumstantial evidence—evidence that does not directly prove or disprove a disputed fact, but raises inferences which tend to prove or disprove the fact. Generally, a "reasonable inference" will qualify as "some evidence" and put the case in the "zone of reasonable disagreement." And an "unreasonable inference" is "merely a scintilla" of evidence. As the *City of Keller* opinion says, "In viewing the evidence in a light most favorable to the verdict, one must assume that jurors made all inferences in favor of the verdict if reasonable minds could, and disregard others." However, if jurors have to guess whether the fact exists, or when circumstances are equally consistent with either of two facts, neither can be inferred. Thus, as *City of Keller* says, "when the circumstantial evidence of a vital fact is meager, a reviewing court must consider not just favorable but all the circumstantial evidence, and competing inferences as well." Furthermore, "the circumstantial evidence must be evaluated in light of all the known circumstances, not merely in isolation."

Although not set out in full here, lawyers should consult the *City of Keller* opinion whenever a legal sufficiency issue arises. It catalogs many types of evidence (e.g. contextual, competency, circumstantial, consciousness and credibility evidence) and attempts to place them in the legal sufficiency analysis.

---

3. Identifying the Zone of Reasonable Disagreement

a. Products liability cases

GENIE INDUSTRIES, INC.
v.
MATAK
2015 WL 2173786
(Tex. 2015)

Opinion

CHIEF JUSTICE HECHT delivered the opinion of the Court, in which JUSTICE GREEN, JUSTICE JOHNSON, JUSTICE WILLETT, JUSTICE GUZMAN, and JUSTICE BROWN joined.

A product manufacturer is not liable for a design defect unless a safer alternative design exists and the defect renders the product unreasonably dangerous—that is, its risks outweigh its utility. The issue is usually one of fact for the jury but may nevertheless be a legal one when the evidence is such that reasonable minds cannot differ on the risk-utility balancing considerations.

In this case, the users of an aerial lift supporting a worker 40' in the air attempted to move the machine. Signs on the machine and instructions in the user manual warned of the obvious danger: the machine would tip over and the worker would fall to the ground. And that is what happened. So obvious was the danger that although over 100,000 lifts of the same general model have been sold all over the world, the jury was provided with evidence of only three similar accidents involving similar AWP lifts over the past decade—none of which involved the intentional destabilization of a fully-extended 40' lift. The lift cannot be said in any sense to be unreasonably dangerous.

The jury reached a different conclusion. The respective roles of courts and juries must be carefully guarded. The right to trial by jury in civil cases is constitutionally protected because we have, as a polity, determined to lay the resolution of factual disputes at the feet of our peers. But when the facts admit of only one reasonable conclusion, it is the rule of law that must supply the decision, lest jurors be given the very power from which they are intended to protect us, deciding for whatever reasons seem good to them who should and should not prevail.

As we will explain in detail, fully mindful of the respect due the verdict of the jury, our careful review of the record in this case has revealed little evidence of a safer alternative design for the product at issue, and no evidence that the product is unreasonably dangerous. Accordingly, we reverse the judgment of the court of appeals and render judgment for Petitioner Genie Industries, Inc.

I

Genie Industries, Inc., manufactures and sells a wide variety of aerial lifts throughout the world. An aerial lift is used to raise a worker on a platform to reach the ceilings of tall buildings or other high places. One of these lifts is the Aerial Work Platform-40' SuperSeries, also known as the AWP-40S, pictured here.

Figure 1: AWP 40S

The base of the AWP-40S is small, only about 29″ x 55″—narrower than a standard door—and sits on wheels. A vertical, telescoping mast is mounted on the base. An enclosed platform to hold a worker is attached to the top of the mast. A motor extends the mast, raising the platform up to 40' in the air, thus allowing a worker on the platform to reach objects as high as 45-46' above the ground. The AWP-40S is designed to be lightweight and portable. Though the lift weighs roughly 1,000 pounds, it can be rolled around, set up, and operated by a single person. The lift is well-suited for indoor work not accessible by big, heavy machinery. It can pass through ordinary doorways and can be used in tight spaces.

The base of the AWP-40S is too small to support a worker on the platform without tipping over even when the platform is not fully elevated. Before elevating the platform, the machine must be stabilized using outriggers attached to each of the four comers of the base. Each outrigger extends outward diagonally about 3' from the base. At the end of each outrigger is a leveling jack that can be adjusted up or down so that the outrigger is firmly pressed against the floor. The outriggers increase the lift's footprint and its stability, preventing it from tipping over. When the work is done and the mast lowered, the outriggers can be removed to allow the lift to pass through narrow areas. The removable outriggers contribute to the lift's compact design, which is one of its main selling points.

An electromechanical interlock on the lift prevents the platform from being elevated unless all the outriggers are in place and the leveling jacks pressed against the ground. But if the lift becomes destabilized while elevated, it continues to function. Four green lights signal the proper deployment of the outriggers. Several signs on the lift warn users not to release the lift's outriggers while it is in use. One sign, located at eye level on the machine, displays an image of a man pushing the lift while elevated and in use, and states:

> DANGER: Tip-over hazard. Attempting to move the machine with the platform raised will tip the machine over and cause death or serious injury.

A warning in the lift's manual states: "Do not adjust or remove the outriggers while the platform is occupied or raised." Even without these warnings, the danger is obvious.

Genie has sold more than 100,000 of its AWP-series lifts worldwide. The few, comparable lifts that are sold on the market are virtually identical to Genie's AWP-40S. The lift's design is governed by and complies with the Occupational Safety and Health Administration standards. The AWP-40S also complies with both the non-mandatory American National Standards Institute standards and, due to the size of Genie's world market share, the national standards in Canada, Europe, and Australia. Out of the millions of times Genie's AWP-series lifts have been used, there are apparently only three reported accidents like the one in issue.

The Cathedral in the Pines Church in Beaumont has an AWP-40S that it uses to reach the ceilings of its buildings. The Church hired Gulf Coast Electric to run fiber optic cable in the ceilings and allowed Gulf Coast's employees, James Boggan and Walter Matak, to use the lift. Initially, they used the lift as instructed. They positioned the lift, deployed the outriggers, and then raised the platform with Matak standing on it. Each time they needed to reposition the lift to reach a different area, they lowered the platform and Matak stepped down. They then raised the leveling jacks, rolled the lift to another location, and redeployed the outriggers.

A church employee watching them work, John Adams, suggested the work would go faster if Matak were not lowered each time the lift was moved. With Matak still elevated, the jacks could be raised a few inches, just enough to allow the lift to roll, then re-lowered. When Boggan expressed reservations about this method, Adams reassured him that he and the other church employees did it "all the time." Actually, what they had done all the time was move the lift with the worker still on the platform, but not with the platform fully raised.

Boggan attempted to follow Adams's suggestion, but after he raised two of the leveling jacks only a few inches, the lift—with Matak still on the platform extended to its full 40' height—suddenly tipped over and crashed to the floor. Matak died of massive injuries to his head, and this action for wrongful death and survivor damages ensued.

The jury found that a design defect in the AWP-40S caused the accident. The jury was instructed as follows:

> A "design defect" is a condition of the product that renders it unreasonably dangerous as designed, taking into consideration the utility of the product and the risk involved in its use. For a design defect to exist, there must have been a safer alternative design.

"Safer alternative design" means a product design other than the one actually used that in reasonable probability—

(1) would have prevented or significantly reduced the risk of the occurrence or injury in question without substantially impairing the product's utility and

(2) was economically and technologically feasible at the time the product left the control of Genie Industries Inc. by the application of existing or reasonably achievable scientific knowledge.

The jury apportioned responsibility 55% to Genie, 20% to the Church, 20% to Gulf Coast, and 5% to Matak. The trial court rendered judgment on the verdict, and Genie appealed. The court of appeals affirmed, holding that there was legally sufficient evidence to support the jury's design defect finding.

We granted Genie's petition for review.

II

"The law of products liability does not guarantee that a product will be risk free" but imposes liability only for defective products that are "unreasonably dangerous to the user or consumer."

> To recover for a products liability claim alleging a design defect, a plaintiff must prove that (1) the product was defectively designed so as to render it unreasonably dangerous; (2) a safer alternative design existed; and (3) the defect was a producing cause of the injury for which the plaintiff seeks recovery.

A product is unreasonably dangerous when its risk outweighs its utility. Genie argues that the plaintiffs produced no evidence that a safer alternative design for the AWP-40S existed or that the risk of an accident like Matak's outweighs the lift's utility. In assessing the evidence, we cannot, of course, "substitute [our] judgment for that of the [jury], so long as the evidence falls within [the] zone of reasonable disagreement." But "[w]here reasonable minds cannot differ, the issue is one of law rather than one of fact."

* * *

[The court concluded that the record contained some evidence of a safer alternative design and causation.]

IV

Whether a defective design renders a product unreasonably dangerous depends on whether the product's risks outweigh its utility, considering:

> (1) the utility of the product to the user and to the public as a whole weighed against the gravity and likelihood of injury from its use; (2) the availability of a substitute product which would meet the same need and not be unsafe or unreasonably expensive; (3) the manufacturer's ability to eliminate the unsafe character of the product without seriously impairing its usefulness or significantly increasing its costs; (4) the user's anticipated awareness of the dangers inherent in the product and their avoidability because of the general public knowledge of the obvious condition of the product, or of the existence of suitable warnings or instructions; and (5) the expectations of the ordinary consumer.

This balancing is for the jury unless the evidence allows but one reasonable conclusion.

* * *

The five factors to be considered in determining whether a product's risk outweighs its utility, with which we began this discussion, conclusively establish that the AWP-40S is not, on this record, unreasonably dangerous. The first is whether the gravity and likelihood of injury outweighs the lift's utility. While misuse of the lift can result in the most serious injury, as this case illustrates, the likelihood of its occurrence is all but nonexistent. In [another case, the result was different because there was evidence that] the likelihood of injury was greater, and more importantly, even an experienced user might not appreciate the danger in a particular circumstance. Here, the danger was patent. The second factor asks whether there is a substitute that would meet the same need and not be unsafe or unreasonably expensive. There is no evidence of one. The third factor is whether there is a safer alternative design. As we have already explained at length, there is only slight evidence of such a design. The fourth factor is whether the danger of misuse is obvious and readily avoidable. The risk of tip-over is both. One need only look at the machine to appreciate this truth. And the lift's history of use in the world further confirms this fact. The last factor considers ordinary consumers' expectations. Again, the danger of misuse is obvious, even to someone not trained in handling the AWP-40S. These factors require the conclusion that the AWP-40S is not unreasonably dangerous.

We agree with the dissent that it is completely irrelevant what we would have done had we been jurors in the case, although it seems odd that the dissenting Justices would feel constrained to repeat three times that they probably would have sided with Genie. The dissent acknowledges that the AWP-40S cannot be unreasonably dangerous absent evidence that the gravity and likelihood of injury outweighs its utility, but then it concludes that a single accident is enough to show likelihood. The evidence here shows that while it is very likely that users of the lift will not read or follow the user manual or the warning signs on the machine, and likely that they will try to release the outriggers and move the lift with someone on a partially elevated platform, the chance that anyone would attempt to do so with the platform fully elevated is only one in millions. The risk of misuse in this case cannot in any sense be said to be likely.

As we said in *Caterpillar,* "[t]he law of products liability does not guarantee that a product will be risk free," only that it will not be unreasonably dangerous. There is no evidence in the record before us that the AWP-40S is unreasonably dangerous.

* * *

Accordingly, we reverse the judgment of the court of appeals and render judgment for Petitioner.

JUSTICE BOYD, joined by JUSTICE LEHRMANN and JUSTICE DEVINE, dissenting.

* * *

A. The Risk–Utility Analysis

To decide whether a product design is unreasonably dangerous, the jury must balance the product's utility against the risks involved in its use. . . .

We have made it very clear that the fluid process that this risk-utility analysis requires is not susceptible to absolutes. . . .

It used to be the law in Texas that the plaintiff's awareness and appreciation of the risk, whether due to warnings or to the obviousness of the risk, was an absolute defense against a defective-design claim. . . . We have rejected such absolute rules in favor of the more fluid risk-utility analysis because that analysis provides a more effective way to "encourage manufacturers to reach an optimum level of safety in designing their products." . . .

In this case, the Court concludes, as a matter of law, that the Genie lift was not unreasonably dangerous because its risks were both obvious and warned against. While those facts are certainly important to the risk-utility analysis, the Court's own precedent rejects the idea that they make the lift safe *as a matter of law.* "The fact that a product user is or should be aware of the existence and avoidability of dangers inherent in a product's use that are obvious, commonly known, or warned against, . . . may . . . be decisive in a particular case." But such a determination cannot be based merely on the existence of a warning or obviousness of the dangers, as if either were "an absolute bar—like certain affirmative defenses—to liability for a defective design." We must therefore review the record in this case to determine whether it contains any evidence that would allow a reasonable juror to conclude that the risks of the Genie lift outweigh its utility, in spite of the warnings and the allegedly obvious nature of its risks.

* * *

[T]he jurors in this case were capable of forming their own opinions based on the evidence. They did so, and they did not all agree. Ten members of the jury found that the risks of Genie's lift outweigh its utility, making it unreasonably dangerous and thus defectively designed. But they did so thoughtfully, assigning only 55 percent of the responsibility for Matak's death to Genie, while assigning 20 percent to the church, 20 percent to Matak's employer, and 5 percent to Matak himself. Because some evidence supports the jury's findings, we are bound by the law to respect its decision.

. . . Thanking all twelve jurors for their service in this case, I respectfully dissent.

Note on Expert Testimony and Legal Sufficiency

Often expert testimony is essential to a plaintiff's case—particularly in a product's liability case. Expert testimony introduced by the plaintiff is often attacked as not being "reliable,"[1] resulting in a no evidence challenge to a plaintiff's verdict. In *Whirlpool Corp. v. Camancho*,[2] the Texas Supreme Court explained the process as follows:

> Generally, rulings on objections as to admissibility of evidence, including whether expert testimony is reliable, are reviewed for abuse of discretion. But a party may assert on appeal that unreliable scientific evidence or expert testimony is not only inadmissible, but also that its unreliability makes it legally insufficient to support a verdict.
>
> Unlike review of a trial court's ruling as to admissibility of evidence where the ruling is reviewed for abuse of discretion, in a no-evidence review we independently consider whether the evidence at trial would enable reasonable and fair-minded jurors to reach the verdict. *City of Keller v. Wilson,* 168 S.W.3d 802, 827 (Tex. 2005). Further, a no-evidence review encompasses the entire record, including contrary evidence tending to show the expert opinion is incompetent or unreliable. *Id.* at 814.

1 *See* TRE 401.

2 298 S.W.3d 631, 638 (Tex. 2009).

In determining whether expert testimony is reliable, a court may consider the factors set out by the Court in [*E.I. du Pont de Nemours & Co. v.*] *Robinson*[3] and the expert's experience. *See Gammill v. Jack Williams Chevrolet, Inc.*, 972 S.W.2d 713, 724 (Tex. 1998).

In *Comancho*, the Court determined that the plaintiff's expert opinion was not reliable, was legally insufficient to support the jury's verdict, and, therefore, the judgment based on the jury's verdict favoring the plaintiff was reversed and rendered for the defendant.

---

b. ***Slip and fall cases***

WAL-MART STORES, INC.
v.
GONZALEZ
968 S.W.2d 934
(Tex. 1998)

GONZALEZ, JUSTICE.

The question in this slip-and-fall case is what quantum of circumstantial evidence is legally sufficient to support a finding that an unreasonably dangerous condition has existed long enough to charge a proprietor with constructive notice of the condition. The court of appeals held that there was legally sufficient evidence that some macaroni salad had existed on the Wal-Mart floor long enough to charge Wal-Mart with constructive notice of the condition. We hold that when circumstantial evidence is relied upon to prove constructive notice, the evidence must establish that it is more likely than not that the dangerous condition existed long enough to give the proprietor a reasonable opportunity to discover the condition. Because we conclude that the circumstantial evidence in this case supports only the *possibility* that the dangerous condition existed long enough to give Wal-Mart a reasonable opportunity to discover it, we reverse and render judgment for Wal-Mart.

Flora Gonzalez visited the Rio Grande City Wal-Mart with her daughter and two granddaughters. While walking in a busy aisle from the cafeteria toward a store refrigerator, Gonzalez stepped on some cooked macaroni salad that came from the Wal-Mart cafeteria. Gonzalez slipped and fell, sustaining painful injuries to her back, shoulder, and knee. Gonzalez sued Wal-Mart for negligence. A jury awarded her $100,000 and the trial court rendered judgment on the verdict. The court of appeals, with one justice dissenting, reduced Gonzalez's damages to $96,700 and affirmed the judgment as modified.

Gonzalez was Wal-Mart's invitee. As such, Wal-Mart owed her a duty to exercise reasonable care to protect her from dangerous conditions in the store known or discoverable to it. However,

[3] *Robinson* set out the following list of nonexclusive factors: (1) the extent to which the theory has been or can be tested, (2) the extent to which the technique relies upon the subjective interpretation of the expert, (3) whether the theory has been subjected to peer review and/or publication, (4) the technique's potential rate of error, (5) whether the theory or technique has been generally accepted as valid by the relevant scientific community, and (6) the non-judicial uses which have been made of the theory or technique. *Robinson,* 923 S.W.2d at 557.

a land possessor's duty toward its invitee does not make the possessor an insurer of the invitee's safety. To recover damages in a slip-and-fall case, a plaintiff must prove:

(1) Actual or constructive knowledge of some condition on the premises by the owner/operator;

(2) That the condition posed an unreasonable risk of harm;

(3) That the owner/operator did not exercise reasonable care to reduce or eliminate the risk; and

(4) That the owner/operator's failure to use such care proximately caused the plaintiff's injuries.

Keetch v. Kroger Co., 845 S.W.2d 262, 264 (Tex. 1992); *Corbin v. Safeway Stores, Inc.,* 648 S.W.2d 292, 296 (Tex. 1983).

The central issue in this case is whether Wal-Mart had constructive knowledge of the spilled macaroni. Wal-Mart argues that the evidence is legally insufficient to show that the macaroni had been on the floor long enough to charge Wal-Mart with constructive notice. When reviewing a legal sufficiency point, this court "must consider only the evidence and inferences tending to support the trial court's finding, disregarding all contrary evidence and inferences." However, meager circumstantial evidence from which equally plausible but opposite inferences may be drawn is speculative and thus legally insufficient to support a finding.

No witnesses testified that they had seen or were aware of the spilled macaroni before Gonzalez slipped on it. However, as evidence that the macaroni had been on the floor for a prolonged period of time, Gonzalez testified that the macaroni had mayonnaise in it, was "fresh," "wet," "still humid," and contaminated with "a lot of dirt." Gonzalez's daughter testified that the macaroni had footprints and cart track marks in it and "seemed like it had been there a while." The court of appeals held this evidence legally sufficient to support the verdict, apparently calling for a relaxed burden of proof in slip-and-fall cases when the evidence is scant:

> A plaintiff has the obligation to produce the evidence that exists. If a court requires more than is possible to prove, the court has taken over the legislative function of simply deciding that there will be no negligence cause of action for slip and falls. No court has done this, and the cause of action exists. The great majority of slip-and-fall cases are lost at the trial level and, no doubt, always will be. But this court is not willing to say that an injured person must go beyond the evidence that is created by the operative facts, which would be an impossibility. Of course, there may be cases where there is simply not enough evidence to make a case, even if it is all produced. This is not such a case though.

However, "[t]he fact that proof of causation is difficult does not provide a plaintiff with an excuse to avoid introducing some evidence of causation." As the dissent in the court of appeals explained, "[t]he harsh reality is that if the plaintiff cannot prove facts to support her cause of action, there is simply no recovery. This is true not only in slip and fall cases, but in all cases."

Dirt in macaroni salad lying on a heavily-traveled aisle is no evidence of the length of time the macaroni had been on the floor. That evidence can no more support the inference that it accumulated dirt over a long period of time than it can support the opposite inference that the macaroni had just been dropped on the floor and was quickly contaminated by customers and carts traversing the aisle. In *Furr's Supermarkets, Inc. v. Arellano,* 492 S.W.2d 727 (Tex. Civ. App.—El Paso 1973, writ ref'd n.r.e.), another spilled-macaroni case, the court held that testimony that the dried macaroni noodles that caused the plaintiff's fall were "soiled, scattered and appeared as though other persons had passed through the area and had been run over presumably by another cart or carts" was no evidence of the length of time the macaroni noodles had been there. *See also H.E. Butt Grocery Co. v. Rodriguez,* 441 S.W.2d 215, 217 (Tex. Civ. App.—Corpus Christi 1969, no writ) (holding that testimony that the grape on which plaintiff slipped was squashed and muddy, that the floor was dirty, and that pieces of paper were strewn around nearby was no evidence that the grape had been on the floor long enough to charge the store with notice); *H.E. Butt Grocery Store v. Hamilton,* 632 S.W.2d 189, 191 (Tex. App.—Corpus Christi 1982, no writ) (holding that testimony that grapes were stepped on and that the juices from both red and green grapes had blended together was no evidence of how long the grapes were on the floor). There were no comparisons between the dirt on the macaroni salad and the dirt on the surrounding floor space that would justify the inference, relied on in *H.E. Butt Grocery Co. v. Heaton,* 547 S.W.2d 75, 76 (Tex. Civ. App.—Waco 1977, no writ), that the macaroni salad had been on the floor as long as the surrounding dirt on the floor, or that the dirt on the macaroni salad had dried, suggesting that it had been there for a prolonged period of time.

The presence of footprints or cart tracks in the macaroni salad equally supports the inference that the tracks were of recent origin as it supports the opposite inference, that the tracks had been there a long time. In *Kimbell, Inc. v. Roberson,* 570 S.W.2d 587, 590 (Tex. Civ. App.—Tyler 1978, no writ), the court rejected testimony that two or three tracks that had been made through a syrupy or jelly-like substance on which plaintiff slipped tended to show that the substance had been there long enough to charge the store with constructive notice. The court explained, "It is just as likely that the tracks were made by customers traversing the aisle only minutes or even seconds before plaintiff's fall." *Id.* at 590; *see also Robledo v. Kroger Co.*, 597 S.W.2d 560, 560-61 (Tex. Civ. App.—Eastland 1980, writ ref'd n.r.e.) (recognizing that cart tracks through dirty water was no evidence of constructive notice because they could have been made by another customer minutes before the fall); *Kimbell, Inc. v. Blount,* 562 S.W.2d 10, 13 (Tex. Civ. App.—Austin 1978, no writ) (holding that drying footprints and tracks leading away from puddle of liquid was no evidence that the puddle had been there long enough to put the store on constructive notice).

The testimony that the macaroni salad "seemed like it had been there awhile" is mere speculative, subjective opinion of no evidentiary value. The witnesses had not seen the macaroni salad prior to the fall and had no personal knowledge of the length of time it had been on the floor. *See Robledo,* 597 S.W.2d at 561 (holding that the trial court committed no error in sustaining objection to plaintiff's testimony that the water "had been there for some time" because the plaintiff had no personal knowledge of how long the puddle had been there); *Roberson,* 570 S.W.2d at 589 (rejecting the assertion of plaintiff—who had been in the store for only ten to fifteen minutes when he fell—that the substance on which he slipped had been there for thirty to forty minutes, stating that "[h]is opinion as to the length of time that it had been there amounts to nothing more than conjecture and therefore does not amount to any evidence at all").

We hold that the evidence that the macaroni salad had "a lot of dirt" and tracks through it and the subjective testimony that the macaroni salad "seemed like it had been there awhile" is no evidence that the macaroni had been on the floor long enough to charge Wal-Mart with constructive notice of this condition. *Compare with Corbin,* 648 S.W.2d at 296 (Tex. 1983) ("Corbin's testimony that the grapes lying around him were discolored and ruptured does not tend to prove that the grapes had been on the floor a sufficient time to impute knowledge of their location to Safeway."). Gonzalez had to demonstrate that it was *more likely than not* that the macaroni salad had been there for a long time; Gonzalez proved only that the macaroni salad *could possibly* have been there long enough to make Wal-Mart responsible for noticing it. *See Henderson v. Pipkin Grocery Co.,* 268 S.W.2d 703, 705 (Tex. Civ. App.—El Paso 1954, writ dism'd w.o.j.) ("This rule, while harsh and demanding on plaintiffs, is nevertheless well established and plaintiffs must always discharge the burden of proving that the dangerous condition was either known to the defendant or had existed for such a length of time that he should have known it.").

Because there is no evidence that Wal-Mart had constructive notice of the actual existence of spilled macaroni, this Court grants Wal-Mart's petition for review, and under Texas Rule of Appellate Procedure 59.1, without hearing oral argument, reverses the court of appeals' judgment and renders judgment that Flora Gonzalez take nothing.

PHILLIPS, C.J., and SPECTOR, ABBOTT and HANKINSON, JUSTICES, noted their dissent.

BROOKSHIRE BROTHERS, LTD.
v.
ALDRIDGE

2014 WL 2994435
(Tex. 2014)

* * *

IV. Legal Sufficiency Challenge

Finally, we address Brookshire Brothers' assertion that it is entitled to rendition of judgment in its favor on legal sufficiency grounds. Brookshire Brothers argues that, regardless of whether the spoliation instruction is taken into account, the evidence is legally insufficient to support the constructive notice element of Aldridge's claim. One of the grounds on which we will uphold a legal sufficiency challenge is if " 'the evidence offered to prove a vital fact is no more than a scintilla.' " "Evidence does not exceed a scintilla if it is so weak as to do no more than create a mere surmise or suspicion that the fact exists." In reviewing evidence in the context of a legal sufficiency challenge, "we credit evidence that supports the verdict if reasonable jurors could have done so and disregard contrary evidence unless reasonable jurors could not have done so."

As is relevant here, to show Brookshire Brothers had constructive notice of the "condition" (*i.e.,* a slippery substance on the floor), Aldridge had to prove that "it is more likely than not that the condition existed long enough to give the premises owner a reasonable opportunity to discover it." Temporal evidence is the best indicator of whether the owner could have discovered and remedied the condition.

As noted above, the exact area of the floor where Aldridge fell was obscured by a table in the video footage that was preserved, but the video does not appear to show a spill or leak occurring during the seven minutes before the fall. Tyler testified that substances reasonably should not remain on the floor of the store for longer than five minutes without being noticed and cleaned up. The video showed store employees walking past the area approximately three minutes and five minutes before Aldridge fell. It also showed an employee signaling for help to clean up the spill right before the video ended, suggesting the spill was too large to be cleaned by paper towels. This evidence, even without the spoliation instruction, amounts to more than a scintilla favoring a finding that Brookshire Brothers had constructive notice of the condition.

* * *

HENKEL
v.
NORMAN
441 S.W.3d 249
(Tex. 2014)

Opinion

PER CURIAM.

At issue in this premises liability case is whether a homeowner's "don't slip" statement to a mail carrier was adequate as a matter of law to warn him of an icy sidewalk. The trial court determined that it was and granted summary judgment to the homeowner defendants. The court of appeals reversed. Because we agree with the trial court, we reverse the court of appeals' judgment and remand to the court of appeals for it to consider the issues it did not reach.

The trial court granted summary judgment for the defendants in this case, so our standard of review is de novo. *See Buck v. Palmer,* 381 S.W.3d 525, 527 (Tex. 2012). We examine the record in the light most favorable to the nonmovant, indulge every reasonable inference against the motion and likewise resolve any doubts against it. *Id.* Accordingly, our recitation of facts resolves all doubts in favor of Christopher Norman, the plaintiff and nonmovant.

On Saturday, January 9, 2010, mail carrier Norman was delivering mail in Houston. The day was colder than normal and the National Weather Service had issued a hard freeze warning for Friday through Sunday. Neither rain, sleet, nor snow was reported in the area, although Lisa Henkel, one of the homeowner defendants, testified both that she was aware of icy conditions in her neighborhood and that her daughter had slipped on some ice in the road that morning before Norman delivered the mail.

As Norman delivered mail he would walk on the sidewalks of some houses and through the lawns of others. On the morning he fell, he walked through the lawn of the house of Christopher and Lisa Henkel in order to deliver their mail. Lisa was standing at the door so Norman handed her the mail. As he turned to leave and continue on his route, she said "don't slip." Nevertheless, as Norman began walking away on the Henkels' sidewalk he slipped and fell. He denied having seen ice on his route that morning and denied seeing any on the Henkels' property before he fell.

Norman sued the Henkels, alleging that he was injured by the fall and the Henkels were aware of ice on the sidewalk, yet they took no action to prevent the unnatural accumulation of ice, remove the ice, or otherwise remedy the slick conditions. The Henkels filed a Motion for Summary Judgment. By their motion the Henkels asserted that there was no genuine issue of material fact as to whether they failed to warn Norma of any potential danger because "all evidence presented by either side shows . . . Lisa . . . explicitly warned [Norman] regarding potentially icy conditions just seconds before he fell." In response, Norman argued that any warning by Lisa was general, nonspecific, and inadequate.

A traditional summary judgment motion is properly granted where a defendant conclusively negates at least one essential element of a cause of action. *Frost Nat'l Bank v. Fernandez,* 315 S.W.3d 494, 508 (Tex. 2010). The trial court granted the Henkels motion and Norman appealed.

By a two to one decision the court of appeals reversed, holding that "[a] general instruction not to slip or trip or fall is not conclusive evidence of a warning, let alone an adequate warning." *Norman v. Henkel,* 407 S.W.3d 502, 505 (Tex. App.—Houston [14th Dist.] 2013, pet. granted). The dissenting Justice would have held that Lisa's warning was adequate as a matter of law because it "specifically informed Norman of the particular hazard—the slippery ground." *Id.* at 506 (BROWN, J., dissenting).

In their petition for review the Henkels argue that Lisa's statement was an adequate warning as a matter of law because she informed Norman about the condition of the property on which he bases his claim. Norman counters that Lisa's warning was a general instruction and was not adequate because she was required to warn him of the particular condition—the ice.

The parties agree that Norman was an invitee. Generally, premises owners such as the Henkels have a duty to protect invitees from, or warn them of, conditions posing unreasonable risks of harm if the owners knew of the conditions or, in the exercise of reasonable care, should have known of them. *See TXI Operations, L.P. v. Perry,* 278 S.W.3d 763, 764-65 (Tex. 2009). To prevail on a premises liability claim against a property owner, an injured invitee must establish four elements: (1) the property owner had actual or constructive knowledge of the condition causing the injury; (2) the condition posed an unreasonable risk of harm; (3) the property owner failed to take reasonable care to reduce or eliminate the risk; and (4) the property owner's failure to use reasonable care to reduce or eliminate the risk was the proximate cause of injuries to the invitee. *CMH Homes, Inc. v. Daenen,* 15 S.W.3d 97, 99 (Tex. 2000).

The third element is negated if the property owner either adequately warned the invitee about the condition or took reasonable actions designed to make it reasonably safe. *See TXI Operations,* 278 S.W.3d at 765. If the evidence conclusively establishes that the property owner adequately warned the injured party of the condition, then the property owner was not negligent as a matter of law. *Bill's Dollar Store, Inc. v. Bean,* 77 S.W.3d 367, 369 (Tex. App.—Houston [14th Dist.] 2002, pet. denied). To be adequate, a warning must be more than a general instruction such as "be careful"; the warning must notify of the particular condition. *TXI Operations,* 278 S.W.3d at 765. In *TXI,* for example, a speed limit sign was not an adequate warning of a pothole. *Id.* We held that the sign "neither informed the driver of road hazards generally, nor did it identify the particular hazard." *Id; see State v. McBride,* 601 S.W.2d 552, 556-57 (Tex. Civ. App.—Waco 1980, writ ref'd n.r.e.) (holding signs that read "35 MPH" and "SLOW" were insufficient to warn of the actual condition of the construction area, which was that it was muddy and slick when wet). In contrast, a warning by a cashier to a customer to "watch the wet spot" was an adequate warning as a matter of law. *Bill's Dollar Store,* 77 S.W.3d at 370. And a wet floor warning sign and verbal warning to " 'be careful' because the 'floor may be a little damp' " was adequate as a matter of law to discharge a property owner's duty to an invitee. *Brooks v. PRH Invs., Inc.,* 303 S.W.3d 920, 925 (Tex. App.—Texarkana 2010, no pet.).

Turning to the facts of this case, Norman testified in his deposition that Lisa told him "don't slip."[2] He asserts that this warning was a general instruction similar in nature to the general in-

2 In Lisa's deposition she said she told Norman "be careful. It's icy out there today," but as noted previously, we review the evidence in Norman's favor.

struction in *TXI* and did not adequately warn him of the dangerous condition. We disagree. Warnings must be taken in context of the totality of the circumstances. The warning in *TXI*—a speed limit sign—did not inform the driver of the actual condition that caused the injury—a pothole. *TXI Operations,* 278 S.W.3d at 765. But Lisa's statement was not a general "be careful" or "go slow" warning. Under the circumstances the statement Norman heard her make, "don't slip," could only have been taken by a reasonable person as a warning of a specific condition—a slippery walking surface.

Norman also argues that Lisa's warning was inadequate because she did not specifically warn him of ice on the walkway, asserting that ice was the dangerous condition, not the potential for slipping. He says that because one might slip for any number of reasons such as water, paper, freshly mowed grass, potter's clay, loose tile, or even the proverbial banana peel on the ground, Lisa's warning to not slip actually conveyed "everything and nothing." Again, we disagree. Under the circumstances Lisa was not required to warn of the ice itself as opposed to the slippery condition. *See Keetch v. Kroger,* 845 S.W.2d 262, 264 (Tex. 1992) (referencing the dangerous condition as "the slippery spot" on the floor). A warning of the specific material causing a condition is not required, so long as the existence of the condition itself is conveyed. For example, warnings in *Bill's Dollar Store* and *Brooks* were held to have been adequate even though they identified only the dangerous condition (wet floors), not the specific substances that made them wet. *Brooks,* 303 S.W.3d at 925; *Bill's Dollar Store,* 77 S.W.3d at 370.

In sum, absent special circumstances which are not present here, a property owner's warning to an invitee of an unreasonably dangerous condition is adequate if, given the totality of the surrounding circumstances, the warning identifies and communicates the existence of the condition in a manner that a reasonable person would perceive and understand. Here, temperatures had been and were well below freezing and there is no evidence of any other circumstance that a reasonable person might have contemplated would precipitate Lisa's "don't slip" warning. Norman heard her statement and it was adequate in light of the totality of the circumstances to alert a reasonable person in his position that there were slippery conditions caused by the freezing temperatures.

Assuming, without deciding, that ice on the Henkels' sidewalk created an unreasonably dangerous condition, Lisa adequately warned Norman of it. Norman requests that if we reverse the court of appeals' judgment, we remand the case to the court of appeals for it to consider his alternate points raised in, but not addressed by, that court. Accordingly, we reverse the judgment of the court of appeals and remand the case to that court for it to consider Norman's additional issues.

JUSTICE BROWN did not participate in the decision.

---

c. *Fraud cases*

FORD MOTOR COMPANY
v.
CASTILLO
444 S.W.3d 616
(Tex. 2014)

Opinion on Rehearing

PER CURIAM.

At issue in this appeal is the legal sufficiency of circumstantial evidence. A jury determined that a settlement agreement was procured by fraud, and the trial court rendered judgment setting the agreement aside. The court of appeals, however, reversed that judgment, holding the circumstantial evidence of fraud in the case legally insufficient. *Castillo v. Ford Motor Co.,* ——S.W.3d —— (Tex. App.—Corpus Christi-Edinburg 2013) (mem. op.). We conclude that the circumstantial evidence in this case is legally sufficient and accordingly reverse the court of appeals' judgment and remand to the court of appeals for further proceedings consistent with this opinion. The cause is remanded to that court for consideration of the factual sufficiency of the evidence.

In 2004, Ezequiel Castillo and other occupants of his Ford Explorer sued Ford Motor Company for injuries sustained in a roll-over accident. The plaintiffs asserted design defects in the Explorer's roof and in its handling or stability. The products-liability trial lasted approximately four weeks. The case was submitted to the jury on a Friday, late in the afternoon. The jury charge included separate liability questions on the two alleged design defects. A damages question was conditioned on an affirmative answer to one or both of the liability questions.

Cynthia Cruz Cortez, a member of the jury, was very interested in being selected foreperson, and the other jurors acquiesced. The jury was dismissed for the weekend less than an hour after deliberations began. The jury resumed deliberations the following Monday morning.

Within two hours, eleven of the twelve jurors had decided the first liability question in Ford's favor. Cortez was the only juror voting against Ford, but she eventually relented, making the first question a unanimous decision. By the end of Monday's deliberations, eight jurors had decided the second question in Ford's favor. Cortez was one of two jurors who voted against Ford, and two jurors remained undecided.

On Tuesday morning, Cortez failed to return for deliberations. According to other jurors and trial counsel for Ford, Presiding Judge Abel C. Limas[1] informed everybody that Cortez had been in the hospital all night with a sick child. Judge Limas dismissed the jurors for the day and announced that deliberations would resume the following morning.

After the recess was announced, Mark Cantu, one of Castillo's attorneys, called Pete Tassie, Ford's managing counsel, in Michigan to discuss settlement. The two had discussed settlement over several months, but Cantu had refused to budge from his $15 million demand, which Tassie

[1] Judge Limas is currently serving a 72-month sentence in federal prison for taking bribes from attorneys in exchange for favorable rulings. *Former Judge Abel Limas Gets 72 Months in Prison for Taking Bribes,* FBI.GOV (August 21, 2013), http://www.fbi.gov/sanantonio/press-releases/2013/former-judge-abellimas-gets-72-months-inprison-for-taking-bribes.

viewed as unreasonable. This day, however, Cantu asked for $8 million to settle, and later reduced his demand to $4 million. Tassie countered with an offer of $1 million. By the end of the day, the parties were less than $500,000 apart, with Cantu demanding $1.96 million, and Tassie willing to pay $1.5 million.

Tassie recalled from the lengthy negotiations that Cantu repeatedly stated that his demand would increase to $3 million if the jury were to send a note about damages. Tassie, who had ten years of experience negotiating for Ford, including several prior dealings with Cantu, found Cantu's comment odd, not only as to its frequency, but also its specificity. Tassie was accustomed to opposing negotiators stating generally that their demands would increase if certain things were to happen, but had never heard such a specific contingency, let alone one that was repeated several times. At the conclusion of the day's negotiations, Cantu told Tassie he would talk to the judge in the morning and that he could expect the judge to put some pressure on him to settle the case.

The next morning, Tassie called Ford's trial counsel, Eduardo Rodriguez, to update him on the significant progress that had been made in negotiations. Tassie, however, did not hear from the judge or Cantu before the jury began deliberating the next morning. Rodriguez informed Tassie that Cantu was not at the courthouse. Tassie thought this was odd because Cantu had not missed a day during the four week trial. He tried to reach Cantu by phone but was unsuccessful.

About 9 a.m., the jury sent a note to the judge asking for clarification on the burden of proof. Then, about 10:30 a.m., the second note of the day was sent to the judge, inquiring: "What is the maximum amount that can be awarded?" Rodriguez immediately called Tassie in Michigan, and, without hesitation, Tassie obtained authority from his supervisor to settle the case for $3 million—the amount Cantu had said the day before he would demand if the jury were to ask a question about damages. About this same time, Cantu, who had been unavailable all morning, called Tassie. Cantu initially stated that his demand should be $10 or $15 million, but quickly agreed to settle the case for $3 million.

Tassie called Rodriguez to tell him the case had settled, and, because of the disturbing note, asked Rodriguez to speak with members of the jury. Ford's attorneys were able to talk to eleven of the jurors, but Cortez left the courthouse without speaking to them. Discussing the case with the other jurors, Ford learned that the jury had not been discussing damages before the settlement, and did not know that Cortez had sent the damages note to the judge. Ford subsequently tried to obtain a statement from Cortez but was not successful. Ford did obtain affidavits from most of the other jurors, who repeated what they told Ford on the day the case settled. After completing its investigation, Ford refused to pay the $3 million to Castillo, who then sued Ford for breach of contract.

In its defense to the settlement, Ford asserted fraudulent inducement, unilateral mistake, and mutual mistake. However, Judge Limas prohibited Ford from conducting discovery or offering evidence of the jury's deliberations in the products-liability trial, including the signed affidavits from the jurors. Judge Limas subsequently granted summary judgment, and the court of appeals affirmed. *Ford Motor Co. v. Castillo,* 200 S.W.3d 217 (Tex. App.—Corpus Christi-Edinburg 2006, pet. granted). This Court reversed and remanded to permit Ford to conduct discovery and offer evidence from the jurors in the products-liability suit, because, *inter alia,* the circumstantial evidence indicated outside influence. *Ford Motor Co. v. Castillo,* 279 S.W.3d 656, 666 (Tex. 2009) ("Discovery involving jurors will not be appropriate in most cases, but in this case there was more than just a suspicion that something suspect occurred—there was some circumstantial evidence that it did.").

On remand, a new jury heard testimony from, among others, Tassie, Cantu, Rodriguez, and most of the jurors from the products-liability trial, including Cortez. Several of the jurors testified that Cortez kept trying to bring up the damages issue on her own, and sent the note against their specific requests that she not do so. These jurors also testified that all other notes were sent by unanimous agreement. One juror testified that on the morning the case settled—after the day-long recess caused by Cortez's absence—Cortez arrived in a "very happy, very upbeat" mood, and told the other jurors, "This will be settled today."

Unlike the other jurors who testified, Cortez could not recall any of the pertinent details of the trial or the jury deliberations. Notably, Cortez could not recall why she sent the note in question, why exactly she did not show up for the second full day of deliberations, or why she had left the courtroom so quickly after the settlement was announced. Cortez also could not recall her cell phone number or carrier at the time, but signed a release permitting Ford to search for all cell-phone records registered to Cortez during the time of the products-liability trial, using her name, address, and date of birth. After denying that she spoke with any attorneys during the trial, Cortez was asked to explain a phone call on September 21, 2004 to the purported private cell phone of attorney and State Representative Jim Solis.[2] Initially, Cortez explained that her husband probably made the call. When other evidence made that explanation unlikely,[3] she speculated that the phone records were those of another Cynthia Cortez.

After hearing all of the evidence, the jury found the settlement agreement invalid because of fraudulent inducement and mutual mistake. The trial court rendered a take-nothing judgment and Castillo appealed. The court of appeals reversed the judgment, concluding that the evidence was legally insufficient to support a jury verdict. . . .

When reviewing all of the evidence in a light favorable to the verdict, "courts must assume jurors made all inferences in favor of their verdict if reasonable minds could, and disregard all other inferences in their legal sufficiency review." [citing *City of Keller v. Wilson*.] When reviewing circumstantial evidence that favors the verdict, we must "view each piece of circumstantial evidence, not in isolation, but in light of all the known circumstances." If circumstantial evidence, when viewed in light of all the known circumstances, is equally consistent with either of two facts, then neither fact may be inferred. But where the circumstantial evidence is not equally consistent with either of two facts, and the inference drawn by the jury is within the "zone of reasonable disagreement," a reviewing court cannot substitute its judgment for that of the trier-of-fact.

---

[2] Jim Solis is currently serving a 47-month sentence in federal prison after confessing to his role in Judge Limas' extortion scheme, wherein Solis would operate as a middle man between Judge Limas and the attorneys trying cases in Limas' court. *Former Texas Representative Jim Solis Gets 47 Months in Prison for Limas Extortion Scheme,* FBI.GOV (August 02, 2013), http://www.fbi.gov/sanantoni o/press-releases/2013/former-texas-representative-jim-solis-gets-47-months-in-prison-for-limas-extortion-scheme.

[3] Because Cortez's husband was a high school football coach at the time, Ford pointed out to Cortez that the same number making the purported call to Jim Solis also made five different phone calls between 6:50 and 8:00 p.m. on Friday, September 24. Cortez admitted that, as a high school football coach, her husband should not have been making and receiving phone calls during a game, but explained that he could still do so because he was an assistant coach, who worked from a box, rather than on the sidelines.

To find fraudulent inducement, the jury was instructed that it needed to find evidence of five elements: (1) a material misrepresentation; (2) sent by or at the direction of the plaintiffs or their agents or representatives with knowledge it was false; (3) with the intent that Ford Motor Company rely on the representation; (4) that Ford Motor Company did not know the representation was false and actually and justifiably relied upon the representation; and (5) that Ford Motor Company detrimentally relied on the representation by entering into the settlement agreement. Only the first three elements are in dispute.

On the first element, the jury was instructed that a material misrepresentation is a "false statement of fact." Castillo argues that the note sent by Cortez asked a question, and therefore cannot be a false statement of fact. Although the note does ask a question, statements of fact are clearly implied. A jury note, asking about the maximum amount of damages, implies that the jury is deliberating damages and that it intends to award the maximum amount. It also implies that the note is from the jury collectively. The evidence indicates that neither implication was true. According to the testimony of several jurors, the jury was not actually deliberating damages at the time of Cortez's note, and several jurors specifically told Cortez not to send a note about damages. Because the note implies material statements that were false, we conclude that some evidence exists of the first element of fraudulent inducement.

On the second element, Ford was required to produce evidence establishing that the note was sent by or at the direction of the plaintiffs or their agents or representatives with knowledge it was false. Ford's theory was that Cantu, as plaintiffs' representative, directed Cortez to send the note.

* * *

As to the sufficiency of the evidence, the court of appeals held that the only evidence supporting the jury's finding on this element was Cantu's statement the night before that his demand would increase to $3 million in the event of a jury note about damages. The court of appeals found this circumstantial evidence too meager to support the verdict because Cantu's statement was "consistent with the custom of plaintiff's attorneys," and was just as likely coincidence as it was knowledge that Cortez would be sending the fraudulent note. . . .

. . . But here, there is enough circumstantial evidence to establish a pattern—a pattern that reasonably implicates Cantu in Cortez's fraudulent scheme to send the note. . . .

Contrary to the court of appeals' view, the trial evidence did not establish that Cantu's comments the day before the settlement were customary of plaintiff's attorneys, but rather the opposite. Tassie, who had negotiated for Ford for more than ten years, including several prior dealings with Cantu, had never heard such a specific contingency. Moreover, neither Cantu nor any of the other attorneys involved in the case had ever seen such a jury note before. Yet Cantu's comments forecast such a note and elaborated on the effect it would have on settlement negotiations. But the unusual nature and prescient timing of Cantu's statement is not the only circumstantial evidence supporting the jury's finding.

On the brink of a Ford victory, Cortez precipitated a day-long recess because of some serious illness or injury to one of her two children. At the trial of this case, however, Cortez could not recall the illness or injury that kept her at the hospital all night. The same day, Cantu, who had refused to lower his settlement demand below $15 million during weeks of previous negotiations, became more agreeable, reducing his demand to less than $2 million in just a matter of hours. Moreover, even after the surprising jury note inquiring as to the maximum amount of damages it could award in a case alleging damages of $35 million, Cantu remained agreeable to a settlement of less than ten percent of that amount. Viewing this circumstantial evidence in light of all the surrounding circumstances, the jury could reasonably infer from the evidence that Cortez initiated the recess in order to give Cantu more time to negotiate a settlement before the jury foreclosed that possibility.

The inferences become stronger when the circumstantial evidence raises the inference of fraud, and the parties alleged to have engaged in the fraud fail to offer any proof of their legitimate or honest motives. Here, the explanations offered for Cantu and Cortez's unusual and apparently coordinated conduct were lacking.

For instance, Cortez was unwilling to offer any explanation for her actions. Even when she was summoned to testify, she offered no explanation, claiming instead that she could not remember any of the relevant details of the trial or deliberations. As for Cantu, he denied ever making the prediction about the note, instead admitting that it would have been unreasonable to make such a statement. He further justified his willingness to discount the extremely favorable note, and accept a fraction of his original demand, on fear that one of his expert's testimony might provide Ford a fruitful appellate argument. While this concern possibly explains his settlement preference, it does not explain his willingness to give Ford such an extreme discount of the damages pled. The circumstantial evidence here is some evidence from which the jury could have reasonably inferred collusion between Cortez and Cantu in producing the fraudulent note.

Having found evidence that Cortez colluded with Cantu, who unquestionably knew that jury notes would be shown to Ford's attorneys, we necessarily find evidence of the third element—that Cortez sent the fraudulent note with the intent that Ford rely upon it.

As to the fourth element—that Ford did not know the representation was false and actually and justifiably relied upon the representation—there is legally sufficient evidence of reliance for the same reasons we have found some evidence of a material misrepresentation. Castillo argues that any reliance on the note which induced Ford to enter the settlement was unjustified because Ford could not assume that the note containing the damages question indicated that the jury had reached any particular determination in the sequence of its deliberations nor could Ford assume that the note indicated the views of the jury collectively. As discussed above, however, the note did impliedly state these very facts that the jury was deliberating damages and intended to award the maximum amount, as well as that the note was from the jury collectively. Accordingly, because there is some evidence that Ford had no knowledge that these implications were false, there was some evidence that Ford was justified to rely on these implications in entering the settlement agreement.

Because the evidence is legally sufficient to support the jury's verdict, we grant the petition for review and, without hearing oral argument, reverse the court of appeals' judgment and remand to the court of appeals for review of Castillo's factual sufficiency challenge. TEX .R. APP. P. 59.1.

---

4. *Conclusive Evidence*

The concept of "conclusive evidence"—evidence that is so strong that it cannot be disbelieved—can arise in two different situations under *City of Keller*'s analysis. The Powers & Ratliff article discussed "*undisputed* conclusive evidence"—when the plaintiff's undisputed conclusive evidence supports a vital fact and the plaintiff is entitled to judgment as a matter of law ("Zone 5" evidence). But *City of Keller* also discusses "*disputed* conclusive evidence"—when a defendant's conclusive contrary evidence destroys the plaintiff's evidence, rendering the plaintiff's evidence "no evidence" and the defendant is entitled to judgment as a matter of law. Here, the opinion discusses when a reviewing court must consider contrary conclusive evidence:

> . . . There are several types of conclusive evidence. First, an appellate court conducting a legal sufficiency review cannot "disregard undisputed evidence that allows of only one logical inference." By definition, such evidence can be viewed in only one light, and reasonable jurors can reach only one conclusion from it. Jurors are not free to reach a verdict contrary to such evidence; indeed, uncontroverted issues need not be submitted to a jury at all.
>
> Reviewing legal sufficiency in such cases encompasses a general no-evidence review, because if some evidence supports the verdict then the contrary evidence was not "undisputed." But the review does not stop there; the evidence must also have only one logical inference. Undisputed evidence that reasonable jurors could disbelieve has two: (1) it is true, or (2) it is not.
>
> Most often, undisputed contrary evidence becomes conclusive (and thus cannot be disregarded) when it concerns physical facts that cannot be denied. . . .
>
> Undisputed contrary evidence may also become conclusive when a party admits it is true. Thus, a claimant's admission that he was aware of a dangerous premises condition is conclusive evidence he needed no warning about it. Similarly, an ex-employee's admission that she obtained other employment may prove conclusively that she did not detrimentally rely on a defendant's promise to re-hire her. . . .
>
> It is impossible to define precisely when undisputed evidence becomes conclusive. . . Evidence is conclusive only if reasonable people could not differ in their conclusions, a matter that depends on the facts of each case.
>
> There is another category of conclusive evidence, in which the evidence *is* disputed. Undisputed evidence and conclusive evidence are not the same—undisputed evidence may or may not be conclusive, and conclusive evidence may or may not be undisputed.
>
> * * *
>
> Of course, there are few instances in which disputed evidence is conclusive, and many instances in which undisputed evidence is not. As our sister court has noted, testimony by a paid informant is legally sufficient to support a conviction, even if "[t]wenty nuns testify that the defendant was with them at the time, far from the scene of the crime . . . [and] [t]wenty more nuns testify that they saw the informant commit the crime." . . .
>
> While jurors may generally believe either sinners or saints, their discretion is limited when it is proved beyond question that an "eyewitness" was actually far away in prison or totally blind on the day of the crime.
>
> Proper legal-sufficiency review prevents reviewing courts from substituting their opinions on credibility for those of the jurors, but proper review also prevents jurors from substituting their opinions for undisputed truth. When evidence contrary to a verdict is conclusive, it cannot be disregarded. . . .

Both situations—a plaintiff's Zone 5 conclusive evidence and a defendant's conclusive evidence moving a plaintiff's evidence from "some evidence" to "no evidence" are illustrated by the opinions below.

MURDOCK
v.
MURDOCK

811 S.W.2d 557
(Tex. 1991)

OPINION

GONZALEZ, JUSTICE.

This divorce case involves the pleading and proof required of an alleged father who seeks to disprove paternity by means of blood tests. During the trial, the alleged father introduced evidence that blood tests ordered by the trial court excluded him as the biological father of a child born during the marriage. Nonetheless, the trial court found him to be the father and ordered him to pay child support. The court of appeals held that the evidence was legally insufficient to establish that the tests were "properly conducted" and affirmed the judgment of the trial court. *Doe v. Doe,* 796 S.W.2d 506 (Tex. App.—Dallas 1990). We reverse the judgment of the court of appeals and remand the cause to the trial court for further proceedings, if any, which may be necessary to render judgment in accordance with this opinion.

FACTS

Vernie Lucritus "Luke" Murdock, petitioner, married Chere Denise "Chere" Murdock, respondent, in 1982. Chere gave birth to a son in 1987. Luke treated the child as his own until the couple's separation in 1988. Shortly after the separation, Chere filed for divorce and requested custody of the child and also sought child support from Luke. Luke denied paternity and requested pretrial proceedings and blood tests pursuant to chapter 13 of the Texas Family Code. The trial court ordered the parties to submit to blood testing at the Wadley Blood Center for a minimum of seven blood tests to determine whether Luke fathered the child in question. The tests excluded Luke as the biological father and they were filed with the trial court. . . .

At trial, Chere testified that Luke was the father of the child and that she never had sexual relations with any other man during the marriage. She also testified that Luke had always treated the child as his own and only disclaimed paternity on the date of separation. The child's birth certificate lists Luke as the father although there was no testimony as to whether he signed it. Chere's father and a friend of Chere's testified that Luke was the father and that the child looked like Luke.

Luke responded by testifying that he had a vasectomy prior to his marriage to Chere and he offered into evidence the blood tests establishing nonpaternity. In explaining why he treated the child as his own during the marriage, Luke stated that he always believed the child to be his own until his sister reminded him that he had had a vasectomy. Luke attributes his absence of memory to a car accident that caused him to forget many things from his past. Luke's ex-wife from a prior marriage testified that she was aware of the vasectomy and that it had been performed in August 1977. An expert witness from the Wadley Blood Center's tissue typing lab and paternity section testified that pursuant to the trial court's order seven tests were performed on the blood samples of the mother, child and alleged father. The tests showed that the child is blood type B while Chere and Luke are blood type O. Since both Chere and Luke are type O, the B, which is dominant over the recessive O, had to come from someone else. Because certain properties of the blood components are inheritable, detectible and varied, based on the aforementioned tests and the other tests, it was her expert opinion that Luke was not the father. Chere did not challenge the expert's qualifications and these tests were admitted without objection.

On cross-examination, the expert testified that there was no probability of error because duplicate testing is performed. She stated that the results are double-checked by three different people and if any discrepancies are found the tests are repeated. Even after persistent questioning by Chere's counsel, the witness maintained there was no possibility of a mistake in the test results—Luke was not the father.

After considering all of the evidence, the trial court found that Luke was the biological father of the child and ordered him to pay child support. The court of appeals affirmed.

* * *

ADMISSION OF BLOOD TEST RESULTS

When blood testing was first introduced as a means of establishing nonpaternity it was greeted with skepticism by the courts. In fact, it is because of this skepticism and the nature of the tests themselves that evidentiary procedures only permit the tests to be used to establish nonpaternity and not for use to prove paternity. . . .

The court of appeals held that the blood test evidence was inconclusive of non-paternity because Luke failed to establish that the tests had been properly conducted . . . . We disagree.

The "properly conducted" requirement is subsumed within the evidentiary predicate that must be established *prior* to the admission of the test results into evidence. Once the trial court receives blood test results into evidence, they are admitted for all relevant purposes just like any other piece of evidence. In the present case, the test results were admitted into evidence without objection. From all of the test data, it was established that there was a zero probability of paternity. Thus, Luke conclusively proved that he was not the father of the child and is entitled to judgment in his favor.

For the reasons stated above, we reverse the judgment of the court of appeals. Because this issue is involved in the pending action, we remand the cause to the trial court for further proceedings, if any, which may be necessary to render judgment in accordance with this opinion.

BARNES
v.
MATHIS
353 S.W.3d 760
(Tex. 2011)

Opinion

PER CURIAM.

At issue in this case is whether the court of appeals erred in rendering judgment for a plaintiff who received an adverse verdict and take-nothing judgment after a jury trial. When a party with the burden of proof loses at trial and asks an appellate court to render judgment in his favor, that party must show that the evidence conclusively established his entitlement to judgment. Because the court of appeals incorrectly applied this standard and Mathis did not conclusively prove his nuisance and trespass claims, we reverse in part its judgment and remand the case to the court of appeals to determine factual sufficiency issues raised below.

Dr. Lee Roy Mathis and H.E. "Buster" Barnes own adjoining property in Anderson County. Lake Creek runs through both tracts, and Mathis's 1,254 acre property is located upstream from Barnes's. Mathis maintained a wetlands complex on much of his land, which attracted beavers, waterfowl, and other wildlife. Barnes's tract was used predominantly as a pasture. In September 2006, Barnes constructed an earthen road across the creek to more easily access his back pasture. To accommodate water flow in the creek, Barnes installed two twenty-eight-inch culverts, or drainage pipes, into the structure. In October 2006, Mathis noticed an elevated water level in the creek, which he suspected was caused by Barnes's road. By November, Mathis noticed that creek water encroached onto his property, and he asked Barnes to modify the road. Barnes later installed an additional culvert into the structure. In December 2006, Mathis returned to his property after a twelve-day absence to discover that Barnes's road was washed away. The flooding—and subsequent drainage—also affected over four hundred acres of Mathis's property, damaging beaver dams, affecting the wildlife population, and draining the wetlands.

Mathis sued Barnes, alleging negligence, gross negligence, nuisance, and trespass. At trial, Mathis argued that Barnes's road acted as a dam, causing a large amount of water to accumulate, which eventually destroyed Barnes's road and damaged much of Mathis's land. Barnes countered that an upstream event caused the flooding and produced evidence that Mathis's property did not lose value and Mathis did not suffer non-economic damages. After a jury answered "No" as to each of Mathis's causes of action, the trial court entered a take-nothing judgment.

On appeal, Mathis argued that, despite the jury's verdict, the evidence conclusively established nuisance, trespass, and negligence. The court of appeals reversed the trial court's judgment in part, holding that "the evidence is legally insufficient to support the jury's 'No' answer[s]" to the nuisance and trespass issues. 316 S.W.3d at 802-04. The court nevertheless remanded the case for trial because, when "liability is contested, we cannot order a separate trial solely on damages. *See* TEX. R. APP. P. 44.1(b)."

The court of appeals concluded that the following material facts were established as a matter of law: (1) Barnes constructed the road across Lake Creek, (2) the road disrupted the creek's flow, and (3) water from the creek crossed the parties' property line, flooding Mathis's land. Regarding the nuisance claim, the court pointed to evidence that Mathis maintained some of his property as a wetlands area and that after the large flood, the property retained much less water. Thus, the court held that Mathis had conclusively established nuisance. As to the trespass claim, the court observed that Barnes was aware that water encroached on Mathis's property after Barnes built the road. The court held that because damage is presumed after a trespass, that claim, too, was established conclusively.

Barnes contends that the court of appeals erred by focusing on evidence that failed to persuade the jury. We agree. Uncontested evidence may establish a fact as a matter of law—as when scientific proof yields only one conclusion—even if a jury disagrees. *See, e.g., City of Keller v. Wilson,* 168 S.W.3d 802, 816 (Tex. 2005) (citing *Murdock v. Murdock,* 811 S.W.2d 557, 560 (Tex. 1991) (holding that no evidence supported paternity verdict because blood test conclusively proved defendant was not the child's father)). In this case, however, the jury was required to evaluate the cause of an otherwise natural occurrence. Mathis stated the central issue appropriately: "the parties did contest whether the rush of floodwaters was caused by Barnes' structure breaking or, as Barnes argued, some unknown, upstream event. Barnes also posited that the destruction of the beaver dams might have been caused by wild hogs rooting around at their base."

As the plaintiff, Mathis was required to prove nuisance and trespass. A nuisance is a condition that substantially interferes with the use and enjoyment of land by causing unreasonable discomfort or annoyance to persons of ordinary sensibilities.[2] The jury refused to find that Barnes created a nuisance that damaged Mathis's land. In order to have judgment rendered for him despite the jury's verdict, Mathis must show that the evidence establishes conclusively that Barnes substantially interfered with his land and caused unreasonable discomfort. We conclude that Mathis did not do so.

* * *

The conflicting theories, each supported by evidence, presented a classic case for a jury's resolution. A jury could reasonably have found that Mathis did not prove Barnes's road caused a flooding event unique from natural circumstances. We therefore conclude the court of appeals erred in holding that liability was established as a matter of law as to Mathis's nuisance claim. . . .

In the court of appeals, Mathis also asserted that the evidence was factually insufficient to support the jury's verdict, an issue the court of appeals declined to reach. Accordingly, without hearing oral argument, TEX. R. APP. P. 59. 1, we grant Barnes's petition for review, reverse in part the court of appeals' judgment, and remand the case to the court of appeals to consider Mathis's argument that the jury's failure to find nuisance and trespass was against the great weight of the evidence.

---

5. *"No duty" as Legal Sufficiency*

The chapter on summary judgment discussed situations where summary judgment is appropriate because a case presents a pure question of law. These types of situations also present themselves after trial begins, but sometimes they are referred to as "no duty" cases. Professor Powers has described them as follows:[1]

---

2 A similar definition of nuisance was provided in the jury charge.

1 W. Powers, *Judge and Jury in the Texas Supreme Court*, 75 TEX. L. REV. 1699 (1997).

To place this issue in context, it is important to recognize that there are two very different types of no evidence cases in Texas. In one type of case the law is clear, but the facts are not. A typical example would be a dispute about whether a driver was negligent for failing to stop at a red light. No one disagrees that failing to stop at a red light constitutes statutory negligence. If three witnesses testified that the light was green and one witness testified that the light was red, there would be some evidence—more than a scintilla—that the light was red. On the other hand, if three witnesses testified that the light was green and one witness testified that the sun made it impossible to tell one way or the other, there would be no evidence from which a jury could rationally conclude that the light was red. The question in this type of case is about the probative value of the evidence and the permissible inferences a jury can draw.

In a different type of no evidence case the facts are clear, but the law is not. *Fisher v. Carrousel Motor Hotel, Inc.* is an example. The plaintiff was an African-American engineer at NASA who went to lunch with some of his colleagues. The manager of the restaurant where they tried to eat grabbed a plate from the plaintiff's hand and told him he was not welcome at the restaurant. No one disputed the facts. Nevertheless, the trial court granted judgment for the defendant notwithstanding the verdict on the ground that there was no evidence of a battery. The supreme court reversed, holding that there was evidence of a battery. The no evidence issue, however, did not turn on the permissible inferences that could be drawn from the evidence. Instead, it depended on a substantive rule about battery. If the manager's grabbing the plate, rather than the plaintiff's arm, constituted bodily contact, then the manager committed a battery. The court held that it did. This was purely a determination of the correct legal standard. It had nothing to do with what inferences could reasonably be drawn from the evidence.

Under the traditional roles of the judge and jury, it is clear that the jury should ascertain the credibility of witnesses and determine whether a light was red or green. On the other hand, it is equally clear that the court should determine whether grabbing a plate constitutes bodily contact under the law of battery. That is what we generally mean when we say that the jury should decide the facts and the court should decide the law. This distinction is obscured in most tort cases, however, because we allow the jury to determine mixed questions of law and fact. When we ask a jury to determine whether a defendant acted "outrageously" in intentional infliction of emotional distress, when we ask a jury to determine whether a product was "unreasonably" dangerous, or when we ask a jury in a negligence case to determine whether a defendant exercised "ordinary care," we ask the jury to decide both what happened and whether the defendant's behavior was appropriate. The second determination is about how people should behave. It is clear that the jury's role is to determine what happened; that is a descriptive task. It is not so clear that it is the jury's role to determine how people should behave; that is a normative task. Broad, amorphous duty rules, with mixed questions of law and fact, put more of the normative work in the hands of the jury. Particularized duty rules put more of the normative work in the hands of judges. The question is how much of that normative work should be assigned to judges or juries.

Professor Powers and Ratliff, in their article excerpted earlier in this section had also described the *Fisher* case, using the "Zones" vocabulary, as follows:[2]

> Zone 1 also embraces an entirely different type of case. Sometimes little dispute exists about the facts; instead, the opponent claims that the facts do not constitute a cause of action. An example of this type of "no evidence" case is *Fisher v. Carrousel Motor Hotel, Inc.* The defendant's servant grabbed a plate from the plaintiff's hand, and the plaintiff sued for battery. The trial court granted defendant's motion for judgment notwithstanding the verdict and the court of appeals affirmed. Those courts held that grabbing a plate did not constitute harmful or offensive bodily contact, which is a necessary element of battery. Consequently, the record contained no evidence of harmful or offensive bodily contact, and those courts placed the case in zone 1. However, the Texas Supreme Court reversed, holding that contact with an item intimately associated with the plaintiff's body does constitute the requisite bodily contact. Because no dispute existed about whether the defendant's servant actually grabbed the plate, the supreme court's substantive ruling not only removed the case from zone 1, it effectively moved the case all the way to zone 5. Consequently, the court rendered judgment in favor of the plaintiff. In negligence cases these determinations are expressed in terms of the legal duty owed by the defendant and thus have come to be known as "no duty" cases. "No duty" cases are a subset of "no evidence" cases.
>
> This "no duty" variation of the "no evidence" point is qualitatively different from a "no evidence" point where the law is clear but the facts are not. The *Carrousel* court was not required to evaluate specific evidence to determine whether the record contained a quantum of evidence which would support a jury finding. Instead, the court made a legal determination about the substantive elements of a specific cause of action. Nevertheless, Texas courts currently treat the two types of determinations as "no evidence" points; each falls into zone 1.

***El Chico Corp. v. Poole*, 732 S.W.2d 306 (Tex. 1987):**

In *El Chico* the Supreme Court created a common-law cause of action for the negligent serving of alcohol. El Chico had served liquor to an intoxicated customer, who went forth and injured the plaintiff in an automobile wreck. The Supreme Court allowed the plaintiff to sue not only the drunk driver but also the El Chico restaurant, whose liquor had helped get the driver drunk. The court summarized its new common-law cause of action and stated that the elements of proof were: (1) the serving of a patron that the server knew or should have known was intoxicated, and (2) the serving proximately caused damage to the victim. The Court said:

> [W]e hold an alcoholic beverage licensee owes a duty to the general public not to serve alcoholic beverages to a person when the licensee *knows or should know* the patron is intoxicated. A licensee who violates that duty by serving alcoholic beverages to an intoxicated person is negligent as a matter of law. Whether a licensee breached his duty and whether that breach *proximately caused* a plaintiff's injuries are issues of fact for a jury to resolve.

---

[2] William Powers, Jr. and Jack Ratliff, *Another Look at "No Evidence" and "Insufficient Evidence,"* 69 TEX. L. REV. 515 (1991).

(emphasis added). The Court then recognized that the Legislature had recently created a similar cause of action, which required different, more demanding proof:

> In recognizing the cause of action announced today, we are mindful that the legislature has this week enacted a statute creating a civil remedy for persons injured by a licensee's intoxicated patron. The legislature amended the Alcoholic Beverage Code to include a civil cause of action against an alcoholic beverage licensee when "at the time . . . [the licensee-provider served the alcohol] . . . it was *apparent* to the provider that the individual being . . . served . . . was *obviously intoxicated* to the extent he presented a *clear danger* to himself and others." Act of June 1, 1987; § 3 (to be codified at TEX. ALCO. BEV. CODE ANN. § 2.02)

(emphasis added). The Court observed, "The legislature appears to have created a much more onerous burden of proof for an injured plaintiff than we have in this opinion." It is easy to envision cases in which the injured motorist's proof will raise a fact issue on the court's common-law cause of action but not on the legislature's statutory cause of action.

***Montgomery County Hosp. Dist. v. Brown*, 965 S.W.2d 501 (Tex. 1998):**

Brown sued the Hospital (her former employer) for terminating her without cause. The Hospital asserted the employment-at-will doctrine, which gives employers the right to fire employees at will—for any reason, good or bad, or for no reason—unless there is a contract that modifies the at-will principle. (There are also statutory exceptions to the at-will doctrine not at issue in this case.) Brown alleged that the Hospital assured her "that I would be able to keep my job at the Hospital as long as I was doing my job and that I would not be fired unless there was a good reason or good cause to fire me." If oral unspecific promises were enough to prove a contract to modify the at-will doctrine, Brown would have raised a fact issue of modification. But the court agreed with the Hospital that its assurances to Brown, accepted as true for purposes of summary judgment, were too indefinite to constitute an agreement limiting the Hospital's right to discharge Brown at will. "General statements like those made to Brown simply do not justify the conclusion that the speaker intends by them to make a binding contract of employment. For such a contract to exist, the employer must unequivocally indicate a definite intent to be bound not to terminate the employee except under clearly specified circumstances. General comments that an employee will not be discharged as long as his work is satisfactory do not in themselves manifest such an intent. Neither do statements that an employee will be discharged only for 'good reason' or 'good cause' when there is no agreement on what those terms encompass. Without such agreement the employee cannot reasonably expect to limit the employer's right to terminate him. An employee who has no formal agreement with his employer cannot construct one out of indefinite comments, encouragements, or assurances." Brown's evidence was therefore legally insufficient to raise a fact issue on oral modification of the at-will relationship. If the court had defined the substantive law of contract differently—to allow contracts based on general oral assurances of continued employment as long as the employee performed well—Brown's evidence would have been legally sufficient.

---

6. *Motions Presenting Legal Sufficiency*

Read Rules 268, 270, 301.

The first opportunity that a litigant has to obtain a judgment as a matter of law in the Texas trial courts, or to preserve a legal sufficiency point of error for appeal, is the motion for directed verdict. But it is not the last. Recall that a legal sufficiency point can be preserved also by an objection to the charge for reasons of "no evidence" or "conclusive evidence." And after the verdict, the parties can attack it for legal sufficiency reasons through a motion to disregard the jury's answers or a motion for judgment notwithstanding the verdict. You may recall that in federal court, a litigant asserts legal sufficiency through the motion for judgment as a matter of law, original and renewed. The Texas rules continue to use the old nomenclature—directed verdicts and judgments notwithstanding the verdict (or JNOV). The motion for new trial is also available for attacking legal sufficiency of a verdict, but the remedy is a new trial, or remand on appeal. A party attacking a judgment through the means for legal sufficiency is entitled to *rendition* of judgment. We have studied the standard by which the trial and appellate courts consider such motions. The notes below concern the technicalities.

Notes & Questions

1. M*otion for directed verdict.* Plaintiff must have had an opportunity to put on a case-in-chief before defendant may move for a directed verdict. Thus, the first opportunity will be when the plaintiff rests, but motions may also be made when the plaintiff closes (concludes all evidence, including rebuttal) and when all parties close. The federal courts require a motion for JMOL as a predicate for a later renewed motion for JMOL. *See* Federal Rule 50(b). In Texas courts, however, a no evidence point can be raised for the first time on motion for judgment n.o.v. after the jury has been discharged. The "sandbagging" possibilities under the Texas practice have been criticized but there seems to be little sentiment for change. Most motions for directed verdict are made orally—dictated to the court reporter out of the presence of the jury.[1]

2. *Waiver of motion for directed verdict by going forward with the evidence.* Defendant customarily moves for directed verdict when Plaintiff concludes its case-in-chief and "rests." If D thinks its motion is good but the judge overrules it, D has something of a dilemma. It can stand on the motion and refuse to put on evidence of its own, counting on a reversal on appeal (that is, if the judge does not later relent and grant a judgment n.o.v.). But if the appellate court upholds the judge's ruling, the jury verdict—reached without the jury having heard D's case-in-chief—will stand. If, on the other hand, D goes forward with its own evidence and in the process the gaps in P's proof are filled (whether by D's presentation of evidence or by P's cross-examination), then D's right to a directed verdict is lost. D is said to have "waived" the earlier motion.[2] Of course, if P *fails* to plug the gaps, D may again move for directed verdict after the close of all the evidence and that motion will be good. It is surprising how often defense counsel will routinely make the motion after P first rests,

---

1 *See* Dillard v. Broyles, 633 S.W.2d 636 (Tex. App.—Corpus Christi 1982, writ ref'd n.r.e.).

2 *See* McElreath v. McElreath, 542 S.W.2d 206 (Tex. Civ. App.—Tyler 1976, no writ).

but will fail to reurge it, as required, at the close of all the evidence. But, it is not as bad as it sounds. D has an opportunity to raise the same point on motion for judgment n.o.v.

3. *Statement of specific grounds for motion.* A tiny tempest bubbles away in the procedural teapot, generated by the confluence of two imperatives. The first—provided by Rule 268—requires the party moving for directed verdict to "state the specific grounds therefor." The second is based on the long-standing power of a court to direct a verdict on its own motion without stating the grounds.[3] Suppose that a directed verdict is appropriate, but the motion fails to state specific grounds or states the wrong grounds and the judge grants it anyway. If the result is right, who cares about the motion's form? After all, the judge could have acted without any motion at all. The important underlying question is whether or not there are fact issues for the jury. This is the reasoned approach we have seen elsewhere—in connection with rulings on evidence, for example—and is one clearly mandated by the harmless error rule[4] and a number of leading cases.[5] Nevertheless, confusion persists as to whether there must be at least one correct ground in such a motion—even if it is not the one the court relies on.[6] It is clear that no *denial* of a motion for directed verdict will be overturned unless the motion has stated valid, specific ground, supporting it.[7] But why should anyone be concerned about the motion's correctness if the trial court *grants* the motion and it turns out that the court has stumbled onto the right action? One leading commentator suggests that a policy reason for a strict approach to Rule 268 is to prevent the movant's "sandbagging" by concealing the real defects in proof until it is too late to cure them.[8] But the opportunity for "sandbagging" is present in the Texas practice anyway. D does not have to move for directed verdict at all but can wait until it is too late for P to reopen and then move for judgment n.o.v. Therefore, is there a reason to reverse a trial judge who directed a verdict and got it right for the wrong reasons?

4. *Reopening under Rule 270.* You represent the Plaintiff P in an exploding widget products liability case. You have just rested, having concluded your case-in-chief. D's counsel moves for directed verdict, and you listen attentively. To your dismay, she states a valid ground—namely that you have failed to show that the manufacturer, Widget Co., manufactured the widget in question, proof that is

---

[3] *See* McDONALD, Section 21:51 at p. 132; Rudco O. & G. Co. v. Gulf Oil Corp., 169 S.W.2d 791 (Tex. Civ. App.—Austin 1943, writ ref'd w.o.m.); *and* Wilson v. Goodyear Tire & Rubber Co., 753 S.W.2d 442 (Tex. App.—Texarkana 1988, writ denied).

[4] Incorporated, as we have seen, in TRAP Rules 44 & 61.

[5] *See* T.E.I.A. v. Page, 553 S.W.2d 98 (Tex. 1977); Prather v. McNally, 757 S.W.2d 124 (Tex. App.—Dallas 1988, no writ); *and* Maxwell v. Cardinal Petroleum Co., 460 S.W.2d 436 (Tex. Civ. App.—Beaumont 1970), *rev'd o. g.* 471 S.W.2d 785 (Tex. 1971). Because of the requirements of Rule 166a summary judgments are different. There it is clear that the judgment cannot be granted on a ground not included in the motion. *See* Carlisle v. Philip Morris, Inc., 805 S.W.2d 498, 517 (Tex. App.—Austin 1991, writ denied) (citing authority *and* holding in addition that a summary judgment can be upheld only on the ground specified in the *judgment*).

[6] *See*, 4 McDONALD, Section 12:51 *and, e.g.,* Prather v. McNally, 757 S.W.2d 124 (Tex. App.—Dallas 1988, no writ) ("We follow the rule that a directed verdict should be affirmed if it is supported by any ground *asserted in the motion* even though the rationale assigned by the courts...was erroneous.") (Emphasis added.)

[7] *See, e.g.,* Southwest General Construction Co., v. Price, 267 S.W.2d 855 (Tex. Civ. App.—Dallas 1954, no writ); *and see, generally*, McDONALD, Section 21:51 at p. 131.

[8] *See* 4 McDONALD, § 21:51 at p. 133. One case holds that the party losing on the motion for directed verdict waives the right to have specific grounds stated by failing to object to the generality of the motion. *See* Routte v. Guarino, 216 S.W.2d 607 (Tex. Civ. App.—Galveston 1948, writ ref'd n.r.e.), *cited in* McDONALD, Section 21:52 at p. 134.

contained in the deposition of Widget's president. What can you do? Remember Rule 270. You can move to reopen and offer the additional testimony. The decision will be within the trial court's discretion,[9] but policy favors a liberal application of the rule if it creates no delay or injustice.[10] However, the trial court may take into account any want of diligence on your part.[11] As a practical matter the earlier such a motion is made the better one's chances.[12] Even so, it is worth remembering *McRoy v. Riverlake Country Club, Inc.*,[13] which holds that, though the judge has already granted the motion for directed verdict, he may grant a Rule 270 motion and reopen the evidence to allow a party to cure the defect. What if you do not realize at the time of the motion that you have left gaps in your proof? How late can you act to correct your oversight? Obviously, if you have evidence as to which there will be a dispute, you must act before the jury returns its verdict. The jury cannot act on evidence it does not have. But, in your case, the missing proof is not disputed. Opposing counsel concedes that Widget Co. manufactured the product, but maintains that you are out of luck because you produced no proof to that effect. In such instances, the court may allow one to reopen and present uncontroverted evidence *even after the jury has returned a verdict and has been discharged.*[14]

5. *Motions for JNOV.* Rule 301 allows a trial court, on motion, to ignore jury findings that are not supported by the evidence and render judgment notwithstanding the verdict. Thus, the court can ignore a material jury answer because there is no evidence or conclusive evidence on the issue. Note, that a motion is required—the trial court cannot disregard material findings on its own motion.[15] However, it is easy enough for the judge to indicate that he or she would be inclined to grant a motion for judgment n.o.v. should one be filed.

While motions for judgment n.o.v. and for judgment on the verdict are customarily made before judgment, nothing prevents these motions from accompanying a motion to vacate or set aside an initial judgment which has already been signed. The trial court may act on such motions during the period of plenary jurisdiction following the signing of the original judgment—30 days unless extended by motions for new trial or motions to modify the judgment.[16]

---

[9] *See* 4 MCDONALD, Section 21:34 at p. 101, footnote 284 (citing numerous cases), *and, e.g.*, Turner v. Lone Star Industries, Inc., 733 S.W.2d 242 (Tex. App.—Houston [1st Dist.] 1987, writ ref'd n.r.e.).

[10] *See, e.g.,* Canyon Credit Union v. Coleman, 450 S.W.2d 368 (Tex. Civ. App.—Amarillo 1970, no writ).

[11] *See, e.g.,* McCarthy v. George, 623 S.W.2d 772 (Tex. App.—Fort Worth 1981, writ ref'd n.r.e.).

[12] *See* 4 MCDONALD, at Section 21:34.

[13] 426 S.W.2d 299 (Tex. Civ. App.—Dallas 1968, writ ref'd n.r.e.).

[14] *See* McAdams v. Dallas Railway & Terminal Co., 229 S.W.2d 1012 (Tex. 1950); *and see* also T.E.I.A. v. Elder, 282 S.W.2d 371 (Tex. 1955) (Rule 270 contemplates admission of only conclusive evidence, which leaves no decision for a jury; and even uncontroverted evidence is too late if offered after a judgment has been affirmed on appeal.).

[15] *See* Olin Corp. v. Cargo Carriers, Inc., 673 S.W.2d 211 (Tex. App.—Houston [14th Dist.] 1984, no writ). If a motion is required, does that mean that the court cannot grant judgment n.o.v. on grounds not included in the motion? This is the same problem we encountered in connection with motions for directed verdict, and the case law seems similarly divided. *Compare* McDade v. Texas Commerce Bank N.A., 822 S.W.2d 713 (Tex. App.—Houston [1st Dist.] 1991, writ denied)(can grant on grounds outside motion) *with* Most Worshipful Prince Hall Grand Lodge v. Jackson, 732 S.W.2d 407 (Tex. Civ. App.—Dallas 1987, writ ref'd n.r.e.)(cannot grant on grounds outside motion).

[16] These time periods are covered in Chapter 11. *See* Spiller v. Lyons, 737 S.W.2d 29 (Tex. App.—Houston [14th Dist.] 1987, no writ).

6. *JNOV and the appeal.* When the plaintiff rests and the defendant makes a plausible motion for directed verdict, the trial judge must balance two competing interests. If the plaintiff's case really is legally insufficient, the motion should be granted because it will save time and expense for the lawyers, jurors, witnesses and the court to grant the motion and not continue with the defendant's case in chief, jury deliberations, etc. But there is always the chance that an appellate court might disagree with the trial judge's assessment of the legal sufficiency; in that event, if the directed verdict is reversed the case will have to be tried again. If the court had just allowed the jury to decide the case it might have returned a defense verdict. A plaintiff's verdict could be set aside by judgment n.o.v. The appellate court could then reinstate the verdict and avoid a retrial. The following two opening paragraphs from Supreme Court opinions illustrate how an erroneous directed verdict requires a new trial while an erroneous JNOV allows reinstatement of the verdict and rendition of judgment.

***Jones v. Tarrant Utility Co.*, 638 S.W.2d 862 (Tex. 1982):**

> Earl and Lucille Jones brought this suit against Tarrant Utility Company (hereinafter T. U. C.) to recover damages allegedly caused by water overflowing from two T. U. C. water storage tanks. The trial court directed a verdict in favor of T. U. C. The court of appeals affirmed. We reverse the judgments of both courts and remand the cause to the trial court for new trial. The issue before us is whether the trial court correctly withdrew the case from the jury and rendered judgment as a matter of law for T. U. C.

***Dodd v. Texas Farm Products Co.*, 576 S.W.2d 812 (Tex. 1979):**

> The issue to be resolved in this case is whether or not the trial court erred in granting the defendant's motion for judgment notwithstanding the jury verdict. Suit was instituted by Bernard Dodd, plaintiff in the trial court, against Texas Farm Products Company ("Texas Farm"), defendant below, for personal injuries sustained while working on the premises of Texas Farm. The case was tried to a jury, which found in favor of Dodd, awarding him damages in the amount of $86,000. The trial court, however, granted Texas Farm's motion for judgment non obstante veredicto and rendered a take-nothing judgment against Dodd. The court of civil appeals affirmed the judgment of the trial court, holding that there was no evidence to support the jury finding of Texas Farm's negligence. 567 S.W.2d 919. Because we find that there was some evidence to support the jury findings, we reverse the judgments of the court of civil appeals and the trial court and render judgment on the jury verdict for Dodd.

---

7. *Factual Sufficiency Review*

POOL
v.
FORD MOTOR COMPANY
715 S.W.2d 629
(Tex. 1986)

* * *

And even as to factual insufficiency, it has been the supreme court that has delineated the role of the courts of appeals. *In re King's Estate* mandated those courts to consider and weigh all of the evidence in the case in determining whether the evidence is insufficient or if the verdict is so against the great weight and preponderance of the evidence as to be manifestly unjust. This court, in that opinion, recognized that in performing this task, it was not simple to describe the intellectual process to be followed by the court of appeals; how it was that there could be probative evidence to support the verdict and at the same time not be sufficient evidence. 150 Tex. at 666, 244 S.W.2d at 662.

CHIEF JUSTICE CALVERT opined that a court of appeals "should analyze the evidence on both sides of the issue, at least in a brief and general way, and point out why the finding is regarded as being contrary to the great weight and preponderance of the evidence." JUSTICE GARWOOD enumerated a few of the many instances when a verdict should be set aside and a new trial granted. He cited examples of "such as to shock the conscience," "so as to be clearly unjust," "to clearly indicate bias." He suggested that in arriving at an insufficiency holding, the court of appeals "must, up to a point, follow the same kind of mental process that a jury does." Recognizing the inexact standard set for the courts of appeals, JUSTICE GARWOOD allowed that "[m]aybe some day we will develop more rules to aid trial courts and courts of civil appeals in dealing with this troublesome question."

Our continuing review of courts of appeals decisions in which factual insufficiency points are discussed convinces us that the overwhelming majority of those opinions represent honest efforts by their scriveners to adhere to the guidelines of *In re King's Estate*. However, there occasionally appears an opinion in which it seems that the court of appeals has merely substituted its judgment for that of the jury. Those opinions couch their holdings with the necessary "factual insufficiency" or "against the great weight and preponderance" language without providing analyses of the evidence or stating bases for the conclusions drawn. One recent opinion is particularly noteworthy in this regard. In it the court of appeals reversed a judgment on factual insufficiency grounds, saying "[t]he jury evidently believed Appellee's argument; we do not." It may well be that the court of appeals in that case and other courts in similar cases considered and weighed all the evidence before arriving at a decision of insufficiency. But, without that mental process being reflected by the opinion, it is impossible for this court to be certain that the requirements of *In re King's Estate* have been followed.

In order that this court may in the future determine if a correct standard of review of factual insufficiency points has been utilized, courts of appeals, when reversing on insufficiency grounds, should, in their opinions, detail the evidence relevant to the issue in consideration and clearly state why the jury's finding is factually insufficient or is so against the great weight and preponderance as to be manifestly unjust; why it shocks the conscience; or clearly demonstrates bias. Further, those courts, in their opinions, should state in what regard the contrary evidence greatly outweighs the evidence in support of the verdict. It is only in this way that we will be able to determine if the requirements of *In re King's Estate* have been satisfied.

FORD MOTOR COMPANY
v.
POOL

718 S.W.2d 910 (Tex. App.—Texarkana 1986),
pet. dism'd by agr., 749 S.W.2d 489 (Tex. 1988)

ON REMAND

CORNELIUS, CHIEF JUSTICE.

The Supreme Court has remanded this cause for us to consider, on a common law negligence basis, Ford's insufficient evidence points attacking the jury's findings relating to Pool's alleged excessive speed and intoxication, and its points contending that the damage awards are excessive.

Ronnie Pool suffered brain injuries when his Ford pickup truck ran off the road and into a tree. Pool's theory of liability was that the fastening of the right rear U-bolt on the rear suspension came off, causing the truck to go out of control. The jury found that Pool was not contributorily negligent and assigned no percentage of comparative causation to him. The contributory negligence issue was submitted in a checklist form. Two of the alleged negligent acts were driving while intoxicated and speeding. Ford attacked the factual sufficiency of the jury's answer to this special issue in arguing that such findings are against the great weight and preponderance of the evidence.

We do not find the jury's answer on excessive speed to be against the great weight and preponderance of the evidence.

Officer Waldy said that in his opinion Pool was traveling more than seventy miles per hour when he lost control of his truck and that such a speed was not reasonable at any place, but Pool's accident reconstruction expert testified that he believed Pool was traveling at sixty miles per hour at the time he lost control, and that such a speed was not unreasonable on an "open highway" in Texas. Whether the highway at the point of the accident was an open highway according to the expert's definition is uncertain, but we conclude that the jury could reasonably believe from this evidence that Pool was traveling at only sixty miles per hour and that such a speed, although in excess of the posted limits, was not unreasonable or excessive in the circumstances then existing.

We conclude, however, that the jury's failure to find Pool negligent by reason of driving while intoxicated was so against the great weight and preponderance of the evidence as to be manifestly wrong and unjust.

The following evidence supported Ford's position on this issue: While at the American Legion Hall from about 10:30 p.m. to about 11:30 p.m., Pool was seen to drink two or three beers. He was alone in his truck when the accident occurred, and at the scene there was found with him an open container partially filled with cold beer, together with several other beer cans in and near the truck. Pool did not have a beer with him when he left the American Legion Hall, a fact which indicates that he drank after leaving there. At the accident site, Officer Waldy smelled alcohol on Pool's breath and concluded that alcohol contributed to the wreck. Pool's blood alcohol content at approximately 2:15 a.m. was .119, and the doctor testified that if Pool had been conscious at that time he would have been intoxicated.[2] The highway where the accident occurred was a narrow, unlighted blacktop road with soft shoulders and timber on both sides. A defense expert witness, Mr. McDonald, testified that a person of Pool's size and weight would be intoxicated and have impairment of his skills and reactions if he had .119 alcohol in his blood, and that in his opinion Pool was intoxicated. McDonald also testified that according to the standard rate of absorption a person whose blood alcohol content was .119 at 2:15 a.m. and who had not had anything to drink since 11:30 p.m. (Pool left the legion hall somewhere between 11:00 and 11:30, the accident happened at 12:15, and Pool was unconscious from the time of the accident until after the blood test) would have had a blood alcohol content of approximately .160 at 12:15, and that such a condition would constitute very gross intoxication. There was no objection to the evidence of the blood alcohol content or to the testimony of Mr. McDonald.

Pool's evidence on this issue was the following: The ambulance driver and wrecker driver did not smell alcohol on Pool's breath at the accident scene. It was undisputed, however, that Pool had in fact been drinking. An office receptionist testified she saw Pool at 4:30 p.m. in her office and he was not drinking then. His brother saw him just before dark and he was not drinking. Pool's wife said she spoke to him by telephone at 8:15 p.m. and she did not notice anything unusual about his speech and did not think that he had been drinking. Pool's brother and the manager of the legion hall testified they observed Pool intermittently from about 10:30 p.m. when he arrived until he left at about 11:30 p.m., and that he drank two or three beers but they saw nothing unusual about his actions and did not think he was intoxicated. There was testimony that Pool's signature when he signed in at the legion hall appeared to be normal, and that he left the legion hall, went down some steps, drove down a winding road to a traffic circle and through two red lights, some 2.5 miles to the accident site, apparently without incident.

There was no accounting for Pool's whereabouts and activities between 8:15 p.m. and 10:30 p.m. when he arrived at the legion hall, and from 11:30 p.m. when he left to 12:15 p.m. when the accident occurred.

Considering all the evidence, we conclude that a failure to find Pool negligent by reason of driving while intoxicated is so against the great weight and preponderance of the evidence as to be manifestly wrong and unjust. Not only does the evidence of intoxication overwhelmingly preponderate, but the other evidence even if accepted as true, does not contradict the evidence showing that Pool was intoxicated *at the time of the accident.*

* * *

For the reasons stated, the judgment of the trial court is reversed and the cause is remanded for a new trial.

GRANT, J., not participating.

---

[2] The doctor explained that Pool was unconscious when the test was taken, and that in technical medical terms a person had to be conscious in order to be classified as intoxicated.

In re A.B.
437 S.W.3d 498
(Tex. 2014)

Opinion

JUSTICE GUZMAN delivered the opinion of the Court.

In parental termination cases, our courts of appeals are required to engage in an exacting review of the entire record to determine if the evidence is factually sufficient to support the termination of parental rights. And to ensure the jury's findings receive due deference, if the court of appeals reverses the factfinder's decision, it must detail the relevant evidence in its opinion and clearly state why the evidence is insufficient to support the termination finding by clear and convincing evidence. Today, we are asked to extend this requirement well beyond its previous parameters—requiring courts to detail the evidence even when affirming the jury's decision. Because the current standard appellate courts must adhere to in conducting a factual sufficiency review in a termination case protects the fundamental interests at stake, we decline the invitation to unnecessarily expand it.

This protracted parental termination case dates back to 2008. There have been two trials resulting in termination of parental rights, two court of appeals opinions reversing and remanding for new trial on factual sufficiency grounds, and finally, an en banc court of appeals decision affirming termination. But despite the protracted history of this case, this appeal only requires us to decide whether the court of appeals, in affirming the termination, adhered to the proper standard for conducting a factual sufficiency review. Because the court of appeals' opinion and the record demonstrate the court of appeals considered the record in its entirety—as a proper factual sufficiency review requires—we affirm.

I. Background

Mother and Father married in 2005 in Missouri. Their son, A.B., was born later that year, and their daughter, H.B., was born in 2006. By the time Mother and Father separated in July 2007, the family had relocated to Texas. Following the parents' separation, the children remained primarily in Mother's care. There are varying accounts as to how often Father cared for the children following the parents' separation.

The Texas Department of Family and Protective Services ("DFPS") became involved when H.B. was admitted to the intensive care unit at Cook Children's Hospital in September 2007, after Mother reported H.B. had been having seizures. Her seizures were attributed to hyponatremia—inadequate sodium levels in the blood—which can be caused by inadequate nutrition. H.B. was fifteen months old, and weighed fifteen pounds upon admission to the hospital. Testimony at trial indicated H.B. had dropped from the fiftieth percentile in weight on February 2007, to the third percentile by April, and fell off the growth chart entirely by May. Her treating physicians also observed significant developmental delays, noting that H.B. could not crawl, walk, or sit up on her own. She was subsequently diagnosed with failure to thrive, which DFPS concluded was a result of physical neglect.

Rather than return the children to Mother and Father after H.B. was discharged from the hospital, DFPS placed both children with maternal relatives so Mother and Father could complete services with DFPS. Father completed his services, and the children were returned to his care in

June 2008. Roughly one month later, in July 2008, a caseworker visited the children at Father's home and discovered A.B. with injuries to his face and bruising on his left ear extending to his cheek. The children were removed from Father's care, placed with a foster family, and DFPS filed suit to terminate both parents' rights the following day.

After a bench trial in 2009, the trial court found, by clear and convincing evidence, grounds for termination under subsections (D) and (E) of 161.001(1) of the Texas Family Code. Specifically, the court held Father had knowingly placed or allowed the children to remain in conditions and surroundings that endangered their physical and emotional well-being, and that Father engaged in conduct and knowingly placed the children with persons who engaged in conduct that endangered the physical and emotional well-being of the children.[1] The court also concluded termination of Father's parental rights was in the children's best interest.

Father appealed the trial court's 2009 decision, challenging, among other things, the legal and factual sufficiency of the evidence to support the court's endangerment findings. The court of appeals held the evidence was legally sufficient but factually insufficient to support the finding of endangerment. The court reversed and remanded the case for a new trial.

In February 2011, the case was retried before a jury. The jury made the same findings as the trial court had in 2009, including the endangerment findings under section 161.001(1)(D) and (E) and that termination was in the children's best interest. The trial court entered a decree of termination pursuant to the jury's findings in June 2011.

Father appealed the termination order, once again arguing the State failed to present legally and factually sufficient evidence to support the jury verdict. The court of appeals, finding that DFPS did not present enough new evidence to change its holding from the prior case, once again held there was factually insufficient evidence of endangerment.

Both DFPS and Intervenors[2] filed motions for en banc reconsideration in the court of appeals. The court of appeals granted the motion and, in a per curiam opinion, found the evidence of endangerment was factually sufficient to support termination under section 161.001(1)(E) and affirmed the termination of Father's parental rights. Two justices dissented, arguing the court misapplied the standard in conducting its factual sufficiency review and that, under the correct standard in which the entire record is accounted for, the evidence remained factually insufficient to terminate Father's rights under subsection (E).

Here, Father echoes the concerns raised by the dissent, namely that the court failed to conduct a proper factual sufficiency review because, though its opinion analyzed the evidence favorable to DFPS, it failed to review evidence favorable to Father. As such, Father argues the court improperly disregarded relevant, probative evidence in performing its factual sufficiency review, and erred when it "failed to detail the conflicting evidence." We granted Father's petition for review.

II. Discussion

The authority to conduct a factual sufficiency review lies exclusively with the courts of appeals. TEX. CONST. art. V, § 6. Because proper application of the standard involves a legal question, this Court may review a court of appeals' factual sufficiency analysis to ensure the court of appeals adhered to the correct legal standard. Nevertheless, this Court must refrain from trans-

---

[1] Mother voluntarily relinquished her rights in June 2009 and is not a party to this appeal.

[2] In December 2010, A.B. and H.B.'s foster parents filed a motion to intervene in the second suit pursuant to sections 102.003(12) and 102.005(3) of the Family Code.

forming such authority into a guise for conducting its own independent review of the facts. *See* TEX. GOV'T CODE § 22.225(a) ("A judgment of a court of appeals is conclusive on the facts of the case in all civil cases.").

A factual sufficiency review pits two fundamental tenets of the Texas court system against one another: the right to trial by jury[3] and the court of appeals' exclusive jurisdiction over questions of fact.[4] And, in the context of parental termination cases, a third interest must also be accounted for—that is, parents' fundamental right to make decisions concerning "the care, the custody, and control of their children." Thus, in *In re C.H.,* we articulated a factual sufficiency standard to strike an appropriate balance between these competing principles. 89 S.W.3d 17, 25 (Tex. 2002).

Because the termination of parental rights implicates fundamental interests, a higher standard of proof—clear and convincing evidence—is required at trial. Given this higher burden at trial, in *C.H.* we concluded a heightened standard of appellate review in parental termination cases is similarly warranted. Specifically, a proper factual sufficiency review requires the court of appeals to determine whether "the evidence is such that a factfinder could reasonably form a firm belief or conviction about the truth of the State's allegations." "If, in light of the entire record, the disputed evidence that a reasonable factfinder could not have credited in favor of the finding is so significant that a factfinder could not reasonably have formed a firm belief or conviction, then the evidence is factually insufficient." And in making this determination, the reviewing court must undertake "an exacting review of the entire record with a healthy regard for the constitutional interests at stake."

But, as we also recognized in *C.H.,* while parental rights are of a constitutional magnitude, they are not absolute. Consequently, despite the heightened standard of review as articulated in *C.H.,* the court of appeals must nevertheless still provide due deference to the decisions of the factfinder, who, having full opportunity to observe witness testimony first-hand, is the sole arbiter when assessing the credibility and demeanor of witnesses. For this reason, we concluded that if a court of appeals is *reversing* the jury's finding based on insufficient evidence, the reviewing court must "detail the evidence relevant to the issue of parental termination and clearly state why the evidence is insufficient to support a termination finding by clear and convincing evidence." This requirement ensures the reviewing court appropriately respects the jury's fact-finding function.

Though we have repeatedly articulated the above standard—requiring courts of appeals to detail the evidence—in cases *reversing* a jury verdict based on insufficient evidence, we have never similarly required appellate courts to detail the evidence in this manner when the court *affirms* the judgment of termination. In fact, we have expressly held to the contrary for preponderance cases—that is, "a court of appeals must detail the evidence . . . and clearly state why the jury's finding is factually insufficient when *reversing* a jury verdict, *but need not do so when affirming a jury verdict.*" In *Ellis County State Bank v. Keever,* we recognized that the effort of detailing the evidence is required of the courts of appeals when reversing a jury verdict to discourage the reviewing court from "merely substituting its judgment for that of the jury." 888 S.W.2d 790,

---

[3] *See* TEX. CONST. art. I, § 15 ("The right of trial by jury shall remain inviolate."); TEX. CONST. art. V, § 10 ("In the trial of all causes in the District Courts, the plaintiff or defendant shall, upon application made in open court, have the right of trial by jury.").

[4] *See* TEX. CONST. art. V, § 6 ("[T]he decision of [courts of appeals] shall be conclusive on all questions of fact brought before them on appeal or error.").

794 (Tex. 1994). Indeed, our courts of appeals walk a very fine line in conducting an appropriate factual sufficiency review. But when the reviewing court *affirms* the jury verdict, the risk that the court has usurped the role of the jury disappears. . . .

Since our decision in *Keever*, we have established one exception to the general rule that appellate courts need not "detail the evidence" when affirming a jury finding: exemplary damages. In *Transportation Insurance Co. v. Moriel,* we reasoned:

> We have already held in *Pool [v. Ford Motor Co.,* 715 S.W.2d 629 (Tex.1986)*]* that courts of appeals, when reversing on insufficiency grounds, should detail the evidence in their opinions and explain why the jury's finding is factually insufficient or is so against the great weight and preponderance of the evidence as to be manifestly unjust. Due to the jury's broad discretion in imposing [exemplary] damages, we believe that a similar type of review is appropriate when a court of appeals is *afirming* such an award over a challenge that it is based on insufficient evidence or is against the great weight and preponderance of the evidence.

879 S.W.2d 10, 31 (Tex. 1994) (citation omitted). Thus, we concluded that "the court of appeals, when conducting a factual sufficiency review of [an exemplary] damages award, must hereafter detail the relevant evidence in its opinion, explaining why that evidence either supports or does not support the [exemplary] damages award in light of the *[Alamo National Bank v.] Kraus* [616 S.W.2d 908 (Tex.1981)] factors." The Legislature subsequently codified this requirement.[6]

In both exemplary damages and parental termination cases, the standard of proof at trial is heightened—the plaintiff (or in the case of parental termination, the State) must prove the claim by clear and convincing evidence. But the similarities essentially end there. The purpose of an award of exemplary damages is to punish and deter, "similar to that for criminal punishment." But exemplary damage awards have been plagued by concerns that, due to the broad discretion afforded juries in deciding these damages, such awards are unpredictable with little basis in fact, amounting to "unjust punishment." As the United States Supreme Court has explained, "[a] jury's assessment of the extent of a plaintiff's injury is essentially a factual determination, whereas its imposition of [exemplary] damages is an expression of its moral condemnation." *Cooper Indus., Inc. v. Leatherman Tool Grp., Inc.,* 532 U.S. 424, 432, 121 S.Ct. 1678, 149 L.Ed.2d 674 (2001). Such discretion has prompted both this Court and the Legislature to enact substantial procedural safeguards to ensure that jury awards for exemplary damages are properly calculated against defendants. And as one of these procedural safeguards, we concluded in *Moriel* that a court of appeals conducting a factual sufficiency review of an exemplary damages award must detail all relevant evidence in its opinion, whether it ultimately affirms or reverses the award.

The purpose of terminating parental rights, in contrast, is not to punish parents or deter their "bad" conduct, but rather to protect the interests of the child. Unlike exemplary damages awards, which leave much to the jury's discretion, the Family Code provides a detailed statutory framework to guide the jury in making its termination findings.

* * *

---

[6] *See* Act of Apr. 11, 1995, 74th Leg., R.S., ch. 19, § 1, sec. 41.013(a) (current version at TEX. CIV. PRAC. & REM. CODE § 41.013(a)) ("[A]n appellate court that reviews the evidence with respect to a finding by a trier of fact concerning liability for exemplary damages or with respect to the amount of exemplary damages awarded shall state, in a written opinion, the court's reasons for upholding or disturbing the finding or award.").

As such, the rationale which persuaded us to require courts of appeals to detail relevant evidence in affirming exemplary damage awards in *Moriel* does not likewise persuade us to require the same in termination proceedings. This is not to suggest that courts of appeals should not detail the evidence in their opinions affirming a jury's decision to terminate. To the contrary, we encourage courts to do so, and we reaffirm that they must in any event conduct an exacting review of the evidence regardless of how they dispose of the case before them. But in light of the difference in purposes and the limits that the statute already places on the jury's decision to terminate, we decline to mandate that courts of appeals detail the evidence when affirming a jury verdict.[7]

Here, the court of appeals cited the correct standard—that is, whether "*on the entire record,* a factfinder could reasonably form a firm conviction or belief that the parent violated subsection (D) or (E) of section 161.001(1)" and "[i]f, *in light of the entire record,* the disputed evidence that a reasonable factfinder could not have credited in favor of the finding is so significant that a factfinder could not reasonably have formed a firm belief or conviction in the truth of its finding."[8] The court of appeals subsequently devoted six pages of its opinion to articulating the evidence presented at trial.

As the en banc court concluded, there was some evidence tending to support the jury's termination finding under section 161.001(1)(E) that Father engaged in conduct or knowingly placed the children with persons who engaged in conduct that endangered the physical or emotional well-being of the child. For example, as to H.B.'s failure to thrive diagnosis, there was medical testimony that H.B. was "severely malnourished" and suffered from "significant developmental delays." There was also evidence that H.B.'s condition would take months to develop, and thus her growth problems began well before Father and Mother separated. Regarding A.B.'s injuries in 2008, there was medical testimony opining that such injuries "were not of a kind that a child would sustain accidentally," that the linear bruises on A.B.'s face were likely caused by a slap, and that the injury to A.B.'s ear was more consistent with a pinch or "blow."

The record also contains some evidence favorable to Father's position. . . . The court of appeals undoubtably considered this evidence, for it was thoroughly articulated in the court of appeals' earlier decisions in the case, which were included as appendices to the dissent. Thus, from the court of appeals' decision, as well as the record before us, it is evident that the en banc court of appeals, though it did not specifically detail all evidence favorable to Father in its majority opinion, did in fact comply with the standard articulated in *C.H.* when it considered the record in its entirety.

---

7 Father expresses concern that without requiring the court of appeals to detail the evidence it considered in making its decision to affirm termination, this Court surrenders its ability to determine whether the court of appeals did in fact adhere to the correct standard in conducting its factual sufficiency review. But as a practical matter, this Court has the record available when reviewing the court of appeals' opinion. If the record contains evidence that would tend to cast serious doubt on the outcome, and there is no indication in the court of appeals' opinion that this relevant evidence was considered, this Court may conclude the reviewing court did not adhere to the correct standard and remand accordingly. But when the unmentioned evidence does not rise to this level, or when the Court can readily discern from the opinion before it that the court of appeals did in fact review the record in its entirety, this Court has no reason to question whether the reviewing court adhered to the proper factual sufficiency standard.

8 Additionally, in considering the best interests of the children, the court of appeals concluded "viewing the entire record in a neutral light, we hold that the evidence is factually sufficient for the jury to form a firm conviction or belief that termination was in the children's best interest." 412 S.W.3d at 607.

III. Conclusion

For over a decade, we have required courts of appeals conducting factual sufficiency reviews in parental termination cases to engage in a thorough review of the entire record. This exacting review safeguards the constitutional rights of parents, while simultaneously ensuring the emotional and physical interests of the child are appropriately considered. But the court of appeals' authority to conduct a factual sufficiency analysis does not permit the court to stand in the role of a thirteenth juror. Thus, if the reviewing court is to reverse the factfinder, it must detail the evidence supporting its decision. Here, by considering the record in its entirety, the court of appeals executed an appropriate factual sufficiency review. Because the court ultimately affirmed the jury's termination findings, it was not required to detail the evidence. Accordingly, we affirm.

Notes & Questions

1. *Motion for New Trial.* The only method to made a factual sufficiency attack on the jury's verdict is to file a motion for new trial. We will discuss those motions in the chapter on Judgments and Post-Judgment Motions.

2. *Legal vs. Factual Sufficiency.* What is different about the factual sufficiency analysis in this case and the legal sufficiency analysis that we have been looking at in previous cases? For one thing, it is clear that the court is to look at "all of the evidence", not just that favoring the jury's verdict, and is not to look at the evidence and inferences in a light that favors the non-moving party.

3. *Remedy*. Recall that the remedy for a successful factual sufficiency challenge is remand for a new trial, not rendition of judgment.

4. *No Supreme Court jurisdiction.* Remember that only courts of appeals have jurisdiction to conduct factual sufficiency review. The Supreme Court has jurisdiction only over legal issues, not facts.

Chapter 16. Judgments and Post Judgment Motions

A. Civil Judgments Generally

Read Rules 300, 301, 304-306a.

1. *What is a judgment?* How is it different from a "decree" or an "order"? A "decree" is used to describe any court order. An "order" is defined as "a judge's written direction." A "judgment" is "the final decisive act of a court in defining the rights of the parties."[1] Thus, all judgments are orders, but an order is not necessarily a judgment. Often you will find the words "Ordered, adjudged, and decreed" in forms of judgments. "In many American jurisdictions, this wordy phrase routinely appears in court orders. The simple word *ordered* is generally much preferable—e.g. 'It is therefore *ordered, adjudged, and decreed* [read *ordered*] that the Plaintiff take nothing by her suit.' "[2]

2. *Rendition, signing and entry.* Typically, judgments go through three stages—rendition, signing and entry. "Judgment is rendered when the trial court officially announces it decision in open court or by written memorandum filed with the clerk."[3] Therefore, judgment may be orally rendered before there is a written document memorializing it. Nevertheless, under the Texas Rules of Civil Procedure, the deadlines for appeal and trial court jurisdiction do not begin to run until the written memorandum of judgment is signed. Often the judge will make a notation of the judgment on the docket sheet when orally rendering the judgment. The docket entry itself is not the judgment, although it can provide some evidence that the court's announcement was a rendition of judgment.

The date the judgment is "signed" is extremely important in every case as it is the time at which all deadlines begin to run concerning appeal and trial court jurisdiction over the case. Therefore, it is essential that all judgments contain a notation of the date it was signed.[4] Some forms of judgment have one blank for the date the judgment is "rendered, signed and entered." When presented with one of these forms, the clerk or the judge should strike out the words "rendered" and "entered" before it is signed.[5]

Judgment is "entered" in the clerk's minutes at the date it is "pronounced."[6] As a practical matter, this may occur some time after the judgment is signed. Technically, there is nothing from which to appeal until the judgment is "entered." Nevertheless, the failure to enter judgment within the prescribed time does not destroy the appellate court's jurisdiction or the effectiveness of the decision between the parties.[7]

---

[1] B. Garner, Dictionary of Modern Legal Usage, 2d Edition at 625 (1995).

[2] Garner, *supra* (emphasis in original).

[3] S & A Restaurant Corp. v. Leal, 892 S.W.2d 855 (Tex. 1995).

[4] *See* Rule 306a(2).

[5] *See* Walker v. Harrison, 597 S.W.2d 913, 916 (Tex. 1980); Burrell v. Cornelius, 570 S.W.2d 382, 384 (Tex. 1978).

[6] Rule 304.

[7] McDonald, Texas Civil Practice, §27.15 (1992).

3. *Types of judgments.*

a. *Nonsuit.* At any time before the plaintiff has introduced all its evidence other than rebuttal evidence, it may voluntarily dismiss its case, known as taking a "nonsuit."[8] A nonsuit taken as to the entire proceeding is a final judgment, but is ordinarily without prejudice to the right to refile the action. The right to take a nonsuit is an important right and is absolute.[9]

b. *Involuntary dismissal.* There is no rule specifically authorizing a "dismissal" in the Texas Rules of Civil Procedure. Nevertheless, Texas courts often dismiss cases after sustaining a plea in abatement, a plea to the jurisdiction of the court, motion for dismissal on grounds of forum non conveniens, or a special exception without subsequent amendment. Dismissal is also available in some situations as a sanction against a party.

c. *Dismissal for Want of Prosecution.* A party that institutes an action but fails to prosecute it with reasonable diligence may find that the case is dismissed for want of prosecution. Rule 165a contains specific provisions concerning dismissal for want of prosecution, and the circumstances for reinstatement of a case that has been dismissed.

d. *Agreed or consent judgments.* These judgments are rendered pursuant to a compromise or settlement agreement between the parties. The judge cannot render the consent judgment absent the present agreement of all parties. Therefore, a party can withdraw consent to the judgment at any time before rendition.[10] In these cases, the time at which the judgment is "rendered" as opposed to "signed" is often significant.

e. *Default judgments.* A no-answer default judgment is a judgment rendered after the defendant who has been properly served with citation fails to file an answer by appearance day.[11] A judgment "nihil dicit" is rendered when the defendant has appeared (for example, having filed a motion to transfer venue or other dilatory plea that is overruled) but has not filed an answer putting the merits of the case at issue. In both of these situations, since the defendant has not answered, the plaintiff is entitled to a default judgment on the pleadings, subject to presenting evidence on damages if the plaintiff's claim is unliquidated.[12] A post-answer default is rendered when the defendant has answered, putting the merits of the case at issue, but fails to appear at trial. Judgment cannot be entered on the pleadings, but the plaintiff must present evidence and prove its case as with any judgment after trial.

f. *Summary judgment.* A summary judgment is rendered before trial when one of the parties shows through written evidence that it is entitled to judgment as a matter of law because there is no controversy over the facts. When summary judgment is granted, there is no need for a trial. Summary judgment can be granted as to the entire case (a final summary judgment) or as to particular claims or parties (a partial summary judgment).

---

8 TRCP 162.

9 BHP Petroleum Co. v. Millard, 800 S.W.2d 838, 840 (Tex. 1990).

10 *S & A v. Leal, supra.*

11 Rule 239; *see also* Rule 107 (requiring officer's return of service to be on file for 10 days before the default judgment is rendered).

12 Rules 241, 243.

g. *Judgment after trial.* A judgment rendered after trial must conform to the pleadings, the evidence, and the jury's verdict.[13]

h. *Judgment notwithstanding the verdict* (or judgment n.o.v.). A judgment n.o.v. is rendered if the evidence presented at trial is so weak or so strong that a contrary jury's verdict is legally wrong and should be disregarded. Judgment is therefore rendered contrary to the jury's verdict.

4. *Costs of court.* Rule 131 requires the trial court to award all costs of court to the successful party. Thus, the successful party will have judgment against its adversary for the costs of court the successful party paid during the pendency of the law suit. Costs of court include filing fees, service fees, court reporter fees (including the cost of original deposition transcripts) and any other fees paid to court officers. Rule 141 allows the trial court to refuse to order that the winning party recover costs "for good cause, to be stated on the record." The Supreme Court has held that a party's inability to pay court costs, and an unsuccessful plaintiff's "fragile emotional state" that would result in her experiencing "emotional harm" if costs were assessed against her are not good cause as a matter of law.[14]

5. *Notice of Judgment.* TRCP 306a(3) requires the clerk to give notice of the judgment by first class mail to the parties or their attorneys immediately after the judgment is signed. Failure to provide the statutory notice of the judgment does not prevent the judgment from becoming final, although it may affect the time periods for finality and appeals. If a party does not learn of the judgment within 20 days after the judgment is signed, the time periods begin to run on the date that the party proves that it actually learned of the judgment, but in no event later than 90 days after the date the judgment was signed. TRCP 306a(4). The clerk is also required to provide additional notices in particular cases. In uncontested divorce actions resting on waiver of citation, the clerk must mail a certified copy of the final divorce decree or order of dismissal to the party that waived service. TRCP 119a. Moreover, the clerk must send notice of the taking of a default (whether final or interlocutory) to the defendant at the last known mailing address, as certified by the party taking the default. TRCP 239a.

6. *Plenary Power.* For a period of time, initially 30 days after the judgment is signed, the trial court has "plenary" or absolute power over the judgment. Pursuant to Rule 329b(d), the trial court "has plenary power to grant a new trial or to vacate modify, correct, or reform the judgment within thirty days after the judgment is signed." Rules 329b(e) and (g) extend the period of plenary power when a party has filed a timely motion for new trial or motion to modify, correct or reform the judgment to thirty days after the motions are overruled. Calculating the period of the trial court's plenary power, which is important and can get complicated, will be discussed in Section C.3. of this chapter.

---

[13] Rule 301.

[14] Furr's Supermarkets, Inc. v. Bethune, 53 S.W.3d 375 (Tex. 2001). Three justices dissented because they felt that the majority was micro-managing the trial court's exercise of discretion, which should be upheld when the record supports the decision.

B. Motions for Judgment and Judgment N.O.V.

Read Rules 301 and 305.

In most routine cases, once the verdict comes in, there will be no dispute about what judgment results.[1] Typically, the judge will order the victor to prepare a judgment. He or she is well advised to act promptly before the judge is distracted elsewhere. A few hours or days later, the victor submits the judgment form to the loser who will sign—as the victor has already done—in the appropriate signature blank under "approved as to form." The victor then takes the judgment to the judge who signs it, and the original signed judgment is photocopied, and the original is then filed in the court papers. To protect against a later controversy over the starting date for the appellate timetable, the victor should give formal notice to the loser of the date the judgment was signed (usually by supplying a signed copy showing the date). All this assumes that there is no dispute about who is entitled to judgment. If there *is* a dispute, then both parties are likely to file motions. Because there can be questions about who wins even if no jury finding is attacked, both might file motions for judgment on the verdict and either might file a motion for judgment n.o.v. There are waiver hazards in this process and, where the legal effect of findings is not clear, a party might want to file a motion for judgment on the verdict and, alternatively, for judgment n.o.v.[2] Suppose, for example, the jury has found, contrary to the evidence, that P failed to give a required notice under the UCC. P thinks that the notice was not legally required but also thinks that the jury's finding was contrary to the conclusive evidence. P might then move for judgment on the verdict, arguing that the no-notice finding should be disregarded as immaterial and, in the alternative, if the court should conclude that notice *was* required (and thus that the finding is material,) for judgment n.o.v. asking the court to disregard the no-notice finding as contrary to the conclusive evidence.[3]

---

[1] The judgment form should always incorporate the entire verdict for future reference on appeal and in connection with res judicata and collateral estoppel.

[2] *See* Burbridge v. Rich Properties, 365 S.W.2d 657 (Tex. Civ. App.—Houston [1st Dist.] 1963, no writ) (alternative motion does not result in waiver).

[3] This hypothetical is similar to the facts in Miner-Dederick Const. Corp. v. Mid-County Rental Service, Inc., 603 S.W.2d 193 (Tex. 1980). In that case, the Supreme Court held that Miner-Dederick could move for judgment on the verdict and then for judgment n.o.v. without waiver. The better course is to advance both positions in the alternative by way of a single motion.

HOLLAND
v.
WAL-MART STORES, INC.

1 S.W.3d 91
(Tex. 1999)

PER CURIAM.

* * *

The issue in this case is whether a claimant can recover attorney's fees in a worker's compensation discrimination case under former article 8307c of the Texas Revised Civil Statutes. (now TEX. LAB. CODE § 451.002). The court of appeals held that a plaintiff may recover attorney's fees under article 8307c and affirmed the award in this case. In the alternative, the court of appeals held that the defendant waived or invited any error in the award of attorney's fees to the plaintiff. *Id.* at 600. We conclude that both holdings are in error. Therefore, we reverse the judgment of the court of appeals in part, reforming the judgment to delete the award of attorney's fees.

Bettie Jo Holland worked as a stocker in the Palestine, Texas, warehouse of Wal-Mart Stores, Inc. She suffered a back injury after lifting an eighty-pound box of wrenches. She alleges that, after she reported the injury to her supervisor, he retaliated by assigning her to an even more demanding lifting job that he knew might further injure her. After performing that assignment, Holland claimed that she indeed suffered further injury to her back and took several months off to recuperate. During this time, she filed a worker's compensation claim with National Union Fire Insurance Co. of Pittsburgh, Pennsylvania, Wal-Mart's worker's compensation insurance carrier.

Before settling her worker's compensation case, Holland filed this lawsuit against National Union, Corporate Services, Inc. (an independent claims adjuster), and Wal-Mart. Asserting claims under the Insurance Code and the Texas Deceptive Trade Practices Act (DTPA), she alleged that the defendants acted in bad faith and conspired to wrongfully deny or delay her compensation benefits. Holland also asserted a worker's compensation discrimination claim against Wal-Mart under former article 8307c of the Revised Civil Statutes, alleging that Wal-Mart retaliated against her for reporting a work-related injury.

In connection with her discrimination suit against Wal-Mart, Holland sought actual damages, exemplary damages, and attorney's fees. At the charge conference, Wal-Mart objected to submitting a jury question about attorney's fees on the ground that there was no evidence to support its submission in connection with the discrimination claim. Wal-Mart did not object to the question on the ground that such fees are not recoverable under article 8307c as a matter of law. Instead, Wal-Mart specifically requested that the attorney's fee question be submitted with an instruction limiting recovery of attorney's fees to only those fees incurred in connection with the discrimination claim. Noting that the attorney's fee issue was already conditionally submitted on an affirmative finding of liability on the discrimination claim, the trial judge overruled both of Wal-Mart's objections.

The jury found no liability on the DTPA, Insurance Code, and bad faith claims. However, it did find Wal-Mart liable for discrimination and awarded Holland $250,000 for physical impairment in the future, $1,500,000 as exemplary damages, $5,000 for mental anguish, and attorney's fees of one-third of Holland's total recovery. Wal-Mart moved for judgment notwithstanding the verdict. In its motion, Wal-Mart argued for the first time that attorney's fees are not recoverable under Article 8307c as a matter of law. Alternatively, it also renewed its objection that there was no evidence to support such an award, and further in the alternative urged that any such evidence was factually insufficient to support the amount awarded. After hearing argument on the motion, the trial court rendered judgment for Holland, awarding her all damages assessed by the jury.

Wal-Mart appealed. The court of appeals held in pertinent part that a plaintiff may recover attorney's fees under article 8307c, stating that "the causation standard under 8307c allows for the recovery of attorney's fees . . . [because it] permits the victim of retaliation to recover all reasonable damages suffered *as a result of the retaliatory discrimination*." In the alternative, the court of appeals held that Wal-Mart either "waived error in the submission of the attorney's fees question to the jury by failing to object to its submission at the charge conference" or invited error by arguing that the question on attorney's fees should be specifically tied to a finding of liability in the discrimination action.

To preserve a complaint for appellate review, a party must present to the trial court a timely request, motion, or objection, state the specific grounds therefore, and obtain a ruling. *See* TEX. R. APP. P. 52(a), *superseded* September 1, 1997 (current version at TEX. R. APP. P. 33.1(a)). The court of appeals held that Wal-Mart failed to preserve error on its claim that attorney's fees are not available for statutory retaliatory discrimination. We disagree.

The availability of attorney's fees under a particular statute is a question of law for the court. Consequently, the jury's finding about the amount of reasonable attorney's fees is immaterial to the ultimate legal issue of whether such fees are recoverable under former article 8307c as a matter of law. By asserting nonrecoverability in its motion for j.n.o.v., Wal-Mart gave the trial court ample opportunity to rule on the availability of attorney's fees before an erroneous judgment was rendered.

This is not a case in which the trial court had to resolve a legal issue before the jury could properly perform its fact-finding role. In such instances, a party must lodge an objection in time for the trial court to make an appropriate ruling without having to order a new trial. *See, e.g., St. Paul Surplus Lines Ins. Co. v. Dal-Worth Tank Co.*, 974 S.W.2d 51, 53 (Tex. 1998) (to preserve error resulting from a Mary Carter agreement, the defendant must object at trial to give the trial court an opportunity to cure any error resulting from the effect of the agreement); *Carnation Co. v. Borner*, 610 S.W.2d 450, 454-55 & nn. 6-7 (Tex. 1980) (defendant waived argument that exemplary damages were not recoverable under former Article 8307c because defendant failed to object to a definition of exemplary damages that included damages for the plaintiff's inconvenience and mental anguish, which clearly were recoverable). A jury can determine the amount of attorney's fees whether or not they can be recovered under the theory of law submitted to the jury.

Likewise, Wal-Mart did not invite error merely because it requested that the attorney's fee question be submitted with an instruction limiting recovery of attorney's fees to those fees incurred in connection with the discrimination case. The Texas Rules of Civil Procedure state that "[a] claim that the evidence was legally or factually insufficient to warrant the submission of any question may be made for the first time after verdict, *regardless of whether the submission of such question was requested by the complainant.*" TEX. R. CIV. P. 279 (emphasis added). Because the availability of attorney's fees is purely a legal question, this situation is analogous to a legal sufficiency challenge. There is no logical reason to treat a post-verdict legal availability challenge differently than a post-verdict legal sufficiency challenge.

. . . Wal-Mart did raise a timely and specific objection in the trial court that attorney's fees are not recoverable under article 8307c as a matter of law. Moreover, Wal-Mart argues only that attorney's fees are not available under the legal theory submitted to the jury. . . . Because the availability of attorney's fees is solely a question of law for the court, error did not occur until the trial court rendered judgment awarding such fees to Holland. Wal-Mart specifically challenged the availability of attorney's fees under article 8307c before the error resulted. The court of appeals, therefore, erred in concluding that Wal-Mart waived its right to challenge the propriety of an award of attorney's fees under article 8307c.

* * *

Accordingly, without hearing oral argument,[1] we reverse that part of the court of appeals' judgment awarding Holland attorney's fees and render judgment that Holland take nothing on her claim for attorney's fees.

Notes & Questions

1. *What motion to file?* After verdict, parties may file a motion for judgment on the verdict, a motion for judgment notwithstanding the verdict (j.n.o.v.), or a motion to disregard certain of the jury's answers to the charge and motion for judgment pursuant thereto. What is the difference between all of these motions?

2. *Accept the jury's verdict.* When a party accepts the jury's verdict, and seeks judgment thereon, the party will file a motion for judgment on the verdict.

3. *No evidence challenge.* A no evidence challenge to a jury's answer may be made by motion for j.n.o.v. or a motion to disregard on no-evidence grounds. Both methods preserve the no-evidence point for appeal and allow the movant to tell the judge that one or more particular findings (or failures to find) are supported by no evidence (Zone 1) or are established conclusively (Zone 5). The only difference is in the form of the motion. The motion for judgment notwithstanding the verdict asks for a judgment. The motion to disregard must be accompanied by a motion for judgment.

4. *Defective jury charge and sufficiency of the evidence.* Suppose the jury charge defectively submits the legal theory. There are no objections to the charge. No evidence and insufficient evidence challenges made by JNOV and motion for new trial are overruled. On appeal, is the sufficiency of the evidence reviewed against the correct law or the law as submitted in the charge without objection? In *Osterberg v. Peca*, the Supreme Court held that sufficiency of the evidence is reviewed against the charge as submitted without objection.[1]

5. *Immaterial jury answer*. Often the jury is asked a question that one party believes is immaterial to the judgment. In other words, the answer has no legal significance and should be ignored, with judgment rendered accordingly. This was the situation in *Holland*. In *Holland*, the Supreme Court found that Wal-Mart properly raised the immaterial issue in its motion for judgment notwithstanding the verdict. In *Wal-Mart Stores, Inc. v. McKenzie*,[2] the Supreme Court found that the issue was properly raised in the defendant's response to the plaintiff's motion for judgment. In *McKenzie*, Wal-Mart asked the judge to ignore the verdict on certain elements of damages (in-

---

1 *See* TEX. R. APP. P. 59.1.

1 12 S.W.3d 31, 55 (Tex. 2000).

2 997 S.W.2d 278 (Tex. 1999).

cluding mental anguish and exemplary damages) because they were not recoverable under the applicable statute. Other opinions have held that a party may ask the court to ignore an immaterial answer in a motion for judgment on the verdict.[3] Thus, it appears that an immaterial jury answer may be raised in a number of ways, so long as the method "was timely and sufficiently specific to give the trial court an opportunity to resolve the legal issue before rendering judgment."[4]

6. *Motion to disregard.* Remember that a true motion for judgment notwithstanding the verdict seeks to ignore a material finding because there is no evidence or conclusive evidence. How is a motion to disregard different? One court of appeals has said:[5] "There are three necessary elements which must be included in a motion to disregard findings. The motion must (1) designate the finding and/or findings which the court is called upon to disregard; (2) specify the reason why the finding or findings should be disregarded; (3) contain a request that judgment be entered on the remaining findings after the specified findings have been set aside or disregarded."

In *Southeastern Pipe Line Co. v. Tichacek*,[6] the Texas Supreme Court noted that a jury's answers to questions in the charge "may only be disregarded if they have no support in the evidence or if they are immaterial. A question is immaterial when it should not have been submitted, it calls for a finding beyond the province of the jury (such as a question of law), or when it was properly submitted but has been rendered immaterial by other findings."[7] In the first instance—when a legal sufficiency determination trumps the jury's material finding—a motion is required under Rule 301 because the resulting judgment will be n.o.v. In the second instance—when the jury finding is immaterial—the judge can render judgment on his or her own motion because the judge is, in fact, rendering judgment *on* the verdict. The court can, on its own motion, disregard immaterial jury findings and grant judgment on other answers in the verdict.

7. *Distinguish defective charge.* Remember the distinction between a defective question and an immaterial one when determining whether to render judgment or remand on appeal. A question is defective "if it plainly attempts to request a finding on a recognized cause of action, but does so improperly."[8] A defective question may not be disregarded if it is material. Instead, if the error is properly preserved, a new trial will be ordered.[9] Obviously, the motion for judgment, motion for judgment n.o.v. and motion to disregard are not the appropriate vehicles for preserving errors in the charge. *Holland* presents a legal issue concerning the materiality of questions submitted to the jury that need not be raised until after the verdict, not a classic charge error question that must

---

[3] *See* Clear Lake City Water Authority v. Winograd, 695 S.W.2d 632, 639 (Tex. App.—Houston [1st Dist.] 1985, writ ref'd n.r.e.); Guerrero v. Standard Alloys Mfg. Co., 598 S.W.2d 656 (Tex. Civ. App.—Beaumont 1980, writ ref'd n.r.e.).

[4] Wal-Mart Stores, Inc. v. McKenzie, 997 S.W.2d at 280.

[5] Dupree v. Piggly Wiggly Shop Rite Foods, Inc., 542 S.W.2d 882 (Tex. Civ. App.—Corpus Christi 1976, writ ref'd n.r.e.).

[6] 997 S.W.2d 166 (Tex. 1999).

[7] *Id.* (citations omitted.)

[8] Southeastern Pipe Co. v, Tichacek, 997 S.W.2d 166, 172 (Tex. 1999)..

[9] *Id.*

be raised at the charge conference. Consider once again *Burbage v. Burbage*,[10] from the chapter on the jury charge. And consider this excerpt from the Tyler Court of Appeals:[11]

> In its cross-issue three, Big M complains that the trial court erred when it entered judgment awarding Tallyho the difference in market value of the injection molding machine before and after the accident without predicating the damage issue upon Big M's breach. Tallyho submitted the case to the jury and requested issues on multiple theories of liability, including DTPA, negligence and contract. If the jury found liability under any of those theories, it was directed to answer Question Number 9, which reads as follows:
>
> > What is the difference in the market value in Cherokee County, Texas of the injection molding machine immediately before and immediately after the truck wreck occurred on April 6, 1995?
> >
> > 'Market Value' means the amount that would be paid in cash by a willing buyer who desires to buy, but is not required to buy, to a willing seller, who desires to sell, but is under no necessity of selling.
> >
> > Answer in dollars and cents for damages, if any.
> >
> > ANSWER: $97,000.00
>
> We note that this measure of damages is recoverable . . . .
>
> We agree that the above-quoted damage question is defective in that the jury is not required to find that the breach caused the damages inquired about in Question Number 9. However, it is axiomatic that to complain on appeal, an appellant must have brought the charge error to the court's attention. On a review of the record, we note that Big M did not object during the charge conference that the submission on damages was incorrect.
>
> Big M argues that it did not waive error because it complained of the charge error in post-verdict motions. In support of its position, it cites *Wal-Mart Stores, Inc. v. McKenzie*, 997 S.W.2d 278 (Tex. 1999), in which the Supreme Court held that the appellant did not waive his complaint by not objecting to the submission of jury issues on compensatory and punitive damages in a wrongful discharge case. That case is distinguishable, however, because whether a particular remedy is available under a statute is a question of law for the court. Therefore, the jury's findings were immaterial to the ultimate issue of whether compensatory and punitive damages were available under the statute as a matter of law. In the instant case, the jury's finding on damages is not immaterial. It is essential to a judgment on the case that the amount of damages be determined by the jury. It is not a matter for the court; therefore, it was incumbent upon Big M to bring the error to the trial court's attention before it charged the jury. We hold that Big M waived error and overrule its cross-issue three.

8. *Conflicting findings*. Where there are conflicting findings, if either finding is material, they both are. That is, the court may not resolve conflicting findings on a material issue by disregarding one

---

[10] 447 S.W.3d 249 (Tex. 2014).

[11] Tallyho Plastics, Inc. v. Big M Construction Co. 8 S.W.3d 789 (Tex. App.—Tyler 1999, no pet.). *See also* Equistar Chemicals, L.P. v. Dresser-Rand Co., 2007 WL 1299161 (Tex. 2007)(holding that no evidence points in trial court did not preserve error to erroneous measure of damages in jury charge).

of the findings and entering judgment on the verdict.[12] However, if only one of the findings has no support in the evidence, then the court may resolve the conflict by disregarding it under the procedure prescribed by Rule 301.[13]

9. *Mandamus*. A reluctant judge may be compelled by *mandamus* to proceed to judgment.[14] The *mandamus* order will not ordinarily compel a specific judgment but will "direct the trial court to render judgment for the party in whose favor the verdict points unless on appropriate proceedings it is found that judgment n.o.v. should be rendered."[15]

10. *Alternate theories of recovery for single injury*. What if the verdict entitles your client to judgment under your DTPA theory for $300K or a judgment under your negligence theory for $100K? Must you formally elect a remedy in the trial court and waive your right to recover under the other? No. In *Birchfield v. Texarkana Memorial Hospital*,[16] the Supreme Court held that no such election is required, noting that Rule 301 requires a judgment to be "so framed as to give the party all the relief to which he may be entitled." "We hold that where the prevailing party fails to elect between alternative measures of damages, the court should utilize the findings affording the greater recovery and render judgment accordingly."

Suppose that the trial court grants judgment on the plaintiff's DTPA claim and then the court of appeals reverses that judgment because there is no evidence of causation. Has the plaintiff lost the chance to have a judgment based on the jury's negligence findings? No. In *Boyce Iron Works, Inc. v. Southwestern Bell Telephone Co.*,[17] the Supreme Court held that the plaintiff is entitled to seek recovery under the alternate theory if the judgment is reversed on appeal. Because the plaintiff obtained judgment, the plaintiff had no reason to complain in the trial court, and therefore, need not do anything to preserve this right for appeal. Note that nothing in *Birchfield* or *Boyce* allows a plaintiff to recover on both of the alternative theories even though the jury findings support both—generally, a party is entitled to only one recovery for a single injury.[18] *Birchfield* and *Boyce* deal with when and how an election is made (or forced) and do not authorize a double recovery.

11. *Role of motion for directed verdict*. Note that Rule 301 permits a judgment n.o.v. if a directed verdict would have been proper. However, as we noted in connection with motions for directed verdict, no motion for directed verdict is required in Texas in order to preserve the right to a motion for judgment n.o.v.[19] Furthermore, since a factual insufficiency complaint (based on Zone 2 or Zone

---

[12] Recall, however, that some apparently conflicting findings may be reconcilable, as in *Lewis v. Yaggi*, 584 S.W.2d 487 (Tex. Civ. App.—Tyler 1979, writ ref'd n.r.e.).

[13] *See* 4 MCDONALD, TEXAS CIVIL PRACTICE, p. 150 and Faulkner v. Kleinman, 158 S.W. 891 (Tex. Civ. App.—Austin 1942, writ ref'd w.o.m.). As indicated in the chapter on jury deliberations and the verdict, some cases hold that a specific finding will control over a more general one, though they are in conflict.

[14] *See* 4 MCDONALD, TEXAS CIVIL PRACTICE, at 142; Government Code §§ 22.221 and 22.002; *and e.g.*, Goffney v. Lowry, 554 S.W.2d 157 (Tex. 1977).

[15] *See* MCDONALD at p. 146, n. 669, *citing* American Nat. Ins. Co. v. Sutton, 130 S.W.2d 441 (Tex. Civ. App.—El Paso 1939, no writ). The idea, apparently, is that *any* judgment puts the case in a posture for a routine appeal which can attack the propriety of the judgment.

[16] 747 S.W.2d 361 (Tex. 1987).

[17] 747 S.W.2d 785 (Tex. 1988).

[18] Chisholm v. Chisholm, 209 S.W.3d 96 (Tex. 2006).

[19] Most Worshipful Prince Hall v. Jackson, 732 S.W.2d 407 (Tex. App.—Dallas 1987, writ ref'd n.r.e.).

4 evidence) cannot support a directed verdict, it cannot support a judgment n.o.v. Only legal sufficiency points (based on Zone 1 and Zone 5 evidence) qualify because the judge must be able to act solely on controlling questions of law.[20] If, therefore, the terms "insufficient evidence" or "contrary to the great weight and preponderance of the evidence" appear in a motion for judgment n.o.v., it might—as to that part—be recharacterized under Rule 71 as a motion for new trial.

12. *Timing.* While motions for judgment n.o.v. and for judgment on the verdict are customarily made before judgment, nothing prevents these motions from accompanying a motion to vacate or set aside an initial judgment which has already been signed. The trial court may act on such motions during the period of plenary jurisdiction following the signing of the original judgment—30 days unless extended by motions for new trial or motions to modify the judgment.[21]

13. *Motion for judgment on the verdict as a waiver of judgment n.o.v.* It is often said that a motion for judgment on the verdict is an affirmation that the material jury findings are supported by competent evidence. Thus, as a general rule, one may not move for judgment on the verdict and then later claim that a finding essential to that judgment was unsupported. The rule is based on the idea that the movant may not take inconsistent positions. However, the Supreme Court has allowed parties to take consistent but alternative positions under certain circumstances where the motion clearly states the alternative position.[22] These opinions involve complex fact situations and are, unfortunately, not models of clarity. Here, the courts' policy rationale may serve the advocate best. Courts will not ordinarily permit the litigant to have it both ways—to urge the trial court to render judgment based on a fact-finding and, if the court declines to render the movant's judgment, to attack the same finding as unsupported in the evidence. But, if the movant acts consistently, each action supporting the same theory, the approach may succeed. For the uncertain movant, the best solution may be to move for judgment on the verdict and, *in the alternative*, for judgment n.o.v., an approach which has been held not to waive either.[23] Do not confuse the waiver occasioned by a motion for judgment on the verdict with the earlier "inconsistent" action of requesting a jury question on a given issue. It is clear that one may request a jury question on an issue and later claim that there was no evidence to support the answer (or that conclusive evidence governs the answer).[24]

14. *Problem.* Suppose you represent P in a case where D contends that a UCC provision required you to give written notice before filing what D characterizes as a UCC breach of warranty action. You think the notice is not required but introduce evidence (solely your client's testimony) that, in any event, your client gave notice. The jury finds for your client P on all jury questions, including damages, *but*, in answer to Jury Question No. 1, "Did P give timely notice?" the jury answers "no." (You had the burden of proof on this question.) It is your position that (a) no notice was required; (b) even if it was required the jury's answer to the notice question is contrary to the conclusive (Zone 5) evidence or, in the alternative, contrary to the great weight and preponderance of the evi-

---

[20] Alm v. Aluminum Co. of America, 717 S.W.2d 588 (Tex. 1986).

[21] The time periods for a trial court's plenary power are covered later in this chapter. *See* Spiller v. Lyons, 737 S.W.2d 29 (Tex. App.—Houston [14th Dist.] 1987, no writ).

[22] See Miner-Dederick Const. Corp. v. Mid-County Dental Service, Inc., 603 S.W.2d 193 (Tex. 1980) *and* Litton Indus. Products v. Gammage, 668 S.W.2d 319 (Tex. 1984).

[23] *See* Rodgers v. Cook, 115 S.W.2d 1148 (Tex. Civ. App.—Eastland 1938, writ dism'd w.o.j.) *and* Burbridge v. Rich Properties, 365 S.W.2d 657 (Tex. Civ. App.—Houston [1st Dist.] 1963, no writ). *See also* Employers Casualty Co. v. Glens Falls Ins. Co., 484 S.W.2d 570 (Tex. 1972).

[24] *See* Rule 279 (last sentence).

dence. Your opponent asks if you will sign off, approving D's judgment. What do you do? Your agreement would be a bad idea. You would want to move for judgment on the verdict (because you say that the notice finding is immaterial) and, alternatively (in case the court thinks the notice finding *is* material), for judgment n.o.v., the court being asked to disregard the no notice finding because the evidence is conclusive that notice was given (your client's testimony being "clear, direct, positive . . . etc."). If that fails, you would want to move for new trial based on the Zone 4 support for a "yes" answer to the notice question, as Rule 324(b) prescribes. We discuss Rule 324 and the motion for new trial in a later section of this chapter.

C. Remittitur

Read Rule 315.

POPE
v.
MOORE
711 S.W.2d 622
(Tex. 1986)

PER CURIAM.

The question is whether the court of appeals applied the proper remittitur standard. The court of appeals remitted $50,000 in damages in a personal injury suit, although the court found the evidence for these damages legally and factually sufficient. Because we believe the court of appeals applied an improper remittitur standard, we modify its judgment.

On February 28, 1982, Ronnie Moore rode in a motorcycle race at the Flying-P Ranch and Cycle Park in Parker County, Texas. While riding, he fell off his motorcycle, collided head first with a railroad tie, and broke his neck. Moore and his wife, Sandra, filed suit against Pope, individually and d/b/a Flying-P Ranch and Cycle Park; Dallas Emergency Corps. d/b/a Lifecare Ambulance Service; and Cross-Country of Texas, Inc. The Moores alleged that the defendants were negligent in failing to properly design the racetrack, in failing to advise of known dangers at the racetrack (the railroad tie), and in failing to properly ensure that the racetrack was safe for its intended purposes. Pope was served but did not answer.

The trial court rendered a no-answer default judgment against Pope, and after hearing evidence on damages, awarded the Moores $289,000. The trial court then severed the Moores' claims against the other defendants. In an unpublished opinion, the court of appeals affirmed the judgment, but remitted $17,000 in past medical expenses and $50,000 in future damages, including future medical expenses, lost wages, pain and suffering, and loss of consortium.

The Moores contest the court of appeals' standard in remitting $50,000 in future damages, including medical expenses, lost wages, pain and suffering, and loss of consortium. In remitting these damages, the court of appeals reviewed all the evidence on damages and then stated:

> [W]e hold the evidence was legally and factually sufficient to support awards for [future medical expenses], future lost wages, and future pain and suffering suffered by Ronnie and for the $10,000 awarded to Sandra for future loss of consortium. Nevertheless, in light of the entire record, we find and hold that the awards for future damages, which would include

medical expenses, lost wages, pain and suffering and loss of consortium were excessive in the amount of $50,000.

The Moores contend that the proper remittitur standard is factual sufficiency, and therefore, the court of appeals could not order a remittitur after finding the evidence for their damages factually sufficient. We agree.

TEX. R. CIV. P. 440 [currently TRAP 46] states:

> In civil cases appealed to a Court of Appeals, if such court is of the opinion *that the verdict and judgment of the trial court is excessive and that said cause should be reversed for that reason only*, then said appellate court shall indicate to such party, or his attorney, within what time he may file a remittitur of such excess. If such remittitur is so filed, then the court shall reform and affirm such judgment in accordance therewith; if not filed as indicated then the judgment shall be reversed. (emphasis added)

We have jurisdiction because determining the proper remittitur standard is a question of law. The often cited remittitur standard is set forth in *Wilson v. Freeman*:

> All the Court of Civil Appeals can do, and all that is required of it to do, by said statute, is to exercise its sound judicial judgment and discretion in ascertaining what amount would be reasonable compensation for the injury sustained, and treat the balance as excess. The court must first determine what amount would be reasonable, before it can determine what amount would be unreasonable . . . . [I]t should authorize a remittitur of the excess above the amount which would be reasonable compensation for the injury, in accordance with its sound judgment.

185 S.W. 993, 994 (Tex. 1916). The court of appeals interpreted *Wilson* to mean that a court must decide, on its own and outside the record, upon a reasonable amount of damages, then remit the excess regardless of the factual or legal sufficiency of the evidence. Courts of appeals do not use this approach in determining any other fact question.

Wilson indicates that the proper remittitur standard is factual sufficiency: "[t]he question of the excessiveness of a verdict in this character of a suit is *purely a question of fact*, upon which the judgment of the Court of Civil Appeals is final." Moreover, in *Wilson* we construed the court of appeals' opinion as finding the evidence factually insufficient to support the jury's award, holding therefore, that it was mandatory for the court of appeals to determine the amount of excess.

Factual sufficiency is the sole remittitur standard for actual damages. We disapprove of other remittitur standards, such as applied here by the court of appeals. In determining whether damages are excessive, trial courts and courts of appeals should employ the same test as for any factual insufficiency question.

Lower courts should examine all the evidence in the record to determine whether sufficient evidence supports the damage award, remitting only if some portion is so factually insufficient or so against the great weight and preponderance of the evidence as to be manifestly unjust. Courts of appeals also should detail the relevant evidence, and if remitting, state clearly why the jury's finding is so factually insufficient or so against the great weight and preponderance of the evidence as to be manifestly unjust. *Pool v. Ford Motor Co.*, 715 S.W.2d 629 (Tex. 1986). Lower courts need not find passion, prejudice, or other improper motive on the jury's part to order a remittitur.

Since the proper remittitur standard is factual sufficiency, it was improper for the court of appeals to order a remittitur after finding factual sufficiency. The court of appeals' holding is contrary to *Wilson v. Freeman*; therefore, pursuant to TEX. R. CIV. P. 483, we grant Moore's application for writ of error and without hearing oral argument, reform the court of appeals' judgment and reinstate $50,000 plus prejudgment interest. Because the court of appeals has already found factual sufficiency, we render judgment rather than remand the cause.

RANCHO LA VALENCIA, INC.
v.
AQUAPLEX, INC.
383 S.W.3d 150
(Tex. 2012)

Opinion

PER CURIAM.

This case is before us a second time. It concerns a business dispute between Rancho La Valencia, Inc. and Aquaplex, Inc. In the earlier appeal, we held that the evidence of fraudulent intent by Rancho in connection with the execution of a memorandum of settlement agreement (MSA) was legally sufficient. 297 S.W.3d 768, 775 (*Rancho I*). We next analyzed the court of appeals' treatment of damages for fraudulent inducement of the MSA, and held that "some evidence supported an award of damages for fraud under the MSA, just not at the level awarded by the trial court." *Id.* at 777. We remanded the case to the court of appeals to "determine whether to remand for a new trial on damages, or whether to suggest a remittitur," *id.* (citations omitted), and to consider other issues.

On remand, the court of appeals addressed certain previously unaddressed issues, and remanded the case to the trial court for a new trial on the issue of damages including punitive damages. The court declined to suggest a remittitur in light of the state of the record. 357 S.W.3d 137, 144.

Rancho now complains to us that the court of appeals should have remanded the case to the trial court for a new trial on both liability and damages, as Rancho requested in a motion for rehearing to the court of appeals. We agree. Texas Rule of Appellate Procedure 44.1 addresses reversible error in civil cases. Rule 44.1(b) provides in part: "The court [of appeals] may not order a separate trial solely on unliquidated damages if liability is contested." In this case, Rancho contested liability and the alleged damages are unliquidated. We stated in *Rancho I* that the court of appeals, on remand, must decide whether "to remand for a new trial on damages" or instead suggest a remittitur. We did not expressly state that, if the court of appeals concluded a remand to the trial court for a new trial was warranted, it must remand for a new trial on both liability and damages, but Rule 44.1(b) requires this result. Failure to comply with this rule is reversible error. *Estrada v. Dillon,* 44 S.W.3d 558, 562 (Tex. 2001); *Redman Homes, Inc. v. Ivy,* 920 S.W.2d 664, 669 (Tex. 1996) (interpreting prior rule). Further, the Supreme Court, like the courts of appeals, "may not order a separate trial solely on unliquidated damages if liability is contested." TEX. R. APP. P. 61.2. Texas Rule of Appellate Procedure 2 provides that for good cause a rule of appellate procedure in a particular case may be suspended. But we did not indicate in *Rancho I* an intent to suspend the operation of Rule 44.1(b) or Rule 61.2, and we do not see any good cause in this particular case for suspending the Rules.

The court of appeals has already decided not to suggest a remittitur in light of the state of the record; instead it simply remanded the case for a new trial. Accordingly, without hearing oral argument, *see* TEX. R. APP. P. 59.1, we grant the petition for review, reverse the court of appeals' judgment insofar as it ordered a new trial on damages only, and remand the case to the trial court for a new trial on damages and liability on the claim for fraud under the MSA.

Notes & Questions

1. *Trial courts*. The Supreme Court held, in *Larson v. Cactus Utility Co.*,[1] that the *Pope* standard for remittitur applies to trial courts as well as appellate courts. It summarized the court of appeals remittitur practice as follows:

> If a court of appeals holds that there is no evidence to support a damages verdict, it should render a take nothing judgment as to that amount. If part of a damage verdict lacks sufficient evidentiary support, the proper course is to suggest a remittitur of that part of the verdict. The party prevailing in the trial court should be given the option of accepting the remittitur or having the case remanded. If a remand is ordered by the court of appeals, then, in doing so, it should detail and analyze the evidence as required by *Pool v. Ford Motor Co.*

2. *Damage verdict not supported as a matter of law*. The remittitur process and standard applies only to claims that a jury's damages award is supported by some, but insufficient evidence (that is, Zone 2). If the claim is that there is no evidence to support an element of damages (for example, no evidence of future lost wages) or that the law does not allow recovery of an element (for example, attorney's fees are not recoverable for common law fraud), the issue is treated as any "matter of law" issue. That is, the opponent moves for directed verdict, judgment notwithstanding the verdict, or to disregard the jury's verdict, or objects to the submission of the jury question, and the court ignores the verdict and renders judgment accordingly, lowering the total damage award by the amount that is not recoverable. What if the jury is asked one damages question and the question includes elements for which the plaintiff may not recover as a matter of law? Reconsider *Harris County v. Smith* from the chapter on Jury Charge.

3. *Exemplary damages*. When the jury is asked to award exemplary damages, the amount actually awarded must conform to due process standards.[2] The procedure for attacking the amount of exemplary damages is the remittitur. On appropriate motion, when the evidence justifies exemplary damages of some amount, the court must evaluate the jury's award with constitutional ratio analysis and, if it exceeds constitutional standards, offer the plaintiff a lowered award or a new trial.

---

[1] 730 S.W.2d 640 (Tex. 1987).

[2] Bennett v. Reynolds, 2010 WL 2541096 (Tex. June 25, 2010); Tony Gullo Motors L.L.P., 212 S.W.3d 299 (Tex. 2006).

D. Motions for New Trial and Motions to Modify

Read Rules 320-329b.

There are several reasons why the losing litigant might file a motion for new trial. (1) *Second chance.* Occasionally the losing party in a jury case thinks there are reasons for the judge to set aside the verdict and grant a new trial. (2) *Modification of judgment.* In nonjury cases, the losing side sometimes asks the court to take a second look at the evidence and issues and reconsider its decision. (3) *Extension of appellate deadlines.* When the losing party plans to appeal, it will usually file a motion for new trial to extend the appellate deadlines. *See* TRAP 26.1. (4) *Preservation of error.* A motion is required to preserve error in some circumstances, such as jury misconduct and newly discovered evidence.

---

1. *Grounds*

1. *When motion for new trial is required.* Rule 324(b) requires motion for new trial to preserve error for appeal only when the complaint is of factual insufficiency of the evidence (zones 2 and 4), inadequate or excessive damages, incurable jury argument if not otherwise ruled upon, and any complaint on which evidence must be heard. Thus, the motion for new trial is required to preserve errors for which there has been no prior opportunity to present them to the trial judge. For example, because complaints of factual insufficiency and to the amount of damages are complaints about the jury's verdict, the error must be preserved through some post-verdict motion. The motion for new trial is the proper method to preserve these errors because the appropriate remedy is a new trial, not rendition of judgment (in which case a motion for j.n.o.v. might be appropriate). Similarly, because the errors of jury misconduct, newly discovered evidence, or lack of notice of a default judgment appear after the verdict is returned or judgment is rendered, the error must be presented in a motion for new trial which provides an opportunity to present evidence relevant to the issue. A motion for new trial may be used to present any error to the judge, even if the judge has previously ruled on the issue. Occasionally, the judge may decide an error is more egregious than originally thought, and grant a new trial on that basis.

2. *Motions requiring evidence*. Rule 324(b)(1) requires a motion for new trial to preserve errors on matters requiring new evidence for decision—that is, not already included in a bill of exceptions made during the trial. The rule specifically requires a motion for new trial regarding newly discovered evidence, jury misconduct, and setting aside a default judgment, but the rule is not exhaustive. The case law adds such matters as lack of consent to an agreed judgment[1] and a challenge to the amount of a guardian ad litem's award.[2] Note that the affidavits required in connection with jury misconduct are only the predicates entitling the complainant to a hearing. At the hearing, conventional evidence will be required.[3]

---

1 Hensley v. Salinas, 583 S.W.2d 617, 618 (Tex. 1979).

2 Navistar v. Valles, 740 S.W.2d 4 (Tex. App.—El Paso 1987, no writ).

3 Hemsell v. Summers, 153 S.W.2d 305 (Tex. Civ. App.—Amarillo 1941, no writ).

3. *Legal sufficiency*. Recall that a motion for new trial, if denied, can preserve a no evidence point.[4] The rule is, however, that, though a "no evidence" point[5] can be urged in a motion for new trial, the trial court *cannot* grant the appropriate relief; that is, a judgment n.o.v. It can only grant a new trial.[6] This seems a strange approach. Why not apply the misnomer rule to the motion for new trial, consider it as properly a motion for judgment n.o.v., and then grant the appropriate relief, i.e. rendition of judgment?[7]

---

2. *Trial Court Authority*

Read Rules 315, 320 and 326.

a. *Mandamus*

In re TOYOTA MOTOR SALES, U.S.A., INC.
407 S.W.3d 746
(Tex. 2013)

Opinion

CHIEF JUSTICE JEFFERSON delivered the opinion of the Court.

We have recently held that a trial court must explain with reasonable specificity why it has set aside a jury verdict and granted a new trial.[1] Without such an explanation, parties in the case can only speculate about why the court ostensibly circumvented a critical constitutional right. The parties—and the public—are entitled to know why the trial court believes an injustice would occur if the jury's verdict were to stand. In this case, the jury returned a verdict, and the trial court rendered a judgment in conformity with it. The trial court then ordered a new trial. The order is reasonably specific. Its stated reasons are superficially sound. The question is whether an appellate court may, in an original proceeding, determine whether the reasonably specific and legally sound rationale is actually true. And if it is not true, we must decide whether the trial court abuses its discretion by granting a new trial.

We hold that an appellate court may conduct a merits review of the bases for a new trial order after a trial court has set aside a jury verdict. If the record does not support the trial court's rationale for ordering a new trial, the appellate court may grant mandamus relief. We conditionally grant relief.

---

4 *See* Aero Energy, Inc. v. Circle C Drilling Co., 699 S.W.2d 821 (Tex. 1985); *and* Steve's Sash & Door Co. v. Ceco Corp., 751 S.W.2d 473, 477 (Tex. 1988) (both questioned at 863 S.W.2d 697, writ denied).

5 An assertion that Zone 1 or Zone 5 evidence controls over a jury finding.

6 *See* Cecil v. Smith, 804 S.W.2d 509 (Tex. 1991).

7 The trial court can do this at any time before its plenary jurisdiction expires. There is no reason to favor a new trial over a rendition because of any time constraints.

1 In re Columbia Med. Ctr. of Las Colinas, Subsidiary, L.P., 290 S.W.3d 204 (Tex. 2009).

I. Background

A. Facts

Richard King was driving his Toyota 4Runner along a highway when a commercial truck turned onto the road in front of him. King swerved to avoid the truck but lost control of his car, which rolled over several times. King was ejected from the vehicle and died a few hours later.

B. Procedural History

1. Trial Court

King's family sued Toyota and the local Toyota dealership for strict products liability, negligence, wrongful death, and survivorship. The Kings contended that the 4Runner's allegedly defective seat belt system caused his ejection from the car and his subsequent death.

The family asserted that King was wearing his seat belt at the time of the accident. But in a videotaped pretrial deposition, State Trooper Justin Coon, who responded to the emergency call and arrived on the scene to investigate, testified that he believed that King was not wearing the belt at the time of the rollover. . . .

The Kings filed a motion to preclude at trial "[a]ny reference to the purported opinions of Officer Justin Coon . . . since [he] ha[d] never been identified by Defendants as [an] expert witness in this case." At a pretrial hearing, the Kings clarified that they would not object to Officer Coon's testifying about his observations of the accident scene as long as he did not offer his opinion that King had not been wearing a seat belt when the car rolled over. The Kings later filed an additional motion in limine to bar "[a]ny testimony from any purported fact witness including law enforcement officials, investigators, emergency personnel, medical personnel and bystanders that Richard King was not wearing his seatbelt . . . before or during the [ac]cident." The trial court granted these motions.

The case proceeded to trial in May 2009. Despite the limine orders, Officer Coon's statement found its way into the record, in front of the jury, three times before the close of evidence. Because the trial court's order cites Toyota's "prejudicial," "brazen," and "inflammatory" reference to Officer Coon's seat belt testimony as a basis for granting a new trial, it is important to detail precisely the manner in which the information was conveyed to the jury.

The initial instance occurred when Toyota's counsel introduced Officer Coon's video deposition. To comply with the court's limine orders, Toyota had redacted portions of the officer's testimony [the opinions were redacted], and the relevant passage was edited and played into the record . . . .

Immediately after this testimony, in front of the jury, the Kings' attorney introduced [a] portion of the statement into the record. . . .

Toyota's attorney was quick to alert the trial court that *the plaintiffs' counsel* had just introduced Officer Coon's suggestion that King was not wearing a seat belt.

* * *

The Kings' attorney did not move to strike the testimony or seek a mistrial, nor did he request a curative or limiting instruction after quoting the statement. He did not revisit the seat belt issue during his subsequent tender of designated testimony from Officer Coon's deposition.

During Toyota's direct examination of expert witness Lee S. Carr, the statement was again read into the record. Carr, an accident reconstructionist, built a scale model of the accident scene.

Before trial, he surveyed the accident site, read available police reports, and reviewed Officer Coon's deposition. [Toyota's counsel again read the portion of Coon's deposition suggesting that King was not wearing a seatbelt. King's attorney objected, and admitted that he had mistakenly referenced the testimony the previous day, and the court asked Toyota's counsel not to refer to it again.] . . . .

The jury returned, and Toyota's counsel resumed questioning Carr, without publishing Coon's statement again. Later, the statement resurfaced during Toyota's direct examination of William Van Arsdell, Ph.D., another of Toyota's expert witnesses. Dr. Van Arsdell testified that he had been retained to evaluate the seat belt's design and performance, and to investigate whether King's seat belt functioned properly and whether he was wearing it when the accident occurred. Dr. Van Arsdell reviewed the depositions of all witnesses, including Officer Coon. [During his testimony, Ardsell referenced Coon's conclusion that King was not wearing a seatbelt.] . . . .

After the close of evidence, but before arguments commenced, the Kings' attorney asked the trial court for guidance on the point with respect to Officer Coon's testimony, [and the court stated "I don't believe it was read in the record at all."]

During Toyota's closing argument, Toyota's counsel quoted the previously admitted line of questioning from Officer Coon's deposition. . . .

The Kings' attorney objected, arguing that Toyota violated the trial court's limine order. The trial judge sustained the objection. But despite the objection, the Kings' attorney did not move to strike and did not request a curative or limiting instruction. Toyota's attorney responded, "You heard that, and it was read into the record by [the Kings' own attorney] when Mr. Coon's deposition testimony was offered," and continued with closing argument.

The jury returned a verdict in Toyota's favor, and the trial court signed a corresponding judgment. A few weeks later, the Kings moved for new trial, alleging that Toyota's counsel had violated the trial court's limine rulings by reading, during closing argument, the disputed portion of Officer Coon's deposition. . . .

Nevertheless, the trial court granted the Kings' motion on two grounds. First, the trial court stated that Toyota had violated the limine order and "purported to present evidence outside the record." The court explained that its decision was based on Toyota's reference during closing to Coon's testimony. . . . The court [also] granted a new trial "in the interest of justice."

Second, the trial court reasoned that a new trial was warranted to sanction Toyota for violating the limine order, because a limiting instruction could not eliminate the harm. *See* TEX. R. CIV. P. 320 ("New trials may be granted and judgment set aside for good cause, on motion or on the court's own motion on such terms as the court shall direct.").

2. Court of Appeals

Toyota sought a writ of mandamus from the court of appeals, which denied relief. 327 S.W.3d 302. The court evaluated the trial court's order in light of *In re Columbia.* The court of appeals recognized that after *Columbia,* a new trial order must include the basis for the trial court's decision. *Id.* at 305. But after considering the trial court's order—reproduced in its entirety in the court of appeals' opinion—the court concluded that "there is no question that the trial court . . . *specified the reasons* for its decision to grant the Kings' motion [for new trial], and thereby satisfied the specificity requirements of *Columbia.*" *Id.* (emphasis added). The court of appeals rejected the notion that "*Columbia* supports further review of the *merits* of the grounds specified," and was "unpersuaded that the language Toyota relie[d] upon [in requesting mandamus relief] supports such an expansion of *Columbia.*" *Id.* at 305-06 (emphasis added).

* * *

II. Discussion

A. An appellate court may conduct merits-based mandamus review of a trial court's articulated reasons for granting new trial.

In the decades leading up to *Columbia,* our jurisprudence gave trial courts broad deference in granting new trials and, specifically, "approved the practice of trial courts failing to specify reasons for setting aside jury verdicts." *Columbia,* 290 S.W.3d at 208. We generally precluded review of new trial orders, except in two narrow instances. *Id.; see also Johnson v. Court of Civil Appeals,* 162 Tex. 613, 350 S.W.2d 330, 331 (1961) (recognizing that "[t]here are only two instances where any appellate court of this state has ever directed the trial judge to set aside its order granting motion for new trial": when the order was void or when the trial court erroneously concluded that the jury's answers to special issues conflicted irreconcilably).

But in *Columbia,* we emphasized that the discretion given trial courts was "not limitless." *Columbia,* 290 S.W.3d at 210. In that case, the jury returned a verdict in favor of the hospital-defendants after a four-week trial. *Id.* at 206. The trial judge granted the plaintiffs' new trial motion "in the interests of justice and fairness," without further elaboration. *Id.* We held that this was inadequate, noting that "such a vague explanation [whe]n setting aside a jury verdict does not enhance respect for the judiciary or the rule of law, detracts from transparency we strive to achieve in our legal system, and does not sufficiently respect the reasonable expectations of parties and the public when a lawsuit is tried to a jury." *Id.* at 213.

We disapproved of our prior approach under *Johnson v. Fourth Court of Appeals,* 700 S.W.2d 916 (Tex. 1985), and held that "just as appellate courts that set aside jury verdicts are required to detail reasons for doing so, trial courts must give more explanation than 'in the interest of justice' for setting aside a jury verdict." *Columbia,* 290 S.W.3d at 205. We held that "the parties and public are entitled to an *understandable, reasonably specific explanation* [of] why their expectations are frustrated by a jury verdict being disregarded or set aside, the trial process being nullified, and the case having to be retried." *Id.* at 213 (emphasis added). We did not detail exactly what such an explanation would require, although it would have to be more than a bare assertion of "in the interests of justice and fairness." *Id.*

More recently, we decided *In re United Scaffolding, Inc.,* 377 S.W.3d 685 (Tex. 2012), which presented a related, but narrower, question. There, we were asked to decide whether a trial court that gave four reasons for granting a new trial, including "in the interest of justice and fairness," and linked them by "and/or" satisfied *Columbia.*

In concluding that it did not, we noted that *Columbia*'s purpose "w[ould] be satisfied so long as the order provides a *cogent* and *reasonably specific* explanation of the reasoning that led the court to conclude that a new trial was warranted." *Id.* at 688 (emphases added). We acknowledged that *Columbia* focused "not on the length or detail of the reasons a trial court gives, but on how well those reasons serve the general purpose of assuring the parties that the jury's decision was set aside only after careful thought and *for valid reasons.*" We held that the trial court's "use of 'and/or' le[ft] open the possibility that 'in the interest of justice and fairness' [could be] the sole rationale." That possibility, if true, would have violated our *Columbia* standard.

We held that "a trial court does not abuse its discretion[6] so long as its stated reason for granting a new trial (1) is a reason for which a new trial is *legally appropriate* (such as a well-defined legal standard or a defect that probably resulted in an improper verdict); and (2) is *specific enough* to indicate that the trial court did not simply parrot a pro forma template, but rather derived the articulated reasons from the particular facts and circumstances of the case at hand." Applying this new standard to the new trial order, we concluded that because, under *Columbia,* "in the interests of justice or fairness" or similar language "is never an independently sufficient reason for granting new trial," the "and/or" order failed the test's first prong.

This case represents the next step in that progression. We must decide whether, on mandamus review, an appellate court may evaluate the merits of a new trial order that states a clear, legally appropriate, and reasonably specific reason for granting a new trial. Stated differently, if a trial court's order facially comports with *Columbia* and *United Scaffolding,* may an appellate court review the correctness of the stated reasons for granting a new trial? Absent further guidance from this Court, our courts of appeals have generally been reluctant to engage in merits-based review of new trial orders.

To answer this question, we consider *Columbia* and *United Scaffolding* together. A new trial order must be "understandable," "reasonably specific," "cogent," "legally appropriate," "specific enough to indicate that the trial court did not simply parrot a pro forma template," and issued "only after careful thought and *for valid reasons.*" An order that does not satisfy these requirements may be corrected by mandamus.

Having already decided that new trial orders must meet these requirements and that noncompliant orders will be subject to mandamus review, it would make little sense to conclude now that the correctness or validity of the orders' articulated reasons cannot also be evaluated. To deny merits-based review would mean that a trial court could set aside a verdict for reasons that are unsupported by the law or the evidence, as long as those reasons are facially valid. *Columbia's* requirements would be mere formalities, lacking any substantive "checks" by appellate courts to ensure that the discretion to grant new trials has been exercised appropriately. Transparency without accountability is meaningless. While we reiterate our "faith in the integrity of our trial bench as well as that of the appellate bench," we decline to hold that their decisions are immune from substantive review.

We have recognized two narrow instances in which new trial orders are reviewable, on the merits, by mandamus: when the trial court's order was void or when the trial court erroneously concluded that the jury's answers to special issues were irreconcilably in conflict. As to the latter, since at least 1926, we have granted mandamus relief to correct a trial court's erroneous ruling. In such cases, merits-based mandamus review is relatively straightforward—an appellate court may compare the jury charge against the jury's answers, and decide whether the trial court correctly concluded that they conflicted irreconcilably.

This case is analogous. Appellate courts must be able to conduct merits-based review of new trial orders. If, despite conformity with the procedural requirements of our precedent, a trial

---

[6] We also provided a non-exhaustive list of examples of new trial orders that would be clear abuses of discretion, including: giving a reason (specific or not) that was not a legally valid reason; plain statements that the trial court merely substituted its own judgment for the jury's; statements that the trial court simply disliked one party's lawyer; invidious discrimination; an explanation that provides little or no insight into the trial judge's reasoning; and pro forma template language absent a trial judge's analysis. United Scaffolding, 377 S.W.3d at 689.

court's articulated reasons are not supported by the underlying record, the new trial order cannot stand.

While this review is new to us, it is old hat to our colleagues on the federal bench. Federal appellate courts regularly conduct record-bound, merits-based review of new trial orders to evaluate their validity. [Note that in the federal system, the procedure is different. The new trial order is appealed from the judgment in the second trial. Therefore, when the federal court of appeals reverses a district court's ruling granting a new trial, it vacates the judgment rendered after a jury verdict in a second trial, and reinstates the first trial's results.] . . . .

. . . Relevant for our purposes is the fact that the Fifth Circuit has long engaged in merits-based review of new trial orders, looking to the records available on a case-by-case basis. Though not binding on this Court, this approach supports our decision today that the reasons articulated in a new trial order are subject to merits-based mandamus review.

B. Under this standard, the trial court abused its discretion in granting a new trial.

1. Merits–Based Review of This Order

Having concluded that the reasons articulated in a new trial order are reviewable on the merits by mandamus, we now evaluate the trial court's grant of new trial against the underlying record.

The new trial order complies with *Columbia*'s procedural "form" requirements. The trial judge's three-page order, which pinpointed Toyota's reference to Officer Coon's testimony in closing argument as the basis for granting new trial, is distinguishable from the *Columbia* order's bare assertion of "in the interests of justice and fairness." This order, on its face, comports with *Columbia.*

Similarly, the trial court's explanation of and reference to the specific grounds for new trial from Toyota's closing argument satisfy, facially, *United Scaffolding*'s requirements that the reasons listed (if accurate) would have been "legally appropriate" grounds for new trial, and are "specific enough" that they are not simply pro forma.

The trouble is that the record squarely conflicts with the trial judge's expressed reasons for granting new trial. Simply articulating understandable, reasonably specific, and legally appropriate reasons is not enough; the reasons must be valid and correct. Having undertaken our own " 'cumbersome review' of the multi-volume trial record," we conclude that the record does not support the new trial order.

The trial court initially granted the Kings' motion in limine to preclude Officer Coon's deposition testimony regarding King's seat belt usage at the time of the crash. But a protective limine order alone does not preserve error. Furthermore, where, as here, the party that requested the limine order *itself* introduces the evidence into the record, and then fails to immediately object, ask for a curative or limiting instruction or, alternatively, move for mistrial, the party waives any subsequent alleged error on the point.

Even if the attorney's actions were inadvertent, the Kings introduced the point into evidence and waived the point of error. . . .

We acknowledge that appellate courts benefit from the hindsight that a complete record provides. Trial courts, on the other hand, must make difficult, often dispositive, decisions based on their recollection and best judgment alone, frequently without the aid of full records, transcripts, or briefing. Nevertheless, having thoroughly reviewed the record here, we conclude that the trial court's articulated reason for granting new trial—that Toyota's counsel "willfully disregarded, brazenly and intentionally violated" the limine orders in closing—is unsupported. The record directly contravenes the order, including the trial court's acknowledgment during trial that the Kings' attorney "ha[d] read into the record what [Toyota] wanted published."

Because the record does not support the articulated reason, the trial court abused its discretion by granting a new trial on that ground.

* * *

III. Conclusion

On mandamus review, an appellate court may conduct a merits-based review of the reasons given for granting a new trial. That review compels us to conclude that the trial court abused its discretion in granting a new trial here. The stated reasons, though complying in form with the requirements of *Columbia* and *United Scaffolding,* lacked substantive merit. Further, a new trial was an improper sanction.

We conditionally grant relief and order the trial court to withdraw its order and render judgment on the verdict. We are confident the trial court will comply, and the writ will issue only if it does not.

JUSTICE BOYD did not participate in the decision.

JUSTICE LEHRMANN, joined by JUSTICE DEVINE, concurring.

"The right of trial by jury shall remain inviolate." TEX. CONST. art. I, § 15. The importance of protecting that right was the underpinning of the Court's recent holding that mandamus relief is appropriate when a trial court fails to explain with reasonable specificity the reasons it has set aside a jury verdict and granted a new trial. *In re Columbia Med. Ctr. of Las Colinas, Subsidiary, L.P.,* 290 S.W.3d 204, 209 (Tex. 2009). Today the Court takes another step along that path by authorizing appellate courts to conduct merits-based review of such new-trial orders. It is essential to remember in conducting this review, however, that the trial court's authority to grant a new trial " 'is not in derogation of the right of trial by jury but is one of the historic safeguards of that right.' " I thus concur in the Court's opinion, but write separately to emphasize the significant discretion trial courts are, and must continue to be, afforded in determining whether good cause exists to grant a new trial following a jury verdict.

* * *

I agree that, in this case, determining whether the order granting a new trial was an abuse of discretion is "relatively straightforward." . . . [B]oth the motion and order focused solely on Toyota's counsel's referencing the testimony during his closing argument, and the order clarified the trial court's conclusion that Toyota's counsel "purported to present evidence outside the record, and commented on matters in violation of [the trial c]ourt's order in limine." The trial transcript dispositively reveals, however, that the complained—of and unobjected—to evidence discussed by Toyota's counsel during closing argument was *not* outside the record and thus was not improper.

But while review of a cold record appears to be exactly what was needed in this case to evaluate the substantive merit of the new-trial order, that limitation frequently places appellate courts at a disadvantage in evaluating whether there is good cause to grant a new trial. As we recognized in *Columbia,* "there are differences between the review that can be accomplished by appellate judges who have only the record to consider and trial judges who have seen the parties and witnesses and sensed the [e]ffect of certain evidence or occurrences on the trial." . . .

. . . Often, the trial court's presence and observations throughout the trial will be indispensable in evaluating whether the requisite good cause exists to justify setting aside a jury verdict and granting a new trial. *See Columbia,* 290 S.W.3d at 212 ("We do not retreat from the position that trial courts have significant discretion in granting new trials."). Recognizing the need to defer to trial courts with respect to such determinations is crucial to ensuring that parties receive a fair trial.

Notes & Questions

1. *The traditional rule: No review!* Traditionally, the trial court's discretion to grant a new trial is such that any reason (even a wrong one) or no reason at all will suffice. This latitude appeared to grow, in part, from the court's authority to grant a new trial on its own motion,[1] and a frank desire to let judges overrule "runaway" juries.

2. *Matter of right.* The filing of a motion for new trial solely in order to extend the appellate deadlines is a matter of right whether or not there is a reasonable basis for it.[2]

3. *When mandamus is allowed, even before* Columbia. However, as the Supreme Court notes, there were two situations where new trial orders rendered during the time a trial court has plenary power were reviewable by an appellate court: when the trial court's order was void and when the trial court erroneously concluded that the jury's answers to special issues were irreconcilably in conflict. A "void" motion for new trial order was one that was granted when the court had no power to do so—for example, when the court is without subject matter jurisdiction, or after the trial court's plenary power had expired. *Plenary power* is the time period during which the trial court has power to modify, correct, vacate, or reform a judgment, which expires a certain number of days after the judgment is signed, according to the rules. We will study the important concept of plenary power next.

4. *Is mandamus required?* The Texas Supreme Court has not decided whether Texas courts can review new trial orders as the federal courts do—after judgment is rendered in the second trial.[3]

5. *Merits review.* The Court has not clarified the standard by which merits review is conducted. It has said that it has not suggested that it "should be conducted under anything other than the abuse-of-discretion standard that is familiar and inherent to mandamus proceedings." And it has referenced the Fifth Circuit's opinions that "do not hesitate to review new-trial orders based on factual-sufficiency analyses."[4]

6. *Some additional restrictions.* As we have seen, Rule 320 allows the trial court to order partial new trials on points "clearly separable without unfairness," but it may not separate contested liability and damages questions in unliquidated damages cases.[5] Furthermore, Rule 326 limits the number of retrials based on factual sufficiency to two. The rule is silent on what happens the third time

---

[1] *See* Rule 320.

[2] *See* Old Republic Ins. Co. v. Scott, 846 S.W.2d 832, 833 (Tex. 1993).

[3] United Scaffolding, Inc. v. Levine, 537 S.W.3d 463, 482–83 (Tex. 2017).

[4] In re Bent, 487 S.W.3d 170, 177-78 (Tex. 2016).

[5] *See* Rancho La Valencia, Inc. v. Aquaplex, Inc., 383 S.W.3d 150 (Tex. 2012); Iley v. Hughes, 311 S.W.2d 648 (Tex. 1958).

the case is tried with the same insufficient evidence. However, this ambiguity seems to have presented no practical problem, probably because (a) new trials are usually granted on the basis of numerous complaints in addition to the factual sufficiency complaint; and (b) one so short of proof would likely settle before a third trial.

E. Timing and Plenary Power

Read Rules 329b, 316

In re BROOKSHIRE GROCERY COMPANY

250 S.W.3d 66
(Tex. 2008)

JEFFERSON, CHIEF JUSTICE.

In this mandamus action, we determine whether a motion for new trial filed within thirty days of judgment, but after a preceding motion for new trial has been overruled, extends the trial court's plenary power under Texas Rule of Civil Procedure 329b. Because we hold that it does not, we deny relator Brookshire Grocery Company's petition for writ of mandamus.

Background

In the underlying tort action, the jury returned a verdict for Barbara Goss in her action against Brookshire. On December 3, 2004, after the verdict but before the trial court signed the judgment, Brookshire filed a "Motion for Judgment Notwithstanding the Verdict and in the Alternative Motion for New Trial." In these motions, Brookshire argued that there was no evidence to support the verdict and urged the court to render judgment in its favor; alternatively, Brookshire sought a new trial based on an alleged error in the court's charge. On December 9, 2004, the court heard the motions and signed a judgment conforming to the jury verdict. The next day, December 10, 2004, the court signed an order denying not only Brookshire's motion for judgment notwithstanding the verdict, but also its alternative motion for new trial. Specifically, the order stated that "[h]aving considered the pleadings and the evidence presented, and having heard and considered the arguments of counsel, the Court finds that said *Motions* are DENIED." (Emphasis added.)

On January 7, 2005, twenty-nine days after judgment, Brookshire filed a second motion for new trial, which again argued, in considerably more detail, that there was insufficient evidence to support the judgment and that the court's charge was erroneous. Goss countered that the December 10, 2004 order "terminated the period for filing amended or supplemental motions for new trial under TEX. R. CIV. P. 329b(b), and triggered the final thirty days of the Court's plenary power under TEX. R. CIV. P. 329b(e)." After a January 25 hearing, the trial court granted Brookshire's motion for new trial in an order signed on February 1.

Goss sought mandamus relief from the court of appeals, arguing that the trial court lacked jurisdiction on February 1 to grant the second motion for new trial, because its plenary power expired on January 10, thirty days after the court overruled the first motion for new trial.[2] The court of appeals agreed and ordered the trial court to vacate the February 1 order; the trial court has complied. Brookshire now seeks a writ of mandamus directing the trial court to reinstate the order granting new trial.

II

Standard of Review

Mandamus relief is appropriate when a trial court issues an order after its plenary power has expired. When the mandamus proceeding arises out of the interpretation of legal rules, we give limited deference to the lower courts' analysis.

III

Discussion

Texas Rule of Civil Procedure 329b governs the filing of motions for new trial (as well as motions to modify, correct, or reform the judgment) and outlines their effect on the trial court's plenary power. The rule provides, in relevant part:

> (a) *A* motion for new trial, if filed, shall be filed prior to or within thirty days after the judgment or other order complained of is signed.
>
> (b) *One or more amended motions* for new trial may be filed *without leave of court* before any preceding motion for new trial filed by the movant is overruled *and* within thirty days after the judgment or other order complained of is signed.
>
> * * *
>
> (e) If a motion for new trial is timely filed by any party, the trial court, regardless of whether an appeal has been perfected, has plenary power to grant a new trial or to vacate, modify, correct, or reform the judgment until thirty days after *all such timely-filed motions* are overruled, either by a written and signed order or by operation of law, whichever occurs first.

TEX. R. CIV. P. 329b (emphasis added).

We must decide whether a motion for new trial filed within thirty days of judgment, but after a prior motion for new trial has been overruled, is "timely" for purposes of extending plenary power under Rule 329b(e). If Brookshire's second motion for new trial was indeed "timely filed," the trial court's plenary power extended until thirty days after that motion was overruled either by signed order or by operation of law. *See* TEX. R. CIV. P. 329b(e). Under this scenario, the trial court would have had plenary power when it granted the second motion for new trial on February 1, 2005. If, however, the only "timely filed" motion-as governed by Rule 329b(e)-was Brookshire's first motion for new trial,[3] the trial court's plenary power expired January 10, 2005, thirty days after the court overruled that motion. Consequently, the trial court would have lacked jurisdiction on February 1 to grant the second motion for new trial.

---

[2] January 10, 2005 is actually the thirty-first day after the December 10, 2004 order; because the thirtieth day (January 9, 2005) was a Sunday, however, the first day after the thirtieth day that was not a Saturday, Sunday, or legal holiday became the last day of the trial court's plenary power. *See* TEX. R. CIV. P. 4 (governing computation of time under the rules).

[3] Brookshire filed its first motion for new trial before the trial court signed the judgment; thus, the motion was deemed filed on the date of, but subsequent to the time of, the signing of the judgment. TEX. R. CIV. P. 306c.

We conclude the latter interpretation is correct. Subsection (b) of Rule 329b provides that an amended motion may be filed without leave of court when: (1) no preceding motion for new trial has been overruled *and* (2) it is filed within thirty days of judgment. TEX. R. CIV. P. 329b(b). "And" is conjunctive: an amended new-trial motion is timely filed only *before* the court overrules a prior one. An amended motion filed afterwards: (1) need not be considered by the trial court and (2) does not extend the trial court's plenary power. A contrary interpretation would effectively substitute the word "or" for "and," so that a litigant's motion for new trial, filed after a preceding motion has been overruled, would extend the trial court's plenary power. But "ordinarily the words 'and' and 'or' are not interchangeable," and they should not be here.

* * *

Rule 329b's history supports our conclusion that a motion for new trial filed after a preceding motion has been overruled is not "timely" for purposes of extending the trial court's plenary power. . . . . [T]hroughout the history of Rule 329b, timely amended motions for new trial have always been limited to those filed before the trial court overruled a preceding motion, regardless of whether leave of court was required.

Following this pattern, the 1981 rule amendments revised subsection (b) to allow for both original and amended motions to be freely filed within thirty days of judgment, but the rule once again retained the restriction that all such motions must be filed prior to the court overruling a preceding motion for new trial. Therefore, an amended motion for new trial filed after the court has ruled on a prior motion is not "timely" for purposes of extending the trial court's plenary power under Rule 329b(c), *even if* leave of court is obtained and it is filed within thirty days of judgment.[8]

Our holding today does not preclude a party whose motion for new trial has been overruled from continuing to seek a new trial while the trial court is still empowered to act. Pursuant to Rule 329b(e), the trial court retains plenary power for thirty days after overruling a motion for new trial; thus, the losing party may ask the trial court to reconsider its order denying a new trial-or the court may grant a new trial on its own initiative—so long as the court issues an order granting new trial within its period of plenary power. *See Moritz v. Preiss,* 121 S.W.3d 715, 720 (Tex. 2003) (noting that a trial court can always "grant a new trial, or vacate, modify, correct or reform the judgment" during this time); *see also* TEX. R. CIV. P. 5 (trial court may not enlarge period for granting new trials except as stated in the rules).

Additionally, under Rule 329b, a trial court's plenary power to grant a new trial expires thirty days after it overrules a motion for new trial, only provided no other *type* of 329b motion (such as a motion to modify, correct, or reform the judgment) is "timely filed." *See* TEX. R. CIV. P. 329b(e), (g). Thus, a party whose motion for new trial is overruled within thirty days of judgment may still file a motion to modify, correct, or reform the judgment-provided it is filed within thirty days of judgment-and thereby extend the trial court's plenary power. *See* TEX. R. CIV. P. 329b(g) (deadlines for filing and ruling on a motion to modify, correct, or reform the judgment are the

---

8 As the rule is drafted, a party has the right, within thirty days of judgment, to revise its motion before the court rules; afterwards, the trial court retains discretion either to consider a late motion or not, but may act only during its period of plenary power. Once that power expires, as it did here, the court may neither grant nor deny the motion. The rule simply codifies *Kelly's* sensible proposition that a party should have the ability to amend its motion for new trial up until the time the court rules (provided the amended motion is filed within thirty days of judgment), *see Kelly,* 366 S.W.2d at 923; after the court rules, however, a late motion is subject both to the court's *discretion* to consider the filing and the court's *power* to decide the motion.

same as those prescribed for a motion for new trial); *see also L.M. Healthcare, Inc. v. Childs,* 929 S.W.2d 442, 444 (Tex. 1996) (holding that "a timely filed motion to modify judgment extends the trial court's plenary power, separate and apart from a motion for new trial"). It is this scenario-and not one involving successive rulings on multiple motions for new trial that is referenced in Rule 329b(e), which provides that plenary power expires thirty days after "*all* such timely-filed motions are overruled." TEX. R. CIV. P. 329b(e) (emphasis added); *see also id.* 329b(g) (providing that "[t]he overruling of [a motion to modify, correct, or reform the judgment] shall not preclude the filing of a motion for new trial, nor shall the overruling of a motion for new trial preclude the filing of a motion to modify, correct, or reform").

In this case, because the only 329b motion Brookshire filed was a motion for new trial, the trial court's plenary power expired January 10, 2005, thirty days after it overruled the first motion. Brookshire's second motion for new trial was filed within that thirty-day period, and the trial court could have thus considered the grounds raised in it and granted a new trial on that basis or on its own motion; however, the court could only act while it had plenary power. The February 1, 2005 order granting a new trial was signed after the court's plenary power period expired, and, therefore, that order was void.

* * *

IV

Conclusion

In response to the court of appeals' conditional grant of mandamus, the trial court properly vacated its February 1, 2005 order granting new trial. We deny Brookshire's petition for writ of mandamus. TEX. R. APP. P. 52.8(d).

JUSTICE HECHT, joined by JUSTICE WAINWRIGHT, JUSTICE BRISTER, and JUSTICE GREEN, dissenting.

Procedural rules exist to subserve the presentation and resolution of cases on their merits. As Rule 1 of the Texas Rules of Civil Procedure states, "[t]he proper objective of rules of civil procedure is to obtain a just, fair, equitable and impartial adjudication of the rights of litigants under established principles of substantive law." The rules are written to achieve this purpose and must be construed accordingly.

This court has labored long and hard to remove as many procedural traps from our rules as possible. Litigants are entitled to have their disputes resolved on the merits, not on unnecessary and arcane points that can sneak up on even the most diligent of attorneys.

Tricky procedural rules threaten substantive rights. Take this case in point.

* * *

Notes & Questions

1. *Plenary power*. The trial court has power to modify, correct, vacate, or reform the judgment (called "plenary power") for 30 days after a final judgment is signed. Rule 329b(d). However, if a motion for new trial (or appropriate motion to modify, discussed below) is filed within 30 days after the judgment is signed, the trial court's plenary power is extended until 30 days after all such timely filed motions are overruled. Rule 329b(e).

2. *Time to file motion for new trial*. Because the trial court's plenary power expires 30 days after a final judgment is signed, Rule 329b specifies that a motion for new trial shall be filed within 30 days after the date the judgment (or other order complained of) is signed. Rule 329b(a). This deadline is extremely important because if no motion for new trial (or appropriate motion to modify) is filed after a judgment is final,[1] plenary power expires. If no motion is filed within the 30 day period, a motion filed after the 30 day period is a nullity.[2] Why? The trial court has no jurisdiction to hear it. Note that Rule 5, which allows for enlargements of time, does not allow the trial court to extend the time to file a motion for new trial.

3. *Ruling on motions*. If a timely motion is filed, the trial court can rule on it anytime during the court's extended plenary power. Motions for new trial can be overruled by a written and signed order, or if there is not written and signed order,[3] the motion is overruled by operation of law 75 days after the judgment was signed. Rule 329b(c). The trial court's plenary power expires 30 days after the order overruling the motion is signed, or at most 105 days after the judgment is signed (30 days after the motion is overruled as a matter of law). If the motion is *granted*, the court's plenary jurisdiction does not expire. The original judgment is vacated, and if no other judgment is signed, "no plenary clock is ticking."[4] Accordingly, after a motion for new trial is granted, a trial judge can reconsider the new trial order as long as the case is still pending (her order or perhaps the order of a predecessor judge), "ungrant" it, and reinstate the judgment.[5]

4. *Extended time to file in certain cases*. In cases where the defendant was served by publication and did not appear in person or by an attorney of his own selection, Rule 329(a) provides that the defendant has two years to file a motion for new trial, thus significantly extending the trial court's period of plenary power over the default judgment. Furthermore, under Rule 306a(4), a party with late notice of judgment—having first learned of the judgment between 20 and 90 days after the judgment is signed—has additional time to file a motion for new trial. In such a case, time periods run from the date the party proves at a hearing that it learned of the judgment instead of the date the judgment was signed. In effect, the date of first notice of the judgment is substituted for the date that the judgment was signed for determining plenary power deadlines. Appellate deadlines, discussed in a later chapter, are affected as well.

---

[1] Finality is discussed in the chapter on appeals.

[2] *See e.g.,* Smith v. Comm'n for Lawyer Discipline, 42 S.W.3d 362 (Tex. App.—Houston [14th Dist.] 2001, no pet.).

[3] *See* In re Lovito-Nelson, 278 S.W.3d 773, 775-76 (Tex. 2009) (holding that because docket entry or scheduling order setting a trial date will not suffice as an order ruling on the motion for new trial, plenary jurisdiction expired before order signed).

[4] In re Baylor Med. Ctr., 280 S.W.3d 227, 230 (Tex. 2008).

[5] *Id.* at 228.

5. *Amended motions for new trial*. As *Brookshire* holds, under Rule 329b(b), if a timely motion for new trial is filed, amended motions may be filed without leave of court if filed within 30 days of the date the judgment complained of is signed *and* before the original motion is overruled. New grounds for new trial added in a *timely* amended motion are preserved for appeal.

6. *Untimely motions filed within plenary power*. Can a party file and a trial court consider an *untimely* motion for new trial—a motion filed more than 30 days after the judgment, but within the court's plenary power that was previously extended, or an untimely amended motion? Yes, because, as *Brookshire* points out, nothing precludes a party "from continuing to seek a new trial while the trial court is still empowered to act." It is important to remember, however, that the trial court can grant the motion only within the time of its plenary power (which is not extended further by the filing of an untimely motion). And although the trial court may consider any new grounds added in the late-filed motion as it exercises its discretion during its period of plenary power after judgment, the new grounds added in a late-filed motion are not preserved for appeal.

For example, in *Moritz v. Preiss*,[6] cited in *Brookshire*, the defendants prevailed with the jury, and the plaintiff filed a timely motion for new trial. As one ground, the timely motion urged jury misconduct. More than thirty days after the judgment had been signed, the plaintiff filed an amended motion for new trial adding as an additional ground that one of the jurors was legally disqualified. The trial court overruled the motion. The Supreme Court held that the trial court could have considered the late-filed juror-disqualification ground in exercising its discretion, but that the appellate court could not consider it because the late motion was ineffective to preserve the new ground for appeal. The Supreme Court said:

> A party may file an amended motion for new trial without leave of court before any earlier motion for new trial is overruled and within thirty days after the judgment. TEX. R. CIV. P. 329b(b). The court may not enlarge the period for taking any action under the rules relating to new trials except as the rules allow. TEX. R. CIV. P. 5.
>
> Nothing in the express language of Rule 329b or Rule 5 suggests that a party receives appellate review of a trial court's decision to deny an untimely amended motion for new trial simply because the trial court grants a party leave to file the untimely amended motion. Rather, Rule 329b(b) merely allows a party to file an amended motion without the trial court's permission so long as the trial court has not yet ruled on an earlier new trial motion, and the party files the amended motion within thirty days after the trial court signs the judgment. TEX. R. CIV. P. 329b(b). If a party timely files a motion for new trial, the trial court's plenary power extends an additional thirty days after the motion is overruled. During that time, the court may grant a new trial, or vacate, modify, correct or reform the judgment. TEX. R. CIV. P. 329b(e). And Rule 5 prohibits a trial court from enlarging the period for taking any action under the rules relating to new trials. TEX. R. CIV. P. 5.
>
> Read together, Rules 5, 329b(b) and 329b(e) demonstrate that an amended motion for new trial filed more than thirty days after the trial court signs a final judgment is untimely. The trial court's inherent power does not allow a trial court to disregard the plain language of Rule 5 and enlarge the time for filing new trial motions. A trial court's order overruling an untimely new trial motion cannot be the basis of appellate review, even if the trial court acts within its plenary power period. But, the trial court may, at its discretion, consider the

---

[6] 121 S.W.3d 715 (Tex. 2003).

grounds raised in an untimely motion and grant a new trial under its inherent authority before the court loses plenary power.

To summarize the purpose of an untimely motion or amended motion for new trial:

> If the trial court ignores the tardy motion, it is ineffectual for any purpose. The court, however, may look to the motion for guidance in the exercise of its inherent power and acting before its plenary power has expired, may grant a new trial; but if the court denies a new trial, the belated motion is a nullity and supplies no basis for consideration upon appeal of grounds which were required to be set forth in a timely motion.

Here, Preiss filed the amended motion for new trial thirty-five days after the trial court signed the original judgment. We have concluded that this judgment was final for purposes of appeal. Accordingly, Preiss's amended motion for new trial was untimely. See Tex. R. Civ. P. 329b(b). The untimely motion's only purpose was to guide the trial court in the exercise of its inherent authority, and it is a nullity for purposes of preserving issues for appellate review. The court of appeals, therefore, erred in reviewing Preiss's contention that the trial court abused its discretion in denying the amended motion for new trial and reversing the trial court's judgment based on the juror disqualification issue raised for the first time in that motion.

7. *Premature motion.* A motion for new trial or motion to modify filed before the judgment is signed is a "premature motion." A premature motion is deemed timely filed immediately after the trial court judgment is signed, extending plenary power and appellate deadlines.[7]

8. *Motions to modify: timing.* As we have seen, the trial court may act to withdraw ("set aside") or change a judgment at any time during the court's plenary jurisdiction. The court may be prompted to do so by a motion to modify, correct, or reform the judgment. Such a motion is a proper way to complain of any judgment defect, including the scope of relief granted by the trial court with respect to such matters a prejudgment interest[8] or attorneys' fees.[9] A motion for JNOV or a motion for remittitur also can be a motion to modify if it seeks to change a judgment previously signed. Under Rule 329b(g) such a motion extends deadlines in the same way that a motion for new trial does; that is, the court's plenary power runs for 30 days following the overruling of a motion (which overruling occurs by operation of law if the court has not acted within 75 days of the signing of the judgment). Like a motion for new trial—under Rule 329b(g), the court's denial of one does not prejudice the other. A motion to modify differs from a motion for new trial in that when a trial court grants a motion to modify, it results in a new judgment. Of course, the trial court has jurisdiction to sign a new judgment only during its plenary power (unless the new judgment is *nunc pro tunc*, discussed below).

9. *Motions to modify: Substantive and non-substantive modifications.* Importantly, but perhaps somewhat incomprehensibly, a motion to modify will extend the timetables only if it seeks a "*substantive*" change in the judgment. But *any* new judgment (even if the only change is a non-substantive, minor and trivial one) will *re-start* the timetable.[10] In other words, a motion to modify

---

7 Rule 306c, T.R.A.P. 27.2. Wilkins v. Methodist Health Care System, 160 S.W.3d 559, 562 (Tex. 2005).

8 *See* Miller v. Kendall, 804 S.W.2d 933, 945 (Tex. App.—Houston [1st Dist.] 1990, no writ).

9 *See* W.L.R., Inc. v. Borders, 690 S.W.2d 663, 668-669 (Tex. App.—Waco 1985, writ ref'd n.r.e.).

10 Lane Bank Equipment Co. v. Smith Southern Equipment, Inc., 10 S.W.3d 308 (Tex. 2000).

seeking to correct a caption or a misspelling would not extend the timetable; but if the court corrects the caption or the spelling in a new judgment, that change will re-start the timetables. And a motion seeking a change in the *substantive* relief that the court has granted will extend the timetable, like a motion for new trial, even if the court denies the motion or never acts on it.

10. *Distinguish nunc pro tunc orders.* The modification of a judgment *nunc pro tunc* ("now for then") under Rule 316—sometimes confused with the motion to modify—is quite different. A trial court can make *nunc pro tunc* changes at any time after it has lost jurisdiction of the judgment, but only in order to correct clerical errors.[11] As the Texas Supreme Court explained:[12]

> A judgment nunc pro tunc can correct a clerical error in the original judgment, but not a judicial one. An attempted nunc pro tunc judgment entered after the trial court loses plenary jurisdiction is void if it corrects judicial rather than clerical errors. "A clerical error is one which does not result from judicial reasoning or determination." Even a significant alteration to the original judgment may be accomplished through a judgment nunc pro tunc so long as it merely corrects a clerical error. If "the signed judgment inaccurately reflects the true decision of the court," then "the error is clerical and may be corrected."

"Indeed, clerical errors frequently concern matters of substance; they are simply errors "made in *entering* final judgment" and not "in *rendering* a final judgment."[13]

While a motion to modify seeking a non-substantive change in the judgment does not extend deadlines, if the modification sought is the correction of a non-substantive clerical error, the motion can be granted after plenary power with a *nunc pro tunc* correction order. If the court acts within its period of plenary jurisdiction, there is no reason to employ a *nunc pro tunc* correction and, even if a motion is so characterized, an appellate court will treat the new judgment as a new judgment after a motion to modify.[14]

Although there is no specific time limit on *nunc pro tunc* corrections, a concept of laches has been applied to prevent corrections when rights of strangers to the litigation have intervened following the judgment.[15] The *nunc pro tunc* correction may be made while the case is pending on appeal[16] but not after an appellate court has remanded for new trial.[17] Outside these special cases, a court's authority to correct clerical errors is not limited in time.

The timetables on a *nunc pro tunc* order begin to run on the day the order is signed, and a party may appeal the order. However, the issues on appeal are limited to those newly raised in the *nunc pro tunc* order (such as whether the order is correcting a judicial rather than a clerical mistake, or whether the order actually reflects the order rendered at the time of the original judgment). Rule 306a.6 precludes complaints that would be applicable to the original judgment.

---

11 *See* Rule 316 and Rule 329b(b) and (g).

12 Tex. Dept. of Transp. v. A.P.I. Pipe and Supply, LLC, 397 S.W.3d 162, 167 (Tex. 2013).

13 *Id.* at 171 (LEHRMANN, J., concurring).

14 *See* Mathes v. Kelton, 569 S.W.2d 876 (Tex. 1978).

15 *See* King v. Cash, 174 S.W.2d 503 (Tex. Civ. App.—Eastland 1943).

16 Williams v. Pitts, 251 S.W.2d 148 (Tex. 1952).

17 King v. Cash, 174 S.W.2d 503 (Tex. Civ. App.—Eastland 1943).

Whether judgment errors are clerical or judicial is a question of law,[18] and it should not be surprising that there has been a good deal of litigation about which is which.[19] Depending on the state of the record, it can be difficult for an appellate court to discern which of two conflicting judgments accurately reflects the trial court's true decision. Clerical errors embrace such omissions or misstatements as those regarding names of parties, amounts in the judgment, the date from which interest is to be calculated, miscalculations of interest and erroneous property descriptions.[20] By contrast, a judicial error is made when the court has considered a legal issue and made a decision on it.[21] Such errors as an unsupported award of prejudgment interest[22] or a finding that the defendant failed to appear (recited in a default judgment "corrected" three years later)[23] have been pronounced "judicial" and outside the reach of a *nunc pro tunc* correction. Also, provisions inadvertently included in the judgment due to an attorney's mistake, have been held to be judicial errors, and not correctable through a *nunc pro tunc* order.[24]

11. *Various perturbations*. The general rules are set out above. Of course, they have been applied in ways that you might not anticipate, and that you are not to be expected to memorize because the issues are amazingly confusing. But because you might well face these situations in practice, here are at least some of them.

a. What if a losing party files a motion for new trial, but then *withdraws* the motion? Are the deadlines extended or not? The Supreme Court has held that the deadlines are no longer extended. Plenary power expires 30 days after the judgment was signed.[25]

b. What if a party files a motion for new trial, then the trial court signs a new judgment, but the party does not file another motion for new trial attacking the second judgment? Does the motion assailing the first judgment extend plenary power and appellate deadlines for the subsequent judgment? It is considered a prematurely filed motion for new trial with respect to the subsequent judgment? The Supreme Court has held that if that motion for new trial was granted, it does not affect the subsequent judgment—the granting of the motion for new trial "wiped the slate clean" and it is "as though the first [judgment] never existed."[26] Therefore, the granted motion becomes moot and does not preserve error as to the subsequent judgment. But the court has signaled that if the motion is *denied*, either expressly or by operation of law, the motion would be considered a "premature motion" if grounds

---

[18] *See* Finlay v. Jones, 435 S.W.2d 136, 138 (Tex. 1968).

[19] *See* cases collected at 4 MCDONALD, TEXAS CIVIL PRACTICE, § 27:20 at p. 40.

[20] *See* 4 MCDONALD § 27:20 at p. 40.

[21] *See* Comet Aluminum Co. v. Dibrell, 450 S.W.2d 56, 59 (Tex. 1970).

[22] *See Comet Aluminum*, above.

[23] *See* Lone Star Cement Corp. v. Fair, 467 S.W.2d 402, 406 (Tex. 1971).

[24] In re Daredia, 317 S.W.3d 247 (Tex. 2010). The judgment may be "rendered" when the trial judge announces its judgment orally, on the record in open court, which can occur before the form of judgment is signed.

[25] Rogers v. Clinton, 794 S.W.2d 9 (Tex. 1990).

[26] Wilkins v. Methodist Health Care System, 160 S.W.3d 559, 563 (Tex. 2005) (where trial court granted defendant's motion for summary judgment, then granted plaintiff's motion for new trial, then reconsidered the summary judgment motion with additional evidence and argument from plaintiff, and again granted the motion for summary judgment in defendant's favor).

set out in that judgment apply to the new judgment.[27] The Supreme Court also has held that a motion for new trial filed following the signing of the original judgment continues to be effective as to an amended judgment to preserve error insofar as the motion continues to apply to the new judgment's terms.[28] What is the safest thing to do? File another motion for new trial after the subsequent judgment is signed—you are sure to have preserved error and extended the deadlines.

c. What if a trial judge modifies a judgment, then withdraws the modification in favor of the terms of the original judgment? The Supreme Court has held that the judgment is modified "twice rather than never."[29] Therefore, the deadlines run from the last judgment signed.

d. How do things get so complicated? In one case, the trial judge rendered judgment on a jury verdict, then granted a new trial. A new judge took the bench after an election, and that judge "ungranted" the motion for new trial and reinstated judgment on the jury verdict. But later, on motion to reconsider, the new judge reinstated the new trial order.[30] While mandamus was pending, yet another judge took the bench.[31] Noting that only in Texas does one "ungrant" a motion rather than "vacate" or "reconsider" an order, the Supreme Court held that "as with any other order, a trial judge should be able to reconsider a new trial order as long as the case is still pending.[32]

F. Motions Following Bench Trials

Read Rules 262, 296-299a.

The litigant who loses a nonjury trial faces significant hurdles on appeal. If the trial judge does not make express findings of fact and conclusions of law to lay out the legal and factual basis for the judgment, the appellate court will presume that the court found every fact in a way that will support the judgment. In effect, the appellate court will draft whatever findings are necessary to affirm the judgment, provided those findings are supported by the evidence. The Supreme Court summarized the principles in *Worford v. Stamper*:[1]

> In this case, no findings of fact or conclusions of law were requested or filed. It is therefore implied that the trial court made all the findings necessary to support its judgment. In determining whether some evidence supports the judgment and the implied findings of

---

[27] *See* Wilkins, 160 S.W.3d at 563 (discussing Fredonia State Bank v. General Am. Life Ins. Co., 881 S.W.2d 279 (Tex. 1994) and split between courts of appeals discussed there).

[28] *See* Fredonia State Bank v. Great American Life Ins. Co., 881 S.W.2d 279 (Tex. 1994).

[29] Arkoma Basin Exploration Co. v. FMF Assocs. 1990-A Ltd., 249 S.W.3d 380, 391 (Tex. 2008).

[30] In re Baylor Medical Center, 280 S.W.3d 277 (Tex. 2008).

[31] *Id.* at 229.

[32] *Id.* at 228. *See also* Hidalgo v. Hidalgo, 310 S.W.3d 887 (Tex. 2010) (allowing wife to raise substantive agreements regarding third order ungranting new trial order after *Baylor* decision "unvoided" it.

[1] Worford v. Stamper, 801 S.W.2d 108, 109 (Tex. 1990).

fact, "it is proper to consider only that evidence most favorable to the issue and to disregard entirely that which is opposed to it or contradictory in its nature." The judgment must be affirmed if it can be upheld on any legal theory that finds support in the evidence.

To lower the appellate hurdles, the losing litigant should ask for findings of fact and conclusions of law. If the court makes findings, in all likelihood it will find every fact to support its judgment. But without express findings and conclusions, adverse implied findings are a certainty. The next three cases deal with how detailed the findings must be.

ALVAREZ
v.
ESPINOZA
844 S.W.2d 238
(Tex. App.—San Antonio 1992, writ dism'd w.o.j.)

PER CURIAM.

Pedro Espinoza defeated Adolfo Alvarez by twenty-three votes in the Democratic primary run-off election for Frio County Commissioners Court, Precinct Three. Alvarez filed an election contest alleging that the election officials improperly allowed unqualified voters to vote, improperly rejected the ballots of qualified voters, and violated election code procedures. The trial court found that ten unqualified voters voted in the election, but that Espinoza still had a thirteen-vote margin and that the ten improper votes did not change the outcome. * * *

* * *

Initially Alvarez contends that the trial court's findings of fact and conclusions of law are "confusing, contradictory, and incomplete," which makes it impossible for him to present his appeal properly. Alvarez specified his complaints concerning each of the findings and conclusions and asked the court to make amended or additional findings. But he did not draft and submit proposed additional findings and conclusions.

After the court files original findings of fact and conclusions of law, any party may file "a request for *specified* additional or amended findings or conclusions." TEX. R. CIV. P. 298 (emphasis added). As the supreme court held long ago, "Rule 298 contemplates that the request for further additional or amended findings . . . shall specify the further additional or amended findings that the party making the request desires the trial court to make and file." A bare request is not sufficient; proposed findings must be submitted.

Alvarez also complains that the findings are too general, but we conclude they are specific enough. They resolve the controlling issues and reveal the basis for the court's judgment. * * *

***Rafferty v. Finstad*, 903 S.W.2d 374 (Tex. App.—Houston [1 Dist.] 1995, writ denied):**

TEX. R. CIV. P. 298 requires additional findings of fact and conclusions of law only if they relate to "ultimate or controlling issues." *Associated Tel. Directory Publishers v. Five D's Publishing Co.,* 849 S.W.2d 894, 901 (Tex. App.—Austin 1993, no writ); *Dura-Stilts Co. v. Zachry,* 697 S.W.2d 658, 661 (Tex. App.—Houston [1st Dist.] 1985, writ ref'd n.r.e.). The trial court is not required to make findings that are unsupported in the record, that relate merely to evidentiary matters, or that are contrary to other previous findings. *Simmons v. Compania Financiera Libano,* S.A., 830 S.W.2d 789, 791-92 (Tex. App.—Houston [1st Dist.] 1992, writ denied); *Dura-Stilts,* 697 S.W.2d at 661; *Wallace v. Wallace,* 623 S.W.2d 723, 724 (Tex. App.—Houston [1st Dist.] 1981, writ dism'd w.o.j.). If a party makes a request for additional findings and conclusions and the trial court fails to make such findings, its failure is tantamount to a refusal. *Stretcher v. Gregg,* 542 S.W.2d 954, 958 (Tex. Civ. App.—Texarkana 1976, no writ).

***Gutierrez v. Gutierrez*, 791 S.W.2d 659 (Tex. App.—San Antonio 1990, no writ):**

In this divorce case, the husband complained on appeal about the trial court's division of the community property. To bolster his attack on the trial court's property division, the husband sought specific findings of fact stating the different values that the court had placed on particular items of property. The court of appeals agreed with the trial court that he was not entitled to such specific findings of fact:

> In his supplemental request for findings of fact, Robert asked the court to assign a specific value to each item of personal property awarded to Patsy, which the court failed to do. We hold that the court was not required to make the specific findings. We are not aware of any authority that courts must place a value on every item of personalty in the community estate, and we decline to originate such a rule. Upon proper request, trial courts must make findings only on controlling or ultimate issues, not evidentiary ones. Courts have considerable discretion in determining where to draw the line between detail and generality in their findings of fact, and we find no abuse of that discretion here. Findings of fact are analogous to jury questions, which are submitted in broad form. *See* TEX. R. CIV. P. 277. It would be strange indeed to require judges to make findings in minute detail while requiring jury questions to be framed broadly.

Notes & Questions

1. *Deemed finding rules.* Rule 299 for bench trials is the counterpart of 279 (the "deemed finding" rule), which applies to jury trials. It is very similar but provides no role for objections. The judge's omissions are attacked only by requests for findings of fact. A judge's express finding in a bench trial is simply a finding of fact by the primary fact-finder and not, as in a jury trial, a finding by the judge to fill a gap in the questions submitted to the jury. The role of requests is the same in both rules. The judge's refusal to make a finding of fact (like a refusal to submit a requested question to the jury) will prevent a deemed finding on that issue. Here, however—unlike a jury—the

judge/fact-finder will likely still be on the job. Consequently, one case seems to say that the appropriate action by the appeals court is to stay the appeal and send the unanswered question back to the judge for a finding.[1]

2. *The sequence and the "reminder."* Requests for Findings of Fact and Conclusions of Law are due within 20 days of the signing of the judgment.[2] The judge then has 20 days after the request in which to act, but, if he does not, the requesting attorney must prod the judge within 30 days after filing the original request (10 days after the judge's deadline has passed) by giving notice that the findings and conclusions are past due.[3] The reminder notice extends the judge's deadline to 40 days after the original request.[4] If the attorney fails to send the reminder, any complaint of the judge's failure to find is waived.[5] If, however, the judge is properly reminded and fails thereafter to meet the new deadline, the judge's failure is presumed harmful.[6] And if the judge who tried the case leaves office within the prescribed 40 days available to file the findings and conclusions, but before filing them, that judge must file the findings. The newly elected judge who has since taken office has no authority to do so.[7]

***Cherne Industries, Inc. v. Magallanes*, 763 S.W.2d 768 (Tex. 1989):**

[Plaintiffs (a mother and her minor son) settled a wrongful death case against defendant Cherne for a specified sum of money. Because one plaintiff's law firm represented both the mother and the minor child, the firm was not able to represent both of these clients at the settlement hearing because they had conflicting interests in how to divide the settlement money. The trial court appointed attorney Magallanes as attorney *ad litem* to represent the minor child's interests at settlement. In these situations (i.e. settlement with a minor), trial courts customarily assesses the *ad litem*'s attorney fees against the defendant as part of the court costs. Cherne disagreed with the amount of the fees it was ordered to pay Magallanes, and it appealed. Cherne submitted proposed findings of fact and conclusions of law to the judge, but the court did not sign them.]

> Finally, we must determine if the trial court's error in failing to file findings and conclusions was harmful. TEX. R. APP. P. 184(b) [now T.R.A.P. 61.1 and 61.2]. Because the trial court's duty to file findings and conclusions is mandatory, the failure to respond when all requests have been properly made is presumed harmful, unless 'the record before appellate court affirmatively shows that the complaining party has suffered no injury.'

---

1 *See* Chapa v. Reilly, 733 S.W.2d 236 (Tex. App.—Corpus Christi 1986, writ ref'd n.r.e.). *See also* the *Cherne* case following. There is disagreement on this. One view is that the gap cannot be filled under these circumstances (the same as in a jury trial).

2 Rule 296.

3 Rule 297.

4 Rule 297.

5 *See* Employers' Mut. Cas. Co. v. Walker, 811 S.W.2d 270, 271 (Tex. App.—Houston [14th Dist.] 1991, writ denied).

6 *See* Los Fresnos v. Gonzales, 830 S.W.2d 627 (Tex. App.—Corpus Christi 1992, no writ).

7 Ad Villarai, LLC v. Pak, 519 S.W.3d 132 (Tex. 2017).

In this case, we cannot say that the record affirmatively discloses no injury. At the hearing to approve the settlement, Magallanes testified that he normally charged $60 an hour for research time, $75 an hour for out of court time, and $90 an hour for court time, and that those charges were reasonable and customary, or 'a little under,' for an attorney of his experience in Cameron County. He also testified that, as of the time of the hearing, he had spent twelve to fifteen hours on the matter. We recognize that the duties of a guardian ad litem extend beyond the time a settlement is approved, and that hours expended and normal hourly rates are only two of several factors to be considered in awarding fees to an attorney. We also recognize that the determination of guardian ad litem fees rests within the sound discretion of the trial court. Nevertheless, we cannot say that the award of $15,000.00 to the guardian ad litem in this case was so clearly supported by the undisputed evidence that the trial judge could not, as a matter of law, have abused his discretion in making that award.

Because the trial judge continues to serve on the district court, we believe the error in this case is remediable. We therefore reverse the judgment of the court of appeals and remand to that court, with instructions for it to direct the trial court to correct its error pursuant to TEX. R. APP. P. 81(a) [now T.R.A.P. 44.4].

Notes & Questions

1. *Directed verdict or motion for judgment*. Suppose the trial is to a judge as fact-finder. The P puts on his case and rests. The D moves for judgment, urging correctly that there is no evidence to support vital elements of P's claim. Is D entitled to an immediate judgment? Yes. The motion for judgment at this point serves the same function as a motion for directed verdict in a jury trial. Take a harder case: suppose that there is *some* evidence supporting all elements of P's case—say the evidence is in zone 3—but—even without hearing from D—the judge is unpersuaded by it. Must the judge go ahead and hear the D's case before making fact-findings? At one time that was the required course. Under the infamous "*Lorino* rule,"[1] the judge committed reversible error by deciding the case before sitting through D's case, the procedure being identical to that for a motion for directed verdict. In 1988, the supreme court decided *Qantel Business Systems, Inc. v. Custom Control Co.*,[2] in which it abandoned the *Lorino* rule and held that the trial judge may grant judgment in such circumstances without hearing the rest of the case.

2. *Motion for new trial*. A motion for new trial is not required in a non-jury case except to present matters not already in the record.[3] A complaint regarding the legal or factual sufficiency of a finding may be made for the first time on appeal.[4]

3. *Effect of findings*. On appeal, findings of fact have the same status as a jury's verdict and will be reviewed on the same legal sufficiency and factual sufficiency standards.[5]

---

1 From Lorino v. Crawford Packing Co., 169 S.W.2d 235 (Tex. Civ. App.—Galveston), *aff'd* 175 S.W.2d 410 (1943).

2 761 S.W.2d 302 (Tex. 1988).

3 Owen v. Porter, 796 S.W.2d 265, 268 (Tex. App.—San Antonio 1990, no writ).

4 TRAP 33.1(d).

5 *See* Anderson v. City of Seven Points, 806 S.W.2d 791 (Tex. 1991); Alamo Bank of Texas v. Palacios, 804 S.W.2d 291, 295 (Tex. App.—Corpus Christi 1991, no writ); *and* Powers and Ratliff, 65 TEX. L. REV. 564 (1991).

4. *Effect of failure to request findings.* If the court makes no findings of fact (and does not refuse to make any), the appellate court will affirm the judgment if it can be upheld on any legal theory that has support in the evidence.[6] The effect of findings of fact is to convert a judgment which is, in effect, based on a general verdict (D wins or P wins) into a judgment based on a special verdict (specifics given in the findings of fact). Suppose you represent P. The judge has signed a judgment in your favor and you are happy with it. Will you request findings of fact and conclusions of law? Will your opponent?

5. *Request for findings and extending deadlines.* A request for findings and conclusions does not extend the court's period of plenary power. Not all requests for findings and conclusions extend appellate deadlines. TRAP 26.1(a)(4) extends appellate deadlines if the requested findings and conclusions "are required by the Rules of Civil Procedure or, if not required, could properly be considered by the appellate court." What does that mean? In *IKB*, which follows, the Supreme Court interpreted former TRAP 41, the predecessor of the current rule, on which the current rule is based.[7]

In re GILLESPIE
124 S.W.3d 699
(Tex. App.—Houston [14th Dist.] 2004)

GUZMAN, JUSTICE.

In this original proceeding, relator, Clyde E. Gillespie, seeks a writ of mandamus ordering the respondent, the Honorable Gladys B. Burwell, to vacate her November 27, 2002 order setting aside a divorce decree. Relator challenges the trial court's plenary power to set aside the decree. Real parties in interest, Lora E. Gillespie and intervenor, Jerry Hayes, filed a motion to dismiss this mandamus proceeding. We deny the writ of mandamus and the motion to dismiss.

BACKGROUND

After a trial on the merits, a final divorce decree was entered on September 20, 2002, dissolving the marriage of relator and Lora Gillespie. Intervenor Hayes filed a timely request for findings of fact and conclusions of law, and on October 22, 2002, the trial court signed its findings and conclusions. Hayes then filed a "Request for Amended and/or Additional Findings of Fact and Conclusions of Law." A conference regarding this request was conducted on November 6, 2002. On that date, the trial judge ordered a judgment nunc pro tunc be prepared and set for entry on November 22, 2002.

The record contains a subsequent letter addressed to Judge Burwell, from relator's counsel, advising the judge that the perceived error in the original judgment was not a clerical error, but a judicial error; the trial court's plenary power expired thirty days after the signing of the original

---

6 Point Lookout West, Inc. v. Whorton, 742 S.W.2d 277, 279 (Tex. 1987).

7 The language of the new rule is different from that of the former rule. But the change adopts the standard articulated in *IKB*. Therefore, *IKB* is still valid. *See* John Hill Cayce, Jr., et al., *Civil Appeals in Texas: Practicing Under the New Rules of Appellate Procedure*, 49 BAYLOR L. REV. 867, 878 (1997). *See also* Gene Duke Builders v. Abilene Housing Authority, 2004 WL 422492 (Tex. 2004) (holding request after grant of plea to jurisdiction extended deadlines).

judgment, on October 21, 2002; and plenary power had not been extended by the request for findings of fact and conclusions of law filed by Hayes. On November 27, 2002, the trial court, on its own motion, signed an order setting aside the previous judgment and granting a new trial.

Relator filed a petition for writ of mandamus and a motion for temporary relief in this court. On March 10, 2003, we issued an order, staying all proceedings in the trial court pending our disposition of this mandamus proceeding.

I. PLENARY POWER

Relator claims the November 27, 2002 order, setting aside the original judgment and granting a new trial, is void because the trial court acted outside its plenary power. Contrarily, relying upon our decision in *Electronic Power Design, Inc. v. R.A. Hanson Co.,* 821 S.W.2d 170 (Tex. App.—Houston [14th Dist.] 1991, no writ), real parties in interest claim the trial court's plenary power was extended by the request for findings of fact and conclusions of law.

In *Electronic Power,* this court held:

> Texas Rule of Civil Procedure 329b(e) extends the trial court's plenary power over the judgment when a motion for new trial or to vacate, modify, correct, or reform the judgment is filed. We see no reason why, under the current rules, the extension of the trial court's plenary power over its judgment should not also be triggered by the filing of a request for findings of fact and conclusions of law. We hold that the trial court had plenary power over its judgment until 90 days after the signing of the judgment.

Real parties argue the holding in *Electronic Power* is correct because if plenary power were not extended, the trial court may be prevented from rendering the properly requested findings of fact and conclusions of law. Thus, we revisit our holding in *Electronic Power.*

Plenary power refers to that period of time in which a trial court may vacate its judgment by granting a new trial, or in which it may modify or correct its judgment.

By its plain language, Rule 329b sets forth specifically the types of post-judgment action that will extend a trial court's plenary power:

> (d) The trial court, regardless of whether an appeal has been perfected, has plenary power to grant a new trial or to vacate, modify, correct, or reform the judgment within thirty days after the judgment is signed.
>
> (e) If a motion for new trial is timely filed by any party, the trial court, regardless of whether an appeal has been perfected, has plenary power to grant a new trial or to vacate, modify, correct, or reform the judgment until thirty days after all such timely-filed motions are overruled, either by a written and signed order or by operation of law, whichever occurs first.
>
> (g) A motion to modify, correct, or reform a judgment (as distinguished from motion to correct the record of a judgment under Rule 316), if filed, shall be filed and determined within the time prescribed by this rule for a motion for new trial and shall extend the trial court's plenary power and the time for perfecting an appeal in the same manner as a motion for new trial.

TEX.R. CIV. P. 329b(d)-(e).

In *Lane Bank Equipment Co. v. Smith Southern Equipment, Inc.,* the Texas Supreme Court addressed the types of post-judgment motions extending a trial court's plenary power, and stated in no uncertain terms that "any change to a judgment made by the trial court while it retains plenary jurisdiction will restart the appellate timetable under Rule 329b(h), but *only a motion seeking a substantive change* will extend the appellate deadlines and the court's plenary power under Rule 329b(g)." 10 S.W.3d 308, 313 (Tex. 2000) (citations omitted) (emphasis added).

Applying *Lane,* the First Court of Appeals stated a trial court's plenary power is extended only by the filing of appropriate post-judgment motions, such as, motions for new trial or motions to modify, correct, or reform the judgment under rule 329b(g). Specifically, the First Court of Appeals noted:

> [a]lthough any change in the trial court's judgment will restart the appellate-timetable and plenary-power rules under 329b(h), a rule 329b motion for new trial or to modify, correct, or reform the judgment, or a motion that has the same effect, is the only means by which a party may extend the . . . trial court's plenary power over its judgment.

A request for findings of fact and conclusions of law does not seek a substantive change in the judgment. This was recognized in *Pursley v. Ussery,* 982 S.W.2d 596, 599 (Tex. App.—San Antonio 1998, pet. denied), in which the San Antonio Court of Appeals held that a request for findings and conclusions does *not* extend the trial court's plenary power. In reaching this conclusion, the *Pursley* court first noted that a request for findings and conclusions is not included in Rule 329b as one of the post-judgment motions that extends a trial court's plenary power. The court also observed that, because Rule 329b does not mention a request for findings and conclusions, many prominent commentators have concluded that a trial court's plenary power is not extended by requests for findings of fact and conclusions of law.

Findings of fact and conclusions of law, if made by the trial court, do not vacate or change the judgment, they merely explain the reasons for the judgment. Thus, even if a trial court's plenary power has expired, the trial court is not prevented from entering properly requested findings and conclusions.

Also, we note that although Texas Rule of Appellate Procedure 26.1 includes a timely filed request for findings and conclusions as extending the deadline for filing a notice of appeal, this does not mean that the request also extends a trial court's plenary power. *Cf. Pursley,* 982 S.W.2d at 599 n. 2 (distinguishing a case based upon its discussion of extending the appellate timetable as opposed to extending plenary power).

Guided by these authorities and the plain language of Rule 329b, we conclude that a trial court's plenary power is extended by the timely filing of (1) a motion for new trial; (2) motion to vacate, modify, or correct the judgment; or (3) any motion seeking a substantive change in the court's judgment. This does not include, however, a request for findings of fact and conclusions of law.

Further, we find the holding in *Electronic Power* conflicts with the above-quoted sections of Rule 329b to the extent it concludes a request for findings of fact and conclusions of law extends the trial court's plenary power. Moreover, there is no indication in the text of Rule 329b to suggest that a request for findings and conclusions operates to extend the trial court's plenary jurisdiction. Because plenary power is the time within which a trial court may change or withdraw its judgment, there is no reason to extend this period when a motion challenging the judgment has not been filed and instead, only a request for an explanation of the bases for the court's judgment is made. Finding a portion of *Electronic Power* wrongly decided, the en banc court overrules it to the extent it holds that a request for findings of fact and conclusions of law extends the trial court's plenary power.

* * *

IKB INDUSTRIES (NIGERIA) LTD
v.
PRO-LINE CORP.

938 S.W.2d 440
(Tex. 1997)

HECHT, JUSTICE.

Here, the sole question is whether requesting findings of fact and conclusions of law following dismissal of a case as a sanction for discovery abuse extends the time for perfecting appeal under Rule 41(a)(1) of the Texas Rules of Appellate Procedure. The court of appeals answered no. Under the circumstances of this case, as we explain, we disagree.

IKB Industries (Nigeria) Limited sued Pro-Line Corporation. Pro-Line moved to dismiss IKB's action as a sanction for discovery abuse. *See* TEX. R. CIV. P. 215. After a hearing, for which there is no statement of facts, the district court granted the motion, struck IKB's pleadings, and dismissed the action with prejudice. The court's judgment recites that the court considered "the Court's file--including all pleadings, affidavits, and deposition excerpts filed with the Court (and of which the Court takes judicial notice) *and .. . the testimony* and argument *of counsel.*" (Emphasis added.) The judgment contains seven pages of findings that the court made, as the judgment recites, "from the evidence before it."

Notwithstanding these findings, IKB filed a request for findings of fact and conclusions of law, referencing Rule 296 of the Texas Rules of Civil Procedure. Rule 296 states in part:

> In any case tried in the district or county court without a jury, any party may request the court to state in writing its findings of fact and conclusions of law. Such request . . . shall be filed within twenty days after judgment is signed. . . .

IKB's request was filed eight days after the dismissal order was signed. The district court did not respond to IKB's request.

A timely filed request for findings of fact and conclusions of law extends the deadline for perfecting appeal from 30 to 90 days after the judgment is signed "in a case tried without a jury." TEX. R. APP. P. 41(a)(1). Since IKB filed a cost bond 49 days after the dismissal order was signed, IKB perfected appeal only if its request for findings and conclusions extended the deadline for doing so from 30 to 90 days—that is, only if the case was "tried without a jury" within the meaning of Rule 41(a)(1).

Not every case finally adjudicated without a jury trial is "a case tried without a jury" within the meaning of Rule 41(a)(1). For instance, we held in *Linwood v. NCNB Texas,* 885 S.W.2d 102, 103 (Tex. 1994), that a request for findings in a case concluded by summary judgment does not extend appellate deadlines. . . .

. . . *Linwood* takes a functional approach to Rule 41(a)(1). It holds, not that a summary judgment is not a trial within the meaning of the rule, but that "findings of fact and conclusions of law have no place in a summary judgment proceeding". The reason findings and conclusions "have no place" in a summary judgment proceeding is that for summary judgment to be rendered, there cannot be a "genuine issue as to any material fact", TEX. R. CIV. P. 166a(c), and the legal grounds are limited to those stated in the motion and response. In other words, if summary judgment is proper, there are no facts to find, and the legal conclusions have already been stated in the motion and response. The trial court should not make, and an appellate court cannot consider, findings of fact in connection with a summary judgment. Because a request for findings and conclusions following summary judgment can have no purpose, should not be filed, and if filed, should be ignored by the trial court, such a request should not extend appellate deadlines. *Linwood* rejects a broad construction of Rule 41(a)(1) that would cause the filing of a request for findings and conclusions to extend the time for perfecting appeal in every case adjudicated without a jury.

. . . A party is not entitled to findings of fact and conclusions of law following summary judgment, *Linwood,* 885 S.W.2d at 103, judgment non obstante veredicto, *Fancher v. Cadwell,* 159 Tex. 8, 314 S.W.2d 820, 822 (1958), *or judgment after directed verdict, Ditto v. Ditto Investment Co.,,* 158 Tex. 104, 309 S.W.2d 219, 220 (1958), again, not because these adjudications are in no sense trials. Indeed, judgment non obstante veredicto is rendered after a full trial and verdict. Rather, a party is not entitled to findings and conclusions in such instances because judgment must be rendered as a matter of law. . . .

* * *

To summarize: A request for findings of fact and conclusions of law does not extend the time for perfecting appeal of a judgment rendered as a matter of law, where findings and conclusions can have no purpose and should not be requested, made, or considered on appeal. Examples are summary judgment, judgment after directed verdict, judgment non obstante veredicto, default judgment awarding liquidated damages, dismissal for want of prosecution without an evidentiary hearing, dismissal for want of jurisdiction without an evidentiary hearing, dismissal based on the pleadings or special exceptions, and any judgment rendered without an evidentiary hearing. A timely filed request for findings of fact and conclusions of law extends the time for perfecting appeal when findings and conclusions are required by Rule 296, or when they are not required by Rule 296 but are not without purpose—that is, they could properly be considered by the appellate court. Examples are judgment after a conventional trial before the court, default judgment on a claim for unliquidated damages, judgment rendered as sanctions, and any judgment based in any part on an evidentiary hearing.

In the present case, although sanctions were imposed largely on the basis of discovery requests and responses that are a matter of record and indisputable, there appears to be a factual dispute over IKB's explanations for its alleged discovery abuse. The trial court's extensive findings themselves indicate a resolution of disputed factual matters apart from the filings included in the transcript. Applying the rule we have adopted, we hold that IKB's request for findings and conclusions extended the deadline for perfecting appeal. Thus, the court of appeals erred in dismissing the appeal.

* * *

CHAPTER 17. APPEALS

A. Court of Appeals Jurisdiction

Read Rules 301, 329b; Tex. Govt. Code §§ 22.220; CPRC §§ 51.012, 51.014

As discussed in the chapter on judgments, the courts of appeals generally have jurisdiction only over final judgments (judgments that dispose of all parties and all claims, and on which the trial court has lost its plenary power). CPRC 51.012. A court of appeals has no appellate jurisdiction if the judgment is not final, unless a statute (CPRC 51.014, plus some others) provides for interlocutory review. Remember that a trial court's plenary power expires 30 days after a final judgment is signed, or if a timely post-judgment motion is filed, 30 days after the motion is overruled by order or by operation of law. TRCP 329b(d)&(e). A trial court does not lose power over a judgment that is not final, because the time periods do not begin to run.

VAUGHN
v.
DRENNON
324 S.W.3d 560
(Tex. 2011)

PER CURIAM.

In this dispute between neighbors, we must decide whether the trial court's judgment issued after a conventional trial on the merits was final for purposes of appeal. We conclude that it was. The Drennons' grandchildren were joined as parties due to their shared interest in the subject property, but no claims against the grandchildren were addressed at trial nor were any jury questions submitted on the grandchildren. The grandchildren were not mentioned in the trial court's judgment, and this raised finality concerns in the court of appeals. Under the *Aldridge* presumption, any judgment following a conventional trial on the merits creates a presumption that the judgment is final for purposes of appeal. *See Ne. Indep. Sch. Dist. v. Aldridge,* 400 S.W.2d 893, 897-98 (Tex. 1966). A judgment following a conventional trial on the merits need not dispose of every party and claim for the *Aldridge* presumption of finality to apply. Accordingly, we conclude that the *Aldridge* presumption applied in this case, and it was error for the court of appeals to dismiss the appeal for want of jurisdiction.

Millard and Barbara Vaughn and Paul and Mary Drennon had repeated disputes about water drainage off the Vaughns' property. The Vaughns sued the Drennons for blocking and diverting the natural flow of water off the Vaughn property with a concrete fence, also alleging trespass and intentional infliction of emotional distress. The Drennons filed a separate lawsuit against the Vaughns for intentional infliction of emotional distress, and the trial court consolidated the two cases.

The Vaughns' first amended petition added the Drennons' grandchildren, Chase Atwood and Taylor Atwood, as defendants, because the Drennons had executed a deed in favor of the Atwoods. The Drennons' attorney then filed a general denial on behalf of the Atwoods. At trial, the Drennons stipulated that there had been a deed reserving a life estate in the Drennons. The

Vaughns proceeded with their claims against the Drennons only, based on their understanding that the Drennons remained in sole possession of the property throughout the duration of the events giving rise to the suit. The Vaughns did not pursue any claims against the Atwoods at trial, and they did not request the submission of any jury questions regarding the Atwoods, nor were any given.

The jury found that the Drennons' fence and diversion of the natural flow of water caused $4,000 in damages to the Vaughns' property, and that Paul Drennon's intentional infliction of emotional distress had caused Millard Vaughn $25,000 in damages, but the jury awarded no damages for trespass. The jury also awarded each of the Drennons $25,000 for their emotional distress. The trial court, in its judgment, disregarded the jury's findings regarding the diversion of the natural flow of water, offset Millard Vaughn's and Paul Drennon's emotional distress damages, and awarded Mary Drennon $25,000. The judgment made no mention of the Atwoods.

The Vaughns appealed, and from the outset the court of appeals expressed concern about whether the trial court's judgment was final. The court requested that the Vaughns produce evidence of jurisdiction before full briefing, which they did, and the court of appeals then notified both parties in a letter that, in its opinion, the Vaughns had established jurisdiction. Nevertheless, the question of finality and jurisdiction was again raised at oral argument. The Vaughns argued in a post-submission letter that the *Aldridge* presumption applied to the trial court's judgment following a conventional trial on the merits and that, in the alternative, the court of appeals should abate the appeal to allow the trial court to clarify the judgment's finality or to issue a more definitive judgment. Instead, the court of appeals denied the request for abatement and dismissed the appeal for want of jurisdiction. 324 S.W.3d 617, 618 (Tex. App.—Tyler 2009) (mem.op.).

This is exactly the kind of delay in the appellate process that this Court has sought to avoid in continuously enforcing the *Aldridge* presumption. We have long recognized a presumption of finality for judgments that follow a conventional trial on the merits. *Moritz v. Preiss*, 121 S.W.3d 715, 718-19 (Tex. 2003); *see Lehmann v. Har-Con Corp.*, 39 S.W.3d 191, 205 (Tex. 2001) ("[W]e have tried to ensure that the right to appeal is not lost by an overly technical application of the law .... Simplicity and certainty in appellate procedure are nowhere more important than in determining the time for perfecting appeal."). As a general rule, "an appeal may be taken only from a final judgment." But a trial court's judgment need not expressly dispose of all issues and claims in order to be final. In *Aldridge*, we held that:

> When a judgment, not intrinsically interlocutory in character, is rendered and entered in a case regularly set for a conventional trial on the merits, no order for a separate trial of issues having been entered . . . it will be presumed for appeal purposes that the Court intended to, and did, dispose of all parties legally before it and of all issues made by the pleadings between such parties.

This presumption arose out of our concern that too often the right to appeal was abridged by judgments that were drafted poorly or were unclear. Therefore, unless a trial court orders a separate trial to resolve a specific issue, there is a presumption that the trial court's judgment disposes of all claims and issues in the case. . . .

* * *

Because the trial court's judgment after a conventional trial on the merits was final for purposes of appeal, we reverse the court of appeals' judgment dismissing for want of jurisdiction and remand the case to the court of appeals to determine the merits of the Vaughns' appeal.

HOUSTON HEALTH CLUBS, INC.
v.
FIRST COURT OF APPEALS

722 S.W.2d 692
(Tex. 1987)

PER CURIAM.

The issue in this original mandamus proceeding is whether a trial court's order granting a new trial is voidable because it was signed after that court lost plenary jurisdiction over its default judgment. Whether the trial court retained jurisdiction to grant the new trial depends on whether the default judgment is interlocutory or final. In a previous mandamus proceeding, the court of appeals concluded that the default judgment was final and that the trial court's order granting new trial was voidable. In an unpublished opinion, the court of appeals directed the trial court to vacate its order of new trial. We hold that the trial court's order of new trial is not voidable because the default judgment is interlocutory. The court of appeals therefore abused its discretion in ordering the trial court to vacate its order, and we conditionally grant the writ of mandamus.

The lawsuit underlying the present mandamus is a landlord-tenant dispute. The landlord filed suit seeking possession of the leased premises, damages for waste, punitive damages and attorney's fees. The tenant, who is our present relator, failed to answer, and a default judgment was rendered for the landlord. The default judgment granted the landlord all the relief sought except for punitive damages which the judgment did not mention either expressly or by implication.

Seven months later, the tenant filed its motion for new trial in which it argued that the default judgment was interlocutory because it did not dispose of all the issues or claims in the case. The tenant also argued improper service under the Texas Long-Arm Statute, TEX. CIV. PRAC. & REM. CODE Ann. § 17.041 et seq., as well as the requisite elements for a new trial. *See Craddock v. Sunshine Buslines, Inc.*, 134 Tex. 388, 133 S.W.2d 124 (1939). The trial court agreed that the default judgment was interlocutory, agreed that service under the Long-Arm Statute was defective, and agreed that tenant was entitled to a new trial.

Landlord then filed for mandamus relief with the court of appeals. The court of appeals held that the default judgment was final, that the trial court lost jurisdiction over its judgment thirty days after its signing, TEX. R. CIV. P. 329b(d), and that the tenant's claim of defective service could only be pursued by bill of review or appealed by writ of error. We do not agree that the default judgment was final.

A final judgment is one that disposes of all parties and all issues in a lawsuit. In determining whether a judgment is final, different presumptions apply depending on whether the judgment follows a conventional trial on the merits or results from default or a motion for summary judgment. Following a conventional trial on the merits, the judgment is presumed final. This is the rule from *Northeast Independent School District v. Aldridge*, 400 S.W.2d 893, 898 (Tex. 1966):

> When a judgment . . . is rendered and entered in a case regularly set for a conventional trial on the merits, . . . it will be presumed for appeal purposes that the court intended, and did, dispose of all parties legally before it and of all issues made by the pleadings between such parties . . . . Of course, the problem can be eliminated entirely by . . . a simple statement that all relief not expressly granted is denied.

However, the *Aldridge* presumption does not apply to summary judgments or default judgments.

The default judgment in the present case did not dispose of the punitive damage issue, thus, it is not final. Because the default judgment is interlocutory, the trial court retained jurisdiction to set it aside and grant a new trial. The action of the court of appeals in directing the trial court to vacate its order of new trial is contrary . . . constitutes an abuse of discretion. Without oral argument and pursuant to TEX. R. APP. P. 122 [now T.R.A.P. 52.8], we conditionally grant the writ of mandamus.

Notes & Questions

1. *One final judgment.* Only one final judgment may be rendered in any cause.[1] And a final judgment is one that disposes of all parties and all issues in a lawsuit. After a final judgment is signed, a second judgment does not vacate the first (absent language to that effect)[2] and is a nullity. It is extremely important to know when a judgment becomes final for at least two reasons: (1) unless otherwise allowed by statute, a party can only appeal a final judgment because the court of appeals has jurisdiction only over final judgments;[3] and (2) the deadline for the expiration of the trial court's plenary power over the cause runs from the date the final judgment is signed.[4]

2. *Interlocutory judgments.* A judgment that does not dispose of all parties and all claims, "leaving something further to be determined and adjudicated by the court in disposing of the parties and their rights," is "interlocutory."[5] For example, a judgment that specifically reserves issues for later disposition is interlocutory. A default judgment rendered against one of several defendants is interlocutory. A summary judgment in favor of one of several defendants is interlocutory. These judgments do not dispose of all the claims against all parties. The court of appeals has jurisdiction over an interlocutory judgment only if a statute gives the court of appeals jurisdiction. Most interlocutory appeals are listed in CPRC § 51.014. The venue statute enacted in 1995 also allows an interlocutory appeal from an order granting or denying intervention or joinder under CPRC §15.003.

3. *Doctrine of presumed disposition.* Often it is difficult to determine whether a judgment is final or interlocutory just by looking at it. A judgment may expressly address each of the claims and parties at issue in the lawsuit and recite the disposition of each. In such a case, which is rare, after one has compared the pleadings to the judgment, one will see that the judgment expressly disposes of all claims and parties and, of course, is final. But most judgments do not expressly

---

1 *See* Rule 301.

2 Hammett v. Lee, 730 S.W.2d 350, 351 (Tex. App.—Dallas 1987, writ dism'd w.o.j.).

3 CPRC § 51.012.

4 Rule 329b(d) & (e).

5 5 MCDONALD TEXAS CIVIL PRACTICE, § 27:4 (1992).

dispose of all claims and parties. To make things easier in many cases, we have the doctrine of presumed disposition—if the judgment is rendered after a conventional trial on the merits, it is presumed that the court disposed of all issues and parties, unless the terms of the judgment make clear that it is not.[6]

4. *No presumed disposition for judgments rendered without a conventional trial on the merits.* If a default judgment is rendered, it is not presumed that the court disposed of all issues and parties. Thus, the judgment must expressly dispose of them for the judgment to be a final judgment. Similarly, if the judgment is rendered in response to a motion for summary judgment, it is not presumed that the court disposed of all issues and parties. In fact, the court can only address the issues and parties that are expressly presented in the motion for summary judgment. Therefore, all issues and parties may not be before the court and the court cannot grant a final summary judgment in response to the motion. Therefore, a summary judgment that does not expressly dispose of all issues is not a final judgment. The difficulty in determining whether these judgments are final or not has generated substantial litigation over the court of appeals' jurisdiction in particular cases.

5. *The Mother Hubbard Clause*. *Aldridge*, quoted in *Houston Health Clubs*, notes that the problem of determining whether a judgment is final or not can be eliminated by inserting in the judgment a "simple statement that all relief not expressly granted is denied." This statement, which expressly denies all claims not specifically disposed of in the judgment (and thus expressly disposes of all claims), is called a "Mother Hubbard" clause. For a while, but no longer, any judgment containing a Mother Hubbard clause was deemed final. The following case reviews some of the problems caused by improper use of Mother Hubbard clauses and gives guidance to the bench and bar as to their proper wording and use.

LEHMANN
v.
HAR-CON CORPORATION

39 S.W.3d 191
(Tex. 2001)

HECHT, JUSTICE.

In these two consolidated cases we revisit the persistent problem of determining when a judgment rendered without a conventional trial on the merits is final for purposes of appeal. We consider only cases in which one final and appealable judgment can be rendered and not cases, like some probate and receivership proceedings, in which multiple judgments final for purposes of appeal can be rendered on certain discrete issues. And we consider a judgment's finality only for purposes of appeal and not for other purposes, such as issue and claim preclusion. In *Mafrige v. Ross*,[3] we held that a summary judgment is final if it contains language purporting to dispose of all claims and parties. We gave as one example of such language what we have called a "Mother

[6] *See* Moritz v. Preiss, 121 S.W.3d 715 (Tex. 2003); John v. Marshall Health Serv., Inc., 58 S.W.3d 738, 740 (Tex. 2001); N.E. Indep. Sch. Dist. v. Aldridge, 400 S.W.2d 893, 897 (Tex. 1966).

[3] 866 S.W.2d 590 (Tex. 1993).

Hubbard" clause—a recitation that all relief not expressly granted is denied. Since then, the routine inclusion of this general statement in otherwise plainly interlocutory orders and its ambiguity in many contexts have rendered it inapt for determining finality when there has not been a conventional trial. We no longer believe that a Mother Hubbard clause in an order or in a judgment issued without a full trial can be taken to indicate finality. We therefore hold that in cases in which only one final and appealable judgment can be rendered, a judgment issued without a conventional trial is final for purposes of appeal if and only if either it actually disposes of all claims and parties then before the court, regardless of its language, or it states with unmistakable clarity that it is a final judgment as to all claims and all parties. In the two cases before us, the court of appeals concluded that judgments that do not meet this test were final and dismissed the appeals as having been untimely perfected. We reverse and remand for consideration of the merits of the appeals.

I

Lehmann v. Har-Con Corp.

Douglas and Virginia Lehmann sued the University of St. Thomas and Har-Con Corp. in the district court in Harris County to recover damages for injuries Douglas suffered in a construction accident. The University cross-claimed against Har-Con for indemnity. The Lehmanns settled with Har-Con and executed a release, agreeing in part to indemnify Har-Con against certain claims which had been or could be asserted by or through them. Virginia then filed an amended petition on behalf of her minor son against both defendants, claiming damages for loss of parental consortium because of his father's injuries. In response, Har-Con filed a counterclaim against Virginia and a third-party petition against Douglas, seeking indemnity from them under the terms of their prior release.

The Lehmanns and Har-Con all moved for summary judgment on Har-Con's indemnity claims. The district court denied the Lehmanns' motion and granted Har-Con's motion. The court's order granting Har Con's motion stated in full:

> ORDER
>
> On this *12* day of *March,* 1998 came on to be considered the Motion for Summary Judgment of HAR-CON CORPORATION. After considering the motion, the response, the summary judgment evidence and the argument of counsel, the Court is of the opinion that the motion should be in all things granted. It is therefore,
>
> ORDERED, ADJUDGED AND DECREED that the Motion for Summary Judgment by HAR-CON CORPORATION be and it is hereby GRANTED.
>
> All relief not expressly granted herein is denied.
>
> Signed this the *12* day of *March,* 1998
>
> s/________________
>
> JUDGE PRESIDING
>
> [s/ Attorneys for Har-Con Corporation]

The order did not reference Virginia's claims on behalf of her son against Har-Con, although it would appear that Har Con's summary judgment on its indemnity claim would effectively bar recovery for Virginia's son. The order also did not reference Virginia's son's claims against the University, which would not appear to be affected by Har-Con's summary judgment. The order contained a "Mother Hubbard" clause stating that "[a]ll relief not expressly granted herein is denied."

The district clerk advised the Lehmanns by postcard that an interlocutory summary judgment order had issued. The record does not reflect whether the parties received a copy of the actual order after it was signed. The Lehmanns tell us that the practice of the district clerk in Harris County is not to send copies of orders to the parties but to give parties notice by postcard when orders are signed. The notice does not completely describe the content of the order.

The Lehmanns appear to have believed that the summary judgment order was interlocutory because they moved to sever it and Har-Con's claims into a separate action, ostensibly to make the summary judgment final. The court granted the motion to sever on the twenty-fifth day after the summary judgment order was signed. Twenty-eight days after the severance order was signed, the Lehmanns noticed their appeal from the summary judgment order.

If the summary judgment was not final until the severance order was signed, then the Lehmanns' appeal was timely. But the court of appeals held that the summary judgment order was final when it issued because of the Mother Hubbard clause and that the order was not modified by the severance so as to restart the time for perfecting appeal. Because the Lehmanns did not perfect appeal within thirty days of the signing of the order as prescribed by the rules of appellate procedure,[8] the court dismissed the appeal for want of jurisdiction. In holding that the summary judgment order was final, the court followed our decision in *Mafrige,* although the court expressed concerns that the inclusion of a Mother Hubbard clause in an otherwise plainly interlocutory order should not make the order final.

We granted the Lehmanns' petition for review and consolidated it for argument and decision with *Harris v. Harbour Title Co.*

Harris v. Harbour Title Co.

Melvin and Helena Harris sued five defendants—Greenfield Financial Corp. and Larry J. Greenfield ("the Greenfield defendants"), Tim Rice and Rice Development, Inc. ("the Rice defendants"), and Harbour Title Co.—in the district court in Harris County on breach-of-contract and tort claims arising from a conveyance of real property. The court granted an interlocutory default judgment against Tim Rice on liability only, leaving for later a determination of the damages to be assessed against him. The Harrises nonsuited their claims against the Greenfield defendants. The fifth defendant, Harbour Title Co., moved for summary judgment, which the court granted with the following order:

> Order Granting Harbour Title Company's
> Motion for Summary Judgment
>
> On August 28, 1998, came on to be heard the Motion for Summary Judgment of one of the defendants, Harbour Title Company, and the Court having considered the Motion, together with any response, and the supplemental briefing filed by the parties to date is of the opinion that said Motion is with merit and should be granted. It is therefore
>
> ORDERED that defendant Harbour Title Company's Motion for Summary Judgment is in all things granted; it is further

---

[8] *See* TEX. R. APP. P. 26.1 (appellate time limits).

ORDERED that the Plaintiffs, Melvin G. Harris and Helena M. Harris take nothing as to any of their claims against Harbour Title Company.

All relief requested and not herein granted is denied.

SIGNED this 15 day of October 1998.

s/______________________

JUDGE PRESIDING

APPROVED AND ENTRY REQUESTED:

[s/ Attorneys for Harbour Title Company]

Although the order did not reference the Harrises' pending claims against the Rice defendants, it nevertheless contained a Mother Hubbard clause stating that "[a]ll relief requested and not herein granted is denied."

The Harrises assert that they received notice of the order by a postcard that described the order as an interlocutory summary judgment, but the postcard is not in our record. The record does not reflect whether the parties obtained a copy of the order after it was signed. It appears that the district clerk followed her usual procedure of notifying the parties by postcard in lieu of providing copies of the order.

The district court apparently did not consider the summary judgment order to be final; forty-six days after it was signed, the court generated a form order setting the case for trial the next year. The Harrises, too, appear to have believed the summary judgment to be interlocutory; two weeks after the order issued setting the case for trial, the Harrises obtained what was captioned a "Final Default Judgment" against the Rice defendants. Twenty-five days later the Harrises noticed their appeal from Harbour Title's summary judgment.

If Harbour Title's summary judgment did not dispose of the Harrises' claims against the Rice defendants, and the default judgment against those defendants was the final order in the case, then the Harrises' appeal was timely. But following *Mafrige,* as it had done in *Lehmann,* the court of appeals concluded that the summary judgment order was final and therefore dismissed the appeal as not having been timely perfected. We granted the Harrises' petition for review and consolidated it with *Lehmann* for argument and decision.

II

A

Though its origins are obscure and its rationale has varied over time, the general rule, with a few mostly statutory exceptions, is that an appeal may be taken only from a final judgment. A judgment is final for purposes of appeal if it disposes of all pending parties and claims in the record, except as necessary to carry out the decree. (An order that does not dispose of all pending parties and claims may also be final for purposes of appeal in some instances, such as orders that resolve certain discrete issues in some probate and receiverships cases, but we exclude those cases from consideration here. Nor do we consider when a judgment may be final for purposes other than appeal, such as claim and issue preclusion.) Because the law does not require that a final judgment be in any particular form, whether a judicial decree is a final judgment must be determined from its language and the record in the case. Since timely perfecting appeal (as well as filing certain post-judgment motions and requests) hangs on a party's making this determination correctly, certainty is crucial.

From the beginning, however, certainty in determining whether a judgment is final has proved elusive. What has vexed courts in this State and elsewhere is this: must a final judgment dispose of all parties and claims specifically, or may it do so by general language or even by inference? If a specific disposition of each party and claim is strictly required, a judgment apparently intended by the parties and the trial court to be final and appealable may not be. An appeal from such a judgment must be dismissed or at least abated, resulting in delay and a waste of the courts' and the parties' resources. More importantly, if a judgment intended to be final did not meet the strict requirements, then the case would remain open, allowing the possibility of further proceedings and appeal years later. On the other hand, if a judgment may dispose of all parties and claims by general language or inference, a party or trial court may think that a judgment is interlocutory, only to be told later by the appellate court after the time for appeal has passed that the judgment was final. A party who is uncertain whether a judgment is final must err on the side of appealing or risk losing the right to appeal.

* * *

In 1966, we [decided] *Northeast Independent School District v. Aldridge*,[35] [in which] . . . we stated the following rule

> for determining, in most instances, whether judgments in which parties and issues made by the pleadings are not disposed of in express language are, nevertheless, final for appeal purposes. When a judgment, not intrinsically interlocutory in character, is rendered and entered in a case regularly set for conventional trial on the merits, no order for a separate trial of issues having been entered . . . , it will be presumed for appeal purposes that the Court intended to, and did, dispose of all parties legally before it and of all issues made by the pleadings between such parties.

We added: "Of course, the problem [of determining whether judgments are final] can be eliminated entirely by a careful drafting of judgments to conform to the pleadings or by inclusion in judgments of a simple statement that all relief not expressly granted is denied." Inclusion of a catch-all statement—which we later denominated a "Mother Hubbard" clause—would make clear that a post-trial judgment on the merits, presumed to have disposed of all claims, did indeed do so.

B

The presumption that a judgment rendered after a conventional trial on the merits is final and appealable has proved fairly workable for nearly a century, but we have never thought that it could be applied in other circumstances, ... [W]e expressly acknowledged in *Aldridge,* that "[i]t will not be presumed that a judgment dismissing a plaintiff's suit on nonsuit, plea to the jurisdiction, plea in abatement, for want of prosecution, etc., also disposed of the issues in an independent cross-action."

We have since held that "etc." includes default judgments and summary judgments. The reason for not applying a presumption in any of these circumstances is that the ordinary expectation that supports the presumption that a judgment rendered after a conventional trial on the merits will comprehend all claims simply does not exist when some form of judgment is rendered without such a trial. On the contrary, it is quite possible, perhaps even probable these days in cases involving multiple parties and claims, that any judgment rendered prior to a full-blown trial is

35 400 S.W.2d 893 (Tex. 1966).

intended to dispose of only part of the case. Accordingly, the finality of the judgment must be determined without the benefit of any presumption.

A judgment that finally disposes of all remaining parties and claims, based on the record in the case, is final, regardless of its language. A judgment that actually disposes of every remaining issue in a case is not interlocutory merely because it recites that it is partial or refers to only some of the parties or claims. Thus, if a court has dismissed all of the claims in a case but one, an order determining the last claim is final. This is settled law in Texas, and while there have been proposals to change it by rule, proposals that are currently pending consideration by this Court's Advisory Committee, we are not inclined to depart from it here. The language of an order or judgment cannot make it interlocutory when, in fact, on the record, it is a final disposition of the case.

But the language of an order or judgment *can* make it final, even though it should have been interlocutory, if that language expressly disposes of all claims and all parties. It is not enough, of course, that the order or judgment merely use the word "final". The intent to finally dispose of the case must be unequivocally expressed in the words of the order itself. But if that intent is clear from the order, then the order is final and appealable, even though the record does not provide an adequate basis for rendition of judgment. So, for example, if a defendant moves for summary judgment on only one of four claims asserted by the plaintiff, but the trial court renders judgment that the plaintiff take nothing on all claims asserted, the judgment is final—erroneous, but final. A judgment that grants more relief than a party is entitled to is subject to reversal, but it is not, for that reason alone, interlocutory.

Texas appellate courts, this Court included, have had difficulty determining when a judgment is final on its face—by its own express terms, in other words—even though it should not have been because no sufficient basis for rendering a final judgment was presented.

* * *

In sum, our opinions have not been entirely consistent on whether the inclusion or omission of a Mother Hubbard clause does or does not indicate that a summary judgment is final for purposes of appeal. This ambivalence has resulted in considerable confusion in the courts of appeals.

III

A

Much confusion can be dispelled by holding, as we now do, that the inclusion of a Mother Hubbard clause—by which we mean the statement, "all relief not granted is denied," or essentially those words—does not indicate that a judgment rendered without a conventional trial is final for purposes of appeal. We overrule *Mafrige* to the extent it states otherwise. If there has been a full trial on the merits either to the bench or before a jury, the language indicates the court's intention to finally dispose of the entire matter, assuming that a separate or bifurcated trial is not ordered. But in an order on an interlocutory motion, such as a motion for partial summary judgment, the language is ambiguous. It may mean only that the relief requested *in the motion*—not all the relief requested by anyone in the case—and not granted by the order is denied. The clause may also have no intended meaning at all, having been inserted for no other reason than that it appears in a form book or resides on a word processor. For whatever reason, the standard Mother Hubbard clause is used in interlocutory orders so frequently that it cannot be taken as any indication of finality.

As we have already explained, an order can be a final judgment for appeal purposes even though it does not purport to be if it actually disposes of all claims still pending in the case. Thus, an order that grants a motion for partial summary judgment is final if in fact it disposes of the only remaining issue and party in the case, even if the order does not say that it is final, indeed, even if it says it is not final. (Again, we do not consider here the various kinds of cases in which there may be more than one final judgment for purposes of appeal.) Also, an order can be final and appealable when it should not be. For example, an order granting a motion for summary judgment that addressed all of the plaintiff's claims when it was filed but did not address claims timely added by amendment after the motion was filed may state unequivocally that final judgment is rendered that the plaintiff take nothing by his suit. Granting more relief than the movant is entitled to makes the order reversible, but not interlocutory.

While the present problems in determining whether an order is a final judgment should be lessened significantly by denying the standard Mother Hubbard clause of any indicia of finality in any order not issued after a conventional trial, the difficulty in determining what does make an order final and appealable remains. One solution would be stricter requirements for the form of a final judgment. Rule 58 of the Federal Rules of Civil Procedure takes this approach by requiring that to be final a judgment must "be set forth on a separate document" and be entered by the clerk on the civil docket. The separate-document requirement was added to the rule in 1963 to remove uncertainty over whether a trial judge's opinion or order constituted a final judgment. Rule 58, with its dual requirements, "enhances certainty by insisting on formality." The United States Supreme Court has insisted on strict compliance with the rule, quoting Professor Moore's observation that the rule

> "would be subject to criticism for its formalism were it not for the fact that something like this was needed to make certain when a judgment becomes effective, which has a most important bearing, inter alia, on the time for appeal and the making of post-judgment motions that go to the finality of the judgment for purposes of appeal."

The one recognized exception is a party's failure to object.

The price of certainty, however, as federal rulemakers have come to realize, is that in many cases the failure to comply with Rule 58 means that no final judgment was ever rendered, and the time for appeal remains open. A proposed amendment to Rule 58 would provide that if final judgment is not rendered on a separate document, it is deemed rendered on the sixtieth day after the clerk's entry on the civil docket. While this proposal helps ensure that every case will be closed, it also makes it more likely that a party will not be aware that the time for appeal is running—the problem the 1963 amendment to Rule 58 was meant to cure—because he does not know of the clerk's entry on the civil docket.

There may be other solutions to these dilemmas which could be implemented by changes in our own rules, and this Court's Advisory Committee is presently studying the issues. But we do not write rules by opinion. We must decide what Texas law requires for finality given the present rules.

In the past we have tried to ensure that the right to appeal is not lost by an overly technical application of the law. Fundamentally, this principle should guide in determining whether an order is final. Simplicity and certainty in appellate procedure are nowhere more important than in determining the time for perfecting appeal. From the cases we have reviewed here, we conclude that when there has not been a conventional trial on the merits, an order or judgment is not final for purposes of appeal unless it actually disposes of every pending claim and party or unless it clearly and unequivocally states that it finally disposes of all claims and all parties. An order that adjudicates only the plaintiff's claims against the defendant does not adjudicate a counterclaim, cross-claim, or third party claim, nor does an order adjudicating claims like the latter dispose of the plaintiff's claims. An order that disposes of claims by only one of multiple plaintiffs or against one of multiple defendants does not adjudicate claims by or against other parties. An order does not dispose of all claims and all parties merely because it is entitled "final", or because the word "final" appears elsewhere in the order, or even because it awards costs. Nor does an order completely dispose of a case merely because it states that it is appealable, since even interlocutory orders may sometimes be appealable. Rather, there must be some other clear indication that the trial court intended the order to completely dispose of the entire case. Language that the plaintiff take nothing by his claims in the case, or that the case is dismissed, shows finality if there are no other claims by other parties; but language that "plaintiff take nothing by his claims against X" when there is more than one defendant or other parties in the case does not indicate finality.

To determine whether an order disposes of all pending claims and parties, it may of course be necessary for the appellate court to look to the record in the case. Thus, in the example just given, if the record reveals that there is only one plaintiff and only one defendant, X, the order is final, but if the record reveals the existence of parties or claims not mentioned in the order, the order is not final. On the other hand, an order that expressly disposes of the entire case is not interlocutory merely because the record fails to show an adequate motion or other legal basis for the disposition. The record may help illumine whether an order is made final by its own language, so that an order that all parties appear to have treated as final may be final despite some vagueness in the order itself, while an order that some party should not reasonably have regarded as final may not be final despite language that might indicate otherwise.

One may argue after *Aldridge* and *Mafrige* that it is perilous to suggest any particular language that will make a judgment final and appealable because that language can then be inserted in orders intended to be interlocutory. But to leave in doubt the degree of clarity required for finality creates its own problems. The Mother Hubbard clause proved to give no indication of finality not just because it found its way into every kind of order, but because it was inherently ambiguous, as we have explained. A statement like, "This judgment finally disposes of all parties and all claims and is appealable", would leave no doubt about the court's intention. An order must be read in light of the importance of preserving a party's right to appeal. If the appellate court is uncertain about the intent of the order, it can abate the appeal to permit clarification by the trial court.[92] But if the language of the order is clear and unequivocal, it must be given effect despite any other indications that one or more parties did not intend for the judgment to be final. An express adjudication of all parties and claims in a case is not interlocutory merely because the record does not afford a legal basis for the adjudication. In those circumstances, the order must be appealed and reversed.

B

Nothing in the order in *Lehmann* indicates that it is a final judgment, and it did not dispose of all pending claims and parties. The order in *Harris* states that plaintiffs take nothing as to "one of the defendants", but that language does not suggest that all of the plaintiffs' claims were denied. As the order recites and as the record demonstrates, the defendant named in the order was not the

92 TEX. R. APP. P. 27.2.

only defendant remaining in the case. Thus, we conclude that a final and appealable judgment was not rendered in either case.

We are concerned that in neither case were the non-movants provided a copy of the court's signed order but were merely sent notice by postcard that an order had been signed. The Rules of Civil Procedure do not require clerks to send all parties copies of all orders, only final orders.[93] Nevertheless, the practice of courts in some counties is to require that a party seeking an order provide copies and addressed, postage-paid envelopes for all other parties. The Court's Advisory Committee should consider whether the rules should require that all parties be given copies of all orders signed in a case.

IV

We must respond briefly to the concurring opinion. It would hold that no "type of conclusory finality language can ever be read to grant more relief than requested by the parties." This goes too far. The legitimate problem with Mother Hubbard clauses, which we failed to appreciate in *Mafrige,* is that they are ambiguous: one cannot be sure whether the denial of all relief other than what has been expressly granted is limited to relief requested in a motion or extends to all relief requested in the litigation. But it is a long way from the now well-established fact that Mother Hubbard clauses can understandably be misread to the concurring opinion's conclusion that clear language should be given no meaning. We require certainty for finality, but we cannot say that certainty is impossible.

* * *

For the reasons we have explained, the judgments of the court of appeals in these cases are reversed, and the cases are remanded to that court for further proceedings.

In re ELIZONDO

544 S.W.3d 824

(Tex. 2018)

Opinion

PER CURIAM

This is a mandamus action. After its plenary power had expired, the trial court issued an amended order omitting a *Lehmann*-like finality phrase that it had included in its original order. *See generally Lehmann v. Har-Con Corp.*, 39 S.W.3d 191, 205-06 (Tex. 2001) (discussing finality phrases). The court of appeals directed the trial court to vacate the amended order. Here, the relator seeks a writ directing the court of appeals to vacate its opinion. For seventeen years, we have relied on *Lehmann* to mitigate the mischief and chaos that can arise when the prospect of appeal rears its head long after the parties believed a judgment to be final. We see no need to reduce *Lehmann*'s ambit, and we deny Elizondo's petition for writ of mandamus. *See* TEX. R. APP. P. 52.8(d).

Paul Elizondo, Cynthia Elizondo, and Eagle Fabricators, Inc. (collectively, Elizondo) hired M & O Homebuilders, Inc., Orlando Cuello, Maria De Jesus Gamez, and Texas Homebuilders, LLC

---

93 *See* TEX. R. CIV. P. 306a(3).

(collectively, the Builders) to build a home. A cost dispute arose. Elizondo sued the Builders, asserting breach of contract, fraud, negligence, and other claims. Elizondo placed a lien on the Builders' property on the theory that the Builders had improved it using funds intended for his home. For good measure, he also applied for a temporary injunction to prevent the Builders from selling the property until the underlying litigation ended. The trial court granted the temporary injunction.

The Builders argued the lien was invalid and they filed a motion to remove it. The Builders drafted and submitted an order titled "Order on Defendants' Summary Motion to Remove Invalid Lien." The trial court signed the order, which included at the bottom of its first and only page a finality phrase that stated: "This judgment is final, disposes of all claims and all parties, and is appealable. All relief not granted herein is denied." The order left lots of relief not granted—namely, all other relief Elizondo sought against the Builders. Thirty days elapsed, marking the end of the trial court's plenary power. *See* TEX. R. CIV. P. 329b(d). Several weeks later, Elizondo noticed the original order had disposed of his entire case. He requested an amended order, which the trial court issued, this time omitting the finality phrase.

The Builders sought mandamus relief in the court of appeals, requesting a writ directing the trial court to vacate the amended order. The Builders argued that the original order was final, and that the amended order was void since the trial court issued it after the court's plenary power had expired. *See id.* ("The trial court . . . has plenary power to grant a new trial or to vacate, modify, correct, or reform the judgment within thirty days after the judgment is signed."). Elizondo argued that the original order was not final, and that even if it was, the finality phrase constituted a clerical error the likes of which a trial court can modify even after its plenary power expires. *See id.* 329b(f) (clarifying that "the [trial] court may at any time correct a *clerical* error in the *record* of a judgment and render judgment nunc pro tunc under Rule 316" (emphasis added)).

A divided panel conditionally granted the writ in favor of the Builders. *In re M & O Homebuilders, Inc.*, 516 S.W.3d 101, 110 (Tex. App.—Houston [1st Dist.] 2017, orig. proceeding).

* * *

We conclude that the court of appeals correctly applied *Lehmann*. Elizondo had thirty days to examine the one-page order and notice that it included a finality phrase. Even if he disagreed that the order was final, he should have treated it as though it was. *See id.* at 196 ("A party who is uncertain whether a judgment is final must err on the side of appealing or risk losing the right to appeal."). Had he examined the order within the thirty-day window, he could have sought an amended order or pursued an appeal. Since Elizondo waited more than thirty days to contend that the order improperly disposed of his other claims, he has lost them. Though jarring for Elizondo, this outcome reflects *Lehmann*'s reasoning and comports with this Court's subsequent application of *Lehmann*'s finality tests.

* * *

The court of appeals was correct that *Lehmann* instructs reviewing courts to look at the record "only if the order [i]s not clear and unequivocal." *See Homebuilders*, 516 S.W.3d at 106. *Lehmann* said:

- "[W]hether a judicial decree is a final judgment must be determined from its language *and* the record in the case." *Lehmann*, 39 S.W.3d at 195 (emphasis added).
- "[W]hen there has not been a conventional trial on the merits, an order or judgment is not final for purposes of appeal unless it actually disposes of every pending claim and par-

ty *or* unless it clearly and unequivocally states that it finally disposes of all claims and all parties." Id. at 205 (emphasis added).

• "To determine *whether* an order *disposes of all pending claims and parties*, it may of course be necessary for the appellate court to look to the record in the case." *Id.* at 205-06 (emphasis added).

Elizondo relies on the first sentence. The Builders rely on the second and third, and those sentences more accurately convey *Lehmann*'s holding. While the first sentence appears in *Lehmann*'s discussion of finality's history, id. at 195, the second and third sentences appear within the body of *Lehmann*'s analysis, *Id.* at 205-06. By implication, the second and third sentences mean that a reviewing court confronting an order that includes a finality phrase cannot look at the record. Instead, it must take the order at face value. That makes sense. If it were otherwise, finality phrases would serve no purpose. That is, if both of *Lehmann*'s tests allow a reviewing court to look at the record, then a reviewing court may always look at the record. That would distill *Lehmann*'s joint tests into a simple rule: when there has not been a conventional trial on the merits, a court must look to the record to determine whether the judgment is final. That is not *Lehmann*'s rule. Had it lacked the finality phrase, the original order in this case would not have disposed of all claims and parties. However, since the original order included a finality phrase, it was clear and unequivocal.

Elizondo urges the Court to conclude that the original order is ambiguous. He contrasts the finality phrase with the original order's title, which addressed the summary removal of a lien—a proceeding he argues is not intended to be final or appealable. *See* TEX. PROP. CODE § 53.160(e). The trouble is that the title and the finality phrase admit of only one construction: the order (correctly) removes a lien and (incorrectly) disposes of Elizondo's other claims. Elizondo's ambiguity argument also errs in attempting to create an ambiguity from language that *Lehmann* describes as clear and unequivocal. *See Lehmann*, 39 S.W.3d at 206. The order may lack a basis in law, but it is not ambiguous. Rather, the order clearly purports to dispose of all claims and all parties. Error is not the same as ambiguity.

Nor did the court of appeals reach an absurd result. Elizondo contends that *Lehmann* embraced the absurdity doctrine as a limit without explicitly referring to it. Even if that were true, the absurdity doctrine does not decide this case. The reason is that the doctrine is merely a presumption against absurdity, and presumptions must yield to clear and unequivocal language. But even accepting Elizondo's view of *Lehmann*, the outcome here was not absurd. Elizondo argues that the order could not reasonably be read as final, and that it would therefore be absurd to conclude that it was final. To the contrary, the absurd thing would be to hold that a clear and unequivocal finality phrase does not trigger *Lehmann*'s directive that "[a] party who is uncertain whether a judgment is final must err on the side of appealing." Id. at 196. Elizondo also urges that the court of appeals' opinion generates absurdity by encouraging unscrupulous attorneys to sneak finality phrases into commonplace orders. The *Lehmann* rule actually helps on this front. No rule, alas, can altogether prevent unethical attorneys from acting unethically, but *Lehmann* discourages trickery by making it easier to spot.

* * *

Our conclusion that the original order was final also decides the issue whether the amended order was void as an attempt to correct judicial error. A trial court may correct clerical errors in a judgment even after its plenary power has expired. *See* TEX. R. CIV. P. 329b(d), (f). But it must correct judicial errors within thirty days of judgment or not at all. *See Escobar v. Escobar*, 711

S.W.2d 230, 231 (Tex. 1986) ("After the trial court loses its jurisdiction over a judgment, it can correct only *clerical* errors in the judgment by judgment nunc pro tunc." (emphasis added)).

The trial court's inclusion of the finality phrase in the original order constituted judicial error. It is settled that "only errors made in entering a judgment are clerical; an error in rendition is judicial." *Daredia*, 317 S.W.3d at 249 (citing *Escobar*, 711 S.W.2d at 231). Here, as in *Daredia*, the trial court signed an order that one of the parties submitted. *See Daredia*, 317 S.W.3d at 249. As such, the finality phrase was part of the judgment that the trial court rendered. *See id.* ("[P]rovisions alleged to have been inserted by mistake of the attorney nevertheless become a part of the court's judgment and therefore are judicial errors when thus rendered in writing by the court." (quoting *Dikeman v. Snell*, 490 S.W.2d 183, 185-86 (Tex.1973))). Since the amended order sought to correct judicial error after the trial court's plenary power had expired, the amended order was void.

In sum, we conclude that the original order's finality phrase was clear, unequivocal, and neither ambiguous nor absurd. The court of appeals correctly reasoned that the finality phrase rendered the record irrelevant to determining whether the order was final. Consequently, the original order was final—"erroneous, but final." *Lehmann*, 39 S.W.3d at 200. The trial court's amended order was an attempt to correct judicial error beyond the period of that court's plenary power. The amended order was therefore void. Elizondo should have raised the error while the trial court still had plenary power over the case. Alternatively, Elizondo should have appealed. Having done neither, he has lost his claims. We emphasize that parties may avoid this result by following *Lehmann*'s admonition to "err on the side of appealing or risk losing the right to appeal." *Id.* at 196.

When a trial court issues an order or judgment without a conventional trial on the merits, *Lehmann* remains the rule for identifying whether the order or judgment is final. It is a rigid rule, but that is why it is useful. Although no rule can altogether prevent parties from using finality as a sword, the requirement of clear and unequivocal language makes offensive blows easy to spot. Blunting *Lehmann*'s blade would neither cushion finality's cuts nor reduce their number. Accordingly, we deny Elizondo's petition for writ of mandamus. *See* TEX. R. APP. P. 52.8(d).

Notes & Questions

1. *How can an interlocutory or partial judgment become final?* After *Lehman*, an interlocutory, partial judgment will be final if any of the following occurs:

a. *The judgment "clearly and unequivocally" states that it disposes of all claims and parties.* Even if the judge and the parties do not intend the judgment to be final, if it contains clear and unequivocal language, such as the "*Lehman* magic language" clause, it expressly disposes of all claims and parties and is a final judgment.

b. *The other claims and parties in the lawsuit are disposed of in subsequent judgments or orders*, such as a judgment rendered after a conventional trial on the merits, or subsequent partial default judgments, summary judgments or nonsuits. Therefore, it is possible that one would have to assemble several documents to determine the final disposition of all the claims in a single suit. Attorneys are encouraged to draft one "Final Judgment" that includes all of the previous interlocutory judgments and the *Lehman* clause.

c. *The cause is severed.* If all of the claims against one defendant are resolved in an interlocutory judgment and are separated from those against other defendants and put into a separate cause, the original judgment will be final upon severance. The interlocutory judgment will become final when the severance order is signed. Again, several orders may be required to show finality. A party often will seek severance in such a situation specifically to achieve finality.

2. *When one movant's motion is granted and opponent's motion denied.* The *denial* of a summary judgment is not a final judgment and is not ordinarily appealable.[1] However, when there are cross-motions for summary judgment and the court grants one and denies the other, both orders (the grant and the denial of summary judgment) may be appealed at the same time,[2] and the appellate court will determine all questions presented and render the judgment the trial court should have rendered.[3] Where there are cross motions for motions for summary judgment, the court will deny both if there are fact questions to be decided.[4] When the party resisting summary judgment appeals, it cannot be granted its own summary judgment in the appellate court unless it has made its own motion for summary judgment.[5]

3. *The severance trap.* The trap that can catch the would-be appellant dozing and cut off appellate remedies has a counterpart which appears in connection with severance. When part of a case is severed, the case becomes two separate cases with separate cause numbers. Often the new cause number is simply the old one with an "A" added. So cause number 1445 remains 1445 and the severed cause becomes 1445-A. A judgment that is not final can be made final by a severance, which removes the unresolved claims into another cause. Suppose, for example, P sues D1 and D2. D1 defaults and P makes proof establishing P's right to a default judgment. The court grants a default judgment against D1. Is the judgment final and unappealable? No. P's claims against D2 are still pending in the same case. Suppose that P moves to sever P's claims against D1 from the rest of the case (that being P's claims against D2) and the court grants the motion, assigning a new cause number to the severed P v. D1 claims. Is P's judgment against D1 now appealable? Yes. There are no longer any unresolved claims in the new cause. Now the appeals deadlines are running in the new P v. D1 cause number and D1 must take timely action to perfect an appeal on it. The judgment becomes final and appellate deadlines begin to run from the date the order of severance is signed.[6]

Suppose that D1 revives and hires a new attorney to appeal the default judgment. The new attorney inadvertently files a motion for new trial in the *wrong cause number* (the still pending claims of P v. D2). No one points out the error and the time expires for appeal. Is D1 out of luck? Until recently, he was. This is an error easily made in such circumstances and the problem was not infrequent. It is clear nowadays that the errant counsel in such a case gets a second chance.[7] When an

---

1 *See* Valencia v. Garza, 765 S.W.2d 893 (Tex. App.—San Antonio 1989, no writ).

2 Jones v. Strauss, 745 S.W.2d 898 (Tex. 1988).

3 Dow Chemical Co. v. Bright, 89 S.W.3d 602 (Tex. 2002); City of Garland v. Dallas Morning News, 22 S.W.3d 351, 356 (Tex. 2000).

4 *See* Cove Invest., Inc. v. Manges, 602 S.W.2d 512 (Tex. 1980).

5 *See* CU Lloyds v. Feldman, 977 S.W.2d 568, 569 (Tex. 1998); Tobin v. Garcia, 316 S.W.2d 396 (Tex. 1958).

6 Park Place Hospital v. Estate of Milo, 909 S.W.2d 508 (Tex. 1995).

7 *See* Blankenship v. Robins, 878 S.W.2d 138 (Tex. 1994).

appellate step taken under the wrong cause number is a bona fide attempt to invoke the jurisdiction of the court of appeals, the appellant must have an opportunity to cure before having the case dismissed.[8]

But other severance traps have arisen. Suppose the trial judge grants D1's summary judgment, and the order says "All claims against Defendant are severed from this cause into cause number *to be assigned* on the docket of this Court *upon compliance with the District Clerk's procedure.*" (all italicized portions are handwritten). Does that order make the summary judgment final? The parties agreed that the order was conditional and not final, but the court of appeals disagreed and dismissed the appeal as untimely. The Supreme Court disagreed, holding that the handwritten condition applied to the severance, keeping it from being final until the conditions were met. The Court cautioned, however, that "this practice, though permitted, should be avoided because of the potential for confusion."[9]

4. *Finality decisions are not easy.* In *Briscoe v. Goodmark Corp.*,[10] the trial court rendered judgment and the appellant filed a notice of appeal, but pointed out in the notice of appeal that he was not sure he had a final judgment. The court of appeals agreed and dismissed the appeal for want of jurisdiction. The trial court signed a new judgment that was clearly final, and the appellant once again appealed. But this time the court of appeals held that the original judgment had been final, so the subsequent appeal was untimely. Thus, the second appeal was dismissed for want of jurisdiction. The Supreme Court reversed, noting that under the "law of the case doctrine" a court of appeals is ordinarily bound by its initial decision if there is a subsequent appeal in the same case. However, if the first decision is "clearly erroneous" the court of appeals can refuse to follow its previous decision. The Court said:

> Because application of the law of the case doctrine is discretionary, the court of appeals had the authority to re-visit its jurisdictional decision. Finding clear error in its first decision, it had the power to overturn that first decision on the second appeal. Based on the incomplete record before it at the time of the first appeal, and because it did not receive any additional briefing from the parties, the court of appeals dismissed for want of jurisdiction because it did not appear that there was a final judgment in the case. On the second appeal, armed with a complete record and more extensive briefing, as well as a positive statement from the trial court that its July 14, 2000, judgment was indeed final, the court of appeals was then able to hold that a final, appealable order had indeed been issued on July 14, 2000. Because its first decision was clearly erroneous, the law of the case doctrine did not apply and the court of appeals was not bound by its first decision.
>
> Being incorrect in that decision, however, does not mean that the court of appeals was correct in dismissing this appeal for want of jurisdiction. As incorrect as that decision was, as a matter of law, the judgment was then interlocutory. Consequently, the court should have asserted jurisdiction over Briscoe's second appeal and considered his issues on the merits. This is consistent with our oft-repeated position that a party should not lose the right to ap-

---

8 *See* Mueller v. Saravia, 826 S.W.2d 608 (Tex. 1992), *citing* San Antonio v. Rodriguez, 828 S.W.2d 417 (Tex. 1992) *and* Blankenship v. Robins, 878 S.W.2d 138 (Tex. 1994).

9 Doe v. Pilgrim Rest Baptist Church, 218 S.W.3d 81 (Tex. 2007).

10 102 S.W.3d 714 (Tex. 2003).

> peal because of an "overly technical" application of the law.[11] Here, Briscoe did everything that he possibly could to preserve his appellate rights. The court of appeals originally held that the July 2000, judgment was not final. Briscoe should not now have to lose his appellate rights because the court of appeals later found that its original decision was erroneous.

5. *Interest.* The Texas Finance Code provides for the recovery of prejudgment and postjudgment interest. Prejudgment interest and postjudgment interest both compensate a judgment creditor for her lost use of the money due her as damages. Prejudgment interest accrues from the earlier of: (1) 180 days after the date a defendant receives written notice of a claim, or (2) the date suit is filed, and until the day before the judgment.[12] Postjudgment interest accrues from the judgment date through the date the judgment is satisfied. Prejudgment interest is computed as simple interest and does not compound.[13] Postjudgment interest compounds annually.[14]

Determining the finality of the judgment is essential to making the interest calculation. As the Texas Supreme Court discussed in *Long v. Castle Texas Production Limited Partnership*[15]:

> Under the Texas Finance Code, "postjudgment interest on a money judgment of a court in this state accrues during the period beginning on the date the judgment is rendered and ending on the date the judgment is satisfied." TEX. FIN. CODE § 304.005(a). The Finance Code defines a money judgment as "a judgment for money" which "includes legal interest or contract interest, if any, that is payable to a judgment creditor under a judgment." *Id.* § 301.002(a)(12).
>
> We assess a judgment's finality differently, depending upon the context. For example, the finality test for the purpose of appeal differs from the finality test for when a court's power to alter a judgment ends or when the judgment becomes final for the purpose of claim and issue preclusion. [F]inality for the purpose of appeal bears the closest resemblance to finality for the purpose of accruing postjudgment interest. A judgment is final for the purpose of appeal "if it disposes of all pending parties and claims in the record, except as necessary to carry out the decree." A judgment that disposes of all parties and claims begins appellate deadlines and generally triggers the accrual of postjudgment interest. *See* TEX. FIN. CODE § 304.005(a). But if an appellate court reverses that final judgment and remands for further proceedings, the original, erroneous trial court judgment is no longer final because it no longer disposes of all parties and claims. Generally then, if a remand results in multiple trial court judgments, postjudgment interest accrues from the date of the *final* judgment (rather than the original, erroneous judgment).
>
> [T]he general rule is that postjudgment interest accrues from the date of the judgment, which is the final judgment in a case where the trial court issues multiple judgments. TEX. FIN. CODE § 304.005(a); TEX. R. CIV. P. 301. The exception is when the appellate court renders (or could have rendered) judgment, in which case postjudgment interest accrues from the date of trial court's original, erroneous judgment. TEX. R. APP. P. 43.3.

---

[11] Lehmann v. Har-Con Corp., 39 S.W.3d 191, 205 (Tex. 2001); Verburgt v. Dorner, 959 S.W.2d 615, 616-617 (Tex. 1997).

[12] TEX. FIN. CODE § 304.104.

[13] TEX. FIN. CODE § 304.104.

[14] TEX. FIN. CODE at § 304.006.

[15] 426 S.W.3d 73 (Tex. 2014).

But when an appeal instead results in a retrial or a remand for further proceedings where new evidence is required, postjudgment interest will accrue from the trial court's subsequent judgment.

6. *Statutory jurisdiction over interlocutory orders*. TEX. CIV. PRAC. & REM. CODE ANN. § 51.014 gives courts of appeals jurisdiction over several kinds of interlocutory orders. Common examples are: orders that (1) grant or deny a temporary injunction, (2) grant or deny a special appearance, (3) deny summary judgment to a media defendant, (4) deny summary judgment to a government official claiming immunity, and (5) certify or refuse to certify a class action.[16] If a trial court signs one of these listed orders, a party may appeal the order without waiting for a final judgment. Interlocutory appeals are taken on the accelerated appeal timetable.

---

16 *See* Rusk State Hospital v. Black, 392 S.W.3d 88 (Tex. 2012) (holding that immunity, an issue of subject matter jurisdiction, can be raised for the first time in an interlocutory appeal).

B. Timetables in the Court of Appeals

1. *Timetable: No Motion for New Trial*

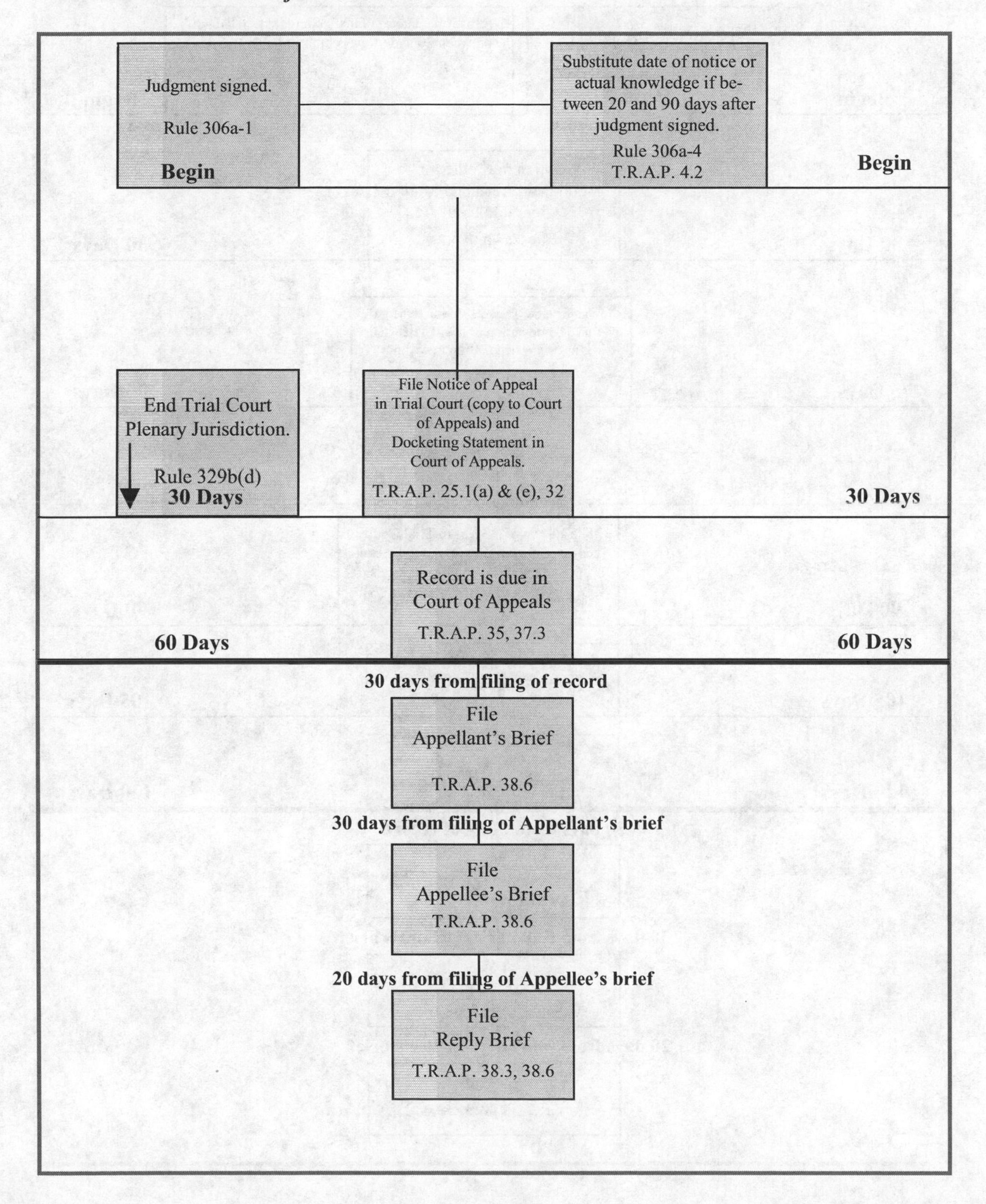

2. *Timetable: Motion for New Trial or Motion to Modify*

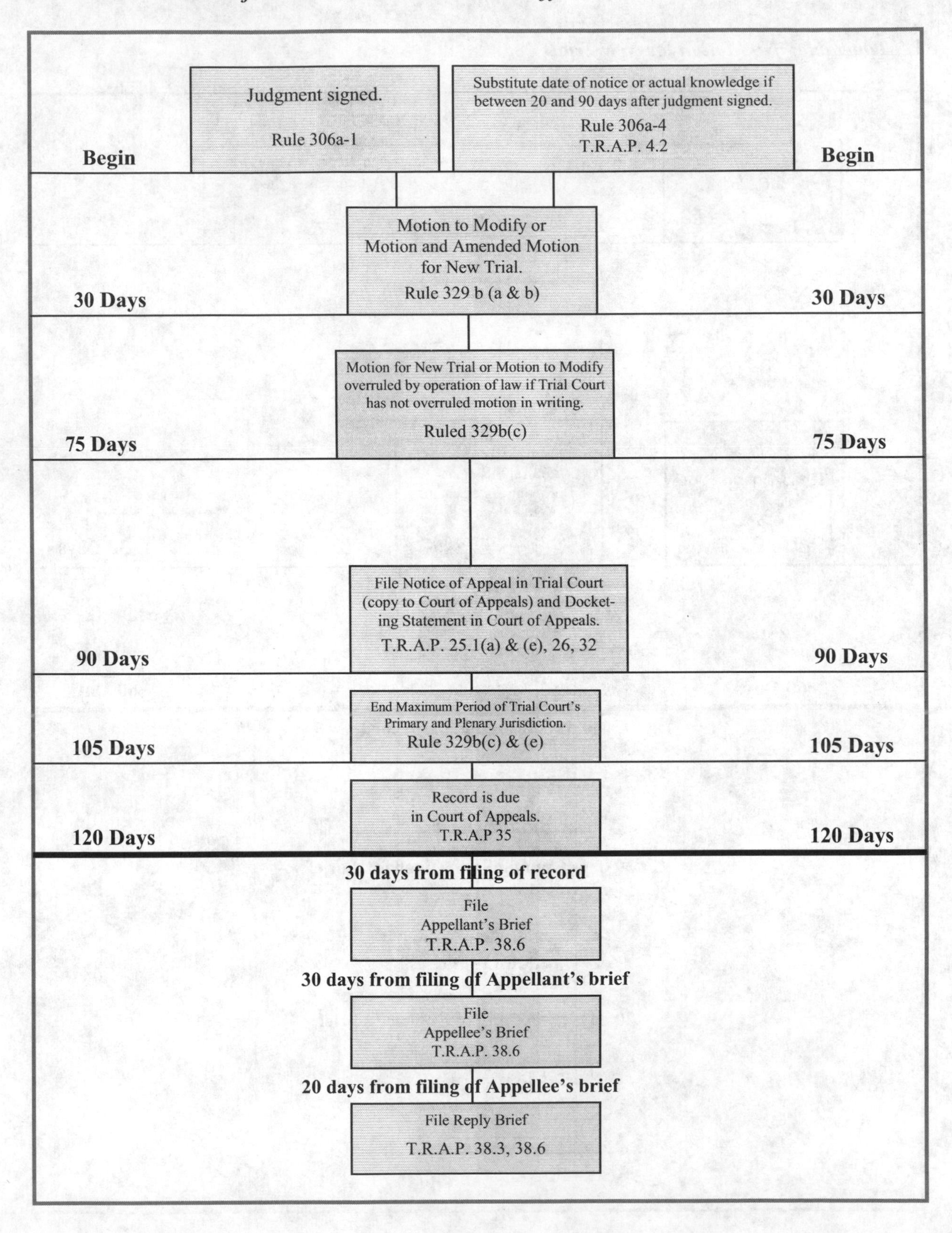

ARKOMA BASIN EXPLORATION COMPANY, INC.
v.
FMF ASSOCIATES 1990-A, LTD.

349 S.W.3d 380
(Tex. 2008)

JUSTICE BRISTER delivered the opinion of the Court in which CHIEF JUSTICE JEFFERSON, JUSTICE HECHT, JUSTICE WAINWRIGHT, JUSTICE GREEN, JUSTICE MEDINA, JUSTICE JOHNSON, and JUSTICE WILLETT joined.

Eight Virginia limited partnerships hired Arkoma Basin Exploration Company to estimate production from mineral properties in the Arkoma Basin in southeastern Oklahoma. When the properties failed to produce as predicted, they sued.

Based on Virginia law, a Texas jury found clear and convincing evidence of fraud and awarded $5.5 million in damages. The trial court signed a judgment reducing the verdict to $4.7 million, and later reduced that further by remittitur to about $2.9 million. When Arkoma appealed the judgment and the partnerships cross-appealed the remittitur, the court of appeals affirmed in all respects but one, holding part of the remittitur improper and restoring about $1.5 million of the jury's verdict.

We granted Arkoma's petition to consider whether there was legally sufficient evidence of fraud under Virginia law, or of damages under Texas law. Finding that only two of the eight limited partnerships met these standards, we affirm the court of appeals' judgment as to FMF Associates 1988-B, Ltd. and FMF Lazare, Ltd., and reverse the remainder.

I. Evidence of Fraud: Statement of Fact or Opinion?

[The court affirmed the jury's fraud verdicts as to two of the limited partnerships.]

II. Evidence of Damages: Preservation and Legal Sufficiency

Arkoma also challenges the legal sufficiency of the damages evidence. For the reasons stated above, we restrict our review to the two partnerships who proved fraud. They argue Arkoma failed to preserve this error in the trial court because Arkoma's no-evidence objection (1) did not specify why the evidence was legally insufficient, and (2) was not raised before or during trial. As these preservation points concern procedural matters, Texas law governs.

To assert a no-evidence complaint in this Court, a party must preserve error in both the trial court and the court of appeals.[18] The court of appeals held that Arkoma's objections in the trial court were not "specific enough to call the trial court's attention to the precise lack of sufficiency asserted on appeal." We disagree, for two reasons.

First, Arkoma's post-trial motion explicitly asserted that "there is no evidence . . . to support the jury's answers to each part of Question 4," the damages question. Generally, a no-evidence objection directed to a single jury issue is sufficient to preserve error without further detail. Thus, as Justice Calvert wrote for this Court 50 years ago, while a single such objection to all 79 jury answers is too general, the same objection addressed to each individual issue is adequate. Several commentators suggest this is precisely what careful practitioners should do.

---

[18] *See* TEX. R. APP. P. 53.2(f).

Second, the cardinal rule for preserving error is that an objection must be clear enough to give the trial court an opportunity to correct it. Here, the trial judge not only had that opportunity, he took it. The trial judge conducted a post-trial hearing on the sufficiency of the damages evidence, received letter briefs on the issue, and wrote a four-page single-spaced letter granting remittitur. Though damages were not reduced as much as Arkoma had hoped, there is no question the trial court was aware of its objection.

Of course, stock objections may not always preserve error. If a single jury question involves many issues, it is possible that a general objection may not tell the trial court where to start. But post-trial objections will rarely be as detailed as an appellate brief because time is short, the record may not be ready, and the trial court is already familiar with the case. In that context, an objection is not necessarily inadequate because it does not specify every reason the evidence was insufficient. Like all other procedural rules, those regarding the specificity of post-trial objections should be construed liberally so that the right to appeal is not lost unnecessarily. We hold the court of appeals erred in holding that Arkoma's objection was too general.

* * *

III. Deadlines for Appeal: From Judgment or Remittitur?

In its original judgment, the trial court reduced the jury's damages verdict for the 1988-B partnership to $2,090,000 and for Lazare to $930,000, a matter they never appealed. But they did challenge by cross-appeal the trial court's remittitur reducing damages further to $1,302,302 for 1988-B and $579,492.76 for Lazare. The court of appeals reversed the remittitur and reinstated the former amounts. Arkoma asserts the court had no jurisdiction to reinstate anything because the partnerships' cross-appeal was two days late.

The trial court's original judgment was signed January 29, 2002. Arkoma's motion for new trial extended the time for appeal to April 29th, 90 days after judgment.[36] When Arkoma filed its notice of appeal on the last possible day, the deadline for a cross-appeal was further extended an additional 14 days to May 13th.[37] The partnerships filed two days later, May 15th.

But the partnerships argue their cross-appeal was timely because the original judgment was modified by remittitur. "If a judgment is modified in any respect," appellate deadlines do not run from the original judgment but "from the date when the modified judgment is signed."[38] According to the partnerships, the trial court's order granting remittitur on April 15, 2002 restarted the appellate timetables, rendering their cross-appeal filed 30 days later timely.[39]

Technically, neither trial nor appellate courts can order remittitur; they can only suggest a remittitur on condition that a new trial will be granted if it is refused. We have held that if a court directly orders a reduction in damages, that order necessarily modifies the judgment even if it is incorrectly called a remittitur. By contrast, we have also held that if a party files a purely voluntary remittitur (without any order or suggestion from the court), the judgment has not been modified. If the latter rule were otherwise, a party could extend appellate deadlines indefinitely by remitting a dollar at a time.

---

36 *See* TEX. R. APP. P. 26.1(a).

37 *See id.* 26.1(d).

38 *Id. 4.3(a); see also* TEX. R. CIV. P. 329b(h).

39 *See* TEX. R. APP. P. 26.1.

We have never addressed whether an order that properly suggests remittitur modifies a judgment "in any respect," and thus restarts appellate deadlines. But we have explained that the deadlines are restarted by "*any* change, whether or not material or substantial." Thus, appellate deadlines are restarted by an order that does nothing more than change the docket number or deny all relief not expressly granted.

By this standard, we think a signed order suggesting remittitur must restart the appellate deadlines as well. By its very nature, such an order allows only two options: a smaller judgment or a new trial. While it may not be clear when the order is signed which option a claimant will select, it is immediately clear that the original judgment will change. In many cases, the order itself will immediately change which party, if any, should begin preparing for an appeal. Given the relative impacts of an order adding a docket number and an order suggesting remittitur, it would be anomalous if the former restarted appellate deadlines but the latter did not.

It is conceivable, of course, that a judgment might be reinstated after a suggestion of remittitur because the trial judge withdraws the latter. But that does not mean the judgment was not modified "in any respect" in the interim; a trial judge who modifies a judgment and then withdraws the modification has modified the judgment *twice* rather than never.

Because appellate timetables restarted when the trial court signed its remittitur order, the court of appeals had jurisdiction to consider the remittitur. Because Arkoma asserts no other objection to it, it is affirmed.

* * *

Notes & Questions

1. *Preserving error*. Remember that proper and timely preservation of error is the initial and most crucial step in the appellate process. TRAP 33.1 states the basic requirement—to complain of any error on appeal, the record must reflect that the complaint was timely and properly made by request, objection or motion and ruled on by the trial court. Throughout this course we have discussed requirements for preserving error in different contexts.

2. *Timetables*. Generally speaking, all appellate time periods run from the date the judgment is signed. This approach is used so that one can know and calendar all critical deadlines immediately following the signing of judgment. There are two exceptions, however. As the tables show, the deadlines for the filing of appellate briefs run from the date the record is filed in the court of appeals. T.R.A.P. 38.6.

In Table 2, applicable to cases in which a motion for new trial or motion to modify judgment is filed, the period of trial court plenary jurisdiction runs from the date the motion for new trial (or to motion to modify) is overruled. The table assumes that the trial court does not act on the motion and that it is therefore overruled by operation of law after 75 days, at which time the 30 day period of plenary jurisdiction begins and runs to the 105th day. This timetable—Table 2—shows the maximum possible time for the trial court's exercise of plenary jurisdiction. The plenary jurisdiction period can be greatly compressed, however, if the trial court overrules the motion by written order. For example, suppose that the court signs a judgment, the loser files a motion for new trial and the court overrules it, all on the same day. That starts the plenary period which expires 30 days later, as in Table 1. However, the appellate deadlines which were extended by the motion (time for filing the record, for example) remain, giving more time to the appellant. For this reason, appellants often take advantage of their unfettered procedural right to file a motion for new trial. Keep in mind also that although these tables assume that no step is taken prematurely, an appellant can avoid tripping over a deadline by taking critical steps in advance.

3. *Restarting the clock.* The rules on late notice of judgment—Rule 306a(4) and (5) duplicated by T.R.A.P. 4.2(a), (b) and (c)—provide relief when the clerk fails to give prompt notice of the signing of a judgment required by 306a(3). When a party receives notice of a judgment between 20 and 90 days after the judgment is signed, the party can file a sworn motion in the trial court setting out the date that the party actually got notice of the judgment, asking that the deadlines start from the date of notice rather than the date of the judgment.[1] Unless the parties agree, the court will have a hearing and grant or deny the Rule 306a motion. Therefore, using these provisions, plenary power will expire and motions for new trial must be filed up to 120 days after the judgment is signed, rather than 30 days after the judgment is signed as provided in the ordinary timetables. The supreme court has held the motion must be filed within 90 days after the judgment is signed.[2] If the notice is more than 90 days late, the rule provides no way to "restart the clock" and the party's remedy is by restricted appeal to the court of appeals in a default judgment case or equitable bill of review (perhaps based on official mistake).[3] The idea seems to be that a diligent attorney will have inquired and discovered the judgment at some point before the 90th day and that grace periods must have some ending point.

If the notice is received within 20 days, the assumption seems to be that the party is not harmed. A motion for new trial—filed, in a worst case, in the ten-day window between the 20th and 30th days—will extend critical deadlines. Obviously, the recipient of notice after, say, 19 days have passed, must move quickly, as the time for action has been compressed.

Restarting the clock requires a sworn motion, notice and hearing, at which the afflicted party must prove the first date of actual notice.[4] Although TRAP 4.2 requires an express finding of the date of actual notice, TRCP 306a(5) does not. The Supreme Court has suggested that trial courts issue a finding of the notice date as a matter of course, and held that when the trial court fails to make a finding the date of notice is implied from the order unless there is no evidence from which to imply the finding.[5]

There is a second way to restart the clock. A new judgment which, by its terms, vacates an earlier judgment starts the timetable running again from the beginning.[6] Recall, however, that a trial court can vacate its previous judgment only during its period of plenary jurisdiction.

4. *Accelerated Appeals.* The timetables above show only deadlines for ordinary appeals. The rules provide for certain accelerated appeals, which have a different timetable. Accelerated appeals are governed by TRAP 28. Appeals are accelerated in appeals from interlocutory orders (as allowed

---

1 *See* In Interest of J.Z.P., 484 S.W.3d 924 (Tex. 2016) (holding that failure to caption the motion as a motion filed under Rule 306a was not fatal to the motion, citing Rule 71).

2 *See* Levit v. Adams, 850 S.W.2d 469 (Tex. 1993).

3 *See id.*

4 In Cantu v. Longoria, 878 S.W.2d 131 (Tex. 1994), mandamus issued because trial court failed to make finding required in response to "motion for designation of date notice received" and "motion to designate date of judgment."

5 In re The Lynd Co., 195 S.W.3d 682 (Tex. 2006).

6 *See* Trans-Continental Properties, Ltd. v. Taylor, 717 S.W.2d 890 (Tex. 1986).

by law) and in *quo warranto* proceedings. The notice of appeal must be filed within 20 days after judgment or order appealed from is signed,[7] and a motion for new trial will not extend the deadline.[8] Courts and scholars disagree about whether filing a request for findings of fact and conclusions of law extends the deadline for perfecting an appeal when the appeal is accelerated.[9] The Supreme Court has not decided the issue.[10]

5. *Suspension of rules*. It is important to understand the appellate timetables. But also recognize that TRAP 2 allows an appellate court to suspend the operation of any rule in a particular case (and thus change appellate deadlines, except the deadline for perfecting appeal) for good cause. One commentator cautions that this rule may lead to "appellate anarchy."[11]

6. *Appeal "perfected" by filing notice of appeal*. The most critical of many deadlines is the one governing the filing of a notice of appeal with the trial court clerk under T.R.A.P. 25.1(a). This is the essential act without which there is no appeal,[12] because—absent a timely filing—the appellate court has no jurisdiction over the appeal.[13] TRAP 26 provides that the notice must be filed within 30 days after the judgment is signed, or within 90 days after the judgment is signed if any party files a timely motion for new trial, motion to modify the judgment (if substantive), motion to reinstate, or request for findings of fact and conclusions of law in a bench trial. A timely filed but defective notice that is timely amended will invoke the appellate court's jurisdiction.[14] Notice that the deadlines for expiration of the trial court's plenary power is independent of the appellate deadlines. The trial court may continue to have plenary power after the deadline for perfecting appeal (if motion for new trial overruled by operation of law at day 75, rctains power for 30 more days, until day 105; nevertheless, the appeal must be perfected by day 90).

7. *Request for findings extending deadlines*. What if your judgment is not after a jury trial, but is a summary judgment, default judgment, or even a judgment rendered as a sanction? You may ask the trial judge for findings of fact. TRAP 26.1(a)(4) extends appellate deadlines if the requested findings and conclusions "are required by the Rules of Civil Procedure or, if not required, could properly be considered by the appellate court." What does that mean? The Supreme Court has said:[15]

> A request for findings of fact and conclusions of law does not extend the time for perfecting appeal of a judgment rendered as a matter of law, where findings and conclusions can have no purpose and should not be requested, made, or considered on appeal. Examples

---

[7] TRAP 26.1(b). *See* City of Magnolia 4A Econ. Dev. Corp. v. Smedley, 533 S.W.3d 297, 300 (Tex. 2017) (holding timetable ran from date of summary judgment order that was not a mere reconsideration of previous motion to dismiss).

[8] TRAP 28, cmt.

[9] Hone v. Hanafin, 104 S.W.3d 884, 887 (Tex. 2003).

[10] *Id.* at 885.

[11] *See* William J. Boyce, et al., *Update on the Texas Rules of Appellate Procedure*, The Univ. of Tex. School of Law, 10th Annual Conf. on State and Federal Appeals (June 2000). *See* Ray Ins. Agency v. Jones, 928 S.W.3d 530 (Tex. 2002) (expressing disapproval of use of Rule 2 to suspend pleading rules).

[12] *See* T.R.A.P. 26.1.

[13] *See* Dallas County Appraisal Dist. v. Inst. for Aerobics Research, 751 S.W.2d 860, 861 (Tex. 1988).

[14] In re J.M., 396 S.W.3d 528 (Tex. 2013); Sweed v. Nye, 232 S.W.3d 873 (Tex. 2010).

[15] IKB Industries (Nigeria) Ltd. v. Pro-Line Corp., 938 S.W.2d 440 (Tex. 1997).

> are summary judgment, judgment after directed verdict, judgment non obstante veredicto, default judgment awarding liquidated damages, dismissal for want of prosecution without an evidentiary hearing, dismissal for want of jurisdiction without an evidentiary hearing, dismissal based on the pleadings or special exceptions, and any judgment rendered without an evidentiary hearing. A timely filed request for findings of fact and conclusions of law extends the time for perfecting appeal when findings and conclusions are required by Rule 296, or when they are not required by Rule 296 but are not without purpose—that is, they could properly be considered by the appellate court. Examples are judgment after a conventional trial before the court, default judgment on a claim for unliquidated damages, judgment rendered as sanctions, and any judgment based in any part on an evidentiary hearing.

Findings are not appropriate where the trial court renders judgment as a matter of law because "there are no facts to find, and the legal conclusions have already been stated in the motion and response."[16]

8. *Premature filing*. When a party prematurely files a notice of appeal, the rules treat the premature notice as filed subsequent to the order or judgment to which it applies.[17] Similarly, when a motion for new trial or motion to modify is filed before the final judgment is signed, the party is not required to refile the complaint after the formal judgment to extend the appellate deadlines.[18] And when a court replaces an existing judgment during plenary power, but the new judgment fails to correct an error asserted in a previously filed postjudgment motion, the movant is not required to refile the motion to preserve the error,[19] or to extend the appellate deadlines.[20] But if all relief requested in the postjudgment motion is granted in the subsequent judgment, the motion does not extend the appellate deadlines after the subsequent judgment.[21]

9. *Extensions of time for perfecting appeal*. TRAP 26.3 allows the appellate court to extend the time for perfecting appeal for 15 days, if the party seeking the extension files the notice of appeal *and* a motion to extend time within that 15-day period. The motion must "reasonably explain" the need for the extension. TRAP 10.5(b). Parties may seek additional time for filing other matters as well. For example, TRAP 38.6(d), allows appellate courts to extend the time for filing the appellant's brief.

10. *Implied motions to extend time*. What happens when the appellant perfects the appeal beyond the deadline, but within the 15-day window during which the appellant can seek a motion to extend time, but fails to file the motion? The Supreme Court held that courts of appeals must *imply* a motion to extend time.

---

16 *Id.*

17 TEX. R. APP. P. 27.2.

18 TEX. R. CIV. P. 306c (treating prematurely filed motions for new trial as filed subsequent to the signing of the judgment). *See* Ryland Enter., Inc. v. Weatherspoon, 355 S.W.3d 664, 666 (Tex. 2011) (per curiam) (citing Gomez v. Tex. Dep't of Criminal Justice, Inst'l Div., 896 S.W.2d 176, 176-77 (Tex. 1995) (per curiam) (treating motion for judgment notwithstanding the verdict as a prematurely filed motion to modify or motion for new trial).

19 Fredonia State Bank v. General American Life Insurance Co., 881 S.W.2d 279, 282 (Tex. 1994).

20 Brighton v. Koss, 415 S.W.3d 864 (Tex. 2013); Wilkins v. Methodist Health Care Sys., 160 S.W.3d 559, 562 (Tex. 2005).

21 Wilkins, 160 S.W.3d at 563-64 (Tex.2005).

From VERBURGT v. DORNER, 959 S.W.2d 615 (Tex. 1997):

This Court has never wavered from the principle that appellate courts should not dismiss an appeal for a procedural defect whenever any arguable interpretation of the Rules of Appellate Procedure would preserve the appeal. We have repeatedly held that a court of appeals has jurisdiction over any appeal in which the appellant files an instrument in a bona fide attempt to invoke the appellate court's jurisdiction. Our decisions reflect the policy embodied in our appellate rules that disfavors disposing of appeals based upon harmless procedural defects. Thus, we have instructed the courts of appeals to construe the Rules of Appellate Procedure reasonably, yet liberally, so that the right to appeal is not lost by imposing requirements not absolutely necessary to effect the purpose of a rule.

As the dissenting justice in the court of appeals pointed out, the result the court of appeals reached was not "absolutely necessary" under these facts. Here, the court of appeals acknowledged that Verburgt demonstrated that he had made a bona fide attempt to timely perfect an appeal.

We hold that a motion for extension of time is necessarily implied when an appellant acting in good faith files a bond beyond the time allowed by Rule 41(a)(1), but within the fifteen-day period in which the appellant would be entitled to move to extend the filing deadline under Rule 41(a)(2). Our holding does not indefinitely extend the time in which parties may perfect an appeal. . . . Instead, once the period for granting a motion for extension of time under Rule 41(a)(2) has passed, a party can no longer invoke the appellate court's jurisdiction. It also does not alter the time for perfecting an appeal beyond the period authorized by Rule 41(a). Nor does our holding undermine finality of judgments, as the court of appeals believed. Parties who prevail in the trial court will still know within the time specified in Rule 41(a)(2) whether their opponents will seek to perfect an appeal. We decline to elevate form over substance, as the dissenters would.

Accordingly, we reverse the judgment of the court of appeals and remand to that court to allow it to determine whether Verburgt offered a reasonable explanation for his failure to timely file his bond. *See* TEX. R. APP. P. 41(a)(2).

* * *

11. *Reasonable explanation for extension.* Motions to extend time require a reasonable explanation. The Texas Supreme Court has held that a reasonable explanation means "any plausible statement of circumstances indicating that failure to file within the [required] period was not deliberate or intentional, but was the result of inadvertence, mistake or mischance . . . . Any conduct short of deliberate or intentional noncompliance qualifies as inadvertence, mistake or mischance—even if that conduct can also be characterized as professional negligence"[22] Thus, miscalculations of the appellate timetable,[23] miscommunication between counsel and client,[24] and

---

[22] Garcia v. Kastner Farms, Inc., 774 S.W.2d 668, 669 (Tex. 1989) (interpreting former TEX. R. APP. P. 41(a)(2)). *See also* Hone v. Hanafin, 104 S.W.3d 884, 887 (Tex. 2003) (holding that court of appeals should ordinarily accept appellant's explanations as reasonable absent a finding of deliberate or intentional conduct).

[23] *Hone*, 104 S.W.3d at 888; National Union Fire Ins. Co. v. Ninth Court of Appeals, 864 S.W.2d 58, 60 (Tex. 1993).

[24] Hagaman v. Morgan, 886 S.W.2d 398, 403-04 (Tex. App.—Dallas 1994, writ denied).

confusion about applicable law[25] have been found to be reasonable explanations. In situations where there is an implied motion to extend time, courts of appeals are issuing a notice to the appellant that the appeal will be dismissed absent a reasonable explanation.[26] And the Supreme Court has held that the appellant need not concede untimeliness to obtain an extension of time.[27] In that case the appellant contended the notice was timely, and, accordingly, the court of appeals held that the appellant failed to establish a reasonable explanation for the late filing. The Supreme Court disagreed, noting that the disagreement about the deadline established a plausible explanation.

In the next two cases, notice how the appellants lost their right to appeal by failing to comply with the routine, but essential, appellate procedures set out in the TRAP rules.

DALGLISH
v.
SUTTON
2005 WL 1397204
(Tex. App.—San Antonio 2005, no pet.) (not reported in S.W.3d)

PER CURIAM.

Because Appellant Robert L. Dalglish did not file a timely notice of appeal, we dismiss this appeal for lack of jurisdiction.

The trial court signed a final judgment on September 20, 2004. Dalglish filed a timely motion for new trial on October 5, 2004. Therefore, the notice of appeal was due to be filed on December 20, 2004. *See* TEX. R. APP. P. 26.1(a). A motion for extension of time to file the notice of appeal was due on January 4, 2005. *See* TEX. R. APP. P. 26.3. Dalglish, however, did not file his notice of appeal until January 12, 2005. Therefore, on March 25, 2005, we ordered Dalglish to show cause why this appeal should not be dismissed for lack of jurisdiction.

On April 13, 2005, Dalglish filed a response, raising several arguments. In our order of April 20, 2005, we explained why those arguments have no merit. First, Dalglish argued that the trial court's judgment of September 20, 2004, was not a final judgment. In our order of April 20, 2005, we explained that a judgment is final for purposes of appeal if it disposes of all pending parties and claims in the record. Whether a judicial decree is a final judgment must be determined from its language and the record in the case. Here, Dalglish sued Bill Sutton and Allstate

---

[25] McLendon v. McLendon, 862 S.W.2d 662, 669 (Tex. App.—Dallas 1994, writ denied) *disapproved on other grounds*, Dallas Mkt. Center Dev. Co. v. Liedecker, 958 S.W.2d 382 (Tex. 1997).

[26] *See* Coronado v. Farming Technology, Inc. 994 S.W.2d 901, *appeal dismissed*, 1999 WL 548703 (Tex. App.—Houston [14th Dist.] 1999); Smith v. Houston Lighting & Power co., 7 S.W.3d 287 (Tex. App.—Houston [14th Dist.] 1999, no pet.)(affidavit stating inability to obtain pro bono counsel until after deadline accepted as reasonable explanation).

[27] Hone v. Hanafin, 104 S.W.3d 884 (Tex. 2003).

Insurance Company for various claims. The trial court's judgment grants Bill Sutton and Allstate Insurance Company's no-evidence and traditional motion for summary judgment:

> IT IS THEREFORE ORDERED, ADJUDGED AND DECREED, that Defendants' No-Evidence and Traditional Motion for Summary Judgment *as to all of Plaintiff's claims* is GRANTED and that Plaintiff *take nothing by way of against Defendants*, ALLSTATE INSURANCE COMPANY and BILL SUTTON.

(emphasis added). This judgment, disposing of all pending parties and claims, is a final judgment.

Dalglish also argued that the trial court's order denying the motion for new trial was a second judgment, thereby extending appellate deadlines. According to Dalglish, the trial court heard new "substantive issues" during the motion for new trial. Thus, Dalglish argued that the trial court's order denying the motion for new trial was a new judgment. In our order of April 20, 2005, we again explained why Dalglish's argument was incorrect. In its order, the trial court merely states that appellant's motion for new trial is "DENIED based on the findings herein that Plaintiff does not raise a cause of action." This language does not modify, vacate, correct, or reform the judgment. It merely gives the reason why the trial court denied the motion for new trial.

Although Dalglish's response did not raise any meritorious arguments, it did, as noted in our order April 20, 2005, state that his notice of appeal was mailed on January 3, 2005. If true, then pursuant to Texas Rule of Civil Procedure 5, the notice of appeal would be deemed filed within the fifteen-day grace period allowed by Texas Rule of Appellate Procedure 26.3. Although Dalglish did not file a motion for extension of time to file his notice of appeal, a motion for extension of time is necessarily implied when an appellant, acting in good faith, files a notice of appeal beyond the time allowed by rule 26.1 but within the fifteen-day grace period provided by rule 26.3 for filing a motion for extension of time. However, an appellant must offer a reasonable explanation for failing to file the notice of appeal in a timely manner. *See id.*; TEX. R. APP. P. 26.3, 10.5(b)(1)(C).

Therefore, in our order of April 20, 2005, we ordered Dalglish to file a written response showing proof that the notice of appeal was mailed timely in compliance with Texas Rule of Civil Procedure 5 and presenting a reasonable explanation for failing to file the notice of appeal in a timely manner.

On May 10, 2005, Dalglish filed a written response. On May 13, 2005, we issued an order finding that the response was sufficient to show proof that the notice of appeal was mailed within the fifteen-day grace period and finding Dalglish's explanation reasonable. We, therefore, granted Dalglish's implied motion for extension of time to file the notice of appeal and ordered this appeal retained on the court's docket. We also denied appellees' motion to dismiss for lack of jurisdiction and for want of prosecution.

On May 16, 2005, appellees filed an "Amended Motion to Dismiss for Want of Jurisdiction, or in the Alternative, Motion for Want of Prosecution." In their motion, appellees argue that the affidavits Dalglish attached to his response to this court's show cause order are insufficient. Specifically, appellees argue that the affidavits of Karen Dalglish Seal, attorney for Dalglish, and Seal's legal assistant, Kassandra Levay, do not show compliance with Texas Rule of Civil Procedure 5. We agree. Rule 5 provides the following:

> If any document is sent to the proper clerk by first-class United States mail in an envelope or wrapper properly addressed and stamped and is deposited in the mail on or before the

> last day for filing same, the same, if received by the clerk not more than ten days tardily, shall be filed by the clerk and be deemed filed in time. A legible postmark affixed by the United States Postal Service shall be prima facie evidence of the date of mailing.

TEX. R. CIV. P. 5. Karen Dalglish Seal's affidavit affirms that on January 3, 2005, she gave the notice of appeal to her legal assistant along with a manila envelope and instructed her legal assistant to mail three copies. Kassandra Levay's affidavit affirms that on January 3, 2005, Karen Dalglish Seal "asked me to mail the Notice [of appeal] to the Court which I did that day." The affidavits do not state that the notice was mailed by first-class United States mail, nor do they state that the notice was addressed to the proper clerk. Levay's affidavit merely states that she mailed the notice to the Court. We agree with appellees that the affidavits do not comply with rule 5. And, despite having more than twenty days, Dalglish has failed to respond to appellees' amended motion to dismiss.

Because the affidavits do not comply with rule 5, the notice of appeal was not timely filed. As such, our jurisdiction was not invoked. * * * We dismiss this appeal for lack of jurisdiction.

KAHANEK
v.
GROSS
2005 WL 1277745
(Tex. App.—San Antonio 2005, no pet.) (not reported in S.W.3d)

PER CURIAM.

Appellee Sheldon Gross, M.D., has filed a motion to dismiss this appeal for want of prosecution. Appellants Timothy and Nancy Kahanek, individually and as personal representatives of the estate of their minor child, Kyndil Kahanek, filed their notice of appeal with the trial court clerk on November 7, 2002, seeking to appeal the summary judgment rendered on August 9, 2002, in favor of Dr. Gross. The Kahaneks, however, never filed a copy of the notice of appeal with this court. Thus, it was not until Dr. Gross filed his motion to dismiss for want of prosecution that we had notice of the pending appeal.

As emphasized by Dr. Gross, the Kahaneks did not file a copy of the notice of appeal with this court as required by the Texas Rules of Appellate Procedure. *See* TEX. R. APP. P. 25.1(e); . . . . Nor did the Kahaneks file a docketing statement as required by the rules. *See* TEX. R. APP. P. 32.1; . . . . No clerk's or reporter's record has been filed. Indeed, since they filed their notice of appeal with the trial court clerk in November 2002, more than two years ago, the Kahaneks have taken no action in prosecuting this appeal. We, therefore, ordered the Kahaneks to file a response to Dr. Gross's motion to dismiss for want of prosecution. They have filed no such response. As such, they have failed to comply with a court order. *See* TEX. R. APP. P. 42.3(c) (allowing involuntary dismissal of appeal for failure to comply with a court order).We, therefore, grant Dr. Gross's motion to dismiss and dismiss this appeal. *See* TEX. R. APP. P. 42.3(b), (c).

Notes & Questions

1. *Docketing statement.* Upon perfecting the appeal, the appellant must file a docketing statement with the court of appeals that gives a substantial amount of information about the parties, lawyers, trial court, and dates. TRAP 32. This also gives the court of appeals notice that the appeal may be coming. The docketing statement is not jurisdictional, only informational.

2. *What happens to the judgment pending appeal?* Unless a losing party pays or "supercedes" a judgment pending appeal, the judgment winner can begin to use collection efforts to enforce it. As the Texas Supreme Court noted:[1]

> A judgment debtor is entitled to supersede the judgment while pursuing an appeal; this defers payment until the matter is resolved but does not halt the accumulation of interest on the judgment. If the debtor rejects the supersedeas option and does not otherwise suspend enforcement, the creditor may execute on the judgment by seizing bank accounts or other property. To avoid seizure, the debtor may pay the judgment outright, which stops the accumulation of post-judgment interest. But these alternatives to suspending enforcement put at risk the judgment debtor's ability to recoup the seized assets or payment when the appeal is successful.

Upon successful appeal, rule of "restitution upon reversal" applies, creating an obligation in the party who has received the benefit of the erroneous judgment to make restitution to the other party for what he has lost.[2] In *Miga v. Jensen*,[3] the defendant suffered a judgment of over $25 million, including pre-judgment interest, which increased due to post-judgment interest to almost $30 million. The defendant then tendered $23 million to the plaintiff while appeal to the Supreme Court was pending. The Supreme Court reduced the judgment to almost $2 million. The plaintiff refused to return the excess to the defendant, so the defendant had to file suit. The Supreme Court upheld summary judgment—so the original defendant now has a judgment against the original plaintiff that it must try to collect.

3. *Supercedeas.* TRAP 24 provides for the filing of a bond or deposit that will suspend enforcement of the underlying judgment through the pendency of the appeal. The supersedeas bond guarantees payment of an ultimate judgment against the appellant. The typical bond should be high enough to cover the amount of compensatory damages, interest for the duration of the appeal[4] and costs. The Supreme Court has held that attorney's fees incurred in the prosecution or defense of a claim[5] and interest on those fees[6] are not "compensatory damages" and need not be superceded.

---

[1] Miga v. Jensen, 299 S.W.3d 98, 100 (Tex. 2009).

[2] *Id.*

[3] *Id.*

[4] One commentator has suggested that because it is hard to estimate the duration of an appeal, it is appropriate to add two years of post-judgment interest to the bond. The additional premium is generally minimal and it saves the trouble of having to renew and increase the bond after the first year has passed. Julia F. Pendery, et al., *Calming a Rottweiler—Miscellaneous Challenges in Supercedeas Bond Practice*, State Bar of Texas, Advanced Civil Appellate Course (1997*), quoted in* Lowe v. Monsanto Co., 965 S.W.2d 741, 742 n.2 (Tex. App.—El Paso 1998, no pet.)

[5] In re Nalle Plastics Family Limited Partnership, 406 S.W.3d 168 (Tex. 2013).

[6] In re Corral-Lerma, 451 S.W.3d 385 (Tex. 2015).

Posting a bond can be quite onerous where large judgments have been rendered, and there has been some discussion about its adverse effect upon a defendant's right to appeal, especially in the wake of huge judgments. Therefore, the rule limits the maximum amount of the bond, and TRAP 24.2(b) allows a trial court to order a lower bond under certain circumstances (including irreparable harm to the judgment debtor). The trial court retains jurisdiction over the bond, and the trial court's exercise of discretion concerning the bond is reviewable on appeal.

In re SMITH

192 S.W.3d 564
(Tex. 2006)

PER CURIAM.

Judgment debtors Ron Smith and Main Place Custom Homes, Inc. filed motions seeking review of the trial court's order setting aside their cash deposits in lieu of supersedeas bond to suspend enforcement of the trial court's judgment and sustaining the judgment creditors' challenge to their net worth affidavits. We treat the motions as petitions for writ of mandamus and conditionally grant in part and deny in part the relief sought.

Texas law provides that when a judgment is for money, the amount of security required to suspend enforcement of the judgment pending appeal may not exceed the lesser of: (1) fifty percent of the judgment debtor's net worth; or (2) twenty-five million dollars. TEX CIV. PRAC. & REM. CODE § 52.006(b); TEX. R. APP. P. 24.2(a)(1). Under Texas Rule of Appellate Procedure 24.2(c)(1), a judgment debtor who provides a bond, deposit, or security based upon its net worth "must simultaneously file an affidavit that states complete, detailed information concerning the debtor's assets and liabilities from which net worth can be ascertained." A judgment creditor may challenge the debtor's affidavits, and the trial court must hear the judgment creditor's challenge promptly after reasonable discovery concerning the judgment debtor's net worth is complete. TEX. R. APP. P. 24.2(c)(2)-(3). Following the hearing, "[t]he trial court must issue an order that states the debtor's net worth and states with particularity the factual basis for that determination." TEX. R. APP. P. 24.2(c)(3).[1]

Richard and Ginger Honaker obtained a judgment against Smith and Main Place in the total amount of $800,820.44, plus post-judgment interest. Smith and Main Place filed notices of appeal in September of 2004 with the Second Court of Appeals. In March of 2005, the Honakers began conducting post-judgment discovery in an effort to enforce the judgment. The parties then entered into protracted negotiations over the date for Smith's deposition. On June 14, 2005, two days before the agreed upon date for Smith's deposition, Smith and Main Place filed cash deposits in lieu of bond in the amount of $10.00 each and net worth affidavits to supersede enforcement of the trial court's judgment and to stay post-judgment discovery. In the affidavits, Smith averred that his net worth was negative $167,206.00 and that Main Place's net worth was $0.00.

The Honakers immediately filed a contest to the affidavits of net worth and moved the trial court to set aside the cash deposits in lieu of bond. They also filed a motion for sanctions and to compel discovery responses in aid of the judgment. The Honakers contended that the net worth affidavits were "manipulative and false" and that Smith's affidavit testimony that Main Place had

---

1 Texas Rule of Appellate Procedure 24.2(c)(1)-(c)(3) [text omitted].

no assets was not verifiable without discovery. Nevertheless, the Honakers claimed that they had obtained sufficient information through discovery to establish that Smith's closely held corporation, R.A. Smith & Company, Inc. (an entity not named in the Honakers' lawsuit), was Smith's alter ego. Therefore, the Honakers argued, all of that company's assets should be included in the calculation of Smith's net worth.

The trial court held hearings on the Honakers' motions in August of 2005. On October 14, 2005, the trial court issued two separate orders which Smith and Main Place challenge here. In the first order, the trial court sustained the Honakers' contest. The trial court found that the net worth affidavits were insufficient to adequately describe Smith's and Main Place's net worth. The trial court also found that the affidavits were designed to mislead the court and work an injustice on the Honakers by inappropriately staying execution and post-judgment discovery efforts. Without stating the basis for its calculation, the trial court found that Smith's net worth as of June 14, 2005 was $1,142,951; however, the court did not determine Main Place's net worth. The trial court further ordered that any future attempts by Smith and Main Place to stay enforcement of the judgment or post-judgment discovery must be approved in advance and must comply with the finding that R.A. Smith & Company, Inc. is Smith's alter ego. In the second order, the trial court reiterated its alter ego finding, granted the Honakers' motion to compel, ordered Smith and Main Place to respond to the Honakers' discovery requests, and sanctioned Smith $11,275 for expenses, plus attorney's fees.

As Texas Rule of Appellate Procedure 24.4 permits, Smith and Main Place filed a motion with the court of appeals seeking review of the trial court's order setting aside their cash deposits in lieu of bond and determining Smith's net worth. They subsequently filed a separate appeal of the discovery order. . . .

When a judgment creditor files a contest to the judgment debtor's affidavit of net worth, the trial court must hold a hearing and "issue an order that states the debtor's net worth and states with particularity the factual basis for that determination." TEX. R. APP. P. 24.2(c)(3). The trial court abused its discretion here because it failed to state with particularity the factual basis for its determination that Smith's net worth was $1,142,951. The trial court did not make any findings that would permit a reviewing court to ascertain the basis for that determination. Further, the trial court found that R.A. Smith & Company, Inc. was Smith's alter ego without stating the factual or legal basis for that conclusion.

Smith argues that the trial court abused its discretion by basing the determination that he had a net worth of $1,142,951 on the alter ego finding. He argues that the Honakers were foreclosed from raising that theory post-judgment and presented legally and factually insufficient evidence to support it. Because we conclude that the trial court must enter additional findings to support its alter ego determination, and because post-judgment discovery is still ongoing,[2] we reserve judgment on whether the trial court abused its discretion in determining that R.A. Smith & Company, Inc. is Smith's alter ego for purposes of Rule 24.2(c).[3]

However, as to Smith's argument that the trial court abused its discretion by considering the alter ego theory in the post-judgment net worth proceeding, we disagree. Because "[a]lter ego

[2] We stayed enforcement of the judgment pending review of this matter but declined to stay post-judgment discovery.

[3] As we recently stated, factual sufficiency has been the sole domain of the intermediate appellate courts in Texas since 1891. *City of Keller v. Wilson*, 168 S.W.3d 802, 822 (Tex. 2005). Therefore, we could not conduct a factual sufficiency review of the evidence even if we were inclined to do so.

applies when there is such unity between corporation and individual that the separateness of the corporation has ceased," *Castleberry v. Branscum,* 721 S.W.2d 270, 272 (Tex. 1986), an alter ego finding is relevant to the determination of the judgment debtor's net worth. Therefore, the trial court did not abuse its discretion by considering the alter ego theory in determining Smith's net worth pursuant to Rule 24.

Although the trial court did not abuse its discretion by considering the alter ego theory, that does not mean that the trial court's alter ego finding may be used to hold R.A. Smith & Company, Inc. or any other nonparty liable for the judgment. A judgment may not be amended to include an alter ego that was not named in the suit. *Matthews Const. Co., Inc. v .Rosen*, 796 S.W.2d 692, 693 (Tex. 1990). Therefore, an alter ego finding in a post-judgment net worth proceeding may not be used to enforce the judgment against the unnamed alter ego or any other nonjudgment debtor, but only to determine the judgment debtor's net worth for the purposes of Rule 24.

In addition to the failure to make adequate fact findings supporting its determination of Smith's net worth, the trial court failed to determine Main Place's net worth as required by Rule 24.2(c)(3). Even though the Honakers did not complete discovery concerning Smith's and Main Place's net worth before the hearing, under Rule 24.2(c)(3) "[t]he trial court must hear a judgment creditor's contest promptly after any discovery has been completed." Rule 24.2(c)(3) clearly provides that after the hearing the trial court must issue an order that states the judgment debtor's net worth. To the extent that a judgment debtor is uncooperative with reasonable discovery concerning the judgment debtor's net worth, the trial court may take appropriate steps (e.g. compel responses, issue sanctions, etc.) to ensure that discovery is completed before the hearing on the judgment creditor's contest. *See Arndt v. Farris,* 633 S.W.2d 497 (Tex. 1982) (trial court had jurisdiction to enter sanctions order for failure to comply with post-judgment discovery requests).

Smith and Main Place also argue that the trial court abused its discretion by compelling responses to the Honakers' post-judgment enforcement discovery requests because the Honakers were foreclosed by Texas Rule of Civil Procedure 621a from seeking responses to the requests after Smith and Main Place superseded the judgment by filing affidavits of net worth and cash deposits in lieu of bond. We disagree. Smith and Main Place refused to answer much of the written post-judgment enforcement discovery even though it was relevant to determining what assets were available to satisfy the judgment. Further, the parties had been engaged in post-judgment enforcement discovery for several months, and it was not until the eve of Smith's deposition that Smith and Main Place filed their cash deposits in lieu of bond and affidavits of net worth to supersede enforcement of the judgment. The trial court's conclusion that Smith and Main Place were attempting to avoid answering post-judgment enforcement discovery by filing the cash deposits in lieu of bond and affidavits of net worth was reasonable. In addition, Rule 24.2(c)(2) allows the judgment creditor to conduct reasonable discovery concerning the judgment debtor's net worth. The discovery in question sought information regarding assets owned by Smith and Main Place; therefore, the discovery was reasonably calculated to lead to information relevant to the net worth proceeding. In these circumstances, the trial court did not abuse its discretion by ordering Smith and Main Place to respond to the discovery requests.

We decline Smith's and Main Place's requests to review the discovery sanctions order in this proceeding. A sanctions order is appealable when the judgment is signed. Arndt, 633 S.W.2d at 500. Smith and Main Place filed a separate appeal of the trial court's sanctions order; accordingly, they have an adequate remedy by appeal. Walker v. Packer, 827 S.W.2d 833, 840 (Tex.

1992)(orig.proceeding). In addition, Rule 24.4 does not provide a basis for reviewing a discovery sanctions order.

Finally, Smith and Main Place argue that the court of appeals erred in not conducting a legal and factual sufficiency analysis of the trial court's net worth determination. We agree that the court of appeals should have conducted a legal and factual sufficiency analysis of the trial court's net worth determination, but the trial court's failure to make the required findings prevented the court of appeals from conducting the necessary sufficiency review. We trust that if it is called upon to do so again, the court of appeals will review the trial court's net worth determinations for legal and factual sufficiency. *See City of Keller v. Wilson,* 168 S.W.3d 802, 822 (Tex. 2005) (discussing standards for legal sufficiency review)*; Pool v. Ford Motor Co.,* 715 S.W.2d 629, 635 (Tex. 1986) (discussing standards for factual sufficiency review); *cf. Beaumont Bank v. Buller,* 806 S.W.2d 223, 226 (Tex. 1991) (noting court of appeals should have reviewed turnover order under an abuse of discretion standard instead of reversing on the ground that there was "no evidence" to support issuance of the order).

We hold that the trial court abused its discretion by issuing an order that did not state with particularity the factual basis for its determination of Smith's net worth and that did not state Main Place's net worth as required by Rule 24. Accordingly, without hearing oral argument, we conditionally grant the writ and direct the trial court to enter additional findings as to Smith's net worth and the determination that R.A. Smith & Company, Inc. is Smith's alter ego. TEX. R. APP. P. 52.8(c). We further direct the trial court to determine Main Place's net worth and to issue an order that states with particularity the factual basis for that determination. All other relief is denied. We are confident that the trial court will comply, and our writ will issue only if the trial court fails to do so.

Notes & Questions

1. *Requesting and filing the record.* The court of appeals must have a record from the trial court to determine the issues on appeal. The appellate record is made up of the "clerk's record"—selected trial court pleadings, orders, notices, and other papers—which is requested from the clerk, and "reporter's record"—the Q and A transcript of court proceedings made by the court reporter—which is requested from the court reporter. TRAP 34. Under the former rules, the clerk's record was called the "transcript" and the reporter's record was called the "statement of facts." It is now the duty of the court reporter and the clerk, not the appellant, to file the record. No longer will appellants have to mandamus court reporters to obtain an appellate record.[1] Late filing is a matter for the appellate court to take up with the clerk and court reporter. Technically, the clerk's record need not be requested. But the parties need to pay the fee for preparing the record and must be sure that any papers not listed as automatically included, but needed for the appeal, are included. The appellant must request the reporter's record from the official court reporter at or before the time for perfecting the appeal, and must make satisfactory arrangements for paying for it. TRAP 34.6(b).[2] Although there may be more than one appellant, there is only one appellate record in a

---

[1] *See, e.g.,* Wolters v. Wright, 623 S.W.2d 301, 305 (Tex. 1981); Click v. Tyra, 867 S.W.2d 406 (Tex. App.—Houston [14th Dist.] 1993, orig. proceeding).

[2] *See* In re Marriage of Spiegel, 6 S.W.3d 643 (Tex. App.—Amarillo 1999, no pet.)(holding appellant has duty to request and pay for the reporter's record); Utley v. Marathon Oil Co., 958 S.W.2d 960 (Tex. App.—

case. TRAP 34.1. The record must be filed with the court of appeals within 60 days after the judgment is signed or 120 days after the judgment is signed if there was a timely filed motion for new trial (or other motion that extends deadlines). TRAP 35.

2. *Partial record.* The rules allow parties to rely on a partial record, instead of having the court reporter transcribe the entire record of the trial. TRAP 34(6)(c). In many cases, reliance upon a partial record can be risky, and it is generally recognized that an appellant should ordinarily request a full record, unless it is absolutely necessary to cut costs by cutting the record down to size. However, the 1997 rules do make it easier to proceed on a partial record. For example, TRAP 34.6(d) allows the record to be supplemented, and requires appellate courts to file records even though they were requested late. Moreover, the new rules now permit an appeal on a partial record if the appellant provides a statement of the points or issues to be presented on appeal. Thus, TRAP 34.6(c) contains a presumption that a partial record is the entire record for purposes of the appeal for the issues identified. This overrules a 1968 opinion,[3] which held that a complaint about legal or factual sufficiency of evidence could not be successfully raised without a complete statement of facts. But the failure to provide a statement of the points or issues to be presented resurrects this presumption that the "omitted portions support the trial court's findings."[4] The statement of points or issues "need not be exact [but] should describe the nature of the complained of error with reasonably particularity."[5] However, the Supreme Court has taken a "flexible approach" to certain cases "when a rigid application of Rule 34.6 would result in denying review on the merits, even though the appellee has not established any prejudice from a slight relaxation of the rule."[6] Thus, the appellant's delay did not preclude appellate review of the appellant's legal and factual sufficiency points.[7]

3. *Briefs.* TRAP 9 sets out technical requirements and length limits for all briefs. TRAP 38 details the requirements for briefs in the court of appeals. The appellant's brief to the court of appeals is due 30 days after the record is filed, and the appellee's brief 30 days after the appellant's brief is filed. The appellant may file a reply brief within 20 days after the date the appellee's brief was filed. TRAP 38.6. Appellant and appellee briefs are limited to 15,000 words or 50 pages and a reply brief is limited to 7,500 words or 25 pages. There is an additional aggregate limit of 27,000 words or 90 pages of briefing per party (because both parties can be appellant and appellee). TRAP 9.4(i). If the appellant fails to file its brief, the appeal can be dismissed for want of prosecution. If the appellee fails to file its brief, the appellate court cannot simply grant the relief requested by the appellant—the appellant must satisfy the burden of showing error and harm. This result is somewhat analogous to the situation where the non-movant fails to file a response to a motion for summary judgment.

4. *Issues presented or points of error.* Rule 38.1 allows parties to use the federal courts' "issues presented" practice rather than the traditional Texas "point of error" practice. The point of error practice required specific and individual enumeration of each error complained of, with record

---

Waco 1998, no pet.) (holding that duties of trial court clerk, court reporter and appellate clerk with respect to the record do not arise until appellant has requested and arranged for payment of the record).

3 Englander Co. v. Kennedy, 428 S.W.2d 806 (Tex. 1968).

4 *See* Richards v. Schion, 969 S.w.2d 131 (Tex. App.—Houston [1st Dist.] 1998, no pet.).

5 CMM Grain Co. v. Ozgunduz, 991 S.W.2d 437, 439 (Tex. App.—Ft. Worth 1999, no pet.).

6 Bennett v. Cochran, 96 S.W.3d 227, 229 (Tex. 2003).

7 *Id.* at 231.

references to where the error occurred. Some courts took a literal and strict view of points of error, finding that points were waived because they were stated improperly. The 1997 rules reaffirm the Supreme Court's expressions of concern about using technicalities to waive valid points of error.[8] Thus, the new issues practice signals an intention to have all appeals judged on the merits of controversies rather than hyper-technical waiver issues. Appellate courts must now look to the argument part of the brief to determine the nature of complaints, including any subsidiary issues, rather than the points or issues alone. If the court is able to ascertain the nature of the complaint from the argument, the issue will be preserved for appellate review.[9] Nevertheless, it is important to carefully, clearly and concisely specify the complained of error in a point of error or issue. Failure to complain to the court of appeals of errors preserved in the trial court waives error.[10]

5. *Oral argument*. TRAP 39 governs oral argument. If a party desires oral argument, the party must include a request for oral argument on the front cover of its brief. Even when both parties request oral argument, the court of appeals may decide to submit the case without argument because it doubts that argument would "significantly aid the court in determining the legal and factual issues presented in the appeal."[11] The clerk must give written notice to all parties at least 21 days before the submission date telling the parties whether argument will be allowed or not, the submission date, time allowed for argument (if any), and the names of panel members.[12]

6. *Who has to perfect appeal to the court of appeals?* Under TRAP 25.1(c), any party who wishes to alter the trial court's judgment must perfect an appeal. This is a big change from the former rules, because under the former rules an ordinary appeal to the court of appeals was unlimited in scope unless a party filed a proper "limitation of appeal." Thus, once one party perfected an appeal, other parties could bring up their own complaints about the judgment in the appellee's brief by "cross-point." But these cross-points are not allowed under the current rules. Instead, every party that has a complaint about the judgment must file a notice of appeal and file an appellant's brief, bringing up points of error or issues on appeal, to which the appellee responds in the appellee's brief. In most cases, there is only one appellant and one appellee. However, confusion can result when several litigants have different objections to the judgment below. Every party on appeal then becomes an appellant, and every party will file briefs as an appellant and as a appellee.

7. *Crosspoints*. TRAP 38.2 retains cross-points in one situation, also discussed in TRCP 324(c), where the judgment is granted notwithstanding the verdict, and the verdict-winner (now judgment-loser) appeals. The judgment winner (verdict loser) can raise cross-points attacking the verdict should the jnov be reversed on appeal.[13] The rules do not address other situations where

---

8 *See* Pool v. Ford Motor Co., 715 S.W.2d 629 (Tex. 1986).

9 *See, e.g.* Perry v. Cohen, 272 S.W.3d 585, 586 (Tex. 2008)(holding that right to appellate review is preserved where raised in body of appellate brief but not in issues section of brief); Hutchison v. Pharris, 158 S.W.3d 554, 564 (Tex. App.—Ft. Worth, no pet.)(holding that although ordinarily issue raised for first time in reply brief is waived, where parties fully brief and respond to it, appellate court can treat as properly presented).

10 Ontiveros v. Flores, 218 S.W.3d 70, 71 (Tex. 2007).

11 TRAP 39.8.

12 TRAP 39.9.

13 *See* Dudley Constr., Ltd. v. Act Pipe & Supply, Inc., 545 S.W.3d 532, 539 (Tex. 2018) (holding that appellee successfully raised a "cross-point," erroneously called a "counter-point" in the brief, that preserved an alternative argument proscribing the jury's original verdict).

an appellee may seek a less favorable judgment in the event of reversal. Under the former rules, this could be raised for the first time in a motion for rehearing, filed after the court of appeals issued its opinion reversing the trial court's judgment.[14] To be safe, the appellee should raise this as a cross-point in the appellee's brief. To be really safe, since the point will "alter" the trial court's judgment, the appellee should file a conditional notice of appeal.

8. *Relief in the court of appeals*. The appellant will request that the court of appeals reverse the trial court's judgment and either render judgment for the appellant, or remand for a new trial. When an appellant presents remand and rendition points, the court of appeals should address the rendition points first, as an error that requires rendering judgment may make the remand points moot.[15] TRAP 43.2 sets forth the types of judgment that the court of appeals can issue. When reversing a trial court's judgment, TRAP 43.3 requires the appellate court to render the judgment that the trial court should have rendered, except when a remand is necessary for further proceedings or when the interests of justice require a remand. For example, rendition is appropriate:

(1) when a no evidence point that is properly preserved (not solely by a motion for new trial) is sustained; and
(2) when the trial court's judgment notwithstanding the verdict is reversed (and judgment on the jury's verdict is rendered).

9. *Opinions*. The courts of appeals must write an opinion in every appeal "that is as brief as possible but that addresses every issue raised and necessary to final disposition of the appeal."[16] Each opinion must be designated as an "Opinion" or a "Memorandum Opinion." Memorandum opinions are favored and are to be used when issues in the appeal are settled. Opinions are to be used *only* when the opinion "(a) establishes a new rule of law, alters or modifies an existing rule, or applies an existing rule to a novel fact situation likely to recur in future cases; (b) involves issues of constitutional law or other legal issues important to the jurisprudence of Texas; (c) criticizes existing law; or (d) resolves an apparent conflict of authority."[17] Different from the prior rule, all opinions are open to the public and made available to all reporting services. Opinions in civil cases can no longer be designated "not for publication" and those previously so designated still have no precedential value, but may be cited.[18]

10. *Motion for rehearing*. Within 15 days after the court of appeals issues its judgment, any party can file a motion for rehearing to try to convince the appellate court to revise its judgment or

---

[14] *See e.g.*, Oak Park Townhouses v. Brazosport Bank, 851 S.W.2d 189, 190 (Tex. 1993); Boyce Iron Works, Inc. v. Southwestern Bell Tel. Co., 747 S.w.2d 785, 787 (Tex. 1988).

[15] *See* Bradley's Electric Inc. v. Cigna Lloyds Ins. Co., 995 S.W.2d 675 (Tex. 1999).

[16] TRAP 47.1. *But see* Gonzalez v. McAllen Medical Center, Inc. 195 S.W.3d 680 (Tex. 2006) and Citizens National Bank v. Scott, 195 S.W.3d 94 (Tex. 2006)(both chastising courts of appeals for writing opinions that are too brief, not explaining why the court substituted its judgment for the trial court's).

[17] TRAP 47.4.

[18] TRAP 47.7. The earlier rule prohibiting citation to unpublished opinions was quite problematic. One court noted:

> At the time of the hearing on the motion to dismiss, R & M alluded to Rule 47.7 by specifically noting it was prohibited from citing the Austin opinion as "authority," and indicating it was only providing the trial court with the citation as a "hint" in case the trial court was "curious."

Robbins & Myers, Inc. v. J.M. Huber Corp., 2002 WL 418206 (Tex. App.—Dallas 2002, no pet.) (not designated for publication).

opinion. TRAP 49. Under the 1997 rules, a motion for rehearing is no longer required to preserve points of error or issues for obtaining review in the Supreme Court. Nevertheless, there may good reasons to file the motion. First, courts of appeal like to have the opportunity to correct opinions before they go to the Supreme Court, and thus often give motions for rehearing considered review. Second, because the majority of cases do not merit Supreme Court review, rehearing may be the last opportunity for review. Finally, the motion extends time for filing the petition for review to the Supreme Court.

11. *Plenary power of the court of appeals.* TRAP 19 for the first time defines the plenary power of the courts of appeals. The court of appeals' jurisdiction automatically ceases 60 days after the judgment if no timely motion for rehearing or motion to extend time is filed, or 30 days after all timely filed motions for rehearing and motions to extend time are overruled.[19] The court of appeals retains plenary power until the expiration of the time period even after the petition for review is filed.[20]

12. *Frivolous appeals.* TRAP 45 gives the courts of appeals broad powers to award sanctions for frivolous appeals. A similar rule, TRAP 62, applies to proceedings in the Supreme Court. One court of appeals has discussed the standard for imposing sanctions as follows:[21]

> Rule 45 replaces the former Rule 84, entitled "Damages for Delay in Civil Cases," which applied "where the court of appeals shall determine that an appellant has taken an appeal for delay and without sufficient cause." A showing of "bad faith" was required. Under the new rule, "bad faith" is not required. However, it may be relevant in determining the amount of damages.
>
> Damages have been awarded when, looking at the record from the viewpoint of the appellant, there was no reasonable expectation of reversal. Other courts have . . . kept the "bad faith" requirement. Damages have also been awarded when an appeal is objectively frivolous and injures the appellee. Finally, one Houston court considered whether the appellant legitimately argued for a change in the law or merely presented his distorted version of the law
>
> The fundamental principle in these cases is that "[a] party's decision to appeal should be based on professional judgment made after careful review of the record for preserved error in light of the applicable standards of review." The record of the hearing on the plea to the jurisdiction shows that TxDOT's appellate division had already decided to appeal if the trial court denied the plea. Evidently TxDOT thought it might prevail on a novel issue. We conclude, as the trial court did, that this is a close call, but we will give TxDOT's motives the benefit of the doubt. We deny the Rule 45 motion for sanctions.

---

19 A motion for rehearing en banc is included as a motion that will extend the plenary power deadlines. Rule 19.1(b); Yzaguirre v. Gonzalez, 989 S. W.2d 111 (Tex. App.—San Antonio 1999, pet. denied).

20 *See* City of San Antonio v. Hartman, 201 S.W.3d 667 (Tex. 2006)(motion for rehearing en banc is a motion for rehearing that extends deadlines for petition for review).

21 Texas Dept. of Transp. v. Beckner, 74 S.W.3d 98 (Tex. App.—Waco 2002, no pet.).

13. *Other sanctions in the appellate courts*. Consider the following from *Merrill Dow Pharmaceuticals, Inc. v. Havner*:[22]

ON MOTION FOR REHEARING

ORDER

The motion for rehearing filed on behalf of the Havners is overruled. However, the tenor of that motion requires that we address the conduct of Respondents' counsel.

* * *

In assessing the appropriate response to the motion for rehearing that has now been filed by [counsel] and his co-counsel in this Court, we agree with another of our courts of appeals who recently found it necessary to address attacks on the integrity of that court:

> A distinction must be drawn between respectful advocacy and judicial denigration. Although the former is entitled to a protected voice, the latter can only be condoned at the expense of the public's confidence in the judicial process. Even were this court willing to tolerate the personal insult levied by [counsel], we are obligated to maintain the respect due this Court and the legal system we took an oath to serve.

Courts possess inherent power to discipline an attorney's behavior. "Courts of justice are universally acknowledged to be vested, by their very creation, with power to impose silence, respect, and decorum, in their presence."

The Disciplinary Rules governing the conduct of a lawyer provide:

> A lawyer should demonstrate respect for the legal system and for those who serve it, including judges, other lawyers and public officials. While it is a lawyer's duty, when necessary, to challenge the rectitude of official action, it is also a lawyer's duty to uphold legal process.

TEX. DISCIPLINARY R. PROF'L CONDUCT preamble & 4. Rule 8.02(a) of the Disciplinary Rules specifically states:

> A lawyer shall not make a statement that the lawyer knows to be false or with reckless disregard as to its truth or falsity concerning the qualifications or integrity of a judge, adjudicatory official or public legal officer, or of a candidate for election or appointment to judicial or legal office.

The Legislature has also provided a mechanism for courts to sanction counsel who file pleadings presented for an improper purpose or to harass. TEX. CIV. PRAC. & REM.CODE §§ 10.001-10.005. In addition, one of the lawyers for the Havners . . . is a non-resident attorney. His appearance in Texas courts is subject to the Rules Governing Admission to the Bar, including Rule XIX.

. . . Counsel for Respondents . . . are hereby afforded the opportunity to respond as to why the Court should not

(1) refer each of them to the appropriate disciplinary authorities;

(2) prohibit [non-resident] attorney from practicing in Texas courts; and

---

22 953 S.W.2d 706, 732-33 (Tex. 1997).

(3) impose monetary penalties as sanctions.

14. *Appeals by indigents*. Someone unable to pay the costs of appeal may file an affidavit of indigence with or before the notice of appeal, pursuant to TRAP 20. If no contest to the affidavit is filed and sustained, the party can proceed with the appeal without paying the costs for the record or any filing fees. The person most likely to challenge the affidavit is the court reporter, who may be the most affected by the decision to allow an appeal without cost. Because the affidavit is filed with the "trial court" and no notice is given directly to the court reporter, it is possible that the court reporter may not get notice of the affidavit until after the deadline for challenging it.[23]

15. *Motion practice in the appellate courts*. TRAP 9 and 10 govern motions filed in appellate courts. The requirements are spelled out clearly.

16. *Rehearing en banc*. TEX. CIV. PRAC. & REM. CODE 22.223 and TRAP 41.2 authorize courts of appeals to consider a case en banc upon a vote of a majority of the court's members. A justice can request a vote on en banc reconsideration with or without a motion filed by a party (rehearing before the panel requires a motion).[24] A motion for en banc reconsideration may requested at any time while the court of appeals has plenary power.[25] En banc consideration is disfavored, and "should not be ordered unless necessary to secure or maintain uniformity of the court's decisions or unless extraordinary circumstances require en banc consideration."[26] Apparently, a party has no right to argue the case before the en banc court or to get notice of reconsideration en banc.[27] Chief justices of the courts of appeals are not required to submit cases en banc unless the court has adopted rules that require it.[28]

---

23 *See In re* B.A.C., 4 S. W.3d 322 (Tex. App.—Houston [1st Dist.] 1999, pet. dism'd); Ford v. Whitehead, 2 S.W.3d 304 (Tex. App.—San Antonio 1999, no pet.). *See also* Morris v. Aguilar, 369 S.W.3d 168 (Tex. 2012) (holding that indigent party does not waive objection to late filed challenge by failure to make it in the trial court); In the Interest of C.H.C., 331 S.W.3d 426 (Tex. 2011)(holding that when pro se party filed sufficient and unchallenged affidavit establishing indigency, a free record is mandated).

24 City of San Antonio v. Hartman, 201 S.W.3d 667, 671 (Tex. 2006).

25 *Id.*

26 TRAP 41.2(c). *See* Wal-Mart Stores, Inc. v. Miller, 102 S.W.3d 706, 709 n.1 (Tex. 2003).

27 *Id.*

28 *In re* Yates, 960 S.W.3d 652 (Tex. 1997).

C. Jurisdiction of the Supreme Court of Texas

Read Tex. Const. Art. V, § 3; Tex. Govt. Code 22.001.

POOL
v.
FORD MOTOR COMPANY
715 S.W.2d 629
(Tex. 1986)

[Pool suffered a brain injury when his pickup truck left the road and hit a tree. He brought a product liability case against Ford, which defended the design and manufacture of its truck and also presented evidence that Pool caused the wreck by driving drunk and speeding. The jury found Ford liable and rejected its contention that Pool was at fault. The trial court rendered judgment on the verdict, but the court of appeals concluded that the jury's failure to find Pool contributorily negligent was against the weight of the evidence and ordered a new trial. The supreme court reversed that decision, remanded the case to the appellate court for further review, and required appellate courts in the future to explain in detail their reasoning when they reverse a jury finding on factual insufficiency/against-the-weight grounds.]

KILGARLIN, JUSTICE.

* * *

As a further argument as to why this cause should not be remanded for factual sufficiency determination, the Pools allege that the court of appeals exercised its fact jurisdiction in such a way as to undermine the jury verdict in contravention of the constitutional guarantee of right of trial by jury. It is true that Texas Constitution article I, section 15, provides that the right of trial by jury shall remain inviolate, but it is the same Constitution in article V, section 6, that states that decisions of courts of appeals shall be conclusive on all questions of fact. The Pools' argument is not a novel one. Indeed, shortly after the 1891 adoption of the amendment creating the then courts of civil appeals and delineating their jurisdiction, this court recognized the potential constitutional conflict and sought to strike a balance. *Choate v. San Antonio & A.P. Ry. Co.*, 91 Tex. 406, 44 S.W. 69 (1898).

In essence, CHIEF JUSTICE GAINES, speaking for the court in *Choate*, wrote that it was in the province of the jury to determine questions of fact but it was in the power of courts of civil appeals to set aside the finding and to award a new trial. He stated: It is contrary to the genius of our institutions, as well as to the letter and spirit of every constitution ever adopted in this State, to suppose that it was ever intended to substitute the judgment of the appellate courts upon the facts of a case in place of that of the jury, and to make the determination of these courts final. But, *Choate*, as did so many scholarly opinions which followed, sought to harmonize the two constitutional provisions by stating that while appellate courts could not find facts, if the jury finding was so against the great weight and preponderance of the evidence, the court of appeals could unfind facts and reverse the judgment and remand the matter for a new trial.

A case probably as often cited as any other before this court, *In re King's Estate*, 150 Tex. 662, 244 S.W.2d 660 (1951), alluded to the seeming conflict by saying: But Article 5, § 6 of the Constitution, VERNON'S ANN. ST., is no more to be ignored than any other part of that document, and that provision, with the decisions, statutes and rules based upon it, requires the Court of Civil Appeals, upon proper assignment, to consider the fact question of weight and preponderance of all the evidence and to order or deny a new trial accordingly as to the verdict may thus appear to it clearly unjust or otherwise.

* * *

However, *In re King's Estate* established that the supreme court might take jurisdiction, notwithstanding the finality of judgments of the courts of civil appeals on fact questions, in order to determine if a correct standard had been applied by the intermediate courts. A litany of subsequently decided cases serve as examples of a variety of situations in which the supreme court has reviewed factual insufficiency points because the court of appeals had utilized an incorrect test.

And even as to factual insufficiency, it has been the supreme court that has delineated the role of the courts of appeals. *In re King's Estate* mandated those courts to consider and weigh all of the evidence in the case in determining whether the evidence is insufficient or if the verdict is so against the great weight and preponderance of the evidence as to be manifestly unjust. This court, in that opinion, recognized that in performing this task, it was not simple to describe the intellectual process to be followed by the court of appeals; how it was that there could be probative evidence to support the verdict and at the same time not be sufficient evidence.

CHIEF JUSTICE CALVERT opined that a court of appeals "should analyze the evidence on both sides of the issue, at least in a brief and general way, and point out why the finding is regarded as being contrary to the great weight and preponderance of the evidence." Calvert, *supra*, at 368. JUSTICE GARWOOD enumerated a few of the many instances when a verdict should be set aside and a new trial granted. He cited examples of "such as to shock the conscience," "so as to be clearly unjust," "to clearly indicate bias." He suggested that in arriving at an insufficiency holding, the court of appeals "must, up to a point, follow the same kind of mental process that a jury does." Garwood, *supra*, at 811. Recognizing the inexact standard set for the courts of appeals, JUSTICE GARWOOD allowed that "[m]aybe some day we will develop more rules to aid trial courts and courts of civil appeals in dealing with this troublesome question." *Id.* at 812.

Our continuing review of courts of appeals decisions in which factual insufficiency points are discussed convinces us that the overwhelming majority of those opinions represent honest efforts by their scriveners to adhere to the guidelines of *In re King's Estate*. However, there occasionally appears an opinion in which it seems that the court of appeals has merely substituted its judgment for that of the jury. Those opinions couch their holdings with the necessary "factual insufficiency" or "against the great weight and preponderance" language without providing analyses of the evidence or stating bases for the conclusions drawn. One recent opinion is particularly noteworthy in this regard. In it the court of appeals reversed a judgment on factual insufficiency grounds, saying "[t]he jury evidently believed Appellee's argument; we do not." It may well be that the court of appeals in that case and other courts in similar cases considered and weighed all the evidence before arriving at a decision of insufficiency. But, without that mental process being reflected by the opinion, it is impossible for this court to be certain that the requirements of *In re King's Estate* have been followed.

In order that this court may in the future determine if a correct standard of review of factual insufficiency points has been utilized, courts of appeals, when reversing on insufficiency grounds, should, in their opinions, detail the evidence relevant to the issue in consideration and clearly state why the jury's finding is factually insufficient or is so against the great weight and preponderance as to be manifestly unjust; why it shocks the conscience; or clearly demonstrates bias. Further, those courts, in their opinions, should state in what regard the contrary evidence greatly outweighs the evidence in support of the verdict. It is only in this way that we will be able to determine if the requirements of *In re King's Estate* have been satisfied.

* * *

GONZALEZ, JUSTICE, concurring.

I concur with the court's opinion except that portion which deals with *In re King's Estate*. The majority acknowledges that: Our continuing review of courts of appeals decisions in which factual insufficiency points are discussed convinces us that the *overwhelming majority* of those opinions represent honest efforts by the scriveners to adhere to the guidelines of *In re King's Estate*. However, there occasionally appears an opinion in which is seems that the court of appeals has merely substituted its judgment for that of the jury. So, if the system "ain't broke, don't fix it."

* * *

Although the court's discussion does not directly violate the well established rules of *In re King's Estate*, the court is implicitly trying to prevent the court of appeals from second guessing the jury. I am fearful that this opinion may in turn be used to allow this court to second guess the courts of appeal. We cannot interfere with the fact jurisdiction of the court of appeals in contravention of our constitution. TEX. CONST. art. V, §§ 3, 6.

For the above reasons, I disagree with that portion of the majority opinion.

Notes & Questions

1. *Constitutional jurisdiction*. The Texas Constitution limits the Supreme Court's jurisdiction to questions of law (court of appeals' decision is conclusive on all questions of fact) in civil cases (the court of appeals have criminal and civil jurisdiction). Because the Supreme Court has no jurisdiction over facts, and the court of appeals' decision is conclusive on all questions of fact, the Supreme Court has no jurisdiction to address factual sufficiency points (Zones 2 and 4). The Supreme Court cannot review the record and determine whether the court of appeals correctly determined whether the evidence is factually sufficient of not to support the jury's verdict. The Supreme Court can, however, review the legal standard by which the court of appeals reviews factual sufficiency points, and if the wrong legal standard was applied, remand for reconsideration with the correct legal standard.

2. *Summary and review of legal and factual sufficiency.* Legal and factual sufficiency review can be confusing, but it is extremely important to understand. What follows is a series of questions and answers going through all possibilities of legal and factual sufficiency review in a particular case. Assume a misrepresentation case. Question #1 to the jury, an essential element for plaintiff's recovery, is "Did Plaintiff rely on Defendant's misrepresentation?" This is the question at issue below.

1. Verdict for Plaintiff. (All jury questions answered "yes.")
   Judgment for Plaintiff.
   Defendant's motion for judgment notwithstanding the verdict is denied.
   On appeal D claims jury answer to misrepresentation question 1 was based on zone 1 evidence.
   Court of Appeals finds evidence is zone 1.
   Court of Appeals result: Render judgment for Defendant.
   (Same result in Supreme Court.)

2. Verdict for Plaintiff.
   Judgment for Plaintiff.
   Defendant's motion for judgment notwithstanding the verdict and alternative motion for new trial are denied say evidence is zone 1 or zone 2 on Q #1.
   Court of Appeals finds it is zone 2.
   Court of Appeals result: Remand for new trial.
   (Supreme Court cannot make this determination.).

3. Verdict for Plaintiff.
   Judgment for Plaintiff.
   Defendant moves for judgment notwithstanding the verdict and is denied.
   Court of Appeals determines evidence is in zone 3.
   Court of Appeals result: Judgment for Plaintiff affirmed.
   What if Court of Appeals determined evidence in zone 4 or 5?
   Same result.

4. Verdict for Defendant.
   Judgment for Defendant.
   (Jury answered "no" to Q1, "yes" to all others and awarded damages).
   Plaintiff's motion for new trial is denied.
   Court of Appeals finds evidence in zone 4.
   Result in Court of Appeals: Remand for new trial.

5. Verdict for Defendant (as above).
   Judgment on verdict for D (same jury answers as above).
   Plaintiff's motion for judgment notwithstanding the verdict and alternate motion for new trial are denied.
   Court of Appeals finds evidence in zone 4.
   Court of Appeals result: Remand for new trial.
   Defendant appeals to Supreme Court (asserting evidence in Zone 2 or 3, not 4).
   Supreme Court result: No jurisdiction.

6. Verdict for Defendant (as above).
   Judgment on verdict for Defendant.
   Plaintiff's motion for judgment notwithstanding the verdict and motion for new trial are denied.
   Court of Appeals finds evidence in zone 5.
   Court of Appeals result: Render judgment for Plaintiff.

Defendant appeals to Supreme Court.
Supreme Court finds Plaintiff's evidence falls short of zone 5 but is in zone 2, 3 or 4.
Supreme Court result: Remand to Court of Appeals for further determination.
On remand, Court of Appeals finds evidence in zone 4.
Court of Appeals result: Remand to Trial Court for new trial.

7. Defendant's motion for directed verdict at close of Plaintiff's evidence granted based on Trial Court's conclusion that evidence supporting Q1 was zone 1.
   Court of Appeals finds evidence is actually zone 3.
   Court of Appeals result: Remand for new trial.
   Suppose Court of Appeals found evidence was zone 5?
   Result: Reverse and remand so Defendant can present evidence and court can rule again.
   Suppose Court of Appeals found evidence was zone 2?
   Result: Remand for new trial.
   Suppose Court of Appeals found evidence was zone 4?
   Result: Remand for new trial.
   Suppose Court of Appeals found evidence was zone 1?
   Result: Affirm Trial Court judgment.

3. *Statutory jurisdiction.* The Supreme Court's jurisdiction is also limited by statute. Section 22.001 of the Government Code, amended in 2017, provides that the court has jurisdiction over an appeal where "if the court determines that the appeal presents a question of law that is important to the jurisprudence of the state," except where the judgment of the court of appeals is made final by statute. This includes interlocutory appeals.[1]

4. *Discretionary review.* The Supreme Court does not have to exercise its jurisdiction in every case presented. Instead, when the Supreme Court has jurisdiction over a particular case, review is discretionary.[2]

5. *Petition for review.* The 1997 rules drastically changed practice in the Supreme Court of Texas as it replaced the old writ of error practice with the petition for review. The petition for review, governed by TRAP 53, is not intended to serve as the brief on the merits of all issues presented for review. Instead, it is designed principally to tell the Court why it should exercise jurisdiction in the case. The petition for review is limited to 4,500 words or 15 pages, and, in theory, is designed to allow each justice time to read all petitions filed and to decide whether to grant each petition on that basis, rather than on summaries prepared by staff attorneys. The decision whether to grant or deny the petition is purely a matter of judicial discretion.[3] In exercising its discretion, the court may consider, among other things, whether there is a dissenting opinion in the court of appeals, whether there is a conflict among courts on the issue, whether the case involves constitutional issues, whether the case presents issues concerning the construction or validity of a statute,

---

1 GOVT. CODE § 22.225, which made the court of appeals' judgment conclusive on the law and the facts in five types of cases, including appeals from most interlocutory orders that can be appealed, was repealed in 2017.

2 *See* TRAP 56.1.

3 TRAP 56.1(a).

whether the error "is of such importance to the state's jurisprudence that it should be corrected," and whether it presents an issue of first impression for the Supreme Court.[4]

6. *Who must file a petition for review and when.* Any party aggrieved by the judgment of the court of appeals (who seeks to alter the judgment of the court of appeals) must file a petition for review. TRAP 53. The petition must be filed within 45 days after the date the court of appeals rendered judgment if no timely motion for rehearing is filed, or 45 days after the date all motions for rehearing were overruled. Once one party has filed a petition for review, others must file within this 45-day period, or within 30 days after any preceding petition is filed, whichever is later. TRAP 53.7. The petition is filed with the Clerk of the Supreme Court. The issues or points raised in the petition must have been preserved in the trial court and assigned as error in the court of appeals. Thus, one cannot raise an error of the trial court for the first time in the Supreme Court.

7. *Disposition of the petition.* The Supreme Court may grant the petition or choose from four different orders when it chooses not to grant, as set out in TRAP 56. (a) The court most often "denies" the petition, which means that the court of appeals opinion may contain an error, but not of such importance that it requires correction. The denial or dismissal of a petition gives no indication of the Supreme Court's decision on the merits of the case.[5] (b) If the Court lacks jurisdiction, it will dismiss the case with the notation "dismissed w.o.j." (c) If the petition is "refused," the Court has determined that the Court of Appeals judgment and the legal principles announced in the opinion are correct. A "pet. ref'd" notation gives the court of appeals opinion the same precedential value as an opinion of the Supreme Court. (d) If the Court grants the petition, but then determines that review should not have been granted, it may set aside the order granting review, and either deny or refuse review. A vote of 4 justices will grant the petition, and the petition can be granted on some issues or points of error and not others. Within 15 days after the court issues its order disposing of the petition for review, or its judgment if the petition was granted, the parties may file a motion for rehearing pursuant to TRAP 64.

8. *Record.* TRAP 54.2(a) mandates that the court of appeals not send the original record of the trial court proceedings to the Supreme Court unless requested. Unless and until the Supreme Court requests the record, the appendix to the petition for review serves the purpose of the record. Thus, the appendix is very important. TRAP 53.2(k) mandates the contents of the appendix—the trial court judgment or appealable order, the jury verdict or findings of fact and conclusions of law, the opinion of the court of appeals, and the text of any rule, statute or other law on which argument is based and the text of any contract or document central to the argument. Other items may be included in the appendix as well.

9. *The response.* A response to the petition is not required, and some parties may choose not to file one. A party may expedite disposition of the petition for review by filing a "waiver" of response.[6] The Supreme Court may then act on the petition for review without waiting until the time has expired for filing the response. If no response is filed, the Court can deny or dismiss the petition. However, it may not grant or refuse the petition without first requesting a response. If

---

[4] *Id.*

[5] *See* Loram Maintenance of Way, Inc. v. Ianni, 210 S.W.3d 593 (Tex. 2006)(holding that the "law of the case" doctrine does not prevent Supreme Court from deciding issue presented in prior petition for review that was denied).

[6] TRAP 53.3.

the respondent chooses to file a response, it must be filed within 30 days after the petition is filed, and any reply must be filed within 15 days after the response is filed.

The response primarily responds to the points or issues asserted in the petition for review. If the respondent has complaints about anything that the court of appeals did, it is not sufficient simply to present those complaints in the response to the petition.[7] TRAP 53.3 requires the respondent to assert as separate points or issues any independent grounds for affirmance overruled or rejected by the court of appeals, and any independent grounds for alternative but lesser relief overruled or rejected by the court of appeals, in the event of reversal of the court of appeals' judgment (e.g. a remand for new trial rather than rendition of judgment favoring petitioner). The parties may raise at any time (even on motion for rehearing) points briefed but not decided by the court of appeals to obtain a remand to the court of appeals to consider those issues or have the Supreme Court decide them.

10. *Reply*. TRAP 53.5 expressly permits the petitioner to file a reply within 15 days of the filing of the response.

11. *Briefs on the merits*. After the petition for review has been filed, with or without granting the petition, and in addition to its option to request a response, the Supreme Court may request full briefs on the merits under TRAP 55.1. The schedule for briefing will be set out in the notice requesting briefs on the merits. Both petitioner's and respondent's briefs are limited to 50 pages, and a reply brief of 25 pages is also allowed.

12. *Submission and argument*. TRAP 59 governs submission and argument. The Supreme Court may grant a petition for review and hand down an opinion without oral argument upon a vote of at least six members of the court. The court will set argument in those cases where it feels that argument will aid the court.

13. *Direct appeals*. TRAP 57 provides for direct appeals to the Supreme Court in cases allowed by Constitution or statute. Section 22.001(c) of the Government Code allows direct appeals when the trial court grants or denies an injunction on the ground of the constitutionality of a Texas statute. The direct appeal is perfected the same way as ordinary appeals to the courts of appeals; thus, those deadlines must be followed.

14. *Certifications*. Federal appellate courts can certify questions of law to the Texas Supreme Court under TRAP 58 which the Supreme Court can answer or decline to answer.

Problem

P pleads and gets jury questions (broad form) on negligence and DTPA causes of action. The jury finds favorably to the P on the negligence theory, but fails to find a violation of the DTPA. The jury finds P's actual damages of $100,000, and the attorney's fees (recoverable under the DTPA) of $300,000. The trial court awards judgment on the verdict to the P for $100,000. P files a motion for judgment notwithstanding the verdict on grounds of conclusive evidence and a motion for new trial on grounds that the verdict is against the great weight of the evidence on the failure to find a DTPA violation. D files a motion for judgment notwithstanding the verdict on no

[7] See The Center for Health Care Services v. Qunitanilla, 121 S.W.3d 733 (Tex. 2003) (holding that issue was waived when raised only in responsive brief on the merits, not in a petition for review or response to petition for review.).

evidence grounds and motion for new trial on insufficient evidence grounds on the negligence finding. D had also objected to a large part of P's evidence because it was "prejudicial," but the trial court overruled the objection. D files a timely notice of appeal in the court of appeals. What are D's issues on appeal? What are P's issues in response? Does P have to perfect its own appeal?

If the Court of Appeals decides that there was insufficient evidence to support the finding of negligence and that the failure to find a DTPA violation was not against the great weight and preponderance of the evidence, what is the judgment of the court of appeals? Who would file petitions for review? What issues should be in the response(s)?

D. Original Jurisdiction in the Appellate Courts

In re PRUDENTIAL INSURANCE COMPANY
148 S.W.3d 124
(Tex. 2004)

HECHT, JUSTICE.

* * *

Having concluded that the parties' contractual jury waiver is enforceable, we turn to whether Prudential is entitled to relief by mandamus. Prudential must meet two requirements. One is to show that the trial court clearly abused its discretion. *E.g., Walker v. Packer,* 827 S.W.2d 833, 840 (Tex. 1992). We have concluded as a matter of law that Prudential was entitled to enforcement of the jury waiver. Since "[a] trial court has no 'discretion' in determining what the law is or applying the law to the facts," even when the law is unsettled, the trial court's refusal to enforce the jury waiver was a clear abuse of discretion. Thus, Prudential has met the first requirement.

The other requirement Prudential must meet is to show that it has no adequate remedy by appeal. The operative word, "adequate", has no comprehensive definition; it is simply a proxy for the careful balance of jurisprudential considerations that determine when appellate courts will use original mandamus proceedings to review the actions of lower courts. These considerations implicate both public and private interests. Mandamus review of incidental, interlocutory rulings by the trial courts unduly interferes with trial court proceedings, distracts appellate court attention to issues that are unimportant both to the ultimate disposition of the case at hand and to the uniform development of the law, and adds unproductively to the expense and delay of civil litigation. Mandamus review of significant rulings in exceptional cases may be essential to preserve important substantive and procedural rights from impairment or loss, allow the appellate courts to give needed and helpful direction to the law that would otherwise prove elusive in appeals from final judgments, and spare private parties and the public the time and money utterly wasted enduring eventual reversal of improperly conducted proceedings. An appellate remedy is "adequate" when any benefits to mandamus review are outweighed by the detriments. When the benefits outweigh the detriments, appellate courts must consider whether the appellate remedy is adequate.

This determination is not an abstract or formulaic one; it is practical and prudential. It resists categorization, as our own decisions demonstrate. Although this Court has tried to give more concrete direction for determining the availability of mandamus review, rigid rules are necessarily inconsistent with the flexibility that is the remedy's principal virtue. Thus, we wrote in *Walker v. Packer* that "an appellate remedy is not inadequate merely because it may involve more expense or delay than obtaining an extraordinary writ." While this is certainly true, the word "merely" carries heavy freight. In *In re E.I. duPont de Nemours & Co.,* 92 S.W.3d 517, 523-524 (Tex. 2002), we concluded that defending the claims of more than 8,000 plaintiffs in litigation that would last for years was not *mere* expense and delay, and that mandamus review of the denial of duPont's special appearance was justified, even though duPont could eventually appeal and did not appear to be in any danger of succumbing to the burden of the litigation. In *Travelers Indemnity Co. v. Mayfield,* 923 S.W.2d 590, 595 (Tex. 1996), we granted mandamus review of an order requiring a carrier to pay the plaintiff's attorney fees as incurred in a compensation case, even though the carrier could have appealed from the final judgment and won recovery for the amounts paid, because the order not only cost the carrier money but "radically skew[ed] the procedural dynamics of the case" by requiring the defendant to fund the plaintiff's prosecution of her claims. In *In re Masonite Corp.,* 997 S.W.2d 194, 195-196 (Tex. 1999), the trial court on its own motion and without any authority whatever, split two cases into sixteen and transferred venue of fourteen of them to other counties. We held that the defendants were not required to wait until appeal to complain:

> *Walker* does not require us to turn a blind eye to blatant injustice nor does it mandate that we be an accomplice to sixteen trials that will amount to little more than a fiction. Appeal may be adequate for a particular party, but it is no remedy at all for the irreversible waste of judicial and public resources that would be required here if mandamus does not issue.

These cases, among a great many others that could be cited, serve to illustrate that whether an appellate remedy is "adequate" so as to preclude mandamus review depends heavily on the circumstances presented and is better guided by general principles than by simple rules.[1]

Nor is the consideration whether to grant mandamus review confined to private concerns. No one suggested in *Masonite* that any individual party would suffer more by waiting to complain on appeal of the venue order than would any other party complaining of any other venue order in any other case. Two factors drove our decision in *Masonite*: the complete lack of authority for the trial court's order, and the impact on the legal system. We simply could not justify putting the civil justice system itself to the trouble of grinding through proceedings that were certain to be "little more than a fiction." The trial court's ruling in *Travelers* was novel but might easily have become a repeated error. Either way, the error was clear enough, and correction simple enough, that mandamus review was appropriate.

Prudent mandamus relief is also preferable to legislative enlargement of interlocutory appeals.[2] The unavailability of mandamus relief increases the pressure for expanded interlocutory

---

1 *See also* 16 CHARLES ALAN WRIGHT, ARTHUR R. MILLER, & EDWARD H. COOPER, FEDERAL PRACTICE AND PROCEDURE § 3934.1, at 572, 574 (1996) (stating that "[w]rit review that responds to occasional special needs provides a valuable ad hoc relief valve for the pressures that are imperfectly contained by the statutes permitting appeals from final judgments and interlocutory orders", and that "[i]mportant questions of procedure often are difficult to review by appeal, and at times may demand appellate intervention to secure uniformity between different judges, or simply to bring the balancing perspective that appellate review is intended to provide in controlling the practices as well as the substantive decisions of trial courts.").

appeals. For example, when this Court refused to review venue decisions by mandamus, the Legislature responded by authorizing mandamus review of all decisions involving mandatory venue provisions. When we held that the denial of a special appearance would ordinarily not warrant mandamus review, the Legislature responded by creating an interlocutory appeal from the denial of a special appearance. When questions arose concerning the availability of mandamus to review the sufficiency of expert reports required in medical malpractice cases, the Legislature responded by creating an interlocutory appeal from the denial of dismissals of such cases for insufficient expert reports. Interlocutory appeals lie as of right and must be decided on the merits, increasing the burden on the appellate system. "Mandamus," on the other hand, "is an extraordinary remedy, not issued as a matter of right, but at the discretion of the court. Although mandamus is not an equitable remedy, its issuance is largely controlled by equitable principles." As a selective procedure, mandamus can correct clear errors in exceptional cases and afford appropriate guidance to the law without the disruption and burden of interlocutory appeal. Appellate courts must be mindful, however, that the benefits of mandamus review are easily lost by overuse.

The issue before us in the present case—whether a pre-suit waiver of trial by jury is enforceable—fits well within the types of issues for which mandamus review is not only appropriate but necessary. It is an issue of law, one of first impression for us, but likely to recur (it has already arisen in another case in the court of appeals, also on petition for mandamus. It eludes answer by appeal. In no real sense can the trial court's denial of Prudential's contractual right to have the Secchis waive a jury ever be rectified on appeal. If Prudential were to obtain judgment on a favorable jury verdict, it could not appeal, and its contractual right would be lost forever. If Prudential suffered judgment on an unfavorable verdict, Prudential could not obtain reversal for the incorrect denial of its contractual right "unless the court of appeals concludes that the error complained of ... probably caused the rendition of an improper judgment".[10] Even if Prudential could somehow obtain reversal based on the denial of its contractual right, it would already have lost a part of it by having been subject to the procedure it agreed to waive.

* * *

---

2 *See also* George C. Pratt, *Extraordinary Writs,* in 19 MOORE'S FEDERAL PRACTICE § 204.01[2][b], at 204-7 (3d ed. 2004) ("In order to meet the demands of justice in individual cases, discretionary review is preferable to enlarging by judicial interpretation the categories of interlocutory orders that are appealable as of right. General categories of orders that are appealable as of right often include many orders that should not be appealable at all. Review by extraordinary writ allows the circuit courts to retain the final judgment rule and avoid piecemeal appeals, yet be able to respond to the exceptional case that should be reviewed prior to final judgment. Thus, [mandamus] affords an avenue of relief to litigants and a tool for the courts to supervise the proper administration of justice.").

10 TEX. R. APP. P. 44.1(a)(1). *Cf.* Mercedes-Benz Credit Corp. v. Rhyne, 925 S.W.2d 664, 667 (Tex. 1996) ("The wrongful denial of a jury trial is harmful when the case contains material fact questions."); Halsell v. Dehoyos, 810 S.W.2d 371, 372 (Tex. 1991) (per curiam) ("A refusal to grant a jury trial is harmless error only if the record shows that no material issues of fact exist and an instructed verdict would have been justified."); William. D. Cleveland & Sons v. Smith, 102 Tex. 490, 119 S.W. 843, 843-844 (1909) (same).

Notes & Questions

1. *Original jurisdiction*. Note that mandamus proceedings originate in the Supreme Court. The trial judge is the respondent. Under Article 5, Sections 3 and 7 of the Texas Constitution (and by statute), both the supreme court and appellate courts have jurisdiction to issue writs of mandamus and habeas corpus[1] and other writs "as provided by law."[2] Any Texas court has statutory authority to issue writs in aid of its jurisdiction.[3] The Supreme Court alone may issue writs of *procedendo*, *quo warranto*[4] and mandamus or injunction against an officer of the executive branch of Texas government.[5] Since 1983, the courts of appeals have had the power to issue mandamus as to district and county court judges.[6]

With both the Supreme Court and the courts of appeals hearing mandamus petitions, is there not a danger that parties will file in both places and that confusion will result? No. When both have jurisdiction, the mandamus should be filed first in the court of appeals. However, the Supreme Court can bypass the court of appeals when there is a "compelling reason" to do so.[7]

2. *Mandamus*. By far the most used writ is the writ of mandamus, by which the court issues an order to a public official, including a trial court judge, in an attempt to get immediate review of the judge's orders. Both the court of appeals and the Supreme Court have mandamus jurisdiction over a trial court judge. These mandamus actions must, therefore, be filed first in the court of appeals. Only after the court of appeals has decided the issue may mandamus be filed in the Supreme Court. Absent a compelling reason, the Supreme Court will not hear a mandamus matter until a court of appeals has acted on it.[8] If the court of appeals issued the writ, the mandamus will be filed against the court of appeals rather than the district judge. Mandamus is available only when the judge has clearly abused its discretion and the remedy of an ordinary appeal is inadequate. This is a difficult showing, as it requires a showing that the parties are in danger of losing

---

1 The Supreme Court's habeas corpus jurisdiction is limited to confinements resulting from the violation of an order or decree in a civil case. The Court of Criminal Appeals deals with other confinements. *See Ex parte McDonald*, 441 S.W.2d 828 (Tex. 1969).

2 *See* §§ 22.002; 22.221 GOV'T CODE.

3 § 21.001 GOV'T CODE.

4 A writ of quo warranto requires an official to say by what authority he or she is proceeding. A writ of procedendo requires a trial court to go forward (usually to proceed to trial). These functions are now handled routinely by mandamus or injunction. Though these writs are rarely used, they are still appropriate in some cases. *See* State ex. rel. Angelini v. Hardberger, 932 S.W.2d 489 (Tex. 1996) (declaring that a resigning judge continues in office until the date of his resignation, despite the Governor's appointment of another judge for a term beginning before the stated resignation date).

5 § 22.002 GOV'T CODE.

6 *See* § 22.221, GOV'T CODE and Welder v. Fritz, 750 S.W.2d 930 (Tex. App.—Corpus Christi 1988, orig. proceeding) (court of appeal's mandamus authority limited to county and district court judges within its district). The supreme court's authority does not extend to county court judges. *See* § 22.002(a), GOV'T CODE. Note that district courts, when acting as appellate courts, have mandamus authority with respect to inferior courts. *See, e.g.*, Alice National Bank v. Edwards, 383 S.W.2d 482, 483-484 (Tex. Civ. App.—Corpus Christi 1964, writ ref'd n.r.e.).

7 In re State Bar of Texas, 113 S.W.3d 730 (Tex. 2003).

8 *See* T.R.A.P. 52.3(d)(5).

substantial rights. A showing that an appeal would involve more expense and delay is not sufficient.[9]

3. *Requirements*. TRAP 52 governs all original proceedings in the appellate courts. The rule sets out in specific detail the form and content of the documents parties are required to file. The original proceeding is commenced by filing a petition with the clerk.[10] The timetables for ordinary appeals do not apply—thus there is no specific time by which the writ must be filed. The party seeking relief is the "relator." The judge, court or officer against whom relief is sought is the "respondent." In contrast to prior practice, the name of the respondent will not appear in the style of the proceeding. Instead, the petition will read "*In re* [name of the relator]."

---

[9] Walker v. Packer, 827 S.W.2d 833 (Tex. 1992). *Compare* Canadian Helicopters v. Wittig, 876 S.W.2d 304 (Tex. 1994)(no mandamus for erroneous refusal to grant special appearance) *with* National Industrial Sand Ass'n v. Gibson, 897 S.W.2d 769 (Tex. 1995)(allowing mandamus for erroneous refusal to grant special appearance).

[10] The former rules' requirement that the party must first seek leave to file the writ has been eliminated. *See* TRAP 52, cmt.

CHAPTER 18. DEFAULTS AND DISMISSALS

A. Obtaining and Overturning a Default Judgment

Read Rules 239-244.

When a defendant is served with process, he is obligated to respond by answer or other appearance by the Monday next following 20 days after service of process.[1] If he does not, the plaintiff may ask the court to render a judgment by default, a "no-answer" default judgment. The non-answering party "is said to have admitted both the truth of facts set out in the petition and the defendant's liability on any cause of action properly alleged by those facts, but a trial may still be necessary if the plaintiff's damages are unliquidated."[2]

To obtain a default judgment, the plaintiff should file a motion for default judgment, informing the court that the return of service has been on file for more than 10 days,[3] and providing the defendant's last known address.[4] The best practice is to have the court sign the default judgment on liability as soon as possible, and if damages are unliquidated, schedule a hearing and present evidence of damages.[5] Usually, the defendant will not appear at this hearing, although he is entitled to if he learns of it.[6]

After the hearing, the judge awards damages according to the evidence, and renders a final default judgment. The clerk is supposed to send notice of the judgment to the defendant at the defendant's last known address, but the clerk's failure to do so, is not grounds for overturning the default.[7] The plaintiff can begin the process of executing on the judgment.

Sometimes a defendant will file an answer, but will not show up for trial, setting up a post-answer default. The post-answer default differs from the no-answer default because the answer puts the merits of the claim in issue. Therefore, judgment cannot be rendered on the pleadings, and the plaintiff must prove liability as well as damages in the default judgment hearing.[8]

The procedure by which defendants seek to overturn a default judgment is largely dependent upon when the defendant learns of the judgment and acts upon that knowledge. Earlier is almost always better—overturning a judgment that has become finally final (it disposes of all claims and all parties, and the time periods for appeal have expired) is more difficult because of a fundamental public policy favoring the finality of judgments.[9]

---

1 TRCP 99(b).

2 Paradigm Oil, Inc. v. Retamco Operating, Inc., 372 S.W.3d 177, 183 (Tex. 2012). Unliquidated damages are damages that are uncertain in amount, and cannot be established from the pleadings by a mathematical calculation. Liquidated damages are damages of a sum certain, or an amount that can be mathematically calculated from information set forth in the pleadings. For example, personal injury damages are unliquidated. Principal and interest due on a promissory note are liquidated damages.

3 Rules 239, 107.

4 Rule 239a.

5 Rule 243.

6 Paradigm, 372 S.W.3d at 183.

7 Rule 239a.

8 Paradigm, 372 S.W.3d at 183.

9 Mabon Limited v. Afri-Carib Enterprises, Inc., 369 S.W.3d 809 (Tex. 2012).

Defendants learn of default judgments at different times and in a variety of ways. Sometimes they receive the notice from the clerk fairly soon after the judgment is signed, in which case, the defendant will have a plethora of methods by which to overturn the default, and is likely to be fairly successful at doing so.

Sometimes they do not hear of the judgment until the plaintiff begins to attempt execution, which can be long after the judgment was signed and becomes finally final. In one of the Texas Supreme Court's opinions, the plaintiff "waited six years to abstract the judgment and about nine years to attempt execution" of a $1.5 million default judgment, which by then "had more than doubled" to about $3.5 million due to the accumulation of post-judgment interest.[10] As that opinion makes clear, the methods available to challenge a finally final default are limited, as are the chances of success.

B. Void or Voidable Judgment & Direct or Collateral Attack?

The first thing one should ask when faced with a default judgment (after determining that it is a final judgement, disposing of all parties and all issues) is whether it is "void" or merely "voidable." If the judgment is void, it can be attacked anytime, using any available procedure. If the judgment is "merely voidable," one is limited in the time and procedures available to challenge it.

As the Supreme Court tells us, a judgment is void when "the court rendering judgment had no jurisdiction of the parties or property, no jurisdiction of the subject matter, no jurisdiction to enter the particular judgment, or no capacity to act."[1] In other words, the judgment is void when the court rendering that judgment had no power over the parties or the controversy, and it is merely voidable when the court did have such power.

The failure to fill out the certificate of service properly under Rules 106 and 107, and other technical problems with service of process are not jurisdictional, and do not render a judgment void.[2] But publication notice in a parental termination case, given to a mother who was in touch with CPS, is a violation of due process, rendering the judgment void.[3]

"A judgment entered without notice or service is constitutionally infirm."[4] And "some form of attack must be available when defects in personal jurisdiction violate due process."[5]

A void judgment may be attacked either directly *or* collaterally.[6] A direct attack, such as an appeal, is a proceeding brought for the purpose of attacking a judgment, and must be filed within strict deadlines. In contrast, a collateral attack is an attack on a judgment brought in a proceeding

---

10 PNS Stores, Inc. v. Rivera, 379 S.W.3d 267, 269 (Tex. 2012).

1 *Id.* at 272.

2 *Id.* at 273.

3 In the Interest of E.R., 385 S.W.3d 552, 563-66 (Tex. 2012).

4 Peralta v. Heights Medical Center, Inc., 485 U.S. 80, 84 (1988).

5 PNS, 379 S.W.3d at 272-73.

6 *Id.* at 271.

brought for some other purpose.[7] For example, when a judgment creditor brings an enforcement action, the judgment debtor may collaterally attack the judgment by claiming it is void and convincing the court that the judgment is not enforceable. There is no time limit for collaterally attacking a void judgment—a void judgment is void, is always void, and can never be enforced.

If the judgment is not void, it nevertheless may be "voidable," which means that it is erroneous and reversible.

While a voidable judgment cannot be collaterally attacked, it may be attacked directly. "A direct attack—such as an appeal, a motion for new trial, or a bill of review—attempts to correct, amend, modify or vacate a judgment and must be brought within a definite time period after the judgment's rendition."[8]

There are three methods to directly attack a default judgment in Texas: (1) the motion for new trial filed in the trial court, which if denied will be appealed; (2) writ of error review, which is a special appeal to the court of appeals; and (3) the bill of review, an equitable proceeding filed in the trial court. Remember, a defaulting defendant also may use these procedures to directly attack a judgment for an error that renders the judgment void within the time allowed.

C. Motion for New Trial and the *Craddock* Test

The Motion for New Trial must be filed within 30 days after the date a final judgment is signed.[1] But, if the defendant got notice of the judgment between 20 and 90 days after the judgment was signed, the time is extended as the Rules restart the clock. The judgment is not final, and a motion for new trial may be filed, until 30 days after the date that the defendant learned of the judgment.[2] And if the defendant was served by publication, a motion for new trial may be filed until 2 years after the date the judgment was signed.[3]

It is almost impossible to reverse a trial judge's order *granting* a timely motion for new trial, primarily because new trial orders are not appealable.[4] But all is not lost if the trial court denies the motion, because the order can be reversed for abuse of discretion if the defendant satisfies the venerable *Craddock* test, which has three parts:.[5]

> Under *Craddock*, a trial court is required to set aside a default judgment if (1) "the failure of the defendant to answer before judgment was not intentional, or the result of conscious indifference on his part, but was due to a mistake or an accident"; (2) "the motion for a

---

7 *Id.* at 272.

8 *Id.* at 271.

1 Rule 329b.

2 Rule 306a(4); E.R., 385 S.W.3d at 557.

3 Rule 329.

4 In re Columbia Medical Center, 290 S.W.3d 204 (Tex. 2009).

5 *See* Craddock v. Sunshine Bus Lines, Inc., 133 S.W.2d 124, 126 (Tex. 1939).

new trial sets up a meritorious defense"; and (3) granting the motion "will occasion no delay or otherwise work an injury to the plaintiff." *Craddock,* 133 S.W.2d at 126.[6]

As the Supreme Court has noted, the "critical question" in any default judgment challenge is "Why did the defendant not appear?"[7] If the defendant never received the suit papers (and got no notice of the proceeding), the trial court should generally set aside the default judgment without regard to the other *Craddock* elements.

But proving lack of service can be extremely difficult because the recitations in a return of service carry significant weight.[8] My favorite case illustrating this is *Caldwell v. Barnes,*[9] where the process server and his girlfriend both testified that they were in Las Vegas instead of in Wyoming on the day the return said that process was served, directly contradicting his return of service. But the trial judge, questioning all of the witness' credibility, refused to find no service, and upheld the default judgment.

If the defendant did receive the suit papers, but has some other reason for not appearing, *Craddock* must be satisfied. Of course, the first *Craddock* element is the one usually at issue. What excuse is "good enough"?

SUTHERLAND
v.
SPENCER
376 S.W.3d 752
(Tex. 2012)

Opinion

JUSTICE GREEN delivered the opinion of the Court, in which JUSTICE HECHT, JUSTICE WAINWRIGHT, JUSTICE MEDINA, JUSTICE JOHNSON, JUSTICE GUZMAN and JUSTICE LEHRMANN joined.

In this case, we consider whether the excuse offered by defendants for failing to answer a lawsuit timely is sufficient to satisfy the first element of the *Craddock* test for setting aside a no-answer default judgment; *i.e.,* that the failure to appear was not intentional or the result of conscious indifference but was the result of a mistake or an accident. *See Craddock v. Sunshine Bus Lines, Inc.,* 134 Tex. 388, 133 S.W.2d 124, 126 (Tex. Com. App. 1939). Because the affidavits attached to the defendants' motion established the first *Craddock* element, the defendants' motion for new trial could not be denied on the ground that the excuse was insufficient. Accordingly, we reverse the court of appeals' judgment and remand the case to that court.

I

Robert Spencer contracted with Southern Customs Paint and Body to paint and perform a frame-off restoration on his 1965 Chevrolet Corvette for $7,500. Spencer alleged that when he went to pick up his car five months later, he found that the work was incomplete and that irre-

---

6 Sutherland, 376 S.W.3d at 754

7 Sutherland at 755; Milestone at 309.

8 Primate Constr., Inc. v. Silver, 884 S.W.2d 151, 152 (Tex. 1994).

9 975 S.W.2d 535 (Tex. 1998).

placeable parts and pieces of the vehicle were missing. In accordance with the notice provision of the Deceptive Trade Practices Act (DTPA), Spencer sent Southern Customs and its co-operators, Jesus "Jesse" De La Garza and Robert Sutherland, (collectively, Southern Customs) a demand letter alerting them to the possibility of a suit. *See* TEX. BUS. & COM. CODE § 17.505 (requiring a consumer to give written notice to the defendant at least sixty days before filing suit). Upon receipt, Southern Customs responded to that letter.

A year later, Spencer brought a DTPA suit against Southern Customs for violating the terms of the automobile repair service contract. Spencer complained of an incomplete and inadequate paint job on his Corvette, lost car parts, and false representations regarding the time and cost for completing the work. Through a process server, Spencer served all three named defendants with citations. One citation named "Jesse Garza" as the defendant for service, but the return stated that the citation was served on "Jesse De La Garza." Another citation named "Southern Customs Paint and Body" as a defendant, while the return stated the citation was served on "Southern Custom's by delivering to Robert Sutherland." De La Garza pointed out the citation's error in his name to the process server, who then offered to take the citation back to correct the mistake. De La Garza declined that offer and told the process server that regardless of the error, he knew he was the person being sued and to leave the documents with him.

Southern Customs failed to file a timely answer. Spencer obtained a default judgment that awarded him nearly $150,000, which included the trebling of Spencer's economic and mental anguish damages due to alleged intentional conduct under the DTPA, as well as attorney's fees.

Southern Customs filed a timely motion for new trial, arguing that service on De La Garza was improper, and that Southern Customs established the necessary *Craddock* elements to set aside the default judgment. Under *Craddock,* a trial court is required to set aside a default judgment if (1) "the failure of the defendant to answer before judgment was not intentional, or the result of conscious indifference on his part, but was due to a mistake or an accident"; (2) "the motion for a new trial sets up a meritorious defense"; and (3) granting the motion "will occasion no delay or otherwise work an injury to the plaintiff." *Craddock,* 133 S.W.2d at 126. The trial court denied the motion for new trial. The court of appeals affirmed the trial court's judgment, holding that the default judgment was not void for defective service, and that Southern Customs was not entitled to a new trial because it failed to satisfy the first *Craddock* element. 377 S.W.3d 1, 5-6 (Tex. App.—Corpus Christi-Edinburg 2010). Because Southern Customs asserted facts that, if true, negate intentional or consciously indifferent conduct, we reverse the court of appeals' judgment and remand the case for consideration of the second and third elements of the *Craddock* test.

II

Southern Customs asserts that service of process was invalid because one of the citations misstated the name of Jesse De La Garza and the return on the other citation did not show proper service on Southern Customs Paint and Body. Southern Customs states that "[t]here are no presumptions in favor of valid issuance, service, and return of citation," citing *Fidelity & Guaranty Insurance Co. v. Drewery Construction Co.,* 186 S.W.3d 571, 573-74 (Tex. 2006). That is true when attacking a default judgment by restricted appeal, but our analysis is different when, as here, a default judgment is attacked by a motion for new trial. In this circumstance, we focus on "the critical question in any default judgment: 'Why did the defendant not appear?' " If the defendant did not appear because he or she never received the suit papers, then the court should generally set aside the default judgment. But if the defendant received the suit papers and has some other reason for not appearing, then the default judgment must be set aside if the defendant proves the three elements of the *Craddock* test. Here, De La Garza and Sutherland acknowledged in their affidavits that they received the suit papers. Thus, to determine whether the trial court erred by refusing to set aside the default judgment and order a new trial, we must determine whether Southern Customs satisfied the *Craddock* test. *Id.* Because the court of appeals addressed only *Craddock* 's first element, we limit our review to that determination.

A defendant satisfies its burden as to the first *Craddock* element when its factual assertions, if true, negate intentional or consciously indifferent conduct by the defendant and the factual assertions are not controverted by the plaintiff. Consciously indifferent conduct occurs when "the defendant knew it was sued but did not care." Generally, "some excuse, although not necessarily a good one, will suffice to show that a defendant's failure to file an answer was not because the defendant did not care." Here, Southern Customs offered an excuse that was not controverted and, if true, negated intentional or consciously indifferent conduct on its part. Specifically, Southern Customs alleged, among other reasons, that the citation was left in a stack of papers on a desk and forgotten about because of limited time spent at the office due to weather conditions over a nearly three-week period during the Christmas holiday season. *See Craddock,* 133 S.W.2d at 126 (holding that the effect of weather on business "certainly constituted some excuse for the oversight"). Spencer made no attempt to controvert Southern Customs's claims regarding the weather conditions during this time period or the weather's adverse effect on Southern Customs's business. We conclude that this excuse is sufficient to show that the failure to answer was not the result of intentional or consciously indifferent conduct.

Contrary to the dissent's assertion, this decision does not alter our default judgment jurisprudence. We do not hold that forgetfulness alone is sufficient to satisfy the first *Craddock* element; rather, we simply conclude that the excuse presented here is so similar to that which we accepted as sufficient in *Craddock* that the same result is required. Southern Customs provided some excuse for its oversight, which satisfies the first element of *Craddock.* In *Craddock,* weather conditions altered a company's ordinary course of business, which ultimately led to the misplacement of a citation among less urgent mail and the failure to answer the lawsuit before judgment. Similarly, weather conditions were alleged in this case to have altered the ordinary course of business for Southern Customs, ultimately leading Sutherland and De La Garza to misplace the citations in a pile of ordinary papers and to fail to answer the lawsuit before judgment. This *Craddock*-like situation, coupled with time spent out of the office for the holidays and the defendants' forgetfulness, combine to create "some excuse, although not necessarily a good one" and demonstrate that the failure to answer was not intentional or the result of conscious indifference. As we stated in *Craddock,* "the absence of an intentional failure to answer rather than a real excuse for not answering was the controlling fact." Because of the similarity of the excuse asserted in *Craddock* and the uncontroverted excuse in this case, our holding does not extend *Craddock;* it merely follows it. Moreover, our holding not only conforms to existing law, it also comports with the policy that "an adjudication on the merits is preferred in Texas."

III

Southern Customs provided a sufficient excuse for failing to answer the suit timely, thus satisfying the first element of the *Craddock* standard. The trial court's denial of Southern Customs's motion for new trial, therefore, cannot be affirmed on the ground that its excuse for not answering was insufficient. The court of appeals erred when it held otherwise. Accordingly, we grant the petition for review and, without hearing oral argument, we reverse the court of appeals' judgment and remand the case to that court for consideration of the second and third Craddock elements. TEX. R. APP. P. 59.1.

CHIEF JUSTICE JEFFERSON, joined by JUSTICE WILLETT, dissenting.

"I forgot."

We reject this excuse when tax returns are late, or when homework is missing, but a defendant can now use it to disregard an official directive by the State of Texas that he either answer a lawsuit or risk a judgment against him. The defendants here received and reviewed the citation and petition, placed the papers on their office desk, stopped thinking about the lawsuit because of the holidays and "weather conditions," and ultimately forgot about it. If those facts constitute a sufficient excuse for neglecting to answer a lawsuit, the rules and precedent governing default judgments have been displaced by a simple command: no default judgment will stand if the defendant asserts that the mundane distractions of everyday life destroyed his cognition.

Because we prefer a merits determination to a procedural forfeit, we have been reluctant to uphold a default judgment if it is clear that the defendant intended to answer the lawsuit. This policy should always inform our analysis, but that does not mean we can simply ignore procedural commands. A rule of procedure is a rule of law. We should tread carefully before we tolerate its disregard based on the tenuous rationale presented here.

Our precedent and rules have warned about the risk of default for more than a century. It functions primarily to spur quick action when a defendant is served with a lawsuit. Our legal system is built around deadlines. Deadlines ensure the orderly process of litigation. Statutes of limitations force the plaintiff to act, and the risk of default induces the defendant to answer.

* * *

We recently held "that *some* excuse, although not necessarily a good one, will suffice to show that a defendant's failure to file an answer was not because the defendant did not care." Respondents have argued that *any* excuse is sufficient. But that cannot be so because we subsequently upheld a default judgment because the offered excuse was wholly insufficient. *See Levine v. Shackelford, Melton & McKinley, L.L.P.,* 248 S.W.3d 166, 168-69 (Tex. 2008) (upholding a default judgment based on the defense attorney's "pattern of ignoring deadlines and warnings from the opposing party" despite the defendants' claim "that their attorney placed the answer, along with a filing letter, in his 'outgoing mail bin' four days before the trial court signed the original default judgment"). If any excuse negated conscious indifference then *Craddock* 's command would lose all meaning. Thus, there will always be a question of whether the facts reveal a sufficient excuse. And our prior cases show what types of excuses qualify:

- Not receiving the citation is always a sufficient excuse for not answering. *See, e.g., Estate of Pollack v. McMurrey,* 858 S.W.2d 388, 391 (Tex. 1993) (noting that no evidence established that the defense attorney knew that his clients had been served and that the failure to answer under these circumstances "could not have been intentional or the result of conscious indifference"); *cf. Mathis v. Lockwood,* 166 S.W.3d 743, 745 (Tex. 2005) (per curiam) (accepting a defendant's excuse that she failed to appear at trial because she never received notice of the setting).

- Losing the service papers can be a sufficient excuse if it is "supported by some explanation from the person most likely to have seen them, or of the efforts made to find them." *Fidelity,* 186 S.W.3d at 575-76 (setting a default judgment aside based on the defendant's excuse of losing the citation because the defendant's affidavits showed no intent or indifference but instead detailed its "efforts to establish a system that would avoid precisely what happened").

• Misplacing the citation is sufficient when it is the result of a turnover in staff or a breakdown in communication. *See, e.g., Dir., State Emp. Workers' Comp. Div. v. Evans,* 889 S.W.2d 266, 269 (Tex. 1994) (setting aside a post-answer default judgment when the attorney failed to appear because her predecessor, whom she replaced after trial had been set, misdated the trial date on his calendar and conveyed the wrong information to her); *Old Republic Ins. Co. v. Scott,* 873 S.W.2d 381, 382 (Tex. 1994) (per curiam) (accepting a workers' compensation carrier's excuse that the citation was misplaced because it was inadvertently included with files that were being transferred from one adjustment company to another); *Strackbein,* 671 S.W.2d at 39 (finding no conscious indifference when the failure to answer was the result of a "breakdown of communication" between two individuals, each of whom thought the other was going to forward the relevant materials to the attorney).

• Some mistakes of law suffice if the mistake is the result of a defendant's prior interactions with the law. *See, e.g., In re R.R.,* 209 S.W.3d at 115 (holding that a mother's mistake of law that was "based on her prior experiences with the court system and her contacts with CPS," along with her action of "staying in regular contact with the caseworker about the progress of the case" was sufficient to "negate the element of conscious indifference to proceedings designed to terminate the parent-child relationship between [her] and her children"); *Bank One, Tex.,* 830 S.W.2d at 84-85.

This list is not exhaustive, but it is a useful point of reference when analyzing a default judgment. None of these cases, however, address the type of excuse presented in this case. Both De La Garza and Sutherland explain their failure to answer as follows:

> I remember someone coming to my shop on or about December 19, 2008, and leaving some papers with me and my partner. This was a Friday. The person who gave the papers to me did not explain what they were for or that I had any obligation to do anything in response. I had never been sued before like this and have no experience with the legal system. I briefly reviewed the papers and the[n] placed them on a desk in my office. My desk is covered in papers, concerning various matters. We do not employ a secretary or have any administrative help. My partner and I do everything. When we received the papers, it was less than a week before the Christmas holidays. The weather conditions during this period made it difficult for me to perform much labor for any customers because weather conditions adversely affect paint work on automobiles. I did return to the shop on Monday and worked part of the day. However, the work was limited to mostly returning automobiles to customers. I spent little time in my office. I also worked briefly on Tuesday, December 23, 2008, again, just returning automobiles and scheduling work. By this time, and due, in part, to the holidays, I was not thinking about the papers that had been delivered to me at my shop. The papers had been placed on my desk but were not on my mind and were camouflaged with other papers;
>
> I did not return to the shop again after December 23, 2008, until January 5, 2009. During this period, the shop was closed for the holidays and, in part, because of the weather conditions. I also spent a lot of time during this period in San Antonio, Texas, to visit friends for the holidays. Also during this period, my thoughts were on the holidays

and things I had to do to plan and prepare for the holidays. Therefore, my thoughts were not on the papers that had been delivered to me;

Between January 5, 2009, and January 16, 2009, I resumed a regular schedule at the shop. During this period, I was working and not thinking about the papers that had been delivered to me. In fact, by this time, I had forgotten that [sic] about them. I also did not understand or realize that I had any obligation to do anything, including filing an answer to the papers within any time period. This was clearly a mistake on my part;

I now understand that a default judgment was entered because an answer to the suit was not filed within the time allowed. My failure to review the documents and understand what they must have been was an accident or mistake by me because I did not understand the significance of the documents and even failed to remember that I had gotten them. Further, the papers were given to me during the Christmas and New Year's holiday period, when my mind was focused elsewhere and not on the papers. I have never been sued before. Nor did I consciously disregard answering the suit because I did not even realize that the papers that had been delivered required any attention by me. Had I realized what the documents must have been, I would have immediately retained the services of an attorney to represent me, as I did as soon as I received notice of the default judgment. The notice received by me in the mail was the first indication that I had that a lawsuit had been filed against me that required affirmative action by me.

This excuse cannot suffice. The defendants did not lose the citation. They knew where it was. De La Garza placed it on his desk upon receipt. Nor is this a case where a mistake of law justifies the failure to answer. The only mistake the defendants offer is that they did not know that they had to respond to the citation. Yet they read the citation when the process server delivered it. The citation said: "You have been sued. You may employ an attorney. If you or your attorney do not file a written answer with the clerk who issued this citation by 10:00 a.m. on the Monday next following the expiration of twenty days after you were served this citation and petition, a default judgment may be taken against you." *See* TEX. R. CIV. P. 99(c). Even putting aside the citation's clear warning, we have held that "[n]ot understanding a citation and then doing nothing following service does not constitute a mistake of law that is sufficient to meet the *Craddock* requirements."

This case is distinct from *Craddock,* where inclement weather caused the defendant to misplace the citation. There, an insurance company fell behind in its work because of an influx of claims due to a recent hail and wind storm. To catch up, the company began separating important mail "from that which was not so important." In the process, the citation was inadvertently placed with the unimportant mail, despite being marked "urgent," and was not discovered until the day the default judgment was rendered.

In this case, the affidavits obliquely speak of "weather conditions." There is no assertion that the weather impeded access to the courthouse, precluded the retention of a lawyer, or (as in *Craddock*) overburdened the defendants' business with an influx of work. Indeed, according to the affidavits, the defendants had more time on their hands as business subsided due to the weather.

That leaves "the holidays." We are lenient when deadlines fall on legal holidays. *See* TEX. R. CIV. P. 4. But the rules nevertheless require that litigants answer lawsuits, request a jury, move for new trial, perfect an appeal—all within prescribed time limits and even when holidays intervene. In any event, the defendants offer no particular reason why the holidays prevented them from answering the lawsuit. Rather, they assert that their minds were preoccupied by the holidays, to the exclusion of the lawsuit. Consequently, this case comes down to one proposition: that a defendant who says he forgot about being sued is not indifferent to the risk of default.

* * *

We will one day see a case in which a defendant served with citation is so overwhelmed with events that a trial judge exercises sound discretion to order a new trial. In this case, however, the period from the defendants' receipt of the citation to notice of the default is marked with contempt for their obligation to the rule of law. The trial court was not required to accept the defendants' excuse on these facts. Because the Court holds otherwise, I respectfully dissent.

Notes & Questions

1. *"I don't recall being served."* In one case,[1] the parties hotly disputed whether the defendant's registered agent had actually been served in a suit that resulted in a $1.8 million default judgment. Thus, the issue was whether the judgment was void for lack of notice as required by due process. The trial judge found that there was service and denied the motion for new trial. But the Supreme Court reversed, holding that because there was uncontroverted testimony establishing that the agent for service did not *recall* being served with process in this particular case, the first Craddock element was satisfied. The evidence established that the agent was familiar with being served, and had a routine procedure for responding to service, that being turning the papers over to counsel. So the Court held that the testimony provided a sufficient excuse to show that the failure to answer was neither intentional or the result of consciously indifferent conduct. The served party's testimony of appreciation of the significance of service of process with no memory of receiving this one in particular is difficult to contradict and almost certainly will satisfy the first *Craddock* element.

2. *Constitutional limitation.* If the movant had no notice of the proceedings he is not required to show a meritorious defense in order to obtain a new trial. That would violate federal due process protection. The other *Craddock* requirements would still apply.[2]

3. *Trial court discretion.* Though the granting or denial of an equitable motion for new trial is said to be within the trial court's discretion, it is an abuse of discretion to refuse to grant a new trial after a default when the *Craddock* requirements have been satisfied.[3] A trial court may err in denying a motion for new trial on legal grounds as well—for example, a defect in service of process.

4. *Burden.* Once the movant has shown by affidavits that the *Craddock* criteria are met the burden shifts to the plaintiff to produce evidence to the contrary.[4] Evidence is presented at the hearing on the motion.

5. *Special appearance and waiver.* Suppose an out-of-state D wishes to try to set aside the default judgment but has a strong basis for contesting the court's personal jurisdiction. Can a motion for

---

[1] Milestone Operating, Inc. v. ExxonMobil Corp., 388 S.W.3d 307 (Tex. 2012).

[2] *See* Lopez v. Lopez, 757 S.W.2d 721 (Tex. 1988) *and* Peralta v. Heights Medical Center, Inc., 485 U.S. 80, 108 S.Ct. 896, 99 L.Ed. 2d 75.

[3] *See* Old Republic Ins. Co. v. Scott, 837 S.W.2d 381 (Tex. 1994).

[4] *See* Director, State Employee Workers' Compensation Division v. Evans, 889 S.W.2d 266-B (Tex. 1994).

new trial be pursued without waiving the jurisdictional point? Yes. The D may participate for the purpose of setting aside the default after resisting jurisdiction through a special appearance if he is careful to pursue the special appearance first and to offer the motion for new trial conditionally.[5]

6. *Late notice of judgment.* Recall that a party with late notice of a judgment (actual notice between 20 and 90 days after the date the judgment is signed) can move to restart the appellate clock, giving substantial additional time for an equitable motion for new trial.[6]

7. *Limits to application of* Craddock *test.* In *Carpenter v. Cimarron Hydrocarbons Corp.*,[7] the Texas Supreme Court refused to apply the *Craddock* test to a motion for new trial after summary judgment based upon the failure to timely respond. The Court said:

> In this case, Cimarron learned two days before the summary-judgment hearing, well before judgment was rendered, that a timely response to the motion for summary judgment had not been filed. Our summary-judgment rules afford a party in this situation an opportunity to obtain additional time to file a response, either by moving for leave to file a late response or by requesting a continuance of the summary-judgment hearing. *See* TEX. R. CIV. P. 166a(c), 251. Cimarron actually availed itself of these remedies by filing a motion for leave to file a late response and, alternatively, requesting a continuance. That the trial court denied these remedies does not mean that they were not available; rather, the trial court's rulings on Cimarron's pre summary-judgment motions are, like most other trial court rulings, subject to review for an abuse of discretion.
>
> Our purpose in adopting the *Craddock* standard was to alleviate unduly harsh and unjust results at a point in time when the defaulting party has no other remedy available. *See Craddock,* 133 S.W.2d at 126. But when our rules provide the defaulting party a remedy, *Craddock* does not apply. Thus, we hold that *Craddock* does not apply to a motion for new trial filed after judgment has been granted on a summary-judgment motion to which the nonmovant failed to timely respond when the movant had an opportunity to seek a continuance or obtain permission to file a late response.

---

[5] Koch Graphics, Inc. v. Avantech, Inc., 803 S.W.2d 432, 433 (Tex. App.—Dallas 1991, no writ).

[6] Rule 306a(4), 329a(b).

[7] 98 S.W.3d 682, 685-86 (Tex. 2002).

D. Restricted Appeal

Read TRAP 30, CPRC § 51.013.

If a party misses the deadline for filing a motion for new trial and for a conventional appeal, she may be able to use the restricted appeal procedure in the court of appeals to attack a default, dismissal, or other judgment. This procedure was known as the "writ of error" to the court of appeals until the 1997 amendments to the Texas Rules of Appellate Procedure changed its name. The restricted appeal must be filed within six months of the date of the judgment, and is available only to parties who did not participate in the hearing in which the judgment was rendered. The error must be apparent from the face of the record from the trial court.

GENERAL ELECTRIC COMPANY
v.
FALCON RIDGE APARTMENTS, JOINT VENTURE

811 S.W.2d 942
(Tex. 1991)

DOGGETT, JUSTICE.

We consider whether in an appeal by writ of error [now restricted appeal] the absence from the record of proof of notice of the trial court's dismissal constitutes error on the face of the record. The court of appeals reversed the dismissal by the trial court and remanded for further proceedings. Because lack of notice is not apparent from the face of the record and must be established by extrinsic evidence, we reverse the judgment of the court of appeals and affirm the trial court's dismissal.

The record provided by the parties to the court consists of the transcript that contains the written pleadings and motions filed in the trial court, the court's orders and the clerk's notations on the docket sheet of events in the cause. In its original petition filed in August 1984, Respondent Falcon Ridge Apartments sought recovery for substantial property damage resulting from a fire allegedly caused by a defective heating and air conditioning unit manufactured by General Electric. An amended petition filed in May 1985 added as plaintiffs four individual residents of the apartment complex. Although rulings on various motions between June 1985 and April 1986 are noted on the docket sheet, no further action is reflected in the transcript until February 1988, when the plaintiffs' attorney sought leave to withdraw as counsel for the individual residents, which the trial court granted by four separate orders signed in late February and early March. Second and third amended petitions were filed on February 17, 1988 and April 18, 1988. The action was dismissed for want of prosecution by an order dated May 9, 1988. The transcript further shows that two months after the dismissal Falcon Ridge filed a notice of substitution of counsel.

On appeal by writ of error to the court of appeals, Falcon Ridge alleged that it received no notice of the trial court's intention to dismiss for want of prosecution, as required by Rule 165a, Texas Rules of Civil Procedure, or of the order of dismissal, as required by Rule 306a. To prove lack of notice, Falcon Ridge filed in the appellate court affidavits from both the district clerk and its counsel averring respectively that notice was neither given nor received, and that counsel for Falcon Ridge first learned of the dismissal order on October 4, 1988.

Based in part on these affidavits, the court of appeals reversed the dismissal and remanded to the trial court for reinstatement. We reverse.

A direct attack on a judgment by writ of error must: (1) be brought within six months after the judgment was signed, TEX. CIV. PRAC. & REM. CODE ANN. § 51.013 (Vernon 1986); TEX. R. APP. P. 45 [now T.R.A.P. 25.1, 26.1 and 30]; (2) by a party to the suit, TEX. R. APP. P. 45 [now T.R.A.P. 25.1, 26.1 and 30]; (3) who did not participate in the actual trial, *id.*; (4) and the error complained of must be "apparent from the face of the record." Only the last of these requirements is at issue here.

Rule 165a, Texas Rules of Civil Procedure, which governs dismissals for want of prosecution, directs the district clerk to mail to counsel of record and to each party not represented by counsel a notice containing the date and place of the hearing at which the court intends to dismiss. A similar notice of the signing of the order of dismissal is also required. TEX. R. CIV. P. 165a, 306a. The rules do not, however, impose upon the clerk the duty to note on the docket sheet the fact of mailing such notices. Consequently, in cases dismissed for want of prosecution, the record is ordinarily silent as to whether or not the required notices were given.

There is thus nothing in the transcript before us that affirmatively indicates that notice was given, nor any notation to establish that notice was omitted. . . . The absence from the record of affirmative proof that notice of intent to dismiss or of the order of dismissal was provided does not establish error. . . .

The rule has long been that evidence not before the trial court prior to final judgment may not be considered in a writ of error proceeding. Our system is founded upon a belief that trial courts should first be given the opportunity to consider and weigh factual evidence. Permitting challenge to a judgment based on affidavits first filed in the appellate court undermines this judicial structure. The appropriate remedy when extrinsic evidence is necessary to the challenge of a judgment is by motion for new trial, TEX. R. CIV. P. 320, or by bill of review filed in the trial court. *See* TEX. R. CIV. P. 329b(f).

Falcon Ridge acknowledges that appeal by writ of error is not the exclusive method available to it of attacking the dismissal of its cause without proper notice.[2] It asserts, however, that the alternative procedure of bill of review is more burdensome than a challenge on appeal by writ of error. A party suffering an adverse judgment rendered without notice may not, consistent with concepts of due process, be hampered with undue burdens in attacking the judgment. *Peralta v. Heights Medical Center, Inc.*, 485 U.S. 80, 86, 108 S.Ct. 896, 899-900, 99 L.Ed.2d 75, 82 (1988).[3] Unlike the defaulted defendant in *Peralta*, however, Falcon Ridge has failed to demonstrate that no alternative remedy is available and that an undue burden has been imposed. In the absence of such a showing, we are unwilling to encroach upon the traditional role of the trial court by permitting new evidence to be first tendered to the court of appeals.

---

2 Falcon Ridge asserted that it could not attack the dismissal by bill of review so long as appeal by writ of error was available. This court having concluded that appeal is not available, there is no bar to Falcon Ridge seeking bill of review in the district court.

3 Peralta v. Heights Medical Center, Inc., 485 U.S. 80 (1988), eliminated the requirement of proving that a dismissed claim or defense has probable merit in a bill of review attacking a judgment rendered without proper notice.

We hold that no reversible error is evident on the face of the record when the transcript is silent as to notice of the trial court's intention to dismiss, as required by Rule 165a, Texas Rules of Civil Procedure, or of the order of dismissal, as required by Rule 306a. We reverse the judgment of the court of appeals and affirm the trial court's order of dismissal.

Notes & Questions

1. *Face of the record.* It should not be surprising that there is a great deal of case law on what is or is not an error "apparent" from the "face of the record."[1] Generally speaking, the appeals court cannot consider documents or evidence that were not before the trial court at the time it rendered judgment.[2] The reviewing court may, however, consider all of the papers on file in the appeal, including any court reporter's record.[3] As *Falcon Ridge* demonstrates, error is not "on the face of the record" when it must be shown by extrinsic evidence—new evidence presented to the court of appeals.

2. *No extension of time for late notice.* Note that TRAP 4.2(a)(2) provides that the deadlines for restricted appeal are not extended by Rule 306a's provisions for late notice of judgment, as are other appellate deadlines.

E. Bill of Review & Extrinsic Fraud

If the deadline for filing a motion for new trial and restricted appeal are past, the defaulting defendant should consider filing a bill of review, an equitable proceeding that must be brought within four years of the rendition of judgment.[1]

The bill of review plaintiff (the defaulting defendant) must plead and prove: (1) a meritorious defense; (2) that he was prevented from making by the fraud, accident or wrongful act of his opponent or official mistake, (3) unmixed with any fault or negligence on his own part. The parties have a right to a jury determination of the fact issues presented, and if established, the bill of review plaintiff gets a new trial on the underlying claim.[2]

As you would expect, if the default judgment is void, the bill of review plaintiff does not have to satisfy all of these requirements.[3] When a bill of review plaintiff claims a due process violation

---

1 *See* Ginn v. Forrester, 282 S.W.3d 430 (Tex. 2009)(affirming *Falcon Ridge,* and holding that clerk's notation indicating no documents were available showing notice or hearing was not sufficient for restricted appeal proof).

2 *See* General Elec. v. Falcon Ridge Apts., 811 S.W.2d 942, 944 (Tex. 1991).

3 *See* DSC Fin. Corp. v. Moffitt, 815 S.W.2d 551 (Tex. 1991). This means that legal and factual sufficiency of the evidence may be reviewed by writ of error. Norman Communications v. Texas Eastman Co., 955 S.W.2d 269 (Tex. 1997).

1 Valdez v. Hollenbeck, 465 S.W.3d 217, 222 (Tex. 2015). Note that a statute may prescribe an express limitations period that overcomes the four-year residual statute. *Id.* (finding that Probate Code's 2-year statute barred the heirs' bill of review).

2 Caldwell v. Barnes, 154 S.W.3d 93 (Tex. 2004).

3 Mabon, 369 S.W.3d at 811.

for no service or notice, it is relieved of proving the first two bill of review elements and the third is conclusively established upon proof of lack of service of process.[4] For example, in one case,[5] the defendant's attorney answered but failed to notify his client of the trial setting. When no one appeared for trial, the court rendered a post-answer default judgment. The court held that the client was denied due process when it was not notified of the trial setting, so it was not required to prove a meritorious defense or fraud. The court further held that the client had no duty to diligently monitor a case after hiring a lawyer and once the client learned of the default, it diligently sought to contest it. Thus, the client successfully established its right to relief under the bill of review.

Of course, a party facing a voidable (rather than void) judgment has a more difficult burden. And the burden is more difficult than that imposed by the motion for new trial—the bill of review plaintiff may not avoid the judgment with a simple excuse. Instead, he must show that the judgment was procured by "fraud" or "official mistake."

The fraud required for the bill of review is "extrinsic fraud"—"fraud that denies a litigant the opportunity to fully litigate at trial all the rights or defenses that could have been asserted. It occurs when a litigant has been misled by his adversary by fraud or deception, or was denied knowledge of the suit."[6] It is contrasted with intrinsic fraud, which "relates to the merits of the issues which were presented . . . . Within that term are included such matters as fraudulent instruments, perjured testimony, or any matter which was actually presented to and considered by the court in rendering the judgment assailed."[7]

Extrinsic fraud justifies a direct attack on a final judgment because it "distorts the judicial process to such an extent that confidence in the ability to discover the fraudulent conduct through the regular adversarial process is undermined."[8] It also tolls the four-year statute of limitations, so that it runs from the time the bill of review plaintiff knew or should have known about the default judgment.[9]

My favorite opinion on extrinsic fraud is *King Ranch, Inc. v. Chapman*,[10] where descendants of Helen Chapman filed a bill of review claiming that an 1883 judgment was procured by Richard King's fraud, which they attempted to prove through a 1957 history of the King Ranch and a 1992 newspaper article. They "cobbled together a series of interesting historical tidbits and Texas folklore,"[11] but suffered a no-evidence summary judgment for failure to present more than a scintilla of real evidence. Evidence of fraud is difficult to find, and as the Chapman heirs discovered, it becomes even more difficult to find as time passes.

---

4 *Id.*at 812.

5 *Id.*

6 Sutherland, 376 S.W.3d at 275.

7 *Id.*

8 *Id.*

9 PNS, 379 S.W.3d at 275, 277 n. 16.

10 118 S.W.3d 742 (Tex. 2003).

11 *Id.* at 755.

The following opinion provides additional commentary on the extrinsic fraud requirement and the difference between void and voidable judgments.

PNS STORES, INC.
v.
RIVERA
379 S.W.3d 267
(Tex. 2012)

Opinion

JUSTICE GUZMAN delivered the opinion of the Court.

In this appeal from a summary judgment dismissal of a direct and collateral attack, the petitioner, PNS Stores, Inc., contends the underlying judgment is void and subject to collateral attack at any time. In this regard, PNS argues that the trial court rendering the default judgment never acquired personal jurisdiction over it because the service of process was defective. Alternatively, PNS argues that its adversary's extrinsic fraud prevented it from learning about the underlying default judgment and that limitations was thereby tolled, making its direct attack through a bill of review timely.

The court of appeals affirmed the summary judgment, concluding that the underlying default judgment was not void and that there was no evidence of extrinsic fraud that would toll limitations. 335 S.W.3d 265, 277. We agree with the court below that the alleged defects in service of process were not sufficient to render the default judgment void, but we hold that summary judgment was improperly granted because there is some evidence of extrinsic fraud. Accordingly, we reverse the court of appeals' judgment and remand the case to the trial court for further proceedings.

I. Factual and Procedural Background

On December 29, 1998, Rachael Rivera filed suit against PNS Stores, Inc. in state court for injuries she allegedly sustained when she slipped and fell at a MacFrugal's Bargain Closeouts Store, owned by PNS. PNS removed the case to federal court, and after discovery, the federal district court granted PNS's motion for summary judgment and dismissed the case "without prejudice on January 7, 2000."[2] No appeal was taken.

Three months later, Rivera, through her attorney Oscar Tamez, sued again in state court for the same slip and fall claims,[3] serving PNS through its registered agent for service of process, Prentice Hall Corporation. PNS failed to answer, and Rivera obtained a no-answer default judgment for $1,480,677.74 plus post-judgment interest. Rivera then waited six years to abstract the

---

[2] The federal district court granted summary judgment on the ground that Rivera had not raised a genuine issue of material fact to show PNS had actual or constructive knowledge of the dangerous condition in its store, an essential element of her premises-liability claim.

[3] Other than a modified date, Rivera's re-filed state court pleadings were identical to her initial state court pleadings that PNS had prevailed against in federal court.

judgment and about nine years to attempt execution.[4] By then, the judgment had more than doubled to $3,513,070.55. The writ of execution was served at the PNS corporate headquarters in Columbus, Ohio and at its place of business in San Antonio on February 10, 2009.

Thirteen days later, PNS filed a bill of review seeking to set aside the default judgment and quash the writ. After limited discovery, both Rivera and PNS moved for summary judgment. Rivera moved for summary judgment based on the four-year statute of limitations applicable to a bill of review. In its summary judgment motion, PNS argued that the default judgment was barred by res judicata[5] and void due to errors in service of process. Alternatively, PNS argued that if the judgment was merely voidable, its bill of review was nonetheless timely filed because its adversary's extrinsic fraud tolled limitations.

The trial court granted Rivera's motion for summary judgment and denied PNS's. PNS appealed. The court of appeals affirmed the summary judgment, concluding that: (1) PNS's attack was a direct attack; (2) PNS's only possible means of direct attack was by bill of review that would be barred by limitations unless there was evidence of extrinsic fraud sufficient to toll the bill's four-year limitations period; and (3) there was no evidence of extrinsic fraud.[6] 335 S.W.3d 265, 275-77.

II. Analysis

PNS argues the court of appeals erred in affirming Rivera's summary judgment because (1) defects in service rendered the default judgment void, and therefore assailable at any time, and (2) even if the judgment was merely voidable, the summary judgment was nevertheless erroneous because fact issues remained regarding the existence of extrinsic fraud sufficient to toll the bill of review's limitations period. Although we disagree that the alleged defects in service render the default judgment void, we agree there is some evidence of extrinsic fraud sufficient to raise a fact issue about whether PNS's bill of review is barred by limitations.

A. Void and Voidable Judgments

* * *

PNS argues that defects in service prevented the trial court from acquiring personal jurisdiction over it and asserts that the citation: (1) fails to list the exact time service was performed; (2) fails to state that PNS was served through its registered agent; (3) states that Prentice Hall was served "VIA USPS" as well as "in person;" (4) does not state that service was by certified mail; (5) does not recite that Prentice Hall was served by registered or certified mail; and (6) lacks any

4 Between the time the judgment was taken and executed, Tamez was disbarred and filed for bankruptcy, listing Rivera as a creditor. Rachael Rivera signed a general power of attorney in favor of her daughter, Anna Rivera, in 2005 and was found *non compos mentis* early in this bill of review action.

5 PNS had obtained a *nunc pro tunc* order from the federal district court stating that "the Court's ruling was clearly an adjudication of Plaintiff's claims on the merits and the words 'without prejudice' were obviously a clerical mistake." Rivera appealed, the Fifth Circuit affirmed, Rivera v. PNS Stores, Inc., 647 F.3d 188, 202 (5th Cir. 2011), and the United States Supreme Court denied certiorari, Rivera v. PNS Stores, Inc., — U.S. —, 132 S.Ct. 1741, 182 L.Ed.2d 529 (2012).

6 The court of appeals held that the federal court's corrected judgment *nunc pro tunc, see supra* n. 6, did not render the default judgment void because res judicata and collateral estoppel are affirmative defenses that constitute pleas in bar, not pleas to the jurisdiction. 335 S.W.3d 265, 274.

proof that it was on file for ten days preceding the default judgment. *See generally* TEX. R. CIV. P. 106, 107. PNS concludes that the default judgment is void and therefore must be set aside because of these defects.

* * *

In sum, a judgment is void if the defects in service are so substantial that the defendant was not afforded due process. None of the defects at issue here deprived PNS of a meaningful opportunity to appear and answer Rivera's claims. When a defective citation is served, but the citation puts the defendant on notice of asserted claims in a pending suit, and the technical defects are not of the sort that deprive a litigant of the opportunity to be heard, we reject them as grounds sufficient to support a collateral attack. Because the trial court had jurisdiction over the subject matter of Rivera's claims and the technical defects in service at best render the default judgment voidable, not void, PNS may not collaterally attack the judgment.

B. Extrinsic Fraud

Having rejected PNS's collateral attack on the judgment, PNS must rely on its bill of review to attack the default judgment directly. A direct attack can be in the form of a motion for new trial, appeal, or bill of review. *Frost Nat'l Bank v. Fernandez,* 315 S.W.3d 494, 504 (Tex. 2010). A bill of review is an equitable proceeding to set aside a prior judgment that is no longer subject to challenge by a motion for new trial or direct appeal. *Id.* It must, however, be brought within four years of the rendition of the judgment. *Caldwell v. Barnes,* 975 S.W.2d 535, 537 (Tex. 1998) (citing TEX. CIV. PRAC. & REM. CODE § 16.051). Here, PNS did not file its bill of review until approximately nine years after the default was rendered. If PNS can prove extrinsic fraud, however, the bill of review's four-year limitations period may be tolled. In affirming the summary judgment, the court of appeals concluded that there was no evidence of extrinsic fraud. We disagree.

A direct attack on "a judgment on the basis of extrinsic fraud is allowed because such fraud distorts the judicial process to such an extent that confidence in the ability to discover the fraudulent conduct through the regular adversarial process is undermined." *Browning,* 165 S.W.3d at 348. Extrinsic fraud is fraud that denies a litigant the opportunity to fully litigate at trial all the rights or defenses that could have been asserted.[14] *King Ranch,* 118 S.W.3d at 752. It occurs when a litigant has been misled by his adversary by fraud or deception, or was denied knowledge of the suit. *Alexander,* 226 S.W.2d at 1001. PNS argues that Tamez's failure to comply with Texas Rule of Civil Procedure 239a, his violations of the Texas Lawyer's Creed, and his extensive history of unethical conduct, including his disbarment, are indicative of extrinsic fraud.

We first address PNS's argument that Tamez misled the trial court by providing the clerk with PNS's registered agent's address as the last known address for PNS. Texas Rule of Civil Procedure 239a requires in relevant part:

> At or immediately prior to the time . . . [a] final default judgment is rendered, the party taking the same or his attorney shall certify to the clerk in writing the last known mailing address of the party against whom the judgment is taken . . . . Immediately upon the sign-

[14] Intrinsic fraud, by contrast, "relates to the merits of the issues which were presented . . . . Within that term are included such matters as fraudulent instruments, perjured testimony, or any matter which was actually presented to and considered by the trial court in rendering the judgment assailed." *Tice v. City of Pasadena,* 767 S.W.2d 700, 702 (Tex. 1989) (orig. proceeding). Only extrinsic fraud will support a bill of review because each party must guard against an adverse finding on issues directly presented. *Id.*

ing of the judgment, the clerk shall mail written notice thereof to the party against whom the judgment was rendered at the address shown in the certificate . . . .

TEX. R. CIV. P. 239a. PNS argues that Tamez knew: (1) PNS's contact information including the address of its corporate headquarters and its local store in San Antonio; (2) the name and address of the local attorneys who had defended PNS in the previous case involving the same claim; and (3) that PNS would certainly defend any refiled claim. This knowledge, according to PNS, is some evidence that Tamez purposefully provided the clerk with Prentice Hall's address instead of PNS's last known address to prevent PNS from discovering the default. This is especially so, PNS argues, in light of PNS's failure to appear after the previous service through Prentice Hall. Rule 239a is intended to ensure that the party in default receives personal notice.

Rivera responds that Tamez's violation of Rule 239a is not evidence of extrinsic fraud and points us to two cases. In *Layton,* Layton provided the clerk with the address she had been given by defendant Nationsbanc as the place to receive her payments. 141 S.W.3d at 764. The court of appeals stated that Nationsbanc had failed to demonstrate why that address would be fraudulent for the purpose of receiving notices of judgment. *Id.* In *Alderson v. Alderson,* the defendant failed to provide any evidence to show that the plaintiff engaged in a purposeful act of deception, because although the motion for summary judgment was mailed to the wrong address, there was no evidence that this was due to anything other than mistake or accident. 352 S.W.3d 875, 878 (Tex. App.—Dallas 2001, pet. denied).

We conclude that under the specific circumstances presented in this case, Tamez's failure to provide the clerk with PNS's last known address, which he knew, is some evidence of extrinsic fraud. In contrast to *Layton* and *Alderson,* Tamez knew PNS's mailing address, had corresponded with PNS and its counsel at this last known address only months earlier and instead chose to provide the clerk with the address of PNS's registered agent, Prentice Hall.

Next, PNS argues that Tamez's violations of the Texas Lawyer's Creed is evidence of extrinsic fraud. The Texas Lawyer's Creed, promulgated by this Court and the Court of Criminal Appeals, was intended to encourage lawyers to be mindful that abusive tactics—ranging from hostility to obstructionism—do not serve the justice we pursue. The Texas Lawyer's Creed–A Mandate for Professionalism, *reprinted in* TEXAS RULES OF COURT 865, 865 (West 2012). The Lawyer's Creed serves as an important reminder that the conduct of lawyers "should be characterized at all times by honesty, candor, and fairness." *Id.* The Lawyer's Creed states that an attorney "will not take advantage, by causing any default or dismissal to be rendered, when [he] know[s] the identity of an opposing counsel, without first inquiring about that counsel's intention to proceed." *Id.* at 867.

PNS argues that Tamez, in blatant violation of the Texas Lawyer's Creed, purposefully took a default judgment against PNS without contacting PNS's known attorneys and that he did so only three months after the federal court granted summary judgment in the first suit with full knowledge that PNS would defend the second lawsuit as vigorously as it had the first. The Lawyer's Creed, however, is aspirational. It does not create new duties and obligations enforceable by the courts beyond those existing as a result of (1) the courts' inherent powers and (2) the rules already in existence.[15] *Id.* at 865. The failure to notify opposing counsel of an intent to take a

[15] *See also* The Texas Lawyer's Creed—A Mandate for Professionalism, *reprinted in* TEXAS RULES OF COURT 865, 865 (West 2012) ("These standards are not a set of rules that lawyers can use and abuse to incite ancillary litigation or arguments over whether or not they have been observed.").

default judgment does not trigger the courts' inherent powers. *See Cont'l Carbon Co. v. Sea–Land Serv., Inc.,* 27 S.W.3d 184, 189 (Tex. App.—Dallas 2000, pet. denied). A lawyer's failure to adhere to the Texas Lawyer's Creed may be evidence of a lack of professionalism or character, but Tamez's failure to adhere to the spirit and letter of this aspirational standard in this case is not itself evidence of extrinsic fraud.

Finally, PNS argues that Tamez's history of unethical conduct, including grievances filed against him, his subsequent disbarment, and his refusal to give deposition testimony, is evidence of extrinsic fraud. But "[e]vidence of other wrongs or acts is not admissible to prove character in order to show 'action in conformity therewith.' " *Serv. Corp. Int'l v. Guerra,* 348 S.W.3d 221, 235 (Tex. 2011) (*quoting* TEX. R. EVID. 404(a)). Such evidence may be admissible to show intent, however, if "the prior acts are 'so connected with the transaction at issue that they may all be parts of a system, scheme or plan.' " *Id.* (quoting *Oakwood Mobile Homes, Inc. v. Cabler,* 73 S.W.3d 363, 375 (Tex. App.—El Paso 2002, pet. denied)). Unless some connection can be drawn between PNS's failure to assert its rights in this case and Tamez's grievances and disbarment, they will not suffice as evidence of extrinsic fraud. *See King Ranch,* 118 S.W.3d at 752. Because PNS offers no connection here, these prior acts are not evidence of extrinsic fraud.

In sum, although Tamez's failure to abide by the Texas Lawyer's Creed and his unethical conduct are not evidence of extrinsic fraud, under the specific facts of this case, his failure to comply with Texas Rule of Civil Procedure 239a is sufficient to raise a genuine issue of material fact regarding extrinsic fraud and its effect on limitations.[16]

III. Conclusion

The alleged technical defects in service render the judgment voidable, not void. Therefore, PNS cannot collaterally attack the judgment. But because there is some evidence of extrinsic fraud, a material fact issue remains regarding Rivera's limitations defense. Accordingly, we reverse the judgment of the court of appeals and remand the case to the trial court for further proceedings.

Notes & Questions

It is interesting to consider how PNS could have approached this had it learned of the judgment in time to file a motion for new trial. Because PNS claimed that it never got the documents, it seems likely that PNS could have come up with testimony that would provide an excuse satisfying *Craddock's* "not intentional or with conscious disregard" standard. But PNS learned of the judgment far too late to avail itself of the motion for new trial, perhaps purposefully on the part of

[16] Evidence of extrinsic fraud does not toll the bill of review's limitations period indefinitely. *See Defee v. Defee,* 966 S.W.2d 719, 722 (Tex. App.—San Antonio 1998, no pet.); *Maddux v. Brownen,* 759 S.W.2d 183, 185 (Tex. App.—Waco 1988, writ denied). A bill of review's four-year limitations period begins to run when the litigant knew or should have known about the default judgment. Rivera argues that because there is some record evidence that PNS acknowledged receipt of the judgment, PNS's bill of review was untimely. PNS responds that a letter from PNS's attorneys, dated at least six months after the default was taken, informed PNS that there had been no additional litigation pertaining to Rivera's slip and fall claim after the federal court granted PNS's summary judgment. PNS additionally cites testimony from its representative that PNS had no notice of the default judgment until it was served with the writ of execution. Because there is a factual dispute over when PNS learned of the default judgment, we do not resolve this issue.

plaintiff's counsel (who was disbarred between the time the judgment was taken and executed). PNS, therefore, was left only with the bill of review, and had to prove extrinsic fraud to overturn the judgment.

F. Dismissal for Want of Prosecution and Motion to Reinstate

Read Rule 165a.

Rule 165a gives the trial court the power to dismiss a case for want of prosecution under two circumstances: (1) when a party seeking affirmative relief fails to appear for any hearing or trial of which the party had notice; or (2) when the case is not disposed of within the time standards promulgated by the Supreme Court. In addition, the court has the inherent power to dismiss a case when the plaintiff fails to prosecute his or her case with due diligence.[1] Thus, the Supreme Court has affirmed dismissals of cases remaining on the docket for several years without satisfactory explanation.[2]

However, a party must be provided with notice and an opportunity to be heard before a court can dismiss the case either under Rule 165a or its inherent authority.[3] Thus, many courts have a practice of sending dismissal notices in cases that have been pending on the docket for a certain amount of time without a request for a trial setting. This is often referred to as a "DWOP notice." The notice form used by the San Antonio courts was the subject of a recent Supreme Court opinion.[4] There The Supreme Court held that the notice form used by the San Antonio courts gave a plaintiff notice of the possibility of dismissal for want of prosecution if the plaintiff did not appear at the hearing. However, the dismissal was reversed because the notice did not tell a plaintiff that the case could be dismissed for want of prosecution if the plaintiff failed to show good cause for keeping the case on the docket under Rule 165a(1).

When a case is dismissed for want of prosecution, Rule 165a(3) provides that the court "shall reinstate the case upon finding after a hearing that the failure of the party or his attorney was not intentional or the result of conscious indifference but was due to an accident or mistake or that the failure has been otherwise reasonably explained." The Supreme Court has held that this standard is "essentially the same" as the *Craddock* standard for setting aside a default judgment by equitable motion for new trial.[5] Therefore, the trial court abused its discretion in failing to reinstate a case when the attorney did not appear because of he was in trial in another county, and, based up-

---

1 Villarreal v. San Antonio Truck & Equipment, 994 S.W.2d 628 (Tex. 1999); Veterans' Land Board v. Williams, 543 S.W.2d 89, 90 (Tex. 1976).

2 *See id.* (affirming dismissal when case pending for over seven years without explanation for the delay); Bevil v. Johnson, 157 Tex. 621, 307 S.W.2d 85 (1957) (affirming dismissal of case pending for eight years without satisfactory explanation for delay).

3 *Villareal*, 994 S.W.2d at 629.

4 *Id.*

5 Smith v. Babcock & Wilcox Construction Co., 913 S.W.2d 467 (Tex. 1995).

on the judge's comments in a telephone conference call, he believed the judge would grant a continuance.[6]

The dismissal order is a judgment and the motion for reinstatement is like the motion for new trial. Thus, Rule 165a(3) provides for deadlines for filing the motion and the court's plenary power that are like those for motions for new trial in Rule 306a.

G. Collateral Attacks

A collateral attack on a judgment is an attempt to avoid its effect in a proceeding brought for some other purpose.[1] For example, when one party attempts to avoid the res judicata effect of a prior judgment, it is collaterally attacking the judgment. Unlike a direct attack, which is made under specific time constraints in the court in which the original judgment was rendered (or in an appellate court for that trial court), a collateral attack may be made at any time[2] and in any court of competent jurisdiction. The basis for a collateral attack is far more limited than a direct attack—a collateral attack claims that the court which rendered the judgment lacked jurisdiction.[3] Other errors are immaterial in a collateral attack.[4] Following are several examples of collateral attacks.

The TRAVELERS INSURANCE COMPANY v. JOACHIM

315 S.W.3d 860
(Tex. 2010)

JUSTICE GREEN delivered the opinion of the Court.

In this procedural dispute, we must decide whether a trial court's erroneous dismissal of a suit with prejudice, following the plaintiff's filing of a nonsuit, operates to bar a later suit because of res judicata. We conclude that it does. Therefore, we reverse the court of appeals' judgment and order the case dismissed.

I

Barry Joachim sued his insurer, The Travelers Insurance Company, alleging he was entitled to benefits from Travelers for damages caused by Joachim's accident with an underinsured driver. On the day before trial, Joachim filed a "Notice of Non-Suit" stating that he "no longer wishes to

---

6 *Id.* at 468.

1 Austin Indep. School Dist. v. Sierra Club, 495 S.W.2d 878 (Tex. 1973).

2 *See* Cook v. Cameron, 733 S.W.2d 137 (Tex. 1987).

3 *Id.*

4 Empire Gas & Fuel Co. v. Albright, 87 S.W.2d 1092 (Tex. 1935). For a general discussion of collateral attacks, *see* 5 MCDONALD, TEXAS CIVIL PRACTICE, § 29:18 et. seq.

pursue his claims against Defendants," and therefore "gives notice to all parties that his claims against the same are hereby dismissed without prejudice." No motions or counterclaims were pending at that time. Several months later, the trial court sent notice that if a final order was not filed within 10 days of the notice, the court would dismiss the case for want of prosecution. Joachim asserts he did not receive this notice. The trial court then entered an order that the case "is hereby dismissed in full with prejudice for want of prosecution." Joachim claims he did not receive a copy of that order either. Unaware of the dismissal order, Joachim neither contested it while the court retained plenary power, *see* TEX.R. CIV. P. 329b, nor perfected an appeal.

Joachim later refiled the same cause of action, and the case was assigned to a different trial court. Travelers filed a motion for summary judgment based on res judicata. The second trial court granted Travelers' motion and ordered that Joachim take nothing by his suit. Joachim appealed that judgment. The court of appeals reversed, holding that a nonsuit removes a trial court's jurisdiction to enter a dismissal with prejudice. The court of appeals therefore determined that the first trial court's order was void, not merely voidable. Thus, it concluded that Travelers failed to establish the defense of res judicata.

II

We review a trial court's summary judgment de novo. The party relying on the affirmative defense of res judicata must prove (1) a prior final determination on the merits by a court of competent jurisdiction; (2) identity of parties or those in privity with them; and (3) a second action based on the same claims as were or could have been raised in the first action. *See* TEX.R. CIV. P. 94 (identifying res judicata as an affirmative defense). "The judgment in the first suit precludes a second action by the parties and their privies on matters actually litigated and on causes of action or defenses arising out of the same subject matter that might have been litigated in the first suit." *Gracia v. RC Cola-7-Up Bottling Co.,* 667 S.W.2d 517, 519 (Tex. 1984). Only the first element-prior final determination on the merits-is contested in this appeal.

"At any time before the plaintiff has introduced all of his evidence other than rebuttal evidence, the plaintiff may . . . take a non-suit, which shall be entered in the minutes. Notice of the . . . non-suit shall be served ... on any party who has answered or who has been served with process without necessity of court order." TEX.R. CIV. P. 162. A party has an absolute right to file a nonsuit, and a trial court is without discretion to refuse an order dismissing a case because of a nonsuit unless collateral matters remain. A nonsuit "extinguishes a case or controversy from 'the moment the motion is filed' or an oral motion is made in open court; the only requirement is 'the mere filing of the motion with the clerk of the court.' " It renders the merits of the nonsuited case moot.

The parties agree that the first trial court's order, which dismissed the case with prejudice, was erroneous because Joachim's nonsuit was without prejudice to refiling. *See generally* TEX.R. CIV. P. 301 ("The judgment of the court shall conform to the pleadings, the nature of the case proved and the verdict, if any, and shall be so framed as to give the party all the relief to which he may be entitled either in law or equity."). The question of whether Travelers established its res judicata defense turns on the issue of whether the trial court's erroneous order was void, or merely voidable. "A judgment is void only when it is apparent that the court rendering judgment had no jurisdiction of the parties or property, no jurisdiction of the subject matter, no jurisdiction to enter the particular judgment, or no capacity to act." *Browning v. Prostok,* 165 S.W.3d 336, 346 (Tex. 2005) (internal quotation omitted). A void order is subject to collateral attack in a new lawsuit, while a voidable order must be corrected by direct attack; unless successfully attacked, a voidable judgment becomes final. After a nonsuit, a trial court retains jurisdiction to address collateral matters, such as motions for sanctions, even when such motions are filed after the nonsuit, as well as jurisdiction over any remaining counterclaims. *See Scott & White Mem'l Hosp. v. Schexnider,* 940 S.W.2d 594, 596 (Tex. 1996) (per curiam) (holding that a trial court has authority to decide a motion for sanctions while it retains plenary power, even after a nonsuit is taken); TEX.R. CIV. P. 162 ("Any dismissal pursuant to this rule shall not prejudice the right of an adverse party to be heard on a pending claim for affirmative relief or excuse the payment of all costs taxed by the clerk."). We must determine, then, whether filing a nonsuit strips a trial court of jurisdiction to dismiss a case with prejudice.

We have held that an order dismissing a case with prejudice for want of prosecution, though mistaken, is merely voidable and must be attacked directly in order to prevent the order from becoming final for purposes of establishing res judicata. That the order happens to follow a nonsuit does not make it void. Many litigants use a nonsuit as a procedural device to effectuate a settlement agreement, intentionally dismissing claims with prejudice. Indeed, in this case Joachim had taken a nonsuit with the first trial court "dismissing with prejudice all of Plaintiff's claims" against another defendant with whom Joachim had settled, before he filed the nonsuit as to Travelers. Just as the trial court has jurisdiction to enter a dismissal with prejudice upon the filing of a nonsuit to effectuate a settlement agreement, it must also have jurisdiction to enter a dismissal with prejudice in other nonsuit situations. Accordingly, we conclude that the trial court's order in this case was voidable, not void. Therefore, the order was subject only to direct attack to avoid becoming a final judgment.

* * *

The question remains whether the trial court's voidable order of dismissal is sufficient to establish Travelers' affirmative defense of res judicata. We conclude it is. Because Joachim failed to attack the trial court's order directly, it became a final judgment for purposes of res judicata. Joachim alleges that he never received notice of the judgment dismissing his cause of action with prejudice. Certainly, if this is true, the lack of notice would not bind him to the effects of the first trial court's erroneous judgment without some potential remedy. However, there is a remedy: an equitable bill of review is a direct attack on a judgment. *See* TEX.R. CIV. P. 329b(f) (providing that a judgment may be set aside by the trial court by bill of review for sufficient cause). Had the trial court set aside the judgment, either by timely motion for new trial or by bill of review, Joachim's underlying claim would no longer be barred by res judicata, as there would no longer be a final determination on the merits. Yet, because the first trial court's order stands, Joachim's claim is barred. Accordingly, we reverse the court of appeals' judgment and render judgment dismissing Joachim's cause of action with prejudice based on Travelers' defense of res judicata.

III.

We hold that because a trial court has jurisdiction to enter orders dismissing a case with prejudice upon filing of a nonsuit, the trial court's order here was voidable, not void, and subject only to direct attack. Because Joachim failed to attack the trial court's order directly, it became a final determination on the merits for purposes of res judicata. Therefore, we reverse the court of appeals' judgment and render judgment dismissing the case with prejudice.

H. Foreign Judgments

1. *Full faith and credit.* The judgments of the United States federal courts or of the courts of the other states of the United States are entitled to full faith and credit in the Texas courts under the United States Constitution. U.S. CONST. art. IV, § 1. This means that a party that has a final judgment from one of these courts has a constitutional right to bring that judgment to the Texas courts for enforcement. The judgment creditor must first get the Texas courts to recognize the foreign judgment, after which the judgment is treated exactly as a Texas judgment for enforcement purposes. Judgments of other countries are not entitled to full faith and credit under the Constitution. Nevertheless, courts of the United States recognize and enforce judgments rendered in the courts of many foreign countries, in effect giving these judgments full faith and credit. There are three different procedures by which one can seek recognition of a foreign judgment in the Texas courts.

2. *Filing under the Uniform Enforcement of Foreign Judgments Act, Ch. 35, TEX. CIV. PRAC. & REM. CODE ["UEFJA"].* Under this statute, the judgment creditor files an authenticated copy of the foreign judgment in the clerk's office, and upon filing, the clerk is to treat the foreign judgment in the same manner as a judgment of the court in which it is filed.[1] The judgment creditor must also file an affidavit showing the name and last known post office address of the judgment creditor and judgment debtor in the clerk's office, which allows the clerk to "promptly" mail notice of the filing of the judgment to the judgment debtor.[2] The judgment creditor can also send notice, in which case the clerk's failure to send the notice will not affect the enforcement proceedings. Section 35.007 sets out provisions for the payment of filing fees when the judgment is filed. Significantly, under this statute, a properly authenticated and filed foreign judgment immediately has the same effect as a Texas judgment. As the Texas Supreme Court has said, "[W]hen a judgment creditor proceeds under the UEFJA, the filing of the foreign judgment comprises both a plaintiff's original petition and a final judgment."[3] Appellate deadlines begin to run on the day the judgment is filed. The judgment debtor can seek a stay of enforcement[4] or present defenses to enforcement of the judgment by motion for new trial or other motion contesting recognition within 30 days of the filing.[5] The judgment can be attacked through the same procedures that are available for attacking a Texas judgment—motion for new trial (within 30 days of the filing), restricted appeal, and bill of review.

3. *Filing under the Uniform Foreign Country Money Judgment Recognition Act, Ch. 36, TEX. CIV. PRAC. & REM. CODE [the "Recognition Act"].* This statute provides for the same filing procedure as provided for the judgments of sister states, making a final money-judgment of the courts of a foreign country enforceable in Texas upon filing an authenticated copy with the clerk.[6] This act applies only to judgments of a foreign country (a governmental unit other than the United

[1] TEX. CIV. PRAC. & REM. CODE §35.003.

[2] TEX. CIV. PRAC. & REM. CODE §35.004.

[3] Walnut Equipment Leasing Co. v. Wu, 920 S.W.2d 285 (Tex. 1996).

[4] *See* TEX. CIV. PRAC. & REM. CODE § 35.006.

[5] Moncrief v. Harvey, 805 S.W.2d 20 (Tex. App.—Dallas 1991, no writ).

[6] TEX. CIV. PRAC. & REM. CODE §§ 36.004-.0043.

States or its states, districts, territories and possessions) "granting or denying a sum of money," and specifically does not include a judgment for taxes, a fine, or other penalty, or for support in a matrimonial or family matter.[7] Unlike the UEFJA, the Recognition Act contains two provisions specifically setting out grounds for nonrecognition of the foreign judgment[8] and a procedure whereby the judgment debtor can contest the recognition within 30 days after service of the notice of filing (60 days if the party is domiciled in a foreign country).

4. *An action to enforce a judgment.* Section 35.008 of the UEFJA retains the common law action to enforce a judgment instead of proceeding under the statute. In such an action, the judgment creditor files a lawsuit in the Texas court asking the Texas court to render a Texas judgment recognizing and incorporating the foreign judgment. The judgment debtor is given the opportunity to answer and present any defenses to the foreign judgment. The judgment is given effect in Texas only after the trial court renders judgment, sometimes after a trial on whether the judgment should be given full faith and credit.[9] The Recognition Act has a similar provision.[10]

RUSSO
v.
DEAR
105 S.W.3d 43
(Tex. App.—Dallas 2003, pet. denied)

CORNELIUS, JUSTICE (Retired).

This case involves a suit to enforce a foreign judgment. Barbara Russo appeals from a district court judgment giving full faith and credit to an Ohio judgment filed in Texas pursuant to chapter 35 of the Texas Civil Practice and Remedies Code. We affirm.

In 1987, Russo hired William C. Dear, Jr., a private investigator, to investigate a friend's death. Dear's investigation took him to Ohio. In 1990, Russo sued Dear in Texas for overcharging her and for acting fraudulently and negligently in his investigation. Dear filed a counterclaim against Russo for slander and notified his insurance carrier of her suit.

On October 7, 1992, shortly before the trial was held in the Texas suit, Dear sued Russo in Ohio, alleging causes of action for libel, slander, and interference with business. Russo appeared with counsel in the Ohio suit and filed a motion to dismiss based in part on lack of personal jurisdiction, res judicata, and collateral estoppel. Specifically, Russo argued that Dear was precluded from litigating his claims in Ohio because he could or should have raised them in his counterclaim in the Texas suit. Dear responded, and the trial court held a hearing. On November 16, 1993, the Ohio trial court denied Russo's motion to dismiss, stating: (1) Russo had sufficient minimum contacts with Ohio for the trial court to have personal jurisdiction over her, and (2) because the bases for Dear's slander claim in Ohio were not in existence at the time he filed his an-

---

7 TEX. CIV. PRAC. & REM. CODE § 36.001(2).

8 TEX. CIV. PRAC. & REM. CODE § 36.005, Grounds for Nonrecognition.

9 *See* Moncreif v. Harvey, 805 S.W.2d 20 (Tex. App.—Dallas 1991, no writ) (comparing the two procedures).

10 TEX. CIV. PRAC. & REM. CODE § 36.008.

swer in the Texas suit, his counterclaim in Texas was not compulsory, and his failure to assert the same slander claim in Texas did not preclude his assertion of it in a later suit in Ohio. The Ohio case was set for a jury trial. In October 1994, Dear appeared in the Ohio court for trial, but Russo did not. Dear sought and recovered a postanswer default judgment against Russo. Russo did not file a direct appeal of the Ohio judgment.

Dear then sought to enforce the Ohio judgment in Texas pursuant to chapter 35 of the Texas Civil Practice and Remedies Code. Russo responded with a motion to vacate or stay execution of the Ohio judgment based in part on lack of finality. In July 1996, the Texas trial court rendered judgment declaring the Ohio judgment not final, and this Court affirmed. *See Dear v. Russo,* 973 S.W.2d 445 (Tex. App.—Dallas 1998, no pet.).

In response to this Court's opinion, Dear obtained two nunc pro tunc orders from the Ohio trial court, one dated June 11, 1996 and the other dated February 19, 1996. Dear then again sought to enforce the Ohio judgment in Texas. Russo responded with another motion to dismiss or stay execution of judgment, alleging lack of finality, res judicata, and collateral estoppel. In the alternative, she filed a motion for new trial, asserting that the Ohio court lacked personal and subject matter jurisdiction, the Ohio judgment was not final, the judgment was barred by res judicata and collateral estoppel, and that she had received no notice of the Ohio trial court's final hearing on Dear's motion for the postanswer default judgment. The Texas trial court granted Russo's motion to dismiss, and Dear appealed. This Court reversed and remanded for further proceedings, holding that the nunc pro tunc orders made the Ohio judgment final. *See Dear v. Russo,* WL 953396 (Tex. App.—Dallas Aug.23, 2001, no pet.) (not designated for publication) [*Dear v. Russo II*]. This Court also held that Ohio law did not require its trial court to provide Russo with either notice of the hearing on the postanswer default judgment or notice that it was issuing the nunc pro tunc orders.

On remand from this Court, the trial court held a hearing on Russo's previously filed motion for new trial and a supplement to that motion, in both of which she argued the merits of how the Ohio trial court erred in rendering its postanswer default judgment. The trial court denied Russo's motion for new trial without stating a reason. This appeal ensued.

On appeal, Russo contends the grounds for her motion for new trial were not the subject of any previous appeal and may therefore be decided now. In her first four points, she contends (in order) the Ohio trial court erred by: (1) failing to find that collateral estoppel barred its judgment; (2) failing to find that res judicata barred its judgment; (3) rendering judgment based on insufficient evidence to support a judgment or jury verdict; and (4) denying her due process in rendering its judgment without providing her with notice. In her fifth point, she argues the Texas trial court erred in not reviewing the Ohio trial court's denial of her special appearance.

The United States Constitution requires each state to give full faith and credit to the public acts, records, and judicial proceedings of every other state. *See* U.S. CONST. art. IV, § 1. In Texas, the enforcement of foreign judgments is governed by the Texas version of the Uniform Enforcement of Foreign Judgments Act. *See* TEX. CIV. PRAC. & REM. CODE ANN. §§ 35.001-.008 (Vernon 1997 & Supp.2003); Under the full faith and credit clause, a valid foreign judgment is entitled to the same recognition in this state as the judgment would receive in the state where it was rendered. A properly filed foreign judgment has the same effect and is subject to the same procedures, defenses, and proceedings for reopening, vacating, staying, enforcing, or satisfying a judgment as a judgment of the court in which it is filed. *See* TEX. CIV. PRAC. & REM. CODE ANN. § 35.003(c). The party seeking to enforce a foreign judgment has the initial burden to present a judgment that appears on its face to be a final, valid, and subsisting judgment. Thereafter, the defendant has the burden of collaterally attacking the judgment by establishing a recognized exception to the full faith and credit requirements, *e.g.*, when a decree is interlocutory or subject to modification under the law of the rendering state, when the rendering court lacks jurisdiction, when the judgment was procured by fraud or is penal in nature, or when limitations has expired under Texas Civil Practice and Remedies Code section 16.066. However, in a collateral attack on a sister state's judgment, no defense may be set up that goes to the merits of the original controversy.

When this Court decided in the previous appeal that the Ohio judgment was final, Dear fulfilled his initial burden of presenting a facially valid and final judgment. The burden then shifted to Russo to show a legal reason for the Texas trial court to deny the Ohio judgment full faith and credit. Russo's points one through three do not fall within one of the exceptions to full faith and credit; instead, they impermissibly attempt to collaterally attack the merits of the Ohio judgment. To the extent the trial court did not grant Russo's motion for new trial on these grounds, it did not err.

In her fourth point complaining of no notice of either the Ohio trial setting or the nunc pro tunc orders, Russo presents the same argument this Court previously addressed and decided in [*Dear v. Russo II*]. We find no need to revisit this point.

[Russo next complains that the Ohio court did not have personal jurisdiction over her.] She may not raise that argument now in Texas because the Ohio trial court fully and fairly litigated that issue. The Texas court's scope of inquiry into the foreign court's jurisdiction is limited to whether questions of jurisdiction were fully and fairly litigated and finally decided by the sister state, and if so, personal jurisdiction may not be raised again in the Texas court.

For the reasons stated, we affirm the judgment.

CHAPTER 19. COMPLEX LITIGATION

A. Severance, Separate Trials and Consolidation

Read Rules 40(b), 41, 174.

In re ETHYL CORPORATION
975 S.W.2d 606
(Tex. 1998)

JUSTICE OWEN delivered the opinion of the Court, in which CHIEF JUSTICE PHILLIPS, JUSTICE ENOCH, JUSTICE SPECTOR, JUSTICE BAKER, JUSTICE ABBOTT and JUSTICE HANKINSON joined.

In this original proceeding, we are called upon to determine whether the trial court abused its discretion by grouping for trial the premises liability claims of twenty-two workers or their family members against five defendants for deaths or injuries allegedly caused by exposure to asbestos. Because the record is silent with regard to many factors that would inform our decision on the commonality or conversely the dissimilarity of these claims, the relators have not demonstrated that the trial court abused its discretion. Accordingly, we deny the petition for writ of mandamus.

I

The underlying suit was brought by numerous plaintiffs who were represented by the same counsel, and at one time, this single suit encompassed the claims of 459 workers or their families, each of whom sued one or more of sixty-nine defendants. All claims are against premise owners or occupiers for the injuries or deaths of workers allegedly exposed to asbestos or asbestos-containing materials at industrial sites. The workers were employed by various independent contractors and were sent onto these sites. Settlements and summary judgments reduced the number of claims remaining for trial to those of 111 workers or their families against one or more of five defendants. Those defendants are Ethyl Corporation, USX Corporation, Todd Shipyards, Texas City Refining, Inc., and Associated Metals, doing business as Tex-Tin. Each plaintiff has also asserted claims for the same injuries or deaths in separate suits against manufacturers of asbestos-containing products. All asbestos products suits in Harris County have been assigned to a special asbestos docket, but at the time this case was submitted for argument, the premises cases had not been included in that docket.

In an attempt to pare down the diverse premises liability claims at issue in this proceeding to manageable numbers of plaintiffs for trial, the trial court directed the parties to attempt to agree on the first grouping. When no agreement was reached, the court selected twenty-five claims with one predominant factor in common—the separate actions against products manufacturers had been resolved. The defendants objected to trying these twenty-five claims together, contending that each should be tried separately. The defendants filed written objections and motions, which the trial court denied. The number of claims ultimately set for trial was reduced to twenty-two when counsel for the plaintiffs determined that three of the corresponding but separate products liability actions had not been resolved.

The twenty-two workers whose claims or derivative claims were chosen for trial were allegedly exposed to asbestos or asbestos-containing products at varying times from 1941 to 1981. The lengths of exposure ranged from just over one year to more than thirty-eight years. None of the workers had been on the premises of all five defendants. Of the twenty-two workers, eleven had been on the premises of only one defendant, six worked at the premises of two defendants, four worked at the premises of three defendants, and one worked at the premises of four defendants. All of the workers had also been exposed to asbestos at one or more of forty-one sites other than those of the defendants.

The nature of the injuries allegedly suffered by these workers differ in severity, ranging from thickening of the pleural lining, to asbestosis, lung cancer, and mesothelioma. Seven of the workers were deceased at the time these claims were set for trial.

Four of the five defendants sought writ of mandamus from the court of appeals, which denied any relief in an unpublished per curiam opinion. These defendants now seek mandamus relief from this Court. . . .

II

The mass tort litigation that has proliferated over the last two decades has caused departures from traditional ways in which cases have been filed, discovery has proceeded, and trials have been set. As already noted, the case before us is a single suit in which a large number of plaintiffs have asserted separate claims against one or more of five defendants. Technically speaking, this mandamus proceeding does not concern consolidation, because all plaintiffs and all defendants were already parties to the same suit when certain of the claims were selected for a separate trial. The record indicates that counsel for the plaintiffs did not contend that all 111 claims should be tried at once. Rather, plaintiffs' counsel as well as the trial court contemplated that the separate claims would be aggregated into groups for trial purposes.

Consolidation is governed by Rule 174(a) of the Texas Rules of Civil Procedure, which provides:

> (a) Consolidation. When actions involving a common question of law or fact are pending before the court, it may order a joint hearing or trial of any or all the matters in issue in the actions; it may order all the actions consolidated; and it may make such orders concerning proceedings therein as may tend to avoid unnecessary costs or delay.

Subpart (b) of the same rule governs separate trials:

> (b) Separate Trials. The court in furtherance of convenience or to avoid prejudice may order a separate trial of any claim, cross-claim, counterclaim, or third-party claim, or of any separate issue or of any number of claims, cross-claims, counterclaims, third-party claims, or issues.

In their briefing in this Court, the defendants at times refer to "consolidation," and at other times refer to the trial court's failure to order "separate trials." The plaintiffs refer only to the "consolidation" of their claims and rely on Rule 174(a) as authority for the trial court's action rather than on Rule 174(b). The record in the trial court reflects that the defendants made it abundantly clear that they objected to a single trial of twenty-two claims. Regardless of whether the issue is denominated one of consolidation, separate trials, or severance, the merits of the controversy were fully presented to and ruled upon by the trial court when it repeatedly denied the defendants' objections to "consolidation" and motions for "separate trials." The question squarely before us is whether the trial court abused its discretion in setting these twenty-two claims for a single trial.

III

Before the dawn of mass torts, this Court considered the extent of a trial court's discretion under Rule 174(b) to decline to order separate trials. In *Womack v. Berry*, 291 S.W.2d 677 (Tex. 1956), we held that although the word "may" in Rule 174(b) indicates that the trial court has discretion, that discretion is not unlimited. A trial court "is required to exercise a sound and legal discretion within limits created by the circumstances of the particular case." *Id.* We observed that the express purpose of Rule 174(b) was to further convenience, to avoid prejudice, and to promote the ends of justice. The trial court has no discretion to deny separate trials when an injustice will result:

> When all of the facts and circumstances of the case unquestionably require a separate trial to prevent manifest injustice, and there is no fact or circumstance supporting or tending to support a contrary conclusion, and the legal rights of the parties will not be prejudiced thereby, there is no room for the exercise of discretion. The rule then is peremptory in operation and imposes upon the court a duty to order a separate trial.

Many considerations under Rule 174(b) are shared under Rule 174(a), and the paramount objective of preventing injustice obtains whether the question is one of separate trials or of consolidation.

The principles we espoused in *Womack* remain sound, but over the last twenty years, our legal system has been faced with new challenges. The advent of mass torts necessitates that our courts devise a systematic means of resolving large numbers of cases that have issues in common. We must resolve such claims in a timely manner while ensuring that justice is dispensed to each individual plaintiff and defendant in the process. The rights of the parties to a fair trial cannot be compromised in the name of judicial economy.

Scholars and courts have recognized that a mass tort has a life cycle. *See, e.g.*, McGovern, *An Analysis of Mass Torts for Judges*, 73 TEX. L. REV. 1821, 1841-45 (1995). Professor McGovern opines that a mass tort reaches maturity when

> there has been full and complete discovery, multiple jury verdicts, and a persistent vitality in the plaintiffs' [contentions]. Typically at the mature stage, little or no new evidence will be developed, significant appellate review of any novel legal issues has been concluded, and at least one full cycle of trial strategies has been exhausted.

Asbestos litigation, particularly asbestos products cases, has achieved maturity. Our state trial courts have gained considerable experience in managing the thousands of claims asserted in asbestos litigation. By and large, our courts appear to be coordinating pretrial discovery and scheduling trials in a satisfactory manner, given the paucity of appeals challenging trial settings of multiple claims. We have found only one reported decision of a Texas court in which the propriety of a consolidation of claims was raised. *See Owens-Corning Fiberglas Corp. v. Martin*, 942 S.W.2d 712, 715-20 (Tex. App.—Dallas 1997, no writ) (holding that consolidation of the claims and derivative claims of twelve workers against a single manufacturer of asbestos products was not error). Because of the experience our trial courts have gained over time in asbestos litigation, they now have a track record on which to base decisions about consolidation and separate trials. We can glean from the experiences of our Texas courts and those reported by federal courts that it is possible to try more than one asbestos-related claim in a single trial. The question in each proposed consolidation is how many more.

The court of appeals in *Martin* identified several factors that it and other courts have found useful. These are known as the Maryland factors. They were first articulated in an unreported federal district court decision, *In re All Asbestos Cases Pending in the United States District Court for the District of Maryland*, slip op. at 3 (D. Md. Dec. 16, 1983) (en banc). The Maryland factors are "(1) common worksite; (2) similar occupation; (3) similar time of exposure; (4) type of disease; (5) whether plaintiffs were living or deceased; (6) status of discovery in each case; (7) whether all plaintiffs were represented by the same counsel; and (8) type of cancer alleged." As the number of *Maryland* factors that different cases have in common increases, the number of those claims that can be tried together may increase. But there is no mathematical formula, and some of the *Maryland* factors should be given more weight than others. The maximum number of claims that can be aggregated is not an absolute, and the particular circumstances determine the outer limits beyond which trial courts cannot go.

The experiences of the federal courts in reviewing consolidations in asbestos litigation is enlightening. The federal rules governing consolidation and separate trials are similar to our rules of procedure. Our Rule 174 was modeled after federal Rule 42. The federal courts have recognized, as have our courts, that the discretion to consolidate is not unfettered. A court contemplating or reviewing consolidation must weigh the risk of prejudice or confusion against economy of scale:

> [T]he court must determine "[w]hether the specific risks of prejudice and possible confusion [are] overborne by the risk of inconsistent adjudications of common factual and legal issues, the burden on parties, witnesses and available judicial resources posed by multiple lawsuits, the length of time required to conclude multiple suits as against a single one, and the relative expense to all concerned of the single-trial, multiple-trial alternatives."

Hendrix v. Raybestos-Manhattan, Inc., 776 F.2d 1492, 1495 (11th Cir. 1985). While considerations of judicial economy are a factor, "[c]onsiderations of convenience and economy must yield to a paramount concern for a fair and impartial trial."

* * *

The facts presented in this mandamus proceeding lie on a continuum somewhere between *Malcolm* (48 plaintiffs, 25 defendants, and over 200 third-party defendants) and *Consorti* (4 workers with the same disease but multiple defendants and worksites). We now turn to whether the trial court abused its discretion in grouping for trial the particular claims before us.

IV

We first recognize the practicalities involved in setting cases for trial and the difficulties encountered by trial courts. A court may join cases for a single trial with the expectation that some will settle before trial commences. The number of cases initially set might exceed the number that can be tried together without confusion or prejudice. But, by the time the trial date is reached, the number and character of claims that remain to be tried may be within the bounds of the trial court's discretion to group them for a single trial.

Trial courts must be very cautious both in choosing the cases that are initially set and in proceeding with the actual trial to ensure that the process remains fair to all. Even when a court sets cases for trial with the expectation that some will settle, the process cannot be abused. Setting far more cases than can be tried would present a serious issue. *Cf. In re Rhone-Poulenc Rorer Inc.*, 51 F.3d 1293, 1299 (7th Cir.) (holding that the trial court abused its discretion in forcing the "defendants to stake their companies on the outcome of a single jury trial, or be forced by fear of the risk of bankruptcy to settle"), *cert. denied* 516 U.S. 867 (1995); *see also* Friendly, *Federal Jurisdiction: A General View* 120 (1973) (condemning "blackmail settlements"), *quoted in In re Rhone-Poulenc Rorer Inc.*, 51 F.3d at 1298. On the other hand, trial courts must set enough cases for trial to ensure that those cases that do not settle will be reached on a timely basis. Plaintiffs in asbestos suits who do not survive their wait for a trial date will be denied justice. In recognizing this reality, we also recognize that there is some tension between the principle of law that a court has no discretion to consolidate claims for trial when that will result in an injustice, *see Womack v. Berry*, 291 S.W.2d 677, 683 (Tex. 1956), and the possibility that an abuse of discretion in joining many disparate claims may evaporate before trial if cases were to settle.

We emphasize, however, that once the trial date arrives, a trial court should reassess the claims that have been aggregated to make certain that the requisite commonality is present and that the sheer number of claims, parties, or worksites will not overwhelm or confuse the jury. The lesson learned by the court in *Cain v. Armstrong World Industries* bears repeating: "The 'Try-as-many-as-you-can-at-one-time' approach is great if they all, or most, settle; but when they don't, and they didn't here, [the plaintiffs] got a chance to do something not many other civil litigants can do—overwhelm a jury with evidence." 785 F. Supp. 1448, 1457 (S.D. Ala. 1992).

The *Maryland* factors are designed to assist courts in determining if the consolidation of claims is likely to prejudice or confuse the jury. In some cases, the probability that prejudice or confusion will result may be apparent when only one factor is examined. It may be that the number or diversity of worksites, for example, would create such confusion that it would be an abuse of discretion to consolidate. In other cases, no single factor may clearly indicate that prejudice or confusion is probable, but when the evidence that will be presented is considered in the aggregate, the cumulative effect would result in an unacceptably high risk of prejudice or juror confusion. In the final analysis, the dominant consideration in every case is whether the trial will be fair and impartial to all parties.

This case presents a close call. On balance, however, we cannot conclude that the trial court abused its discretion because the record is silent with regard to many aspects of the *Maryland* factors. In utilizing the *Maryland* factors, we caution that they are not exclusive and may not be the best indicia in other types of mass tort litigation. For example, *see In re Bristol-Myers Squibb Co.*, 975 S.W.2d 601 (Tex. 1998), which we also decide today. They are, however, appropriate in this case:

1) Worksites

As already noted, there is not a single worksite at issue, and the worksites are not of the same type. . . . It is questionable whether, in determining causation and liability, jurors could reach reasoned decisions regarding the extent to which each worker was exposed to asbestos fibers at each site.

* * *

While premises cases such as these hold the potential for juror confusion because of the fact issues that may arise with regard to each individual worker and his employer, the record is devoid of any evidence whether disputed fact issues exist regarding the right of control by an owner or occupier of the premises or whether the injured party or his employer created the alleged premise defect. Nevertheless, on balance, the diversity and sheer number of worksites weigh against consolidation.

2) Similar Occupations

The twenty-two individuals allegedly exposed to materials that contained asbestos were engaged in a wide variety of occupations, and therefore, some may have had more intensive exposure to asbestos than others. Decisions that have applied the Maryland factors indicate that a disparity in occupations weighs against consolidation. We agree that if the nature or extent of exposure qualitatively varied among the different occupations, this would be significant. However, the record is silent as to whether these various occupations resulted in differing exposure levels, and we cannot simply presume that material differences exist.

3) Time of Exposure

This factor has two aspects, the dates on which exposure occurred and the length of exposure. The dates on which each worker came into contact with materials that contained asbestos and the length of that contact varies substantially from worker to worker and from worksite to worksite, including worksites owned or occupied by more than forty entities that are not parties to this suit. . . .

Although logically one would suspect that the state of a given defendant's knowledge about asbestos-containing products would be different at different points in time and that the evidence regarding causation would vary depending on the length of exposure and the dates of exposure, the record is silent on these matters. Defendants argue that the varying dates and degrees of exposure are significant, but the record provides no evidence of how or why. We cannot say, based on this record, that evidence admissible and probative against some defendants would be inadmissible and unduly prejudicial as to others or that the jury would be confused by the fact that different workers were exposed at different points in time and for different lengths of time.

4) Disease types and types of cancer

The courts that have considered the question of consolidation or separate trials in asbestos litigation have focused on whether the diseases alleged have the same or similar etiologies. The diseases allegedly suffered by the twenty-two workers in this case run the gamut from mesothelioma at one end of the spectrum to pleural thickening at the other and include asbestosis and lung cancer. Again, one might surmise that there are indeed differences in the etiologies of these conditions, but we cannot say that the trial court abused its discretion on the basis of surmise. The record in this case contains no stipulation, expert testimony, or affidavits stating that the evidence regarding these various diseases will vary significantly.

5) The living and the deceased

Some courts have expressed concern that permitting the consolidation of claims by living workers with claims of the families of deceased workers would unduly prejudice the trial because there is a danger that the claims regarding deceased workers or those who have life-ending diseases will boot-strap the claims of workers who do not have fatal conditions:

"[T]he presence of wrongful death claims and personal injury actions in a consolidated trial is somewhat troublesome. . . . [T]he dead plaintiffs may present the jury with a powerful demonstration of the fate that awaits those claimants who are still living."

Malcolm, 995 F.2d at 351-52 (alterations in original) (*quoting In re Joint E. & S. Dists. Asbestos Litig.*, 125 F.R.D. 60, 65-66 (E.& S.D.N.Y. 1989)).

This concern has considerable force when the types of diseases suffered by the workers vary and it is disputed whether these diseases are likely to result in death. However, when all of the claimants suffer from an inevitably fatal disease, the prejudice from consolidating the cases of living claimants with those of decedents generally diminishes. The record does not inform us whether the prognoses for pleural thickening, asbestosis, mesothelioma, and lung cancer differ among the twenty-two surviving workers or whether there is a substantial dispute about the prognoses of those who suffer from any of these diseases.

The remaining Maryland factors, which are the status of discovery and whether the workers or their families are represented by the same counsel, are not at issue and favor a single trial. However, we agree with the Second Circuit that these factors are far less important than the other considerations identified by the Maryland criteria. *See In re Repetitive Stress Injury Litig.*, 11 F.3d 368, 374 (2d Cir. 1993).

At least one other consideration should be added to the Maryland factors in asbestos litigation and that is the type of asbestos-containing product to which the worker was exposed. In some products, the asbestos is embedded and fibers are not likely to become loose or airborne. In other products, the asbestos is friable. This, of course, bears on the extent and intensity of exposure to asbestos and could be considered a subset of the worksite or occupation factors. There is no evidence in this record regarding the types of asbestos products that the workers encountered.

The defendants contend that whether there is evidence that is admissible against one defendant would be inadmissible against others should be given overriding weight. They cite *Lone Star Ford, Inc. v. McCormick*, 838 S.W.2d 734 (Tex. App.—Houston [1st Dist.] 1992, writ denied), in which the court of appeals observed that consolidation is proper only if the claims are "so related that evidence presented will be material, relevant, and admissible in each case." We agree that this is an important consideration in determining if consolidation or separate trials are in order. Use of the *Maryland* factors assists in identifying evidence that would be inadmissible against a particular defendant but that could come into evidence against another defendant. The prejudicial effect of such evidence should be weighed very carefully, but the fact that some evidence may be inadmissible against some defendants is not necessarily outcome-determinative on the issue of separate trials or consolidation. The degree of prejudice and the potential that the jury would not be able to keep track of what evidence applies to which defendant must be considered.

The ultimate question under our rules of procedure and decisions interpreting them is whether the undisputed facts and circumstances of this case require a separate trial of fewer than the twenty-two claims at issue to prevent prejudice and manifest injustice. In this mandamus proceeding, we cannot say, based on this record, that a party's ability to present a viable claim or defense will be vitiated or severely compromised. Accordingly, we deny the petition for a writ of mandamus.

JUSTICE HECHT, joined by JUSTICE GONZALEZ, dissenting.

Having canvassed the reported decisions of every jurisdiction in the United States and correctly concluded that none has ever come close to approving a single trial of as many different claims of injury due to exposure to asbestos against as many separate defendants involving as widely disparate allegations as the district court has done in the present case, the Court still holds that the district court has not been shown to have abused its discretion because defendants did not adduce more proof of likely confusion and prejudice. Requiring additional evidence of confusion and prejudice in mature mass-tort litigation like this is unnecessary. The purpose of the Maryland factors that the Court adopts is to determine when prejudice is likely without a mini-trial before the real trial. If defendants' evidence of prejudice in this case is weak—I do not think it is—

evidence of the possibility of a fair and impartial trial under the consolidation order in this case is scant, and evidence of any real judicial efficiency or economy to be achieved is nonexistent.

Trying multiple claims in a single trial can avoid unnecessary expense and delay without prejudice to the parties. The rules of procedure provide for consolidation as a useful tool for resolving numerous claims involving common issues. But it cannot simply be presumed, as the district court and this Court have done, that consolidated trials are more efficient and non-prejudicial absent evidence to the contrary. Having shown that some prejudice is likely, absent evidence that prejudice is unlikely and that any real efficiency can be achieved, and most especially, absent any supporting authority from any jurisdiction, defendants are entitled to have the consolidation order set aside. Accordingly, I respectfully dissent.

Notes & Questions

1. *In re Bristol-Myers Squibb Co.*[1] The Texas Supreme Court issued an opinion in this case on the same day as *In re Ethyl Corp*. Applying the reasoning used in *Ethyl*, the Court held that the trial judge did not abuse his discretion in consolidating all of the breast implant cases pending in his court into a single trial. Although 23 cases were originally consolidated, only 4 cases with 9 plaintiffs remained to be tried. The Supreme Court concluded that the breast implant litigation was not a mature tort, unlike the asbestos litigation at issue in *Ethyl*. The plaintiffs had different implants and different injuries. Like *Ethyl*, however, the majority determined that the record was not sufficient to conclude that the trial court abused its discretion. The court concluded:

> In sum, if the defendants had demonstrated that the disparities among the claims would actually affect the trial of the case and the evidence that the jury would consider, we would be inclined to agree with the manufacturers that a jury would be confused and that the parties would be prejudiced by a single trial of these nine claims. But evidence has not been provided to support the claims of prejudice and confusion. . . .
>
> We recognize that the trial court made no attempt to assess whether confusion or prejudice would result if these claims were tried together. The only criterion utilized by the trial court was that these cases were all of the breast implant cases pending at the time in its court. We further recognize that even counsel for the plaintiffs stated repeatedly at oral argument that the selection process employed by the court was "arbitrary." But in determining whether mandamus should issue, we cannot plumb the subjective reasoning of the trial court. We must focus on the record that was before the court and whether the decision was not only arbitrary but also amounted "to clear and prejudicial error of law."

2. *Mandamus relief appropriate*. In 2004, the Supreme Court found a case where mandamus relief was appropriate.[2] The court applied the "Maryland factors" and found that they weighed strongly against trying 20 plaintiffs' claims together in a mass tort suit. The court said:[3]

> Given the totally unrelated claims of plaintiffs exposed to entirely different chemicals produced by different defendants, consolidation risks the jury finding against a defendant based on sheer numbers, on evidence regarding a different plaintiff, or out of reluctance to

---

[1] 975 S.W.2d 601 (Tex. 1998).

[2] In re Van Waters & Rogers, Inc. 145 S.W.3d 203 (Tex. 2004).

[3] *Id.* at 211.

find against a defendant with regard to one plaintiff and not another. The defensive theories as to many of these plaintiffs may also differ given the varying sources of exposure. The confusion created by multiple defensive theories is augmented in this case because there are fifty-five original defendants and at least nine remaining defendants. Similarly, confusion and prejudice could subsume the valid claim of a plaintiff based on an unrelated flaw or defense applicable to a different plaintiff's claim. Juror confusion and prejudice, under these facts, is almost certain, and it would be impossible for an appellate court to untangle the confusion or prejudice on appeal. [footnote omitted]

We conclude that the consolidation of these twenty plaintiffs' claims against the defendants was an abuse of discretion for which there is no adequate remedy by appeal. Whatever advantage may be gained in judicial economy or avoidance of repetitive costs is overwhelmed by the greater danger an unfair trial would pose to the integrity of the judicial process.

In re TEXAS DEPARTMENT OF FAMILY AND PROTECTIVE SERVICES
255 S.W.3d 613
(Tex. 2008)

PER CURIAM.

The Yearning for Zion Ranch is a 1,700-acre complex near Eldorado, Texas, that is home to a large community associated with the Fundamentalist Church of Jesus Christ of Latter Day Saints. On March 29, 2008, the Texas Department of Family Protective Services received a telephone call reporting that a sixteen-year-old girl named Sarah was being physically and sexually abused at the Ranch. On April 3, about 9:00 p.m., Department investigators and law enforcement officials entered the Ranch, and throughout the night they interviewed adults and children and searched for documents. Concerned that the community had a culture of polygamy and of directing girls younger than eighteen to enter spiritual unions with older men and have children, the Department took possession of all 468 children at the Ranch without a court order.[1] The Department calls this "the largest child protection case documented in the history of the United States." It never located the girl Sarah who was the subject of the March 29 call.

---

[1] *See* TEX. FAM. CODE § 262.104(a) ("If there is no time to obtain a temporary restraining order or attachment before taking possession of a child consistent with the health and safety of that child, an authorized representative of the Department of Family and Protective Services . . . may take possession of a child without a court order under the following conditions, only: (1) on personal knowledge of facts that would lead a person of ordinary prudence and caution to believe that there is an immediate danger to the physical health or safety of the child; (2) on information furnished by another that has been corroborated by personal knowledge of facts and all of which taken together would lead a person of ordinary prudence and caution to believe that there is an immediate danger to the physical health or safety of the child; (3) on personal knowledge of facts that would lead a person of ordinary prudence and caution to believe that the child has been the victim of sexual abuse; (4) on information furnished by another that has been corroborated by personal knowledge of facts and all of which taken together would lead a person of ordinary prudence and caution to believe that the child has been the victim of sexual abuse . . . .").

The Department then filed several suits affecting the parent-child relationship ("SAPCRs")[2] requesting emergency orders removing the children from their parents and limiting the parents' access to the children. The Department also requested appointment as temporary sole managing conservator of the children, genetic testing, and permanent relief. On April 17-18, the district court conducted the adversary hearing required by section 262.201(a) of the Texas Family Code.[3] Subsections (b) and (c) state in relevant part:

> (b) At the conclusion of the full adversary hearing, the court shall order the return of the child to the parent . . . entitled to possession unless the court finds sufficient evidence to satisfy a person of ordinary prudence and caution that:
>
> (1) there was a danger to the physical health or safety of the child which was caused by an act or failure to act of the person entitled to possession and for the child to remain in the home is contrary to the welfare of the child;
>
> (2) the urgent need for protection required the immediate removal of the child and reasonable efforts, consistent with the circumstances and providing for the safety of the child, were made to eliminate or prevent the child's removal; and
>
> (3) reasonable efforts have been made to enable the child to return home, but there is a substantial risk of a continuing danger if the child is returned home.
>
> (c) If the court finds sufficient evidence to satisfy a person of ordinary prudence and caution that there is a continuing danger to the physical health or safety of the child and for the child to remain in the home is contrary to the welfare of the child, the court shall issue an appropriate temporary order under Chapter 105.

The hearing was attended by scores of attorneys for the parties, attorneys ad litem, guardians ad litem, Texas Court Appointed Special Advocates (CASA), and many others. The hearing was conducted in the courtroom in San Angelo with overflow participants in the city auditorium. At the conclusion of the hearing, the district court issued temporary orders continuing the Department's custody of the children and allowing for visitation by the parents only with the Department's agreement.

Thirty-eight mothers petitioned the court of appeals for review by mandamus, seeking return of their 126 children. The record reflects that at least 117 of the children are under 13 and that two boys are 13 and 17. The ages of the other seven, at least two of whom are boys, are not shown. Concluding that the Department had failed to meet its burden of proof under section 262.201(b)(1), the court of appeals directed the district to vacate its temporary orders granting the Department custody.

The Department petitioned this Court for review by mandamus. Having carefully examined the testimony at the adversary hearing and the other evidence before us, we are not inclined to disturb the court of appeals' decision. On the record before us, removal of the children was not warranted. The Department argues without explanation that the court of appeals' decision leaves

---

[2] *See* TEX. FAM. CODE § 262.105(a) ("When a child is taken into possession without a court order, the person taking the child into possession, without unnecessary delay, shall: (1) file a suit affecting the parent-child relationship; (2) request the court to appoint an attorney ad litem for the child; and (3) request an initial hearing to be held by no later than the first working day after the date the child is taken into possession.").

[3] Section 262.201(a) provides: "Unless the child has already been returned to the parent, managing conservator, possessory conservator, guardian, caretaker, or custodian entitled to possession and the temporary order, if any, has been dissolved, a full adversary hearing shall be held not later than the 14th day after the date the child was taken into possession by the governmental entity."

the Department unable to protect the children's safety, but the Family Code gives the district court broad authority to protect children short of separating them from their parents and placing them in foster care. The court may make and modify temporary orders "for the safety and welfare of the child," including an order "restraining a party from removing the child beyond a geographical area identified by the court." The court may also order the removal of an alleged perpetrator from the child's home and may issue orders to assist the Department in its investigation. The Code prohibits interference with an investigation, and a person who relocates a residence or conceals a child with the intent to interfere with an investigation commits an offense.

While the district court must vacate the current temporary custody orders as directed by the court of appeals, it need not do so without granting other appropriate relief to protect the children, as the mothers involved in this proceeding concede in response to the Department's motion for emergency relief. The court of appeals' decision does not conclude the SAPCR proceedings.

Although the SAPCRs involve important, fundamental issues concerning parental rights and the State's interest in protecting children, it is premature for us to address those issues. The Department's petition for mandamus is denied.

JUSTICE O'NEILL, joined by JUSTICE JOHNSON and JUSTICE WILLETT, concurring in part and dissenting in part.

In this case, the Department of Family and Protective Services presented evidence that "there was a danger to the physical health or safety" of pubescent girls on the Yearning for Zion (YFZ) Ranch from a pattern or practice of sexual abuse, that "the urgent need for protection required the immediate removal" of those girls, and that the Department made reasonable efforts, considering the obstacles to information-gathering that were presented, to prevent removal and return those children home. TEX. FAM.CODE § 262.201(b)(1)-(3). As to this endangered population, I do not agree with the Court that the trial court abused its discretion in allowing the Department to retain temporary conservatorship until such time as a permanency plan designed to ensure each girl's physical health and safety could be approved. On this record, however, I agree that there was no evidence of imminent "danger to the physical health or safety" of boys and pre-pubescent girls to justify their removal from the YFZ Ranch, and to this extent I join the Court's opinion.

Evidence presented in the trial court indicated that the Department began its investigation of the YFZ Ranch on March 29th, when it received a report of sexual abuse of a sixteen-year-old girl on the property. On April 3rd, the Department entered the Ranch along with law-enforcement personnel and conducted nineteen interviews of girls aged seventeen or under, as well as fifteen to twenty interviews of adults. In the course of these interviews, the Department learned there were many polygamist families living on the Ranch; a number of girls under the age of eighteen living on the Ranch were pregnant or had given birth; both interviewed girls and adults considered no age too young for a girl to be "spiritually" married; and the Ranch's religious leader, "Uncle Merrill," had the unilateral power to decide when and to whom they would be married. Additionally, in the trial court, the Department presented "Bishop's Records"—documents seized from the Ranch-indicating the presence of several extremely young mothers or pregnant "wives"[1]

---

1 Although referred to as "wives" in the Bishop's Records, these underage girls are not legally married; rather, the girls are "spiritually" married to their husbands, typically in polygamous households with multiple other "spiritual" wives. Subject to limited defenses, a person who "engages in sexual contact" with a child younger than seventeen who is not his *legal* spouse is guilty of a sexual offense under the Texas Penal Code. *See* TEX. PENAL CODE § 21.11(a)-(b). Those who promote or assist such sexual contact, *see id.* § 7.02(a)(2), or cause the child to engage in sexual contact, *see id.* § 21.11(a)(1), may also be criminally liable.

on the Ranch: a sixteen-year-old "wife" with a child, a sixteen-year-old pregnant "wife," two pregnant fifteen-year-old "wives," and a thirteen-year-old who had conceived a child. The testimony of Dr. William John Walsh, the families' expert witness, confirmed that the Fundamentalist Church of Jesus Christ of Latter Day Saints accepts the age of "physical development" (that is, first menstruation) as the age of eligibility for "marriage." Finally, child psychologist Dr. Bruce Duncan Perry testified that the pregnancy of the underage children on the Ranch was the result of sexual abuse because children of the age of fourteen, fifteen, or sixteen are not sufficiently emotionally mature to enter a healthy consensual sexual relationship or a "marriage."

Evidence presented thus indicated a pattern or practice of sexual abuse of pubescent girls, and the condoning of such sexual abuse, on the Ranch[2]—evidence sufficient to satisfy a "person of ordinary prudence and caution" that other such girls were at risk of sexual abuse as well. *Id.* § 262.201(b). This evidence supports the trial court's finding that "there was a danger to the physical health or safety" of pubescent girls on the Ranch. *Id.* § 262.201(b)(1); *see id.* § 101.009 (" 'Danger to the physical health or safety of a child' includes exposure of the child to loss or injury that jeopardizes the physical health or safety of the child without regard to whether there has been an actual prior injury to the child."); *cf. Tex. Dep't of Human Servs. v. Boyd,* 727 S.W.2d 531, 533 (Tex. 1987) (affirming the termination of parental rights for "endanger[ing] . . . the physical well-being of [a] child," and holding: "While we agree that 'endanger' means more than a threat of metaphysical injury or the possible ill effects of a less-than-ideal family environment, it is not necessary that the conduct be directed at the child or that the child actually suffers injury. Rather, 'endanger' means to expose to loss or injury; to jeopardize."). Thus, the trial court did not abuse its discretion in finding that the Department met section 262.201(b)(1)'s requirements.

Notwithstanding this evidence of a pattern or practice of sexual abuse of pubescent girls on the Ranch, the court of appeals held-and the Court agrees today—that the trial court abused its discretion in awarding temporary conservatorship to the Department because the Department failed to attempt legal steps, short of taking custody, to protect the children. Based on the language of section 262.201 of the Family Code, I disagree. Subsections (b)(2) and (b)(3) of section 262.201 require the Department to demonstrate that "reasonable efforts, consistent with the circumstances and providing for the safety of the child, were made to eliminate or prevent the child's removal," TEX. FAM. CODE § 262.201(b)(2), and that "reasonable efforts have been made to enable the child to return home," *id.* § 262.201(b)(3). The Court suggests, consistent with the mothers' arguments in the court of appeals below, that the Department failed to adequately justify its failure to seek less-intrusive alternatives to taking custody of the children: namely, seeking restraining orders against alleged perpetrators under section 262.1015 of the Family Code, or other temporary orders under section 105.001 of the Family Code. *Id.* §§ 262.1015, 105.001.

However, the Family Code requires only that the Department make "reasonable efforts, consistent with the circumstances" to avoid taking custody of endangered children. *Id.* § 262.201(b)(2). Evidence presented in the trial court indicated that the actions of the children and mothers precluded the Department from pursuing other legal options. When the Department

---

[2] The Family Code defines "abuse" to include "sexual conduct harmful to a child's mental, emotional, or physical welfare"-including offenses under section 21.11 of the Penal Code-as well as "failure to make a reasonable effort to prevent sexual conduct harmful to a child." TEX. FAM. CODE § 261.001(1)(E)-(F). In determining whether there is a "continuing danger to the health or safety" of a child, the Family Code explicitly permits a court to consider "whether the household to which the child would be returned includes a person who . . . has sexually abused another child." *Id.* § 262.201(d).

arrived at the YFZ Ranch, it was treated cordially and allowed access to children, but those children repeatedly pled "the Fifth" in response to questions about their identity, would not identify their birth-dates or parentage, refused to answer questions about who lived in their homes, and lied about their names-sometimes several times. Answers from parents were similarly inconsistent: one mother first claimed that four children were hers, and then later avowed that they were not. Furthermore, the Department arrived to discover that a shredder had been used to destroy documents just before its arrival.

Thwarted by the resistant behavior of both children and parents on the Ranch, the Department had limited options. Without knowing the identities of family members or of particular alleged perpetrators, the Department could not have sought restraining orders under section 262.1015 as it did not know whom to restrain. Likewise, it could not have barred any family member from access to a child without filing a verified pleading or affidavit, which must identify clearly the parent and the child to be separated. *See id.* § 105.001(c)(3) ("Except on a verified pleading or an affidavit . . . an order may not be rendered . . . excluding a parent from possession of or access to a child."). Furthermore, the trial court heard evidence that the mothers themselves believed that the practice of underage "marriage" and procreation was not harmful for young girls; the Department's witnesses testified that although the Department "always wants kids to be with their parents," they will only reunify children with their parents after "it's determined that [their parents] know and can express what it was in the first place that caused harm to their children." This is some evidence that the Department could not have reasonably sought to maintain custody with the mothers. Thus, evidence presented to the trial court demonstrated that the Department took reasonable efforts, consistent with extraordinarily difficult circumstances, to protect the children without taking them into custody.

The record demonstrates that there was evidence to support the trial court's order as it relates to pubescent female children. Although I agree with the Court that the trial court abused its discretion by awarding custody of male children and pre-pubescent female children to the Department as temporary conservator, I would hold that the trial court did not abuse its discretion as to the demonstrably endangered population of pubescent girls, and to this extent would grant the Department's petition for mandamus. Because the Court does not, I respectfully dissent.

B. Multi-District Litigation

Read Tex. Gov't Code 74.161-.164; Court Administration Rule 13

In re CANO PETROLEUM, INC., et al.
283 S.W.3d 179
(Tex. 2008)

PRESIDING JUDGE PEEPLES delivered the opinion of the MDL Panel.

In March 2006 wildfire swept across 480,000 acres in the Texas Panhandle east of Amarillo, causing the death of several individuals and also destroying ranch land, barns, homes, fences, equipment, and livestock. Eventually ninety-one individuals filed seven lawsuits against four oil and gas operators in four contiguous counties (Roberts, Gray, Hutchinson, and Carson). Plaintiffs allege that the defendants' electrical lines and equipment caused an initial fire, which spread to other areas and lasted several days.

Defendants have asked this panel to appoint one pretrial judge for these cases. Pursuant to Rule 13.3(b), the four trial judges in whose courts the cases are pending, joined by the Presiding Judge of the Ninth Administrative Judicial Region in the Panhandle, have concurred in that request and asked the panel to assign the cases to one pretrial judge. The vast majority of the plaintiffs oppose the request for an MDL pretrial judge, though one small group of plaintiffs does not oppose it. After the matter was briefed, on September 25, 2007 the panel granted the motion and assigned a pretrial judge. This opinion states the panel's reasons for granting the motion.

Rule 13 authorizes us "to transfer 'related' cases from different trial courts to a single pretrial judge if transfer will (1) serve the convenience of the parties and witnesses and (2) promote the just and efficient conduct of the litigation." *See In re Ad Valorem Tax Litigation,* 216 S.W.3d 83, 84 (Tex. M.D.L. Panel 2006); TEX.R. JUD. ADMIN. 13.2(f), 13.3(a), 13.3(*l*).

These cases are clearly related within the meaning of rule 13. Like the *Hurricane Rita* cases, they will explore negligence and causation issues in one enormous event. *See In re Hurricane Rita Evacuation Bus Fire,* 216 S.W.3d 70 (Tex. M.D.L. Panel 2006). The fact that ninety-one plaintiffs have been joined in seven cases (seventy-eight property-damage plaintiffs in five cases) suggests a certain degree of relatedness. The various plaintiffs' pleadings allege essentially the same thing: that a fire was caused by the defendants' "electrical distribution system," or their "electrical wiring and equipment," or their "equipment and/or electrical lines." The damages resulting from the wildfire will of course differ with each individual plaintiff, as damages usually do. *See id.* at 72. But the negligence and causation issues will be substantially related in all the cases. We conclude that the cases involve common issues of fact and are related within the meaning of rule 13.

We also conclude that assigning the cases to one judge for pretrial matters will minimize inconvenience to the witnesses and parties and promote the just and efficient handling of the cases. The core issue that runs through all the cases is whether Cano was negligent and whether that negligence proximately caused damages. Movants assert that in these cases there will be many common expert and fact witnesses who should not have to respond to duplicative discovery obligations. In addition, they argue, there will be other common pretrial issues, such as challenges to expert testimony, rulings on dispositive motions, allegations of evidence spoliation, efforts to disregard the corporate form, and motions to disqualify one of the plaintiffs' law firms in four cases. Respondents have not convincingly rebutted these assertions. We are persuaded that discovery in the different cases will involve many of the same witnesses, such as eyewitnesses, firefighters and other first responders, and defense employees and that discovery issues would be best handled by a single pretrial judge as would the common legal issues.

Here the local issues do not predominate over the common ones, as they did in *In re Ad Valorem Tax Litigation,* 216 S.W.3d at 86 (referring to "the overwhelmingly local nature of these cases"). And of course an MDL movant need not show that witnesses have already been inconvenienced or subjected to multiple similar discovery requests, *In re Silica Prods. Liability Litig.,* 166 S.W.3d 3, 5 (Tex. M.D.L. Panel 2004), or that discovery has already been characterized by conflict instead of agreement, *id.* at 5-6, 7-8 (no reason to suspect that agreement and cooperation will cease when pretrial judge is assigned). "Rule 13 seeks to prevent the occurrence of problems in the future and is not limited to correcting ongoing problems from the past." *In re Ocwen Loan Servicing Litigation,* No. 07-0037 (Tex. M.D.L. Panel 2007), slip op. at 3.

Plaintiffs make four principal arguments in opposition to the motion for a pretrial judge: (1) defendants filed this motion for delay; (2) defendants have waived their right to file the motion; (3) the wrongful death and property damage cases are so unrelated that they should not be consolidated for pretrial purposes; and (4) inefficiencies outweigh any efficiencies. Concerning the first two objections, it is not at all clear that rule 13 contemplates inquiry into a movant's subjective state of mind or its promptness in asserting its rights. Assuming, without deciding, that delay motive and waiver are proper arguments in opposition to a rule 13 motion, we address them below. The other two arguments clearly contend that appointing a pretrial judge will not promote efficiency, convenience, or justice.

1. Delay.

When this matter was briefed, plaintiffs argued that appointing one pretrial judge would delay an October 29 trial setting and that delay was the real motive behind the MDL motion. We understand that the trial setting was indeed continued and the case reset for a later date. Nevertheless the delay argument fails to take into account two fundamental truths about MDL procedures.

First, appointment of a pretrial judge has no direct effect on existing settings. It does not necessarily cause delay; it simply puts a different judge in place to make decisions about pretrial matters, including whether and when to remand cases for trial and whether to postpone and reschedule existing trial settings. When an MDL motion is filed, there is no stay of trial court proceedings unless the panel or the trial court expressly issues one. *See* TEX.R. JUD. ADMIN 13.4. Existing trial settings are not affected unless the pretrial judge makes such a ruling and postpones a trial setting.

Second, the granting of an MDL motion does not mean that all cases must proceed at the pace of the slowest. When an individual case is ready for trial, the pretrial judge will ordinarily remand it for trial after consulting with the original trial court about docket realities. The readiness of one case for remand should not be affected by the readiness of other cases because appointment of a pretrial judge does not consolidate cases for purposes of trial; it brings them together for pretrial purposes only. There is no reason why *all* related cases must be ready for trial before *any* may be remanded. Nothing in this opinion or our order granting the MDL motion prevents the pretrial judge from remanding any case for trial at any time he deems the case ready. Whether a case is ready for remand and trial is a decision for the pretrial court to make in its broad discretion.

2. Waiver.

Several plaintiffs argue that defendants have in effect waived their right to seek MDL treatment by waiting too long to make that request. It goes without saying that as cases mature from just-filed to fully-discovered and ready for trial, there will be a smaller pretrial portion remaining for a pretrial judge to supervise. This seems to have been the situation in *In re Vanderbilt Mortgage and Finance, Inc.,* 166 S.W.3d 12 (Tex. M.D.L. Panel 2005), in which two of six very similar cases were substantially discovered and set for trial. If an MDL movant has waited until many cases have progressed through discovery and reached maturity, that fact might *weigh against* an MDL assignment. But it does not follow that waiting until there has been considerable pretrial discovery means that a movant has *waived* its right to file an MDL motion. We respectfully reject the suggestion that a litigant must act promptly or it waives its right under rule 13 to ask for a pretrial judge.

3. Wrongful death and property damage differences.

Plaintiffs argue that property damage cases and wrongful death cases are so different that they should not be handled together. Wrongful death cases, they say, are usually more complicated and require more discovery. And the damages in the two kinds of cases are of course completely different. This much is true. But the liability part of each case will be substantially similar. On balance it makes sense to have one judge handle the pretrial phase of all these enormous wildfire cases arising from a common disaster, giving consistent, unified treatment to the common issues and individualized treatment to the issues that are different. To hold otherwise would in effect require separate pretrial treatment of mass disaster cases whenever there is damage to both property and person.

4. Inefficiencies.

Plaintiffs are concerned that if a pretrial judge is assigned they will have to attend hearings and depositions on matters that may be of minimal importance to them. Not knowing in advance whether their interests will be implicated, they may have to err on the side of caution and attend, wasting attorney time and increasing costs.[6] We are confident that the pretrial judge, upon request, will address these concerns. The pretrial judge might, for example, ensure that parties with property damage cases need not participate in damages-only discovery in injury and death cases and vice versa. The court could order that parties with cases in only one county need not participate in specified localized discovery in other counties. And the court could allow any lawyer who thinks his client will not be interested in a deposition to e-mail the lawyer who noticed the deposition and seek assurances about the scope of the questioning; the court could grant the right to re-depose the witness if the assurances were not accurate or something unexpected occurred. These suggestions are illustrative only; lawyers should be creative in asking for efficiency-seeking relief that is tailored to the situation. The pretrial judge has ample discretion to fashion such relief.

* * *

For the reasons stated, Cano's motion to transfer these cases to a pretrial court is granted.

JUSTICES LANG, HANKS, STONE, and MCCLURE join.

---

6 In the *Ad Valorem Tax* cases, if a pretrial judge had been assigned, the attorneys and witnesses for forty-two taxing districts would have faced the prospect of having to travel significant distances to attend common hearings and depositions. We said:

> Valero has not shown that any witnesses except its own corporate witnesses may be exposed to multiple demands. Appraisal district personnel and their witnesses, however, will clearly be inconvenienced if they must travel to one central court for pretrial matters instead of to their forty-two local courthouses or to nearby conference rooms. Several of the districts are located in smaller counties, and the amount of tax revenue in their cases is small; to them there is a great difference between pretrial hearings in their own county and hearings in a distant central county for all these cases. Attorneys for the districts often will not know whether a pretrial hearing will implicate their interests, and they will therefore have to attend the distant hearing or risk being bound by the result. On balance, any inconvenience to Valero's witnesses pales in comparison to the potential inconvenience to the local officials, their appraisal personnel, and their attorneys.

216 S.W.3d at 86. These convenience issues are not as salient in the present litigation, in which the cases are pending in four adjacent counties and involve a common disaster.

Notes & Questions

Consolidation for pretrial proceedings. In 2003, the Legislature included multidistrict litigation in its tort reform bill. Subchapter H was added to Section 74 of the Government Code, establishing a judicial panel on multidistrict litigation (members to be appointed by the Chief Justice of the Texas Supreme Court), and giving the panel the power to transfer "civil actions involving one or more common questions of fact pending in the same or different . . . courts . . . to any district court for consolidated or coordinated pretrial proceedings, including summary judgment or other dispositive motions, but not for trial on the merits."[1] Transfer is to be predicated upon a determination that the transfer will "be for the convenience of the parties and witnesses" and "promote the just and efficient conduct of the actions."[2] Rules of practice and procedure have been adopted.[3] The MDL Panel, which decides what cases will be consolidated, has issued orders in several types of cases, such as those alleging asbestos exposure, silicosis exposure, and Firestone/Ford rollover injury cases. Consolidated cases are sent to a "pretrial court" for pretrial matters, and then sent back to the "trial court" for trial.

C. Class Actions

Read Rule 42.

Complex cases involving multiple parties present vexing problems for our civil justice system. Some of these complex cases arise under the traditional procedural rules. As we have seen, multiple plaintiffs can join together under Rule 40 to jointly sue defendants, so long as their claims arise from the same transaction, occurrence or series of transactions or occurrences. Furthermore, if multiple plaintiffs have filed multiple suits, cases can be consolidated under Rules 174 and 41.

The class action procedure, which is found in Rule 42, is another procedural device for these types of suits. The Texas Supreme Court has explained the class action as follows:[1]

> Rule 42 is a form of joinder, a procedural mechanism established to increase judicial economy and efficiency for suits with parties too numerous for conventional joinder. *See Hansberry v. Lee,* 311 U.S. at 42-43, 61 S.Ct. 115 ("[t]he class suit was an invention of equity to enable it to proceed to a decree [when parties are so numerous as to make joinder] in conformity to usual rules of procedure . . . impracticable"). Rule 42 is intended to eliminate or reduce the threat of repetitive litigation, prevent inconsistent resolution of similar cases, and provide an effective means of redress for individuals whose claims are

---

[1] TEX. GOV'T CODE §§ 74.161; 74.162.

[2] *Id.*

[3] *See* Tex. R. Judicial Admin. 13.

[1] Citizens Ins. of American v. Daccach, 217 S.W.3d 430, 449 (Tex. 2007); *see also generally, e.g.*, Sw. Bell Tel. Co. v. Mktg. on Hold Inc., 308 S.W.3d 909 (Tex. 2010); Heckman v. Williamson Cty., 369 S.W.3d 137 (Tex. 2012).

> too small to make it economically viable to pursue them in independent actions. Although intended to be an efficient device, "there is no right to litigate a claim as a class action." A Texas court may certify a class action only if the plaintiff satisfies the requirements of Rule 42.

Texas Rule 42 was amended in 2003 largely in response to a statute requiring the Supreme Court to "adopt rules to provide for the fair and efficient resolution of class actions."[2] And, in 2005, the Class Action Fairness Act (CAFA),[3] was signed into law. CAFA moves many class actions from state court to federal court by expanding federal jurisdiction to include most class actions where plaintiffs as a group seek more than $5 million and have "minimal diversity," meaning at least one plaintiff and one defendant are citizens of different states. Previously, a class action filed in state court could only be removed to federal court if the amount in controversy per plaintiff was greater than $75,000 and complete diversity existed between all plaintiffs and all defendants. The Act's jurisdictional provisions are extraordinarily complex and rife with ambiguities that are beyond the subject of this course. However, because of CAFA, there are fewer class actions filed in Texas state court. Therefore, we leave class actions to other law school courses.

D. Limiting the Scope of Discovery in Complex Cases

In re ALLIED CHEMICAL CORP.

227 S.W.3d 652
(Tex. 2007)

JUSTICE BRISTER delivered the opinion of the Court, in which JUSTICE HECHT, JUSTICE MEDINA, JUSTICE GREEN, and JUSTICE WILLETT joined.

Trial judges have broad discretion in scheduling discovery and trial, but that discretion has never been unlimited. As we stated in 1847, trial courts may set trials as they wish, but not so indiscriminately that the parties are "deprived of any just defense, or that their rights would in any manner be jeopardized."

Since 1847, new kinds of litigation have emerged that require new applications of this rule. Eleven years ago in *Able Supply Co. v. Moye*, we held that in mass tort cases involving hundreds of parties and complicated causation questions, a trial judge could not postpone responses to basic discovery until shortly before trial.[2] Finding that is precisely what has occurred here, we again grant mandamus relief.

I. The Proceedings and Mootness

Roughly 1,900 plaintiffs sued 30 defendants in Hidalgo County, alleging exposure to chemical fumes and leaks from several sites where pesticides were mixed or stored before the sites were placed in receivership in 1967 and remediated in 1980. The plaintiffs identified no particular incidents or products, instead alleging exposure to a "toxic soup" of emissions in the air

---

2 TEX. CIV. PRAC. & REM. CODE § 26.001.

3 28 U.S.C. § 1332, 1335, 1453, 1603, and 1711-1715.

2 898 S.W.2d 766, 772 (Tex. 1995).

for many decades. As we recently noted, no such claim "has ever been tried or appealed in Texas," and thus "the tort is immature."[3]

Five years after filing, the trial court set the first trial for little more than six months away. Despite our admonitions that trial courts should "proceed with extreme caution" in setting consolidated trials in immature mass torts,[4] the trial court consolidated five claims for the initial trial. The five plaintiffs had little in common—ranging in age from 29 to 74, residing in various directions from two different sites, alleging exposure over different parts of seven decades, and suffering injuries from asthma and arthritis to miscarriages and heart disease, and in two cases damaged property. Shortly after the trial court's order, we issued *In re Van Waters & Rogers, Inc.*, reversing the same kind of order in the same kind of case in the same county.[5] The defendants brought the opinion to the trial judge's attention, but he changed nothing. Neither did the Thirteenth Court of Appeals, where the defendants sought mandamus relief to no avail.

But when we granted a stay and requested full briefing, the plaintiffs retreated, asking the trial court to (1) sever out the property claims, (2) drop one plaintiff, and eventually (3) withdraw its consolidation order and proceed to trial on just one plaintiff's claims. The trial court granted these requests, ordering that "the personal injury claims of Plaintiff Guadalupe Garza proceed to trial."

* * *

II. The Trial Setting and *Able Supply*

In *Able Supply*, more than 3,000 plaintiffs sued nearly 300 defendants for toxic exposure. After 8 years, the plaintiffs still had not named anyone who could connect their injuries to any defendant's product. Instead, each plaintiff responded in discovery that this basic and crucial element of their claims "has not been determined at this time, but will be supplemented at a later date." As here, the plaintiffs asserted that the trial court had "broad discretion to manage its own docket, and . . . has acted well within that discretion in determining that no answers are required at the present time."[10] We disagreed, holding that the trial court's apparent indifference as to when such information might be disclosed was a clear abuse of discretion with no adequate remedy by appeal.

The issue in this case is the same. The defendants made the same request as in *Able Supply*, asking for medical experts who could connect the plaintiffs' diseases to the defendants' products.[12] Although five years had passed since filing, the plaintiffs all responded either "not applicable" or that "none of their treating physicians" could do so. But the interrogatory did not ask about treating physicians, but any expert; as we noted in *Merrell Dow Pharmaceuticals, Inc.*

---

[3] In re Van Waters & Rogers, Inc., 145 S.W.3d 203, 208 (Tex. 2004).

[4] *Id.* at 208 (citation omitted); In re Ethyl Corp., 975 S.W.2d 606, 614 (Tex. 1998) (allowing consolidated trial as asbestos claims were mature tort).

[5] 145 S.W.3d at 211.

[10] Able Supply Co. v. Moye, 898 S.W.2d 766, 770 (Tex. 1995).

[12] Specifically, the defendants' interrogatory stated:

Please state the name and address of each and every doctor, physician, psychiatrist, psychologist, counselor, or other medical practitioner who has attributed your alleged injury made the basis of this lawsuit to exposure to the Defendants' products or Defendants' conduct, including the dates of treatment or examination of each such doctor, physician, or other medical practitioner, and the name or identity of the products to which your alleged injury is attributed.

v. Havner, treating physicians usually cannot make this kind of connection.[13] By changing the defendants' question, the plaintiffs were able to respond with almost nothing.

The plaintiffs point out that their supplemental answers included a long list of chemicals to which they were "potentially exposed," and medical articles and expert reports suggesting some of those chemicals were "capable of causing" or "significantly contributed" to some of their diseases. But as this Court explained in *Havner*, "[t]o raise a fact issue on causation . . . a claimant must do more than simply introduce into evidence epidemiological studies." Evidence that a chemical can cause a disease is no evidence that it probably caused the plaintiff's disease. And as *Havner* illustrated, an expert's assurance that a study establishes causation does not make it so. Claimants must have an expert who can answer why a study is reliable, and how the plaintiff's exposure is similar to that of the study's subjects. An expert must also exclude other causes with reasonable certainty, a special problem here as the plaintiffs allege exposure to so many different chemicals. By failing to list any expert who could make this vital connection, the plaintiffs' responses were, for all practical purposes, just like those in *Able Supply*: "We'll tell you later."

We recognize this evidence is hard to obtain, but courts cannot "embrace inferences that good science would not draw." Without it, no one can prepare for trial. Accordingly, we have repeatedly granted mandamus in mass toxic tort cases when plaintiffs have refused to produce basic information like this.[19]

The plaintiffs point out that this case comes to us in a different posture than *Able Supply*, in which the trial court had refused to compel discovery. Here, although the defendants have moved to compel discovery several times, the order they challenge merely sets the case for trial. But that does not make this case different for two reasons.

First, unless we assume the interrogatory was answered in bad faith, there is nothing more to compel. The discovery rules have been amended since *Able Supply*, now requiring that "a party must make a complete response, based on all information reasonably available to the responding party or its attorney at the time the response is made."[20] Parties and attorneys certify this to be true when they sign a discovery response;[21] they can no longer simply choose to delay disclosure until the last minute.[22] Taking their responses at face value, the plaintiffs here and their attorneys certified that no one could make the causal connection they needed. Given the short time remaining before trial, the defendants properly objected that this rendered the trial setting premature; they did not have to spend the few remaining weeks begging for better answers.

---

[13] 953 S.W.2d 706, 719-20 (Tex. 1997).

[19] *See* Van Waters, 62 S.W.3d 197, 201 (Tex. 2001); In re Colonial Pipeline Co., 968 S.W.2d 938, 942 (Tex. 1998); Able Supply, 898 S.W.2d at 768.

[20] TEX. R. CIV. P. 193.1; *see also* Alex Wilson Albright, *New Discovery Rules: The Supreme Court Advisory Committee's Proposal*, 15 REV. OF LITIG. 275, 292-93 (1996) ("The proposed rules, therefore, require parties to respond, amend, and supplement discovery earlier than required under the current rules. While parties now may wait until as few as thirty days before trial to disclose important requested discovery, Proposed Rule [193.1] requires a party to make full disclosure upon the initial response to written discovery.").

[21] *See* TEX. R. CIV. P. 191.3 ("The signature of an attorney or party on a disclosure constitutes a certification that to the best of the signer's knowledge, information, and belief, formed after a reasonable inquiry, the disclosure is complete and correct as of the time it is made.")

[22] *See id.* 193.5(b) (requiring supplemental responses "reasonably promptly after the party discovers the necessity for such a response"), 193.6(a) (requiring exclusion of untimely supplements except on showing of good cause and no unfair surprise or prejudice).

Second, *Able Supply* addressed not just inadequate responses but inadequate time for discovery. There, the trial court never barred discovery completely, as the plaintiffs promised to give better answers 30 days before trial. But we held that was not enough:

> In a suit of this massive nature, which includes disparate exposures to a multitude of products, requiring defendants to wait until 30 days before trial to obtain crucial and probative evidence of a causal connection between their products and plaintiffs' injuries is such a denial of their rights as to go to the heart of the case.[23]

Here, the plaintiffs never promised better answers any earlier; to the contrary, they claimed to have "fully and accurately" responded already.

Thus, the problem here is the same as that in *Able Supply*: too little time between adequate responses and trial for the defendants to have a fair chance to mount a defense. This problem can be addressed from either end: the defendants in *Able Supply* sought to move discovery responses up; the defendants here sought to move the trial setting back. Defendants are not required to seek both. Instead, the trial court abused its discretion by doing neither.

III. Mandamus and Appeal

Of course, we generally do not consider interlocutory complaints about trial settings.[24] But we generally do not review orders refusing to compel discovery either. Yet we did so in *Able Supply* for three reasons.

First, we have granted mandamus when a discovery order imposes a burden on one party far out of proportion to any benefit to the other.[25] Here, as in *Able Supply*, the burden of making 30 defendants prepare in the dark for 1,900 claims is far out of proportion to the benefit of giving the plaintiffs more time (after five years) to decide who or what injured them. Filing thousands of claims like those here requires only a reasonable inquiry and belief that they are not groundless;[26] recovering on them requires considerably more. In the meantime, thousands of hours and millions of dollars may be needlessly wasted if the claims can never be proved. Mandamus is appropriate in such cases to avoid this "monumental waste of judicial resources."

Second, we have granted mandamus when a denial of discovery goes to the heart of a party's case. There are many cases in which it is perfectly reasonable to conduct discovery up until 30 days before trial.[29] But in suits like this one, denying discovery until then goes to the very heart of this case, as well as what our justice system is supposed to be about.[30]

Third, we have granted mandamus when a discovery order severely compromises a party's ability to present any case at all at trial. No trial was set in *Able Supply*, but the plaintiffs' intention to withhold responses until shortly before then meant the defendants could not prepare a viable defense. Late disclosure may not compromise a defendant when the complaint is minor or

[23] Able Supply, 898 S.W.2d at 772.

[24] *See* Gen. Motors Corp. v. Gayle, 951 S.W.2d 469, 477 (Tex. 1997) ("[T]he denial of a motion for continuance is an incidental trial ruling ordinarily not reviewable by mandamus.").

[25] *See* Able Supply, 898 S.W.2d at 771 (*citing* Walker v. Packer, 827 S.W.2d 833, 843 (Tex. 1992)).

[26] *See* TEX. R. CIV. P. 13.

[29] *See, e.g.*, TEX. R. CIV. P. 190.2 (allowing discovery until 30 days before trial in cases involving up to $50,000).

[30] *See* Able Supply, 898 S.W.2d at 772.

causation obvious; but the connection between chemical fumes and cancer is quite different, as is a bellwether trial that may affect thousands of others.

We cannot ignore the trial court's order here without ignoring *Able Supply*. If mandamus was proper there, it must be here too.

IV. Conclusion

Since *Able Supply*, we have intervened to compel discovery only in complex mass tort cases like this one.[32] Similarly, today's holding is no indication that we intend to intervene in more trial settings. There are good reasons to schedule trial settings well in advance, and few reasons to postpone doing so until discovery is fully complete. But trial settings, like discovery orders, cannot be used to hold the parties hostage.[33]

It has long been the rule in Texas that plaintiffs bear the burden of pleading and proving how they were injured and by whom.[34] They cannot simply file suit against everyone in the vicinity and demand that the defendants prove otherwise.

Therefore, we direct the trial court to vacate its order setting any of the plaintiffs' claims for trial until the defendants have a reasonable opportunity to prepare for trial after learning who will connect their products to plaintiffs' injuries. The writ will issue only if the trial court fails to comply.

Notes & Questions

1. In *In re Colonial Pipeline*,[1] the Court granted mandamus relief to defendants who were precluded from obtaining discovery from plaintiffs other than the ten in the first trial group. The court said:

> In this case, relators are precluded from obtaining even the most basic information from 3,265 plaintiffs until after the claims of the initial trial group of ten are resolved. Given that three and a half years have already passed since the incident underlying this case occurred, it could be many months or even years before any discovery is available. Unfortunately but inevitably, memories fade with time and evidence may be lost or corrupted. Documents may be destroyed in compliance with document retention programs. More importantly, there were four different pipelines with different substances involved. Certain illnesses or damage may conceivably be attributable to one but not all of the substances involved. The defendants have not been provided, among other things, with descriptions of the plaintiffs' alleged injuries, the names of treating physicians, or the names of the substances that caused the alleged injuries. Without discovery of basic medical information from all the plaintiffs, each defendant is put in the position of

---

32 *See* In re Van Waters & Rogers, Inc., 62 S.W.3d 197, 201 (Tex. 2001); In re Colonial Pipeline Co., 968 S.W.2d 938, 943 (Tex. 1998).

33 *See* Able Supply, 898 S.W.2d at 772.

34 *See* Gaulding v. Celotex Corp., 772 S.W.2d 66, 68 (Tex. 1989) ("A fundamental principle of traditional products liability law is that the plaintiff must prove that the defendants supplied the product which caused the injury.").

1 968 S.W.2d 938 (Tex. 1998). *See also* In re Van Waters & Rogers, 62 S.W3d 197 (Tex. 2001) (granting mandamus on order that for seven years prevented discovery in complex case).

> preparing to defend itself against claims that may not involve the substance that was contained in its pipeline. While we encourage trial courts to manage litigation actively, to try test cases to establish benchmark results, and to prohibit needless or repetitive discovery in thousands of cases that might never be tried, "[e]ach defendant is entitled to discover whether there has been a medical determination that an illness has been caused by that defendant's product." We therefore conclude that the trial court's order abating all discovery from such a large group of parties constitutes an abuse of discretion.

2. *Proportionality, e-discovery, and complex repeating claims.* In *In re State Farm*[12] (excerpted in Chapter 8, Discovery Mechanics), the Supreme Court addressed the discoverability of native data formats in an insurance-claims-underpayment case. The Court applied the proportionality factors (benefits v. burdens) to the discovery requests at issue, and in the process, included this explication of the first factor (benefits of the requested discovery):

> Courts should consider cumulative effects rather than viewing benefits and burdens in a vacuum. Here, for example, many similar cases arising from the same extreme weather event are currently pending against State Farm. The identification and retrieval process State Farm would have to develop for native-form production may be a ticket for one train only—exponentially increasing the burden when considered in the context of repeated litigation—or have broader utility, which could have a cumulatively reductive effect. The record does not tell us, but if there are likely uses for the identification and retrieval process beyond the instant mandamus cases, initial burden and expense may be substantially ameliorated, and if not, the burden and expense may be significantly enhanced.

Is this approach just? Should a plaintiff in one case face restricted discovery because of "cumulative" burdens in other pending (or even unfiled) cases? Is the risk of repeated litigation and cumulative discovery burdens a cost of doing business for large companies? Or is it fair to look outside the confines of a particular case to the actual effects of an order compelling discovery in a complex case?

E. Complex Cases and Summary Judgment

In re MOHAWK RUBBER COMPANY

982 S.W.2d 494

(Tex. App.—Texarkana 1998, pet. ref'd)

CORNELIUS, CHIEF JUSTICE.

Mohawk Rubber Company has filed a petition for a writ of mandamus ordering the Honorable Jimmy White, Judge of the 76th Judicial District of Texas, to (1) properly consider and rule on its no-evidence motion for summary judgment, (2) rescind the court's order that abated discovery as to all plaintiffs not yet set for trial and abated the filing of no-evidence summary judgment motions as to each group of plaintiffs until that group is set for trial, and (3) rescind the court's scheduling order and enter a proper case management order.

---

[2] 520 S.W.3d 595.

This lawsuit was filed on June 24, 1988. There are 205 plaintiffs who allege generally that they suffered actual or potential injuries because of their exposure to rubber products manufactured by some defendants and to rubber fumes created by the use of machines built by other defendants. There are currently four defendants remaining after others have settled.

Mohawk filed its motion for summary judgment under TEX. R. CIV. P. 166a(i) based on its contention that there was no evidence that it had in any way caused injury to the plaintiffs. The motion, commonly known as a no-evidence summary judgment motion, alleged that adequate time for discovery had elapsed and that plaintiffs had no evidence of causation.[1] The trial court signed an order overruling the motion for summary judgment, but Mohawk contends that the court did not properly interpret Rule 166a(i) and that, in reality, the court failed to rule on the merits of the summary judgment motion.

Mohawk also filed a motion asking the court to enter a *Lone Pine*-type case management order directing the plaintiffs to provide individualized information specifying their claimed injuries and to state in what manner Mohawk's activities caused such injuries. The court overruled the motion, and instead entered an order for generalized discovery that does not require the plaintiffs to provide proof of causation.

There are two separate and, in some respects, overlapping orders that are the subject of our review. We first address Mohawk's motion for summary judgment.

On June 5, 1998, the trial court issued an order denying Mohawk's motion for summary judgment. In the order the trial court acknowledged that there currently is no evidence that any defendant caused any injury to any plaintiff. The trial court further stated that there had not been adequate time for discovery and that plaintiffs had "provided adequate evidence to indicate that further discovery *may lead* to discovery of factual evidence needed to prove causation in these cases" (emphasis added).

The court also noted that it had, after the motion for summary judgment was filed, issued a case management scheduling order setting various deadlines and giving plaintiffs "a reasonable opportunity to complete discovery . . . ."[2]

In the final paragraph of the order, the court expressly stated that the denial was without prejudice and went on to state that "Mohawk may reassert a specific no evidence motion for summary judgment relating to 'a single, fine point concerning one element of a cause of action' after discovery relating to the causation issues are (sic) completed."

Thus, the trial court denied the motion for summary judgment and ordered that the deadline on further discovery be directed to the sequential groups as they become ready for trial and that

---

[1] An identical case was filed involving a large number of other plaintiffs against the same defendants. It was removed to Federal District Court. Judge David Folsom entered a *Lone Pine* order directing the plaintiffs to provide medical evidence to support their claim that the defendants had caused them harm. *See* Lore v. Lone Pine Corp., No. L-33606-85 (N.J. Super. Ct. Law Div.1986). Plaintiffs failed to do so, and less than eighteen months later, Judge Folsom dismissed the case pursuant to a no-evidence summary judgment motion.

[2] In Paragraph 18, the court held as follows:

> Furthermore, the Court is of the opinion that no evidence summary judgments in this case should be dealt with in the context of the scheduling order deadlines for plaintiffs whose cases are actually set for trial. For the sake of judicial efficiency, logistical feasibility and to avoid unnecessary and oppressive burdens on the parties or the Court, representative plaintiffs, rather than all of the plaintiffs should be selected for a scheduling order, discovery deadlines, trial dates and "no evidence" summary judgment motions. That is what this court has done through its January 2, 1998 Scheduling Order.

additional no-evidence summary judgment motions on each group could not be filed until that time. The court further concluded that causation was not an element of the causes of action, but rather that there are several separate components of causation, each of which is an "element" of plaintiffs' causes of action and which must be attacked by separate no-evidence summary judgment motions. The court thus ordered that the defendants not file any additional motions based on a failure to submit evidence of causation, but instead file any new motions for summary judgment based on a failure to provide proof of some subdivision of causation, such as duration of exposure.

Ordinarily, mandamus is not available to review an order denying a motion for summary judgment. Mohawk, however, asserts first that mandamus is appropriate here because the trial court did not actually rule on its motion for summary judgment. This is incorrect. Although the order signed contains a large amount of extraneous material, it also contains the necessary decretal language denying the motion.

Second, Mohawk argues that the trial court improperly analyzed and improperly applied the no-evidence summary judgment rule. TEX. R. CIV. P. 166a(i). We agree. We conclude that we cannot order the court to rescind its order overruling the summary judgment motion because, in the circumstances here, that order is not reviewable on mandamus. But for the guidance of the trial court in ruling on future motions for summary judgment (which under our ruling may now be filed at any time), we set out the proper application and interpretation of the no-evidence summary judgment rule in the context of this case.

The main basis that the trial court used to overrule Mohawk's motion for summary judgment was that the motion was too general because it only alleged there was no evidence of causation. The court concluded that causation in toxic tort cases is not a single element of the cause of action, but is a combination of several specific facts (plaintiffs suggested eight) that together make up causation, and that each of these factual components must be attacked in a specific summary judgment motion. This view misinterprets the element of causation as well as the requirements of the summary judgment rule.

In tort cases, the elements of the cause of action are (1) a duty to the plaintiff, (2) a breach of that duty, and (3) proximate cause of damages.

In product liability cases, causation is called producing cause. In both negligence and strict liability cases, proximate cause or producing cause is an essential element of recovery. Although causation is made up of several evidentiary components, causation itself is a single essential element of tort liability.

The plaintiffs here alleged repeatedly in their petition that their injuries were "proximately caused" by the products manufactured by the defendants. Mohawk had a right to move for summary judgment on the causation alleged by the plaintiffs, and it did so in its motion by alleging that the plaintiffs had no evidence of "causation."

We believe the plaintiffs and the learned trial court have also misinterpreted the intent of the no-evidence summary judgment rule and the comments that have been written and stated about it. The rule requires a motion to be specific in alleging a lack of evidence on an essential element of the plaintiffs' alleged cause of action, but it does not require that the motion specifically attack the evidentiary components that may prove an element of the cause of action. The specificity requirement is designed to avoid conclusory no-evidence challenges to an opponent's cause of action. The rule requires a specific challenge to the evidentiary support for an element of a claim or defense. Causation is a specific element of tort liability.

The plaintiffs also argued, and the trial court found, that Mohawk's motion would require plaintiffs to "marshal all of their evidence" to resist it, a result that the official comment to Rule 166a(i) forbids. But this argument misunderstands the term "marshal the evidence." To marshal one's evidence is to arrange all of the evidence in the order that it will be presented at trial. A party is not required to present or arrange all of its evidence in response to a summary judgment motion. But Rule 166a(i) explicitly provides that, in response to a no-evidence summary judgment motion, the respondent must present some summary judgment evidence raising a genuine issue of material fact on the element attacked, or the motion must be granted.

The trial court also found that the motion for summary judgment should be overruled because adequate time for discovery had not been allowed and because further discovery might lead to additional discovery. The court also found that discovery had not been completed. The rule, however, does not require that discovery must have been completed. It provides that a no-evidence summary judgment may be granted "after adequate time for discovery."

This case has been pending for ten years. Extensive discovery has been conducted. Interrogatories have long since been served; nearly 200 plaintiffs' depositions have been taken; and personal and employment records of the plaintiffs have been obtained. Plaintiffs have had nearly a year since Mohawk's motion for summary judgment was filed to conduct additional discovery. There has been more than "adequate time for discovery."

Mohawk also asked the trial court to issue a scheduling order that, among other things, set a timetable for discovery of facts showing a causal relationship between the defendants' products and any harm to the plaintiffs. Mohawk asked the trial court for an order substantially identical to the order issued by Judge Folsom in the federal case. The trial court denied this motion. In its order of denial, the court characterized the motion as nothing more than a second, back-door attempt at a no-evidence motion for summary judgment. The court then granted the plaintiffs' proposed scheduling order, which contains no requirement for discovery of such facts.

In the case of *In re Colonial Pipeline Co.*, 968 S.W.2d 938 (Tex. 1998), the Supreme Court addressed a situation very similar to the situation here. In that case, three and a half years had passed without discovery adequate to show causation. The trial court then entered orders abating further discovery on causation for the remaining plaintiffs until after termination of trial involving the first group of ten plaintiffs.

The Supreme Court found the order improper and ordered the restrictive language removed. The court also voiced its displeasure with the order because of its interference with the use of the no-evidence summary judgment rule because, with discovery so restricted, a no-evidence motion could not be brought until shortly before trial, which could be years in coming. The court then reiterated its holding in *Able Supply Co. v. Moye*, 898 S.W.2d 766 (Tex. 1995), that "[e]ach defendant is entitled to discover whether there has been a medical determination that an illness has been caused by that defendant's product."

In *Able Supply*, the Court discussed the same kinds of problems as those presented in this case. The court held that the denial of discovery going to the heart of the plaintiffs' case can render appellate remedies inadequate, that mandamus is proper in such a case, and that defendants are entitled to timely discover whether there has been a medical determination that an illness has been caused by that defendant's product.

The court stated:

> The refusal [or inability] of the plaintiffs to provide a medical link between a particular plaintiff and a particular product at this point in time puts every defendant in the position

> of having to defend every case until all are tried, which constitutes a monumental waste of judicial resources. The burden imposed by requiring 294 defendants to continue to defend the claims of over 3,000 plaintiffs while awaiting a thirty-day window prior to trials that have yet to be scheduled before discovering which defendants are implicated is far out of proportion to any benefit to the plaintiffs in withholding this basic information.

Mohawk's motion asked the trial court to enter a scheduling order similar to the one in *Lone Pine*, and it provided a proposed order for the court to review. The court reviewed it, but denied the motion and, rather, issued a generic order for discovery as to Trial Group No. 1 and Trial Group No. 2. The order provides a sliding deadline for various types of discovery as to only those trial groups, but it also provides that all plaintiffs are to be submitted for deposition by March 31, 1998.

The scheduling order fails to require the production of causation information, except as might be obtained through designation of all fact and expert witnesses and summaries of their expected testimony and opinions. The testimony and opinions, however, are limited only to the trial groups. The order provides that the parties are to complete discovery as to Group No. 1 before December 1, 1998, and that all pending pleas, motions, and exceptions will be considered at the final pretrial hearing on January 4, 1999, with jury selection to begin on January 12, 1999.

The scheduling order is different from the one condemned in *Colonial Pipeline*. In that case, discovery on all but the first trial group of ten plaintiffs was wholly abated, while here the court did order completed depositions of the plaintiffs before a certain date. That distinction, however, does not address the concerns of the *Colonial Pipeline* opinion. The opinion in that case explicitly addressed the problem of a failure to provide any proof of causation at a relatively early stage in the proceeding. This case has already existed for years beyond the age of the case in *Colonial Pipeline*. In addition, the court in *Colonial Pipeline* also explicitly approved the concept that a plaintiff should not even file a suit until he has adequate reason to believe that he is injured and that the defendant caused the injury.

In *Colonial Pipeline*, the Supreme Court, in the interest of judicial economy, revised through mandamus the provisions in the scheduling order. The court held that arbitrarily lengthening the time for a group of plaintiffs to file a discovery response on the issue of causation, without a showing of good cause, was an abuse of discretion. The scheduling order here does not show good cause.

Accordingly, we conditionally grant the petition for writ of mandamus and direct the trial court to issue a new case management order similar to the one issued by Judge Folsom in the federal case. Only if the court fails to do so will the writ issue.

[illegible]

[illegible]

[illegible]

[illegible]

[illegible]

A. Release

McMILLEN
v.
KLINGENSMITH

467 S.W.2d 193
(Tex. 1971)

POPE, JUSTICE.

Joyce Lynn McMillen and husband sued Dr. William Klingensmith and Dr. Henry E. Martinez for negligence in the treatment of Joyce McMillen's injuries which she suffered in an automobile collision with a car driven by William Robert Perkins. Mrs. McMillen and her husband released Perkins from all claims upon his payment of $7,900. The McMillens then instituted suit against the two physicians who moved for summary judgment grounded upon the release. The trial court and the court of civil appeals rendered judgment for the defendant doctors, holding that the release of the original tort-feasor operated to release the subsequent tort-feasors also. 454 S.W.2d 424. We reverse those judgments and remand the cause to the trial court.

The collision occurred on June 2, 1967. Mrs. McMillen was hospitalized in Clarendon, Texas, for emergency treatment, including an emergency tracheotomy. She was then transferred to an Amarillo hospital where the two defendant physicians treated her. On June 9, 1967, Mrs. McMillen was released from the hospital, and accompanied by a nurse, returned to her home in California.

On May 2, 1968, Mrs. McMillen and her husband, upon receipt of $7,900, signed a release which named Perkins only and discharged him

> 'from any and all actions, causes of action, claims, demands, damages, costs, loss of services, expenses and compensation, on account of, or in any way growing out of, any and all known AND UNKNOWN personal injuries and property damage resulting or to result from the accident that occurred on or about the 2nd day of June, 1967, at or near Clarendon, Texas.
>
> I/we hereby declare and represent that the injuries sustained are permanent and progressive and that recovery therefrom is uncertain and indefinite, and in making this release and agreement it is understood and agreed that I/we rely wholly upon my/our own judgment, belief and knowledge of the nature, extent and duration of said injuries, ...
>
> This release contains the ENTIRE AGREEMENT between the parties hereto, and the terms of this release are contractual and not a mere recital.'

On May 22, 1969, the McMillens filed suit against Doctors Klingensmith and Martinez, asserting that their negligent diagnoses and treatment resulted in permanent damage to her larynx. The two doctors answered and moved for summary judgment, contending that the release of Perkins was also a release of them. The legal question presented is whether the McMillens may maintain an action for damages against the doctors for malpractice after releasing from liability the named tort-feasor whose conduct made the services of the doctors necessary.

Both parties before us recognize the significance of *Cannon v. Pearson*, 383 S.W.2d 565 (Tex. 1964), in deciding the issue in this case. We granted the application for writ of error in that case believing that the issue stated above was presented for decision. However, we ultimately concluded that the trial pleadings and the summary judgment proofs were not directed to that issue.

In *Cannon v. Pearson*, *supra*, we reviewed the rule that a release of an original named tort-feasor also operates to release an unnamed negligent doctor, citing three Texas cases which had followed the rule. . . . We then said that the rule had been disavowed by a number of jurisdictions and wrote that the modern tendency 'is to treat the older rule as an illegitimate off-spring of the rule that release of one joint tort-feasor releases all, which rule is itself condemned by some of our ablest scholars on the theory that the courts have confused release of a party with satisfaction of a cause of action.'

We cited a number of precedents which had adopted or changed to the rule that the release of the original named tort-feasor did not necessarily release an unnamed subsequent tort-feasor. . . .

* * *

The rule that a release of an original tort-feasor also releases a malpracticing physician finds its basis in the broader common-law rule known as the unity of release rule. The unity of release rule is based upon the idea that there is such a unity of the obligation or injury that a release of one is release of all. After a re-examination of this common-law rule, we have now determined to place our decision in this case upon a broader base than that expressed by our dictum in *Cannon v. Pearson.*

The legal basis for the unity of release rule has been challenged by every legal scholar who has examined it. . . .

* * *

Underlying much of the criticism is the idea mentioned in *Cannon v. Pearson*, *supra*, that there has been a confusion of satisfaction of a claim with release of a cause of action. As expressed by Prosser: 'A satisfaction is an acceptance of full compensation for the injury; a release is a surrender of the cause of action, which might be gratuitous, or given for inadequate consideration.' Prosser, *Joint Torts and Several Liability*, 25 CAL. L. REV. 413, 423 (1937). Unless the settlement with one of the tort-feasors fully satisfies the injured party, the release of one party should, according to Prosser, release only the tort-feasor who makes the partial settlement.

Those jurisdictions which purport to follow the unity of release rule have, nevertheless, looked with favor upon devices, such as the 'covenant not to sue' or a reservation of a cause against others, which are used to skirt the rule. Texas is among those jurisdictions which hold that such devices will save the cause against another tort-feasor when a release would be fatal to it. [Citing authority]

* * *

These judicial efforts to avoid the harsh common-law rule have also been challenged for their artificial reasoning. They have been declared . . . to be less than forthright, judicial fudging, and a trap for the unwary who do not notice in a document such nice distinctions. [Citing authority]

Mr. Justice Rutledge, while serving on the court of appeals for the District of Columbia wrote *McKenna v. Austin*, 77 U.S. App. D.C. 228, 134 F.2d 659, 148 A.L.R. 1253 (1943). He thoroughly examined the foundation and rationale of the unity of release rule. He said that it arose historically by an inappropriate transference of the metaphysics of the property concepts of joint estates and survivorship to the law of obligations independent of property. He summarized the practical reasons for abandoning the rule by saying:

> The rule's results are incongruous. More often than otherwise they are unjust and unintended. Wrongdoers who do not make or share in making reparation are discharged, while one

> willing to right the wrong and no more guilty bears the whole loss. Compromise is stifled, first, by inviting all to wait for the others to settle and, second, because claimants cannot accept less than full indemnity from one when doing that discharges all. Many, not knowing this, accept less only to find later they have walked into a trap. The rule shortchanges the claimant or overcharges the person who settles, as the recurring volume and pattern of litigation show. Finally, it is anomalous in legal theory, giving tort-feasors an advantage wholly inconsistent with the nature of their liability.

The Supreme Court of Alaska, writing in *Young v. State*, 455 P.2d 889 (Alaska 1969), reviewed the several alternatives which that jurisdiction could adopt, and it chose the path of simplicity. It wrote:

> In our opinion the rule which will bring most clarity to this area of ambiguous and conflicting release rules is one under which a release of one tort-feasor does not release other joint tort-feasors unless such tort-feasors are specifically named in the release. We are of the further view that adoption of this rule will insure that the intent of the parties to the release is given effect and will greatly minimize the possibility of any party being misled as to the effect of the release.

The rule is a simple one. Unless a party is named in a release, he is not released. A rule of this type is fairer and easier to apply. It avoids many of the problems arising from the present rule which often requires proof by parole evidence of the releasor's subjective intent at the time the release was executed. With a slight modification we adopt the rule suggested by the Alaska court. We hold that a release of a party or parties named or otherwise specifically identified fully releases only the parties so named or identified, but no others. Our holding in this case shall not affect releases presently in existence where it appears from the language of the release and other circumstances that it was the intention of the releasor to release the named parties and other persons generally identified. The release presently before us names only William Robert Perkins and makes no reference to any other parties.

In holding as we do, we preserve the rule that a claimant in no event will be entitled to recover more than the amount required for full satisfaction of his damages. *Bradshaw v. Baylor University*, 126 Tex. 99, 84 S.W.2d 703 (1935). One of the problems considered by the court in *McKenna v. Austin*, *supra*, was that of disturbing the law concerning the adjustment of rights between tort-feasors after a release of one tort-feasor. In deciding *McKenna* both Justice Rutledge for the majority and Judge Stephens in dissent, discussed this problem in connection with their choice of the better rule. We regard this as less a problem in Texas than in *McKenna* by reason of our decision in *Palestine Contractors, Inc. v. Perkins*, 386 S.W.2d 764 (Tex. 1965) which concerned true joint tort-feasors. *See also*, Hodges, *Contribution and Indemnity Among Tort-feasors*, 26 TEX. L. REV. 150, 170-172 (1947). We feel that these authorities are also instructive on the effects of a release on the relative rights and liabilities of successive tort-feasors. The impact of a release effective only as to the named original tort-feasor on the extent of the liability of the successive tort-feasor is not yet before us. We reserve judgment on that problem.

* * *

This case is before us as a result of the trial court's judgment sustaining the defendant physicians' motion for summary judgment. This judgment was based solely on the conclusion that the release, which named only Perkins, released all other tort-feasors including the doctors. Under our present decision disapproving the unity of release rule, this conclusion was erroneous and the summary judgment for the doctors must fall. The judgments of the courts below are reversed and the cause is remanded for trial.

Notes & Questions

1. Duncan v. Cessna. In *Duncan v. Cessna Aircraft Co.*,[1] the Supreme Court said: "We hold that under Texas law, the mere naming of a general class of tort-feasors in a release does not discharge the liability of each member of that class. A tort-feasor can claim the protection of a release only if the release refers to him by name or with such descriptive particularity that his identity or his connection with the tortious event is not left in doubt. In this case the release does not name Cessna, nor does it provide some specific description of Cessna. Since the reference to 'all corporations' does not supply the descriptive particularity necessary to specifically identify Cessna, the release does not bar Duncan's action if Texas law applies to its construction."

2. *Old Form.* An old form of release, not yet out of circulation, looks something like this: "P releases X Corporation and all other persons, firms, or corporations whether named herein or not." You represent X corporation and its officers and are settling with P in a wrongful discharge case. X's president is reluctant to suggest that the release name her and other officers personally for fear that P will decide to sue them individually if the settlement falls through. Won't the "all other persons" language suffice? Your advice?

3. *The single release trap.* Recall that Rule 97a, which grants res judicata effect to compulsory counterclaims, does not extend to *agreed* judgments or settlements. The rule provides that "a judgment based upon a settlement or compromise of a claim of one party to . . . occurrence *prior to a disposition on the merits* shall not operate as a bar to the . . . claims of any other party to the . . . occurrence" absent written consent that the judgment shall act as a bar. The moral? Settle with mutual releases; that is, have each party release the other as part of the settlement consideration.

4. *Practical information.* A typical settlement will be accomplished through a release (perhaps included in a document called "settlement agreement"), and an agreed order of dismissal with prejudice reciting that the case has been settled. Sometimes, a joint motion to dismiss is used but most judges will accept the agreed order bearing signatures showing approval of all counsel. Taxable costs of suit are customarily borne by defendant, but this is a matter of negotiation which should be resolved by agreement. A plaintiff's attorney must give careful consideration to the tax aspects of the settlement, as it is sometimes possible to apportion the bulk of the settlement to non-taxable recoveries. Consultation with a tax specialist may be a good idea. If a minor's interests are involved in the settlement, the court typically appoints an attorney not previously involved in the case as *guardian ad litem* to review the settlement from the minor's standpoint and to report to the court as to its fairness. (The court's duty is to protect the interest of the minor and the court may, in its discretion, reject a settlement unfair to the minor. The careful defendant will insist on the appointment of a guardian ad litem). When the funds are received, usually by a draft if an insurance company is involved, the plaintiff's attorney must disburse the proceeds. The money goes into the attorney's trust account, not his personal account. It is a breach of ethics for an attorney to place a client's funds in his own personal account, however briefly. The careful attorney will prepare a settlement

---

[1] 665 S.W.2d 414 (Tex. 1984) (*Duncan's* comparative-causation scheme was abrogated by statute as recognized in Sky View at Las Palmas, LLC v. Mendez, No. 17-0140, 2018 WL 2449349, at *3 n.7 (Tex. June 1, 2018)).

statement showing exactly the amount received, the costs paid from the amounts, the attorney's share and the client's share, and will explain the statement to the client and have the client sign it.

5. *Indemnity.* A defendant will almost always insist that any party from whom it is obtaining a release provide it with indemnity from any future claims that arise "by, through or under" the party. For example, a defendant who settles with a corporation might insist that the corporation (and perhaps certain individuals) indemnify the defendant for any claims made by corporate subsidiaries or other members of the corporate family concerning the same transaction or occurrence. Some defense lawyers also want protection in case the plaintiff has assigned part of the cause of action, and they will get an indemnity agreement from plaintiff to protect against this possibility. Typically, an indemnity agreement is a promise to safeguard or hold the indemnitee harmless against either existing and/or future loss liability. The agreement creates a potential cause of action in the indemnitee against the indemnitor.[2] This agreement protects the defendant from cross-claims and other claims that may be pending or claims asserted in the future that are derivative of the plaintiff. Hence the "by, through or under" language typically controls the scope of the claims for which the plaintiff agrees to assume should any such claims be pursued against the defendant. Another way to address this issue if the plaintiff has remaining claims is to have the plaintiff assign its claims to the defendant so that those remaining claims are now subject to the defendant's control. Frequently a settlement agreement will contain both provisions.

6. *Confidentiality.* Can the parties agree that the terms of the settlement agreement remain confidential? Yes, usually so. What if the confidentiality agreement extends to documents or other information generated in discovery, are there any restrictions then? Rule 76a(2)(b) restricts the sealing of court records as defined by the rule.

7. *The holding in* Stowers Furniture Co. v. American Indemnity Co.[3] The *Stowers* case vests a right in the insured to sue his liability insurer for a negligent refusal to settle a claim within the limits of the policy. The *Stowers* doctrine was extended in *Ranger County Mut. Ins. Co. v. Guin*[4] so that the insurer's obligation to act as an ordinarily prudent person in business management extends to claim investigation, trial defense, and settlement negotiations. The primary insurance carrier has the same obligation to an excess carrier (one providing coverage which takes up where the primary policy's limits stop) as it does to the insured. *See American Centennial Ins. Co. v. Canal Ins. Co.*[5]

What does the *Stowers* line of cases have to do with settlement? The *Stowers* threat is a great incentive to settlement because, by refusing an offer within the policy limits, the insurer may be saddled with whatever the judgment amount may be, even though it exceeds the policy limits. The insurance company's position is made worse by the fact that, in the second suit in which the insured claims that the company negligently failed to settle a claim, the insurance company will be the named defendant. Furthermore, it will then be clear that refusing settlement was a mistake as the results of the first case will be known. The second suit will often be brought by the original plaintiff who has released the original defendant in return for an assignment of his *Stowers* and bad faith claims against the insurer.

---

2 *See* Dresser Industries Inc. v. Page Pet., Inc., et al., 853 S.W.2d 505 (Tex. 1993).

3 15 S.W.2d 544 (Tex. Comm'n App. 1929, opinion adopted).

4 723 S.W.2d 656, 659 (Tex. 1987).

5 843 S.W.2d 480 (Tex. 1992).

B. Enforcement

Settlement agreements are often reached immediately before or during trial with little time for the preparation of detailed settlement documents. The agreements are customarily "handshake deals." What if there is a misunderstanding about the terms before the judge can enter the judgment? What if the client has a change of heart and wants to back out after the jury has been dismissed, the setting lost and the witnesses sent home? Read Rule 11 and see the next two cases.

KNAPP MEDICAL CENTER
v.
DE LA GARZA

238 S.W.3d 767

(Tex. 2007)

Opinion

PER CURIAM.

In this case, we must decide whether Texas Rule of Civil Procedure 11 bars enforcement of a disputed oral settlement agreement. Rule 11 requires that agreements between attorneys or parties touching any pending suit be in writing, signed and filed of record, or be made in open court and entered of record as a condition to enforcement. The court of appeals found the rule to be no impediment when it affirmed a trial court judgment for damages in contract and fraud arising out of an oral settlement dispute. Because the court's judgment is contrary to the requirements of Rule 11, we reverse and render.

Dr. Javier De La Garza, M.D., sued Knapp Medical Center, a hospital in Weslaco, for defamation, business disparagement, interference with business relations, and civil conspiracy. The case went to trial in September, 2000. During that trial, De La Garza's attorney offered to settle the case for the hospital's insurance policy limits of $1,000,000. When this settlement demand was made, De La Garza's attorney understood that the hospital would contribute an additional $200,000 to the settlement. After making the policy limits demand, he learned that the hospital did not plan to contribute to the settlement, but that the insurer had agreed to settle for the $1,000,000 policy limits.

During recorded proceedings held just before jury arguments on September 15, 2000, De La Garza's attorney, Ramon Garcia, explained to the court that he had offered to settle for the policy limits based upon his understanding that the hospital would contribute $200,000, and that he was now in a quandary as to what should be done because of the hospital's disagreement with that understanding. The hospital's attorney, Rex Leach, acknowledged that the insurer had agreed to settle the case for policy limits. He further acknowledged that an additional contribution from the hospital had been discussed, but that no agreement had been reached and that the hospital would, in fact, not contribute anything further to the settlement. Despite the disagreement about what had been promised, De La Garza agreed on the record to settle the underlying claims for $1,000,000, while purporting to reserve his right to collect an additional $200,000 from the hospital in another lawsuit. The court accepted the agreement and discharged the jury. De La Garza thereafter signed a Release, acknowledging the settlement funds as complete satisfaction of the claims asserted in the underlying litigation.

De La Garza then sued the hospital for the disputed $200,000, alleging fraud and breach of an oral agreement that pre-dated the September 15 hearing at which the settlement terms were dictated into the record and accepted by the court. A bench trial ensued with the trial court rendering judgment for De La Garza's damages and attorney's fees. The hospital appealed this judgment, contending that Rule 11 barred De La Garza's claims because they were based on an alleged oral settlement agreement. Instead of addressing this Rule 11 argument, the court of appeals concluded that the parol testimony of one of the attorneys was sufficient to support the existence and breach of the settlement agreement, and affirmed the trial court's judgment. We, however, agree with the hospital's unaddressed argument below that the failure to comply with Rule 11 bars the present claims.

As we said in *Kennedy v. Hyde,* 682 S.W.2d 525, 528 (Tex.1984): "Rule 11 is a minimum requirement for enforcement of all agreements concerning pending suits." The rule provides, with certain exceptions not relevant here, that "no agreement between attorneys or parties touching any suit pending will be enforced unless it be in writing, signed and filed with the papers as part of the record, or unless it be make in open court and entered of record." TEX. R. CIV. P. 11. The rule has long been a part of Texas jurisprudence. One hundred and fifty years ago, we recognized the wisdom of eschewing the verbal agreements of counsel in favor of written ones, noting that the vicissitudes of memory would otherwise "beget misunderstandings and controversies." *Birdwell v. Cox,* 18 Tex. 535, 537 (1857). The rule continues to be an effective tool for finalizing settlements by objective manifestation so that the agreements "do not themselves become sources of controversy." *Kennedy,* 682 S.W.2d at 530. In short, settlement agreements "must comply with Rule 11 to be enforceable." *Padilla v. LaFrance,* 907 S.W.2d 454, 460 (Tex. 1995).

The trial court's findings of fact included a finding that the parties' oral settlement agreement was read into the record of the court on September 15, 2000. The record conclusively shows, however, that there was no agreement between the parties to settle the lawsuit for any amount other than the $1,000,000 policy limits. Because the hospital's alleged agreement to contribute an additional $200,000 to settle the underlying suit was neither in writing nor made in open court and entered of record, it is not enforceable. The court of appeals' judgment to the contrary conflicts both with Rule 11 and our decision in *Kennedy v. Hyde.* Accordingly, pursuant to Texas Rule of Appellate Procedure 59. 1, we grant the petition for review, and, without hearing oral argument, we reverse the court of appeals' judgment and render judgment that De La Garza take nothing.

* * *

From *The Wall Street Journal*:

Unsolicited Advice to the Plaintiff:
Next Time Around, Try Takeout.

By Andrea Gerlin

After accepting a $2 million settlement for injuries allegedly suffered at a restaurant, Annie Marie Leal rose out of her wheelchair and walked-in high heels.

That seems to have proved costly.

It all began in 1989, when a waiter at a Steak & Ale in Houston dropped a tray full of dinners on Ms. Leal's head. She sued, alleging that the Texas-sized steaks had caused her serious head, neck and back injuries.

During much of her trial in a Texas state court in 1991, Ms. Leal sat in a wheelchair. In the middle of the trial, the chain offered her a $2 million settlement. She accepted. The judge orally approved but as a matter of procedure didn't immediately sign the judgment. Shortly afterward, Ms. Leal was spotted—by a paralegal from a firm representing Steak & Ale—walking around another restaurant without apparent difficulty.

The restaurant chain hired private investigators, who videotaped Ms. Leal driving an unmodified vehicle (which an expert witness had testified she couldn't do) and walking unaided. Based on the new evidence, Steak & Ale tried to withdraw from the settlement agreement, claiming it could legally do so because the judge hadn't signed the judgment. But the judge refused to hear new evidence, holding that his oral approval was a final judgment. Steak & Ale appealed, but a state appeals court affirmed the settlement, reasoning that the parties understood the case was over when the judge orally approved it.

Steak & Ale took the case to the Supreme Court of Texas, which yesterday reversed the appeals-court ruling and sent the case back to the trial court. The high court said that when the judge orally approved the settlement, he explained that the case wasn't "full, final and complete" until the judgment was signed.

An attorney for Ms. Leal, Tim Maloney of San Antonio, defends the settlement. He says Ms. Leal periodically used a wheelchair during the trial because of pain from surgery. He says she never claimed total and permanent dependence on the wheelchair. Another attorney for Ms. Leal said a decision hasn't yet been made whether to seek another hearing.

Ms. Leal is back at work, Mr. Maloney says and "has good days and bad days." Yesterday, he says, was expected to be one of her bad days.

S & A RESTAURANT CORPORATION
v.
LEAL

892 S.W.2d 855
(Tex. 1995)

PER CURIAM.

The question presented by this appeal is whether S & A Restaurant Corporation d/b/a Steak & Ale Restaurant (Steak & Ale) revoked its consent to a settlement agreement with Annie Marie Leal prior to the trial court's rendition of judgment. The trial court purported to render an agreed judgment on the settlement agreement. The court of appeals determined that the trial court rendered judgment before Steak & Ale's revocation of consent, but remanded the case to the trial court for a hearing on Steak & Ale's motion for new trial. 883 S.W.2d 221, 228-30. A majority of this Court reverses the judgment of the court of appeals and remands this case for a new trial.

Leal filed this personal injury suit against Steak & Ale claiming that she sustained serious head, back, and neck injuries when a waiter at a Steak & Ale Restaurant dropped a large tray of double-plated dinners on her. According to Leal's testimony at trial and the depositions of Leal's doctors, Leal was confined to a wheelchair as a result of the accident. At a hearing on May 14, 1991, the parties agreed to settle for $2 million, at which time the following exchange took place:

THE COURT: Yes. We need to go on the record.

[PLAINTIFF'S ATTORNEY]: And I would say to you, just listen to this. So that we have now asked the Court to approve a settlement in the total sum of $2 million. Before doing that, however, and we need to know that you understand it, that you want it settled, that you approve of it, and that you understand that forever concludes your claim against Steak & Ale. Do you understand all of that?

MS. LEAL: Yes, sir.

[PLAINTIFF'S ATTORNEY]: And do you ask the Judge and want the Judge to approve the conclusion and settlement?

MS. LEAL: Yes, sir.

THE COURT: You realize that once this Judgment is signed and I approve it, everything else, it's full, final and complete? You can't come back later and say, "Well I made a mistake," or "We should have gone for more?" Whatever? Do you understand?

MS. LEAL: Yes, I do.

THE COURT: Are the court costs going to be paid by Defendants?

[PLAINTIFF'S ATTORNEY]: Yes.

[DEFENDANT'S ATTORNEY]: Normally we pay for the court costs. Yes, we'll agree to pay the costs.

THE COURT: You realize now, and you are sufficiently aware of the facts now, and there isn't any question about your understanding the total settlement is $2 million? Do you understand that?

MS. LEAL: Yes, sir. I understand that. Mike and I—

THE COURT: And you want me to approve the settlement and sign the Judgment?

MS LEAL: Yes, sir.

[PLAINTIFF'S ATTORNEY]: And you understand that once you settle the claim you will be responsible for paying all of your medical bills?

THE COURT: And the attorneys' fees come out of that. Do you understand?

MS. LEAL: Yes, sir.

THE COURT: I'll approve the settlement.

One month after the May 14 hearing, a legal assistant employed by Steak & Ale's counsel in this case, saw Leal walking without apparent difficulty in a San Antonio restaurant. Steak & Ale hired private investigators who watched and videotaped Leal for five days. During that time, none of the investigators saw Leal use a cane, walker, or wheelchair. On June 18, Steak & Ale sent letters to the trial court and to Leal's counsel advising that Steak & Ale was withdrawing its consent to the settlement agreement based on its newly discovered evidence that Leal was not confined to a wheelchair. At a hearing on June 19, the trial court refused to allow Steak & Ale to present its new evidence and signed a judgment against Steak & Ale and for Leal for $2 million.

A party may revoke its consent to a settlement agreement at any time before judgment is rendered on the agreement. *Quintero v. Jim Walter Homes, Inc.*, 654 S.W.2d 442, 444 (Tex. 1983); *Samples Exterminators v. Samples*, 640 S.W.2d 873, 874-75 (Tex. 1982). A judgment rendered after one of the parties revokes his consent is void. *Samples*, 640 S.W.2d at 875. Thus, the question before us is whether the trial court rendered judgment before or after Steak & Ale revoked its consent to the settlement agreement on June 18.

Leal argues that the trial court rendered judgment on May 14 at the time the settlement agreement was dictated into the record, and that the trial court rendered judgment before Steak & Ale's revocation of consent. Both parties agree that the trial court approved the settlement agreement at the May 14 hearing.[1] However, approval of a settlement does not necessarily constitute rendition of judgment. *Buffalo Bag Co. v. Joachim*, 704 S.W.2d 482, 484 (Tex. App.—Houston [14th Dist.] 1986, writ ref'd n.r.e.). Judgment is rendered when the trial court officially announces its decision in open court or by written memorandum filed with the clerk. *Samples*, 640 S.W.2d at 875; *Comet Aluminum Co. v. Dibrell*, 450 S.W.2d 56, 59 (Tex. 1970). As we explained in *Reese v. Piperi*:

> The judge's intention to render judgment in the future cannot be a present rendition of judgment. The rendition of judgment is a present act, either by spoken word or signed memorandum, which decides the issues upon which the ruling is made. The opportunities for error and confusion may be minimized if judgments will be rendered only in writing and signed by the trial judge after careful examination. Oral rendition is proper under the present rules, but orderly administration requires that form of rendition to be in and by spoken words, not in mere cognition, and to have effect only insofar as those words state the pronouncement to be a present rendition of judgment. 534 S.W.2d 329, 330 (Tex. 1976). The words used by the trial court must clearly indicate the intent to render judgment at the time the words are expressed.

---

1 Steak & Ale acknowledges that Leal could sue Steak & Ale for breach of the settlement agreement, but that Leal's claim would be subject to Steak & Ale's defense of fraudulent inducement.

The application of these principles leads us to the conclusion that the trial court did not render judgment during the May 14 settlement hearing. The trial court distinguished between the acts of approving the settlement and rendering judgment, as evidenced by the following statements to Leal: You realize that once this judgment is signed and I approve it, everything else, it's full, final and complete? . . . And you want me to approve the settlement and sign the judgment? . . . I'll approve the settlement. Although the trial court expressly approved the settlement, he did not clearly indicate that he intended to render judgment during the May 14 hearing. Rather, the trial court stated that the case would not be "full, final, and complete" until the signing of the judgment, which did not occur until June 19. The fact that the trial court believed that he had rendered judgment during the May 14 hearing is not dispositive.[2] As we stated in Reese, "orderly administration requires [a] rendition [in open court] to be in and by spoken words, not in mere cognition." 534 S.W.2d at 330.

The court of appeals, however, determined that there was a rendition on May 14 because everyone at the May 14 hearing "clearly understood that the case was all over ('full, final, and complete') and that thereafter [Leal] could not come back seeking further recovery." 883 S.W.2d at 228. But the words of the trial court do not evince, as they must, such a "clear" understanding. In fact, the trial court's express words were that the case was not to be "full, final and complete" until after the judgment was signed.

Therefore, a majority of this Court holds that the trial court did not render judgment during the May 14 settlement hearing, and that the trial court did not render judgment until after Steak & Ale's revocation of consent.[3] The judgment of the court of appeals is reversed and this case is remanded to the trial court for a new trial. *See* TEX. R. APP. P. 122 [now T.R.A.P. 52.8].

Notes & Questions

1. *Was judgment rendered or not?* As *S & A* points out, when a party decides it no longer wants to be bound by the settlement agreement, there may be a controversy over whether the trial judge in fact orally "rendered" judgment.[1]

If the judge has rendered judgment, no party can withdraw consent. If the judgment was rendered orally, the signing of an order that strictly complies with the agreement is a ministerial act that simply memorializes the settlement agreement and judgment which was dictated into the record.[2]

---

2 At the motion for new trial hearing on July 25, 1992, the trial court described the events at the May 14 hearing: "I approved the settlement. I also rendered Judgment."

3 We note that our holding today does not affect TEX. R. CIV. P. 306a, which provides that the appellate timetable begins to run on the date that the judgment is signed.

1 *See* Formby's KOA v. BHP Water Supply Corp., 730 S.W.2d 428 (Tex. App.—Dallas 1987, no writ) (docket notation "Agreement announced & read into the record. approved. Instruments to be drawn . . . . (This is a final disposition of the case)" expressed future, not present, judgment and was not a rendition); Buffalo Bag Co. v. Joachim, 704 S.W.2d 482 (Tex. App.—Houston [14th Dist.] 1986, writ ref'd n.r.e.) (docket sheet notation "Judgment to be entered accordingly." is not a rendition). *See also* Goledetz Trading Corp. v. Curland, 886 S.W.2d 503 (Tex. App.—Houston [1st Dist.] 1994, no writ) *and* Wharton v. Gonzales, 761 S.W.2d 72 (Tex. App.—Houston [1st Dist.] 1988, no writ) for close cases on what constitutes a rendition on the record.

2 Vickrey v. American Youth Camps, Inc., 532 S.W.2d 292 (Tex. 1976) (*per curiam*).

Judgment has been rendered and the party's only recourse is to use appropriate procedures to attack that judgment. As the Dallas Court of Appeals has noted:[3]

> Hawkins and Dallas Juice argue Howard materially breached the settlement agreement entitling them to rescission of both the agreement and the agreed judgment stemming from it. Even if Hawkins and Dallas Juice could show the judgment was dependent upon the agreement and there was a material breach of the agreement after the judgment was signed, this would not entitle them to a new trial. An agreed judgment is not invalidated by a subsequent failure to perform a condition on which the consent was based. *See Routon v. Phillips*, 246 S.W.2d 223, 225 (Tex. Civ. App.—Fort Worth 1952, writ ref'd n.r.e.). The validity and correctness of a judgment is not called into question by a subsequent breach because the breach did not occur until after the judgment was signed. *Cf. Compania Financiara Libano, S.A. v. Simmons*, 53 S.W.3d 365, 367 (Tex. 2001). Although breach of the settlement agreement may give rise to new claims between the parties, it does not affect the correctness of the judgment at the time it was rendered. Accordingly, Hawkins's and Dallas Juice's argument is without merit.

2. *Contract rules of interpretation.* A settlement agreement or an agreed judgment is interpreted as if it were a contract and the rules governing interpretation of contracts will apply. As in contracts, the court's primary concern is to ascertain the intent of the parties expressed in the instrument. If the intention is ambiguous, the court may resort to parol evidence.[4] Also as in contracts, only the parties joining the agreement are bound.[5]

3. *Remedy if no rendition.* Suppose the parties entered into a settlement agreement, there is no consent judgment rendered, and one backs out of the agreement. Does the party seeking to enforce the agreement have any remedy considering that the court cannot render a consent judgment on the agreement under *Burnaman*? Yes. As pointed out in footnote 1 of *S & A*, that party may amend its pleadings to bring an action on the underlying settlement agreement, and perhaps obtain specific enforcement of it. So long as the agreement satisfies Rule 11 (or is undisputed) and is an enforceable contract under contract law, the agreement may be enforced by a judgment on the contract, perhaps by a summary judgment.[6]

4. *Time of filing.* In *Padilla v. LaFrance*, 907 S.W.2d 454 (Tex. 1995), the Supreme Court held that an exchange of letters between lawyers was enough to satisfy the "writing" requirement *and* that the letters complied with Rule 11 even though they were filed after one of the parties refused to go through with the agreed judgment.

5. *Discovery Agreements.* Under rule 191.1, "An agreement of the parties [to modify discovery procedures] is enforceable if it complies with Rule 11 or, as it affects an oral deposition, it if is made a part of the record of the deposition."

---

[3] Hawkins v. Howard, 97 S.W.3d 676, 678 (Tex. App.—Dallas 2003, no pet.).

[4] Miller v. Miller, 700 S.W.2d 941, 951 (Tex. 1985)(contract interpretation law applies); Hutchings v. Bates, 406 S.W.2d 419, 420 (Tex. 1966) (parol evidence admissible to resolve doubt).

[5] Edwards v. Gifford, 155 S.W.2d 786 (Tex. 1941); see also Chavez v. Kansas City S. Ry. Co., 520 S.W.3d 898, 901 (Tex. 2017) (reversing summary judgment that established validity of settlement absent evidence that putatively settling party "actually authorized her counsel to enter into a settlement agreement on her behalf.").

[6] Cothron Aviation, Inc. v. Avco Corp., 843 S.W.2d 260 (Tex. App.—Ft. Worth 1992, writ denied).

6. *Problem.* In the third day of trial you, as attorney for P and P's minor child, and opposing counsel agree that you will settle the case for "$10,000 and costs." You announce the settlement to the judge in open court after the jury has been retired. To be safe you dictate it to the court reporter in the presence of the judge. Before you can prepare the settlement papers your opponent calls to say that his client has backed out. No deal. Now the jury has been finally dismissed and you are looking at another year before a trial setting and your client needs the money now. Can you enforce the settlement? Does it matter what the trial judge has said on the record following the dictation of the settlement?

CHISHOLM
v.
CHISHOLM
209 S.W.3d 96
(Tex. 2006)

PER CURIAM.

In this divorce case, petitioner Qi Wu Chisholm complains that the trial court, after a bench trial, rendered judgment based on an alleged agreement between the parties to which she had not consented. The only issue before us is whether Ms. Chisholm agreed to the property division in the judgment.

When the case was called for trial, counsel for respondent Gary Bruce Chisholm recited into the record what she said was the parties' agreement, containing terms on custody of the parties' minor child and the division of property. Counsel then tendered an exhibit she described as "the division of the personal property that the clients have approved." The exhibit listed pre-marital household items and items acquired after marriage to be divided to either Mr. or Ms. Chisholm. Without objection by Ms. Chisholm's attorney, the court received the exhibit in evidence.

Almost immediately, Ms. Chisholm, whose ability to speak and understand English is disputed, stated that she didn't understand what had been read into the record. Testifying with the occasional aid of an interpreter, Ms. Chisholm acknowledged that she and Mr. Chisholm had reached an agreement on custody, but said they had only discussed, not decided, everything else. After further questioning, she appeared to assent to the sale of the marital residence, but when asked if she understood the agreement, still maintained she did not. Although there was further discussion between the attorneys, the parties, and the court on other portions of the agreement, Ms. Chisholm was never asked whether she understood or consented to the agreement as a whole. No other evidence was admitted.

After Mr. Chisholm moved for a final decree, stating that "the parties [had] read an agreement into the record for full and final settlement of all issues in this case," the trial court rendered a judgment containing most but not all of the recited terms, as well as additional terms never discussed at trial, such as the division of tax liability.

The court of appeals affirmed, concluding that "despite Ms. Chisholm's statements indicating a lack of understanding during the proceeding, she participated with her attorney in reaching the agreement and understood it sufficiently for the trial court to enter a judgment." [214 S.W.3d 463, 464]. We disagree. Even if Ms. Chisholm consented to the custody arrangements and the sale of the marital residence, nothing in the record shows she consented to the property division. A court "cannot render a valid agreed judgment absent consent at the time it is rendered." *Padilla v. LaFrance,* 907 S.W.2d 454, 461-62 (Tex. 1995); *see also Mantas v. Fifth Court of Appeals,* 925 S.W.2d 656, 658 (Tex. 1996) (per curiam). Moreover, the judgment was not "in strict or literal compliance" with the terms recited into the record; the judgment improperly removed and added material terms. *Vickrey v. Am. Youth Camps, Inc.,* 532 S.W.2d 292, 292 (Tex. 1976)(per curiam); *see also Matthews v. Looney,* 132 Tex. 313, 123 S.W.2d 871, 872 (Tex. 1939). When a consent judgment is rendered without consent or is not in strict compliance with the terms of the agreement, the judgment must be set aside. *See Burnaman v. Heaton,* 150 Tex. 333, 240 S.W.2d 288, 291-292 (1951).

Mr. Chisholm argues in his brief in this Court:

> While certainly not a work of art, the court's proceedings were very typical of family law cases in Bexar County, Texas where there is a hodge podge of agreements recited into the record and various orders entered by the court to resolve disputes between the parties. The record ultimately shows that the order was not based purely on the agreement of the parties, rather the decree consisted of part agreement, part orders from the court which were incorporated into the composition of the parties' decree of divorce.

Whether the characterization of practice is accurate, there was no basis in this case for the trial court to make the findings necessary to divide the marital estate and render final judgment.

Accordingly, we grant Ms. Chisholm's petition for review and, without hearing oral argument, TEX. R. APP. P. 59.1, reverse the court of appeals' judgment and remand the case to the trial court for further proceedings.

KENNEDY
v.
HYDE
682 S.W.2d 525
(Tex. 1984)

ROBERTSON, JUSTICE

The question presented in this case is whether Texas Rule of Civil Procedure 11 bars enforcement of a disputed oral settlement agreement. Herman J. Smith sold capital stock in the Mansfield State Bank to a number of buyers, including Forrest L. Kennedy, Richard J. Hyde, and the other respondents in this cause. Subsequently, some of these purchasers, including Hyde, sued Kennedy and other defendants not appealing, seeking to recover interest paid to Smith for defendants' benefit. Kennedy counterclaimed and also brought a third party action against Smith, alleging misrepresentation in the original stock sale.

Thereafter, the parties to the suit met for depositions, but instead became involved in settlement discussions. These discussions resulted in the drafting, revisions and eventual signing of documents settling the suit. All parties save Kennedy ultimately signed these documents.

Smith, Hyde and the other plaintiffs then amended their pleadings, alleging that although Kennedy refused to sign any of the settlement documents, he had nonetheless entered into an oral contract of settlement. As amended, the pleadings introduced the oral settlement as a basis for affirmative relief, seeking damages for breach of contract or specific performance. The oral agreement was also pleaded as a defense to Kennedy's claims, on theories of accord and satisfaction, novation, waiver and estoppel, among others. Kennedy likewise amended his pleadings to deny entering into any settlement agreement, and to point out the noncompliance of any alleged agreement with Rule 11 of the Texas Rules of Civil Procedure.

The trial court ordered a separate trial on the existence and validity of the alleged oral agreement. Pursuant to jury findings of an oral agreement to settle the lawsuit, the trial court rendered judgment against Kennedy, effectively enforcing the agreement according to its terms. The court of appeals affirmed, holding that Rule 11 does not prohibit the enforcement of disputed oral settlement agreements. 666 S.W.2d 325. We reverse the decisions of the courts below and remand the cause for trial.

For reasons soon apparent, a historical review of Rule 11 is in order. TEX. R. CIV. P. 11 states:

> "No agreement between attorneys or parties touching any suit pending will be enforced unless it be in writing, signed and filed with the papers as part of the record, or unless it be made in open court and entered of record."

This rule is not of recent origin, but can be traced in substantially its present form to District Court Rule 28, adopted in 1840 under the laws of the Republic of Texas, 1 Tex. 849, 852 (1848), and recodified as District and County Court Rule 47 in 1877 by authority of article V, section 25 of the Texas Constitution. *See* 47 Tex. 597, 625 (1877).[1]

* * *

Rule 11 of the Texas Rules of Civil Procedure became effective on September 1, 1941. By its wording, Rule 11 mandates that "[n]o agreement between attorneys or parties touching any suit pending will be enforced unless it be in writing . . . ." The rule has been held applicable to a wide variety of agreements concerning lawsuits, including stipulations as to the testimony of absent witnesses, *Austin v. Austin*, 603 S.W.2d 204 (Tex. 1980), and agreements to limit the issues in dispute. *City of Houston v. Clear Creek Basin Authority*, 589 S.W.2d 671 (Tex. 1979); *see also* 3 R. MCDONALD, TEXAS CIVIL PRACTICE IN DISTRICT AND COUNTY COURTS § 10.12.3 n. 6 (1983). On at least two recent occasions, this court has strongly implied that a settlement agreement is also to be judged by Rule 11 standards. *Williams v. Hollingsworth*, 568 S.W.2d 130, 131 (Tex. 1978); *Vickrey v. American Youth Camps, Inc.*, 532 S.W.2d 292, 292 (Tex. 1976).

The court of appeals in the instant case attempts to avoid application of Rule 11 by making a fine distinction, stating that "the purpose of rule 11 is to authorize rendition of agreed judgments." 666 S.W.2d at 327. As we understand the opinion, an agreement in compliance with Rule 11 would authorize an agreed judgment on the merits of the underlying suit. An agreement in violation of Rule 11 would support the same result in the same suit. The sole distinction would be that in the latter case, the judgment would recite that it was based on breach of the contract to settle the suit, rather than incorporating the terms of the contract to settle the suit.

Given this interpretation, no "agreement between attorneys or parties touching any suit pending" need comply with Rule 11. For example, since any stipulation could be characterized as a contract, *see, e.g., Keller Industries, Inc. v. O. O. Reeves*, 656 S.W.2d 221, 228 (Tex. App.—Austin 1983,

[1] Rule 47 was amended in 1892 by adding the phrase "or unless it be made in open court and entered of record." 84 Tex. 695, 715. The portion of TEX. R. CIV. P. 11 at issue in this cause, though, is unchanged since 1877.

writ ref'd n.r.e.), any stipulation failing to comply with Rule 11 could nonetheless be enforced as a contract.

This court will not eviscerate Rule 11. Nor does the authority cited by the court of appeals support such a narrow interpretation. In *Burnaman v. Heaton*, 150 Tex. 333, 240 S.W.2d 288 (1951), this court refused to sanction a consent judgment where consent was withdrawn prior to rendition of judgment. The agreement in *Burnaman*, however, complied with the requirements of Rule 11. The face of the opinion in *Stewart v. Mathes*, 528 S.W.2d 116 (Tex. Civ. App.—Beaumont 1978, no writ) does not reveal whether the agreement complied with Rule 11, nor was the rule mentioned in the court of civil appeals' opinion. Neither opinion speaks authoritatively to the question of enforcing a settlement agreement not in compliance with Rule 11.

It is not surprising to find discussion of Rule 11 and settlement agreements in appeals challenging consent judgments, as such a judgment is a normal method of effectuating a settlement. This does not, however, warrant the court of appeals' conclusion that "the *purpose* of rule 11 is to authorize rendition of agreed judgments only if the agreement for judgment is memorialized . . . ." 666 S.W.2d at 327 (emphasis added).

A better statement of the general rule is that Rule 11 is a minimum requirement for enforcement of all agreements concerning pending suits, including, but not limited to, agreed judgments. *Burnaman* stands for the proposition that, notwithstanding a valid Rule 11 agreement, consent must exist at the time an agreed judgment is rendered. . . . *Matthews v. Looney*, 132 Tex. 313, 123 S.W.2d 871 (1939), demonstrates that an agreement not in compliance with the rule will not support a consent judgment. Thus it may be said that as a general rule compliance with Rule 11 is necessary, but not sufficient for an agreed judgment. The clear language of the rule indicates, and this court holds, that compliance with Rule 11 is a general prerequisite for any judgment enforcing an agreement touching a pending suit.

* * *

Our holding, that Rule 11 means precisely what it says, should not be interpreted as requiring "slavish adherence" to the literal language of the rule in all cases. *Sone v. Braunig*, 469 S.W.2d 605, 611 (Tex. Civ. App.—Beaumont 1971, writ ref'd n.r.e.). To the contrary, there are well recognized exceptions to the rule in this state, and in other jurisdictions with similar requirements. *See generally* Annot., 7 A.L.R.3d 1394 (1966). For example, an undisputed stipulation may be given effect despite literal noncompliance with the rule. *Thomas v. Smith*, 60 S.W.2d 514, 516 (Tex. Civ. App.—Texarkana 1933, writ dism'd). Likewise, an agreement in compliance with the rule is subject to attack on the grounds of fraud or mistake, *Burnaman v. Heaton*, 150 Tex. 333, 240 S.W.2d 288 (1951), and a nonconforming agreement may be enforced for similar equitable reasons. *Williams v. Huling*, 43 Tex. 113, 120 (1875). Quite recently, this court has interpreted the requirements of Rule 11 liberally to conform to modern trial practice. *City of Houston v. Clear Creek Basin Authority*, 589 S.W.2d 671 (Tex. 1979).

In determining whether a particular situation warrants an exception to Rule 11, an examination of the policy behind the rule is always paramount. *Fidelity & Cas. Co. of N.Y. v. McCollum*, 656 S.W.2d 527 (Tex. App.—Dallas 1983, writ ref'd n.r.e.). The reason for Rule 11 is clear. As already observed, oral agreements concerning suits "are very liable to be misconstrued or forgotten, and to beget misunderstandings and controversies." *Birdwell*, 18 Tex. at 537. "The purpose of this rule is evident, and its wisdom will be readily conceded. Agreements of counsel in the course of a judicial proceeding which affect the interests of their clients should not be left to the fallibility of human recollection. *This is especially true with reference to agreed judgments which finally dispose of the rights of the litigants.*" *Wyss v. Bookman*, 235 S.W. 567, 569 (Tex. Comm'n App. 1921, holding approved) (emphasis added).

The rationale underlying Rule 11 is sensible and contributes to efficient court administration. Agreements and stipulations are welcomed by courts because they limit the matters in controversy and expedite trial proceedings. Rule 11 ensures that such agreements do not themselves become sources of controversy, impeding resolution of suits. The requirements of Rule 11 are not onerous; the benefits are substantial.

The instant case illustrates the wisdom of the rule. The purported oral settlement agreement with Forrest Kennedy could easily have been reduced to writing and signed. In fact, all other parties to the suit did sign agreements comporting with Rule 11. Forrest Kennedy's pleadings clearly, emphatically and unequivocally denied entering into an oral settlement agreement. Nonetheless, the existence and terms of the alleged agreement were litigated, consuming some six days of court time and generating well over $100,000 in attorneys' fees on a $12,000 claim.

Respondents attempt to bring this case within an exception to Rule 11 by claiming that the oral agreement is "undisputed." They point this court to reams of testimony and eventual favorable jury findings. This argument begs the question. The oral agreement was disputed and unenforceable at the moment its existence was denied in the pleadings; Rule 11 prohibits further inquiry.

While judicial efficiency and the wish to avoid disputes over the credibility of opposing counsel may well have been the original rationale for Rule 11's requirements, changing times provide an additional benefit from the rule. In a day of burgeoning litigation and crowded dockets, the amicable settlement of lawsuits is greatly to be desired. This court has recognized both a public policy favoring settlements and the need for reasonable safeguards on the settlement process. *See, e.g., Cypress Creek Utility Service Co., Inc. v. Muller*, 640 S.W.2d 860 (Tex. 1982); *General Motors Corp. v. Simmons*, 558 S.W.2d 855 (Tex. 1977). Similar considerations are present in this case. A requirement that an out-of-court settlement be memorialized by a writing should aid the settlement process, permitting free and frank discussion and negotiation without fear that a careless word or mistake of meaning will itself become the basis for further litigation.

For the reasons stated, we reverse the judgments of the courts below and remand the cause for trial.

GONZALEZ, JUSTICE, dissents with opinion that is joined by WALLACE, JUSTICE.

GONZALEZ, JUSTICE, dissenting.

I respectfully dissent. I am of the opinion that the court of appeals rendered the correct judgment and that the writ should be dismissed as improvidently granted. TEX. R. CIV. P. 500.

I perceive a fundamental difference between an agreement concerning a suit and a suit concerning an agreement. In my judgment, TEX. R. CIV. P. 11 does not apply to an oral agreement concerning a suit when a party does not in good faith dispute the terms of that agreement. Since neither Kennedy nor his first attorney, who negotiated the settlement disputes the terms of the agreement, I am puzzled by my colleagues' characterization of this case as one involving a "disputed" agreement. The only dispute concerns Kennedy's refusal to be bound by the agreement.

The lack of dispute is evident in some brief excerpts of Kennedy's deposition which were introduced into evidence in his trial in 1982.

(Questions by Attorney Friedman, representing Herman Smith, Third Party Defendant):

Q Did you have any question in your mind about what you were doing when you agreed to settle; that is, you understood that you were agreeing to pay twelve thousand dollars that would end this lawsuit, as far as you knew; your claims and the claims against you? You understood that, didn't you?

A Yes. (S.F., p. 45)

* * *

Q ... But, when you left there that day, you believed it was settled and that there were no suits pending, going to be pending by you, or against you, as a result of the matters involved in this litigation, didn't you?

A I presumed that was the case that day.

Q Well, you know it was the case, don't you?

A I presume so. I didn't question it.

* * *

Q Now, in reference to the fact that as you've mentioned awhile ago, that after the agreement had been reached, and so forth, that you, in fact, changed your mind. I'm talking about the October 5, 1978 transaction. If you hadn't changed your mind, you probably would have gone and signed the papers along with everybody else, isn't that right?

A Yes, probably. (S.F., p. 54)

* * *

Q Okay, admit or deny this: That you agreed to execute a promissory note in the amount of twelve thousand dollars, payable to the Plaintiffs herein in the presence of Carl G. Quisenberry in exchange for all parties to the lawsuit at that time agreeing to relinquish all claims to each other arising from the subject matter of this litigation?

A As of precisely that date that's true, but of course, as we testified earlier, there were a lot of reservations and discussions, but as of precisely that date, I would say yes. (S.F., p. 59).

* * *

As the court correctly recognizes, the purpose of Rule 11 is to require that agreements concerning suits "not be left to the fallibility of human recollection." *Wyss v. Bookman*, 235 S.W. 567 (Tex. Comm'n App. 1921, holding approved); *Matthews v. Looney*, 132 Tex. 313, 319, 123 S.W.2d 871, 873 (1939). This is not a suit to construe the language of an unclear agreement, or one in which the court would be forced to supply absent terms. *See Sergeant v. Goldsmith Dry Goods Co.*, 110 Tex. 482, 221 S.W. 259 (1920). The excerpts from Kennedy's own testimony reveal that the terms were not in dispute. It is, therefore, my opinion that the underlying purpose of Rule 11 has been satisfied.

In *Birdwell v. Cox*, 18 Tex. 535, 537 (1857) this court stated that the rule requiring agreements concerning causes to be in writing "is a salutary one, and ought to be adhered to *whenever counsel disagrees as to what has transpired between them*." (emphasis added). Further, this court has stated that the enforcement of an oral agreement lies within the discretion of the trial court, and such an agreement may be enforced to prevent unjust enrichment. *Jenkins v. Adams*, 71 Tex. 1, 8 S.W. 603 (1888). *Williams v. Huling*, 43 Tex. 113 (1875). Where the terms of an oral agreement or stipulation are undisputed or expressly admitted, the agreement should be enforceable even in the absence of a writing.

The court states that this case closely parallels *Matthews v. Looney*, 123 S.W.2d 871. This reliance is misplaced because in Matthews there was a dispute between the parties and the attorneys that negotiated the agreement as to the terms of the agreement. There is no such dispute by the parties in our case.

To buttress its opinion, the court says that the "purported oral settlement agreement with Kennedy could easily have been reduced to writing and signed." This assumption ignores the practical realities of modern trial practice. There is nothing easy about settling a multi-party, multi-suit controversy where charges and counter-charges have been exchanged. Suits are generally settled on broad terms on a "gentleman's agreement." Out-of-state witnesses may be released and juries discharged while the lawyers commence the process of drafting and getting the necessary signatures on the documents. Thereafter, the parties must arrange for court approval of the agreement. It is virtually impossible to complete these tasks in the space of one day or even a week. In a case such as this the process often takes several months.

This case has already been tried once to a jury. The jury answered special issues against Kennedy, and the trial court rendered judgment against him. The court of appeals correctly affirmed the judgment of the trial court. Once the announced purpose of Rule 11 has been satisfied, further adherence to its literal requirements becomes a "slavish adherence" to empty legal technicalities. I cannot condone the nullification by the majority of the results of a six day trial and a subsequent appellate review to require compliance with a procedural rule which, in this case, serves no apparent purpose. I would allow enforcement of this oral agreement and bring this matter to an end, avoiding further costly trials and appeals on this six-year old claim.

It used to be that a man's word was his bond. I regret that the court's opinion facilitates a further erosion of this value.

WALLACE, JUSTICE, joins in this dissenting opinion.

Notes & Questions

1. *Consent at time of judgment.* Even though there is an agreement or order complying with Rule 11, the court may not enter a judgment unless the parties are in agreement *at the time the judgment is entered.* This is the holding in the landmark case of *Burnaman v. Heaton*[1] cited by the majority. Therefore, until the judgment is rendered, any party with a change of heart can prevent its rendition.[2] For this reason, seasoned lawyers will give top priority to completing settlement documents and obtaining an agreed judgment or order of dismissal.

Ordinarily, when a case settles at the courthouse, the lawyers will finalize their settlement in one of two ways before anyone has a change of mind. *(1) Written agreement.* In simple cases lawyers will often prepare a handwritten Rule 11 agreement They will then have it signed by the parties and lawyers, and will ask the judge to indicate on the agreement that judgment is rendered. A formal judgment will be prepared later on the word processor and signed. *(2) Agreement on the record.* Another method is to appear in person before the court and state the terms of the set-

---

[1] 240 S.W. 288 (Tex. 1951).

[2] This is not to say that there is no remedy. The appropriate remedy would be suit for breach of the settlement agreement.

tlement on the record. Careful judges and lawyers have all parties and lawyers announce their consent to the terms, and the judge will then approve the settlement and render judgment. Many lawyers will make sure that the judge says, "The agreement is approved and judgment rendered," or words to similar effect. Either of these methods will comply with Rule 11 (written, signed, and filed, or on the record in open court) and with the case law that requires rendition of judgment at a time when all parties agree on all material terms. If a party later tries to back out of the agreement, the judge will be able to rule that it is too late to withdraw consent because judgment was rendered earlier when everyone consented.

2. *Confusion.* Often students and litigants confuse the requirements for an agreed judgment with those for an enforceable settlement agreement. Consider the following from *Padilla v. LaFrance*:[3]

> The LaFrances, however, confuse the requirements for an agreed judgment with those for an enforceable settlement agreement. Although a court cannot render a valid agreed judgment absent consent at the time it is rendered, this does not preclude the court, after proper notice and hearing, from enforcing a settlement agreement complying with Rule 11 even though one side no longer consents to the settlement. The judgment in the latter case is not an agreed judgment, but rather is a judgment enforcing a binding contract.
>
> In *Burnaman*, for example, the plaintiff wanted to repudiate a settlement that her attorney had agreed to on the record in open court, claiming that she had not authorized such settlement. Although aware of the plaintiff's objection, the court subsequently rendered a consent judgment incorporating the terms of the settlement. We held that the consent judgment was improper since contemporaneous consent was lacking. "It is not sufficient to support the judgment that a party's consent thereto may at one time have been given; consent must exist at the very moment the court undertakes to make the agreement the judgment of the court." 240 S.W.2d at 291. In reversing the agreed judgment, however, we noted as follows:
>
>> Since the judgment of the trial court is reversed, we cannot pass on the effect of the agreement made by the attorneys or the notation of that agreement on the docket. We can only say that the announcement of the agreement in open court and its notation on the docket cannot give it the force of a judgment. It follows that the reversal of the judgment should be without prejudice to the right of defendants to plead the agreement in bar of plaintiff's suit and without prejudice also to plaintiff's right to avoid the agreement by pleading that her attorney was without authority to make it. These are issues to be settled by the jury or the court in a trial of the case.
>>
>> 240 S.W.2d at 292. Similarly in *Quintero v. Jim Walter Homes, Inc.*, 654 S.W.2d 442 (Tex. 1983), we held that the trial court erred by rendering an agreed judgment of dismissal based on a release signed by plaintiff because plaintiff did not consent to the judgment at the time it was rendered. We noted, however, that "our reversal of the judgment of dismissal is without prejudice to the rights of the Jim Walter Homes in its attempt to plead and prove an enforceable settlement agreement under the release."

* * *

[3] 907 S.W.2d 454 (Tex. 1995).

An action to enforce a settlement agreement, where consent is withdrawn, must be based on proper pleading and proof. *See Quintero*, 654 S.W.2d at 444; *Browning*, 620 S.W.2d at 615. In this case, for example, Padilla filed a counterclaim seeking enforcement of the parties' agreement, and both sides moved for summary judgment on that claim. As previously discussed, the summary judgment evidence established an enforceable settlement agreement as a matter of law. The trial court therefore should have granted Padilla's motion for summary judgment and enforced the agreement.

3. *When to file Rule 11 agreement?* The Supreme Court has held that the agreement need not be filed until after the dispute arises, before it is sought to be enforced. "To require the parties to immediately rush to the courthouse with a signed document in order to quickly comply with the requirements of Rule 11 before the other party reneges on his agreement goes against the grain of the policy in Texas jurisprudence which favors the settlement of lawsuits."[4]

4. *Tying down settlements*. JUSTICE GONZALEZ'S dissent points out a practical problem in real-world litigation where settlements often occur immediately before or during a trial. What can be done to tie down a settlement before the jury is dismissed and the wholesome effect of the oncoming trial is lost? Some judges, recognizing the complexity of settlements in some large cases, will agree to declare a recess of the ongoing trial, telling the jury to wait in the hall or perhaps to return the next day. The parties use this time to iron out the settlement details, reduce the settlement to writing, have it signed, and present the court with an agreed judgment. If one party backs out of the agreement during this recess, the trial will simply proceed. In most cases, however, the settlement terms are simpler and judges are unwilling to keep the jury on call for any length of time. What can the parties do at the courthouse that will satisfy the *Burnaman* rule and Rule 11? *See* discussion in note 1, *supra*.

5. *Pre-suit exceptions*. The foregoing observations refer to agreements made after suit has been filed. "Confessions of judgment" made as part of a contract or other transaction signed *before suit commences* are invalid.[5] Conversely, some *oral* agreements concerning compromise of disputed claims made before trial commences may be enforceable.[6]

6. *Summary*.

As a preliminary matter, we know that a judgment can be *rendered* by an oral pronouncement of the judge. Therefore, there is sometimes a question as to whether the comment by the judge was a *rendition* of judgment or simply an announcement of an *intention* to review a settlement and approve or disapprove it by judgment at the appropriate time. That problem is discussed in the *Leal* case. In *Kennedy v. Hyde*, however, we deal with the problem of enforceability of settlement agreements under Rule 11.

---

4 Padilla v. LaFrance, 907 S.W.3d 454, 461 (Tex. 1995).

5 *Compare* Rule 314 (Rules 563, 564 in Justice Courts) permitting a party to confess judgment in open court *with* Section 30.001 Civil Practices and Remedies Code: "In an instrument executed before suit is brought, a person may not accept service and waive process, enter an appearance in open court, or confess a judgment."

6 *See* Estate of Pollack v. McMurrey, 858 S.W.2d 388 (Tex. 1993):

> McMurrey contends that because the alleged compromise agreement was not reduced to writing, it is not enforceable and therefore does not constitute a meritorious defense. McMurrey relies on TEX. R. CIV. P. 11. . . . Rule 11, however, applies only to agreements concerning a pending suit; it does not apply to a pre-existing agreement asserted as a defense to a suit.

First Proposition: If a judgment *is* rendered while all parties are in agreement, the judgment is valid, even though the agreement does not comply with Rule 11 (or the "undisputed" exception to Rule 11).

Second Proposition: It is only when one party attempts to obtain a judgment based on a settlement and the other party has backed out (resists for other reasons) that the Rule 11 problem surfaces. In such a case where one party disagrees or resists at the time the other party seeks rendition of judgment the judge *cannot* render a judgment.

Third Proposition: When a judge cannot render a judgment because one party is in disagreement at the time the other seeks a rendition, the case takes one of two courses:

(1) If Rule 11 (or the undisputed exception) *has been complied with*, the party seeking to enforce the judgment must file a separate suit (or amend pleadings in the instant suit) and sue in contract on the settlement agreement for specific performance. If the proponent of the settlement wins, judgment will be rendered in accordance with the settlement. *But*, the resistor may be claiming that the original settlement was obtained by a fraudulent representation so that, after full litigation of the issues and the defense of fraud in the inducement, the proponent of the settlement may lose. That consequence does not dispose of the underlying litigation which may then go forward.

(2) If Rule 11 (or the undisputed exception) *has not been complied with*, the proponent of the settlement is out of luck. This is true even though the settlement might arguably be enforceable as an oral agreement under contract law. Rule 11 superimposes a phantom addition to the statute of frauds so that settlement agreements must be in writing to be enforceable. Even though the proponent of the settlement is out of luck and cannot enforce the settlement under these conditions, the underlying suit remains and can go forward just as if there had been no attempt at settlement.

In re VAISHANGI, Inc.
442 S.W.3d 256
(Tex. 2014)

Opinion

PER CURIAM.

In this mandamus proceeding, we must decide whether the trial court had jurisdiction to enforce a Rule 11 agreement when the defendant filed a motion to enforce almost one year after the case had been dismissed. We hold that the Rule 11 agreement was not an agreed judgment. Because the trial court's plenary power expired thirty days after the dismissal order, the court lacked power to enforce the agreement. We conditionally grant relief.

The relators, Vaishangi, Inc., Shivangi, Inc., Meena Patel, and Vinayak K. Patel (collectively, Vaishangi), entered into a commercial real estate lien note and related security instruments with Southwestern National Bank to finance a hotel. After disagreement regarding the note, the Bank accelerated the note and began proceedings to foreclose on the hotel property. In response, Vaishangi filed suit for breach of contract and wrongful foreclosure in Harris County. The parties reached a settlement, memorialized in a handwritten Rule 11 agreement,[1] which the parties and the trial court signed. The agreement provided that Vaishangi "agree[d] to execute" a referenced loan-modification agreement. The Bank filed the Rule 11 agreement with the trial court that same day and attached an unsigned loan-modification agreement. The parties disagree whether Vaishangi had an opportunity to review and approve the referenced loan-modification agreement before the Bank filed the Rule 11 agreement with the court.

Four days later, the trial court signed an agreed order dismissing all claims. The order of dismissal did not incorporate the entire Rule 11 agreement. The parties soon disagreed on the principal amount remaining on the note and the terms of the settlement, ultimately resulting in the Bank's foreclosure of the hotel property. Vaishangi filed suit in Bexar County for wrongful foreclosure.

In response, the Bank filed a motion to transfer the case to Harris County, the venue of the previously dismissed lawsuit. The Bank also filed a "Motion to Enforce Settlement Agreement" in the Harris County lawsuit, which had been dismissed eleven months prior. Because Vaishangi had not yet executed the loan-modification agreement, the motion to enforce requested that the court order Vaishangi to pay damages, costs, and attorney's fees. Alternatively, the Bank requested that the court order Vaishangi to execute the loan-modification agreement. Vaishangi argued in response that the trial court had no jurisdiction to enforce the Rule 11 agreement because the trial court's plenary power expired thirty days after signing the dismissal order. Vaishangi also argued that a genuine issue of material fact existed regarding the balance owed under the modification agreement that should be resolved by trial.

Without hearing evidence, the Harris County court issued an order granting the Bank's motion to enforce the Rule 11 agreement, awarding the Bank damages and attorney's fees and ordering Vaishangi to execute the modification agreement. Vaishangi filed a petition for writ of mandamus with the Fourteenth Court of Appeals, seeking to set aside the trial court's enforcement

---

[1] The handwritten Rule 11 agreement reads as follows:

Re: 2010-40753; Vaishangi Inc., Shivangi Inc., Meena Patel,
Vinayak K. Patel v. Southwestern National Bank

The Parties in the above-referenced matter, in resolution of this lawsuit, agree to the following terms:

1. Plaintiffs agree to dismiss their claims against Southwestern National Bank with prejudice;
2. Southwestern National Bank agrees to dismiss its claims against Plaintiffs without prejudice;
3. All parties agree to pay their own attorney's fees and costs;
4. Southwestern National Bank agrees to provide Plaintiffs with a copy of the March 2010 appraisal and related invoice;
5. Plaintiffs agree to execute the modified loan documents attached hereto;
6. All parties agree that Southwestern National Bank is entitled to and may withdraw all funds held in the Court's registry;
7. Plaintiffs agree to have the check from Cramer Johnson Wiggins and Assoc. re-issued payable solely to Southwestern National Bank, and to have said check mailed to Leyh [*sic*] & Payne LLP, 9545 Katy Freeway, Suite 200, Houston, Texas, 77024;
8. The District Clerk is ordered to prepare a check made payable to Southwestern National Bank in the amount of all principal plus interest currently held in the Court's Registry, less any administrative fees. Southwestern National Bank's attorneys can pick up the check on its behalf.
9. All parties agree that all defaults other than payment prior to the date of the modification agreement are settled including the alleged defaults on this loan relating to the La Porte Property;
10. All parties agree that the Settlement Agreement at issue in this lawsuit dated May 27, 2010, is valid and enforceable.

order by contending that the trial court lacked jurisdiction. The court of appeals denied relief. --- S.W.3d ----, ----.

If the Rule 11 agreement is a final judgment, as the Bank argues, the trial court maintains continuing jurisdiction to enforce that judgment. If, however, the agreement is simply an interlocutory order, and the dismissal order signed four days later is the court's final judgment, as Vaishangi argues, the trial court was without jurisdiction to enforce the Rule 11 agreement because its plenary power had expired. *See* TEX. R. CIV. P. 329b(d) (providing that a trial court's plenary power runs for thirty days after judgment is signed).

Texas Rule of Civil Procedure 11 provides that "no agreement between attorneys or parties touching any suit pending will be enforced unless it be in writing, signed and filed with the papers as part of the record, or unless it be made in open court and entered of record." TEX. R. CIV. P. 11. We have generally treated Rule 11 agreements as separate and distinct from agreed judgments entered thereon. *See, e.g., Mantas v. Fifth Court of Appeals,* 925 S.W.2d 656, 658 (Tex. 1996) (per curiam) (discussing when a court can "render an agreed judgment on the settlement agreement"); *Padilla v. LaFrance,* 907 S.W.2d 454, 462 (Tex. 1995) ("[T]he announcement of the agreement in open court and its notation on the docket cannot give it the force of a judgment." (quoting *Burnaman v. Heaton,* 150 Tex. 333, 240 S.W.2d 288, 292 (Tex. 1951))); *Kennedy v. Hyde,* 682 S.W.2d 525, 528 (Tex. 1984) ("[N]otwithstanding a valid Rule 11 agreement, consent must exist at the time an agreed judgment is rendered."). But nothing in the rules of procedure prohibits a Rule 11 agreement from being, itself, an agreed judgment, so long as the agreement meets the requirements for a final judgment. A judgment is final "if and only if either it actually disposes of all claims and parties then before the court, regardless of its language, or it states with unmistakable clarity that it is a final judgment as to all claims and all parties." However, a trial court's "approval of a settlement does not necessarily constitute rendition of judgment," because rendition of judgment requires a "present act" to "decide the issues." *S & A Rest. Corp. v. Leal,* 892 S.W.2d 855, 857-58 (Tex. 1995) (per curiam) When parties dictate a settlement agreement on the record (creating an enforceable agreement under Rule 11) and the trial court approves it on the record, such a settlement agreement does not constitute an agreed judgment unless "[t]he words used by the trial court . . . clearly indicate the intent to render judgment at the time the words are expressed." *Id.* at 858.

The Bank argues that fact issues regarding whether the Rule 11 agreement disposed of all claims and all parties preclude us from determining this issue in a mandamus proceeding. Although fact issues about the scope and terms of the Rule 11 agreement may remain, those issues do not prevent the Court from determining as a matter of law whether the Rule 11 agreement constitutes an agreed judgment. Additionally, we are not precluded from deciding if the trial court exceeded its jurisdiction, as we need not resolve any fact issues to reach that determination. The Bank's concerns go to the question of whether the parties agreed to dispose of all claims; the issue before the Court is whether the trial court intended to dispose of all claims and all parties through the entry of this agreement, thereby rendering final judgment, at that moment.

The Rule 11 agreement here provides that Vaishangi and the Bank agree to dismiss all claims. Additionally, the agreement states that "[a]ll parties agree that the Settlement Agreement at issue in this lawsuit dated May 27, 2010, is valid and enforceable." Although the trial court signed the agreement, nowhere did the trial court indicate the "intent to render judgment at the time the words [were] expressed." In fact, we note that the Rule 11 agreement contains no decretal language typically seen in a judgment (i.e., "ordered, adjudged, and decreed"), while the dismissal order repeatedly recites the decretal language of "ordered, adjudged, and decreed." The signed agreement may be a binding and enforceable settlement as between the parties, but we cannot conclude that it is a judgment.

Additionally, if the Rule 11 agreement were a final judgment, the dismissal order would have been useless and unnecessary because a trial court can render only one judgment in a case, TEX. R. CIV. P. 301. Thus, the trial court here likely would not have entered the dismissal order had it intended the Rule 11 agreement to be a final judgment. Further, a later judgment supersedes a prior one, *see Old Republic Ins. Co. v. Scott,* 846 S.W.2d 832, 833 & n. 2 (Tex. 1993), so the dismissal order would have nullified any effect of the Rule 11 agreement as a judgment. The only reasonable conclusion is that the dismissal order is the trial court's final judgment and the Rule 11 agreement is not.

While a party can certainly pursue a claim for breach of a settlement agreement even when that settlement agreement is not an agreed judgment, the "[t]he party seeking enforcement of the settlement agreement must pursue a separate claim for breach of contract." When, as here, the trial court's plenary power had expired, a party could not "reinvest the trial court that dismissed the case with jurisdiction to enforce the settlement agreement" by filing a post-judgment motion to enforce the agreement. When the trial court nevertheless heard the motion and issued an order enforcing the settlement agreement, the trial court exceeded its jurisdictional authority. In these instances, mandamus is proper even without a showing that the relator lacks an adequate remedy on appeal. Therefore, we conditionally grant the petition for writ of mandamus without hearing oral argument, *see* TEX. R. APP. P. 52.8(c), and direct the trial court to vacate its order granting Southwestern National Bank's motion to enforce the settlement agreement. As we are confident that the trial court will comply, the writ will issue only if the trial court fails to do so.

C. Mary Carter Agreements

ELBAOR
v.
SMITH

845 S.W.2d 240
(Tex. 1992)

GONZALEZ, JUSTICE.

[A short time before his medical malpractice trial began, plaintiff Smith entered into Mary Carter agreements with three defendants, Dr. Syrquin, Dr. Stephens, and Arlington Community Hospital (ACH).] Under the terms of the agreements, the settling defendants were required to participate in the trial of the case. The agreements also contained pay-back provisions whereby Dr. Syrquin and ACH would be reimbursed for all or part of the settlement money paid to Ms. Smith out of the recovery against another defendant, Dr. Elbaor.

Dr. Syrquin had performed emergency surgery on Ms. Smith's ankle. Testimony at trial revealed that Dr. Syrquin, who was not an orthopedic specialist, committed malpractice by closing the ankle too soon after debriding it. Eight days after the surgery, Dr. Syrquin recommended transferring Ms. Smith to ACH where she came under the care of, among others, Dr. Elbaor, an orthopedic specialist. At ACH, Dr. Elbaor observed but did not participate in two additional debridements of Ms. Smith's ankle which were performed by Dr. Stephens, a plastic surgeon. Dr. Stephens sought to explore and alleviate any infection in Ms. Smith's ankle. Additional expert medical testimony elicited during the trial demonstrated that, in all probability, Ms. Smith's ankle was beyond restoration by the time she arrived at ACH. Arguably neither the subsequent surgeries performed at ACH nor the care she received there could have remedied the damage caused by Dr. Syrquin's malpractice.

Although the Mary Carter agreements were not entered into evidence, the trial judge was troubled by them and he took remedial measures to mitigate their harmful effects by reapportioning the peremptory challenges, changing the order of proceedings to favor Dr. Elbaor, allowing counsel to explain the agreements to the jury, and instructing the jury regarding the agreements.

During the trial, the settling defendants' attorneys, who sat at the table with Dr. Elbaor's attorneys, vigorously assisted Ms. Smith in pointing the finger of culpability at Dr. Elbaor. This created some odd conflicts of interest and some questionable representations of fact. For example, although Ms. Smith's own experts testified that Dr. Syrquin committed malpractice, her attorney stated during voir dire and in her opening statement that Dr. Syrquin's conduct was "heroic" and that Dr. Elbaor's negligence caused Ms. Smith's damages. And during her closing argument, Ms. Smith's attorney urged the jury to find that Dr. Syrquin had not caused Ms. Smith's damages. This is hardly the kind of statement expected from a plaintiff's lawyer regarding a named defendant. ACH and Drs. Syrquin and Stephens had remained defendants of record, but their attorneys asserted during voir dire that Ms. Smith's damages were "devastating," "astoundingly high," and "astronomical." Furthermore, on cross examination they elicited testimony from Ms. Smith favorable to her and requested recovery for pain and mental anguish. The settling defendants' attorneys also abandoned their pleadings on Ms. Smith's contributory negligence, argued that Ms. Smith should be awarded all of her alleged damages, and urged that Dr. Elbaor was 100 percent liable.

A.

The term 'Mary Carter agreement' has been defined in different ways by various courts and commentators.[13] This Court has yet to definitively define the requisite elements of a Mary Carter agreement—our prior pronouncements utilized different definitions of the term. *Compare General Motors Corp. v. Simmons*, 558 S.W.2d 855 (Tex. 1977) (a Mary Carter agreement is a settlement where the settling defendant remains a party at trial and retains a financial stake in the plaintiff's recovery), overruled on other grounds by *Duncan v. Cessna Aircraft Co.*, 665 S.W.2d 414 (Tex. 1984) *with Bristol-Myers Co. v. Gonzales*, 561 S.W.2d 801, 805 (Tex. 1978) (a Mary Carter agreement is a settlement where the settling defendant retains a financial interest in the plaintiff's recovery). Today we clarify what we mean by the term 'Mary Carter agreement.' A Mary Carter agreement exists when the settling defendant retains a financial stake in the plaintiff's recovery and re-

[13] The majority of cases and commentators define "Mary Carter agreement" as one in which the settling defendant possesses a financial stake in the outcome of the case and the settling defendant remains a party to the litigation. * * * Many cases also describe other requisite elements of a Mary Carter agreement, such as secrecy. *See, e.g.,* Ward, 284 So.2d at 387. Other cases and commentators argue that a Mary Carter agreement exists any time the settling defendant possesses a financial interest in the plaintiff's recovery. *See* Bristol-Myers Co. v. Gonzales, 561 S.W.2d 801, 805 (Tex. 1978); Robin Renee Green, Comment, *Mary Carter Agreements: The Unsolved Evidentiary Problems in Texas*, 40 BAYLOR L. REV. 449, 451 (1988).

mains a party at the trial of the case.[14] This definition comports with both the present majority view[15] and the original understanding of the term.[16]

A Mary Carter agreement exists, under our definition, when the plaintiff enters into a settlement agreement with one defendant and goes to trial against the remaining defendant(s). The settling defendant, who remains a party, guarantees the plaintiff a minimum payment, which may be offset in whole or in part by an excess judgment recovered at trial. *See General Motors Corp. v. Simmons*, 558 S.W.2d 855, 858 (Tex. 1977), overruled on other grounds by *Duncan v. Cessna Aircraft* Co., 665 S.W.2d 414, 427 (Tex. 1984). This creates a tremendous incentive for the settling defendant to ensure that the plaintiff succeeds in obtaining a sizable recovery, and thus motivates the defendant to assist greatly in the plaintiff's presentation of the case (as occurred here). Indeed, Mary Carter agreements generally, but not always, contain a clause requiring the settling defendant to participate in the trial on the plaintiff's behalf.

Given this Mary Carter scenario, it is difficult to surmise how these agreements promote settlement. Although the agreements do secure the partial settlement of a lawsuit, they nevertheless nearly always ensure a trial against the non-settling defendant. *Bedford School Dist. v. Caron Constr. Co.*, 116 N.H. 800, 367 A.2d 1051, 1054 (1976) (agreement required plaintiff to prosecute claim against remaining defendant and plaintiff could not settle the claim for under $20,000 without the consent of the settling defendant); *Lum v. Stinnett*, 87 Nev. 402, 488 P.2d 347, 348 (1971) (same). Mary Carter agreements frequently make litigation inevitable, because they grant the settling defendant veto power over any proposed settlement between the plaintiff and any remaining defendant. *See Bass v. Phoenix Seadrill*/78 Ltd., 749 F.2d 1154, 1156 (5th Cir. 1985) (Mary Carter agreement gave settling defendant veto power). Thus, '[o]nly a mechanical jurisprudence could characterize Mary Carter arrangements as promoting compromise and discouraging litigation—they plainly do just the opposite.' *Stein v. American Residential Mgmt.*, 781 S.W.2d 385, 389 (Tex. App.—Houston [14th Dist.] 1989), *writ denied per curiam*, 793 S.W.2d 1 (Tex. 1990).

In his concurring opinion in *Scurlock Oil Co. v. Smithwick*, 724 S.W.2d 1, 8 (Tex. 1986) (on motion for rehearing), Justice Spears pointed out that 'Mary Carter agreements should be prohibited because they are inimical to the adversary system, and they do not promote settlement—their primary justification.' The truth of this statement has been recognized by commentators and has been proven by the subsequent history regarding the use of Mary Carter agreements.[17]

---

14 A Mary Carter agreement does not have to expressly state that the settling defendant must participate in the trial. The participation requirement is satisfied by the mere presence of the settling defendant as a party in the case. Obviously, a Mary Carter agreement would not exist if a settling defendant acquires a financial interest in the outcome of the trial and then testifies at trial as a non-party witness. However, Rule 3.04(b) of the Texas Disciplinary Rules of Professional Conduct prohibits a lawyer from paying or offering to pay a witness contingent upon the content of the testimony of the witness or the outcome of the case. Certainly Rule 3.04(b) mandates that an attorney has an ethical duty to refrain from making a settlement contingent, in any way, on the testimony of a witness who was also a settling party.

15 *See supra* note 13.

16 The first case to utilize the term "Mary Carter agreement" was Ward v. Ochoa, 284 So.2d 385, 386 (Fla. 1973). The Florida Supreme Court defined a Mary Carter agreement as "a contract by which one co-defendant secretly agrees with the plaintiff that, if such defendant will proceed to defend himself in court, his own maximum liability will be diminished proportionately by increasing the liability of the other co-defendants." *Id.* at 387.

17 Numerous commentators have criticized Mary Carter agreements. [Citations omitted.]

The dissent approves of the supervisory guidelines suggested in the Smithwick concurrence, but his opinion misses the point. These guidelines were suggested as a stop-gap measure to ameliorate the harmful effects of Mary Carter agreements until this Court finally ruled on the agreements' propriety. Our inaction has created confusion, because the question as to whether Mary Carter agreements are valid has remained open . . . ."

* * *

B.

Many jurisdictions have decided to tolerate the ill effects of Mary Carter agreements, presumably because they believe that the agreements promote settlement. Some have sought to mitigate the agreements' harmful skewing of the trial process by imposing prophylactic protection.[18] Indeed, Texas previously has taken such an approach. *See Stein*, 781 S.W.2d at 389 (problematic incentives created by Mary Carter agreements require supervisory guidelines enabling trial judges to 'keep a short leash on Mary Carter agreements' potential for wreaking havoc on the civil justice system'); *Smithwick*, 724 S.W.2d at 8-12 (SPEARS, J., concurring).[19] These protective measures generally seek to remove the secrecy within which Mary Carter agreements traditionally have been shrouded. *See Slusher v. Ospital*, 777 P.2d 437, 440 (Utah 1989) (secrecy is the essence of a Mary Carter agreement).

Justice Spears rightly noted in *Smithwick* the falsity of the premise upon which the prophylactic protection approach is founded, namely, the promotion of equitable settlements. *Id.* at 8. Mary Carter agreements instead: present to the jury a sham of adversity between the plaintiff and one codefendant, while these parties are actually allied for the purpose of securing a substantial judgment for the plaintiff and, in some cases, exoneration for the settling defendant. June F. Entman, *Mary Carter Agreements: An Assessment of Attempted Solutions*, 38 U. FLA. L. REV. 521, 574 (1986); *see also General Motors Corp. v. Lahocki*, 286 Md. 714, 410 A.2d 1039, 1046 (1980). The agreements pressure the 'settling' defendant to alter the character of the suit by contributing discovery material, peremptory challenges, trial tactics, supportive witness examination, and jury influence to the plaintiff's cause. *See* John E. Benedict, Note, *It's A Mistake to Tolerate the Mary Carter Agreement*, 87 COLUMBIA L. REV. 368, 372-73 (1987). These procedural advantages distort the case presented before a jury that came 'to court expecting to see a contest between the plaintiff and the defendants [and] instead see[s] one of the defendants cooperating with the plaintiff.' *Smithwick*, 724 S.W.2d at 9 (SPEARS, J., concurring).

Mary Carter agreements not only allow plaintiffs to buy support for their case,[20] they also motivate more culpable defendants to 'make a 'good deal' [and thus] end up paying little or nothing in damages.' *Id.*; *cf. Slayton v. Ford Motor Co.*, 140 Vt. 27, 435 A.2d 946, 947 (1981) (jury may infer that non-settling defendant was the most culpable defendant because plaintiff did not settle with that defendant). Remedial measures cannot overcome nor sufficiently alleviate the malignant effects that Mary Carter agreements inflict upon our adversarial system. No persuasive public policy justifies

---

[18] [Citations omitted.]

[19] The guidelines provided in the *Smithwick* concurrence require that Mary Carter agreements: (1) are discoverable; (2) should be fully disclosed "to the trial court before trial or immediately after the agreement is formed;" (3) should be considered by the trial court in allowing jury strikes and ruling on witness examination; and (4) should be fully disclosed to the jury at the start of the trial. *Smithwick*, 724 S.W.2d at 8-11.

[20] We previously condemned the practice of buying a witness' testimony in order to silence testimony. Tom L. Scott, Inc. v. McIlhany, 798 S.W.2d 556, 560 (Tex. 1990).

them, and they are not legitimized simply because this practice may continue in the absence of these agreements. The Mary Carter agreement is simply an unwise and champertous device that has failed to achieve its intended purpose. *See Lum*, 488 P.2d at 351 (Mary Carter agreements essentially champertous because settling defendant retains financial interest in plaintiff's success against non-settling defendant); *cf. Monjay v. Evergreen School Dist.*, 13 Wash. App. 654, 537 P.2d 825, 830 (1975).

IV.

The case before us reveals yet another jury trial and verdict distorted by a Mary Carter agreement. The trial judge, who fully grasped the detrimental effect these agreements could have on the outcome, attempted to monitor the lawsuit by assiduously applying the guidelines suggested in the *Smithwick* concurrence. The conduct of this trial, however, confirms the apprehension expressed by Justice Spears in *Smithwick*: that these remedial measures would only mitigate and not eliminate the unjust influences exerted on a trial by Mary Carter agreements. Equalizing peremptory strikes, reordering proceedings, thoroughly disclosing the true alignment of the parties, and revealing the agreement's substance cannot overcome collusion between the plaintiff and settling defendants who retain a financial interest in the plaintiff's success. In fact, Mary Carter agreements may force attorneys into questionable ethical situations under Rule 3.05 of the Texas Disciplinary Rules of Professional Conduct, which is titled 'Maintaining the Impartiality of the Tribunal.' Comment 2 to that rule notes, regarding alternate methods of dispute resolution (like Mary Carter agreements), that 'a lawyer should avoid any conduct that is or could reasonably be construed as being intended to corrupt or to unfairly influence the decision-maker.' *See Supreme Court of Texas, Texas Disciplinary Rules of Professional Conduct* art. X, § 9 (1990); *cf. Model Code of Professional Responsibility* EC-720 (1979) (attorneys responsible for upholding adversarial system). The dissent acknowledges that Mary Carter agreements skew the trial process. This effect reasonably could be construed as unfairly influencing the decision-maker.

As a matter of public policy, this Court favors settlements, but we do not favor partial settlements that promote rather than discourage further litigation. And we do not favor settlement arrangements that skew the trial process, mislead the jury, promote unethical collusion among nominal adversaries, and create the likelihood that a less culpable defendant will be hit with the full judgment. The bottom line is that our public policy favoring fair trials outweighs our public policy favoring partial settlements.

This case typifies the kind of procedural and substantive damage Mary Carter agreements can inflict upon our adversarial system. Thus, we declare them void as violative of sound public policy."

* * *

[The court deals with whether or not today's decision should be applied retroactively.]

DOGGETT, JUSTICE, dissenting, joined by MAUZY and GAMMAGE, JUSTICES.

* * *

The chief problem associated with a Mary Carter agreement is that a hidden alteration of the relationship of some of the parties will give the jury a misleading and incomplete basis for evaluating the evidence. As is true in so many areas of jurisprudence, secrecy is the first enemy of justice. To address this concern, trial judges have appropriately implemented several procedural safeguards that remove the veil of secrecy from such settlements. Accordingly, we have emphasized the importance of complete disclosure of these arrangements. *General Motors Corp. v. Simmons*, 558 S.W.2d 855, 858-59 (Tex. 1977), overruled on other grounds by *Duncan v. Cessna Aircraft Co.*, 665 S.W.2d 414, 427 (Tex. 1984). A concurrence to *Smithwick* suggested a number of specific protection regarding such agreements: discovery of them by the non-settling parties; their pretrial disclosure to the court; thorough explanation of the nature of their terms to the jury at the beginning of the trial; and restriction of a settling defendant's leading questions of the plaintiff's witnesses. 724 S.W.2d at 9-11 (SPEARS and GONZALEZ, JUSTICES, concurring).[6]

In the instant case the trial court took great care to safeguard procedurally the adversarial nature and fairness of its proceedings. Nothing about the agreements now under attack was hidden from anyone.[7] * * *

Notes & Questions

1. *Mary Carter's origins.* The term "Mary Carter" comes from a Florida case, *Booth v. Mary Carter Paint Co.*[1]

2. Elbaor *foreshadowed.* In *Scurlock Oil Co. v. Smithwick*,[2] decided in 1986, the Supreme Court majority suggested that a trial court might refuse to give collateral estoppel effect to an earlier case because of the unfairness to the Case 1 defendant caused by a Mary Carter agreement. JUSTICE SPEARS, in a persuasive concurring opinion, condemned Mary Carter agreements in the following aspects:

> Mary Carter agreements . . . threaten the non-settling defendant's due process right to a fair trial. First, settling defendants have an incentive to perjure themselves, since they have a financial interest in the plaintiff's recovery . . . . Second, Mary Carter agreements skew the presentation of the case to the jury. Jurors, unfamiliar with court proceedings, come to court expecting to see a contest between the plaintiff and the defendants, but instead see one of the defendants cooperating with the plaintiff or standing mute. Such cooperation is certainly detrimental to the non-settling defendant. Third, Mary Carter agreements give plaintiffs and settling defendants procedural advantages, the most egregious example being that plaintiffs can lead friendly settling defendants on cross-examination, and vice versa.

3. *The disclosure approach.* In 1977, the Supreme Court decided *General Motors Corp. v. Simmons*.[3] The case involved a typical variant of the many Mary Carter versions. P had sued GM and Feld. P and Feld agreed that Feld would receive half of any plaintiff's judgment against GM up to $200,000 and that P's recovery against Feld would be capped at $200,000. Thus, if Feld could assist

---

6 [Citations omitted.]

7 The settling parties appear to have been open regarding these Mary Carter agreements from the outset, fully disclosing their arrangements to Elbaor and the court prior to trial. While ruling on pretrial motions, the trial court explained its intent to "minimize [any] possible adverse effect [by making] known the essential elements of the Mary Carter agreement to the jury."

1 202 So.2d 8 (Fla. App. 1967).

2 724 S.W.2d 1 (Tex. 1986).

3 558 S.W.2d 855 (Tex. 1977) (overruled on other grounds by Duncan v. Cessna Aircraft Co., 665 S.W.2d 414, 427 (Tex. 1984)).

P so that the judgment against GM reached at least $200,000, Feld's liability would be a maximum of $100,000.

Noting that "there is no contention in this case that the [Mary Carter] agreement was void" the Court held that GM should have been permitted to place the agreement before the jury in order to show Feld's true interest in the litigation. This holding is an exception to the usual rule that settlement offers and agreements should be withheld from the jury because they might be taken as an admission of liability.[4] Settlements may become admissible as impeachment (to show that a witness's interest in the case is not what it seems)[5] and are, therefore, discoverable under Rule 192.3(g). The court identifies Mary Carter agreements as those giving a defendant a financial stake in plaintiff's recovery.

4. *Evidentiary problems with introducing Mary Carters.* The disclosure approach was not without problems. Mary Carter agreements between P and D1 frequently contained self-serving recitations about the egregious conduct of D2, so that D2, encountering a "best evidence" objection to summaries of the agreement sometimes found itself forced to choose between introducing the harmful recitations or foregoing the impeachment.[6]

5. *Problem.* Suppose P sues Retailer and Manufacturer for defects in a widget which has exploded. Retailer cross-claims against the manufacturer for indemnity.[7] P dismisses Retailer after Retailer "lends" P $200,000 which P agrees to repay only out of any recovery against Manufacturer. (Retailer will be paid 50% of P's recovery until he has recovered his $200,000). Retailer agrees only to "tell the truth" if subpoenaed by P for trial. You prudently serve a request for production about "all settlements" which exposes a written agreement to this effect. What do you do? Is this a Mary Carter agreement forbidden under *Elbaor*? Can you prevent Retailer from testifying? Will your answer change if you discover a later agreement which requires, as part of the agreement, that Retailer testify that the widget was defective? In a footnote to *Elobaor* not reproduced here Justice Gonzalez observed that an attorney making an arrangement to provide specific testimony would violate an ethical duty.

6. *Waiver.* It now appears that a failure to object to a Mary Carter arrangement may result in waiver.[8]

---

[4] *See* Texas Rule of Evidence 408; City of Houston v. Sam P. Wallace & Co., 585 S.W.2d 669 (1979); 2 MCCORMICK & RAY, TEXAS LAW OF EVIDENCE § 1142 (2d ed. 1956).

[5] *See* General Motors Corp. v. Simmons, 558 S.W.2d 855 (Tex. 1977).

[6] The court *should* allow the self-serving portions to be redacted by the offeror.

[7] An innocent retailer has a right of indemnity against the manufacturer. *See* Bonniwell v. Beech Aircraft Corp., 663 S.W.2d 816 (Tex. 1984).

[8] *See* St. Paul Surplus Lines Ins. Co. v. Dal-Worth Tank Co., 974 S.W.2d 51 (Tex. 1998).

CITY OF HOUSTON
v.
SAM P. WALLACE & CO.
585 S.W.2d 669
(Tex. 1979)

POPE, JUSTICE.

City of Houston complains of the trial court's denial of its motions for mistrial and new trial. It says the basis for the motions was that Maurice Little, its co-plaintiff in a suit against Sam P. Wallace Company, Inc., secretly made a settlement with Wallace Company just before final arguments and then changed his posture by arguing that City of Houston, rather than defendant Wallace Company, was at fault in causing City of Houston's property damages and Little's personal injuries. While the jury was deliberating and counsel for City of Houston was absent from the courtroom, Little asked for a nonsuit. City of Houston did not discover the secret settlement nor learn of the nonsuit until one week later. The jury answered special issues adversely to both City of Houston and Little and the trial court rendered judgment that City of Houston take nothing. The court of civil appeals affirmed the judgment. 574 S.W.2d 864. We reverse the judgments of the courts below and remand the cause for another trial.

City of Houston sued Wallace Company and Precision Insulation Company, Inc. for property damages to its water cooling plant at the Houston Intercontinental Airport which resulted from an explosion and fire on October 19, 1971. Wallace Company had a contract with City of Houston to construct certain additions to its water cooling plant and Precision Insulation had a subcontract with Wallace Company to perform certain insulation work. Little, an employee of Precision Insulation, in a separate suit against Wallace Company, claimed damages for personal injuries he suffered in the same accident. The trial court consolidated the City's suit seeking damages for its property loss and Little's suit seeking damages for his personal injuries. Wallace Company's answer asked for indemnity against Precision Insulation and Precision Insulation prayed for judgment against City of Houston. The trial court aligned City of Houston and Little as co-plaintiffs and Wallace Company and Precision Insulation as defendants.

Little, an insulator, was assigned the task of insulating some water pipes that were located a few feet above a large metal box-like container in which was housed an electrical switch gear. Little had to use a roll scaffold to climb on top of the switch gear box so he could reach the water pipes that he had to insulate. While Little was standing on a board that someone had laid across the top of the switch gear box, there was a series of electrical explosions followed by a fire which destroyed the City's plant and seriously injured Little.

At trial, all the parties had closed their evidence and the court was preparing its charge when Little and Wallace Company settled their differences. They did not tell the court or City of Houston about the settlement; so the court submitted special issues by which both City of Houston and Little sought to establish Wallace Company's negligence. Another series of issues asked about Precision Insulation's negligence. Other issues inquired about contributory negligence on the part of City of Houston and also Little. Each party was allowed forty-five minutes to argue to the jury, and each party used the time allotted. City of Houston made the first argument, followed in turn by Little, Wallace Company and Precision Insulation.

City of Houston opened the jury arguments by explaining its theory for fixing liability upon Wallace Company. It read to the jury and urged answers to certain specific issues that would fix responsibility upon Wallace Company.[1] Counsel closed his argument by explaining to the jury that Little's attorney would follow him, saying: "The reason that is done that way is because the Rules of Civil Procedure provided that we have the burden of proof, Mr. Barker (Little's counsel) and I . . . after the defendants tell their story we get to have a few more minutes with you to rebut anything they may have said."

Little's counsel began his argument by explaining why his client was not contributorily negligent and by urging the severity of Little's injuries. He then wholly switched his direction. He argued that Wallace Company, his ostensible adversary, did not know about the presence of the dangerous condition, did not fail to inspect the premises in the area of the switch gear, did not operate the water lines that ran over the switch gear box, did not fail to perform its work in a good and workmanlike manner, and that the evidence would not support a finding against Wallace Company on those issues. Little's argument also urged the defeat of his co-plaintiff's right of recovery against Wallace Company by his argument that City of Houston was operating the electrical equipment in an overloaded condition, as Wallace Company had contended during trial. Little's counsel told the jury that the overloading issue should be answered against City of Houston, "We do," and that similar answers should be made to the accompanying negligence and proximate cause issues. Little's counsel also argued that the jury should answer affirmatively the issue which asked if the water was being run through the pipes at the request and for the benefit of City of Houston. The jury returned a favorable verdict for the defendants, Wallace Company and Precision Insulation, as Little had argued.

The judgment form that was circulated for approval of the attorneys one week after the jury returned its verdict contained a recital that Little had announced to the court during jury deliberations that he wished to take a nonsuit. That was when City of Houston learned for the first time about the settlement and the nonsuit. It promptly filed a motion asking for a mistrial. At the mistrial hearing, counsel for plaintiff Little admitted that "the real consideration for my settlement is the fact that I would not argue negligence against Sam P. Wallace Company." The court overruled the motion for mistrial and later overruled City's motion for a new trial based on the same complaint.

At the commencement of the trial, both City of Houston and Little had actions against Wallace Company as their common adversary. The trial court properly and fairly cast them as plaintiffs after the consolidation of the two cases. Rule 174(a), TEX. R. CIV. P. The fairness of the alignment turned into unfairness when, unknown to City of Houston, its ally and confederate became its adversary. City of Houston, under an adversary proceeding, had the burden to develop and present its own case, but it did not have the additional burden to defeat the Trojan Horse that had secretly invaded City's camp. Counsel for Little switched sides and then undermined his co-plaintiff's and his own case as alleged.

In *Degen v. Bayman*, 200 N.W.2d 134 (S.D. 1972), the plaintiff settled with one co-defendant who then changed positions and argued for the plaintiff and against his co-defendant, saying:

---

[1] Special Issue No. 12

Do you find from a preponderance of the evidence that the chilled water lines over the area of the switchgear box were operated by Sam P. Wallace & Co. prior to the occurrence in question without being insulated?

Special Issue No. 15

Do you find from a preponderance of the evidence that by allowing the chilled water lines over the switchgear to be operated prior to being insulated, the contractor, Sam P. Wallace Co., failed to perform its work in a good and workmanlike manner?

> I have no doubt, ladies and gentlemen, that in this case you're going to give Billy Degen a verdict and believe me, in this argument and particularly in a case like this, I think the attorneys have a real responsibility to be candid with the jury, and I'm trying to be with you because this is a very serious case.
>
> There isn't any doubt in my mind but what you're going to give Billy Degen a verdict. There isn't any doubt in my mind that it's going to be a substantial one.

In reversing the case, the court said:

> Not knowing the motive for the evaporation of adversary vigor between plaintiff and Bayman, this benevolent candor coming from a joint tort-feasor could only appear to the jury as a shattering admission.
>
> The protective order was a proper exercise of discretion. However, the responsibility to assure a fair trial is continuous. The court should not have allowed it to be used as a collusive advantage. When that appeared, a limited rescission was necessary to let the adversary process put the issues in perspective.

Little's counsel had no business making an argument to the jury at all. After his settlement with Wallace Company, Little had no further claim against anybody and no other party had any claim against him. Findings on Little's issues in no way would affect the claims for indemnity. This was not a comparative negligence case. Candor required a disclosure to the court that Little had no further interest in the case; so the trial judge would not have submitted meaningless special issues that inquired about Wallace Company's negligence toward Little, Little's contributory negligence, and his damages. * * *

Defendant Wallace Company contends that City of Houston waived its complaint because it failed to object to the jury argument, relying upon *Turner v. Turner*, 385 S.W.2d 230 (Tex. 1964), which holds that jury arguments may be cured by instruction after a timely objection is sustained. In *Turner*, counsel heard and knew about the error but failed to object. The error in this instance was a secret one; it was concealed from City of Houston. Just what objection the City might have made except that it was surprised, is not suggested. As soon as City of Houston learned that Little had secretly settled and had been dismissed, it moved for a mistrial, and it was in that post-trial hearing that it learned for the first time that "the real consideration for my settlement is the fact that I would not argue negligence against Sam P. Wallace Company."

* * *

It is our conclusion that the trial court erred in refusing to grant City of Houston's motions for mistrial and for new trial by reason of the misalignment of the parties at the argument stage of the trial. The error was such a denial of the rights of City of Houston as was reasonably calculated to cause and probably did cause the rendition of an improper judgment in the case. Rule 503, TEX. R. CIV. P. From the whole record we conclude that the jury received a distorted and unfair portrayal of the posture of the parties.

* * *

Texas adheres to the rule that information about settlement agreements should be excluded from the jury, because the agreement may be taken as an admission of liability. *McGuire v. Commercial Union Ins. Co.*, 431 S.W.2d 347 (Tex. 1968); 2 MCCORMICK & RAY, TEXAS LAW OF EVIDENCE § 1142 (2d ed. 1956). We recently recognized that an exception to that general rule will be made when a plaintiff and one defendant settle a cause on an agreement that the settling defendant will receive back a percentage of what the plaintiff recovers from the other defendant. *General Motors Corp. v. Simmons*, 558 S.W.2d 855 (Tex. 1977). Defendant General Motors complained and this court held that it should have been permitted to introduce evidence of the "Mary Carter" agreement so it could discredit witnesses for the settling defendant who actually had a financial stake in the success of the plaintiff's recovery. Defendant Wallace Company insists that the settlement agreement it made is not a Mary Carter agreement, for which reason, *General Motors Corporation v. Simmons* should not control this case. The Mary Carter agreements and the misalignment of the plaintiffs in this case both possess a more basic vice. Both of them are false and misleading portrayals to the jury of the real interests of the parties and witnesses.

* * *

The trial was not a fair adversary proceeding.

We reverse the judgments of the courts below and remand the cause to the trial court for another trial.

Notes & Questions

1. *Preventive action.* Was the agreement in this case a Mary Carter? What course of action would have been open to opposing counsel if he had learned of the agreement *before* the jury argument in question?

2. *Ethics.* When does permitted cooperation between litigants with common interests become deception or collusion which corrupts the process? Mary Carter-style agreements, when concealed, have been condemned as ethical violations. In a law review article critical of Mary Carters[1] one author suggests that they create the appearance of professional impropriety, diminish public confidence in the judicial process, are prejudicial to the administration of justice, and violate the lawyer's traditional ethical obligation of candor and fairness. But attorneys are often required by their role as advocates to be something less than candid, as when they seek to withhold certain information from the jury—a client's old conviction, for example, or the outcome of an earlier trial of the same dispute. What is the difference between that and the sub-rosa Mary Carter agreement or the "deal" made in *Wallace*?

---

[1] J. Benedict, *It's a Mistake to Tolerate the Mary Carter Agreement*, 87 COLUMBIA L. REV. 368 (1987).

D. Alternative Dispute Resolution

While not officially part of the rules of civil procedure, students should be aware of the significant move towards requiring the use of some mechanism of ADR before courts will allow a case to proceed to trial. Many local rules and statutory provisions require parties to participate in mediation before trial; therefore, many settlements will occur in the context of mediation. Both trial courts and appellate courts have the power to refer parties to ADR.[1]

Besides mediation, parties can use a moderated settlement conference, summary jury trial, nonbinding or binding arbitration and, if by agreement, mini-trial or a special judge trial. A party not wanting to participate in ADR does have the power to file a written objection to the referral to ADR and can have that objection heard by the trial court, just as a party desiring to compel ADR can file a written request for referral.

E. Offer of Settlement

AMEDISYS, INC.
v.
KINGWOOD HOME HEALTH CARE
437 S.W.3d 507
(Tex. 2014)

Opinion

JUSTICE BOYD delivered the opinion of the Court.

The parties in this case dispute the validity of the plaintiff's attempt to accept the defendant's settlement offer under chapter 42 of the Civil Practice & Remedies Code and rule 167 of the Texas Rules of Civil Procedure. We hold that the plaintiff presented uncontroverted evidence that it accepted the material terms of the defendant's offer. We therefore reverse the court of appeals' judgment and remand for that court to consider the defendant's remaining challenges to the trial court's summary judgment in favor of the plaintiff.

I.
Background

Amedisys, Inc. and Kingwood Home Health Care, L.L.C. are competitors. After two Amedisys employees left to work for Kingwood and allegedly began soliciting business from Amedysis clients, Amedisys sued Kingwood for tortious interference with Amedisys's non-solicitation agreements with the employees. Kingwood alleges that in subsequent settlement discussions Amedysis repeatedly stated that it would not accept anything less than a "six-figure" offer. Believing that amount was significantly more than Amedisys could recover at trial, King-

---

1 CPRC 154.021(a). *See also* Downey v. Gregory, 757 S.W.2d 524 (Tex. App.—Houston [1st Dist.] 1988, orig. proceeding).

wood invoked rule 167, which authorizes a party to recover certain litigation costs if the party made, and the party's opponent rejected, a settlement offer that was significantly more favorable than the judgment obtained at trial. *See* TEX. R. CIV. P. 167.2(a), 167.4(a). Kingwood then delivered a written offer, "in accordance with" rule 167 and chapter 42 of the Civil Practice & Remedies Code, to pay Amedisys $90,000 within fifteen days after Amedisys's acceptance of the offer. Consistent with rule 167.2(b)(5), Kingwood gave Amedisys fourteen days to accept the offer or it would be "deemed rejected and can serve as the basis for litigation costs under Texas Civil Practice & Remedies Code Chapter 42 and Texas Rule of Civil Procedure 167."

Five days after receiving the settlement offer, Amedisys filed its designation of expert witnesses. After another five days, Kingwood filed its own expert designations and moved to strike Amedisys's designations on the ground that, because Amedisys was the party seeking affirmative relief, its deadline to designate experts had passed nearly a month earlier. Four days later, apparently to Kingwood's surprise, Amedisys sent a letter, by facsimile and as an email attachment, "accepting" Kingwood's $90,000 offer. As it turns out, Kingwood did not want Amedisys to accept the offer and made it only because Amedisys said it would not accept an offer under six figures. Instead, Kingwood made the offer merely to trigger a right to recover its litigation costs under rule 167.

During the next two weeks, Amedisys's attorney emailed Kingwood's attorney twice, suggesting they "discuss the terms of the settlement agreement." Kingwood did not respond to the first email but did respond to the second, stating that it would send "a letter shortly explaining [Kingwood's] position on why the consideration fails for the offer that was previously extended to [Amedisys]." When no such letter arrived and the deadline for payment under the settlement had passed, Amedisys demanded payment and threatened to file an emergency motion to enforce the settlement agreement. Kingwood responded that the agreement "failed for consideration" because Amedisys had missed its expert designation deadline, and asserted that Amedisys had "fraudulently induced" Kingwood's settlement offer by repeatedly stating "that it would 'never settle' for less than six figures."

A few days later, Kingwood attended the previously scheduled hearing on its motion to strike Amedisys's expert designations. Believing that the settlement mooted that motion, Amedisys did not file a response or attend the hearing. When it learned that Kingwood had appeared at the hearing and the trial court had granted Kingwood's motion to strike, Amedisys filed an emergency motion asking the court to enforce the settlement agreement, reconsider the order striking its expert designations, and stay the case until the settlement dispute was resolved. In response, Kingwood argued that the agreement was unenforceable because it lacked consideration and was fraudulently induced. Kingwood later filed a "Notice of Withdraw[al] of Consent to Alleged Settlement Agreement," and on the same day, Amedisys filed a "Notice of Rule 11 Agreement."

Amedisys amended its pleadings to assert a breach of contract claim based on the alleged settlement agreement and moved for summary judgment on that claim. In support of its motion, Amedisys submitted copies of the offer and acceptance letters and argued that the settlement agreement was binding on Kingwood as a settlement offer under rule 167, as a contract under general contract law, and as an agreement between attorneys under rule 11 of the Texas Rules of Civil Procedure. In its response, Kingwood agreed that general contract law applies but asserted that the agreement failed for lack of consideration because Amedisys failed to timely designate experts and that Amedisys fraudulently induced the offer by stating that it would not accept an offer less than six figures. Kingwood also argued that the settlement was unenforceable because it had withdrawn its consent. In reply, Amedisys asserted that Kingwood's fraud and failure of consideration defenses were legally inapplicable, that Kingwood had waived them by not pleading them, and that Kingwood had failed to support them with any competent summary judgment evidence. Amedisys disputed Kingwood's contention that withdrawal of consent relieved Kingwood of its contractual obligations.

The trial court granted Amedisys's summary judgment motion without stating its grounds for doing so. Kingwood appealed, arguing that it had created fact issues regarding its affirmative defenses of fraudulent inducement and failure of consideration. Addressing this argument in its appellate brief, Kingwood included a paragraph in which it contended no agreement existed because "an acceptance that does not mirror the terms of the offer is both a rejection of the original offer and a counteroffer." Kingwood pointed out that it had offered in its letter "to pay a total sum of $90,000 to settle all claims asserted *or which could have been asserted* by Amedisys," while Amedisys's letter had accepted Kingwood's "offer to settle all monetary *claims asserted* against [Kingwood] for the total sum of $90,000." Because Amedisys's acceptance letter "omitted the idea that a settlement would not only resolve all claims asserted but also all claims not asserted," Kingwood argued that the letter "constituted a rejection of Kingwood's offer." In its brief, Amedisys argued that Kingwood had not challenged the validity or effectiveness of the acceptance letter in the trial court and could not do so for the first time on appeal.

A majority of the court of appeals agreed with Kingwood and reversed the trial court's judgment, concluding that no settlement agreement existed because Amedisys had not accepted all of the offer's material terms. 375 S.W.3d 397, 400-01. . . . We granted Amedisys's petition for review.

II.

Burdens of Proof and Preservation of Error

* * *

In this case, Amedisys had the burden to submit sufficient evidence to support each element of its breach of contract claim, and this burden required evidence that a contract in fact exists. Kingwood contends that the letter and email that Amedisys submitted to prove its acceptance of Kingwood's offer prove no such thing, but instead prove that Amedisys made a counteroffer by changing a material term of the offer. We therefore review Amedisys's letter and email to determine whether they constitute evidence that Amedisys accepted Kingwood's settlement offer. If they constitute evidence of acceptance, they were uncontroverted evidence because Kingwood did not present any evidence to disprove or create a fact issue on the acceptance element. But if the letter and email constitute no evidence of acceptance, Amedisys did not satisfy its burden of proof and was not entitled to summary judgment.

III.

Acceptance

We now turn to the issue of whether the summary judgment evidence establishes that Amedisys accepted Kingwood's settlement offer. Amedisys contends that, in resolving this issue, the court of appeals erred by applying common law contract principles of offer and acceptance because rule 167 and chapter 42 govern the parties' dealings and displace the common law. Alternatively, Amedisys contends that, even under the common law, it accepted Kingwood's settlement offer. We hold that the common law governs Amedisys's breach of contract claim, but we agree with Amedisys that its email and letter constituted uncontroverted evidence of acceptance.

A. Common Law Principles of "Acceptance" Apply

Amedisys first argues that the court of appeals erred by applying the common law rule that an acceptance is effective only if it matches the material terms of the offer to which it responds. *See, e.g., United Concrete Pipe Corp. v. Spin-Line Co.,* 430 S.W.2d 360, 364 (Tex. 1968) ("It is well settled that an acceptance must not change or qualify the terms of the offer. If it does, the offer is rejected."). In support, Amedisys contends that chapter 42 and rule 167 govern the validity of the parties' settlement agreement, and they do not expressly require an acceptance to match the terms of the offer. Amedisys argues that imposing general contract law's acceptance doctrine on settlement offers under chapter 42 and rule 167 would undermine their purpose by impeding, rather than facilitating, settlement agreements. We disagree that chapter 42 and rule 167 govern here, and hold that Amedisys was required to prove a valid "acceptance" under contract law to prevail on its breach of contract claim.

When applicable, chapter 42 and rule 167 provide a method by which parties in certain cases who make certain offers to settle certain claims can recover certain litigation costs, if the offeree rejects the offer and "the judgment to be awarded [on those claims] is significantly less favorable to the offeree than was the offer." TEX. R. CIV. P. 167.4(a); *see* TEX. CIV. PRAC. & REM. CODE §§ 42.002-.005; TEX. R. CIV. P. 167.1-167.7. This applies only to "an offer made substantially in accordance with this rule," TEX. R. CIV. P. 167. 1, and "[a] settlement offer not made in compliance with this rule, or a settlement offer not made under this rule, or made in an action to which this rule does not apply, cannot be the basis for awarding litigation costs under this rule as to any party." TEX. R. CIV. P. 167.7. If the issue in this case were whether Kingwood is entitled to recover its litigation costs, rule 167 and chapter 42 would govern the resolution of that issue. But the issue here is whether Amedisys submitted sufficient evidence to obtain summary judgment on its claim for breach of a settlement agreement, not whether it can recover its litigation costs. Therefore, contract law governs resolution of the issue.

Certainly, the Legislature can alter, and in some circumstances has altered, the legal requirements for enforcing a settlement agreement. But chapter 42 and rule 167 govern the requirements for awarding litigation costs, not the requirements for breach of contract claims. To the contrary, they expressly provide that they do "not limit or affect a party's right to make a settlement offer that does not comply with this rule," but a non-conforming offer "cannot be the basis for awarding litigation costs under this rule[.]" TEX. R. CIV. P. 167.7; *see also* TEX. CIV. PRAC. & REM. CODE § 42.002(d).

We agree with Amedisys that Texas has a public policy preference for the settlement of legal disputes, and that chapter 42 and rule 167 encourage such settlements. But more fundamental Texas policies prohibit us from binding parties to contracts to which they never agreed. *See Nafta Traders, Inc. v. Quinn,* 339 S.W.3d 84, 95-96 (Tex. 2011) (observing that freedom of contract is a fundamental Texas policy and that "contracts when entered into freely and voluntarily shall be held sacred") (quoting *Fairfield Ins. Co. v. Stephens Martin Paving, LP,* 246 S.W.3d 653, 664 (Tex. 2008)). We find that the authorities on which Amedisys relies are not persuasive in this case. *See, e.g., Poster v. S. Cal. Rapid Transit Dist.,* 52 Cal.3d 266, 276 Cal.Rptr. 321, 801 P.2d 1072, 1075 (1990) (holding that judgment could be entered under California statute based on acceptance of offer during statutory 30-day period, even though the accepting party made counteroffers before accepting the original offer). Here, Amedisys sought to enforce a contract, not to recover litigation costs, and to prevail on that claim it had to establish the existence of a valid contract under the common law, including the elements of offer and acceptance.

B. Amedisys Accepted Kingwood's Settlement Offer

Under the common law, an acceptance may not change or qualify the material terms of the offer, and an attempt to do so results in a counteroffer rather than acceptance. But the materiality of the altered term is key, and an immaterial variation between the offer and acceptance will not prevent the formation of an enforceable agreement.

. . . We agree . . . that, under the summary judgment record in this case, the variation in language between Kingwood's offer and Amedisys's acceptance is not material and did not convert Amedisys's acceptance into a counteroffer.

The offer letter that Kingwood sent to Amedisys, titled "Rule 167 Statutory Offer of Settlement," stated:

> Please accept this letter as an offer of settlement regarding the above referenced matter. Specifically, my client, [Kingwood] makes this offer to pay your client, [Amedisys] to settle *all monetary claims between the parties* in accordance with Texas Civil Practice & Remedies Code Chapter 42 and Texas Rule of Civil Procedure 167.
>
> * * *
>
> ***Offer of Settlement***
>
> [Kingwood] offers to settle with Amedisys the following claims in accordance with Texas Civil Practice & Remedies Code Chapter 42 and Texas Rule of Civil Procedure 167:
>
> [Kingwood] offers a total sum of $90,000 to settle *all claims asserted or which could have been asserted* by Amedisys against [Kingwood] in the above referenced case. This full and final offer is for *all monetary damages claimed*—including attorney[']s fees, costs and interest that were recoverable as of the date of this offer by [Kingwood]. A lump-sum payment in the amount of $90,000 will be made by [Kingwood] within fifteen (15) days after acceptance. If your client agrees, please indicate so by affixing your signature below and returning to me.
>
> Amedisys may accept this settlement offer by serving written notice on [Kingwood's] counsel before June 25, 2010, which is at least fourteen (14) days after this offer is served. If this offer is not accepted by 5:00 p.m. on June 25, 2010, it is deemed rejected and can serve as the basis for litigation costs under Texas Civil Practice & Remedies Code Chapter 42 and Texas Rule of Civil Procedure 167.

(Emphasis added.)

Amedisys responded in a letter that it delivered both by facsimile and as an attachment to an email. The email stated: "Attached please find Amedisys' acceptance *of the settlement offer you sent* pursuant to Rule 167. Please let me know when you are available Monday to discuss the terms of the settlement agreement." (Emphasis added.) The attached letter stated:

> Pursuant to Rule 167.3(b) of the Texas Rules of Civil Procedure, [Amedisys] hereby accepts [Kingwood's] offer to settle *all monetary claims asserted* against [Kingwood] for the total sum of $90,000, for which a lump sum payment shall be tendered to Amedisys by [Kingwood] within fifteen days after acceptance.
>
> I will contact you early next week to discuss the preparation and execution of settlement agreement that memorializes all necessary settlement terms.

(Emphasis added.)

Kingwood argues that Amedisys did not accept Kingwood's offer because "[c]onspicuously missing from Amedisys' letter was its acceptance to settle any claim that *could have been asserted* against [Kingwood] as well as all *non-monetary claims* such as the injunctive relief as had been asserted by Amedisys." We begin with an analysis of the materiality of the offer's reference to claims that "could have been asserted," and then address the reference to "non-monetary" claims.

* * *

Under these circumstances, we cannot conclude that the slight variation in language from Kingwood's offer to Amedisys's acceptance is sufficient, on its face, to convert Amedisys's purported acceptance into a counteroffer. The uncontroverted evidence demonstrates that Amedisys intended to accept Kingwood's offer, did not intend to make a counteroffer, and did not intend that the settlement be dependent on any alteration of the offer's terms. And Kingwood does not appear to have doubted Amedisys's intent to accept its settlement offer until this case was on appeal.

The shifting burden of proof in the summary judgment context is important to the disposition of this case. If the divergence in language between Kingwood's offer and Amedisys's purported acceptance was material on its face, Amedisys's letter and email would have been no evidence of acceptance and Amedisys would not have been entitled to summary judgment. *Cf. Schriver v. Tex. Dep't of Transp.,* 293 S.W.3d 846, 851 (Tex. App.—Fort Worth 2009, no pet.) (holding that settlement offer to purchase all interests in property for specified amount was not accepted by response agreeing to convey only party's own interest in property when record demonstrated that parties had different understandings of whether settlement required conveyance of third parties' leasehold interests). Or if Amedisys's communications had been patently ambiguous about whether Amedisys intended to accept Kingwood's offer, the communications would have, themselves, created a fact issue on acceptance and Amedisys would not have been entitled to summary judgment. *See Coleman v. Reich,* 417 S.W.3d 488, 493-94 (Tex. App.—Houston [14th Dist.] July 2, 2013, no pet.) (holding that ambiguity prevented summary judgment when purported acceptance repeatedly stated that it constituted an offer to settle, rather than acceptance of previous offer, and included a place for other party to sign if accepted).

Here, however, Amedisys's email and letter constitute prima facie evidence of a clear intent to accept Kingwood's settlement offer and did not indicate that acceptance was conditioned on the alteration of any material terms. Amedisys thus satisfied its initial summary judgment burden, and the burden shifted to Kingwood to produce evidence raising an issue of fact. *See Kerlin v. Arias,* 274 S.W.3d 666, 668 (2008) (upholding summary judgment in favor of party who produced prima facie evidence of a valid deed and noting that party did not have burden to prove age or marital status of grantor because opposing party did not produce evidence raising a fact question on those issues) (citing *Centeq Realty, Inc. v. Siegler,* 899 S.W.2d 195, 197 (Tex. 1995) ("Once the defendant produces sufficient evidence to establish the right to summary judgment, the plaintiff must present evidence sufficient to raise a fact issue.")). But Kingwood did not submit any contrary evidence, nor did it challenge the validity of the acceptance at all until after the trial court granted summary judgment. Under these circumstances, we conclude that Amedisys conclusively established through its summary judgment evidence that it accepted Kingwood's settlement offer.

IV.
Conclusion

Because we hold that the summary judgment evidence established that Amedisys accepted Kingwood's settlement offer, we reverse the court of appeals' judgment. Amedisys urges us to reinstate the trial court's judgment, but Kingwood argued to the court of appeals that fact issues regarding its fraudulent inducement and failure of consideration defenses also preclude summary judgment, even if Amedisys accepted Kingwood's offer. Because the court of appeals did not reach or address those issues, Kingwood requests that we remand this case to that court "to consider the outstanding undecided issues." Because neither of the parties has briefed those issues to this Court, we remand to the court of appeals for further proceedings consistent with this opinion.

Notes & Questions

Applies only to monetary claims. Note that that chapter 42's settlement procedures "apply only to claims for monetary relief," TEX. CIV. PRAC. & REM. CODE § 42.002(a), and an offer under rule 167 "must not include non-monetary claims." TEX. R. CIV. P. 167.2(d). Therefore, the Supreme Court noted in Amedisys that because Kingwood repeatedly stated that its offer was made pursuant to chapter 42 and rule 167, the offer's reference to "all claims" did not include non-monetary claims.[1]

---

[1] 437 S.W.3d 507 at n.8.

TABLE OF CASES